Pep Boys	www.pepboys.com
PetsMart	www.petsmart.com
Publix	www.publix.com
QVC	www.qvc.com
Radio Shack	www.radioshack.com
Raleys	www.raleys.com
Rite Aid	www.riteaid.com
Ross Stores	www.rossstores.com
Safeway	www.safeway.com
Saks, Inc.	www.saksincorporated.com
Schnucks	www.schnucks.com
Sears	www.sears.com
Sherwin-Williams	www.sherwin-williams.com
Shopko	www.shopko.com
Smart & Final	www.smartandfinal.com
Sonic Automotive	www.sonicautomotive.com
Spiegel	www.spiegel.com
Staples	www.staples.com
Starbucks	www.starbucks.com
Stater Bros.	www.staterbros.com
Super Valu	www.supervalu.com
Target	www.target.com
Tiffany	www.tiffany.com
TJX Companies	www.tjx.com
Toys "R" Us	www.tru.com
United Auto Group	www.uag.com
Walgreens	www.walgreens.com
Wal-Mart	www.walmart.com
Wegman's	www.wegmans.com
Wendy's	www.wendys.com
Whole Foods Market	www.wholefoods.com
Williams-Sonoma	www.williams-sonoma.com
Winn-Dixie	www.winndixie.com
Yum! Brands	www.yum.com
Zales	www.zales.com

JAPAN (J MEANS SITE IS IN JAPANESE)

Aeon (Jusco)	www.aeon.info/aeoncorp/english
Best Denki	www.bestdenki.ne.jp J
Co-op Kobe	www.kobe.coop.or.jp J
Daiei	www.daiei.co.jp J
Daimaru	www.daimaru.co.jp/english/index.html
Edion	www.edion.co.jp/english/index.html
Hankyu Department Stores	www.hankyu-dept.co.jp J
Heiwado	www.heiwado.co.jp J
Isetan	www.isetan.co.jp J
Ito-Yokado	www.itoyokado.co.jp/company/index1_e.htm
Izumi	www.izumi.co.jp J
Izumiya	www.izumiya.co.jp J
Kintetsu	www.kintetsu.co.jp/english/index.html
Kojima	www.kojima.net J
Maruetsu	www.maruetsu.co.jp/recruit/indexe.html
Marui	www.marui-imai.co.jp/sapporo J
Matsuzakaya	www.matsuzakaya.co.jp J
Mitsukoshi	www.mitsukoshi.co.jp J
Odakyu Electric Railway	www.odakyu.jp.english
Seibu	www.seibu.co.jp J
Seiyu	www.seiyu.co.jp/english/index.shtml
Shimamura Music	www.shimamura.co.jp/english
Skylark	www.skylark.co.jp J
Takashimaya	www.takashimaya.co.jp J
Tokyu Department Store	www.tokyu-dept.co.jp J
Tokyu Store Corporation	www.tokyu-store.co.jp J
Uniqlo	www.uniqlo.co.jp/english/index_f.html
Uny	www.uny.co.jp J
Yamada Denki	www.yamada-denki.jp/company_e/index.html
Yodobashi Camera	www.yodobashi.com J

GREAT BRITAIN

Arcadia Group	www.arcadiagroup.co.uk
Boots Group	www.boots-plc.com
Compass Group	www.compass-group.com
Cooperative Group (CWS)	www.co-op.co.uk

Retail Management

A STRATEGIC APPROACH

TENTH EDITION

Barry Berman
Hofstra University

Joel R. Evans
Hofstra University

PEARSON
Prentice
Hall

Upper Saddle River, NJ 07458

Library of Congress Cataloging-in-Publication Data

Berman, Barry.
 Retail management : a strategic approach / Barry Berman, Joel R. Evans.—10th ed.
   p. cm.
 Includes bibliographical references and indexes.
 ISBN 0-13-187016-5
   1. Retail trade—Management.   I. Evans, Joel R. II. Title.

HF5429.B45 2006
658.8'7—dc22   2005057977

Senior Acquisitions Editor: Katie Stevens
VP/Editorial Director: Jeff Shelstad
Product Development Manager: Ashley Santora
Editorial Assistant: Christine Ietto
Media Project Manager: Peter Snell
Marketing Manager: Ashaki Charles
Managing Editor, Production: Renata Butera
Production Editor: Suzanne Grappi
Permissions Coordinator: Charles Morris
Manufacturing Buyer: Diane Peirano
Design/Composition Manager: Christy Mahon
Composition Liaison: Suzanne Duda
Art Director: Pat Smythe
Interior Design: Blair Brown
Cover Design: Marjory Dressler
Cover Photo: Veer/Digital Vision
Director, Image Resource Center: Melinda Reo
Manager, Rights and Permissions: Zina Arabia
Manager, Visual Research: Beth Brenzel
Image Permission Coordinator: Cynthia Vincenti
Composition: GGS Book Services
Full-Service Project Management: GGS Book Services
Printer/Binder: Quebecor-Dubuque
Typeface: 10/12 Palatino

Credits and acknowledgments borrowed from other sources and reproduced, with permission, in this textbook appear on the appropriate page within the text.

Microsoft® and Windows® are registered trademarks of the Microsoft Corporation in the U.S.A. and other countries. Screen shots and icons reprinted with permission from the Microsoft Corporation. This book is not sponsored or endorsed by or affiliated with the Microsoft Corporation.

Pearson Education LTD.   Pearson Education Australia PTY, Limited
Pearson Education Singapore, Pte. Ltd   Pearson Education North Asia Ltd
Pearson Education, Canada, Ltd   Pearson Educación de Mexico, S.A. de C.V.
Pearson Education–Japan   Pearson Education Malaysia, Pte. Ltd.

10 9 8 7 6 5 4 3
ISBN: 0-13-187016-5

To Linda; Glenna, Paul, Danielle, and Sophie;
and Lisa and Ben

To Linda, Stacey, and Jennifer

Thank you for your enduring
patience and understanding.

Brief Contents

v

Contents

6 PART SIX

MERCHANDISE MANAGEMENT AND PRICING   405

Preface

This edition marks a major milestone for *Retail Management: A Strategic Approach*—a Tenth Edition. We are both pleased and truly thankful to have produced a book that has been so enduringly popular. As we move further into the new millennium, our goal is to seamlessly meld the traditional framework of retailing with the realities of the competitive environment and the emergence of high-tech as a backbone for retailing. We have worked hard to produce a cutting-edge text, while retaining the coverage and features most desired by professors and students.

The concepts of a strategic approach and a retail strategy remain our cornerstones. With a strategic approach, the fundamental principle is that the retailer has to plan for and adapt to a complex, changing environment. Both opportunities and constraints must be considered. A retail strategy is the overall plan or framework of action that guides a retailer. Ideally, it will be at least one year in duration and outline the mission, goals, consumer market, overall and specific activities, and control mechanisms of the retailer. Without a pre-defined and well-integrated strategy, the firm may flounder and be unable to cope with the environment that surrounds it. Through our text, we want the reader to become a good retail planner and decision maker and to be able to adapt to change.

Retail Management is designed as a one-semester text for students of retailing or retail management. In many cases, such students will have already been exposed to marketing principles. We feel retailing should be viewed as one form of marketing and not distinct from it.

HOW THE TEXT IS ORGANIZED

Retail Management: A Strategic Approach has eight parts. Part One introduces the field of retailing, the basics of strategic planning, the importance of building and maintaining relations, and the decisions to be made in owning or managing a retail business. In Part Two, retail institutions are examined in terms of ownership types, as well as store-based, nonstore-based, electronic, and nontraditional strategy mixes. The wheel of retailing, scrambled merchandising, the retail life cycle, and the Web are covered. Part Three focuses on target marketing and information-gathering methods, including discussions of why and how consumers shop and the retailing information system and data warehouse. Part Four presents a four-step approach to location planning: trading-area analysis, choosing the most desirable type of location, selecting a general locale, and deciding on a specific site.

Part Five discusses the elements involved in managing a retail business: the retail organization structure, human resource management, and operations management (both financial and operational). Part Six deals with merchandise management—developing and implementing merchandise plans, the financial aspects of merchandising, and pricing. In Part Seven, the ways to communicate with customers are analyzed, with special attention paid to retail image, atmosphere, and promotion. Part Eight deals with integrating and controlling a retail strategy.

At the end of the text, Appendix A highlights career opportunities in retailing, Appendix B explains the components of the Web site and how to use it, and Appendix C is a comprehensive glossary.

NEW TO THE TENTH EDITION

Since the first edition of *Retail Management: A Strategic Approach*, we have sought to be as contemporary and forward-looking as possible. We are proactive rather than reactive in our preparation of each edition. That is why we still take this adage of Wal-Mart's founder, the late Sam Walton, so seriously: "Commit to your business. Believe in it more than anybody else."

For the Tenth Edition, there are many changes in *Retail Management*:

1. These Substantive Chapter Changes Have Been Made

- Chapter 1, "An Introduction to Retailing"—We introduce the National Retail Federation's career Web site and look, in-depth, at Target Corporation's current retail strategy.
- Chapter 2, "Building and Sustaining Relationships in Retailing"—There is enhanced coverage of "value" and relationships in retailing—with both customers and other channel members.
- Chapter 3, "Strategic Planning in Retailing"—There is a new section of the chapter that demonstrates how a strategic plan can be developed. This section is keyed to the *Computer-Assisted Strategic Retail Management Planning* template that appears at our Web site (**www.prenhall.com/bermanevans**).
- Chapter 4, "Retail Institutions by Ownership"—All of the data on retail ownership formats have been updated. The appendix on franchising opportunities presents current data on the costs of setting up a new franchised outlet.
- Chapter 5, "Retail Institutions by Store-Based Strategy Mix"—All of the data on store-based retail strategies have been updated, and the chapter is keyed to today's economic conditions and trends.
- Chapter 6, Web, "Nonstore-Based, and Other Forms of Nontraditional Retailing"—There is an all-new appendix on multi-channel retailing and its impact. The Internet discussion reflects the present state of Web retailing.
- Chapter 7, "Identifying and Understanding Consumers"—There is a strong emphasis on the retailing ramifications of consumer characteristics, attitudes, and behavior. We include current data on where U.S. and foreign consumers shop, as well as global demographics.
- Chapter 8, "Information Gathering and Processing in Retailing"—We have strengthened the section on "Information Flows in a Retail Distribution Channel."
- Chapter 9, "Trading-Area Analysis"—There is new material on geographic information systems and many new applications. The *American Community Survey* is introduced as a data source.
- Chapter 10, "Site Selection"—We include many new retail applications.
- Chapter 11, "Retail Organization and Human Resource Management"—There is more strategic emphasis on the human resource environment in retailing.
- Chapter 12, "Operations Management: Financial Dimensions"—We have new material on events relating to asset management, including mergers, consolidations, and spinoffs; bankruptcies and liquidations; questionable accounting and financial reporting practices; and other topics.
- Chapter 13, "Operations Management: Operational Dimensions"—There is updated material on operations issues in retailing.
- Chapter 14, "Developing Merchandise Plans"—We make a sharp distinction between the roles of buyers and sales managers, with illustrative (and real)

career ladders. There is current coverage of private brands and a description of commercial merchandising software.

- Chapter 15, "Implementing Merchandise Plans"—There is new coverage of RFID (radio frequency identification).
- Chapter 16, "Financial Merchandise Management"—There is updated coverage of financial merchandise management.
- Chapter 17, "Pricing in Retailing"—We focus on the retailer's need to provide value to customers, regardless of its price orientation.
- Chapter 18, "Establishing and Maintaining a Retail Image"—We place more focus on the total retail experience, retail positioning, and atmospherics and Web-based retailers, as well as how to increase shopping time.
- Chapter 19, "Promotional Strategy"—There are many new examples and a strong strategic emphasis on the retail promotional strategy.
- Chapter 20, "Integrating and Controlling" the Retail Strategy—There is a compelling discussion on integrating the retail strategy and how to assess it, with many new tables.
- Appendix A, "Careers in Retailing"—We dispel several negative myths about retailing careers.

2. The Opening Vignettes Are All Updated and Highlight the Titans of Retailing

Chapter 1—Wal-Mart	Chapter 11—Nordstrom
Chapter 2—Stew Leonard's	Chapter 12—Federated Department Stores
Chapter 3—Limited Brands	Chapter 13—Starbucks
Chapter 4—McDonald's	Chapter 14—Gap Inc.
Chapter 5—Ikea	Chapter 15—Pearle Vision
Chapter 6—Amazon.com	Chapter 16—eBay
Chapter 7—Staples	Chapter 17—Costco
Chapter 8—Mrs. Fields	Chapter 18—Target
Chapter 9—Blockbuster	Chapter 19—Mary Kay
Chapter 10—Dunkin' Donuts	Chapter 20—Home Depot

3. All of the Applied Boxes in Each Chapter Are New. Here Are Some Examples of the Topics We Look At

a. *Technology in Retailing:* "PayPass Comes to Retailing," "Power Sellers on eBay," "Hyperactive Bob: Predictive Technology Comes to Fast Food," "Sportsman's Warehouse: Optimizing Logistics," and "Casual Male's In-Stock Guarantee."

b. *Retailing Around the World:* "Upscale Retail Slowly Enters China," "How Popular Are Convenience Stores Outside the United States?" "Understanding Eastern European Shoppers," "Times Square in Hong Kong," and "J.C. Penney's New Japanese-Inspired Inventory System."

c. *Ethics in Retailing:* "McDonald's Introduces a More Well-Rounded Menu," "Blockbuster Removes Late Fees," "Selling to the Poor Can Be Good—for the Consumer and for Business," "Home Depot Is Now Green," and "Is 'Free' Really Free?"

d. *Careers in Retailing:* The National Retail Federation has graciously permitted us to reprint material from the career section of its Web site throughout our book. This material encompasses the broad range of career opportunities available in retailing.

4. All of the Cases Are New

There are 30 shorter cases, as well as 8 comprehensive cases. Every case is based on real companies and real situations. Among the popular companies featured in the cases are Abercrombie's Ruehl No. 925, Albertson's, Amazon.com, Bed Bath & Beyond, Ben & Jerry's, eBay, Home Depot, Limited Brands, Neiman Marcus, Netflix, Sony, Starbucks, Stop & Shop, Subway, and Trader Joe's.

BUILDING ON A STRONG TRADITION

Besides introducing the new features just mentioned, *Retail Management*, Tenth Edition, carefully builds on its heritage. At the request of our reviewers, these features have been retained from earlier editions of *Retail Management*:

- A strategic decision-making orientation, with many illustrative flowcharts, figures, tables, and photos. The chapter coverage is geared to the six steps used in developing and applying a retail strategy, which are first described in Chapter 1.
- Full coverage of all major retailing topics—including merchandising, consumer behavior, information systems, store location, operations, logistics, service retailing, the retail audit, retail institutions, franchising, human resource management, computerization, and retailing in a changing environment.
- A real-world approach focusing on both small and large retailers.
- Real-world boxes on current retailing issues in each chapter. These boxes further illustrate the concepts presented in the text by focusing on real firms and situations.
- A numbered summary keyed to chapter objectives, a key terms listing, and discussion questions at the end of each chapter.
- Both short cases involving a wide range of retailers and retail practices and comprehensive cases.
- Up-to-date information from such sources as *Advertising Age*, *Business Week*, *Chain Store Age*, *Direct Marketing*, *DSN Retailing Today*, *Entrepreneur*, *Fortune*, *Inc.*, *Journal of Retailing*, *Progressive Grocer*, *Stores*, and *Wall Street Journal*.
- "How to Solve a Case Study" (now online at **www.prenhall.com/bermanevans**).
- End-of-chapter appendixes on service retailing (following Chapter 2), global retailing (following Chapter 3), and franchising (following Chapter 4).
- Three end-of-text appendixes: "Careers in Retailing," "About the Web Site," and "Glossary."

BUILDING ON THE EVOLUTION OF *RETAIL MANAGEMENT: A STRATEGIC APPROACH*

From a retailer perspective, we see four formats—all covered in *Retail Management*—competing in the new millennium (cited in descending order of importance): combined "bricks-and-mortar" and "clicks-and-mortar" retailers—store-based retailers that also offer Web shopping, thus providing customers the ultimate in choice and convenience; clicks-and-mortar retailers—the new breed of Web-only retailers that have emerged in recent years; direct marketers with clicks-and-mortar retailing operations—firms relying on traditional nonstore media such as print catalogs, direct selling in homes, and TV infomercials that have recently added Web sites to enhance their businesses; and bricks-and-mortar retailers—companies that rely on their physical facilities to make sales.

Retail Management: A Strategic Approach, Tenth Edition, incorporates a host of Web-related features throughout the book—and at our Web site (**www.prenhall.com/ bermanevans**). This book has a very strong integration with its Web site:

- Every chapter concludes with a short Web exercise.
- We have moved some material to our Web site for better currency and visualization, including hints for solving cases, a listing of key online secondary data sources, and descriptions of retail job opportunities and career ladders.
- The end papers show the Web addresses for more than 225 retailers around the globe.
- A number of "Technology in Retailing" boxes cover E-applications.
- Many cases have E-components.

A WEB SITE FOR THE 21ST CENTURY:
www.prenhall.com/bermanevans

The Web site that accompanies *Retail Management: A Strategic Approach*, Tenth Edition is a lively learning, studying, interactive tool. It is easy to use (see Appendix B for more details), provides hands-on applications, and has easy downloads and hot links. We believe the supplement will be of great value to you. It is completely revamped for the Tenth Edition and has separate student and instructor sections.

The student section of the Web site has several elements, including:

- **Important "Hot Links":** Applications broken down by chapter of *Retail Management*.
- **Career and Company Information:** Advice on résumé writing, how to take an interview, jobs in retailing, retail career ladders, and a comprehensive listing of retailers. There are "hot links" that go directly to the career sections of the Web sites of numerous retailers.
- **Study Materials:** Chapter objectives and summaries and chapter-by-chapter listings of key terms with their definitions.
- **Interactive Study Guide:** More than 1,000 questions in all. You can get page references for wrong answers, check your score, and send the results to yourself or your professor.
- **Glossary:** All of the key terms from *Retail Management* with their definitions. Terms may be accessed alphabetically through an easy-to-use search feature.
- **Web Site Directory:** Hundreds of retailing-related Web sites, divided by topic. The sites range from search engines to government agencies to retail firms to trade associations.
- **Computer-Based Exercises in Retail Management:** 16 hands-on exercises to reinforce your knowledge of key concepts. An icon in the text shows the best use for each exercise.
- **Strategic Planning Template for Retail Management**: Places the retail planning process into a series of steps that are integrated with the discussion at the end of Chapter 3. This template is built around several scenarios involving different types of retailers. Each retailer has unique strengths and weaknesses and faces a different set of opportunities and threats.
- **Web Exercises:** Dozens of user-friendly exercises. These are keyed to parts in the text and involve real company Web materials.
- **Free Downloads and Demos:** Encourage you to visit specific Web sites to gather useful information and try out innovative software.
- **Extra Math Problems:** For Chapters 9, 12, 16, and 17. These exercises help you to better understand complex retail mathematical concepts.

The instructor's section of the Web site includes teaching notes, hundreds of colorful PowerPoint slides, and a whole lot more at the password-protected section of our Web site.

ABOUT THE VIDEOS ACCOMPANYING *RETAIL MANAGEMENT*

Retail Management is accompanied by a lively video package on both VHS and DVS, which consists of 10 videos that comprise about 90 minutes of viewing. All of the videos are new to this edition. The videos involve a variety of retailers and their suppliers: American Express, DDB Worldwide, Dunkin' Donuts, Federated Direct, Hasbro, iWon.com, Marriott, Song Airlines, Starbucks, and Subaru.

FOR THE CLASSROOM

A complete teaching package is available. It includes:

- A detailed, password-protected section of our Web site devoted to instructor materials. Please visit **www.prenhall.com/bermanevans** for more details. The site contains student material, as well.
- A comprehensive, several-hundred-page instructor's manual, complete with sample syllabi, lecture notes, and a lot more.
- Hundreds of colorful PowerPoint slides.
- A large computerized test bank.
- Teaching notes on the videos noted above.
- A companion book, *Great Ideas in Retailing*, with additional cases, exercises, and more to use in the classroom with your students. Contact your local Prentice Hall representative for the ISBN.

As always, the authors have remained extremely "hands on" in the development of these instructor materials. Please feel free to send us comments regarding any aspect of *Retail Management* or its package: Barry Berman (E-mail at **mktbxb@hofstra.edu**) or Joel R. Evans (E-mail at **mktjre@hofstra.edu**), Department of Marketing and International Business, Hofstra University, Hempstead, N.Y., 11549. We promise to reply to any correspondence.

About the Authors

Barry Berman

Joel R. Evans

Barry Berman (Ph.D. in Business with majors in Marketing and Behavioral Science) is the Walter H. "Bud" Miller Distinguished Professor of Business and Professor of Marketing and International Business at Hofstra University. He is also the director of Hofstra's Executive M.B.A. program. **Joel R. Evans** (Ph.D. in Business with majors in Marketing and Public Policy) is the RMI Distinguished Professor of Business and Professor of Marketing and International Business at Hofstra University. He is also the coordinator for Hofstra's Master of Science programs in Marketing and Marketing Research.

While at Hofstra, each has been honored as a faculty inductee in Beta Gamma Sigma honor society, received multiple Dean's Awards for service, and been selected as the Teacher of the Year by the Hofstra M.B.A. Association. For several years, Drs. Berman and Evans were co-directors of Hofstra's Retail Management Institute and Business Research Institute. Both regularly teach undergraduate and graduate courses to a wide range of students.

Barry Berman and Joel R. Evans have worked together for nearly 30 years in co-authoring several best-selling texts, including *Retail Management: A Strategic Approach*, Tenth Edition. They have also consulted for a variety of clients, from "mom-and-pop" retailers to *Fortune 500* companies. They are co-founders of the American Marketing Association's Special Interest Group in Retailing and Retail Management. They have co-chaired the Academy of Marketing Science/ American Collegiate Retailing Association's triennial conference. They have been featured speakers at the annual meeting of the National Retail Federation, the world's largest retailing trade association. Each has a chapter on retailing in Dartnell's *Marketing Manager's Handbook*.

Barry and Joel are both active Web practitioners (and surfers), and they have written and developed all of the content for the comprehensive, interactive Web site that accompanies *Retail Management* (**www.prenhall.com/bermanevans**). They may be reached through the Web site or by writing to **mktbxb@hofstra.edu** (Barry Berman) and **mktjre@hofstra.edu** (Joel R. Evans).

Acknowledgments

Many people have assisted us in the preparation of this book, and to them we extend our warmest appreciation.

We thank the following reviewers, who have reacted to this or earlier editions of the text. Each has provided us with perceptive comments that have helped us to crystallize our thoughts and to make *Retail Management* the best book possible:

M. Wayne Alexander, Morehead State University

Larry Audler, University of New Orleans

Ramon Avila, Ball State University

Betty V. Balevic, Skidmore College

Stephen Batory, Bloomsburg University

Joseph J. Belonax, Western Michigan University

Ronald Bernard, Diablo Valley College

Charlane Bomrad, Onondaga Community College

John J. Buckley, Orange County Community College

David J. Burns, Youngstown State University

Joseph A. Davidson, Cuyahoga Community College

Peter T. Doukas, Westchester Community College

Blake Escudier, San Jose State University

Jack D. Eure, Jr., Southwest Texas State University

Phyllis Fein, Westchester Community College

Letty Fisher, Westchester Community College

Myron Gable, Shippensburg University

Linda L. Golden, University of Texas at Austin

James Gray, Florida Atlantic University

Barbara Gross, California State University— Northridge

J. Duncan Herrington, Radford University

Mary Higby, University of Detroit, Mercy

Terence L. Holmes, Murray State University

Charles A. Ingene, University of Mississippi

Marvin A. Jolson, University of Maryland

David C. Jones, Otterbein College

Marilyn Jones, Bond University

Carol Kaufman-Scarborough, Rutgers University

Ruth Keyes, SUNY College of Technology

Maryon King, Southern Illinois University

Stephen Kirk, East Carolina University

John Lanasa, Duquesne University

J. Ford Laumer, Jr., Auburn University

Richard C. Leventhal, Metropolitan State College

Michael Little, Virginia Commonwealth University

John Lloyd, Monroe Community College

James O. McCann, Henry Ford Community College

Frank McDaniels, Delaware County Community College

Ronald Michman, Shippensburg University

Jihye Park, Iowa State University

Howard C. Paul, Mercyhurst College

Roy B. Payne, Purdue University

Susan Peters, California State Polytechnic University, Pomona

Dawn I. Pysarchik, Michigan State University

Curtis Reierson, Baylor University

Barry Rudin, Loras College

Julie Toner Schrader, North Dakota State University

Steven J. Shaw, University of South Carolina

Ruth K. Shelton, James Madison University

Gladys S. Sherdell, Bellarmine College

Jill F. Slomski, Gannon University

John E. Swan, University of Alabama, Birmingham

Ruth Taylor, Texas State University—San Marcos

Anthony Urbanisk, Northern State University

Lillian Werner, University of Minnesota

Kaylene C. Williams, California State University, Stanislaus

Terrell G. Williams, Western Washington State University

Yingjiao Xu, Ohio University

Ugur Yucelt, Penn State University, Harrisburg

Special recognition is due to the National Retail Federation, Retail Forward, and Retail Image Consulting for their cooperation and assistance in providing career materials, case studies, and photos for this edition. We also appreciate the efforts of our Prentice Hall colleagues who have worked diligently on this edition. As always, thank you to Diane Schoenberg for the editorial assistance and Linda Berman for compiling the indexes.

Barry Berman
Joel R. Evans
HOFSTRA UNIVERSITY

An Overview of Strategic Retail Management

Welcome to *Retail Management: A Strategic Approach*, 10e. We hope you find this book to be both informative and reader-friendly. Please visit our Web site (**www.prenhall.com/bermanevans**) for interactive, useful, up-to-date features that complement the text—including chapter hot links, a study guide, and much more! The complete Web features are highlighted on the end pages of the print book.

In Part One, we explore the field of retailing, establishing and maintaining relationships, and the basic principles of strategic planning and the decisions made in owning or managing a retail business.

- **Chapter 1** describes retailing, shows why it should be studied, and examines its special characteristics. We note the value of strategic planning, including a detailed review of Target Corporation (a titan of retailing). The retailing concept is presented, along with the total retail experience, customer service, and relationship retailing. The focus and format of the text are detailed.

- **Chapter 2** looks at the complexities of retailers' relationships—with both customers and other channel members. We examine value and the value chain, customer relationships and channel relationships, the differences in relationship-building between goods and service retailers, the impact of technology on retailing relationships, and the interplay between ethical performance and relationships in retailing. The chapter ends with an appendix on planning for the unique aspects of service retailing.

- **Chapter 3** shows the usefulness of strategic planning for all kinds of retailers. We focus on the planning process: situation analysis, objectives, identifying consumers, overall strategy, specific activities, control, and feedback. We also look at the controllable and uncontrollable parts of a retail strategy. Strategic planning is shown as a series of interrelated steps that are continuously reviewed. A detailed computerized strategic planning template, available at our Web site, is described. At the end of the chapter, there is an appendix on the strategic implications of global retailing.

Chapter 1
AN INTRODUCTION TO RETAILING

A perfect example of a dream come true is the story of Sam Walton, the founder of Wal-Mart (**www.walmart.com**). From a single store, Wal-Mart has grown to become the largest company in the United States in terms of revenues. And today it dwarfs every other retailer. In 2005, Wal-Mart was rated as one of America's top five most admired corporations by *Fortune* magazine.

Reprinted by permission.

As a store owner in Bentonville, Arkansas, Sam Walton had a simple strategy: to take his retail stores to rural areas of the United States and then sell goods at the lowest prices around. Sam was convinced that a large discount format would work in rural communities. Wal-Mart's strategy is based on everyday low prices (which reduces its advertising costs), having the lowest prices on 1,500 key items, and on a low-cost distribution system (based on scanning and a satellite communications system).

Walton's first discount store opened in 1962 and used such slogans as "We sell for less" and "Satisfaction guaranteed," two of the retailer's current hallmarks. By the end of 1969, Wal-Mart had expanded to 31 locations. Within a year, Wal-Mart became a public corporation and rapidly grew on the basis of additional discount stores and global expansion. Wal-Mart has become a true textbook example of how a retailer can maintain growth without losing sight of its original core values of low overhead, the use of innovative distribution systems, and customer orientation—whereby employees swear to serve the customer. "So help me, Sam."[1]

chapter objectives

1. To define retailing, consider it from various perspectives, demonstrate its impact, and note its special characteristics
2. To introduce the concept of strategic planning and apply it
3. To show why the retailing concept is the foundation of a successful business, with an emphasis on the total retail experience, customer service, and relationship retailing
4. To indicate the focus and format of the text

OVERVIEW

Retailing encompasses the business activities involved in selling goods and services to consumers for their personal, family, or household use. It includes every sale to the *final* consumer—ranging from cars to apparel to meals at restaurants to movie tickets. Retailing is the last stage in the distribution process.

Retailing today is at a fascinating crossroads. On the one hand, retail sales are at their highest point in history. Wal-Mart is now the leading company in the world in terms of sales—ahead of ExxonMobil, General Motors, and other manufacturing giants. New technologies are improving retail productivity. There are lots of opportunities to start a new retail business—or work for an existing one—and to become a franchisee. Global retailing possibilities abound. On the other hand, retailers face numerous challenges. Many consumers are bored with shopping or do not have much time for it. Some locales have too many stores, and retailers often spur one another into frequent price cutting (and low profit margins). Customer service expectations are high at a time when more retailers offer self-service and automated systems. At the same time, some retailers remain unsure what to do with the Web; they are still grappling with the emphasis to place on image enhancement, customer information and feedback, and sales transactions.

These are the key issues that retailers must resolve: "How can we best serve our customers while earning a fair profit?" "How can we stand out in a highly competitive environment where consumers have so many choices?" "How can we grow our business while retaining a core of loyal customers?" Our point of view: Retail decision makers can best address these questions by fully understanding and applying the basic principles of retailing in a well-structured, systematic, and focused retail strategy. That is the philosophy behind *Retail Management: A Strategic Approach.*

Can retailers flourish in today's tough marketplace? You bet! Just look at your favorite restaurant, gift shop, and food store. Look at the growth of Costco, Starbucks, and Lowe's. What do they have in common? A desire to please the customer and a strong market niche. To prosper in the long term, they all need a strategic plan and a willingness to adapt, both central thrusts of this book. See Figure 1-1.

Visit Lowe's Web site (www.lowes.com) and see what drives one of the world's "hot" retailers.

FIGURE 1-1
Boom Times for Lowe's

Lowe's has been very successful with its enhanced focus on women, a neglected segment in the home improvement business.

Photo reprinted by permission of Susan Berry, Retail Image Consulting, Inc.

In Chapter 1, we look at the framework of retailing, the importance of developing and applying a sound retail strategy, and the focus and format of the text.

THE FRAMEWORK OF RETAILING

To better appreciate retailing's role and the range of retailing activities, let us view it from three different perspectives:

- Suppose we manage a manufacturing firm that makes vacuum cleaners. How should we sell these items? We could distribute via big chains such as Best Buy or small neighborhood appliance stores, have our own sales force visit people in their homes (as Aerus—formerly Electrolux—does), or set up our own stores (if we have the ability and resources to do so). We could sponsor TV infomercials or magazine ads, complete with a toll-free phone number.

- Suppose we have an idea for a new way to teach first graders how to use computer software for spelling and vocabulary. How should we implement this idea? We could lease a store in a strip shopping center and run ads in a local paper, rent space in a Y and rely on teacher referrals, or do mailings to parents and visit children in their homes. In each case, the service is offered "live." But there is another option: We could use an animated Web site to teach children online.

- Suppose that we, as consumers, want to buy apparel. What choices do we have? We could go to a department store or an apparel store. We could shop with a full-service retailer or a discounter. We could go to a shopping center or order from a catalog. We could look to retailers that carry a wide range of clothing (from outerwear to jeans to suits) or look to firms that specialize in one clothing category (such as leather coats). We could surf around the Web and visit retailers around the globe.

Service businesses such as Lawn Doctor (www.lawndoctor.com) often engage in retailing.

There is a tendency to think of retailing as primarily involving the sale of tangible (physical) goods. However, retailing also includes the sale of services. And this is a big part of retailing! A service may be the shopper's primary purchase (such as a haircut) or it may be part of the shopper's purchase of a good (such as furniture delivery). Retailing does not have to involve a store. Mail and phone orders, direct selling to consumers in their homes and offices, Web transactions, and vending machine sales all fall within the scope of retailing. Retailing does not even have to include a "retailer." Manufacturers, importers, nonprofit firms, and wholesalers act as retailers when they sell to final consumers.

Let us now examine various reasons for studying retailing and its special characteristics.

Reasons for Studying Retailing

Learn more about the exciting array of retailing career opportunities (www.allretailjobs.com).

Retailing is an important field to study because of its impact on the economy, its functions in distribution, and its relationship with firms selling goods and services to retailers for their resale or use. These factors are discussed next. A fourth factor for students of retailing is the broad range of career opportunities, as highlighted with a "Careers in Retailing" box in each chapter, Appendix A at the end of this book, and our Web site (www.prenhall.com/bermanevans). See Figure 1-2.

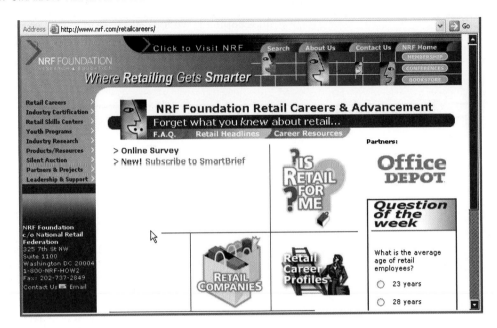

The Impact of Retailing on the Economy

Retailing is a major part of U.S. and world commerce. Retail sales and employment are vital economic contributors, and retail trends often mirror trends in a nation's overall economy.

According to the Department of Commerce, annual U.S. retail store sales exceed $4 trillion—representing one-third of the total economy. Telephone and mail-order sales by nonstore retailers, vending machines, direct selling, and the Web generate hundreds of billions of dollars in additional yearly revenues. And personal consumption expenditures on financial, medical, legal, educational, and other services account for another several hundred billion dollars in annual retail revenues. Outside the United States, retail sales are several trillions of dollars per year.

Careers in RETAILING
The Tremendous Opportunities in Retailing

In each chapter of *Retail Management*, career material from the National Retail Federation (NRF) is presented. Included are an overview of retailing careers, illustrative retail career profiles (Chapters 2–7), and specific kinds of retailing jobs (Chapters 8–20). At the NRF's Web site (**www.nrf.com/retailcareers**), a wealth of additional information may also be found.

Retailing offers perhaps the greatest variety of opportunities for ambitious and hardworking employees. Some of the major retail career areas are marketing and advertising; store operations; loss prevention; store management; finance; human resources; IT and E-commerce; sales and sales related; distribution, logistics, and supply chain management; merchandise planning and buying; entrepreneurship; and retail industry support.

Career paths in the dynamic, expanding retail industry are exciting, varied, and lucrative. At the store level alone, a general manager of a department store oversees an average sales volume of $25 million to $30 million and employs an average of 150 people. Average department store manager salaries start at $80,000 and exceed $100,000. Most retail companies encourage employees at all levels of the company, even management and corporate employees, to have solid, store-level (i.e., sales associate) experience. Some even require it. And, most of the skills you are using to succeed as a sales associate are needed as you move up the ladder—skills such as: problem solving and decision making, teamwork, dedication to courtesy and customer service, "people skills" (the ability to interact effectively with different personalities), good work ethic and reliability, enthusiasm and initiative, cross-cultural awareness, and communication skills (listening, speaking, and writing).

Source: Reprinted by permission of the National Retail Federation.

Durable goods stores—including motor vehicles and parts dealers; furniture, home furnishings, electronics, and appliances stores; and building materials and hardware stores—make up 38 percent of U.S. retail store sales. Nondurable goods and services stores—including general merchandise stores; food and beverage stores; health and personal care stores; gasoline stations; clothing and accessories stores; sporting goods, hobby, book, and music stores; eating and drinking places; and miscellaneous retailers—together account for 62 percent of U.S. retail store sales.

The world's 100 largest retailers generate more than $2.4 trillion in annual revenues. They represent 17 nations. Forty-three of the 100 are based in the United States, 12 in Great Britain, 9 in France, 9 in Germany, and 9 in Japan.[2] Table 1-1 shows the 10 largest U.S. retailers. In 2004, they produced more than $700 billion in sales, operated about 25,000 stores, and had 3.5 million employees. Visit our Web site for links to a lot of current information on retailing (**www.prenhall.com/bermanevans**).

The *Occupational Outlook Handbook* (**www.bls.gov/oco**) is a great source of information on employment trends.

Retailing is a major source of jobs. In the United States alone, 25 million people—about one-sixth of the total labor force—work for traditional retailers (including food and beverage places). Yet this figure understates the true number of people who work in retailing because it does not include the several million persons employed by service firms, seasonal employees, proprietors, and unreported workers in family businesses or partnerships.

From a cost perspective, retailing is a significant field of study. In the United States, on average, 30 cents of every dollar spent in department stores, 44 cents spent in furniture and home furnishings stores, and 28 cents spent in grocery stores go to the retailers to cover operating costs, activities performed, and profits. Costs include rent, displays, wages, ads, and maintenance. Only a small part of each dollar is profit. In 2004, the 10 largest U.S. retailers' after-tax profits averaged

TABLE 1-1		The 10 Largest Retailers in the United States					
Rank	Company	Web Address	Major Retail Emphasis	2004 Sales (millions)	2004 After-Tax Earnings (millions)	2005 Number of Stores	2005 Number of Employees
1	Wal-Mart	www.walmart.com	Full-line discount stores, supercenters, membership clubs	$289,189	$10,267	5,200+	1,500,000+
2	Home Depot	www.homedepot.com	Home centers, design centers	73,094	5,001	1,800+	300,000+
3	Kroger	www.kroger.com	Supermarkets, convenience stores, jewelry stores	56,434	(128)	3,800+	290,000+
4	Target	www.target.com	Full-line discount stores, supercenters	49,934	3,198	1,350+	295,000+
5	Costco	www.costco.com	Membership clubs	48,107	882	450+	110,000+
6	Albertson's	www.albertsons.com	Supermarkets, drugstores	40,052	444	2,300+	230,000+
7	Walgreens	www.walgreens.com	Drugstores	37,508	1,350	4,750+	160,000+
8	Lowe's	www.lowes.com	Home centers	36,464	2,176	1,100+	160,000+
9	Sears Roebuck	www.sears.com	Department stores, specialty stores	36,099	(507)	2,400+	240,000+
10	Safeway	www.safeway.com	Supermarkets	35,823	560	1,800+	190,000+

Sources: "Largest U.S. Corporations," *Fortune* (April 18, 2005); and company annual reports.

FIGURE 1-3
The High Costs and Low Profits of Retailing—Where the Typical $100 Spent with Walgreens Went in 2004

Source: Computed by the authors from *Walgreens 2004 Annual Report*.

Manufacturer's costs and profits	Retailer's operating, personnel, advertising, and other costs	Retailer's income taxes	Retailer's after-tax profits
$72.75	$21.50	$2.15	$3.60

3.3 percent of sales.[3] Figure 1-3 shows costs and profits for Walgreens, a drugstore chain.

Retail Functions in Distribution

Retailing is the last stage in a **channel of distribution**—all of the businesses and people involved in the physical movement and transfer of ownership of goods and services from producer to consumer. A typical distribution channel is shown in Figure 1-4. Retailers often act as the contact between manufacturers, wholesalers, and the consumer. Many manufacturers would like to make one basic type of item and sell their entire inventory to as few buyers as possible, but consumers usually want to choose from a variety of goods and services and purchase a limited quantity. Retailers collect an assortment from various sources, buy in large quantity, and sell in small amounts. This is the **sorting process**. See Figure 1-5.

Another job for retailers is communicating both with customers and with manufacturers and wholesalers. Shoppers learn about the availability and characteristics of goods and services, store hours, sales, and so on from retailer ads, salespeople, and displays. Manufacturers and wholesalers are informed by their retailers with regard to sales forecasts, delivery delays, customer complaints, defective items, inventory turnover, and more. Many goods and services have been modified due to retailer feedback.

For small suppliers, retailers can provide assistance by transporting, storing, marking, advertising, and pre-paying for products. Small retailers may need the same type of help from their suppliers. The tasks performed by retailers affect the percentage of each sales dollar they need to cover costs and profits.

Retailers also complete transactions with customers. This means having convenient locations, filling orders promptly and accurately, and processing

FIGURE 1-4
A Typical Channel of Distribution

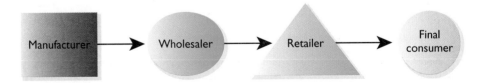

FIGURE 1-5
The Retailer's Role in the
Sorting Process

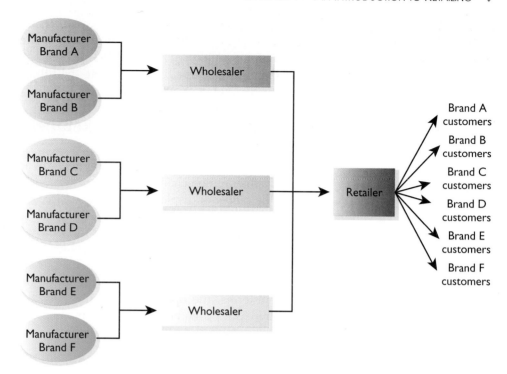

credit purchases. Some retailers also provide customer services such as gift wrapping, delivery, and installation. To make themselves even more appealing, many firms now engage in **multi-channel retailing**, whereby a retailer sells to consumers through multiple retail formats (points of contact). Most large retailers operate both physical stores and Web sites to make shopping easier and to accommodate consumer desires. Some firms even sell to customers through retail stores, mail-order catalogs, a Web site, and a toll-free phone number. See Figure 1-6.

For these reasons, products are usually sold through retailers not owned by manufacturers (wholesalers). This lets the manufacturers reach more customers,

FIGURE 1-6
Brooks Brothers and Multi-Channel Retailing

Brooks Brothers clothing can be purchased at its stores in shopping centers, through its Web site (**www.brooksbrothers. com**), and at its outlet stores—such as the one shown here. This makes it quite convenient for customers.

Photo reprinted by permission.

Sherwin-Williams (www.sherwin-williams. com) is not only a designer but also a retailer.

reduce costs, improve cash flow, increase sales more rapidly, and focus on their area of expertise. Select manufacturers such as Sherwin-Williams and Polo Ralph Lauren do operate retail facilities (besides selling at traditional retailers). In running their stores, these firms complete the full range of retailing functions and compete with conventional retailers.

The Relationships Among Retailers and Their Suppliers

Relationships among retailers and suppliers can be complex. Because retailers are part of a distribution channel, manufacturers and wholesalers must be concerned about the caliber of displays, customer service, store hours, and retailers' reliability as business partners. Retailers are also major customers of goods and services for resale, store fixtures, computers, management consulting, and insurance.

These are some issues over which retailers and suppliers have different priorities: control over the distribution channel, profit allocation, the number of competing retailers handling suppliers' products, product displays, promotion support, payment terms, and operating flexibility. Due to the growth of chains, retailers have more power than ever. Unless suppliers know retailers' needs, they cannot have good rapport with them; and as long as retailers have a choice of suppliers, they will pick those that offer more.

Channel relations tend to be smoothest with **exclusive distribution**, whereby suppliers make agreements with one or a few retailers that designate the latter as the only ones in specified geographic areas to carry certain brands or products. This stimulates both parties to work together to maintain an image, assign shelf space, allot profits and costs, and advertise. It also usually requires that retailers limit their brand selection in the specified product lines; they might have to decline to handle other suppliers' brands. From the manufacturers' perspective, exclusive distribution may limit their long-run total sales.

Channel relations tend to be most volatile with **intensive distribution**, whereby suppliers sell through as many retailers as possible. This often maximizes suppliers' sales and lets retailers offer many brands and product versions.

FIGURE 1-7
Comparing Exclusive, Intensive, and Selective Distribution

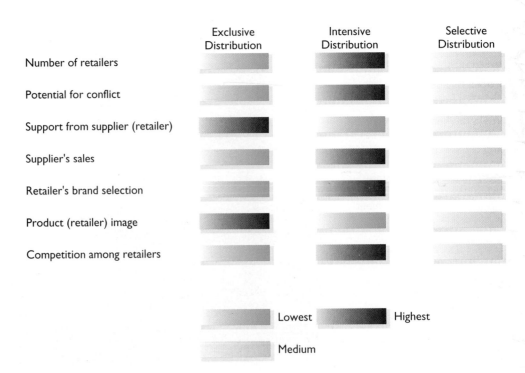

RETAILING
Around the World   Upscale Retailer Slowly Enters China

Even though there is no Louis Vuitton (**www.vuitton.com**) store in either Philadelphia or Nashville, the luxury leather goods retailer just opened its 338th boutique in Qingdao, a Chinese sea resort. According to some market analysts, the China market may become the new Japan. While Japanese consumers account for approximately 41 percent of global luxury sales, the Chinese (including residents of Hong Kong) already account for 12 percent. A Goldman Sachs analyst predicts that the Chinese will account for one-fifth of total luxury sales by 2008 and become as important as the Japanese market by 2015.

Since there are no glossy magazines in China, Vuitton used a touring exhibition on the history of luxury goods to build awareness for its brand when it first entered the Chinese market. Later, Vuitton sponsored a five-day classic car China Run from Dalian to Beijing, which attracted over 6 million people.

Giorgio Armani (**www.giorgioarmani.com**) already has several stores in China and plans a total of 30 as of 2008. Prada (**www.prada.com**) planned to have 13 stores in China by the end of 2005.

Source: Sarah Raper Larenaudie, "Luxury for the People!" *Time Style & Design* (Spring 2005).

Competition among retailers selling the same items is high; and retailers may use tactics not beneficial to individual suppliers, as they are more concerned about their own results. Retailers may assign little shelf space to specific brands, set very high prices on them, and not advertise them.

With **selective distribution**, suppliers sell through a moderate number of retailers. This combines aspects of exclusive and intensive distribution. Suppliers have higher sales than in exclusive distribution, and retailers carry some competing brands. It encourages suppliers to provide some marketing support and retailers to give adequate shelf space. See Figure 1-7.

The Special Characteristics of Retailing

Three factors that distinguish retailing from other types of business are noted in Figure 1-8 and discussed here. Each factor imposes unique requirements on retail firms.

The average amount of a sales transaction for retailers is much less than for manufacturers. The average sales transaction per shopping trip is well under $100 for department stores, specialty stores, and supermarkets. This low amount creates a need to tightly control the costs associated with each transaction (such as credit verification, sales personnel, and bagging); to maximize the number of customers drawn

FIGURE 1-8
Special Characteristics
Affecting Retailers

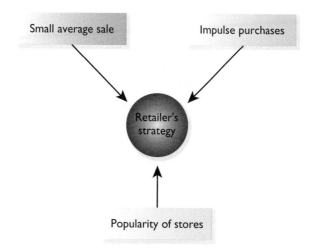

to the retailer, which may place more emphasis on ads and special promotions; and to increase impulse sales by more aggressive selling. However, cost control can be tough. For instance, inventory management is often expensive due to the many small transactions to a large number of customers. A typical supermarket has several thousand customer transactions *per week*, which makes it harder to find the proper in-stock level and product selection. Thus, retailers are expanding their use of computerized inventory systems.

Final consumers make many unplanned or impulse purchases. Surveys show that a large percentage of consumers do not look at ads before shopping, do not prepare shopping lists (or deviate from the lists once in stores), and make fully unplanned purchases. This behavior indicates the value of in-store displays, attractive store layouts, and well-organized stores, catalogs, and Web sites. Candy, cosmetics, snack foods, magazines, and other items are sold as impulse goods when placed in visible, high-traffic areas in a store, catalog, or Web site. Because so many purchases are unplanned, the retailer's ability to forecast, budget, order merchandise, and have sufficient personnel on the selling floor is more difficult.

Bloomingdale's (**www.bloomingdales.com**) has a Web site to accompany its traditional stores and catalogs.

Retail customers usually visit a store, even though mail, phone, and web sales have increased. Despite the inroads made by nonstore retailers, most retail transactions are still conducted in stores—and will continue to be in the future. Many people like to shop in person; want to touch, smell, and/or try on products; like to browse for unplanned purchases; feel more comfortable taking a purchase home with them than waiting for a delivery; and desire privacy while at home. This store-based shopping orientation has implications for retailers; they must work to attract shoppers to stores and consider such factors as store location, transportation, store hours, proximity of competitors, product selection, parking, and ads.

THE IMPORTANCE OF DEVELOPING AND APPLYING A RETAIL STRATEGY

A **retail strategy** is the overall plan guiding a retail firm. It influences the firm's business activities and its response to market forces, such as competition and the economy. Any retailer, regardless of size or type, should utilize these six steps in strategic planning:

1. Define the type of business in terms of the goods or service category and the company's specific orientation (such as full service or "no frills").
2. Set long-run and short-run objectives for sales and profit, market share, image, and so on.
3. Determine the customer market to target on the basis of its characteristics (such as gender and income level) and needs (such as product and brand preferences).
4. Devise an overall, long-run plan that gives general direction to the firm and its employees.
5. Implement an integrated strategy that combines such factors as store location, product assortment, pricing, and advertising and displays to achieve objectives.
6. Regularly evaluate performance and correct weaknesses or problems when observed.

To illustrate these points, the background and strategy of Target Stores—one of the world's foremost retailers—are presented. Then the retailing concept is explained and applied.

Target Stores: The Successful Saga of an Upscale Discounter![4]

Company Background

See the mass/class approach of Target Stores (**www.target.com**).

Target Stores is the leading division of Target Corporation. A brief history of Target Stores appears at its Web site (**www.target.com**):

> Unlike most other mass merchandisers, we have department store roots. Back in 1961, Dayton's department store identified a demand for a store that sold less expensive goods in a quick, convenient format. Target was born. In 1962, the first Target store opened in Roseville, Minnesota. We were the first retail store to offer well-known national brands at discounted prices. We paved new ground by implementing electronic cash registers storewide to monitor inventory and speed up guest service. We also began hosting an annual shopping event for seniors and people with disabilities, plus a toy safety campaign. Opening new stores all the time, we rolled out electronic scanning nationwide. In the 1990s, we launched our first Target Greatland store. Our Club Wedd bridal gift registry went nationwide in 1995, and Lullaby Club soon followed. We next opened our first SuperTarget store, which combined groceries and special services with a Target Greatland store. We introduced our credit card, the Target Guest Card.

After divesting itself of the underperforming Mervyn's and Marshall Field's chains, today Target Corporation "is an upscale discounter that provides quality merchandise at attractive prices in clean, spacious, and guest-friendly stores" through its various Target Stores and its Target.com Web site. Target Corporation has nearly 1,400 stores in 47 states with almost 300,000 employees. Besides operating a popular Web shopping site of its own, the firm is a partner of Amazon.com. Target Corporation is the fourth largest U.S. retailer (in terms of revenues).

The Target Stores' Strategy: Keys to Success

Throughout its existence, Target Stores has adhered to a consistent, far-sighted, customer-oriented strategy—one that has paved the way for its long-term achievements:

- *Growth-oriented objectives.* "Target Corporation has long been guided by principles that are designed to enhance our long-term financial performance and we remain steadfastly committed to strategies that fuel consistent growth and profitable market share gains. We believe that by managing our business like this, we can continue to deliver average annual growth in earnings per share of 15 percent or more over time and generate substantial value for our shareholders."

- *Appeal to a prime market.* The firm is strong with middle-income, well-educated adults, who have an average income that is about 20 percent higher than the typical Wal-Mart shopper. It is quite popular among female shoppers, parents with children under 18, and 25- to 54-year-olds.

FIGURE 1-9

"Pay Less + Expect More" at Target

This very successful chain projects a strong image through a combination of low prices and plentiful, quality merchandise.

Photo reprinted by permission of Susan Berry, Retail Image Consulting, Inc.

- *Distinctive company image.* Target Stores has done a superb job of positioning itself: "Pay Less + Expect More." See Figure 1-9. It is a true discount department store chain with everyday low prices. Along with Wal-Mart and Kmart, Target Stores makes up the "big three" of discounting. It has linoleum floors, shopping carts, and a simple store layout. But Target is also perceived as an "upscale discounter." It carries products from such designers as Mossimo (apparel), Isaac Mizrahi (apparel and home products), Michael Graves (home products), Liz Lange (maternity clothes), and Amy Coe (baby's nursery).

- *Focus.* The chain never loses sight of its discount store niche: "Our strategic direction at Target is clear: to continue to delight our guests with differentiated merchandising and exceptional value while we continue to invest in our technology and leverage our resources throughout our organization to enhance our performance."

- *Strong customer service for its retail category.* The firm prides itself on offering excellent customer service for a discount store. For example, at the end of many aisles, there is a red service phone so shoppers can check a price or ask a question.

- *Multiple points of contact.* Target reaches its customers through extensive advertising, stores in 47 states, a toll-free telephone service center (open 7 days a week, 17 hours per day), and a Web site.

- *Employee relations.* These are some of the awards recently won by Target: "Top 30 Companies for Executive Women" by the National Association for Female Executives, "Best for Latinas" in *Latina Style* magazine's "50 Best Companies for Latinas," "Top Work Place for Women" in *Working Mother* magazine's "100 Best Companies for Working Women," "100 Best Corporate Citizens" by *Business Ethics* magazine (for diversity efforts), and "Top in Training" in *Training* magazine's "Training Top 100" list.

- *Innovation.* The firm "has long embraced the concepts of innovation and newness, recognizing the importance of creating unique ways to delight our guests every time they visit our stores."

- *Commitment to technology.* Target is devoted to new technologies. Consider the Target Visa card: It "has a built-in computer chip, called a smart chip. Today, you can use your Target Visa with an in-home smart card reader to access exclusive offers. And soon, you'll see exciting new smart chip features popping up! The chip makes the Target Visa smart."
- *Community involvement.* Target believes in giving back. One of its popular programs is School Fundraising: "You can support your school just by shopping with your Target Visa or Target Guest Card. Target will donate an amount equal to one percent of your qualifying purchases at Target Stores or target.com to the eligible K–12 school of your choice."
- *Constantly monitoring performance.* Two years ago, Target sold off two divisions: "Both Marshall Field's and Mervyn's were saddled with declining sales and most experts believed Target would be better off getting rid of both and flying solo." Today, "Target is on its own with a lighter load and more free cash after selling the two chains for a total of $4.9 billion."

The Retailing Concept

As we just described, Target Stores has a sincere long-term desire to please customers. In doing so, it uses a customer-centered, chainwide approach to strategy development and implementation; it is value-driven; and it has clear goals. Together, these four principles form the **retailing concept** (depicted in Figure 1-10), which should be understood and applied by all retailers:

1. *Customer orientation.* The retailer determines the attributes and needs of its customers and endeavors to satisfy these needs to the fullest.
2. *Coordinated effort.* The retailer integrates all plans and activities to maximize efficiency.
3. *Value-driven.* The retailer offers good value to customers, whether it be upscale or discount. This means having prices appropriate for the level of products and customer service.
4. *Goal orientation.* The retailer sets goals and then uses its strategy to attain them.

Unfortunately, this concept is not grasped by every retailer. Some are indifferent to customer needs, plan haphazardly, have prices that do not reflect the value offered, and have unclear goals. Some are not receptive to change, or they blindly

FIGURE 1-10
Applying the Retailing Concept

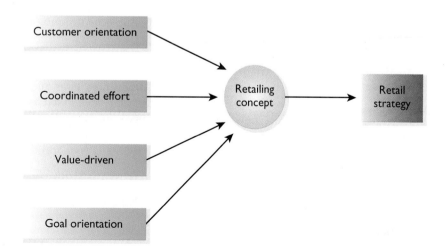

follow strategies enacted by competitors. Some do not get feedback from customers; they rely on supplier reports or their own past sales trends.

The retailing concept is straightforward. It means communicating with shoppers and viewing their desires as critical to the firm's success, having a consistent strategy (such as offering designer brands, plentiful sales personnel, attractive displays, and above-average prices in an upscale store), offering prices perceived as "fair" (a good value for the money) by customers, and working to achieve meaningful, specific, and reachable goals. However, the retailing concept is only a strategic guide. It does not deal with a firm's internal capabilities or competitive advantages but offers a broad planning framework.

Let's look at three issues that relate to a retailer's performance in terms of the retailing concept: the total retail experience, customer service, and relationship retailing.

The Total Retail Experience

While one consumer may shop at a discount retailer, another at a neighborhood store, and a third at a full-service firm, these diverse customers all have something crucial in common: They each encounter a total retail experience (including everything from parking to checkout counter) in making a purchase. According to the director of IBM's global retail consulting practice, "Consumers are clearly telling retailers that they want a personalized and interactive shopping experience. They want immediate access to promotions based on past purchases and loyalty, as well as precise details on product availability or items that are out-of-stock. They also want helpful sales associates, fast service, and a store that is easy to shop, sometimes even more than they want low prices."[5]

The **total retail experience** includes all the elements in a retail offering that encourage or inhibit consumers during their contact with a retailer. Many elements, such as the number of salespeople, displays, prices, the brands carried, and inventory on hand, are controllable by a retailer; others, such as the adequacy of on-street parking, the speed of a consumer's modem, and sales taxes, are not. If some part of the total retail experience is unsatisfactory, consumers may not make a purchase—they may even decide not to patronize a retailer again: "Recently, I was in a store and couldn't find my charge card fast enough to apparently make

Ethics in RETAILING
McDonald's Introduces a More Well-Rounded Menu

McDonald's (**www.mcdonalds.com**) now offers sliced apples, called Apple Dippers, as an alternative to french fries in its Happy Meals. McDonald's has also recently added a line of premium salads and a specialty salad consisting of grapes, walnuts, and apples to its menu. While McDonald's has offered salads on its menu since the late 1980s, these new salads are among its most successful new products in the past 10 years.

The company hopes that the healthy new menu additions will reduce criticism that McDonald's offers fat- and salt-laden foods to an unsuspecting public, including small children. What remains to be seen is the extent to which these healthier alternatives result in positive changes in consumer tastes.

Implementing the healthy options menu items has not been easy. Although a large percentage of consumers say they want healthy foods, less than 10 percent of McDonald's customers actually buy the salads. The healthy items are also more costly for McDonald's to purchase, as well as to store. The apple dippers and salads, for example, must be delivered several times per week to be fresh since McDonald's does not use any preservatives or additives in these items.

Sources: Melanie Warner, "You Want Any Fruit with That Big Mac?" *New York Times* (February 20, 2005); and "Fruit & Walnut Salad," **www. mcdonalds.com/usa/eat/features/fruitnwalnut.html** (November 19, 2005).

my clerk happy. As I searched through my wallet, I apologized for the delay—apologized several times. All the while she was visibly annoyed with my lack of organization and remained unresponsive to my conversation. My experience with that store was impacted by this salesperson. Her bad attitude could easily translate into a substantial loss of revenue for the store. She wasn't the owner, and her behavior may not have reflected the attitude of the management, but the fact remains, she does represent the management."[6]

In planning its strategy, a retailer must be sure that all strategic elements are in place. *For the shopper segment to which it appeals*, the total retail experience must be aimed at fulfilling that segment's expectations. A discounter should have ample stock on hand when it runs sales but not plush carpeting; and a full-service store should have superior personnel but not have them perceived as haughty by customers. Various retailers have not learned this lesson, which is why some theme restaurants are in trouble. The novelty has worn off, and many people believe the food is only fair while prices are high.

A big challenge for retailers is generating customer "excitement" because many people are bored with shopping or have little time for it. Here is what one retailer, highlighted in Figure 1-11, is doing:

Build-A-Bear Workshop (**www.buildabear.com**) even offers a great online shopping experience.

Build-A-Bear Workshop is a unique and exceptional approach to the entertainment retail industry. The teddy bear theme is carried throughout the store with original teddy bear fixtures, murals, and artwork. The store associates, known as master Bear Builder associates, share the experience with Guests at each phase of the bear-making process. Regardless of age, Guests enjoy the highly visual environment, the sounds, and the fantasy of this special place while they create a memory with their friends and family. Guests who visit a Build-A-Bear Workshop store enter a lighthearted teddy-bear-themed environment consisting of eight bear-making stations: Choose Me, Hear Me (sounds), Stuff Me and Heart Stuff, Stitch Me, Fluff Me, Name Me, Dress Me, and Take Me Home.[7]

FIGURE 1-11
Eliminating Shopper Boredom

Shopper interactivity and involvement at Build-A-Bear Workshop make this chain a fun place to shop.

Photo reprinted by permission of Retail Forward, Inc.

Customer Service

Customer service refers to the identifiable, but sometimes intangible, activities undertaken by a retailer in conjunction with the basic goods and services it sells. It has a strong impact on the total retail experience. Among the factors comprising a customer service strategy are store hours, parking, shopper friendliness of the store layout, credit acceptance, salespeople, amenities such as gift wrapping, rest rooms, employee politeness, delivery policies, the time shoppers spend on check-out lines, and customer follow-up. This list is not all inclusive, and it differs in terms of the retail strategy undertaken. Customer service is discussed further in Chapter 2, "Building and Sustaining Relationships in Retailing."

At L.L. Bean (www.llbean.com), customer service means satisfaction is guaranteed. 100%.

Satisfaction with customer service is affected by expectations (based on the type of retailer) and past experience, and people's assessment of customer service depends on their perceptions—not necessarily reality. Different people may evaluate the same service quite differently. The same person may even rate a firm's customer service differently over time due to its intangibility, though the service stays constant:

> Costco shoppers don't expect anyone to help them to their car with bundles of commodities. Teens at Abercrombie & Fitch would be pretty turned off if a tuxedo clad piano player serenaded them while they shopped. And Wal-Mart customers would protest loudly if the company traded its shopping carts for oversized nylon tote bags. On the other hand, helping shoppers to their cars when they have an oversized purchase is part of the service package at P.C. Richard & Sons, piano music sets the mood at Nordstrom, and nylon totes jammed full of value-priced apparel are in sync with the Old Navy image. Service varies widely from one retailer to the next, and from one shopping channel to the next. The challenge for retailers is to ask shoppers what they expect in the way of service, listen to what they say, and then make every attempt to satisfy them.[8]

Interestingly, despite a desire to provide excellent customer service, a number of outstanding retailers now wonder if "the customer is always right." Are there limits? Ponder this scenario: Companies such as Home Depot, Saks Fifth Avenue, and Old Navy are among those that have tightened their return policies. Furthermore, "Burlington Coat Factory gives only store credit, not cash, when accepting any kind of return. Don't have a receipt? Then you can't get cash or store credit at Kmart stores. Changed your mind about your new laptop? You're stuck with it after 14 days at Circuit City. Returning 20 pieces of clothing you bought at Express in a week? You may be stuck with all of it when your return is 'declined.'" Why the policy change? About 6 percent of retail purchases are returned annually.[9]

Relationship Retailing

As with the retailers profiled in this book, we want to engage in relationship retailing. So please visit our Web site (www.prenhall.com/bermanevans).

The best retailers know it is in their interest to engage in **relationship retailing**, whereby they seek to establish and maintain long-term bonds with customers, rather than act as if each sales transaction is a completely new encounter. This means concentrating on the total retail experience, monitoring satisfaction with customer service, and staying in touch with customers. Figure 1-12 shows a customer respect checklist that retailers could use to assess their relationship efforts.

To be effective in relationship retailing, a firm should keep two points in mind: (1) Because it is harder to lure new customers than to make existing ones happy, a "win-win" approach is critical. For a retailer to "win" in the long run

FIGURE 1-12
A Customer Respect
Checklist

Source: Adapted by the authors
from Leonard L. Berry, "Retailers
with a Future," *Marketing
Management* (Spring 1996), p. 43.
Reprinted by permission of the
American Marketing Association.

✓ Do we trust our customers?

✓ Do we stand behind what we sell? Are we easy to deal with if a customer has a problem? Are frontline workers empowered to respond properly to a problem? Do we guarantee what we sell?

✓ Is keeping commitments to customers—from being in stock on advertised goods to being on time for appointments—important in our company?

✓ Do we value customer time? Are our facilities and service systems convenient and efficient for customers to use? Do we teach employees that serving customers supersedes all other priorities, such as paperwork or stocking shelves?

✓ Do we communicate with customers respectfully? Are signs informative and helpful? Is advertising above reproach in truthfulness and taste? Are contact personnel professional? Do we answer and return calls promptly—with a smile in our voice? Is our voice mail caller-friendly?

✓ Do we treat all customers with respect, regardless of their appearance, age, race, gender, status, or size of purchase or account? Have we taken any special precautions to minimize discriminatory treatment of certain customers?

✓ Do we thank customers for their business? Do we say "thank you" at times other than after a purchase?

✓ Do we respect employees? Do employees, who are expected to respect customers, get respectful treatment themselves?

(attract shoppers, make sales, earn profits), the customer must also "win" in the long run (receive good value, be treated with respect, feel welcome by the firm). Otherwise, that retailer loses (shoppers patronize competitors) and customers lose (by spending time and money to learn about other retailers). (2) Due to the advances in computer technology, it is now much easier to develop a customer database with information on people's attributes and past shopping behavior. Ongoing customer contact can be better, more frequent, and more focused. This topic is covered further in Chapter 2, "Building and Sustaining Relationships in Retailing."

THE FOCUS AND FORMAT OF THE TEXT

There are various approaches to the study of retailing: an institutional approach, which describes the types of retailers and their development; a functional approach, which concentrates on the activities that retailers perform (such as buying, pricing, and personnel practices); and a strategic approach, which centers on defining the retail business, setting objectives, appealing to an appropriate customer market, developing an overall plan, implementing an integrated strategy, and regularly reviewing operations.

We will study retailing from each perspective but center on a *strategic approach*. Our basic premise is that the retailer has to plan for and adapt to a complex, changing environment. Both opportunities and threats must be considered. By engaging in strategic retail management, the retailer is encouraged to study competitors, suppliers, economic factors, consumer changes, marketplace trends, legal restrictions, and other elements. A firm prospers if its competitive strengths match the opportunities in the environment, weaknesses are eliminated or minimized, and plans look to the future (as well as the past).

Technology in RETAILING — Lillian Vernon: Keeping Things Running 24/7

For Lillian Vernon, any downtime on its Web site (**www.lillianvernon.com**) can be quite detrimental as the site accounts for 40 percent of the firm's total retail sales. According to Ellis Admire, Lillian Vernon's director of emerging technology, "We can't afford for our Web store to go down for even a few minutes."

Until recently, Lillian Vernon monitored its Web site with load-testing software that simulated the effect of a large number of Lillian Vernon customers accessing the site at one time. Now, Lillian Vernon is able to constantly assess its Web site's performance. This is especially helpful since the amount of Web site traffic is highly variable. Although the firm's average Web traffic is 30,000 page views per hour, customer visits can increase to 350,000 page views within 10 minutes of a banner ad appearing on a major Web portal or search engine.

As Admire says, "because our site operates 24/7, we want immediate notification if the site isn't performing properly. That's what the monitoring solution tells us. We don't want to have to wait for the customers to tell us the site isn't working."

Source: Dan Scheraga, "Better Safe Than Sorry," *Chain Store Age* (March 2005), p. 77.

Retail Management: A Strategic Approach is divided into eight parts. The balance of Part One looks at building relationships and strategic planning in retailing. Part Two characterizes retailing institutions on the basis of their ownership, store-based strategy mix, and Web, nonstore-based, and other nontraditional retailing format. Part Three deals with consumer behavior and information gathering in retailing. Parts Four to Seven discuss the specific elements of a retailing strategy: planning the store location; managing a retail business; planning, handling, and pricing merchandise; and communicating with the customer. Part Eight shows how a retailing strategy may be integrated, analyzed, and improved. These topics have special end-of-chapter appendixes: service retailing (Chapter 2), global retailing (Chapter 3), franchising (Chapter 4), and multi-channel retailing (Chapter 6). There are three end-of-text appendixes: retailing careers, about the Web site accompanying *Retail Management*, and a glossary. And our Web site includes "How to Solve a Case Study" (**www.prenhall.com/bermanevans**), which will aid you in your case analyses.

To underscore retailing's exciting nature, four real-world boxes appear in each chapter: "Careers in Retailing," "Ethics in Retailing," "Retailing Around the World," and "Technology in Retailing."

Summary

In this and every chapter, the summary is related to the objectives stated at the beginning of the chapter.

1. *To define retailing, consider it from various perspectives, demonstrate its impact, and note its special characteristics.* Retailing comprises the business activities involved in selling goods and services to consumers for personal, family, or household use. It is the last stage in the distribution process. Today, retailing is at a fascinating crossroads, with many challenges ahead.

Retailing may be viewed from multiple perspectives. It includes tangible and intangible items, does not have to involve a store, and can be done by manufacturers and others—as well as retailers.

Annual U.S. store sales exceed $4 trillion, with other forms of retailing accounting for hundreds of billions of dollars more. The world's 100 largest retailers generate $2.4 trillion in yearly revenues. About 25 million people in the United States work for retailers (including food and beverage places), which understates the number of those actually employed in a retailing capacity. Retail firms receive up to 40 cents or more of every sales dollar as compensation for operating costs, the functions performed, and the profits earned.

Retailing encompasses all of the businesses and people involved in physically moving and transferring ownership of goods and services from producer to consumer. In a distribution channel, retailers do valuable functions as the contact for manufacturers, wholesalers, and final consumers. They collect assortments from various suppliers and offer them to customers. They communicate with both customers and other channel members. They may ship, store, mark, advertise, and pre-pay for items. They complete transactions with customers and often provide customer services. They may offer multiple formats (multi-channel retailing) to facilitate shopping.

Retailers and their suppliers have complex relationships because retailers serve in two capacities. They are part of a distribution channel aimed at the final consumer, and they are major customers for suppliers. Channel relations are smoothest with exclusive distribution; they are most volatile with intensive distribution. Selective distribution is a way to balance sales goals and channel cooperation.

Retailing has several special characteristics. The average sales transaction is small. Final consumers make many unplanned purchases. Most customers visit a store location.

2. *To introduce the concept of strategic planning and apply it.* A retail strategy is the overall plan guiding the firm. It has six basic steps: defining the business, setting objectives, defining the customer market, developing an overall plan, enacting an integrated strategy, and evaluating performance and making modifications. Target Stores' strategy has been particularly well designed and enacted.

3. *To show why the retailing concept is the foundation of a successful business, with an emphasis on the total retail experience, customer service, and relationship retailing.* The retailing concept should be understood and used by all retailers. It requires a firm to have a customer orientation, use a coordinated effort, and be value-driven and goal-oriented. Despite its straightforward nature, many firms do not adhere to one or more elements of the retailing concept.

The total retail experience consists of all the elements in a retail offering that encourage or inhibit consumers during their contact with a retailer. Some elements are controllable by the retailer; others are not. Customer service includes identifiable, but sometimes intangible, activities undertaken by a retailer in association with the basic goods and services sold. It has an effect on the total retail experience. In relationship retailing, a firm seeks long-term bonds with customers rather than acting as if each sales transaction is a totally new encounter with them.

4. *To indicate the focus and format of the text.* Retailing may be studied by using an institutional approach, a functional approach, and a strategic approach. Although all three approaches are covered in this book, our focus is on the strategic approach. The underlying principle is that a retail firm needs to plan for and adapt to a complex, changing environment.

Key Terms

retailing (p. 4)
channel of distribution (p. 8)
sorting process (p. 8)
multi-channel retailing (p. 9)

exclusive distribution (p. 10)
intensive distribution (p. 10)
selective distribution (p. 11)
retail strategy (p. 12)

retailing concept (p. 15)
total retail experience (p. 16)
customer service (p. 18)
relationship retailing (p. 18)

Questions for Discussion

1. What is your favorite consumer electronics retailer? Discuss the criteria you have used in making your selection. What can a competing firm do to lure you away from your favorite firm? Apply your answer to retailing in general.

2. What kinds of information do retailers communicate to customers? To suppliers?

3. What are the pros and cons of a firm such as Nine West having its own retail facilities and E-commerce Web site (**www.ninewest.com**), as well as selling through traditional retailers?

4. Why would one retailer seek to be part of an exclusive distribution channel while another seeks to be part of an intensive distribution channel?

5. Describe how the special characteristics of retailing offer unique opportunities and problems for gift stores.

6. What is the purpose of developing a formal retail strategy? How could a strategic plan be used by a local delicatessen?

7. On the basis of the chapter description of Target Stores, present five suggestions that a new retailer should consider.

8. Explain the retailing concept. Apply it to a local Dunkin' Donuts store.

9. Define the term "total retail experience." Then describe a recent retail situation in which your expectations were surpassed and state why.

10. Do you believe that customer service in retailing is improving or declining? Why?

11. How could a small Web-only retailer engage in relationship retailing?

12. What checklist item(s) in Figure 1-12 do you think would be most difficult for Ikea, as the world's largest furniture retailer, to address? Why?

Web-Based Exercise

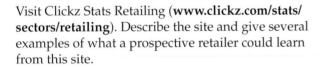

Visit Clickz Stats Retailing (**www.clickz.com/stats/ sectors/retailing**). Describe the site and give several examples of what a prospective retailer could learn from this site.

Note: Stop by our Web site (**www.prenhall.com/bermanevans**) to experience a number of highly interactive, appealing Web exercises based on actual company demonstrations and sample materials related to retailing.

Chapter Endnotes

1. Various company sources.

2. Estimated by the authors from data in "2005 Global Powers of Retailing," *Stores* (January 2005), special section.

3. *Annual Benchmark Report for Retail and Food Services* (Washington, DC: U.S. Census Bureau, March 2005); and retailer annual reports.

4. The material in this section is drawn from **www.target.com**; **www.targetcorp.com**; *Target Corporation Annual Report 2005*; Doug Desjardins, "Simple Merchandising Sells Toys at Target," *DSN Retailing Today* (May 23, 2005), p. 20; "Right on the Mark: Target Excels in Apparel," *DSN Retailing Today* (April 11, 2005), pp. 12, 14; Laura Heller, "Target Fine-Tuning the Right Formula for Success," *DSN Retailing Today* (April 11, 2005), p. 31; Doug Desjardins, "Cash from M&M Sale Pays Way to Stock Buyback, Debt Reduction," *DSN Retailing Today* (April 11, 2005), pp. 32–33; "Target Merchandising,"

DSN Retailing Today (April 11, 2005), pp. 38, 43; and Laura Heller, "Innovative Thinking Permeates Entire Business Model," *DSN Retailing Today* (April 11, 2005), pp. 40, 43.

5. IBM, "Retailers Offering a 'One Size Fits All' Shopping Experience Will Lose Customer Loyalty," **www.marketwire.com** (May 24, 2005).

6. Terri Murphy, "What Customers Don't Tell You Can Hurt," **http://realtytimes.com/rtapages/20050530_ customersatisfaction.htm** (May 30, 2005).

7. "Fact Sheet," **www.buildabear.com/aboutUs/Our Company/FactSheet.pdf** (February 3, 2006).

8. Susan Reda, "Saving Customer Service: Are Retailers Up to the Challenge?" *Stores* (January 2001), p. 50.

9. Tenisha Mercer, "Retailers Rein in Returns," **www. detnews.com/2005/business/0502/03/C01-78357.htm** (February 3, 2005); and Linda Stern, "Rite of Return," *Newsweek* (January 10, 2005), p. 61.

Chapter 2
BUILDING AND SUSTAINING RELATIONSHIPS IN RETAILING

Stew Leonard's (**www.stewleonards. com**) is a four-store supermarket chain with units in Connecticut and New York. Each square foot of selling space yields over $1,400 in sales; that's among the highest figures of any retail store in the country and about 2.5 times higher than the average supermarket. In addition, its stores have a 2.5 percent profit margin versus 1 percent or so for the average supermarket.

Reprinted by permission.

Stew Leonard's bases its store strategy on "retailtainment" and on building and maintaining customer relationships. One of Stew Leonard's strategies is to be known as the "Disneyland of Dairy Stores" by being as exciting as possible for shoppers of all ages. For example, Stew Leonard's processes milk in full view of customers while the "Farm Fresh Five," a band of milk-carton robots, sing. The parking lot even has a petting zoo. Day in, day out, Stew Leonard's offers free samples from its in-house bakeries and dairies. There are also special activities on major holidays. For example, local music groups and dancers perform on St. Patrick's Day and at Halloween, and the chain features hayrides and pumpkin-carving contests.

Stew Leonard's really prides itself on its customer service. The retailer's shopper relationships are built on the concept that the "Customer Is Always Right." Carved into 6-foot-high, 6,000-pound boulders at the entrance to the firm's Norwalk and Danbury, Connecticut, stores are two rules: "Rule 1: The customer is always right. Rule 2: If the customer is wrong, reread Rule 1."[1]

chapter objectives

1. To explain what "value" really means and highlight its pivotal role in retailers' building and sustaining relationships
2. To describe how both customer relationships and channel relationships may be nurtured in today's highly competitive marketplace
3. To examine the differences in relationship building between goods and service retailers
4. To discuss the impact of technology on relationships in retailing
5. To consider the interplay between retailers' ethical performance and relationships in retailing

OVERVIEW

Dillard's (www.dillards.com) is—first and foremost—a value-driven retailer.

To prosper, a retailer must properly apply the concepts of "value" and "relationship" so (a) customers strongly believe the firm offers a good value for the money and (b) both customers and channel members want to do business with that retailer. Some firms grasp this well. Others still have some work to do. Consider the forward-thinking view of Dillard's, a department store chain:

Fundamentally, our business model is to offer the customer a compelling price/value relationship through the combination of high-quality goods and services at a competitive price. Our stores are located in suburban shopping malls and open-air lifestyle centers and offer a broad selection of fashion apparel and home furnishings. We offer an appealing and attractive assortment of merchandise to our customers at a fair price. We seek to enhance our income by maximizing the sale of this merchandise to our customers. We do this by promoting and advertising our merchandise and by making our stores an attractive and convenient place for our customers to shop.[2]

As retailers look to the future, this is the looming bottom line on value: "Consumers will demand more for less from the shopping experience. Time and budget constrained consumers will spend less time shopping, make fewer trips, visit fewer stores, and shop more purposefully. Different strokes will satisfy different folks. Consumers will shop different formats for different needs. Specifically, they will split the commodity shopping trip from the value-added shopping trip. Consumers are becoming more skeptical about price. Under the barrage of sales, price has lost its meaning; gimmicks have lost their appeal. To regain consumer confidence, pricing by retailers and manufacturers alike will become clearer, more sensible, and more sophisticated."[3] See Figure 2-1.

This chapter looks at value and the value chain, relationship retailing with regard to customers and channel partners, the differences in relationship building

FIGURE 2-1

Best Buy: Providing Extra Value for Customers

Best Buy offers shoppers a tremendous assortment, plentiful sales help, and fully integrated home entertainment systems.

Photo reprinted by permission of Susan Berry, Retail Image Consulting, Inc.

between goods and service retailers, technology and relationships, and ethics and relationships. There is also a chapter appendix on service retailing.

VALUE AND THE VALUE CHAIN

In many channels of distribution, there are several parties: manufacturer, wholesaler, retailer, and customer. These parties are most apt to be satisfied with their interactions when they have similar beliefs about the value provided and received, and they agree on the payment for that level of value.

From the perspective of the manufacturer, wholesaler, and retailer, **value** is embodied by a series of activities and processes—a value chain—that *provides* a certain value for the consumer. It is the totality of the tangible and intangible product and customer service attributes offered to shoppers. The level of value relates to each firm's desire for a fair profit and its niche (such as discount versus upscale). Where firms may differ is in rewarding the value each provides and in allocating the activities undertaken.

From the customer's perspective, **value** is the *perception* the shopper has of a value chain. It is the customer's view of all the benefits from a purchase (formed by the total retail experience). Value is based on the perceived benefits received versus the price paid. It varies by type of shopper. Price-oriented shoppers want low prices, service-oriented shoppers will pay more for superior customer service, and status-oriented shoppers will pay a lot to patronize prestigious stores.

Why is "value" such a meaningful concept for every retailer in any kind of setting?

- Customers must always believe they get their money's worth, whether the retailer sells $20,000 Rolex watches or $40 Casio watches.
- A strong retail effort is required so that customers perceive the level of value provided in the manner the firm intends.
- Value is desired by all customers; however, it means different things to different customers.
- Consumer comparison shopping for prices is easy through ads and the World Wide Web. Thus, prices have moved closer together for different types of retailers.
- Retail differentiation is essential so a firm is not perceived as a "me too" retailer.
- A specific value/price level must be set. A retailer can offer $100 worth of benefits for a $100 item or $125 worth of benefits (through better ambience and customer service) for the same item and a $125 price. Either approach can work if properly enacted and marketed.

Peapod (**www.peapod.com**) offers a unique value chain with its home delivery service.

A retail **value chain** represents the total bundle of benefits offered to consumers through a channel of distribution. It comprises store location and parking, retailer ambience, the level of customer service, the products/brands carried, product quality, the retailer's in-stock position, shipping, prices, the retailer's image, and other elements. As a rule, consumers are concerned with the results of a value chain, not the process. Food shoppers who buy online via Peapod care only that they receive the brands ordered when desired, not about the steps needed for home delivery at the neighborhood level.

Some elements of a retail value chain are visible to shoppers, such as display windows, store hours, sales personnel, and point-of-sale equipment. Other elements are not visible, such as store location planning, credit processing, company warehouses, and many merchandising decisions. In the latter case, various cues are surrogates for value: upscale store ambience and plentiful sales personnel for high-end retailers; shopping carts and self-service for discounters.

There are three aspects of a value-oriented retail strategy: expected, augmented, and potential. An *expected retail strategy* represents the minimum value chain elements a given customer segment (e.g., young women) expects from a type of retailer (e.g., a mid-priced apparel retailer). In most cases, the following are expected value chain elements: store cleanliness, convenient hours, well-informed employees, timely service, popular products in stock, parking, and return privileges. If applied poorly, expected elements cause customer dissatisfaction and relate to why shoppers avoid certain retailers.

Compare Sears (www.sears.com) and Saks (www.saks.com).

An *augmented retail strategy* includes the extra elements in a value chain that differentiate one retailer from another. As an example, how is Sears different from Saks? The following are often augmented elements: exclusive brands, superior salespeople, loyalty programs, delivery, personal shoppers and other special services, and valet parking. Augmented features complement expected value chain elements, and they are the key to continued customer patronage with a particular retailer.

A *potential retail strategy* comprises value chain elements not yet perfected by a competing firm in the retailer's category. For example, what customer services could a new upscale apparel chain offer that no other chain offers? In many situations, the following are potential value chain elements: 24/7 store hours (an augmented strategy for supermarkets), unlimited customer return privileges, full-scale product customization, instant fulfillment of rain checks through in-store orders accompanied by free delivery, and in-mall trams to make it easier for shoppers to move through enormous regional shopping centers. The first firms to capitalize on potential features gain a head start over their adversaries. Barnes & Noble and Borders accomplished this by opening the first book superstores, and Amazon.com has become a major player by opening the first online bookstore. Yet, even as pioneers, firms must excel at meeting customers' basic expectations and offering differentiated features from competitors if they are to grow.

Today Barnes & Noble (www.bn.com) relies on both its stores and its Web site for revenues.

Careers in RETAILING — Maxine: Chief Executive Officer

Maxine began her full-time career with a national department store operator in the executive training program and quickly progressed to assistant buyer, buyer, and merchandise manager. Maxine then became marketing communications manager, executive vice-president of marketing and merchandising, and ultimately executive vice-president of stores.

At that point, after spending most of her career "working for someone else," Maxine decided it was time to build her own business. She had a unique idea for a specialty store and wanted to invest her time and resources to develop her own new concepts to take to market. The idea was successful and the one specialty store grew to 10. Maxine has not taken a salary. She is investing all of the profits into growing her business.

As an entrepreneur and owner, ultimate responsibility for the company's success or failure belongs to Maxine. Running a business requires long hours, but she loves the changing environment. Though her schedule is unpredictable and full of surprises, Maxine often works 12- to 14-hour days. She spends a great deal of time in meetings, on the phone, and visiting stores. Maxine does a lot of business planning—evaluating store sales, reviewing financial reports, researching where the next store(s) should be opened, and negotiating those deals. She also performs much of the human resource function, hiring team members for all positions from district manager and above.

Source: Reprinted by permission of the National Retail Federation.

There are five potential pitfalls to avoid in planning a value-oriented retail strategy:

- *Planning value with just a price perspective:* Value is tied to two factors: benefits and prices. Most discounters now accept credit cards because shoppers want to purchase with them.
- *Providing value-enhancing services that customers do not want or will not pay extra for:* Ikea knows most of its customers want to save money by assembling furniture themselves.
- *Competing in the wrong value/price segment:* Neighborhood retailers generally have a tough time competing in the low-price part of the market. They are better off providing augmented benefits and charging somewhat more than large chains.
- *Believing augmented elements alone create value:* Many retailers think that if they offer a benefit not available from competitors that they will automatically prosper. Yet, they must never lose sight of the importance of expected benefits. A movie theater with limited parking will have problems even if it features first-run movies.
- *Paying lip service to customer service:* Most firms say, and even believe, that customers are always right. Yet, they act contrary to this philosophy—by having a high turnover of salespeople, charging for returned goods that have been opened, and not giving rain checks if items are out of stock.

To sidestep these pitfalls, a retailer could use the checklist in Figure 2-2, which poses a number of questions that must be addressed. The checklist can be answered by an owner/corporate president, a team of executives, or an independent consultant. It should be reviewed at least once a year or more often if a major development, such as the emergence of a strong competitor, occurs.

FIGURE 2-2
A Value-Oriented Retailing Checklist

Answer yes or no to each question.

✓ Is value defined from a consumer perspective?

✓ Does the retailer have a clear value/price point?

✓ Is the retailer's value position competitively defensible?

✓ Are channel partners capable of delivering value-enhancing services?

✓ Does the retailer distinguish between expected and augmented value chain elements?

✓ Has the retailer identified meaningful potential value chain elements?

✓ Is the retailer's value-oriented approach aimed at a distinct market segment?

✓ Is the retailer's value-oriented approach consistent?

✓ Is the retailer's value-oriented approach effectively communicated to the target market?

✓ Can the target market clearly identify the retailer's positioning strategy?

✓ Does the retailer's positioning strategy consider trade-offs in sales versus profits?

✓ Does the retailer set customer satisfaction goals?

✓ Does the retailer periodically measure customer satisfaction levels?

✓ Is the retailer careful to avoid the pitfalls in value-oriented retailing?

✓ Is the retailer always looking out for new opportunities that will create customer value?

RETAILER RELATIONSHIPS

In Chapter 1, we introduced the concept of *relationship retailing*, whereby retailers seek to form and maintain long-term bonds with customers, rather than act as if each sales transaction is a new encounter with them. For relationship retailing to work, enduring value-driven relationships are needed with other channel members, as well as with customers. Both jobs are challenging. See Figure 2-3. Visit our Web site for links related to relationship retailing issues (**www.prenhall.com/bermanevans**).

Customer Relationships

Loyal customers are the backbone of a business. For example,

> Besides having strong and able franchisees, nothing is more important to the well-being of a restaurant or retail franchisor than a loyal customer. In fact, nothing probably even comes close. A chain's most loyal customers are those who are "highly satisfied" and they bring with them considerably more clout to a franchisor's bottom line than customers who are just "satisfied." According to the *Harvard Business Review*, an exceptionally-satisfied customer is six times more likely to buy again as one who is merely satisfied. And only a five percent increase in customer loyalty can boost profits 25 percent to 85 percent.[4]

In relationship retailing, there are four factors to keep in mind: the customer base, customer service, customer satisfaction, and loyalty programs and defection rates. Let's explore these next.

FIGURE 2-3
J.C. Penney: An Emphasis on Solid Retail Relationships

J.C. Penney wants its customers to be fully satisfied with the shopping experience—and to return over and over. It also seeks to have strong relationships with the many suppliers from which it buys merchandise.

Photo reprinted by permission of Susan Berry, Retail Image Consulting, Inc.

The Customer Base

Retailers must regularly analyze their customer base in terms of population and lifestyle trends, attitudes toward and reasons for shopping, the level of loyalty, and the mix of new versus loyal customers.

The U.S. population is aging. One-fourth of households have only one person, one-sixth of people move annually, most people live in urban and suburban areas, the number of working women is high, middle-class income has been rising slowly, and African-American, Hispanic-American, and Asian-American segments are expanding. Thus, gender roles are changing, shoppers demand more, consumers are more diverse, there is less interest in shopping, and time-saving goods and services are desired.

There are various factors that influence shopping behavior. Here are some examples:

- In 1985, women bought 70 percent of men's products; today, they buy only 25 percent due to the increased shopping done by men. Women do more product research before shopping and are less apt to be influenced by ads than are men.
- On a typical mall shopping trip, women spend about 10 percent more than their male counterparts.
- Due to time constraints, consumers now spend an average of only 75 minutes when visiting a shopping mall.
- Consumers' most important reasons to shop at a given *food store* are high-quality fresh foods, good value, and healthy food alternatives.
- Consumers give *department stores* high marks for the brands and styles they carry but lower marks for prices.
- Consumers at *supercenters* and *discount department stores* tend to be households in the family life stages, often in the down- and middle-income brackets. These retailers are popular for many different product categories.[5]

It is more worth nurturing relationships with some shoppers than with others; they are the retailer's **core customers**—its best customers. And they should be singled out:

> Most firms have a mix of good, better, and best customers. Unfortunately, there are bad customers as well, and they can be a time and money drain. Good customers might be good because they spend lots of money. They might be good because they come back often. It might be that they're easy to look after. Bad customers are those who are never satisfied and almost always cost you more to serve than they spend. The trick is in identifying the best customers, determining what characteristics differentiate these profitable customers from all the rest, learning what these customers want, and working hard to keep them happy.[6]

A retailer's desired mix of new versus loyal customers depends on that firm's stage in its life cycle, goals, and resources, as well as competitors' actions. A mature firm is more apt to rely on core customers and supplement its revenues with new shoppers. A new firm faces the dual tasks of attracting shoppers and building a loyal following; it cannot do the latter without the former. If goals are growth-oriented, the customer base must be expanded by adding stores, increasing advertising, and so on; the challenge is to do this in a way that does not deflect attention from core customers. Although it is more costly to attract new customers than to serve existing ones, core customers are not cost-free. If competitors try to take away a firm's existing customers with price cuts and special promotions, a retailer may feel it must pursue competitors' customers in the same way. Again, it must be careful not to alienate core customers.

Customer Service

As described in Chapter 1, *customer service* refers to the identifiable, but sometimes intangible, activities undertaken by a retailer in conjunction with the goods and services it sells. It impacts on the total retail experience. Consistent with a value chain philosophy, retailers must apply two elements of customer service: **Expected customer service** is the service level that customers want to receive from any retailer, such as basic employee courtesy. **Augmented customer service** includes the activities that enhance the shopping experience and give retailers a competitive advantage. AutoZone does a good job with both expected and augmented customer services:

AutoZone (**www.autozone. com**) has a unique style of customer service.

> AutoZone offers thousands of parts and accessories in its stores. But the best product we offer is our customer service—and you get that free of charge. "AutoZoners always put customers first." That's the first line of AutoZone's pledge and it's the most important thing we do. We go the extra mile to make sure you get the help you need. Our AutoZoners are friendly, knowledgeable, and eager to help you with your vehicle. We created our shopping experience with the customer in mind. Many of our services are free of charge. We're constantly changing our stores to bring you the newest and most exciting products. And you always know when you enter our stores you'll find a great selection of quality merchandise at low prices.[7]

The attributes of personnel who interact with customers (such as politeness and knowledge), as well as the number and variety of customer services offered, have a strong effect on the relationship created. Consider this consumer perception (by the editor-in-chief of *Sales & Marketing Management*) related to a recent hotel stay:

> While vacationing in Hawaii, I experienced what it feels like to be on the receiving end of two different manifestations of customer service. My husband and I stayed on two islands, at two well-known luxury hotels. Both were exquisite but in subtle ways, we felt that one hotel outdid the other in terms of customer service. The employees at Hotel A referred to us by name and never made us feel rushed in its restaurants. Hotel A had complimentary coffee waiting for us in the lobby each morning, and bottles of water available near the gym. It felt as though Hotel A and its employees believed our contentment was worth whatever expense such complimentary offerings would incur. And that made us like the hotel— so much so that we're planning to go back. Whereas we enjoyed Hotel B very much, we feel as if we now have a relationship with Hotel A.[8]

Planning the best customer service strategy can be complex. That is why Home Depot now has a senior executive, John Costello, who functions as the firm's chief customer officer. As he says, "My job is to make sure I understand what the customer wants, put together the very best team, and then create an environment where they can accomplish what it takes to make Home Depot, and them, successful."[9]

Some retailers realize that customer service is better when they utilize **employee empowerment**, whereby workers have the discretion to do what they believe is necessary—within reason—to satisfy the customer, even if this means bending some rules. At Nordstrom, "Taking care of the customer is our number one priority. It's all about people. People who have the freedom to make spot decisions—big or small—in order to grow their business and make the customer happy. Much of what one does here can't be taught in a training room. We have only one rule—'Use good judgment in all situations.'"[10] At Home Depot, every worker on the selling floor gets several weeks training prior to meeting customers. They have wide latitude in making on-the-spot decisions. They can act as consultants and problem solvers.

To apply customer service effectively, a firm must first develop an overall service strategy and then plan individual services. Figure 2-4 shows one way a retailer may view the customer services it offers.

DEVELOPING A CUSTOMER SERVICE STRATEGY. A retailer must make the following vital decisions.

What customer services are expected and what customer services are augmented for a particular retailer? Examples of expected customer services are credit for a furniture retailer, new-car preparation for an auto dealer, and a liberal return policy for a gift shop. Those retailers could not stay in business without them. Because augmented customer services are extra elements, a firm could serve its target market without such services; yet, using them enhances its competitive standing. Examples are delivery for a supermarket, an extra warranty for an auto dealer, and gift wrapping for a toy store. Each firm needs to learn which customer services are expected and which are augmented for its situation. Expected customer services for one retailer, such as delivery, may be augmented for another. See Figure 2-5.

What level of customer service is proper to complement a firm's image? An upscale retailer would offer more customer services than a discounter because people expect the upscale firm to have a wider range of customer services as part of its basic strategy. Performance would also be different. Customers of an upscale retailer may expect elaborate gift wrapping, valet parking, a restaurant, and a ladies' room attendant, whereas discount shoppers may expect cardboard gift boxes, self-service parking, a lunch counter, and an unattended ladies' room. Customer service categories are the same; performance is not.

Nordstrom (www.nordstrom.com) really believes in empowering its employees to better serve customers.

FIGURE 2-4
Classifying Customer Services

Source: Adapted by the authors from Albert D. Bates, "Rethinking the Service Offer," *Retailing Issues Letter* (December 1986), p. 3. Reprinted by permission.

| | Cost of Offering the Customer Service | |
	High	**Low**
High Value of the Customer Service to the Shopper **Low**	**Patronage Builders** High-cost activities that are the primary factors behind customer loyalties. Examples: transaction speed, credit, gift registry	**Patronage Solidifiers** The "low-cost little things" that increase loyalty. Examples: courtesy (referring to the customer by name and saying thank you), suggestion selling
	Disappointers Expensive activities that do no real good. Examples: weekday deliveries for two-earner families, home economists	**Basics** Low-cost activities that are "naturally expected." They don't build patronage, but their absence could reduce patronage. Examples: free parking, in-store directories

FIGURE 2-5
Augmented Services: Going
Above and Beyond

At this Home Depot store in
Manhattan, there is a doorman
who helps shoppers with their
packages and helps to hail a
cab—not your typical customer
service from a home supply
store.

Photo reprinted by permission.

Staples (www.staples.com)
offers free delivery on
orders of $50 or more.

Should there be a choice of customer services? Some firms let customers select
from various levels of customer service; others provide only one level. A retailer
may honor several credit cards or only its own. Trade-ins may be allowed on some
items or all. Warranties may have optional extensions or fixed lengths. A firm may
offer one-, three-, and six-month payment plans or insist on immediate payment.

Should customer services be free? Two factors cause retailers to charge for some
customer services: (1) Delivery, gift wrapping, and some other customer services
are labor intensive. (2) People are more apt to be home for a delivery or service call
if a fee is imposed. Without a fee, a retailer may have to attempt a delivery twice.
In settling on a free or fee-based strategy, a firm must determine which customer
services are expected (these are often free) and which are augmented (these may
be offered for a fee), monitor competitors and profit margins, and study the target
market. In setting fees, a retailer must also decide if its goal is to break even or to
make a profit on certain customer services.

*How can a retailer measure the benefits of providing customer services against their
costs?* The purpose of customer services is to enhance the shopping experience in
a manner that attracts and retains shoppers—while maximizing sales and profits.

Thus, augmented customer services should not be offered unless they raise total sales and profits. A retailer should plan augmented customer services based on its experience, competitors' actions, and customer comments; and when the costs of providing these customer services increase, higher prices should be passed on to the consumer.

How can customer services be terminated? Once a customer service strategy is set, shoppers are likely to react negatively to any customer service reduction. Nonetheless, some costly augmented customer services may have to be dropped. In that case, the best approach is to be forthright by explaining why the customer services are being terminated and how customers will benefit via lower prices. Sometimes a firm may use a middle ground, charging for previously free customer services (such as clothing alterations) to allow those who want the services to still receive them.

PLANNING INDIVIDUAL CUSTOMER SERVICES. Once a broad customer service plan is outlined, individual customer services are planned. A department store may offer credit, layaway, gift wrapping, a bridal registry, free parking, a restaurant, a beauty salon, carpet installation, dressing rooms, clothing alterations, pay phones, restrooms and sitting areas, the use of baby strollers, delivery, and fur storage. The range of typical customer services is shown in Table 2-1 and described next.

Most retailers let customers make credit purchases; and many firms accept personal checks with proper identification. Consumers' use of credit rises as the purchase amount goes up. Retailer-sponsored credit cards have three key advantages: (1) The retailer saves the fee it would pay for outside card sales. (2) People are encouraged to shop with a given retailer because its card is usually not accepted elsewhere. (3) Contact can be maintained with customers and information learned about them. There are also disadvantages to retailer cards: Startup costs are high, the firm must worry about unpaid bills and slow cash flow, credit checks and follow-up tasks must be performed, and customers without the firm's card may be discouraged from shopping. Bank and other commercial credit cards enable small and medium retailers to offer credit, generate added business for all types of retailers, appeal to mobile shoppers, provide advertising support from the sponsor, reduce bad debts, eliminate startup costs for the retailer, and provide

TABLE 2-1	Typical Customer Services		
Credit	Miscellaneous		
Delivery	• Bridal registry	• Restrooms
Alterations and installations	• Interior designers	• Restaurant
Packaging (gift wrapping)	• Personal shoppers	• Baby-sitting
Complaints and returns handling	• Ticket outlets	• Fitting rooms
Gift certificates	• Parking	• Beauty salon
Trade-ins	• Water fountains	• Fur storage
Trial purchases	• Pay phones	• Shopping bags
Special sales for regular customers	• Baby strollers	• Information
Extended store hours		
Mail and phone orders		

data. Yet, these cards charge a transaction fee and do not yield loyalty to the retailer.

All bank cards and most retailer cards involve a **revolving credit account**, whereby a customer charges items and is billed monthly on the basis of the outstanding cumulative balance. An **option credit account** is a form of revolving account; no interest is assessed if a person pays a bill in full when it is due. Should a person make a partial payment, he or she is assessed interest monthly on the unpaid balance. Some credit card firms (such as American Express) and some retailers offer an **open credit account**, whereby a consumer must pay the bill in full when it is due. Partial, revolving payments are not permitted. A person with an open account also has a credit limit (although it may be more flexible).

For a retailer that offers delivery, there are three decisions: the transportation method, equipment ownership versus rental, and timing. The shipping method can be car, van, truck, rail, mail, and so forth. The costs and appropriateness of the methods depend on the products. Large retailers often find it economical to own their delivery vehicles. This also lets them advertise the company name, have control over schedules, and use their employees for deliveries. Small retailers serving limited trading areas may use personal vehicles. Many small, medium, and even large retailers use shippers such as United Parcel Service if consumers live away from a delivery area and shipments are not otherwise efficient. Finally, the retailer must decide how quickly to process orders and how often to deliver to different locales.

For some retailers, alterations and installations are expected customer services—although more retailers now charge fees. However, many discounters have stopped offering alterations of clothing and installations of heavy appliances on both a free and a fee basis. They feel the services are too ancillary to their business and not worth the effort. Other retailers offer only basic alterations: shortening pants, taking in the waist, and lengthening jacket sleeves. They do not adjust jacket shoulders or width. Some appliance retailers may hook up washing machines but not do plumbing work.

Within a store, packaging (gift wrapping)—as well as complaints and returns handling—can be centrally located or decentralized. Centralized packaging counters and complaints and returns areas have key advantages: They may be situated in otherwise dead spaces; the main selling areas are not cluttered; specialized personnel can be used; and a common policy is enacted. The advantages of

RETAILING Around the World — London's Topshop: Pulling Out All the Stops

The United States has plenty of stores aimed at fashion-loving young women—but there is nothing in America that directly compares with Topshop's (**www.topshop.co.uk**) megastore located on Oxford Street in London. What makes the store so appealing is that it feels more like an underground club than a traditional retailer with its witty signs and eye-appealing graphics. And unlike most retailers that have their front display window filled with fashions, Topshop's window recently featured windup bunnies that bumped into each other. To further instill humor, a sign in the window reads: "All our fur is fake."

While the store's street-level floor is filled with accessories, fun gifts, and novelty items, the basement (where the ladies' clothing and accessories departments are located) is clearly where the action is. The basement even contains a Vintage Shop that features secondhand clothing. In addition, Topshop has a manicure bar, restaurant, style advisors, and personal shoppers. These amenities are unusual for a mass-market retailer that attracts young shoppers. To keep the excitement going and the merchandise fresh, the store gets two deliveries each day.

Sources: Marianne Wilson, "Mad for Topshop," *Chain Store Age* (January 2005), p. 104; and "Topshop," **www.topshop.co.uk** (January 29, 2006).

decentralized facilities are that shoppers are not inconvenienced; people are kept in the selling area, where a salesperson may resolve a problem or offer different merchandise; and extra personnel are not required. In either case, clear guidelines as to the handling of complaints and returns are needed.

Gift certificates encourage shopping with a given retailer. Many firms require certificates to be spent and not redeemed for cash. Trade-ins also induce new and regular shoppers to shop. People may feel they are getting a bargain. Trial purchases let shoppers test products before purchases are final to reduce risks.

Retailers increasingly offer special customer services to regular customers. Sales events (not open to the general public) and extended hours are provided. Mail and phone orders are handled for convenience.

Other useful customer services include a bridal registry, interior designers, personal shoppers, ticket outlets, free (or low-cost) and plentiful parking, water fountains, pay phones, baby strollers, restrooms, a restaurant, baby-sitting, fitting rooms, a beauty salon, fur storage, shopping bags, and information counters. A retailer's willingness to offer some or all of these services indicates to customers a concern for them. Therefore, firms need to consider the impact of excessive self-service.

Customer Satisfaction

Customer satisfaction occurs when the value and customer service provided through a retailing experience meet or exceed consumer expectations. If the expectations of value and customer service are not met, the consumer will be dissatisfied: "Retail satisfaction consists of three categories: shopping systems satisfaction which includes availability and types of outlets; buying systems satisfaction which includes selection and actual purchasing of products; and consumer satisfaction derived from the use of the product. Dissatisfaction with any of the three aspects could lead to customer disloyalty, decrease in sales, and erosion of the market share."[11]

Only "very satisfied" customers are likely to remain loyal in the long run. How well are retailers doing in customer satisfaction? Many have much work to do. The American Customer Satisfaction Index annually questions thousands of people to link customer expectations, perceived quality, and perceived value to satisfaction. Overall, retailers consistently score only about 75 on a scale of 100. Fast-food firms usually rate lowest in the retailing category (with scores around 70). To improve matters, retailers should engage in the process shown in Figure 2-6.

Most consumers do not complain when dissatisfied. They just shop elsewhere. Why don't shoppers complain more? (1) Because most people feel complaining produces little or no positive results, they do not bother to complain.

FIGURE 2-6
Turning Around Weak Customer Service

Source: Figure and its discussion developed by the authors from information in Jeff Mowatt, "Keeping Customers When Things Go Wrong," *Canadian Manager* (Summer 2001), pp. 23, 28.

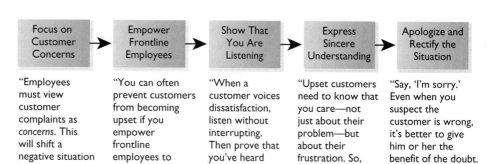

(2) Complaining is not easy. Consumers have to find the party to whom they should complain, access to that party may be restricted, and written forms may have to be completed.

To obtain more feedback, retailers must make it easier for shoppers to complain, make sure shoppers believe their concerns are being addressed, and sponsor ongoing customer satisfaction surveys. As suggested by consulting firm CustomerSat.com at its Web site, retailers should ask such questions as these and then take corrective actions:

Try out some of CustomerSat.com's (www.customersat.com) tools for measuring customer satisfaction.

1. "Please rate our customer service."
2. "How often does our customer service exceed expectations?"
3. "What do you like most about our customer service?" "What do you like least?"

Loyalty Programs

Consumer loyalty (frequent shopper) programs reward a retailer's best customers, those with whom it wants long-lasting relationships. According to A.C. Nielsen surveys, more than 80 percent of all U.S. households participate in at least one loyalty program.[12] And here's what consumers want:

> For almost two-thirds of the public, receiving "a percentage discount on all purchases" is the feature that would "most likely" encourage them to participate. One-third would be attracted by "advance notice of upcoming sales"; 31 percent would look for either "special coupons for new products" or "coupons or discounts on goods and services from other vendors"; 29 percent are attracted by "cash-back offers"; and almost a quarter want a "free gift with purchase." Relatively few overall are attracted by invitations to special events or parties (10 percent), preferred parking (10 percent), or personal shopping assistance (9 percent). Just as important as the attractions are the turnoffs. In a time when headlines often are devoted to privacy issues, it should come as no surprise that the top consumer negative has to do with this topic.[13]

Great Britain's Tesco (www.tesco.com/clubcard) has a strong loyalty program (Tesco Clubcard) for its supermarket customers.

What do good customer loyalty programs have in common? Their rewards are useful and appealing, and they are attainable in a reasonable time. The programs honor shopping behavior (the greater the purchases, the greater the benefits). A database tracks behavior. There are features that are unique to particular retailers and not redeemable elsewhere. Rewards stimulate both short- and long-run purchases. Customer communications are personalized. Frequent shoppers feel "special." Participation rules are publicized and rarely change.

When a retailer studies customer defections (by tracking databases or surveying consumers), it can learn how many customers it is losing and why they no longer patronize the firm. Customer defections may be viewed in absolute terms (people who no longer buy from the firm at all) and in relative terms (people who shop less often). Each retailer must define its acceptable defection rate. Furthermore, not all shoppers are "good" customers. A retailer may feel it is okay if shoppers who always look for sales, return items without receipts, and expect fee-based services to be free decide to defect. Unfortunately, too few retailers review defection data or survey defecting customers because of the complexity of doing so and an unwillingness to hear "bad news."

Channel Relationships

Within a value chain, the members of a distribution channel (manufacturers, wholesalers, and retailers) jointly represent a **value delivery system**, which comprises all the parties that develop, produce, deliver, and sell and service particular goods and services. The ramifications for retailers follow:

- Each channel member is dependent on the others. When consumers shop with a certain retailer, they often do so because of both the retailer and the products it carries.
- All value delivery systems activity must be enumerated and responsibility assigned for them.
- Small retailers may have to use suppliers outside the normal distribution channel to get the products they want and gain adequate supplier support. Although large retailers may be able to buy directly from manufacturers, smaller retailers may have to buy through wholesalers handling such accounts.
- A value delivery system is as good as its weakest link. No matter how well a retailer performs its activities, it will still have unhappy shoppers if suppliers deliver late or do not honor warranties.
- The nature of a given value delivery system must be related to target market expectations.
- Channel member costs and functions are influenced by each party's role. Long-term cooperation and two-way information flows foster efficiency.
- Value delivery systems are complex due to the vast product assortment of superstores, the many forms of retailing, and the use of multiple distribution channels by some manufacturers.
- Nonstore retailing (such as mail order, phone, and Web transactions) requires a different delivery system than store retailing.
- Due to conflicting goals about profit margins, shelf space, and so on, some channel members are adversarial—to the detriment of the value delivery system and channel relationships.

When they forge strong positive channel relationships, members of a value delivery system better serve each other and the final consumer. Here's how:

> If you are interested in becoming a supplier for your locally-based Wal-Mart Store or Supercenter and do not want to distribute product on a national level, you then qualify for our Local Purchases Program. You may acquire the Local Supplier Questionnaire at any Wal-Mart store from the Store Manager or Food Merchandiser (only). This guide includes step-by-step instructions and requirements needed to become a local supplier with Wal-Mart Stores, Inc. Merchandise presented for re-sale must first be approved at store level and then authorized by a purchasing agent at the Wal-Mart Stores, Inc. Home Office. All final decisions are made by this agent and approved. Only through this process will you receive a supplier number. We have committed resources to education and training in order to establish new relationships with diverse businesses. We do this because we know the more products and services we provide through our suppliers translates into customer satisfaction—and that's our No. 1 commitment.[14]

Ace (www.acehardware. com) prides itself on strong relationships with its suppliers.

For Ace Hardware, the benefits of cooperation are real. By allowing both retailer and partner to see the same data, sales increases are a result. "Our vendors that have been on the program for more than a year had a 10.3 percent annual sales increase versus our corporate sales rates, which were basically flat," said Ace's collaborative project leader. Ace has also seen expense reduction on the traffic side, with one manufacturer reducing freight cost as a percentage of the production cost from 7 to 2.5 percent. "I firmly believe when you have more than one person looking at a business decision and you

FIGURE 2-7
Elements Contributing to
Effective Channel
Relationships

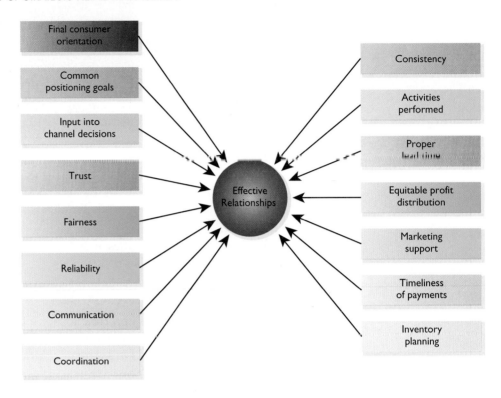

take a team approach, you really come up with a better decision," the project leader added.[15]

One relationship-oriented practice that some manufacturers and retailers use, especially supermarket chains, is *category management*, whereby channel members collaborate to manage products by category rather than by individual item. Category management is based on these principles: (1) Retailers listen more to customers and stock what they want. (2) Profitability is improved because inventory matches demand more closely. (3) By being better focused, shoppers find each department to be more desirable. (4) Retail buyers are given more responsibilities and accountability for category results. (5) Retailers and suppliers must share data and be more computerized. (6) Retailers and suppliers must plan together. Category management is discussed further in Chapter 14.

Figure 2-7 shows various factors that contribute to effective channel relationships.

THE DIFFERENCES IN RELATIONSHIP BUILDING BETWEEN GOODS AND SERVICE RETAILERS

The consumer interest in services makes it crucial to understand the differences in relationship building between retailers that market services and those that market goods. This applies to store-based and nonstore-based firms, those offering only goods *or* services, and those offering goods *and* services.

Goods retailing focuses on the sale of tangible (physical) products. **Service retailing** involves transactions in which consumers do not purchase or acquire ownership of tangible products. Some retailers engage in either goods retailing (such as hardware stores) or service retailing (such as travel agencies); others offer a combination of the two (such as video stores that rent, as well as sell, movies). The latter format is the fastest-growing. Consider how many pharmacies offer film developing, how many department stores have beauty salons, how many hotels have gift shops, and so on.

Service retailing encompasses such diverse businesses as personal services, hotels and motels, auto repair and rental, and recreational services. In addition, although several services have not been commonly considered a part of retailing (such as medical, dental, legal, and educational services), they should be when they entail final consumer sales. There are three kinds of service retailing:

- **Rented-goods services**, whereby consumers lease and use goods for specified periods of time. Tangible goods are leased for a fixed time, but ownership is not obtained and the good must be returned when the rental period is up. Examples are Hertz car rentals, carpet cleaner rentals at a supermarket, and video rentals at a 7-Eleven.
- **Owned-goods services**, whereby goods owned by consumers are repaired, improved, or maintained. In this grouping, the retailer providing the service never owns the good involved. Illustrations include watch repair, lawn care, and an annual air-conditioner tune-up.
- **Nongoods services**, whereby intangible personal services are offered to consumers who then experience the services rather than possess them. The seller offers personal expertise for a specified time in return for a fee; tangible goods are not involved. Some examples are stockbrokers, travel agents, real-estate brokers, and personal trainers.

Please note: The terms *customer service* and *service retailing* are not interchangeable. Customer service refers to the activities undertaken *in conjunction with* the retailer's main business; they are part of the total retail experience. Service retailing refers to situations in which services *are sold to* consumers.

Cheap Tickets (www.cheaptickets.com) makes itself more tangible through its descriptive name.

There are four unique aspects of service retailing that influence relationship building and customer retention: (1) The intangibility of many services makes a consumer's choice of competitive offerings tougher than with goods. (2) The service provider and his or her services are sometimes inseparable (thereby localizing marketing efforts). (3) The perishability of many services prevents storage and increases risks. (4) The aspect of human nature involved in many services makes them more variable.

The intangible (and possibly abstract) nature of services makes it harder for a firm to develop a clear consumer-oriented strategy, particularly because many retailers (such as opticians, repairpeople, and landscapers) start service businesses on the basis of their product expertise. The inseparability of the service provider and his or her services means the owner-operator is often indispensable and good customer relations are pivotal. Perishability presents a risk that in many cases cannot be overcome. Thus, revenues from an unrented hotel room are forever lost. Variability means service quality may differ for each shopping experience, store, or service provider. See Figure 2-8.

Service retailing is much more dependent on personal interactions and word-of-mouth communication than goods retailing:

Relationship marketing benefits the customer, as well as the firm. For services that are personally important, variable in quality, and/or complex, many customers will desire to be "relationship customers." Medical, banking, insurance, and hairstyling services illustrate some or all of the significant factors—importance, variability, and complexity—that would cause many customers to desire continuity with the same provider, a proactive service attitude, and customized service delivery. The intangible nature of services makes them difficult for customers to evaluate prior to purchase. The heterogeneity of labor-intensive services encourages

FIGURE 2-8

Characteristics of Service Retailing That Differentiate It from Goods Retailing and Their Strategic Implications

Sources: Adapted by the authors from Valarie A. Zeithaml, A. Parasuraman, and Leonard L. Berry, "Problems and Strategies in Service Marketing," *Journal of Marketing*, Vol. 49 (Spring 1985), p. 35. Reprinted by permission of the American Marketing Association.

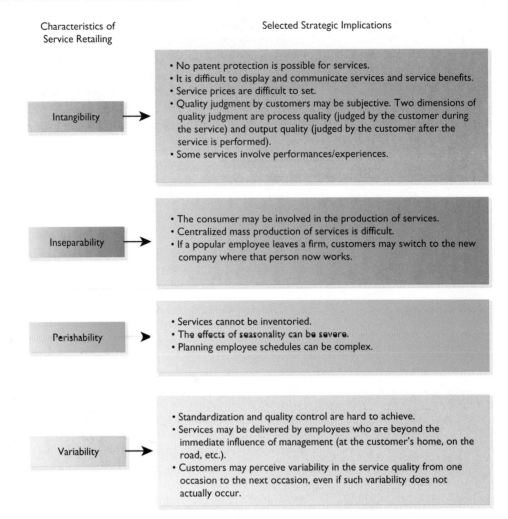

Characteristics of Service Retailing | Selected Strategic Implications

Intangibility
• No patent protection is possible for services.
• It is difficult to display and communicate services and service benefits.
• Service prices are difficult to set.
• Quality judgment by customers may be subjective. Two dimensions of quality judgment are process quality (judged by the customer during the service) and output quality (judged by the customer after the service is performed).
• Some services involve performances/experiences.

Inseparability
• The consumer may be involved in the production of services.
• Centralized mass production of services is difficult.
• If a popular employee leaves a firm, customers may switch to the new company where that person now works.

Perishability
• Services cannot be inventoried.
• The effects of seasonality can be severe.
• Planning employee schedules can be complex.

Variability
• Standardization and quality control are hard to achieve.
• Services may be delivered by employees who are beyond the immediate influence of management (at the customer's home, on the road, etc.).
• Customers may perceive variability in the service quality from one occasion to the next occasion, even if such variability does not actually occur.

customer loyalty when excellent service is experienced. Not only does the auto repair firm want to find customers who will be loyal, but customers want to find an auto repair firm that evokes their loyalty. Knowledge of the customer combined with social rapport built over a series of service encounters facilitate the tailoring of service to customer specifications. Relationship marketing does not apply to every service situation. However, for those services distinguished by the characteristics discussed here, it is potent.[16]

Figure 2-9 highlights several factors that consumers may consider in forming their perceptions about the caliber of the service retailing experience offered by a particular firm. The appendix at the end of this chapter presents an additional discussion on the unique aspects of operating a service retailing business.

TECHNOLOGY AND RELATIONSHIPS IN RETAILING

Technology is beneficial to retailing relationships if it facilitates a better communication flow between retailers and their customers, as well as between retailers and their suppliers, and there are faster, more dependable transactions.

These two points are key in studying technology and its impact on relationships in retailing: (1) In each firm, the roles of technology and "humans" must be

FIGURE 2-9
Selected Factors Affecting Consumer Perceptions of Service Retailing

Sources: Adapted by the authors from Leonard L. Berry, Kathleen Seiders, and Dhruv Grewal, "Understanding Service Convenience," *Journal of Marketing*, Vol. 66 (July 2002), pp. 1–17; and Hung-Chang Chiu, "A Study on the Cognitive and Affective Components of Service Quality," *Total Quality Management*, Vol. 13 (March 2002), pp. 265–274.

clear and consistent with the goals and style of that business. Although technology can facilitate customer service, it may become overloaded and break down. It is also viewed as impersonal by some consumers. New technology must be set up efficiently with minimal disruptions to suppliers, employees, and customers. (2) Shoppers expect certain operations to be in place, so they can rapidly complete credit transactions, get feedback on product availability, and so on. Firms have to deploy some advances (such as a computerized checkout system) simply to be competitive. By enacting other advances, they can be distinctive. For instance, consider the paint store with computerized paint-matching equipment for customers who want to touch up old jobs.

Throughout this book, we devote a lot of attention to technological advances via "Technology in Retailing" boxes and in-chapter discussions. Here, we look at technology's effects in terms of electronic banking and customer/supplier interactions.

Electronic Banking

Electronic banking involves both the use of automatic teller machines (ATMs) and the instant processing of retail purchases. It allows centralized recordkeeping and lets customers complete transactions 24 hours a day, 7 days a week at bank and nonbank locations—including home or office. Besides its use in typical financial transactions (such as check cashing, deposits, withdrawals, and transfers), electronic banking is now used in retailing. Many retailers accept some form of electronic debit payment plan (discussed further in Chapter 13) whereby the purchase price is immediately deducted from a consumer's bank account by computer and transferred to the retailer's account.

Worldwide, there are more than 1.1 billion ATMs—400,000 in the United States alone—and people make billions of ATM transactions yearly.[17] ATMs are located in banks, shopping centers, department stores, supermarkets, convenience stores, hotels, and airports; on college campuses; and at other sites. With sharing systems, such as the Cirrus and Plus networks, consumers can make transactions at ATMs outside their local banking areas and around the world.

A highly touted, but thus far limited in use, new version of electronic payment is called the *smart card* by industry observers. The smart card contains an electronic strip that stores and modifies customer information as transactions take place. It is similar to pre-paid phone cards, whereby consumers buy computer-coded cards in denominations of $10, $20, $50, $100, and more. As they shop, card readers deduct the purchase amount from the cards. After they are used up, the cards are thrown away or are recoded. However, unlike with cash payments, retailers pay a fee for smart card transactions. In the future, "smarter" smart cards are expected to be more permanent and store more information (such as frequent shopper points).[18]

Customer and Supplier Interactions

Technology is changing the nature of retailer-customer and retailer-supplier interactions. If applied well, benefits accrue to all parties. If not, there are negative ramifications. Here are several illustrations.

Retailers widely use point-of-sale scanning equipment. Why? By electronically scanning products (rather than having cashiers "ring up" each product), retailers can quickly complete transactions, amass sales data, give feedback to suppliers, place and receive orders faster, reduce costs, and adjust inventory. There is a downside to scanning: the error rate. This can upset consumers, especially if they perceive scanning to be inaccurate. Yet, according to a Federal Trade Commission (FTC) study, scanner errors in reading prices occurred only 3.4 percent of the time; and although consumers believe that most errors result in overcharges, the FTC found that overcharges and undercharges were equally likely.[19] One way to assure consumers is to display more information at the point of purchase.

An increasingly popular point-of-sale system involves self-scanning (which is discussed further in Chapter 13). Here's how a basic system works:

> A supermarket customer scans the groceries and sacks them. The sacking area is built atop a scale linked to the scanner that alerts the customer if an item was scanned twice or not at all. After all items are scanned, the customer scans in any coupons and selects a payment method. The machine accepts cash, credit, and debit cards, and electronic benefits transfers. Customers can use checks and food stamps but may need assistance from a cashier. Additionally, a cashier monitoring the checkout stations will be required to enter the birth date of customers purchasing alcohol or cigarettes.[20]

Other technological innovations are also influencing retail interactions. Here are three examples:

Neiman Marcus (**www.neimanmarcus.com**) pioneered the electronic gift card.

- Many retailers think they have the answer to the problem of finding the perfect gift—the electronic gift card. They have become so popular that two-thirds of U.S. adults buy or receive at least one gift card each year: "Gift cards have done more than revolutionize the practice of gift giving. They redefine how consumers shop, employers motivate, parents manage spending, and retailers boost sales. The leading occasion for gift card purchases is birthdays and, second, the winter holidays.[21]
- Interactive electronic kiosks (discussed further in Chapter 6) are gaining in use: "It's a shame to waste a minute in Honolulu, so that may be why Hilton Hotels chose that city's airport to demo its new off-site check-in kiosk.

FIGURE 2-10
Interactive Marketing at McDonald's

Through this kiosk, parents can place a food order for their children and themselves, and the completed order will be delivered to the McDonald's play area.

Photo reprinted by permission of Susan Berry, Retail Image Consulting, Inc.

Arriving fliers can use it to get their magnetic keys, so when they get to the hotel they can go straight to their rooms. The kiosks expand the efforts of several hotel chains, including Hilton and Hyatt, which are each adding kiosks to hotel lobbies. Hilton's also reversing the deal, letting American Airlines put a kiosk in the lobby of the O'Hare Hilton."[22] Figure 2-10 shows a McDonald's interactive kiosk.

● More retailers are using Web portals to exchange information with suppliers: "ChainDrugStore.net (**www.chaindrugstore.net**) is a secure online communications network connecting suppliers, wholesalers, and retailers in the retail pharmacy industry with vital information critical to business operations of each." The site "provides hundreds of companies of all sizes with new ways to build, sustain, and enhance trading relationships while increasing efficiencies and reducing costs. ChainDrugStore.net is a wholly-owned subsidiary of the National Association of Chain Drug Stores."[23]

Technology in RETAILING — PayPass Comes to Retailing

Mastercard's PayPass (**www.paypass.com**) is a relatively new credit card with a built-in radio frequency identification chip (RFID) that sends payment information to a merchant's point-of-sale system. Already, McDonald's (**www.mcdonalds.com**), CVS (**www.cvs.com**), Subway (**www.subway.com**), and several other retailers have agreed to accept PayPass at some of their locations.

According to McDonald's management, there are key advantages for PayPass over traditional credit cards and cash. Unlike traditional credit cards that are based on magnetic strips, the PayPass system can be swiped from any direction and does not require a signature for transactions of $25 or less. And unlike cash, there is no small change to be counted or exchanged. These characteristics speed PayPass-based transactions.

Like other forms of payment systems, PayPass faces an interesting problem in generating greater use by consumers and widespread acceptance by merchants. Consumers typically have little use for a technology that's not widely accepted by merchants. Merchants also have little interest in using a payment form without a large customer base. A MasterCard executive calls this a "chicken-and-the-egg" type problem.

Sources: Ken Clark, "PayPass Touches Down at McDonald's," *Retail Technology Quarterly* (October 2004), pp. 24A, 28A; and "MasterCard PayPass," **www.mastercard.com/aboutourcards/paypass.html** (April 9, 2006).

ETHICAL PERFORMANCE AND RELATIONSHIPS IN RETAILING

Ethical challenges fall into three interconnected categories: *Ethics* relates to the retailer's moral principles and values. *Social responsibility* involves acts benefiting society. *Consumerism* entails protecting consumer rights. "Good" behavior depends not only on the retailer but also on the expectations of the community in which it does business.

Throughout this book, in "Ethics in Retailing" boxes and chapter discussions, we look at many ethical issues. Here we study the broader effects of ethics, social responsibility, and consumerism. Visit our Web site for links on retailers' ethical challenges (**www.prenhall.com/bermanevans**).

Ethics

In dealing with their constituencies (customers, the general public, employees, suppliers, competitors, and others), retailers have a moral obligation to act ethically. Furthermore, due to the media attention paid to firms' behavior and the high expectations people have today, a failure to be ethical may lead to adverse publicity, lawsuits, the loss of customers, and a lack of self-respect among employees.

When a retailer has a sense of **ethics**, it acts in a trustworthy, fair, honest, and respectful manner with each of its constituencies. Executives must articulate to employees and channel partners which kinds of behavior are acceptable and which are not. The best way to avoid unethical acts is for firms to have written ethics codes, to distribute them to employees and channel partners, to monitor behavior, and to punish poor behavior—and for top managers to be highly ethical in their own conduct. See Figure 2-11.

Society often may deem certain behavior to be unethical even if laws do not forbid it. Most observers would agree that practices such as these are unethical (and sometimes illegal, too):

- Raising prices on scarce products after a natural disaster such as a hurricane.
- Not having adequate stock when a sale is advertised.

FIGURE 2-11
Eddie Bauer: Strong Ethical
Sensibilities

Reprinted by permission of Eddie
Bauer, Inc.

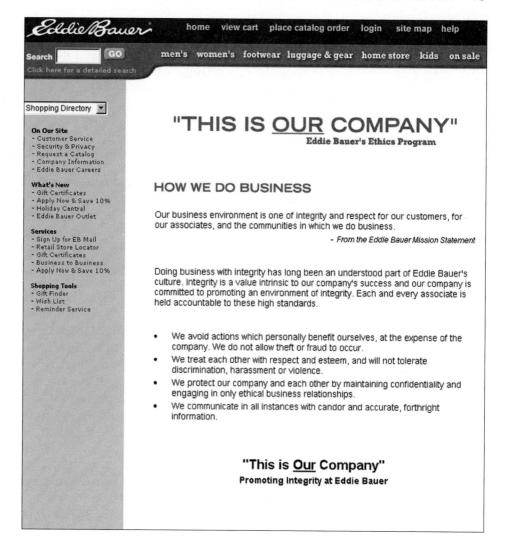

- Charging high prices in low-income areas because consumers there do not have the transportation mobility to shop out of their neighborhoods.
- Selling alcohol and tobacco products to children.
- Having a salesperson pose as a market researcher when engaged in telemarketing.
- Defaming competitors.
- Selling refurbished merchandise as new.
- Pressuring employees to push high-profit items, even if these items are not the best products.
- Selling information from a customer database.

The Direct Marketing Association makes its complete ethics code available at its Web site (**www.the-dma.org/ guidelines/ethicalguidelines. shtml**).

    Many trade associations promote ethics codes to member firms. For example, here are some provisions of the Direct Marketing Association's ethics code: *Article 1:* All offers should be clear, honest, and complete. *Article 5:* Disparagement of any person or group on grounds addressed by federal or state laws that prohibit discrimination is unacceptable. *Article 8:* All contacts should disclose the name of the sponsor and each purpose of the contact; no one should make offers or solicitations in the guise of one purpose when the intent is a different one. *Article 24:* No sweepstakes promotion should represent that a recipient or entrant has won a prize or that any entry stands a greater chance of winning a prize than any other entry when this is not the case. *Article 28:* Merchandise or services should not be provided without having first received the customer's permission. *Article 43:* A firm should not knowingly call or send a voice solicitation message to a consumer who has an unlisted or unpublished phone number except where the number was provided by the consumer to that marketer for that purpose.[24]

Social Responsibility

A retailer exhibiting **social responsibility** acts in the best interests of society—as well as itself. The challenge is to balance corporate citizenship with a fair level of profits for stockholders, management, and employees. Some forms of social responsibility are virtually cost-free, such as having employees participate in community events or disposing of waste products in a more careful way. Some are more costly, such as making donations to charitable groups or giving away goods and services to a school. Still others mean going above and beyond the letter of the law, such as having free loaner wheelchairs for persons with disabilities besides legally mandated wheelchair accessibility to retail premises.

Most retailers know socially responsible acts do not go unnoticed. Though the acts may not stimulate greater patronage for firms with weak strategies, they can be a customer inducement for those otherwise viewed as "me too" entities. It may also be possible to profit from good deeds. If a retailer donates excess inventory to a charity that cares for the ill, it can take a tax deduction equal to the cost of the goods plus one-half the difference between the cost and the retail price. To do this, a retailer must be a corporation and the charity must use the goods and not sell or trade them.

The Ronald McDonald House program (www.rmhc.org) is one of the most respected community outreach efforts in retailing.

This is what some retailers are doing. McDonald's founded Ronald McDonald House so families can stay at a low-cost facility instead of a costly hotel when their seriously ill children get medical treatment away from home. Target Stores no longer sells cigarettes. In 2005, Wal-Mart announced an "Acres for America program and committed $35 million for the next 10 years to conserve at least one acre of priority wildlife habitat for every acre developed for company use."[25] J.C. Penney requires all suppliers to sign a code of conduct that underage labor is not used. Hannaford Bros.' pledge sums up the role of a socially involved retailer:

> Our business depends on the people who shop at our stores and the people who work for our firm. When we help our communities—the places where our customers and associates and their families live and work— become better, healthier, and more prosperous, we grow along with them. Hannaford has a long history of being a good neighbor and a good corporate citizen. Wherever we do business, we take time to support schools, community groups, and charitable organizations that enrich our communities and the lives of the people who reside there. We do this with corporate and foundation giving, numerous fundraisers, and sponsorships carried out year round by our stores, and through the strong commitment of our associates who willingly volunteer their time, energy, and enthusiasm.[26]

Consumerism

Consumerism involves the activities of government, business, and other organizations to protect people from practices infringing upon their rights as consumers. These actions recognize that consumers have basic rights that should be

Ethics in RETAILING

Red Lobster: In Sync with Its Customers

Michael Friedman, Red Lobster's (**www.redlobster.com**) interactive marketing manager, believes that Overboard Club, the firm's loyalty program, needs to adhere to the highest ethical principles. At the time he first took over the loyalty program, customers complained of pop-up ads from other vendors when they entered Red Lobster's Web site. So, he discontinued this practice. According to Friedman, "We asked ourselves, 'Are we abusing the privilege of data that is given to us when people sign up for the Overboard Club?'" Red Lobster also does not trade or sell its loyalty program members' e-mail addresses.

When Friedman joined Red Lobster in 2004, Overboard Club (**www.redlobster.com/overboard**) had 32,000 members—mostly employees. A year later, Overboard Club had more than 800,000 members; and it is growing at 50 to 60 percent per year. Overboard Club e-mails 13 communications per year to each member. These messages are tailored based on members' dining choices, buying patterns, and geographic region. Thus, a consumer with a history of wine purchases may be offered a special wine promotion.

Sources: Mila N. D'Antonio, "Red Lobster Goes Overboard for Its Customers," *1to1* (January–February 2005); and "Red Lobster Overboard Club," **www.redlobster.com/overboard** (February 19, 2006).

safeguarded. As President Kennedy said about 45 years ago, consumers have the *right to safety* (protection against unsafe conditions and hazardous goods and services), the *right to be informed* (protection against fraudulent, deceptive, and incomplete information, advertising, and labeling), the *right to choose* (access to a variety of goods, services, and retailers), and the *right to be heard* (consumer feedback, both positive and negative, to the firm and to government agencies).

Retailers and their channel partners need to avoid business practices violating these rights and to do all they can to understand and protect them. These are some reasons why:

Learn more about the ADA (www.usdoj.gov/crt/ada/adahom1.htm).

- Some retail practices are covered by legislation. One major law is the **Americans with Disabilities Act (ADA)**, which mandates that persons with disabilities be given appropriate access to retailing facilities. As Title III of the Act states: "Public accommodations [retail stores] must comply with basic nondiscrimination requirements that prohibit exclusion, segregation, and unequal treatment. They also must comply with specific requirements related to architectural standards for new and altered buildings; reasonable modifications to policies, practices, and procedures; effective communication with people with hearing, vision, or speech disabilities; and other access requirements. Additionally, public accommodations must remove barriers in existing buildings where it is easy to do so without much difficulty or expense, given the public accommodation's resources." ADA affects entrances, vertical transportation, width of aisles, and store displays.[27] See Figure 2-12.

- People are more apt to patronize firms perceived as customer-oriented and not to shop with ones seen as greedy.

- Consumers are more knowledgeable, price-conscious, and selective than in the past.

- Large retailers may be viewed as indifferent to consumers. They may not provide enough personal attention for shoppers or may have inadequate control over employees.

- The use of self-service is increasing, and it can cause frustration for some shoppers.

FIGURE 2-12
Understanding the
Americans with
Disabilities Act

- Innovative technology is unsettling to many consumers, who must learn new shopping behavior (such as how to use electronic video kiosks).
- Retailers are in direct customer contact, so they are often blamed for and asked to resolve problems caused by manufacturers (such as defective products).

One troublesome issue for consumers involves how retailers handle *customer privacy*. A consumer-oriented approach, comprising these elements, can reduce negative shopper feelings: (1) Notice—"A company should provide consumers with a clear and conspicuous notice regarding its information practices." (2) Consumer choice—"A company should provide consumers with an opportunity to decide whether it may disclose personal information about them to unaffiliated third parties." (3) Access and correction—"Companies should provide consumers with an opportunity to access and correct personal information that they have collected about the consumers." (4) Security—"Companies should adopt reasonable security measures to protect the privacy of personal information." (5) Enforcement—"The firm should have in place a system by which it can enforce its privacy policy."[28]

To avoid customer relations problems, many retailers have devised programs to protect consumer rights without waiting for government or consumer pressure to do so. Here are examples.

For more than 90 years, J.C. Penney has adhered to the "Penney Idea":

> To serve the public, as nearly as we can, to its complete satisfaction; to expect for the service we render a fair remuneration and not all the profit the traffic will bear; to do all in our power to pack the customer dollar with value, quality, and satisfaction; to continue training ourselves and our associates so the service we give will be more intelligently performed; to improve constantly the human factor in our business; to reward men and women in our firm by participation in what the business produces; and to test our every policy, method, and act—"Does it square with what is right and just?"[29]

About 40 years ago, the Giant Food supermarket chain devised a consumer bill of rights (based on President Kennedy's), which it still follows today: (1) Right to safety—Giant's product safety standards, such as age-labeling toys, go beyond those required by the government. (2) Right to be informed—Giant has a detailed labeling system. (3) Right to choose—Consumers who want to purchase possibly harmful or hazardous products (such as foods with additives) can do so. (4) Right to be heard—A continuing dialogue with reputable consumer groups is in place. (5) Right to redress—There is a money-back guarantee policy on products. (6) Right to service—Customers should receive good in-store service.[30]

A number of retailers have enacted their own programs to test merchandise for such attributes as value, quality, misrepresentation of contents, safety, and durability. Sears, Wal-Mart, A&P, Macy's, and Target Stores are just a few of those doing testing. See Figure 2-13. Among the other consumerism activities undertaken by many retailers are setting clear procedures for handling customer complaints, sponsoring consumer education programs, and training personnel to interact properly with customers.

Consumer-oriented activities are not limited to large chains; small firms can also be involved. A local toy store can separate toys by age group. A grocery store can set up displays featuring environmentally safe detergents. A neighborhood restaurant can cook foods in low-fat vegetable oil. A sporting goods store can give a money-back guarantee on exercise equipment, so people can try it at home.

FIGURE 2-13
Voluntary Product Testing at Target Stores

Reprinted by permission of Target Stores.

Target's Responsibility
At Target, toys are an important part of our business. We want the toys you buy to meet Target's and the U.S. Government's high standards of quality, value, and safety. Therefore, we abide by all U.S. Consumer Product Safety Regulations. Target also utilizes an independent testing agency. They test samples of all toys we sell to help ensure your child's safe play.

All toys sold at Target are tested to be certain they are free from these dangers:

Sharp edges

Toys of brittle plastic or glass can be broken to expose cutting edges. Poorly made metal or wood toys may have sharp edges.

Small parts

Tiny toys and toys with removable parts can be swallowed or lodged in child's windpipe, ears, or nose.

Loud noises

Noise-making guns and other toys can produce sounds at noise levels that can damage hearing.

Sharp points

Broken toys can expose dangerous points. Stuffed toys can have barbed eyes or wired limbs that can cut.

Propelled objects

Projectiles and similar flying toys can injure eyes in particular. Arrows or darts should have protective soft tips.

Electrical shock

Electrically operated toys that are improperly constructed can shock or cause burns. Electric toys must meet mandatory safety requirements.

Wrong toys for the wrong age

Toys that may be safe for older children can be dangerous when played with by little ones.

Summary

1. *To explain what "value" really means and highlight its pivotal role in retailers' building and sustaining relationships.* Sellers undertake a series of activities and processes to provide a given level of value for the consumer. Consumers then perceive the value offered by sellers, based on the perceived benefits received versus the prices paid. Perceived value varies by type of shopper.

   A retail value chain represents the total bundle of benefits offered by a channel of distribution. It comprises store location, ambience, customer service, the products/brands carried, product quality, the in-stock position, shipping, prices, the retailer's image, and so forth. Some elements of a retail value chain are visible to shoppers. Others are not. An expected retail strategy represents the minimum value chain elements a given customer segment expects from a given retailer type. An augmented retail strategy includes the extra elements that differentiate retailers. A potential retail strategy includes value chain elements not yet perfected in the retailer's industry category.

2. *To describe how both customer relationships and channel relationships may be nurtured in today's highly competitive marketplace.* For relationship retailing to work, enduring relationships are needed with other channel members, as well as with customers. More retailers now realize loyal customers are the backbone of their business.

   To engage in relationship retailing with consumers, these factors should be considered: the customer base, customer service, customer satisfaction, and loyalty programs and defection rates. In terms of the customer base, all customers are not equal. Some shoppers are more worth nurturing than others; they are a retailer's core customers.

   Customer service has two components: expected services and augmented services. The attributes of personnel who interact with customers, as well as the number and variety of customer services offered, have a big impact on the relationship created. Some firms have improved customer service by empowering personnel, giving them the authority to bend some rules. In devising a strategy, a retailer must make broad decisions and then enact specific tactics as to credit, delivery, and so forth.

   Customer satisfaction occurs when the value and customer service provided in a retail experience meet or exceed expectations. Otherwise, the consumer will be dissatisfied.

   Loyalty programs reward the best customers, those with whom a retailer wants to develop long-lasting relationships. To succeed, they must complement a sound value-driven retail strategy. By studying defections, a firm can learn how many customers it is losing and why they no longer patronize it.

   Members of a distribution channel jointly represent a value delivery system. Each one depends on the others; and every activity must be enumerated and responsibility assigned. Small retailers may have to use suppliers outside the normal channel to get the items they want and gain supplier support. A delivery system is as good as its weakest link. A relationship-oriented technique that some manufacturers and retailers are trying, especially supermarket chains, is category management.

3. *To examine the differences in relationship building between goods and service retailers.* Goods retailing focuses on selling tangible products. Service retailing involves transactions where consumers do not purchase or acquire ownership of tangible products.

   There are three kinds of service retailing: rented-goods services—consumers lease goods for a given time; owned-goods services—goods owned by consumers are repaired, improved, or maintained; and nongoods services—consumers experience personal services rather than possess them. Customer service refers to activities that are part of the total retail experience. With service retailing, services are sold to the consumer.

   The unique features of service retailing that influence relationship building and retention are the intangible nature of many services, the inseparability of some service providers and their services, the perishability of many services, and the variability of many services.

4. *To discuss the impact of technology on relationships in retailing.* Technology is advantageous when it leads to an improved information flow between retailers and suppliers, and between retailers and customers, and to faster, smoother transactions.

   Electronic banking involves both the use of automatic teller machines and the instant processing of retail purchases. It allows for centralized records and lets customers complete transactions 24 hours a day, 7 days a week at various sites. Technology is also changing the nature of supplier/retailer/customer interactions via point-of-sale equipment, self-scanning, electronic gift cards, interactive kiosks, and other innovations.

5. *To consider the interplay between retailers' ethical performance and relationships in retailing.* Retailer challenges fall into three related categories: Ethics

relates to a firm's moral principles and values. Social responsibility has to do with benefiting society. Consumerism entails the protection of consumer rights. "Good" behavior is based not only on the firm's practices but also on the expectations of the community in which it does business.

Ethical retailers act in a trustworthy, fair, honest, and respectful way. Firms are more apt to avoid unethical behavior if they have written ethics codes,

communicate them to employees, monitor and punish poor behavior, and have ethical executives. Retailers perform in a socially responsible manner when they act in the best interests of society through recycling and conservation programs and other efforts. Consumerism activities involve government, business, and independent organizations. Four consumer rights are basic: to safety, to be informed, to choose, and to be heard.

Key Terms

value (p. 25)

value chain (p. 25)

core customers (p. 29)

expected customer service (p. 30)

augmented customer service (p. 30)

employee empowerment (p. 30)

revolving credit account (p. 34)

option credit account (p. 34)

open credit account (p. 34)

customer satisfaction (p. 35)

consumer loyalty (frequent shopper) programs (p. 36)

value delivery system (p. 36)

goods retailing (p. 38)

service retailing (p. 38)

rented-goods services (p. 39)

owned-goods services (p. 39)

nongoods services (p. 39)

electronic banking (p. 41)

ethics (p. 44)

social responsibility (p. 46)

consumerism (p. 46)

Americans with Disabilities Act (ADA) (p. 47)

Questions for Discussion

1. When a consumer shops at an upscale furniture store, what factors determine whether the consumer feels that he or she got a fair value? How does the perception of value differ when that same consumer shops at a discount furniture store?

2. What are the expected and augmented value chain elements for each of these retailers?
   a. Roadside diner.
   b. Resort hotel.
   c. Local bank.

3. Why should a retailer devote special attention to its core customers? How should it do so?

4. What is the connection between customer service and employee empowerment? Is employee empowerment always a good idea? Why or why not?

5. How would you measure the level of customer satisfaction with your college's bookstore?

6. Devise a consumer loyalty program for a national hardware store chain.

7. What are the unique aspects of service retailing? Give an example of each.

8. What are the pros and cons of ATMs? As a retailer, would you want an ATM in your store? Why or why not?

9. Will the time come when most consumer purchases are made with self-scanners? Explain your answer.

10. Describe three unethical, but legal, acts on the part of retailers that you have encountered. How have you reacted in each case?

11. Differentiate between social responsibility and consumerism from the perspective of a retailer.

12. How would you deal with consumer concerns about privacy in their relationships with retailers?

Web-Based Exercise

Visit the Web site of Kohl's (**www.kohls.com**). Click on "customer service" at the top of the home page. Comment on the information you find there. Does Kohl's have customer-oriented policies? Explain your answer.

Note: Stop by our Web site (**www.prenhall.com/bermanevans**) to experience a number of highly interactive, appealing Web exercises based on actual company demonstrations and sample materials related to retailing.

Chapter Endnotes

1. Various company sources.

2. *Dillards, Inc. Quarterly Report* (April 30, 2005).

3. Retail Forward, *Retailing 2005*, p. 9.

4. Jack Mackey, "Franchisors Reap Multiple Benefits From Increasing Customer Loyalty," *Franchising World* (May 2005), p. 49.

5. Linda Tucci, "Men Conquer a New Frontier: The Mall," *Boston.com* (April 10, 2005); Pallavi Gogoi and Patricia O'Connell, "I Am Woman, Hear Me Shop," *Business Week Online* (February 14, 2005); *Strategic Focus: Global Food, Drug, Mass Shopper Update* (Columbus, OH: Retail Forward, April 2005); *Industry Outlook: Value Department Stores* (Columbus, OH: Retail Forward, March 2005); and *Industry Outlook: Mass Channel* (Columbus, OH: Retail Forward, May 2005).

6. Third Wave Research Group, "How to Identify Good and Bad Clients, and Focus our Efforts," **www.bcentral.co.uk/marketing/customerservice/know-your-customers.mspx** (February 7, 2006).

7. "Our Company, Our Culture," **www.autozoneinc.com/about_us/our_company/index.html** (March 2, 2006).

8. Jennifer Rooney, "Why Orchids Matter," *Sales & Marketing Management* (June 2005), p. 6.

9. John Galvin, "Chief Customer Officer," *Point* (April 2005), pp. 11–15.

10. "A Company of Entrepreneurs," **http://careers.nordstrom.com/story2.html** (February 27, 2006).

11. Rose Otieno, Chris Harrow, and Gaynor Lea-Greenwood, "The Unhappy Shopper, A Retail Experience: Exploring Fashion, Fit, and Affordability," *International Journal of Retail & Distribution Management*, Vol. 33 (Number 4, 2005), pp. 298–309.

12. John Chesak and Jim Dippold, "Frequent Doesn't Mean Loyal: Using Segmentation to Build Shopper Loyalty," *Consumer Insight* (Spring 2004), pp. 18–23.

13. Carolyn Setlow, "The Benefits of Frequent Shopper Clubs," *DSN Retailing Today* (March 25, 2002), p. 11.

14. "Supplier Information," **www.walmartstores.com/wmstore/wmstores/Mainsupplier.jsp** (March 2, 2006).

15. Ken Clark, "Collaborators, and Proud of It," *Chain Store Age* (March 2002), p. 76.

16. Leonard L. Berry, "Relationship Marketing of Services—Growing Interest, Emerging Prospects," *Journal of the Academy of Marketing Science*, Vol. 23 (Fall 1995), pp. 237–38. See also Charlene Pleger Bebko, "Service Intangibility and Its Impact on Consumer Expectations of Service Quality," *Journal of Services Marketing*, Vol. 14, Number 1 (2000), pp. 9–26.

17. *ATM & Debit News' EFT Data Book 2005.*

18. Charlene O'Hanlon, "Smart Cards Keep Getting Smarter All the Time," *CRN* (May 2, 2005), p. 1.

19. Federal Trade Commission, "Price Check II Shows Scanner Accuracy Has Improved Since 1996" (December 16, 1998), press release.

20. "Omaha, Neb., Grocery Joins Growing Number to Add Self-Checkout Stands," *Omaha World-Herald* (February 18, 2002).

21. Ken Clark, "Much Ado About Gift Cards," *Chain Store Age* (December 2004), p. 142; and "Industry News," **www.storedvalue.com/industrynews.html** (November 17, 2005).

22. "No-Wait Check-Ins," *Newsweek* (May 9, 2005), p. E2.

23. "ChainDrugStore.net—the First Real-time Network That Connects Suppliers with Retailers," **https://www.chaindrugstore.net/CDSInfo/pages/aboutUs.htm** (March 9, 2006).

24. *Direct Marketing Association Guidelines for Ethical Business Practices* (New York: Direct Marketing Association, revised November 2004).

25. "Wal-Mart Good. Works." **www.walmartfoundation.org** (December 9, 2005).

26. "Hannaford Helps Communities," **www.hannaford.com/Contents/Our_Company/Community/index.shtml** (March 11, 2006).

27. See Marianne Wilson, "ADA: Open to Interpretation," *Chain Store Age* (July 2002), p. 110.

28. Susan Haller, "Privacy: What Every Manager Should Know," *Information Management Journal*, Vol. 36 (May–June 2002), pp. 38–39.

29. J.C. Penney, public relations.

30. Giant Food, public relations.

Appendix on Planning for the Unique Aspects of Service Retailing

We present this appendix because service retailing in the United States and around the world is growing steadily and represents a large portion of overall retailing. In the United States, consumers spend 60 percent of their after-tax income on such services as travel, recreation, personal care, education, medical care, and housing. Well over 75 percent of the labor force works in services. Consumers spend billions of dollars each year to rent such products as power tools and party goods (coffee urns, silverware, wine glasses, etc.). People annually spend $150 billion to maintain their cars. There are 80,000 beauty and barber shops, 42,000 laundry and cleaning outlets, 55,000 hotels and motels, 17,000 video-rental stores, and 25,000 sports and recreation clubs. During the past 30 years, the prices of services have risen more than the prices of many goods. Due to technological advances, automation has substantially reduced manufacturing labor costs, but many services remain labor-intensive due to their personal nature.[1]

Here we will look at the abilities required to be a successful service retailer, how to improve the performance of service retailers, and the strategy of a recent Baldrige Award winner.

ABILITIES REQUIRED TO BE A SUCCESSFUL SERVICE RETAILER

The personal abilities required to succeed in service retailing are usually quite distinct from those in goods retailing:

- With service retailing, the major value provided to the customer is some type of retailer service, not the ownership of a physical product produced by a manufacturer.

- Specific skills are often required, and these skills may not be transferable from one type of service to another. TV repairpeople, beauticians, and accountants cannot easily change businesses or transfer skills. The owners of appliance stores, cosmetics stores, and toy stores (all goods retailers) would have an easier time than service retailers in changing and transferring their skills to another area.

- More service operators must possess licenses or certification to run their businesses. Barbers, real-estate brokers, dentists, attorneys, plumbers, and others must pass exams in their fields.

- Owners of service businesses must enjoy their jobs and have the aptitude for them. Because of the close personal contact with customers, these elements are essential and difficult to feign.

Many service retailers can operate on lower overall investments and succeed on less yearly revenues than goods retailers. A firm with four outdoor tennis courts can operate with one worker who functions as clerk/cashier and maintenance person. A tax-preparation firm can succeed with one accountant. A watch repair business needs one repairperson. In each case, the owner may be the only skilled worker. Operating costs can be held down accordingly. On the other hand, a goods retailer needs a good product assortment and inventory on hand, which may be costly and require storage facilities.

The time commitment of a service retailer differs by type of business opportunity. Some businesses, such as a self-service laundromat or a movie theater, require a low time commitment. Other businesses, such as house painting or a travel agency, require a large time commitment because personal service is the key to profitability. More service firms are in the high rather than the low time-investment category.

IMPROVING THE PERFORMANCE OF SERVICE RETAILERS[2]

Service tangibility can be increased by stressing service provider reliability, promoting a continuous theme (the Hertz #1 Club Gold), describing specific results (a car tune-up's improving gas consumption by one mile per gallon), and offering warranties (hotels giving automatic refunds to unhappy guests). Most airlines have Web sites where customers can select flights and make their reservations interactively. These sites are a tangible representation of the airlines and their logos.

Demand and supply can be better matched by offering similar services to market segments with different demand patterns (Manhattan tourists versus residents), new services with demand patterns that are countercyclical from existing services (cross-country skiing during the winter at Denver golf resorts), new services that complement existing ones (beauty salons adding tanning booths), special deals during nonpeak times (midweek movie theater prices), and new services not subject to existing capacity constraints (a 10-table restaurant starting a home catering service).

Standardizing services reduces their variability, makes it easier to set prices, and improves efficiency. Services can be standardized by clearly defining each task, determining the minimum and maximum times needed to complete each task, selecting the best order for tasks to be done, and noting the optimum time and quality of the entire service. Standardization has been successfully applied to such firms as quick-auto-service providers (oil change and tune-up firms), legal services (for house closings and similar proceedings), and emergency medical care centers. If services are standardized, there is often a trade-off (e.g., more consistent quality and convenience in exchange for less of a personal touch).

Besides standardizing services, retailers may be able to make services more efficient by automating them and substituting machinery for labor. Thus, attorneys often use computerized word-processing templates for common paragraphs in wills and house closings. This means more consistency in the way documents look, time savings, and neater documents with fewer errors. Among the service firms that automate at least part of their operations are banks, car washes, bowling alleys, airlines, phone services, real-estate brokers, and hotels.

The location of a service retailer must be carefully considered. Sometimes, as with TV repairs, house painting, and lawn care, the service is "delivered" to the customer. The firm's location becomes a client's home, and the actual retail office is rather insignificant. Many clients might never even see a service firm's office; they make contact by phone or personal visits, and customer convenience is optimized. The firm incurs travel expenses, but it also has low (or no) rent and does not have to maintain store facilities, set up displays, and so on. Other service retailers are visited on "specific-intent" shopping trips. Although a customer may be concerned about the convenience of a service location, he or she usually does not select a skilled practitioner such as a doctor or a lawyer based on the location. It is common for doctors and attorneys to have offices in their homes or near hospitals or court buildings. A small store can often be used because little or no room is needed for displaying merchandise. A travel agency may have six salespeople and book millions of dollars in trips but fit into a 500-square-foot store.

To improve their pricing decisions, service retailers can apply these principles to "capture and communicate value through their pricing"[3]: Satisfaction-based pricing recognizes and reduces customer perceptions of uncertainty that service intangibility magnifies. It involves service guarantees, benefit-driven pricing, and flat-rate pricing. Relationship pricing encourages long-term relationships with valuable customers. It entails long-term contracts and price bundling. Efficiency pricing shares cost savings with customers that arise from the firm's efficiently executing service tasks. It is related to the concept of cost leadership.

Negotiated pricing occurs when a retailer works out pricing arrangements with individual customers because a unique or complex service is involved and a one-time price must be agreed on. Unlike traditional pricing (whereby each consumer pays the same price for a standard service), each consumer may pay a different price under negotiated pricing (depending on the nature of the unique service). A moving company charges different fees, depending on the distance of the move, who packs the breakable furniture, the use of stairs versus an elevator, access to highways, and the weight of furniture.

Contingency pricing is an arrangement whereby the retailer does not get paid until after the service is performed and payment is contingent on the service's being satisfactory. A real-estate broker earns a fee only when a house purchaser (who is ready, willing, and able to buy) is presented to the house seller. Several brokers may show a house to prospective buyers, but only the broker who actually sells the house earns a commission. This technique presents risks to a retailer because considerable time and effort may be spent without payment. A broker may show a house 25 times, not sell it, and, therefore, not be paid.

One customer type is often beyond the reach of some service firms: the do-it-yourselfer. And the number of do-it-yourselfers in the United States is growing, as service costs increase. The do-it-yourselfer does a car tune-up, paints the house, mows the lawn, makes all vacation plans, and/or sets up a darkroom for developing film. Goods-oriented discount retailers do well by selling supplies to these people, but service retailers suffer because the labor is done by the customer.

Figure A2-1 highlights 10 lessons that service retailers can learn from the best in the business, such as Walt Disney Company, Marriott International, Ritz-Carlton, and Southwest Airlines.

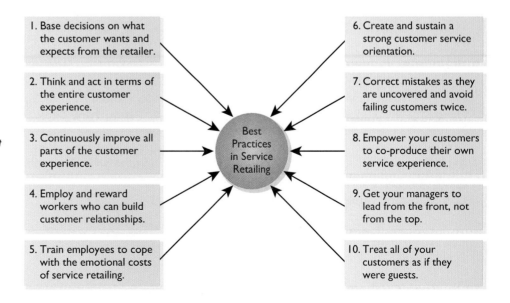

FIGURE A2-1

Lessons in Service Retailing from the Best Firms

Source: Figure developed by the authors based on information in Robert C. Ford, Cherrill P. Heaton, and Stephen W. Brown, "Delivering Excellent Service: Lessons from the Best Firms," *California Management Review*, Vol. 44 (Fall 2001), pp. 39–56.

1. Base decisions on what the customer wants and expects from the retailer.
2. Think and act in terms of the entire customer experience.
3. Continuously improve all parts of the customer experience.
4. Employ and reward workers who can build customer relationships.
5. Train employees to cope with the emotional costs of service retailing.
6. Create and sustain a strong customer service orientation.
7. Correct mistakes as they are uncovered and avoid failing customers twice.
8. Empower your customers to co-produce their own service experience.
9. Get your managers to lead from the front, not from the top.
10. Treat all of your customers as if they were guests.

Best Practices in Service Retailing

THE STRATEGY OF PAL'S SUDDEN SERVICE: A BALDRIGE AWARD WINNER[4]

The Baldrige Award is given by the president of the United States to businesses—manufacturing and service, small and large—and to education and health care organizations that apply and are judged to be outstanding in seven areas: leadership; strategic planning; customer and market focus; measurement, analysis, and knowledge management; human resource focus; process management; and business results. One of the few retailers to win this award is Pal's Sudden Service, a privately owned, quick-service restaurant chain with 18 locations (as of mid-2005), all within 60 miles of Kingsport, Tennessee. The firm distinguishes itself by offering competitively priced food of consistently high quality, delivered rapidly, cheerfully, and without error.

Hop over to Pal's Sudden Service (**www.palsweb. com**). See why it's a big winner!

For everything organizational and operational, Pal's has a process. Its Business Excellence Process is the key integrating element; it ensures that customer requirements are met in each transaction. Carried out under the leadership of Pal's two top executives and its owner-operators, the Business Excellence Process spans all facets of operations from strategic planning (done annually) to online quality control.

Pal's goal is to provide the "quickest, friendliest, most accurate service available." Achieving this is a challenge in an industry with annual employee turnover rates of more than 200 percent. The company's success in reducing turnover among frontline production and service personnel, most of whom are between the ages of 16 and 32, has become a key advantage. Owner-operators and assistant managers have primary responsibility for training based on a four-step model: show, do it, evaluate, and perform again. Employees must demonstrate 100 percent competence before they can work at a specific job task.

Pal's order handout speed has improved more than 30 percent since 1995, decreasing to 20 seconds, almost four times faster than its top competitor. Order errors are rare, averaging less than one for every 2,000 transactions. The firm aims to reduce its error rate to one in 5,000 transactions. In addition, Pal's has consistently received the highest health inspection scores in its market.

Appendix Endnotes

1. Estimated by the authors based on data in *2002 Economic Census Industry Series Reports* (Washington, DC: U.S. Department of Commerce).

2. See Duncan Dickson, Robert C. Ford, and Bruce Laval, "The Top Ten Excuses for Bad Service (and How to Avoid Needing Them)," *Organizational Dynamics*, Vol. 34 (2005), pp. 168–184; and Marukei Nunez and Corey M. Yulinsky, "Better Customer Service in Banks," *McKinsey Quarterly Online* (Number 1, 2005).

3. Leonard L. Berry and Manjit S. Yadav, "Capture and Communicate Value in the Pricing of Services,"

Sloan Management Review, Vol. 37 (Summer 1996), pp. 41–51.

4. The material in this section is excerpted from "Baldrige Award Recipient Profile: Pal's Sudden Service," **www.nist.gov/public_affairs/pals.htm** (January 21, 2003); "Criteria for Excellence," **www. quality.nist.gov/Business_Criteria.htm** (January 14, 2006); "Pal's," **www.palsweb.com** (January 14, 2006); and Leo Jacobson, "Fast and Happy," *Incentive* (November 2004), p. 22.

Chapter 3
STRATEGIC PLANNING IN RETAILING

While working at his father's general clothing store, Leslie Wexner urged his father to concentrate on sportswear due to its higher sales rates. His father insisted that a clothing store needed a wide variety of merchandise, including formal and business clothes. He angrily told Leslie, "You'll never be a merchant." So, at age 26, Leslie Wexner founded The Limited— which is now known as Limited Brands (**www.limitedbrands.com**). He started in 1963 with one small store after getting a $5,000 loan from an aunt.

Clearly, Wexner's focused strategy has worked. Today, Limited Brands operates thousands of stores in the United States (including Express, Lerner New York, The Limited, Structure, and Victoria's Secret). Recently, Limited Brands announced a reorganization of the company into three

Reprinted by permission.

groups made up of apparel, lingerie (including Victoria Secret), and beauty and personal care (including Bath & Body Works). A group president is now in charge of each of the three groups. Leslie Wexner oversees the Victoria's Secret brand.

Wexner has certainly been an ace merchant. He was one of the first retailing executives to understand the importance of developing a network of foreign suppliers that could manufacture goods at low cost and at blazing speed. This enabled his stores to rapidly respond to hot fashion trends without the risks associated with large inventories. Wexner also had the insight to reposition Victoria's Secret, which was a rather sleazy six-store chain based in San Francisco at the time Wexner bought it. Today, it is the leader in intimate apparel.[1]

chapter objectives

1. To show the value of strategic planning for all types of retailers
2. To explain the steps in strategic planning for retailers: situation analysis, objectives, identification of consumers, overall strategy, specific activities, control, and feedback
3. To examine the individual controllable and uncontrollable elements of a retail strategy, and to present strategic planning as a series of integrated steps
4. To demonstrate how a strategic plan can be prepared

OVERVIEW

In this chapter, we cover strategic retail planning—the underpinning of our book—in detail. As noted in Chapter 1, a **retail strategy** is the overall plan or framework of action that guides a retailer. Ideally, it will be at least one year long and outline the retailer's mission, goals, consumer market, overall and specific activities, and control mechanisms. Without a defined and well-integrated strategy, a firm may be unable to cope with the marketplace: "Despite the critical importance of a business plan, many entrepreneurs drag their feet when it comes to preparing one. They argue that their marketplace changes too fast for a plan to be useful or that they just don't have enough time. But just as a builder won't begin construction without a blueprint, eager business owners shouldn't rush into new ventures without a business plan."[2]

All Business (www. allbusiness.com) has a lot of useful planning tools for retailers at its Web site.

The process of strategic retail planning has several attractive features:

- It provides a thorough analysis of the requirements for doing business for different types of retailers.
- It outlines retailer goals.
- A firm determines how to differentiate itself from competitors and develop an offering that appeals to a group of customers.
- The legal, economic, and competitive environment is studied.
- A firm's total efforts are coordinated.
- Crises are anticipated and often avoided.

Strategic planning can be done by the owner of a firm, professional management, or a combination of the two. Even among family businesses, the majority of high-growth companies have strategic plans.

The steps in planning and enacting a retail strategy are interdependent; a firm often starts with a general plan that gets more specific as options and payoffs become clearer. In this chapter, we cover each step in developing a retail strategy, as shown in Figure 3-1. Given the importance of global retailing, a chapter appendix explores the special dimensions of strategic planning in a global retailing environment. Visit our Web site (**www.prenhall.com/bermanevans**) for several links on strategic planning.

SITUATION ANALYSIS

Situation analysis is a candid evaluation of the opportunities and threats facing a prospective or existing retailer. It seeks to answer two general questions: What is the firm's current status? In which direction should it be heading? Situation analysis means being guided by an organizational mission, evaluating ownership and management options, and outlining the goods/service category to be sold.

A good strategy anticipates and adapts to both the opportunities and threats in the changing business environment. **Opportunities** are marketplace openings that exist because other retailers have not yet capitalized on them. Ikea does well because it is the pioneer firm in offering a huge selection of furniture at discount prices. **Threats** are environmental and marketplace factors that can adversely affect retailers if they do not react to them (and, sometimes, even if they do). Single-screen movie theaters have virtually disappeared since they have been unable to fend off the inroads made by multi-screen theaters.

FIGURE 3-1
Elements of a Retail Strategy

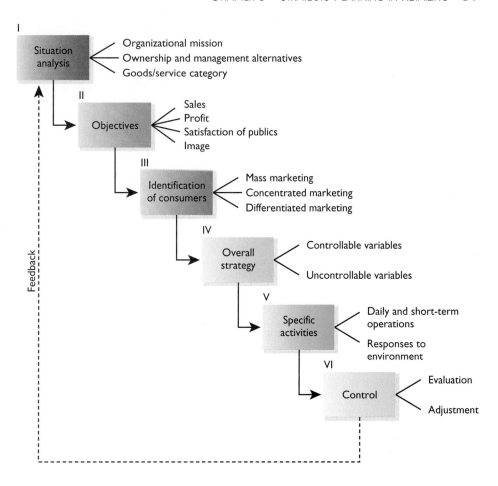

A firm needs to spot trends early enough to satisfy customers and stay ahead of competitors, yet not so early that shoppers are not ready for changes or that false trends are perceived. Merchandising shifts—like stocking fad items—are more quickly enacted than changes in a firm's location, price, or promotion strategy. A new retailer can adapt to trends easier than existing firms with established images, ongoing leases, and space limitations. Small firms that prepare well can compete in a market with large retailers.

During situation analysis, especially for a new retailer or one thinking about making a major strategic change, an honest, in-depth self-assessment is vital. It is all right for a person or company to be ambitious and aggressive, but overestimating one's abilities and prospects may be harmful—if the results are entry into the wrong retail business, inadequate resources, or misjudgment of competitors.

Organizational Mission

An **organizational mission** is a retailer's commitment to a type of business and to a distinctive role in the marketplace. It is reflected in the firm's attitude toward consumers, employees, suppliers, competitors, government, and others. A clear mission lets a firm gain a customer following and distinguish itself from competitors. See Figure 3-2.

One major decision is whether to base a business around the goods and services sold or around consumer needs. A person opening a hardware business must decide if, in addition to hardware products, a line of bathroom vanities should be stocked. A traditionalist might not carry vanities because they seem unconnected to the proposed business. But if the store is to be a do-it-yourself

FIGURE 3-2

The Focused Organizational Mission of Frisch's Restaurants

The company operates and licenses family restaurants under the trade name Frisch's Big Boy. These facilities are located in Ohio, Indiana, and Kentucky. Additionally, the firm operates two hotels with restaurants in metropolitan Cincinnati, where it is headquartered. Trademarks that the company has the right to use include "Frisch's," "Big Boy," "Quality Hotel," and "Golden Corral."

Reprinted by permission.

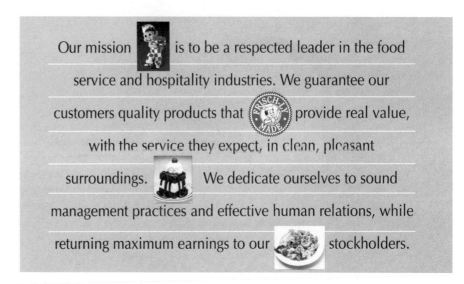

Our mission is to be a respected leader in the food service and hospitality industries. We guarantee our customers quality products that provide real value, with the service they expect, in clean, pleasant surroundings. We dedicate ourselves to sound management practices and effective human relations, while returning maximum earnings to our stockholders.

home improvement center, vanities are a logical part of the mix. That store would carry any relevant items the consumer wants.

A second major decision is whether a retailer wants a place in the market as a leader or a follower. It could seek to offer a unique strategy, such as Taco Bell becoming the first national quick-serve Mexican food chain. Or it could emulate the practices of competitors but do a better job in executing them, such as a local fast-food Mexican restaurant offering five-minute guaranteed service and a cleanliness pledge.

See how Sam Goody's Web site (www.samgoody.com) is consistent with its mission.

A third decision involves market scope. Large chains often seek a broad customer base (due to their resources and recognition). It is often best for small retailers and startups to focus on a narrower customer base, so they can compete with bigger firms that tend not to adapt strategies as well to local markets.

Although the development of an organizational mission is the first step in the planning process, the mission should be continually reviewed and adjusted to

Careers in RETAILING — Bob: General Store Manager

Bob worked as a commissioned salesperson at an international department store chain for four years while in college, where he earned a Master of Business Administration after receiving an undergraduate degree with a major in economics. Bob then became a manager trainee for one year. He attended a company-sponsored program that prepared management candidates for salaried positions.

Automotive sales manager was the first salaried position Bob held in this company. He had 72 people working for him. Bob held this position for one year. As a national account representative, Bob called on approximately 100 stores in the Northeast to promote the product line. Bob rounded out his internal résumé by taking a position as a home furnishings sales manager. He

worked in this position for two years. As appliance electronics sales manager, Bob managed a very large organization of commission sales associates within the overall international department store chain. He attributes his success to properly motivating his employees. He is now a general store manager.

Bob's salary is competitive with other international department store chains. The industry range for a store manager is $60,000–$100,000, plus benefits. As he says, "You'd like my job if you like an environment that is fast paced, constantly changing, and seasonally driven. You must like people and be able to maintain the morale of your employees."

Source: Reprinted by permission of the National Retail Federation.

reflect changing company goals and a dynamic retail environment. Here are examples of well-conceived retail organizational missions:[3]

> Burlington Coat Factory is a national department store chain, which offers current, high-quality, designer merchandise at prices up to 60 percent below those at other department stores. It features coats, apparel, shoes, accessories for the entire family, baby clothes, furniture, toys, home décor items, and gifts.

> PetsMart is the nation's leading retail supplier of products, services, and solutions for the lifetime needs of pets. The company operates pet super-stores, as well as a large pet supply catalog business, and the Internet's leading pet product Web site. Stores carry the industry's broadest line of products for every stage of a pet's life. PetsMart offers exclusive products at good values, a proposition supported by our solid relationships with suppliers around the world and our cost-control initiatives.

> For years, the Sam Goody name has been synonymous with music. The stores are stocked with an overwhelming selection of music in a store that screams ENTERTAINMENT. From new releases and best sellers to classics, the store is filled with all the products music lovers can't get enough of.

Ownership and Management Alternatives

An essential aspect of situation analysis is assessing ownership and management alternatives, including whether to form a sole proprietorship, partnership, or corporation—and whether to start a new business, buy an existing business, or become a franchisee.[4] Management options include owner-manager versus professional manager and centralized versus decentralized structures. Consider that "There is no single best form of ownership. That's partly because the limitations of a particular form of ownership can often be compensated for. For instance, a sole proprietor can often buy insurance coverage to reduce liability exposure, rather than form a limited liability entity. Even after you have established your business as a particular entity, you may need to re-evaluate your choice of entity as the business evolves."[5]

A **sole proprietorship** is an unincorporated retail firm owned by one person. All benefits, profits, risks, and costs accrue to that individual. It is simple to form, fully controlled by the owner, operationally flexible, easy to dissolve, and subject to single taxation by the government. It makes the owner personally liable for legal claims from suppliers, creditors, and others; and it can lead to limited capital and expertise.

A **partnership** is an unincorporated retail firm owned by two or more persons, each with a financial interest. Partners share benefits, profits, risks, and costs. Responsibility and expertise are divided among multiple principals, there is a greater capability for raising funds than with a proprietorship, the format is simpler to form than a corporation, and it is subject to single taxation by the government. Depending on the type of partnership, it, too, can make owners personally liable for legal claims, can be dissolved due to a partner's death or a disagreement, binds all partners to actions made by any individual partner acting on behalf of the firm, and usually has less ability to raise capital than a corporation.

A **corporation** is a retail firm that is formally incorporated under state law. It is a legal entity apart from individual officers (or stockholders). Funds can be raised through the sale of stock, legal claims against individuals are not usually allowed, ownership transfer is relatively easy, the firm is assured of long-term existence (if a founder leaves, retires, or dies), the use of professional managers is encouraged, and unambiguous operating authority is outlined. Depending on the type of corporation, it is subject to double taxation (company earnings and stock-holder dividends), faces more government rules, can require a complex process when established, may be viewed as impersonal, and may separate ownership from management. A closed corporation is run by a limited number of persons who control ownership; stock is not available to the public. In an open corporation, stock is widely traded and available to the public.

Sole proprietorships account for 72 percent of all U.S. retail firms that file tax returns, partnerships for 8 percent, and corporations for 20 percent. In terms of sales volume, sole proprietorships account for just 5 percent of total U.S. retail store sales, partnerships for 11 percent, and corporations for 84 percent.[6]

Starting a new business—being entrepreneurial—offers a retailer flexibility in location, operating style, product lines, customer markets, and other factors; and a strategy is fully tailored to the owner's desires and strengths. There may be high construction costs, a time lag until the business is opened and then until profits are earned, beginning with an unknown name, and having to form supplier relationships and amass an inventory of goods. Figure 3-3 presents a checklist to consider when starting a business.

Buying an existing business allows a retailer to acquire an established company name, a customer following, a good location, trained personnel, and

FIGURE 3-3
A Checklist to Consider When Starting a New Retail Business

Source: Adapted by the authors from *Small Business Management Training Instructor's Guide*, No. 109 (Washington, DC: U.S. Small Business Administration, n.d.).

Name of Business _____

A. Self-Assessment and Business Choice
✓ Evaluate your strengths and weaknesses.
✓ Commitment paragraph: Why should you be in business for yourself? Why open a new business rather than acquire an existing one or become a member of a franchise chain?
✓ Describe the type of retail business that fits your strengths and desires. What will make it unique? What will the business offer customers? How will you capitalize on the weaknesses of competitors?

B. Overall Retail Plan
✓ State your philosophy of business.
✓ Choose an ownership form (sole proprietorship, partnership, or corporation).
✓ State your long- and short-run goals.
✓ Analyze your customers from their point of view.
✓ Research your market size and store location.
✓ Quantify the total retail sales of your goods/service category in your trading area.
✓ Analyze your competition.
✓ Quantify your potential market share.
✓ Develop your retail strategy: store location and operations, merchandising, pricing, and store image and promotion.

C. Financial Plan
✓ What level of funds will you need to get started and to get through the first year? Where will they come from?
✓ Determine the first-year profit, return on investment, and salary that you need/want.
✓ Project monthly cash flow and profit-and-loss statements for the first two years.
✓ What sales will be needed to break even during the first year? What will you do if these sales are not reached?

D. Organizational Details Plan
✓ Describe your personnel plan (hats to wear), organizational plan, and policies.
✓ List the jobs you like and want to do and those you dislike, cannot do, or do not want to do.
✓ Outline your accounting and inventory systems.
✓ Note your insurance plans.
✓ Specify how day-to-day operations would be conducted for each aspect of your strategy.
✓ Review the risks you face and how you plan to cope with them.

FIGURE 3-4
A Checklist for Purchasing
an Existing Retail Business

NAME OF BUSINESS _____

✓ Why is the seller placing the business up for sale?

✓ How much are you paying for goodwill (the cost of the business above its tangible asset value)?

✓ Have sales, inventory levels, and profit figures been confirmed by your accountant?

✓ Will the seller introduce you to his or her customers and stay on during the transition period?

✓ Will the seller sign a statement that he or she will not open a directly competing business in the same trading area for a reasonable time period?

✓ If sales are seasonal, are you purchasing the business at the right time of the year?

✓ In the purchase of the business, are you assuming existing debts of the seller?

✓ Who receives proceeds from transactions made prior to the sale of the business but not yet paid by customers?

✓ What is the length of the lease if property is rented?

✓ If property is to be purchased along with the business, has it been inspected by a professional engineer?

✓ How modern are the storefront and store fixtures?

✓ Is inventory fresh? Does it contain a full merchandise assortment?

✓ Are the advertising policy, customer service policy, and pricing policy of the past owner similar to yours? Can you continue old policies?

✓ If the business is to be part of a chain, is the new unit compatible with existing units?

✓ How much trading-area overlap is there with existing stores?

✓ Has a lawyer examined the proposed contract?

✓ What effect will owning this business have on your lifestyle and on your family relationships?

facilities; to operate immediately; to generate ongoing sales and profits; and to possibly get good lease terms or financing (at favorable interest rates) from the seller. Fixtures may be older, there is less flexibility in enacting a strategy tailored to the new owner's desires and strengths, and the growth potential of the business may be limited. Figure 3-4 shows a checklist to consider when purchasing an existing retail business.

By being a franchisee, a retailer can combine independent ownership with franchisor support: strategic planning assistance; a known company name and loyal customer following; cooperative advertising and buying; and a regional, national, or global (rather than local) image. However, a franchisee contract may specify rigid operating standards, limit the product lines sold, and restrict supplier choice; the franchisor company is usually paid continuously (royalties); advertising fees may be required; and there is a possibility of termination by the franchisor if the agreement is not followed satisfactorily.

Strategically, the management format also has a dramatic impact. With an owner-manager, planning tends to be less formal and more intuitive, and many tasks are reserved for that person (such as employee supervision and cash management). With professional management, planning tends to be more formal and systematic. Yet, professional managers are more constrained in their authority than an owner-manager. In a centralized structure, planning clout lies with top management or ownership; managers in individual departments have major input into decisions with a decentralized structure.

A comprehensive discussion of independent retailers, chains, franchises, leased departments, vertical marketing systems, and consumer cooperatives is included in Chapter 4.

Entrepreneur Magazine (www.entrepreneurmag. com) addresses many of the issues facing new and growing firms as they plan their strategies.

Goods/Service Category

Before a prospective retail firm can fully design a strategic plan, it selects a **goods/service category**—the line of business—in which to operate. Figure 3-5 shows the diversity of goods/service categories. Chapter 5 examines the attributes of food-based and general merchandise store retailers. Chapter 6 focuses on Web, nonstore, and other forms of nontraditional retailing.

It is advisable to specify both a general goods/service category and a niche within that category. Jaguar dealers are luxury auto retailers catering to upscale customers. Wendy's is an eating and drinking chain known for its quality fast food with a menu that emphasizes hamburgers. Motel 6 is a chain whose forte is inexpensive rooms with few frills.

A potential retail business owner should select a type of business that will allow him or her to match personal abilities, financial resources, and time availability with the requirements of that kind of business. Visit our Web site (**www.prenhall.com/bermanevans**) for links to many retail trade associations, which represent various goods/service categories.

Personal Abilities

Personal abilities depend on an individual's aptitude—the preference for a type of business and the potential to do well; education—formal learning about retail practices and policies; and experience—practical learning about retail practices and policies.

An individual who wants to run a business, likes to use initiative, and has the ability to react quickly to competitive developments will be suited to a different type of situation than a person who depends on others for advice and does not

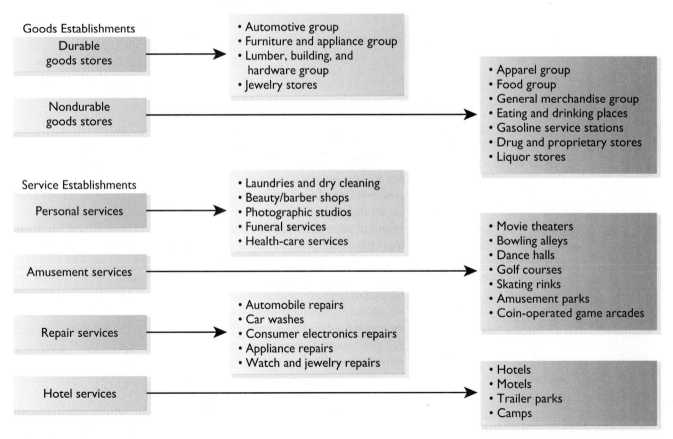

FIGURE 3-5
Selected Kinds of Retail Goods and Service Establishments

like to make decisions. The first individual could be an independent operator, in a dynamic business such as apparel; the second might seek partners or a franchise and a stable business, such as a stationery store. Some people enjoy customer interaction; they would dislike the impersonality of a self-service operation. Others enjoy the impersonality of mail-order or Web retailing.

In certain fields, education and experience requirements are specified by law. Stockbrokers, real-estate brokers, beauticians, pharmacists, and opticians must all satisfy educational or experience standards to show competency. For example, real-estate brokers are licensed after a review of their knowledge of real-estate practices and their ethical character. The designation "broker" does not depend on the ability to sell or have a customer-oriented demeanor.

Some skills can be learned; others are inborn. Accordingly, potential retail owners have to assess their skills and match them with the demands of a given business. This involves careful reflection about oneself. Partnerships may be best when two or more parties possess complementary skills. A person with selling experience may join with someone who has the operating skills to start a business. Each partner has valued skills, but he or she may be unable to operate a retail entity without the expertise of the other.

Financial Resources

Many retail enterprises, especially new, independent ones, fail because the owners do not adequately project the financial resources needed to open and operate the firm. Table 3-1 outlines some of the typical investments for a new retail venture.

Novice retailers tend to underestimate the value of a personal drawing account, which is used for the living expenses of the owner and his or her family in the early, unprofitable stage of a business. Because few new ventures are immediately profitable, the budget must include such expenditures. In addition, the costs of renovating an existing facility often are miscalculated. Underfunded firms usually invest in only essential renovations. This practice reduces the initial investment, but it may give the retailer a poor image. Merchandise assortment, as well as the types of goods and services sold, also affects the financial outlay. Finally, the use of a partnership, corporation, or franchise agreement will affect the investment.

TABLE 3-1	Some Typical Financial Investments for a New Retail Venture
Use of Funds	**Source of Funds**
Land and building (lease or purchase)	Personal savings, bank loan, commercial finance company
Inventory	Personal savings, manufacturer credit, commercial finance company, sales revenues
Fixtures (display cases, storage facilities, signs, lighting, carpeting, etc.)	Personal savings, manufacturer credit, bank loan, commercial finance company
Equipment (cash register, marking machine, office equipment, computers, etc.)	Personal savings, manufacturer credit, bank loan, commercial finance company
Personnel (salespeople, cashiers, stockpeople, etc.)	Personal savings, bank loan, sales revenues
Promotion	Personal savings, sales revenues
Personal drawing account	Personal savings, life insurance loan
Miscellaneous (equipment repair, credit sales [bad debts], professional services, repayment of loans)	Personal savings, manufacturer and wholesaler credit, bank credit plan, bank loan, commercial finance company

Note: Collateral for a bank loan may be a building, fixtures, land, inventory, or a personal residence.

TABLE 3-2	Financial Requirements for a Used-Car Dealer	

Total investments (first year)

Lease (10 years, $60,000 per year)		$ 60,000
Beginning inventory (32 cars, average cost of $12,500)		400,000
Replacement inventory (32 cars, average cost of $12,500)[a]		400,000
Fixtures and equipment (painting, paneling, carpeting, lighting, signs, heating and air-conditioning system, electronic cash register, service bay)		60,000
Replacement parts		75,000
Personnel (one mechanic)		45,000
Promotion (brochures and newspaper advertising)		35,000
Drawing account (to cover owner's personal expenses for one year; all selling and operating functions except mechanical ones performed by the owner)		40,000
Accountant		15,000
Miscellaneous (loan payments, etc.)		100,000
Profit (projected)		40,000
		$1,270,000

Source of funds

Personal savings		$ 300,000
Bank loan		426,000
Sales revenues (based on expected sales of 32 cars, average price of $17,000)		544,000
		$1,270,000

[a]Assumes that 32 cars are sold during the year. As each type of car is sold, a replacement is bought by the dealer and placed in inventory. At the end of the year, inventory on hand remains at 32 units.

Table 3-2 illustrates the financial requirements for a hypothetical used-car dealer. The initial personal savings investment of $300,000 would force many potential owners to rethink the choice of product category and the format of the firm: (1) The plans for a 32-car inventory reflect this owner's desire for a balanced product line. If the firm concentrates on subcompact, compact, and intermediate cars, it can reduce inventory size and lower the investment. (2) The initial investment can be reduced by seeking a location whose facilities do not have to be modified. (3) Fewer financial resources are needed if a partnership or corporation is set up with other individuals, so that costs—and profits—are shared.

The U.S. Small Business Administration (**www.sba.gov/financing**) assists businesses by guaranteeing tens of thousands of loans each year. Such private companies as Wells Fargo and American Express also have financing programs specifically aimed at small businesses.

American Express (**http:// home.americanexpress. com/home/open.shtml**) offers financial support and advice for small firms.

Time Demands

Time demands on retail owners (or managers) differ significantly by goods or service category. They are influenced both by consumer shopping patterns and by the ability of the owner or manager to automate operations or delegate activities to others.

Many retailers must have regular weekend and evening hours to serve time-pressed shoppers. Gift shops, toy stores, and others have extreme seasonal shifts in their hours. Mail-order firms and those selling through the Web, which can process orders during any part of the day, have more flexible hours.

Some businesses require less owner involvement, including gas stations with no repair services, coin-operated laundries, and movie theaters. The emphasis on automation, self-service, standardization, and financial controls lets the owner reduce the time investment. Other businesses, such as hair salons, restaurants, and jewelry stores, require more active owner involvement.

Intensive owner participation can be the result of several factors:

- The owner may be the key service provider, with patrons attracted by his or her skills (the major competitive advantage). Delegating work to others will lessen consumer loyalty.

- Personal services are not easy to automate.

- Due to limited funds, the owner and his or her family must often undertake all operating functions for a small retail firm. Spouses and children work in 40 percent of family owned businesses.

- In a business that operates on a cash basis, the owner must be around to avoid being cheated.

Off-hours activities are often essential. At a restaurant, some foods must be prepared in advance of the posted dining hours. An antique dealer spends non-store hours hunting for goods. An owner of a small computer store cleans, stocks shelves, and does the books during the hours the firm is closed. A prospective retail owner also has to examine his or her time preferences regarding stability versus seasonality, ideal working hours, and personal involvement.

OBJECTIVES

Kroger (www.kroger.com) is the leading food-based retailer in the United States.

After situation analysis, a retailer sets **objectives**, the long-run and short-run performance targets it hopes to attain. This helps mold a strategy and translates the organizational mission into action. A firm can pursue goals related to one or more of these areas: sales, profit, satisfaction of publics, and image. Some retailers strive to achieve all the goals fully; others attend to a few and want to achieve them really well. Think about this array of goals for the Kroger Company:

> We will conduct our business to produce financial returns that reward investment by shareowners and allow us to grow. Investments in retailing, distribution, and food processing will be continually evaluated for their contribution to our corporate return goals. We will strive to satisfy the needs of customers as well as, or better than, our best competitors. We value America's diversity and will strive to reflect that diversity in our work force, the companies with which we do business, and the customers we serve. We will encourage our associates to be active and responsible citizens and will allocate resources for activities that enhance the quality of life for the communities we serve.[7]

Sales

Sales objectives are related to the volume of goods and services a retailer sells. Growth, stability, and market share are the sales goals most often sought.

Some retailers set sales growth as a top priority. They want to expand their business. There may be less emphasis on short-run profits. The assumption is that investments in the present will yield future profits. A firm that does well often becomes interested in opening new units and enlarging revenues. However, management skills and the personal touch are sometimes lost with overly fast expansion.

Stability is the goal of retailers that emphasize maintaining their sales volume, market share, price lines, and so on. Small retailers often seek stable sales that enable the owners to make a satisfactory living every year without downswings or upsurges. And certain firms develop a loyal customer following and are intent not on expanding but on continuing the approach that attracted the original consumers.

For some firms, market share—the percentage of total retail-category sales contributed by a given company—is another goal. It is often an objective only for large retailers or retail chains. The small retailer is more concerned with competition across the street than with total sales in a metropolitan area.

Sales objectives may be expressed in dollars and units. To reach dollar goals, a retailer can engage in a discount strategy (low prices and high unit sales), a moderate strategy (medium prices and medium unit sales), or a prestige strategy (high prices and low unit sales). In the long run, having unit sales as a performance target is vital. Dollar sales by year may be difficult to compare due to changing retail prices and inflation; unit sales are easier to compare. A firm with sales of $350,000 three years ago and $500,000 today might assume it is doing well, until unit sales are computed: 10,000 then and 8,000 now.

Profit

With profitability objectives, retailers seek at least a minimum profit level during a designated period, usually a year. Profit may be expressed in dollars or as a percentage of sales. For a firm with yearly sales of $5 million and total costs of $4.2 million, pre-tax dollar profit is $800,000 and profits as a percentage of sales are 16 percent. If the profit goal is equal to or less than $800,000, or 16 percent, the retailer is satisfied. If the goal is higher, the firm has not attained the minimum desired profit and is dissatisfied.

Firms with large capital expenditures in land, buildings, and equipment often set return on investment (ROI) as a goal. ROI is the relationship between profits and the investment in capital items. A satisfactory rate of return is pre-defined and compared with the actual return at the end of the year or other period. For a retailer with annual sales of $5 million and expenditures (including payments for capital items) of $4 million, the yearly profit is $1 million. If the total capital investment is $10 million, ROI is $1 million/$10 million, or 10 percent per year. The goal must be 10 percent or less for the firm to be satisfied.

Operating efficiency may be expressed as $1 -$ (operating expenses/company sales). The higher the result, the more efficient the firm. A retailer with sales of $2 million and operating costs of $1 million has a 50 percent efficiency rating ([1 − ($1 million/$2 million)]). Of every sales dollar, 50 cents goes for nonoperating costs and profits and 50 cents for operating expenses. The retailer might set a goal to increase efficiency to 60 percent. On sales of $2 million, operating costs would have to drop to $800,000 ([1 − ($800,000/$2 million)]). Sixty cents of every sales dollar would then go for nonoperating costs and profits and 40 cents for operations, which would lead to better profits. If a firm cuts expenses too much, customer service may decline; this may lead to a decline in sales and profit.

Satisfaction of Publics

Retailers typically strive to satisfy their publics: stockholders, customers, suppliers, employees, and government. Stockholder satisfaction is a goal for any publicly owned retailer. Some firms set policies leading to small annual increases in sales and profits (because these goals can be sustained over the long run and indicate good management) rather than ones based on innovative ideas that may lead to peaks and valleys in sales and profits (indicating poor management). Stable earnings lead to stable dividends.

Customer satisfaction with the total retail experience is a well-entrenched goal at most firms now. A policy of *caveat emptor* ("Let the buyer beware") will not work in today's competitive marketplace. Retailers must listen to criticism and adapt. If shoppers are pleased, other goals are more easily reached. Yet, for many retailers, other objectives rate higher in their list of priorities.

Good supplier relations is also a key goal. Retailers must understand and work with their suppliers to secure favorable purchase terms, new products, good return policies, prompt shipments, and cooperation. Relationships are very important for small retailers due to the many services that suppliers offer them.

Cordial labor relations is another goal that is often critical to retailers' performance. Good employee morale means less absenteeism, better treatment of customers, and lower staffing turnover. Relations can be improved by effective selection, training, and motivation.

Because all levels of government impose rules affecting retailing practices, another goal should be to understand and adapt to these rules. In some cases, firms can influence rules by acting as members of large groups, such as trade associations or chambers of commerce.

Image (Positioning)

An **image** represents how a given retailer is perceived by consumers and others. A firm may be seen as innovative or conservative, specialized or broad-based, discount-oriented or upscale. The key to a successful image is that consumers view the retailer in the manner the firm intends.

Through **positioning**, a retailer devises its strategy in a way that projects an image relative to its retail category and its competitors and that elicits a positive consumer response. A firm selling women's apparel could generally position itself as an upscale or mid-priced specialty retailer, a department store, a discount department store, or a discount specialty retailer, and it could specifically position itself with regard to other retailers carrying women's apparel.

Two opposite positioning philosophies have gained popularity in recent years: mass merchandising and niche retailing. **Mass merchandising** is a positioning approach whereby retailers offer a discount or value-oriented image, a wide and/or deep merchandise selection, and large store facilities. Wal-Mart has a wide, deep merchandise mix whereas Sports Authority has a narrower, deeper assortment. These firms appeal to a broad customer market, attract a lot of customer traffic, and generate high stock turnover. Because mass merchants have relatively low operating costs, achieve economies in operations, and appeal to value-conscious shoppers, their continuing popularity is forecast.

In **niche retailing**, retailers identify specific customer segments and deploy unique strategies to address the desires of those segments rather than the mass market. Niching creates a high level of loyalty and shields retailers from more conventional competitors. Babies "R" Us appeals to parents with very young children whereas Catherine's Stores has fashions for plus-size women. This approach will have a strong future since it lets retailers stress factors other than price and have a better focus. See Figure 3-6.

Because both mass merchandising and niche retailing are popular, some observers call this the era of **bifurcated retailing**. They believe this may mean the decline of middle-of-the-market retailing. Firms that are neither competitively priced nor particularly individualistic may have difficulty competing.

Babies "R" Us (www.babiesrus.com) has a very focused strategy and an online partnership with Amazon.com.

FIGURE 3-6
Niche Retailing by Hear Music

Starbucks is opening up a new chain, called Hear Music Coffeehouses. These shops are targeted at the real music aficionado, who can visit the listening stations to explore numerous musical selections and then burn personalized CDs. As the Starbucks' Web site (**www.starbucks.com**) notes: The stores place "a premium on exploration and discovery, with a staff of music lovers on hand to provide assistance." Yes, you can buy coffee there.

Photo reprinted by permission of Susan Berry, Retail Image Consulting, Inc.

Let us further examine the concept of positioning through these examples:

- bebe (the apparel store chain) "designs, develops, and produces a distinctive line of contemporary women's apparel and accessories, which it markets under the bebe, BEBE SPORT, and bebe O brand names. The firm was founded as a San Francisco boutique at a time when three categories dominated the women's wear market: junior, bridge, and missy. Having discovered a demographic that was neither junior nor bridge, bebe aimed to break the mold by offering this underrepresented population of stylish women distinctive and inspirational fashion bearing an unmistakable hint of sensuality. bebe's influence on fashion continued to thrive when the company debuted a private collection—featuring originally designed, impeccably made suits. bebe currently operates more than 200 stores."[8]

Trader Joe's (**www.traderjoes.com**) is a shopping haven for consumers looking for distinctive, fairly priced food items.

- At Trader Joe's food stores, "you'll find interesting products with our label. We buy products we think are winners and that will find a following among

---

Technology in RETAILING | **Bad Boy: Improving the Delivery Experience for Customers**

Bad Boy (**www.nooobody.com**) is a five-store, Toronto-based retail chain that sells furniture, appliances, and electronics. Bad Boy uses 12 independent contractors to deliver its products to customers' homes from the firm's distribution center. Until recently, Bad Boy relied on these contractors to estimate delivery times for customers, who were then called the morning of each delivery and given a four-hour delivery window. Now, Bad Boy relies on software developed by Cube Route (**www.cuberoute.com**) to handle route optimization, dispatch management, and customer notification functions. After a $2,500 up-front setup charge, Cube Route bills retailers on the basis of the number of deliveries.

Each evening, the drivers upload information concerning the next day's deliveries to Cube Route's Web site. Cube Route's system then generates routes for each driver and calculates an estimated arrival time with a two-hour range for each customer. The following morning, Cube Route contacts each customer via an automated telephone system with an estimated delivery time. Customers can also track their order through Bad Boy's Web site, which is linked to the Cube Route system.

Sources: Merrill Douglas, "Bad Boy Makes Good with Customers," *Inbound Logistics* (December 2004), pp. 59–61; and "Our History," **www.nooobody.com/history.php** (March 27, 2006).

FIGURE 3-7
Selected Retail Positioning
Strategies

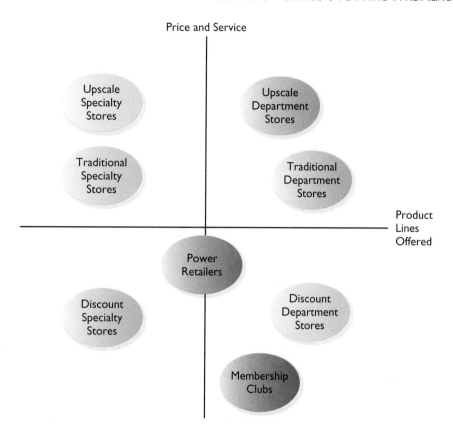

our customers. Sometimes it's a product which we intend to stock as long as it sells well; sometimes we buy a product which is in limited supply. Our mission is to bring you the best quality products at the best prices. We don't have deep promotional discount programs. Each product must meet certain sales criteria to earn its way onto our shelves. If it doesn't sell well, we know our customers don't embrace it. So products that aren't selling well need to gang way to make room for new and exciting products we hope our customers will love. We also have limited quantities of some items such as wines, nuts, or dried fruits, which change vintages each year. We don't change our prices unless our costs change."[9]

Figure 3-7 shows a retail positioning map based on two shopping criteria: (1) price and service and (2) product lines offered. Our assumption: There is a link between price and service (high price equals excellent service). Upscale department stores (Neiman Marcus) offer outstanding customer service and carry several product lines. Traditional department stores (Sears) carry more electronics and other product lines than upscale stores. They have a trained sales staff to help customers. Discount department stores (Wal-Mart) carry a lot of product lines and rely on self-service. Membership clubs (Costco) have a limited selection in a number of product categories. They have very low prices and plain surroundings. Upscale specialty stores (Tiffany) offer outstanding customer service and focus on one general product category. Traditional specialty stores (Gap) have a trained sales staff to help customers and focus on one general product category. Discount specialty stores (Old Navy) rely more on self-service and focus on one general product category. Power retailers (Home Depot) offer moderate service and prices and a huge assortment within one general product category.

Selection of Objectives

A firm that clearly sets its goals and devises a strategy to achieve them improves its chances of success.

An example of a retailer with clear goals and a proper strategy to attain them is Papa John's, the nearly 3,000-outlet pizza chain. As reported at its Web site (**www.papajohns.com**):

Customers: Papa John's will create superior brand loyalty—raving fans—through (a) authentic, superior-quality products, (b) legendary customer service, and (c) exceptional community service. *Team Members:* People are our most important asset. Papa John's will provide clear, consistent, strategic leadership and career opportunities for team members who (a) exhibit passion toward their work, (b) uphold our core values, (c) take pride of ownership in building the long-term value of the Papa John's brand, and (d) have ethical business practices. *Franchisees:* We will partner with our franchisees to create continued opportunity for outstanding financial returns to those franchisees who (a) adhere to Papa John's proven core values and systems, (b) exhibit passion in running their businesses, and (c) take pride of ownership in building the long-term value of the Papa John's brand. *Shareholders:* We will produce superior long-term value for our shareholders.

IDENTIFICATION OF CONSUMER CHARACTERISTICS AND NEEDS

The customer group sought by a retailer is called the **target market**. In selecting its target market, a firm may use one of three techniques: **mass marketing**, selling goods and services to a broad spectrum of consumers; **concentrated marketing**, zeroing in on one specific group; or **differentiated marketing**, aiming at two or more distinct consumer groups, with different retailing approaches for each group.

Supermarkets and drugstores define their target markets broadly. They sell a wide assortment of medium-quality items at popular prices. In contrast, a small upscale men's shoe store appeals to a specific consumer group by offering a narrow, deep product assortment at above-average prices (or in other cases, below-average prices). A retailer aiming at one segment does not try to appeal to everyone.

Department stores are among the retailers seeking multiple market segments. They cater to several customer groups, with unique goods and services for each. Apparel may be sold in a number of distinctive boutiques in the store. Large chains frequently have divisions that appeal to different market segments. Darden Restaurants operates Red Lobster (seafood), Olive Garden (Italian), Smoky Bones (barbeque-style), and Bahama Breeze (Caribbean-style) restaurants for customers with different food preferences.

After choosing the target market, a firm can determine its best competitive advantages and devise a strategy mix. See Table 3-3. The significance of **competitive advantages**—the distinct competencies of a retailer relative to competitors—must not be overlooked. Some examples will demonstrate this.

Tiffany seeks affluent, status-conscious consumers. It places stores in prestigious shopping areas, offers high-quality products, uses elegant ads, has extensive customer services, and sets rather high prices. Kohl's targets middle-class, value-conscious shoppers. It locates mostly in suburban shopping areas, offers national brands and Kohl's brands of medium quality, features good values in ads, has some customer services, and charges below-average to average prices. T.J. Maxx, a chain of off-price stores, aims at extremely price-conscious consumers. It locates in low-rent strip shopping centers or districts, offers national brands (sometimes overruns and seconds) of average to below-average quality, emphasizes low prices, offers few customer services, and sets very low prices. The key to the success of each of these retailers is its ability to define customers and cater to their needs in a distinctive manner. See Figure 3-8.

Is the T.J. Maxx Web site (www.tjmaxx.com) on target for the customers it wants to reach?

TABLE 3-3	**Target Marketing Techniques and Their Strategic Implications**		
	TARGET MARKET TECHNIQUES		
Strategic Implications	**Mass Marketing**	**Concentrated Marketing**	**Differentiated Marketing**
Retailer's location	Near a large population base	Near a small or medium population base	Near a large population base
Goods and service mix	Wide selection of medium-quality items	Selection geared to market segment—high- or low-quality items	Distinct goods/services aimed at each market segment
Promotion efforts	Mass advertising	Direct mail, E-mail, subscription	Different media and messages for each segment
Price orientation	Popular prices	High or low	High, medium, and low—depending on market segment
Strategy	One general strategy for a large homogeneous (similar) group of consumers	One specific strategy directed at a specific, limited group of customers	Multiple specific strategies, each directed at different (heterogeneous) groups of consumers

FIGURE 3-8

Jean-Philippe Patisserie: A Shop of Distinction

The Bellagio Hotel & Casino (**www.bellagio.com**) in Las Vegas wants to stand out in a competitive environment. One way it does so is through this upscale food shop: "A mesmerizing fountain of cascading liquid chocolate awaits you at the Jean-Philippe Patisserie. Delight the imagination as well as the appetite, with an incredible selection of sweet and savory items including chocolates, cookies, cakes, crepes, salads, sandwiches, and much more."

Photo reprinted by permission of Susan Berry, Retail Image Consulting, Inc.

A retailer is better able to select a target market and satisfy customer needs if it has a good understanding of consumer behavior. This topic is discussed in Chapter 7.

OVERALL STRATEGY

Next, the retailer develops an in-depth overall strategy. This involves two components: the aspects of business the firm can directly affect and those to which the retailer must adapt. The former are called **controllable variables**, and the latter are called **uncontrollable variables**. See Figure 3-9.

A strategy must be devised with both variables in mind. The ability of retailers to grasp and predict the effects of controllable and uncontrollable variables is greatly aided by the use of suitable data. In Chapter 8, information gathering and processing in retailing are described.

Controllable Variables

The controllable parts of a retail strategy consist of the basic categories shown in Figure 3-9: store location, managing a business, merchandise management and pricing, and communicating with the customer. A good strategy integrates these areas. These elements are covered in depth in Chapters 9 to 19.

Store Location

A retailer has several store location decisions to make. The initial one is whether to use a store or nonstore format. Then, for store-based retailers, a general location and a specific site are determined. Competitors, transportation access, population density, the type of neighborhood, nearness to suppliers, pedestrian traffic, and store composition are considered in picking a location. See Figure 3-10.

The terms of tenancy (such as rent and operating flexibility) are reviewed and a build, buy, or rent decision is made. The locations of multiple outlets are considered if expansion is a goal.

Managing a Business

Two major elements are involved in managing a business: the retail organization and human resource management, and operations management. Tasks, policies, resources, authority, responsibility, and rewards are outlined via a retail organization structure. Practices regarding employee hiring, training, compensation, and supervision are instituted through human resource management. Job descriptions and functions are communicated, along with the responsibility of all personnel and the chain of command.

Operations management oversees the tasks that satisfy customer, employee, and management goals. The financial aspects of operations involve asset management, budgeting, and resource allocation. Other elements include store format

FIGURE 3-9
Developing an Overall Retail Strategy

FIGURE 3-10

Barrington Plaza: An Appealing Shopping Center

Because of its convenient location and appealing shopper demographics, a broad mix of retailers find Barrington Plaza in Massachusetts to be a desirable place to locate their stores.

Photo reprinted by permission.

and size, personnel use, store maintenance, energy management, store security, insurance, credit management, computerization, and crisis management.

Merchandise Management and Pricing

In merchandise management, the general quality of the goods and services offering is set. Decisions are made as to the width of assortment (the number of product categories carried) and the depth of assortment (the variety of products carried in any category). Policies are set with respect to introducing new items. Criteria for buying decisions (how often, what terms, and which suppliers) are established. Forecasting, budgeting, and accounting procedures are outlined, as is the level of inventory for each type of merchandise. Finally, the retailer devises procedures to assess the success or failure of each item sold.

With regard to pricing, a retailer chooses from among several techniques; and it decides what range of prices to set, consistent with the firm's image and the quality of goods and services offered. The number of prices within each product category is determined, such as how many prices of luggage to carry. And the use of markdowns is planned in advance.

Communicating with the Customer

An image can be created and sustained by applying various techniques.

The physical attributes, or atmosphere, of a store and its surrounding area greatly influence consumer perceptions. The impact of the storefront (the building's exterior or the home page for a Web retailer) should not be undervalued, as it is the first physical element seen by customers. Once inside, layouts and displays,

RETAILING
Around the World
How Popular Are Convenience Stores Outside the United States?

The convenience store sector in Great Britain has undergone considerable change as two of the largest chains, T&S Stores and Alldays, were recently acquired by Tesco (**www.tesco.com**) and the Co-operative Group (**www.co-op.co.uk**) respectively. In addition, competition has also increased in this sector since new planning restrictions have forced many superstore operators to build smaller-format outlets such as convenience stores.

In 2003, sales of convenience stores in Great Britain equaled £18.6 billion (approximately $34.8 billion); and the average British convenience store had sales of £430,000 (about $804,000). By 2008, according to one industry expert, annual sales at British convenience stores should reach £25 billion. Furthermore, the frequency with which British residents shop at convenience stores has been increasing, with 18 percent of shoppers stating that they now use such stores on a daily basis. Frequent convenience store shoppers are generally under 35, less affluent, and more likely to be male.

When asked about improvements sought for convenience stores, the most frequently cited consumer suggestion is that these stores need to offer more value for the money. The second most popular suggestion is for convenience stores to be open 24 hours.

Sources: Amanda Lintott, "Convenience Retailing," *Design Week* (June 2004), pp. 18–19; and "Convenience Is King in the U.K.," **www. nacsonline.com** (May 23, 2005).

floor colors, lighting, scents, music, and the kind of sales personnel also contribute to a retailer's image. Customer services and community relations generate a favorable image for the retailer.

The right use of promotional tools enhances sales performance. These tools range from inexpensive flyers for a take-out restaurant to an expensive national ad campaign for a franchise chain. Three forms of paid promotion are available: advertising, personal selling, and sales promotion. In addition, a retailer can obtain free publicity when stories about it are written, televised, or broadcast.

While the preceding discussion outlined the controllable parts of a retail strategy, uncontrollable variables (discussed next) must also be kept in mind.

Uncontrollable Variables

The uncontrollable parts of a strategy consist of the factors shown in Figure 3-9: consumers, competition, technology, economic conditions, seasonality, and legal restrictions. Farsighted retailers adapt the controllable parts of their strategies to take into account elements beyond their immediate control.

Consumers

A skillful retailer knows it cannot alter demographic trends or lifestyle patterns, impose tastes, or "force" goods and services on people. The firm learns about its target market and forms a strategy consistent with consumer trends and desires. It cannot sell goods or services that are beyond the price range of customers, that are not wanted, or that are not displayed or advertised in the proper manner.

Competition

There is often little that retailers can do to limit the entry of competitors. In fact, a retailer's success may encourage the entry of new firms or cause established competitors to modify their strategies to capitalize on the popularity of a successful retailer. A major increase in competition should lead a company to re-examine its strategy, including its target market and merchandising focus, to ensure that it sustains a competitive edge. A continued willingness to satisfy customers better than any competitor is fundamental.

Technology

Computer systems are available for inventory control and checkout operations. There are more high-tech ways to warehouse and transport merchandise. Toll-free 800 numbers are popular for consumer ordering. And, of course, there is the Web. Nonetheless, some advancements are expensive and may be beyond the reach of small retailers. For example, although small firms might have computerized checkouts, they will probably be unable to use fully automated inventory systems. As a result, their efficiency may be less than that of larger competitors. They must adapt by providing more personalized service.

Economic Conditions

Economic conditions are beyond any retailer's control, no matter how large it is. Unemployment, interest rates, inflation, tax levels, and the annual gross domestic product (GDP) are just some economic factors with which a retailer copes. In outlining the controllable parts of its strategy, a retailer needs to consider forecasts about international, national, state, and local economies.

Seasonality

A constraint on certain retailers is their seasonality and the possibility that unpredictable weather will play havoc with sales forecasts. Retailers selling sports equipment, fresh food, travel services, and car rentals cannot control the seasonality of demand or bad weather. They can diversify offerings to carry a goods/service mix with items that are popular in different seasons. Thus, a sporting goods retailer can emphasize ski equipment and snowmobiles in the winter, baseball and golf equipment in the spring, scuba equipment and fishing gear in the summer, and basketball and football supplies in the fall.

Legal Restrictions

The Federal Trade Commission has a section of its Web site (www.ftc.gov/ftc/business. htm) devoted to do's and don'ts for business.

Table 3-4 shows how each controllable aspect of a retail strategy is affected by the legal environment.

Retailers that operate in more than one state are subject to federal laws and agencies. The Sherman Act and the Clayton Act deal with monopolies and restraints of trade. The Federal Trade Commission deals with unfair trade practices and consumer complaints. The Robinson-Patman Act prohibits suppliers from giving unjust merchandise discounts to large retailers that could adversely affect small ones. The Telemarketing Sales Rule protects consumers.

At the state and local levels, retailers have to deal with many restrictions. Zoning laws prohibit firms from operating at certain sites and demand that building specifications be met. Blue laws limit the times during which retailers can conduct business. Construction, smoking, and other codes are imposed by the state and city. The licenses to operate some businesses are under state or city jurisdiction.

For more information, contact the Federal Trade Commission (**www.ftc.gov**), state and local bodies, the Better Business Bureau (**www.bbb.org**), the National Retail Federation (**www.nrf.com**), or a specialized group such as the Direct Marketing Association (**www.the-dma.org**).

Integrating Overall Strategy

At this point, the firm has set an overall strategy. It has chosen a mission, an ownership and management style, and a goods/service category. Goals are clear. A target market has been designated and studied. Decisions have been made about

TABLE 3-4	**The Impact of the Legal Environment on Retailing**[a]
Controllable Factor Affected	**Selected Legal Constraints on Retailers**
Store Location	*Zoning laws* restrict the potential choices for a location and the type of facilities constructed. *Blue laws* restrict the days and hours during which retailers may operate. *Environmental laws* limit the retail uses of certain sites. *Door-to-door (direct) selling laws* protect consumer privacy. *Local ordinances* involve fire, smoking, outside lighting, capacity, and other rules. *Leases and mortgages* require parties to abide by stipulations in tenancy documents.
Managing the Business	*Licensing provisions* mandate minimum education and/or experience for certain personnel. *Personnel laws* involve nondiscriminatory hiring, promoting, and firing of employees. *Antitrust laws* limit large firm mergers and expansion. *Franchise agreements* require parties to abide by various legal provisions. *Business taxes* include real-estate and income taxes. *Recycling laws* mandate that retailers participate in a recycling process for various materials.
Merchandise Management and Pricing	*Trademarks* provide retailers with exclusive rights to the brand names they develop. *Merchandise restrictions* forbid some retailers from selling specified goods or services. *Product liability laws* allow retailers to be sued if they sell defective products. *Lemon laws* specify consumer rights if products, such as autos, require continuing repairs. *Sales taxes* are required in most states, although *tax-free days* have been introduced in some locales to encourage consumer shopping. *Unit-pricing laws* require price per unit to be displayed (most often applied to supermarkets). *Collusion laws* prohibit retailers from discussing selling prices with competitors. *Sales prices* must be a reduction from the retailer's normal selling prices. *Price discrimination laws* prohibit suppliers from offering unjustified discounts to large retailers that are unavailable to smaller ones.
Communicating with the Customer	*Truth-in-advertising* and *-selling laws* require retailers to be honest and not omit key facts. *Truth-in-credit laws* require that shoppers be informed of all terms when buying on credit. *Telemarketing laws* protect the privacy and rights of consumers regarding telephone sales. *Bait-and-switch laws* make it illegal to lure shoppers into a store to buy low-priced items and then to aggressively try to switch them to higher-priced ones. *Inventory laws* mandate that retailers must have sufficient stock when running sales. *Labeling laws* require merchandise to be correctly labeled and displayed. *Cooling-off laws* let customers cancel completed orders, often made by in-home sales, within three days of a contract date.

[a]This table is broad in nature and omits a law-by-law description. Many laws are state or locally oriented and apply only to certain locations; the laws in each place differ widely. The intent here is to give the reader some understanding of the current legal environment as if affects retail management.

Ethics in RETAILING
Blockbuster Removes (?) Late Fees

According to critics of Blockbuster's (**www.blockbuster.com**) "end of late fees" advertising campaign, its claims were only partially true. While Blockbuster no longer charges late fees for those returning a movie up to seven days late, consumers who keep a movie for eight days or longer are charged the full purchase price, less the original rental fee.

Blockbuster has defended its advertising on several grounds: Its employees were trained to explain the exact details of its policy. Each customer with an overdue film was to be called to explain the late fees. And even if a customer was charged for a VCR or DVD video, Blockbuster gave the customer 30 days to return it for a credit for the selling price charged, less a $1.25 restocking fee.

On March 29, 2005 (three months after its introduction), Blockbuster announced that it had reached agreement with 47 states and the District of Columbia to modify its no-late-fees policy. The firm also paid $630,000 to cover the states' legal costs. The revised policy requires Blockbuster to clearly stipulate this information on receipts: due dates, the end dates for grace periods, and how much renters will be charged if items are not returned.

Sources: T. L. Stanley, "Blockbuster Erases Its Late Fees—Sort Of," *Advertising Age* (January 17, 2005), p. 6; and Jill Kipnis, "Blockbuster Agrees to Pay for 'No Late Fee' Confusion," *Billboard* (April 9, 2005), p. 7.

What do you think about the overall strategy of Enterprise (www.enterprise.com)?

store location, managing the business, merchandise management and pricing, and communications. These factors must be coordinated to have a consistent, integrated strategy and to account for uncontrollable variables (consumers, competition, technology, economy, seasonality, and legal restrictions). The firm is then ready to do the specific tasks to carry out its strategy productively.

SPECIFIC ACTIVITIES

Short-run decisions are now made and enacted for each controllable part of the strategy in Figure 3-9. These actions are known as **tactics** and encompass a retailer's daily and short-term operations. They must be responsive to the uncontrollable environment. Here are some tactical moves a retailer may make:

Stores (www.stores.org) tracks all kinds of tactical moves made by retailers.

- Store location: Trading-area analysis gauges the area from which a firm draws its customers. The level of competition in a trading area is studied regularly. Relationships with nearby retailers are optimized. A chain carefully decides on the sites of new outlets. Facilities are actually built or modified.

- Managing the business: There is a clear chain of command from managers to workers. An organization structure is set into place. Personnel are hired, trained, and supervised. Asset management tracks assets and liabilities. The budget is spent properly. Operations are systemized and adjusted as required.

- Merchandise management and pricing: The assortments within departments and the space allotted to each department require constant decision making. Innovative firms look for new merchandise and clear out slow-moving items. Purchase terms are negotiated and suppliers sought. Selling prices reflect the firm's image and target market. Price ranges offer consumers some choice. Adaptive actions are needed to respond to higher supplier prices and react to competitors' prices.

- Communicating with the customer: The storefront and display windows, store layout, and merchandise displays need regular attention. These elements help gain consumer enthusiasm, present a fresh look, introduce new products, and reflect changing seasons. Ads are placed during the proper time and in the proper media. The deployment of sales personnel varies by merchandise category and season.

The essence of retailing excellence is building a sound strategy and fine-tuning it. A firm that stands still is often moving backward. Tactical decision making is discussed in detail in Chapters 9 through 19.

CONTROL

In the **control** phase, a review takes place (Step VI in Figure 3-1), as the strategy and tactics (Steps IV and V) are assessed against the business mission, objectives, and target market (Steps I, II, and III). This procedure is called a retail audit, which is a systematic process for analyzing the performance of a retailer. The retail audit is covered in Chapter 20.

The strengths and weaknesses of a retailer are revealed as performance is reviewed. The aspects of a strategy that have gone well are continued; those that have gone poorly are revised, consistent with the mission, goals, and target market. The adjustments are reviewed in the firm's next retail audit.

FEEDBACK

During each stage in a strategy, an observant management receives signals or cues, known as **feedback**, as to the success or failure of that part of the strategy. Refer to Figure 3-1. Positive feedback includes high sales, no problems with the government, and low employee turnover. Negative feedback includes falling sales, government sanctions (such as fines), and high turnover.

Retail executives look for positive and negative feedback so they can determine the causes and then capitalize on opportunities or rectify problems.

A STRATEGIC PLANNING TEMPLATE FOR RETAIL MANAGEMENT

A comprehensive, user-friendly strategic planning template, *Computer-Assisted Strategic Retail Management Planning*, appears at our Web site (**www.prenhall. com/bermanevans**). This template uses a series of drop-down menus, based on Figure 3-1, to build a strategic plan. You may apply the template to one of the retail

TABLE 3-5	Outline of the Computerized Strategic Planning Template

1. **Situation Analysis**
   - Current organizational mission
   - Current ownership and management alternatives
   - Current goods/service category

2. **SWOT Analysis**
   - Strengths: Current and long term
   - Weaknesses: Current and long term
   - Opportunities: Current and long term
   - Threats: Current and long term

3. **Objectives**
   - Sales
   - Profit
   - Positioning
   - Satisfaction of publics

4. **Identification of Consumers**
   - Choice of target market
     - Mass marketing
     - Concentrated marketing
     - Differentiated marketing

5. **Overall Strategy**
   - Controllable variables
     - Goods/services strategy
     - Location strategy
     - Pricing strategy
     - Promotion strategy
   - Uncontrollable variables
     - Consumer environment
     - Competitive environment
     - Legal environment
     - Economic environment
     - Technological environment

6. **Specific Activities**
   - Daily and short-term operations
   - Responses to environment

7. **Control**
   - Evaluation
   - Adjustment

business scenarios that are provided—or devise your own scenario. You have the option of printing each facet of the planning process individually or printing the entire plan as an integrated whole.

Table 3-5 highlights the steps used in *Computer-Assisted Strategic Retail Management Planning* as the basis for preparing a strategic plan. Table 3-6 presents an example of how the template may be used.

TABLE 3-6	**Sample Strategic Plan: A High-Fashion Ladies Clothing Shop**

Sally's is a small, independently-owned, high-fashion ladies clothing shop located in a suburban strip mall. It is a full-price, full-service store for fashion-forward shoppers. Sally's carries sportswear from popular designers, has a personal shopper for busy executives, and has an on-premises tailor. The store is updating its strategic plan as a means of getting additional financing for an anticipated expansion.

1. **Situation Analysis**
   - Current organizational mission: A high-fashion clothing retailer selling high-quality and designer-label clothing and accessories in an attractive full-service store environment.
   - Current ownership and management alternatives: Sole proprietor, independent store.
   - Current goods/service category: Ladies coats, jackets, blouses, and suits from major designers, as well as a full line of fashion accessories (such as scarves, belts, and hats).

2. **SWOT Analysis**
   - Strengths
     - Current
       - A loyal customer base.
       - An excellent reputation for high-fashion clothing and accessories within the community.
       - Little competition within a target market concerned with high fashion.
       - Acceptance by a target market more concerned with fashion, quality, and customer service than with price.
       - Unlike shoppers favoring classic clothing, Sally's fashion-forward shopper spends a considerable amount of money on clothing and accessories per year.
       - Sally's has a highly regarded personal shopper (who assembles clothing based on customer preferences, visits customers, and arranges for a tailor to visit customers).
     - Long term
       - A fashion-forward image with the store's target market.
       - Exclusive relationships with some well-known and some emerging designers.
       - A low-rent location in comparison to a regional shopping center.
       - Excellent supplier relationships.
       - Loyal employees.
       - Excellent relationships within the community.
   - Weaknesses
     - Current
       - Difficulty in recruiting appropriate part-time personnel for peak seasonal periods.
       - The store's small space limits assortment and depth. Too often, the tailor has to perform major alterations.
       - Delivery times for certain French and Italian designers are too long.
       - The retailer does not have a computer-based information system which would better enable it to access key information concerning inventory, sales, customer preferences, and purchase histories.
     - Long term
       - Sally's small orders limit bargaining power with vendors. This affects prices paid, as well as access to "hot-selling" clothing.
       - The store's suburban strip mall location substantially reduces its trading area. The store gets little tourist trade.
       - Over-reliance on the owner/manager, and on several key employees.
       - No long-term management succession plan.
   - Opportunities
     - Current
       - Sally's can hire another experienced tailor with a following to create a custom-made clothing department.
       - The store can hire an assistant to better coordinate trunk and fashion shows. This would solidify Sally's reputation among fashion-forward shoppers and in the community.
       - An adjacent store is vacant. This would enable Sally's to increase its size by 50 percent.
       - Sally's is considering developing a Web site. This would enable it to appeal to a larger trading area, offer a medium to announce events (such as a fashion show), and provide links to designers.

(Continued)

TABLE 3-6	*Continued*

- ○ Long term
  - ■ The larger store would allow Sally's to expand the number of designers, as well as the product lines carried. This would also improve Sally's bargaining power with suppliers.
  - ■ A custom-made clothing department would enable Sally's to appeal to customers who dislike "ready-to-wear apparel" and to customers with highly individualized tastes.
  - ■ The Web site should expand Sally's market.
- • Threats
  - ○ Current
    - ■ There are rumors that Bloomingdale's, a fashion-based department store, may soon locate a new store within 10 miles of Sally's. This could affect relationships with suppliers, as well as customers. Bloomingdale's offers one-stop shopping and has a flexible return policy for unaltered merchandise with its labels intact.
    - ■ The current local recession has reduced revenues significantly as many customers have cut back on purchases.
  - ○ Long term
    - ■ Many of Sally's customers are in their 50s and 60s. Some are close to retirement; others intend to spend more time in Florida and Arizona during the winter. The store needs to attract and hold on to younger shoppers.

3. Objectives
- • Sales: Achieve sales volume of $4 million per year.
- • Profit: (1) Achieve net profit before tax of $300,000. (2) Increase inventory turnover from 4 times a year to 6 times a year. (3) Increase gross margin return on inventory (GMROI) by 50 percent through more effective inventory management.
- • Positioning: (1) Reposition store to appeal to younger shoppers without losing current clientele. (2) Increase acceptance by younger shoppers. (3) Establish more of a Web presence.
- • Satisfaction of publics: (1) Maintain store loyalty among current customers. (2) Increase relationship with younger designers selling less-costly, younger apparel. (3) Maintain excellent relationship with employees.

4. Identification of Consumers
- • Choice of target market
  - ○ Mass marketing: This is not a mass market store.
  - ○ Concentrated marketing: This is Sally's current target market strategy.
  - ○ Differentiated marketing: Sally's might consider attracting multiple target markets: its current fashion-forward customers seeking designer apparel and accessories in a full-service environment; younger, professional customers who desire more trendy clothing; and fashion-forward customers who desire custom-made clothing.

5. Overall Strategy
- • Controllable variables
  - ■ Goods/services strategy: Clothing is fashion-forward from established and emerging designers. The fashion accessories sold include such items as scarves, belts, and hats. The retailer has no plans to sell ladies shoes, or pocketbooks. Most of the designer merchandise is selectively distributed. A planned custom-made clothing department would enable Sally's to attract hard-to-fit and hard-to-please shoppers. Custom-made clothing shoppers would have a wide variety of swatches and fashion books from which to choose.
  - ■ Location strategy: Sally's currently occupies a single location in a suburban strip mall. This site has comparatively low rent, is within 10 miles of 80 percent of the store's customers, has adequate parking, and has good visibility from the road.
  - ■ Pricing strategy: Sally's charges list price for all of its goods. Included in the price are full-tailoring service, as well as a personal shopper for important customers. Twice a year, the store has a 50 percent off sale on seasonal goods. This is followed by 70 percent off sales to clear the store of remaining off-season inventory.
  - ■ Promotion strategy: Sally's sales personnel are well-trained and highly motivated. They know key customers by name and by their style, color, and designer preferences. Sally's plans to upgrade its regular fashion and trunk shows where new styles are exhibited to important customers. Sally's also maintains a customer data base. The best customers are called when suitable merchandise arrives and allowed to preview it. Some other customers are contacted by mail. The new Web site will feature the latest styles, the Web address of major designers, and color availability. Sally's has a display listing in the Yellow Pages.
- • Uncontrollable variables
  - ■ Consumer environment: Business is subject to the uncertainty of the acceptance of new fashions by the target market. Although Sally's wants to attract two additional segments (custom-made clothing buyers and younger buyers), there is no assurance that it will be successful with these target markets. The store needs to be careful that in seeking these new segments, that it does not alienate its current shoppers.
  - ■ Competitive environment: The rumored opening of a fashion-oriented department store in the area would significantly impact sales.
  - ■ Legal environment: Sally's is careful in fully complying with all laws. Unlike some competitors, it does not eliminate sales taxes for cash purchases or ship empty boxes out-of-state to avoid sales tax.
  - ■ Economic environment: Local recessions can reduce sales substantially.
  - ■ Technological environment: Sally's is in the process of investigating a new retail information system to track purchases, inventories, credit card transactions, and more.

TABLE 3-6	*Continued*

6. Specific Activities
- Daily and short-term operations: Sally's policy is to match competitors' prices, correct alteration problems immediately, have longer store hours during busy periods, and offer exclusive merchandise.
- Responses to environment: Sally's acts appropriately with regard to trends in the economy, competitor actions, and so forth.

7. Control
- Evaluation: The new retail information system will better enable Sally's to ascertain fashion trends, adjust inventories to reduce markdowns, and contact customers with specific offerings. Sales by color, size, style, and designer will be more carefully monitored.
- Adjustment: The retail information system will enable Sally's to reduce excess inventories, maximize sales opportunities, and better target individual customers.

Summary

1. *To show the value of strategic planning for all types of retailers.* A retail strategy is the overall plan that guides a firm. It consists of situation analysis, objectives, identification of a customer market, broad strategy, specific activities, control, and feedback. Without a well-conceived strategy, a retailer may be unable to cope with environmental factors.

2. *To explain the steps in strategic planning for retailers.* Situation analysis is the candid evaluation of opportunities and threats. It looks at the firm's current marketplace position and where it should be heading. This analysis includes defining an organizational mission, evaluating ownership and management options, and outlining the goods/service category.

   An organizational mission is a commitment to a type of business and a place in the market. Ownership/management options include sole proprietorship, partnership, or corporation; starting a business, buying an existing one, or being a franchisee; owner management or professional management; and being centralized or decentralized. The goods/service category depends on personal abilities, finances, and time resources.

   A firm may pursue one or more of these goals: sales (growth, stability, and market share); profit (level, return on investment, and efficiency); satisfaction of publics (stockholders, consumers, and others); and image/positioning (customer and industry perceptions).

   Next, consumer characteristics and needs are determined, and a target market is selected. A firm can sell to a broad spectrum of consumers (mass marketing); zero in on one customer group (concentrated marketing); or aim at two or more distinct groups of consumers (differentiated marketing), with separate retailing approaches for each.

   A broad strategy is then formed. It involves controllable variables (aspects of business a firm can directly affect) and uncontrollable variables (factors a firm cannot control and to which it must adapt).

   After a general strategy is set, a firm makes and implements short-run decisions (tactics) for each controllable part of that strategy. Tactics must be forward-looking and respond to the environment.

   Through a control process, strategy and tactics are evaluated and revised continuously. A retail audit systematically reviews a strategy and its execution on a regular basis. Strengths are emphasized and weaknesses minimized or eliminated.

   An alert firm seeks out signals or cues, known as feedback, that indicate the level of performance at each step in the strategy.

3. *To examine the individual controllable and uncontrollable elements of a retail strategy, and to present strategic planning as a series of integrated steps.* There are four major controllable factors in retail planning: store location, managing the business, merchandise management and pricing, and communicating with the customer. The principal uncontrollable factors affecting retail planning are consumers, competition, technology, economic conditions, seasonality, and legal restrictions.

   Each stage in the strategic planning process needs to be performed, undertaken sequentially, and coordinated in order to have a consistent, integrated, unified strategy.

4. *To demonstrate how a strategic plan can be prepared.* A comprehensive, user-friendly strategic planning template, *Computer-Assisted Strategic Retail Management Planning*, appears at our Web site. This template uses a series of drop-down menus to build a strategic plan.

Key Terms

retail strategy (p. 58)	objectives (p. 67)	differentiated marketing (p. 72)
situation analysis (p. 58)	image (p. 69)	competitive advantages (p. 72)
opportunities (p. 58)	positioning (p. 69)	controllable variables (p. 74)
threats (p. 58)	mass merchandising (p. 69)	uncontrollable variables (p. 74)
organizational mission (p. 59)	niche retailing (p. 69)	tactics (p. 79)
sole proprietorship (p. 61)	bifurcated retailing (p. 69)	control (p. 79)
partnership (p. 61)	target market (p. 72)	feedback (p. 80)
corporation (p. 61)	mass marketing (p. 72)	
goods/service category (p. 64)	concentrated marketing (p. 72)	

Questions for Discussion

1. Why is it necessary to develop a thorough, well-integrated retail strategy? What could happen if a firm does not develop such a strategy?

2. How would situation analysis differ for a major appliance store chain and an online major appliance retailer?

3. What are the pros and cons of starting a new bakery versus buying an existing one?

4. Develop a checklist to help a prospective service retailer choose the proper service category in which to operate. Include personal abilities, financial resources, and time demands.

5. Why do retailers frequently underestimate the financial and time requirements of a business?

6. Draw and explain a positioning map showing the kinds of retailers selling cell phones and cell phone monthly service plans.

7. Discuss local examples of retailers applying mass marketing, concentrated marketing, and differentiated marketing.

8. Marsha Hill is the store manager at a popular greeting card store. She has saved $100,000 and wants to open her own store. Devise an overall strategy for Marsha, including each of the controllable factors listed in Figure 3-9 in your answer.

9. A competing gift store has a better location than yours. It is in a modern shopping center with a lot of customer traffic. Your store is in an older neighborhood and requires customers to travel farther to reach you. How could you use a merchandising, pricing, and communications strategy to overcome your disadvantageous location?

10. Describe how a retailer can use fine-tuning in strategic planning.

11. How are the control and feedback phases of retail strategy planning interrelated? Give an example.

12. Should a store-based TV set retailer use the strategic planning process differently from a catalog retailer? Why or why not?

Web-Based Exercise

Visit the Web site of Carrefour (**www.carrefour.com**), the largest retailer outside the United States. Describe and evaluate the company based on the information you find there. What U.S. firm does it most resemble? Why?

Note: Stop by our Web site (**www.prenhall.com/bermanevans**) to experience a number of highly interactive, appealing Web exercises based on actual company demonstrations and sample materials related to retailing.

Chapter Endnotes

1. Various company sources.

2. "Business Plan Basics," **www.sba.gov/starting_ business/planning/basic.html** (April 4, 2006).

3. "Burlington Company Profile," **http://corporate. burlingtoncoatfactory.com/corpinfo** (April 5, 2006); "PetsMart Company Profile," **www.petsmart.com/ about_us/index.shtml** (April 5, 2006); and "Sam

Goody Company Info," **www.samgoody.com/Help/mCompany.aspx** (April 5, 2006).

4. For additional information about business owner-ship formats, go to *Inc.'s* "Legal Issues-Buying/Selling a Business" site (**www.inc.com/articles_by_topic/legal-biz_finance-legal_buy_sell**).

5. "Choosing an Entity for Your Business," **www.360financialliteracy.org/Life+Stages/Entrepreneurs** (April 2, 2006).

6. Estimated by the authors from data in *Statistical Abstract of the United States 2004–2005* (Washington, DC: U.S. Department of Commerce, 2004).

7. "Corporate News & Info," **www.kroger.com/corpnewsinfo_mission.htm** (March 20, 2006).

8. "Company Background," **www.bebe.com/Company/background.jsp** (March 20, 2006).

9. "How We Do Business," **www.traderjoes.com/about/wedobiz.asp** (March 20, 2006).

Appendix on the Special Dimensions of Strategic Planning in a Global Retailing Environment

Michigan State University's CIBER (**http://ciber.bus.msu.edu**) is an excellent source of information on global business practices.

There are about 270 countries—with 6.5 billion people and a $55 trillion economy—in the world. The United States accounts for less than 5 percent of the world's population and more than one-fifth of the worldwide economy. Although the United States is an attractive marketplace, there are also many other appealing markets. Annual worldwide retailing sales have already reached $9 trillion—and they are growing.[1] When we talk about the global environment of retailing, we mean both U.S. firms operating in foreign markets and foreign retailers operating in U.S. markets.

The strategic planning challenge is clear: "The constant state of flux in the retail world keeps many retailers feverishly planning to stay ahead of the game. By its nature, the industry is driven by newness, excitement, and variability. It's what keeps customers excited and willing to buy. However, because of the fast pace of change, it doesn't take long for a retailer to fall behind. And when this happens, it's not always easy to regain momentum. Consumers are fickle. There's very little allegiance. Shoppers quickly are engaged by the latest sensation, fad, or fashion. To stay on top, retailers need to be mindful of many aspects of the business—the competition, consumers, technology, and their own operations."[2] In embarking on an international retailing strategy, firms should consider the factors shown in Figure A3-1.

THE STRATEGIC PLANNING PROCESS AND GLOBAL RETAILING

Retailers looking to operate globally should follow these four steps *in conjunction with* the strategic planning process described in Chapter 3:

1. *Assess Your International Potential:* "You must first focus on assessing your international potential to get a picture of the trends in your industry, your domestic position in that industry, the effects that international activity may have on current operations, the status of your resources, and an estimate of your sales potential. Find out about candidate countries by using research. It's easy to ruin a good plan by making fundamental cultural, partnering, or resource allocation mistakes."

2. *Get Expert Advice and Counseling:* "Many groups in the private sector and government provide guidance to those planning to go international. Trade associations are also useful, as are consulting firms and the business departments of universities. If you are entirely new to international retailing, contact the U.S. Trade

FIGURE A3-1
Factors to Consider When
Engaging in Global
Retailing

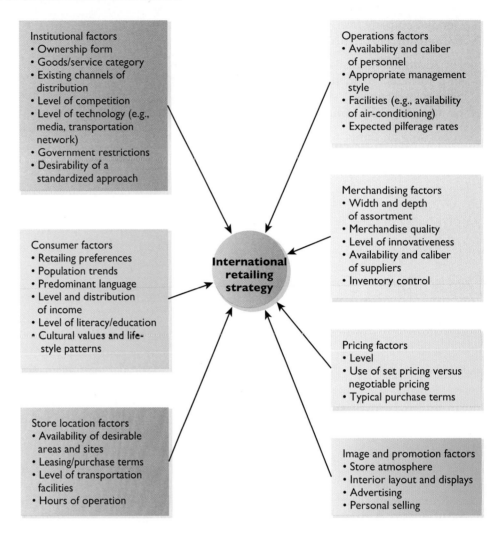

Institutional factors
• Ownership form
• Goods/service category
• Existing channels of distribution
• Level of competition
• Level of technology (e.g., media, transportation network)
• Government restrictions
• Desirability of a standardized approach

Operations factors
• Availability and caliber of personnel
• Appropriate management style
• Facilities (e.g., availability of air-conditioning)
• Expected pilferage rates

Merchandising factors
• Width and depth of assortment
• Merchandise quality
• Level of innovativeness
• Availability and caliber of suppliers
• Inventory control

Consumer factors
• Retailing preferences
• Population trends
• Predominant language
• Level and distribution of income
• Level of literacy/education
• Cultural values and lifestyle patterns

International retailing strategy

Pricing factors
• Level
• Use of set pricing versus negotiable pricing
• Typical purchase terms

Store location factors
• Availability of desirable areas and sites
• Leasing/purchase terms
• Level of transportation facilities
• Hours of operation

Image and promotion factors
• Store atmosphere
• Interior layout and displays
• Advertising
• Personal selling

The United Nations (www.un.org) has a wealth of useful data about the international environment.

Information Center (**www.ita.doc.gov/tic**) at (800) USA-TRADE (800-872-8723). If you are further along, contact a district office of the Commerce Department's International Trade Administration (**www.ita.doc.gov**). State governments are another source of assistance."

3. *Select Your Countries:* "You need to prioritize information about each country's economic strength, political stability, regulatory environment, tax policy, infrastructure development, population size, and cultural factors. For example, the economy of a country is generally considered critical to most businesses. Equally critical are political factors, particularly government regulations. Others are more dependent on which product you market. The technological stage of a country has a more influential role for computers than for cosmetics."

4. *Develop, Implement, and Review the International Retailing Strategy:* "In general, a successful strategy identifies and manages your objectives, both immediate and long range; specifies tactics you will use; schedules activities and deadlines; and allocates resources among those activities. The plan should cover a two- to five-year period, depending on what you are selling, competitors' strength, conditions in target countries, and other factors. Keep your strategy flexible because often it is only after entering a country that you realize that your way of doing business needs modification. The best strategies can be changed to exploit unique local conditions and circumstances. Don't underestimate the local competition, but don't overestimate it either."[3]

OPPORTUNITIES AND THREATS IN GLOBAL RETAILING

For participating firms, there are wide-ranging opportunities and threats in global retailing.

Opportunities

- Foreign markets may be used to supplement domestic sales.
- Foreign markets may represent growth opportunities if domestic markets are saturated or stagnant.
- A retailer may be able to offer goods, services, or technology not yet available in foreign markets.
- Competition may be less in foreign markets.
- There may be tax or investment advantages in foreign markets.
- Due to government and economic shifts, many countries are more open to the entry of foreign firms.
- Communications are easier than before. The Internet enables retailers to reach customers and suppliers well outside their domestic markets.

Threats

- There may be cultural differences between domestic and foreign markets.
- Management styles may not be easily adaptable.
- Foreign governments may place restrictions on some operations.
- Personal income may be poorly distributed among consumers in foreign markets.
- Distribution systems and technology may be inadequate (for example, poor roads and lack of refrigeration). This may minimize the effectiveness of the Web as a selling tool.
- Institutional formats vary greatly among countries.
- Currencies are different. The countries in the European Union have sought to alleviate this problem by introducing the euro, a common currency, in most of their member nations.

Standardization: An Opportunity and a Threat

When devising a global strategy, a retailer must pay attention to the concept of *standardization*. Can the home market strategy be standardized and directly applied to foreign markets, or do personnel, physical facilities, operations, advertising messages, product lines, and other factors have to be adapted to local conditions and needs? Table A3-1 shows how the economies differ in 15 countries. And consider this:

> If you intend to enter a foreign market, you must be very sensitive to local cultural issues, and then be humble enough to accept that no matter how well you have prepared, some aspect of local culture will probably surprise you. Your entry plans must consist of some measure of humility and flexibility. You will inevitably be facing execution challenges that you had not adequately considered in the planning stage of your market entry.[4]

| TABLE A3-1 | The Global Economy, Selected Countries |

Country	2005 Population (millions)	2005 Population Density (per sq. kilometer)	2004 Per Capita GDP (U.S. $)	2003 Per Capita Retail Sales— Excluding Autos (U.S. $)	2003–2008 Projected Annual Retail Growth Rate— After Inflation (%)	2004 World Competitiveness Ranking Among the 15 Countries Listed
Brazil	186	23	8,100	400	3.3	13
Canada	33	3	31,500	5,500	4.7	2
China	1,300	135	5,600	440	9.0	6
France	61	109	28,700	6,465	4.0	7
Germany	82	231	28,700	4,455	1.5	3
Great Britain	60	244	29,600	6,750	6.5	4
India	1,080	325	3,100	210	3.8	8
Indonesia	242	128	3,500	135	6.1	15
Italy	58	195	27,700	4,655	2.5	11
Japan	127	336	29,400	7,700	1.0	5
Mexico	106	54	9,600	425	2.7	14
Philippines	88	290	5,000	130	5.9	12
Russia	144	8	9,800	1,025	6.5	10
South Korea	49	493	19,200	2,590	3.3	9
United States	296	31	40,100	9,850	5.2	1

GDP is a country's gross domestic product. Per capita GDP is expressed in terms of purchasing power parity.
World Competitiveness Ranking is based on a country's economic performance, government efficiency, business efficiency, and infrastructure.

Sources: Compiled by the authors from *World Factbook*, **www.odci.gov/cia/publications/factbook/index.html** (updated online as of June 14, 2005); Retail Forward, *Global Retail Outlook* (November 2004); and *IMD World Competitiveness Yearbook 2004*.

FACTORS AFFECTING THE SUCCESS OF A GLOBAL RETAILING STRATEGY

Several factors can affect the level of success of an international retailing strategy:

● *Timing:* "Being first in a market doesn't ensure success, but being there before the serious competition does increase one's chances."

● *A balanced international program:* "Market selection is critical."

● *A growing middle class:* "A rapidly growing middle class means expendable income, which translates into sales."

● *Matching concept to market:* "In *developed* markets, where quality and fashion are more appreciated, specialty operations are entering with success. In *developing* markets, discount/combination (food and general merchandise) retailers have been successful. Consumers there are more interested in price, assortment, value, and convenience." See Table A3-2.

● *Solo or partnering:* "When establishing a presence, retailers have often chosen the route of joint ventures with local partners. This makes it easier to establish government contacts and learn the ways of getting things done."

TABLE A3-2   Preparing for Different Global Markets

Developed, Mature Markets

Issues
- Increasing competition, deteriorating margins, and saturation
- Consolidation and rationalization (cost cutting), forcing poor performers out of the market
- New enabling technologies
- Demanding customers
- Limited growth

Implications
- Retailers must focus on maximizing operational efficiencies, vendor relationships, infrastructure, and technology
- For growth, large retailers are expanding regionally and then globally into developed or developing markets

Developing, Immature Markets

Issues
- Minimal purchasing power per capita, yet strong economic growth and pent-up demand
- Huge customer base, representing up to 70 percent of the world's population
- Infrastructure issues—transportation, communication, etc.—may pose problems
- Disorganized, fragmented retail structures that are vulnerable to new entrants
- The number of indigenous large retailers is small to none
- Strong protectionist measures may exist

Implications
- Tremendous opportunity for large retailers, limited competition, huge growth potential
- Initial entry may need to be through intermediary; joint venture, etc.

Source: Deloitte & Touche, "Global Powers of Retailing," *Stores* (January 1998), Section 3, p. S15. Reprinted by permission.

- *Store location and facilities:* "Foreign retailers often have to adapt their concepts to different real-estate configurations in other markets." Shopping malls may be rare in some places.
- *Product selection:* "Consumers in most parts of the world would be overwhelmed by the product assortment in North American stores."
- *Service levels:* "Consumers in some areas do not expect anything close to the level of service American shoppers demand." This can be a real point of distinction.[5]

U.S. RETAILERS IN FOREIGN MARKETS

Here are examples of U.S. retailers with high involvement in foreign markets.

Toys "R" Us has been active internationally for years and now has about 570 stores abroad. Among the nearly 30 nations in which it has well-established stores are Australia, Canada, France, Germany, Great Britain, Japan, Singapore, Spain, and Sweden. In some of its markets, such as Indonesia, South Africa, Turkey, and United Arab Emirates, the firm emphasizes franchising rather than direct corporate ownership. Why? This enables Toys "R" Us to better tap the local knowledge of franchisees in certain markets while still setting corporate policies.[6]

For two decades, the majority of McDonald's new restaurants have opened outside the United States. Sales at the 17,000 outlets in 120 foreign nations account for two-thirds of total revenues. Besides Western Europe, McDonald's has outlets in such nations as Argentina, Australia, Brazil, Bulgaria, Canada, China, Colombia, Czech Republic, Egypt, Hungary, India, Japan, Malaysia, Mexico, New Zealand, Russia, South Africa, Turkey, and Yugoslavia. The restaurants in India are distinctive: "McDonald's worked with its local Indian partners to adapt the menu to meet local tastes and needs. As the old advertising jingle goes, the 'Maharaja Mac' is made of: 'two all lamb patties, special sauce, lettuce, cheese, pickles, onions on a sesame seed bun.' The famous sandwich's main ingredient, beef, was replaced out of respect for the local Hindu population of India."[7]

Many of the world's leading mail-order retailers are U.S.-based, including American Express, Avon, Franklin Mint, and Reader's Digest. They are efficient and have a clear handle on customers and distribution methods. Because total worldwide mail-order sales (for both U.S. and foreign firms) outside the United States are less than those in the United States, there is great potential in foreign markets.

Amazon.com has rapidly expanded globally by introducing dedicated Web sites for specific nations. They include Canada (**www.amazon.ca**), China (**www.joyo.com**), France (**www.amazon.fr**), Germany (**www.amazon.de**), Great Britain (**www.amazon.co.uk**), and Japan (**www.amazon.co.jp**). While these sites all have the familiar Amazon Web design, they differ by language, products offered, and currency.

FOREIGN RETAILERS IN THE U.S. MARKET

A large number of foreign retailers have entered the United States to appeal to the world's most affluent mass market. Here are three examples.

Ikea is a Swedish-based home-furnishings retailer operating in 35 nations. In 1985, Ikea opened its first U.S. store in Pennsylvania. Since then, it has added more than 25 other U.S. stores in such cities as Baltimore, Chicago, Elizabeth (New Jersey), Hicksville (Long Island, New York), Houston, Los Angeles, San Francisco, Seattle, and Washington, D.C. The firm offers durable, stylish, ready-to-assemble furniture at low prices. Stores are huge, have enormous selections, and include a playroom for children and other amenities. Today, Ikea generates 93 percent of its sales from international operations, and 16 percent of total company sales (more than $2 billion per year) are from its North American stores.[8]

The Netherlands' Royal Ahold ranks among the world's top retailers with annual worldwide retail sales exceeding $50 billion. It has food stores in more than 20 countries and serves 40 million shoppers weekly. In the United States, Royal Ahold has acquired several chains, making it the leading supermarket firm on the East Coast. Its 1,600 U.S. stores include Stop & Shop, Giant Food, Bruno's, and Bi-Lo. The firm also owns Peapod, the online food store.[9]

Body Shop International is a British-based chain that sells natural cosmetics and lotions that "cleanse, beautify, and soothe the human form." There are 2,000 Body Shop stores in 50 countries, including the United States. The firm has more than 430 U.S. stores (60 percent company-owned and 40 percent franchised), which generate 23 percent of total revenues.[10]

Although the revenues of U.S.-based retailers owned by foreign firms are hard to measure, they exceed $175 billion dollars annually. Foreign ownership in U.S. retailers is highest for general merchandise stores, food stores, and apparel and accessory stores. Examples of U.S.-based retailers owned by foreign firms are shown in Table A3-3.

TABLE A3-3	Selected Ownership of U.S. Retailers by Foreign Firms		
U.S. Retailer	**Principal Business**	**Foreign Owner**	**Country of Owner**
Brooks Pharmacy	Drugstores	Jean Coutu	Canada
Circle K	Convenience stores	Couche-Tard	Canada
Crate & Barrel	Housewares stores	Otto Group	Germany
Eckerd (eastern U.S.)	Drugstores	Jean-Coutu	Canada
Food Lion	Supermarkets	Delhaize Group	Belgium
Giant Food	Supermarkets	Royal Ahold	Netherlands
Great Atlantic & Pacific (A&P)	Supermarkets	Tengelmann	Germany
Hannaford Bros.	Supermarkets	Delhaize Group	Belgium
LensCrafters	Optical stores	Luxottica	Italy
Motel 6	Economy motels	Accor	France
7-Eleven (Southland)	Convenience stores	Seven & I Holdings	Japan
Stop & Shop	Supermarkets	Royal Ahold	Netherlands
Sunglass Hut	Sunglass stores	Luxottica	Italy
Talbots	Apparel	Aeon	Japan

Appendix Endnotes

1. *World Factbook*, **www.odci.gov/cia/publications/factbook/index.html** (updated online as of August 30, 2005).

2. "2005 Global Powers of Retailing," *Stores* (January 2005), p. G38.

3. William J. McDonald, "Five Steps to International Success," *Direct Marketing* (November 1998), pp. 32–36.

4. John C. Koopman, "Successful Global Retailers a Rare Breed," *Canadian Manager* (Spring 2000), p. 25.

5. "Global Powers of Retailing," *Chain Store Age* (December 1996), Section 3, pp. 10B–13B.

6. *Toys "R" Us 2005 Annual Report*.

7. *McDonald's 2005 Annual Report*; and "Maharaja Mac," **www.media.mcdonalds.com/secured/products/international/maharajamac.html** (August 18, 2002).

8. "Inter Ikea Systems," **http://franchisor.ikea.com** (March 2, 2006).

9. "About Ahold," **www.ahold.com** (March 2, 2006).

10. "The Body Shop," **www.thebodyshopinternational.com** (March 2, 2006).

part one
Short Cases

CASE 1: BED BATH & BEYOND'S PLAN FOR GROWTH[c-1]

Bed Bath & Beyond (BB&B) (**www.bedbathandbeyond.com**), the power retailer of domestics and home furnishings, has annual sales of $6 billion and a net income of $600 million (up a compounded rate of 28 percent and 33 percent, respectively, over the prior decade). As of this writing, BB&B has delivered 15 consecutive years of record profits. As one retailing consultant says, BB&B is viewed as "the most powerful specialty home-décor merchant in the country, much more than anyone else. They are more imaginative in creating value than anyone I know of."

The firm's profitability can be explained by its increasing gross profit margins at the same time it is decreasing selling, general, and administrative (SG&A) expenses as a percent of sales. BB&B is able to increase its gross profit margins due to its excellent atmosphere, wide assortments, and deep variety within most merchandise lines. Its control over SG&A expenses is partly due to the outsourcing of its distribution centers to a third party.

BB&B anticipates growing via three ways. One, it is consistently able to secure greater sales on a year-to-year basis from comparable store sales. In a recent quarter, the chain increased comparable store sales by 11 percent.

Two, BB&B has opened hundreds of stores over the last few years, ranging in size from 30,000 to 80,000 square feet. Since it uses a flexible real-estate strategy, BB&B is able to locate in a variety of locations. According to one expert, "Because BB&B isn't a cookie-cutter operation, it can shoehorn itself in anywhere the opportunities are." Furthermore, BB&B is now being allowed into large shopping centers. In the past, department store anchor tenants blocked BB&B.

Three, BB&B recently purchased the Christmas Tree Shops, a chain of nearly 30 stores specializing in giftware and household items. Although the Christmas Tree Shops' name suggests that it concentrates on Christmas merchandise, the chain is positioned against Pier 1.

BB&B management (as well as many retail analysts) also attributes the chain's strong sales performance to its superior customer service. As one retail analyst states, BB&B's "management likes to tell the staff that 70 percent of customer reorders rests on their shoulders." Store-level and regional managers spend a lot of time on the sales floor to determine customer trends, as well as to help customers.

BB&B is obsessive about its consumers receiving a consistently high level of customer service whether they are in Boca Raton or New York City. A recent shopper at a suburban Long Island store reported that a sales clerk was highly attentive. When the shopper asked the clerk where she could find a set of dishes listed on a bridal registry, the clerk immediately dropped what she was doing. The clerk then located the dishes, stood by the shopper as she decided whether to purchase the set, and even had the dishes delivered to a nearby checkout, so that the shopper could continue buying at the store. The sales clerk then met the shopper at the checkout to facilitate the transaction.

Questions

1. Explain how Bed Bath & Beyond practices the retailing concept.
2. Evaluate Bed Bath & Beyond's growth plans.
3. How can Bed Bath & Beyond increase the overall quality of its customer service?
4. Explain the concept of value from the perspective of a Bed Bath & Beyond customer.

CASE 2: NETFLIX: COMPETING IN A TOUGH MARKETPLACE[c-2]

In 1999, Netflix (**www.netflix.com**) introduced its online DVD rental service; this has been its major offering ever since. For a flat monthly fee, Netflix subscribers can order as many movies as they desire, up to three movies at a time, and they can keep the movie rentals for as long as they want. Unlike other services at that time, such as Blockbuster, Netflix had no due dates or no late fees. The movie rentals generally arrived the next day and titles were rarely out of stock. As of 2005, Netflix had more than 3 million subscribers; and subscriber turnover was extremely low.

According to Reed Hastings, Netflix's chief executive officer, "What you have here is a $500 million market growing 100 percent a year. And any market that big, growing that fast, is bound to attract competitors." Wal-Mart began offering online rentals of DVDs in June 2003 and in summer 2004, Blockbuster invested $100 million in an online rental service. In December 2004, Amazon launched an online rental service in Great Britain. Many analysts saw this move as a test for a possible entry by Amazon into the U.S. market.

Hastings sees the competitive environment as a "classic case where our competitors have size, but we have focus." Hastings believes that his firm's major asset is its subscriber base. He also feels that new features such as Netflix Friends, which enables users to share movie reviews with each other, is another important competitive advantage.

Of its competitors, Hastings is most concerned about Blockbuster. Netflix has 35 distribution centers (which enable it to reach more than 85 percent of its customers overnight). Blockbuster (**www.blockbuster.com**) has 25 centers and plans to add more. Hastings recognizes that Netflix has attacked Blockbuster's core business and that Blockbuster will strongly defend it.

[c-1]The material in this case is drawn from Isadore Barmash, "A Hotbed of Home Décor," *Chain Store Age* (March 2005), pp. 60, 62; and *Bed Bath & Beyond 2005 Annual Report*.

[c-2]The material in this case is drawn from John Heilemann, "Showtime for Netflix," *Business 2.0* (March 2005), pp. 36, 38; and "Wal-Mart's Film Flop," *Newsday* (May 20, 2005), p. A59.

In contrast, Hastings does not know if Amazon will invest the resources to build and maintain sufficient distribution centers. Competition from Amazon, however, cannot be dismissed. Unlike Blockbuster, Amazon is an Internet firm, has a huge base of customers, and has a logistics infrastructure to efficiently distribute DVD rentals.

In May 2005, Wal-Mart decided to exit the online DVD business, a rare defeat for the retailing giant. Wal-Mart worked out an arrangement with Netflix that gave Wal-Mart's DVD customers the chance to continue their subscriptions with Netflix at their current price for one year. Netflix will promote Wal-Mart as a place to purchase DVDs, and Wal-Mart will publicize its arrangement with Netflix.

Many retail analysts are concerned not only with the size and retail backgrounds of Netflix's competitors but also worry about the possibility of a price war. To stay competitive, Netflix cut the price of its basic subscription plan from $21.99 to $17.99. A few weeks later, Blockbuster cut its main plan (allowing up to three rentals at a time) by $2.50 to $14.99.

Hastings believes that a price war with Blockbuster is unlikely because a price war will cut into the profitability of Blockbuster's store operations. Netflix also has existing software and logistics systems that give it a significant cost advantage over its competitors: "Our favorite analogy is Dell, which makes money on prices that no one else in the industry can profit from."

Questions

1. Develop specific objectives for Netflix's strategic plan over the next five years.
2. What target market strategy is most appropriate for Netflix? Explain your answer.
3. Describe Netflix's competitive advantages and disadvantages relative to Blockbuster and Amazon.com.
4. Explain why retail analysts are so concerned about a price war for online DVD rentals.

CASE 3: WHAT LOYALTY PROGRAMS WORK IN BRAZIL?[c-3]

Peppers & Rogers Group Brazil (**www.1to1.com.br**), a subsidiary of Carlson Marketing (**www.carlsonmarketing.com**), recently completed a study of loyalty programs in Brazil. Fifty-three retailers with 21 million loyalty program participants (out of the 186 million population for Brazil) were surveyed. Among the retailers represented were firms in the financial services, telecommunications, travel, transportation, and healthcare industries. Peppers & Rogers focused on Brazil due to its economic growth. Brazil's gross domestic product is now growing by 4 to 5 percent annually, the highest growth rate in a decade.

[c-3]The material in this case is drawn from Weslyeh Mohriak and Fernando Pierry, "Loyalty Programs in Micro: Brazil Study Shows Advanced Strategy," *Inside 1to1 Strategy* (November 23, 2004); and "Brazil," *World Factbook 2005*.

Six different types of loyalty programs were studied:

- Points: Members receive points, credits, miles, or other units based on purchases.
- Affinity: Members receive special services not available to nonmembers.
- Discount: Members receive "members only" discounts.
- Partnership: Members receive offers from other firms.
- Fee: Members are required to pay a fee to maintain their membership.
- Communications: Members can send periodic communications based upon their stated interest, past purchases, and demographics.

Here are some of the findings of the study:

- All of the retailers collected basic personal data to develop consumer profiles on loyalty program members. Eighty-seven percent kept transaction-based data to identify purchase amounts and frequency. Eighty-two percent recorded credits and redemptions. Interestingly, 76 percent of the companies restrict access of the data base to the loyalty program.
- Most firms seek to differentiate membership benefits by the value of members. Criteria include the purchase of a given good or service, the frequency of purchase, and the communication channel (for customers that furnish their E-mail address).
- Eighty-nine percent of the firms manage their own loyalty programs. The others sponsor shared programs, are partners in third-party programs, or belong to programs that use a common currency that rewards loyalty.

Retailers were asked to what degree their loyalty program attained specific program goals. The highest levels of goal attainment were associated with member satisfaction, the use of benefits by members, increased profitability, and higher sales by members. For example, two-thirds of the firms that measure trading-up indicators of success and 58 percent that monitor cross-selling indicated that they met or exceeded their goals. Firms reported much lower levels of goal attainment relative to program costs, member cancellation rates, and offering additional goods and services to members.

The study concluded that Brazil's loyalty programs have evolved from short-term means of increasing sales to longer-term customer retention strategies that provide important customer data to retailers. It also found large differences between ineffective and effective loyalty programs. Ineffective programs are thinly disguised advertising messages sent to groups of customers, while effective programs establish a meaningful dialogue between the retailer and the consumer.

Questions

1. Are the six loyalty programs outlined in the case mutually exclusive? Can a retailer have elements of multiple forms of loyalty program? Explain your answers.

2. Describe the pros and cons of restricting the program data to the loyalty program division.
3. Explain this statement: "Brazil's loyalty programs have evolved from short-term means of increasing sales to longer-term customer retention strategies that provide important customer data to retailers."
4. What material from this case can be used by a U.S. supermarket chain considering a loyalty program?

CASE 4: eBAY EXPANDS AROUND THE GLOBE[c-4]

While as recently as 2000, eBay (**www.ebay.com**) had virtually no international operations, by 2005, the firm had sites in 31 countries around the world ranging from Brazil to Germany and China. eBay's 2005 foreign operations generated well over $1 billion in revenues, accounting for 46 percent of eBay's trading revenues. And of eBay's 135 million registered users, about half live outside the United States. Since eBay's international sales are growing at twice the rate as its domestic operations, its international sales will soon surpass domestic sales.

eBay has succeeded abroad because its global strategy is flexible enough to adapt to countries with vastly different cultures, while retaining the core elements of its business model. The global strategy is based on a playbook that is a how-to manual that covers such topics as online marketing, category management, and community outreach. The playbook, which is constantly updated, consists of several hundred Web pages that summarize the collective wisdom of all of eBay's worldwide managers.

The playbook details how to drive traffic to the local eBay site through online ads at a country's most popular Web sites and search engines. The playbook also dictates that products, information, and chat groups be created by buyers and sellers in that country. Thus, eBay looks and feels like a particular foreign country's Web site brand. This strategy also

[c-4]The material in this case is drawn from Erick Schonfeld, "The World According to eBay," *Business 2.0* (January/February 2005), pp. 76–84.

avoids problems associated with a cookie-cutter approach to Web site planning on a global basis.

Meg Whitman, who became eBay's CEO in 1998, originally wanted to perfect eBay's concept in the United States before going abroad. However, she soon realized that many small competitors were springing up around the world. She became concerned that unless eBay went global, she would forfeit many opportunities to these small local firms or to major firms such as Amazon and Yahoo!.

eBay's first foreign country was Germany, chosen in part due to the country's 40 million Internet users. eBay purchased Alando, an eBay copycat site, for $47 million in June 1999. A German business student had started Alando four months earlier. From the start, eBay was careful to adapt its sites to a country's culture. For example, a lot of time and effort went into figuring out how to structure categories based on German customers' needs. Today, Germany is eBay's largest international site, with estimated annual total sales of $7 billion versus $20 billion for the United States.

Shortly after purchasing Alando, eBay launched its own sites in Great Britain and Australia. In 2001, eBay purchased Korea's Internet Auction Co. and Europe's iBazar (which gave eBay immediate access to Italy, the Netherlands, and Spain). eBay then purchased a minority interest in MercadoLibre, Latin America's leading auction firm. In total, eBay has invested nearly $2 billion in its international acquisitions.

Questions

1. Comment on the choice of Germany as eBay's first international market.
2. Evaluate the pros and cons of eBay's playbook strategy.
3. Describe the pros and cons of eBay's entering an international market by purchasing a foreign firm rather than building an operation from scratch.
4. Comment on this statement: "eBay has succeeded abroad because its global strategy is flexible enough to adapt to countries with vastly different cultures, while retaining the core elements of its business model."

part one
Comprehensive Case
Mining for Growth*

INTRODUCTION

Growth does not usually find you. You need to find it. Or even mine for it. For many firms, the question is not "How fast can you grow?" It's "How do you keep growing—at all?" In today's saturated retail environment, it is harder to grow the tried-and-true way, by rolling out more stores and more products.

Planned growth requires a framework—from optimizing the business, to expanding the business, to redefining the business. It requires a superior consumer value proposition to drive economic advantage. It requires a process for investigating, generating, evaluating, and initiating growth opportunities.

Profitable growth is the mission of every retailer, whose prospects for long-term profitable growth drive share price appreciation. People want to work for a company that is growing. Vendors want to do business with growth companies. No matter how the retail marketplace evolves, there is one constant—success is all about profitable growth. But, growth has become more difficult to find.

The Growth Opportunity Matrix

In the abstract, growth is a pretty simple concept. You can sell more to the customers you already have, or you can sell more customers (or both). To sell more customers, you can target consumers in your existing target market who are not current customers, or you can target a different segment. Theoretically, retail growth opportunities can be classified into a number of different types based on the desired outcome or goal of the growth strategy and the growth levers that are used to achieve the goal. See Figure 1.

Growth Strategy Objectives

Growth can focus on the existing business, striving to do it better, providing intensification of the present market situation. It can focus on expanding the scope or reach of the current operation, doing more of it or doing it in more ways, resulting in the logical extension of the existing business. Or, growth can focus on wholly new areas that transcend traditional competitive boundaries, daring to do things differently, providing strategic diversification of the business. The spectrum of growth strategy objectives—from intensification to extension to

Growth Strategy Objectives		Geography/Location	Product/Service Offer	Target Customer	Format/Channel
	Intensity	Leverage relationships with existing customers by increasing penetration of existing geographic markets	Optimize existing offer to better serve existing customers	Build/maintain loyalty/satisfaction with current customers: discover areas of untapped potential to sell more to existing customers	Enhance the shopping experience of existing customers through store modernization/ new store prototypes and/or better integration of existing channels
	Extend	Reach more target customers by expanding into new geographic markets/locations with similar market characteristics	Expand existing offer to leverage relationships with existing customers and attract new customers	Target consumer sub-segments within existing customer base	Develop multiple format/channel business model to reach more target customers in more shopping situations and/or satisfy different shopping needs of same customer
	Diversity	Expand into new geographic markets/locations with different market characteristics	Converge into other business sectors to create new value for new and existing customers in wholly new areas	Target new customer groups	Create new concepts to reach new customer segments

(Top axis label: Growth Levers)

FIGURE 1
Retail Growth Opportunity Matrix

Source: Retail Forward, Inc.

diversification—creates the vertical axis for the growth opportunity matrix.

Growth Levers

The growth levers that retailers can control to achieve a growth objective appear along the horizontal axis of the matrix. They represent the market opportunity in terms of geography/location, product/service offer, target customer, and format/channel.

The growth opportunity matrix graphically depicts the scope of potential retail growth initiatives, with the resulting 12 cells representing the options that firms can pursue. Within each cell or type, there are multiple growth initiatives that may make sense for many retailers to consider. The value of this framework is not so much where a particular strategy fits but that all opportunities are considered.

Geography/Location Growth Opportunities

Despite the slowdown in new store expansion many retailers face in the years ahead, companies pursuing geographic growth have a number of productive opportunities.

Geographic Intensification: Strengthen position in existing markets by increasing market penetration. A retailer can explore opportunities to fill in gaps in existing markets. Retailers such as Wal-Mart (**www.walmart.com**), Walgreens (**www.walgreens.com**), Home Depot (**www.homedepot.com**), and Costco (**www.costco.com**) are locating stores much closer together, expanding market share while alleviating pressures on high-volume stores that have become almost too successful.

Geographic Extension: Expand into more geographic markets with similar market characteristics to reach more customers in target segment. For retailers facing saturation in major metropolitan markets, small markets and urban markets provide new geographic growth opportunities. A number of retailers see that there is plenty of money to be made in less-competitive, smaller towns and in densely populated urban neighborhoods where real estate is at a premium and consumers' options are often limited. Before 1999, Best Buy (**www.bestbuy.com**) built only 45,000-square-foot stores in large markets. Since then, it has begun to tap into smaller market areas. Staples (**www.staples.com**) has opened stores in a smaller format. These stores are two-thirds the size of the standard format and are designed to address smaller markets, as well as smaller areas of potential in existing markets.

More consumers are abandoning the mall, with its confusing layout and sprawling parking lot, in favor of easier-to-reach, easier-to-shop alternatives. The pathway to continued growth for mall-based retailers will require new types of locations that have better growth prospects than the regional mall. Unlike in the past, today only 30 percent of Chico's (**www.chicos.com**) hundreds of apparel stores are mall-based, while half are in specialty or strip centers and 20 percent are street-front locations.

As the department store industry continues to consolidate and more anchor space sits empty, retailers that have traditionally been nonmall players will take advantage of opportunities to anchor regional malls. Attractive lease arrangements make it more feasible for value retailers such as Kohl's (**www.kohls.com**), Target (**www.target.com**), and T.J. Maxx (**www.tjmaxx.com**)/Marshalls (**www.marshallsonline.com**), as well as other big-box retailers, to take an anchor position, encouraging more to explore this alternative.

Geographic Diversification: Expand into new geographies/locations with different market characteristics to reach new customers. Opening stores in alternative locations (e.g., airports and transportation hubs, entertainment venues, mixed-use developments, off-mall locations) allows retailers to reach customers who are not shopping their stores and leads to increased shopping frequency among existing customers by intercepting them in a variety of situations. As part of its rapidly growing wholesale business, Sharper Image (**www.sharperimage.com**) entered into a partnership with Circuit City (**www.circuitcity.com**) that features Sharper Image brand products in Circuit City stores and on its Web site. This provides an opportunity for Sharper Image to build its brand name and its sales with a wider audience and provides a way for Circuit City to differentiate itself from competitors.

For some retailers, going beyond conventional locations might also extend to "pop-up" sites and mobile opportunities. Temporary locations provide opportunities to get in front of consumers at peak selling times or places (e.g., sporting events) when and where consumers are most likely to be receptive.

Product/Service Growth Opportunities

There are many opportunities to grow by better aligning the product/service offer with the needs and expectations of the best customers. At the same time, retailers can explore opportunities to add new goods and services that leverage existing relationships into new areas while also gaining new customers.

Product/Service Intensification: Optimize existing offer to better serve existing customers. One of the biggest merchandising opportunities is growth that can be achieved by capturing the unsatisfied desires in the consumer marketplace. Often, this is driven by an aspirational desire to trade up, an emotional desire for products that are more personally meaningful, an aesthetic desire for form, as well as function, or simply a desire for the latest and greatest. Lowe's (**www.lowes.com**) continues to see strong results from its "up-the-continuum" merchandising strategy. Based on research, Lowe's concluded several years ago that 80 percent of home improvement decisions were made by women. In addition to making its stores cleaner and brighter to better appeal to female customers, Lowe's has been upscaling by narrowing the breadth and increasing the depth of its product lines and adding more designer-name goods.

Product/Service Extension: Expand existing offer to leverage relationships with existing customers and attract new customers. Services designed to enhance the physical product offer are becoming a key differentiating factor with huge growth potential as retailers seek to create solution-driven concepts. Best Buy is working with several home builders, installing video and computer network wiring. Its plan is to have the builder include a basic wiring package in every home in a development and then to try to sell additional features, such as in-wall speakers, security cameras, and even a big-screen television, all bundled into the home buyer's mortgage.

Product/Service Diversification: Converge into other business sectors to create new value for new and existing customers in wholly new areas. Going forward, market share will no longer suffice as the measure by which some companies gauge growth and performance. Instead, they will look to capture a larger share of life. They will forge partnerships with firms in other business sectors to enter new markets and/or offer new services outside their core businesses (e.g., media, finance, travel, healthcare, telecom services). In the process, they will create new value for customers by expanding their brands well beyond traditional boundaries to generate new revenue streams. Virgin Group (**www.virgingroup.com**) is involved in planes, trains, finance, soft drinks, music, mobile phones, holidays, cars, wines, publishing, bridal wear, and more. What ties all these businesses together are the values of the brand—good value for the money, quality, innovation, fun, and a sense of competitive challenge.

Target Customer Growth Opportunities

Retailers have many opportunities to grow their business by intensifying and extending their customer relationships and diversifying into new segments. For established retailers, often the fastest, easiest, and least risky path to increased sales and profitability starts with existing customers. Most customers would gladly give a retailer "permission" to sell more things to them if it simply offered more of what they want.

Customer Intensification: Build and maintain current customer loyalty and satisfaction. High-growth retailers recognize that their "best customers" are not only those spending the most with them but also those who are the most "open to spend" with them. Finding these customers and giving them what they want is the key to incremental sales. Chico's Passport Club marketing and loyalty program is acknowledged for building strong customer relationships that have resulted in significant increases in the apparel retailer's average transaction size—the average transaction for Passport members is 50 percent higher than for nonmembers. About three-quarters of Chico's total sales are derived from its more than 900,000 permanent Passport members.

Customer Extension: Discover areas of untapped potential to sell more to existing customers. Broaden appeal to consumer subsegments. Retailers searching for relevant ways to connect with target customers are integrating content and commerce through ownership or control of highly targeted

media or specific programming opportunities. In some cases, they create their own value-added content around the goods and services they offer as a way to gain credibility and drive greater consumer involvement with their brands. Arts-and-crafts chain Michaels Stores (**www.michaels.com**) launched *Michaels Create!*, a magazine dedicated to providing inspirational ideas to crafters and decorators at all skill levels. The magazine is available at newsstands, in Michaels stores, and by subscription. Michaels' partner, Krause Publishing, is in charge of editorial staffing and receives all revenues from circulation and advertising. Michaels benefits because all projects featured in the magazine are available in its stores.

Pottery Barn (**www.potterybarn.com**) launched the *Pottery Barn Design Library*, a series of source books for home decorating—including Pottery Barn Bedrooms, Pottery Barn Living Rooms, Pottery Barn Bathrooms, etc. The series, for sale at Pottery Barn and through bookstores, is scheduled to continue its expansion into many areas of the home as a source of ideas and inspiration for consumers.

Customer Diversification: Target new customer groups. Retailers committed to understanding their customers as individuals (or groups of like-minded individuals) rather than averages have been able to move the growth needle significantly. The ability to recognize the needs and wants of different market segments becomes increasingly critical as the marketplace changes. Today, nearly one-third of the U.S. population is represented by Hispanic-Americans, African-Americans, and Asian-Americans. Walgreens became the first national pharmacy retailer with a Web site designed specifically for Hispanics. WalgreensEspanol.com provides drug information, an online prescription refill form, a store locator, and directions on how to use some of the services on walgreens.com. Walgreens also pioneered a chainwide multilanguage prescription label service to help its customers completely understand how they should take their medicine. The service has been expanded to 10 languages—Spanish, Chinese, French, Polish, Portuguese, Russian, Vietnamese, German, Italian, and Tagalog (for Filipinos).

Tesco's (**www.tesco.com**) focus on its customers and gaining their loyalty has been at the heart of the firm's growth and vision. It is widely credited with having one of the best, if not the best, customer-driven data-base marketing programs in existence. Tesco's Clubcard loyalty program boasts 10 million active households and captures 85 percent of the retailer's weekly sales. The program has made Tesco the number one grocer in Great Britain. Tesco has also fine-tuned its ability to segment its customers into "lifestyle" groups whose spending patterns are distinct, recognizable, and actionable. Every quarter, a 10-million-piece mailing with nearly 4 million variants is tailored to the needs, interests, and potential interests of Clubcard members. For Tesco, the media effectiveness of the Clubcard program has allowed the retailer to save money on promotions and increase sales at the same time.

Business-to-business is proving to be a growing customer opportunity for many retailers. Wholesale, commercial, and institutional sales can provide significant incremental volume by leveraging the retailer's expertise and existing supply and service networks. Looking to grow its commercial business, AutoZone (**www.autozone.com**) is taking over Midas' (**www.midas.com**) parts distribution. The agreement calls for AutoZone to distribute parts and accessories to Midas' franchised and company-owned U.S. service shops. The contract is expected to add at least $100 million annually to AutoZone's revenue.

BestBuyBiz (**www.bestbuybiz.com**) is the commercial sales division of Best Buy, putting the retailer's buying power to work for businesses and institutions of all types and sizes— from schools to small businesses to worldwide firms. Lands' End Business Outfitters (**www.landsend.com/business**) offers company incentives, rewards, gifts, and logo apparel and accessories to firms of all sizes, including 9 out of 10 *Fortune 500* companies. Regional Lands' End field sales representatives call directly on medium- to large-size companies with a substantial apparel program in mind. In addition to its store, catalog, and Internet operations, Sharper Image has a business-to-business operation for marketing its proprietary products for corporate incentive and reward programs. For a minimum purchase of reward cards or certificates, the retailer also offers private shopping events in its stores for corporate customers.

Format/Channel Growth Opportunities

To maintain sales growth in a retail environment characterized by accelerating format life cycles, firms must strive for a balance between updating existing formats and creating dynamic new ones. The strategies of migrating the brand into new channels, along with better channel integration, also remain important growth opportunities.

Format/Channel Intensification: Enhance the shopping experience of existing customers with updated formats. As store expansion opportunities grow scarce, what they lack in quantity they must make up for in quality by investing more in existing stores. Best Buy has a new "digital life" store prototype where shoppers can test fully functioning display products throughout the store. Products are displayed in settings that look more like a residence than a retail store. Shoppers can test video games from the comfort of a sofa that faces a large-screen TV. The appliance department features a model kitchen setup that features a drop-down LCD TV screen highlighting the connection between the company's electronics and appliance offerings. "Project Living Room" includes several living room-style arrangements to promote sales of high-end home theater equipment.

Format/Channel Extension: Develop multiple format/channel business model to reach more target customers in more shopping situations and/or satisfy different shopping needs of same customer. Striving to increase their market share, retailers are developing multi-format strategies in response to the needs of different customer groups or to satisfy different shopping needs of the same customer at different times. Williams-Sonoma's (**www.williams-sonoma.**

com) multi-channel strategy uses catalogs to test new concepts prior to making the commitment to opening stores. They are also a key marketing tool for driving interest and traffic to retail stores and Web sites. Pottery Barn Kids (**www.potterybarnkids.com**) was the first "new" brand to experience this multi-channel treatment. It was launched and refined as a catalog, then developed into a retail concept. The stores benefit from a product mix that has already gone through several direct marketing cycles to determine what sells and what doesn't. And the firm can refine its site selection to precisely locate stores in the areas that match their best pockets of direct response.

Diversification: Embrace creative use of all available consumer touchpoints. The exhortation to offer multiple points of access to cater to the growing number of "multi-modal" shoppers needs to go beyond thinking about leveraging the three primary distribution channels generally thought of as "multi-channel." To grow in a mature environment, retailers must go beyond multi-channel to "omni-channel," embracing a wider variety of customer touchpoints—which may or may not offer a way to engage in a transaction.

Sharper Image has been an omni-channel innovator, embracing the creative and liberal use of all available touchpoints to maximize sales—including stores, catalogs, Internet, online auction sites, and a partnership with in-flight co-op cataloger Sky Mall (**www.skymall.com**). In addition to its own Web site, Sharper Image offers its products via Internet marketing agreements with Google (**www.google. com**), eBay (**www.ebay.com**), MSN Shopping (**www.msn shopping.com**), Amazon.com (**www.amazon.com**), Linkshare (**www.linkshare.com**), Yahoo! Shopping (**http://shopping. yahoo.com**), Catalog City (**www.catalogcity.com**), and AOL (**www.aol.com**), enabling the retailer to expand and diversify its existing customer base. It also offers international Web sites where Internet shoppers get local delivery of Sharper Image branded products, which in some cases have been specifically adapted for use throughout Europe. The company has also increased the circulation of single product mailers, radio and print ads, and infomercial advertising to maximize the sales potential of individual products such as Ionic Breeze.

Questions

1. What can *any* retailer learn from this case?
2. How can the principles in this case enable a retailer to better apply the retailing concept? Be specific in your answer.
3. Where does your local supermarket fit in the retail growth matrix highlighted in Figure 1? What are the implications of this?
4. Why is product/service intensification a good approach for a retailer interested in relationship retailing?
5. Visit the Tesco Web site (**www.tesco.com**) and describe why its loyalty program is so widely praised.

6. Discuss why this suggestion is so hard to implement: "To maintain sales growth in a retail environment characterized by accelerating format life cycles, firms must strive for a balance between updating existing formats and creating dynamic new ones."
7. For each of three different retail growth opportunity matrix strategies, set one objective that a retailer could monitor to determine whether it has been successful with that strategy.

*The material in this case is adapted by the authors from *Growth Mining: The New Imperative for Retailers* (Columbus, OH: Retail Forward, May 2004). Reprinted by permission of Retail Forward, Inc. (**www.retailforward.com**).

part two

Situation Analysis

In Part Two, we present the organizational missions, ownership and management alternatives, goods/service categories, and objectives of a broad range of retail institutions. By understanding the unique attributes of these institutions, better retail strategies can be developed and implemented.

- **Chapter 4** examines the characteristics of retail institutions on the basis of ownership type: independent, chain, franchise, leased department, vertical marketing system, and consumer cooperative. We also discuss the methods used by manufacturers, wholesalers, and retailers to obtain control in a distribution channel. A chapter appendix has additional information on franchising.

- **Chapter 5** describes retail institutions in terms of their strategy mix. We introduce three key concepts: the wheel of retailing, scrambled merchandising, and the retail life cycle. Strategic responses to the evolving marketplace are noted. Several strategy mixes are then studied, with food and general merchandise retailers reviewed separately.

- **Chapter 6** focuses on nonstore retailing, electronic retailing, and nontraditional retailing approaches. We cover direct marketing, direct selling, vending machines, the World Wide Web, video kiosks, and airport retailing. The dynamics of Web-based retailing are featured. A chapter appendix covers the emerging area of multi-channel retailing in more depth.

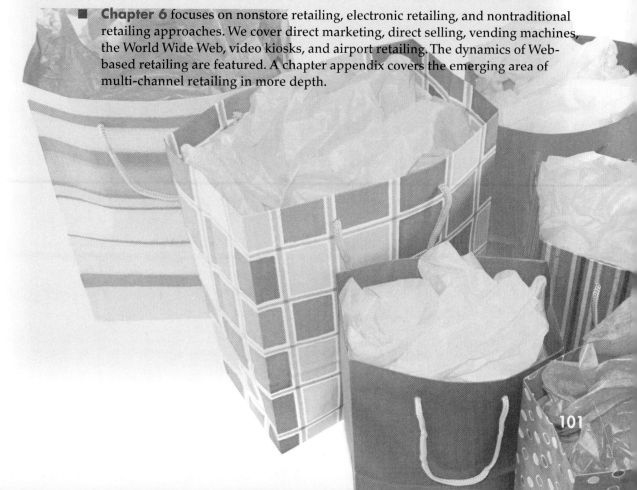

Chapter 4
RETAIL INSTITUTIONS BY OWNERSHIP

In 1954, Ray Kroc, then a salesman of milkshake mixers, visited two of his best customers—Maurice and Richard McDonald—in San Bernadino, California. The McDonald brothers had just purchased eight Multimixers, one of Kroc's largest orders, and he wanted to observe their operations in action. What Kroc saw astounded him. Although many burger places of that era were

Reprinted by permission.

dirty and had poor reputations, the McDonald brothers' operation was clean and modern, and there was even a burger production line.

The following day, Kroc approached the brothers and came to an agreement with them whereby he would sell franchises for $950 each and 1.4 percent of the sales while the brothers received 0.5 percent. Kroc became so obsessed with the business that he was often quoted as saying, "I believe in God, family, and McDonald's." He soon bought out the McDonald brothers.

As the chain expanded, Kroc was careful to ensure that the eating experience was identical at each restaurant. McDonald's (**www.mcdonalds.com**) controlled franchisees' menu items and décor, automated many of the operations, instituted training programs at its Hamburger University, and developed precise operating standards. Kroc passed on his obsession with quality and cleanliness to franchisees. An often quoted motto was, "if you have time to lean, you have time to clean."

Recently, McDonald's was voted "Marketer of the Year" by *Advertising Age* magazine in recognition of the chain's global marketing achievements associated with its international "I'm lovin' it" campaign. The campaign had awareness levels as high as 86 percent in the top 10 countries where McDonald's has a franchising presence.[1]

chapter objectives

1. To show the ways in which retail institutions can be classified
2. To study retailers on the basis of ownership type and examine the characteristics of each
3. To explore the methods used by manufacturers, wholesalers, and retailers to exert influence in the distribution channel

OVERVIEW

A **retail institution** is the basic format or structure of a business. In the United States, there are 2.3 million retail firms (including those with no payroll, whereby only the owner and/or family members work for the firm), and they operate 3 million establishments. An institutional discussion shows the relative sizes and diversity of different kinds of retailing and indicates how various retailers are affected by the external environment. Institutional analysis is important in strategic planning when selecting an organizational mission, choosing an ownership alternative, defining the goods/service category, and setting objectives.

We examine retail institutions from these perspectives: ownership (Chapter 4); store-based strategy mix (Chapter 5); and nonstore-based, electronic, and nontraditional retailing (Chapter 6). Figure 4-1 shows a breakdown. An institution may be correctly placed in more than one category: A department store may be part of a chain, have a store-based strategy, accept mail-order sales, and operate a Web site.

Please interpret the data in Chapters 4 to 6 carefully. Because some institutional categories are not mutually exclusive, care should be taken in combining statistics so double counting does not occur. We have drawn in the data in these chapters from a number of government and nongovernment sources. Although data are as current as possible, not all information corresponds to a common date. *Census of Retail Trade* data are only collected twice a decade. Furthermore, our numbers are based on the broad interpretation of retailing used in this book, which includes auto repair shops, hotels and motels, movie theaters, real-estate brokers, and others who sell to the final consumer.

FIGURE 4-1
A Classification Method for Retail Institutions

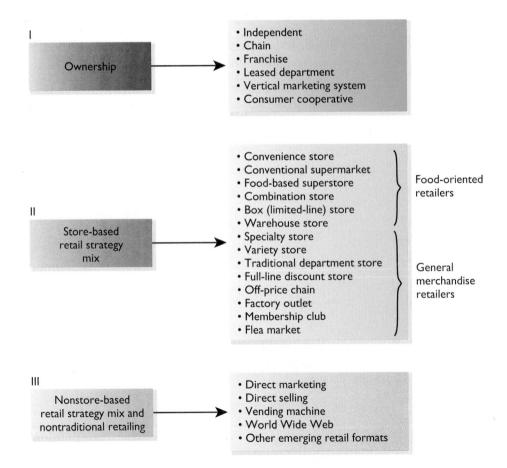

RETAIL INSTITUTIONS CHARACTERIZED BY OWNERSHIP

Retail firms may be independently owned, chain-owned, franchisee-operated, leased departments, owned by manufacturers or wholesalers, or consumer-owned.

Although retailers are primarily small (three-quarters of all stores are operated by firms with one outlet and over one-half of all firms have two or fewer paid employees), there are also very large retailers. The five leading U.S. retailers total more than $550 billion in sales and employ 2.5 million people. Ownership opportunities abound. For example, according to the U.S. Census Bureau (**www.census. gov**), women own about 1 million retail firms, African-Americans (men and women) about 100,000 retail firms, and Asian-Americans (men and women) about 200,000 retail firms.

Each ownership format serves a marketplace niche, if the strategy is executed well:

- Independent retailers capitalize on a very targeted customer base and please shoppers in a friendly, folksy way. Word-of-mouth communication is important. These retailers should not try to serve too many customers or enter into price wars.

- Chain retailers benefit from their widely known image and from economies of scales and mass promotion possibilities. They should maintain their image chainwide and not be inflexible in adapting to changes in the marketplace.

- Franchisors have strong geographic coverage—due to franchisee investments—and the motivation of franchisees as owner-operators. They should not get bogged down in policy disputes with franchisees or charge excessive royalty fees.

- Leased departments enable store operators and outside parties to join forces and enhance the shopping experience, while sharing expertise and expenses. They should not hurt the image of the store or place too much pressure on the lessee to bring in store traffic.

- A vertically integrated channel gives a firm greater control over sources of supply, but it should not provide consumers with too little choice of products or too few outlets.

- Cooperatives provide members with price savings. They should not expect too much involvement by members or add facilities that raise costs too much.

Independent

The CCH Business Owner's Toolkit (http://toolkit. cch.com) is an excellent resource for the independent retailer.

An **independent** retailer owns one retail unit. There are 2.2 million independent U.S. retailers—accounting for about 35 percent of total store sales. Seventy percent of independents are run by the owners and their families; these firms generate just 3 percent of U.S. store sales (averaging under $100,000 in annual revenues) and have no paid workers (there is no payroll).

The high number of independents is associated with the **ease of entry** into the marketplace, due to low capital requirements and no, or relatively simple, licensing provisions for many small retail firms. The investment per worker in retailing is usually much lower than for manufacturers, and licensing is pretty routine. Each year, tens of thousands of new retailers, mostly independents, open in the United States.

The ease of entry—which leads to intense competition—is a big factor in the high rate of failures among newer firms. One-third of new U.S. retailers do not survive the first year and two-thirds do not continue beyond the third year. Most

Careers in RETAILING

Kathi: Senior Vice-President and General Manager

Kathi ended up in retail right out of college. She wasn't able to get a job in journalism (her college major) because she didn't have any experience. So, she began working in a family-owned department store, thinking she would stay there until she got a job in her field. But, she was promoted for her good work and decided to stay. She went from sales associate to department manager to assistant buyer to gourmet food buyer.

Kathi's upward progression at the department store gave her opportunities to build her knowledge and skills. As gourmet food buyer, she knew the cookware department's products inside and out. As a result, the store's biggest cookware supplier recruited her to their company, where Kathi was in charge of the company's recipes, magazine, and testing program.

Kathi then joined an international specialty store chain, which was the second largest vendor at her original department store. She became the wholesale sales representative, selling to department store buyers in stores like the one in which she began her career. Kathi was successful in this position because she had retail experience; she knew the buyers' business, and she could understand and address their needs. She has been promoted several times at this company, where she is currently senior vice-president and general manager, retail division. Kathi's current salary exceeds $100,000 annually, plus benefits.

Source: Reprinted by permission of the National Retail Federation.

failures involve independents. Annually, thousands of U.S. retailers (of all sizes) file for bankruptcy protection besides the thousands of small firms that simply close.[2]

The U.S. Small Business Administration (SBA) has a Small Business Development Center (SBDC) to assist current and prospective small business owners (**www.sba.gov/sbdc**). There are 63 lead SBDCs (at least 1 in every state) and 1,100 local SBDCs, satellites, and specialty centers. The purpose "is to provide basic business counseling and management assistance to current and prospective small business owners." Centers offer individual counseling, seminars and training sessions, conferences, information through the Internet, as well as in person and by phone, and "assist anyone seeking advice about running a small business." The SBA also has many free downloadable publications at its Web site. See Figure 4-2.

FIGURE 4-2
Useful Online Publications for Small Retailers

Go to **www.sba.gov/ library/pubs.html** and download any of the U.S. Small Business Administration publications at this Web site. They're free!

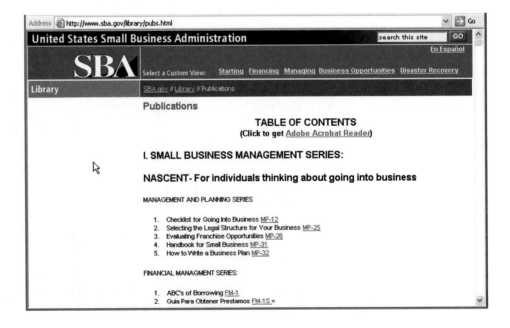

Competitive Advantages and Disadvantages of Independents

Independent retailers have a variety of advantages and disadvantages. These are among their advantages:

Read the Mrs. Fields story (www.mrsfields.com)— from one cookie store to a worldwide chain.

- There is flexibility in choosing retail formats and locations, and in devising strategy. Because only one location is involved, detailed specifications can be set for the best site and a thorough search undertaken. Uniform location standards are not needed, as they are for chains, and independents do not have to worry about company stores being too close. Independents have great latitude in selecting target markets. Because they often have modest goals, small segments may be selected rather than the mass market. Assortments, prices, hours, and other factors are then set consistent with the segment.
- Investment costs for leases, fixtures, workers, and merchandise can be held down; and there is no duplication of stock or personnel functions. Responsibilities are clearly delineated within a store.
- Independents frequently act as specialists in a niche of a particular goods/service category. They are then more efficient and can lure shoppers interested in specialized retailers.
- Independents exert strong control over their strategies, and the owner-operator is typically on the premises. Decision making is centralized and layers of management personnel are minimized.
- There is a certain image attached to independents, particularly small ones, that chains cannot readily capture. This is the image of a personable retailer with a comfortable atmosphere in which to shop.
- Independents can easily sustain consistency in their efforts because only one store is operated.
- Independents have "independence." They do not have to fret about stockholders, board of directors meetings, and labor unrest. They are often free from unions and seniority rules.
- Owner-operators typically have a strong entrepreneurial drive. They have made a personal investment and there is a lot of ego involvement. According to a recent National Small Business Poll, "Two-thirds of Americans hold the view that if you want to get ahead, own a small business."[3]

These are some of the disadvantages of independent retailing:

- In bargaining with suppliers, independents may not have much power because they often buy in small quantities. Suppliers may even bypass them. Reordering may be hard if minimum order requirements are high. Some independents, such as hardware stores, belong to buying groups to increase their clout.
- Independents generally cannot gain economies of scale in buying and maintaining inventory. Due to financial constraints, small assortments are bought several times per year. Transportation, ordering, and handling costs per unit are high.
- Operations are labor intensive, sometimes with little computerization. Ordering, taking inventory, marking items, ringing up sales, and bookkeeping may be done manually. This is less efficient than computerization. In many cases, owner-operators are unwilling or unable to spend time learning how to set up and apply computerized procedures.

● Due to the relatively high costs of TV ads and the broad geographic coverage of magazines and some newspapers (too large for firms with one outlet), independents are limited in their access to certain media. Yet, there are various promotion tools available for creative independents (see Chapter 19).

● A crucial problem for family-run independents is overdependence on the owner. Often all decisions are made by that person, and there is no management continuity when the owner-boss is ill, on vacation, or retires. Long-run success and employee morale can be affected by this. As one small business consultant says, "Running a family owned or closely held business is a challenge. It is difficult to keep it up and running."[4]

● A limited amount of time is allotted to long-run planning, since the owner is intimately involved in daily operations of the firm.

Chain

A **chain** retailer operates multiple outlets (store units) under common ownership; it usually engages in some level of centralized (or coordinated) purchasing and decision making. In the United States, there are roughly 110,000 retail chains that operate about 800,000 establishments.

The relative strength of chain retailing is great, even though the number of firms is small (less than 5 percent of all U.S. retail firms). Chains today operate more than one-quarter of retail establishments, and because stores in chains tend to be considerably larger than those run by independents, chains account for roughly 65 percent of total U.S. store sales and employment. Although the majority of chains have 5 or fewer outlets, the several hundred firms with 100 or more outlets account for more than 60 percent of U.S. retail sales. Some big U.S. chains have at least 1,000 outlets each. There are also many large foreign chains. See Figure 4-3.

The dominance of chains varies by type of retailer. Chains generate at least 75 percent of total U.S. category sales for department stores, discount department stores, and grocery stores. On the other hand, stationery, beauty salon, furniture,

There are 7,000 U.S. Radio Shack (www.radioshack.com) stores and 500 Radio Shack kiosks in Sam's Club outlets. See if there is one near you.

FIGURE 4-3
The Body Shop: A Powerhouse of Retailing

The Body Shop (**www.thebodyshop.com**) is a huge British-based chain with stores in 50 different markets around the world—covering 25 languages and 12 time zones. The company is "a global operation with thousands of people working towards common goals and sharing common values."

Photo reprinted by permission.

In any given month, eBay (**www.ebay.com**) draws tens of millions of visitors to its site, even exceeding Amazon. com's (**www.amazon.com**) average number of visitors. Many of eBay's "power sellers," firms that sell $1,000 of goods each month, are traditional retailers that use this channel to expand their trading area beyond their store-based locations. Other power sellers sell goods only online and use eBay to supplement their regular jobs or as a main source of income. Let's look at the lives of one of eBay's power sellers.

Sheryl Williams specializes in the sale of Precious Moments porcelain figurines on eBay. Ms. Williams uses Sellathon (**www.sellathon.com**) software that highlights the search terms that bring the most customer traffic, the keywords used, the categories browsed, and the time a visitor spends on each item and page.

eBay has several programs to increase the income of its power sellers. PayPal (**www.paypal.com**), a payment program owned by eBay, now enables sellers to pay for postage online so they can avoid waiting at the post office. eBay has also increased its insurance coverage to $1,000 to protect customers from misrepresentation and fraud.

Sources: Lisa Guernsey, "eBay Sellers Do the Holiday Sprint," *New York Times* (November 25, 2004); and "Selling Resources," **http://pages.ebay.com/sell/resources.html** (April 4, 2006).

and liquor store chains produce far less than 50 percent of U.S. retail sales in their categories.

Competitive Advantages and Disadvantages of Chains

There are abundant competitive advantages for chain retailers:

Sears' Kenmore brand (www.kenmore.com) is so powerful that many different appliances are sold under the Kenmore name.

- Many chains have bargaining power due to their purchase volume. They receive new items when introduced, have orders promptly filled, get sales support, and obtain volume discounts. Large chains may also gain exclusive rights to certain items and have goods produced under the chains' brands.

- Chains achieve cost efficiencies when they buy directly from manufacturers and in large volume, ship and store goods, and attend trade shows sponsored by suppliers to learn about new offerings. They can sometimes bypass wholesalers, with the result being lower supplier prices.

- Efficiency is gained by sharing warehouse facilities; purchasing standardized store fixtures; centralized buying and decision making; and other practices. Chains typically give headquarters executives broad authority for personnel policies and for buying, pricing, and advertising decisions.

- Chains use computers in ordering merchandise, taking inventory, forecasting, ringing up sales, and bookkeeping. This increases efficiency and reduces overall costs.

- Chains, particularly national or regional ones, can take advantage of a variety of media, from TV to magazines to newspapers.

- Most chains have defined management philosophies, with detailed strategies and clear employee responsibilities. There is continuity when managerial personnel are absent or retire because there are qualified people to fill in and succession plans in place. See Figure 4-4.

- Many chains expend considerable time on long-run planning and assign specific staff to planning on a permanent basis. Opportunities and threats are carefully monitored.

Chain retailers do have a number of disadvantages:

- Once chains are established, flexibility may be limited. New nonoverlapping store locations may be hard to find. Consistent strategies must be maintained throughout all units, including prices, promotions, and product assortments. It may be difficult to adapt to local diverse markets.

- Investments are higher due to multiple leases and fixtures. The purchase of merchandise is more costly because a number of store branches must be stocked.

- Managerial control is complex, especially for chains with geographically dis-persed branches. Top management cannot maintain the control over each branch that independents have over their single outlet. Lack of communica-tion and delays in making and enacting decisions are particular problems.

- Personnel in large chains often have limited independence because there are several management layers and unionized employees. Some chains empower personnel to give them more authority.

Franchising[5]

Franchising involves a contractual arrangement between a *franchisor* (a manufac-turer, wholesaler, or service sponsor) and a retail *franchisee*, which allows the fran-chisee to conduct business under an established name and according to a given pattern of business. The franchisee typically pays an initial fee and a monthly per-centage of gross sales in exchange for the exclusive rights to sell goods and ser-vices in an area. Small businesses benefit by being part of a large, chain-type retail institution.

In **product/trademark franchising**, a franchisee acquires the identity of a fran-chisor by agreeing to sell the latter's products and/or operate under the latter's name. The franchisee operates rather autonomously. There are certain operating rules; but the franchisee sets store hours, chooses a location, and determines facil-ities and displays. Product/trademark franchising represents two-thirds of retail franchising sales. Examples are auto dealers and many gasoline service stations.

The International Franchise Association (**www.franchise.org**) is a leading source of information about franchising.

With **business format franchising**, there is a more interactive relationship between a franchisor and a franchisee. The franchisee receives assistance on site location, quality control, accounting systems, startup practices, management training, and responding to problems besides the right to sell goods and services. Prototype stores, standardized product lines, and cooperative advertising foster a level of coordination previously found only in chains. Business format franchising arrangements are common for restaurants and other food outlets, real-estate, and service retailing. Due to the small size of many franchisees, business formats account for about 80 percent of franchised outlets, although just one-third of total sales.

McDonald's (**www.mcdonalds.com/corp/franchise/franchisinghome.html**) is a good example of a business format franchise arrangement. The firm provides franchisee training at "Hamburger U," a detailed operating manual, regular visits by service managers, and brush-up training. In return for a 20-year franchising agreement with McDonald's, a traditional franchisee must put up a minimum of $200,000 of nonborrowed personal resources and pays ongoing royalty fees totaling at least 12.5 percent of gross sales to McDonald's. See Figure 4-5.

Size and Structural Arrangements

Although auto and truck dealers provide more than one-half of all U.S. retail franchise sales, few sectors of retailing have not been affected by franchising's growth. In the United States, there are 3,000 retail franchisors doing business with 325,000 franchisees. They operate 750,000 franchisee- and franchisor-owned outlets, employ several million people, and generate one-third of total store sales. In addition, hundreds of U.S.-based franchisors have foreign operations, with tens of thousands of outlets.

Nearly 80 percent of U.S. franchising sales and franchised outlets involve franchisee-owned units; the rest involve franchisor-owned outlets. If franchisees operate one outlet, they are independents; if they operate two or more outlets, they are chains. Today, a large number of franchisees operate as chains.

Three structural arrangements dominate retail franchising. See Figure 4-6:

1. *Manufacturer-retailer.* A manufacturer gives independent franchisees the right to sell goods and related services through a licensing agreement.

FIGURE 4-5
McDonald's Qualifications for Potential Franchisees

Source: Figure developed by the authors based on information in McDonald's "Frequently Asked Questions—Qualifications," **www.mcdonalds.com/corp/franchise/faqs2/qualifications.html** (February 22, 2006)

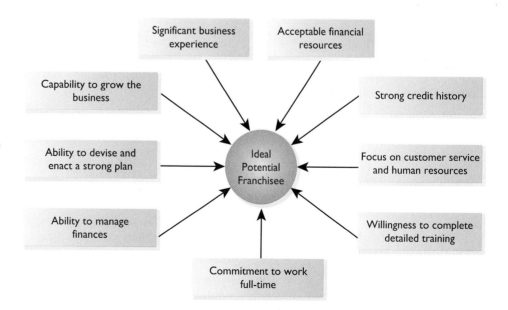

FIGURE 4-6
Structural Arrangements
in Retail Franchising

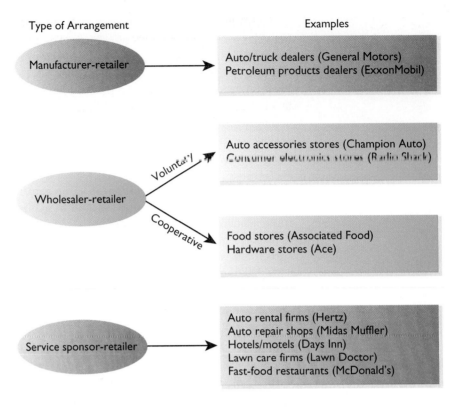

2. *Wholesaler-retailer.*
   a. *Voluntary.* A wholesaler sets up a franchise system and grants franchises to individual retailers.
   b. *Cooperative.* A group of retailers sets up a franchise system and shares the ownership and operations of a wholesaling organization.

3. *Service sponsor-retailer.* A service firm licenses individual retailers so they can offer specific service packages to consumers.

Competitive Advantages and Disadvantages of Franchising

Want to learn more about what it takes to be a franchisee? Check out the Jazzercise Web site (**www.jazzercise.com/ become_franchise.htm**).

Franchisees receive several benefits by investing in successful franchise operations:

- They own a retail enterprise with a relatively small capital investment.
- They acquire well-known names and goods/service lines.
- Standard operating procedures and management skills may be taught to them.
- Cooperative marketing efforts (such as national advertising) are facilitated.
- They obtain exclusive selling rights for specified geographical territories.
- Their purchases may be less costly per unit due to the volume of the overall franchise.

Some potential problems do exist for franchisees:

- Oversaturation could occur if too many franchisees are in one geographic area.
- Due to overzealous selling by some franchisors, franchisees' income potential, required managerial ability, and investment may be incorrectly stated.
- They may be locked into contracts requiring purchases from franchisors or certain vendors.

- Cancellation clauses may give franchisors the right to void agreements if provisions are not satisfied.
- In some industries, franchise agreements are of short duration.
- Royalties are often a percentage of gross sales, regardless of franchisee profits.

The preceding factors contribute to **constrained decision making**, whereby franchisors limit franchisee involvement in the strategic planning process.

The Federal Trade Commission (FTC) has a recently revised rule regarding disclosure requirements and business opportunities that applies to all U.S. franchisors. It is intended to provide adequate information to potential franchisees prior to their making an investment. Though the FTC does not regularly review disclosure statements, several states do check them and may require corrections. Also, a number of states (including Arizona, California, Indiana, New Jersey, Virginia, Washington, and Wisconsin) have fair practice laws that do not permit franchisors to terminate, cancel, or fail to renew franchisees without just cause. The FTC has an excellent franchising Web site (**www.ftc.gov/bcp/franchise/netfran. htm**), as highlighted in Figure 4-7.

Franchisors accrue lots of benefits by having franchise arrangements:

- A national or global presence is developed more quickly and with less franchisor investment.
- Franchisee qualifications for ownership are set and enforced.
- Agreements require franchisees to abide by stringent operating rules set by franchisors.
- Money is obtained when goods are delivered rather than when they are sold.
- Because franchisees are owners and not employees, they have a greater incentive to work hard.
- Even after franchisees have paid for their outlets, franchisors receive royalties and may sell products to the individual proprietors.

Franchisors also face potential problems:

- Franchisees harm the overall reputation if they do not adhere to company standards.

FIGURE 4-7
Franchise and Business Opportunities

At the FTC's franchising site, **www. ftc.gov/bcp/ franchise/netfran.htm**, there are many free downloads about opportunities—and warnings, as well.

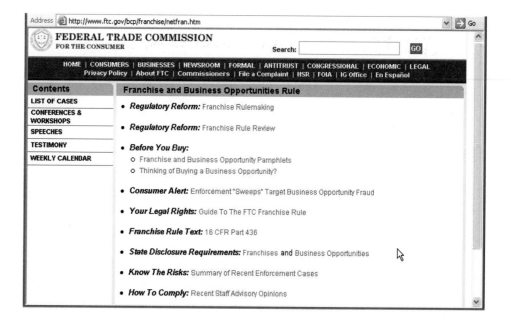

- A lack of uniformity among outlets adversely affects customer loyalty.
- Intrafranchise competition is not desirable.
- The resale value of individual units is injured if franchisees perform poorly.
- Ineffective franchised units directly injure franchisors' profitability that results from selling services, materials, or products to the franchisees and from royalty fees.
- Franchisees, in greater numbers, are seeking to limit franchisors' rules and regulations.

Additional information on franchising is contained in the appendix at the end of this chapter. Also, visit our Web site for a lot of links on this topic (**www.prenhall. com/bermanevans**).

Leased Department

A **leased department** is a department in a retail store—usually a department, discount, or specialty store—that is rented to an outside party. The leased department proprietor is responsible for all aspects of its business (including fixtures) and normally pays a percentage of sales as rent. The store sets operating restrictions for the leased department to ensure overall consistency and coordination.[6]

Leased departments are used by store-based retailers to broaden their offerings into product categories that often are on the fringe of the store's major product lines. They are most common for in-store beauty salons, banks, photographic studios, and shoe, jewelry, cosmetics, watch repair, and shoe repair departments. Leased departments are also popular in shopping center food courts. They account for $18 billion in annual department store sales. Data on overall leased department sales are not available.

Meldisco Corporation (**www.footstar.com**) runs leased shoe departments in 2,300 stores (especially Kmart and Rite Aid) and has annual leased department sales of $1 billion. It owns the inventory and display fixtures, staffs and merchandises the departments, and pays a fee for the space occupied. The stores where Meldisco operates typically cover the costs of utilities, maintenance, advertising, and checkout services.

Competitive Advantages and Disadvantages of Leased Departments

From the *stores' perspective*, leased departments offer a number of benefits:

- The market is enlarged by providing one-stop customer shopping.
- Personnel management, merchandise displays, and reordering items are undertaken by lessees.
- Regular store personnel do not have to be involved.
- Leased department operators pay for some expenses, thus reducing store costs.
- A percentage of revenues is received regularly.

There are also some potential pitfalls, from the stores' perspective:

- Leased department operating procedures may conflict with store procedures.
- Lessees may adversely affect stores' images.
- Customers may blame problems on the stores rather than on the lessees.

Ethics in RETAILING
Simon Property: Resolving a Gift Card Dispute

Simon Property Group (**www.simon.com**), the largest shopping center developer in the United States, has agreed to change its gift card program (**www.simon.com/giftcard**) after New York's attorney general called the program misleading and costly for consumers. Simon, which operates 10 malls and outlet centers in New York State, originally charged consumers a $2.50 monthly administrative fee for gift cards that were not redeemed as of the seventh month. This plan violates New York State law that bans monthly service fees on gift cards until after 12 months of nonuse. The state also noted that Simon's policy of charging a $5 fee to replace a lost or stolen card and a $7.50 fee to reissue an expired card was not legal since it was not conspicuously disclosed on the card. Simon agreed to pay $100,000 to New York State in penalties and $25,000 in legal costs.

Three other states—Massachusetts, Connecticut, and New Hampshire—have also sued Simon over these fees. And more than 25 states have enacted or introduced similar legal protections for gift card recipients.

Sources: Patricia Odell, "Simon Property Settles with NY; to Pay $125,000 in Penalties," *Promo* (March 2, 2005); and "Simon to Alter Gift-Card Rules," *Wall Street Journal* (March 2, 2005), p. D2.

For *leased department operators*, there are these advantages:

- Stores are known, have steady customers, and generate immediate sales for leased departments.
- Some costs are reduced through shared facilities, such as security equipment and display windows.
- Their image is enhanced by their relationships with popular stores.

Lessees face these possible problems:

- There may be inflexibility as to the hours they must be open and the operating style.
- The goods/service lines are usually restricted.
- If they are successful, stores may raise rent or not renew leases when they expire.
- In-store locations may not generate the sales expected.

CPI (**www.cpicorp.com**) has flourished with its leased department relationship at Sears.

An example of a thriving long-term lease arrangement is one between CPI Corporation and Sears. In exchange for space in more than 1,000 U.S. and Canadian Sears stores, CPI pays 15 percent of its sales. Its annual sales per square foot are much higher than Sears' overall average. CPI's agreement with Sears has been renewed several times. Annual revenues through Sears exceed $290 million.[7]

Vertical Marketing System

A **vertical marketing system** consists of all the levels of independently owned businesses along a channel of distribution. Goods and services are normally distributed through one of these systems: independent, partially integrated, and fully integrated. See Figure 4-8.

In an *independent vertical marketing system*, there are three levels of independently owned firms: manufacturers, wholesalers, and retailers. Such a system is most often used if manufacturers or retailers are small, intensive distribution is sought, customers are widely dispersed, unit sales are high, company resources are low, channel members seek to share costs and risks, and task specialization is desirable. Independent vertical marketing systems are used by many stationery

FIGURE 4-8
Vertical Marketing Systems:
Functions and Ownership

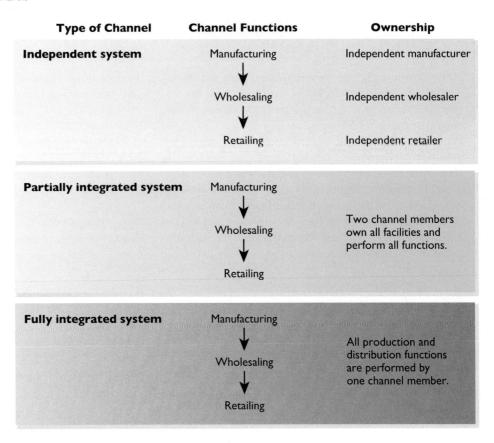

Type of Channel	Channel Functions	Ownership
Independent system	Manufacturing ↓ Wholesaling ↓ Retailing	Independent manufacturer / Independent wholesaler / Independent retailer
Partially integrated system	Manufacturing ↓ Wholesaling ↓ Retailing	Two channel members own all facilities and perform all functions.
Fully integrated system	Manufacturing ↓ Wholesaling ↓ Retailing	All production and distribution functions are performed by one channel member.

stores, gift shops, hardware stores, food stores, drugstores, and many other firms. They are the leading form of vertical marketing system.

With a *partially integrated system,* two independently owned businesses along a channel perform all production and distribution functions. It is most common when a manufacturer and a retailer complete transactions and shipping, storing, and other distribution functions in the absence of a wholesaler. This system is most apt if manufacturers and retailers are large, selective or exclusive distribution is sought, unit sales are moderate, company resources are high, greater channel control is desired, and existing wholesalers are too expensive or unavailable. Partially integrated systems are often used by furniture stores, appliance stores, restaurants, computer retailers, and mail-order firms.

Through a *fully integrated system,* one firm performs all production and distribution functions. The firm has total control over its strategy, direct customer contact, and exclusivity over its offering; and it keeps all profits. This system can be costly and requires a lot of expertise. In the past, vertical marketing was employed mostly by manufacturers, such as Avon and Sherwin-Williams. At Sherwin-Williams, its own 2,600 paint stores account for two-thirds of total company sales.[8] Today, more retailers (such as Kroger) use fully integrated systems for at least some products.

Some firms use **dual marketing** (a form of *multi-channel retailing*) and engage in more than one type of distribution arrangement. In this way, firms appeal to different consumers, increase sales, share some costs, and retain a good degree of strategic control. Here are two examples. (1) Sherwin-Williams sells Sherwin-Williams paints at company stores. It sells Dutch Boy paints in home improvement stores, full-line discount stores, hardware stores, and others. See Figure 4-9. (2) In addition to its traditional standalone outlets, Dunkin' Donuts and Baskin-Robbins share facilities in a number of locations, so as to attract more customers and increase the revenue per transaction.

Kroger, the food *retailer,* manufactures more than 3,500 food and nonfood products in its 42 plants (**www.kroger.com/ operations.htm**).

FIGURE 4-9
Sherwin-Williams' Dual Vertical Marketing System

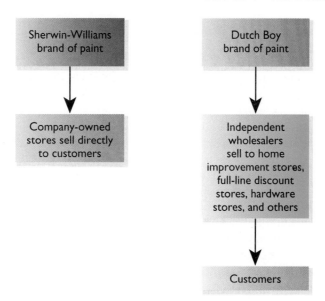

Besides partially or fully integrating a vertical marketing system, a firm can exert power in a distribution channel because of its economic, legal, or political strength; superior knowledge and abilities; customer loyalty; or other factors. With **channel control**, one member of a distribution channel dominates the decisions made in that channel due to the power it possesses. Manufacturers, wholesalers, and retailers each have a combination of tools to improve their positions relative to one another.

Manufacturers exert control by franchising, developing strong brand loyalty, pre-ticketing items (to designate suggested prices), and using exclusive distribution with retailers that agree to certain standards in exchange for sole distribution rights in an area. *Wholesalers* exert influence when they are large, introduce their own brands, sponsor franchises, and are the most efficient members in the channel for tasks such as processing reorders. *Retailers* exert clout when they represent a large percentage of a supplier's sales volume and when they foster their own brands. Private brands let retailers switch vendors with no impact on customer loyalty, as long as the same product features are included.

Strong long-term channel relationships often benefit all parties. They lead to scheduling efficiencies and cost savings. Advertising, financing, billing, and other tasks are dramatically simplified.

Consumer Cooperative

A **consumer cooperative** is a retail firm owned by its customer members. A group of consumers invests, elects officers, manages operations, and shares the profits or savings that accrue.[9] In the United States, there are several thousand such cooperatives, from small buying clubs to Recreational Equipment Inc. (REI), with nearly $1 billion in annual sales. Consumer cooperatives have been most popular in food retailing. Yet, the 500 or so U.S. food cooperatives account for less than 1 percent of total grocery sales.

Consumer cooperatives exist for these basic reasons: Some consumers feel they can operate stores as well as or better than traditional retailers. They think existing retailers inadequately fulfill customer needs for healthful, environmentally safe products. They also assume existing retailers make excessive profits and that they can sell merchandise for lower prices.

REI sells outdoor recreational equipment to more than 2 million members. It has 80 stores, a mail-order business, and a Web site (**www.rei.com**). Unlike other

As an REI member (**www.rei.com/shared/help/membership.html**), look at what $15 will get you!

Frank Polzler and Walter Schneider are Canadian investors who believe that the European market is ready for Re/Max (**www.remax.com**), a United States-based real-estate brokerage franchise company. Polzler and Schneider have sold the rights to open over 1,000 Re/Max real-estate brokerage franchises in 21 countries, starting with Spain in 1994. They now plan to increase the number of Re/Max offices fivefold over the next 10 years, and they see the former Soviet bloc countries as an attractive opportunity for additional growth.

Unlike in Canada, where Polzler and Schneider sold franchises directly to real-estate brokers, in Europe, they are selling regional rights to local businesspeople who then sell the franchises. They have also had to change the Re/Max model to adapt to the European marketplace. For example, real-estate salespeople in Europe commonly receive 80 percent of the total commissions and pay the balance as a desk and management fee to their brokerage firms. In contrast, in Canada, the salespeople commonly receive 95 percent of the total commission. There is also no multiple listing service throughout Europe and little cooperation among brokers.

Source: Andy Holloway, "European Invasion," *Canadian Business* (February 14, 2005), pp. 42–45.

cooperatives, REI is run by a professional staff that adheres to policies set by the member-elected board. There is a $15 one-time membership fee, which entitles customers to shop at REI, vote for the board of directors, and share in profits (based on the amount spent by each member). REI's goal is to distribute a 10 percent dividend to members.

Cooperatives are only a small part of retailing because they involve consumer initiative and drive, consumers are usually not experts in retailing functions, cost savings and low selling prices are often not as expected, and consumer boredom in running a cooperative frequently occurs.

Summary

1. *To show the ways in which retail institutions can be classified.* There are 2.3 million retail firms in the United States operating 3 million establishments. They can be grouped on the basis of ownership, store-based strategy mix, and nonstore-based and nontraditional retailing. Many retailers can be placed in more than one category. This chapter deals with retail ownership. Chapters 5 and 6 report on the other classifications.

2. *To study retailers on the basis of ownership type and examine the characteristics of each.* Nearly three-quarters of U.S. retail establishments are independents, each with one store. This is mostly due to the ease of entry. Independents' competitive advantages include their flexibility, low investments, specialized offerings, direct strategy control, image, consistency, independence, and entrepreneurial spirit. Disadvantages include limited bargaining power, few economies of scale, labor intensity, reduced media access, overdependence on owner, and limited planning.

Chains are multiple stores under common ownership, with some centralized buying and decision making. They account for just over one-quarter of U.S. retail outlets but 65 percent of retail sales. Chains' advantages are bargaining power, functional efficiencies, multiple-store operations, computerization, media access, well-defined management, and planning. They face these potential problems: inflexibility, high investments, reduced control, and limited independence of personnel.

Franchising embodies arrangements between franchisors and franchisees that let the latter do business under established names and according to detailed rules. It accounts for one-third of U.S. store sales. Franchisees benefit from small investments, popular company names, standardized operations and training, cooperative marketing, exclusive selling rights, and volume purchases. They may face constrained decision making, resulting in oversaturation, lower than promised profits, strict contract terms, cancellation clauses, short-term contracts, and royalty fees. Franchisors benefit by expanding their businesses, setting franchisee qualifications, improving cash flow, outlining procedures, gaining motivated franchisees, and receiving ongoing royalties. They may suffer if franchisees hurt the company image, do not operate uniformly, compete with one another, lower resale values and franchisor profits, and seek greater independence.

Leased departments are in-store locations rented to outside parties. They usually exist in categories on the fringe of their stores' major product lines. Stores gain from the expertise of lessees, greater traffic, reduced costs, merchandising support, and revenues. Potential store disadvantages are conflicts with lessees and adverse effects on store image. Lessee benefits are well-known store names, steady customers, immediate sales, reduced expenses, economies of scale, and an image associated with the store. Potential lessee problems are operating inflexibility, restrictions on items sold, lease nonrenewal, and poorer results than expected.

Vertical marketing systems consist of all the levels of independently owned firms along a channel of distribution. Independent systems have separately owned manufacturers, wholesalers, and retailers. In partially integrated systems, two separately owned firms, usually manufacturers and retailers, perform all production and distribution functions. With fully integrated systems, single firms do all production and distribution functions. Some firms use dual marketing, whereby they are involved in more than one type of system.

Consumer cooperatives are owned by their customers, who invest, elect officers, manage operations, and share savings or profits. They account for a tiny piece of retail sales. Cooperatives are formed because consumers think they can do retailing functions, traditional retailers are inadequate, and prices are high. They have not grown because consumer initiative is required, expertise may be lacking, expectations have frequently not been met, and boredom occurs.

3. *To explore the methods used by manufacturers, wholesalers, and retailers to exert influence in the distribution channel.* Even without an integrated vertical marketing system, channel control can be exerted by the most powerful firm(s) in a channel. Manufacturers, wholesalers, and retailers each have ways to increase their impact. Retailers' influence is greatest when they are a large part of their vendors' sales and private brands are used.

Key Terms

retail institution (p. 104)
independent (p. 105)
ease of entry (p. 105)
chain (p. 108)
franchising (p. 110)

product/trademark franchising (p. 110)
business format franchising (p. 111)
constrained decision making (p. 113)
leased department (p. 114)
vertical marketing system (p. 115)

dual marketing (p. 116)
channel control (p. 117)
consumer cooperative (p. 117)

Questions for Discussion

1. What are the characteristics of each of the ownership forms discussed in this chapter?

2. Do you believe that independent retailers will soon disappear with the retail landscape? Explain your answer.

3. Why does the concept of ease of entry usually have less impact on chain retailers than on independent retailers?

4. How can an independent retailer overcome the problem of overdependence on the owner?

5. What difficulties might an independent encounter if it tries to expand into a chain?

6. What competitive advantages and disadvantages do regional chains have in comparison with national chains?

7. What are the similarities and differences between chains and franchising?

8. From the franchisee's perspective, under what circumstances would product/trademark franchising be advantageous? When would business format franchising be better?

9. Why would a department store want to lease space to an outside operator rather than run a business, such as shoes, itself? What would be its risks in this approach?

10. What are the pros and cons of Sherwin-Williams using dual marketing?

11. How could a small independent restaurant increase its channel power?

12. Why have consumer cooperatives not expanded much? What would you recommend to change this?

Web-Based Exercise

Visit the Web site of Dunkin' Brands (**www.dunkin-baskin-togos.com/html/home.asp**), one of the largest retail franchisors in the world. Based on the information you find there, would you be interested in becoming a Dunkin' Brands franchisee? Why or why not?

Note: Stop by our Web site (**www.prenhall.com/bermanevans**) to experience a number of highly interactive, appealing Web exercises based on actual company demonstrations and sample materials related to retailing.

Chapter Endnotes

1. Various company sources.

2. *Statistical Abstract of the United States 2004–2005* (Washington, DC: U.S. Department of Commerce, 2004).

3. "2004 in Review: Small Business Gets Rave Reviews," **www.nfib.com/object/IO_19303.html** (December 21, 2004).

4. Paul Rich, "Succession Strategies for Family-Owned or Closely Held Businesses," **www.nfib.com/object/IO_19333.html** (December 28, 2004).

5. For a good overview of franchising and franchising opportunities, see *Entrepreneur's* "Annual Franchise 500" issue, which appears each January.

6. For more information on leased departments, see Connie Robbins Gentry, "Retailers as Landlords," *Chain Store Age* (May 2002), pp. 55–58.

7. "Investor Relations," **www.cpicorp.com** (March 8, 2006).

8. *Sherwin-Williams 2005 Annual Report*.

9. For more information on cooperatives, visit the Web site of the National Cooperative Business Association (**www.ncba.coop**).

Appendix on the Dynamics of Franchising

This appendix is presented because of franchising's strong growth and exciting opportunities. Over the past two decades, annual U.S. franchising sales have more than tripled! We go beyond the discussion of franchising in Chapter 4 and provide information on managerial issues in franchising and on franchisor–franchisee relationships.

Consider: In 1986, the Serruya brothers (Aaron, Michael, and Simon—who then ranged in age from 14 to 20) opened their first Yogen Früz frozen yogurt stand in Toronto. Now, due to franchising, CoolBrands International (**www.coolbrandsinternational.com**) has thousands of outlets, most of which are franchised—including Yogen Früz, I Can't Believe It's Yogurt, Bresler's Ice Cream & Yogurt, Swensen's Ice Cream, and Java Coast Fine Coffees. Its outlets have revenues in the hundreds of millions of dollars, and there are stores throughout the United States and Canada, as well as in 80 other nations.

How about Blockbuster? Although it has a base of company-owned outlets, it also has nearly 1,500 franchised stores. Consider this:

Click on "About Blockbuster" and then look at Blockbuster's "Franchise" section of its Web site (www.blockbuster.com).

If you become a Blockbuster franchisee, you will be in very good company. Today, we have more than 8,500 corporate and franchise stores in 28 countries. The Blockbuster franchising initiative is one of the fastest and most exciting ways to grow in attractive new markets and in underserved existing markets. Our franchisees get to associate with a world leader in home entertainment. In return, we're assured high-quality, on-site management to service Blockbuster customers. Financial requirements are a minimum net worth of $400,000 and a minimum liquidity of $100,000.[1]

U.S. franchisors are situated in well over 160 countries, a number that keeps on rising due to these factors: U.S. firms see the potential in foreign markets. Franchising is accepted as a retailing format in more nations. Trade barriers are fewer due to such pacts as the North American Free Trade Agreement, which makes it easier for firms based in the United States, Canada, and Mexico to operate in each other's marketplaces.

Here are four Web sites for you to get more information on franchising. And, remember, we have a special listing of franchising links at our Web site (**www.prenhall.com/bermanevans**):

- Federal Trade Commission (**www.ftc.gov/bcp/conline/pubs/invest/buy fran.pdf**).
- International Franchise Association (**www.franchise.org**).
- Franchising.org (**www.franchising.org**).
- Small Business Administration Franchise Workshop (**www.sba.gov/gopher/ Business-Development/Business-Initiatives-Education-Training/Franchise-Plan**).

MANAGERIAL ISSUES IN FRANCHISING

Franchising appeals to franchisees for several reasons. Most franchisors have easy-to-learn, standardized operating methods that they have perfected. New franchisees do not have to learn from their own trial-and-error method. Franchisors often have facilities where franchisees are trained to operate equipment, manage employees, keep records, and improve customer relations; there are usually follow-up field visits.

A new outlet of a nationally advertised franchise (such as Subway fast food) can attract a large customer following rather quickly and easily because of the reputation of the firm. And not only does franchising result in good initial sales and profits, it also reduces franchisees' risk of failure *if the franchisees affiliate with strong, supportive franchisors*.

What kind of individual is best suited to being a franchisee? This is what one expert says:

One of the myths that has been perpetuated is that franchise ownership is easy. This is just simply not true! While the franchisor will give the startup training and offer ongoing support, you, the franchisee, must be prepared to manage the business. While some franchises may lend themselves to absentee ownership, most are best run by hands-on management. You must be willing to work harder than you have perhaps ever worked before. Forty-hour weeks are also a myth, particularly in the start-up phase of the business. It is more like 60- to 70-hour weeks. You must also be willing to mop floors, empty garbage, fire employees, and handle upset customers.[2]

What makes McDonald's such an admired franchise operator? Read on:

> McDonald's is successful because it involves a mixture of system standards and individual opportunities. As a franchisee, you agree to work within the McDonald's system. McDonald's franchisees must personally devote their full time and best efforts to day-to-day operations. McDonald's does not grant franchises to corporations or partnerships. The franchise agreement allows you to operate a specific McDonald's restaurant, according to McDonald's standards, for a period of years (usually 20). McDonald's locates, develops, and constructs the restaurant under its own direction based on a nationwide development plan which seeks to be responsive to changing demographic factors, customer convenience, and competition. McDonald's retains control of the restaurant facilities it has developed. You equip the restaurant at your own expense with kitchen equipment, lighting, signage, seating, and décor. While none of this equipment is purchased from the company, it must meet McDonald's specifications. To maintain uniformity, franchisees must use McDonald's formulas and specifications for menu items; methods of operation, inventory control, bookkeeping, accounting, and marketing; trademarks and service marks; and concepts for restaurant design, signage, and equipment layout.[3]

Investment and startup costs for a franchised outlet can be as low as a few thousand dollars for a personal service business to as high as several million dollars for a hotel. In return for its expenditures, a franchisee gets exclusive selling rights for an area; a business format franchisee gets training, equipment and fixtures, and support in site selection, supplier negotiations, advertising, and so on. One-half of U.S. business format franchisors require franchisees to be owner-operators and work full-time. Besides receiving fees and royalties from franchisees, franchisors may sell goods and services to them. This may be required; more often, for legal reasons, such purchases are at the franchisees' discretion (subject to franchisor specifications). Each year, franchisors sell billions of dollars worth of items to franchisees.

Table A4-1 shows the franchise fees, startup costs, and royalty fees for new franchisees at 10 leading franchisors in various business categories. Financing support—either through in-house financing or third-party financing—is offered by most of the firms cited in Table A4-1. In addition, with its guaranteed loan program, the U.S. Small Business Administration is a good financing option for prospective franchisees, and some banks offer special interest rates for franchisees affiliated with established franchisors.

Franchised outlets can be bought (leased) from franchisors, master franchisees, or existing franchisees. Franchisors sell either new locations or company-owned outlets (some of which may have been taken back from unsuccessful franchisees). At times, they sell the rights in entire regions or counties to master franchisees, which then deal with individual franchisees. Existing franchisees usually have the right to sell their units if they first offer them to their franchisor, if potential buyers meet all financial and other criteria, and/or if buyers undergo training. Of interest to prospective franchisees is the emphasis a firm places on franchisee-owned outlets versus franchisor-owned ones. This indicates the commitment to franchising. As indicated in Table A4-1, leading franchisors typically own a small percentage of outlets.

One last point regarding managerial issues in franchising concerns the failure rate of new franchisees. For many years, it was believed that success as a franchisee was a "sure thing"—and much safer than starting a business—due to the franchisor's well-known name, its experience, and its training programs.

TABLE A4-1	The Costs of Becoming a New Franchisee with Selected Franchisors (as of 2005)				
Franchising Company	Total Startup Costs (Including Franchise Fee)	Franchise Fee	Royalty Fee as a % of Sales	Franchisee-Owned Outlets as a % of All Outlets	Offers Financing Support
Aamco Transmissions	$192,600–$212,600	$30,000	7	100	Third party
Dunkin' Donuts	$255,700–$1,100,000	$40,000–$80,000	5.9	99+	Third party
Fantastic Sams	$138,000–$188,000	$25,000	$236/week	100	Third party
Jazzercise	$2,600–$32,800	$325–$650	up to 20	99+	None
Medicine Shoppe	$74,300–253,400	$10,000–$18,000	2–5.5	99+	In-house
Moto Photo	$16,000–$220,000	$5,300	6	99+	None
Pearle Vision	$115,800–$372,800	$10,000–$30,000	7	30	In-house and third party
Petland	$334,000–$913,700	$25,000	4.5	97	Third party
Super 8 Motels	$297,000–$2,300,000	Varies	5	100	In-house
UPS Store[a]	$143,300–$247,000	$19,950–$29,950	5	100	In-house and third party

[a]Formerly Mail Boxes Etc.

Source: Computed by the authors from "26th Annual Franchise 500,"*Entrepreneur* (January 2005), various pages.

However, some recent research has shown franchising to be as risky as opening a new business. Why? Some franchisors have oversaturated the market and not provided promised support, and unscrupulous franchisors have preyed on unsuspecting investors.

With the preceding in mind, Figure A4-1 has a checklist by which potential franchisees can assess opportunities. In using the checklist, franchisees should

FIGURE A4-1

A Checklist of Questions for Prospective Franchisees Considering Franchise Opportunities

✓ What are the required franchise fees: initial fee, advertising appropriations, and royalties?
✓ What degree of technical knowledge is required of the franchisee?
✓ What is the required investment of time by the franchisee? Does the franchisee have to be actively involved in the day-to-day operations of the franchise?
✓ How much control does the franchisor exert in terms of materials purchased, sales quotas, space requirements, pricing, the range of goods sold, required inventory levels, and so on?
✓ Can the franchisee tolerate the regimentation and rules of the franchisor?
✓ Are the costs of required supplies and materials purchased from the franchisor at market value, above market value, or below market value?
✓ What degree of name recognition do consumers have of the franchise? Does the franchisor have a meaningful advertising program?
✓ What image does the franchise have among consumers and among current franchisees?
✓ What are the level and quality of services provided by the franchisor: site selection, training, bookkeeping, human relations, equipment maintenance, and trouble-shooting?
✓ What is the franchisor policy in terminating franchisees? What are the conditions of franchise termination? What is the rate of franchise termination and nonrenewal?
✓ What is the franchisor's legal history?
✓ What is the length of the franchise agreement?
✓ What is the failure rate of existing franchises?
✓ What is the franchisor's policy with regard to company-owned and franchisee-owned outlets?
✓ What policy does the franchisor have in allowing franchisees to sell their business?
✓ What is the franchisor's policy with regard to territorial protection for existing franchisees? With regard to new franchisees and new company-owned establishments?
✓ What is the earning potential of the franchise during the first year? The first five years?

also obtain full prospectuses and financial reports from all franchisors under consideration, and talk to existing franchise operators and customers.

FRANCHISOR–FRANCHISEE RELATIONSHIPS

Taco John's (**www.tacojohns.com**) prides itself on its collegial relationships with franchisees.

Many franchisors and franchisees have good relationships because they share goals for company image, operations, the goods and services offered, cooperative ads, and sales and profit growth. This two-way relationship is illustrated by the actions of Taco John's International (**www.tacojohns.com**), a firm with more than 400 franchised pizza restaurants in about 27 states. As the franchisor says at its Web site:

Our customers are our franchisees, their employees, and their customers. Everything we do is aimed at helping franchisees better serve customers:

- *Franchise Development.* The design of our restaurants is the result of careful, independent research and hands-on development with company prototypes. We provide conceptual floor plans and site sketches. We also provide construction consultation.

- *Marketing and Advertising.* The marketing department is responsible for planning, producing, and distributing effective and impactful programs and materials to help you grow your business and build the Taco John's brand image. Our national campaign is funded by Taco John's, suppliers, and franchisees. Each restaurant also belongs to a regional marketing co-op to participate in advertising that would otherwise not be cost-effective. Special promotions for individual restaurants are part of Taco John's local store marketing program.

- *Franchise Business Consultants.* Each restaurant is assigned a franchise business consultant.

- *Human Resources and Training.* Our human resources department will provide you with materials to help attract, motivate, and retain people. The training department teaches franchisees and their team members our operating system and how to best deliver the Taco John's promise to every customer.

- *Your New Restaurant Opening.* A grand opening team will work with you in your restaurant, just before and during your opening.

- *Research and Development.* The research and development department's focus is consumer research, operations testing, and customer feedback.

- *Purchasing and Distribution.* Purchasing and distribution personnel negotiate with manufacturers and distribution centers to make sure our system receives the best possible quality, service, and purchase prices. A nationwide system of approved distributors warehouse all products necessary to operate a restaurant. Weekly orders are delivered to each restaurant's door.

Nonetheless, for several reasons, tensions do sometimes exist between various franchisors and their franchisees:

- The franchisor–franchisee relationship is not one of employer to employee. Franchisor controls are often viewed as rigid.

- Many agreements are considered too short by franchisees. Nearly half of U.S. agreements are 10 years or less (one-sixth are 5 years or less), usually at the franchisor's request.

- The loss of a franchise generally means eviction, and the franchisee gets nothing for "goodwill."

- Some franchisors believe their franchisees do not reinvest enough in their outlets or care enough about the consistency of operations from one outlet to another.
- Franchisors may not give adequate territorial protection and may open new outlets near existing ones.
- Franchisees may refuse to participate in cooperative advertising programs.
- Franchised outlets up for sale must usually be offered first to franchisors, which also have approval of sales to third parties.
- Some franchisees believe franchisor marketing support is low.
- Franchisees may be prohibited from operating competing businesses.
- Restrictions on suppliers may cause franchisees to pay higher prices and have limited choices.
- Franchisees may band together to force changes in policies and exert pressure on franchisors.
- Sales and profit expectations may not be realized.

Tensions can lead to conflicts—even litigation. Potential negative franchisor actions include terminating agreements; reducing marketing support; and adding red tape for orders, information requests, and warranty work. Potential negative franchisee actions include terminating agreements, adding competitors' products, refusing to promote goods and services, and not complying with data requests. Each year, business format franchisors terminate the contracts of 10 percent of the franchisee-owned stores that opened within the preceding five years.

Although franchising has been characterized by franchisors having more power than franchisees, this inequality is being reduced. First, franchisees affiliated with specific franchisors have joined together. For example, the Association of Kentucky Fried Chicken Franchisees, Supercuts Franchisee Association, and Vision Care Franchisee Association represent thousands of franchisees. Second, large umbrella groups, such as the American Franchisee Association (**www.franchisee. org**) and the American Association of Franchisees & Dealers (**www.aafd.org**), have been formed. Third, many franchisees now operate more than one outlet, so they have greater clout. Fourth, there has been a substantial rise in litigation.

Better communication and better cooperation are necessary to resolve problems. Here are two progressive approaches: First, the International Franchise Association has an ethics code for its franchisor and franchisee members, founded on these principles (**www.franchise.org/content.asp?contentid=781**):

> Every franchise relationship is founded on the mutual commitment of both parties to fulfill their obligations under the franchise agreement. Each party will fulfill its obligations, will act consistent with the interests of the brand, and will not act so as to harm the brand and system. This willing interdependence between franchisors and franchisees, and the trust and honesty upon which it is founded, has made franchising a worldwide success as a strategy for business growth. Honesty embodies openness, candor, and truthfulness. Franchisees and franchisors commit to sharing ideas and information and to face challenges in clear and direct terms. Our members will be sincere in word, act, and character—reputable and without deception.

Second, the National Franchise Mediation Program ("Franchise," **www. cpradr.org**) was established "by a group of franchisors who sought a way to resolve disputes with franchisees without the rancor, uncertainty, and cost of litigation, wherever possible. The goal is to encourage all members of the franchise community—and those who counsel them—to resolve such conflicts fairly, amicably, and cost-effectively." The program has worked quite well: "Thus far, a success rate of 90 percent has been achieved in cases in which the franchisee agreed to participate, and in which a mediator was needed. Many more disputes have been resolved prior to a mediator's intervention."

Appendix Endnotes

1. "About Blockbuster," **www.blockbuster.com/ corporate/displayAboutBlockbuster.action** (March 7, 2006).

2. Robert McIntosh, "Self-Evaluation: Is Franchising for You?" **www.franchise.org/content.asp?contentid= 616** (July 8, 2005).

3. *McDonald's 2005 Franchising Brochure*, p. 3.

Chapter 5
RETAIL INSTITUTIONS BY STORE-BASED STRATEGY MIX

Ikea (**www.ikea.com**) is the world's leading home furnishing retailer with more than 220 stores in 35 countries, including 30 U.S. stores. In the past 10 years, its sales have tripled. Since the firm's founding, Ikea has offered a wide range of home furnishings and accessories of good design at attractive price levels.

Although Ikea has had stores in the United States for just over 20 years, Ingvar Kamprad began selling furniture in Almhult, Sweden, under the Ikea name about 60 years ago. Kamprad got the idea for producing ready-to-assemble furniture to reduce his delivery costs when the milk wagon that was used to ship his small orders changed its route. In 1953, he purchased an empty factory and opened a showroom. Five years later, when he opened a large store, Kamprad cleverly added roof racks to the inventory mix so that customers could take their purchases home.

Reprinted by permission.

Today, Ikea strives to facilitate the shopping process. Most stores have a spacious, open layout, a cafeteria, and even a playroom that offers baby-sitting assistance for customers. The layout encourages browsing and increases impulse purchases. The inexpensive cafeteria, which serves Swedish-style delicacies at cost, encourages customers to spend more time on the premises. The playroom enables shoppers to go through the store without their children tagging behind them.

Recently, Ikea was again named to *Working Mother* magazine's annual listing of "100 Best Companies for Working Mothers," due to its family-friendly program for workers.[1]

chapter objectives

1. To describe the wheel of retailing, scrambled merchandising, and the retail life cycle and show how they can help explain the performance of retail strategy mixes
2. To discuss ways in which retail strategy mixes are evolving
3. To examine a wide variety of food-oriented retailers involved with store-based strategy mixes
4. To study a wide range of general merchandise retailers involved with store-based strategy mixes

OVERVIEW

In Chapter 4, retail institutions were described by type of ownership. In this chapter, we discuss three key concepts in planning retail strategy mixes: the wheel of retailing, scrambled merchandising, and the retail life cycle. We then look at how retail strategies are evolving and study the basic strategies of several store-based institutions. Chapter 6 deals with nonstore-based, electronic, and nontraditional strategies.

CONSIDERATIONS IN PLANNING A RETAIL STRATEGY MIX

A retailer may be categorized by its **strategy mix**, the firm's particular combination of store location, operating procedures, goods/services offered, pricing tactics, store atmosphere and customer services, and promotional methods.

Store location refers to the use of a store or nonstore format, placement in a geographic area, and the kind of site (such as a shopping center). Operating procedures include the kinds of personnel employed, management style, store hours, and other factors. The goods/services offered may encompass several product categories or just one; and quality may be low, medium, or high. Pricing refers to a retailer's use of prestige pricing (creating a quality image), competitive pricing (setting prices at the level of rivals), or penetration pricing (underpricing other retailers). Store atmosphere and customer services are reflected by the physical facilities and personal attention provided, return policies, delivery, and other factors. Promotion involves activities in such areas as advertising, displays, personal selling, and sales promotion. By combining these elements, a retailer can develop a unique strategy.

To flourish today, a retailer should strive to be dominant in some way. The firm may then reach **destination retailer** status—whereby consumers view the company as distinctive enough to become loyal to it and go out of their way to shop there. We tend to link "dominant" with "large." Yet, both small and large retailers can dominate in their own way. As follows, there are many ways to be a destination retailer, and combining two or more approaches can yield even greater appeal for a given retailer:

- Be price-oriented and cost-efficient to attract price-sensitive shoppers.
- Be upscale to attract full-service, status-conscious consumers.
- Be convenient to attract those wanting shopping ease, nearby locations, or long hours.
- Offer a dominant assortment in the product lines carried to appeal to consumers interested in variety and in-store shopping comparisons.
- Offer superior customer service to attract those frustrated by the decline in retail service.
- Be innovative or exclusive and provide a unique way of operating (such as kiosks at airports) or carry products/brands not stocked by others to reach people who are innovators or bored.

Before looking at specific strategy mixes, let us look at three concepts that help explain the use of these mixes: the wheel of retailing, scrambled merchandising, and the retail life cycle—as well as the ways in which retail strategies are evolving.

Careers in RETAILING
Jeff: Senior Vice-President, Human Resources and Training

Shortly before graduating from college (with a degree in liberal arts), Jeff was offered a job at an international department store chain in its executive training program. He felt that the retail environment was one that would allow him to excel as quickly as his own performance would warrant.

Part of Jeff's training included direct experience on the sales floor. He interrupted his retail career for three years of Army service. There was an opportunity to advance to store management when he returned because of the leadership skills he learned while in the Army, as well as his previous success on the sales floor. Jeff loved the pace and the intensity of a store, but after assignments in the human resource side, he wanted his experience to focus more on people development and management. Through a contact and friendship he had developed with another senior executive, he was recruited to a department store chain that afforded him the opportunity to specialize on the human resource side of the business.

Jeff developed a specialty in managing in a union environment. His firm had 22 separate unions. One of his biggest challenges was negotiating simultaneously 17 labor agreements over a one-year period. During his seven-year tenure in the position, he intensified his knowledge of the realities of operating in a unionized structure. Many successes were achieved relative to organizational development and executive development, which resulted in a much broader perspective of the role of human resources.

Jeff was then recruited by a specialty store chain, where he worked for 12 years. At that point, an opportunity arose for Jeff to move to another specialty store chain, focusing on electronics. He welcomed the challenge of designing a sophisticated, people-intensive human resources strategy. Jeff's current salary is more than $100,00 annually. Some years, his income has been as high as a million dollars because of the stock options provided by the company as a part of his compensation.

Source: Reprinted by permission of the National Retail Federation.

The Wheel of Retailing

According to the **wheel of retailing** theory, retail innovators often first appear as low-price operators with low costs and low profit margin requirements. Over time, the innovators upgrade the products they carry and improve their facilities and customer service (by adding better-quality items, locating in higher-rent sites, providing credit and delivery, and so on), and prices rise. As innovators mature, they become vulnerable to new discounters with lower costs, hence, the wheel of retailing.[2] See Figure 5-1.

FIGURE 5-1
The Wheel of Retailing

As a low-end retailer upgrades its strategy to increase sales and profit margins, a new form of discounter takes its place.

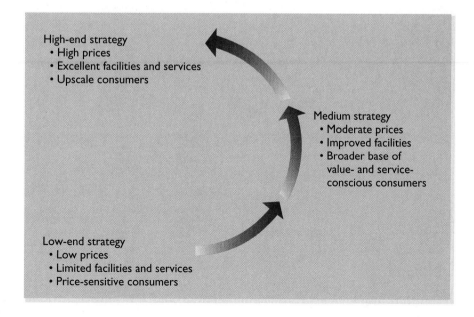

High-end strategy
• High prices
• Excellent facilities and services
• Upscale consumers

Medium strategy
• Moderate prices
• Improved facilities
• Broader base of value- and service-conscious consumers

Low-end strategy
• Low prices
• Limited facilities and services
• Price-sensitive consumers

The wheel of retailing is grounded on four principles: (1) There are many price-sensitive shoppers who will trade customer services, wide selections, and convenient locations for lower prices. (2) Price-sensitive shoppers are often not loyal and will switch to retailers with lower prices. However, prestige-sensitive customers like shopping at retailers with high-end strategies. (3) New institutions are frequently able to have lower operating costs than existing institutions. (4) As retailers move up the wheel, they typically do so to increase sales, broaden the target market, and improve their image.

For example, when traditional department store prices became too high for many consumers, the growth of the full-line discount store (led by Wal-Mart) was the result.[3] The full-line discount store stressed low prices because of such cost-cutting techniques as having a small sales force, situating in lower-rent store locations, using inexpensive fixtures, emphasizing high stock turnover, and accepting only cash or check payments for goods. Then, as full-line discount stores prospered, they typically sought to move up a little along the wheel. This meant enlarging the sales force, improving locations, upgrading fixtures, carrying a greater selection of merchandise, and accepting credit. These improvements led to higher costs, which led to somewhat higher prices. The wheel of retailing again came into play as newer discounters, such as off-price chains, factory outlets, and permanent flea markets, expanded to satisfy the needs of the most price-conscious consumer. More recently, we have witnessed the birth of discount Web retailers, some of which have very low costs because they do not have "bricks-and-mortar" facilities.

As indicated in Figure 5-1, the wheel of retailing reveals three basic strategic positions: low end, medium, and high end. The medium strategy may have some difficulties if retailers in this position are not perceived as distinctive: "With specialty stores siphoning customers from above and discounters siphoning from below, J.C. Penney and Sears are stuck in the very skinny middle."[4] Figure 5-2 shows the opposing alternatives in considering a strategy mix.

The wheel of retailing suggests that established firms should be wary in adding services or converting a strategy from low end to high end. Because price-conscious shoppers are not usually loyal, they are apt to switch to lower-priced firms. Furthermore, retailers may then eliminate the competitive advantages that

Where would you place Michael's arts and crafts stores (www.michaels.com) along the wheel of retailing?

FIGURE 5-2
Retail Strategy Alternatives

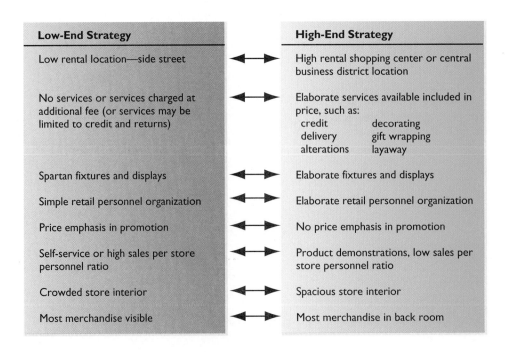

Low-End Strategy		High-End Strategy
Low rental location—side street	⟷	High rental shopping center or central business district location
No services or services charged at additional fee (or services may be limited to credit and returns)	⟷	Elaborate services available included in price, such as: credit / delivery / alterations — decorating / gift wrapping / layaway
Spartan fixtures and displays	⟷	Elaborate fixtures and displays
Simple retail personnel organization	⟷	Elaborate retail personnel organization
Price emphasis in promotion	⟷	No price emphasis in promotion
Self-service or high sales per store personnel ratio	⟷	Product demonstrations, low sales per store personnel ratio
Crowded store interior	⟷	Spacious store interior
Most merchandise visible	⟷	Most merchandise in back room

have led to profitability. This occurred with the retail catalog showroom, which is now a defunct format.

Scrambled Merchandising

Whereas the wheel of retailing focuses on product quality, prices, and customer service, scrambled merchandising involves a retailer increasing its width of assortment (the number of different product lines carried). **Scrambled merchandising** occurs when a retailer adds goods and services that may be unrelated to each other and to the firm's original business. See Figure 5-3.

Scrambled merchandising is popular for many reasons: Retailers want to increase overall revenues; fast-selling, highly profitable goods and services are usually the ones added; consumers make more impulse purchases; people like one-stop shopping; different target markets may be reached; and the impact of seasonality and competition is reduced. In addition, the popularity of a retailer's original product line(s) may fall, causing it to scramble to maintain and grow the customer base. Blockbuster, due to the advent of pay-per-view and premium movie channels on cable and satellite TV, now carries CDs, magazines, movie merchandise, candy, video games, game players, DVD players, and more.

How much of a practitioner of scrambled merchandising is Hammacher Schlemmer (www.hammacher schlemmer.com)?

Scrambled merchandising is contagious. Drugstores, bookstores, florists, video stores, and photo-developing firms are all affected by supermarkets' scrambled merchandising. About one-fifth of U.S. supermarket sales are from general merchandise, health and beauty aids, and other nongrocery items, such as pharmacy products, magazines, flowers, and video rentals. In response, retailers such as drugstores are pushed into scrambled merchandising to fill the sales void caused by supermarkets. They have added toys and gift items, greeting cards, batteries, and cameras. This then creates a void for other retailers, which are also forced to scramble.

The prevalence of scrambled merchandising means greater competition among different types of retailers and that distribution costs are affected as sales are dispersed over more retailers. There are other limitations to scrambled

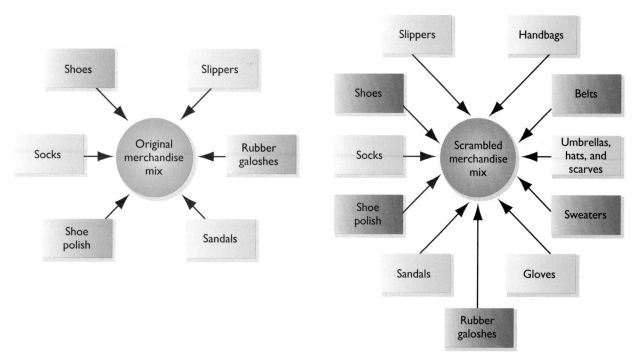

FIGURE 5-3
Scrambled Merchandising by a Shoe Store

FIGURE 5-4
The Retail Life Cycle

Source: Retail Forward, "Mall Retailers—The Search for Growth," *Industry Outlook* (October 2001), p. 3. Reprinted by permission of Retail Forward, Inc. (**www.retailforward.com**).

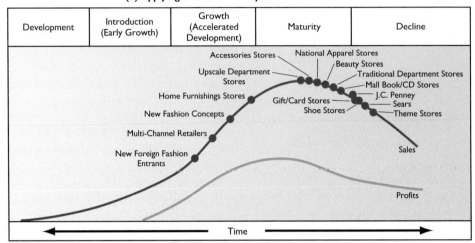

(a) Key Business Characteristics During the Stages of the Retail Life Cycle

	Life Cycle Stage			
	Introduction	Growth	Maturity	Decline
Sales	Low/growing	Rapid acceleration	High, leveling off	Dropping
Profitability	Negative to break even	High yield	High/declining	Low to break even
Positioning	Concept innovation	Special need	Broad market	Niche
Competition	None	Limited	Extensive/ saturation	Intensive/ consolidated

(b) Applying the Retail Life Cycle to Mall Retailers

Development	Introduction (Early Growth)	Growth (Accelerated Development)	Maturity	Decline

Accessories Stores
National Apparel Stores
Beauty Stores
Upscale Department Stores
Traditional Department Stores
Mall Book/CD Stores
Home Furnishings Stores
Gift/Card Stores
J.C. Penney
Sears
New Fashion Concepts
Shoe Stores
Theme Stores
Multi-Channel Retailers
New Foreign Fashion Entrants

Sales

Profits

Time

merchandising, including the potential lack of retailer expertise in buying, selling, and servicing unfamiliar items; the costs associated with a broader assortment (including lower inventory turnover); and the possible harm to a retailer's image if scrambled merchandising is ineffective.

The Retail Life Cycle

The **retail life cycle** concept states that retail institutions—like the goods and services they sell—pass through identifiable life stages: introduction (early growth), growth (accelerated development), maturity, and decline. The direction and speed of institutional changes can be interpreted from this concept. Take a look at Figure 5-4. The Figure 5-4(a) shows the business characteristics of the four stages, and Figure 5-4(b) indicates the stages in which several mall-based retail formats are now operating.

Let us examine the stages of the retail life cycle as they apply to individual institutional formats and show specific examples. During the first stage of the cycle (introduction), there is a strong departure from the strategy mixes of existing retail institutions. A firm in this stage significantly alters at least one element of the strategy mix from that of traditional competitors. Sales and then profits often rise sharply for the first firms in a category. There are risks that new institutions will not be accepted by shoppers, and there may be large initial losses due to heavy investments. At this stage, long-run success is not assured.

One institution in the introduction stage is the online grocery store. How will the format do?

The online grocery business is littered with failures—notably Webvan, which raised $1 billion before collapsing in 2001. At New York startup FreshDirect (**www.freshdirect.com**), overaggressive marketing and service problems led to smashed tomatoes and red ink. But a management shakeup could lead it to profitability. In late 2004, FreshDirect tapped Dean Furbush as chief executive. Furbush joined as chief operating officer earlier in the year, a few months before flamboyant co-founder

Joseph Fedele stepped down. Already, Furbush has increased delivery fees and is adding new routes cautiously to concentrate on keeping the company's existing 100,000 customers happy. FreshDirect's revamped strategy calls for adding a national mail-order service and business catering in New York, while delaying a push into other cities. That contrasts with rivals such as Peapod and Safeway, which are pursuing national reach. FreshDirect's eventual goal is to quintuple revenues over the next several years. "We have to make sure we have a consistently positive experience," Furbush says. That means keeping an eye first and foremost on the tomatoes.[5]

In the second stage (growth), both sales and profits exhibit rapid growth. Existing firms expand geographically, and newer companies of the same type enter. Toward the end of accelerated development, cost pressures (to cover a larger staff, a more complex inventory system, and extensive controls) may begin to affect profits.

See TouchVision's (**www.touchvision.com**) view of the future for video kiosks.

The interactive electronic video kiosk is an institution in the growth stage. Today, kiosks sell everything from clothing to magazines to insurance to PCs. According to *Kiosk* and Jupiter Media Metrix, U.S. retail sales revenues generated by kiosks were expected to rise from $370 million in 1996 and $1.1 billion in 2001 to $6.5 billion in 2006. Worldwide, the number of installed kiosks was projected to go from 246,000 in 2001 to 598,000 in 2006.[6] This institution is examined further in Chapter 6.

The third stage (maturity) is characterized by slow sales growth for the institutional type. Though overall sales may continue to go up, that rise is at a much lower rate than during prior stages. Profit margins may have to be reduced to stimulate purchases. Maturity is brought on by market saturation caused by the high number of firms in an institutional format, competition from newer institutions, changing societal interests, and inadequate management skills to lead mature or larger firms. Once maturity is reached, the goal is to sustain it as long as possible and not to fall into decline.

The liquor store, a form of specialty store, is an institution in the maturity stage; sales are rising, but very slowly as compared to earlier years. From 1992 to 2005, U.S. liquor store sales went up an average of 3 percent annually, which was far less than the rate for all U.S. retailers. This is due to competition from membership clubs, mail-order wine retailers, and supermarkets (in states allowing wine or liquor sales); changing lifestyles and attitudes regarding liquor; the national 21-year-old drinking age requirement; and limits on the nonalcoholic items that liquor stores are permitted to sell in some locales.

The final stage in the retail life cycle is decline, whereby industrywide sales and profits for a format fall off, many firms abandon the format, and newer formats attract consumers previously committed to that retailer type. In some cases, a decline may be hard or almost impossible to reverse. In others, it may be avoided or postponed by repositioning the institution.

With the retail catalog showroom, consumers chose items from a catalog, shopped in a warehouse setting, and wrote up orders. After peaking in the 1980s, the format declined thereafter, and it vanished in 1998. The leading firms went out of business. Why? Many other retailers cut costs and prices, so showrooms were no longer low-price leaders. Catalogs had to be printed far in advance. Many items were slow-sellers or had low margins. Some consumers found showrooms crowded and disliked writing orders, the lack of displays reduced browsing time, and the paucity of apparel goods also held down revenues.[7]

On the other hand, conventional supermarkets have slowed their decline by placing new units in suburban shopping centers, redesigning interiors, lengthening store hours, having low prices, expanding the use of scrambled merchandising, closing unprofitable smaller units, and converting to larger outlets.

The life cycle concept highlights the proper retailer response as institutions evolve. Expansion should be the focus initially, administrative skills and operations become critical in maturity, and adaptation is essential at the end of the cycle.

HOW RETAIL INSTITUTIONS ARE EVOLVING

Forward-looking firms know their individual strategies must be modified as retail institutions evolve over time. Complacency is not desirable. Many retailers have witnessed shrinking profit margins due to intense competition and consumer interest in lower prices. This puts pressure on them to tighten internal cost controls and to promote higher-margin goods and services while eliminating unprofitable items. Let us see how firms are reacting to this formidable environment through mergers, diversification, and downsizing, as well as cost containment and value-driven retailing.

Mergers, Diversification, and Downsizing

Some firms use mergers and diversification to sustain sales growth in a highly competitive environment (or when the institutional category in which they operate matures). For stronger firms, this trend is expected to carry over into the future.

Mergers involve the combination of separately owned retail firms. Some mergers take place between retailers of different types, such as the ones between Sears (the department store chain) and Kmart (the full-line discount store chain). Other mergers occur between similar types of retailers, such as two local banks or two video rental chains (as took place when Movie Gallery acquired Hollywood Entertainment). By merging, retailers hope to jointly maximize resources, enlarge their customer base, improve productivity and bargaining power, limit weaknesses, and gain competitive advantages. This is a way for resourceful retailers to grow more rapidly and for weaker ones to enhance their long-term prospects for survival (or gain some return on investment by selling assets).

Through its various divisions, Limited Brands (www.limitedbrands.com) is an apparel retailing dynamo.

With **diversification**, retailers become active in businesses outside their normal operations—and add stores in different goods/service categories. To expand beyond its core business, Limited Brands (parent of The Limited) developed Express (targeting young women), Bath & Body Works (toiletries), and White Barn Candle (high-quality candles, home fragrances, and accessories.). It also acquired Victoria's Secret (a mail-order, store, and Web lingerie business) and Henri Bendel (upscale women's clothing). Figure 5-5 illustrates a new Williams-Sonoma concept: west elm.

The size of many retail chains has grown due to mergers and diversification. All have not done well with that approach. Thus, even though stronger firms are expanding, we are also witnessing **downsizing**—whereby unprofitable stores are closed or divisions are sold off—by retailers unhappy with performance. Because Kmart's diversification efforts had poor results, it closed or sold its ventures outside the general merchandise store field (including Borders bookstores, Builders Square, OfficeMax, Pay Less drugstores, and Sports Authority). It also closed a number of Kmart stores after merging with Sears.

The interest in downsizing should continue. Various retailers have overextended themselves and do not have the resources or management talent to succeed without retrenching. In their quest to open new stores, certain firms have chosen poor sites (having already saturated the best locations). Retailers such as

FIGURE 5-5
west elm from Williams-Sonoma

Five years ago, Williams-Sonoma (**www.williams-sonomainc.com**) launched west elm as a new store concept to "draw in design-savvy customers with stylish, high-quality furnishings for every room in their apartment, loft, or second home. With price points from $19 to $399, west elm has earned a reputation for affordable style and grown into a destination lifestyle concept known for unique, exclusive products."

Photo reprinted by permission of Susan Berry, Retail Image Consulting, Inc.

Barnes & Noble are more interested in operating fewer, but much larger, stores and using the Web. Retailers such as supermarkets are finding they can do better if they are regional rather than national.

Cost Containment and Value-Driven Retailing

With a cost-containment approach, retailers strive to hold down both initial investments and operating costs. Many firms use this strategy because of intense competition from discounters, the need to control complicated chain or franchise operations, high land and construction costs, the volatility of the economy, and a desire to maximize productivity. Today, "retailers are examining every aspect of their businesses in order to streamline processes and costs."[8]

Cost containment can be accomplished through one or more of these approaches:

The 99¢ Only Stores chain has a cost-containment approach that even extends to its austere Web site (www.99only.com).

- Standardizing operating procedures, store layouts, store size, and product offerings.
- Using secondary locations, freestanding units, and locations in older strip centers and by occupying sites abandoned by others (second-use locations).
- Placing stores in smaller communities where building regulations are less strict, labor costs are lower, and construction and operating costs are reduced.
- Using inexpensive construction materials, such as bare cinder-block walls and concrete floors.
- Using plainer fixtures and lower-cost displays.
- Buying refurbished equipment.
- Joining cooperative buying and advertising groups.
- Encouraging manufacturers to finance inventories.

A driving force behind cost containment is the quest to provide good value to customers:

> Value remains a retailing buzzword. The word's meaning, however, is subjective; it can mean price, quality, service, convenience, or a combination thereof. Price clearly plays a big role in what consumers buy and where they buy it. Indeed, retailers' pricing policies—particularly those of discounters—have encouraged consumers to shop for bargains and to distrust traditional sales and sale prices. Pragmatic consumers have discovered they can get reasonable quality at everyday low prices. Price is no longer an accurate reflection of value.[9]

RETAIL INSTITUTIONS CATEGORIZED BY STORE-BASED STRATEGY MIX

Selected aspects of the strategy mixes of 14 store-based retail institutions, divided into food-oriented and general merchandise groups, are highlighted in this section and Table 5-1. Although not all-inclusive, the strategy mixes do provide a good overview of store-based strategies. Please note that *width of assortment* is the number of different product lines carried by a retailer; *depth of assortment* is the selection within the product lines stocked. Visit our Web site (**www.prenhall.com/bermanevans**) for many links related to retail institutions' strategies.

Food-Oriented Retailers

The following food-oriented strategic retail formats are described next: convenience store, conventional supermarket, food-based superstore, combination store, box (limited-line) store, and warehouse store.

Convenience Store

A **convenience store** is typically a well-located, food-oriented retailer that is open long hours and carries a moderate number of items. The store facility is small (only a fraction of the size of a conventional supermarket), has average to above-average prices, and average atmosphere and customer services. The ease of shopping at convenience stores and the impersonal nature of many large supermarkets make convenience stores particularly appealing to their customers, many of whom are male.

7-Eleven (**www.7-eleven. com**) dominates the convenience store category.

There are 140,000 U.S. convenience stores (excluding the stores where food is a small fraction of revenues), and their total annual sales are $130 billion (excluding gasoline).[10] 7-Eleven, Circle K, and Casey's General Store are major food-based U.S. convenience store chains. Speedway SuperAmerica is a leading gasoline service station-based convenience store chain with more than 1,700 outlets.

Items such as milk, eggs, and bread once represented the major portion of sales; now sandwiches, tobacco products, snack foods, soft drinks, newspapers and magazines, beer and wine, video rentals, ATMs, and lottery tickets are also key items. And gasoline generates 30 percent or more of total sales at most of the convenience stores that carry it. See Figure 5-6.

The convenience store's advantages are its usefulness when a consumer does not want to travel to or shop at a supermarket, the availability of both fill-in items and gas, long hours, and drive-through windows. Many customers shop there

TABLE 5-1	Selected Aspects of Store-Based Retail Strategy Mixes				
Type of Retailer	**Location**	**Merchandise**	**Prices**	**Atmosphere and Services**	**Promotion**
Food-Oriented					
Convenience store	Neighborhood	Medium width and low depth of assortment; average quality	Average to above average	Average	Moderate
Conventional supermarket	Neighborhood	Extensive width and depth of assortment; average quality; manufacturer, private, and generic brands	Competitive	Average	Heavy use of newspapers, flyers, and coupons; self-service
Food-based superstore	Community shopping center or isolated site	Full assortment of supermarket items, plus health and beauty aids and general merchandise	Competitive	Average	Heavy use of newspapers and flyers; self-service
Combination store	Community shopping center or isolated site	Full selection of supermarket and drugstore items or supermarket and general merchandise; average quality	Competitive	Average	Heavy use of newspapers and flyers; self-service
Box (limited-line) store	Neighborhood	Low width and depth of assortment; few perishables; few national brands	Very low	Low	Little or none
Warehouse store	Secondary site, often in industrial area	Moderate width and low depth; emphasis on manufacturer brands bought at discounts	Very low	Low	Little or none
General Merchandise					
Specialty store	Business district or shopping center	Very narrow width and extensive depth of assortment; average to good quality	Competitive to above average	Average to excellent	Heavy use of displays; extensive sales force
Traditional department store	Business district, shopping center, or isolated store	Extensive width and depth of assortment; average to good quality	Average to above average	Good to excellent	Heavy ad and catalog use; direct mail; personal selling
Full-line discount store	Business district, shopping center, or isolated store	Extensive width and depth of assortment; average to good quality	Competitive	Slightly below average to average	Heavy use of newspapers; price-oriented; moderate sales force
Variety store	Business district, shopping center, or isolated store	Good width and some depth of assortment; below average to average quality	Average	Below average	Heavy use of newspapers; self-service

(Continued)

TABLE 5-1		Selected Aspects of Store-Based Retail Strategy Mixes *(Continued)*				
Type of Retailer	Location	Merchandise	Prices	Atmosphere and Services	Promotion
Off-price chain	Business district, suburban shopping strip, or isolated store	Moderate width but poor depth of assortment; average to good quality; lower continuity	Low	Below average	Use of newspapers; brands not advertised; limited sales force
Factory outlet	Out-of-the-way site or discount mall	Moderate width but poor depth of assortment; some irregular merchandise; lower continuity	Very low	Very low	Little; self-service
Membership club	Isolated store or secondary site (industrial park)	Moderate width but poor depth of assortment; lower continuity	Very low	Very low	Little; some direct mail; limited sales force
Flea market	Isolated site, racetrack, or arena	Extensive width but poor depth of assortment; variable quality; lower continuity	Very low	Very low	Limited; self-service

multiple times a week, and the average transaction is small. Due to limited shelf space, stores receive frequent deliveries and there are high handling costs. Customers are less price-sensitive than those at other food-oriented retailers.

The industry does have problems: Some areas are saturated with stores; supermarkets have longer hours and more nonfood items; some stores are too big, making shopping less convenient; the traditional market (blue-collar workers) has shrunk; and some chains have had financial woes.

Conventional Supermarket

A **supermarket** is a self-service food store with grocery, meat, and produce departments and minimum annual sales of $2 million. Included are conventional

The Food Marketing Institute (www.fmi.org) is the leading industry association for food retailers.

FIGURE 5-6
Jack in the Box Restaurants and Quick Stuff Convenience Stores: A New Combination

Jack in the Box (www.jackinthebox.com) has begun opening co-branded stores in a number of locations. The Quick Stuff shops are about 2,000 square feet in size; and they are open 24 hours. They include ATMs and branded gasoline pumps, complete with pay-at-the-pump credit-card readers.

Photo reprinted by permission of Susan Berry, Retail Image Consulting, Inc.

FIGURE 5-7
Supermarkets Have Come a Long Way

Kroger (**www.kroger.com**) has been introducing a number of new Kroger Marketplace stores: "These multi-department stores offer full-service grocery, pharmacy, and expanded general merchandise—including outdoor living products, electronics, home goods, and toys." They range in size from 80,000 square feet to 125,000 square feet.

Photo reprinted by permission of Susan Berry, Retail Image Consulting, Inc.

supermarkets, food-based superstores, combination stores, box (limited-line) stores, and warehouse stores. See Figure 5-7.

A **conventional supermarket** is a departmentalized food store with a wide range of food and related products; sales of general merchandise are rather limited. This institution started 75 years ago when it was recognized that large-scale operations would let a retailer combine volume sales, self-service, and low prices. Self-service enabled supermarkets to both cut costs and increase volume. Personnel costs were reduced, and impulse buying increased. The car and the refrigerator contributed to the supermarket's success by lowering travel costs and adding to the life span of perishables.

For several decades, overall supermarket sales have been about 70 to 75 percent of U.S. grocery sales, with conventional supermarkets now yielding 26 percent of total supermarket sales. There are 19,000 conventional units, with annual sales of $125 billion.[11] Chains account for the majority of sales. Among the leaders are Kroger, Safeway, Albertson's, and Ahold USA. Many independent supermarkets are affiliated with cooperative or voluntary organizations, such as IGA and Supervalu.

Conventional supermarkets generally rely on high inventory turnover (volume sales). Their profit margins are low. In general, average gross margins (selling price less merchandise cost) are 20 to 22 percent of sales and net profits are 1 to 3 percent of sales.

These stores face intense competition from other food stores: Convenience stores offer greater customer convenience; food-based superstores and combination stores have more product lines and greater variety within them, as well as better margins; and box and warehouse stores have lower operating costs and prices. Membership clubs (discussed later), with their low prices, also provide competition—especially now that they have much expanded food lines. Variations of the supermarket are covered next.

Food-Based Superstore

A **food-based superstore** is larger and more diversified than a conventional supermarket but usually smaller and less diversified than a combination store.

This format originated in the 1970s as supermarkets sought to stem sales declines by expanding store size and the number of nonfood items carried. Some supermarkets merged with drugstores or general merchandise stores but more grew into food-based superstores. There are 9,500 food-based U.S. superstores, with sales of $200 billion.[12]

The typical food-based superstore occupies at least 30,000 to 50,000 square feet of space and 20 to 25 percent of sales are from general merchandise, including garden supplies, flowers, small appliances, and film developing. It caters to consumers' complete grocery needs, along with fill-in general merchandise.

Like combination stores, food-based superstores are efficient, offer a degree of one-stop shopping, stimulate impulse purchases, and feature high-profit general merchandise. But they also offer other advantages: It is easier and less costly to redesign and convert supermarkets into food-based superstores than into combination stores. Many consumers feel more comfortable shopping in true food stores than in huge combination stores. Management expertise is better focused.

Over the past two decades, U.S. supermarket chains have turned more to food-based superstores. They have expanded and remodeled existing supermarkets and built numerous new stores. Many independents have also converted to food-based superstores.

Combination Store

A **combination store** unites supermarket and general merchandise in one facility, with general merchandise accounting for 25 to 40 percent of sales. The format began in the late 1960s and early 1970s, as common checkout areas were set up for separately owned supermarkets and drugstores or supermarkets and general merchandise stores. The natural offshoot was integrating operations under one management. There are 3,500 U.S. combination stores (including supercenters), and annual sales are $100 billion.[13] Among those with combination stores are Meijer, Fred Meyer, and Albertson's.

Meijer's (www.meijer.com) combination stores are quite popular with shoppers. They carry 120,000 items.

Combination stores are large, from 30,000 up to 100,000 or more square feet. This leads to operating efficiencies and cost savings. Consumers like one-stop shopping and will travel to get there. Impulse sales are high. Many general merchandise items have better margins than food items. Supermarkets and drugstores have commonalities in the customers served and the low-price, high-turnover items sold. Drugstore and general merchandise customers are drawn to the store more often.

A **supercenter** is a combination store blending an economy supermarket with a discount department store. It is the U.S. version of the even larger **hypermarket** (the European institution pioneered by firms such as Carrefour that did not succeed in the United States). As a rule, the majority of supercenter sales are from nonfood items. Stores usually range from 75,000 to 150,000 square feet in size and they stock up to 50,000 and more items, much more than the 30,000 or so items carried by other combination stores. Wal-Mart, Kmart, and Target all operate some supercenters.

Box (Limited-Line) Store

The **box (limited-line) store** is a food-based discounter that focuses on a small selection of items, moderate hours of operation (compared to other supermarkets), few services, and limited manufacturer brands. It carries fewer than 2,000 items, few refrigerated perishables, and few sizes and brands per item. Prices are on shelves or overhead signs. Items are displayed in cut cases. Customers bag purchases. Box stores rely on low-priced private-label brands. Their prices are 20 to 30 percent below supermarkets.

The box store originated in Europe and was exported to the United States in the mid-1970s. The growth of these stores has not been as anticipated, as sales rose modestly over the last decade. Some other food stores have matched box-store prices. Many people are loyal to manufacturer brands, and box stores cannot fulfill one-stop shopping needs. There are 3,350 box stores in the United States, with sales of $20 billion.[14] The leading box store operators are Save-A-Lot and Aldi.

Warehouse Store

A **warehouse store** is a food-based discounter offering a moderate number of food items in a no-frills setting. It appeals to one-stop food shoppers, concentrates on special purchases of popular brands, uses cut-case displays, offers little service, posts prices on shelves, and locates in secondary sites. Warehouse stores began in the late 1970s. There are now 1,400 U.S. stores with $35 billion in annual sales.[15]

The largest warehouse store is known as a super warehouse. There are more than 600 of them in the United States. They have annual sales exceeding $20 million each and they contain a variety of departments, including produce. High ceilings accommodate pallet loads of groceries. Shipments are made directly to the store. Customers pack their own groceries. Super warehouses are profitable at gross margins far lower than for conventional supermarkets. The leading super warehouse chain is Cub Foods.

Many consumers do not like shopping in warehouse settings. Furthermore, because products are usually acquired when special deals are available, brands may be temporarily or permanently out of stock.

Table 5-2 shows selected operating data for the food-oriented retailers just described.

General Merchandise Retailers

We now examine these general merchandise strategic retail formats highlighted in Table 5-1: specialty store, traditional department store, full-line discount store, variety store, off-price chain, factory outlet, membership club, and flea market.

TABLE 5-2	Selected Typical Operating Data for Food-Oriented Retailers, as of 2005					
Factor	Convenience Stores	Conventional Supermarkets	Food-Based Superstores	Combination Stores	Box (Limited-Line) Stores	Warehouse Stores
Number of stores	140,000	19,000	9,500	3,500	3,350	1,400
Total annual sales	$130 billion[a]	$125 billion	$200 billion	$100 billion[b]	$20 billion	$35 billion[c]
Average store selling area (sq. ft.)	5,000 or less	15,000–20,000	30,000–50,000+	30,000–100,000+	5,000–9,000	15,000+
Number of checkouts per store	1–3	6–10	10+	10+	3–5	5+
Gross margin	25–30%	20–22%	20–25%	25%	10–12%	12–15%
Number of items stocked per store	3,000–4,000	12,000–17,000	20,000+	30,000+	Under 2,000	2,500+
Major emphasis	Daily fill-in needs; dairy, sandwiches, tobacco, gas, beverages, magazines	Food; only 5–10% of sales from general merchandise	Positioned between supermarket and combo store; 20–25% of sales from general merchandise	One-stop shopping; general merchandise is 25–40% of sales (higher at supercenters)	Low prices; few or no perishables	Low prices; variable assortments; may or may not stock perishables

[a]Excluding gasoline.

[b]Including supermarket-item sales at the supercenters of Wal-Mart, Kmart, and Target (which are more heavily oriented to general merchandise than other combination stores).

[c]Including supermarket-item sales at Sam's, Costco, and other membership clubs.

Sources: Various issues of *Progressive Grocer*; Food Marketing Institute, "Facts & Figures," **www.fmi.org/facts_figs/superfact.htm**; *Convenience Store News Online,* **www.csnews.com**; and authors' estimates.

Specialty Store

A **specialty store** concentrates on selling one goods or service line, such as young women's apparel. It usually carries a narrow but deep assortment in the chosen category and tailors the strategy to a given market segment. This enables the store to maintain a better selection and sales expertise than competitors, which are often department stores. Investments are controlled, and there is a certain amount of flexibility. Among the most popular categories of specialty stores are apparel, personal care, auto supply, home furnishings, electronics, books, toys, home improvement, pet supplies, jewelry, and sporting goods.

Consumers often shop at specialty stores because of the knowledgeable sales personnel, the variety of choices within the given category, customer service policies, intimate store size and atmosphere (although this is not true of the category killer store), the lack of crowds (also not true of category killer stores), and the absence of aisles of unrelated merchandise that they must pass through. Some specialty stores have elaborate fixtures and upscale merchandise for affluent shoppers, whereas others are discount-oriented and aim at price-conscious consumers.

Total specialty store sales are difficult to determine because these retailers sell virtually all kinds of goods and services, and aggregate specialty store data are not compiled by the government. We do estimate that annual nonfood specialty store sales in the United States exceed $1.3 trillion (including auto dealers). The top 100 specialty store chains (excluding auto dealers) have sales of more than $275 billion and operate about 115,000 outlets. Among those chains, about one-third are involved with apparel. Specialty store leaders include Best Buy and Circuit City (consumer electronics), Toys "R" Us (toys), The Limited and Gap (apparel), and Barnes & Noble and Borders (books).[16]

As noted earlier in the chapter, one type of specialty store—the category killer—has gained particular strength. A **category killer** (also known as a **power retailer**) is an especially large specialty store. It features an enormous selection in its category and relatively low prices. Consumers are drawn from wide geographic areas. Toys "R" Us, The Limited, Old Navy, Sam Goody, and Barnes & Noble are just some of the specialty store chains that have category killer stores to complement existing stores. See Figure 5-8. Blockbuster, Sephora, Home Depot, Sports Authority, and Staples are among the chains almost fully based on the concept. At Sephora's 525 stores around the world, the "unique, open-sell environment features more than 250 classic and emerging brands across a broad range of product categories including skincare, color, fragrance, makeup, bath and body, and hair care, in addition to Sephora's own private label."[17]

Nonetheless, smaller specialty stores (even ones with under 1,000 square feet of space) can prosper if they are focused, offer strong customer service, and avoid imitating larger firms. Many consumers do not like shopping in category killer stores: "Shoppers looking for just one or a few basic items and a quick checkout may not want to scour a cavernous warehouse to find what they need." That is why we are seeing the emergence of another specialty store format: "Nicknamed 'gnategory killers,' these retailers specialize in a single item or a narrow range of related items. Their extremely narrow focus allows them to stock deep assortments of a particular item while operating small stores. A pioneer of this concept is Sunglass Hut, which now has 1,500 stores. It also operates over 100

Sometimes the focus of specialty stores is as narrow as the Joy of Socks (www.joyofsocks.com).

FIGURE 5-8

Old Navy: A Discount Power in Apparel

At many of its stores, Old Navy carries a huge selection of casual apparel and accessories, all under the Old Navy brand.

Photo reprinted by permission of Susan Berry, Retail Image Consulting, Inc.

Watch Station and Watch World stores, which sell wristwatches. Gnategory killers are particularly suited to malls, which allow them to operate small stores cost-effectively."[18]

Any size specialty store can be adversely affected by seasonality or a decline in the popularity of its product category. This type of store may also fail to attract consumers who are interested in one-stop shopping for multiple product categories.

Traditional Department Store

A **department store** is a large retail unit with an extensive assortment (width and depth) of goods and services that is organized into separate departments for purposes of buying, promotion, customer service, and control. It has the most selection of any general merchandise retailer, often serves as the anchor store in a shopping center or district, has strong credit card penetration, and is usually part of a chain. To be classified as a department store, a retailer must sell a wide range of products—such as apparel, furniture, appliances, and home furnishings; and selected other items, such as paint, hardware, toiletries, cosmetics, photo equipment, jewelry, toys, and sporting goods—with no one merchandise line predominating.

Two basic types of retailers meet the preceding criteria: the traditional department store and the full-line discount store. They account for more than $415 billion in annual sales (including supercenters where general merchandise sales exceed food sales and leased departments), about one-tenth of all U.S. retail sales.[19] The traditional department store is discussed here; the full-line discount store is examined next.

Belk, Inc. (www.belk.com) operates three department store chains in 14 states: Belk, McRae's, and Profitt's.

At a **traditional department store**, merchandise quality ranges from average to quite good. Pricing is moderate to above average. Customer service ranges from medium levels of sales help, credit, delivery, and so forth to high levels of each. For example, Macy's targets middle-class shoppers interested in assortment and moderate prices, whereas Bloomingdale's aims at upscale consumers through more trendy merchandise and higher prices. Few traditional department stores sell all of the product lines that the category used to carry. Many place greater emphasis on apparel and may not carry such lines as furniture, electronics, and major appliances.

Over its history, the traditional department store has contributed many innovations, such as advertising prices, enacting a one-price policy (whereby all shoppers pay the same price for the same item), developing computerized checkouts, offering money-back guarantees, adding branch stores, decentralizing management, and moving into suburban shopping centers. However, in recent years, the performance of traditional department stores has lagged far behind that of full-line discount stores. Today, traditional department store sales ($90 billion annually) represent less than one-quarter of total department store sales. These are some reasons for traditional department stores' difficulties:

- They no longer have brand exclusivity for a lot of the popular items they sell.
- Instead of creating more of their own brands, they have signed exclusive licensing agreements with fashion designers to use the designers' names. This generates loyalty to the designer, not the retailer.
- Price-conscious consumers are more attracted to discounters than to traditional department stores.
- The popularity of shopping centers has aided specialty stores since consumers can engage in one-stop shopping at several specialty stores in the

same shopping center. Department stores do not dominate the smaller stores around them as they once did.

- Specialty stores often have better assortments in the lines they carry.
- Customer service has deteriorated. Often, store personnel are not as loyal, helpful, or knowledgeable.
- Some stores are too big and have too much unproductive selling space and low-turnover merchandise.
- Many department stores have had a weak focus on market segments and a fuzzy image.
- Such chains as Sears have repeatedly changed strategic orientation, confusing consumers as to their image. (Is Sears a traditional department store chain or a full-line discount store chain?)
- Some companies are not as innovative in their merchandise decisions as they once were.

Traditional department stores need to clarify their niche in the marketplace (retail positioning); place greater emphasis on customer service and sales personnel; present more exciting, better-organized store interiors; use space better by downsizing stores and eliminating slow-selling items (such as J.C. Penney dropping consumer electronics); and open outlets in smaller, less-developed towns and cities (as Sears has done). They can also centralize more buying and promotion functions, do better research, and reach customers more efficiently (by such tools as targeted mailing pieces).

Full-Line Discount Store

A **full-line discount store** is a type of department store with these features:

- It conveys the image of a high-volume, low-cost outlet selling a broad product assortment for less than conventional prices.
- It is more apt to carry the range of product lines once expected at department stores, including electronics, furniture, and appliances—as well as auto accessories, gardening tools, and housewares.
- Shopping carts and centralized checkout service are provided.

Technology in RETAILING — Hudson's Bay: Improving Supplier Relationships

Hudson's Bay Company (**www.hbc.com**) is a Canadian-based department, discount, and home-goods retailer. Under Gary Davenport, its vice-president and chief information officer, Hudson Bay has invested heavily to transform its IT operations. According to Davenport, until recently, "our technology was supporting the company, but not advancing it. It was not serving the company's needs well." Davenport and his colleagues identified a dozen core capabilities that needed enhancement.

As part of its technology planning, Hudson's Bay placed all of its suppliers into one of three tiers: transactional vendors, preferred vendors, and key suppliers (such as Microsoft, IBM, Oracle, and Cisco) that Hudson Bay considered the best to nurture relationships.

Here are some of the highlights of its technology partnership. Hudson's Bay's alliance partners offer the retailer pre-negotiated prices, discounts, and terms to facilitate reordering throughout the year. Hudson's Bay holds two to three meetings each year with its partners to encourage the exchange of information. At each meeting, partners are asked to evaluate their technology offerings and to recommend solutions to specific problems and opportunities.

Source: Dan Scheraga, "All for One, One for All," *Retail Technology Quarterly* (January 2005), pp. 24A–28A.

- Customer service is not usually provided within store departments but at a centralized area. Products are normally sold via self-service with minimal assistance in any single department.
- Nondurable (soft) goods feature private brands, whereas durable (hard) goods emphasize well-known manufacturer brands.
- Less fashion-sensitive merchandise is carried.
- Buildings, equipment, and fixtures are less expensive; and operating costs are lower than for traditional department stores and specialty stores.

Annual U.S. full-line discount store revenues are $325 billion (including general merchandise-based supercenters and leased departments), more than three-quarters of all U.S. department store sales. Together, Wal-Mart, Kmart, and Target Stores operate 6,000 full-line discount stores (including supercenters) with $250 billion in full-line discount store sales.[20]

The success of full-line discount stores is due to many factors. They have a clear customer focus: middle-class and lower-middle-class shoppers looking for good value. The stores feature popular brands of average- to good-quality merchandise at competitive prices. They have expanded their goods and service categories and often have their own private brands. Firms have worked hard to improve their image and provide more customer services. The average outlet (not the supercenter) tends to be smaller than a traditional department store and sales per square foot are usually higher, which improves productivity. Some full-line discount stores are located in small towns where competition is less intense. Facilities may be newer than those of many traditional department stores.

The greatest challenges facing full-line discount stores are the competition from other retailers (especially lower-priced discounters and category killers), too rapid expansion of some firms, saturation of prime locations, and the dominance of Wal-Mart, Kmart, and Target Stores. The industry has undergone a number of consolidations, bankruptcies, and liquidations.

Variety Store

A **variety store** handles an assortment of inexpensive and popularly priced goods and services, such as apparel and accessories, costume jewelry, notions and small wares, candy, toys, and other items in the price range. There are open displays and few salespeople. The stores do not carry full product lines, may not be departmentalized, and do not deliver products. Although the conventional variety store format has faded away, there are two successful spin-offs from it: dollar discount stores and closeout chains.

Dollar discount stores sell similar items to those in conventional variety stores but in plainer surroundings and at much lower prices. They generate $16 to $18 billion in yearly sales. Dollar General and Family Dollar are the two leading dollar discount store chains. The two firms operate a total of 13,500 stores and have $14 billion in annual sales. *Closeout chains* sell similar items to those in conventional variety stores but feature closeouts and overruns. They account for $7 billion annually. Big Lots is the leader in that category with 1,600 stores and annual sales of $4.5 billion.[21]

The conventional variety store format (led by Woolworth and McCrory) disappeared from the U.S. marketplace in the mid-1990s after a long, successful run. What happened? There was heavy competition from specialty stores and discounters, most of the stores were older facilities, and some items had low profit margins. At one time, Woolworth had 1,200 variety stores with annual sales of $2 billion.

Off-Price Chain

An **off-price chain** features brand-name (sometimes designer) apparel and accessories, footwear (primarily women's and family), linens, fabrics, cosmetics, and/or housewares and sells them at everyday low prices in an efficient, limited-service environment. It frequently has community dressing rooms, centralized checkout counters, no gift wrapping, and extra charges for alterations. The chains buy merchandise opportunistically, as special deals occur. Other retailers' canceled orders, manufacturers' irregulars and overruns, and end-of-season items are often purchased for a fraction of their original wholesale prices. The total sales of U.S. off-price apparel stores are $35 billion. The biggest chains are T.J. Maxx and Marshalls (both owned by TJX), Ross Stores, and Burlington Coat Factory.

TJX (www.tjx.com) operates two of the biggest off-price apparel chains: T.J. Maxx and Marshall's.

Off-price chains usually aim at the same shoppers as traditional department stores but with prices reduced by 40 to 50 percent. Shoppers are also lured by the promise of new merchandise on a regular basis. At T.J. Maxx, "Our off-price mission is to deliver a rapidly changing assortment of quality, branded merchandise at prices that are up to 60 percent less than department and specialty store regular prices, every day. Our target customer is a middle- to upper-middle income shopper, who is fashion and value conscious."[22] Off-price shopping centers now appeal to people's interest in one-stop shopping.

The most crucial strategic element for off-price chains involves buying merchandise and establishing long-term relationships with suppliers. To succeed, the chains must secure large quantities of merchandise at reduced wholesale prices and have a regular flow of goods into the stores. Sometimes manufacturers use off-price chains to sell samples, products that are not doing well when they are introduced, and merchandise remaining near the end of a season. At other times, off-price chains employ a more active buying strategy. Instead of waiting for close-outs and canceled orders, they convince manufacturers to make merchandise during off-seasons and pay cash for items early. Off-price chains are less demanding in terms of the support requested from suppliers, they do not return products, and they pay promptly.

Off-price chains face some market pressure because of competition from other institutional formats that run frequent sales throughout the year, the discontinuity of merchandise, poor management at some firms, insufficient customer service for some shoppers, and the shakeout of underfinanced companies.

Factory Outlet

A **factory outlet** is a manufacturer-owned store selling closeouts, discontinued merchandise, irregulars, canceled orders, and, sometimes, in-season, first-quality merchandise. Manufacturers' interest in outlet stores has risen for four basic reasons: (1) Manufacturers can control where their discounted merchandise is sold. By placing outlets in out-of-the-way spots with low sales penetration of the firm's brands, outlet revenues do not affect sales at key specialty and department store accounts. (2) Outlets are profitable despite prices up to 60 percent less than customary retail prices due to low operating costs—few services, low rent, limited displays, and plain store fixtures. (3) The manufacturer decides on store visibility, sets promotion policies, removes labels, and ensures that discontinued items and irregulars are disposed of properly. (4) Because many specialty and department stores are increasing private label sales, manufacturers need revenue from outlet stores to sustain their own growth.

More factory stores now operate in clusters or in outlet malls to expand customer traffic, and they use cooperative ads. Large outlet malls are in Connecticut, Florida, Georgia, New York, Pennsylvania, Tennessee, and other states. There are

16,000 U.S. factory outlet stores representing hundreds of manufacturers, many in the 225 outlet malls nationwide. These stores have $16 billion in yearly sales, with three-quarters from apparel and accessories.[23] Manufacturers with a major outlet presence include Bass (footwear), Brooks Brothers (apparel), Harry & David (fruits and gift items), Levi's (apparel), Liz Claiborne (apparel), Pepperidge Farm (food), Samsonite (luggage), and Totes (rain gear). See Figure 5-9.

When deciding whether to utilize factory outlets, manufacturers must be cautious. They must evaluate their retailing expertise, the investment costs, the impact on existing retailers that buy from them, and the response of consumers. Manufacturers do not want to jeopardize their products' sales at full retail prices.

Membership Club

A **membership (warehouse) club** appeals to price-conscious consumers, who must be members to shop there. It straddles the line between wholesaling and retailing. Some members are small business owners and employees who pay a membership fee to buy merchandise at wholesale prices. They make purchases for use in operating their firms or for personal use and yield 60 percent of club sales. Most members are final consumers who buy for their own use; they represent 40 percent of club sales. They also pay a fee and must belong to a union, be municipal employees, work for educational institutions, or belong to other specific groups to be members (in reality, eligibility is so broad as to exclude few people). Prices may be slightly more than for business customers. There are 1,300 U.S. membership clubs, with annual sales to final consumers of nearly $40 billion. Costco and Sam's Club generate 90 percent of industry sales.[24]

Sam's (www.samsclub.com) is Wal-Mart's membership club division. It has lower prices and plainer settings than Wal-Mart's full-line discount stores.

The operating strategy of the modern membership club centers on large stores (up to 100,000 or more square feet), inexpensive isolated or industrial locations, opportunistic buying (with some merchandise discontinuity), a fraction of the items stocked by full-line discount stores, little advertising, plain fixtures, wide aisles to give forklift trucks access to shelves, concrete floors, limited delivery, fewer credit options, and very low prices. A typical club carries general merchandise, such as consumer electronics, appliances, computers, housewares, tires, and apparel (35 to 60 percent of sales); food (20 to 35 percent of sales); and sundries, such as health and beauty aids, tobacco, liquor, and candy (15 to 30 percent of sales). It may also have a pharmacy, photo developing, a car-buying service, a gasoline service station, and other items once viewed as frills for this format. Inventory turnover is several times that of a department store.

The major retailing challenges relate to the allocation of company efforts between business and final consumer accounts (without antagonizing one group or the other and without presenting a blurred store image), the lack of interest by many consumers in shopping at warehouse-type stores, the power of the two industry leaders, and the potential for saturation caused by overexpansion.

Flea Market

At a **flea market,** many retail vendors sell a range of products at discount prices in plain surroundings. It is rooted in the centuries-old tradition of street selling—shoppers touch and sample items and haggle over prices. Vendors used to sell only antiques, bric-a-brac, and assorted used merchandise. Today, they also frequently sell new goods, such as clothing, cosmetics, watches, consumer electronics, housewares, and gift items. Many flea markets are located in nontraditional sites such as racetracks, stadiums, and arenas. Some are at sites abandoned by other retailers. Typically, vendors rent space. A flea market might rent individual spaces for $30 to $100 or more per day, depending on location. Some flea markets impose a parking fee or admission charge for shoppers.

There are a few hundred major U.S. flea markets, but overall sales data are not available. The credibility of permanent flea markets, consumer interest in bargaining, the broader product mix, the availability of brand-name goods, and the low prices all contribute to the format's appeal. The Rose Bowl Flea Market has 2,000 vendors and attracts 20,000 shoppers a day:

> The flea market is held the second Sunday of every month. The only restricted items are food, animals, guns, ammunition, and pornography. The price of available selling space is as follows: Our best available high-traffic spaces are $100.00 pink spaces located around the main perimeter. These spaces are considered best for new merchandise, and arts and crafts. Also, for new merchandise sellers, we have $70.00 yellow spaces located in a section by the front of the main entrance. However, no cars may remain in the space. We have $80.00 reserved white spaces located across a bridge from our other flea market areas, in the front half and prime areas of the white section. The $50.00 unreserved white spaces are unnumbered and assigned the morning of the event. They are located in the rear portion of the white section. Regular admission for the general public is $7.00 per person; children under 12 are admitted free with an adult.[25]

At a flea market, price haggling is encouraged, cash is the predominant currency, and many vendors gain their first real experience as retail entrepreneurs. The newest trend involves nonstore, Web-based flea markets such as eBay (**www.ebay.com**) and Amazon.com (**www.auctions.amazon.com**). Online auction sites account for several billion dollars in sales annually and are quite popular.

Many traditional retailers believe flea markets represent an unfair method of competition because the quality of merchandise may be misrepresented, consumers may buy items at flea markets and return them to other retailers for higher refunds, suppliers are often unaware their products are sold there, sales taxes can be easily avoided, and operating costs are quite low. Flea markets may also cause traffic congestion.

The Army and Air Force Exchange Service (AAFES) (**www.aafes.com**), also referred to as PX for post exchange, is a U.S.-government-run retail chain that is unknown to many traditional consumers. These 3,000 PXs account for retail sales of $8 billion a year and serve as community centers for 11.5 million active or retired military personnel and their families. Military personnel stationed overseas often see the PX as a place to shop that reflects contemporary American culture and values. For example, compact discs, DVDs, and electronics goods are popular sellers. The motto of AAFES is "We go where you go." AAFES currently operates dozens of outlets in Iraq, Kuwait, and Afghanistan.

The PXs are efficiently operated by the Department of Defense. A recent study found that its prices were only 2.5 percent higher than Wal-Mart's. And AAFES' net profit margin was 4.6 percent of sales. AAFES is also a model of logistics speed. The military PXs were operational on Iraqi military bases before the post office and mess halls were set up.

Sources: Ann Zimmerman, "Christmas at the PX," *Wall Street Journal* (December 13, 2004), pp. B1, B5; and "AAFES Homepage," **www.aafes.com** (March 5, 2006).

The high sales volume from off price chains, factory outlets, membership clubs, and flea markets is explained by the wheel of retailing. These institutions are low-cost operators appealing to price-conscious consumers who are not totally satisfied with other retail formats that have upgraded their merchandise and customer service, raised prices, and moved along the wheel.

Summary

1. *To describe the wheel of retailing, scrambled merchandising, and the retail life cycle and show how they can help explain the performance of retail strategy mixes.* In Chapter 4, retail institutions were examined by ownership. This chapter uses a store-based strategic retailing perspective. A retail strategy mix involves a combination of factors: location, operations, goods/services offered, pricing, atmosphere and customer services, and promotion. To flourish, a firm should strive to be dominant in some way and, thus, reach destination retailer status.

Three important concepts help explain the performance of diverse retail strategies. According to the wheel of retailing, retail innovators often first appear as low-price operators with low costs and low profit margins. Over time, they upgrade their offerings and customer services and raise prices. They are then vulnerable to new discounters with lower costs that take their place along the wheel. With scrambled merchandising, a retailer adds goods and services that are unrelated to each other and its original business to increase overall sales and profits. Scrambled merchandising is contagious and often used in self-defense. The retail life cycle states that institutions pass through identifiable stages of introduction, growth, maturity, and decline. Strategies change as institutions mature.

2. *To discuss ways in which retail strategy mixes are evolving.* Many institutions are adapting to marketplace dynamics. These approaches have been popular for various firms, depending on their strengths, weaknesses, and goals: mergers—by which separately owned retailers join together; diversification—by which a retailer becomes active in businesses outside its normal operations; and downsizing—whereby unprofitable stores are closed or divisions sold. Sometimes, single companies use all three approaches. More firms also utilize cost containment and value-driven retailing. They strive to hold down both investment and operating costs. There are many ways to do this.

3. *To examine a wide variety of food-oriented retailers involved with store-based strategy mixes.* Retail institutions may be classified by store-based strategy mix and divided into food-oriented and general merchandise groups. Fourteen store-based strategy mixes are covered in this chapter.

These are the food-oriented store-based retailers: A convenience store is well located, is open long hours, and offers a moderate number of fill-in items at average to above-average prices. A conventional supermarket is departmentalized and carries a wide range of food and related items, there is little general merchandise, and prices are competitive. A food-based superstore is larger and more diversified than a conventional supermarket but smaller and less diversified than a combination store. A combination store unites supermarket and general merchandise in a large facility and sets competitive prices; the food-based supercenter (hypermarket) is a type of combination store. The box (limited-line) store is a discounter focusing on a small selection, moderate hours, few services, and few manufacturer brands. A warehouse store is a discounter offering a moderate number of food items in a no-frills setting that can be quite large.

4. *To study a wide range of general merchandise retailers involved with store-based strategy mixes.* A specialty store concentrates on one goods or service line and has a tailored strategy; the category killer is a special kind of specialty store. A department store is a large retailer with an extensive assortment of goods and services. The traditional one has a range of customer services and average to above-average prices. A full-line discount store is a department store with a low-cost, low-price strategy. A variety store has inexpensive and popularly priced items in a plain setting. An off-price chain features brand-name items and sells them at low prices in an austere environment. A factory outlet is manufacturer-owned and sells closeouts, discontinued merchandise, and irregulars at very low prices. A membership club appeals to price-conscious shoppers who must be members to shop. A flea market has many vendors offering items at discount prices in nontraditional venues.

Key Terms

strategy mix (p. 128)
destination retailer (p. 128)
wheel of retailing (p. 129)
scrambled merchandising (p. 131)
retail life cycle (p. 132)
mergers (p. 134)
diversification (p. 134)
downsizing (p. 134)
convenience store (p. 136)

supermarket (p. 138)
conventional supermarket (p. 139)
food-based superstore (p. 139)
combination store (p. 140)
supercenter (p. 141)
hypermarket (p. 141)
box (limited-line) store (p. 141)
warehouse store (p. 141)
specialty store (p. 142)

category killer (power retailer) (p. 143)
department store (p. 144)
traditional department store (p. 144)
full-line discount store (p. 145)
variety store (p. 146)
off-price chain (p. 147)
factory outlet (p. 147)
membership (warehouse) club (p. 148)
flea market (p. 149)

Questions for Discussion

1. Describe how a small shoe repair store could be a destination retailer.

2. Explain the wheel of retailing. Is this theory applicable today? Why or why not?

3. Develop a low-end retail strategy mix for a shoe store. Include location, operating procedures, goods/services offered, pricing tactics, and promotion methods.

4. How could these retailers best apply scrambled merchandising? Explain your answers.
   a. Burger King.
   b. Circuit City.
   c. Jiffy Lube.
   d. Ben & Jerry's.

5. What strategic emphasis should be used by institutions in the introduction stage of the retail life cycle compared with the emphasis by institutions in the decline stage?

6. Contrast the strategy mixes of convenience stores, conventional supermarkets, food-based superstores, and warehouse stores. Is there room for each? Explain your answer.

7. Do you think U.S. combination stores (supercenters) will dominate grocery retailing? Why or why not?

8. What are the pros and cons of Sephora carrying 250 brands of personal care products?

9. Contrast the strategy mixes of specialty stores, traditional department stores, and full-line discount stores.

10. What must the off-price chain do to succeed in the future?

11. Do you expect factory outlet stores to keep growing? Explain your answer.

12. Comment on the decision of many membership clubs to begin selling gasoline.

Web-Based Exercise

Visit the Web site of eBay (**www.ebay.com**). In your view, (a) where is eBay positioned along the wheel of retailing and (b) how would you describe its use of scrambled merchandising? Explain whether you think that eBay is doing the right thing in terms of these two concepts.

Note: Stop by our Web site (**www.prenhall.com/bermanevans**) to experience a number of highly interactive, appealing Web exercises based on actual company demonstrations and sample materials related to retailing.

Chapter Endnotes

1. Various company sources.
2. The pioneering works on the wheel of retailing are Malcolm P. McNair, "Significant Trends and Developments in the Postwar Period," in A. B. Smith (Editor), *Competitive Distribution in a Free High Level Economy and Its Implications for the University* (Pittsburgh: University of Pittsburgh Press, 1958), pp. 17–18; and Stanley Hollander, "The Wheel of Retailing," *Journal of Marketing*, Vol. 25 (July 1960), pp. 37–42. For further analysis of the concept, see Stephen Brown, "The Wheel of Retailing: Past and Future," *Journal of Retailing*, Vol. 66 (Summer 1990), pp. 143–149; Stephen Brown, "Postmodernism, the Wheel of Retailing, and Will to Power," *International Review of Retail, Distribution, and Consumer Research*, Vol. 5 (July 1995), pp. 387–414; and Don E. Schultz, "Another Turn of the Wheel," *Marketing Management* (March-April 2002), pp. 8–9.
3. For an interesting review of Wal-Mart's founding and evolution, see "The Class of '62," *Chain Store Age* (August 2002), pp. 41–79; and Katherine Bowers, "Wal-Mart CEO Scott, on the Hot Seat, Navigates New Course," *Women's Wear Daily* (May 24, 2005), pp. 1ff.
4. Dina Elboghdady, "Sears, J.C. Penney Taking Different Paths to Survival," *Houston Chronicle* (April 21, 2002), p. 6.
5. Heather Green and Brian Hindo, "FreshDirect Keeps on Truckin'," *Business Week* (September 13, 2004), p. 13.
6. "Projected Retail Revenues Earned Via Kiosks, 2000–2006," **www.kiomag.com/sf9** (October 17, 2002).
7. "Last Catalog Showroom Retailer Now in Liquidation," *Knight Ridder/Tribune Business News* (February 3, 2002).
8. "Retailing: General," *Standard & Poor's Industry Surveys* (May 19, 2005), p. 9.
9. Ibid., p. 14.
10. "Convenience Store Industry Fact Sheet," **http://cstorecentral.com/NACS/Resource/PRToolkit/FactSheets/prtk_fact_ecoimpact.htm** (February 26, 2006).
11. Various issues of *Progressive Grocer*; and Food Marketing Institute, "Facts & Figures," **www.fmi.org/facts_figs/superfact.htm**.
12. Ibid.
13. Ibid.
14. Ibid.
15. Ibid.
16. Computed by the authors from "Top 100 Specialty Stores," **www.stores.org** (August 2005).
17. "Sephora," **www.sephora.com/help/about_sephora.jhtml?location=sephora** (March 18, 2006).
18. "Retailing: Specialty," *Standard & Poor's Industry Surveys* (January 13, 2005), p. 19.
19. *Soft Goods Economic Forecast: Outlook to 2009* (Columbus, OH: Retail Forward, April 2005); and "Annual Industry Report," *DSN Retailing Today* (June 13, 2005), various pages.
20. "Annual Industry Report."
21. Ibid.
22. "About Our Company," **www.tjx.com/about/about.html** (March 16, 2006).
23. "Outlet Industry Data," **www.valueretailnews.com/research/research_index.htm** (March 18, 2006).
24. "Annual Industry Report."
25. "Rose Bowl Flea Market," **www.pasadena.com/adView.asp?ad_id=320** (March 19, 2006).

Chapter 6
WEB, NONSTORE-BASED, AND OTHER
FORMS OF NONTRADITIONAL RETAILING

A decade ago, after learning that Web usage was growing at 2,300 percent per year, Jeff Bezos analyzed a list of the 20 best products to sell online. Books topped the list, in large part due to the vast number of available titles. After deciding to sell books, Bezos moved to Seattle, due to the large number of computer professionals located there. He created an online strategy based on the

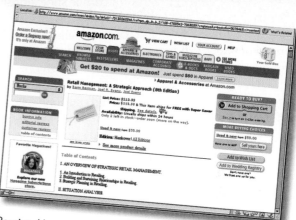

Reprinted by permission.

concept of creating a place where people could not only find and buy any book they wanted but also get great customer service. To Bezos, the three most important components of this strategy were and still are service, selection, and price.

Sales for the company that Bezos named Amazon.com (**www.amazon.com**) took off immediately, as the firm concentrated on books and sought to have the largest selection of books that could be found anywhere. Almost from the start, industry analysts believed that Amazon.com's Web site had several distinctive advantages: an emphasis on information over graphics; a separate page for each book, including a brief description; customer reviews; and, sometimes, author interviews. Although Amazon.com started off selling only books, it has since branched out into many other product lines, such as electronics, small appliances, a bridal registry, and toys. Amazon.com also operates Web sites for Target Stores, Bombay Company, Borders, and the NBA, among others. In essence, it is now an online department store.

Under a relatively new shipping plan called Amazon Prime, customers who pay an annual $79 membership fee can get unlimited two-day shipping. These members will also be eligible for overnight shipping for $3.99 per item.[1]

chapter objectives

1. To contrast single-channel and multi-channel retailing
2. To look at the characteristics of the three major retail institutions involved with nonstore-based strategy mixes: direct marketing, direct selling, and vending machines—with an emphasis on direct marketing
3. To explore the emergence of electronic retailing through the World Wide Web
4. To discuss two other nontraditional forms of retailing: video kiosks and airport retailing

OVERVIEW

From its roots as a full-line discount store chain, Wal-Mart (www.walmart.com) has become a master of multi-channel retailing.

In this chapter, we contrast single-channel and multi-channel retailing and then examine nonstore-based retailing, electronic retailing, and two other types of non-traditional retailing: video kiosks and airport retailing. These formats influence the strategies of current store retailers and newly formed retailers. Visit our Web site (**www.prenhall.com/bermanevans**) for links on a variety of nonstore and nontraditional topics.

When it begins, a retailer often relies on **single-channel retailing**, whereby it sells to consumers through one retail format. That one format may be store-based (a corner shoe store) or nonstore-based (catalog retailing, direct selling, or Web retailing). As the firm grows, it may turn to **multi-channel retailing**, whereby a retailer sells to consumers through multiple retail formats.

Multi-channel retailing enables a firm to reach different customer groups, share costs among various formats, and diversify its supplier base. Retail leader Wal-Mart sells through stores (including Wal-Mart stores, Sam's Club, and Neighborhood Market) and a Web site (**www.walmart.com**). Figure 6-1 shows examples of single-channel and multi-channel retailing. An appendix at the end of this chapter explores multi-channel retailing in much greater detail.

Why have we introduced this concept here? Because even though some nonstore-based firms are "pure players" (single-channel retailers), a rapidly grow-ing number of firms are combining store and nonstore retailing to actively pursue multi-channel retailing:

The value of a Web site to the multi-channel retailer's bottom line is far greater than just the online purchases being generated. A large proportion of multi-channel shoppers—86 percent of those surveyed in a recent study—prefer to make purchases offline. Yet this statistic dramatically understates the influence of the Web channel. Nearly 40 percent of multi-channel shop-pers prefer to use the Web for browsing and researching their purchases. Of this group of people who would typically be viewed as unconverted browsers or "shopping-cart abandoners," 71 percent complete their pur-chase in the store. In addition, shoppers are consistently less satisfied with the store experience than with the Web sites of the same multi-channel retailers,

FIGURE 6-1
Approaches to Retailing Channels

Examples of Single-Channel Retailing

Store-based retailer, such as a local apparel store, operating only one store format	Mail-order sporting goods retailer selling only through catalogs	Online CD/DVD retailer that only does business through the Web

Examples of Multi-Channel Retailing

Store-based retailer, such as a local gift store, also selling through catalogs	Store-based retailer, such as a jewelry store, also selling through the Web	Store-based retailer, such as Toys "R" Us, affiliating with a Web-based firm, such as Amazon.com
Store-based retailer, such as a local gift store, also selling through catalogs and the Web	Store-based retailer, such as a jewelry store, also selling through the Web and leased departments in select department stores	Store-based retailer, such as Toys "R" Us, affiliating with a Web-based firm, such as Amazon.com, and operating multiple store formats (Kids "R" Us)

FIGURE 6-2

Costco: Combining Bricks-and Mortar with Clicks-and-Mortar

Costco uses a carefully constructed Web site, **www.costco.com**, to complement its chain of membership clubs. The Web site helps to promote Costco's member services (as do its stores, as highlighted here); and the firm also sells some items in the stores that are not carried at the Web site—and vice versa. The Web site is a growing part of Costco's business.

Photo reprinted by permission of Susan Berry, Retail Image Consulting, Inc.

suggesting that positive perceptions generated online are being undermined at the point of sale.[2]

The ever-popular eBay (www.ebay.com) is a pure Web retailer.

Retailers—single-channel or multi-channel—engage in **nonstore retailing** when they use strategy mixes that are not store-based to reach consumers and complete transactions. U.S. nonstore retailing sales exceed $375 billion annually, with 80 percent of that from direct marketing (hence, the direct marketing emphasis in this chapter). The fastest-growing form of direct marketing involves electronic (Web-based) retailing. From sales of $500 million in 1996, Web retailing revenues were expected to exceed $100 billion in 2006.[3] See Figure 6-2.

Nontraditional retailing also comprises video kiosks and airport retailing, two key formats not fitting neatly into "store-based" or "nonstore-based" retailing. Sometimes they are store-based; other times they are not. What they have in common is their departure from traditional retailing strategies.

DIRECT MARKETING

Direct (www.directmag.com) is a vital source of direct marketing information.

In **direct marketing,** a customer is first exposed to a good or service through a nonpersonal medium (direct mail, TV, radio, magazine, newspaper, or computer) and then orders by mail, phone, or fax—and increasingly by computer. Annual U.S. sales are more than $300 billion (including the Web), and more than half of adults make at least one such purchase a year. Japan, Germany, Great Britain, France, and Italy are the among the direct marketing leaders outside the United States.[4] Popular products are gift items, apparel, magazines, books and music, sports equipment, home accessories, food, and insurance.

In the United States, direct marketing customers are more apt to be married, upper middle class, and 35 to 50 years of age. Mail shoppers are more likely to live in areas away from malls. Phone shoppers are more likely to live in upscale metropolitan areas, and they want to avoid traffic and save time. The share of direct marketing purchases made by men has grown: The average consumer who buys

direct spends several hundred dollars per year; and he or she wants convenience, unique products, and good prices.[5]

Direct marketers can be divided into two broad categories: general and specialty. General direct marketing firms offer a full line of products and sell everything from clothing to housewares. J.C. Penney (with its mail-order and Web businesses) and QVC (with its cable TV and Web businesses) are general direct marketers. Specialty direct marketers focus on more narrow product lines. L.L. Bean, Publishers Clearinghouse, and Franklin Mint are among the thousands of U.S. specialty firms. See Figure 6-3.

Direct marketing has a number of strategic business advantages:

● Many costs are reduced—low startup costs are possible; inventories are reduced; no displays are needed; a prime location is unnecessary; regularly staffed store hours are not important; a sales force may not be needed; and business may be run out of a garage or basement.

● It is possible for direct marketers to have lower prices (due to reduced costs) than store-based retailers with the same items. A huge geographic area can be covered inexpensively and efficiently.

● Customers shop conveniently—without crowds, parking congestion, or checkout lines. And they do not have safety concerns about shopping early in the morning or late at night.

● Specific consumer segments are pinpointed through targeted mailings.

● Consumers may sometimes legally avoid sales tax by buying from direct marketers not having retail facilities in their state (however, some states want to eliminate this loophole).

● A store-based firm can supplement its regular business and expand its trading area (even becoming national or global) without adding outlets.

Direct marketing also has its limits, but they are not as critical as those for direct selling:

● Products cannot be examined before purchase. Thus, the range of items purchased is more limited than in stores, and firms need liberal return policies to attract and keep customers.

- Prospective firms may underestimate costs. Catalogs can be expensive. A computer system is required to track shipments, monitor purchases and returns, and keep mailing lists current. A 24-hour phone staff may be needed.

- Even successful catalogs often draw purchases from less than 10 percent of recipients.

- Clutter exists. Each year, billions of catalogs are mailed in the United States alone.

- Printed catalogs are prepared well in advance, causing difficulties in price and style planning.

- Some firms have given the industry a bad name due to delivery delays and shoddy goods.

The full 30-day rule is available online (**www.ftc.gov/bcp/conline/ pubs/buspubs/mailorder. htm**).

The Federal Trade Commission's "30-day rule" is a U.S. regulation that affects direct marketers. It requires firms to ship orders within 30 days of their receipt or notify customers of delays. If an order cannot be shipped in 60 days, the customer must be given a specific delivery date and offered the option of canceling an order or waiting for it to be filled. The rule covers mail, phone, fax, and computer orders.

Despite its limitations, good long-run growth for direct marketing is projected. Consumer interest in convenience and the difficulty in setting aside shopping time will continue. More direct marketers will offer 24-hour ordering and improve their efficiency. Greater product standardization and the prominence of well-known brands will reduce consumer perceptions of risk when buying from a catalog or the Web. Technological breakthroughs, such as purchases on the Web, will attract more consumer shopping.

Due to its vast presence and immense potential, our detailed discussion is intended to give you an in-depth look into direct marketing. Let us study the domain of direct marketing, emerging trends, steps in a direct marketing strategy, and key issues facing direct marketers.

The Domain of Direct Marketing

As defined earlier, *direct marketing* is a form of retailing in which a consumer is exposed to a good or service through a nonpersonal medium and then orders by mail, phone, fax, or computer. It may also be viewed as "an interactive system that uses one or more advertising media to effect a measurable response and/or transaction at any location, with this activity stored on a data base."[6]

Accordingly, we *do* include these as forms of direct marketing: any catalog; any mail, TV, radio, magazine, newspaper, phone directory, fax, or other ad; any computer-based transaction; or any other nonpersonal contact that stimulates customers to place orders by mail, phone, fax, or computer.

We *do not* include these as forms of direct marketing: (1) Direct selling—Consumers are solicited by in-person sales efforts or seller-originated phone calls and the firm uses personal communication to initiate contact. (2) Conventional vending machines, whereby consumers are exposed to nonpersonal media but do not complete transactions via mail, phone, fax, or computer; they do not interact with the firm in a manner that allows a data base to be generated and kept.

Direct marketing *is* involved in many computerized kiosk transactions; when items are mailed to consumers, there is a company-customer interaction and a data base can be formed. Direct marketing is also in play when consumers originate phone calls, based on catalogs or ads they have seen.

The Customer Data Base: Key to Successful Direct Marketing

Because direct marketers initiate contact with customers (in contrast to store shopping trips that are initiated by the consumer), it is imperative that they develop and maintain a comprehensive customer data base. They can then pinpoint their best customers, make offers aimed at specific customer needs, avoid costly mailings to nonresponsive shoppers, and track sales by customer. A good data base is the major asset of most direct marketers, and *every* thriving direct marketer has a strong data base.

Data-base retailing is a way to collect, store, and use relevant information about customers. Such information typically includes a person's name, address, background data, shopping interests, and purchase behavior. Though data bases are often compiled through large computerized information systems, they may also be used by small firms that are not overly computerized.

Here's an example of how data-base retailing can be beneficial:

> Your family clothing store is going to have a sale on children's clothing. Rather than mail a postcard to the whole customer list (both men and women), you mail the postcard only to customers who have purchased children's clothing from you in the past. The result of that targeting effort will be reduced promotion costs and increased return on your investment.[7]

Data-base retailing is discussed further in Chapter 8.

Emerging Trends

Several trends are relevant for direct marketing: the evolving activities of direct marketers, changing consumer lifestyles, increased competition, the greater use of dual distribution channels, the newer roles for catalogs and TV, technological advances, and the interest in global direct marketing.

Evolving Activities of Direct Marketers

Over the past 30 years, these direct marketing activities have evolved:

- Technology has moved to the forefront in all aspects of direct marketing—from lead generation to order processing.
- Multi-channel retailing is utilized by many more firms today.
- There is an increased focus on data-base retailing.
- Many more firms now have well-articulated and widely communicated privacy policies.

Changing Consumer Lifestyles

Consumer lifestyles in America have shifted dramatically over the past several decades, mostly due to the large number of women who are now in the labor force and the longer commuting time to and from work for suburban residents. Many consumers no longer have the time or inclination to shop at stores. They are attracted by the ease of purchasing through direct marketing.

These are some of the factors consumers consider in selecting a direct marketer:

- Company reputation (image).
- Ability to shop whenever the consumer wants.
- Types of goods and services, as well as the assortment and brand names carried.
- Availability of a toll-free phone number or Web site for ordering.
- Credit card acceptance.
- Speed of promised delivery time.
- Competitive prices.
- Satisfaction with past purchases and good return policies.

Increased Competition Among Firms

As direct marketing sales have risen, so has competition; and although there are a number of big firms, such as J.C. Penney and Spiegel, there are also thousands of small ones. The Direct Marketing Association estimates that there are over 10,000 U.S. mail-order companies.

Intense competition exists because entry into direct marketing is easier and less costly than entry into store retailing. A firm does not need a store; can operate with a small staff; and can use low-cost one-inch magazine ads, send brochures to targeted shoppers, and have an inexpensive Web site. It can keep a low inventory and place orders with suppliers after people buy items (as long as it meets the 30-day rule).

About one out of every two new direct marketers fails. Direct marketing lures many small firms that may poorly define their market niche, offer nondistinctive goods and services, have limited experience, misjudge the needed effort, have trouble with supplier continuity, and attract many consumer complaints.

Spiegel (www.spiegel.com) has largely been a direct marketer since the early 1900s. It faces more competition now than ever before.

Greater Use of Multi-Channel Retailing

Today, many stores add to their revenues by using ads, brochures, catalogs, and Web sites to obtain mail-order, phone, and computer-generated sales. They see that direct marketing is efficient, targets specific segments, appeals to people who might not otherwise shop with those firms, and needs a lower investment to reach other geographic areas than opening branch outlets.

Bloomingdale's is a store-based retailer that has flourished with a multi-channel approach. Bloomingdale's by Mail has a loyal target market and a data base of 3 million people. Bloomingdale's Web site (**www.bloomingdales.com**) capitalizes on the firm's strong product mix and customer service reputation: "Bloomingdale's is committed to leading the way with exclusive merchandise, customized services, and alternative shopping venues. We'll also be expanding our Web site to bring more of the 59th & Lex store experience closer to you."[8]

Newer Roles for Catalogs and TV

Direct marketers are recasting the ways in which they use their catalogs and their approach to TV retailing. Here's how.

We are witnessing three key changes in long-standing catalog tactics: (1) Many firms now print "specialogs" in addition to or instead of the annual catalogs showing all of their products. With a **specialog**, a retailer caters to a particular customer segment, emphasizes a limited number of items, and reduces production and postage costs (as a specialog is much shorter than a general catalog). Each year, such firms as Spiegel, L.L. Bean, and Travelsmith send out separate specialogs by market segment or occasion. (2) To help defray costs, some companies accept ads from noncompeting firms that are compatible with their image. For instance, Bloomingdale's by Mail has had ads for fine liquors and luxury cars. (3) To stimulate sales and defray costs, some catalogs are sold in bookstores, supermarkets, and airports, and at company Web sites. The percentage of consumers buying a catalog who actually make a product purchase is many times higher than that for those who get catalogs in the mail.

TV retailing has two components: shopping networks and infomercials. On a *shopping network*, the programming focuses on merchandise presentations and their sales (usually by phone). The two biggest players are cable giants QVC and Home Shopping Network (HSN), with combined annual worldwide revenues of $8.5 billion. Each firm has access to a global TV audience of more than 125 million households. About 10 percent of U.S. consumers buy goods through TV shopping programs each year. Once regarded as a medium primarily for shut-ins and the lower middle class, the typical TV-based shopper is now younger, more fashion-conscious, and as apt to be from a high-income household as the overall U.S. population. QVC and HSN feature jewelry, women's clothing, and personal-care items, and do not stress nationally known brands. Most items must be bought as they are advertised to encourage shoppers to act quickly. The firms also have active Web sites (**www.qvc.com** and **www.hsn.com**).[9]

An **infomercial** is a program-length TV commercial (typically, 30 minutes) for a specific good or service that airs on cable or broadcast television, often at a fringe time. As they watch an infomercial, shoppers call in orders, which are delivered to them. Infomercials work well for products that benefit from demonstrations. Good infomercials present detailed information, include customer testimonials, are entertaining, and are divided into timed segments (since the average viewer watches only a few minutes at a time) with ordering information displayed in every segment. Infomercials account for $5 billion in annual U.S. revenues. Extremely popular infomercials have included those for the Ronco Showtime Rotisserie, the George Forman Grill, "Fitness Made Simple," and a variety of exercise equipment. The Electronic Retailing Association (**www.retailing.org**) is the trade association for infomercial firms.

Ron Popeil has become a very rich man through his Ronco (**http://shop.ronco.com**) infomercials.

Ethics in
RETAILING   The Flood of Junk Mail: No End in Sight

Since the Can Spam Act (**www.spamlaws.com/federal/ can-spam.shtml**), a major federal antispam law that went into effect in January 2004, the amount of unsolicited junk E-mail has increased by 50 to 60 percent. According to some estimates, unsolicited E-mail accounts for 80 percent or perhaps even more of all E-mail sent.

To many observers, the increase in junk E-mail has come as no surprise. Antispam groups argue that the new law effectively gave spammers permission to send junk E-mails if they followed several guidelines. The Can Spam Act requires that advertising messages be identified in the E-mail's subject line. It also prohibits the use of a phony return E-mail address. The real weakness of the law, to these critics, is that it puts the burden on recipients to be removed from an E-mailer's mailing list through an "opt-out" feature. However, the "opt-out" message is often used by spammers as a means of verifying that the E-mail address used is current. In contrast, bulk E-mailers in Europe and Australia need to receive "opt-in" authorization from recipients before sending unwanted messages.

Sources: Tom Zeller Jr., "Law Barring Junk E-Mail Allows a Flood Instead," *New York Times* (February 1, 2005); and "Spam Laws," **www.spamlaws.com/federal/can-spam.shtml** (January 9, 2006).

Technological Advances

A technological revolution is improving operating efficiency and offering enhanced sales opportunities:

- Market segments can be better targeted. Through selective binding, longer catalogs are sent to the best customers and shorter catalogs to new prospects.
- Firms inexpensively use computers to enter mail and phone orders, arrange for shipments, and monitor inventory on hand.
- It is simple to set up and maintain computerized data bases using inexpensive software.
- Huge, automated distribution centers efficiently accumulate and ship orders.
- Customers dial toll-free phone numbers or visit Web sites to place orders and get information. The cost per call for the direct marketer is quite low.
- Consumers can conclude transactions from more sites, including kiosks at airports and train stations.
- Cable TV programming and the Web offer 24-hour shopping and ordering.
- Both in-home and at-work Web-based shopping transactions can be conducted.

Mounting Interest in Global Direct Marketing

Lands' End has many different Web sites to service customers around the world, such as its German site (www. landsend.de). Because of Lands' End's customer commitment, this site is in German.

More retailers are involved with global direct marketing because of the growing consumer acceptance of nonstore retailing in other countries. Among the U.S.-based direct marketers with a significant international presence are Eddie Bauer, Lands' End, Sharper Image, and Williams-Sonoma.

Outside the United States, annual direct marketing sales (by both domestic and foreign firms) are hundreds of billions of dollars. Direct marketing trade associations—each representing numerous member firms—exist in such diverse countries as Australia, Brazil, China, France, Germany, Japan, Russia, and Spain. In Europe alone, there are well over 10,000 direct marketing companies. Korean shoppers can view a TV shopping channel from Japan on the Internet and order through their computers.[10]

FIGURE 6-4
Executing a Direct Marketing Strategy

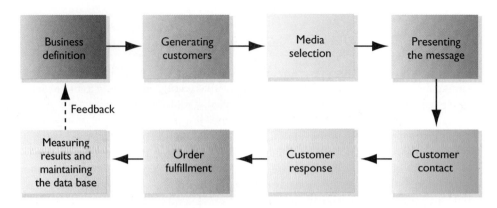

The Steps in a Direct Marketing Strategy

A direct marketing strategy has eight steps: business definition, generating customers, media selection, presenting the message, customer contact, customer response, order fulfillment, and measuring results and maintaining the data base. See Figure 6-4.

Business Definition

First, a company makes two decisions regarding its business definition: (1) Is the firm going to be a pure direct marketer or is it going to engage in multi-channel retailing? If the firm chooses the latter, it must clarify the role of direct marketing in its overall retail strategy. (2) Is the firm going to be a general direct marketer and carry a broad product assortment, or will it specialize in one goods/service category?

Generating Customers

A mechanism for generating business is devised next. A firm can

- Buy a printed mailing list from a broker. For one mailing, a list usually costs $50 to $100 or more per 1,000 names and addresses; it is supplied in mailing-label format. Lists may be broad or broken down by gender, location, and so on. In purchasing a list, the direct marketer should check its currency.
- Download a mailing list from the Web that is sold by a firm such as infoUSA (**www.infousa.com**), which has data on 105 million U.S. households. With a download, a firm can use the list multiple times, but it is responsible for selecting names and printing labels.
- Send out a blind mailing to all the residents in a particular area. This method can be expensive (unless done through E-mail) and may receive a very low response rate.
- Advertise in a newspaper, magazine, Web site, or other medium and ask customers to order by mail, phone, fax, or computer.
- Contact consumers who have bought from the firm or requested information. This is efficient, but it takes a while to develop a data base. To grow, a firm cannot rely solely on past customers.

Media Selection

Several media are available to the direct marketer:

- Printed catalogs.
- Direct mail ads and brochures.

- Inserts with monthly credit card and other bills ("statement stuffers").
- Freestanding displays with coupons, brochures, or catalogs (such as magazine subscription cards at the supermarket checkout counter).
- Ads or programs in the mass media—newspapers, magazines, radio, TV.
- Banner ads or "hot links" on the World Wide Web.
- Video kiosks.

In choosing among media, costs, distribution, lead time, and other factors should be considered.

Presenting the Message

Now, the firm prepares and presents its message in a way that engenders interest, creates (or sustains) the proper image, points out compelling reasons to purchase, and provides data about goods or services (such as prices and sizes). The message must also contain ordering instructions, including the payment method, how to designate the chosen items, shipping fees, and a firm's address, phone number, and Web address.

The message, and the medium in which it is presented, should be planned in the same way that a traditional retailer plans a store. The latter uses a storefront, lighting, carpeting, the store layout, and displays to foster an image. In direct marketing, the headlines, message content, use of color, paper quality, personalization of mail, space devoted to each item, and other elements affect a firm's image.

Customer Contact

For each campaign, a direct marketer decides whether to contact all customers in its data base or to seek specific market segments (with different messages and/or media for each). It can classify prospective customers as *regulars* (those who buy continuously); *nonregulars* (those who buy infrequently); *new contacts* (those who have never been sought before by the firm); and *nonrespondents* (those who have been contacted but never made a purchase).

Regulars and nonregulars are the most apt to respond to a firm's future offerings, and they can be better targeted since the firm has their purchase histories. For example, customers who have bought clothing before are prime prospects for specialogs. New contacts probably know little about the firm. Messages to them must build interest, accurately portray the firm, and present meaningful reasons for consumers to buy. This group is important if growth is sought.

Nonrespondents who have been contacted repeatedly without purchasing are unlikely to ever buy. Unless a firm can present a very different message, it is inefficient to pursue this group. Firms such as Publishers Clearinghouse send mailings to millions of people who have never bought from them; this is okay since they sell inexpensive impulse items and need only a small response rate to succeed.

Customer Response

Customers respond to direct marketers in one of three ways: (1) They buy through the mail, phone, fax, or computer. (2) They request further information, such as a catalog. (3) They ignore the message. Purchases are generally made by no more than 2 to 3 percent of those contacted. The rate is higher for specialogs, mail-order clubs (e.g., for music), and firms focusing on repeat customers.

Order Fulfillment

A system is needed for order fulfillment. If orders are received by mail or fax, the firm must sort them, determine if payment is enclosed, see whether the item is in stock, mail announcements if items cannot be sent on time, coordinate shipments, and replenish inventory. If phone orders are placed, a trained sales staff must be available when people may call. Salespeople answer questions, make suggestions, enter orders, note the payment method, see whether items are in stock, coordinate shipments, and replenish inventory. If orders are placed by computer, there must be a process to promptly and efficiently handle credit transactions, issue receipts, and forward orders to a warehouse. In all cases, names, addresses, and purchase data are added to the data base for future reference.

In peak seasons, additional warehouse, shipping, order processing, and sales workers supplement regular employees. Direct marketers that are highly regarded by consumers fill orders promptly, have knowledgeable and courteous personnel, do not misrepresent quality, and provide liberal return policies.

Measuring Results and Maintaining the Data Base

The last step is analyzing results and maintaining the data base. Direct marketing often yields clear outcomes:

- Overall response rate—The number and percentage of people who make a purchase after receiving or viewing a particular brochure, catalog, or Web site.
- Average purchase amount—By customer location, gender, and so forth.
- Sales volume by product category—Revenues correlated with the space allotted to each product in brochures, catalogs, and so forth.
- Value of list brokers—The revenues generated by various mailing lists.

After measuring results, the firm reviews its data base and makes sure that new shoppers are added, address changes are noted for existing customers, purchase and consumer information is current and available in segmentation categories, and nonrespondents are purged (when desirable).

This stage provides feedback for the direct marketer as it plans each new campaign.

Key Issues Facing Direct Marketers

In planning and applying their strategies, direct marketers must keep the following in mind.

Many people dislike one or more aspects of direct marketing. They are the most dissatisfied with late delivery or nondelivery, deceptive claims, broken or damaged items, the wrong items being sent, and the lack of information. Nonetheless, in most cases, leading direct marketers are rated well by consumers.

Most U.S. households report that they open all direct mail, but many would like to receive less of it. Since the average American household receives numerous catalogs each year, besides hundreds of other mailings, firms must be concerned about marketplace clutter. It is hard to be distinctive in this environment.

A lot of consumers are concerned that their names and other information are being sold by list brokers, as well as by some retailers. They feel this is an invasion of privacy and that their decision to purchase does not constitute permission to pass on personal data. To counteract this, members of the Direct Marketing Association remove people's names from list circulation if they make a request.

Multiple-channel retailers need a consistent image for both store-based and direct marketing efforts. They must also perceive the similarities and differences in each approach's strategy. The steady increase in postal rates makes mailing catalogs, brochures, and other promotional materials costly for some firms. Numerous direct marketers are turning more to newspapers, magazines, and cable TV—and the Web.

Direct marketers must monitor the legal environment. They must be aware that, in the future, more states will probably require residents to pay sales tax on out-of-state direct marketing purchases; the firms would have to remit the tax payments to the affected states.

DIRECT SELLING

The Direct Selling Association (**www.dsa.org**) is working hard to promote the image and professionalism of this retail format.

Direct selling includes both personal contact with consumers in their homes (and other nonstore locations such as offices) and phone solicitations initiated by a retailer. Cosmetics, jewelry, vitamins, household goods and services (such as carpet cleaning), vacuum cleaners, and magazines and newspapers are among the items sometimes sold in this way. The industry has $31 billion in annual U.S. sales and employs 14 million people (more than 80 percent part-time). Annual foreign direct selling revenues exceed $65 billion, generated by 40 million salespeople.[11] Table 6-1 shows an industry overview.

The direct selling strategy mix emphasizes convenient shopping and a personal touch, and detailed demonstrations can be made. Consumers often relax more in their homes than in stores. They are also likely to be attentive and are not exposed to competing brands (as they are in stores). For some shoppers, such as

TABLE 6-1	A Snapshot of the U.S. Direct Selling Industry

Major Product Groups (as a percent of sales dollars)

Home/family care products (cleaning products, cookware, cutlery, etc.)	32.0
Personal care products (cosmetics, jewelry, skin care, etc.)	29.4
Services/miscellaneous/other	15.4
Wellness products (weight loss products, vitamins, etc.)	15.3
Leisure/educational products (books, encyclopedias, toys/games, etc.)	7.9

Place of Sales (as a percent of sales dollars)

In the home	61.9
Over the phone	15.6
Over the Internet	10.8
In a workplace	6.7
At a temporary location (such as a fair, exhibition, shopping mall, etc.)	3.9
Other locations	1.1

Sales Approach (method used to generate sales, as a percent of sales dollars)

Individual/one-to-one selling	69.0
Party plan/group sales	28.5
Customer placing order directly with firm	1.7
Other	0.8

Demographics of Salespeople (as a percent of all salespeople)

Independent contractors/Employees	99.9/0.1
Female/Male	79.9/20.1
Part-time/Full-time (30 hours and up per week)	85.1/14.9

Source: Direct Selling Association, "Selling by the Numbers," **www.dsa.org/research/numbers.htm** (August 23, 2005).

older consumers and those with young children, in-store shopping is hard due to limited mobility. For the retailer, direct selling has lower overhead costs because stores and fixtures are not necessary.

Despite its advantages, direct selling in the United States is growing slowly:

- More women work, and they may not be interested in or available for in-home selling.
- Improved job opportunities in other fields and the interest in full-time careers have reduced the pool of people interested in direct selling jobs.
- A firm's market coverage is limited by the size of its sales force.
- Sales productivity is low since the average transaction is small and most consumers are unreceptive—many will not open their doors to salespeople or talk to telemarketers.
- Sales force turnover is high because employees are often poorly supervised part-timers.
- To stimulate sales personnel, compensation is usually 25 to 50 percent of the revenues they generate. This means average to above-average prices.
- There are various legal restrictions due to deceptive and high-pressure sales tactics. One such restriction is the FTC's Telemarketing Sales Rule (**www.ftc.gov/bcp/rulemaking/tsr**), which mandates that firms must disclose their identity and that the purpose of the call is selling.
- Because *door-to-door* has a poor image, the industry prefers the term *direct selling*.

Firms are reacting to these issues. Avon places greater emphasis on workplace sales, offers free training to sales personnel, rewards the best workers with better territories, pursues more global sales, and places cosmetics kiosks in shopping centers. Mary Kay hires community residents as salespeople and has a party atmosphere rather than a strict door-to-door approach; this requires networks of family, friends, and neighbors. And every major direct selling firm has a Web site to supplement revenues.

Among the leading direct sellers are Avon and Mary Kay (cosmetics), Amway (household supplies), Tupperware (plastic containers), Shaklee (health products),

Technology in RETAILING — Direct Selling: Using the Internet to Improve Performance

The use of Web-based technology has simplified the life of many direct sellers by facilitating the recruitment of sales representatives and better enabling firms to expand their territories.

Nadine Thompson owns Warm Spirit Inc. (**www.warmspirit.com**), a company with annual sales of $6 million, that sells shampoos and herbal extracts targeted at African-American women. Recently, Thompson held a national sales meeting with her 9,100 sales consultants from her home office. According to Ms. Thompson, "I didn't have to put on a Donna Karan suit or set up a PowerPoint presentation. I didn't have to pay and pull a whole convention together."

Andrew Shure, owner of Shure Pets (**www.shurepets.com**), uses direct selling to sell his natural pet lifestyle products that include Aromutt Therapy spray, Devine Canine Breath drops, and Purr-fect Wheat Grass. He now uses Google and Yahoo! to attract sales reps. New reps pay $99 for a "New Puppy on the Block" starter kit and then receive a 25 percent commission from each sale they make. Sales reps also benefit from purchases from Shure's own Web site, if they identify their sales representative.

Sources: Gwendolyn Bounds, "Direct-Sales Operations Gain, With Boost from the Internet," *Wall Street Journal* (October 26, 2004), B4; and "Our Company," **www.warmspirit.com/fam_abo_divetext.jsp** (May 1, 2006).

FIGURE 6-5
Direct Selling and Mary Kay

Throughout the world (in 33 countries), Mary Kay Cosmetics employs more than 1 million direct sales "consultants," who mostly visit customers in their homes and account for $1 billion in revenues. Through its Web site, **www.marykay.com**, the company even provides links to the home pages of its U.S. consultants.

Reprinted by permission of Mary Kay Cosmetics.

Fuller Brush (small household products), Kirby (vacuum cleaners), and Welcome Wagon (greetings for new residents sponsored by groups of local retailers). Some stores, such as J.C. Penney, also use direct selling. Penney's decorator consultants sell a complete line of furnishings, not available in its stores, to consumers in their homes. See Figure 6-5.

VENDING MACHINES

A **vending machine** is a cash- or card-operated retailing format that dispenses goods (such as beverages) and services (such as electronic arcade games). It eliminates the use of sales personnel and allows 24-hour sales. Machines can be placed wherever convenient for consumers—inside or outside stores, in motel corridors, at train stations, or on street corners.

The Canteen Corporation (www.canteen.com) has vending machines at 18,500 client locations.

Although there have been many attempts to "vend" clothing, magazines, and other general merchandise, 95 percent of the nearly $45 billion in annual U.S. vending machine sales involve hot and cold beverages and food items. Because of health issues, over the past 25 years, cigarettes' share of sales has gone from 25 to just 3 percent. The greatest sales are achieved in factory, office, and school lunchrooms and refreshment areas; public places such as service stations are also popular sites. Newspapers on street corners and sidewalks, various machines in hotels and motels, and candy machines in restaurants and at train stations are visible aspects of vending but account for a small percentage of U.S. vending machine sales.[12] Leading vending machine operators are Canteen Corporation and Aramark Refreshment Services.

Items priced above $1.50 have not sold well; too many coins are required and some vending machines do not have dollar bill changers. Consumers are reluctant to buy more expensive items that they cannot see displayed or have explained. However, their expanded access to and use of debit cards are expected to have a major impact on resolving the payment issue, and the video-kiosk type of vending machine lets people see product displays and get detailed information (and then place a credit or debit card order). Popular brands and standardized nonfood items are best suited to increasing sales via vending machines.

To improve productivity and customer relations, vending operators are applying several innovations. Popular products such as french fries are being made fresh in vending machines. Machine malfunctions are reduced by applying electronic mechanisms to cash-handling controls. Microprocessors track consumer preferences, trace malfunctions, and record receipts. Some machines have voice synthesizers that are programmed to say "Thank you, come again" or "Your change is 25 cents."

Operators must still deal with theft, vandalism, stockouts, above-average prices, and the perception that vending machines should be patronized only when a fill-in convenience item is needed.

ELECTRONIC RETAILING: THE EMERGENCE OF THE WORLD WIDE WEB

We are living through enormous changes from the days when retailing simply meant visiting a store, shopping from a printed catalog, greeting the Avon lady in one's home, or buying candy from a vending machine. Who would have thought that a person could "surf the Web" to research a stock, learn about a new product, search for bargains, save a trip to the store, and complain about customer service? Well, these activities are real and they're here to stay. Let's take a look at the World Wide Web from a retailing perspective, remembering that selling on the Web is a form of direct marketing.

Let us define two terms that may be confusing: The **Internet** is a global electronic superhighway of computer networks that use a common protocol and that are linked by telecommunications lines and satellite. It acts as a single, cooperative virtual network and is maintained by universities, governments, and businesses. The **World Wide Web (Web)** is one way to access information on the Internet, whereby people work with easy-to-use Web addresses (sites) and pages. Web users see words, charts, pictures, and video, and hear audio—which turn their computers into interactive multimedia centers. People can easily move from site to site by pointing at the proper spot on the monitor and clicking a mouse button. Browsing software, such as Microsoft Internet Explorer and Mozilla Firefox, facilitate Web surfing.

Both *Internet* and *World Wide Web* convey the same central theme: online interactive retailing. Since almost all online retailing is done by the World Wide Web, we use *Web* in our discussion, which is comprised of these topics: the role of the Web, the scope of Web retailing, characteristics of Web users, factors to consider in planning whether to have a Web site, and examples of Web retailers. Visit our Web site (**www.prenhall.com/bermanevans**) for several valuable links on E-retailing.

The Role of the Web

From the vantage point of the retailer, the World Wide Web can serve one or more roles:

- Project a retail presence and enhance the retailer's image.
- Generate sales as the major source of revenue for an online retailer or as a complementary source of revenue for a store-based retailer.
- Reach geographically dispersed consumers, including foreign ones.
- Provide information to consumers about products carried, store locations, usage information, answers to common questions, customer loyalty programs, and so on.
- Promote new products and fully explain and demonstrate their features.
- Furnish customer service in the form of E-mail, "hot links," and other communications.

- Be more "personal" with consumers by letting them point and click on topics they choose.
- Conduct a retail business in a cost-efficient manner.
- Obtain customer feedback.
- Promote special offers and send coupons to Web customers.
- Describe employment opportunities.
- Present information to potential investors, potential franchisees, and the media.

The role a retailer assigns to the Web depends on (1) whether its major goal is to communicate interactively with consumers or to sell goods and services, (2) whether it is predominantly a traditional retailer that wants to have a Web presence or a newer firm that wants to derive most or all of its sales from the Web, and (3) the level of resources the retailer wants to commit to site development and maintenance. There are millions of Web sites worldwide and hundreds of thousands in retailing.

The Scope of Web Retailing

Internet Retailer (http://internetretailer.com/contents.asp) tracks online retailing.

The potential of the Web is enormous: As of 2007, there are expected to be 235 million Web users in North America, 265 million in Europe, 330 million in Asia-Pacific, 90 million in Latin America, and 30 million in the Middle East/Africa. One-third of all U.S. households purchase online at least once a year. Less than a decade ago, U.S. shoppers generated 75 percent of worldwide online retail sales; the amount is now less than 40 percent and falling. U.S. retail Web sales have doubled over the past five years; and three-quarters of current purchases are made by those with broadband connections (rather than dialup). At least 5 percent or more of the U.S. sales of these goods and services are made online: apparel, banking, books, computer hardware and software, consumer electronics, gifts, greeting cards, insurance, music, newspapers/magazines, sporting goods, toys, travel, and videos. A real milestone in Web retailing was achieved just a few years ago, when—for the first time—the majority of U.S. E-retailers reported a profit.[13] Figure 6-6 indicates the percentage of projected 2010 online sales by product category.

Despite the foregoing data, the Web accounts for only 3 to 4 percent of U.S. retail sales! It will not be the death knell of store-based retailing but another choice for shoppers, like other forms of direct marketing. There is much higher sales growth for "clicks-and-mortar" Web retailing (multi-channel retailing) than "bricks-and-mortar" stores (single-channel retailing) and "clicks only" Web firms (single-channel retailing). Store-based retailers account for more than three-quarters of U.S. online sales:

> Consumers might be shopping online more than ever, but that doesn't mean the physical stores will soon be sitting empty. Online retailing has evolved differently than first predicted, said Steve Mullen, senior public relations representative for Circuit City Stores: "In the 1990s, when Web shopping was on the rise, some said it was the end of brick-and-mortar stores. That hasn't been the case at all." Instead, virtual stores have complemented their real counterparts. According to Mullen, "One thing we're definitely seeing an increase in people doing is they check the Web site, do all their research, then go to the store and buy it." As a result, many retailers like Circuit City are coordinating their online and brick-and-mortar retailers so they work well together to benefit the customer. Circuit City allows shoppers to order online and pick up in their local store.[14]

FIGURE 6-6
Web-Based Retail Sales
Projections for Selected
Product Categories

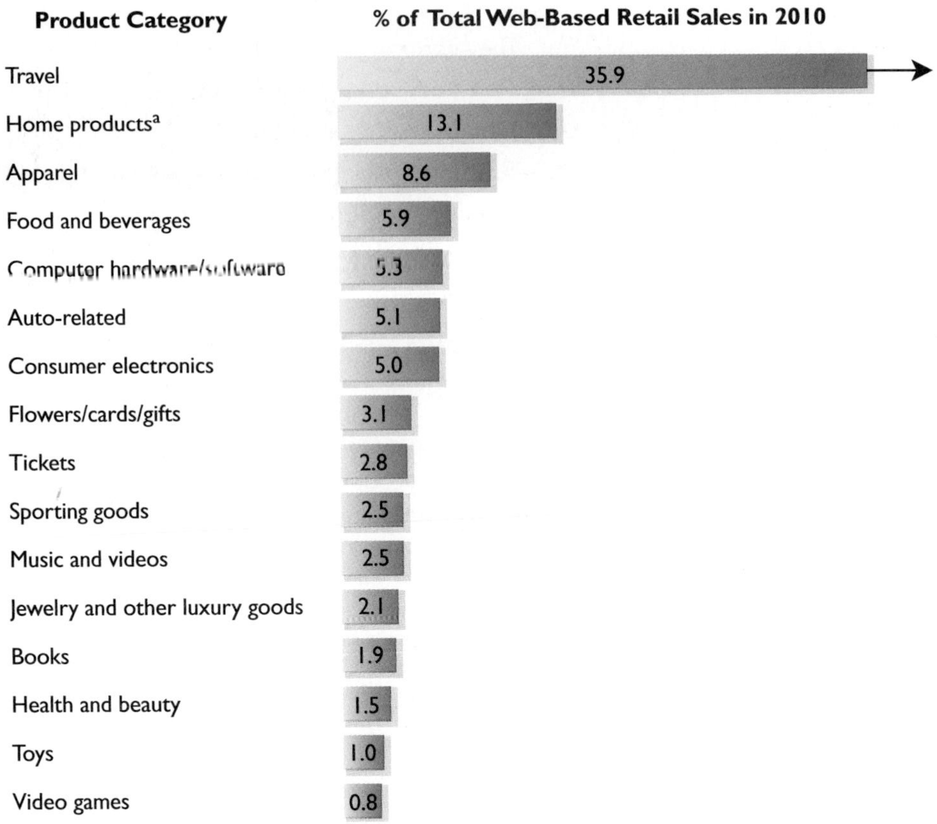

Product Category	% of Total Web-Based Retail Sales in 2010
Travel	35.9
Home products[a]	13.1
Apparel	8.6
Food and beverages	5.9
Computer hardware/software	5.3
Auto-related	5.1
Consumer electronics	5.0
Flowers/cards/gifts	3.1
Tickets	2.8
Sporting goods	2.5
Music and videos	2.5
Jewelry and other luxury goods	2.1
Books	1.9
Health and beauty	1.5
Toys	1.0
Video games	0.8

[a]Including furniture, garden supplies, home décor, appliances, office supplies, pet supplies,
and tools/hardware.

Source: Chart developed by the authors from data by Forrester Research, 2004.

Characteristics of Web Users

U.S. Web users have these characteristics, many of which are highlighted in
Figure 6-7:

- Gender and age—There are about as many males as females on the Web; however, females shop more often. Eighteen- to 29-year-olds are the most likely to
  use the Web; those 65 and older are the least likely.

- Income and education—Less than one-half of households with an annual
  income under $30,000 use the Web; in contrast, 92 percent of households with
  an annual income of at least $75,000 use the Web. Those who have graduated
  from college are more than three times as likely to use the Internet as those
  who have not graduated from college.

- Purchase behavior—The average monthly spending online for those making
  Web purchases is nearly $200. Men spend slightly more than women (even
  though more women shop online).

- Reasons for *using* the Web—People seek information, entertainment, and
  interactive communications.

- Reasons for *shopping* on the Web—Shoppers are attracted by the convenience,
  prices, and product selection of Web retailing.

- Reasons for *not shopping* on the Web—Nonshoppers do not trust online retailers, worry about their privacy, like to see and handle products, like talking to
  salespeople, like taking purchases with them, and do not want to be surprised
  by the lack of shipping cost information.

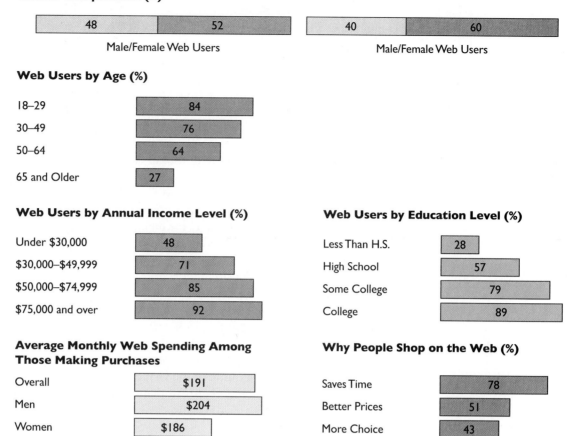

FIGURE 6-7
A Snapshot of U.S. Web Users

Sources: Charts developed by the authors from data in Eric Chabrow, "Report Finds Women Behind Surge in Online Retail Sales," *Information Week Online* (May 24, 2005); "Ethnic Groups Online," **www.emarketer.com** (June 20, 2005); "Statistics: U.S. Online Shoppers," **www.shop.org/learn/stats_usshop_general.asp** (July 25, 2005); and Bart Kittle, "Online Christmas 2004: Tenth Anniversary Celebration," *Retail Education Today* (May 2005), pp.13–15.

Shoppers say the most important factors in their continued patronage are value and customer service: "If an online retailer is true to its value proposition, shopper loyalty will follow. But today's shoppers are fickle, eclectic, value-driven, and searching for new experiences. That puts pressure on retailers to be consistent in their value propositions and vigilant of the fulfillment activities that weigh heavily on the likelihood to buy again. Loyalty on the Web remains suspect. If online firms want to turn the tide, they must offer loyalty programs based on rewards, personalization, quality customer support for the online shopping experience, and privacy policies that protect customers and establish trust."[15]

Web users can be enticed to shop more often if they are assured of privacy, retailers are perceived as trustworthy, sites are easy to maneuver, prices are lower than at stores, there are strong money-back guarantees, they can return a product to a store, shipping costs are not hidden until the end of a purchase, transactions are secure, they can speak with sales representatives, and download time is faster.

Factors to Consider in Planning Whether to Have a Web Site

The Web generally offers many *advantages* for retailers. It is usually less costly to have a Web site than a store. The potential marketplace is huge and dispersed, yet relatively easy to reach. Web sites can be quite exciting, due to their multimedia capabilities. People can visit Web sites at any time, and their visits can be as short or long as they desire. Information can be targeted, so that, for example, a person visiting a toy retailer's Web site could click on the icon labeled "Educational Toys—ages three to six." A customer data base can be established and customer feedback obtained.

The Web also has *disadvantages* for retailers: If consumers do not know a firm's Web address, it may be hard to find. For various reasons, many people are not yet willing to buy online. There is tremendous clutter with regard to the number of Web sites. Because Web surfers are easily bored, a Web site must be regularly updated to ensure repeat visits. The more multimedia features a Web site has, the slower it may be for people with dialup connections to access. Some firms have been overwhelmed with customer service requests and questions from E-mail. It may be hard to coordinate store and Web transactions. There are few standards or rules as to what may be portrayed at Web sites. Consumers expect online services to be free and are reluctant to pay for them.

There is a large gulf between full-scale, integrated Web selling and a basic "telling"—rather than "selling"—Web site. To better understand this gulf, the model highlighted in Figure 6-8 was introduced at a National Retail Federation Information Technology Power Summit so that retailers can envision Web site development as a five-step process: "Many large, successful retailers are happy to be at Stage 2, and find that it brings them new customers and increased visibility. Stage 3, where the Web becomes simply another channel, was, for a time, the ideal that retailers sought. Stages 4 and 5 represent the next steps on the road to retail nirvana—the total integration of the virtual with the physical. Yet, as history tells us, Stages 6, 7, 8, and beyond are out there, waiting for technology to mature and new applications."[16]

FIGURE 6-8

The Five Stages of Developing a Retail Web Presence

Source: Chart developed by the authors from the discussion in Tracy Mullin, "Determining Web Presence," *Chain Store Age* (October 1999), p. 42.

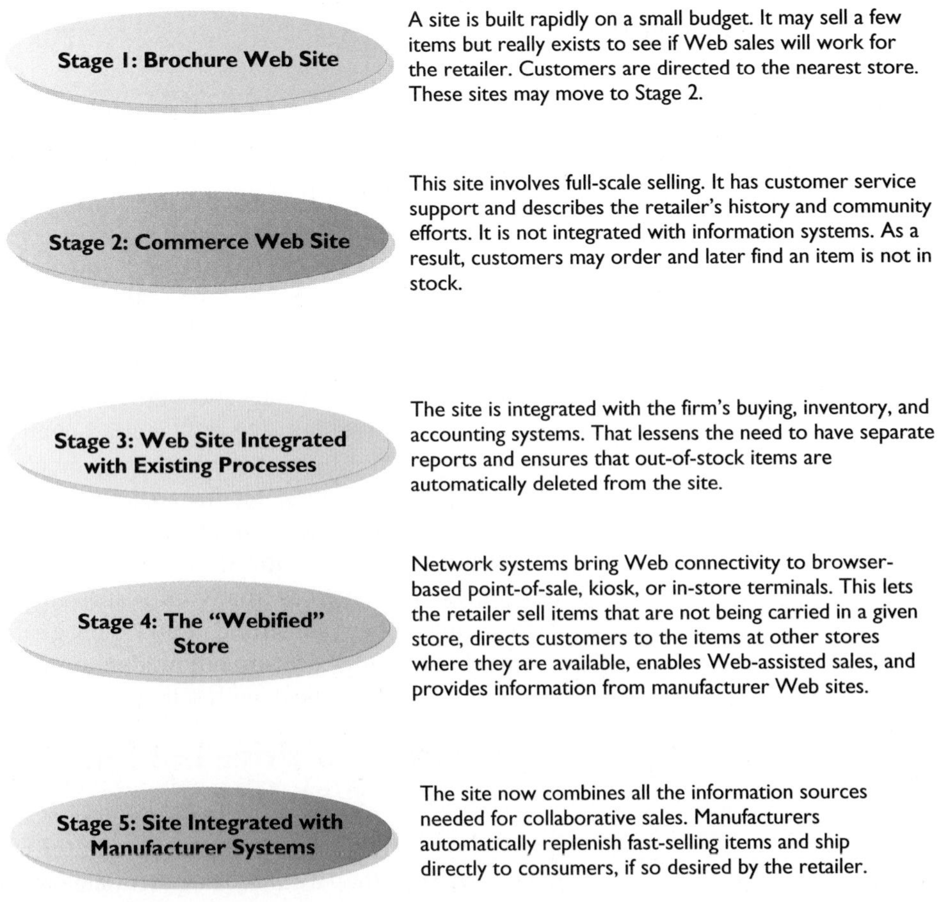

Stage 1: Brochure Web Site

A site is built rapidly on a small budget. It may sell a few items but really exists to see if Web sales will work for the retailer. Customers are directed to the nearest store. These sites may move to Stage 2.

Stage 2: Commerce Web Site

This site involves full-scale selling. It has customer service support and describes the retailer's history and community efforts. It is not integrated with information systems. As a result, customers may order and later find an item is not in stock.

Stage 3: Web Site Integrated with Existing Processes

The site is integrated with the firm's buying, inventory, and accounting systems. That lessens the need to have separate reports and ensures that out-of-stock items are automatically deleted from the site.

Stage 4: The "Webified" Store

Network systems bring Web connectivity to browser-based point-of-sale, kiosk, or in-store terminals. This lets the retailer sell items that are not being carried in a given store, directs customers to the items at other stores where they are available, enables Web-assisted sales, and provides information from manufacturer Web sites.

Stage 5: Site Integrated with Manufacturer Systems

The site now combines all the information sources needed for collaborative sales. Manufacturers automatically replenish fast-selling items and ship directly to consumers, if so desired by the retailer.

Keep current on E-retailing news with Retail Forward's information-rich Web site (http://eretail.retailforward.com).

Web retailers should carefully consider these recommendations, compiled from several industry experts:

- Develop (or exploit) a well-known, trustworthy retailer name.
- Tailor the product assortment for Web shoppers, and keep freshening the offerings.
- With download speed in mind, provide pictures and ample product information.
- Enable the shopper to make as few clicks as possible to get product information and place orders.
- Provide the best possible search engine at the firm's Web site.
- Capitalize on customer information and relationships.
- Integrate online and offline businesses, and look for partnering opportunities.
- With permission, save customer data to make future shopping trips easier.
- Indicate shipping fees upfront and be clear about delivery options.
- Do not promote items that are out of stock; and let shoppers know immediately if items will not be shipped for a few days.
- Offer online order tracking.
- Use a secure order entry system for shoppers.
- Prominently state the firm's return and privacy policies.

See Figure 6-9.

Consistent with the preceding discussion, a firm has many decisions to make if it wants to utilize the Web (as enumerated in Figure 6-9). A firm cannot just put up a site and wait for consumers to visit it in droves and then expect them to happily return. In many cases: (1) It is still difficult for people to find exactly what they are looking for. (2) Once the person finds what he or she wants, it may be hard to envision the product. "Subtleties of color and texture often don't come across well on the Web. Until someone figures out how to send a cashmere scarf digitally, you won't be able to touch it." (3) Customer service is sometimes lacking. (4) Web sites and their store siblings may not be in sync. "Send someone a gift from CompanyA.com and the recipient may be surprised to find it can't be returned or exchanged at a Company A store." (5) Privacy policies may not be consumer-oriented. "Order from a site, fill out a survey, or merely browse, and you find your E-mail box swamped with unsolicited ads and other junk."[17]

Examples of Web Retailing in Action

These examples show the breadth of retailing on the World Wide Web.

Amazon.com (**www.amazon.com**) is probably the most famous pure Web retailer in the world, with revenues exceeding $8 billion and tens of millions of customers purchasing from the firm each year. See Figure 6-10. This is how *Hoover's Online* sums up the Amazon.com phenomenon:

What started as Earth's biggest bookstore is rapidly becoming Earth's biggest anything store. Expansion has propelled Amazon.com in many directions. The firm's main Web site offers millions of books, CDs, DVDs, and videos (which still account for the majority of the firm's sales), not to mention toys, tools, electronics, home furnishings, apparel, health and beauty goods, prescription drugs, gourmet foods, and services including

FIGURE 6-9
A Checklist of Retailer
Decisions in Utilizing
the Web

✓ What are the company's Web goals? At what point is it expected that the site will be profitable?
✓ What budget will be allocated to developing and maintaining a Web site?
✓ Who will develop and maintain the Web site, the retailer itself or an outside specialist?
✓ Should the firm set up an independent Web site for itself or should it be part of a "cybermall?"
✓ What features will the Web site have? What level of customer service will be offered?
✓ What information will the Web site provide?
✓ How will the goods and services assortment differ at the Web site from the firm's store?
✓ Will the Web site offer benefits not available elsewhere?
✓ Will prices reflect a good value for the consumer?
✓ How fast will the user be able to download the text and images from the Web site, and point and click from screen to screen?
✓ How often will Web site content be changed?
✓ What staff will handle Web inquiries and transactions?
✓ How fast will turnaround time be for Web inquiries and transactions?
✓ How will the firm coordinate store and Web transactions and customer interactions?
✓ What will be done to avoid crashes and slow site features during peak shopping hours and seasons?
✓ How will online orders be processed?
✓ How easy will it be for shoppers to enter and complete orders?
✓ What online payment methods will be accepted?
✓ What search engines (such as Yahoo!) will list the retailer's Web site?
✓ How will the site be promoted: (a) on the Web and (b) by the company?
✓ How will Web data be stored and arranged? How will all of the firm's information systems be integrated?
✓ How will Web success be measured?
✓ How will the firm determine which Web shoppers are new customers and which are customers who would otherwise visit a company store?
✓ How will the firm ensure secure (encrypted) transactions?
✓ How will consumer privacy concerns be handled?
✓ How will returns and customer complaints be handled?

FIGURE 6-10
Amazon.com: A Pure Web
Retailer

"Amazon.com opened its virtual doors in July 1995 with a mission to use the Internet to transform book buying into the fastest, easiest, and most enjoyable shopping experience possible. While our customer base and product offerings have grown considerably since our early days, we still maintain our founding commitment to customer satisfaction and the delivery of an educational and inspiring shopping experience." [**www.amazon.com**]

Reprinted by permission.

film processing. Long a model for Internet firms that put market share ahead of profits and made acquisitions funded by meteoric market capitalization, Amazon.com is now focusing on profits. Founder Jeff Bezos owns about 25 percent of the firm.[18]

At the opposite end of the spectrum from Amazon.com is the tiny business of Tony Roeder, the owner and proprietor of RedWagons.com (**www.redwagons.com**):

> Roeder is living proof that "small guys can win the online game." He launched Redwagons.com in 1998, selling the classic American childhood toy—the Radio Flyer wagons. He found a good break, and went on to start an online store at Yahoo! from his home, armed only with a keen sense of business acumen. With hardly any capital and no programming skills, the online store grew into a million dollar business in just three years. Roeder credits much of his success to the strategy of concentrating on a small area of the toy market: "We focused our attention on Radio Flyer Wagons and became an Internet toy store primarily selling their products." As a result, "We have the advantage because we have a wide product line whereas most online stores only carry two or three models of the products. We're filling a niche and answering the problem that there was no selection since most stores carry only 2 to 3 percent of that selection."[19]

Netflix (**www.netflix.com**) is a very successful online service retailer that was started in September 1999. It rents DVDs in a customer-friendly way:

> Netflix is the world's largest online DVD movie rental service, offering more than three million members access to 45,000 titles. Our appeal and success are built on providing the most expansive selection of DVDs, an easy way to choose movies; and fast, free delivery. Members have the choice of eight subscription plans, starting at $9.99 per month for unlimited rentals with one DVD out at a time. With the most popular plan of $17.99 a month, members rent as many DVDs as they want and keep them as long as they want, with three movies out at a time. Members enjoy fast and free delivery: We reach more than 90 percent of our members with generally one-business-day delivery and provide free, pre-paid

RETAILING
Around the World — Online Shopping: Opportunities Abroad

According to Forrester Research (**www.forrester.com**), from 2004 to 2009, European Web-based sales are forecast to grow at an annual rate that is more than double the rate in the United States. While the number of Europeans with online capability continues to expand each year, growth potential in the United States is more limited since most residents are already online. Some analysts attribute the current interest among retailers in expanding their online operations overseas to the increased sales by Amazon.com's (**www.amazon.com**) foreign operations. In one recent year, the firm's British, German, French, Japanese, and Chinese sites reported annual sales growth of 52 percent.

eBags (**www.ebags.com**), a seller of luggage, handbags, and shoes, is an example of online overseas expansion by a U.S. retailer. The firm plans to add a German and a French site to its recently introduced British site (**www.ebags.co.uk**). According to Peter Cobb, eBags' senior vice-president and co-founder, most European luggage retailers are "small family-run operations with maybe 100 or 200 items," and have more limited hours than a typical U.S. retailer. In contrast, eBags sells 1,200 products representing over 70 brands on its British site.

Source: Bob Tedeschi, "Online Retailers Look Overseas," *New York Times* (January 10, 2005); and "eBags," **www.ebags.co.uk** (March 12, 2006).

FIGURE 6-11
Priceline.com: Online
Auctions for Travel

At Priceline.com
(**www.priceline.com**), "you
can now choose your exact
flights and times for incredible
travel savings or Name Your
Own Price and save even more!
All it takes is a little flexibility
with your travel plans. If you
can fly any time of day, agree
to fly on any major airline, stay
in any name-brand hotel, or
rent from any of the top 5 U.S.
rental car agencies—you can
save a lot of money with
Priceline!"

Reprinted by permission.

return envelopes. With no commitments, members can cancel anytime.
Our "no late fees, no due dates" online movie rental model has elimi-
nated the hassle involved in choosing, renting, and returning movies.
New members can try Netflix for free by visiting netflix.com.[20]

Finally, here are two other exciting Web retailing illustrations: First, eBay
(**www.ebay.com**), Priceline.com (**www.priceline.com**), and uBid.com (**www.ubid.
com**) are just three of the retailers with online auctions, featuring everything from
consumer electronics and textbooks to hotel rates and air fares. See Figure 6-11. Even
nonprofit Goodwill has an auction Web site (**www.shopgoodwill.com**) to sell
donated items. Second, Starbucks is offering high-speed wireless Internet service at
thousands of its outlets: "Travel at blazing speeds on the Internet—all from the comfort of your favorite cozy chair. With high-speed wireless Internet service from
T-Mobile HotSpot, your search for phone jacks is over and the opportunity to stay
connected has just begun. The T-Mobile HotSpot service at Starbucks gives you the
speed you need to quickly and easily check your E-mail, download that file you need
for your next meeting, surf the Web, and get work done in coffeehouse comfort."[21]

OTHER NONTRADITIONAL FORMS OF RETAILING

Two other nontraditional institutions merit discussion: video kiosks and airport
retailing. Although both formats have existed for years, they are now much more
noteworthy. They appeal to retailers' desires to use new technology (video kiosks)
and to locate in sites with high pedestrian traffic (airports).

Video Kiosks

Kiosks.org
(**www.kiosks.org**)
tracks the trends with
video kiosks.

The **video kiosk** is a freestanding, interactive, electronic computer terminal that
displays products and related information on a video screen; it often has a touch-
screen for consumers to make selections. Some kiosks are located in stores to
enhance customer service; others let consumers place orders, complete transactions (typically with a credit card), and arrange for shipping. Kiosks can be linked
to retailers' computer networks or to the Web. There are 2 million video kiosks in
use throughout the world, 750,000 of which are Internet-connected. In the United

States, they generate $5 billion in annual retail sales. Worldwide, it is estimated that kiosks *influence* $50 to $100 billion in retail sales—by providing product and warranty information, showing product assortments, displaying out-of-stock products, listing products by price, and so forth—and *generate* $8 billion in retail sales annually. North America accounts for the bulk of kiosk sales, followed by the Pacific Rim, Europe, and the rest of the world.[22]

How exactly do video kiosks work?

These kiosks are self-contained computing terminals that provide access to on-demand information and transactions. Some examples include airport self-check-in systems, retail product locators, and bill pay terminals. Interactive kiosks typically utilize a touchscreen for data entry, along with an on-screen keyboard and other peripherals, such as card readers and barcode scanners. A thermal printer is the most common output device. Some interactive kiosks are even equipped to burn custom CDs or DVDs on demand, or download multimedia files to handheld media players. Interactive kiosks may have a customized, hardened enclosure, or may simply be a standard PC that has been repurposed for interactive kiosk duties. Some kiosks even serve multiple purposes, e.g., a product catalog for customers and a job application center for potential employees. Kiosks may be found in a growing number of industries, including retail, automotive, education, food service, and banking.[23]

Video kiosks can be placed almost anywhere (from a store aisle to the lobby of a college dormitory to a hotel lobby), require few employees, and are an entertaining and easy way to shop. See Figure 6-12. Many shopping centers and individual

FIGURE 6-12
Borders' Title Sleuth Video Kiosk

At each of Borders' 500 book superstores, there are 5 to 10 Title Sleuth kiosks. Each week, nearly 1 million searches are conducted at these kiosks as customers track down the books they are most interested in buying. Shoppers can locate nearby stores that have their selections in stock or place an order for delivery.

Photo reprinted by permission.

stores are putting their space to better, more profitable use by setting up video kiosks in previously underutilized areas. These kiosks carry everything from gift certificates to concert tickets to airline tickets. Take the case of Best Buy, which has more than 9,000 kiosks in stores (ranging from 8 to 20 per store). Its kiosks provide shoppers with "easy access to a variety of products that Best Buy sells, deep product information, the ability to interact with digital products before purchasing them, and the ability to sign up for a variety of services (including broadband service, wireless plans, and digital cable). They are frequently used to access Bestbuy.com, as well. Often, a customer's interaction with a kiosk is supplemented by employee assistance. Employees like the kiosks because they offer the ability to showcase some of our exciting digital products and because they can easily sign customers up for services online."[24]

The average hardware cost to a retailer per video kiosk is $5,750. This does not include content development and kiosk maintenance. Hardware prices range from under $500 per kiosk to $10,000 to $15,000 per kiosk, depending on its functions—the more "bells and whistles," the higher the price.[25]

Airport Retailing

In the past, the leading airport retailers were fast-food outlets, tiny gift stores, and newspaper/magazine stands. Today, airports are a major mecca of retailing. At virtually every large airport, as well as at many medium ones, there are full-blown shopping areas. And most small airports have at least a fast-food retailer and vending machines for newspapers, candy, and so forth. See Figure 6-13.

The potential retail market is huge. U.S. airports alone fly up to 3 million passengers a day and employ nearly 2 million people (who often buy something for their personal use at the airport). There are almost 420 primary commercial U.S. airports, 31 of which are large hubs, 35 of which are medium hubs, 71 of which are small hubs, and 282 of which are nonhubs. Overall, U.S. airport retailing generates

New York's Kennedy Airport (**www.panynj. gov/aviation/jfkshopsframe. htm**) typifies the retailing environment at the world's major airports.

FIGURE 6-13
Airport Retailing and Borders

As airport retailing has grown, more nationally recognized retailers have located stores there. This Borders bookstore is situated at Orlando Airport in Florida.

Photo reprinted by permission of Susan Berry, Retail Image Consulting, Inc.

$6 billion in sales annually, and 10 airports have annual revenues of at least $50 million.[26] Consider this:

> At one of New York City's toniest retail venues, shoppers can browse in boutiques featuring merchandise from DKNY, H. Stern Jewelers, and Danish designer Sand. But these shoppers aren't on Fifth or Madison Avenues. They're at The Shops at Terminal 4, at John F. Kennedy International Airport, in Queens, NY. The Shops occupies 100,000 square feet at the 1.5-million-square-foot terminal. Those involved with the project say they are particularly impressed by the success of its high-end offerings, which may extend its reach beyond the typical airport retail customers—travelers, meeters and greeters, and employees—to the surrounding neighborhood. A key factor toward this goal is the fact that shoppers do not need to pass through security checkpoints to reach The Shops.[27]

These are some of the distinctive features of airport retailing:

- There is a large group of prospective shoppers. In an average year, a big airport may have 20 million people passing through its concourses. In contrast, a typical regional shopping mall attracts 5 million to 6 million annual visits.
- Air travelers are a temporarily captive audience at the airport and looking to fill their waiting time, which could be up to several hours. They tend to have above-average incomes.
- Sales per square foot of retail space are much higher than at regional malls. Rent is about 20 to 30 percent higher per square foot for airport retailers.
- Airport stores are smaller, carry fewer items, and have higher prices than traditional stores.
- Replenishing merchandise and stocking shelves may be difficult at airport stores because they are physically removed from delivery areas and space is limited.
- The sales of gift items and forgotten travel items, from travelers not having the time to shop elsewhere, are excellent. Brookstone, which sells garment bags and travel clocks at airport shops, calls these products "I forgot" merchandise.
- Passengers are at airports at all times of the day. Thus, longer store hours are possible.
- International travelers are often interested in duty-free shopping.
- There is much tighter security at airports than before, which has had a dampening effect on some shopping.

Summary

1. *To contrast single-channel and multi-channel retailing.* A new retailer often relies on single-channel retailing, whereby it sells to consumers through one retail format. As the firm grows, it may turn to multi-channel retailing and sell to consumers through multiple retail formats. This allows the firm to reach different customers, share costs among various formats, and diversify its supplier base.

2. *To look at the characteristics of the three major retail institutions involved with nonstore-based strategy* mixes: *direct marketing, direct selling, and vending machines—with an emphasis on direct marketing.* Firms employ nonstore retailing to reach customers and complete transactions. Nonstore retailing encompasses direct marketing, direct selling, and vending machines.

In direct marketing, a consumer is exposed to a good or service through a nonpersonal medium and orders by mail, phone, fax, or computer. Annual U.S. retail sales from direct marketing exceed $300 billion. Direct marketers fall into two categories: general and specialty. Among the strengths of direct marketing are its reduced operating costs, large geographic coverage, customer convenience, and targeted segments. Among the weaknesses are the shopper's inability to examine items before purchase, the costs of printing and mailing, the low response rate, and marketplace clutter. Under the "30-day rule," there are legal requirements that a firm must follow as to shipping speed. The long-run prospects for direct marketing are strong due to consumer interest in reduced shopping time, 24-hour ordering, the sales of well-known brands, improvements in operating efficiency, and technology.

The key to successful direct marketing is the customer data base, with data-base retailing being a way to collect, store, and use relevant information. Several trends are vital to direct marketers: their attitudes and activities, changing consumer lifestyles, increased competition, the use of dual distribution, the roles for catalogs and TV, technological advances, and the growth in global direct marketing. Specialogs and infomercials are two tools being used more by direct marketers.

A direct marketing plan has eight stages: business definition, generating customers, media selection, presenting the message, customer contact, customer response, order fulfillment, and measuring results and maintaining the data base. Firms must consider that many people dislike shopping this way, feel overwhelmed by the amount of direct mail, and are concerned about privacy.

Direct selling includes personal contact with consumers in their homes (and other nonstore sites) and phone calls by the seller. It yields $31 billion in annual U.S. retail sales, covering many goods and services. The strategy mix stresses convenience, a personal touch, demonstrations, and relaxed consumers. U.S. sales are not going up much due to the rise in working women, the labor intensity of the business, sales force turnover, government rules, and the poor image of some firms.

A vending machine uses coin- and card-operated dispensing of goods and services. It eliminates salespeople, allows 24-hour sales, and may be put almost anywhere. Beverages and food represent 95 percent of the $45 billion in annual U.S. vending revenues. Efforts in other product categories have met with customer resistance, and items priced above $1.50 have not done well.

3. *To explore the emergence of electronic retailing through the World Wide Web.* The Internet is a global electronic superhighway that acts as a single, cooperative virtual network. The World Wide Web (Web) is a way to access information on the Internet, whereby people turn their computers into interactive multimedia centers. The Web can serve one or more retailer purposes, from projecting an image to presenting information to investors. The purpose chosen depends on the goals and focus. There is a great contrast between store retailing and Web retailing.

The growth of Web-based retailing has been enormous. U.S. revenues from retailing on the Web were expected to surpass $100 billion in 2006. Nonetheless, the Web still garners only 3 to 4 percent of total U.S. retail sales.

Somewhat more females than males shop on the Web. Web usage declines by age group and increases by income and education level. Shoppers are attracted by convenience, prices, and selection. Nonshoppers worry about the trustworthiness of online firms, want to see and handle products first, and do not like shipping cost surprises.

The Web offers these positive features for retailers: It can be inexpensive to have a Web site. The potential marketplace is huge and dispersed, yet easy to reach. Sites can be quite exciting. People can visit a site at any time. Information can be targeted. A customer data base can be established and customer feedback obtained. Yet, if consumers do not know a firm's Web address, it may be hard to find. Many people will not buy online. There is clutter with regard to the number of retail sites. Because Web surfers are easily bored, a firm must regularly update its site to ensure repeat visits. The more multimedia features a site has, the slower it may be to access. Some firms have been deluged with customer service requests. Improvements are needed to coordinate store and Web transactions. There are few standards or rules as to what may be portrayed at Web sites. Consumers expect online services to be free and are reluctant to pay for them.

A Web strategy can move through five stages: brochure site, commerce site, site integrated with existing processes, "Webified" store, and site integrated with manufacturer systems.

4. *To discuss two other nontraditional forms of retailing: video kiosks and airport retailing.* The video kiosk is a freestanding, interactive computer terminal that displays products and other information on a video screen; it often has a touchscreen for people to make selections. Although some kiosks are in stores to upgrade customer service, others let consumers place orders, complete transactions, and arrange shipping. Kiosks can be put almost anywhere, require few personnel, and are an entertaining and easy way for people to shop. They yield $5 billion in annual U.S. revenues.

Due to the huge size of the air travel marketplace, airports are popular as retail shopping areas. Travelers (and workers) are temporarily captive at the airport, often with a lot of time to fill. Sales per square foot, as well as rent, are high. Gift items and "I forgot" merchandise sell especially well. Annual retail revenues are $6 billion at U.S. airports.

Key Terms

single-channel retailing (p. 154)
multi-channel retailing (p. 154)
nonstore retailing (p. 155)
direct marketing (p. 155)
data-base retailing (p. 158)

specialog (p. 160)
infomercial (p. 160)
direct selling (p. 165)
vending machine (p. 167)
Internet (p. 168)

World Wide Web (Web) (p. 168)
video kiosk (p. 176)

Questions for Discussion

1. Contrast single-channel and multi-channel retailing. What do you think are the advantages of each?
2. Do you think nonstore retailing will continue to grow faster than store-based retailing? Explain your answer.
3. How would you increase a direct marketer's response rate from less than 1 percent of those receiving E-mail sales offers by the firm to 3 percent?
4. Explain the "30-day rule" for direct marketers.
5. What are the two main decisions to be made in the business definition stage of planning a direct marketing strategy?
6. How should Amazon.com handle consumer concerns about their privacy?
7. Differentiate between direct selling and direct marketing. What are the strengths and weaknesses of each?
8. Select a product not heavily sold through vending machines and present a brief plan for doing so.
9. From a consumer's perspective, what are the advantages and disadvantages of the World Wide Web?
10. From a retailer's perspective, what are the advantages and disadvantages of having a Web site?
11. What must retailers do to improve customer service on the Web?
12. What future role do you see for video kiosks? Why?

Web-Based Exercise

Visit the Stats Toolbox section of ClickZ's Web site (**www.clickz.com/stats/stats_toolbox**). Describe four key facts that a retailer could learn from this site.

Note: Stop by our Web site (**www.prenhall.com/ bermanevans**) to experience a number of highly interactive, appealing Web exercises based on actual company demonstrations and sample materials related to retailing.

Chapter Endnotes

1. Various company sources.
2. "Retail Web Sites Are Powerful Drivers of In-Store Sales, Brand Loyalty, and Customer Satisfaction, Says Groundbreaking Study of Multi-Channel Shoppers," *Business Wire* (January 19, 2005).
3. "Quarterly Retail E-Commerce Sales: 1st Quarter 2006" (Washington, DC: U.S. Department of Commerce, 2006).
4. Direct Marketing Association, *Economic Impact: Direct Marketing in 30 Countries Worldwide* (New York: DMA, 2002).
5. Sherry Chiger, "Consumer Catalog Shopping Survey: Parts I to III," *Catalog Age* (August, October, and November 2001).
6. "Direct Marketing: An Aspect of Total Marketing," *Direct Marketing* (March 2004), p. 2.

7. "Data-Base Marketing Defined," **www.itsallgood webdesign.com/html/database_marketing.html** (March 11, 2006).

8. "Bloomingdale's—Our History," **www.blooming dales.com/media/about/history.jsp** (March 12, 2006).

9. "QVC Corporate Facts," **www.qvc.com/mainhqfact. html** (March 19, 2006); and "HSN Company Info," **www.hsn.com/corp/info/default.aspx** (March 19, 2006).

10. "Direct Marketing Associations Around the World," **www.the-dma.org/affiliates/dmintl.shtml** (as of 2003); "Federation of European Direct and Interactive Marketing Press Pack," **www.fedma.org/img/db/ PressPackJan2005.pdf** (January 2005); and "Japanese Shopping Channel to Debut in Korea," **www.atimes. com** (June 10, 2005).

11. *2005 Direct Selling Industrywide Growth & Outlook Survey* (Washington, DC: Direct Selling Association, 2005); and "Worldwide Direct Sales Data," **www. wfdsa.org** (April 28, 2005).

12. "About Vending," **www.vending.org/vending/index. php?page=main** (February 19, 2006); and "Vending Industry Trends," **www.vencoa.com/vending_trends. html** (December 19, 2005).

13. "Online Global Populations," **www.clickz.com/stats/ statstoolbox** (March 16, 2005); "The Top 400 Guide," **http://internetretailer.com/article.asp?id= 15099** (June 2005); Bart Kittle, "Online Christmas 2004: Tenth Anniversary Celebration," *Retail Education Today* (May 2005), pp. 12–19; and "More Than Two-Thirds of Online Retail Purchases Are Transacted via Broadband," **www.nielsen-netratings.com/pr/ pr_050119.pdf** (January 19, 2005).

14. Melissa L. Jones, "Christmas Shopping Often Means Braving Malls and Battling Crowds," *Arkansas Democrat-Gazette Online* (January 16, 2005).

15. Susan Reda, "Research Probes Links Between Online Satisfaction and Customer Loyalty," *Stores* (August 1999), p. 65.

16. Tracy Mullin, "Determining Web Presence," *Chain Store Age* (October 1999), p. 42.

17. Jodi Mardesich, "The Web Is No Shopper's Paradise," *Fortune* (November 8, 1999), pp. 188–198.

18. "Amazon.com, Inc." **www.hoovers.com/co/capsule/ 3/0,2163,51493,00.html** (November 17, 2005).

19. Isabel M. Isidiro, "Riding High on the Wagon of Success: RedWagons.com," **www.powerhomebiz. com/OnlineSuccess/redwagons.htm** (October 9, 2005).

20. "About Netflix," **www.netflix.com/PressRoom?id= 1005** (January 11, 2006).

21. "High-Speed Internet Access at Starbucks," **www. starbucks.com/retail/wireless.asp** (January 11, 2006).

22. Authors' projections, based on "Stats N' Facts Research Area," **www.kiomag.com/statfactoptions** (January 18, 2006); and *Kiosk Industry Sector Report—Retail* (Rockville, MD: Summit Research Associates, September 2004).

23. "Interactive Kiosks," **www.wirespring.com/ Solutions/interactive_kiosks.html** (February 23, 2006).

24. "On Dasher! On Dancer! On Kiosk!" **www. kioskmarketplace.com/mag.php** (January–February 2005).

25. Vineeta Kommineni, "State of the Retail Kiosk Market," **www.kioskmarketplace.com/mag.php** (May–June 2004).

26. Authors' projections, based on *The Economic Impact of U.S. Airports* (Washington, DC: Airports Council International—North America, 2002); and *Airport Revenue News 2005 Fact Book*.

27. Jacqueline T. DeLise, "Elaborate Retail Environments Taking Off at U.S. Airports," *Brandweek* (April 10, 2000).

Appendix on Multi-Channel Retailing*

As we noted at the beginning of Chapter 6, a retail firm relies on single-channel retailing if it sells to consumers through one format. A firm uses multi-channel retailing if it sells to consumers through multiple formats. We devote this appendix to multi-channel retailing because so many firms are combining store and non-store retailing—as well as using multiple store formats.

*The material in this appendix is adapted by the authors from Barry Berman and Shawn Thelen, "A Guide to Developing and Managing a Well-Integrated Multi-Channel Retail Strategy," *International Journal of Retail & Distribution Management*, Vol. 32 (Number 3, 2004), pp. 147–156. Reprinted by permission of Barry Berman and Shawn Thelen.

Multi-channel retailing enables consumers to conveniently shop in a number of different ways, including stores, catalogs, a Web site, kiosks, and even PDAs (personal digital assistants) with Web access. Some firms have even developed advanced multi-channel retailing systems that enable consumers to examine products at one format, buy them at another format, and pick them up—and possibly return them—at a third format. Consider REI:

> Millions of hiking, climbing, camping, and paddling enthusiasts make Recreational Equipment, Inc. (REI) their first stop whenever they head for the great outdoors. An important factor behind the success of REI has been its efforts to make itself as accessible as possible to customers through multiple shopping channels. The firm has retail stores in 25 states and Washington, D.C., an online store at **www.rei.com**, a Web-based discount outlet at **www.rei-outlet.com**, a call center, and catalog sales. While there is no doubt as to the success of REI's online business, the firm has focused on synchronizing its retail channels rather than pitting them against each other. In the recent enhancement of its Web site, REI deployed an in-store pickup service for items ordered on the Web and a multi-channel gift registry to involve customers in both online and brick-and-mortar stores.[1]

In recognition of the increasing importance of multi-channel retailing, *Catalog Age* was recently renamed and repositioned as *Multi-Channel Merchant* (**www.multichannel merchant.com**).

Planning and maintaining a well-integrated multi-channel strategy is not easy. At a minimum, it requires setting up an infrastructure that can effectively link multiple channels. A retailer that accepts a Web purchase for exchange at a retail store needs an information system to verify the purchase, the price paid, the method of payment, and the date of the transaction. That firm also needs a mechanism for delivering goods regardless of which channel was used by a customer to purchase the goods.

These are just some of the strategic and operational issues for multi-channel retailers to address:

- What multi-channel cross-selling opportunities exist? A firm could list its Web site on its business cards, store invoices, and shopping bags. It could also list the nearest store locations when a consumer inputs a ZIP code at the Web site.
- How should the product assortment/variety strategy be adapted to each channel? How much merchandise overlap should exist across channels?
- Should prices be consistent across channels (except for shipping and handling, as well as closeouts)?
- How can a consistent image be devised and sustained across all channels?
- What is the role of each channel? Some consumers prefer to search the Web to determine pricing and product information, and then they purchase in a store due to their desire to see the product, try it on, and gain the immediacy that accompanies an in-store transaction.
- What are the best opportunities for leveraging a firm's assets through a multi-channel strategy? Many catalog-based retailers have logistics systems that can be easily adapted to Web-based sales.
- Do relationships with current suppliers prevent the firm from expanding into new channels?

ADVANTAGES OF MULTI-CHANNEL RETAIL STRATEGIES

There are several advantages to a retailer's enacting a multi-channel approach, including the selection of specific channels based upon their unique strengths, opportunities to leverage assets, and opportunities for increased sales and profits by appealing to multi-channel shoppers.

Selecting Among Multiple Channels Based on Their Unique Strengths

A retailer with a multi-channel strategy can use the most appropriate channels to sell particular goods or services or to reach different target markets. Because each channel has a unique combination of strengths, a multi-channel retailer has the best opportunities to fulfill its customers' shopping desires.

Store-based shopping enables customers to see an item, feel it, smell it (e.g., candles or perfumes), try it out, and then pick it up and take it home on the same shopping trip without incurring shipping and handling costs. Catalogs offer high visual impact, a high-quality image, and portability (they can be taken anywhere by the shopper). The Web offers high-quality video/audio capabilities, an interactive format, a personalized customer interface, virtually unlimited space, the ability for a customer to verify in-stock position and order status, and, in some cases, tax-free shopping. In-store kiosks are helpful for shoppers not having Web access, can lead to less inventory in the store (and reduce the need to stock low-turnover items in each store), facilitate self-service by providing information, and offer high video/audio quality.

To plan an appropriate channel mix and the role of each channel, retailers must recognize how different channels complement one another. J.C. Penney (**www.jcpenney.com**) posts circulars on its Web site for consumers to use in stores, and it has a broader selection of items such as small appliances in catalogs to encourage consumers to shop in multiple ways.

Opportunities to Leverage Assets

Multi-channel retailing presents opportunities for firms to leverage both tangible assets and intangible assets. A store-based retailer can leverage tangible assets by using excess capacity in its warehouse to service catalog or Web sales; and that same firm can leverage its well-known brand name (an intangible asset) by selling online in geographic areas where it has no stores.

Retailers can work with channel partners to leverage their collective assets. Under a strategic partnership between Office Depot (**www.officedepot.com**) and Amazon.com (**www.amazon.com**), Amazon.com processes customer transactions (including credit-card processing) and develops and maintains the Web site. Office Depot manages its own inventory and handles all order fulfillment activities. In addition, merchandise ordered online can be picked up at Office Depot's U.S. stores.

Opportunities for Increased Sales and Profits by Appealing to Multi-Channel Shoppers

Research indicates that multi-channel consumers spend more than those who confine their shopping to a single channel. At J.C. Penney, customers who only shop online spend $150 per year, those who only shop in a Penney store spend $195, and those who shop only by catalog spend $200. Penney customers who shop at all three channels spend nearly $900 yearly. At Saks Fifth Avenue, customers who shop at both Saks.com and a Saks store spend five times as much annually as those who shop at just one channel.[2]

Multi-channel shoppers may also be quite profitable. According to an Aberdeen Group (**www.aberdeen.com**) report, *Multi-Channel Retailers Must Integrate Their Enterprises*, "60 percent of retailers see more profit from multi-channel customers than from their single-channel counterparts. The difference is significant: On average, multi-channel customers are 20 to 25 percent more profitable."[3]

DEVELOPING A WELL-INTEGRATED MULTI-CHANNEL STRATEGY

A well-integrated multi-channel strategy requires linkages among all of the channels. Customers should be able to easily make the transition from looking up products on the Web or in a catalog to picking up the products in a retail store. There should be some commonality in the description and appearance of each item regardless of channel. In-store personnel should be able to verify a Web or catalog purchase and arrange for returns or exchanges. At Brooks Brothers' Web site (**www.brooksbrothers.com**), shoppers can access copies of catalogs by page number. In addition, salespeople in the stores have copies of the catalogs available so that customers can place orders for items not carried in that particular outlet.

These are characteristics common to superior multi-channel strategies: integrated promotions across channels; product consistency across channels; an integrated information system that shares customer, pricing, and inventory data across multiple channels; a store pickup process for items purchased on the Web or through a catalog; and the search for multi-channel opportunities with appropriate partners.

Integrating Promotions Across Channels

Cross promotion enables consumers to use each promotional forum in its best light. Here is a list of some cross-promotion tactics:

- Include the Web site address on shopping bags, in catalogs, and in newspaper ads.
- Use in-store kiosks so customers can order out-of-stock merchandise without a shipping fee.
- Include store addresses, phone numbers, hours, and directions on the Web site and in catalogs.
- Make it possible for customers to shop for items on the Web using the catalog order numbers.
- Distribute store coupons by direct mail and online; and offer catalogs in stores and at the Web site.
- Target single-channel customers with promotions from other channels.
- Send store-based shoppers targeted E-mails (on an opt-in basis) for selected goods and services.

Ensuring Product Consistency Across Channels

Too little product overlap across channels may result in an inconsistent image. However, too much overlap may result in the loss of sales opportunities. For example, although separate buyers and inventory are used with Macy's Web site (**www.macys.com**), all items featured online must be available for sale in at least one Macy's store division. A senior vice-president at Macys.com says that, "The online shopper comes to Macys.com with a mission, a gift to buy or something she needs. It would be neither practical nor profitable to have the same four million stock-keeping units online as we have in the stores. We have to cater to the needs of the online customer if we intend to grow this business."[4]

Multi-channel retailers often use the Web as a way to offer highly specialized merchandise that cannot be profitably offered in store units. For example, at its Web site, Wal-Mart (**www.walmart.com**) complements store sales by selling a greater assortment in such merchandise categories as books, furniture, and jewelry. Some companies offer products online that are not featured in their traditional outlets to reach the same customer base without increasing the cost of operating their stores, such as the Victoria's Secret Web site (**www.victoriassecret.com**) offering apparel and shoes not found in its stores.

Having an Information System That Effectively Shares Data Across Channels

To effectively manage a multi-channel system, a retailer needs an information system that shares customer, pricing, and inventory information across channels:

● REI relies on IBM's WebSphere platform to better utilize its Web site. It can refer new online shoppers to a local store. A person who buys a backpack in a store can also be contacted by E-mail with an offer of a discount on a sleeping bag that can be applied to an online or store-based purchase.

● Home Depot (**www.homedepot.com**) customers in Las Vegas can confirm if a power tool they want to buy is in stock at a particular store in their area.

● Circuit City (**www.circuitcity.com**) and CompUSA (**www.compusa.com**) have Web sites that enable shoppers to not only confirm whether a good is in stock but also set up in-store pickup.

Enacting a Store Pickup Process for Items Purchased on the Web or Through a Catalog

In-store pickup requires that a retailer's inventory data base be integrated and that the firm has a logistics infrastructure that can pick and route merchandise to customers. Increasingly, shoppers order big-ticket items such as digital cameras, computers, and appliances online but pick them up at nearby stores. Consumers favor this approach to avoid shipping and handling charges, to reduce their having to navigate through a large box store, and to avoid wasting time looking for items that may be out of stock. Store pickup also enables shoppers to get items on the same day they are bought.

A recent survey found that more than 80 percent of U.S. consumers who had utilized multi-channel retailers' "Web-to-store" shopping services rated them as good or excellent. Nonetheless, one-third of shoppers reported waiting more than 10 minutes to collect an item. They were willing to accept shoddy service when using online and offline channels in one purchase. They expected seamless shopping.[5]

Searching for Multi-Channel Opportunities with Appropriate Partners

The retailer needs to understand that in almost all cases a multi-channel strategy requires additional resources and competencies that are significantly greater than those demanded by a single-channel strategy. While some retailers may conclude that they do not have these competencies or resources, others look for strategic partnerships with firms having complementary resources.

Besides Office Depot, Amazon.com also has alliances with Babies "R" Us (**www.babiesrus.com**), Target (**www.target.com**), and Toys "R" Us (**www.toysrus.com**)—and others. These firms share tasks and communicate electronically with one another.

SPECIAL CHALLENGES

A multi-channel strategy is not appropriate for every retailer. Not all retailers possess the financial and managerial resources to do so—or have the same potential synergies.

According to consulting firm Retail Forward:

> Once it became clear that online sales were not going to displace stores, retailers began developing online features that enabled customers to use the Web not just as a place to buy, but as a place to shop. But even the largest retailers have only deployed a few of the multi-channel features customers expect. There's a lot of room for improvement just to satisfy customers today and with broadband access on the rise—and customer expectations along with it—retailers have to take a new look at their Web sites and stores—and the space in between them.

- *Multi-channel gaps plague all retail categories.* In an audit of leading multi-channel retailers, not a single one met more than one-half of the criteria associated with a state-of-the-art multi-channel shopping experience.
- *Different strokes for different folks.* There isn't just one "perfect" multi-channel experience. Each retail channel will use the Web differently to influence store shopping, with "high touch" retailers focusing on customer service while commodity brokers better align supply and demand.
- *Manufacturers get into the multi-channel game.* Many manufacturers tried—and failed—to sell products directly online during the early era of E-commerce, but the more advanced thinkers began using their Web site and retail partners' stores to create multi-channel experiences.
- *Consumer expectations grow with broadband adoption.* No doubt about it, broadband penetration is on the rise, with tens of millions of Americans surfing the Web from home using cable, DSL, and satellite. Retailers have a new opportunity to take advantage of high-speed, always-on Internet access in developing the multi-channel experience.[6]

Appendix Endnotes

1. "REI Optimizes Sales with Cross-Channel Commerce Solution," **http://www-306.ibm.com/software/success/cssdb.nsf/CS/BEMY-5ZZM2L?OpenDocument&Site=software** (March 7, 2006).

2. Kortney Stringer, "Style & Substance: Shoppers Who Blend Store, Catalog, and Web Spend," *Wall Street Journal* (September 3, 2004), p. A7; and John Gaffney, "Finding the Right Fit," **www.1to1.com/View.aspx?DocID=28740** (March 2005).

3. Joshua Weinberger, "Multi-Channel Customers Are More Profitable, Analysts Say," **www.destinationcrm. com/default.asp?NewsID=4415** (September 8, 2004).

4. Susan Reda, "Retailers Take Multi-Faceted Approaches to Multi-Channel Success," *Stores* (June 2003), pp. 22–26.

5. Claire Armitt, "Multi-Channel Retailing Proves to Be a Hit with U.S. Consumers," *New Media Age* (January 27, 2005), p. 13.

6. Retail Forward, "Multi-Channel Retailing Benchmarks & Best Practices," *Industry Outlook* (May 2004), pp. 1–2.

part two
Short Cases

CASE 1: THE STRONG COMEBACK OF SMALL RETAILERS[c-1]

Even though some small retailers and many mid-sized chains have been forced out of business by successful big-box chains (such as Wal-Mart and Best Buy) and Web retailers (such as Amazon), many small retailers have survived and even thrived. According to an analyst at one consulting firm, "We see Wal-Mart around for generations to come. But we're seeing on a daily basis a shift in consciousness that there are other choices, that it's not always about the lowest price." In a recent survey of shoppers, 45 percent of respondents said they would pay more for products if they could shop in a nicer environment.

Adds the president of another consulting firm, "Wal-Mart's influence over shoppers has peaked. Maybe consumers need to go to big-box retailers to buy toilet paper, cat food, and such everyday items. But shopping is about more than necessities. More consumers today look for products and experiences that are more unique, more stylish, and more sensory than what Wal-Mart has."

One indication that smaller stores are economically viable is the recent growth of specialty stores in several industries. In 2000, 8 percent of survey respondents stated that they made clothing purchases at specialty stores. By 2005, that percentage grew to more than 21 percent.

Let's look at the strategies used by successful small and mid-sized chains. They:

- Use a niche strategy that Wal-Mart cannot copy. Jim Baum, author of *Challenges of the Future: The Rebirth of the Small Independent Retailer in America*, found that his hometown's best retailers included a fabric store that sells crafts and quilting and gift shops with specialty items. And although 30 percent of all toy dollars go to Wal-Mart, smaller toy stores with unique goods and merchandising strategies can still successfully attract shoppers.
- Offer personalization and customization opportunities. American Girl (www.americangirl.com) and Build-A-Bear Workshop (www.buildabear.com) are among the most successful toy retailers due to their offering customized products. Build-A-Bear lets shoppers choose an animal "skin," watch as it is filled and then dressed, and lets the shopper sign its birth certificate. "Shopping will be more fun if there are more interactive places like Build-A-Bear Workshop," says the firm's "chief executive bear."

- Offer products that discounters do not stock. Many retailers have developed partnerships with leading designers. For example, H&M (www.hm.com), a Swedish clothing chain, sells a line of clothing designed by Karl Lagerfeld. Bath & Body Works (www.bbw.com) sells a $25 Henri Bendel scented candle. Whole Foods (www.wholefoods.com) is very successful selling organic products and ready-to-heat specialty items that traditional groceries do not stock.
- Develop and implement a multi channel strategy. According to a consultant with Kurt Salmon Associates, retailers with store, catalog, and Web operations have significant advantages over single channel-based retailers. To properly implement a multi-channel strategy, some retailers are hiring fulfillment specialists to overcome picking and shipping concerns. Others are using software to reduce downloading time and to facilitate the overall online buying experience.

Questions

1. Discuss the competitive advantages of smaller retail chains as contrasted with large retail chains.
2. What factors could explain the increased popularity of specialty stores in many sectors of retailing?
3. Describe the pros and cons of a smaller retailer's pursuit of a niche strategy.
4. What are the advantages and disadvantages of a retailer's switching from a bricks-only to a bricks-and-clicks (multi-channel) strategy?

CASE 2: SUBWAY IN CHINA: NOT SO EASY[c-2]

In Beijing, Jim Bryant is known as the Franchise King. His office is decorated with awards for being Subway's (www.subway.com) Top International Franchise Salesperson 1997, Highest Percentage Increase in Unit Sales 2002, and Most Franchises Sold in Asia June 2003 to March 2004. Subway is the third-largest U.S. fast-food chain in China, after McDonald's and KFC.

Even though many franchisors have been lured to China by its 1.3 billion people and its strong economy, the Chinese market is an especially difficult one. Many firms—including A&W, Chili's Grill & Bar, Dunkin' Donuts, and Rainforest Café—have closed their stores. And while Bryant has opened 19 Subway stores in Beijing over the past decade, his quota for the time period was 38 stores. Bryant says Subway has charged him $2,000 as damages for not opening the required number of restaurants.

Jim Bryant started doing business in China in the 1970s when he set up a shoe-manufacturing factory in Datong, China's northern coal capital. In 1974, he signed an agreement to be Subway's representative in China. Bryant would be responsible for recruiting local entrepreneurs to become

[c-1]The material in this case is drawn from Amy Tsao, "Retail's Little Guys Come Back," *Business Week Online* (November 22, 2004); and "Build-A-Bear's Fuzzy Future," *Kiplinger's Personal Finance Magazine* (March 2005), p. 67.

[c-2]The material in this case is drawn from Carlye Adler, "How China Eats a Sandwich," *Fortune* (March 21, 2005), pp. F210B–F210D.

Subway franchisees and act as a liaison between the franchisee and Subway. As compensation, Bryant would receive half of the initial $10,000 franchising fee and one-third of the 8 percent royalty fee paid to Subway. Bryant also received the rights to open his own Subway sandwich shops.

Although many Subway restaurants were immediately popular among Americans, the Chinese were confused by the choices. Bryant reduced the confusion by printing signs that explained how to order. Many locals also did not believe that Subway's tuna fish was made from a fish since they could not see the fish's head or tail. Unlike other chains such as KFC that offers shredded carrots, fungus, or bamboo shoots, Subway did not tailor its menus to appeal to the Chinese tastes. According to a Subway franchisee, "Subway should have at least one item tailored to Chinese tastes to show that they are respecting the local culture."

There are a host of other potential difficulties doing business in China. Some franchisees refused to adapt to the franchisor's requirements for consistency. One of Subway's earliest franchisees decided, for example, to change the restaurant's colors and name. Construction costs were severely underestimated on one job. And in a third property, the franchisee was locked out of a location even though it had six months remaining on its lease. Apparently, the property owner found a new tenant who paid two years' rent up front. Now Bryant will only sign leases with business entities, not individuals.

Bryant is currently considering whether to sell his stores and the rights to develop Beijing. Like many entrepreneurs, while he enjoys building a business, he does not like his role of inspecting stores for overall cleanliness, recipe consistency, and décor: "I don't like pruning the tree. I like to plant the seed and watch it grow."

Questions

1. Describe the pros and cons of a Chinese businessperson's investing in a Subway franchise.
2. What are the pros and cons of Subway's developing its own stores versus using franchising as a means of selling to the China market?
3. Should Subway modify its menu to meet Chinese tastes? If yes, how? Explain your answer.
4. Why does a franchisor commonly penalize master franchisees such as Bryant when they do not develop sufficient franchises within a given timetable?

CASE 3: TRADER JOE'S DISTINCTIVE APPROACH[c-3]

In 1979, Joe Coulombe sold Trader Joe's (**www.traderjoes. com**), the chain he started in Southern California, to the German-based Albrecht family (which owns more than 700

[c-3]The material in this case is drawn from Wilbert Jones, "Not Your Average Joe," *Prepared Foods* (June 2004), pp. 29–31; Deborah Kolben, "A Trader Joe's Is on Menu for Brooklyn," *Daily News* (February 17, 2005); and "Where Is Trader Joe's?" **www.traderjoes. com/locations/index.asp** (February 19, 2006).

Aldi supermarkets in the United States and 11 percent of Albertson's, an Idaho-based supermarket chain). Trader Joe's now has 250 stores in 20 states nationwide; and while the company does not disclose its sales, they have been estimated at more than $2 billion annually.

Trader Joe's mission is to provide its customers with the best food and beverage values anywhere. It also seeks to provide nutritional and product information so its customers can make informed decisions. According to Trader Joe's vice-president of marketing, "We keep our promise, which means continuing to deliver interesting, high-quality foods at very good prices. Trader Joe's brand isn't about the products; it's about the customer experience. Our employees are friendly and very knowledgeable about the products." Unlike a typical supermarket with 25,000 or more different products and 60,000 square feet of space, the average Trader Joe's sells 3,000 products in stores that range in size from 8,000 to 15,000 square feet.

There are several cornerstones to Trader Joe's overall retail strategy. These include the importance of customer service, private labels, high sales of imported and organic foods, and use of word-of-mouth promotions.

Trader Joe's really cares about customer service. The chain was among the first to have its cashiers ask all customers if they found everything they wanted. Cashiers are even trained to leave their post and get an item a shopper cannot locate. All items in the store have an unconditional "no questions asked" money-back guarantee. Many stores also feature a sampling area where consumers can snack on freshly prepared products.

About 80 percent of the products at Trader Joe's are private label. Jokingly, it changes its name to "Trader Ming," "Trader Jacques," and "Trader Giotto" depending upon the origin associated with the product. The private-label strategy enables Trader Joe's to achieve store loyalty through product loyalty and to have more power in negotiations with vendors. All of its products are purchased directly from suppliers, not intermediaries. Trader Joe's uses this strategy to reduce costs.

About 20 percent of Trader Joe's suppliers are located overseas. This enables the chain to have distinctive products such as unique pastas imported from Italy, grape leaves from Greece, Eastern European jams and jellies, and French dessert items. Distinctive merchandise sourcing is a difficult strategy for competitors to copy.

Thirty percent of Trader Joe's products are organic. These include bakery items, beverages, cereals, dried fruits and nuts, snacks, and produce. Although other supermarkets such as Whole Foods (**www.wholefoods.com**) and Wild Oats (**www.wildoats.com**) also sell organic foods, Trader Joe's sells these items for 25 to 30 percent less.

Unlike traditional supermarkets that build store traffic with their freestanding advertising inserts and coupon offers, Trader Joe's promotional strategy relies on its quarterly *Fearless Flyer*. This is sent via mail and distributed in its stores. *Fearless Flyer* outlines the features of specific products with a quirky sense of humor. Otherwise, most of Trader Joe's communication is based on word of mouth.

Questions

1. What retail classification in Table 5-1 best fits Trader Joe's store-based strategy mix? Explain your answer.
2. Describe the vertical marketing system used by Trader Joe's.
3. How can a traditional supermarket effectively compete against Trader Joe's?
4. How can Trader Joe's most effectively use the Web?

CASE 4: ONLINE SNAPFISH SEEKS AN OFFLINE PRESENCE[C-4]

With its base of more than 15 million customers, Snapfish (**www.snapfish.com**), an online photofinishing retailer, is firmly entrenched as a major firm in its industry. Snapfish was recently acquired by Hewlett-Packard.

Like many of its competitors, Snapfish enables users to upload or E-mail digital photos and to enhance photos by changing color photos to black and white, by lightening dark images, and by cropping out unwanted images. It also lets users store photos online so they can be ordered by friends and family members. Through its guest book, friends and family members can communicate about the shared photos.

In August 2004, Snapfish opened its first store in suburban Alexandria, Virginia. According to Snapfish's president, "We want to showcase how online and retail can work together." This 1,500-square-foot store, which is located between a drugstore and a restaurant, offers a full line of accessories that go with prints—such as aprons, calendars, key chains, and T-shirts. The store also enables customers to pick up prints at this store that were sent to Snapfish electronically from their home or office.

To expand its store presence, Snapfish is seeking a retail partner such as Costco, Kroger, Target, or Wal-Mart. This would help Snapfish capitalize on the recent growth in ownership of digital cameras, which expanded from 4 percent of all households in 1999 to more than 40 percent of households

in 2005. And the Photo Marketing Association International forecasts that market penetration for digital cameras will continue to expand. While the percent of digital prints processed online has remained flat (at 7.0 percent in 2005 as compared with 6.6 percent in 2003), about 40 percent of digital printing was conducted at retail locations (including self-service kiosks) in 2005 (up from 16 percent in 2003). During the 2003 to 2005 time period, the percent of digital printing done at home dropped from 76 percent to 52 percent. Neither of Snapfish's major competitors, Ofoto (**www.ofoto.com**), a subsidiary of Kodak, and Shutterfly (**www.shutterfly.com**) have store-based locations.

Both Wal-Mart (**www.walmart.com**), the market share leader in on-premises photo processing, and Walgreens (**www.walgreens.com**), the second largest store-based photofinishing firm, currently serve digital customers. Walgreens has installed digital minilabs in one-half of its stores in the past two years; and almost all of its stores offer self-service digital kiosks where consumers can enlarge, crop, edit, and print digital prints. Walgreens also lets customers upload digital photos to its Web site for processing. A partnership with these firms is unlikely.

According to a consultant with a digital photography marketing research firm, mass merchant retailers will decline to partner with Snapfish: "For Snapfish to be setting up a portion of a retailer's footprint—that's a very creative idea that's a little far out for the current market. For starters, these merchants have long-term partnerships with Fuji and Kodak, which also manufacture the digital minilabs now being installed at most retail locations." That consultant speculates that retailers who currently do not offer photofinishing, such as Best Buy (**www.bestbuy.com**) and Radio Shack (**www.radioshack.com**), would be better partners.

Questions

1. Describe the advantages of Snapfish's use of a bricks-and-clicks (multi-channel) strategy.
2. Describe the disadvantages of Snapfish's use of a bricks-and-clicks (multi-channel) strategy.
3. What are the pros and cons of a retailer's partnering with Snapfish?
4. What should be the contract terms in a leased department agreement between a retailer and Snapfish?

[C-4]The material in this case is drawn from Mya Frazier, "Offline Retail," *SCT* (November 2004), pp. 19–20; and *Photo Industry 2005: Review and Forecast*.

part two
Comprehensive Case
The Outlook for Soft Goods Specialty Stores*

Introduction

Soft goods specialty retailers are on a quest to grow, with the high-growth "stars" working to maintain momentum by rolling out successful concepts nationally while investing in new concepts that offer long-term promise. The less stellar performers are reinvigorating tired concepts and strengthening margins via better inventory and promotion management. A saturated marketplace will motivate more specialists at both ends of the spectrum to seek growth by building a portfolio of concepts focused on ever-finer customer groups. Concepts will vie for more attention by developing and applying deep customer insights to their assortment strategy, the shopping experience, and store brand building and communication.

The Retail Landscape

Many soft goods specialty retailers have seen recent improvements in sales and profits, but for most, the recovery is modest in nature and has done little to negate the pervasive price pressure on retail margins. The sustainability of the recovery is questionable given poor comparable store sales performance.

Modest Recovery

Since bottoming out in the first part of this decade, sales have steadily improved in both the apparel and accessories specialty store and shoe specialty store channels. Yet, growth remains modest compared to the late 1990s.

The long-term sales outlook for apparel and accessories specialty stores is stronger than for shoe stores. Apparel stores are forecast to grow in the 4 to 5 percent range annually through 2008, while shoe stores are forecast to grow mostly around 1 percent a year over the same time period. Much of the sales improvement has gone straight to the bottom line for apparel and accessories specialty stores. Though still well below its performance in the late 1990s, the sector has improved another important measure of profitability, return on net worth.

In contrast, the very modest sales improvement among shoe specialty stores has not translated to improved financial performance, with the average net profit margin for publicly held shoe retailers declining. The financial struggles facing the shoe store channel are evident in the closings of individual stores and entire divisions by some of the channel's leading players.

Pervasive price pressure has contributed to the commoditization of apparel and footwear, particularly basic styles that are easily sourced and widely distributed. Commoditization has also been propelled by the growth of Wal-Mart (**www.walmart.com**) and Target (**www.target.com**),

both of which offer wide assortments of basic and fashion-focused soft goods at sharp price points that appeal to a broad swath of consumers. This has increased the pressure on many retailer margins as their increasingly undifferentiated assortment goes head to head with price-driven retailers off the mall.

While apparel price deflation has made it challenging for soft goods specialists, many have proven worthy of the challenge. The availability of cheaper products allowed many of these specialists to improve inventory turns, resulting in a slight increase in their return on inventory ratio since 1998. This improvement reflects a focus by many apparel specialty store retailers on a combination of better markdown strategies, improved inventory management, and introduction of higher-margin fashion items.

A Challenging Environment

Soft goods specialty retailers face a crowded marketplace that is steadily becoming even more competitive. Most shoe specialty stores are faring far worse than the apparel specialists in the competitive wars. Off-mall retailers, including discount department stores/supercenters and Kohl's (**www.kohls. com**), are capturing apparel and shoe share of preference at the expense of mall-based retailers, including specialty stores. Consumer preference for purchasing apparel is strongest at discount stores/supercenters.

The upward trend for discounters contrasts with a decline in spending preference for clothing at apparel specialty stores, value department stores, and traditional/upscale department stores in the same time period. For shoe purchasing, shoe stores are actually gaining spending preference, although the price-driven discount store/supercenter channel is as well. Shoe, discount, and apparel specialty stores are capturing shoe spending preference from value and traditional department stores, particularly Sears (**www. sears.com**) and Dillard's (**www.dillards.com**), as well as Payless (**www.payless.com**).

Although department stores have suffered the most at the hands of off-mall retailer growth, many are reinventing themselves. Key elements of the department store reinvention include a stronger, more exclusive, and more differentiated brand and style assortment supported by upgraded, easier-to-shop stores. Thus, department stores now contribute to more competitive intensity in the apparel and footwear playing field, particularly for upscale customers. The profile of monthly shoppers at traditional/upscale department stores is similar to that of monthly shoppers at apparel specialty stores in terms of higher income and education levels—although apparel store customers skew younger.

Competitive battles are also escalating due to the entry of a number of foreign specialty store retailers to the marketplace. Though most of the new foreign players operate only a handful of U.S. stores at this point in time, several intend to ramp up their store openings after establishing an initial base of stores.

Some suppliers are also branching out to target new customers with new specialty store chains to attain growth in the face of modest prospects at department stores. Polo Ralph

Lauren (**www.polo.com**) is launching Rugby, a new brand and chain of stores targeting college-aged consumers. OshKosh B'Gosh (**www.oshkoshbgosh.com**) is testing a family lifestyle store targeting men and women.

A final factor contributing to heightened competitive pressure is the expansion of full-price specialty store chains by several soft goods suppliers. A number of catalog retailers that are fairly new to retailing are also rapidly building store chains. Although the track record of most soft goods suppliers has been spotty when it comes to operating successful full-price retail stores—and several are closing unsuccessful concepts—it is clear that most of the majors view full-price retail as another avenue for growth that must be pursued as a consequence of overall retail maturity. Suppliers with the most substantial full-price store base include Jones Apparel Group (primarily shoe stores, **www.jny.com**), Liz Claiborne (primarily via Mexx in Europe and Canada, **www.liz.com**), and Polo Ralph Lauren. The two soft goods catalog retailers relatively new to full-price retailing that are most actively building their store chain are Coldwater Creek (**www.coldwatercreek.com**) and J. Jill (**www.jjill.com**).

Growing diversity is making it more difficult for many specialists to adequately address the needs and expectations of all of their target customers—a critical requirement for success in the specialty store arena. Diversity is also propelling more retailers to tailor assortments and adjust merchandising tactics on an individual store basis. Previously, many only altered the offer to reflect regional seasonal variations and market size differences.

Apparel and footwear are steadily capturing less of the consumer's total spending. This is in part due to a shift in consumer spending priorities toward necessities (home, health, and transportation), as well as toward new everyday "luxuries" such as eating out and entertainment—which includes products such as consumer electronics, sporting goods and toys, and the cost of fees/admissions to sporting events, concerts, movies, clubs, and other types of events.

Consumers are increasingly willing to cross channels to shop a growing number of retailers—from mass to class—for apparel. They are more apt to trade down on staple wardrobe elements while trading up on aspirational, ego-intensive purchases and shopping experiences. Thus, value retailers play an even more important role in supplying the core of consumers' wardrobes—from basics like undergarments to wardrobe fashion "staples" such as casual pants, casual shirts, and everyday sweaters. Likewise, a number of soft goods specialty retailers and department stores are taking steps to tap into the shopper's trade-up mindset by upgrading store environments, focusing on stronger aspirational store brand images, and introducing more higher-end and "affordable luxury" products and labels to the assortment.

Looking Forward
Polarizing Playing Field

Although the soft goods specialty store channel is far more fragmented than most other retail channels, it will continue to slowly consolidate as big companies grow bigger, adding more banners to their portfolio. However, the nature of specialty retailing will also ensure the continual entry of new, smaller, usually more flexible niche players able to exploit market gaps not being addressed by the majors. Only 37 percent of total U.S. soft goods channel sales are by the top 15 retailers. This reflects a large number of independent retailers and the presence of smaller firms that operate on a regional or multi-regional basis.

Growth at the ends of the size spectrum will cause the soft goods channel to remain polarized into the very big versus the very small retailers. Those in the middle will continue to be squeezed by the efficiencies and resources of the big retailers and by the flexibility and customer intimacy of smaller retailers and retail chains.

Firms with strong sales growth tend to fall into one of three camps—hot, high-growth youth retailers like Pacific Sunwear (**www.pacsun.com**), Urban Outfitters (**www.urbanoutfitters.com**), Hot Topic (**www.hottopic.com**), and Aeropostale (**www.aeropostale.com**); mature but re-invigorated multi-brand mega-specialists like Gap Inc. (**www.gapinc.com**) and Limited Brands (**www.limitedbrands.com**); and Chico's (**www.chicos.com**), which stands alone within the channel as a result of carving out a very well-defined niche targeting an underserved baby boomer woman.

The strong performance of these retailers indicates that most will be in a position to further propel performance improvements via continued investments in technology and processes that enable them to reduce costs, more effectively allocate and manage inventory, and more strategically manage price and promotional activity. These retailers will also be better positioned than their peers to focus on increasing share of wallet among their highest-prospect customers.

The soft goods specialty store channel will also continue to polarize with respect to new store-opening opportunities, with an expanding number of "tapped-out" retail concepts unable to grow by opening more U.S. stores. With little international experience (or bad experiences in the past), most tapped-out retailers are unlikely to move rapidly or successfully into global apparel retailing, except for opening stores in Canada. Instead, they will focus on growing sales in current concepts by getting more share of wallet from existing customers through a combination of a more well-defined and relevant market position and extending their assortment into new products, brands, and services for the target customer.

Despite overall channel maturity, there are several soft goods specialty store retailers with substantial room to grow, particularly those that have only begun rapid store expansion within recent years. Strong sales growth reflects both a rapid pace of new store openings and, for players such as Chico's and Pacific Sunwear, equally impressive store-to-store sales growth.

Some soft goods specialists that operate a large base of stores and that have struggled will continue to weed out unprofitable, low-prospect stores from their portfolio. In a few cases, retailers will divest or close entire chains to focus resources on higher-profit, higher-growth concepts. This trend has been under way for years, by firms such as Payless, Gap Inc., Limited Brands Inc., Wilsons Leather (**www. wilsonsleather.com**), Charming Shoppes (**www.charming shoppes.com**), Brown Shoe (**www.brownshoe.com**), and Mother's Work (**www.motherswork.com**).

Repositioning for Relevancy

The recent economic downturn has made many retailers loath to invest in major repositioning initiatives. However, as sales gain some momentum and corporate purse strings loosen a bit, more aging soft goods specialty stores will undergo a facelift. For some, this will involve a long overdue re-assessment of the target customer. Perhaps the highest-profile repositioning has been Gap (**www.gap.com**), Old Navy (**www.oldnavy.com**), and Banana Republic (**www. bananarepublic.com**) chains.

Banana Republic has added more trend-driven fashions to better distinguish it from Gap stores. This includes a stronger emphasis on color, more feminine styles, and clothes for social occasions, as well as its standard work-appropriate assortment. Old Navy is more firmly positioned as a value-focused store for the entire family, with more emphasis on serving the needs of each member of the family. The retailer has increased assortment segmentation based on customer group. The chain also has new fixtures that increase selling capacity. Gap has been repositioned as the classic specialty store for a range of fashion "basics" for casual occasions, supplemented by more "occasion-oriented" merchandise for weekends, the workplace, and stepping out. Underperforming Gap stores have been closed, and stores have stricter inventory controls to increase productivity and reduce markdowns. Gap is reinvesting in marketing, including developing a more consistent message across all media.

In line with size-related trends in the overall population, more specialty retailers will expand their standard size range to include larger sizes, as well as petite/small sizes. Some may spin special-size concepts off as their own store banners, but most will choose to simply extend the size range within the existing banner by adding new sizes or by increasing the breadth of assortment within existing special size lines. Ann Taylor (**www.anntaylor.com**) plans an overall focus on petites as one of its growth strategies. Plans include extending the product offering to all categories and more styles, creating a store environment that makes petites a preferred destination, and boosting marketing to generate awareness. The firm has rolled out petite adjacencies in current stores (including some with separate entrances).

To capture more sales from customers already in the store, a growing number of soft goods specialty store retailers will extend their assortments to include products that provide additional style perspectives and meet the needs of additional wearing occasions. Express (**www.expressfashion. com**) strengthened its wear-to-work appeal with the Express Design Studio line of clothing being rolled out to all stores. The line is designed by a New York-based team and focuses on fitted pants, tailored jackets, and key pieces that "add sexy sophistication" and allow the line to move from the "workplace to the weekend." The men's line also includes suits sold as separates, dress shirts, and ties.

Abercrombie & Fitch (**www.abercrombie.com**) is repositioning its brand to be less aggressively sexual in its marketing to customers and to include higher price points and fewer promotions. As part of this strategy, the retailer has a new higher price point collection called Ezra Fitch. The collection includes products such as $118 to $148 jeans and cashmere crew necks at $178.

While the factors having the most influence on trying a new brand or store are the styling and price, followed by the influence of friends and family, monthly specialty store shoppers are far more likely than all shoppers to be influenced to try a brand or shop a store based on fashion magazines and celebrity culture. They are also far more willing than all shoppers to say that wearing designer brands has a positive impact on their self-esteem and self-confidence.

As part of their approach to new customers, most specialists will choose to first move up the age spectrum with the intention of leveraging the knowledge they have about their customers as they "outgrow" the existing concept and enter a new life stage. Where this opportunity has already been tapped out, they will be forced to focus on concepts targeting an entirely new style, lifestyle, or occasion of use.

Driving Growth Through Strategic Investments

More specialty store retailers will invest in initiatives that allow them to not just attain competitive differentiation but to also drive profitable top-line growth via higher purchase conversion levels, more multiple-item transactions, and increased destination store status with targeted customers. Key areas of investment will include new technologies and high-value services, as well as alternative marketing and promotional venues.

New technologies are becoming more mainstream and less cost-prohibitive, a trend that will motivate more specialty store retailers to invest in technological solutions that ensure that the right products are on the selling floor in the right quantities at the right time and price. Technology will also be used to provide more alternative shopping and purchasing options for customers (beyond just online selling). It will also be used to better track the flow of customer traffic in the store on a real-time basis in order to design stores that have higher sell-through levels and staff stores in line with customer needs.

Many specialty store retailers will focus on improving their service programs and associate-customer interaction as a way to build top-of-mind status with target customers. In some cases, this will involve more personal shopping services and stronger customer "clienteling." In others, it will involve creatively responding to the service and shopping experience needs of the best customers in ways that are more meaningful to that customer.

Talbots (**www.talbots.com**) has experimented with a variation on its popular Appointment Shopping service with a service called Wardrobe Express. The service targets busy, time-pressed customers with highly efficient shopping appointments by providing a pre-selected assortment of garments for the customer in the dressing room at the prescribed time—along with a light snack for lunchtime shoppers. During the visit, the store associate completes a "wardrobing sheet" including what was tried on and possible coordinates. Using credit card information that is on file, the associate then completes the purchase after the shopper has left the store and arranges for pickup or delivery.

Questions

1. What can an independent retailer learn from this case?
2. What are the positive implications of this case with respect to the use of leased departments in department stores?

3. How can a mid-priced apparel store become a destination retailer?
4. How is Gap Inc. utilizing the principles of the wheel of retailing through its Gap, Old Navy, and Banana Republic divisions?
5. How can high-priced apparel specialty stores successfully compete against full-line discount stores?
6. What role should the Internet play for apparel retailers?
7. Can an apparel retailer prosper in the future if it does not engage in multi-channel retailing? Explain your answer.

*The material in this case is adapted by the authors from *Industry Outlook: Soft Goods Specialty Stores* (Columbus, OH: Retail Forward, August 2004). Reprinted by permission of Retail Forward, Inc. (**www.retailforward.com**).

part three

Targeting Customers and Gathering Information

In Part Three, we first present various key concepts for retailers to better identify and understand consumers and develop an appropriate target market plan. Information-gathering methods—which can be used in identifying and understanding consumers, as well as in developing and implementing a retail strategy—are then described.

■ **Chapter 7** discusses many influences on retail shoppers: demographics, lifestyles, needs and desires, shopping attitudes and behavior, retailer actions that influence shopping, and environmental factors. We place these elements within a target marketing framework, because it is critical for retailers to recognize what makes their customers and potential customers tick—and for them to act accordingly.

■ **Chapter 8** deals with information gathering and processing in retailing. We first consider the information flows in a retail distribution channel and review the difficulties that may arise from basing a retail strategy on inadequate information. Then we examine in depth the retail information system, its components, and recent advances in information systems—with particular emphasis on data ware-housing and data mining. The last part of the chapter describes the marketing research process.

Chapter 7

IDENTIFYING AND UNDERSTANDING CONSUMERS

Thomas Stemberg, a Harvard M.B.A., was working on a business plan in his home during summer 1985. While printing spreadsheets, he realized that his printer ribbon was broken. Attempts to purchase a new ribbon over the Fourth of July weekend were unsuccessful. His local stationery store and a nearby computer store were both closed, and the nearest BJ's did not carry the correct ribbon. All of a sudden, a thought occurred to Stemberg: What the world needed was a superstore selling nothing but office supplies at great prices.

Reprinted by permission.

On May 1, 1986, Staples (**www.staples.com**) opened its first superstore in Brighton, Massachusetts. The store was so successful that about 20 competitors launched similar store formats within the next two years. Today, Staples is the world's largest office-supply retailer with about 1,600 office superstores in the United States, Canada, and Europe. Staples also has a catalog and Web-based business.

Staples appeals to three distinct market segments: small and large businesses, home offices, and final consumers. Its stores have changed the way each of these consumers purchases supplies. Recently, Staples introduced its Easy Rebates program; this enables consumers to submit their rebates online by entering only two key data points: the rebate offer number and the Easy Rebates identification number. Unlike other programs, Universal Product Codes (UPCs) are not required for rebate redemption. Easy Rebates was a response to comments made by focus groups citing dissatisfaction with completing and monitoring rebates. Staples is promoting Easy Rebates in its stores, catalogs, and Web site.[1]

chapter objectives

1. To discuss why it is important for a retailer to properly identify, understand, and appeal to its customers
2. To enumerate and describe a number of consumer demographics, lifestyle factors, and needs and desires—and to explain how these concepts can be applied to retailing
3. To examine consumer attitudes toward shopping and consumer shopping behavior, including the consumer decision process and its stages
4. To look at retailer actions based on target market planning
5. To note some of the environmental factors that affect consumer shopping

OVERVIEW

The quality of a retail strategy depends on how well a firm identifies and understands its customers and forms its strategy mix to appeal to them. This entails identifying consumer characteristics, needs, and attitudes; recognizing how people make decisions; and then devising the proper target market plan. It also means studying the environmental factors that affect purchase decisions. Consider the following:

> In addition to understanding general demographic and economic trends, it is important to recognize the many motivations that drive consumers to shop, such as browsing, meeting a specific need, having the experience/fun, and comparing prices. Approximately 60 percent to 70 percent of what Americans buy is discretionary, and about two-thirds of their purchases are unplanned. An individual consumer's needs and rationale for purchasing will differ throughout any given day, week, month, or indeed, a lifetime. Retailers will not be able to meet all consumers' needs at all times; however, those that can foresee and adapt to changing consumer needs and tastes will survive and prosper.[2]

In this chapter, we explore—in a retailing context—the impact on shoppers of each of the elements shown in Figure 7-1: demographics, lifestyles, needs and desires, shopping attitudes and behavior, retailer actions that influence shopping, and environmental factors. By studying these elements, a retailer can devise the best possible target market plan and do so in the context of its overall strategy.

Please note: We use *consumer*, *customer*, and *shopper* interchangeably in this chapter.

CONSUMER DEMOGRAPHICS AND LIFESTYLES

Demographics are objective, quantifiable, easily identifiable, and measurable population data. **Lifestyles** are the ways in which individual consumers and families (households) live and spend time and money. Visit our Web site (**www.prenhall.com/bermanevans**) for several useful links on these topics.

FIGURE 7-1
What Makes Retail
Shoppers Tick

TABLE 7-1		Population Demographics: A Global Perspective—Selected Countries						
		Age Distribution (%)			Annual	Life		Principal
Country	Male/ Female (%)	0–14 Years	15–64 Years	65 Years and Over	Population Growth (%)	Expectancy in Years	Literacy Rate (%)	Languages Spoken
Canada	49.5/50.5	18	69	13	0.92	80.0	97	English, French
China	51.5/48.5	22	70	8	0.57	72.0	91	More than a dozen versions of Chinese
Great Britain	49.5/50.5	18	66	16	0.29	78.3	99	English, Welsh
India	51.7/48.3	32	63	5	1.44	64.0	60	Hindi, English, 14 other official languages
Italy	49.0/51.0	14	67	19	0.09	79.5	99	Italian, German, French, Slovene
Japan	49.0/51.0	14	67	19	0.08	81.0	99	Japanese
Mexico	49.0/51.0	31	63	6	1.18	74.9	92	Spanish
Poland	48.5/51.5	17	70	13	0.02	74.9	99+	Polish
South Africa	49.5/50.5	30	65	5	−0.25	44.1	86	Afrikaans, English, 9 other official languages
United States	49.2/50.8	21	67	12	0.92	77.4	97	English, Spanish

The literacy rate is the percentage of people who are 15 and older who can read and write.

Source: Compiled by the authors from *World Factbook*, **www.odci.gov/cia/publications/factbook/index.html** (updated online as of November 2005).

Consumer Demographics

At *The Rite Site* (**www.easidemographics. com**), retailers can access lots of useful demographic data. Take a look at the free reports.

Both groups of consumers and individual consumers can be identified by such demographics as gender, age, population growth rate, life expectancy, literacy, language spoken, household size, marital and family status, income, retail sales, mobility, place of residence, occupation, education, and ethnic/racial background. These factors affect people's retail shopping and retailer actions.

A retailer should have some knowledge of overall trends, as well as the demographics of its own target market. Table 7-1 indicates broad demographics for 10 nations around the world and Table 7-2 shows U.S. demographics by region. Regional data are useful since most retailers are local and regional.

In understanding U.S. demographics, it is helpful to know these facts:

- The typical household has an annual income of $45,000. The top one-fifth of households earn $85,000 or more; the lowest one-fifth earn under $18,000. If income is high, people are apt to have **discretionary income**—money left after paying taxes and buying necessities.
- One-seventh of people move each year, yet 60 percent of all moves are in the same county.
- There are 5 million more females than males, and three-fifths of females aged 20 and older are in the labor force (many full-time).
- Most U.S. employment is in services. In addition, there are now more professionals and white-collar workers than before and fewer blue-collar and agricultural workers.

TABLE 7-2	Selected U.S. Demographics by Region				
Region	Percent of Population	Percent of Household Income	Percent Ages 18–34	Percent Ages 50 and Older	Population Per Square Mile
ENC	15.7	16.1	23.1	28.9	153
ESC	5.9	5.0	23.7	29.7	95
M	6.7	6.4	25.2	27.9	??
MA	13.8	14.8	22.2	30.7	369
NE	4.9	6.0	22.3	30.7	198
P	16.2	16.7	24.7	26.3	48
SA	18.8	18.7	23.4	30.5	185
WNC	6.7	6.8	23.1	29.6	38
WSC	11.3	9.5	24.6	26.3	75

ENC (East North Central) = Illinois, Indiana, Michigan, Ohio, Wisconsin
ESC (East South Central) = Alabama, Kentucky, Mississippi, Tennessee
M (Mountain) = Arizona, Colorado, Idaho, Montana, Nevada, New Mexico, Utah, Wyoming
MA (Middle Atlantic) = New Jersey, New York, Pennsylvania
NE (New England) = Connecticut, Maine, Massachusetts, New Hampshire, Rhode Island, Vermont
P (Pacific) = Alaska, California, Hawaii, Oregon, Washington
SA (South Atlantic) = Delaware, District of Columbia, Florida, Georgia, Maryland, North Carolina, South Carolina, Virginia, West Virginia
WNC (West North Central) = Iowa, Kansas, Minnesota, Missouri, Nebraska, North Dakota, South Dakota
WSC (West South Central) = Arkansas, Louisiana, Oklahoma, Texas

Source: Computed by the authors from U.S. Bureau of the Census data, **www.census.gov** (February 9, 2006).

- More adults have attended some level of college, with more than one-quarter of all U.S. adults aged 25 and older at least graduating from a four-year college.
- The population comprises many ethnic and racial groups. African-Americans, Hispanic-Americans, and Asian-Americans account for 30 percent of U.S. residents—a steadily rising figure. Each of these groups represents a large potential target market; their total annual buying power is $1.4 trillion.[3]

Although the preceding gives an overview of the United States, demographics vary by area (as Table 7-2 indicates). Within a state or city, some locales have larger populations and more affluent, older, and better-educated residents. Because most retailers are local or operate in only part of a region, they must compile data about the people living in their trading areas and those most apt to shop there. *For a given business and location*, the characteristics of the target market (the customer group to be sought by the retailer) can be studied on the basis of some combination of these demographic factors—and a retail strategy planned accordingly:

- Market size—How many people are in the potential target market?
- Gender—Is the potential target market more male or female, or are they equal in proportion?
- Age—What are the prime age groups to which the retailer wants to appeal?

- Household size—What is the average household size of potential consumers?
- Marital and family status—Are potential consumers single or married? Do families have children?
- Income—Is the potential target market lower income, middle income, or upper income? Is discretionary income available for luxury purchases?
- Retail sales—What is the area's sales forecast for the retailer's goods/services category?
- Birth rate—How important is the birth rate for the retailer's goods/services category?
- Mobility—What percent of the potential target market moves into and out of the trading area yearly?
- Where people live—How large is the trading area from which potential customers can be drawn?
- Employment status—Does the potential target market include working women?
- Occupation—In what industries and occupations are people in the area working? Are they professionals, office workers, or of some other designation?
- Education—Are potential customers college-educated?
- Ethnic/racial background—Does the potential target market cover a distinctive racial or ethnic group?

Consumer Lifestyles

Consumer Insight Magazine (http://us.acnielsen.com/pubs/index.shtml) provides a good perspective on emerging consumer trends.

Consumer lifestyles are based on social and psychological factors, and influenced by demographics. As with demographics, a retailer should first have some knowledge of consumer lifestyle concepts and then determine the lifestyle attributes of its own target market.

These *social factors* are useful in identifying and understanding consumer lifestyles:

- A **culture** is a distinctive heritage shared by a group of people that passes on a series of beliefs, norms, and customs. The U.S. culture stresses individuality, success, education, and material comfort; there are also various subcultures

Technology in RETAILING — Reaching Customers in New Ways

Retailers such as QVC.com (www.qvc.com) and Best Buy (www.bestbuy.com) understand that technological advances better enable retailers to interact with customers, as well as change how customers buy merchandise.

QVC is testing an "On Command" program that enables consumers to buy its merchandise from hotels in select regions. QVC is also testing a service in Great Britain that lets shoppers purchase merchandise via their television's remote control. This eliminates the need for customers to write down the product's identification number and to call in the order. During pilot tests, 14 percent of QVC's sales were through the remote controls.

Best Buy is using technology to change the way in which a Web site is viewed by a customer, based on his or her past browsing and buying behavior. A customer who is recognized as a time-pressed mom may be shown promos for digital cameras and DVDs. That customer might also be shown material about a local store and its kids area. In contrast, a customer who likes high-end products but has a limited budget may be shown information relating to the chain's credit plans.

Source: Matthew Haeberle, "Innovation Wins in E-Retail," *Chain Store Age* (December 2004), p. 92.

(such as African-, Hispanic-, and Asian-Americans) due to the many countries from which residents have come.

- **Social class** involves an informal ranking of people based on income, occupation, education, and other factors. People often have similar values in each social class.
- **Reference groups** influence people's thoughts and behavior: aspirational groups—a person does not belong but wishes to join; membership groups—a person does belong; and dissociative groups—a person does not want to belong. Face to face groups, such as families, have the most impact. Within reference groups, there are opinion leaders whose views are well respected and sought.
- The **family life cycle** describes how a traditional family moves from bachelorhood to children to solitary retirement. At each stage, attitudes, needs, purchases, and income change. Retailers must also be alert to the many adults who never marry, divorced adults, single-parent families, and childless couples. The **household life cycle** incorporates life stages for both family and nonfamily households.
- *Time utilization* refers to the activities in which a person is involved and the amount of time allocated to them. The broad categories are work, transportation, eating, recreation, entertainment, parenting, sleeping, and (retailers hope) shopping. Today, many consumers allocate less time to shopping.

These *psychological factors* help in identifying and understanding consumer lifestyles:

Consumer psychology can be studied with tools such as the Keirsey Temperament Sorter. Take the online test (www.keirsey.com/cgi-bin/keirsey/newkts.cgi) to learn about yourself.

- A **personality** is the sum total of an individual's traits, which make that individual unique. They include a person's level of self-confidence, innovativeness, autonomy, sociability, emotional stability, and assertiveness.
- **Class consciousness** is the extent to which a person desires and pursues social status. It helps determine the use of reference groups and the importance of prestige purchases. A class-conscious person values the status of goods, services, and retailers.
- **Attitudes (opinions)** are the positive, neutral, or negative feelings a person has about different topics. They are also feelings consumers have about a given retailer and its activities. Does the consumer feel a retailer is desirable, unique, and fairly priced?
- **Perceived risk** is the level of risk a consumer believes exists regarding the purchase of a specific good or service from a given retailer, whether or not the belief is correct. There are six types: *functional* (Will a good or service perform well?), *physical* (Can a good or service hurt me?), *financial* (Can I afford to buy?), *social* (What will peers think of my shopping here?), *psychological* (Am I doing the right thing?), and *time* (How much effort must I exert in shopping?). Perceived risk is high if a retailer or its brands are new, a person is on a budget, a person has little experience, there are many choices, and a purchase is socially visible or complex. See Figure 7-2. Retailers can reduce perceived risk through information.
- *The importance of a purchase* to the consumer affects the amount of time he or she will spend to make a decision and the range of alternatives considered. If a purchase is important, perceived risk tends to be higher, and the retailer must adapt to this.

A retailer can develop a lifestyle profile of its target market by answering these questions and then use the answers in developing its strategy:

FIGURE 7-2
The Impact of Perceived Risk
on Consumers

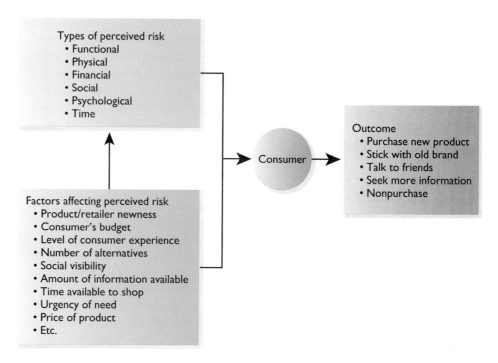

- Culture—What values, norms, and customs are most important to the potential target market?

- Social class—Are potential consumers lower, middle, or upper class? Are they socially mobile?

- Reference groups—To whom do people look for purchasing advice? Does this differ by good or service category? How can a firm target opinion leaders?

- Family (or household) life cycle—In what stage(s) of the cycle are the bulk of potential customers?

- Time utilization—How do people spend time? How do they view their shopping time?

- Personality—Do potential customers have identifiable personality traits?

- Class consciousness—Are potential consumers status-conscious? How does this affect purchases?

- Attitudes—How does the potential target market feel about the retailer and its offerings in terms of specific strategy components?

- Perceived risk—Do potential customers feel risk in connection with the retailer? Which goods and services have the greatest perceived risk?

- Importance of the purchase—How important are the goods/services offered to potential customers?

Retailing Implications of Consumer Demographics and Lifestyles

Demographic and lifestyle factors need to be considered from several perspectives. Here are some illustrations. By no means do the examples cover the full domain of retailing.

Gender Roles: The huge number of working women, who put in 60 to 70 hours or more each week between their job and home responsibilities, is altering lifestyles significantly. Compared to women who have not worked outside the home, they tend to be more self-confident and individualistic, more concerned with convenience, more interested in sharing household and family tasks with spouses or significant others, more knowledgeable and demanding as consumers, more interested in leisure activities and travel, more involved with self-improvement and education, more appearance-conscious, and more indifferent to small price differences among retailers. They are less interested in unhurried shopping trips.

Due to the trend toward working women, the lifestyles of males are also changing. More men now take care of their children, shop for food, do laundry, wash dishes, cook for the family, vacuum the house, and clean the bathroom. Today, 30 percent of U.S. males are either the primary grocery shopper in the family (19 percent) or share that responsibility (11 percent).[4] See Figure 7-3. The future will see still more changes in men's and women's roles—and in the conflicts over them. The clout and duties of husbands and wives will be shared with greater frequency. Retailers need to appreciate this trend.

Consumer Sophistication and Confidence: Many shoppers are now more knowledgeable and cosmopolitan; more aware of trends in tastes, styles, and goods and services; and more sophisticated. Nonconforming behavior is widely accepted since consumers are self-assured and better appreciate the available choices. Confident shoppers will experiment more. For example, "female shoppers want a retail space that's comfortable and has fewer but better choices." Retailers need to see that "it's not just about understanding the functional benefit of the brand or product, but understanding things like personal resonance—what it says about her and how it helps her express herself."[5]

FIGURE 7-3
Blurring Gender Roles

Due to changing lifestyles, more husbands and wives shop together now, as at this A&P store.

Photo reprinted by permission.

RETAILING
Around the World   Understanding Eastern European Shoppers

Years ago, a Russian woman's choices in cosmetics were limited to black-and-white labeled, state-manufactured products. The old shampoo packaging more closely resembled a toothpaste container, and a toothpaste package looked more like soap. Now, the options available to Eastern European consumers are much more appealing. In one recent year, fragrance sales in Eastern Europe increased by over 18 percent; and by the end of 1995, the annual cosmetics and toiletry market in Russia had reached $6 billion.

To capitalize on the market growth, U.S.-based cosmetics firms need to better understand the Eastern European consumer. Unfortunately, there is no single consumer profile that can be applied to the Eastern European consumer. For example, women in some countries purchase cosmetics in department stores, pharmacies, and in specialty stores, while women in other countries purchase cosmetics at roadside vendors and through kiosks.

The Russian cosmetics consumer is focused on her appearance and uses colors to make a bold statement. Some Russian 20-year-olds spend over $300 U.S. a month on cosmetics—even though their monthly income is only several hundred dollars U.S. In contrast, Polish consumers are much more price-conscious and seek lower-priced domestic brands.

Source: Liz Grubow, "Branding Eastern European Shoppers," *GCI* (February 2005), pp. 30–32.

Poverty of Time: The increase in working women, the desire for personal fulfillment, the daily job commute, and the tendency of some people to have second jobs contribute to many consumers feeling time-pressured: "No matter how rich or poor consumers are, time is the great social equalizer. A new priority of making the most of the limited time we have is taking over. Consumers are looking at all the ways they spend their time, including shopping, and demanding a more time-efficient, time-conscious way to shop."[6] There are ways for retailers to respond to the poverty-of-time concept. Firms can add branch stores to limit customer travel time; be open longer hours; add on-floor sales personnel; reduce checkout time; and use mail order, Web sites, and other direct marketing practices. See Figure 7-4.

Component Lifestyles: In the past, shoppers were typecast, based on demographics and lifestyles. Now, it is recognized that shopping is less predictable and more individualistic. It is more situation-based, hence, the term *component lifestyle*: "Have you wondered what's going on with consumers? Why the contradictions

FIGURE 7-4
King Kullen: Addressing the Poverty of Time

To make shopping and food preparation much more convenient for today's time-pressed customers, King Kullen's Web site (**www.kingkullen.com**) offers weekly specials, easy-to-access recipes, a section that describes each in-store department, gift cards, and a lot more.

Reprinted by permission.

when it comes to spending money? Why they will buy a $500 leather jacket at full price but wait for a $50 sweater to go on sale? Will buy a top-line sports utility vehicle then go to Costco for tires? Will pay $3.50 for a cup of coffee but think $1.29 is too much for a hamburger? Will spend $2.00 for a strawberry-smelling bath soap but wait for a coupon to buy a $0.99 twin pack of toilet soap?"[7]

Consumer Profiles

VALS (www.sric-bi.com/VALS) classifies lifestyles into several profiles. Visit the site to learn about the profiles and take the "VALS Survey" to see where you fit.

Considerable research has been aimed at describing consumer profiles in a way that is useful for retailers. Here are three examples:

> Shoppers at Wal-Mart and Kmart skew down-market and older, while shoppers at Target have higher household incomes and are younger. Monthly shoppers at Home Depot and Lowe's, as well as shoppers at Bed Bath & Beyond and Linens 'n Things, typically earn higher household incomes than shoppers in general. Shoppers at Costco, Sam's Club, and Sears are overrepresented in the 55+ age bracket, while Best Buy and Circuit City are much more likely to attract 18- to 34-year-olds.[8]

> What apparel do people buy? The largest percentage of employed shoppers (both men and women) wear somewhat casual clothes such as skirts or slacks without a blazer on a typical workday. A sizeable percentage (both men and women) wear very casual clothes. Only 5 percent typically wear business suits or business dresses. Almost one-half of all workers age 18 to 24 wear very casual clothes on a typical workday. For all other age groups, somewhat casual work attire is the most popular choice. Workers age 65 or older are the most likely to wear somewhat dressy clothes. Work attire also varies by income, with the likelihood of wearing somewhat dressy clothing or business suits/dresses increasing with income. Down-market workers are most likely to wear very casual clothing in the workplace.[9]

> According to the Census Bureau, about 71 million Americans ("Generation Y") were born between 1977 and 1994, representing close to 25 percent of the population. Their numbers are good news for retailers. Today's teens decide for themselves where to spend their money and can wield great influence on their parents' spending. Much of their spending—which likely totals more than $200 billion annually—goes toward clothing items, particularly sportswear, and they are likely to be more adept than older consumers in surfing the Internet for fashion tips and online shopping.[10]

CONSUMER NEEDS AND DESIRES

Catherines (http://catherines.charming shoppes.com/home.asp), a retailer of plus-size women's apparel, works hard to satisfy both consumer needs and desires, especially the latter.

When developing a target market profile, a retailer should identify key consumer needs and desires. From a retailing perspective, *needs* are a person's basic shopping requirements consistent with his or her present demographics and lifestyle. *Desires* are discretionary shopping goals that have an impact on attitudes and behavior. A person may need a new car to get to and from work and seek a dealer with Saturday service hours. The person may desire a Porsche and a free loaner car when the vehicle is serviced but be satisfied with a Saturn that can be serviced on the weekend and fits within the budget.

Consider this: "Consumers today spend proportionately less on basic necessities, such as food, clothing, and shelter, than they did 25, 35, or 50 years ago. But they spend more on discretionary purchases that are motivated by emotion and desire."[11] And this: "Women have felt disrespected and ignored when shopping for consumer electronics products. Yet, it is all about the experience. Some stores generate fun and confidence. How you design your stores is very important. In many cases, women don't like the consumer electronics shopping experience because retailers don't know what they want. Many women want reliable, beautiful products that they are interested in using—and that match the décor of their homes."[12]

When a retail strategy aims to satisfy consumer needs and desires, it appeals to consumer **motives**, the reasons for their behavior. These are just a few of the questions to resolve:

- How far will customers travel to get to the retailer?
- How important is convenience?
- What hours are desired? Are evening and weekend hours required?
- What level of customer services is preferred?
- How extensive a goods/service assortment is desired?
- What level of goods/service quality is preferred?
- How important is price?
- What retailer actions are necessary to reduce perceived risk?
- Do different market segments have special needs? If so, what are they?

Let us address the last question by looking at three particular market segments that attract retailer attention: in-home shoppers, online shoppers, and outshoppers.

In-Home Shopping: The in-home shopper is not always a captive audience. Shopping is often discretionary, not necessary. Convenience in ordering an item, without traveling for it, is important. These shoppers are often active store shoppers, and they are affluent and well-educated. Many in-home shoppers are self-confident, younger, and venturesome. They like in-store shopping but have low opinions of local shopping. For some catalog shoppers, time is not important. In households with young children, in-home shopping is more likely if the woman works part-time or not at all than if she works full-time. In-home shoppers may be unable to comparison shop; may not be able to touch, feel, handle, or examine products firsthand; are concerned about service (such as returns); and may not have a salesperson to ask questions.

Check out the NUA survey site (**www.nua.com/ surveys**) to find out more about Web users. Scroll down to "Demographics."

Online shopping: People who shop online are often well-educated and have above-average incomes (as noted in Chapter 6). Web shopping encompasses more than just purchasing online. At REI, online shoppers can research items, check out prices, and place orders. Some shoppers have items shipped to them, while others go to the store: "REI is respected for its smart approach to multi-channel integration. Especially dazzling is the company's in-store pickup program for online orders. Customers like in-store pickup because they save shipping costs. REI likes it because it brings customers into the store, where they spend even more. About 35 percent of REI.com's sales are designated for customer pickup, and that figure climbs above 40 percent during special sales and promotional events. One in three REI.com online shoppers who opt for store pickup, rather than delivery, buy additional goods on that store visit. This adds $70 to $85 to the purchase."[13]

Outshopping: Out-of-hometown shopping, **outshopping**, is important for both local and surrounding retailers. The former want to minimize this behavior, whereas the latter want to maximize it. Outshoppers are often young, members of a large family, and new to the community. Income and education vary by situation. Outshoppers differ in their lifestyles from those who patronize hometown stores. They enjoy fine foods, like to travel, are active, like to change stores, and read out-of-town newspapers. They also downplay hometown stores and compliment out-of-town stores. This is vital data for suburban shopping centers. Outshoppers have the same basic reasons for out-of-town shopping whether they reside in small or large communities—easy access, liberal credit, store diversity, product assortments, prices, the presence of large chains, entertainment facilities, customer services, and product quality.

SHOPPING ATTITUDES AND BEHAVIOR

In this section, we look at people's attitudes toward shopping, where they shop, and the way in which they make purchase decisions.

Attitudes Toward Shopping

Considerable research has been done on people's attitudes toward shopping. Such attitudes have a big impact on the ways in which people act in a retail setting. Retailers must strive to turn around some negative perceptions that now exist. Let us highlight some research findings.

Shopping Enjoyment: In general, people do not enjoy shopping as much as in the past. So, what does foster a pleasurable shopping experience—a challenge that retailers must address? Many shoppers enjoy bargain hunting ("I get a thrill out of finding a real bargain"), recreational browsing ("window shopping"), being pampered by salespeople (difficult for retailers to accomplish in this era of self-service and cost cutting), and the opportunity to get out of the house or office.[14]

Attitudes Toward Shopping Time: Retail shopping is often viewed as a chore: "Consumers now attempt to limit the time they spend shopping. Time-pressed by family and work responsibilities, they spend fewer hours cruising the mall in search of the perfect item, and look to get what they need as quickly as possible. This trend has been dubbed 'precision shopping.' The upside of precision shopping is that consumers spend more money each time they visit a store."[15]

Shifting Feelings About Retailing: There has been a major change in attitudes toward spending, value, and shopping with established retailers: "The same shopper who buys commodity goods at a BJ's Wholesale Club Inc. may also buy expensive apparel at Nordstrom. This shift does not appear to be transitory, but rather seems to define a more enduring pattern of behavior." In addition, some "Americans seem to be tired of the sameness of malls, with their closed-in, windowless feel and identical cast of retailers and food court vendors."[16]

Why People Buy or Do Not Buy on a Shopping Trip: It is critical for retailers to determine why shoppers leave without making a purchase. Is it prices? A rude salesperson? Not accepting the consumer's credit card? Not having an item in stock? Or some other factor? According to Kurt Salmon Associates, here are the top 10 reasons why shoppers leave an apparel store without buying:

1. Cannot find an appealing style.
2. Cannot find the right size or the item is out of stock.
3. Nothing fits.
4. No sales help is available.
5. Cannot get in and out of the store easily.
6. Prices are too high.
7. In-store experience is stressful.
8. Cannot find a good value.

9. Store is not merchandised conveniently.

10. Seasonality is off.[17]

Attitudes by Market Segment: According to Adjoined Consulting, shoppers can be broken into four types. "Thrifties" are most interested in price and convenience. They are apt to shop at Wal-Mart. "Allures" want a "fun, social shopping experience." They gravitate toward retailers such as Bloomingdale's and Limited Brands. "Speedsters" want to shop quickly. They shop disproportionately at Target and Costco. "Elites" want quality merchandise, an unhurried shopping experience, and the ability to be educated about products. They patronize retailers such as Neiman-Marcus and Amazon.com. Adjoined Consulting believes that many "retailers don't know how their customers prefer their shopping experience and compete by doing what their competitors do. But that doesn't work. Customer insight will allow a retailer not only to survive but to thrive against even the toughest competition."[18]

Attitudes Toward Private Brands: Many consumers believe private (retailer) brands are as good as or better than manufacturer brands: "For American consumers, private brands are brands like any other brands. In a landmark nationwide study, 75 percent of consumers defined store brands as 'brands' and ascribed to them the same degree of positive product qualities and characteristics—such as guarantee of satisfaction, packaging, value, taste, and performance—that they attribute to manufacturer brands. Moreover, more than 90 percent of all consumers polled were familiar with private brands, and 83 percent said that they purchase these products on a regular basis."[19]

Where People Shop

Consumer patronage differs sharply by type of retailer. Thus, it is vital for firms to recognize the venues where consumers are most likely to shop and plan accordingly. Table 7-3 shows where people shop.

Do *you* shop at both Tiffany (www.tiffany.com) and BJ's (www.bjswholesale.com)?

Many consumers do **cross-shopping**, whereby they (a) shop for a product category at more than one retail format during the year or (b) visit multiple retailers on one shopping trip. The first scenario occurs because these consumers feel comfortable shopping at different formats during the year, their goals vary by occasion (they may want bargains on everyday clothes and fashionable items for weekend wear), they shop wherever sales are offered, and they have a favorite format for themselves and another one for other household members. Visiting multiple outlets

---

Ethics in RETAILING — Selling to the Poor Can Be Good—For the Consumer and for Business

Although there is a market of 5 billion people in the world who live on less than $2 per day, many businesses wrongfully assume that this market is not economically viable. Nonetheless, according to various marketing experts, selling to the poor requires a different perspective from selling to middle-class consumers in affluent countries.

Selling to the poor means that retailers should offer small package sizes. India, China, and the Philippines are examples of countries where the sale of single-serve packs of shampoo, detergents, tea, and ketchup are common. Selling to the poor also forces a firm to rethink its cost structure, the size of operations, and the use of capital. Even though the cost of cataract surgery in a developed country can be $3,000, Aravind Eye Care (**www.aravind.org**) is able to provide cataract surgery in Southern India for $25 to $30. Aravind is now the largest eye care facility in the world, performing over 200,000 surgeries per year. Despite its low costs and high quality, Aravind is quite profitable and debt-free.

Sources: C. K. Prahalad, "Why Selling to the Poor Makes for Good Business," *Fortune* (November 15, 2004), pp. 70, 72; and "Aravind Eye Care System," **www.aravind.org** (February 24, 2006).

TABLE 7-3	Retailers Where Primary Household Shoppers Purchase at Least Once per Month (% of primary household shoppers)

Where America Shops:

Supermarkets	72	Traditional department stores	21
Discount department stores/supercenters	66	Deep-discount food stores	20
Drugstores	61	Pet supply stores	18
Convenience stores	59	Shoe stores	17
Apparel stores	36	Toy stores	10
Home improvement centers	31	Factory outlet stores	6
Membership clubs	29	Sporting goods stores	8
Book/music stores	22	Upscale department stores	4
Consumer electronics stores	21	Fine jewelry stores	4

Where the World Shops:

	Canada	China	France	Great Britain	India	Italy	Japan	Mexico	Poland	Russia
Convenience stores	75	75	58	57	63	39	90	67	24	53
Deep-discount food stores	19	73	68	38	47	74	51	31	60	54
Discount department stores	42	65	29	36	53	44	54	41	25	48
Drugstores	78	57	27	57	59	35	79	70	64	58
Membership clubs/cash & carry stores	29	69	11	11	33	28	32	61	19	32
Supercenters/hypermarkets	70	87	90	86	63	85	55	94	78	55
Supermarkets	79	79	49	63	62	68	84	83	50	47

Sources: Compiled by the authors from *Shopper Update: Home Goods* (Columbus, OH: Retail Forward, March 2005), p. 2; *Shopper Update: Soft Goods* (Columbus, OH: Retail Forward, April 2005), p. 2; and *Shopper Insights: Global Food, Drug, Mass Shopper Update* (Columbus, OH: Retail Forward, April 2005), pp. 13–23.

on one trip occurs because consumers want to save travel time and shopping time. Here are cross-shopping examples:

- Some supermarket customers also regularly buy items carried by the supermarket at convenience stores, full-line department stores, drugstores, and specialty food stores.
- Some department store customers also regularly buy items carried by the department store at factory outlets and full-line discount stores.
- The majority of Web shoppers also buy from catalog retailers, mass merchants, apparel chains, and department stores.
- Cross-shopping is high for apparel, home furnishings, shoes, sporting goods, and personal care items.

The Consumer Decision Process[20]

Besides identifying target market characteristics, a retailer should know how people make decisions. This requires familiarity with **consumer behavior**, which is the process by which people determine whether, what, when, where, how, from whom, and how often to purchase goods and services. Such behavior is influenced by a person's background and traits.

The consumer's decision process must be grasped from these different perspectives: (a) what good or service the consumer is thinking about buying and (b) where the consumer is going to purchase that item (if the person opts to buy). A consumer can make the decisions separately or jointly. If made jointly, he or she relies on the retailer for support (information, assortments, and knowledgeable sales personnel) over the entire decision process. If the decisions are made independently—what to buy versus where to buy—the person gathers information and advice before visiting a retailer and views the retailer merely as a place to buy (and probably more interchangeable with other firms).

In choosing whether or not to buy a given item ("*what*"), the consumer considers features, durability, distinctiveness, value, ease of use, and so on. In choosing the retailer to patronize for that item ("*where*"), the consumer considers location, assortment, credit availability, sales help, hours, customer service, and so on. Thus, the manufacturer and retailer have distinct challenges: The manufacturer wants people to buy its brand ("*what*") at any location carrying it ("*where*"). The retailer wants people to buy the product, not necessarily the manufacturer's brand ("*what*"), at its store or nonstore location ("*where*").

The **consumer decision process** has two parts: the process itself and the factors affecting the process. There are six steps in the process: stimulus, problem awareness, information search, evaluation of alternatives, purchase, and post-purchase behavior. The consumer's demographics and lifestyle affect the process. The complete process is shown in Figure 7-5.

The best retailers assist consumers at each stage in the process: stimulus (newspaper ads), problem awareness (stocking new models), information search (point-of-sale displays and good salespeople), evaluation of alternatives (clearly noticeable differences among products), purchase (acceptance of credit cards), and post-purchase behavior (extended warranties and money-back returns). The

The Federal Citizen Information Center facilitates consumer decision making for such products as food by providing free online information (**www.pueblo. gsa.gov/food.htm**).

FIGURE 7-5
The Consumer Decision Process

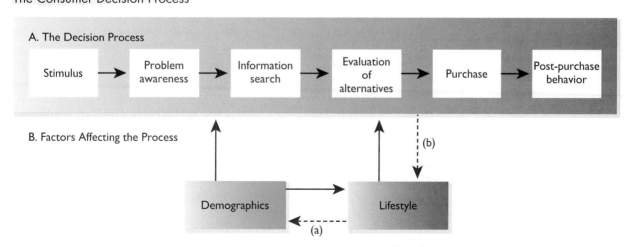

Note: Solid arrows connect all the elements in the decision process and show the impact of demographics and lifestyle upon the process. Dashed arrows show feedback. (a) shows the impact of lifestyle on certain demographics, such as family size, location, and marital status. (b) shows the impact of a purchase on elements of lifestyle, such as social class, reference groups, and social performance.

greater the role a retailer assumes in the decision process, the more loyal the consumer will be.

Each time a person buys a good or service, he or she goes through a decision process. In some cases, all six steps in the process are utilized; in others, only a few steps are employed. A consumer who has previously and satisfactorily bought luggage at a local store may not use the same extensive process as one who has never bought luggage.

The decision process outlined in Figure 7-5 assumes that the end result is a purchase. However, at any point, a potential customer may decide not to buy; the process then stops. A good or service may be unneeded, unsatisfactory, or too expensive. Before we consider the ways in which retail consumers use the decision process, the entire process is explained.

Stimulus: A **stimulus** is a cue (social or commercial) or a drive (physical) meant to motivate or arouse a person to act. When one talks with friends, fellow employees, and others, a social cue is received. The special attribute of a social cue is that it involves an interpersonal, noncommercial source. A commercial cue is a message sponsored by a retailer or some other seller. Ads, sales pitches, and store displays are commercial stimuli. Such cues may not be regarded as highly as social ones by consumers because they are seller-controlled. A third type of stimulus is a physical drive. It occurs when one or more of a person's physical senses are affected. Hunger, thirst, cold, heat, pain, or fear could cause a physical drive. A potential consumer may be exposed to any or all three types of stimuli. If aroused (motivated), he or she goes to the next step in the process. If a person is not sufficiently aroused, the stimulus is ignored—terminating the process for the given good or service.

Problem Awareness: At **problem awareness**, the consumer not only has been aroused by social, commercial, and/or physical stimuli but also recognizes that the good or service under consideration may solve a problem of shortage or unfulfilled desire. It is sometimes hard to learn why a person is motivated enough to move from a stimulus to problem awareness. Many people shop with the same retailer or buy the same good or service for different reasons, they may not know their own motivation, and they may not tell a retailer their real reasons for shopping there or buying a certain item.

Recognition of shortage occurs when a person discovers a good or service should be repurchased. A good could wear down beyond repair or the person might run out of an item such as milk. Service may be necessary if a good such as a car requires a repair. Recognition of unfulfilled desire takes place when a person becomes aware of a good or service that has not been bought before or a retailer that has not been patronized before. An item (such as contact lenses) may improve a person's lifestyle, self-image, and so on in an untried manner, or it may offer new performance features (such as a voice-activated computer). People are more hesitant to act on unfulfilled desires. Risks and benefits may be tougher to see. When a person becomes aware of a shortage or an unfulfilled desire, he or she acts only if it is a problem worth solving. Otherwise, the process ends.

Information Search: If problem awareness merits further thought, information is sought. An **information search** has two parts: (1) determining the alternatives that will solve the problem at hand (and where they can be bought) and (2) ascertaining the characteristics of each alternative.

First, the person compiles a list of goods or services that address the shortage or desire being considered. This list does not have to be formal. It may be a group of alternatives the person thinks about. A person with a lot of purchase experience normally uses an internal memory search to determine the goods or services—and retailers—that are satisfactory. A person with little purchase experience often uses an external search to develop a list of alternatives and retailers. This search can

Nonprofit Consumer World has an online, noncommercial guide catalog with over 2,000 sources to aid the consumer's information search (www. consumerworld.org).

involve commercial sources such as retail salespeople, noncommercial sources such as *Consumer Reports*, and social sources such as friends. Second, the person gathers information about each alternative's attributes. An experienced shopper searches his or her memory for the attributes (pros and cons) of each alternative. A consumer with little experience or a lot of uncertainty searches externally for information.

The extent of an information search depends, in part, on the consumer's perceived risk regarding a specific good or service. Risk varies among individuals and by situation. For some, it is inconsequential; for others, it is quite important. The retailer's role is to provide enough information for a shopper to feel comfortable in making decisions, thus reducing perceived risk. Point-of-purchase ads, product displays, and knowledgeable sales personnel can provide consumers with the information they need.

Once the consumer's search for information is completed, he or she must decide whether a current shortage or unfulfilled desire can be met by any of the alternatives. If one or more are satisfactory, the consumer moves to the next step in the decision process. The consumer stops the process if no satisfactory goods or services are found.

Evaluation of Alternatives: Next, a person selects one option from among the choices. This is easy if one alternative is superior on all features. An item with excellent quality and a low price is a certain pick over expensive, average-quality ones. However, a choice may not be that simple, and the person then does an **evaluation of alternatives** before making a decision. If two or more options seem attractive, the person determines the criteria to evaluate and their importance. Alternatives are ranked and a choice made.

The criteria for a decision are those good or service attributes that are considered relevant. They may include price, quality, fit, durability, and so on. The person sets standards for these characteristics and rates each alternative according to its ability to meet the standards. The importance of each criterion is also determined, and attributes are usually of differing importance to each person. One shopper may consider price to be most important while another places greater weight on quality and durability.

At this point, the person ranks the alternatives from most favorite to least favorite and selects one. For some goods or services, it is hard to evaluate the characteristics of the available alternatives because the items are technical, intangible, new, or poorly labeled. When this occurs, shoppers often use price, brand name, or store name as an indicator of quality and choose based on this criterion. Once a person ranks the alternatives, he or she chooses the most satisfactory good or service. In situations where no alternative proves adequate, a decision not to purchase is made.

Purchase Act: A person is now ready for the **purchase act**—an exchange of money or a promise to pay for the ownership or use of a good or service. Important decisions are still made in this step. For a retailer, the purchase act may be the most crucial aspect of the decision process because the consumer is mainly concerned with three factors, as highlighted in Figure 7-6:

1. Place of purchase—This may be a store or a nonstore location. Many more items are bought at stores than through nonstore retailing, although the latter are growing more quickly. The place of purchase is evaluated in the same way as the good or the service: alternatives are listed, their traits are defined, and they are ranked. The most desirable place is then chosen. Criteria for selecting a store retailer include store location, store layout, service, sales help, store image, and prices. Criteria for selecting a nonstore retailer include image, service, prices, hours, interactivity, and convenience. A consumer will shop with the firm that has the best combination of criteria, as defined by that consumer.

FIGURE 7-6
Key Factors in the
Purchase Act

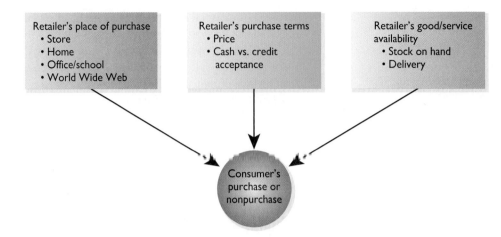

2. Purchase terms—These include the price and method of payment. Price is the dollar amount a person must pay to achieve the ownership or use of a good or service. Method of payment is the way the price may be paid (cash, short-term credit, long-term credit).
3. Availability—This relates to stock on hand and delivery. Stock on hand is the amount of an item that a place of purchase has in stock. Delivery is the time span between placing an order and receiving an item and the ease with which an item is transported to its place of use.

If a person is pleased with all of the aspects of the purchase act, the good or service is bought. If there is dissatisfaction with the place of purchase, the terms of purchase, or availability, the consumer may not buy, although there is contentment with the item itself:

> Karen wanted to buy a stereo. But, after a month of trying, she gave up: "The system I wanted was sold in only three stores and through an online firm. Two stores overpriced the stereo by $75. The third had a good price, but insisted I drive to the warehouse to get the stereo. The Web retailer had a good deal, but it ran out of the model I wanted. When I heard that, I decided to keep my old stereo."

Post-Purchase Behavior: After buying a good or service, a consumer may engage in **post-purchase behavior**, which falls into either of two categories: further purchases or re-evaluation. Sometimes, buying one item leads to further purchases and decision making continues until the last purchase is made. For instance, a car purchase leads to insurance; and a retailer that uses scrambled merchandising may stimulate a shopper to make further purchases, once the primary good or service is bought.

A person may also re-evaluate a purchase. Is the performance as promised? Do actual attributes match the expectations the consumer had of the attributes? Has the retailer acted as expected? Satisfaction typically leads to contentment, a repurchase when a good or service wears out, and favorable ratings to friends. Dissatisfaction may lead to unhappiness, brand or store switching, and unfavorable conversations with friends. The latter situation (dissatisfaction) may result from **cognitive dissonance**—doubt that the correct decision has been made. A consumer may regret that the purchase was made at all or may wish that another alternative had been chosen. To overcome cognitive dissonance and dissatisfaction, the retailer must realize that the consumer decision process does not end with a purchase. After-care (by a phone call, a service visit, or E-mail) may be as important as anything a retailer does to complete the sale. When items are expensive or important, after-care takes on greater significance because the person really wants to be right. In addition, the more alternatives from which to choose, the greater the doubt after a decision is made and the more important the after-care. Department stores pioneered the money-back guarantee so customers could return items if cognitive dissonance occurred.

Realistic sales presentations and ad campaigns reduce post-sale dissatisfaction because consumer expectations do not then exceed reality. If overly high expectations are created, a consumer is more apt to be unhappy because performance is not at the level promised. Combining an honest sales presentation with good customer after-care reduces or eliminates cognitive dissonance and dissatisfaction.

Types of Consumer Decision Making

Every time a person buys a good or service or visits a retailer, he or she uses a form of the decision process. The process is often used subconsciously, and a person is not even aware of its use. Also, as indicated in Figure 7-5, the process is affected by consumer characteristics. Older people may not spend as much time as younger ones in making some decisions due to their experience. Well-educated consumers may consult many information sources before making a decision. Upper-income consumers may spend less time making a decision because they can afford to buy again if they are dissatisfied. In a family with children, each member may have input into a decision, which lengthens the process. Class-conscious shoppers may be more interested in social sources. Consumers with low self-esteem or high perceived risk may use all the steps in detail. People under time pressure may skip steps to save time.

Careers in RETAILING
Chris: Regional Director of Loss Prevention

While in college, Chris worked in mall security—before obtaining an internship at a bank. For the internship, he did internal auditing and operational processes work. Upon college graduation, he was promoted to assistant bank manager.

Shortly thereafter, Chris attended a career fair where he talked with a recruiter for a specialty store chain that specialized in high-end men's suits. He dropped off his résumé because he had a personal interest in the investigative side of the auditing process that had been part of his responsibilities at the bank—digging in and finding the details. He wanted to explore how he could apply this personal interest in his professional life. Chris was hired as a loss prevention (LP) analyst. In this position, he had the opportunity and the challenge to develop the LP department from the ground up. There was only one other person in the department when Chris started. He enjoyed the work.

Chris had been with the company three years when a headhunter called. An up-and-coming specialty store chain was recruiting a District LP Manager, and Chris was offered and accepted this new challenge. Later on, after switching companies again, Chris' boss recognized his responsibility and the initiative Chris took in implementing projects above and beyond his job description. Because of Chris' work ethic and performance, this next position was created for him in order to retain Chris and develop his career path. As Senior Regional LP Manager, Chris had staff reporting directly to him and took on more of an LP-policy role.

At the age of 35, five years ahead of his personal schedule, Chris became Regional Director of LP, thus achieving his goal of a having a director-level title by age 40. He currently earns more than $100,000 per year, plus generous fringe benefits.

Source: Reprinted by permission of the National Retail Federation.

The use of the decision process differs by situation. The purchase of a new home usually means a thorough use of each step in the process; perceived risk is high regardless of the consumer's background. In the purchase of a magazine, the consumer often skips certain steps; perceived risk is low regardless of the person's background. There are three types of decision processes: extended decision making, limited decision making, and routine decision making.

Extended decision making occurs when a consumer makes full use of the decision process. A lot of time is spent gathering information and evaluating alternatives—both what to buy and where to buy it—before a purchase. The potential for cognitive dissonance is great. In this category are expensive, complex items with which the person has had little or no experience. Perceived risk of all kinds is high. Items requiring extended decision making include a house, a first car, and life insurance. At any point in the process, a consumer can stop, and for expensive, complex items, this occurs often. Consumer traits (such as age, education, income, and class consciousness) have the most impact with extended decision making.

Because their customers tend to use extended decision making, such retailers as real-estate brokers and auto dealers emphasize personal selling, printed materials, and other communication to provide as much information as possible. A low-key approach may be best, so shoppers feel comfortable and not threatened. In this way, the consumer's perceived risk is minimized.

With **limited decision making**, a consumer uses each step in the purchase process but does not spend a great deal of time on each of them. It requires less time than extended decision making since the person typically has some experience with both the what and the where of the purchase. This category includes items that have been bought before but not regularly. Risk is moderate, and the consumer spends some time shopping. Priority may be placed on evaluating known alternatives according to the person's desires and standards, although information search is important for some. Items requiring limited decision making include a second car, clothing, a vacation, and gifts. Consumer attributes affect decision making, but the impact lessens as perceived risk falls and experience rises. Income, the importance of the purchase, and motives play strong roles in limited decision making.

This form of decision making is relevant to such retailers as department stores, specialty stores, and nonstore retailers that want to sway behavior and that carry goods and services that people have bought before. The shopping environment and assortment are very important. Sales personnel should be available for questions and to differentiate among brands or models.

Routine decision making takes place when the consumer buys out of habit and skips steps in the purchase process. He or she wants to spend little or no time shopping, and the same brands are usually repurchased (often from the same retailers). This category includes items that are bought regularly. They have little risk because of consumer experience. The key step is problem awareness. When the consumer realizes a good or service is needed, a repurchase is often automatic. Information search, evaluation of alternatives, and post-purchase behavior are unlikely. These steps are not undertaken as long as a person is satisfied. Items involved with routine decision making include groceries, newspapers, and haircuts. Consumer attributes have little impact. Problem awareness almost inevitably leads to a purchase.

This type of decision making is most relevant to such retailers as supermarkets, dry cleaners, and fast-food outlets. For them, these strategic elements are crucial: a good location, long hours, clear product displays, and, most important, product availability. Ads should be reminder-oriented. The major task is completing the transaction quickly and precisely.

Impulse Purchases and Customer Loyalty

Impulse purchases and customer loyalty merit our special attention.

Impulse purchases arise when consumers buy products and/or brands they had not planned on buying before entering a store, reading a mail-order catalog, seeing a TV shopping show, turning to the Web, and so forth. At least part of consumer decision making is influenced by the retailer. There are three kinds of impulse shopping:

- *Completely unplanned*—A consumer has no intention of making a purchase in a goods or service category before he or she comes into contact with a retailer.
- *Partially unplanned*—A consumer intends to make a purchase in a goods or service category but has not chosen a brand or model before he or she comes into contact with a retailer.
- *Unplanned substitution*—A consumer intends to buy a specific brand of a good or service but changes his or her mind about the brand after coming into contact with a retailer.

With the partially unplanned and substitution kinds of impulse purchases, some decision making takes place before a person interacts with a retailer. In these cases, the consumer may be involved with extended, limited, or routine decision making. Completely unplanned shopping is usually related to routine decision making or limited decision making; there is little or no time spent shopping, and the key step is problem awareness.

Impulse purchases are more influenced by retail displays than are pre-planned purchases: "Serving as the last three feet of the marketing plan," point-of-purchase displays are effective "at the critical point where products, consumers, and the money to purchase the product all meet at the same time. It is no coincidence that with 74 percent of all purchase decisions in mass merchandisers made in the store, an increasing number of brand marketers and retailers invest in displays." And for retailers, "a seemingly irresistible price can seal the deal for an impulse buy. If something has been lowered in price, is perceived by the consumer to have real value, and may not be there next week, it might make for an appealing buy on impulse."[21] See Figure 7-7.

In studying impulse buying, these are some of the consumer attitudes and behavior patterns that retailers should take into consideration:

- In-store browsing is positively affected by the amount of time a person has to shop.
- Some individuals are more predisposed toward making impulse purchases than others.
- Those who enjoy shopping are more apt to make in-store purchase decisions.
- Impulse purchases are greater if a person has discretionary income to spend.[22]

L.L. Bean (www.llbean.com) has some of the most loyal customers around. See why.

When **customer loyalty** exists, a person regularly patronizes a particular retailer (store or nonstore) that he or she knows, likes, and trusts. This lets a person reduce decision making because he or she does not have to invest time in learning about and choosing the retailer from which to purchase. Loyal customers tend to be time-conscious, like shopping locally, do not often engage in outshopping, and spend more per shopping trip. In a service setting, such as an auto repair shop, customer satisfaction often leads to shopper loyalty; price has less bearing on decisions.

It can be testing to gain customer loyalty—a retailer's greatest asset: "'What classifies as customer loyalty today only lasts until the next, better deal comes

FIGURE 7-7
Stimulating Impulse
Purchases

Could you pass by this vending
machine without making a
purchase?

Photo reprinted by permission.

along,' said the chairman of America's Research Group. 'More people shop somewhere only because that place has the best selection and price of the moment. If
someone else comes along with a better offer, loyalty just isn't an issue.'"[23]
Applying the retailing concept certainly enhances the chances of gaining and
keeping loyal customers: customer orientation, coordinated effort, value-driven,
and goal orientation. Relationship retailing helps also!

As A.C. Nielsen notes,

> New retail formats are cropping up every day, retail channels overlap
> one another, and thanks to the Internet, nothing is more than a mouse
> click away. Retail technology has given us information on where con-
> sumers shop and what they buy. But the essence of customer loyalty is
> listening to people—finding out why they shop one particular venue
> and avoid others—and creating a satisfying shopping experience with
> repeat business that doesn't depend on having the lowest prices in
> town.[24]

RETAILER ACTIONS

As noted in Chapter 3, in *mass marketing*, a firm such as a supermarket or a drugstore sells to a broad spectrum of consumers; it does not really focus efforts on any
one kind of customer. In *concentrated marketing*, a retailer tailors its strategy to the
needs of one distinct consumer group, such as young working women; it does not
attempt to satisfy people outside that segment. With *differentiated marketing*, a
retailer aims at two or more distinct consumer groups, such as men and boys, with
a different strategy mix for each; it can do this by operating more than one kind of
outlet (such as separate men's and boys' clothing stores) or by having distinct

FIGURE 7-8
Contrasting Target Market Strategies

Lord & Taylor is an upscale department store chain, while Jack's 99¢ Stores appeals to customers looking for deep discounts and no frills.

Photos reprinted by permission.

departments grouped by market segment in a single store (as a department store might do). In deciding on a target market approach, a retailer considers its goods/service category and goals, competitors' actions, the size of various segments, the efficiency of each target market alternative for the particular firm, the resources required, and other factors. See Figure 7-8.

After choosing a target market method, the retailer selects the target market(s) to which it wants to appeal; identifies the characteristics, needs, and attitudes of the target market(s); seeks to understand how its targeted customers make purchase decisions; and acts appropriately. The process for devising a target market strategy is shown in Figure 7-9. Visit our Web site (**www.prenhall.com/bermanevans**) for several useful links on target marketing.

We now present several examples of retailers' target market activities.

Retailers with Mass Marketing Strategies

Murray's Discount Auto Parts and Kohl's Department Stores engage in mass marketing.

Murray's is a Michigan-based regional chain with more than 100 auto parts stores. Unlike many of its competitors, the firm works to attract a broad array of customers—not just experienced male do-it-yourselfers. Murray's offers personal

FIGURE 7-9
Devising a Target Market Strategy

Determine Target Market Approach → Select Specific Target Market(s) → Study Characteristics, Needs, and Attitudes of Target Market(s) → Examine How Consumers Make Decisions—by Product Category → Develop and Enact Appropriate Retail Strategy Mix(es) for the Target Market(s) Chosen

shoppers, computer-assisted ordering, and 10,000-square-foot stores with every-day low prices: "Murray's has just about everything you need to work on your car except the elbow grease. The chain sells only brand-name products, including AC Delco, Bosch, Ford/Motorcraft, Mother's, Quaker State, and Valvoline. In addition to auto parts, the stores provide services such as system and component testing and recycling."[25]

Find out why Kohl's is so popular (www.kohls.com).

Kohl's is one of the fastest-growing general merchandise retailers in the United States. And it is capitalizing on a mass marketing approach: "Our stores are stocked with everything you need for yourself and your home—apparel, shoes, and accessories for women, children, and men, plus home products like small electrics, bedding, luggage, and more." The firm has become a formidable threat to retailers such as Sears. And it is "forcing rivals to fight back with new store formats and services that mimic Kohl's mass marketing, even offering shopping carts and express checkouts near the exits at traditional department stores. Kohl's edge over rivals is an emphasis on big brands including Sag Harbor and Reebok that generally aren't available at discounters. Moreover, its prices are lower than at department stores, and it also avoids regional malls where department stores are based, focusing instead on strip centers that are more convenient for customers."[26]

Retailers with Concentrated Marketing Strategies

Family Dollar and Wet Seal engage in concentrated marketing.

Family Dollar
(www.familydollar.com)
has carved out a distinctive, narrow niche for itself.

Family Dollar operates 6,000 dollar stores (a type of variety store) in 44 states. It has a very focused target market strategy: The average Family Dollar customer is a female with an annual income of less than $35,000 who shops for her family. Customers depend on Family Dollar for the good prices they need to stretch their budgets. Stores are rather small and often situated in rural areas and small towns, as well as in urban areas. "Our merchandise is sold at everyday low prices in a no-frills, low overhead, self-service environment. Most merchandise is priced under $10.00."[27]

Wet Seal is a 425-store apparel chain that caters to young women. According to the company, "Whatever look young women crave, Wet Seal is the first place they go for the last word on style. This group tries on personalities as easily as they try on clothes, and they count on Wet Seal to supply an ever-changing, always fresh array of style choices." Wet Seal brings in new apparel and accessories on a regular basis. This "gives trendy young women the opportunity to explore every look under the sun, from casual to funky to glamorous."[28]

Retailers with Differentiated Marketing Strategies

Through its KFC, Pizza Hut, Taco Bell, Long John Silver's, and A&W restaurants, Yum! (www.yum.com) is another retailer practicing differentiated marketing—by food preference.

Foot Locker and Gap Inc. engage in differentiated marketing.

Besides its mainstream Foot Locker stores, the parent company (Foot Locker, Inc.) also operates chains geared specially toward women and children. Lady Foot Locker "has become the leading national athletic specialty store catering exclusively to women, with its core customer being 14 to 29 years old." Kids Foot Locker "has quickly become the market leader in children's athletic footwear and apparel, carrying the largest selection of merchandise for our core customer, children 5 to 11 years old."[29]

For many years, Gap Inc. has applied differentiated marketing through its Gap ("fashion apparel, accessories, and wardrobe staples—including Gap, Gap Kids, Baby Gap, and Gap Body"), Old Navy ("fun, fashion, and value for the whole family"), and Banana Republic ("an affordable luxury brand offering high-quality apparel and accessories) chains. Today, it has a new chain, Forth & Towne, which offers "fashionable apparel and accessories, targeting women over the age of 35."[30]

ENVIRONMENTAL FACTORS AFFECTING CONSUMERS

Several environmental factors influence shopping attitudes and behavior, including the:

- State of the economy.
- Rate of inflation (how quickly prices are rising).
- Infrastructure where people shop, such as traffic congestion, the crime rate, and the ease of parking.
- Price wars among retailers.
- Emergence of new retail formats.
- Trend toward more people working at home.
- Government and community regulations regarding shopping hours, new construction, consumer protection, and so forth.
- Evolving societal values and norms.

Although all of these elements may not necessarily have an impact on any particular shopper, they do influence the retailer's overall target market.

When considering the strategy that they offer their customers, retailers should also know the following about the U.S. standard of living:

> The standard of living in the United States is one of the highest in the world. Americans are some of the wealthiest people in the world, with a very high income per capita. Americans are top in the world for most material possessions. The number of TVs, vehicles, and other such products per person are considerably higher than in any other country. The United States also consistently has one of the lowest unemployment rates in the world. Nonetheless, much of the extra money in the United States is the result of a much wealthier top section of the population. The United States also has more people below the defined poverty line than several other countries. The wealthiest 10 percent of Americans are 15 times richer than the bottom 10 percent.[31]

Summary

1. *To discuss why it is important for a retailer to properly identify, understand, and appeal to its customers.* So as to properly develop a strategy mix, a retailer must identify the characteristics, needs, and attitudes of consumers; understand how consumers make decisions; and enact the proper target market plan. It must study environmental influences, too.

2. *To enumerate and describe a number of consumer demographics, lifestyle factors, and needs and desires—and to explain how these concepts can be applied to retailing.* Demographics are easily identifiable and measurable population statistics. Lifestyles are the ways in which consumers live and spend time and money.

Consumer demographics include gender, age, life expectancy, literacy, languages spoken, income, retail sales, education, and ethnic/racial background. These data usually have to be localized to be useful for retailers. Consumer lifestyles comprise social and psychological elements and are affected by demographics. Social factors include culture, social class, reference groups, the family life cycle, and time utilization. Psychological factors include personality, class consciousness, attitudes, perceived risk, and purchase importance. As with demographics, a firm can generate a lifestyle profile of its target market by analyzing these concepts.

There are several demographic and lifestyle trends that apply to retailing. These involve gender roles, consumer sophistication and confidence, the poverty of time, and component lifestyles. Research has enumerated consumer profiles in a useful way for retailers.

When preparing a target market profile, consumer needs and desires should be identified. Needs are basic shopping requirements and desires are discretionary shopping goals. A retail strategy geared toward satisfying consumer needs is appealing to their motives—the reasons for behavior. The better needs and desires are addressed, the more apt people are to buy.

3. *To examine consumer attitudes toward shopping and consumer shopping behavior, including the consumer decision process and its stages.* Many people do not enjoy shopping and no longer feel high prices reflect value. Different segments have different attitudes. More people now believe private brands are of good quality. Consumer patronage differs by retailer type. People often cross-shop, whereby they shop for a product category at more than one retail format during the year or visit multiple retailers on the same shopping trip.

Retailers should have an awareness of consumer behavior—the process individuals use to decide whether, what, when, where, how, from whom, and how often to buy. The consumer's decision process must be grasped from two perspectives: (a) the good or service the consumer thinks of buying and (b) where the consumer will buy that item. These decisions can be made separately or jointly.

The consumer decision process consists of stimulus, problem awareness, information search, evaluation of alternatives, purchase, and post-purchase behavior. It is influenced by a person's background and traits. A stimulus is a cue or drive meant to motivate a person to act. At problem awareness, the consumer not only has been aroused by a stimulus but also recognizes that a good or service may solve a problem of shortage or unfulfilled desire. An information search determines the available alternatives and their characteristics. Alternatives are then evaluated and ranked. In the purchase act, a consumer considers the place of purchase, terms, and availability. After a purchase, there may be post-purchase behavior in the form of additional purchases or re-evaluation. The consumer may have cognitive dissonance if there is doubt that a correct choice has been made.

In extended decision making, a person makes full use of the decision process. In limited decision making, each step is used, but not in depth. In routine decision making, a person buys out of habit and skips steps. Impulse purchases occur when shoppers make purchases they had not planned before coming into contact with the retailer. With customer loyalty, a person regularly patronizes a retailer.

4. *To look at retailer actions based on target market planning.* Retailers can deploy mass marketing, concentrated marketing, or differentiated marketing. Several examples are presented.

5. *To note some of the environmental factors that affect consumer shopping.* Consumer attitudes and behavior are swayed by the economy, the inflation rate, the infrastructure where people shop, and other factors. Retailers also need to consider how the standard of living is changing.

Key Terms

demographics (p. 198)
lifestyles (p. 198)
discretionary income (p. 199)
culture (p. 201)
social class (p. 202)
reference groups (p. 202)
family life cycle (p. 202)
household life cycle (p. 202)
personality (p. 202)
class consciousness (p. 202)

attitudes (opinions) (p. 202)
perceived risk (p. 202)
motives (p. 207)
outshopping (p. 207)
cross-shopping (p. 209)
consumer behavior (p. 210)
consumer decision process (p. 211)
stimulus (p. 212)
problem awareness (p. 212)
information search (p. 212)

evaluation of alternatives (p. 213)
purchase act (p. 213)
post-purchase behavior (p. 214)
cognitive dissonance (p. 214)
extended decision making (p. 216)
limited decision making (p. 216)
routine decision making (p. 216)
impulse purchases (p. 217)
customer loyalty (p. 217)

Questions for Discussion

1. Comment on this statement: "Each consumer segment has its own value equation and shops accordingly. Understanding what drives different groups is critical to creating an experience and product offering that satisfies their individual value equations."

2. Analyze the global population data in Table 7-1 from a retailing perspective.

3. How could a national camera store chain use the U.S. population data presented in Table 7-2?

4. Explain how a retailer selling expensive, custom-made jewelry could reduce the six types of perceived risk.

5. Why is it important for retailers to know the difference between needs and desires?

6. Why do some consumers engage in outshopping? What could be done to encourage them to shop closer to home?

7. Is cross-shopping good or bad for a retailer? Explain your answer.

8. Describe how the consumer decision process would operate for these goods and services. Include "what" and "where" in your answers: an iPod, a hedge trimmer, and a used car. Which elements of the decision process are most important to retailers in each instance? Explain your answers.

9. Differentiate among the three types of impulse purchases. Give an example of each.

10. Contrast the mass market approach used by a fast-food restaurant with the concentrated marketing approach used by an upscale restaurant. What is the key to each firm succeeding?

11. Visit a neraby Radio Shack (**www.radioshack.com**) and then describe its target market strategy.

12. Why is it valuable for retailers to know how the standard of living is changing?

Web-Based Exercise

Best Buy has widely promoted its "Geek Squad" as a major customer service initiative. Visit the Geek Squad Web site (**www.geeksquad.com**). Evaluate the target marketing efforts that you find described there, in terms of the concepts in this chapter.

Note: Stop by our Web site (**www.prenhall.com/bermanevans**) to experience a number of highly interactive, appealing Web exercises based on actual company demonstrations and sample materials related to retailing.

Chapter Endnotes

1. Various company sources.

2. 2005 Consumer Trends Report (New York, NY: Ernst & Young Consumer Trends Center), p. 2.

3. Authors' estimates, based on data from the U.S. Census Bureau (**www.census.gov**) and the U.S. Bureau of Labor (**www.bls.gov**) Web sites (February 7, 2006).

4. "Consumer Trends," *Progressive Grocer Annual Report of the Grocery Industry* (April 2005), p. 60.

5. Rebecca Harris, "Shop Psychology," *Marketing Magazine* (May 23, 2005), p. 4.

6. Pamela N. Danziger, "The Lure of Shopping," *American Demographics* (July–August 2002), p. 46.

7. WSL Strategic Retail, *How America Shops 1998.*

8. *Shopper Update: Home Goods Annual Data Review* (Columbus, OH: Retail Forward, March 2005), p. 1.

9. *Shopper Update: Soft Goods Point of View* (Columbus, OH: Retail Forward, June 2005), p. 3.

10. "Retailing: Specialty," *Standard & Poor's Industry Surveys* (January 13, 2005), p. 15.

11. "Desire, Not Necessity, Drives $3 Trillion in Consumer Spending," **http://retailindustry.about.com/library/bl/02q3/bl_um071202.htm** (September 23, 2002).

12. Steve Smith, "What Women Want When Shopping for CE," *Twice* (June 6, 2005), p. 20.

13. Anthony D. Cox, Dena Cox, and Ronald D. Anderson, "Reassessing the Pleasures of Store Shopping," *Journal of Business Research*, Vol. 58 (Number 3, 2005), pp. 250–259.

14. Calmetta Y. Coleman, "Making Malls (Gasp!) Convenient," *Wall Street Journal* (February 8, 2000), pp. B1, B4.

15. "Retailing: General," *Standard & Poor's Industry Surveys* (May 19, 2005), p. 14.

16. Ibid; and "Retailing: Specialty," *Standard & Poor's Industry Surveys* (January 13, 2005), p. 11.

17. Kurt Salmon Associates, "Which Way to the Emerald City?" *Perspective* (February 2000), p. 3.

18. Don Peppers, "Retailers Emphasize Customer Knowledge," **www.1to1.com/View.aspx?DocID=28792** (April 4, 2005).

19. Private Label Manufacturers Association, "Store Brands Today," **www.plma.com/storebrands/sbt02.html** (July 30, 2005).

20. For good background reading, see "Special Issue: Retail Consumer Decision Processes," *Journal of Business Research*, Vol. 54 (November 2001).

21. "The Retail Marketing Industry," **www.popai.com** (February 15, 2006).

22. Sharon E. Beatty and M. Elizabeth Ferrell, "Impulse Buying: Modeling Its Precursors," *Journal of Retailing*, Vol. 74 (Summer 1998), pp. 169–191.

23. Richard Burnett, "Customer Loyalty Is Up for Grabs," *Knight-Ridder/Tribune Business News* (January 27, 2002).

24. Ken Greenberg, "In Search of Loyalty," **http://us.acnielsen.com/pubs/2004_11_fff_loyalty.shtml** (November 2004).

25. "Murray's Discount Auto Stores, Inc.," **www.hoovers.com** (March 1, 2006); and "Murray's Discount Auto Stores: The Auto Parts Supermarket," **www.murraysdiscount.com** (March 1, 2006).

26. "About Kohl's," **www.kohlscorporation.com/About Kohls/AboutKohls01A.htm** (March 1, 2006); and "Kohl's Focus on Big Brands Gives Rivals Fits; Discount Retailer Expanding with Mass-Market Approach," *Bergen County Record* (June 2, 2002).

27. "Family Dollar Stores, Inc.," **www.hoovers.com** (March 3, 2006); and *Family Dollar 2005 Annual Report*.

28. "Corporate Information," **www.wetsealinc.com/corpinfo/corpinfo.asp?id=2** (March 3, 2006).

29. "Our Company," **www.footlocker-inc.com** (March 5, 2006).

30. "Our Brands," **www.gapinc.com/public/OurBrands/brands.shtml** (March 5, 2006).

31. "Standard of Living in the United States," **http://en.wikipedia.org/wiki/Standard_of_living_in_the_United_States** (March 7, 2006).

Chapter 8
INFORMATION GATHERING AND PROCESSING IN RETAILING

When Debbi Fields opened her first cookie store in Palo Alto, California, in 1977, she was a 20-year-old housewife with no business experience. Mrs. Fields Cookies (**www.mrsfields.com**) became popular very quickly, and several new stores were set up. To grow even faster, Mrs. Fields started franchising in 1990. Today the company has 400 stores in the United States and nearly 100 in foreign countries. The firm is the largest retailer of baked-on-premises specialty cookies and brownies in the United States.

Mrs. Fields is among the most widely recognized names in the premium cookie industry with 94 percent brand awareness among consumers. The retailer offers more than 50 different types of cookies, brownies, and muffins. To ensure freshness and quality, products are baked continuously, and all dough is centrally manufactured using only high-quality ingredients.

Reprinted by permission.

Mrs. Fields has several cookie stores in Hong Kong and recently opened its first two stores in Shanghai. In China, where Mrs. Fields targets women aged 20 to 35, 70 percent of its customers are foreign. The retailer is also generating sales by delivering cookies with children's names on them for birthday parties, through catering events at foreign schools, and by donating cookies for fundraising purposes. Although Mrs. Fields Cookies currently sells the same products in Shanghai as in the United States, it is considering adapting its menu in the future to appeal to foreign tastes. For example, Chinese customers generally prefer less sugary foods than Westerners. Mrs. Fields Cookies is experimenting with several marketing promotions such as free samples, joint promotions with local companies, and gift items.[1]

chapter objectives

1. To discuss how information flows in a retail distribution channel
2. To show why retailers should avoid strategies based on inadequate information
3. To look at the retail information system, its components, and the recent advances in such systems
4. To describe the marketing research process

OVERVIEW

When a retailer forms a new strategy or modifies an existing one, gathering and reviewing information is crucial because it reduces the chances of wrong decisions. The firm can study the attributes and buying behavior of current and potential customers, alternative store and nonstore sites, store management and operations, product offerings, prices, and store image and promotion to prepare the best plan.

Research activity should, to a large degree, be determined by the risk involved. Although it may be risky for a department store to open a new branch store, there is much less risk if a retailer is deciding whether to carry a new line of sweaters. In the branch store situation, thousands of research dollars and months of study may be necessary. In the case of the new sweaters, limited research may be sufficient.

iTools (www.itools.com) offers very useful research tools, including multiple search engines, a dictionary, a thesaurus, a language translator, and more.

Information gathering and processing should be conducted in an ongoing manner, yielding enough data for planning and analysis:

Decision makers—merchandisers, financial planners, inventory planners, buyers, and forecasters—throughout retail organizations clamor for the information necessary to gain a competitive advantage. They need the "business intelligence"—the availability of the right information to answer immediate business questions—to improve performance. Today's information systems let retailers interactively investigate performance and trends, and suppliers to assist in managing retail inventory.[2]

Wal-Mart wants suppliers to clean up product data and establish uniform product descriptions based on industry standards, all in the name of improved communications and more-efficient supply chains. The retailer is synchronizing product data such as packaging dimensions, color, and weight with suppliers across 2,000 product categories and 60,000 unique items. Consistency in product descriptions makes it easier to load delivery trucks, reduces discrepancies in orders, and increases the likelihood that the correct products get stocked on shelves. Wal-Mart also plans to expand data synchronization internationally.[3]

This chapter first looks at the information flows in a retail distribution channel and notes the ramifications of inadequate research. We then describe the retail information system, data-base management and data warehousing, and the marketing research process in detail.

INFORMATION FLOWS IN A RETAIL DISTRIBUTION CHANNEL

In an effective retail distribution channel, information flows freely and efficiently among the three main parties: supplier (manufacturer and/or wholesaler), retailer, and consumer. This enables the parties to better anticipate and address each other's performance expectations. We highlight the flows in Figure 8-1 and describe the information needs of the parties next.

A *supplier* needs these kinds of information: (1) from the retailer—estimates of category sales, inventory turnover rates, feedback on competitors, the level of customer returns, and so on; and (2) from the consumer—attitudes toward given styles and models, the extent of brand loyalty, the willingness to pay a premium for superior quality, and so on. A *retailer* needs these kinds of information: (1) from the supplier—advance notice of new models and model changes, training materials

FIGURE 8-1
How Information Flows in a
Retail Distribution Channel

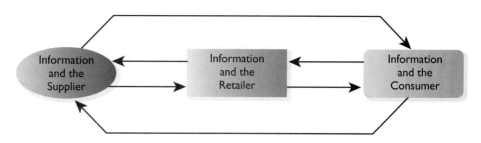

for complex products, sales forecasts, justification for price hikes, and so on; and (2) from the consumer—why people shop with the retailer, what they like and dislike about the retailer, where else people shop, etc. A *consumer* needs these kinds of information: (1) from the supplier—assembly and operating instructions, the extent of warranty coverage, where to send a complaint, and so on; and (2) from the retailer—where specific merchandise is stocked in the store, the methods of payment accepted, the rain check policy when a sale item is out of stock, etc.

Retailers often play a crucial role in collecting data for other members of the value delivery chain because they have the most direct contact with shoppers. Retailers can assist other channel members by:

- Allowing data to be gathered on their premises. Many research firms like to conduct surveys at shopping centers because of the large and broad base of shoppers.

- Gathering specific data requested by suppliers, such as how shoppers react to displays.

- Passing along information on the attributes of consumers buying particular brands and models. Since credit transactions account for a major portion of sales, many retailers link purchases with consumer age, income, occupation, and other factors.

Careers in RETAILING — Is Retail for Me? IT and E-Commerce—Part 1

Technology careers are numerous in retailing. From technology-driven training programs delivered over satellites or the Internet to state-of-the-art cash register and credit systems, from Web design to servers and network systems management, technology careers are only growing in the retail industry:

- *Head of Information Systems and Data Processing:* Top position with overall responsibility for the data-processing efforts within the firm, including systems design, programming, computer operations, and information systems (IS) capital purchasing.

- *Head of Systems Applications Programming:* Top position responsible for coordinating systems planning and programming. This person typically reports to the head of information systems and data processing. In some chains, there may be multiple software heads, responsible separately for merchandising, finance, and operations systems, for example.

- *Systems Development Manager:* Coordinates systems planning and programming with user requirements. This position reports to the head of systems applications programming. Typically responsible for programming one business segment, such as merchandising, finance, or logistics.

- *Head of Computer Operations/Technical Services:* This is the top computer operations/technical service position and reports to the head of information systems and data processing. Establishes operating standards, and may initiate capital budgets. Responsible for coordinating computer operations with workstation networks, telecommunications, and any other data operations.

- *Point of Sales Administrator:* Controls the daily processing of sales and inventory information. Sets procedures for POS applications, reviews store systems, and may maintain a help desk for users.

Source: Reprinted by permission of the National Retail Federation.

For the best information flows, collaboration and cooperation are necessary—especially between suppliers and retailers. This is not always easy, as the view of one senior retail executive indicates: "Traditionally, retailers and suppliers just don't like to share supply-chain information with each other. They're more inclined to guard that valuable data than to give it away, even when sharing it would be in their own best interest. As it is, there's friction between retailer and supplier in every step of the supply chain. That's why we still have a messed-up supply chain."[4]

Fortunately, many retailers are working to improve their information-sharing efforts. And as in many aspects of retailing, Wal-Mart is leading the way. Thousands of suppliers have online access to Wal-Mart's password-protected data base through the firm's Retail Link system (**https://retaillink.wal-mart.com**), which handles more than 150,000 complex information queries weekly. Retail Link was developed more than a decade ago to promote more collaboration in inventory planning and product shipping, and it is a linchpin of Wal-Mart's information efforts today:

> Retail Link provides information and an array of products that allows a supplier to impact all aspects of their business. By using the information available in Retail Link, suppliers can plan, execute, and analyze their businesses—thus providing better service to our common customers. Retail Link is a Web site that is accessible to any area within your company. Wal-Mart requires all suppliers to participate in Retail Link because of the benefits it provides. Should you become a supplier with Wal-Mart, you will be provided with the requirements for accessing Retail Link.[5]

AVOIDING RETAIL STRATEGIES BASED ON INADEQUATE INFORMATION

Retailers are often tempted to rely on nonsystematic or incomplete ways of obtaining information due to time and costs, as well as a lack of research skills. The results can be devastating. Here are examples.

Using intuition—A movie theater charges $10 for tickets at all times. The manager feels that because all patrons are seeing the same movie, prices should be the same for a Monday matinee as a Saturday evening. Yet, by looking at data stored in the theater's information system, she would learn attendance is much lower on Mondays, indicating that because people prefer Saturday evening performances, they will pay $10 to see a movie then. Weekday customers have to be lured, and a lower price is a way to do so.

Continuing what was done before—A toy store orders conservatively for the holiday season because prior year sales were weak. The store sells out two weeks before the peak of the season, and more items cannot be received in time for the holiday. The owner assumed that last year's poor sales would occur again. Yet, a consumer survey would reveal a sense of optimism and an increased desire to give gifts.

Copying a successful competitor's strategy—A local independent bookstore decides to cut the prices of best-sellers to match the prices of a nearby chain bookstore. The local store then loses a lot of money and has to go out of business. Its costs are too high to match the chain's prices. The firm lost sight of its natural strengths (personal service, a more customer-friendly atmosphere, and long-time community ties).

Devising a strategy after speaking to a few individuals about their perceptions—A family-run gift store decides to have a family meeting to determine the product assortment for the next year. Each family member gives an opinion and an overall "shopping list" is then compiled. Sometimes the selections are right on target; other times, they result in a lot of excess inventory. The family would do better by also attending trade shows and reading industry publications.

Automatically assuming that a successful business can easily expand—A Web retailer does well with small appliances and portable TVs. It has a good reputation and wants to add other product lines to capitalize on its customer goodwill. However, the addition of furniture yields poor results. The firm did not first conduct research, which would have indicated that people buy standard, branded merchandise via the Web but are more reluctant to buy most furniture that way.

Not having a good read on consumer perceptions—A florist cuts the price of two-day-old flowers from $17 to $5 a dozen because they have a shorter life expectancy, but they don't sell. The florist assumes bargain-hunting consumers will want the flowers as gifts or for floral arrangements. What the florist does not know (due to a lack of research) is that people perceive the older flowers to be of poor quality. The reduced price actually turns off customers!

What conclusion should we draw from these examples? Inadequate information can cause a firm to enact a bad strategy. These situations can be avoided by using a well-conceived retail information system and properly executing marketing research.

THE RETAIL INFORMATION SYSTEM

A retail information system requires a lot of background information, which makes the SecondaryData.com Web site valuable (**www.secondarydata.com/ marketing/retailing.asp**).

Data gathering and analysis should not be regarded as a one-shot resolution of a single issue. They should be part of an ongoing, integrated process. A **retail information system (RIS)** anticipates the information needs of retail managers; collects, organizes, and stores relevant data on a continuous basis; and directs the flow of information to the proper decision makers.

These topics are covered next: building and using a retail information system, data-base management, and gathering information through the UPC and EDI.

Building and Using a Retail Information System

Figure 8-2 presents a general RIS. The retailer begins with its business philosophy and objectives, which are influenced by environmental factors (such as competitors and the economy). The philosophy and goals provide broad guidelines that direct strategic planning. Some aspects of plans are routine and need little re-evaluation. Others are nonroutine and need evaluation each time they arise.

Once a strategy is outlined, the data needed to enact it are collected, analyzed, and interpreted. If data already exist, they are retrieved from files. When new data are acquired, files are updated. All of this occurs in the information control center. Based on data in the control center, decisions are enacted.

Performance results are fed back to the information control center and compared with pre-set criteria. Data are retrieved from files or further data are collected. Routine adjustments are made promptly. Regular reports and exception reports (to explain deviations from expected performance) are given to the right managers. Sometimes managers may react in a way that affects the overall philosophy or goals (such as revising an old-fashioned image or sacrificing short-run profits to introduce a computer system).

All types of data should be stored in the control center for future and ongoing use, and the control center should be integrated with the firm's short- and long-run

FIGURE 8-2

A Retail Information System

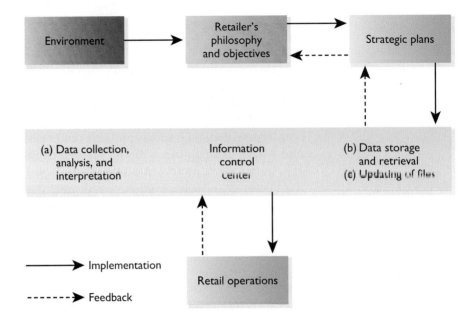

Retail Info Systems News (**www.risnews.com**) provides good insights for retailers.

plans and operations. Information should not be gathered sporadically and haphazardly but systematically.

A good RIS has several strengths. Information gathering is organized and company focused. Data are regularly gathered and stored so that opportunities are foreseen and crises averted. Strategic elements can be coordinated. New strategies can be devised more quickly. Quantitative results are accessible, and cost-benefit analysis can be done. Information is routed to the right personnel. However, deploying an RIS may require high initial time and labor costs, and complex decisions may be needed to set up such a system.

In building a retail information system, a number of decisions have to be made:

- *How active a role should the RIS have?* Will it proactively search for and distribute any relevant information or will it reactively respond to requests from managers when problems arise? The best systems are more proactive, since they anticipate events.

- *Should an RIS be managed internally or be outsourced?* Although many retailers perform RIS functions, some use outside specialists. Either style can work, as long as the RIS is guided by the retailer's information needs. Several firms have their own RIS and use outside firms for specific tasks (such as conducting surveys or managing networks).

- *How much should an RIS cost?* Retailers typically spend 0.5 to 1.5 percent of their sales on an RIS. This lags behind most of the suppliers from which retailers buy goods and services.[6]

- *How technology-driven should an RIS be?* Although retailers can gather data from trade associations, surveys, and so forth, more firms now rely on technology to drive the information process. With the advent of personal computers, inexpensive networks, and low-priced software, technology is easy to use. Even a neighborhood deli can generate sales data by product and offer specials on slow-sellers.

- *How much data are enough?* The purpose of an RIS is to provide enough information, on a regular basis, for a retailer to make the proper strategy choices—not to overwhelm retail managers. This means a balancing act between too

Ethics in RETAILING
The Impact of Negative Customer Service

Amdocs (**www.amdocs.com**), a billing and customer relationship management service provider, recently conducted a national survey of 1,000 consumers about their recent experiences in the banking, cable, retail, and telecommunications industries. The study found that only 13 percent of the respondents reported having a customer service experience they would describe as completely satisfactory. And 45 percent of consumers felt that most companies provide bad customer service. In contrast, the survey found that 93 percent of respondents expected most companies to provide good customer service. Eighty-nine percent of the respondents also felt that good customer service should not be difficult to provide.

The survey cited a number of consumer reactions to poor customer service. Over 75 percent of respondents said they would hang up on a customer service call if they were placed on hold for over five minutes. Three-quarters of respondents stated that they would tell their friends and family members about negative customer experiences with firms. And 85 percent of all respondents stated that negative customer service would drive them to switch service providers.

Sources: Linda Abu-Shalback Zid, "Two Strikes and You're Out," *Marketing Management* (September–October 2004), p. 5; and "Amdocs 2004 Customer Service Survey Results," **www.amdocs.com/documents/survey-results.html** (June 27, 2005).

little information and information overload. To avoid overload, data should be carefully edited to eliminate redundancies.

- *How should data be disseminated throughout the firm?* This requires decisions as to who receives various reports, the frequency of data distribution, and access to data bases. When a firm has multiple divisions or operates in several regions, information access and distribution must be coordinated.

- *How should data be stored for future use?* Relevant data should be stored in a manner that makes information retrieval easy and allows for adequate longitudinal (period-to-period) analysis.

Larger retailers tend to have a chief information officer (CIO) overseeing their RIS. Information systems departments often have formal, written annual plans. Computers are used by most companies that conduct information systems analysis, and many firms use the Web for some RIS functions. Growth in the use of retail information systems is expected. There are many differences in information systems among retailers, on the basis of revenues and retail format.

Twenty-five years ago, most computerized retail systems were used only to reduce cashier errors and improve inventory control. Today they often form the foundation for a retail information system and are used in surveys, ordering, merchandise transfers between stores, and other tasks. These activities are conducted by both small and large retailers. The vast majority of small and medium retailers—as well as large retailers—have computerized financial management systems, analyze sales electronically, and use computerized inventory management systems. Here are illustrations of the ways in which retailers are using the latest technological advances to computerize their information systems.

Island Pacific markets Retail Pro management information software to retailers. See Figure 8-3. This software is used at stores around the world. Although popular with large retailers, Retail Pro software also has an appeal among smaller retailers due to flexible pricing based on the number of users and stores, the type of hardware, and so forth:

To see the various applications of Retail Pro, visit this Web site (**www.islandpacific.com/ RPFeature.htm**).

Retail Pro is the leading point-of-sale and inventory management software used by specialty retailers worldwide. Over 10,000 retail companies have purchased Retail Pro since 1986. Retailers are experiencing the

FIGURE 8-3
Retail Pro Management
Information Software

Reprinted by permission of Retail
Technologies International.

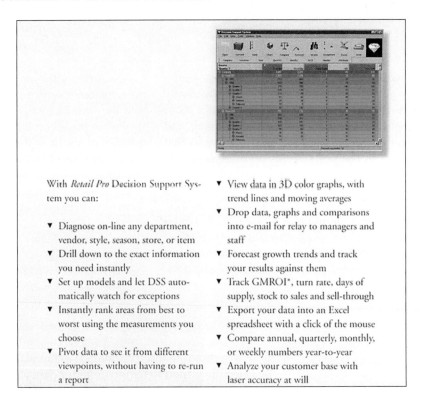

With *Retail Pro* Decision Support System you can:

▼ Diagnose on-line any department, vendor, style, season, store, or item

▼ Drill down to the exact information you need instantly

▼ Set up models and let DSS automatically watch for exceptions

▼ Instantly rank areas from best to worst using the measurements you choose

▼ Pivot data to see it from different viewpoints, without having to re-run a report

▼ View data in 3D color graphs, with trend lines and moving averages

▼ Drop data, graphs and comparisons into e-mail for relay to managers and staff

▼ Forecast growth trends and track your results against them

▼ Track GMROI*, turn rate, days of supply, stock to sales and sell-through

▼ Export your data into an Excel spreadsheet with a click of the mouse

▼ Compare annual, quarterly, monthly, or weekly numbers year-to-year

▼ Analyze your customer base with laser accuracy at will

benefits of Retail Pro on a daily basis, such as a best-of-breed point-of-sale system, sophisticated business intelligence tools for stock replenishment, and an easy-to-use fully integrated report designer module. Retail Pro is currently being used in 73 countries and has been translated into 18 different languages. Retail Pro excels in multi-store management, customer tracking, and is easy to use. Our standard system works flawlessly with all the latest in hardware technology, including touchscreens at the POS, signature capture, and more. With Retail Pro, retailers have been able to take control of their inventory, improve their cash flow, and save time and money.[7]

MicroStrategy typically works with larger retailers—including two-thirds of the top 500 retailers in the world—to prepare computerized information systems. Clients include Ace Hardware, Benetton, eBay, Lowe's, and Wet Seal. One of its leading products is MicroStrategy Desktop:

This business intelligence software provides integrated monitoring, reporting, powerful analytics, and decision support workflow on an intuitive Windows-based interface. MicroStrategy Desktop provides users with the means to easily access and share critical corporate information from the data base in order to make cost-cutting decisions and improve business processes. Even complex reports are easy to create; they can be viewed in various presentation formats, polished into production reports, distributed to other users, and extended through a host of ad hoc features including drilling, pivoting, and data slicing. Developers and power users alike employ MicroStrategy Desktop as the primary development interface for the MicroStrategy platform; however, the interface can also be customized for different users' skill levels and security profiles.[8]

Staples, the office supplies superstore chain with nearly 1,500 stores, recently undertook a major revamping of its information system:

> According to the Data Warehousing Institute, before its recent system overhaul, Staples couldn't identify purchasing trends and lacked the dexterity to make merchandising decisions because of its inability to access customer sales information. Staples turned to IBM to integrate the company's data and provide real-time analysis. Now, Staples' product managers can review sales data from the company's retail, catalog, and online channels. They can evaluate sales performance, collect customer intelligence, and complete reports faster than in the past, without having to access a number of diverse systems. The director of enterprise data management at Staples says that the company can adapt more quickly to changing business conditions and marketplace demands.[9]

Data-Base Management

In **data-base management**, a retailer gathers, integrates, applies, and stores information related to specific subject areas. It is a major element in an RIS and may be used with customer data bases, vendor data bases, product category data bases, and so on. A firm may compile and store data on customer attributes and purchase behavior, compute sales figures by vendor, and store records by product category. Each of these would represent a separate data base. Among retailers that have data bases, most use them for frequent shopper programs, customer analysis, promotion evaluation, inventory planning, trading-area analysis, joint promotions with manufacturers, media planning, and customer communications.

Data-base management should be approached as a series of five steps:

1. Plan the particular data base and its components, and determine information needs.
2. Acquire the necessary information.
3. Retain the information in a usable and accessible format.
4. Update the data base regularly to reflect changing demographics, recent purchases, and so forth.
5. Analyze the data base to determine company strengths and weaknesses.

Information can come from internal and external sources. A retailer can develop data bases internally by keeping detailed records and arranging them. It could generate data bases *by customer*—purchase frequency, items bought, average purchase, demographics, and payment method; *by vendor*—total retailer purchases per period, total sales to customers per period, the most popular items, retailer profit margins, average delivery time, and service quality; and *by product category*—total category sales per period, item sales per period, retailer profit margins, and the percentage of items discounted.

Donnelley (www.donnelleymarketing.com) offers a number of useful products to help small firms build and manage their data bases.

There are firms that compile data bases and make them available for a fee. Donnelley Marketing, a subsidiary of infoUSA, has a comprehensive U.S. data base, with data on more than 95 percent of all households. Its DQI[3] data base is a comprehensive source of demographic and lifestyle information: "Our multi-sourced consumer data base provides you with the best coverage. We offer hundreds of different demographic and lifestyle elements to help you pinpoint exactly the right prospects. Valuable demographic and lifestyle information is compiled using thousands of public, proprietary, and self-reported sources. We help our clients understand everything they need to know about their customers." The data base allows selection by age, income, types of auto, and credit card holders—to name a few."[10]

To effectively manage a retail data base, these are vital considerations:

- Is senior management knowledgeable in data-base strategies and does it know how company data bases are currently being used?
- Is there a person or department responsible for overseeing the data base?
- Does the firm have data-base acquisition and retention goals?
- Is every data-base initiative analyzed to see if it is successful?
- Is there a mechanism to flag data that indicates potential problems or opportunities?
- Are customer purchases of different products or company divisions cross-linked?
- Is there a clear privacy policy that is communicated to those in a data base? Are there opt-out provisions for those who do not want to be included in a data base?
- Is the data base updated each time there is a customer interaction?
- Are customers, personnel, suppliers, and others invited to update their personal data?
- Is the data base periodically checked to eliminate redundant files?[11]

Let us now discuss two aspects of data-base management: Data warehousing is a mechanism for storing and distributing information. Data mining and micromarketing are ways in which information can be utilized. Figure 8-4 shows the interplay of data warehousing with data mining and micromarketing.

Data Warehousing

NCR publishes a useful online *Data Warehousing Report* (**www.teradata. com/dwr**) with timely tips and news.

One recent advance in data-base management is **data warehousing**, whereby copies of all the data bases in a firm are maintained in one location and accessible to employees at any locale. Simply stated, a data warehouse is a collection of data that supports management decision making: "Typically, a data warehouse is housed on an enterprise mainframe server. It is a central repository for all or significant

FIGURE 8-4

Retail Data-Base Management in Action

The data warehouse is where information is collected, sorted, and stored centrally. Information is disseminated to retailer personnel, as well as to channel partners (such as alerting them to what merchandise is hot and what is not hot) and customers (such as telling them about order status). In data mining, retail executives and other employees—and sometimes channel partners—analyze information by customer type, product category, and so forth in order to determine opportunities for tailored marketing efforts. With micromarketing, the retailer applies differentiated marketing. Focused retail strategy mixes are planned for specific customer segments—or even for individual customers.

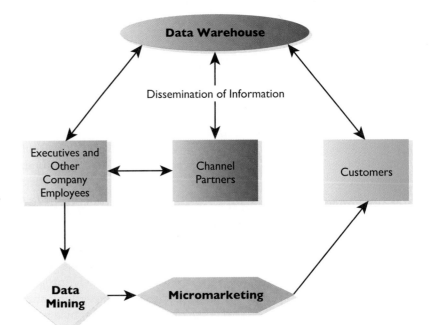

parts of the data that a firm's numerous business systems collect. Data warehousing describes the process of defining, populating, and using a data warehouse." This process "emphasizes the capture of data from diverse sources for useful analysis and access."[12]

A data warehouse has the following components: (1) the data warehouse, where data are physically stored; (2) software to copy original data bases and transfer them to the warehouse; (3) interactive software to process inquiries; and (4) a directory for the categories of information kept in the warehouse.

Data warehousing has several advantages. Executives and other employees are quickly, easily, and simultaneously able to access data wherever they may be. There is more companywide entrée to new data when they are first available. Data inconsistencies are reduced by consolidating records in one location. Better data analysis and manipulation are possible because information is stored in one location.

Computerized data warehouses were once costly to build (an average of $2.2 million a decade ago) and, thus, feasible only for the largest retailers. This has changed. A simple data warehouse can now be put together for less than $25,000, making it affordable to all but very small retailers (which do not have to deal with far-flung executives, making data warehousing less necessary for them).

Federated Department Stores, Hollywood Video, 7-Eleven, and Sears are just a few of the thousands of firms that use data warehousing: "Retailers have collected vast amounts of data for years, but they have not had the means to apply it effectively to their planning and buying because, until a few years ago, no computer or software application could process all of that data. The applications available today offer retailers better results because they incorporate more than just historical sales data."[13] See Figure 8-5.

Fossil is one of many retailers that is positioning itself for long-term growth and focusing on cost reductions through a new data warehousing structure:

> SAP for Retail software is expected to help cut inventory in Fossil's supply chain by fueling collaboration and providing clarity across all its sales channels. As inventory for all sales channels in the United States is consolidated in its 500,000-square-foot warehouse and distribution center in Dallas, Fossil can reduce the amount of available inventory and increase the number of times product flows through the warehouse and

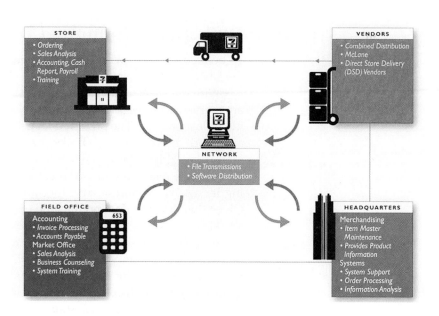

FIGURE 8-5

7-Eleven's Forword-Looking Approach to Data Warehousing

By electronically connecting all parties in the 7-Eleven supply chain, its retail information system creates a higher level of coordination and much better decision making. Store operators have actual sales information presented in logical formats and are able to order more effectively. Receiving exact orders in an organized fashion allows vendors to provide better service to the stores. Field offices are able to reduce administration costs by receiving information in electronic format. Headquarters merchandising staff are able to judge new product acceptance and communicate upcoming advertising and promotions from manufacturers that will affect sales.

Reprinted by permission.

into the stores. SAP for Retail will tie together sales data and inventory information across the 140 Fossil boutique stores and outlets worldwide that sell watches, jeans, shirts, belts, and other accessories, with its wholesale and E-commerce businesses.[14]

Data Mining and Micromarketing

Data mining is the in-depth analysis of information to gain specific insights about customers, product categories, vendors, and so forth. The goal is to learn if there are opportunities for tailored marketing efforts that would lead to better retailer performance. One application of data mining is **micromarketing**, whereby the retailer uses differentiated marketing and develops focused retail strategy mixes for specific customer segments, sometimes fine-tuned for the individual shopper.

For an in-depth discussion, go to About Retail Industry (**http://retailindustry.about. com**) and type "customer data mining" in the search engine.

Data mining relies on special software to sift through a data warehouse to uncover patterns and relationships among different factors. The software allows vast amounts of data to be quickly searched and sorted. That is why many firms such as Bear Creek, the parent of Harry & David (the popular fruit and gift direct marketer), have made the financial commitment to data mining: "We've had to invest in our data bases. They are key to our success in being able to identify and segment customers. They allow us to look at customer purchasing behavior and effectively manage our mailing and E-mail campaigns."[15]

Look at how Fairmont Resort Hotels is using data mining in the firm's micromarketing efforts:

> The hotel chain wanted to learn more about its customers, but there were some questions it couldn't ask them directly. So, the Toronto-based hotel chain decided to use MapInfo's Psyte data mining tool to get a better understanding of who its customers were and what kinds of vacations they were likely to take. As its executive director of marketing services noted, "We were looking for a partner that could provide us with more information about our guests in terms of their lifestyle—things that would be inappropriate to ask directly of our guests." The hotel overlays the information it gets from its customers when they enroll in its loyalty program with information from MapInfo. It has used the data to help it make purchase decisions for new resorts, place ads where they are more likely to reach customers, and send better-targeted advertising brochures to its customers.[16]

Gathering Information Through the UPC and EDI

To be more efficient with their information systems, many retailers now rely on the Universal Product Code (UPC) and electronic data interchange (EDI).

With the **Universal Product Code (UPC)**, products (or tags attached to them) are marked with a series of thick and thin vertical lines, representing each item's identification code. The preferred UPC includes both numbers and lines. The lines are "read" by scanners at checkout counters. Cashiers do not enter transactions manually—although they can, if needed. Because the UPC itself is not readable by humans, the retailer or vendor must attach a ticket or sticker to a product specifying its size, color, and other information (if not on the package or the product). Given that the UPC does not include price information, this too must be added by a ticket or sticker.

By using UPC-based technology, retailers can record data instantly on an item's model number, size, color, and other factors when it is sold, as well as send the data to a computer that monitors unit sales, inventory levels, and so forth. The goals are to produce better merchandising data, improve inventory management, speed transaction time, raise productivity, reduce errors, and coordinate information.

Since its inception, UPC technology has improved substantially. Today, it is the accepted standard in retailing:

> Today there are about five billion scans every day. The UPC has allowed retailers to control their inventory more efficiently, provided a faster and more accurate check out for customers, and made gathering information for accurate and immediate marketing studies incredibly simple.[17]

Virtually every time sales or inventory data are scanned by computer, UPC technology is involved. More than 250,000 U.S. manufacturers and retailers belong to GS1 US (formerly known as the Uniform Code Council), a group that has taken the lead in setting and promoting interindustry product identification and communication standards. Figure 8-6 shows how far UPC technology has

FIGURE 8-6
Applying UPC Technology to Gain Better Information

As this photo montage shows, Symbol Technologies has devised a host of scanning products (some of which are wireless) that make UPC data capture and processing quite simple. For example, Symbol products can be used at the point of sale to enter transaction data and transmit them to a central office, at product displays to verify shelf prices, at storage areas to aid in taking physical inventories, at receiving stations to log in the receipt of new merchandise, and at delivery points to track the movement of customer orders.

Photos reprinted by permission of Symbol Technologies.

Global eXchange Services
is one of the leaders in
EDI technology
(www.gegxs.com).

come. The UPC is discussed further in Chapter 16 ("Financial Merchandise Management").

With **electronic data interchange (EDI)**, retailers and suppliers regularly exchange information through their computers with regard to inventory levels, delivery times, unit sales, and so on of particular items. As a result, both parties enhance their decision-making capabilities, better control inventory, and are more responsive to demand. UPC scanning is often the basis for product-related EDI data. Tens of thousands of firms around the world use some form of EDI system. Consider this scenario:

> Virtually every pair of blue jeans sold in a department store today is tracked through a barcode system. When the retailer's computer system sees that the supply of a particular style and size is low, it automatically generates a purchase order that is transmitted to the apparel manufacturer via EDI. The manufacturer's EDI system imports the information into a computer data base. It is confirmed that the product is in stock, the product is found via barcode, and a trucking company is notified. When the truck picks up the jeans, the EDI system creates an advance shipment notice and sends it via EDI to the retailer. At the same time, a barcode label for the shipping carton is created. When the truck delivers the jeans, the retailer scans the barcode label. The retailer then automatically generates an electronic funds transfer.[18]

Today more retailers are expanding their EDI efforts to incorporate Internet communications with suppliers. One such retailer is the Piggly Wiggly supermarket chain, which has reduced its EDI costs by 20 percent since converting from a conventional to an Internet-based EDI system: "The Internet changed the picture for EDI. Suddenly, it seemed there was a single, low-cost, all-inclusive way to connect computer networks for data exchange. Why absorb high upfront and transaction costs, when you could make use of standard PCs? New standards allow secure, direct connections between supplier and customer, over the Internet."[19]

EDI is covered further in Chapter 15 ("Implementing Merchandise Plans"); CPFR (collaborative planning, forecasting, and replenishment) is also discussed there.

THE MARKETING RESEARCH PROCESS

Marketing research in retailing entails the collection and analysis of information relating to specific issues or problems facing a retailer. At farsighted firms, marketing research is just one element in a retail information system. At others, marketing research may be the only type of data gathering and processing.

The **marketing research process** embodies a series of activities: defining the issue or problem to be studied, examining secondary data, generating primary data (if needed), analyzing data, making recommendations, and implementing findings. It is not a single act; it is a systematic process. Figure 8-7 outlines the research process. Each activity is done sequentially. Secondary data are not examined until after an issue or problem is defined. The dashed line around the primary

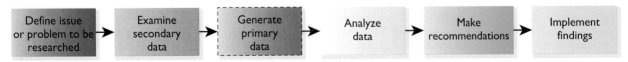

FIGURE 8-7
The Marketing Research Process in Retailing

data stage means these data are generated only if secondary data do not yield actionable information. The process is described next.

Issue (problem) definition involves a clear statement of the topic to be studied. What information does the retailer want to obtain to make a decision? Without clearly knowing the topic to be researched, irrelevant and confusing data could be collected. Here are examples of issue definitions for a shoe store. The first one seeks to compare three locations and is fairly structured; the second is more open-ended:

1. "Of three potential new store locations, which should we choose?"
2. "How can we improve the sales of our men's shoes?"

When **secondary data** are involved, a retailer looks at data that have been gathered for purposes other than addressing the issue or problem currently under study. Secondary data may be internal (such as company records) or external (such as government reports and trade publications). When **primary data** are involved, a retailer looks at data that are collected to address the specific issue or problem under study. This type of data may be generated via survey, observation, experiment, and simulation.

Secondary data are sometimes relied on; other times, primary data are crucial. In some cases, both are gathered. It is important that retailers keep these points in mind: One, there is great diversity in the possible types of data collection (and in the costs). Two, only data relevant to the issue being studied should be collected. Three, primary data are usually acquired only if secondary data are inadequate (thus, the dashed box in Figure 8-7). Both secondary and primary data are described further in the next sections.

These kinds of secondary and primary data can be gathered for the shoe store issues just stated:

Issue (Problem) Definition	Information Needed to Solve Issue (Problem)
1. Which store location?	1. Data on access to transportation, traffic, consumer profiles, rent, store size, and types of competition are gathered from government reports, trade publications, and observation by the owner for each of the three potential store locations.
2. How to improve sales of shoes?	2. Store sales records for the past five years by product category are gathered. A consumer survey in a nearby mall is conducted.

Technology in RETAILING

HyperActive Bob: Predictive Technology Comes to Fast Food

As a result of a robot manager known as "HyperActive Bob" (**www.gohyper.com/Content/HyperActiveBob.aspx**), the term "fast food" may soon take on a new meaning. HyperActive Bob, being tested at select McDonald's, Taco Bell, and Burger King restaurants in the Pittsburgh area, uses rooftop cameras to track vehicles as they enter the restaurant's parking lot. This gives the restaurant one-and-a-half minutes' advance notice of a vehicle's reaching the drive-through window and three to five minutes' notice of a group of customers arriving at the counter.

Bob matches information from its cameras with data bases from each store. This helps restaurants anticipate demand. For example, if Bob knows that one-fifth of the cars entering the drive-in lane typically order a cheeseburger, cheeseburgers will be grilled at the time when six cars are observed entering the restaurant location. In one refinement, Bob will be able to determine if different types of vehicles are associated with different ordering patterns. According to the manager at a McDonald's where Bob was installed, "It's put 10 years on my life and probably saved me from a heart attack."

Sources: Ed McKinley, "We're Not Asking, We Know You Want Fries with That," *Stores* (November 2004); and "HyperActive Bob," **www.hyperactivetechnologies.com/Library/pages/flashversion/products/boboverview.cfm** (April 11, 2006).

After data are collected, data analysis is performed to assess that information and relate it to the defined issue. Alternative solutions are also clearly outlined. For example:

Issue (Problem) Definition	Alternative Solutions
1. Which store location?	1. Each site is ranked for all of the criteria (access to transportation, traffic, consumer profiles, rent, store size, and types of competition).
2. How to improve sales of shoes?	2. Alternative strategies to boost sales are analyzed and ranked

At this point, the pros and cons of each alternative are enumerated. See Table 8-1. Recommendations are then made as to the best strategy for the retailer. Of the available options, which is best? Table 8-1 also shows recommendations for the shoe-store issues discussed in this section.

Last, but not least, the recommended strategy is implemented. If research is to replace intuition in strategic retailing, a decision maker must follow the recommendations from research studies, even if they seem to contradict his or her own ideas.

Let us now look at secondary data and primary data in greater depth.

Through Report Gallery (www.reportgallery.com), a retailer can do competitive intelligence on other firms around the globe. Want the most current annual report? Get it here.

Secondary Data
Advantages and Disadvantages

Secondary data have several advantages:

- Data assembly is inexpensive. Company records, trade journals, and government publications are all rather low-cost. No data collection forms, interviewers, and tabulations are needed.

TABLE 8-1		Research-Based Recommendations	
Issue (Problem)	Alternatives	Pros and Cons of Alternatives	Recommendation
1. Which store location?	Site A.	Best transportation, traffic, and consumer profiles. Highest rent. Smallest store space. Extensive competition.	Site A: the many advantages far outweigh the disadvantages.
	Site B.	Poorest transportation, traffic, and consumer profiles. Lowest rent. Largest store space. No competition.	
	Site C.	Intermediate on all criteria.	
2. How to improve sales of shoes?	Increased assortment.	Will attract and satisfy many more customers. High costs. High level of inventory. Reduces turnover for many items.	Lower prices and increase ads: additional customers offset higher costs and lower margins; combination best expands business.
	Drop some lines and specialize.	Will attract and satisfy a specific consumer market. Excludes many segments. Costs and inventory reduced.	
	Slightly reduce prices.	Unit sales increase. Markup and profit per item decline.	
	Advertise.	Will increase traffic and new customers. High costs.	

- Data can be gathered quickly. Company records, library sources, and Web sites can be accessed immediately. Many firms store reports in their retail information systems.
- There may be several sources of secondary data—with many perspectives.
- A secondary source may possess information that would otherwise be unavailable to the retailer. Government publications often have statistics no private firm could acquire.
- When data are assembled by a source such as *Progressive Grocer*, A.C. Nielsen, *Stores*, or the government, results are usually quite credible.
- The retailer may have only a rough idea of the topics to investigate. Secondary data can then help to define issues more specifically. In addition, background information about a given issue can be gathered from secondary sources before undertaking a primary study.

Secondary data also have several potential disadvantages:

- Available data may not suit the purposes of the current study because they have been collected for other reasons. Neighborhood statistics may not be found in secondary sources.
- Secondary data may be incomplete. A service station owner would want car data broken down by year, model, and mileage driven, so as to stock parts. A motor vehicle bureau could provide data on the models but not the mileage driven.
- Information may be dated. Statistics gathered every two to five years may not be valid today. The *U.S. Census of Retail Trade* is conducted every five years. Furthermore, there is often a long time delay between the completion of a census and the release of information.
- The accuracy of secondary data must be carefully evaluated. Thus, a retailer needs to decide whether the data have been compiled in an unbiased way. The purpose of the research, the data collection tools, and the method of analysis should each be examined—if they are available for review.
- Some secondary data sources are known for poor data collection techniques; they should be avoided. If there are conflicting data, the source with the best reputation for accuracy should be used.
- In retailing, many secondary data projects are not retested and the user of secondary data has to hope results from one narrow study are applicable to his or her firm.

Whether secondary data resolve an issue or not, their low cost and availability require that primary data not be amassed until after studying secondary data. Only if secondary data are not actionable should primary data be collected. We now present various secondary data sources for retailers.

Sources

There are many sources and types of secondary data. The major distinctions are between internal and external sources.

Internal secondary data are available within the company, sometimes from the data bank of a retail information system. Before searching for external secondary data or primary data, the retailer should look at information available inside the firm.

At the beginning of the year, most retailers develop budgets for the next 12 months. They are based on sales forecasts and outline planned expenditures for that year. A firm's budget and its performance in attaining budgetary goals are good sources of secondary data.

Retailers use sales and profit-and-loss reports to judge performance. Many have data from electronic registers that can be studied by store, department, and item. By comparing data with prior periods, a firm gets a sense of growth or contraction. Overdependence on sales data may be misleading. Sales should be examined along with profit-and-loss data to indicate strengths and weaknesses in operations and management and lead to improvements.

Through customer billing reports, a retailer learns about inventory movement, sales by different personnel, and sales volume. For credit customers, sales by location, repayment time, and types of purchases can be reviewed. Purchase invoices show the retailer's own buying history and let it evaluate itself against budgetary goals. See Figure 8-8.

Inventory records indicate the merchandise carried throughout the year and the turnover of these items. Knowing the lead time to place and receive orders from suppliers, as well as the extra merchandise kept on hand to prevent running out at different times during the year, aids planning.

If a firm does primary research, the resultant report should be kept for future use (hopefully in the retail information system). When used initially, a report involves primary data. Later reference to it is secondary in nature since the report is no longer used for its primary purpose.

Written reports on performance are another source of internal secondary data. They may be prepared by senior executives, buyers, sales personnel, or others. All phases of retail management can be improved through formal report procedures.

External secondary data are available from sources outside the firm. They should be consulted if internal information is insufficient for a decision to be made on a defined issue. These sources are comprised of government and nongovernment categories.

To use external secondary data well, appropriate reference guides should be consulted. They contain listings of written (computer-based) materials, usually by subject or topic heading, for a specified time. Here are several guides, chosen for their retailing relevance. Most are available through any college library or other large library or via the Web (for online access, you must use your college or local library Web connection—direct entry to the sites is password protected):

FIGURE 8-8
Internal Secondary Data: A Valuable Source of Information

The sales receipt (invoice) contains a lot of useful data, from the name of the person involved in each sales transaction to the items sold to the selling price. Weekly, monthly, and yearly performance can easily be tracked by carefully storing and retrieving sales receipt data.

Reprinted by permission of Retail Technologies International.

- *Business Periodicals Index.* Monthly, except for July. Cumulations quarterly, semiannually, and annually. Subject index of hundreds of English-language periodicals.
- *Dialog* (data base). Contains hundreds of data bases covering various disciplines. Information on public firms, economic data, financial news, and business news.
- EBSCOhost (data base). Covers hundreds of journals, newspapers, and financial reports in business and other disciplines. Full-text articles and abstracts available.
- *InfoTrac* (data base). Covers hundreds of journals, newspapers, and financial reports in business and other disciplines. Full-text articles and abstracts available.
- LexisNexis Academic Universe (data base). Includes full-text documents from over 5,600 news, business, legal, medical, and reference publications with a variety of flexible search options.
- *ProQuest* (data base). Covers hundreds of journals, newspapers, and financial reports in business and other disciplines. Full-text articles and abstracts available.
- *Wall Street Journal Index.* Monthly, with quarterly and annual cumulations.

The U.S. Census Bureau has a Web site (**www.census. gov/econ/www/retmenu. html**) listing its most recent retailing reports, which can be viewed and downloaded from the site.

The government distributes a wide range of materials. Here are several publications, chosen for their retailing value. They are available in any business library or other large library or through the Web:

- *U.S. Census of Retail Trade.* Every five years ending in 2 and 7. Detailed data by retail classification and metropolitan region.
- *U.S. Census of Service Industries.* Every five years ending in 2 and 7. Similar to *Census of Retail Trade* but covers service industries organized by SIC code.
- *Monthly Retail Trade and Food Services Sales.* Compiled monthly. Data by retail classification.
- *Statistical Abstract of the United States.* Annually. Detailed summary of U.S. statistics.
- *U.S. Survey of Current Business.* Monthly, with weekly supplements. On all aspects of business.
- *Other.* Registration data (births, deaths, automobile registrations, etc.). Available through federal, state, and local agencies.

Government agencies, such as the Federal Trade Commission, provide pamphlets on topics such as franchising, unit pricing, deceptive ads, and credit policies. The Small Business Administration provides smaller retailers with literature and advice. Pamphlets are distributed free or sold for a nominal fee.

Nongovernment secondary data come from many sources, often cited in reference guides. Major nongovernment sources are regular periodicals; books, monographs, and other nonregular publications; channel members; and commercial research houses.

Looking for secondary data on direct marketing (**www.colinear.com/ resource.htm**) or E-commerce (**www. wilsonweb.com/research**)? Check out these sites.

Regular periodicals are available at most libraries or by personal subscription. A growing number are also online; some Web sites provide free information, whereas others charge a fee. Periodicals may have a broad scope (such as *Business Week*) and discuss diverse business topics, or they may have narrower coverage (such as *Chain Store Age*) and deal mostly with retail topics.

Many organizations publish books, monographs, and other nonregular retailing literature. Some, such as Prentice Hall (**www.prenhall.com**), produce textbooks and practitioner-oriented books. Others have more distinct goals. The American Marketing Association (**www.marketingpower.com**) offers information to enhance readers' business knowledge. The Better Business Bureau (**www.bbb.org**) wants to improve the public's image of business and expand industry self-regulation. The International Franchise Association (**www.franchise.org**) and the National Retail Federation (**www.nrf.com**) describe industry practices and trends and act as spokespersons to advocate the best interests of members. Other associations can be uncovered by consulting Gale's *Encyclopedia of Associations*.

Retailers often get information from channel members such as ad agencies, franchise operators, manufacturers, and wholesalers. When these firms do research for their own purposes and present some or all of the findings to their retailers, external secondary data are involved. Channel members pass on findings to enhance their sales and retailer relations. They usually do not charge for the information.

The last external source is the commercial research house that conducts ongoing studies and makes results available to many clients for a fee. This source is secondary if the retailer is a subscriber and does not request tailored studies. Information Resources Inc., A.C. Nielsen, and Standard Rate & Data Service provide subscriptions at lower costs than a retailer would incur if data were collected only for its use.

Our Web site (**www.prenhall.com/bermanevans**) has links to about 50 online sources of free external secondary data—both government and nongovernment.

Primary Data
Advantages and Disadvantages

After exhausting the available secondary data, a defined issue may still be unresolved. In this instance, primary data (collected to resolve a specific topic at hand) are needed. When secondary data are sufficient, primary data are not collected. There are several advantages associated with primary data:

- They are collected to fit the retailer's specific purpose.
- Information is current.
- The units of measure and data categories are designed for the issue being studied.
- The firm either collects data itself or hires an outside party. The source is known and controlled, and the methodology is constructed for the specific study.
- There are no conflicting data from different sources.
- When secondary data do not resolve an issue, primary data are the only alternative.

There are also several possible disadvantages often associated with primary data:

- They are normally more expensive to obtain than secondary data.
- Information gathering tends to be more time consuming.
- Some types of information cannot be acquired by an individual firm.
- If only primary data are collected, the perspective may be limited.
- Irrelevant information may be collected if the issue is not stated clearly enough.

In sum, a retailer has many criteria to weigh in evaluating the use of primary data. In particular, specificity, currency, and reliability must be weighed against high costs, time, and limited access to materials. A variety of primary data sources for retailers are discussed next.

Sources

Want to learn about conducting an Internet survey? Go to this Business Research Lab Web site (www.busreslab.com/onlinesurvey.htm).

The first decision is to determine who collects the data. A retailer can do this itself (internal) or hire a research firm (external). Internal collection is usually quicker and cheaper. External collection is usually more objective and formal. Second, a sampling method is specified. Instead of gathering data from all stores, all products, and all customers, a retailer may obtain accurate data by studying a sample of them. This saves time and money. With a **probability (random) sample**, every store, product, or customer has an equal or known chance of being chosen for study. In a **nonprobability sample**, stores, products, or customers are chosen by the researcher—based on judgment or convenience. A probability sample is more accurate but is also more costly and complex. Third, the retailer chooses among four methods of data collection: survey, observation, experiment, and simulation. All of the methods are capable of generating data for each element of a strategy.

SURVEY. With a **survey**, information is systematically gathered from respondents by communicating with them. Surveys are used in many retail settings. Circuit City surveys thousands of customers monthly to determine their satisfaction with the selling process. Spiegel combines a computer-assisted telephone interviewing system with mail questionnaires and personal surveys to monitor customer tastes and needs. Food Lion uses in-store surveys to find out how satisfied its customers are and what their attitudes are on different subjects.

A survey may be conducted in person, over the phone, by mail, or online. Typically, a questionnaire is used. A *personal survey* is face-to-face, flexible, and able to elicit lengthy responses; unclear questions can be explained. It may be costly, and interviewer bias is possible. A *phone survey* is fast and rather inexpensive. Responses are often short, and nonresponse may be a problem. A *mail survey* can reach a wide range of respondents, has no interviewer bias, and is not costly. Slow returns, high nonresponse rates, and participation by incorrect respondents are potential problems. An *online survey* is interactive, can be adapted to individuals, and yields quick results. Yet, only certain customers shop online or answer online surveys. The technique chosen depends on the goals and requirements of the research project.

A survey may be nondisguised or disguised. In a nondisguised survey, the respondent is told the real purpose of the study. In a disguised survey, the respondent is not told the true purpose so that person does not answer what he or she thinks a firm wants to hear. Disguised surveys use word associations, sentence completions, and projective questions (such as, "Do your friends like shopping at this store?").

The **semantic differential**—a listing of bipolar adjective scales—is a survey technique that may be disguised or nondisguised. The respondent is asked to rate one or more retailers on several criteria, each evaluated by bipolar adjectives (such as unfriendly-friendly). By computing the average rating of all respondents for each criterion, an overall profile can be developed. A semantic differential comparing two furniture retailers appears in Figure 8-9. Store A is a prestige, high-quality store and Store B is a medium-quality, family-run store. The semantic differential graphically portrays the store images.

RETAILING
Around the World　Mystery Shoppers: A Research Tool Comes to Puerto Rico

Puerto Rican retailing is so competitive that shoppers often see the same products at identical prices at different stores throughout the island. As a result, merchants are well aware of the importance of customer service as a differential advantage. The trend of using mystery shoppers to assess a store's customer service is now catching on in Puerto Rico. According to a University of Puerto Rico marketing professor, many fast-food chains, apparel stores, and video rental stores are now using mystery shoppers.

Although mystery shopping can be used to evaluate employee integrity and product quality, its major objective is to help improve customer service. Questionnaires used by mystery shoppers generally include both open-

and closed-ended questions, as well as a comments section where suggestions for improvement can be noted. Among the areas covered are politeness, store cleanliness, and product quality. According to the Mystery Shopping Providers Association (**www.mysteryshop. org**), 69 percent of customers stop buying at businesses due to poor service and 13 percent stop due to dissatisfaction with the products offered.

Sources: Rossie Cortes, "Mystery Shopping Helps Businesses Improve Customer Service," *Caribbean Business* (April 15, 2004), p. 45; and "Mystery Shopping Providers Association: News," **www.mysteryshop. org/news** (April 5, 2006).

OBSERVATION. The form of research in which present behavior or the results of past behavior are noted and recorded is known as **observation**. Because people are not questioned, observation may not require respondents' cooperation, and survey biases are minimized. Many times, observation is used in actual situations. The key disadvantage of using observation alone is that attitudes are not elicited.

Retailers use observation to determine the quality of sales presentations (by having researchers pose as shoppers), to monitor related-item buying, to determine store activity by time and day, to make pedestrian and vehicular traffic counts (to measure the potential of new locations), and to determine the proportion of patrons using mass transit.

With **mystery shoppers**, retailers hire people to pose as customers and observe their operations, from sales presentations to how well displays are maintained to service calls.[20] One research firm, Michelson & Associates (**www. michelson.com/mystery**), has a pool of more than 80,000 mystery shoppers: "We

FIGURE 8-9
A Semantic Differential for Two Furniture Stores

Please check the blanks that best indicate your feelings about Stores A and B.

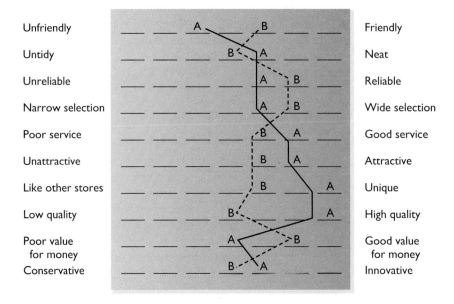

qualify, train, and manage our shoppers to gather factual data and give objective observations. Our people range from 21 to 70 years of age with the majority being women between age 30 and 45. They are pre-selected based on client criteria such as demographics, type of car, shopping habits, etc."[21]

Observation may be disguised or nondisguised, structured or unstructured, direct or indirect, and human or mechanical. In disguised observation, the shopper or company employee is not aware he or she is being watched by a two-way mirror or hidden camera. In nondisguised observation, the participant knows he or she is being observed—such as a department manager watching a cashier's behavior. Structured observation calls for the observer to note specific behavior. Unstructured observation requires the observer to note all of the activities of the person being studied. With direct observation, the observer watches people's present behavior. With indirect observation, the observer examines evidence of past behavior such as food products in consumer pantries. Human observation is carried out by people. It may be disguised, but the observer may enter biased notations and miss behavior. Mechanical observation, such as a camera filming in-store shopping, eliminates viewer bias and does not miss behavior.

EXPERIMENT. An **experiment** is a type of research in which one or more elements of a retail strategy mix are manipulated under controlled conditions. An element may be a price, a shelf display, or store hours. If a retailer wants to find out the effects of a price change on a brand's sales, only the price of that brand is varied. Other elements of the strategy stay the same, so the true effect of price is measured.

An experiment may use survey or observation techniques to record data. In a survey, questions are asked about the experiment: Did you buy Brand Z because of its new shelf display? Are you buying more ice cream because it's on sale? In observation, behavior is watched during the experiment: Sales of Brand Z rise by 20 percent when a new display is used. Ice cream sales go up 25 percent during a special sale.

Surveys and observations are experimental if they occur under closely controlled situations. When surveys ask broad attitude questions or unstructured behavior is observed, experiments are not involved. Experimentation can be difficult since many uncontrollable factors (such as the weather, competition, and the economy) come into play. Yet, a well-controlled experiment yields a lot of good data.

The major advantage is an experiment's ability to show cause and effect (a lower price results in higher sales). It is also systematically structured and enacted. The major potential disadvantages are high costs, contrived settings, and uncontrollable factors.

SIMULATION. A type of experiment whereby a computer program is used to manipulate the elements of a retail strategy mix rather than test them in a real setting is **simulation**. Two kinds are now being applied in retail settings: those based on mathematical models and those involving "virtual reality."

With the first kind of simulation, a model of the expected controllable and uncontrollable retail environment is constructed. Factors are manipulated by computer so their effects on the overall strategy and specific elements of it are learned. No consumer cooperation is needed, and many combinations of factors can be analyzed in a controlled, rapid, inexpensive, and risk-free manner. This format is gaining popularity because good software is available. However, it is still somewhat difficult to use.

In the second kind of simulation, a retailer devises or buys interactive software that lets participants simulate actual behavior in as realistic a format as possible. This approach creates a "virtual shopping environment." At present, there is limited software for these simulations and personnel must be trained to use it. One application of a virtual reality simulation—used by numerous clients—is from IFOP-CMR:

> Visionary Shopper is a computer-generated shopping simulation where you can create the retail environment you want, without the expense of controlling a store or creating a product prototype; vary the marketing stimuli at the touch of a button; send consumers shopping on a touch-screen monitor; and measure purchase behavior in response to changes in the marketing variables; all in a controlled and confidential setting, within a central location facility. Visionary Shopper provides a unique focus on consumer behavior—what they do, not what they say they will do. It allows you to understand buying behavior in the context of realistic store environments, not products in isolation or shelf subsets. It runs faster, and at a lower cost than current in-store research techniques.[22]

Summary

1. *To discuss how information flows in a retail distribution channel.* In an effective retail distribution channel, information flows freely and efficiently among the three main parties (supplier, retailer, and consumer). As a result, the parties can better anticipate and address each other's performance expectations. Retailers often have a vital role in collecting data because they have the most direct contact with shoppers.

2. *To show why retailers should avoid strategies based on inadequate information.* Whether developing a new strategy or modifying an existing one, good data are necessary to reduce a retailer's chances of making incorrect decisions. Retailers that rely on nonsystematic or incomplete research, such as intuition, increase their probabilities of failure.

3. *To look at the retail information system, its components, and the recent advances in such systems.* Useful information should be acquired through an ongoing, well-integrated process. A retail information system anticipates the data needs of retail managers; continuously collects, organizes, and stores relevant data; and directs the flow of information to decision makers. Such a system has several components: environment, retailer's philosophy, strategic plans, information control center, and retail operations. The most important component is the information control center. It directs data collection, stores and retrieves data, and updates files.

   Data-base management is used to collect, integrate, apply, and store information related to specific topics (such as customers, vendors, and product categories). Data-base information can come from internal (company generated) and external (purchased from outside firms) sources. A key advance in data-base management is data warehousing, whereby copies of all the data bases in a firm are kept in one location and can be accessed by employees at any locale. It is a huge repository separate from the operational data bases that support departmental applications. Through data mining and micromarketing, retailers use data warehouses to pinpoint the specific needs of customer segments.

   Retailers have increased their use of computerized retail information systems, and the Universal Product Code (UPC) is now the dominant technology for processing product-related data. With electronic data interchange (EDI), the computers of retailers and their suppliers regularly exchange information, sometimes through the Web.

4. *To describe the marketing research process.* Marketing research in retailing involves these sequential activities: defining the issue or problem to be researched, examining secondary data, gathering primary data (if needed), analyzing the data, making recommendations, and implementing findings. It is systematic in nature and not a single act.

   Secondary data (gathered for other purposes) are inexpensive, can be collected quickly, may have several sources, and may yield otherwise unattainable information. Some sources are very credible. When an issue is ill defined, a secondary data search can clarify it. There are also potential pitfalls: These data may not suit the purposes of the study, units of measurement may not be specific enough, information may be old or inaccurate, a source may be disreputable, and data may not be reliable.

Primary data (gathered to resolve the specific topic at hand) are collected if secondary data do not adequately address the issue. They are precise and current, data are collected and categorized with the units of measures desired, the methodology is known, there are no conflicting results, and the level of reliability can be determined. When secondary data do not exist, primary data are the only option. The potential disadvantages are the costs, time, limited access, narrow perspective, and amassing of irrelevant information.

Key Terms

retail information system (RIS) (p. 229)
data-base management (p. 233)
data warehousing (p. 234)
data mining (p. 236)
micromarketing (p. 236)
Universal Product Code (UPC) (p. 236)
electronic data interchange (EDI) (p. 238)

marketing research in retailing (p. 238)
marketing research process (p. 238)
issue (problem) definition (p. 239)
secondary data (p. 239)
primary data (p. 239)
internal secondary data (p. 241)
external secondary data (p. 242)
probability (random) sample (p. 245)

nonprobability sample (p. 245)
survey (p. 245)
semantic differential (p. 245)
observation (p. 246)
mystery shoppers (p. 246)
experiment (p. 247)
simulation (p. 247)

Questions for Discussion

1. Relate the information flows in Figure 8-1 to a retailer near your college or university.

2. What would you recommend to guard against this comment? "Traditionally, retailers and suppliers just don't like to share supply-chain information with each other."

3. Can a retailer ever have too much information? Explain your answer.

4. How could a small retailer devise a retail information system?

5. Explain the relationship among the terms *data warehouse*, *data mining*, and *micromarketing*. How can Amazon.com apply these concepts?

6. What are the opportunities and potential problems with electronic data interchange (EDI) for a drugstore chain?

7. Cite the major advantages and disadvantages of secondary data.

8. As a gift store owner, what kinds of secondary data would you use to learn more about your industry and consumer trends in leisure activities?

9. Describe the major advantage of each method of gathering primary data: survey, observation, experiment, and simulation.

10. Develop a 10-item semantic differential for a local hair salon to judge its image. Who should be surveyed? Why?

11. Why would a retailer use mystery shoppers rather than other forms of observation? Are there any instances when you would not recommend their use? Why or why not?

12. Why do you think that "virtual shopping" has not taken off faster as a research tool for retailers?

Web-Based Exercise

Visit the Web site of A.C. Nielsen (**www.acnielsen.com**), the world's largest marketing research firm. Describe some of the services it offers for retailers. Which service would you most recommend? Why?

Note: Stop by our Web site (**www.prenhall.com/bermanevans**) to experience a number of highly interactive, appealing Web exercises based on actual company demonstrations and sample materials related to retailing.

Chapter Endnotes

1. Various company sources.

2. Kurt Salmon Associates, "Business Intelligence: An Edge for Retailers and Suppliers," *Online Viewpoint* (reprinted from *Retail Asia*, n.d.).

3. Laurie Sullivan, "Wal-Mart to Suppliers: Clean Up Your Data," *Information Week* (May 30, 2005), p. 24.

4. Dan Scheraga, "Disappointment Reigns," *Chain Store Age* (August 2002), p. 83.

5. "Supplier Information," **www.walmartstores.com/ wmstore/wmstores/Mainsupplier.jsp** (February 1, 2006).

6. "Retail IT and Budgeting Study," *Stores* (June 2005), special section.

7. "Retail Pro," **www.islandpacific.com/RetailPro.htm** (January 29, 2006).

8. "MicroStrategy Desktop," **www.microstrategy. com/Software/Products/User_Interfaces/Desktop** (January 29, 2006).

9. Mila N. D'Antonio, "Searching for Next-Level Value," **www.1to1.com/View.aspx?DocID=28699** (January– February 2005).

10. "Consumer Data Bases: "DQI³," **www.donnelley marketing.com/service/donnelley/consumer_db. aspx** (January 23, 2006).

11. Adapted by the authors from Jeff St. Onge, "Direct Marketing Credos for Today's Banking," *Direct Marketing* (March 1999), p. 56.

12. "Data Warehousing: Putting Your Data to Work," **www.techdivas.com/data.htm** (June 29, 2005).

13. Meridith Levinson, "They Know What You'll Buy Next Summer (They Hope)," *CIO* (May 2002), p. 116.

14. Laurie Sullivan, "ERP Vendors Battle for Retailers," *Information Week* (June 13, 2005), p. 52.

15. "CIOs on CRM," *Chain Store Age* (September 2001), p. 18B.

16. Poonam Khanna, "Hotel Chain Gets Personal with Customers," *Computing Canada* (April 8, 2005), p. 18.

17. "The UPC Code," **www.gs1us.org/upc_background. html** (January 24, 2006).

18. Stuart Swabini, "EDI and the Internet," *Journal of Business Strategy*, Vol. 22 (January–February 2001), p. 42.

19. Scott Bury, "Piggly Wiggly's Doing It," *Manufacturing Business Technology* (February 2005), p. 43.

20. For more information, see Nancy Feig, "Taking the Mystery Out of Good Customer Service," *Community Banker* (March 2005), pp. 66, 68; and Barbara Whitaker, "Yes, There Is a Job That Pays You to Shop," *New York Times* (March 13, 2005), Section 3, p. 8.

21. "Who Are Michelson & Associates' Mystery Shoppers?" **www.michelson.com/mystery/ourshoppers. html** (February 9, 2006).

22. "Virtual Shopper: The Next Generation of Market Research," **www.ifop.com/america/to/shopper_eng. htm** (January 5, 2006).

part three
Short Cases

CASE 1: ABERCROMBIE'S RUEHL NO. 925 TARGETS A DIFFERENT CUSTOMER NICHE[c-1]

Abercrombie & Fitch (**www.abercrombie.com**) hopes that when its current male and female shoppers grow up and graduate from college, they will become shoppers at Ruehl No. 925, its new store concept. As one industry expert says, "It's really exciting that [Abercrombie & Fitch] added this customer that's older than their other businesses, in an area that's really not addressed by others."

The concept of Ruehl No. 925 is based on a lifestyle appropriate to the Ruehls, a German family that settled in New York City in the late 19th century and founded a leather goods company in a Greenwich Street townhouse. The store exterior, for example, resembles a row of three brick townhouses with iron gates. The interior is also laid out like a home. Shoppers enter rooms on each side of an entranceway that leads to a "porch" with the central checkout and fitting rooms. Although the interior is attractive, some shoppers have complained that the compartment-based layout makes going from one section to another difficult. There is no indication that the chain is owned by Abercrombie & Fitch. Noticeably absent from Ruehl are the bright lights, loud music, and large graphics that are characteristic of Abercrombie & Fitch stores. Some customers have even commented that Ruehl's lighting is subdued or even dark.

Retailers such as J. Crew (**www.jcrew.com**), Banana Republic (**www.bananarepublic.com**), and Ralph Lauren (**www.polo.com**)—while selling goods to more-affluent 20-somethings—also serve a much broader target market. According to John C. Schroder, the chief operating officer of a major shopping center in which three Ruehl stores recently opened, "Ruehl, to me, is an edgier version of J. Crew." Whereas J. Crew may feature cable-knit sweaters, Ruehl's clothing may have sequins.

Abercrombie's director of corporate communications says that Ruehl's core customer is "a person in the early stages of a career who can afford better quality but still wants youthful looks." Like Abercrombie & Fitch, Ruehl's merchandise is casual. However, its sweaters, instead of being wool, are cashmere; its jeans are a better grade of denim; and the leather purses are embossed.

The reaction of shoppers to the Ruehl stores is generally positive even though some complained about high prices. Cashmere sweaters, for example, have been selling at more than $160 and some purses are priced at over $900. Ruehl's management believes that the concept's New York feel will definitely work in San Francisco and other northern California markets but may not play out in other areas. However, a lead-ing industry expert feels "Abercrombie may have hit upon a way to hold onto existing customers as they exit their teens."

This is not Abercrombie's first venture beyond its traditional stores. A sister chain of Ruehl's, Hollister, features a California/beach design. Hollister targets teens who prefer more of a surfer look in their apparel. Abercrombie is also rolling out a children's apparel chain.

Questions

1. Is Abercrombie & Fitch following a mass marketing, a concentrated marketing, or a differentiated marketing strategy? Explain your answer.
2. Describe the pros and cons of Ruehl's choice of a target market.
3. How can Ruehl's help shoppers to effectively evaluate alternative products?
4. Discuss how Ruehl's can reduce shoppers' cognitive dissonance.

CASE 2: BEN & JERRY'S: STAYING TRUE TO ITS CORE CUSTOMERS[c-2]

Walt Freese, the chief executive of Ben & Jerry's Homemade (**www.benjerry.com**), is in a tough position. Since Ben & Jerry's is a Unilever (**www.unilever.com**) subsidiary, along with Breyer's, Good Humor, Popsicle, and Klondike, Freese must meet the parent company's profit, sales, and market share goals for his business. On the other hand, at Ben & Jerry's South Burlington, Vermont, headquarters, Freese must deal with the cultural and social values of the firm's employees and customers. These include such concerns as "Should the firm's coffee be organic?" "Should Ben & Jerry's pay a premium price for coffee grown and harvested in a manner fair to a grower's employees?" and "Which rock star's name should be placed on Ben & Jerry's newest flavor of ice cream?"

An important question is whether Ben & Jerry's can be true to its original mission while being owned by a major food-based conglomerate. Even Freese admits that "there are plenty of examples of large companies acquiring brands that are unusual, that occupy a niche, and then homogenizing them until the brands become nothing special."

Ben & Jerry's started when Ben Cohen and Jerry Greenfield found themselves unemployed in Burlington, Vermont, in 1978. The friends debated whether they should open a bagel shop or make ice cream. Having completed a correspondence course in ice cream making, they opened their first store in a converted gas station. Since the beginning of their retail operation, Ben & Jerry's has been known for paying a premium for milk purchased from local dairies and buying milk from farmers whose cows have not been treated with hormones. Ben & Jerry's major competitor, Häagen-Dazs, has revenues that are 10 percent greater than Ben & Jerry's. The latter outsells Häagen-Dazs in convenience stores. In contrast, Häagen-Dazs outsells Ben & Jerry's in supermarkets.

[c-1]The material in this case is drawn from Debra Hazel, "Willkommen," *SCT* (February 2005), pp. 19–20, 22.

[c-2]The material in this case is drawn from Sarah Mahoney, "It Only Looks Easy," *Point* (March 2005), pp. 13–18.

As noted, Freese's biggest challenge is to maintain the corporate culture of Ben & Jerry's while meeting Unilever's sales and profit goals. For instance, every Ben & Jerry's employee gets three free pints of ice cream per day, and employees are allowed to bring their dogs to work. And for the company's fans, Freese has to keep the brand's core values of having a social mission, great tasting ice cream, and a product that is promoted in a fun kind of way.

An example of an innovative Ben & Jerry's promotion was its association with the Dave Matthews Band, which was seeking an innovative way to address global warming concerns. Ben & Jerry's new product launch for One Sweet Whirled, an intense caramel-chocolate mixture, was conducted at the band's concerts. Ben & Jerry's trucks also went to the concerts and distributed global warming literature along with ice cream. According to the president of an event marketing firm, "People at the concerts are aware of the company's heritage, and the DNA. But if Häagen-Dazs (**www. haagen-dazs.com**) did the same thing, it wouldn't work. There's a huge difference between posing as an involved company, and really doing something, and customers can tell."

Questions

1. List important data bases by customer, vendor, and product category that Ben & Jerry's should maintain.
2. List five important sources of internal secondary data that are valuable to Ben & Jerry's.
3. Develop a semantic differential questionnaire comparing the images of Ben & Jerry's and Häagen-Dazs.
4. How can Unilever assure that Ben & Jerry's image will not be changed?

CASE 3: 7-ELEVEN TURNS UPS ITS RETAIL INFORMATION SYSTEM[c-3]

7-Eleven (**www.7-eleven.com**), the convenience store chain widely known for selling gasoline, cigarettes, and the Big Gulp, is now seeking to appeal to a more upscale audience with offerings that include Chardonnay wine, cappuccino, artisan breads, focaccia sandwiches, and even sushi. 7-Eleven has also made strong inroads to female shoppers by being one of the first convenience stores to install credit card readers at the gas pumps (instead of in the store). The chain recognized that mothers do not want to leave their children in the car while they pay for gasoline purchases. Lastly, 7-Eleven has begun to roll out fancier stores located in downtown business districts, at airports, and colleges.

Central to the change in target market focus is 7-Eleven's reliance on a sophisticated marketing information system that isolates trends, forecasts sales, and reorders merchandise. The impetus behind this system was Ito-Yokado, 7-Eleven's licensee in Japan, that owns 70 percent of 7-Eleven.

Now every store manager can tap into 7-Eleven's computer system to determine which products are selling best at his or her location; store managers can also determine best-selling products for the chain as a whole. In addition, the system provides other key information such as weather reports and notifies managers of major local sporting events and special functions at a local school. This information enables store mangers to constantly revise their selections.

7-Eleven stores are equipped with NEC (**www.nec.com**) handheld computers that utilize touchscreen and wireless radio-frequency technologies. The device computes weekly sales for each item stocked and then computes a suggested order size. These units enable store personnel to place orders on a daily basis; many of these orders are directed to the retailer's 25 third-party distribution centers. The orders are arranged by store and route during the afternoon and are delivered as of 5 P.M. the following morning. According to a 7-Eleven store manager based in San Francisco, "All of these tools allow me to provide what my customers really want. Without them, my job would be twice as hard."

The new marketing information system better enables 7-Eleven to directly communicate with its vendors. As a result, 7-Eleven has experienced a growth in sales of Anheuser beer of 6 to 10 percent per year. This occurred in an industry where a 2 percent annual growth is generally considered to be good. Through data mining, David Podeschi, 7-Eleven's senior vice-president for merchandising, is constantly looking for new opportunities. Two years ago, Podeschi noticed that supermarket sales of cleaning wipes were growing at a superfast rate. As a result, 7-Eleven developed a low-cost towelette especially designed to remove coffee stains.

Jim Keyes, 7-Eleven's chief executive officer, feels that the retailer's biggest challenge is to make sure that store managers know how to use the data: "You can supply all the technology in the world, and it won't matter if they don't think like entrepreneurs."

Questions

1. Assess 7-Eleven's retail information system.
2. How can 7-Eleven effectively coordinate its use of marketing research with its retail information system?
3. Discuss how 7-Eleven can use data mining to improve its sales and profitability.
4. Comment on this statement: "You can supply all the technology in the world, and it won't matter if they [store managers] don't think like entrepreneurs."

CASE 4: THE VALUE AND CHALLENGES OF COMPARISON WEB SITES[c-4]

According to Jupiter Research, a leading online marketing research firm, 8 percent of online shoppers used comparison

[c-3]The material in this case is drawn from Elizabeth Esfahani, "7-Eleven Gets Sophisticated," *Business 2.0* (January/February 2005), pp. 93–100.

[c-4]The material in this case is drawn from Heather Ratzlaff, "Shopping Around: Comparison Shopping Websites," *Catalog Age* (January 2005).

shopping engine sites during a recent holiday shopping season, versus 64 percent of online shoppers who used general search engines.

Unlike general search engines such as Google (**www. google.com**) and Yahoo! (**www.yahoo.com**) that provide information on a wide range of topics, comparison shopping engines such as PriceGrabber (**www.pricegrabber.com**), Shopping.com (**www.shopping.com**), MySimon (**www. mysimon.com**), and Shopzilla (**www.shopzilla.com**) enable shoppers to research the price (including sales tax and shipping) and merchant ratings for multiple E-retailers at the same time. After an acceptable price is found, a consumer can then click on a retailer's hot link and he or she is directed to the retailer's Web site to place an order.

Some of these comparison Web sites (such as PriceGrabber, MySimon, and Shopping.com) charge merchants a fee to list their items in a given product category. Typically, the fee is based on the product category. While the fee can be 5 to 10 cents per lead for low-margin products such as books and toys, it can be as high as one dollar or even more for ink cartridges and other high-margin products. Other sites, such as Shopzilla, allow retailers to list products for free but have a separate charge for their listing to appear on the top of the search results.

There are several major benefits for an online retailer to have its products listed on comparison shopping engines. Unlike consumers using a general search engine who may look up a product's consumer reviews, the comparison shopping engine user is further along in the purchasing process. As a result, many retail analysts feel that the comparison shopping engines have a higher success in converting shoppers into buyers.

Alan Rimm-Kaufman, founder of the Rimm-Kaufman Group, states that the cost to acquire a customer from most comparison shopping engines can be as little as half of the cost of acquiring buyers from lists of potential customers. For example, Shopping.com charges merchants between five cents and one dollar per lead and has a conversion rate of between 2 and 10 percent of viewers.

Most comparison shopping sites will also provide merchants with detailed data on the number of viewers and sales in various product categories. The data are unavailable for traditional advertising media such as television.

Retail analysts offer a number of suggestions for merchants that are first deciding whether to use comparison shopping engines. One, it is important to use paid, as well as free, listings—since free listings alone may not significantly increase sales. Two, a merchant should not focus solely on providing the lowest price. Jupiter Research has found that about 70 percent of the clickthroughs on comparison shopping engines are not for the merchant with the lowest price. Such factors as speed of delivery, merchant reputation, and return policy are also important. Lastly, before listing products on comparison shopping engines, merchants need to be sure that their Web sites can effectively handle the increased traffic.

Questions

1. What types of perceived risk can a comparison shopping site effectively reduce?
2. Discuss the role of comparison shopping Web sites in each stage of the consumer decision process (see Figure 7-5).
3. Describe how an effective merchant must maintain and update its data on a comparison shopping Web site.
4. How can a merchant reduce the impact of price as a shopping determinant on a comparison shopping Web site?

part three
Comprehensive Case
The Apparel Shopper*

INTRODUCTION

Several general observations can be offered regarding apparel shoppers:

- High-income shoppers and younger shoppers underlie recent sales growth.
- Spending changes are more likely to be driven by needs, not wants. Although important, the advent of new fashion "looks" is not the main reason shoppers increase—or decrease—their spending. Instead, changes are far more likely to be related to very practical reasons (e.g., a change in size, replacement of worn clothing, lower household incomes, more savings/debt reduction).
- Also important in prompting changes in clothing spending is the need to upgrade/update a work wardrobe or respond to a changed work situation.
- As down-market shoppers feel the need to pinch their pennies for apparel, they spend more of their budget at Wal-Mart. Among these shoppers, Wal-Mart is overwhelmingly seen as offering the best clothing value, while its clothing styles are a good match for their basic style preferences.
- Clothing specialty stores and traditional department stores benefit from consistent or increased spending among up-market shoppers. The brands and styles offered at these retail formats are most preferred by up-market shoppers.
- Much of the spending increases among younger shoppers are funneled to fashion-focused clothing specialty stores, as well as retailers offering credible fashions plus a strong price for the quality value.
- Department stores and clothing specialty stores are the top two choices for offering the most-wanted brands *and* the most-wanted styles, both overall and among key segments.
- The majority of Americans wear ordinary/basic styles at work and at play. However, they seem a bit more stylish on the job than off. Younger and higher-income shoppers skew toward more fashion-driven looks for both wearing occasions.

Who Is Driving Apparel Shopping Growth?

Apparel sales grew 6 percent from 2003 to 2004, following 1.4 percent growth the prior year. We project apparel spending to increase about 4 percent annually during the next several years. Margins, however, will be severely tested by accelerating price pressure. The 2004 sales increase can be explained by our ShopperScape™ data, particularly when viewed through the "lens" of household income. Every month, we survey 4,000 shoppers about their recent and planned spending. We collect purchasing data for over 150 retailers and more than 100 product categories.

The majority of ShopperScape™ respondents say they spent about the same amount on clothes for themselves in 2004 compared with 2003. Twice as many reported reduced spending than reported increased spending. These proportions, however, dramatically varied by upper- versus lower-income households and resulted in a net increase in overall spending.

Consumers with the highest incomes were the most likely to increase their spending for themselves, while those with lower incomes were the most likely to reduce spending. According to U.S. personal consumption expenditure data, the highest-income shoppers account for one-quarter of all apparel spending, although they make up only 12 percent of all households. The lowest-income households account for over one-third of all households but only 18 percent of all apparel spending.

With respect to race/ethnicity, Whites were the most likely to maintain their clothing spending for themselves, compared with African-Americans and Hispanics/Latinos, more of whom reported reduced spending. Spending trends on clothing also varied notably by both gender and age. Changes in spending—both increases and reductions—were more pronounced among women and younger shoppers than among their counterparts. Men and mid-life to older shoppers were most likely to have an unchanged rate of spending on clothing for themselves. Women were more likely to have both increased or decreased spending compared with men. Working-age shoppers (ages 18 to 54) were more likely than older shoppers to have increased their spending on clothing for themselves.

What Underlies Spending Changes?
Spending Increases

Spending increases were most likely to be related to very practical reasons (e.g., a change in clothing size, replacement of worn clothing). Spending decreases were most likely to reflect a shrinking wallet. Work wardrobes also were important to spending changes, whether related to updating the wardrobe or a change in work status.

Among those spending more on clothing, the most commonly cited reasons were related to practical needs for new or replacement clothing rather than to having more discretionary income available to spend on clothing or having a desire for a new fashion look. The need for a new size was mentioned as the most important reason for spending more on clothing by 28 percent of respondents. The replacement of worn-out items was mentioned by 21 percent. Eighteen percent increased spending to upgrade the work wardrobe. Few shoppers (3 percent) increased spending because fashions were of greater interest than previously. A slightly larger percentage (9 percent) attributed the increase in spending to higher income.

Specific reasons for increasing clothing spending were highly related to age but not as much to gender. The only significant gender differences were that women were more likely than men to increase spending on clothing due to a change in size, while men were more likely to increase spending because of the need to replace a worn or torn item. Shoppers in older age groups were more likely to spend more because they were replacing worn-out clothing. Those in their mid-life "work" years were more likely to spend more because they were updating their work wardrobe. Less debt, higher incomes, and more time to shop were more likely to be reasons cited by younger shoppers for higher spending.

Reasons behind increased spending were not well explained by either income or race. The most notable differences by income were among shoppers with household incomes of $25,000 to $49,999 and $75,000 to $99,999. Both groups were more likely than others to spend more to upgrade the work wardrobe. Those with incomes from $25,000 to $49,999 also were more likely than others to spend because they had more income and more free time to shop.

Spending Decreases

Among respondents cutting back on their clothing spending, most did so because their clothing budget shrank, either due to a decrease in income (21 percent) or in an attempt to spend less so as to save more or pay down debt (18 percent). Other frequent responses included a change in a workplace situation that resulted in a decreased need for clothing spending, a spending shift away from clothing to other items, and a desire to wait to make new purchases until the respondent lost weight. Only 2 percent said they reduced spending because they were less interested in the latest fashions.

The most frequently mentioned reasons for reduced clothing spending were closely related to age and gender. Women and shoppers younger than 55 were most likely to say a decrease in income caused them to cut back. Mid-life shoppers were more likely to decrease their budget to save money or pay down debt. Younger shoppers were more likely to reduce spending due to a shift in spending priorities away from clothing toward other types of products. Men and older shoppers were more likely to say a change in their work situation triggered reduced spending, presumably reflecting retirement among the oldest shoppers. Women were more likely to say they were holding off on new clothing purchases until they lost weight.

Income is modestly indicative of the reasons why shoppers cut back on spending. However, race is not a good indicator. Lower-income households were more likely to cut back because of a decrease in income. Shoppers in the lowest-income households also were the least likely to postpone new apparel purchases until they lost weight. Shoppers in the highest-income households that cut back on spending were more likely to say they did so because they had less time to shop or were shifting work wear spending toward less expensive, more casual clothing. African-Americans were much more apt to spend less because they shifted spending away from clothing to other nonclothing items.

What Retailers Are Benefiting from Spending Growth?

Overall, Wal-Mart (**www.walmart.com**) was the biggest direct beneficiary of recent increased spending—although primarily from lower-income or mid-life shoppers. Higher-income shoppers and those at each end of the age spectrum shifted their spending to more fashion-focused apparel retailers. Regardless of whether their budget was going up or down, about one out of four shoppers said they weren't giving more of their clothing budget to any particular retailer. An equal number of shoppers, however, said they were shifting more of their clothing budget to Wal-Mart.

The retail recipient of shifting spending on apparel varied notably by age and gender:

- Wal-Mart gained more of the budget of women than of men, as well as of all but the youngest and oldest shoppers.
- Women were more likely than men to shift their clothing budget toward all types of specialty stores, from full-price to off-price and value-priced Old Navy (**www. oldnavy.com**).
- Men were more likely than women to shift more of their budget to Sears (**www.sears.com**).
- Eighteen- to 34-year-olds formed a distinctive bloc that was especially likely to shift their budgets to all types of specialty stores, as well as to Target (**www.target.com**). They were the most likely to shift their clothing budget among retailers, reflecting less-ingrained shopping patterns and a greater desire to shop at retailers offering trend-right fashions, particularly at value price points.
- Shoppers age 45 or older were more likely to shift their budget toward traditional department stores, long the domain of the mid-life to older shoppers.

Shifts in the budget to various types of retailers also are linked to income and race. Wal-Mart's everyday low prices clearly attracted shoppers on a budget; 40 percent of consumers with incomes less than $25,000 say they spent more on clothing there. Shoppers with incomes of $75,000 or higher were more likely to shift their budget to Kohl's (**www. kohls.com**) and Old Navy. The most-affluent shoppers ($100,000 and above) were more likely than others to shift their budget to traditional department stores.

African-Americans were more likely than Whites or Latinos to shift their budget to Wal-Mart and clothing specialty stores. Latinos were more apt than Whites or African-Americans to shift to Target and Sears. African-Americans and Latinos were more likely than Whites to shift spending to off-price stores and Old Navy. Whites were more apt than African-Americans or Latinos to shift to Kohl's.

Who Has the Right Clothing Quality for the Price?

Apparel shoppers come in all shapes, sizes, ages, incomes, and taste levels. Even though there are clear differences in retailer preferences based largely on age and income, it is safe to say that Wal-Mart is the overall clothing value leader. However, consumers have different criteria for assessing value, which is evident based on the ratings of shoppers by key demographics such as age and income.

The assessment of which retailer offers the best clothing value clearly differs by age but less so by gender. Wal-Mart is seen as a good value by more men than women. Women are more likely to perceive that Target and Old Navy offer a good value, most likely because of the "fashion right" orientation of these retailers, an aspect of value that women are more likely to use in their ratings. Older shoppers are notably more likely than younger shoppers to perceive that J.C. Penney (www.jcpenney.com) and Kohl's offer a good value. Younger shoppers are more likely to perceive that Target and Old Navy offer a good value, again likely including being "fashion right" as a more important component of value.

Income has a direct relationship with shopper rankings of quality for the price paid. Value retailers receive higher ratings among lower-income than upper-income households. Race/ethnicity has less of a relationship to shopper perceptions, although a few differences exist. Wal-Mart's overall top ranking for clothing value is directly linked to its high ranking among lower-income shoppers; no other retailer comes close in terms of perceived clothing value. The gap between Wal-Mart and other retailers also is large in the $25,000 to $49,999 income group but narrows among those with incomes of $50,000 to $74,999.

In the highest income group ($100,000 and over), only 7 percent of shoppers feel Wal-Mart offers the best clothing value. Kohl's is perceived by the highest percentage of shoppers in this group to offer the best clothing value. As income increases, traditional department stores, Old Navy, clothing specialty stores, and Target are more likely to be perceived to offer the best clothing value.

With respect to race/ethnicity, Whites are more likely than African-Americans or Latinos to feel that Kohl's offers the best clothing values. Latinos are more likely to feel that Target offers the best values. This surpasses the percent of Latinos who say that Wal-Mart offers the best clothing values—which is not the case with Whites or African-Americans, who give Wal-Mart the highest rating on this measure.

Who Has the Right Brands and Styles?

The overall ranking of retailers based on whether or not they offer more of the brands shoppers want to buy is very different from retailer rankings based on whether or not they offer the best value. Traditional department stores and clothing specialty stores (excluding Old Navy) are the most likely to offer more of the brands shoppers prefer. A smaller percentage say Wal-Mart has more of the brands they want to buy, followed by J.C. Penney and Kohl's.

Because many brands are aimed at specific age groups and sold at retailers targeting these groups, brand ratings of retailers noticeably vary by age. There are few differences based on gender. Older shoppers are the least likely to know which retailer carries the brands they prefer; they also are the most likely to say that traditional department stores carry the brands they want. J.C. Penney is rated highly on this factor by the oldest shoppers. Clothing specialty stores receive high ratings for carrying the "right" brands by most shoppers, particularly younger ones. Target and Old Navy are more likely to get higher marks for having the "right" brands from younger than older shoppers. Old Navy also gets better marks for its brand assortment from women than from men.

Shopper perceptions of the appropriateness of the brand assortment are clearly linked to income but less to race/ethnicity. The perception that department stores and clothing specialty stores carry the "right" assortment increases with income. Many shoppers in the lowest-income group say they can find more of the clothing brands they want at Wal-Mart. Kohl's brands appeal most strongly to shoppers in the middle-income ranges and are more likely to appeal to high-income shoppers than those of value department store competitors J.C. Penney and Sears.

At Work or Play, Basics Rule

American consumers are not trendy—either at work or play. Regardless of wearing occasion, "ordinary, very basic" styles were preferred by a wide margin over all other styles, although more so for casual/weekend wear than for work. Second in preference for both wearing occasions were classic and traditional styles that never go out of fashion. Slightly more shoppers wear this style for work than for weekend. Less than a third of consumers said they wore "contemporary" or "trendsetting" fashions for work or for casual wear. The percent wearing the more fashion-focused styles for work was higher than the percent wearing these styles for the weekend.

Age has a more noticeable impact than gender on the styles worn by full-time workers. Younger adults are more likely to wear work wardrobes comprised of contemporary or trendsetting styles. Roughly half of those younger than 34 are attracted to fashion-forward types of work wear, compared with less than a third of all workers. Older workers are more likely to stick to classics and basics for work, with 83 percent and 88 percent of workers in the 55-to-64 and 65+ age groups saying they wear one of these two categories. Workers in the oldest age group are twice as likely to favor basic styles for work compared with those in the youngest. Women are more likely than men to wear trendsetting styles for work.

Outside of the office, consumers are even more likely to wear basic styles: Half of all shoppers say this is their favorite style to wear on the weekend or on other casual occasions. As shoppers get older, they are more likely to prefer basic casual looks. More than 60 percent of the oldest shoppers cite basic styles as preferred for weekend/casual wear. Classic/traditional styles are less preferred by younger shoppers for casual wear than for workplace attire. Contemporary looks are most preferred by younger shoppers for their casual wardrobe, with more than a third saying this is their favorite casual style.

There is a direct relationship between income and style preferences for work attire, with preferences becoming less basic as incomes increase. Race/ethnicity is also related to work wardrobe preferences. Higher-income workers are most likely to prefer a classic work wardrobe. They, along with those in the middle-income range, also are more likely to favor contemporary, but not trendy, work wardrobes. The lower workers' incomes, the more likely they are to wear basic styles to work. Basic styles also are more favored by White workers than by African-American and Latino workers. Latino workers are the trendiest race/ethnic group with respect to work clothing.

Questions

1. What overall conclusions do you reach after reading this case?
2. How can apparel retailers compete with Wal-Mart?
3. Does cross-shopping affect apparel retailing? Is this good or bad? Why?
4. What are the retail implications of this statement: "American consumers are not trendy—either at work or play?" Do you agree with the statement? Explain your answer.
5. How could the information cited in the case be used in a retail information system?
6. Devise a questionnaire to determine what improvements the loyal customers of an apparel store chain would like to see in the chain.
7. What additional consumer-related information would you like to review about apparel shoppers besides that stated in the case?

*The material in this case is adapted by the authors from *Soft Goods Shopper Update* (Columbus, OH: Retail Forward, January 2005). Reprinted by permission of Retail Forward, Inc. (**www. retailforward.com**).

part four

Choosing a Store Location

Once a retailer has conducted a situation analysis, set its goals, identified consumer characteristics and needs, and gathered adequate information about the marketplace, it is ready to develop and enact an overall strategy. In Parts Four through Seven, we examine the elements of such a strategy: choosing a store location, managing a business, merchandise management and pricing, and communicating with the customer. Part Four concentrates on store location.

■ **Chapter 9** deals with the crucial nature of store location for retailers and outlines a four-step approach to location planning. In this chapter, we focus on Step 1, trading-area analysis. Among the topics we look at are the use of geographic information systems, the size and shape of trading areas, how to determine trading areas for existing and new stores, and the major factors to consider in assessing trading areas. Several data sources are described.

■ **Chapter 10** covers the last three steps in location planning: deciding on the most desirable type of location, selecting a general location, and choosing a particular site within that location. We first contrast isolated store, unplanned business district, and planned shopping center locales. Criteria for rating each location are then outlined and detailed.

Chapter 9
TRADING-AREA ANALYSIS

Since Blockbuster (**www.block buster.com**) opened its first store in 1985, it has grown into the world's largest provider of rentable home videocassettes, DVDs, and video games. Today, on average, more than 3 million customers walk into a U.S. Blockbuster store each day. Blockbuster has approximately 9,100 stores throughout the United States, its territories, and 25 other countries. Blockbuster estimates that two-thirds of the U.S. population lives within a 10-minute drive of one of its stores.

Reprinted by permission.

In planning new store locations, Blockbuster performs sophisticated trading-area analysis based on its market share, customer transaction, and real-estate data bases. The analysis also includes data on an area's demographics, lifestyles, customer concentration levels, and competition. Through this assessment, Blockbuster's store development team is able to minimize lost sales due to trading-area overlap with its existing stores, to determine whether a new store should be built or an existing one expanded, and to decide upon the appropriate store format. Blockbuster then seeks out locations that are high in customer convenience and visibility.

Blockbuster has developed a comprehensive model that it uses to find suitable locations for its stores. The model uses membership transaction data (including population demographics and customer concentration levels) and real-estate data (including information on competition in each market area) to increase sales at new locations without significantly decreasing sales at existing ones.

Outside the United States, Blockbuster plans to open most of its new company-operated stores in core markets where it already has a significant presence.[1]

chapter objectives

1. To demonstrate the importance of store location for a retailer and outline the process for choosing a store location
2. To discuss the concept of a trading area and its related components
3. To show how trading areas may be delineated for existing and new stores
4. To examine three major factors in trading-area analysis: population characteristics, economic base characteristics, and competition and the level of saturation

OVERVIEW

More than 90 percent of retail sales are made at stores. Thus, the selection of a store location is one of the most significant strategic decisions in retailing. Consider the detailed planning of Wireless Toyz, a specialty retailer that carries numerous brands of cell-phone service, equipment, and accessories, as well as satellite TV. The chain

> looks for corner real-estate at busy intersections. Of course, those same criteria describe what every freestanding retailer hopes to find. The difference is that Wireless Toyz eagerly acquires dilapidated buildings or community eyesores that it transforms into productive, inviting retail stores: "We're looking for sites in middle-class, mostly blue-collar neighborhoods, with a minimum population of 50,000 people within the trade area and positioned at intersections with daily traffic counts of at least 50,000 vehicles." An average Wireless Toyz store is 1,500 to 2,500 square feet, in a market where average household incomes range from $35,000 to $55,000. Sometimes the company will lease a larger space, around 4,000 square feet, and sublease one-half of the area to another retailer. From 63 stores in 2004, the firm's goal is to have 250 stores by December 2006 and 1,000 stores by December 2011. "That's not just opening any store, that's 1,000 stores with great locations."[2]

This chapter and the next explain why the proper store location is so crucial, as well as the steps a retailer should take in choosing a store location and deciding whether to build, lease, or buy facilities. Visit our Web site (**www.prenhall.com/ bermanevans**) for many links on store location.

THE IMPORTANCE OF LOCATION TO A RETAILER

At the Entrepreneur Web site (**www.entrepreneur. com**), type in "Finding a Location" to access a wealth of helpful articles on location planning.

Location decisions are complex, costs can be quite high, there is little flexibility once a site is chosen, and locational attributes have a big impact on a strategy. One of the oldest adages in retailing is that "location, location, location" is the major factor leading to a firm's success or failure. See Figure 9-1.

A good location may let a retailer succeed even if its strategy mix is mediocre. A hospital gift shop may do well, although its assortment is limited, prices are high, and it does not advertise. On the other hand, a poor location may be such a liability that even superior retailers cannot overcome it. A mom-and-pop store may do poorly if it is across the street from a category killer store; although the small firm features personal service, it cannot match the selection and prices. At a different site, it might prosper.

The choice of a location requires extensive decision making due to the number of criteria considered, including population size and traits, the competition, transportation access, parking availability, the nature of nearby stores, property costs, the length of the agreement, legal restrictions, and other factors.

A store location typically necessitates a sizable investment and a long-term commitment. Even a retailer that minimizes its investment by leasing (rather than owning a building and land) can incur large costs. Besides lease payments, the firm must spend money on lighting, fixtures, a storefront, and so on.

Although leases of less than 5 years are common in less desirable retailing locations, leases in good shopping centers or shopping districts are often 5 to 10 years or more. It is not uncommon for a supermarket lease to be 15, 20, or 30 years. Department stores and large specialty stores on major downtown thoroughfares occasionally sign leases longer than 30 years.

FIGURE 9-1
The Importance of Location to Trader Joe's

Trader Joe's (**www.traderjoes.com**) has grown to more than 200 stores in Arizona, California, Connecticut, Delaware, Illinois, Indiana, Maryland, Massachusetts, Michigan, Missouri, Nevada, New Jersey, New Mexico, New York, Ohio, Oregon, Pennsylvania, Virginia, and Washington. "Our future plans call for ongoing development of new, one-of-a-kind food items at value prices, and continued expansion of our chain across the country." Trader Joe's looks for highly visible sites, sometimes for standalone stores and other times for stores in shopping centers.

Photo reprinted by permission of Susan Berry, Retail Image Consulting, Inc.

Due to its fixed nature, the investment, and the length of the lease, store location is the least flexible element of a strategy. A firm cannot easily move to another location or convert to another format. It may also be barred from subleasing to another party during the lease period; and if a retailer breaks a lease, it may be responsible to the property owner for financial losses. In contrast, ads, prices, customer services, and assortment can be altered as the environment (consumers, competition, the economy) changes.

Even a retailer that owns its store's building and land may also find it hard to change locations. It has to find an acceptable buyer, which might take several months or longer; and it may have to assist the buyer with financing. It may incur a loss, should it sell during an economic downturn.

Any retailer moving from one location to another faces three potential problems. (1) Some loyal customers and employees may be lost; the greater the distance between the old and new locations, the bigger the loss. (2) A new site may not have the same traits as the original one. (3) Store fixtures and renovations at an old site usually cannot be transferred to a new site; their remaining value is lost if they have not been fully depreciated.

Store location affects long- and short-run planning. In the *long run*, the choice of location influences the overall strategy. A retailer must be at a site that is consistent with its mission, goals, and target market for an extended time. It also must regularly study and monitor the status of the location as to population trends, the distances people travel to the store, and competitors' entry and exit—and adapt accordingly.

In the *short run*, the location has an impact on the specific elements of a strategy mix. A retailer in a downtown area with many office buildings may have little pedestrian traffic on weekends. It would probably be improper to sell items such as major appliances there (these items are often bought jointly by husbands and wives). The retailer could either close on weekends and not stock certain products or remain open and try to attract customers to the area by aggressive promotion or

RETAILING
Around the World | Chain Stores Grow in Russia

Retail chain electronics and appliance stores (such as M. Video, Eldorado, Tekhnosila, and MIR), sports clothing and equipment chain Sportsmaster, supermarket chain Perekryostok, and other major retailers are all looking for suitable retail space in Russia. According to the development director at MIR, "Modern chain stores need large amounts of retail space to display their array of products, but commercial real-estate with an area of at least 2,500 square meters [8,000-plus square feet per retailer] is a rare find." The director adds, "Now there is little competition between these shopping centers with spacious retail floors, so they charge inordinately high rents, creating obstacles for retailers' expansion. When more new shopping centers open, such obstacles will disappear."

The director of marketing and research at a major Russian shopping center developer notes that many larger spaces are broken up into smaller spaces to achieve higher rents. The competition for the better locations is generally among Moscow-based and Western retailers since local retailers typically lack the financial resources to utilize larger units.

Sources: Maria Levitov, "Chain Stores Help Fuel Regional Boom," *The Moscow Times* (April 27, 2004); and *Russia Country Monitor* (May 2005).

pricing. If the retailer closes on weekends, it adapts its strategy mix to the attributes of the location. If it stays open, it invests additional resources in an attempt to alter shopping habits. A retailer that strives to overcome its location, by and large, faces greater risks than one that adapts.

Retailers should follow these four steps in choosing a store location:

1. Evaluate alternate geographic (trading) areas in terms of the characteristics of residents and existing retailers.
2. Determine whether to locate as an isolated store, in an unplanned business district, or in a planned shopping center within the geographic area.
3. Select the general isolated store, unplanned business district, or planned shopping center location.
4. Analyze alternate sites contained in the specified retail location type.

This chapter concentrates on Step 1. Chapter 10 details Steps 2, 3, and 4. The selection of a store location is a process involving each of these steps.

TRADING-AREA ANALYSIS

The first step in the choice of a retail store location is to describe and evaluate alternate trading areas and then decide on the most desirable one. A **trading area** is "a geographic area containing the customers of a particular firm or group of firms for specific goods or services."[3] After a trading area is picked, it should be reviewed regularly.

A thorough analysis of trading areas provides several benefits:

● Consumers' demographic and socioeconomic characteristics are uncovered. For a new store, the study of proposed trading areas reveals opportunities and the retail strategy necessary to succeed. For an existing store, it can be determined if the current strategy still matches consumer needs.

● The focus of promotional activities is ascertained, and the retailer can look at media coverage patterns of proposed or existing locations. If 95 percent of customers live within three miles of a store, it would be inefficient to advertise in a paper with a citywide audience.

FIGURE 9-2
The Trading Areas of Current and Proposed Supermarket Outlets

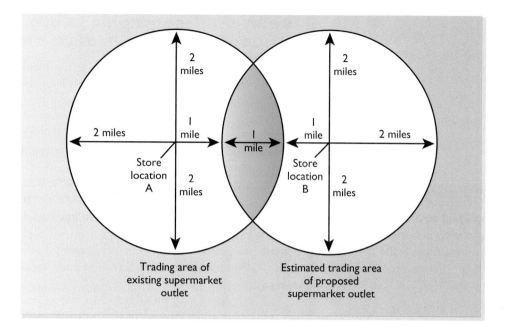

Trading area of existing supermarket outlet

Estimated trading area of proposed supermarket outlet

- A retailer learns whether the location of a proposed branch store will service new customers or take business from its existing stores. Suppose a supermarket chain has a store in Jackson, Mississippi, with a trading area of two miles, and it considers adding a new store, three miles from the Jackson branch. Figure 9-2 shows the distinct trading areas and expected overlap of the stores. The shaded portion represents the **trading-area overlap**, where the same customers are served by both branches. The chain must find out the overall net increase in sales if it adds the proposed store (total revised sales of existing store + total sales of new store − total previous sales of existing store).

- Chains anticipate whether competitors want to open nearby stores if the firm does not do so itself. That is why TJX has two of its chains, T.J. Maxx and Marshalls, situated within 1.5 miles of each other in more than 100 U.S. markets, even though they are both off-price apparel firms.

- The best number of stores for a chain to operate in a given area is calculated. How many outlets should a retailer have in a region to provide good service for customers (without raising costs too much or having too much overlap)? When CVS entered Atlanta, it opened nine new drugstores in one day. This gave it enough coverage of the city to service residents, without placing stores too close together. A major competitive advantage for Canadian Tire Corporation is that four-fifths of the Canadian population live within a 15-minute drive of a Canadian Tire store.

- Geographic weaknesses are highlighted. Suppose a suburban shopping center does an analysis and discovers that most of those residing south of town do not shop there, and a more comprehensive study reveals that people are afraid to drive past a dangerous railroad crossing. Due to its research, the shopping center exerts political pressure to make the crossing safer.

- The impact of the Internet is taken into account. Store-based retailers must examine trading areas more carefully than ever to see how their customers' shopping behavior is changing due to the Web.

- Other factors are reviewed. The competition, financial institutions, transportation, labor availability, supplier location, legal restrictions, and so on can each be learned for the trading area(s) examined.

The Use of Geographic Information Systems in Trading-Area Delineation and Analysis

Increasingly, retailers are using **geographic information systems (GIS)** software, which combines digitized mapping with key locational data to graphically depict trading-area characteristics such as population demographics, data on customer purchases, and listings of current, proposed, and competitor locations. Commercial GIS software lets firms quickly research the attractiveness of different locations and access computer-generated maps. Before, retailers often placed different color pins on paper maps to show current and proposed locales—and competitors' sites—and had to collect and analyze data.[4]

Most GIS software programs are extrapolated from the decennial *Census of Population* and the U.S. Census Bureau's national digital map (known as TIGER—topologically integrated geographic encoding and referencing). TIGER (**www.census.gov/geo/www/tiger**) incorporates all streets and highways in the United States. GIS software can be purchased and accessed through Web site downloads or by CDs.

TIGER maps may be adapted to reflect census tracts, railroads, highways, waterways, and other physical attributes of any U.S. area. They do not show retailers, other commercial entities, or population traits; and the Web site is hard to use. Figure 9-3 shows a sample TIGER map. The federal government is investing $500 million to upgrade the TIGER program, with completion expected by 2008.

Software from private firms has many more enhancements than TIGER. While these firms often offer free demonstrations, they expect to be paid for their software packages. Although GIS software differs by vendor, it generally can be accessed or bought for as little as under a hundred dollars to as much as several thousand dollars, is designed to work with personal computers, and allows for some manipulation of trading-area data. Illustrations appear in Figure 9-4. Private firms that offer mapping software include:

- Autodesk (**http://usa.autodesk.com**).
- Caliper Corporation (**www.caliper.com**).
- Claritas (**www.claritas.com**).
- ESRI (Environmental Systems Research Institute) (**www.esri.com**).
- geoVue (**www.geovue.com**).
- MapInfo (**www.mapinfo.com**).
- MPSI Systems (**www.mpsisys.com**).
- SRC (**www.demographicsnow.com**).
- TeleAtlas (**www.teleatlas.com**).
- Tetrad Computer Applications (**www.tetrad.com**).

At our Web site (**www.prenhall.com/bermanevans**), we provide links to the descriptions of the GIS software for all of these firms. Many of the companies have free demonstrations at their sites.

GIS software can be applied in various ways. A chain retailer could learn which of its stores have trading areas containing households with a median annual income of more than $50,000. That firm could derive the sales potential of proposed new store locations and those stores' potential effect on sales at existing branches. It could use GIS software to determine the demographics of customers at its best locations and set up a computer model to find the potential locations with the most desirable attributes. A retailer could even use the software to pinpoint its geographic areas of strength and weakness.

TIGER (**http://tiger.census.gov/cgi-bin/mapbrowse-tbl**) can map out any U.S. community. At the bottom of the screen, enter a ZIP code.

In the "Company" section of the MapInfo Web site (**www.mapinfo.com**), take a look at the free "Literature" on store location planning.

Do you like *colorful* trading-area maps? Enter SRC's site (**www.demographicsnow.com**) and click "View Sample Reports and Maps" on the left toolbar.

FIGURE 9-3
The TIGER Map Service

Reprinted by permission.

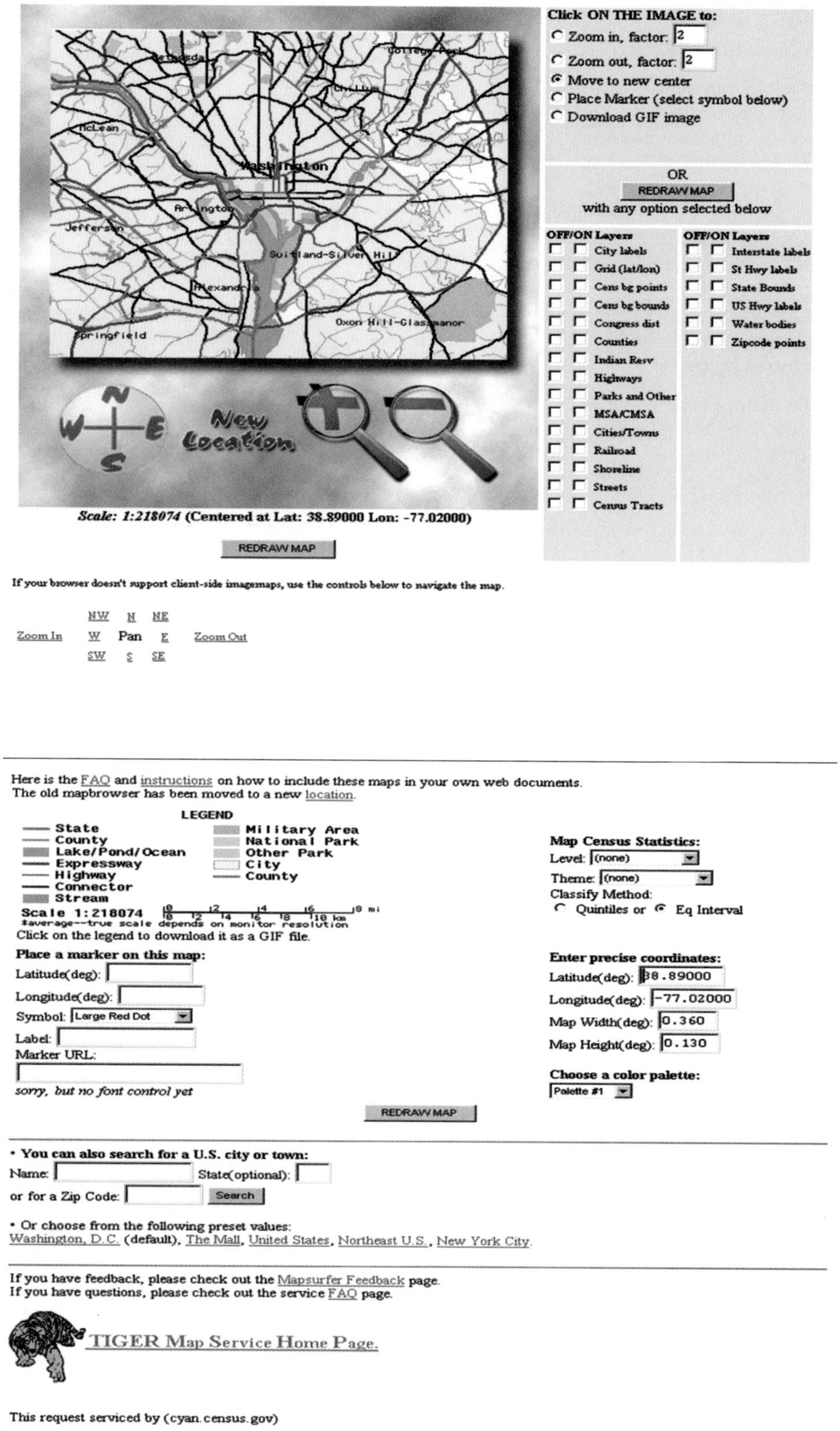

Click ON THE IMAGE to:
- Zoom in, factor: 2
- Zoom out, factor: 2
- Move to new center
- Place Marker (select symbol below)
- Download GIF image

OR

REDRAW MAP

with any option selected below

OFF/ON Layers
- City labels
- Grid (lat/lon)
- Cens bg points
- Cens bg bounds
- Congress dist
- Counties
- Indian Resv
- Highways
- Parks and Other
- MSA/CMSA
- Cities/Towns
- Railroad
- Shoreline
- Streets
- Census Tracts

OFF/ON Layers
- Interstate labels
- St Hwy labels
- State Bounds
- US Hwy labels
- Water bodies
- Zipcode points

Scale: 1:218074 (Centered at Lat: 38.89000 Lon: -77.02000)

REDRAW MAP

If your browser doesn't support client-side imagemaps, use the controls below to navigate the map.

	NW	N	NE	
Zoom In	W	Pan	E	Zoom Out
	SW	S	SE	

Here is the FAQ and instructions on how to include these maps in your own web documents.
The old mapbrowser has been moved to a new location.

LEGEND

State	Military Area
County	National Park
Lake/Pond/Ocean	Other Park
Expressway	City
Highway	County
Connector	
Stream	

Scale 1:218074
*average--true scale depends on monitor resolution
Click on the legend to download it as a GIF file.

Place a marker on this map:
Latitude(deg):
Longitude(deg):
Symbol: Large Red Dot
Label:
Marker URL:

sorry, but no font control yet

Map Census Statistics:
Level: (none)
Theme: (none)
Classify Method:
- Quintiles or ⦿ Eq Interval

Enter precise coordinates:
Latitude(deg): 38.89000
Longitude(deg): -77.02000
Map Width(deg): 0.360
Map Height(deg): 0.130

Choose a color palette:
Palette #1

REDRAW MAP

• You can also search for a U.S. city or town:
Name: State(optional):
or for a Zip Code: Search

• Or choose from the following preset values:
Washington, D.C. (default), The Mall, United States, Northeast U.S., New York City.

If you have feedback, please check out the Mapsurfer Feedback page.
If you have questions, please check out the service FAQ page.

TIGER Map Service Home Page.

This request serviced by (cyan.census.gov)

These two examples show how retailers can employ GIS software:

- Dunkin' Donuts has used geoVue's iSITE software to analyze new store locations for nearly a decade. This replaced a costly, time-consuming manual system. iSITE is "sophisticated market analysis software. By screening trade

FIGURE 9-4

GIS Software in Action

Through GIS mapping software, retailers can pinpoint the trading areas for their stores and the characteristics of the residents in these areas. (A) indicates population density relative to store ★. (B) shows a new store branch ★ relative to other branch stores. (C) presents distinct trading areas with minimal overlap. (D) reveals the level of retail sales by census tract.

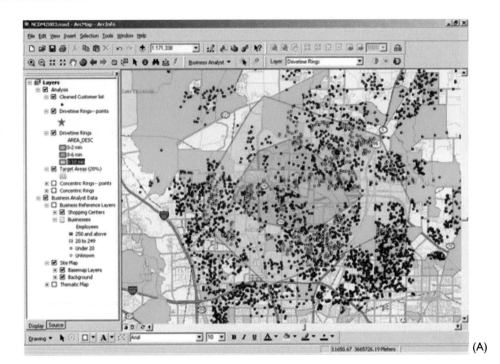

(A)

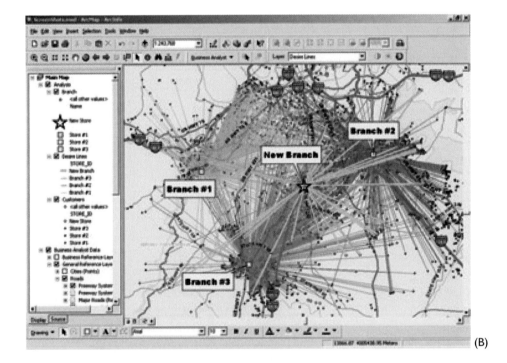

(B)

areas in advance, we can tie up the best locations before others have even started their analysis. geoVue has dramatically cut our time to market."

● Eddie Bauer is a Claritas client. Previously, it "ordered basic reports from a vendor, pulling out Rand McNally maps and photocopying them." The retailer "would mark stores and trace ZIP code areas by hand, and couldn't map the stores or competitors. Today, Eddie Bauer uses online geocoding and GIS mapping software from Claritas, as well as several data bases, to get information

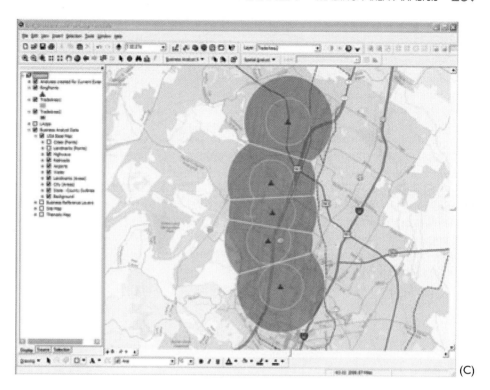

(C)

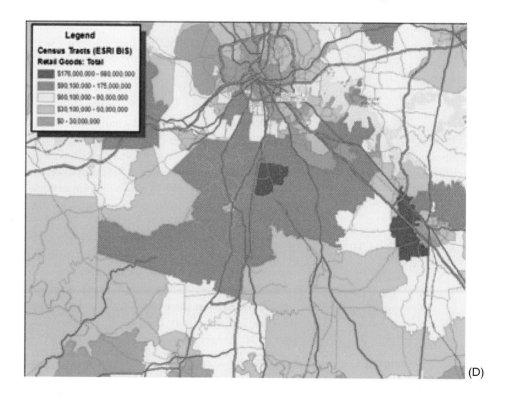

(D)

needed." By using the retail trade data base, Eddie Bauer, "can find area retail expenditures. Then, using Claritas demographics, it gets the household growth rate, the number of housing units, and other detailed consumer information. It has latitudes and longitudes to map each Eddie Bauer store and the ability to map each local competitor."[5]

Technology in RETAILING — Using GIS to Improve Retail Decision Making

At one time, retailers had to rely on ZIP code-based geographic mapping. Although ZIP codes can be easily obtained from consumers, retailers could not determine whether two customers lived one block or three miles from one another. ZIP code-based data could also not determine how many households earning $100,000 or more were within two miles of a planned store location.

Through geographic information software (GIS), retailers can draw or create a territory in digital format. Most detailed maps are generated by governmental agencies, while private service bureaus reorganize maps from multiple agencies in a user-friendly manner. GIS assigns latitude-longitude coordinates to each customer

based upon his or her address. The software is then able to develop demographic profiles of residents in a particular area (block, ZIP code, census tracts, and counties).

By understanding the demographics of a retailer's best customers, that retailer can develop more intelligent retail location decisions. Franchises and chains can also use this information to determine the optimal number of store units in a given market area.

Sources: Jeffrey Davis, "Developing Franchise Territories," *Franchising World* (August 2004), pp. 25–26; Kevin Fogarty, "Primer: Geospatial Analysis," *Baseline* (August 2004), p. 69; and Jonathan W. Lowe, "Web GIS Gets Flashy," *Geospatial Solutions* (May 2005), pp. 33–36.

The Size and Shape of Trading Areas

Each trading area has three parts: The **primary trading area** encompasses 50 to 80 percent of a store's customers. It is the area closest to the store and possesses the highest density of customers to population and the highest per capita sales. There is little overlap with other trading areas. The **secondary trading area** contains an additional 15 to 25 percent of a store's customers. It is located outside the primary area, and customers are more widely dispersed. The **fringe trading area** includes all the remaining customers, and they are the most widely dispersed. A store could have a primary trading area of 4 miles, a secondary trading area of 5 miles, and a fringe trading area of 10 miles. The fringe trading area typically includes some outshoppers who travel greater distances to patronize certain stores.

Visit this site to fully see the complexity of factors in site selection (www.conway.com/cheklist).

Figures 9-5 and 9-6 show the makeup of trading areas and their segments. In reality, trading areas do not usually follow such circular patterns. They adjust to the physical environment. The size and shape of a trading area are influenced by store type, store size, the location of competitors, housing patterns, travel time and traffic barriers (such as toll bridges), and media availability. These factors are discussed next.

Two stores can have different trading areas even if they are in the same shopping district or shopping center. Situated in one shopping center could be a branch of an apparel chain with a distinctive image and people willing to travel up to 20 miles and a shoe store seen as average and people willing to travel up to 5 miles. When one store has a better assortment, promotes more, and/or creates a stronger image, it may then become a **destination store** and generate a trading area much larger than that of a competitor with a me-too appeal. That is why Dunkin' Donuts used the slogan "It's worth the trip" for many years.

A **parasite store** does not create its own traffic and has no real trading area of its own. This store depends on people who are drawn to the location for other reasons. A magazine stand in a hotel lobby and a snack bar in a shopping center are parasites. While they are there, customers patronize these shops.

The extent of a store's or center's trading area is affected by its own size. As a store or center gets larger, its trading area usually increases, because store or center size generally reflects the assortment of goods and services. Yet, trading areas do not grow proportionately with store or center size. As a rule, supermarket trading areas are bigger than those of convenience stores. Supermarkets have a better

FIGURE 9-5
The Segments of a Trading
Area

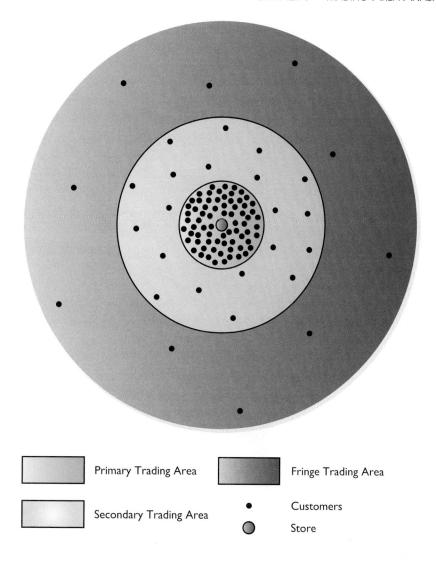

	Primary Trading Area		Fringe Trading Area
	Secondary Trading Area	•	Customers
		◯	Store

FIGURE 9-6
Delineating Trading-Area
Segments

This GIS map clearly depicts
primary, secondary, and fringe
trading areas for a store.
However, the shapes are rarely
so concentric.

Reprinted by permission of ESRI and
GDT.

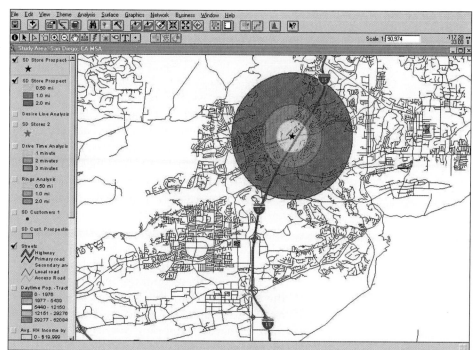

FIGURE 9-7
Broadway Mall: The Draw
of Big-Name Retailers

The Broadway Mall in
Hicksville, New York, has
enlarged its trading area by
having three leading anchor
stores—Ikea, Macy's, and
Target, as well as more than
100 other stores.

Photo reprinted by permission.

product selection and convenience stores appeal to the need for fill-in merchandise. In a regional shopping center, department stores typically have the largest trading areas, followed by apparel stores; gift stores have comparatively small trading areas. See Figure 9-7.

Whenever potential shoppers are situated between two competing stores, the trading area is often reduced for each store. The size of each store's trading area normally increases as the distance between stores grows (target markets do not then overlap as much). On the other hand, when stores are situated very near one another, the size of each store's trading area does not necessarily shrink. This store grouping may actually increase the trading area for each store if more consumers are attracted to the location due to the variety of goods and services. Yet, each store's market penetration (its percentage of sales in the trading area) may be low with such competition. Also, the entry of a new store may change the shape or create gaps in the trading areas of existing stores.

In many urban communities, people are clustered in multi-unit housing near the center of commerce. With such population density, it is worthwhile for a retailer to be quite close to consumers; and trading areas tend to be small because there are several shopping districts in close proximity to one another, particularly for the most densely populated cities. In many suburbs, people live in single-unit housing—which is more geographically spread out. To produce satisfactory sales volume there, a retailer needs to attract shoppers from a greater distance.

The influence of travel or driving time on a trading area may not be clear from the population's geographic distribution. Physical barriers (toll bridges, poor roads, railroad tracks, one-way streets) usually reduce trading areas' size and contribute to their odd shapes. Economic barriers, such as different sales taxes in two towns, also affect the size and shape of trading areas.

In a community where a newspaper or other local media are available, a retailer could afford to advertise and enlarge its trading area. If local media are not available, the retailer would have to weigh the costs of advertising in countywide or regional media against the possibilities of a bigger trading area.

Delineating the Trading Area of an Existing Store

The size, shape, and characteristics of the trading area for an existing store—or shopping district or shopping center—can usually be delineated quite accurately. Store records (secondary data) or a special study (primary data) can measure the trading area. And many firms offer computer-generated maps that can be tailored to individual retailers' needs.

Store records can reveal customer addresses. For credit customers, the data can be obtained from a retailer's billing department; for cash customers, addresses can be acquired by analyzing deliveries, cash sales slips, store contests (sweepstakes), and checks. In both instances, the task is relatively inexpensive and quick because the data were originally collected for other purposes and are readily available.

Since many big retailers have computerized credit card systems, they can delineate primary, secondary, and fringe trading areas in terms of the

- Frequency with which people from various geographic locales shop at a particular store.
- Average dollar purchases at a store by people from given geographic locales.
- Concentration of a store's credit card holders from given geographic locales.

Though it is easy to get data on credit card customers, the analysis may be invalid if cash customers are not also studied. Credit use may vary among shoppers from different locales, especially if consumer characteristics in the locales are dissimilar. A firm reduces this problem if both cash and credit customers are reviewed.

A retailer can also collect primary data to determine trading-area size. It can record the license plate numbers of cars parked near a store, find the general addresses of those vehicle owners by contacting the state motor vehicle office, and then note them on a map. Typically, only the ZIP code and street of residence are provided to protect people's privacy. When using license plate analysis, nondrivers and passengers—customers who walk to a store, use mass transit, or are driven by others—should not be omitted. To collect data on these customers, questions must often be asked (survey).

If a retailer desires more demographic and lifestyle information about consumers in particular areas, it can buy the data. PRIZM NE is Claritas' system for identifying communities by lifestyle clusters. It identifies 66 neighborhood types, including "Gray Power," "Urban Achievers," and "Suburban Sprawl." This system was based on ZIP codes; it now also incorporates census tracts, block groups and enumeration districts, phone exchanges, and postal routes. Online PRIZM NE reports can be downloaded for as little as a few hundred dollars; costs are higher if reports are tailored to the individual retailer.

MetroCount (www.metrocount.com) offers software to provide vehicular traffic counts. Click on "Products."

Visit this site (www.clusterbigip1.claritas.com) to study your area's lifestyles and purchasing preferences. Click on "You Are Where You Live."

No matter how a trading area is delineated, a time bias may exist. A downtown business district is patronized by different customers during the week (those who work there) than on weekends (those who travel there to shop). Special events may attract people from great distances for only a brief time. Thus, an accurate estimate of a store's trading area requires complete and continuous investigation.

After delineating a trading area, the retailer should map people's locations and densities—either manually or with GIS software. In the manual method, a paper map of the area around a store is used. Different color dots or pins are placed on this map to represent *population* locations and densities, incomes, and other factors. *Customer* locations and densities are then indicated; primary, secondary, and fringe trading areas are denoted by ZIP code. Customers can be lured by promotions aimed at particular ZIP codes. With GIS software, vital customer data (such as purchase frequencies and amounts) are combined with other information sources (such as census data) to yield computer-generated digitized maps depicting primary, secondary, and fringe trading areas.

Delineating the Trading Area of a New Store

A new store opening in an established trading area can use the methods just noted. This section refers to a trading area with less-defined shopping and traffic patterns. Such an area must normally be evaluated in terms of opportunities rather than current patronage and traffic (pedestrian and vehicular) patterns. Accordingly, additional tools must be utilized.

Trend analysis—projecting the future based on the past—can be employed by examining government and other data for predictions about population location, auto registrations, new housing starts, mass transportation, highways, zoning, and so on. Consumer surveys can gather information about the time and distance people would be willing to travel to various possible retail locations, the factors attracting people to a new store, the addresses of those most apt to visit a new store, and other topics. Either technique may be a basis for delineating alternate new store trading areas.

Three computerized trading-area analysis models are available for assessing new store locations:

- An **analog model** is the simplest and most popular trading-area analysis model. Potential sales for a new store are estimated on the basis of revenues for similar stores in existing areas, the competition at a prospective location, the new store's expected market share at that location, and the size and density of the location's primary trading area.

- A **regression model** uses a series of mathematical equations showing the association between potential store sales and several independent variables at each location, such as population size, average income, the number of households, nearby competitors, transportation barriers, and traffic patterns.

- A **gravity model** is based on the premise that people are drawn to stores that are closer and more attractive than competitors' stores. The distance between consumers and competitors, the distance between consumers and a given site, and store image are included in this model.[6]

Computerized trading-area models offer several benefits to retailers: They operate in an objective and systematic way. They offer insights as to how each locational attribute should be weighted. They are useful in screening a large number of locations. They can assess management performance by comparing forecasts with results.

More specific methods for delineating new trading areas are described next.

Reilly's Law

The traditional means of trading-area delineation is **Reilly's law of retail gravitation**.[7] It establishes a point of indifference between two cities or communities, so the trading area of each can be determined. The **point of indifference** is the geographic breaking point between two cities (communities) at which consumers are indifferent to shopping at either. According to Reilly's law, more consumers go to the larger city or community because there are more stores; the assortment makes travel time worthwhile. Reilly's law rests on these assumptions: Two competing areas are equally accessible from a major road, and retailers in the two areas are equally effective. Other factors (such as population dispersion) are held constant or ignored.

The law may be expressed algebraically as:[8]

$$D_{ab} = \frac{d}{1 + \sqrt{P_b/P_a}}$$

where

D_{ab} = Limit of city (community) A's trading area, measured in miles along the road to city (community) B

d = Distance in miles along a major roadway between cities (communities) A and B

P_a = Population of city (community) A

P_b = Population of city (community) B

A city with a population of 90,000 (A) would draw people from three times the distance as a city with 10,000 (B). If the cities are 20 miles apart, the point of indifference for the larger city is 15 miles, and for the smaller city, it is 5 miles:

$$D_{ab} = \frac{20}{1 + \sqrt{10,000/90,000}} = 15 \text{ miles}$$

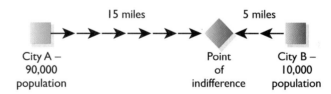

Reilly's law is an important contribution to trading-area analysis because of its ease of calculation. It is most useful when other data are not available or compiling other data is costly. Nonetheless, Reilly's law has three limitations: (1) Distance is only measured by major thoroughfares; some people will travel shorter distances along cross streets. (2) Travel time does not necessarily reflect the distance traveled. Many people are more concerned about time than distance. (3) Actual distance may not correspond with the perceptions of distance. A store with few services and crowded aisles is apt to be a greater perceived distance from the person than a similarly located store with a more pleasant atmosphere.

Huff's Law

Huff's law of shopper attraction delineates trading areas on the basis of the product assortment (of the items desired by the consumer) carried at various shopping locations, travel times from the shopper's home to alternative locations, and the sensitivity of the kind of shopping to travel time. Assortment is rated by the total square feet of selling space a retailer expects all firms in a shopping area to allot to a product category. Sensitivity to the kind of shopping entails the trip's purpose (restocking versus shopping) and the type of good/service sought (such as clothing versus groceries).[9]

Huff's law is expressed as:

$$P_{ij} = \frac{\dfrac{S_j}{(T_{ij})^{\lambda}}}{\displaystyle\sum_{j}^{n} \dfrac{S_j}{(T_{ij})^{\lambda}}}$$

where

P_{ij} = Probability of a consumer's traveling from home i to shopping location j
S_j = Square footage of selling space in shopping location j expected to be devoted to a particular product category
T_{ij} = Travel time from consumer's home i to shopping location j
λ = Parameter used to estimate the effect of travel time on different kinds of shopping trips
n = Number of different shopping locations

λ must be determined through research or by a computer program.

Assume a leased department operator studies three possible locations with 200, 300, and 500 total square feet of store space allocated to men's cologne (by all retailers in the areas). A group of potential customers lives 7 minutes from the first location, 10 minutes from the second, and 15 minutes from the third. The operator estimates the effect of travel time to be 2. Therefore, the probability of consumers' shopping is 43.9 percent for Location 1, 32.2 percent for Location 2, and 23.9 percent for Location 3:

$$P_{i1} = \frac{(200)/(7)^2}{(200)/(7)^2 + (300)/(10)^2 + (500)/(15)^2} = 43.9\%$$

$$P_{i2} = \frac{(300)/(10)^2}{(200)/(7)^2 + (300)/(10)^2 + (500)/(15)^2} = 32.2\%$$

$$P_{i3} = \frac{(500)/(15)^2}{(200)/(7)^2 + (300)/(10)^2 + (500)/(15)^2} = 23.9\%$$

If 200 men live 7 minutes from Location 1, about 88 of them will shop there.

These points should be considered in using Huff's law:

- To determine Location 1's trading area, similar computations would be made for people living at a driving time of 10, 15, 20 minutes, and so on. The number of people at each distance who would shop there are then summed. Thus, stores in Location 1 could estimate their total market, the trading-area size, and the primary, secondary, and fringe areas for a product category.

- If new retail facilities in a product category are added to a locale, the percentage of people living at every travel time from that location who would shop there goes up.

- The probability of people shopping at a location depends on the effect of travel time. If a product is important, such as dress watches, consumers are less travel sensitive. A λ of 1 leads to these figures: Location 1, 31.1 percent; Location 2, 32.6 percent; and Location 3, 36.3 percent (based on the space in the cologne example). Location 3 would be popular for the watches due to its assortment.

- All the variables are rather hard to calculate; for mapping purposes, travel time must be converted to miles. Travel time also depends on the transportation form used.
- Since people buy different items on different shopping trips, the trading area varies by trip.

MPSI Systems offers a PC-based software package called Huff's Market Area Planner.

Access samples of Huff software at MPSI's site (**www.datametrix.com/ website/huff/huff.html**).

Other Trading-Area Research

Over the years, many researchers have examined trading-area size in a variety of settings. They have introduced additional factors and advanced statistical techniques to explain the consumer's choice of shopping location.

In his model, Gautschi added to Huff's analysis by including shopping-center descriptors and transportation conditions. Weisbrod, Parcells, and Kern studied shopping center appeal on the basis of expected population changes, store characteristics, and the transportation network. Ghosh developed a consumer behavior model that takes into account multi-purpose shopping trips. LeBlang demonstrated that consumer lifestyles could be used to predict sales at new department store locations. Schneider, Johnson, Sleeper, and Rodgers studied trading-area overlap and franchisees. Albaladejo-Pina and Aranda-Gallego looked at the effects of competition among stores in different sections of a trading area. Bell, Ho, and Tang devised a model with fixed and variable store choice factors. Ruiz studied

---

Careers in RETAILING   Is Retail for Me? IT and E-Commerce—Part 2

There are many opportunities specifically related to E-commerce:

- *E-Commerce Director:* This person may come from a merchandising, marketing, or information technology (IT) background, but holds the top position over all Internet initiatives. The individual is responsible for the Internet retailing strategies, Web site content and appearance, Internet partnerships, effectiveness, and financial results of the E-tailing effort.
- *Web Site Designer/Art Director:* This is the top designer position responsible for the creative look and feel of the Web site environment. This individual will determine the use and layout of graphics, pictures, placement, and content of copywriting text, etc. She or he may have a graphic arts or advertising background, for example, rather than a technical background installing gifs, jpegs, etc.
- *Web Site Project Manager:* This is a technical position assigning work to programming staff (internal and/or contract staff), ensuring that deadlines, hardware, and programming specifications are met. Has

typical IT project manager responsibilities, but all are related to E-commerce. Duties may include project budgeting and hiring staff or directing an outsourced programming service.
- *Top E-Merchant (Merchandise Manager):* This position is responsible for selecting the merchandise displayed on the Web, and determining the inventory quantities needed for Internet sales. Decides prices, markdowns, and when to remove end-of-stock items from the Web site. May negotiate bulk sales of returns and closeouts with other retailers. May supervise a staff of merchants and/or inventory planners. This person is not responsible for the technical IT part of the Web site.
- *Fulfillment Manager:* This position is responsible for the pick, pack, and send operations for all customer Web orders. May also be responsible for the call center. May manage an internal processing staff or may direct an outsourced distribution center service provider.

Source: Reprinted by permission of the National Retail Federation.

shopping center image and shopper attractiveness. Rogers examined the role of human decision making versus computer-based models in site choice. Smith and Hay reviewed the role of competition in trading areas.[10]

CHARACTERISTICS OF TRADING AREAS

PCensus with MapInfo (www.tetrad.com/new/franchise.html) is a useful tool for scrutinizing potential franchise locations.

After the size and shape of alternative trading areas are determined, the characteristics of those areas are studied. Of special interest are the attributes of residents and how well they match the firm's definition of its target market. An auto repair franchisee may compare opportunities in several locales by reviewing the number of car registrations; a hearing aid retailer may evaluate the percentage of the population 60 years of age or older; and a bookstore retailer may be concerned with residents' education level.

Among the trading-area factors that should be studied by most retailers are the population size and characteristics, availability of labor, closeness to sources of supply, promotion facilities, economic base, competition, availability of locations, and regulations. The **economic base** is an area's industrial and commercial structure—the companies and industries that residents depend on to earn a living. The dominant industry (company) in an area is important since its drastic decline may have adverse effects on a large segment of residents. An area with a diverse economic base, where residents work for a variety of nonrelated industries, is more secure than an area with one major industry. Table 9-1 summarizes a number of factors to consider in evaluating retail trading areas.

Much of the data needed to describe an area can be obtained from the U.S. Bureau of the Census, the *American Community Survey, Editor & Publisher Market Guide, Survey of Buying Power, Rand McNally Commercial Atlas & Market Guide, Standard Rate & Data Service*, regional planning boards, public utilities, chambers of commerce, local government offices, shopping-center owners, and renting agents. In addition, GIS software provides data on potential buying power in an area, the location of competitors, and highway access. Both demographic and lifestyle information may also be included in this software.

Although the yardsticks in Table 9-1 are not equally important in all location decisions, each should be considered. The most important yardsticks should be "knockout" factors: If a location does not meet minimum standards on key measures, it should be immediately dropped from further consideration.

These are examples of desirable trading-area attributes, according to several retailers:

- Walgreens looks to position its drugstores in sites where "evening commuter traffic can make an easy right turn into our parking lots." To one observer, "The moral of this story is that site selection is as much about understanding your shoppers' buying habits as it is about market demographics."
- The fast-growing Petco chain "looks at opportunities market by market." Nonetheless, the majority of its stores are situated in regional power centers with a large food-based superstore and such firms as Home Depot or Best Buy. It "avoids locating on top of a competitor because in this retail niche there needs to be market spacing."
- At Sharper Image: "We have a two-pronged strategy right now in terms of our real-estate. The first is we're looking for grade-A regional malls in urban areas. The other prong is we're looking at drive-up locations in sort of fill-in geographic locations. We believe with our store we can draw people into centers now. That's why we're looking at both prongs."

TABLE 9-1	Chief Factors to Consider in Evaluating Retail Trading Areas

Population Size and Characteristics

Total size and density	Total disposable income
Age distribution	Per capita disposable income
Average educational level	Occupation distribution
Percentage of residents owning homes	Trends

Availability of Labor

Management
Management trainee
Clerical

Closeness to Sources of Supply

Delivery costs	Number of manufacturers and wholesalers
Timeliness	Availability and reliability of product lines

Promotion Facilities

Availability and frequency of media
Costs
Waste

Economic Base

Dominant industry	Freedom from economic and seasonal
Extent of diversification	fluctuations
Growth projections	Availability of credit and financial facilities

Competitive Situation

Number and size of existing competitors	Short-run and long-run outlook
Evaluation of competitor strengths/weaknesses	Level of saturation

Availability of Store Locations

Number and type of locations	Zoning restrictions
Access to transportation	Costs
Owning versus leasing opportunities	

Regulations

Taxes	Minimum wages
Licensing	Zoning
Operations	

- Forty-three hundred of Dollar General's stores serve communities with a population of less than 20,000. This lets it take advantage of its brand awareness, maximize operating efficiencies, and serve untapped markets.
- The Syms off-price apparel chain seeks locations near highways or thoroughfares in suburban areas populated by at least 1 million persons and readily accessible by car. In certain areas, with over 2 million people, Syms has more than one store.[11]

Several stages of the process for gathering data to analyze trading areas are shown in Figure 9-8, which includes not only the attributes of residents but also those of the competition. By studying these factors, a retailer sees how desirable an area is for its business.

We next discuss three elements in trading-area selection: population characteristics, economic base characteristics, and the nature of competition and the level of saturation.

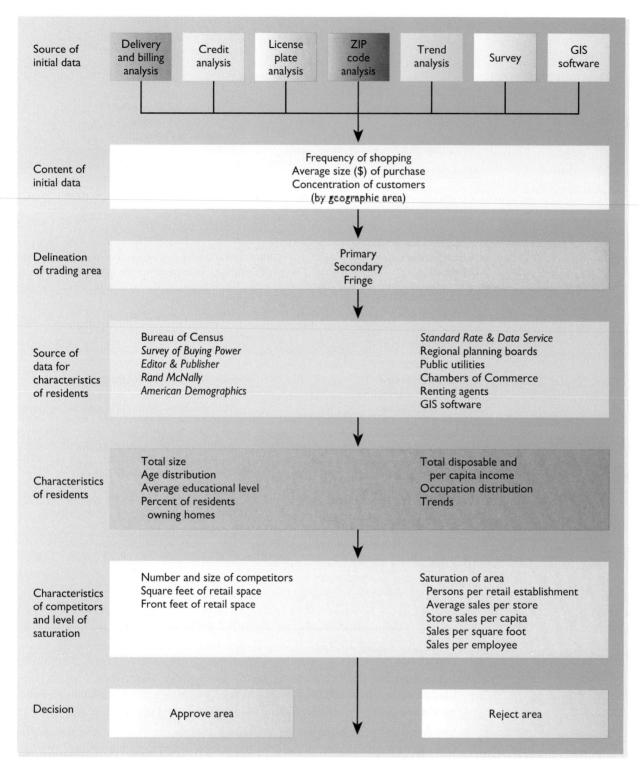

FIGURE 9-8
Analyzing Retail Trading Areas

Characteristics of the Population

Extensive knowledge about an area's population characteristics can be gained from secondary sources. They offer data about the population size, number of households, income distribution, education level, age distribution, and more.

Because the *Census of Population* and other public sources are so valuable, we briefly describe them next.

Census of Population

Find out about the 2000 U.S. Census (www.census.gov/dmd/www/2khome.htm).

The *Census of Population* supplies a wide range of demographic data for all U.S. cities and surrounding vicinities. Data are organized on a geographic basis, starting with blocks and continuing to census tracts, cities, counties, states, and regions. There are less data for blocks and census tracts than for larger units due to privacy issues. The major advantage of census data is the information on small geographic units. Once trading-area boundaries are outlined, a firm can look at data for each of the geographic units in that area and study aggregate demographics. There are also data categories that are especially helpful for retailers interested in segmenting the market—including racial and ethnic data, small-area income data, and commuting patterns. Census data are available on CDs, on computer tapes, and online.

The U.S. Census Bureau's TIGER computerized data base contains extremely detailed physical breakdowns of areas in the United States. The data base has digital descriptions of geographic areas (area boundaries and codes, latitude and longitude coordinates, and address ranges). Because TIGER data must be used in conjunction with population and other data, GIS software is necessary. As noted earlier in this chapter, many private firms have devised location analysis programs, based in large part on TIGER. These firms also usually project data to the present year and into the future.

The major drawbacks of the *Census of Population* are that it is undertaken only once every 10 years and that all data are not immediately available when they are collected. For example, the next Census is not until 2010, and information from the 2000 *Census of Population* was released in phases from 2001 through 2003. Census material can thus be out-of-date and inaccurate—particularly several years after collection. Supplementary sources, such as municipal building departments or utilities, state government offices, other Census reports (including the *Current Population Survey*), and computerized projections by firms such as Dun & Bradstreet must be used to update *Census of Population* data.

The value of the *Census of Population's* actual 2000 census tract data can be shown by an illustration of Long Beach, New York, which is 30 miles east of New York City on Long Island's south shore. Long Beach encompasses six census tracts: 4164, 4165, 4166, 4167.01, 4167.02, and 4168. See Figure 9-9. Although tract 4163 is contiguous with Long Beach, it represents another community. Table 9-2 shows various population statistics for each Long Beach census tract. Resident characteristics in each tract differ; thus, a retailer might choose to locate in one or more tracts but not in others.

Suppose a bookstore chain wants to evaluate two potential trading areas. Because of the demographic differences of tract 4165 from the other tracts, the chain decides not to include this tract in its analysis. Trading area A corresponds with tracts 4164 and 4166. Area B is similar to tracts 4167.01, 4167.02, and 4168. Population data for these areas (extracted from Table 9-2) are presented in Table 9-3. Area A differs from Area B, despite their proximity and similar physical size:

- The population in Area B is 13 percent larger.
- Although the population in both areas rose from 1990 to 2000, Area B grew very little.
- In Area A, a slightly greater percentage of residents aged 25 and older have college degrees.

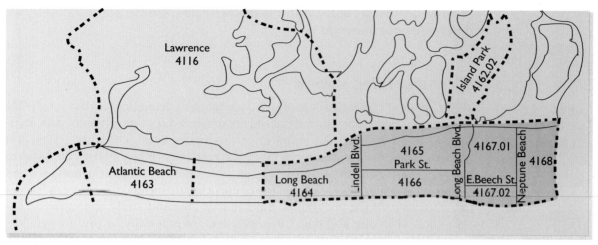

FIGURE 9-9
The Census Tracts of Long Beach, New York

| | | | **TABLE 9-2** | Selected Characteristics of Long Beach, New York, Residents by Census Tract, 1990 and 2000 |

	TRACT NUMBER					
	4164	**4165**	**4166**	**4167.01**	**4167.02**	**4168**
Total Population						
1990	7,082	5,694	5,613	4,162	4,479	6,480
1990 population 25 and older	5,315	3,331	4,306	3,003	3,620	5,074
2000	7,406	6,231	6,326	4,471	4,443	6,585
2000 population 25 and older	5,772	4,073	4,904	3,163	3,739	5,173
Number of Households						
1990	2,735	1,812	2,219	1,465	2,295	3,066
2000	3,138	2,002	2,592	1,601	2,440	3,165
Education						
College graduates (% of population 25 and older), 2000	38.4	18.6	44.9	35.8	35.9	43.7
Income						
Median household income, 2000 (estimate)	$59,188	$46,261	$63,716	$68,680	$52,334	$64,348
Selected Occupations						
Managerial, professional, and related occupations (% of employed persons 16 and older), 2000	42.6	25.2	49.1	45.4	40.9	47.6

Sources: Census of Population (Washington, DC: U.S. Bureau of the Census, 2000); and authors' computations. Data obtained through "American FactFinder," **http://factfinder.census.gov** (January 29, 2006).

TABLE 9-3	Selected Population Statistics for Long Beach Trading Areas A and B	
	Area A (Tracts 4164 and 4166)	Area B (Tracts 4167.01, 4167.02, and 4168)
Total population, 2000	13,732	15,499
Population change, 1990–2000 (%)	+8.2	+2.5
College graduates, 25 and older, 2000 (%)	41.4	39.2
Median household income, 2000	$61,236	$61,242
Managerial and professional specialty occupations (% of employed persons 16 and older), 2000	45.3	45.0

- The annual median income and the proportion of workers who are managers or professionals are roughly equal in Areas A and B.

The bookstore chain would have a tough time selecting between the areas since they are so similar. Thus, the chain might also consider the location of the sites available in Area A and Area B, relative to the locations of its existing stores, before making a final decision.

Other Public Sources

There are many other useful, easily accessible public sources for current population information in addition to the *Census of Population*—especially on a city or county basis. These sources typically update their data annually. They also provide some data not available from the *Census of Population*: total annual retail sales by area, annual retail sales for specific product categories, and population projections. The biggest disadvantage of these sources is their use of geographic territories that are often much larger than a store's trading area and that cannot be broken down easily.

Ethics in RETAILING

Is Wal-Mart Really a Bad Neighbor for Cities?

Although many retail analysts believe that consumers and public officials should embrace the opening of a Wal-Mart store (www.walmart.com) in a hard-pressed urban neighborhood underserved by traditional retailers, opposition to a new Wal-Mart is often fierce. Applications for new Wal-Mart sites in Inglewood, California, Chicago, and New Orleans have recently been turned down due to land use and design issues.

According to a University of Missouri study, five years after a Wal-Mart opens in most markets, there is a small net gain in retail employment in counties where the store is located. The study also found that the number of small businesses drops by 1 percent. As importantly, retail prices for many goods decline by 5 to 10 percent.

When a new Wal-Mart opened in Baldwin Hills Crenshaw Plaza in South Central Los Angeles, it took over space that was vacant for five years. After its opening, local store traffic increased. And many of the stores that were there before Wal-Mart came are still there. Furthermore, Wal-Mart has been an important factor in creating jobs for community residents.

Sources: Robert McNatt, Ronald Grover, and Wendy Zellner, "Who Says Wal-Mart is Bad for Cities?" *Business Week* (May 10, 2004), pp. 77–78; and William Beaver, "Battling Wal-Mart: How Communities Can Respond," *Business & Society Review*, Vol. 110 (Summer 2005), pp. 159–169.

One new national source of annual population data is the *American Community Survey*, which provides "demographic, social, economic, and housing data for over 800 geographical areas." The Survey has an excellent, user-friendly Web site (**www.census.gov/acs/www**). On the state and local level, public data sources include planning commissions, research centers at public universities, county offices, and many other institutions.

Let us demonstrate the usefulness of public sources through the following example. Note: We obtained all of the information for our example on the Internet—free!

Suppose a prospective new car dealer investigates three counties near Chicago: Du Page, Kane, and Lake. The dealer decides to focus on three sources of information: *American Community Survey*, Northeastern Illinois Planning Commission, and the *Illinois Statistical Abstract* (prepared by the Institute of Government and Public Affairs at the University of Illinois). Table 9-4 lists selected population and retail sales data (as well as population projections to the year 2020) for these counties.

| TABLE 9-4 | Selected Data Relating to Three Illinois Counties (2003, unless otherwise specified) |||

	COUNTY		
	Du Page	**Kane**	**Lake**
Total population	909,856	450,692	663,721
Total population, projected 2020	985,704	552,034	806,779
Annual population growth, 2003–2020	0.47%	1.20%	1.15%
Number of households	334,236	148,260	226,074
Number of people 18 and over	670,481	317,760	470,168
Median household income	$67,505	$60,348	$69,670
Households with $50,000 or more in annual income	65.1%	59.0%	65.0%
Total retail sales	$15,925,000,000	$4,998,000,000	$9,706,000,000
Annual per-capita retail sales	$17,503	$11,090	$14,624
Employment in retail trade	52,853	28,240	39,098
Total retail sales by category			
General merchandise sales	$1,819,200,000	$640,100,000	$961,900,000
Retail food sales	$1,714,400,000	$741,800,000	$1,151,700,000
Retail apparel sales	$606,500,000	$161,700,000	$344,400,000
Retail lumber, building, and hardware sales	$838,200,000	$569,400,000	$703,000,000
Auto and recreational vehicle sales	$3,577,500,000	$782,000,000	$2,311,500,000
Percentage of total retail sales by category			
General merchandise sales	11.4%	12.8%	9.9%
Retail food sales	10.8%	14.8%	11.9%
Retail apparel sales	3.8%	3.2%	3.6%
Retail lumber, building, and hardware sales	5.3%	11.4%	7.2%
Auto and recreational vehicle sales	22.5%	15.7%	23.8%

Sources: Computed by the authors from *American Community Survey 2003* (Washington, DC: U.S. Census Bureau); Northeastern Illinois Planning Commission (**www.nipc.org**); and *Illinois Statistical Abstract 2004*.

What can the car dealer learn? Du Page is by far the largest county; Kane is the smallest. However, the population growth rate until 2020 is much higher for Kane. Lake has the highest median household income, slightly ahead of Du Page. On a per-capita basis, Du Page residents account for 58 percent more retail sales than Kane residents and 20 percent more than Lake residents. Lake and Du Page residents both allocate more than one-fifth of their retail spending to autos and recreational vehicles, compared to less than one-sixth for Kane residents.

A Cadillac dealer using these data might select Du Page or Lake, while a Chevrolet dealer might select Kane. But because the data are broad in nature, several subsections of Kane may actually be superior choices to subsections in Du Page or Lake for the Cadillac dealer. The competition in each area also must be noted.

The location decision for a fast-food franchise usually requires less data than for a bookstore or an auto dealer. Fast-food franchisors often seek communities with many people living or working within a three- or four-mile radius of their stores. However, bookstore owners and auto dealers cannot locate merely on the basis of population density. They must consider a more complex set of population factors.

Economic Base Characteristics

The economic base reflects a community's commercial and industrial infrastructure and residents' sources of income. A firm seeking stability normally prefers an area with a diversified economic base (a large number of nonrelated industries) to one with an economic base keyed to a single major industry. The latter area is more affected by a strike, declining demand for an industry, and cyclical fluctuations.

In assessing a trading area's economic base, a retailer should investigate the percentage of the labor force in each industry, transportation, banking facilities, the impact of economic fluctuations, and the future of individual industries (firms). Data can be obtained from such sources as Easy Analytic Software, *Editor & Publisher Market Guide*, regional planning commissions, industrial development organizations, and chambers of commerce.

Easy Analytic Software (**www.easidemographics.com**) provides a wide range of inexpensive economic reports. It also produces several "Census 2000 Reports" that can be downloaded free (after a simple sign-in procedure), including Quick Reports, Ring Studies Site Selection with Maps, Quick Maps, Rank Analysis, and Profile Analysis.

Editor & Publisher Market Guide offers annual economic base data for cities, including employment sources, transportation networks, financial institutions, auto registrations, newspaper circulation, and shopping centers. It also has data on population size and total households. *Editor & Publisher Market Guide* data cover broad geographic areas. The bookstore chain noted earlier would find the information on shopping centers to be helpful. The auto dealer would find the information on the transportation network, the availability of financial institutions, and the number of passenger cars to be useful. *Editor & Publisher Market Guide* is best used to supplement other sources.

The Nature of Competition and the Level of Saturation

Although a trading area may have residents who match the characteristics of the desired market and a strong economic base, it may be a poor location for a new store if competition is too intense. A locale with a small population and a narrow economic base may be a good location if competition is minimal.

When examining competition, these factors should be analyzed: the number of existing stores, the size distribution of existing stores, the rate of new store openings, the strengths and weaknesses of all stores, short-run and long-run trends, and the level of saturation.

Over the past decade, many retailers have expanded into the Southeast and Southwest due to their growing populations. Tiffany, Target Stores, Nordstrom, and Macy's are among those that have entered New Orleans, Dallas, Orlando, Phoenix, Atlanta, and other markets. Yet, there is a concern that these locales may become oversaturated due to all the new stores. Furthermore, although the Northeast population has been declining relative to the Southeast and the Southwest, its high population density (the number of persons per square mile) is crucial for retailers. In New Jersey, there are 1,170 people per square mile; in Massachusetts, 820; in Florida, 320; in Louisiana, 105; and in Arizona, 50.

An **understored trading area** has too few stores selling a specific good or service to satisfy the needs of its population. An **overstored trading area** has so many stores selling a specific good or service that some retailers cannot earn an adequate profit. A **saturated trading area** has the proper amount of stores to satisfy the needs of its population for a specific good or service and to enable retailers to prosper.

Despite the large number of areas in the United States that are overstored, there still remain plentiful opportunities in understored communities. For example,

> Located in Baldwin County between the larger metro areas of Mobile, Alabama, and Pensacola, Florida, Spanish Fort, Alabama, is a small town with a nearby Tanger Outlet Center but few other specialty retail choices. Even though Baldwin has been the fastest-growing county in Alabama, until recently it lacked concentrated traditional retailing because of the size of the market—about 5,500 people. But the market is actually larger than just the population of Spanish Fort. Its primary trade area includes not only all of Baldwin County but also the western section of Escambia County, Alabama. The total population is projected to grow a bit, to nearly 185,000 by 2007. And those residents are affluent: The average yearly household income within Spanish Fort is $75,000 a year; nearby Daphne boasts an average household income of $77,000. Tourists and part-time residents are also important to the trade area, which boasts about 4 million visitors annually.[12]

Measuring Trading-Area Saturation

Because any trading area can support only a given number of stores or square feet of selling space per goods/service category, these ratios can help to quantify retail store saturation:

- Number of persons per retail establishment.
- Average sales per retail store.
- Average sales per retail store category.
- Average store sales per capita or household.
- Average sales per square foot of selling area.
- Average sales per employee.

The saturation level in a trading area can be measured against a goal or compared with other trading areas. An auto accessory chain might find that its current trading area is saturated by computing the ratio of residents to auto accessory stores. On the basis of this calculation, the owner could then decide to expand into a nearby locale with a lower ratio rather than to add another store in its present trading area.

Data for saturation ratios can be obtained from a retailer's records on its performance, city and state records, phone directories, consumer surveys, economic census data, *Editor & Publisher Market Guide*, *County Business Patterns*, trade publications, and other sources. Sales by product category, population size, and number of households per market area can be found with other national and state sources.

When investigating an area's saturation for a specific good or service, ratios must be interpreted carefully. Differences among areas are not always reliable indicators of saturation. For instance, car sales per capita are different for a suburban area than an urban area because suburbanites have a much greater need for cars. Each area's level of saturation should be evaluated against distinct standards—based on optimum per-capita sales figures in that area.

In calculating saturation based on sales per square foot, a new or growing retailer must take its proposed store into account. If that store is not part of the calculation, the relative value of each trading area is distorted. Sales per square foot decline most if new outlets are added in small communities. The retailer should also consider if a new store will expand the total consumer market for a good or service category in a trading area or just increase its market share in that area without expanding the total market.

These are three examples of how retailers factor trading-area saturation into their decisions:

- Home Depot has spent $1 billion to remodel its older stores and has added higher-priced goods such as major appliances (lifting the average sale by more than 7 percent—to about $55). It is also preparing for slowing U.S. sales by adding stores in Mexico and Canada. As one industry expert says, Home Depot is "definitely reaching the point of U.S. store saturation, so it has to diversify into professional services and overseas. Maybe some people are a little bit uncomfortable with that."[13]

- Gottschalks operates department stores in the Pacific Northwest and Alaska. Its stores "are located primarily in diverse, growing, nonmajor metropolitan or suburban areas in the western United States where management believes there is strong demand and fewer competitors offering similar better to moderate branded merchandise and a high level of customer service. The firm has avoided expansion into the center of major metropolitan areas that are served by larger competitors and has instead sought to open new stores in nearby suburban or secondary market areas."[14]

Look at the *Marketing Guidebook* sample (**www.tradedimensions.com/tours/mg_samples.asp**) to see the saturation levels of supermarkets. Click "County Level Data."

- Supermarket chains buy annual data from Trade Dimensions (**www.tradedimensions.com**) that measure the level of saturation by U.S. city, including the number of supermarkets, overall supermarket sales, supermarket sales per capita, weekly sales per square foot, chain supermarkets versus independents, total supermarket space, the number of supermarket employees, and more.

Summary

1. *To demonstrate the importance of store location for a retailer and outline the process for choosing a store location.* The location choice is critical because of the complex decision making, the high costs, the lack of flexibility once a site is chosen, and the impact of a site on the strategy. A good location may let a retailer succeed even if its strategy mix is relatively mediocre.

The selection of a store location includes (1) evaluating alternative trading areas; (2) determining the best type of location; (3) picking a general site; and (4) settling on a specific site. This chapter looks at Step 1. Chapter 10 details Steps 2, 3, and 4.

2. *To discuss the concept of a trading area and its related components.* A trading area is the geographical area from which customers are drawn. When shopping locales are nearby, they may have trading-area overlap.

Many retailers utilize geographic information systems (GIS) software to delineate and analyze trading areas. The software combines digitized mapping with key data to graphically depict trading areas. This lets retailers research alternative locations and display findings on computerized maps. Several vendors market GIS software, based on TIGER mapping by the U.S. government.

Each trading area has primary, secondary, and fringe components. The farther people live from a shopping area, the less apt they are to travel there. The size and shape of a trading area depend on store type, store size, competitor locations, housing patterns, travel time and traffic barriers, and media availability. Destination stores have larger trading areas than parasites.

3. *To show how trading areas may be delineated for existing and new stores.* The size, shape, and characteristics of the trading area for an existing store or group of stores can be learned accurately—based on store records, contests, license plate numbers, surveys, and so on. Time biases must be considered in amassing data. Results should be mapped and customer densities noted.

Potential trading areas for a new store must often be described in terms of opportunities, rather than current patronage and traffic. Trend analysis and consumer surveys may be used. Three computerized models are available for planning a new store location: analog, regression, and gravity. They offer several benefits.

Two techniques for delineating new trading areas are Reilly's law, which relates the population size of different cities to the size of their trading areas; and Huff's law, which is based on each area's shopping assortment, the distance of people from various retail locales, and sensitivity to travel time.

4. *To examine three major factors in trading-area analysis: population characteristics, economic base characteristics, and competition and the level of saturation.* The best sources for population data are the *Census of Population* and other publicly available sources. Census data are detailed and specific but become dated. Information from public sources such as the *American Community Survey* may be more current, but they report on broader geographic areas.

An area's economic base reflects the community's commercial and industrial infrastructure, as well as residents' income sources. A retailer should look at the percentage of the labor force in each industry, the transportation network, banking facilities, the potential impact of economic fluctuations on the area, and the future of individual industries. Easy Analytic and *Editor & Publisher Market Guide* are good sources of data on the economic base.

A trading area cannot be properly analyzed without studying the nature of competition and the level of saturation. An area may be understored (too few retailers), overstored (too many retailers), or saturated (the proper number of retailers). Saturation may be measured in terms of the number of persons per store, average sales per store, average store sales per capita or household, average sales per square foot of selling space, and average sales per employee.

Key Terms

trading area (p. 264)
trading-area overlap (p. 265)
geographic information systems (GIS) (p. 266)
primary trading area (p. 270)
secondary trading area (p. 270)
fringe trading area (p. 270)

destination store (p. 270)
parasite store (p. 270)
analog model (p. 274)
regression model (p. 274)
gravity model (p. 274)
Reilly's law of retail gravitation (p. 275)
point of indifference (p. 275)

Huff's law of shopper attraction (p. 275)
economic base (p. 278)
Census of Population (p. 281)
understored trading area (p. 286)
overstored trading area (p. 286)
saturated trading area (p. 286)

Questions for Discussion

1. Comment on this statement: "A good location may let a retailer succeed even if its strategy mix is mediocre." Is it always true? Give examples.

2. If a retailer has a new 10-year store lease, does this mean the next time it studies the characteristics of its trading area should be 5 years from now? Explain your answer.

3. What is trading-area overlap? Are there any advantages to a chain retailer's having some overlap among its various stores? Why or why not?

4. Describe three ways in which a donut chain could use geographic information systems (GIS) software in its trading-area analysis.

5. How could an off-campus store selling musical instruments near a college campus determine its primary, secondary, and fringe trading areas? Why should the music store obtain this information?

6. How could a parasite store increase the size of its trading area?

7. Explain Reilly's law. What are its advantages and disadvantages?

8. Use Huff's law to compute the probability of consumers' traveling from their homes to each of three shopping areas: square footage of selling space—Location 1, 10,000; Location 2, 12,000; Location 3, 20,000; travel time—to Location 1, 15 minutes; to Location 2, 21 minutes; to Location 3, 25 minutes; effect of travel time on shopping trip—2. Explain your answer.

9. What are the major advantages and disadvantages of *Census of Population* data in delineating trading areas?

10. Look at the most recent online edition of the *American Community Survey* (**www.census.gov/acs/www**) for the area in which your college is located. What retailing-related conclusions do you draw?

11. If a retail area is acknowledged to be "saturated," what does this signify for existing retailers? For prospective retailers considering this area?

12. How could a Web-based retailer determine the level of saturation for its product category? What should this retailer do to lessen the impact of the level of saturation it faces?

Note: At our Web site (**www.prenhall.com/bermanevans**), there are several math questions related to the material in this chapter so that you may review these concepts.

Web-Based Exercise

Visit the Web site of Site Selection Online (**www.siteselection.com**). What could a retailer learn from this site? What site feature do you like best? Why?

Note: Stop by our Web site (**www.prenhall.com/bermanevans**) to experience a number of highly interactive, appealing Web exercises based on actual company demonstrations and sample materials related to retailing.

Chapter Endnotes

1. Various company sources.
2. Connie Robbins Gentry, "Small Chains with Big Growth Plans," *Chain Store Age* (March 2005), pp. 121–124.
3. Peter D. Bennett (Editor), *Dictionary of Marketing Terms*, Second Edition (Chicago: American Marketing Association, 1995), p. 287. See also Bill Simmons, "Defining Trade Areas," **www.marketech.com/articles/definingtradeareas.pdf** (March 9, 2006).
4. See Shawana P. Johnson and J. Edward Kunz, "Private Sector Makes Census Bureau's TIGER Roar," *Geospatial Solutions* (May 2005), pp. 28–32; and Jonathan W. Lowe, "Web GIS Gets Flashy," *Geospatial Solutions* (May 2005), pp. 33–36.
5. "About Dunkin' Donuts," **www.geovue.com/profiles/about_dunkindonuts.htm** (March 30, 2006); and "Eddie Bauer: Making Increasingly Educated Decisions," **www.clusterbigip1.claritas.com** (March 30, 2006).
6. For a good overview of gravity models, see "Store Location," **www.geobusiness.co.uk/products/models/ models.htm** (March 3, 2006).
7. William J. Reilly, *Method for the Study of Retail Relationships*, Research Monograph No. 4 (Austin: University of Texas Press, 1929), University of Texas Bulletin No. 2944. See also MacKenzie S. Bottum, "Reilly's Law," *Appraisal Journal*, Vol. 57 (April 1989), pp. 166–172; Michael D. D'Amico, Jon M. Hawes, and Dale M. Lewison, "Determining a Hospital's Trading Area: An Application of Reilly's Law," *Journal of Hospital Marketing*, Vol. 8 (Number 2, 1994), pp. 121–129; and Matt T. Rosenberg, "Gravity Models," **http://geography.about.com/library/weekly/aa031601a.htm** (July 25, 2005).
8. Richard L. Nelson, *The Selection of Retail Locations* (New York: F.W. Dodge, 1959), p. 149.
9. David L. Huff, "Defining and Estimating a Trading Area," *Journal of Marketing*, Vol. 28 (July 1964),

pp. 34–38; and David L. Huff and Larry Blue, *A Programmed Solution for Estimating Retail Sales Potential* (Lawrence: University of Kansas, 1966). See also Christophe Benavent, Marc Thomas, and Anne Bergue, "Application of Gravity Models for the Analysis of Retail Potential," *Journal of Targeting, Measurement & Analysis for Marketing*, Vol. 1 (Winter 1992–1993), pp. 305–315; and Joseph R. Francica, "Are Retail Attractiveness (Huff) Models Misused?" **www.geoplace.com/gw/2002/0206/0206bgeo.asp** (June 2002).

10. David A. Gautschi, "Specification of Patronage Models for Retail Center Choice," *Journal of Marketing Research*, Vol. 18 (May 1981), pp. 162–174; Glen E. Weisbrod, Robert J. Parcells, and Clifford Kern, "A Disaggregate Model for Predicting Shopping Area Market Attraction," *Journal of Retailing*, Vol. 60 (Spring 1984), pp. 65–83; Avijit Ghosh, "The Value of a Mall and Other Insights from a Revised Central Place Model," *Journal of Retailing*, Vol. 62 (Spring 1986), pp. 79–97; Paul LeBlang, "A Theoretical Approach for Predicting Sales at a New Department-Store Location via Lifestyles," *Direct Marketing*, Vol. 7 (Autumn 1993), pp. 70–74; Kenneth C. Schneider, James C. Johnson, Bradley J. Sleeper, and William C. Rodgers, "A Note on Applying Retail Location Models in Franchise Systems: A View from the Trenches," *Journal of Consumer Marketing*, Vol. 15 (Number 3, 1998), pp. 290–296; Isabel P. Albaladejo-Pina and Joaquin Aranda-Gallego, "A Measure of Trade Centre Position," *European Journal of Marketing*, Vol. 32 (Number 5–6, 1998), pp. 464–479; David R. Bell, Teck-Hua Ho, and Christopher S. Tang, "Determining Where to Shop: Fixed and Variable Costs of Shopping," *Journal of Marketing Research*, Vol. 35 (August 1998), pp. 352–369; Francisco José Más Ruiz, "Image of Suburban Shopping Malls and Two-Stage versus Uni-Equational Modelling of the Retail Trade Attraction," *European Journal of Marketing*, Vol. 33 (Number 5–6, 1999), pp. 512–530; David S. Rogers, "Developing a Location Research Methodology," *Journal of Targeting, Measurement & Analysis for Marketing*, Vol. 13 (March 2005), pp. 201–208; and Howard Smith and Donald Hay, "Streets, Malls, and Supermarkets," *Journal of Economics & Management Strategy*, Vol. 14. (March 2005), pp. 29–59.

11. Connie Robbins Gentry, "Science Validates Art," *Chain Store Age* (April 2005), pp. 83–84; "An Off-the-Mall Attitude," *Chain Store Age* (May 2002), p. 60; *Dollar General 2005 Annual Report*; and *Syms 2005 Annual Report*.

12. Debra Hazel, "A Touch of Class," *Shopping Centers Today* (February 2005), p. 41.

13. Steve Matthews, "Home Depot 4th Qtr. Profit Rises 9.5%; Shares Fall," **www.bloomberg.com** (February 22, 2005).

14. *Gottschalks 2005 Annual Report*.

Chapter 10
SITE SELECTION

Shortly after World War II, William Rosenberg started Industrial Luncheon Services to sell donuts, sandwiches, and coffee to factory workers. He purchased 10 unused cab-and-chassis platforms from the New England Telephone Company and had each outfitted with stainless steel bodies and side flaps that could be lifted. Despite the popularity of the sandwiches, coffee and donuts were the real best-sellers. In 1948, Rosenberg opened his first store, Open Kettle, as an additional outlet for the sale of donuts.

In 1950, Rosenberg changed the Open Kettle name to Dunkin' Donuts (**www.dunkin donuts.com**) and began franchising. Allied Domecq PLC (**www.allieddomecq.com**) acquired the chain in 1990. Today, Dunkin' Donuts has more than 4,400 locations in the United States alone. It is the world's largest seller of donuts, bagels, and muffins.

Reprinted by permission.

Dunkin' Donuts has begun an aggressive expansion program to increase the number of its outlets worldwide from 6,000 to 15,000 over the next 10 years. Currently, 80 percent of its sales come from just 34 percent of the United States. Dunkin' Donuts has almost no outlets in much of the Midwest, Southwest, and West.

Dunkin' Donuts has specific location standards. Its standalone stores generally require a population of 15,000 or more within its drive-time parameters, a median household income of more than $38,000, and the presence of 10,000 or more workers within the trading area. Dunkin' Donuts also has specific site requirements. These include a minimum of 20 parking spots, easy access from all traffic directions, high visibility from major arteries (400 feet or more on the approach side), and a 10-year lease with two 5-year renewal options.[1]

chapter objectives

1. To thoroughly examine the types of locations available to a retailer: isolated store, unplanned business district, and planned shopping center
2. To note the decisions necessary in choosing a general retail location
3. To describe the concept of the one-hundred percent location
4. To discuss several criteria for evaluating general retail locations and the specific sites within them
5. To contrast alternative terms of occupancy

291

OVERVIEW

After a retailer investigates alternative trading areas (Step 1), it determines what type of location is desirable (Step 2), selects the general location (Step 3), and evaluates alternative specific store sites (Step 4). Steps 2, 3, and 4 are discussed in this chapter.

As an example, Bed Bath & Beyond (BBB)

Is there now a Bed Bath & Beyond near you (www. bedbathandbeyond.com)? Click on "Store locator."

expects to open new stores and to expand existing stores as opportunities arise. New stores will be opened in new and existing markets. In determining where to open new BBB stores, the firm evaluates a number of factors, including the availability of prime real-estate and demographic information (such as data relating to income and education levels, age, and occupation). Because BBB does not use central distribution, and since BBB relies on only limited advertising, it has the flexibility to enter a new market with just one or two stores. BBB will consider opening additional stores in that market after the first stores are successful. Stores are mostly located in the suburbs of medium and large cities. They are usually in strip and power strip shopping centers, as well as in major off-price and conventional malls, and freestanding buildings.[2]

TYPES OF LOCATIONS

There are three different location types: isolated store, unplanned business district, and planned shopping center. Each has its own attributes as to the composition of competitors, parking, nearness to nonretail institutions (such as office buildings), and other factors. Step 2 in the location process is to determine which type of location to use.

The Isolated Store

An **isolated store** is a freestanding retail outlet located on either a highway or a street. There are no adjacent retailers with which this type of store shares traffic.

The advantages of this type of retail location are many:

- There is no competition in close proximity.
- Rental costs are relatively low.
- There is flexibility; no group rules must be followed in operations and larger space may be obtained.
- Isolation is good for stores involved in one-stop or convenience shopping.
- Better road and traffic visibility is possible.
- Facilities can be adapted to individual specifications.
- Easy parking can be arranged.
- Cost reductions are possible, leading to lower prices.

There are also various disadvantages to this retail location type:

- Initial customers may be difficult to attract.
- Many people will not travel very far to get to one store on a continuous basis.
- Most people like variety in shopping.
- Advertising expenses may be high.

- Costs such as outside lighting, security, grounds maintenance, and trash collection are not shared.
- Other retailers and community zoning laws may restrict access to desirable locations.
- A store must often be built rather than rented.
- As a rule, unplanned business districts and planned shopping centers are much more popular among consumers; they generate the bulk of retail sales.

Large-store formats (such as Wal-Mart supercenters and Costco membership clubs) and convenience-oriented retailers (such as 7-Eleven) are usually best suited to isolated locations because of the challenge of attracting a target market. A small specialty store would probably be unable to develop a customer following; people would be unwilling to travel to a store that does not have a large assortment of products or a strong image for merchandise and/or prices.

Years ago, numerous shopping centers forbade the entry of discounters because discount operations were frowned on by traditional retailers. This forced the discounters to become isolated stores or to build their own centers, and they have been successful. Today, diverse retailers are in isolated locations, as well as at business district and shopping center sites. Retailers using a mixed location strategy include Krispy Kreme, McDonald's, Target, Sears, Toys "R" Us, Wal-Mart, and 7-Eleven. Some retailers, including many gas stations and convenience stores, still emphasize isolated locations. See Figure 10-1.

The Unplanned Business District

An **unplanned business district** is a type of retail location where two or more stores situate together (or in close proximity) in such a way that the total arrangement or mix of stores is not due to prior long-range planning. Stores locate based on what is best for them, not the district. Four shoe stores may exist in an area with no pharmacy. There are four kinds of unplanned business district: central business

FIGURE 10-1
Site Selection and Target Stores

These days, Target has stores at all types of locations—including standalone sites, power centers, and regional shopping centers (a rather recent trend). In this way, it efficiently reaches different geographic markets.

Photo reprinted by permission of Susan Berry, Retail Image Consulting, Inc.

district, secondary business district, neighborhood business district, and string. A description of each follows.

Central Business District

A **central business district (CBD)** is the hub of retailing in a city. It is synonymous with the term *downtown*. The CBD exists where there is the greatest density of office buildings and stores. Both vehicular and pedestrian traffic are very high. The core of a CBD is often no more than a square mile, with cultural and entertainment facilities surrounding it. Shoppers are drawn from the whole urban area and include all ethnic groups and all classes of people. The CBD has at least one major department store and a number of specialty and convenience stores. The arrangement of stores follows no pre-set format; it depends on history (first come, first located), retail trends, and luck.

Here are some strengths that allow CBDs to draw a large number of shoppers:

- Excellent goods/service assortment.
- Access to public transportation.
- Variety of store types and positioning strategies within one area.
- Wide range of prices.
- Variety of customer services.
- High level of pedestrian traffic.
- Nearness to commercial and social facilities.

In addition, chain headquarters stores are often situated in CBDs.

These are some of the inherent weaknesses of the CBD:

- Inadequate parking, and traffic and delivery congestion.
- Travel time for those living in the suburbs.
- Frail condition of some cities—such as aging stores—compared to their suburbs.
- Relatively poor image of central cities to some potential consumers.
- High rents and taxes for the most popular sites.
- Movement of some popular downtown stores to suburban shopping centers.
- Discontinuity of offerings (such as four shoe stores and no pharmacy).

RETAILING
Around the World | Times Square in Hong Kong

At more than 10 years of age, Hong Kong's Times Square (**www.timessquare.com.hk**) retail development has begun to show signs of aging. While newer centers, such as Langham Place, and other recently remodeled centers have been using image-based advertising, until recently, most of Times Square's promotions focused on its dining options and its annual New Year's Eve countdown party. In addition, Times Square's tenant mix had begun to look tired.

Let's look at the comments by Daniel Kong (the general manager for MediaCom Hong Kong) and Desmond So (the chief executive officer for J. Walter Thompson, Hong Kong) regarding Times Square. Daniel Kong feels

that Times Square is the "superbrand" among shopping malls in Hong Kong with a very high awareness level. He feels that Times Square needs to further build its brand as a superior dining experience location for consumers aged 20 to 39. Desmond So feels that Times Square does not have a clear image in terms of the target market and the lifestyle it seeks to portray despite the New Year's Eve countdown buzz.

Sources: Amy White, "Mall Needs to Move a Step Up to Stay Ahead," *Media Asia* (October 8, 2004), pp. 2–4; and "About Us," **www.times square.com.hk/e/index.html** (April 9, 2006).

The CBD remains a major retailing force, although, in recent decades, its share of overall sales has fallen, as compared to the planned shopping center. Besides the weaknesses cited, much of the drop-off is due to suburbanization. In the first half of the 20th century, most urban workers lived near their jobs. Gradually, many people moved to the suburbs—where they are served by planned shopping centers.

A number of CBDs are doing quite well and others are striving to return to their former stature. Many use such tactics as modernizing storefronts and equipment, forming cooperative merchants' associations, modernizing sidewalks and adding brighter lighting, building vertical malls (with several floors of stores), improving transportation networks, closing streets to vehicular traffic (sometimes with disappointing results), bringing in "razzmatazz" retailers such as Nike Town, and integrating a commercial and residential environment known as mixed-use facilities.

According to one retail location expert, a superior CBD "embodies a character, look, flavor, and heritage that are not found in other locations, especially within the surrounding region. To best enhance its distinct qualities, a downtown should build upon its intrinsic historic, economic, natural, and cultural amenities. Why would a person choose a downtown as a destination with so many other alternatives available? The answer is a strong sense of place, a characteristic rarely associated with regional malls, big box retailers, or suburban commercial corridors."[3]

A good example of the value of a revitalized CBD is Atlanta, where there is a strong effort under way to make the central city more competitive with suburban shopping centers:

> Downtown Atlanta seems poised to become a destination for family fun. Since 2003, nearly $1 billion in projects that promise to transform the CBD have broken ground or are poised to start. Stretches of sidewalks that once were rolled up at night may almost be ready to stay in place for tourists and locals out for an evening on the town. Centennial Olympic Park has solidified its position as the area's main recreational attraction. Its famous fountains are now ringed by the Georgia Aquarium; the Children's Museum; and venues for the Atlanta Falcons and Georgia Force football teams, the Atlanta Hawks, and the Atlanta Thrashers. The Georgia Dome could be in line for a major renovation. The opening date of the New World of Coca-Cola museum is set for April 2007, at a construction cost of almost $100 million. Other nearby downtown destinations are being spruced up. And the central issue of the perception of public safety finally is being addressed.[4]

Boston's Faneuil Hall is another important CBD renovation. When developer James Rouse took over the site containing three 150-year-old, block-long former food warehouses, it had been abandoned for almost 10 years. Rouse used landscaping, fountains, banners, open-air courts, street performers, and colorful graphics to enable Faneuil Hall to capture a festive spirit. Faneuil Hall combines shopping, eating, and watching activities and makes them fun. Today, it has 100 shops and pushcarts, 17 restaurants and pubs, 40 food stalls, and a comedy nightclub. It attracts millions of shoppers and visitors yearly.

Other major CBD revitalization projects include Branson Landing (Missouri), Circle Centre (Indianapolis), Grand Central Terminal (New York City), Harborplace (Baltimore), Horton Plaza (San Diego), New Orleans Centre, Peabody Place (Memphis), Pioneer Place (Portland, Oregon), Riverchase Galleria (Birmingham, Alabama), Tower City Center (Cleveland), and Union Station (Washington, D.C.). See Figure 10-2.

Grand Central Terminal (www.grandcentralterminal.com) is all dressed up and open for business. Check out the "Interactive Directory" tour.

FIGURE 10-2
Harborplace: A Revitalized Central Business District

Large business districts rely on the customer traffic drawn by office buildings, as well as cultural and entertainment facilities. One popular, revitalized business district is depicted here: The Gallery at Harborplace in Baltimore.

Reprinted by permission of The Rouse Company

Visit our Web site (**www.prenhall.com/bermanevans**) for links to all of the CBD projects mentioned in this section.

Secondary Business District

A **secondary business district (SBD)** is an unplanned shopping area in a city or town that is usually bounded by the intersection of two major streets. Cities—particularly larger ones—often have multiple SBDs, each with at least a junior department store (a branch of a traditional department store or a full-line discount store) and/or some larger specialty stores—besides many smaller stores. This format is now more important because cities have "sprawled" over larger geographic areas.

The kinds of goods and services sold in an SBD mirror those in the CBD. However, an SBD has smaller stores, less width and depth of merchandise assortment, and a smaller trading area (consumers will not travel as far) and sells a higher proportion of convenience-oriented items.

The SBD's major strengths include a solid product selection, access to thoroughfares and public transportation, less crowding and more personal service than a CBD, and placement nearer to residential areas than a CBD. The SBD's major weaknesses include the discontinuity of offerings, the sometimes high rent and taxes (but not as high as in a CBD), traffic and delivery congestion, aging facilities, parking difficulties, and fewer chain outlets than in the CBD. These weaknesses have generally not affected the SBD as much as the CBD—and parking problems, travel time, and congestion are less for the SBD.

Neighborhood Business District

A **neighborhood business district (NBD)** is an unplanned shopping area that appeals to the convenience shopping and service needs of a single residential area. An NBD contains several small stores, such as a dry cleaner, a stationery store, a barber shop and/or a beauty salon, a liquor store, and a restaurant. The leading retailer is typically a supermarket or a large drugstore. This type of business district is situated on the major street(s) of its residential area.

An NBD offers a good location, long store hours, good parking, and a less hectic atmosphere than a CBD or SBD. On the other hand, there is a limited selection of goods and services, and prices tend to be higher because competition is less than in a CBD or SBD.

String

A **string** is an unplanned shopping area comprising a group of retail stores, often with similar or compatible product lines, located along a street or highway. There is little extension of shopping onto perpendicular streets. A string may start with an isolated store, success then breeding competitors. Car dealers, antique stores, and apparel retailers often situate in strings.

A string location has many of the advantages of an isolated store site (lower rent, more flexibility, better road visibility and parking, and lower operating costs), along with some disadvantages (less product variety, increased travel for many consumers, higher advertising costs, zoning restrictions, and the need to build premises). Unlike an isolated store, a string store has competition at its location. This draws more people to the area and allows for some sharing of common costs. It also means less control over prices and less loyalty toward each outlet. An individual store's increased traffic flow, due to being in a string rather than an isolated site, may be greater than the customers lost to competitors. This explains why four gas stations locate on opposing corners.

Figure 10-3 shows a map with various forms of unplanned business districts and isolated locations.

FIGURE 10-3
Unplanned Business Districts
and Isolated Locations

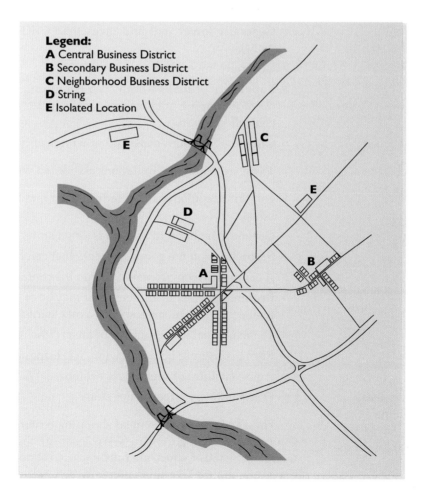

Legend:
A Central Business District
B Secondary Business District
C Neighborhood Business District
D String
E Isolated Location

The Planned Shopping Center

A **planned shopping center** consists of a group of architecturally unified commercial establishments on a site that is centrally owned or managed, designed and operated as a unit, based on balanced tenancy, and accompanied by parking facilities. Its location, size, and mix of stores are related to the trading area served. Through **balanced tenancy**, the stores in a planned shopping center complement each other as to the quality and variety of their product offerings, and the kind and number of stores are linked to overall population needs. To ensure balanced tenancy, the management of a planned center usually specifies the proportion of total space for each kind of retailer, limits the product lines that can be sold by every store, and stipulates what kinds of firms can acquire unexpired leases. At a well-run center, a coordinated and cooperative long-run retailing strategy is followed by all stores.

The planned shopping center has several positive attributes:

- Well-rounded assortments of goods and services based on long-range planning.
- Strong suburban population.
- Interest in one-stop, family shopping.
- Cooperative planning and sharing of common costs.
- Creation of distinctive, but unified, shopping center images.
- Maximization of pedestrian traffic for individual stores.
- Access to highways and availability of parking for consumers.
- More appealing than city shopping for some people.
- Generally lower rent and taxes than CBDs (except for enclosed regional malls).
- Generally lower theft rates than CBDs.
- Popularity of malls—both *open* (shopping area off-limits to vehicles) and *closed* (shopping area off-limits to vehicles and all stores in a temperature-controlled facility).
- Growth of discount malls and other newer types of shopping centers.

There are also some limitations associated with the planned shopping center:

- Landlord regulations that reduce each retailer's flexibility, such as required hours.
- Generally higher rent than an isolated store.
- Restrictions on the goods/services that can be sold by each store.
- A competitive environment within the center.
- Required payments for items that may be of little or no value to an individual retailer, such as membership in a merchants' association.
- Too many malls in a number of areas ("the malling of America").
- Rising consumer boredom with and disinterest in shopping as an activity.
- Aging facilities of some older centers.
- Domination by large anchor stores.

How important are planned shopping centers? According to the International Council of Shopping Centers (**www.icsc.org**), there are 48,000 U.S. shopping centers, about 1,130 of which are fully enclosed shopping malls. Shopping center revenues are about $1.5 trillion annually and account for nearly 40 percent of total

Shopping centers in some form have existed for over 1,000 years. Learn more about this phenomenon (**www.icsc.org/srch/about/ impactofshoppingcenters**).

Shopping Centers Today, in print and online (**www.icsc.org/srch/sct/ current**), is the bible of the industry.

U.S. retail-store sales (including autos and gasoline). About 12.5 million people work in shopping centers. Eighty-five percent of Americans over age 18 visit some type of center in an average month. The Limited, Nordstrom, and Macy's are among the vast number of chains with a substantial presence at shopping centers. Some big retailers have also been involved in shopping center development. Sears has participated in the construction of dozens of shopping centers, and Publix Supermarkets operates centers with hundreds of small tenants. Each year, numerous new centers of all kinds and sizes are built and millions of square feet of retail space are added to existing centers.

To sustain their long-term growth, shopping centers are engaging in these practices:

- Several older centers have been renovated, expanded, or repositioned. The Alderwood Shopping Center in Lynnwood, Washington; East Towne Mall in Madison, Wisconsin; Florida Mall in Orlando; Eaton Centre in Toronto, Canada; Park Place in Tucson, Arizona; Queens Center in New York; and Westfield Shoppingtown in Santa Anita, California, have all been revitalized. See Figure 10-4. Visit our Web site (**www.prenhall.com/bermanevans**) for links to these shopping centers.

- Certain derivative types of centers are fostering consumer interest and enthusiasm. Three of these, megamalls, lifestyle centers, and power centers, are discussed a little later in this chapter.

- Shopping centers are responding to shifting consumer lifestyles. They have made parking easier, added ramps for baby strollers and wheelchairs, and included more distinctive retailers such as Crate & Barrel, Williams-Sonoma, Coach, Hot Topic, Chico's, and Charlotte Russe. They have also introduced more information booths and center directories.

- The retailer mix is broadening at many centers to attract people interested in one-stop shopping. More centers now include banks, stockbrokers, dentists, doctors, beauty salons, TV repair outlets, and/or car rental offices. Many centers also offer "temporary tenants," retailers that lease space (often in mall aisles or walkways) and sell from booths or moving carts. The tenants benefit

FIGURE 10-4
Eaton Centre: Revitalizing a Toronto Star

"Stretching two full city blocks, The Toronto Eaton Centre is a historical landmark, and today one of Canada's best-known retail shopping destinations, attracting approximately 50 million visitors annually. The six-story glass-ceiling structure originated from one man's dream to revolutionize the Canadian retail industry. In recent years, urban developers have redesigned the mall's Yonge Street façade and heavy redevelopment, commonly referred to as the 'Dundas Expansion,' occurred. This has attracted new anchors, such as H&M's Toronto flagship store." [**www. torontoeatoncentre.com**]

Photo reprinted by permission.

from the lower rent and short-term commitment; the centers benefit by creating more excitement and diversity in shopping. Consumers often happen on new vendors in unexpected places.

● Some enclosed malls are uncovering: "We look at these centers with a sort of old-town-square approach. You can drive up to the store you want to visit and leave or you can park at one store and wander around the center doing some old-fashioned window shopping."[5]

● More shopping center developers are striving to build their own brand loyalty. Simon and Westfield are among the developers who have spent millions of dollars to boost their images by advertising their own names—with slogans such as "Simon Malls—More Choices." Simon (**www.simon.com**) owns and manages more than 400 properties in 44 states, Europe, Japan, and elsewhere.

● Some shopping centers are using frequent-shopper programs to retain customers and track spending. Prizes range from pre-paid calling cards to Caribbean vacations.

There are three types of planned shopping centers: regional, community, and neighborhood. Their characteristics are noted in Table 10-1, and they are described next.

Regional Shopping Center

A **regional shopping center** is a large, planned shopping facility appealing to a geographically dispersed market. It has at least one or two department stores (each with a minimum of 100,000 square feet) and 50 to 150 or more smaller retailers. A regional center offers a very broad and deep assortment of shopping-oriented goods and services intended to enhance the consumer's visit. The market is 100,000+ people who live or work up to a 30-minute drive away. On average, people travel less than 20 minutes.

The regional center is the result of a planned effort to re-create the shopping variety of a central city in suburbia. Some regional centers have even become the social, cultural, and vocational focal point of an entire suburban area. Frequently, it is used as a town plaza, a meeting place, a concert hall, and a place for a brisk indoor walk. Despite the declining overall interest in shopping, on a typical visit to a regional shopping center, many people spend an average of an hour or more there.

The first outdoor regional shopping center opened in 1950 in Seattle, anchored by a branch of Bon Marche, a leading downtown department store. Southdale Center (outside Minneapolis), built in 1956 for the Target Corporation (then Dayton Hudson), was the first fully enclosed, climate-controlled mall. Today, there are about 2,350 U.S. regional centers, and this format is popping up around the world (where small stores still remain the dominant force) from Australia to Brazil to India to Malaysia.

Mall of America's attractions (**www.mallofamerica.com**) are as impressive as the mall itself.

One type of regional center is the **megamall**, an enormous planned shopping center with 1 million+ square feet of retail space, multiple anchor stores, up to several hundred specialty stores, food courts, and entertainment facilities. It seeks to heighten interest in shopping and expand the trading area. There are 430 U.S. megamalls, including Mall of America (**www.mallofamerica.com**) in Minnesota. It has four anchors (Bloomingdale's, Macy's, Nordstrom, and Sears), over 500 other stores, a 14-screen movie theater, a health club, 57 restaurants and nightclubs, Camp Snoopy indoor amusement park, and 12,750 parking spaces—on 4.2 million square feet. The mall has stores for every budget, attracts 37 percent of visitors from outside a 150-mile radius, and draws 600,000 to 900,000 visitors weekly.

TABLE 10-1	Characteristics of Typical Neighborhood, Community, and Regional Types of U.S. Planned Shopping Centers		
Features of a Typical Center	**TYPE OF CENTER**		
	Regional	**Community**	**Neighborhood**
Total site area (acres)	30–100+	10–30	3–10
Total sq. ft. leased to retailers	400,001–2,000,000+	100,001–400,000	30,000–100,000
Principal tenant	One, two, or more full-sized department stores	Branch department store (traditional or discount), variety store, and/or category killer store	Supermarket or drugstore
Number of stores	50–150 or more	15–25	5–15
Goods and services offered	Largest assortment for customers, focusing on goods that encourage careful shopping and services that enhance the shopping experience (such as a food court)	Moderate assortment for customers, focusing on a mix of shopping- and convenience-oriented goods and services	Lowest assortment for customers, emphasizing convenience-oriented goods and services
Minimum number of people living/working in trading area needed to support center	100,000+	20,000–100,000	3,000–50,000
Trading area in driving time	Up to 30 minutes	Up to 20 minutes	Fewer than 15 minutes
Location	Outside central city, on arterial highway or expressway	Close to one or more populated residential area(s)	Along a major thoroughfare in a single residential area
Layout	Mall, often enclosed with anchor stores at major entrances/exits	Strip or L-shaped	Strip
Percentage of all centers	5	33	62
Percentage of all centers' selling space	29	46	25
Percentage of all centers' retail sales	29	41	30

Source: Percentage data computed by the authors from *2005 NRB Shopping Center Census.*

Canada's West Edmonton Mall is the largest megamall in the world. See Figure 10-5 for another leading regional center.

Community Shopping Center

A **community shopping center** is a moderate-sized, planned shopping facility with a branch department store (traditional or discount) and/or a category killer store, as well as several smaller stores (similar to those in a neighborhood center). It offers a moderate assortment of shopping- and convenience-oriented goods and services to consumers from one or more nearby, well-populated, residential areas. About 20,000 to 100,000 people, who live or work within a 10- to 20-minute drive, are served by this location.

There is better long-range planning for a community shopping center than a neighborhood shopping center. Balanced tenancy is usually enforced and cooperative

Technology in RETAILING

Customer Relationship Management Software Drives Auto Dealer Sales

According to a Volkswagen of America (**www.vw.com**) executive, "dealerships are looking for software to manage leads because they can't deny the growth in Internet use by consumers." Yet, while 97 percent of Volkswagen's dealers participate in its lead programs, few have the tools to properly manage these leads. The same holds true at Saab Cars USA (**www.saabusa.com**). Even though Saab sends Internet leads to its 250 dealers, many process the leads through spreadsheets rather than contact management software. A dealer's challenge is to find customer relationship software that will augment the Web site for each brand carried by the dealer.

After installing new customer relationship management software, George Matick Chevrolet (**www.**matickchevy.com**) no longer has to re-enter information into its data base. The dealership now closes double the number of leads it did previously. According to George Matick Chevrolet's marketing manager, "About 85 percent of the people that come into the showroom have done their research. We have to embrace technology and make sure it works together with the auto manufacturers [so] everything is integrated to serve the customer."

Sources: Laurie Sullivan, "Car Dealers Rev CRM to Manage Net Leads," *Informationweek.com* (September 13, 2004), p. 40; and "About Us," **www.matickchevy.com/About-Us.aspx** (February 22, 2006).

Centro Watt (**www.centrowatt.com**) is a leading retail-estate developer. Visit its properties online.

promotion is more apt. Store composition and the center's image are kept pretty consistent with pre-set goals.

Two noteworthy types of community center are the power center and the lifestyle center. A **power center** is a shopping site with (a) up to a half-dozen or so category killer stores and a mix of smaller stores or (b) several complementary stores specializing in one product category. A power center usually occupies 200,000 to 400,000 square feet on a major highway or road intersection. It seeks to be quite distinctive to draw shoppers and better compete with regional centers. There are over 2,000 U.S. power centers, such as Pennsylvania's Whitehall Square. That 298,000-square-foot center (operated by Centro Watt) is a category killer center with a 55,000-square-foot Raymour & Flanigan Furniture Store, a 49,000-square-foot Sports Authority, a 30,000-square-foot Ross Dress for Less, and many smaller stores.

A **lifestyle center** is an open-air shopping site that typically includes 150,000 to 500,000 square feet of space dedicated to upscale, well-known specialty stores. The focus is often on apparel, home products, books, and music—as well as

FIGURE 10-5
Festival Walk: Hong Kong Megamall

"Festival Walk is an energized environment of innovation, originality, and pleasure. Boasting a world-class design of natural light and open space, Festival Walk offers an unparalleled environment for business and pleasure: over 200 shops and 25 restaurants, an 11-screen cinema multiplex, Hong Kong's largest ice rink, over 220,000 square feet of office space, an 850-space car park, and direct access to buses, taxis, a train station. Its dramatic setting and accessibility have made it the location of choice for some of the world's best-known retail names and reputable companies."
[**www.festivalwalk.com**]

Photo reprinted by permission of Retail Forward, Inc.

FIGURE 10-6
CocoWalk: A Lifestyle
Center

CocoWalk is an open-air,
lifestyle shopping center in
Coconut Grove, Florida. It is
home to legendary restaurants,
exclusive retailers, and the
AMC 16 "gourmet cinemas."
The vibrant Mediterranean
ambience, unique shopping
and dining experiences, and
visitor-friendly surroundings
have made it one of the most-
frequented destinations in South
Florida with over 3.5 million
visitors every year.

Reprinted by permission of City
Center Retail.

restaurants.[6] Popular stores at lifestyle centers include Ann Taylor, Banana
Republic, Barnes & Noble, Bath & Body Works, Gap, GapKids, Pottery Barn,
Talbots, Victoria's Secret, Williams-Sonoma, and many others. Aspen Grove in
Littleton, Denver; Deer Park Town Center in Illinois; Rookwood Commons in
Norwood, Ohio; and CocoWalk in Coconut Grove, Florida, are examples of
lifestyle shopping centers. See Figure 10-6. At present, there are about 130 such
centers in the United States—a number that is growing rapidly.

Neighborhood Shopping Center

A **neighborhood shopping center** is a planned shopping facility, with the largest
store being a supermarket or a drugstore. Other retailers often include a bakery, a
laundry, a dry cleaner, a stationery store, a barbershop or beauty parlor, a hardware store, a restaurant, a liquor store, and a gas station. This center focuses on
convenience-oriented goods and services for people living or working nearby. It
serves 3,000 to 50,000 people who are within a 15-minute drive (usually less than
10 minutes).

A neighborhood center is usually arranged in a strip. Initially, it is carefully
planned and tenants are balanced. Over time, the planned aspects may lessen and
newcomers may face fewer restrictions. Thus, a liquor store may replace a
barbershop—leaving a void. A center's ability to maintain balance depends on its
attractiveness to potential tenants (expressed by the extent of store vacancies). In
number, but not in selling space or sales, neighborhood centers account for more
than 60 percent of U.S. shopping centers.

THE CHOICE OF A GENERAL LOCATION

The last part of Step 2 in location planning requires a retailer to select a locational
format: isolated, unplanned district, or planned center. The decision depends on
the firm's strategy and a careful evaluation of the advantages and disadvantages
of each alternative.

Next, Step 3, the retailer chooses a broadly defined site. Two decisions are
needed here. First, the specific kind of isolated store, unplanned business district,
or planned shopping center location is picked. If a firm wants an isolated store, it
must decide on a highway or side street. Should it desire an unplanned business

area, it must decide on a CBD, an SBD, an NBD, or a string. A retailer seeking a planned area must choose a regional, community, or neighborhood shopping center—and whether to use a derivative form such as a megamall or power center. Here are the preferences of three retailers:

> At Wendy's, the majority of restaurants are freestanding, one-story brick buildings, substantially uniform in design and appearance, with parking for approximately 45 cars. Some restaurants, located in downtown areas or shopping malls, are of a storefront type and vary according to available locations. The typical new freestanding restaurant contains about 2,900 square feet and has a food preparation area, a dining room capacity for 90 persons, and a double pickup window for drive-through service. Restaurants are generally located in urban or heavily populated suburban areas, and their success depends upon serving a large number of customers. Wendy's provides a facility for rural and less populated areas that has a building size of about 2,100 square feet with 60 seats.[7]

Guitar Center (**www. guitarcenter.com**) has a well-conceived location plan.

> The Guitar Center chain has developed unique and, what historically have been, highly effective selection criteria to identify prospective store sites for our Guitar Center units. In evaluating the suitability of a particular location, we concentrate on the demographics of our target customer, as well as traffic patterns and specific site characteristics such as visibility, accessibility, traffic volume, shopping patterns, and availability of adequate parking. Stores are typically located in freestanding locations to maximize their outside exposure and signage.[8]

> Dillard's, a department store chain that traditionally located units in regional shopping centers, is now truly energized by the changes occurring in retail development. We find the progressive lifestyle centers particularly compelling and we believe they are an ideal complement to our more upscale approach to retailing. These centers feature not only great shopping, but also fine dining and entertainment choices, often in beautiful open-air or village-themed settings. Our new Dillard's locations at Yuma Palms in Yuma, Arizona and The Shoppes at East Chase in Montgomery, Alabama, are located in these remarkable new venues.[9]

Second, a firm must select its general store placement. For an isolated store, this means picking a specific highway or side street. For an unplanned district or planned center, this means picking a specific district (e.g., downtown Los Angeles) or center (e.g., Seminary South in Fort Worth, Texas).

In Step 3, the retailer narrows down the decisions made in the first two steps and then chooses a general location. Step 4 requires the firm to evaluate specific alternative sites, including their position on a block (or in a center), the side of the street, and the terms of tenancy. The factors to be considered in assessing and choosing a general location and a specific site within that location are described together in the next section because many strategic decisions are similar for these two steps.

LOCATION AND SITE EVALUATION

The assessment of general locations and the specific sites contained within them requires extensive analysis. In any area, the optimum site for a particular store is called the **one-hundred percent location**. Since different retailers need different kinds of locations, a location labeled as 100 percent for one firm may be less than optimal for another. An upscale ladies' apparel shop would seek a location unlike

FIGURE 10-7
A Location/Site Evaluation Checklist

Rate each of these criteria on a scale of 1 to 10, with 1 being excellent and 10 being poor.

Pedestrian Traffic	Number of people	_____
	Type of people	_____
Vehicular Traffic	Number of vehicles	_____
	Type of vehicles	_____
	Traffic congestion	_____
Parking Facilities	Number and quality of parking spots	_____
	Distance to store	_____
	Availability of employee parking	_____
Transportation	Availability of mass transit	_____
	Access from major highways	_____
	Ease of deliveries	_____
Store Composition	Number and size of stores	_____
	Affinity	_____
	Retail balance	_____
Specific Site	Visibility	_____
	Placement in the location	_____
	Size and shape of the lot	_____
	Size and shape of the building	_____
	Condition and age of the lot and building	_____
Terms of Occupancy	Ownership or leasing terms	_____
	Operations and maintenance costs	_____
	Taxes	_____
	Zoning restrictions	_____
	Voluntary regulations	_____
Overall Rating	General location	_____
	Specific site	_____

that sought by a convenience store. The apparel shop would benefit from heavy pedestrian traffic, closeness to major department stores, and proximity to other specialty stores. The convenience store would rather be in an area with ample parking and heavy vehicular traffic. It does not need to be close to other stores.

Figure 10-7 contains a location and site evaluation checklist. A retailer should rate every alternative location (and specific site) on all the criteria and develop overall ratings for them. Two firms may rate the same site differently. This figure should be used in conjunction with the trading-area data noted in Chapter 9, not instead of them.

Pedestrian Traffic

The most crucial measures of a location's and site's value are the number and type of people passing by. Other things being equal, a site with the most pedestrian traffic is often best.

Not everyone passing a location or site is a good prospect for all types of stores, so many firms use selective counting procedures, such as counting only those carrying shopping bags. Otherwise, pedestrian traffic totals may include too many nonshoppers. It would be improper for an appliance retailer to count as prospective shoppers all the people who pass a downtown site on the way to work. In fact, much of the downtown pedestrian traffic may be from people who are there for nonretailing activities.

A proper pedestrian traffic count should encompass these four elements:

- Separation of the count by age and gender (with very young children not counted).

Retailers offer a large variety of career opportunities—complete with competitive wages, fringe benefits, positive working conditions, and opportunities for career and educational advancement. In this chapter and the next several chapters, we provide information from the NRF about specific career tracks. This information is general in nature; individual firms will vary in the details based on size, retail format, etc.

Are you a big picture person? Retail professionals in the store operations career area oversee overall store operations and profits. Responsibilities may include managing staff functions like loss prevention and/or human resources. Here are several positions at the top of the store operations career ladder:

- *Head of Store Operations*: Top executive in charge of overall store operation and profits. May supervise some staff functions like loss prevention, distribution, and/or a field human resources group. Does not have buying or accounting responsibility. Typically reports to the head of a chain.

- *Zone Manager*: This position exists only in very large chains to supervise a geographic group of regional managers. This position is the third level above the store managers (store manager to district manager to regional manager to zone manager).
- *Regional Manager*: This manager supervises a geographic group of district managers and is two levels above store managers.
- *District Manager*: This position is the first level above a group of store and/or area managers and does not personally manage a specific store.
- *Area Manager*: This position is a "super store manager" role, running one store as the store manager while supervising one or more other store managers. This arrangement may also be called a district manager trainee or senior store manager, among other titles.

Source: Reprinted by permission of the National Retail Federation.

- Division of the count by time (this allows the study of peaks, low points, and changes in the gender of the people passing by the hour).
- Pedestrian interviews (to find out the proportion of potential shoppers).
- Spot analysis of shopping trips (to verify the stores actually visited).

Vehicular Traffic

The quantity and characteristics of vehicular traffic are very important for retailers that appeal to customers who drive there. Convenience stores, outlets in regional shopping centers, and car washes are retailers that rely on heavy vehicular traffic. And automotive traffic studies are essential in suburban areas, where pedestrian traffic is often limited.

As with pedestrian traffic, adjustments to the raw count of vehicular traffic must be made. Some retailers count only homeward-bound traffic, some exclude vehicles on the other side of a divided highway, and some omit out-of-state cars. Data may be available from the state highway department, the county engineer, or the regional planning commission.

Besides traffic counts, the retailer should study the extent and timing of congestion (from traffic, detours, and poor roads). People normally avoid congested areas and shop where driving time and driving difficulties are minimized.

Parking Facilities

Most U.S. retail stores include some provision for nearby off-street parking. In many business districts, parking is provided by individual stores, arrangements among stores, and local government. In planned shopping centers, parking is shared by all stores there. The number and quality of parking spots, their distances from stores, and the availability of employee parking should all be evaluated.

The need for retailer parking facilities depends on the store's trading area, the type of store, the proportion of shoppers using a car, the existence of other parking, the turnover of spaces (which depend on the length of a shopping trip), the flow of shoppers, and parking by nonshoppers. A shopping center normally needs 4 to 5 parking spaces per 1,000 square feet of gross floor area, a supermarket 10 to 15 spaces, and a furniture store 3 or 4 spaces.

Free parking sometimes creates problems. Commuters and employees of nearby businesses may park in spaces intended for shoppers. This problem can be lessened by validating shoppers' parking stubs and requiring payment from nonshoppers. Another problem may occur if the selling space at a location increases due to new stores or the expansion of current ones. Existing parking may then be inadequate. Double-deck parking or parking tiers save land and shorten the distance from a parked car to a store—a key factor since customers at a regional shopping center may be unwilling to walk more than a few hundred feet from their cars to the center.

Transportation

Mass transit, access from major highways, and ease of deliveries must be examined.

In a downtown area, closeness to mass transit is important for people who do not own cars, who commute to work, or who would not otherwise shop in an area with traffic congestion. The availability of buses, taxis, subways, trains, and other kinds of public transit is a must for any area not readily accessible by vehicular traffic.

Locations dependent on vehicular traffic should be rated on their nearness to major thoroughfares. Driving time is a consideration for many people. In addition, drivers heading eastbound on a highway often do not like to make a U-turn to get to a store on the westbound side of that highway.

The transportation network should be studied for delivery truck access. Many thoroughfares are excellent for cars but ban large trucks or cannot bear their weight.

Store Composition

The number and size of stores should be consistent with the type of location. A retailer in an isolated site wants no stores nearby; a retailer in a neighborhood business district wants an area with 10 to 15 small stores; and a retailer in a regional shopping center wants a location with many stores, including large department stores (to generate customer traffic).

If the stores at a given location (be it an unplanned district or a planned center) complement, blend, and cooperate with one another, and each benefits from the others' presence, **affinity** exists. When affinity is strong, the sales of each store are greater, due to the high customer traffic, than if the stores are apart. The practice of similar or complementary stores locating near each other is based on two factors: (1) Customers like to compare the prices, styles, selections, and services of similar stores. (2) Customers like one-stop shopping and purchase at different stores on the same trip. Affinities can exist among competing stores, as well as among complementary stores. More people travel to shopping areas with large selections than to convenience-oriented areas, so the sales of all stores are enhanced.

One measure of compatibility is the degree to which stores exchange customers. Stores in these categories are very compatible with each other and have high customer interchange:

- Supermarket, drugstore, bakery, fruit-and-vegetable store, meat store.
- Department store, apparel store, hosiery store, lingerie shop, shoe store, jewelry store.

Retail balance, the mix of stores within a district or shopping center, should also be considered. Proper balance occurs when the number of store facilities for each merchandise or service classification is equal to the location's market potential, a range of goods and services is provided to foster one-stop shopping, there is an adequate assortment within any category, and there is a proper mix of store types (balanced tenancy).

Specific Site

Visibility, placement in the location, size and shape of the lot, size and shape of the building, and condition and age of the lot and building should be reviewed for the specific site.

Visibility is a site's ability to be seen by pedestrian or vehicular traffic. A site on a side street or at the end of a shopping center is not as visible as one on a major road or at the center's entrance. High visibility aids store awareness; and some people hesitate to go down a side street or to the end of a center.

Placement in the location is a site's relative position in the district or center. A corner location may be desirable since it is situated at the intersection of two streets and has "corner influence." It is usually more expensive because of the greater pedestrian and vehicular passersby due to traffic flows from two streets, increased window display area, and less traffic congestion through multiple entrances. Corner influence is greatest in high-volume locations. That is why some Pier 1 stores, Starbucks restaurants, and other retailers occupy corner sites. See Figure 10-8.

A convenience-oriented firm, such as a stationery store, is very concerned about the side of the street, the location relative to other convenience-oriented

FIGURE 10-8

Corner Influence and Sean Jean

Consider the pedestrian and vehicular traffic—and the eye-catching appeal—generated by this distinctive Sean Jean clothing store in Manhattan. Yes, it's Sean "Diddy" Combs' store.

Photo reprinted by permission.

stores, nearness to parking, access to a bus stop, and the distance from residences. A shopping-oriented retailer, such as a furniture store, is more interested in a corner site to increase window display space, proximity to wallpaper and other related retailers, the accessibility of its pickup platform to consumers, and the ease of deliveries to the store.

When a retailer buys or rents an existing building, its size and shape should be noted. The condition and age of the lot and the building should also be studied. A department store requires significantly more space than a boutique; and it may desire a square site, while the boutique seeks a rectangular one. Any site should be viewed in terms of total space needs: parking, walkways, selling, nonselling, and so on.

Due to the saturation of many desirable locations and the lack of available spots in others, some firms have turned to nontraditional sites—often to complement their existing stores. TGI Friday, Staples, and Bally have airport stores. McDonald's has outlets in many Wal-Marts and at several gas stations. Some fast-food retailers share facilities to provide more variety and to share costs.

Terms of Occupancy

Terms of occupancy—ownership versus leasing, the type of lease, operations and maintenance costs, taxes, zoning restrictions, and voluntary regulations—must be evaluated for each prospective site.

Ownership versus Leasing

A retailer with adequate funding can either own or lease premises. Ownership is more common in small stores, in small communities, or at inexpensive locations. It has several advantages. There is no chance that a property owner will not renew a lease or double the rent when a lease expires. Monthly mortgage payments are stable. Operations are flexible; a retailer can engage in scrambled merchandising and break down walls. It is also likely that property value will appreciate over time, resulting in a financial gain if the business is sold. Ownership disadvantages are the high initial costs, the long-term commitment, and the inability to readily change sites. Home Depot owns about 85 percent of its store properties.[10]

The Main Street program (**www.mainst.org**) has revitalized communities across the United States.

If a retailer chooses ownership, it must decide whether to construct a new facility or buy an existing building. The retailer should consider the purchase price and maintenance costs, zoning restrictions, the age and condition of existing facilities, the adaptability of existing facilities, and the time to erect a new building. To encourage building rehabilitation in small towns (5,000 to 50,000 people), Congress enacted the Main Street program (**www.mainst.org**) of the National Trust for Historic Preservation. Currently, there is a network of 40 statewide, citywide, and countywide Main Street programs actively serving more than 1,200 towns. These towns benefit from planning support, tax credits, and low-interest loans.

The great majority of stores in central business districts and regional shopping centers are leased, mostly due to the high investment for ownership. Department stores tend to have renewable 30-year leases, supermarkets usually have renewable 20-year leases, and stores such as T.J. Maxx typically have 10-year leases with options to extend. Some leases give the retailer the right to end an agreement before the expiration date—under given circumstances and for a specified payment by the retailer.

Leasing minimizes the initial investment, reduces risk, allows access to prime sites that cannot hold more stores, leads to immediate occupancy and traffic, and reduces the long-term commitment. Many retailers also feel they can open more stores or spend more on other aspects of their strategies by leasing. Firms that lease accept limits on operating flexibility, restrictions on subletting and selling the business, possible nonrenewal problems, rent increases, and not gaining from rising real-estate values.

Through a *sale-leaseback*, some large retailers build stores and then sell them to real-estate investors who lease the property back to the retailers on a long-term basis. Retailers using sale-leasebacks build stores to their specifications and have bargaining power in leasing—while lowering capital expenditures.

Types of Leases

Property owners do not rely solely on constant rent leases, partly due to their concern about interest rates and the related rise in operating costs. Terms can be quite complicated.

Saks Fifth Avenue (**www.saks.com**), a name synonymous with glamour, is one of the cornerstone retailers on New York's high-rent Fifth Avenue.

The simplest, most direct arrangement is the **straight lease**—a retailer pays a fixed dollar amount per month over the life of the lease. Rent usually ranges from $1 to $75 annually per square foot, depending on the site's desirability and store traffic. At some sites, rents can be much higher. On New York's Fifth Avenue, from 48th to 58th Streets, the average yearly rent exceeds $700 per square foot!

A **percentage lease** stipulates that rent is related to sales or profits. This differs from a straight lease, which provides for constant payments. A percentage lease protects a property owner against inflation and lets it benefit if a store is successful; it also allows a tenant to view the lease as a variable cost—rent is lower when its performance is weak and higher when performance is good. The percentage rate varies by type of shopping district or center and by type of store.

Percentage leases have variations. With a specified minimum, low sales are assumed to be partly the retailer's responsibility; the property owner receives minimum payments (as in a straight lease) no matter what the sales or profits. With a specified maximum, it is assumed that a very successful retailer should not pay more than a maximum rent. Superior merchandising, promotion, and pricing should reward the retailer. Another variation is the sliding scale: the ratio of rent to sales changes as sales rise. A sliding-down scale has a retailer pay a lower percentage as sales go up and is an incentive to the retailer.

A **graduated lease** calls for precise rent increases over a stated period of time. Monthly rent may be $4,800 for the first five years and $5,600 for the last five years of a lease. Rent is known in advance by the retailer and the property owner and based on expected increases in sales and costs. There is no problem auditing sales or profits, as there is for percentage leases. This lease is often used with small retailers.

A **maintenance-increase-recoupment lease** has a provision allowing rent to increase if a property owner's taxes, heating bills, insurance, or other expenses rise beyond a certain point. This provision most often supplements a straight rental lease agreement.

A **net lease** calls for all maintenance costs, such as heating, electricity, insurance, and interior repair, to be paid by the retailer. It frees the property owner from managing the facility and gives the retailer control over store maintenance. It is used to supplement a straight lease or a percentage lease.

Other Considerations

After assessing ownership and leasing opportunities, a retailer must look at the costs of operations and maintenance. The age and condition of a facility may cause a retailer to have high monthly costs, even though the mortgage or rent is low. Furthermore, the costs of extensive renovations should be calculated.

What is the sales tax in Utah? California? Go to this site (http://salestaxinstitute.com/sales_tax_rates.jsp) to find out the sales tax in all 50 states.

Differences in sales taxes (those that customers pay) and business taxes (those that retailers pay) among alternative sites must be weighed. Business taxes should be broken down into real-estate and income categories. The highest statewide sales tax is in Mississippi, Rhode Island, and Tennessee (7 percent); Alaska, Delaware, Montana, New Hampshire, and Oregon have no state sales tax.

There may be zoning restrictions as to the kind of stores allowed, store size, building height, the type of merchandise carried, and other factors that have to be hurdled (or another site chosen). For example,

> With its plans to open a store in Rego Park in Queens, New York, thwarted, Wal-Mart may be licking its wounds but the retail giant won't go quietly into the night. Real-estate sources and retail experts said the company will be back, but the next time it may have to tailor its approach to the New York market. Target, a competitor of Wal-Mart, has been successful in New York with stores in the Bronx, Queens, and Brooklyn. "They know how to do it," said the director of the Downtown Brooklyn Council. "They got immediately involved in the community with local elected officials and community groups. They are philanthropic. They manage a good store and have a reputation for being generous." Wal-Mart, however, became a lightning rod for criticism when it was revealed that the chain was part of a proposed mix-use development in Queens with 700,000 square feet of retail space and 450 residential units above the mall. The developer apparently got cold feet when labor unions and some City Council members voiced opposition to Wal-Mart. "I think this was a good eye-opening experience and they'll probably go back to the drawing board and the next time be a little more sensitive to their surroundings," said a retail real-estate broker. "The chains that are always successful in the city are the chains that come in and change for the city and react to New York."[11]

Voluntary restrictions—not mandated by the government—are most prevalent in planned shopping centers and may include required membership in merchant groups, uniform hours, and cooperative security forces. Leases for many stores in regional shopping centers have included clauses protecting anchor tenants from too much competition—especially from discounters. These clauses involve limits on product lines, bans against discounting, fees for common services, and so forth. Anchors have been protected by developers since the developers need their long-term commitments to finance the centers. The Federal Trade Commission discourages "exclusives"—whereby only a particular retailer in a center can carry specified merchandise—and "radius clauses"—whereby a tenant agrees not to operate another store within a certain distance.

Because of overbuilding, some retailers are in a good position to bargain over the terms of occupancy. This differs from city to city and from shopping location to shopping location.

Overall Rating

The last task in choosing a store location is to compute overall ratings: (1) Each location under consideration is given an overall rating based on the criteria in Figure 10-7. (2) The overall ratings of alternative locations are compared, and the best location is chosen. (3) The same procedure is used to evaluate the alternative sites within the location.

Lease agreements used to be so simple that they could be written on a napkin—not today (**www.icsc.org/ srch/sct/current/sct9905/ 16.htm**).

It is often difficult to compile and compare composite evaluations because some attributes may be positive while others are negative. The general location may be a good shopping center, but the site in the center may be poor; or an area may have excellent potential but take two years to build a store. The attributes in Figure 10-7 should be weighted according to their importance. An overall rating should also include *knockout factors*, those that preclude consideration of a site. Possible knockout factors are a short lease, little or no evening or weekend pedestrian traffic, and poor tenant relations with the landlord.

Summary

1. *To thoroughly examine the types of locations available to a retailer: isolated store, unplanned business district, and planned shopping center.* After a retailer rates alternative trading areas, it decides on the type of location, selects the general location, and chooses a particular site. There are three basic locational types.

   An isolated store is freestanding, not adjacent to other stores. It has no competition, low rent, flexibility, road visibility, easy parking, and lower property costs. It also has a lack of traffic, no variety for shoppers, no shared costs, and zoning restrictions.

   An unplanned business district is a shopping area with two or more stores located together or nearby. Store composition is not based on planning. There are four categories: central business district, secondary business district, neighborhood business district, and string. An unplanned district generally has these favorable points: variety of goods, services, and prices; access to public transit; nearness to commercial and social facilities; and pedestrian traffic. Yet, its shortcomings have led to the growth of the planned shopping center: inadequate parking, older facilities, high rents and taxes in popular

CBDs, discontinuity of offerings, traffic and delivery congestion, high theft rates, and some declining central cities.

   A planned shopping center is centrally owned or managed and well balanced. It usually has one or more anchor stores and many smaller stores. The planned center is popular, due to extensive goods and service offerings, expanding suburbs, shared strategic planning and costs, attractive locations, parking facilities, lower rent and taxes (except for regional centers), lower theft rates, the popularity of malls (although some people are now bored with them), and the lesser appeal of inner-city shopping. Negative aspects include operations inflexibility, restrictions on merchandise carried, and anchor store domination. There are three forms: regional, community, and neighborhood centers.

2. *To note the decisions necessary in choosing a general retail location.* First, the specific form of isolated store, unplanned business district, or planned shopping center location is determined, such as whether to be on a highway or side street; in a CBD, an SBD,

an NBD, or a string; or in a regional, community, or neighborhood shopping center. Then the general store location is specified—singling out a particular highway, business district, or shopping center.

3. *To describe the concept of the one-hundred percent location.* Extensive analysis is required when evaluating each general location and specific sites within it. Most importantly, the optimum site for a given store must be determined. This is the one-hundred percent location, and it differs by retailer.

4. *To discuss several criteria for evaluating general retail locations and the specific sites within them.* Pedestrian traffic, vehicular traffic, parking facilities, transportation, store composition, the attrib-

utes of each specific site, and terms of occupancy should be studied. An overall rating is then computed for each location and site and the best one selected.

Affinity occurs when the stores at the same location complement, blend, and cooperate with one another; each benefits from the others' presence.

5. *To contrast alternative terms of occupancy.* A retailer can opt to own or lease. If it leases, terms are specified in a straight lease, percentage lease, graduated lease, maintenance-increase-recoupment lease, and/or net lease. Operating and maintenance costs, taxes, zoning restrictions, and voluntary restrictions also need to be reviewed.

Key Terms

isolated store (p. 292)
unplanned business district (p. 293)
central business district (CBD) (p. 294)
secondary business district (SBD)
    (p. 296)
neighborhood business district (NBD)
    (p. 296)
string (p. 297)
planned shopping center (p. 298)

balanced tenancy (p. 298)
regional shopping center (p. 300)
megamall (p. 300)
community shopping center (p. 301)
power center (p. 302)
lifestyle center (p. 302)
neighborhood shopping center (p. 303)
one-hundred percent location (p. 304)
affinity (p. 307)

retail balance (p. 308)
terms of occupancy (p. 309)
straight lease (p. 310)
percentage lease (p. 310)
graduated lease (p. 311)
maintenance-increase-recoupment lease
    (p. 311)
net lease (p. 311)

Questions for Discussion

1. A restaurant chain has decided to open outlets in a combination of isolated locations, unplanned business districts, and planned shopping centers. Comment on this strategy.

2. From the retailer's perspective, compare the advantages of locating in unplanned business districts versus planned shopping centers.

3. Differentiate among the central business district, the secondary business district, the neighborhood business district, and the string.

4. Develop a brief plan to revitalize a neighborhood business district near your campus.

5. What is a megamall? What is a lifestyle center? Describe the strengths and weaknesses of each.

6. Evaluate a neighborhood shopping center near your campus.

7. Explain why a one-hundred percent location for Pizza Hut may not be a one-hundred percent location for a local pizza restaurant.

8. What criteria should a small retailer use in selecting a general store location and a specific site within it? A large retailer?

9. What difficulties are there in using a rating scale such as that shown in Figure 10-7? What are the benefits?

10. How do the parking needs for a barber shop, a shoe repair store, and an apparel store differ?

11. Under what circumstances would it be more desirable for a retailer to buy or lease an existing facility rather than to build a new store?

12. What are the pros and cons of a straight lease versus a percentage lease for a prospective retail tenant? For the landlord?

Web-Based Exercise

Visit this Web site (**www.brookings.edu/metro/ pubs/20050307_12steps.pdf**) and read the report on *Turning Around Downtown: Twelve Steps to Revitalization*. Discuss the key points you learn from the report.

Note: Stop by our Web site (**www.prenhall.com/bermanevans**) to experience a number of highly interactive, appealing Web exercises based on actual company demonstrations and sample materials related to retailing.

Chapter Endnotes

1. Various company sources.
2. *Bed Bath & Beyond 2005 Annual Report.*
3. Kent Robertson, "Enhancing Downtown's Sense of Place," *Main Street News* (September 1999).
4. James Pendered, "Downtown Dresses Up," *Atlanta Journal-Constitution* (April 4, 2005), p. 1E.
5. Daniel P. Finney, "Open-Air Mall Is Planned for West Omaha," *Knight-Ridder/Tribune Business News* (November 7, 2001), p. ITEM01311003.
6. See Joseph Weber and Ann Therese Palmer, "How the Net Is Remaking the Mall," *Business Week* (May 9, 2005), pp. 60–61; David Moin, "Lifestyle Centers: The New Pitfalls and Potential," *Women's Wear Daily* (May 16, 2005), p. 12; Gregory R. Gunter, "Lifestyle Centers: The Magic Mix," **www.globest.com/retail/ advisor/1_32/advisor/14912-1.html** (May 16, 2005); and Maria Bird Pico, "Lifestyle the Latin Way," *Shopping Centers Today* (May 2005), pp. 149–152.
7. *Wendy's International 2005 Annual Report.*
8. *Guitar Center 2005 Annual Report.*
9. *Dillard's 2004 Annual Report.*
10. *Home Depot 2005 Annual Report.*
11. David Moin and Sharon Edelson, "Wal-Mart Regrouping for Next N.Y. Attempt," *Women's Wear Daily* (February 25, 2005), p. 22.

part four
Short Cases

CASE 1: RETAIL DEVELOPMENT COMES TO HATTIESBURG, MISSISSIPPI[c-1]

Hattiesburg is a small college town (home of the University of Southern Mississippi) that has been losing business to larger surrounding cities such as Mobile, Alabama; New Orleans, Louisiana; and Biloxi, Mississippi, since the late 1970s. Turtle Creek Mall, a new 390,000-square-foot, $38-million power center that features big-box retailers such as Target (**www.target.com**), Bed Bath & Beyond (**www.bed bathandbeyond.com**), and Old Navy (**www.oldnavy.com**), along with smaller stores such as Dress Barn (**www.dressbarn. com**), Books-A-Million (**www.booksamillion.com**), and PetsMart (**www.petsmart.com**), is hoping to change this trend. Turtle Creek Mall (**www.turtlecreekmall.com**) is located on 57 acres next to Hattiesburg's largest regional shopping center. With 938,000 square feet of retail space, the mall is anchored by Dillard's (**www.dillards.com**), Goody's (**www.goodysonline.com**), J.C. Penney (**www.jcpenney. com**), McRae's (**www.mcraes.com**), and Sears (**www.sears.com**).

In total, the new retail facilities will increase retail square footage in Hattiesburg by 30 percent. According to some retail analysts, the arrival of Target in Hattiesburg has spurred economic development. Another factor that increased new retail development has been the city's expanding access roads. Other significant retail developments include the conversion of a former Kmart (**www.kmart.com**), a new $12-million, 14-screen movie theater, and a new Best Buy (**www.bestbuy. com**).

Hattiesburg has excellent demographics, as well as a sound economic base. The University of Southern Mississippi with 15,000+ students is the state's largest college. This explains why 45 percent of the city's population is between 20 and 44. Average household income in 2004 was over $38,000 per year, and the city has a diversified economic base due to the presence of a university, an industrial base, and health-care facilities. The area's unemployment rate was 4.1 percent.

A major objective of Turtle Creek is to reduce the out-shopping behavior of Hattiesburg residents. According to a University of Southern Mississippi study, the Hattiesburg trade area shrank by 40,000 or so residents between 1997 and 2004. In comparison to other areas, outshopping is easier here since Hattiesburg has easy access via four major highways to much larger cities. The loss of shoppers due to outshopping may partially explain why most existing retailers welcome the new power center. According to Bryan LeBlanc, the general manager of Turtle Creek Mall, "The cross traffic with Turtle Creek Mall is a win-win situation."

While sales at Turtle Creek Mall have not increased for a couple of years, LeBlanc estimates that 2004 sales will be higher than those of 2003. Sales per square foot average $313. While Turtle Creek Mall has no plans to change any of its anchor tenants, it plans to change the tenant mix of its smaller retailers as their leases expire.

Rents at the Turtle Creek Mall average between $30 and $35 per square foot and rents for big-box stores in excellent locations range from $14 to $22 per square foot. A new lifestyle center is offering space at $15 per square foot; this location has additional charges for common area maintenance, taxes, and insurance of $2.50 per square foot.

Questions

1. How could shopping center developers in Hattiesburg use geographic information systems in their planning?
2. Analyze the economic base of Hattiesburg using online research data bases, as well as *Editor & Publisher Market Guide* (if available at your college library).
3. Explain how the trading area of Hattiesburg can be delineated for an existing mall. A new mall.
4. Describe the dangers in Hattiesburg's becoming over-stored. How can the level of saturation for Hattiesburg be controlled?

CASE 2: SMALL CHAINS, BIG STORE LOCATION TACTICS[c-2]

In contrast to large national chains that prefer one-hundred percent locations, many smaller retailers seek out lower-quality locations. Let's examine the retail site location strategies of Wireless Toyz (**www.wirelesstoyz.com**), a retailer of all brands of cellular phone service and accessories, as well as satellite television, and Downtown Locker Room (**www. downtownlockerroom.com**) (DTLR), a retailer of fashion apparel, shoes, and music aimed at 15- to 25-year-olds.

Wireless Toyz seeks corner locations at busy intersections. According to Richard Simtob, the retailer's vice-president of franchise and real-estate development, "We're looking for locations in middle-class, predominantly blue-collar neighborhoods, with a minimum population of 50,000 people within the trade area and positioned at intersections with daily traffic counts of at least 50,000 vehicles." Unlike other retailers, however, Wireless Toyz will acquire locations in poor condition or locations requiring significant renovation, such as a vacant former gas station.

An average Wireless Toyz occupies 1,500 to 2,500 square feet. In some cases, the franchise or firm will lease a larger retail space, around 4,000 square feet, and then sublease half of the space to another retailer. While Wireless Toyz can use locations of less than one-half acre, a location of this size is generally too small for drugstore chains or coffee shops such

---

[c-1]The material in this case is drawn from Jill Maunder, "Big-Box Boom," *SCT* (February 2005) pp. 43–44.

[c-2]The material in this case is drawn from Connie Robbins Gentry, "Small Chains with Big Growth Plans," *Chain Store Age* (March 2005), pp. 121–124.

as Starbucks. And while Wireless Toyz will consider corner locations in strip shopping centers, it will not lease stores located in the middle of strip centers or go into centers with Wal-Mart or Target as anchor tenants.

In 2004, Wireless Toyz expanded from 27 to 63 locations. Over 100 new locations are planned as it expands from 12 to 19 states. In 2004, same-store sales increased 30 percent per year for the third year in a row. Its average store has $900,000 in annual gross sales.

DTLR is currently seeking 3,500- to 4,000-square-foot locations in the Mid-Atlantic states and in metropolitan markets. DTLR does not favor college towns due to the low disposable income of many students. The retailer's director of community and corporate outreach says that, "The biggest challenges we face in real-estate are, first, finding the best location in a market's marquee mall or strip shopping center, and second, dealing with exclusive clauses that other tenants may have in place to prevent us from entering the shopping center." While DTLR welcomes competition from national chains, many national chains seek to limit the retailer's growth through these restrictive lease provisions. Over the past five years, DTLR has grown from 18 to 40 stores and plans to grow by adding 10 new stores each year.

Commercial Net Lease Realty (**www.cnlreit.com**) (CNLR) is a real-estate developer that performs fee development projects for many smaller retailers. In contrast to build-to-suit projects where CNLR owns the land and building and then leases it to a retailer, in fee development, a retailer pays CNLR a fee to manage a project in which the retailer owns the land and building. The fee development approach minimizes the developer's risk, while it provides depreciation and capital gains opportunities for the retailer.

Questions

1. Discuss the pros and cons of the use of lower-quality locations by small chains in contrast to the use of one-hundred percent locations by larger chains.
2. Evaluate Wireless Toyz' site selection strategy.
3. Develop a location/site evaluation checklist for DTLR. See Figure 10–7.
4. Describe the pros and cons of ownership versus leasing for a small retail chain.

CASE 3: HOME DEPOT IN NEW YORK CITY[c-3]

Home Depot's (**www.homedepot.com**) first store in Manhattan has the distinction of being the chain's first three-story unit, as well as its first one with a doorman and concierge. The new store caters to multiple markets: decorators, building contractors and superintendents, brownstone owners, and households that own or rent individual apart-

[c-3]The material in this case is drawn from Glenn Collins, "Decks and the City," *New York Times Online* (September 8, 2004); and Mike Duff, "Home Depot Hangs New Shingle in Manhattan," *DSN Retailing Today* (January 10, 2005), pp. 4–5, 38.

ments, as well as suburban commuters. As Home Depot's Eastern Division president notes, this is "the first time we've done all this under one roof."

Before its Manhattan expansion, Home Depot successfully opened and managed stores in downtown Detroit, downtown Seattle, and the Lincoln Park neighborhood of Chicago. These stores are a clear indication that Home Depot is seeking growth opportunities outside suburban markets and that it is able to tailor its merchandise selections to meet the needs of urban customers.

Since the new Manhattan store is in a landmark preservation area, its store exterior cannot be modified. So instead of large permanent signs, the store's signage consists of orange-color banners. The store stocks 20,000 different products; special ordering capability will increase this number to 100,000 products. The selection in many product categories is unparalleled for both Home Depot and for Manhattan shoppers. For example, the store offers 1,000 different varieties of lighting fixtures; 500 of these are in stock. And customers can choose among 2,000 different types of flooring, including area rugs priced from $200 to $8,000. Lastly, the store offers 3,200 different paint colors that can be mixed from its nine paint-mixing stations. Despite the large selection of these items, the store does not have a lumber department and does not stock plasterboard, insulation, or plywood. These items require special orders.

The store's Chelsea neighborhood location, which used to be full of independent retailers, now has such retail category killers as Old Navy (**www.oldnavy.com**), Staples (**www.staples.com**), Bed Bath & Beyond (**www.bedbathandbeyond.com**), and Best Buy (**www.bestbuy.com**). The trend of large retailers coming to this area has some independents concerned. Others, however, feel that stores like the new Home Depot will increase sales for all merchants in the neighborhood due to the cumulative attraction of chain and independent retailers.

The idea of the doorman for Home Depot stemmed from the need to help get customers a taxi or to help load their car. The concierge offers directions to a product's location and sends customers to the proper aisles. All signs in the store are in English, Spanish, and Mandarin to appeal to the diverse clientele.

Home Depot is committed to pricing its products at this location at the same levels as other locations in the New York City area; however, prices will be higher than for its typical suburban locations. According to one retail analyst, "Manhattan is a bit of a different animal. Costs of occupancy and payroll are greater, and the challenges of the Manhattan landscape include traffic, the times that people shop, getting it all into the store, and getting it all out to the customers."

Questions

1. Discuss the differences in trading-area size and characteristics for a downtown versus a suburban location for Home Depot.

2. Describe how location and site selection would vary between downtown versus a suburban location for Home Depot.

3. Beyond the factors mentioned in this case, how should Home Depot adapt its Manhattan stores to the community?

4. Will Home Depot's presence in Manhattan help or hurt existing hardware and lighting stores? Explain your answer.

CASE 4: SHOPPING CENTER UNREST: THE BATTLE OVER LEASES[c-4]

Recent merger, acquisition, and reorganization activity among department store chains, as well as the expanded definition of what constitutes an anchor tenant in a shopping center, has contributed to the increased litigation between retailers and shopping center developers over what types of retailers can fill vacant shopping center space. Often, these disagreements concern reciprocal easement agreements (REAs) between anchor tenants and the developer that specify the type of retailer that can replace an anchor tenant in a shopping center.

One recent example of a major battle occurred between May Department Stores (**www.mayco.com**) and Taubman Centers (**www.taubman.com**), a leading shopping center developer, over the retailer's wish to replace a Lord & Taylor (**www.lordandtaylor.com**) store that was to be closed with a Foley's Men's and Home store. Taubman felt that May Department Stores already had a conventional Foley's department store (**www.foleys.com**) operating at the mall and that the mall would benefit more from a new Nordstrom or other higher-end retailer. Taubman was also concerned that the Foley's Men's and Home store would not attract as many of the center's core female shoppers.

This disagreement stems from how the REA defines a department and/or specialty store. According to the lawsuit, the REA states that the replacement space must "contain a number of departments for the sale of varied merchandise and services [that are] operated as a single, integrated unit." May's attorneys and senior management insisted that the

Foley's Men's and Home store fit within this definition. However, Taubman argued that the existence of the home and men's store as an anchor tenant would jeopardize the mall's positioning as a regional fashion center.

One retail consultant says "dozens and dozens" of reciprocal easement disagreements have occurred recently. As a developer notes, "The reality is, when malls expanded to six, seven, and eight anchors, the number of department stores went the other way. There aren't as many candidates to choose from."

Another issue that has prompted legal actions involves the evolving definition of an anchor store. Originally, the term was used to describe department stores, but it now includes discounters, grocery stores, theaters, and other entertainment-based retailers. In many traditional centers, Costco and Target stores have been used as replacement anchors. The center's developer sees these as traffic-generating stores that complement the offerings of traditional department stores. In contrast, the traditional department stores may see these as retailers that cheapen the image of the center, as well as providing price competition.

Still another source of conflict between anchor tenants and the mall's developer is when an anchor tenant or developer seeks to divide its store into smaller units. One recent case involved Dallas Galleria's decision to break up a former Saks Fifth Avenue location with a grouping of three Gap-owned stores after Saks Fifth Avenue moved its department store space to another location in the same mall.

Questions

1. Develop a series of arguments as to why Foley's Men's and Home store would serve as a suitable replacement for a Lord & Taylor.

2. Develop a series of arguments as to why Foley's Men's and Home store would not serve as a suitable replacement for a Lord & Taylor.

3. Discuss the pros and cons of replacing a traditional department store with a Costco or Target from the perspective of the existing anchors.

4. Describe the pros and cons of replacing a traditional department store with a Costco or Target from the perspective of the shopping center's developer.

[c-4] The material in this case is drawn from Steve McLinden, "Reciprocal Unease," *SCT* (March 2005), pp. 31–34.

part four
Comprehensive Case
Retailing in Germany*

INTRODUCTION

Until deregulation and a shakeout loosen market forces in the retail sector, Germany is likely to remain an unfulfilled opportunity for retailers. With Western Europe's largest population, the world's third-largest economy, and the sixth-largest retail market, Germany should be attractive for its size, if not strong growth. Yet, as Wal-Mart (**www.walmart. com**) has found, regulations that protect the status quo convert the market into a no-growth quagmire. That's true even when retailers take steps to compete successfully in a market unique in its affinity for squeezing suppliers, cutting prices, and pushing private labels.

The Landscape

A Weak Opportunity

Germany is the weakest retail opportunity among the large Western European countries, based on our analysis. Sluggish growth generated in part by a tough regulatory environment dampens Germany's retail prospects compared with countries such as Spain, Great Britain, and France. Germany's $367 billion retail market is smaller than the markets in France and Great Britain but larger than other Western European countries. German retail sales are expected to continue to slowly increase during the next five years. This forecast means that Germany should continue to clock the weakest increase in real sales among the large Western European countries.

Although Germany's retail market is the third biggest in Western Europe, the country's total economy ranks as the largest in the region. Overall, Germany has the third-largest economy in the world behind the United States and Japan. Germany also has the highest living standard among the large Western European nations. However, Germany's living standards are lower than most of the smaller countries in the region and well below those of the United States.

Germany's population of more than 82 million is the largest in Western Europe and the 13th largest globally. The German population is about a third larger than France's population, which is the next largest in Western Europe. Although Great Britain has the greatest population density among the biggest Western European nations, Germany's large population makes it the most population dense among those in continental Europe. Berlin is home to 3.4 million people, making it the largest city in Germany. Other major markets are Hamburg, Munich (i.e., München in German), and Cologne (i.e., Köln), which each have about 1 million people or more. The next nine largest markets each have about 500,000 to 600,000 people. Germany's population is expected to stay flat during the next five years. The population of

Germany, like Spain and Italy, is skewed a bit older than other Western European countries. Only one-fifth of the German population is under age 20, while about one-fourth exceeds 60 years old.

Germany's income distribution is somewhat more concentrated among the top 20 percent of the population compared with other large Western European nations, though it is similar to the income distribution in the United States. Forty-five percent of Germany's total income is earned by the top 20 percent of income earners.

While many European countries have benefited from strong housing markets in recent years, Germany is a notable exception. The stagnant housing market has contributed to the relatively weak pace of consumer spending in recent years, including spending for home-related merchandise.

The Struggle by Food, Drug, and Mass Market (FDM) Retailers

Germany's FDM retailers are among the largest in the world. Yet, their size has not kept them from stumbling in one of the most difficult retail markets. A weak domestic economy, price-sensitive consumers, cumbersome laws, and intense competition will likely continue to hamper growth prospects for these retailers.

Pioneers of the hard discount format, Aldi (**www.aldi. com**) and Schwarz Group's Lidl (**www.lidl.de**), find themselves victims of the beast they created. Germany's larger retailers introduced their own discount formats. Rewe's Penny (**www.rewe.de**) and Tengelmann's Plus (**www.tengel mann.com**) began to cut into the discounters' sales in 2004. So, Lidl and Aldi moved their battleground outside Germany.

Metro AG (**www.metrogroup.de**) is the largest German retailer in the world, although in Germany the company is second to Edeka Gruppe (**www.edeka.de**) in domestic sales. Metro's presence in 30 countries has helped insulate it from the weak domestic market; but at home, price pressure from discounters has cut into the sales of its supermarkets and hypermarkets.

Domestically, Metro plans to add a few stores and modernize several others. Otherwise, its focus is outside of Germany. In the past few years, Metro expanded into one or two new foreign markets each year. Today, Metro plans to concentrate on developing business in these markets. It is increasing its store network in Eastern Europe, China, Russia, and India. According to one company executive, "China has the potential to become our home market [in 20 years]."

As the largest retailer in Germany, Edeka generates 95 percent of its sales there. The firm comprises 14 cooperatives with 4,100 retailer-members. Edeka's store network encompasses nearly 9,100 outlets in five countries. In 2005, the firm continued its privatization campaign and expected to turn over control of 500 of its 2,500 stores to independent retail managers by year-end.

Hard discounter Aldi has whittled away the market shares of Germany's largest retailers over the years to become Germany's third-largest retailer and one of the largest in the world. Recently, Aldi's price and territorial war with Schwarz Group's Lidl and Germany's smaller discount chains cut into Aldi's share. Aldi has sharpened its international focus, with stores in 10 other nations. In 2004, Aldi announced a huge investment to expand its store count by as many as 200 in Great Britain.

In 2004, Wal-Mart (**www.walmartgermany.de**) marked its fifth anniversary in German retailing, but the U.S. retail giant had little to celebrate. The firm had only about 2 percent of the German food market and posted losses. German courts ordered Wal-Mart to publish its financials, which suggested that the firm's accumulated losses were in the hundreds of millions. The retailer also announced it would close several stores by spring 2005. Recently, Wal-Mart Germany has been able to benefit from the firm's worldwide procurement network. Additionally, Wal-Mart has sought to increase sales of private-label goods—namely, Cosies and Equate. Sales growth, however, won't come from new superstores.

In 2004, Wal-Mart opened a new format store in Essen. The smaller-than-average 65,000-square-foot store emphasizes displays to improve merchandise visibility and navigation. Wal-Mart also switched to its U.S.-style everyday-low-price strategy at the Essen store. And in another move, several Wal-Mart stores introduced weekly singles shopping events. Employees welcome customers with champagne and hors d'oeuvres. So far, the events have been a success.

Home Goods Retailers Face a Major Shakeout

Much of the weakness in home goods can be traced to the German housing market. Flat population growth, slow income growth, and high unemployment have dampened demand for homes and associated products. As a result, home-improvement and consumer-electronics chains, particularly those of the major German retail groups, are moving into foreign markets to drive sales. Retailers whose activities are restricted to Germany—such as small, often family-owned domestic retailers—likely will be the first targets in an upcoming wave of consolidation.

The home goods sector already has experienced the first wave of consolidation, in the furniture channel. In the past several years, Ikea's (**www.ikea.com**) dominance prompted an acquisition spree for Kreiger Group, which now runs the Hoeffner, Walther Moebel, and Moebel Kraft chains. The home-improvement sector, however, is not threatened by a single powerful retailer. It is overcrowded. Most of the major German retail groups have introduced a do-it-yourself (DIY) format that competes with family-owned chains. As such, the opportunity for organic growth, even in a better economy, is declining.

Although Tengelmann subsidiary OBI Baumarkt (**www.obi.de**) has slowed its expansion in Germany, it remains the largest home-improvement chain in the country. OBI also has outlets in 10 other countries. OBI wants to increase international sales from 30 percent to 60 percent by 2010. The retailer lists China, Greece, Hungary, and Russia as key markets. OBI also has announced plans to set up shop in Greece.

Swedish furniture retailer Ikea's symbiotic relationship with Germany keeps getting better. Accounting for 20 percent of Ikea's total sales, Germany is the retailer's largest market. With about 9 percent of the German market, Ikea is Germany's largest furniture retailer. To coincide with its 30th anniversary in Germany, Ikea cut prices there by an average 6 percent as of September 2004. The year-long promotion replaced short-term discounts. Although the new pricing strategy cost Ikea an estimated $160 million, the retailer expected to compensate for the investment by increasing sales by 25 percent. However, consumer-protection groups have criticized Ikea's pricing tactics, which they say artificially inflate prices in Germany. Ikea, they say, fools customers by focusing its discounts on cheap pieces while increasing the prices of other products.

According to U.S. retailer Staples (**www.staples.com**), it pioneered the office supply superstore concept in Europe. Staples first entered the German market in the early 1990s after it acquired Maxi-Papier, a small chain of office supply stores. Staples now has 60 locations throughout northern Germany, as well as catalog and E-commerce operations. Although the parent company is pursuing further international expansion amid a nearly saturated domestic market, Staples Germany likely won't benefit much. Of the company's three most recent acquisitions, only Austria-based Pressel Versand International GmbH has operations in Germany.

Internet Giants Push into Germany

Although mail-order catalogers still account for a larger share of retail sales (9 percent in 2003) in Germany, E-commerce sites are gaining ground. Online sales are estimated to have increased to about $6.8 billion in 2004, about 2 percent of retail sales. The largest and best-known Web sites—eBay (**www.ebay.de**), Amazon (**www.amazon.de**), Quelle (**www.quelle.com**), Tchibo (**www.tchibo.com**), and Otto (**www.otto.de**)—have captured the largest share of sales and are attracting the most new customers. Drawn by their success, other foreign retailers such as Pricerunner.com (**www.pricerunner.com**) have launched operations in Germany.

Although 15.7 million German customers (nearly one-fifth of the population) know the way to use eBay, not all like the online auctioneer and retailer's policies. The top civil court in Germany ruled in late 2004 that buyers must be able to return goods purchased from professional traders within two weeks without giving any reason. (The ruling does not apply to direct sales between individual buyers and sellers.) Still, enough customers found good deals on the Web site to boost eBay's gross merchandise sales in the third quarter of 2004 by 39 percent year-over-year to $1.7 billion. The firm continues to introduce new product lines. It also partnered with Deutsche Post to offer an auction service that is accessible even to those without computers. Customers can drop off objects for sale to one of 12 Berlin post offices. The items are then shipped to a logistics center for expert evaluation before each is made available on the Internet. The service costs 11.50 euros plus a 20 percent commission on the sale.

With estimated book sales of $520 million in 2003, Amazon.de overtook its German competitors. In 2004, Amazon.de moved beyond basic bookseller. Though it still lags the U.S. site's breadth of offerings, Amazon.de has added toys, consumer electronics, and most recently a home-and-garden section. Also in 2004, the firm's problems with publishers came to a head. Amazon.de de-listed all of the titles from the independent Swiss publishing house and top German-language publisher Diogenes after a price dispute.

Looking Forward

Shakeout Affects Retailers Large and Small

A persisting weak retail environment and an often weak response to competitive pressures will contribute to ongoing consolidation across all retail sectors in Germany. Regulatory protections should slow the shakeout, but the shakeout will eventually reverberate through some of the country's largest retailers and across many retail sectors. The shakeout should be most notable for the large food and department store retailers that are particularly vulnerable. And it will be notable for the opportunities it may provide Wal-Mart to bolster, if not fix, its undersized German operations.

The shakeout among FDM retailers in Germany is likely to come at the expense of some big players such as Edeka and Rewe and some notable smaller players such as Spar (**www.spar.de**). With Metro also ceding ground to the discounters, led by Aldi and Lidl, the environment will not necessarily benefit Metro. Wal-Mart, however, could encounter opportunities to bolster its prospects, particularly if Metro wavers in the face of the difficult domestic landscape.

The outlook also favors drugstores at the expense of standalone pharmacies in Germany. Recent legislation has opened up sales of prescription and over-the-counter drugs—previously limited only to pharmacies—to drugstores, which had been limited primarily to health-and-beauty categories. At the same time, competition is being fanned by a court decision in 2003 to relax pricing restrictions that, among other things, mandated minimum retail margins.

The soft goods sector in Germany faces an ongoing shakeout across an array of retailers. The fallout has already been evident among the smallest players, but the key question may be which of the big department store players, Karstadt (**www.karstadt.de**) or Kaufhof (**www.kaufhof.de**), is more vulnerable. The woes of the department stores reflect weakness in the middle market that is also felt by apparel stores. The Gap (**www.gap.com**) has already left the market. Karstadt's decision to move its department stores downmarket will prove to be a pivotal and perhaps fatal move. Kaufhof 's decision to move its stores upmarket is equally pivotal but may give the firm greater opportunity to differentiate itself.

In the home goods sector, while Ikea's continued success continues to splinter the otherwise fragmented furniture sector, another force for shakeout in the sector comes from expansion of hard discounters into home goods categories. Tengelmann may already be at a disadvantage with its recent decision to abandon its discount strategy in favor of customer service. And its network of franchised stores makes it more difficult to carry out a uniform response to competitors' challenges. Metro has weathered the stepped-up competition but continues to give mixed signals about its commitment to its DIY format. Ikea's continued success amid stagnant demand in Germany is evident in the struggles of competitors.

The Slow Pace of Deregulation

The growth in the German retail market will be affected by the degree to which Germany deregulates its markets in the coming years. Although some steps have been taken and Chancellor Gerhard Schröder has vowed to modernize the German economy, change can be expected to continue at a slow pace.

Retailers and suppliers in Germany have been constrained by at least four major strands of regulation: mandated union representation on corporate boards, restricted store hours, constrained pricing flexibility, and limits on big-box retail construction. Limited liberalization has occurred on some of these fronts, and the government likely will continue to pursue modest reform of some of the more archaic regulations. The impact of those reforms may be limited unless mandatory union representation on boards is overhauled.

German law entitles workers and union representatives to half the seats on the supervisory boards of big corporations. It gives labor unprecedented power and undermines corporate management. The result is that executives can be unduly influenced by labor, on whom they depend for their positions. The law also serves to stanch the flow of foreign investment in the country because foreign companies taking over German businesses must adopt the union governance structure. Despite the competitive disadvantage and increasing backlash it is creating for Germany, co-determination is likely to stay in some form. As recently as late 2004, the chancellor defended the necessity of co-determination to protect workers' rights.

Restrictions on store hours were liberalized somewhat in 2003. The government extended store hours on Saturdays by four hours from 6 A.M. to 8 P.M. instead of 4 P.M. Stores remain closed on Sundays and open from 6 A.M. to 8 P.M. on weekdays. In response to union demands, workers receive up to 50 percent more money for working longer hours on Saturday. (Workers already were receiving a 20 percent bonus for shifts on weekday evenings and Saturday afternoons.) The longer hours are not enough for retailers and some government officials, including Minister for Economic Affairs Wolfgang Clement, who continue to campaign for the abolition of restrictions on shop opening hours on weekdays.

The Unfair Competition Law includes many of Germany's pricing regulations. It prohibits businesses "with superior market power in relation to small and medium-sized competitors" from pricing below cost, except when such pricing occurs only "occasionally" and there is an "objective justification" for it. The below-cost pricing constraint has been a particular thorn in Wal-Mart's side. It has been blocked from undertaking promotions common in the United States. As much as Wal-Mart and some other retailers might like a repeal of the below-cost pricing regulation, there appears to be little momentum in that direction. Instead, in 2001, a prohibition on loyalty clubs was repealed.

There appears to be little momentum to liberalize land-use regulation that limits big-box retailing and promotes small formats. Originally intended to protect middle-size retail, the regulations on land use have instead fed the rise of hard discounters. In most urban areas, regulations limit shops to a maximum area of about 13,000 square feet, with a maximum sales area of 7,500 square feet. Getting the approvals to build big-box stores or shopping centers has been known to take 5 to 10 years in Germany.

Questions

1. What are the pros and cons of a U.S. retailer opening a store in Germany?

2. Describe the criteria you used in answering Question 1.
3. How could a U.S. retailer become a destination store in Germany?
4. What Internet sources are available for you to learn more about population demographics in Germany?
5. Are the heavy amount of business regulations good or bad for domestic German retailers? Explain your answer.
6. Are the heavy amount of business regulations good or bad for German shoppers? Explain your answer.
7. As a U.S. retailer in Germany, would you prefer a short-term lease or a long-term lease? Cover the pros and cons of each lease length in your answer.

*The material in this case is adapted by the authors from *Strategic Focus: Retailing in Germany* (Columbus, OH: Retail Forward, January 2005). Reprinted by permission of Retail Forward, Inc. (**www.retailforward.com**).

Chapter 11

RETAIL ORGANIZATION AND HUMAN RESOURCE MANAGEMENT

James Nordstrom and Carl Wallin opened their first Wallin & Nordstrom shoe store in downtown Seattle in 1901. Today, Nordstrom (**www. nordstrom. com**) has evolved into a retailing powerhouse with nearly $8 billion in annual sales. The company operates about 95 department stores, 50 Nordstrom Rack outlet stores, and 35 Façonnable boutiques (mainly in Europe), as well as freestanding shoe stores and a

Reprinted by permission.

clearance store. In addition, Nordstrom has an online presence and serves customers through its direct mail catalogs.

Nordstrom began to overhaul its information technology infrastructure in 2001 with upgraded POS solutions, a perpetual inventory system, and a markdown optimization model. According to one report, Nordstrom invested $350 million on technology from 2001 to 2004. The new POS system reduced transaction times and enables Nordstrom to process debit cards and to print gift receipts. Its perpetual inventory system enabled Nordstrom to more easily identify both slow-selling and fast-selling items, as well as to get "the right goods to the right stores." Its markdown software allows Nordstrom to better plan the amount and the timing of markdowns.

Nordstrom attributes these three systems for much of the improvement in its sales and profit performance. Nordstrom's sales per square foot have increased by 10 percent since 2001. Its sales-per-square-foot performance is the second-highest productivity among all department stores. Nordstrom also has increased its gross margins by three percentage points since 2001 and substantially increased its earnings before taxes.[1]

chapter objectives

1. To study the procedures involved in setting up a retail organization
2. To examine the various organizational arrangements utilized in retailing
3. To consider the special human resource environment of retailing
4. To describe the principles and practices involved with the human resource management process in retailing

OVERVIEW

Managing a retail business comprises three steps: setting up an organization structure, hiring and managing personnel, and managing operations—financially and nonfinancially. In this chapter, the first two steps are covered. Chapters 12 and 13 deal with operations management.

SETTING UP A RETAIL ORGANIZATION

Through a **retail organization**, a firm structures and assigns tasks (functions), policies, resources, authority, responsibilities, and rewards to efficiently and effectively satisfy the needs of its target market, employees, and management. Figure 11-1 shows various needs that should be taken into account when planning and assessing an organization structure.

As a rule, a firm cannot survive unless its organization structure satisfies the target market, regardless of how well employee and management needs are met. A structure that reduces costs through centralized buying but that results in the firm's being insensitive to geographic differences in customer preferences would

FIGURE 11-1
Selected Factors That Must Be Considered in Planning and Assessing a Retail Organization

TARGET MARKET NEEDS
Are there sufficient personnel to provide appropriate customer service?
Are personnel knowledgeable and courteous?
Are store facilities well maintained?
Are the specific needs of branch store customers met?
Are changing needs promptly addressed?

EMPLOYEE NEEDS
Are positions challenging and satisfying enough?
Is there an orderly promotion program from within?
Is the employee able to participate in the decision making?
Are the channels of communication clear and open?
Is the authority-responsibility relationship clear?
Is each employee treated fairly?
Is good performance rewarded?

MANAGEMENT NEEDS
Is it relatively easy to obtain and retain competent personnel?
Are personnel procedures clearly defined?
Does each worker report to only one supervisor?
Can each manager properly supervise all of the workers reporting to him or her?
Do operating departments have adequate staff support (e.g., marketing research)?
Are the levels of organization properly developed?
Are the organization's plans well integrated?
Are employees motivated?
Is absenteeism low?
Is there a system to replace personnel in an orderly manner?
Is there enough flexibility to adapt to changes in customers or the environment?

FIGURE 11-2
The Process of Organizing
a Retail Firm

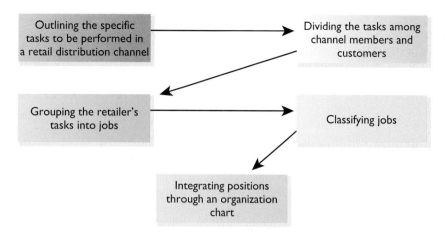

be improper. Although many retailers do similar tasks or functions (buying, pricing, displaying, and wrapping merchandise), there are many ways of organizing to perform these functions. The process of setting up a retail organization is outlined in Figure 11-2 and described next. Visit our Web site (**www.prenhall.com/ bermanevans**) for a variety of links on running a retail business.

Specifying Tasks to Be Performed

The tasks in a distribution channel must be enumerated, and then keyed to the chosen strategy mix, for effective retailing to occur:

- Buying merchandise for the retailer.
- Shipping merchandise to the retailer.
- Receiving merchandise and checking incoming shipments.
- Setting prices.
- Marking merchandise.
- Inventory storage and control.
- Preparing merchandise and window displays.
- Facilities maintenance (e.g., keeping the store clean).
- Customer research and exchanging information.
- Customer contact (e.g., advertising, personal selling).
- Facilitating shopping (e.g., convenient site, short checkout lines).
- Customer follow-up and complaint handling.
- Personnel management.
- Repairs and alteration of merchandise.
- Billing customers.
- Handling receipts and financial records.
- Credit operations.
- Gift wrapping.
- Delivery to customers.
- Returning unsold or damaged merchandise to vendors.
- Sales forecasting and budgeting.
- Coordination.

FIGURE 11-3
The Division of Tasks in a Distribution Channel

Performer	Tasks
Retailer	Can perform all or some of the tasks in the distribution channel, from buying merchandise to coordination.
Manufacturer or Wholesaler	Can take care of few or many functions, such as shipping, marking merchandise, inventory storage, displays, research, etc.
Specialist(s)	Can undertake a particular task: buying office, delivery firm, warehouse, marketing research firm, ad agency, accountant, credit bureau, computer service firm.
Consumer	Can be responsible for delivery, credit (cash purchases), sales effort (self-service), product alterations (do-it-yourselfers), etc.

Dividing Tasks Among Channel Members and Customers

Sysco is a wholesaler serving more than 400,000 restaurants, hotels, schools, and other locales. It offers them a wide range of support services (www.sysco.com/services/services.html).

Although the preceding tasks are typically performed in a distribution channel, they do not have to be done by a retailer. Some can be completed by the manufacturer, wholesaler, specialist, or consumer. Figure 11-3 shows the types of activities that could be carried out by each party. Following are some criteria to consider in allocating the functions related to consumer credit.

A task should be carried out only if desired by the target market. For some retailers, liberal credit policies may provide significant advantages over competitors. For others, a cash-only policy may reduce their overhead and lead to lower prices.

A task should be done by the party with the best competence. Credit collection may require a legal staff and computerized records—most affordable by medium or large retailers. Smaller retailers are likely to rely on bank credit cards. There is a loss of control when an activity is delegated to another party. A credit collection agency, pressing for past-due payments, may antagonize customers.

The retailer's institutional framework can have an impact on task allocation. Franchisees are readily able to get together to have their own private-label brands. Independents cannot do this as easily.

Task allocation depends on the savings gained by sharing or shifting tasks. The credit function is better performed by an outside credit bureau if it has expert personnel and ongoing access to financial data, uses tailored computer software, pays lower rent (due to an out-of-the-way site), and so on. Many retailers cannot attain these savings themselves.

This site (http://retailindustry.about.com/od/retailcareersand training) highlights the range of jobs available in retailing.

Grouping Tasks into Jobs

After the retailer decides which tasks to perform, they are grouped into jobs. The jobs must be clearly structured. Here are examples of grouping tasks into jobs:

Tasks	Jobs
Displaying merchandise, customer contact, gift wrapping, customer follow-up	Sales personnel
Entering transaction data, handling cash and credit purchases, gift wrapping	Cashier(s)
Receiving merchandise, checking incoming shipments, marking merchandise, inventory storage and control, returning merchandise to vendors	Inventory personnel
Window dressing, interior display setups, use of mobile displays	Display personnel
Billing customers, credit operations, customer research	Credit personnel
Merchandise repairs and alterations, resolution of complaints, customer research	Customer service personnel
Cleaning store, replacing old fixtures	Janitorial personnel
Employee management, sales forecasting, budgeting, pricing, coordinating tasks	Management personnel

While grouping tasks into jobs, specialization should be considered, so each employee is responsible for a limited range of functions (as opposed to performing many diverse functions). Specialization has the advantages of clearly defined tasks, greater expertise, reduced training, and hiring people with narrow education and experience. Problems can result due to extreme specialization: poor morale (boredom), people not being aware of their jobs' importance, and the need for more employees. Specialization means assigning explicit duties to individuals so a job position encompasses a homogeneous cluster of tasks.

Once tasks are grouped, job descriptions are constructed. These outline the job titles, objectives, duties, and responsibilities for every position. They are used as a hiring, supervision, and evaluation tool. Figure 11-4 contains a job description for a store manager.

Careers in RETAILING
Is Retail for Me? Human Resources

Human resources is the people side, the legal side, and the detail side of retail. Recruiting and hiring employees are the most obvious parts. But retail careers in human resources also include a wealth of other responsibilities such as training, designing training programs, overseeing compensation and benefits, and planning for and ensuring legal compliance in hiring and employment practices.

- *Head of Human Resources (HR):* Top HR job, responsible for policies in employment, employee relations, wages and benefits, orientation and training, safety and health, and employee services.
- *Compensation and Benefits Manager:* Responsible for plan design recommendations, legal compliance, and administration of both the compensation and employee benefits programs.
- *Benefits Manager:* Responsible for plan design recommendations, legal compliance, and administration of the employee benefits programs.

- *Compensation Manager:* Responsible for plan design recommendations, legal compliance, and administration of the compensation programs.
- *Head of Training and Development:* Responsible for training and development of associates through the creation and management of training programs and the effective communication of information.
- *HR Generalist: Home Office Staff:* Typically responsible for employee relations, recruiting/outplacement, and answering routine employee questions on benefits and HR policies in general, perhaps for specified job levels or operating groups.
- *HR Generalist: Regional or In-Store:* Typically responsible for employee relations, training, recruiting/outplacement, and answering routine questions on benefits and HR policies for a geographic group of stores. Typically reports to store operations management.

Source: Reprinted by permission of the National Retail Federation.

FIGURE 11-4
A Job Description for a Store
Manager

JOB TITLE: Store Manager for 34th Street Branch of Pombo's Department Stores

POSITION REPORTS TO: Senior Vice-President

POSITIONS REPORTING TO STORE MANAGER: All personnel in the 34th Street store

OBJECTIVES: To properly staff and operate the 34th Street store

DUTIES AND RESPONSIBILITIES:
- Sales forecasting and budgeting
- Personnel recruitment, selection, training, motivation, and evaluation
- Merchandise display, inventory management, and merchandise reorders
- Transferring merchandise among stores
- Handling store receipts, preparing bank transactions, opening and closing store
- Reviewing customer complaints
- Reviewing computer data forms
- Semiannual review of overall operations and reports for top management

COMMITTEES AND MEETINGS:
- Attendance at monthly meetings with Senior Vice-President
- Supervision of weekly meetings with department managers

Classifying Jobs

Jobs are then broadly grouped into functional, product, geographic, or combination classifications. *Functional classification* divides jobs by task—such as sales promotion, buying, and store operations. Expert knowledge is utilized. *Product classification* divides jobs on a goods or service basis. A department store hires different personnel for clothing, furniture, appliances, and so forth. This classification recognizes the differences in personnel requirements for different products.

Geographic classification is useful for chains operating in different areas. Employees are adapted to local conditions, and they are supervised by branch managers. Some firms, especially larger ones, use a *combination classification*. If a branch unit of a chain hires its selling staff, but buying personnel for each product line are hired by headquarters, the functional, product, and geographic formats are combined.

Developing an Organization Chart

The format of a retail organization must be designed in an integrated, coordinated way. Jobs must be defined and distinct; yet, interrelationships among positions must be clear. As eBay's chief executive recently noted,

> I think at all good companies, employees are excited by the mission of the company. And at eBay, the mission is about creating this global online marketplace where your next-door neighbor's chance of success is equal to a large corporation's. We look for people who are energized by the mission of the company. Once they're here, we want to make sure that they have a chance to understand the company in a really deep way. I said to our head of strategy when he came to work for us: "Don't do anything for three months. Just absorb, understand, get the counterintuitive nature of the business." We give people a chance to settle in, and then we make sure that they are well managed, that they are focused on high-impact projects, and that they understand the results that they are going to be accountable for.[2]

The **hierarchy of authority** outlines the job interactions within a company by describing the reporting relationships among employees (from the lowest level to

TABLE 11-1	Principles for Organizing a Retail Firm

An organization should show interest in its employees. Job rotation, promotion from within, participatory management, recognition, job enrichment, and so forth improve worker morale.

Employee turnover, lateness, and absenteeism should be monitored, as they may indicate personnel problems.

The line of authority should be traceable from the highest to the lowest positions. In this way, employees know to whom they report and who reports to them (*chain of command*).

A subordinate should only report to one direct supervisor (*unity of command*). This avoids the problem of workers receiving conflicting orders.

There is a limit to the number of employees a manager can directly supervise (*span of control*).

A person responsible for a given objective needs the power to achieve it.

Although a supervisor can delegate authority, he or she is still responsible for subordinates.

The greater the number of organizational levels, the longer the time for communication to travel and the greater the coordination problems.

An organization has an informal structure aside from the formal organization chart. Informal relationships exercise power in the organization and may bypass formal relationships and procedures.

the highest level). Coordination and control are provided by this hierarchy. A firm with many workers reporting to one manager has a *flat organization*. Its benefits are good communication, quicker handling of problems, and better employee identification with a job. The major problem tends to be the number of people reporting to one manager. A *tall organization* has several management levels, resulting in close supervision and fewer workers reporting to each manager. Problems include a long channel of communication, the impersonal impression given to workers regarding access to upper-level personnel, and inflexible rules.

With these factors in mind, a retailer devises an **organization chart**, which graphically displays its hierarchical relationships. Table 11-1 lists the principles to consider in establishing an organization chart. Figure 11-5 shows examples of organization charts.

ORGANIZATIONAL PATTERNS IN RETAILING

An independent retailer has a simple organization. It operates only one store, the owner-manager usually supervises all employees, and workers have access to the owner-manager if there are problems. In contrast, a chain must specify how tasks are delegated, coordinate multiple stores, and set common policies for employees. The organizational arrangements used by independent retailers, department stores, chain retailers, and diversified retailers are discussed next.

Organizational Arrangements Used by Small Independent Retailers

Small independents use uncomplicated arrangements with only two or three levels of personnel (owner-manager and employees), and the owner-manager personally runs the firm and oversees workers. There are few employees, little specialization, and no branch units. This does not mean fewer activities must be

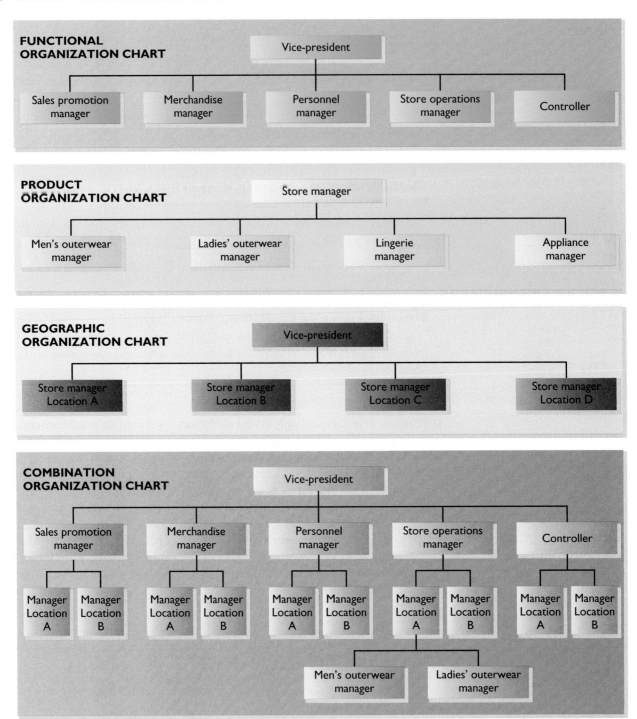

FIGURE 11-5
Different Forms of Retail Organization

performed but that many tasks are performed relative to the number of workers. Each employee must allot part of his or her time to several duties.

Figure 11-6 shows the organizations of two small firms. In A, a boutique is organized by function. Merchandising personnel buy and sell goods and services, plan assortments, set up displays, and prepare ads. Operations personnel are involved with store maintenance and operations. In B, a furniture store is organized on a product-oriented basis, with personnel in each category responsible for selected activities. All products get proper attention, and some expertise is

FIGURE 11-6
Organization Structures
Used by Small Independents

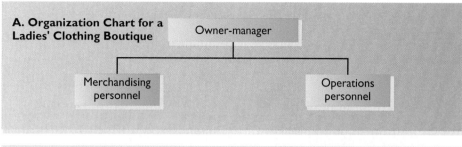

A. Organization Chart for a Ladies' Clothing Boutique
Owner-manager
Merchandising personnel
Operations personnel

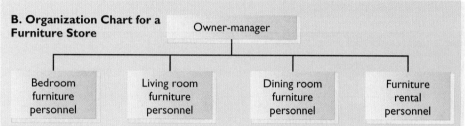

B. Organization Chart for a Furniture Store
Owner-manager
Bedroom furniture personnel
Living room furniture personnel
Dining room furniture personnel
Furniture rental personnel

developed. This is important since different skills are necessary to buy and sell each type of furniture.

Organizational Arrangements Used by Department Stores

Many department stores continue to use organizational arrangements that are a modification of the **Mazur plan**, which divides all retail activities into four functional areas—merchandising, publicity, store management, and accounting and control:

1. Merchandising—buying, selling, stock planning and control, promotion planning.
2. Publicity—window and interior displays, advertising, planning and executing promotional events (along with merchandise managers), advertising research, public relations.
3. Store management—merchandise care, customer services, buying store supplies and equipment, maintenance, operating activities (such as receiving and delivering products), store and merchandise protection (insurance and security), employee training and compensation, workroom operations.
4. Accounting and control—credit and collections, expense budgeting and control, inventory planning and control, recordkeeping.[3]

These areas are organized by *line* (direct authority and responsibility) and *staff* (advisory and support) components. Thus, a controller and a publicity manager provide staff services to merchandisers, but within their disciplines, personnel are organized on a line basis. Figure 11-7 illustrates the Mazur plan.

The merchandising division is responsible for buying and selling. It is headed by a merchandising manager, who is often viewed as the most important area executive. He or she supervises buyers, devises financial controls for each department, coordinates merchandise plans (so there is a consistent image among departments), and interprets the effects of economic data. In some cases, divisional merchandise managers are utilized, so the number of buyers reporting to a single manager does not become unwieldy.

The buyer, in the basic Mazur plan, has complete accountability for expenses and profit goals within a department. Duties include preparing preliminary budgets, studying trends, negotiating with vendors over price, planning the number

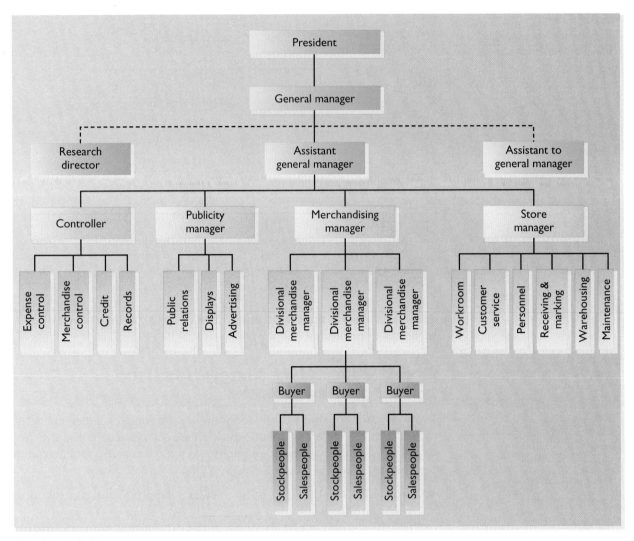

FIGURE 11-7

The Basic Mazur Organization Plan for Department Stores

Source: Adapted from Paul Mazur, *Principles of Organization Applied to Modern Retailing* (New York: Harper & Brothers, 1927), frontispiece. Reprinted by permission.

of salespeople, and informing sales personnel about the merchandise purchased. Grouping buying and selling activities into one job (buyer) may present a problem. Since buyers are not constantly on the selling floor, training, scheduling, and supervising personnel may suffer.

The growth of branch stores has led to three Mazur plan derivatives: *main store control*, by which headquarters executives oversee and operate branches; *separate store organization*, by which each branch has its own buying responsibilities; and **equal store organization**, by which buying is centralized and branches become sales units with equal operational status. The latter is the most popular format.

In the main store control format, most authority remains at headquarters. Merchandise planning and buying, advertising, financial controls, store hours, and other tasks are centrally managed to standardize the performance. Branch store managers hire and supervise employees, but daily operations conform to company policies. This works well if there are few branches and the preferences of their customers are similar to those at the main store. As branch stores increase, buyers, the advertising director, and others may be overworked and give little attention to branches. Since headquarters personnel are not at the branches, differences in customer preferences may be overlooked.

The separate store format places merchandise managers in branch stores, which have autonomy for merchandising and operations. Customer needs are quickly noted, but duplication of tasks is possible. Coordination can also be a problem. Transferring goods between branches is more complex and costly. This format is best if stores are large, branches are dispersed, or local customer tastes vary widely.

In the equal store format, the benefits of both centralization and decentralization are sought. Buying—forecasting, planning, purchasing, pricing, distribution to branches, and promotion—is centralized. Selling—presenting merchandise, selling, customer services, and operations—is managed locally. All stores, including headquarters, are treated alike. Buyers are freed from managing so many workers. Data gathering is critical since buyers have less customer contact.

Organizational Arrangements Used by Chain Retailers

Various chain retailers use a version of the equal store organization, as depicted in Figure 11-8. Although chains' organizations may differ, they generally have these attributes:

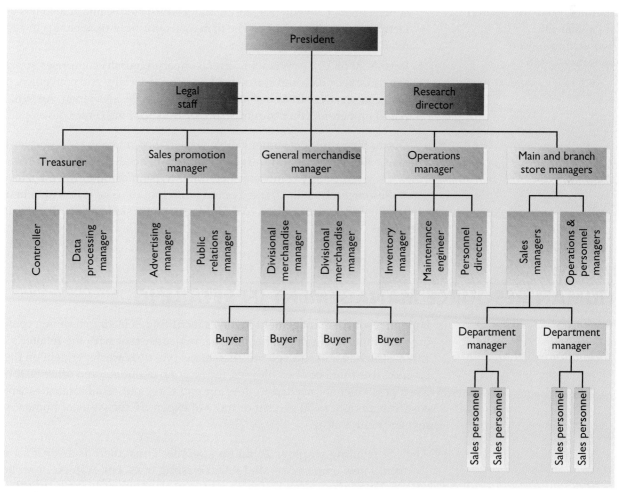

FIGURE 11-8
The Equal Store Organizational Format Used by Many Chain Stores

- There are many functional divisions, such as sales promotion, merchandise management, distribution, operations, real-estate, personnel, and information systems.
- Overall authority is centralized. Store managers have selling responsibility.
- Many operations are standardized (fixtures, store layout, building design, merchandise lines, credit policy, and store service).
- An elaborate control system keeps management informed.
- Some decentralization lets branches adapt to localities and increases store manager responsibility. Though large chains standardize most of the items their outlets carry, store managers often fine-tune the rest of the strategy mix for the local market. This is empowerment at the store manager level.

Organizational Arrangements Used by Diversified Retailers

A **diversified retailer** is a multi-line firm operating under central ownership. Like other chains, a diversified retailer operates multiple stores; unlike typical chains, a diversified firm is involved with different types of retail operations. Here are two examples:

To discover how Kroger operates, go to this section of its Web site (**www.kroger.com/ operations.htm**).

- Kroger Co. (**www.kroger.com**) operates supermarkets, warehouse stores, supercenters, convenience stores, and jewelry stores; and it also has a manufacturing operations group. The firm owns multiple store chains in each of its retail categories. See Figure 11-9.
- Japan's Aeon Co. (**www.aeon.info/aeoncorp/english**) comprises superstores, supermarkets, discount stores, home centers, specialty and convenience stores, financial services stores, restaurants, and more. Besides Japan, Aeon has facilities in numerous other countries. It is also a shopping center developer.

Due to their multiple strategy mixes, diversified retailers face complex organizational considerations. Interdivision control is needed, with operating procedures and goals clearly communicated. Interdivision competition must be coordinated. Resources must be divided among different divisions. Potential image and advertising conflicts must be avoided. Management skills must adapt to different operations.

HUMAN RESOURCE MANAGEMENT IN RETAILING

Human resource management involves recruiting, selecting, training, compensating, and supervising personnel in a manner consistent with the retailer's organization structure and strategy mix. Personnel practices are dependent on the line of business, the number of employees, the location of outlets, and other factors. Since good personnel are needed to develop and carry out retail strategies, and labor costs can amount to 50 percent or more of expenses, the value of human resource management is clear:

- U.S. retailing employs 25 million people. Thus, there is a constant need to attract new employees—and retain existing ones. For example, 2 million fast-food workers are aged 16 to 20, and they stay in their jobs for only short periods. In general, retailers need to reduce the turnover rate; when workers quickly exit a firm, the results can be disastrous. See Table 11-2.

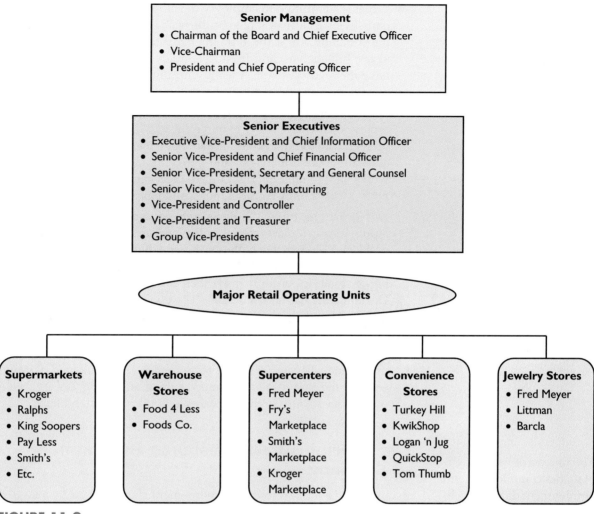

FIGURE 11-9

The Organizational Structure of Kroger Co. (Selected Store Chains and Positions)

Source: Compiled by the authors from the *Kroger Co. 2005 Annual Report.*

TABLE 11-2	The True Cost of Employee Turnover

Costs of using fill-in employees until permanent replacements are found.

Severance pay for exiting employees.

Costs of hiring new employees: advertising, interviewing time, travel expenses, testing, screening.

Training costs: trainers, training materials and technology, trainee compensation, supervisor time (on-the-job training).

Costs of mistakes and lower productivity while new employees gain experience.

Customer dissatisfaction due to the departure of previous employees and the use of inexperienced workers.

Loss of continuity among co-workers.

Poor employee morale when turnover is high.

Lower employee loyalty to retailer when turnover is high.

Pizzeria Uno
(**www.pizzeriauno.com/
employ.html**) has a clear
employee development
plan.

- Target is committed to employee development and retention: "We are a company living a clear vision: to be the best. In everything we do. In every area of the company. We want to be the favorite place to shop. A place with clean aisles, full shelves, and friendly employees. To achieve all of this, we must have the greatest team. A team with unique experiences and differences as people. A team where people bring their personal best every day."[4]

- Pizzeria Uno regularly recruits college graduates for its management training program: "If you're ready to move ahead with a dynamic national chain, team up with Uno today. Each restaurant has a team made up of a general manager, assistant general manager, and 1 to 3 managers. In building this team, Uno works hard to offer the right mix to meet career aspirations, training opportunities, work/family considerations, and pay and benefits expectations."[5]

- At Nordstrom, buying is decentralized and salespeople have considerable input. They can place special orders and are empowered to resolve customer problems: "Taking care of the customer at Nordstrom is our number one priority. It's all about people. People who have the freedom to make spot decisions—big or small—in order to grow their business and make the customer happy. Our company has only one rule—'Use good judgment in all situations.'"[6]

- In *Fortune's* annual "The 100 Best Companies to Work For" listing, retailers usually account for at least 20 of these companies. In 2005, Wegmans Food Markets was rated first: "Salaries aren't the whole story. The company has shelled out $54 million for college scholarships to more than 17,500 full- and part-time employees over the past 20 years. It thinks nothing of sending, say, its cheese manager on a 10-day sojourn to cheesemakers in London, Paris, and Italy."[7]

The Special Human Resource Environment of Retailing

The Bureau of Labor
Statistics compiles current
employment data on such
jobs as retail sales worker
supervisors and managers
(**www.bls.gov/oco**).

Retailers face a human resource environment characterized by a large number of inexperienced workers, long hours, highly visible employees, a diverse workforce, many part-time workers, and variable customer demand. These factors complicate employee hiring, staffing, and supervision.

Ethics in
RETAILING   How Retailers Can Succeed by Doing the Right Thing

Costco (**www.costco.com**), The Container Store (**www.containerstore.com**), Starbucks (**www.starbucks.com**), and Ikea (**www.ikea.com**) are just a few of the retailers that believe treating their employees well is good business. Among the common advantages of providing employees with fair wages, as well as healthcare benefits, are: lower employee turnover, lower costs associated with hiring and firing (such as reduced advertising, lower training costs for new employees, and lower severance costs), as well as a positive corporate culture that is related to employee satisfaction. Some retail analysts feel that reduced employee turnover translates into labor savings of 20 percent.

Ikea, for example, now provides healthcare packages to its part-time workers. At Ikea, employee benefits include full medical/dental insurance for those who work 20 or more hours per week, a fully paid health plan for domestic partners and children, paid maternity/paternity leave, tuition assistance, profit sharing, and flexible work alternatives (including job sharing and telecommuting).

Home Depot (**www.homedepot.com**), McDonald's (**www.mcdonalds.com**), and Sears (**www.sears.com**) have recently joined a group of 45 major firms that are attempting to offer lower-cost health coverage for their uninsured employees (including part-time workers).

Sources: Susan Reda, "Nice Guys Finish First," *Stores* (June 2004); and Stephanie Clifford, "Because Who Knew a Big-Box Chain Could Have a Generous Soul?" *Inc.* (April 2005), p. 88.

The need for a large retail labor force often means hiring those with little or no prior experience. Sometimes a position in retailing represents a person's first "real job." People are attracted to retailing because they find jobs near to home; and retail positions (such as cashiers, stock clerks, and some types of sales personnel) may require limited education, training, and skill. Also, the low wages paid for some positions result in the hiring of inexperienced people. Thus, high employee turnover and cases of poor performance, lateness, and absenteeism may result.

The long working hours in retailing, which may include weekends, turn off certain prospective employees; and many retailers now have longer hours since more shoppers want to shop during evenings and weekends. Accordingly, some retailers require at least two shifts of full-time employees.

Retailing employees are highly visible to the customer. Therefore, when personnel are selected and trained, special care must be taken with regard to their manners and appearance. Some small retailers do not place enough emphasis on employee appearance (neat grooming and appropriate attire).

It is common for retailers to have a diverse labor force, with regard to age, work experience, gender, race, and other factors. This means that firms must train and supervise their workers so that they interact well with one another—and are sensitive to the perspectives and needs of one another. Consider the employee strategy of Home Depot. The firm has "forged hiring partnerships with the U.S. military, AARP (American Association of Retired Persons), and several leading Hispanic organizations, creating a pipeline of skilled associates to meet the diverse communities that Home Depot serves."[8]

Due to their long hours, retailers regularly hire part-time workers. In many supermarkets, over half the workers are part-time, and problems can arise. Some part-time employees are more lackadaisical, late, absent, or likely to quit than full-time employees. They must be closely monitored.

Variations in customer demand by day, time period, or season may cause difficulties. In the United States, 40 percent of shoppers make their major supermarket trips on Saturday or Sunday. So, how many employees should there be on Monday through Friday and how many on Saturday and Sunday? Demand differences by day part (morning, afternoon, evening) and by season (fall, holidays) also affect planning. When stores are very busy, even administrative and clerical employees may be needed on the sales floor.

As a rule, retailers should consider these points:

- Recruitment and selection procedures must efficiently generate sufficient applicants.
- Some training must be short because workers are inexperienced and temporary.
- Compensation must be perceived as "fair" by employees.
- Advancement opportunities must be available to employees who view retailing as a career.
- Employee appearance and work habits must be explained and reviewed.
- Diverse workers must be taught to work together well and amicably.
- Morale problems may result from high turnover and the many part-time workers.
- Full- and part-time workers may conflict, especially if some full-timers are replaced.

Various retail career opportunities are available to women and minorities. There is still some room for improvement.

Women in Retailing

Retailing has made a lot of progress in career advancement for women. These retailers are among the top U.S. public companies in the percentage of women who are corporate officers: Avon, Nordstrom, Target Corporation, Foot Locker, and BJ's Wholesale Club. Restaurateurs such as Carlson, Starbucks, Advantica, and IHOP typically have at least 30 percent of their corporate officers who are women. The female:male mix for managerial jobs in the lodging and food service sectors is nearly 50 percent. More than two-thirds of supervisors at eating and drinking establishments are women. Ikea, Marriott, Sears, Target, and other retailers have been rated as excellent companies for working mothers.

As part of her legacy, Mary Kay Ash left behind a charitable foundation (www.mkacf.org).

Women have more career options in retailing than ever before, as the following examples show. Mary Kay Ash (Mary Kay cosmetics), Debbi Fields (Mrs. Fields Cookies), and Lillian Vernon (the direct marketer) founded retailing empires. At Avon, Andrea Jung, the chairman and chief executive, is an Asian-American woman, and 50 percent of its board of directors are women. Since 1998, the president and chief executive officer at eBay has been Meg Whitman:

> Among Ms. Whitman's many accolades, *Time* named her one of the world's 100 most influential people in 2004 and 2005; *Fortune* ranked her one of the 25 most powerful people in business and the most powerful woman in American business in 2004; *Worth* ranked her number one on its 2002 list of best CEOs; and *Business Week* has included her on its list of the 25 most powerful business managers annually since 2000. Prior to eBay, Ms. Whitman was general manager of Hasbro's Preschool Division. From 1995 to 1997, she was president and chief executive officer of Florists Transworld Delivery (FTD). Before that, Whitman served as president of the Stride Rite Corporation's Stride Rite Division. Ms. Whitman spent 1989 to 1992 at the Walt Disney Company. She also worked for eight years at Bain & Company. Ms. Whitman began her career at Procter & Gamble, where she worked in brand management from 1979 to 1981.[9]

Rite Aid's president and chief executive officer is Mary Sammons. She assumed her current position in 2003, after joining Rite Aid in late 1999 as president and chief operating officer:

> Before joining Rite Aid, Ms. Sammons was President and Chief Executive Officer of Fred Meyer Stores, a food, drug, and general merchandise retailer in the Pacific Northwest and a unit of Fred Meyer, Inc., which was bought by Kroger Co. in 1999. In 26 years at Fred Meyer, she held positions of increasing responsibility in all areas of operations and merchandising before becoming chief executive officer. Sammons is a member of Rite Aid's board of directors, as well as the National Association of Chain Drug Stores, the chain drugstore industry's trade association. She is also a director of First Horizon National Corporation and President of the Rite Aid Foundation.[10]

See why Avon calls itself "The Company for Women" (www.avoncompany.com/women).

Despite recent progress, women still account for less than 15 percent of corporate officers at retail firms. These are some of the issues for retailers to address with regard to female workers:

- Meaningful training programs.
- Advancement opportunities.
- Flex time—the ability of employees to adapt their hours.

- Job sharing among two or more employees who each work less than full-time.
- Child care.

Minorities in Retailing

DiversityInc.com presents a lot of useful information about minorities in the workplace (**www.diversityinc.com**).

As with women, retailers have done many good things in the area of minority employment, with more still to be accomplished. Consider these examples from *Fortune's* "50 Best Companies for Minorities:"[11]

> Fast-food king McDonald's holds on to its first-place crown by having the highest minority employee-retention rate on our list and making a concerted effort to purchase from minorities, who now represent half of its vendors. It also added a third minority to its 16-person board of directors, which oversees a workforce that's 53 percent minority.

> The Hilton hotel empire boasts 61 percent of new hires who are minorities, and its diversity efforts mean making sure those minorities climb the company ladder. Nonwhites make up one-third of employees enrolled in succession plans, and 44 percent of managers must make diversity a priority—their compensation is tied to it.

McDonald's corporate philosophy (**www.mcdonalds.com/corp/values/diversity.html**) encourages diversity and understanding.

> Minority retention rates are a key factor in manager performance evaluations at the Nordstrom department store chain, and in the past year, it has seen a sevenfold increase in the number of minorities enrolled in an expanded succession program. It also has an outreach program to involve minority-owned firms in new store construction.

For Wal-Mart, "diversity is a top priority. Wal-Mart is the largest private employer of people of color with more than 208,000 African-Americans and 139,000 Hispanic associates." According to a J.C. Penney executive, "Today, companies are looking to reflect the demographics of the communities they serve. In retailing, having a diverse workforce helps to provide a competitive advantage in selecting appropriate merchandise and services in support of the customer base." A senior regional vice-president for Sears says that "Retailing is definitely a viable industry for African-American college graduates. Your success is measured by very objective sales and profit results. There is not much subjectivity in analyzing how you are performing."[12]

The results of one study indicate that more minority workers rate career opportunities as favorable than unfavorable and have a better view of retailing than nonminority workers: Asian-Americans, 45.4 percent favorable, 24.6 percent unfavorable; Hispanic-Americans, 37.8 percent favorable, 27.3 percent unfavorable; African-Americans, 36.3 percent favorable, 34.4 percent unfavorable; Caucasian-Americans, 35.5 percent favorable, 34.7 percent unfavorable. As the president of the National Retail Federation observes, "African-Americans, Hispanics, and other minorities will find prime opportunities for career development and advancement in this dynamic industry as retailers recognize the need for diversity to be reflected on the selling floor and in upper management."[13]

These are some of the issues for retailers to address with regard to minority workers:

- Clear policy statements from top management as to the value of employee diversity.
- Active recruitment programs to stimulate minority applications.
- Meaningful training programs.

- Advancement opportunities.
- Zero tolerance for insensitive workplace behavior.

The Human Resource Management Process in Retailing

The **human resource management process** consists of these interrelated personnel activities: recruitment, selection, training, compensation, and supervision. The goals are to obtain, develop, and retain employees. When applying the process, diversity, labor laws, and privacy should be considered.

Diversity involves two premises: (1) that employees be hired and promoted in a fair and open way, without regard to gender, ethnic background, and other related factors; and (2) that in a diverse society, the workplace should be representative of such diversity.

There are several aspects of labor laws for retailers to satisfy. They must not

- Hire underage workers.
- Pay workers "off the books."
- Require workers to engage in illegal acts (such as bait-and-switch selling).
- Discriminate in hiring or promoting workers.
- Violate worker safety regulations.
- Disobey the Americans with Disabilities Act.
- Deal with suppliers that disobey labor laws.

Retailers must also be careful not to violate employees' privacy rights. Only necessary data about workers should be gathered and stored, and such information should not be freely disseminated.

We now discuss each activity in human resource management for sales and middle-management jobs. For more insights on the process, go to our Web site (**www.prenhall.com/bermanevans**).

Recruiting Retail Personnel

Recruitment is the activity whereby a retailer generates a list of job applicants. Table 11-3 indicates the features of several key recruitment sources. In addition to these sources, the Web is playing a bigger role in recruitment. Many retailers have a career or job section at their Web site, and some sections are as elaborate as the overall sites. Visit Target Stores' site (**www.target.com**), for example. Scroll down to the bottom of the home page and click on "Careers."

For entry-level sales jobs, retailers rely on educational institutions, ads, walk-ins (or write-ins), Web sites, and employee recommendations. For middle-management positions, retailers rely on employment agencies, competitors, ads, and current employee referrals. The retailer's typical goal is to generate a list of potential employees, which is reduced during selection. However, retailers that only accept applications from those who meet minimum background standards can save a lot of time and money.

Selecting Retail Personnel

The firm next selects new employees by matching the traits of potential employees with specific job requirements. Job analysis and description, the application blank, interviewing, testing (optional), references, and a physical exam (optional) are tools in the process; they should be integrated.

TABLE 11-3	Recruitment Sources and Their Characteristics
Sources	**Characteristics**

<u>Outside the Company</u>

Sources	Characteristics
Educational institutions	a. High schools, business schools, community colleges, universities, graduate schools. b. Good for training positions; ensure minimum educational requirements are met; especially useful when long-term contacts with instructors are developed.
Other channel members, competitors	a. Employees of wholesalers, manufacturers, ad agencies, competitors; leads from each of these. b. Reduce extent of training; can evaluate performance with prior firm(s); must instruct in company policy; some negative morale if current employees feel bypassed for promotions.
Advertisements	a. Newspapers, trade publications, professional journals, Web sites. b. Large quantity of applicants; average applicant quality may not be high; cost/applicant is low; additional responsibility placed on screening; can reduce unacceptable applications by noting job qualifications in ads.
Employment agencies	a. Private organizations, professional organizations, government, executive search firms. b. Must be carefully selected; must be determined who pays fee; good for applicant screening; specialists in personnel.
Unsolicited applicants	a. Walk-ins, write-ins. b. Wide variance in quality; must be carefully screened; file should be kept for future positions.

<u>Within the Company</u>

Sources	Characteristics
Current and former employees	a. Promotion or transfer of existing full-time employees, part-time employees; rehiring of laid-off employees. b. Knowledge of company policies and personnel; good for morale; honest appraisal from in-house supervisor.
Employee recommendations	a. Friends, acquaintances, relatives. b. Value of recommendations depend on honesty and judgment of current employees.

In **job analysis**, information is amassed on each job's functions and requirements: duties, responsibilities, aptitude, interest, education, experience, and physical tasks. It is used to select personnel, set performance standards, and assign salaries. For example, department managers often act as the main sales associates for their areas, oversee other sales associates, have some administrative duties, report to the store manager, are eligible for bonuses, and are paid from $25,000 to $40,000+ annually.

Job analysis should lead to written job descriptions. A **traditional job description** contains a position's title, relationships (superior and subordinate), and specific roles and tasks. Figure 11-4 showed a store manager job description. Yet, using a traditional description alone has been criticized. This may limit a job's scope, as well as its authority and responsibility; not let a person grow; limit

FIGURE 11-10
A Goal-Oriented Job
Description for a
Management Trainee

Attributes Required	Ability	Desire	In the Retailing Environment
ANALYTICAL SKILLS: ability to solve problems; strong numerical ability for analysis of facts and data for planning, managing, and controlling.			Retail executives are problem solvers. Knowledge and understanding of past performance and present circumstances form the basis for action and planning.
CREATIVITY: ability to generate and recognize imaginative ideas and solutions; ability to recognize the need for and be responsive to change.			Retail executives are idea people. Successful buying results from sensitive, aware decisions, while merchandising requires imaginative, innovative techniques.
DECISIVENESS: ability to make quick decisions and render judgments, take action, and commit oneself to completion.			Retail executives are action people. Whether it's new fashion trends or customer desires, decisions must be made quickly and confidently in this ever-changing environment.
FLEXIBILITY: ability to adjust to the ever-changing needs of the situation; ability to adapt to different people, places, and things; willingness to do whatever is necessary to get the task done.			Retail executives are flexible. Surprises in retailing never cease. Plans must be altered quickly to accommodate changes in trends, styles, and attitudes, while numerous ongoing activities cannot be ignored.
INITIATIVE: ability to originate action rather than wait to be told what to do and ability to act based on conviction.			Retail executives are doers. Sales volumes, trends, and buying opportunities mean continual action. Opportunities for action must be seized.
LEADERSHIP: ability to inspire others to trust and respect your judgment; ability to delegate and to guide and persuade others.			Retail executives are managers. Running a business means depending on others to get the work done. One person cannot do it all.
ORGANIZATION: ability to establish priorities and courses of action for self and/or others; skill in planning and following up to achieve results.			Retail executives are jugglers. A variety of issues, functions, and projects are constantly in motion. To reach your goals, priorities must be set and work must be delegated to others.
RISK-TAKING: willingness to take calculated risks based on thorough analysis and sound judgment and to accept responsibility for the results.			Retail executives are courageous. Success in retailing often comes from taking calculated risks and having the confidence to try something new before someone else does.
STRESS TOLERANCE: ability to perform consistently under pressure, to thrive on constant change and challenge.			Retail executives are resilient. As the above description should suggest, retailing is fast-paced and demanding.

activities to those listed; and not describe how positions are coordinated. To complement a traditional description, a **goal-oriented job description** can enumerate basic functions, the relationship of each job to overall goals, the interdependence of positions, and information flows. See Figure 11-10.

An **application blank** is usually the first tool used to screen applicants; providing data on education, experience, health, reasons for leaving prior jobs, outside activities, hobbies, and references. It is usually short, requires little interpretation, and can be used as the basis for probing in an interview. With a **weighted application blank**, factors having a high relationship with job success are given more weight than others. Retailers that use such a form analyze the performance of current and past employees and determine the criteria (education, experience, and so on) best correlated with job success (as measured by longer tenure, better performance, and so on). After weighted scores are awarded to all job applicants (based on data they provide), a minimum total score becomes a cutoff point for hiring. An effective application blank aids retailers in lessening turnover and selecting high achievers.

An application blank should be used along with a job description. Those meeting minimum job requirements are processed further; others are immediately rejected. In this way, the application blank provides a quick and inexpensive method of screening.

The interview seeks information that can be amassed only by personal questioning and observation. It lets an employer determine a candidate's verbal ability, note his or her appearance, ask questions keyed to the application, and probe career goals. Interviewing decisions must be made about the level of formality, the number and length of interviews, the location, the person(s) to do the interviewing, and the interview structure. These decisions often depend on the interviewer's ability and the job's requirements.

Small firms tend to hire an applicant who has a good interview. Large firms may add testing. In this case, a candidate who does well in an interview then takes a psychological test (to measure personality, intelligence, interest, and leadership) and/or achievement tests (to measure learned knowledge).[14]

Tests must be administered by qualified people. Standardized exams should not be used unless proven effective in predicting job performance. Because achievement tests deal with specific skills or information, like the ability to make a sales presentation, they are easier to interpret than psychological tests; and direct relationships between knowledge and ability can be shown. In administering tests, retailers must not violate any federal, state, or local law. The federal Employee Polygraph Protection Act bars retailers from using lie detector tests in most hiring situations (drugstores are exempt).

CarMax
(www.carmax.com)
encourages potential
employees to submit their
résumés online.

To save time and operate more efficiently, some retailers—large and small—use computerized application blanks and testing. Home Depot and Target are among those with in-store kiosks that allow people to apply for jobs, complete application blanks, and answer several questions. This speeds up the hiring process and attracts a lot of applicants.

Many retailers get references from applicants that can be checked either before or after an interview. References are contacted to see how enthusiastically they recommend an applicant, check the applicant's honesty, and ask why an applicant left a prior job. Mail and phone checks are inexpensive, fast, and easy.

Some firms require a physical exam because of the physical activity, long hours, and tensions involved in many retailing positions. A clean bill of health means the candidate is offered a job. Again, federal, state, and local laws must be followed.

Each step in the selection process complements the others; together they give the retailer a good information package for choosing personnel. As a rule, retailers should use job descriptions, application blanks, interviews, and reference checks. Follow-up interviews, psychological and achievement tests, and physical exams depend on the retailer and the position. Inexpensive tools (such as application blanks) are used in the early screening stages; more costly, in-depth tools (such as interviews) are used after reducing the applicant pool. Equal opportunity, nondiscriminatory practices must be followed.

Training Retail Personnel

Every new employee should receive **pre-training**, an indoctrination on the firm's history and policies, as well as a job orientation on hours, compensation, the chain of command, and job duties. New employees should also be introduced to co-workers: "Effective orientation inspires recruits and provides information that they do not know about their jobs and the retailer. What kind of first impression do orientation programs make? Do they confirm the new hire's choice that XYZ is a good place to work?"[15]

Training programs teach new (and existing) personnel how best to perform their jobs or how to improve themselves. Training can range from one-day sessions on operating a computerized cash register, personal selling techniques, or compliance with affirmative action programs to two-year programs for executive trainees on all aspects of the retailer and its operations:

- For each new employee, The Container Store provides more than 240 hours of formal training during the first year on the job. The training includes learning about how to perform multiple jobs: "New hires spend time unloading delivery trucks and stocking shelves and even cleaning restrooms."[16]

- Big Boy restaurants, a growing fast-food chain, is implementing a Web-based training program for store employees. As one industry expert says, "Online training is an attractive method for multi-unit food operators looking for cost-effective ways to train new employees and give refresher courses for seasoned workers. Web-based programs can reduce the need for travel and time spent in classes."[17]

- Sears University offers retail education courses plus self-study options for Sears' employees. Managers can enroll in hands-on programs ranging from one day to one week. Some programs involve buying, merchandising, and human resource management. Others involve strategic leadership. Courses are taught by seasoned managers, training and development experts, and university faculty consultants.

Training should be an ongoing activity. New equipment, legal changes, new product lines, job promotions, low employee morale, and employee turnover necessitate not only training but also retraining. Federated Department Stores has a program called "clienteling," which tutors sales associates on how to have better long-term relations with specific repeat customers. Core vendors of Federated teach sales associates about the features and benefits of new merchandise when it is introduced.

Technology in RETAILING
How Buzzsaw Software Enables Petco to Save Time and Money

Before switching to a Buzzsaw (**www.buzzsaw.com**) project management software system, Petco's (**www.petco.com**) store designers spent a good deal of their time printing and mailing plans. According to Craig Brown, a Petco store designer, "We were spending too much money plotting floor plans, mailing them, and maintaining our plotters."

Petco now uses Buzzsaw to manage the store design process among its approximately 750 locations in 48 states. Buzzsaw has enabled Petco to consolidate all design information in an easy-to-access centralized location. This reduces the chance for miscommunication that could easily occur when architects, contractors, and electricians each look at a different set of store plans.

Buzzsaw also lets Petco's top management and design personnel review plans and then see the impact of recommended changes in minutes instead of days.

According to Craig Brown, Buzzsaw has resulted in Petco's saving of 180 hours per year that used to be spent managing the paper flow aspects of the design process. It also reduced the review and approval process time by 50 percent.

Sources: "Petco Streamlines Project Management," *Chain Store Age Specs Special Issue* (Mid-December 2004), p. 82; and "About Petco," **www.petco.com/corpinfo.asp?webt=0&** (April 30, 2006).

FIGURE 11-11
A Checklist of Selected
Training Decisions

✓ When should training occur? (At the time of hiring and/or after being at the workplace?)

✓ How long should training be?

✓ What training programs should there be for new employees? For existing employees?

✓ Who should conduct each training program? (Supervisor, co-worker, training department, or outside specialist?)

✓ Where should training take place? (At the workplace or in a training room?)

✓ What material (content) should be learned? How should it be taught?

✓ Should audiovisuals be used? If yes, how?

✓ Should elements of the training program be computerized? If yes, how?

✓ How should the effectiveness of training be measured?

There are several training decisions, as shown in Figure 11-11. They can be divided into three categories: identifying needs, devising appropriate training methods, and evaluation.

Short-term training needs can be identified by measuring the gap between the skills that workers already have and the skills desired by the firm (for each job). This training should prepare employees for possible job rotation, promotions, and changes in the company. A longer training plan lets a firm identify future needs and train workers appropriately.

There are many training methods for retailers: lectures, demonstrations, films, programmed instruction, conferences, sensitivity training, case studies, role playing, behavior modeling, and competency-based instruction. Some techniques may be computerized—as more firms are doing. The methods' attributes are noted in Table 11-4. Retailers often use more than one technique to reduce employee boredom and cover the material better.

To promote its cashier training software, Advanced Learning Systems has an online description of it (**www.retail-training.com/ pub/docs/c-store.html**).

Computer-based training has two formats: personal computer and Web. Advanced Learning Solutions markets all sorts of training software. Its multimedia CD-ROM for convenience stores takes cashiers "through a series of hands-on exercises" that cover "store register procedures and illustrate how to best service your customer." Convergys (**www.convergys.com**), through its DigitalThink acquisition, offers custom E-learning courseware. One of its clients is Circuit City, which uses Convergys "to keep over 40,000 associates and managers current on the latest electronic products. Courses are short and succinct so employees can take them fast and get back to the store floor."[18]

For training to succeed, a conducive environment is needed, based on several principles:

● All people can learn if taught well; there should be a sense of achievement.

● A person learns better when motivated; intelligence alone is not sufficient.

● Learning should be goal-oriented.

● A trainee learns more when he or she participates and is not a passive listener.

● The teacher must provide guidance, as well as adapt to the learner and to the situation.

● Learning should be approached as a series of steps rather than a one-time occurrence.

TABLE 11-4	The Characteristics of Retail Training Methods
Method	**Characteristics**
Lecture	Factual, uninterrupted presentation of material; can use professional educator or expert in the field; no active participation by trainees
Demonstration	Good for showing how to use equipment or do a sales presentation; applies relevance of training; active participation by trainees
Video	Animated; good for demonstration; can be used many times; no active participation by trainees
Programmed instruction	Presents information in a structured manner; requires response from trainees; provides performance feedback; adjustable to trainees' pace; high initial investment
Conference	Useful for supervisory training; conference leader must encourage participation; reinforces training
Sensitivity training	Extensive interaction; good for supervisors as a tool for understanding employees
Case study	Actual or hypothetical problem presented, including circumstances, pertinent information, and questions; learning by doing; exposure to a wide variety of problems
Role playing	Trainees placed into real-life situations and act out roles
Behavior modeling	Trainees taught to imitate models shown on videotape or in role-playing sessions
Competency-based instruction	Trainees given a list of tasks or exercises that are presented in a self-paced format

- Learning should be spread out over a reasonable period of time rather than be compressed.
- The learner should be encouraged to do homework or otherwise practice.
- Different methods of learning should be combined.
- Performance standards should be set and good performance recognized.

A training program must be regularly evaluated. Comparisons can be made between the performance of those who receive training and those who do not, as well as among employees receiving different types of training for the same job. Evaluations should always be made in relation to stated training goals. In addition, training effects should be measured over different time intervals (such as immediately, 30 days later, and six months later), and proper records maintained.

Compensating Retail Personnel

Total **compensation**—direct monetary payments (salaries, commissions, and bonuses) and indirect payments (paid vacations, health and life insurance, and retirement plans)— should be fair to both the retailer and its employees. To better motivate employees, some firms also have profit-sharing. Smaller retailers often pay salaries, commissions, and/or bonuses and have fewer fringe benefits. Bigger ones generally pay salaries, commissions, and/or bonuses and offer more fringe benefits.

The hourly federal minimum wage is $5.15 (which has been in effect for about a decade). In addition, 44 states have their own laws—15 higher than the federal minimum and 2 lower. The minimum wage has the most impact on retailers hiring entry-level, part-time workers. Full-time, career-track retailing jobs are paid an

This site (www.dol.gov/ esa/minwage/america.htm) shows the minimum wage in every state.

attractive market rate; and to attract part-time workers during good economic times, retailers must often pay salaries above the minimum.

At some large firms, compensation for certain positions is set through collective bargaining. According to the U.S. Bureau of Labor Statistics, about 900,000 retail employees are represented by labor unions. However, union membership varies greatly. Unionized grocery stores account for more than one-half of total U.S. supermarket sales, while independent supermarkets are not usually unionized.

With a *straight salary*, a worker is paid a fixed amount per hour, week, month, or year. Advantages are retailer control, employee security, and known expenses. Disadvantages are retailer inflexibility, the limited productivity incentive, and fixed costs. Clerks and cashiers are usually paid salaries. With a *straight commission*, earnings are directly tied to productivity (such as sales volume). Advantages are retailer flexibility, the link to worker productivity, no fixed costs, and employee incentive. Disadvantages are the retailer's potential lack of control over the tasks performed, the risk of low earnings to employees, cost variability, and the lack of limits on worker earnings. Sales personnel for autos, real-estate, furniture, jewelry, and other expensive items are often paid a straight commission—as are direct-selling personnel.

To combine the attributes of salary and commission plans, some retailers pay their employees a *salary plus commission*. Shoe salespeople, major appliance salespeople, and some management personnel are among those paid in this manner. Some bonuses supplement salary and/or commission, normally for outstanding performance. At Finish Line footwear and apparel stores, regional, district, and store managers receive fixed salaries and earn bonuses based on sales, the size of the payroll, and theft rate goals. In certain cases, retail executives are paid via a "compensation cafeteria" and choose their own combination of salary, bonus, deferred bonus, fringe benefits, life insurance, stock options, and retirement benefits.

Sears has a generous employee benefits package (**www.sears.com/sr/misc/ sears/jobsec/careers_ benefits.jsp**).

A thorny issue facing retailers today involves the benefits portion of employee compensation, especially as related to pensions and healthcare. It is a challenging time due to intense price competition, the use of part-time workers, and escalating medical costs as retailers try to balance their employees' needs with company financial needs.

Supervising Retail Personnel

Supervision is the manner of providing a job environment that encourages employee accomplishment. The goals are to oversee personnel, attain good performance, maintain morale, motivate people, control costs, communicate, and resolve problems. Supervision is provided by personal contact, meetings, and reports.

Every firm wants to continually motivate employees so as to harness their energy on behalf of the retailer and achieve its goals. **Job motivation** is the drive within people to attain work-related goals. It may be positive or negative. Sears believes that 10 attitude questions help predict employee behavior, based on their motivation:

1. Do you like the kind of work you do?
2. Does your work give you a sense of accomplishment?
3. Are you proud to say you work at Sears?
4. How does the amount of work expected from you influence your overall job attitude?
5. How do physical working conditions influence your overall job attitude?
6. How does the way you are treated by supervisors influence your overall job attitude?

RETAILING Around the World — How ASDA Motivates Employees

ASDA (**www.asda.co.uk**) is the largest value retailer in Great Britain, with more than 265 stores and 125,000 employees. Several times, ASDA has been voted a leading employee-friendly British employer based on the *Sunday Times'* "Top 100 Best Companies to Work For" survey. ASDA has also received a prize for being the best British company in term of flexible hours. Since ASDA became part of the Wal-Mart (**www.walmart. com**) family in June 1999, its sales have increased dramatically.

An important part of ASDA's human resources management philosophy is based on listening to employees and reacting to their suggestions. There are three central components to this orientation:

- "The We're Listening Survey"—Comments by store, head office, and depot personnel are analyzed on a monthly basis concerning employee management teams, compensation and benefits, training, motivation, and teamwork.
- "Tell Tony"—ASDA receives over 50,000 suggestions, comments, and letters annually from employees based on the Tell Tony suggestion system.
- "Colleague Circles"—These circles meet monthly on a store basis and quarterly on a division basis. There is an annual meeting whereby a representative from each store is invited to meet with the ASDA board of directors.

Source: "About ASDA," **www.asda.co.uk** (March 29, 2006).

7. Do you feel good about the future of the company?
8. Do you think Sears is making the changes necessary to compete effectively?
9. Do you understand Sears' business strategy?
10. Do you see a connection between your work and the company's strategic objectives?[19]

Employee motivation should be approached from two perspectives: What job-related factors cause employees to be satisfied or dissatisfied with their positions? What supervision style is best for both the retailer and its employees? See Figure 11-12.

Tom Holmes

SEARS

TYPE OF STORE:
Department Store

HEADQUARTERS:
Hoffman Estates, Ill.

Upcoming grads anxious to climb to the top might take a look at Tom Holmes. At 29, he has already been general store manager at two Sears stores.

This political science major from the University of Illinois worked retail as an undergrad, but planned a career in investment banking. At graduation, he realized retail offered the chance to develop professionally.

"If you're confused about your direction, find an organization that lets you develop a base foundation of skill sets you can use throughout your career," notes Holmes. "Management and leadership skills are important virtually anywhere."

He contacted Sears, and was brought on board in 1993. He started in an executive development program and became a sales manager. Promotions have been quick to come ever since. He presently manages a Sears in West Dundee, Ill.

Holmes values the adventure of dealing with different personalities. "I really like working with people, both having an impact on customers and being able to coach and mentor teams to success," he says.

He is currently earning his MBA from Northwestern University's Kellogg Graduate School of Management, with a focus on strategy and marketing. Sears has tuition reimbursement for graduate and undergraduate students, which helps its employees contribute more to the company and their mutual futures.

With a college degree, employees start higher up on the food chain, get management responsibilities from square one and a sense of accomplishment as a result.

"The first time you're in charge when you realize your boss is two hours away, it makes you feel really responsible," he adds. "I like it that there are lots of plans, direction from Sears as a company, yet there's autonomy as well."

Holmes also enjoys the variety his position offers. "Yes, it's a cliché, but it really is different every day. Sometimes I do human resources things, sometimes presentations, and on other days customer service is the focus. There's a lot of flexibility day-to-day, and in how you shape your career."

FIGURE 11-12
Sears: Providing a Motivating Career Path for Employees

Reprinted by permission of *DSN Retailing Today*.

Each employee looks at job satisfaction in terms of minimum expectations ("dissatisfiers") and desired goals ("satisfiers"). A motivated employee requires fulfillment of both factors. *Minimum expectations* relate mostly to the job environment, including a safe workplace, equitable treatment for those with the same jobs, some flexibility in company policies (such as not docking pay if a person is 10 minutes late), an even-tempered boss, some freedom in attire, a fair compensation package, basic fringe benefits (such as vacation time and medical coverage), clear communications, and job security. These elements can generally influence motivation in only one way—negatively. If minimum expectations are not met, a person will be unhappy. If these expectations are met, they are taken for granted and do little to motivate the person to go "above and beyond."

Desired goals relate more to the job than to the work environment. They are based on whether an employee likes the job, is recognized for good performance, feels a sense of achievement, is empowered to make decisions, is trusted, has a defined career path, receives extra compensation when performance is exceptional, and is given the chance to learn and grow. These elements can have a huge impact on job satisfaction and motivate a person to go "above and beyond." Nonetheless, if minimum expectations are not met, an employee might still be dissatisfied enough to leave, even if the job is quite rewarding.

There are three basic styles of supervising retail employees:

- Management assumes employees must be closely supervised and controlled and that only economic inducements really motivate. Management further believes that the average worker lacks ambition, dislikes responsibility, and prefers to be led. This is the traditional view of motivation and has been applied to lower-level retail positions.

- Management assumes employees can be self-managers and assigned authority, motivation is social and psychological, and supervision can be decentralized and participatory. Management also thinks that motivation, the capacity for assuming responsibility, and a readiness to achieve company goals exist in people. The critical supervisory task is to create an environment so people achieve their goals by attaining company objectives. This is a more modern view and applies to all levels of personnel.

- Management applies a self-management approach and also advocates more employee involvement in defining jobs and sharing overall decision making. There is mutual loyalty between the firm and its workers, and both parties enthusiastically cooperate for the long-term benefit of each. This is also a modern view and applies to all levels of personnel.

It is imperative to motivate employees in a manner that yields job satisfaction, low turnover, low absenteeism, and high productivity:

> Believe it or not, some of the most effective forms of motivation cost nothing. A sincere word of thanks from the right person at the right time can mean more to an employee than a raise, a formal award, or a wall of certificates or plaques. Part of the power of such rewards comes from the knowledge that someone took the time to notice the achievement, seek out the employee responsible, and personally deliver praise in a timely manner. And the most important things managers can do to develop and maintain motivated employees have no cost, but rather are a function of the daily interactions that managers have with employees pertaining to work. I call these "The Power of I's." There are five of them: (1) Interesting work. (2) Information, communication, and feedback. (3) Involvement and ownership in decisions. (4) Independence, autonomy, and flexibility. (5) Increased visibility, opportunity, and responsibility.[20]

Summary

1. *To study the procedures involved in setting up a retail organization.* A retail organization structures and assigns tasks, policies, resources, authority, responsibilities, and rewards to satisfy the needs of its target market, employees, and management. There are five steps in setting up an organization: outlining specific tasks to be performed in a distribution channel, dividing tasks, grouping tasks into jobs, classifying jobs, and integrating positions with an organization chart.

   Specific tasks include buying, shipping, receiving and checking, pricing, and marking merchandise; inventory control; display preparation; facilities maintenance; research; customer contact and follow-up; and a lot more. These tasks may be divided among retailers, manufacturers, wholesalers, specialists, and customers.

   Tasks are next grouped into jobs, such as sales personnel, cashiers, inventory personnel, display personnel, customer service personnel, and management. Then jobs are arranged by functional, product, geographic, or combination classification. An organization chart displays the hierarchy of authority and the relationship among jobs and coordinates personnel.

2. *To examine the various organizational arrangements utilized in retailing.* Retail organization structures differ by institution. Small independents use simple formats, with little specialization. Many department stores use a version of the Mazur plan and place functions into four categories: merchandising, publicity, store management, and accounting and control. The equal store format is used by numerous chain stores. Diversified firms have very complex organizations.

3. *To consider the special human resource environment of retailing.* Retailers are unique due to the large number of inexperienced workers, long hours, highly visible employees, a diverse work force, many part-time workers, and variations in customer demand. There is a broad range of career opportunities available to women and minorities, although improvement is still needed.

4. *To describe the principles and practices involved with the human resource management process in retailing.* This process comprises several interrelated activities: recruitment, selection, training, compensation, and supervision. In applying the process, diversity, labor laws, and employee privacy should be kept in mind.

   Recruitment generates job applicants. Sources include educational institutions, channel members, competitors, ads, employment agencies, unsolicited applicants, employees, and Web sites.

   Personnel selection requires thorough job analysis, creating job descriptions, using application blanks, interviews, testing (optional), reference checking, and physical exams. After personnel are selected, they go through pre-training and job training. Good training identifies needs, uses proper methods, and assesses results. Training is usually vital for continuing, as well as new, personnel.

   Employees are compensated by direct monetary payments and/or indirect payments. The direct compensation plans are straight salary, straight commission, and salary plus commission and/or bonus. Indirect payments involve such items as paid vacations, health benefits, and retirement plans.

   Proper supervision is needed to sustain superior employee performance. A main task is employee motivation. The causes of job satisfaction/dissatisfaction and the supervisory style must be reviewed.

Key Terms

retail organization (p. 326)
hierarchy of authority (p. 330)
organization chart (p. 331)
Mazur plan (p. 333)
equal store organization (p. 334)
diversified retailer (p. 336)
human resource management (p. 336)

human resource management process (p. 342)
recruitment (p. 342)
job analysis (p. 343)
traditional job description (p. 343)
goal-oriented job description (p. 344)
application blank (p. 344)

weighted application blank (p. 344)
pre-training (p. 345)
training programs (p. 346)
compensation (p. 348)
supervision (p. 349)
job motivation (p. 349)

Questions for Discussion

1. Cite at least five objectives a small independent hardware store should set when setting up its organization structure.

2. Why are employee needs important in developing a retail organization?

3. Are the steps involved in setting up a retail organization the same for small and large retailers? Explain your answer.

4. Describe the greatest similarities and differences in the organization structures of small independents, chain retailers, and diversified retailers.

5. How can retailers attract and retain more women and minority workers?

6. How would small and large retailers act differently for each of the following?
   a. Diversity.
   b. Recruitment.
   c. Selection.

d. Training.
e. Compensation.
f. Supervision.

7. Why are the job description and the application blank so important in employee selection?

8. What problems can occur while interviewing and testing prospective employees?

9. Present a plan for the ongoing training of both existing lower-level and middle-management employees without making it seem punitive.

10. Describe the goals of a compensation plan (both direct and indirect components) in a retail setting.

11. Are the minimum job expectations of entry-level workers and middle-level managers similar or dissimilar? What about the desired goals? Explain your answers.

12. How would you supervise and motivate a 19-year-old supermarket cashier? A 65-year-old cashier?

Web-Based Exercise

Visit the Web site that Federated Department Stores has dedicated to college recruiting (**www.retailology. com/college/home.asp**). What do you think of this site as a mechanism for attracting new college graduates to Federated? Why?

Note: Stop by our Web site (**www.prenhall.com/bermanevans**) to experience a number of highly interactive, appealing Web exercises based on actual company demonstrations and sample materials related to retailing.

Chapter Endnotes

1. Various company sources.

2. Meg Whitman, "How to Manage Growth," *Business 2.0* (December 2004), p. 99.

3. Paul M. Mazur, *Principles of Organization Applied to Modern Retailing* (New York: Harper & Brothers, 1927).

4. "Target: Careers," **http://target.com/targetcorp_ group/careers/index.jhtml** (March 29, 2006).

5. "Employment Opportunities," **www.pizzeriauno. com/employmain.html** (March 29, 2006).

6. "A Company of Entrepreneurs," **http://careers. nordstrom.com/story2.html** (March 29, 2006).

7. Matthew Boyle, "The Wegmans Way," *Fortune* (January 24, 2005), pp. 62–68.

8. "Home Depot's Nardelli Receives Award from Center for Retailing Studies," *Retail Merchandiser Online* (March 30, 2005).

9. "Executive Team," **http://pages.ebay.com/about ebay/thecompany/executiveteam.html** (July 30, 2005).

10. "Rite Aid Management Team," **www.riteaid.com/ company_info/management** (July 30, 2005).

11. "50 Best Companies for Minorities," *Fortune* (June 28, 2004), pp. 140, 142.

12. "Wal-Mart Diversity Fact Sheet," **www.walmart facts.com/doyouknow** (March 22, 2006); and Thelma Snuggs, "Retailing on the Move: An Era of Change," *Black Collegian* (February 2002), p. 52.

13. David P. Schulz, "Employee Attitude Surveys Focus on the Human Side of the Retail Equation," *Stores*

(April 1999), pp. 96–97; and Richard Feinberg, "The Retail Industry: A Giant, Hidden Career Opportunity," **www.black-collegian.com/career/industry-reports/retail.shtml** (July 1, 2005).

14. For a good illustration of the testing resources available for retailers, visit the Web site of Employee Selection & Development Inc. (**www.employeeselect.com**).

15. Marilyn Moats Kennedy, "Setting the Right Tone, Right Away," *Across the Board* (April 1999), pp. 51–52.

16. Alan R. Earls, "Retail Wants You," **http://boston works.boston.com/globe/articles/042405_retail. html** (April 24, 2005).

17. Dina Berta, "Big Boy: Online Training Will Aid Worker Retention," *Nation's Restaurant News* (April 18, 2005), p. 4.

18. "Service Skills: C-Store Cashier," **www.retail-training. com/pub/docs/c-store.html** (March 3, 2006); and "Solution Profiles," **www.digitalthink.com/dtfs/ resources/circuit_city.html** (March 3, 2006).

19. Anthony J. Rucci, Steven P. Kirn, and Richard T. Quinn, "The Employee-Customer-Profit Chain at Sears," *Harvard Business Review*, Vol. 76 (January–February 1998), pp. 82–97.

20. Bob Nelson, "No-Cost Employee Recognition," *Bank Marketing* (September 2002), p. 14. See also Bryan Fisher, "How to Motivate Employees in Tough Financial Times," *Supervision* (April 2002), pp. 9–11; Janet Wiscombe, "Rewards Get Results," *Workforce* (April 2002), pp. 42–48; and Alison Myers, "Motivate to Accumulate," *Financial Management* (April 2002), p. 19.

Chapter 12
OPERATIONS MANAGEMENT: FINANCIAL DIMENSIONS

About 75 years ago, the top management of Lazarus and the John Shillito Company met with senior executives of Abraham & Straus, Filene's, and Bloomingdale's. They agreed to merge and form Federated Department Stores to reduce their vulnerability to economic downturns. Over the years, Federated (**www. federated-fds.com**) acquired such chains as Bon Marche, Burdines, Goldsmith's, Macy's,

Reprinted by permission.

and Rich's, and it closed or divested itself of Shillito, Abraham & Straus, and Filene's. In 2005, Federated Department Stores reached an agreement to purchase May Department Stores for $10.4 billion. Among May's chains were Lord & Taylor, Filene's, and Marshall Field's.

Until recently, the department store sector of retailing was able to attract a large number of customers through one-stop shopping appeals, fashion-forward apparel, and attentive service. Although department store chains were once considered the darlings of retailing, they have been losing market share to discount stores for years. According to the U.S. Department of Commerce, department stores accounted for 50 percent of general merchandise, apparel, and furniture (GAF) sales in 1992. As of now, their share of GAF sales has fallen to 30 percent.

Some analysts believe the purchase of May Department Stores will better enable Federated to achieve economies of scale, and increased bargaining power with its suppliers. As part of its strategy, Federated is converting its regional chains (such as Rich's, Burdines, Marshall Field's, and Goldsmith's) into Macy's stores and selling off Lord & Taylor. There is concern among some analysts that some regional differences in merchandising may become lost due to increased centralization.[1]

chapter objectives

1. To define operations management
2. To discuss profit planning
3. To describe asset management, including the strategic profit model, other key business ratios, and financial trends in retailing
4. To look at retail budgeting
5. To examine resource allocation

OVERVIEW

After devising an organization structure and a human resource plan, a retailer concentrates on **operations management**—the efficient and effective implementation of the policies and tasks necessary to satisfy the firm's customers, employees, and management (and stockholders, if a public company). This has a major impact on sales and profits. High inventory levels, long hours, expensive fixtures, extensive customer services, and widespread advertising may lead to higher revenues. But at what cost? If a store pays night-shift workers a 25 percent premium, is being open 24 hours per day worthwhile (do higher sales justify the costs and add to overall profit)?

This chapter covers the financial aspects of operations management, with emphasis on profit planning, asset management, budgeting, and resource allocation. The operational dimensions of operations management are explored in detail in Chapter 13. A number of useful financial operations links may be found at our Web site (**www.prenhall.com/bermanevans**).

PROFIT PLANNING

Learn more about the profit-and-loss statement (**www.toolkit.cch.com/text/ P06_1578.asp**).

A **profit-and-loss (income) statement** is a summary of a retailer's revenues and expenses over a given period of time, usually a month, quarter, or year. It lets the firm review its overall and specific revenues and costs for similar periods (such as January 1, 2006, to December 31, 2006, versus January 1, 2005, to December 31, 2005) and analyze profitability. By having frequent statements, a firm can monitor progress toward goals, update performance estimates, and revise strategies and tactics.

In comparing profit-and-loss performance over time, it is crucial that the same time periods be used (such as the third quarter of 2006 with the third quarter of 2005) due to seasonality. Some fiscal years may have an unequal number of weeks (53 weeks one year versus 51 weeks another). Retailers that open new stores or expand existing stores between accounting periods should also take into account the larger facilities. Yearly results should reflect total revenue growth and the rise in same-store sales.

A profit-and-loss statement consists of these major components:

- **Net sales**—The revenues received by a retailer during a given period after deducting customer returns, markdowns, and employee discounts.
- **Cost of goods sold**—The amount a retailer pays to acquire the merchandise sold during a given time period. It is based on purchase prices and freight charges, less all discounts (such as quantity, cash, and promotion).
- **Gross profit (margin)**—The difference between net sales and the cost of goods sold. It consists of operating expenses plus net profit.
- **Operating expenses**—The cost of running a retail business.
- **Taxes**—The portion of revenues turned over to the federal, state, and/or local government.
- **Net profit after taxes**—The profit earned after all costs and taxes have been deducted.

Table 12-1 shows the most recent annual profit-and-loss statement for Donna's Gift Shop, an independent retailer. The firm uses a fiscal year (September 1 to August 31) rather than a calendar year in preparing its accounting reports. These observations can be drawn from the table:

TABLE 12-1	Donna's Gift Shop, Fiscal 2006 Profit-and-Loss Statement

Net sales	$330,000
Cost of goods sold	$180,000
Gross profit	$150,000
Operating expenses	
Salaries	$ 75,000
Advertising	4,950
Supplies	1,650
Shipping	1,500
Insurance	4,500
Maintenance	5,100
Other	2,550
Total	$ 95,250
Other costs	$ 20,000
Total costs	$115,250
Net profit before taxes	$ 34,750
Taxes	$ 15,500
Net profit after taxes	$ 19,250

- Annual net sales were $330,000—after deducting returns, markdowns on the items sold, and employee discounts from total sales.
- The cost of goods sold was $180,000, computed by taking the total purchases for merchandise sold, adding freight, and subtracting quantity, cash, and promotion discounts.
- Gross profit was $150,000, calculated by subtracting the cost of goods sold from net sales. This went for operating and other expenses, taxes, and profit.
- Operating expenses totaled $95,250, including salaries, advertising, supplies, shipping, insurance, maintenance, and other expenses.
- Unassigned costs were $20,000.
- Net profit before taxes was $34,750, computed by deducting total costs from gross profit. The tax bill was $15,500, leaving a net profit after taxes of $19,250.

Overall, fiscal 2003 was pretty good for Donna; her personal salary was $43,000 and the store's after-tax profit was $19,250. A further analysis of Donna's Gift Shop's profit-and-loss statement appears in the budgeting section of this chapter.

ASSET MANAGEMENT

Try out the Business Owner's Toolkit's downloadable Excel-based balance sheet template (**www.toolkit.cch.com/tools/balshe_m.asp**).

Each retailer has assets to manage and liabilities to control. This section covers the balance sheet, the strategic profit model, and other ratios. A **balance sheet** itemizes a retailer's assets, liabilities, and net worth at a specific time—based on the principle that assets = liabilities + net worth. Table 12-2 has a balance sheet for Donna's Gift Shop.

Assets are any items a retailer owns with a monetary value. Current assets are cash on hand (or in the bank) and items readily converted to cash, such as inventory on hand and accounts receivable (amounts owed to the firm). Fixed assets are property, buildings (a store, warehouse, and so on), fixtures, and equipment such as cash registers and trucks; these are used for a long period. The major fixed asset

TABLE 12-2	A Retail Balance Sheet for Donna's Gift Shop (as of August 31, 2006)

Assets		Liabilities	
Current		Current	
Cash on hand	$ 19,950	Payroll expenses payable	$ 6,000
Inventory	36,150	Taxes payable	13,500
Accounts receivable	1,650	Accounts payable	32,100
Total	$ 57,750	Short-term loan	1,050
		Total	$ 52,650
Fixed (present value)			
Property	$187,500	Fixed	
Building	63,000	Mortgage	$ 97,500
Store fixtures	14,550	Long-term loan	6,750
Equipment	2,550	Total	$104,250
Total	$267,600		
		Total liabilities	$156,900
Total assets	$325,350		
		Net Worth	$168,450
		Liabilities + net worth	$325,350

for many retailers is real-estate. Unlike current assets, which are recorded at cost, fixed assets are recorded at cost less accumulated depreciation. Thus, records may not reflect the true value of these assets. Many retailing analysts use the term **hidden assets** to describe depreciated assets, such as buildings and warehouses, that are noted on a retail balance sheet at low values relative to their actual worth.

Liabilities are financial obligations a retailer incurs in operating a business. Current liabilities are payroll expenses payable, taxes payable, accounts payable (amounts owed to suppliers), and short-term loans; these must be paid in the coming year. Fixed liabilities comprise mortgages and long-term loans; these are generally repaid over several years.

A retailer's **net worth** is computed as assets minus liabilities. It is also called owner's equity and represents the value of a business after deducting all financial obligations.

In operations management, the retailer's goal is to use its assets in the manner providing the best results possible. There are three basic ways to measure those results: net profit margin, asset turnover, and financial leverage. Each component is discussed next.

Net profit margin is a performance measure based on a retailer's net profit and net sales:

$$\text{Net profit margin} = \frac{\text{Net profit after taxes}}{\text{Net sales}}$$

At Donna's Gift Shop, fiscal year 2006 net profit margin was 5.83 percent—a very good percentage for a gift shop. To enhance its net profit margin, a retailer must either raise gross profit as a percentage of sales or reduce expenses as a percentage of sales.[2] It could lift gross profit by purchasing opportunistically, selling exclusive products, avoiding price competition through excellent service, and adding items with higher margins. It could reduce operating costs by stressing self-service, lowering labor costs, refinancing the mortgage, cutting energy costs, and so on. The firm must be careful not to lessen customer service to the extent that sales and profit would decline.

Asset turnover is a performance measure based on a retailer's net sales and total assets:

$$\text{Asset turnover} = \frac{\text{Net sales}}{\text{Total assets}}$$

Donna's Gift Shop had a very low asset turnover, 1.0143, and it averaged $1.01 in sales per dollar of total assets. To improve the asset turnover ratio, a firm must generate increased sales from the same level of assets or keep the same sales with fewer assets. A firm might increase sales by having longer hours, accepting Web orders, training employees to sell additional products, or stocking better-known brands. None of these tactics requires expanding the asset base. Or a firm might maintain its sales on a lower asset base by moving to a smaller store, simplifying fixtures (or having suppliers install fixtures), keeping a smaller inventory, and negotiating for the property owner to pay part of the costs of a renovation.

By looking at the relationship between net profit margin and asset turnover, **return on assets (ROA)** can be computed:

$$\text{Return on assets} = \text{Net profit margin} \times \text{Asset turnover}$$

$$\text{Return on assets} = \frac{\text{Net profit after taxes}}{\text{Net sales}} \times \frac{\text{Net sales}}{\text{Total assets}}$$

$$= \frac{\text{Net profit after taxes}}{\text{Total assets}}$$

Donna's Gift Shop had an ROA of 5.9 percent ($.0583 \times 1.0143 = 0.059$). This return is below average for gift stores; the firm's good net profit margin does not adequately offset its low asset turnover.

Financial leverage is a performance measure based on the relationship between a retailer's total assets and net worth:

$$\text{Financial leverage} = \frac{\text{Total assets}}{\text{Net worth}}$$

Donna's Gift Shop's financial leverage ratio was 1.9314. Assets were just under twice the net worth, and total liabilities and net worth were almost equal.

Careers in RETAILING — Is Retail for Me? Finance

Are numbers your game? Financial and accounting skills are more than a game in retail; they can be your career! The finance retail career area includes all accounting and treasury functions such as accounting for income, paying expenses, compiling and maintaining financial records, money management and cash flow control, banking, investment, and credit lines. Auditory responsibilities may also fall into this retail career area.

Here are some senior-level positions in finance:

- *Chief Financial Officer (CFO):* The head of all accounting and treasury functions for the firm. May also supervise the information systems department.
- *Controller:* This position is responsible for compiling and maintaining the integrity of the firm's fiscal records and reports. May have accounting department managers as subordinates but is not the CFO; this position reports to the CFO.
- *Treasurer:* Responsible for money management and cash flow control, which includes banking, investment, and credit lines. Responsible for money management and cash flow control, which includes banking, investment, and credit lines.
- *Top Internal Auditor:* Department head responsible for verifying the accuracy of fiscal records and/or policy compliance. May also do operations audits.

Source: Reprinted by permission of the National Retail Federation.

This ratio was slightly lower than the average for gift stores (a conservative group). The store is in no danger.

A retailer with a high financial leverage ratio has substantial debt, while a ratio of 1 means it has no debt—assets equal net worth. If the ratio is too high, there may be an excessive focus on cost-cutting and short-run sales so as to make interest payments, net profit margins may suffer, and a firm may be forced into bankruptcy if debts cannot be paid. When financial leverage is low, a retailer may be overly conservative—limiting its ability to renovate and expand existing stores and to enter new markets. Leverage is too low if owner's equity is relatively high; equity could be partly replaced by increasing short- and long-term loans and/or accounts payable. Some equity funds could be taken out of a business by the owner (stockholders, if a public firm).

The Strategic Profit Model

The relationship among net profit margin, asset turnover, and financial leverage is expressed by the **strategic profit model**, which reflects a performance measure known as **return on net worth (RONW)**. See Figure 12-1. The strategic profit model can be used in planning or controlling assets. Thus, a retailer could learn that the major cause of its poor return on net worth is weak asset turnover or financial leverage that is too low. A firm can raise its return on net worth by lifting the net profit margin, asset turnover, or financial leverage. Because these measures are multiplied to determine return on net worth, doubling *any* of them would double the return on net worth.

This is how the strategic profit model can be applied to Donna's Gift Shop:

$$
\begin{aligned}
\text{Return on net worth} &= \frac{\text{Net profit after taxes}}{\text{Net sales}} \times \frac{\text{Net sales}}{\text{Total assets}} \times \frac{\text{Total assets}}{\text{Net worth}} \\[6pt]
&= \frac{\$19,250}{\$330,000} \times \frac{\$330,000}{\$325,350} \times \frac{\$325,350}{\$168,450} \\[6pt]
&= .0583 \quad\times 1.0143 \quad\times 1.9314 \\[6pt]
&= .1142 \quad= 11.4\%
\end{aligned}
$$

Visit this site (**www.pnwassoc.com/issues/codbanalysis.htm**) to see how the strategic profit model can be applied to a hardware store.

Overall, Donna's return on net worth was above average for gift stores.

Table 12-3 applies the strategic profit model to various retailers. It is best to make comparisons among firms within given retail categories. For example, the net profit margins of general merchandise retailers have historically been higher than those of food retailers. Because financial performance differs from year to year, caution is advised in studying these data. Furthermore, the individual components of the strategic profit model must be analyzed, not just the return on net worth. For example,

- TJX had the highest return on net worth among apparel retailers (and among all 20 retailers shown in Table 12-3). Its net profit margin was lower than other apparel retailers; its asset turnover was quite strong. TJX was also more financially leveraged than the other apparel retailers.

FIGURE 12-1
The Strategic Profit Model

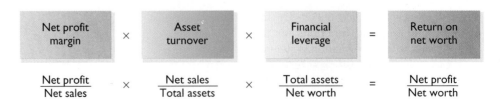

TABLE 12-3	**Application of Strategic Profit Model to Selected Retailers (2004 Data)**			
Retailer	Net Profit Margin ✕	Asset Turnover ✕	Financial Leverage =	Return on Net Worth
Apparel Retailers				
The Limited, Inc.	7.49%	1.55	2.61	30.30%
TJX	4.45%	2.94	3.07	40.16%
Gap, Inc.	7.07%	1.62	2.04	23.36%
Consumer Electronics Retailers				
Best Buy	3.26%	2.84	2.53	23.42%
Circuit City	0.06%	2.76	1.82	00.30%
Drugstore Retailers				
Walgreens	3.62%	2.81	1.62	16.48%
CVS	3.00%	2.10	2.08	13.10%
Food Retailers				
Publix	4.38%	3.13	1.66	22.76%
Albertson's	1.19%	2.18	3.38	8.77%
Safeway	1.56%	2.33	3.57	12.98%
General Merchandise Retailers				
Wal-Mart	3.69%	2.37	2.43	21.25%
Target Corp.	4.02%	1.45	2.48	14.46%
Sears	1.04%	1.61	3.69	6.18%
Costco	1.83%	3.19	1.98	11.56%
Federated Department Stores	4.41%	1.05	2.41	11.16%
J.C. Penney	3.62%	1.30	2.91	13.69%
Home Improvement Retailers				
Home Depot	6.84%	1.88	1.61	20.70%
Lowe's	5.97%	1.72	1.84	18.89%
Office Supplies Retailers				
Staples	4.90%	2.04	1.72	17.19%
Office Depot	2.48%	2.00	2.10	10.42%

Source: Computed by the authors from data in company annual reports.

- Best Buy's profit margins far surpassed those of Circuit City (which had the lowest return on net worth among the 20 retailers listed in Table 12-3).
- Sears' return on net worth lagged well behind that of other general merchandise retailers. Its profit margins were especially low; and Sears was the most highly leveraged general mechandiser.

Other Key Business Ratios

Other ratios can also measure retailer success or failure in reaching performance goals. Here are several key business ratios—besides those covered in the preceding discussion:

- *Quick ratio*—cash plus accounts receivable divided by total current liabilities, those due within one year. A ratio above 1 to 1 means the firm is liquid and can cover short-term debt.
- *Current ratio*—total current assets (cash, accounts receivable, inventories, and marketable securities) divided by total current liabilities. A ratio of 2 to 1 or more is good.

- *Collection period*—accounts receivable divided by net sales and then multiplied by 365. If most sales are on credit, a collection period one-third or more over normal terms (such as 40.0 for a store with 30-day credit terms) means slow-turning receivables.

- *Accounts payable to net sales*—accounts payable divided by annual net sales. This compares how a retailer pays suppliers relative to volume transacted. A figure above the industry average indicates that a firm relies on suppliers to finance operations.

The Census Bureau, online, provides more than a decade of gross profit (gross margin) percentage data by line of business (**www.census.gov/svsd/ retlann/view/table7.txt**).

- *Overall gross profit*—net sales minus the cost of goods sold and then divided by net sales. This companywide average includes markdowns, discounts, and shortages.[3]

Table 12-4 presents key business ratios—including net profit margin, asset turnover, and return on net worth—for several retail categories. From this table, a hardware store owner would learn that the industry average is a marginal quick ratio of 0.9; liquid assets are slightly less than current liabilities. The current ratio of 3.2 is good, mostly due to the value of inventory on hand. The collection period of 15.3 days is moderate, considering the many small sales paid for in cash. Accounts payable of 4.3 percent of sales is good. The overall gross profit of 35.8 percent covers both operating costs and profit. The net profit margin of 1.5 percent

TABLE 12-4	Median Key Business Ratios for Selected Retailer Categories						
Line of Business	QR (times)	CR (times)	CP (days)	AP (%)	OGP (%)[a]	NPM (%)	AT (times)	RONW (%)
Auto & home supply stores	0.8	2.0	23.7	6.2	35.6	1.4	2.9	8.2
Car dealers (new and used)	0.2	1.2	5.5	0.7	13.7	1.0	4.2	16.4
Catalog & mail-order firms	0.7	1.8	8.4	5.6	40.9	1.8	3.2	10.2
Department stores	0.5	2.7	8.4	6.6	34.2	1.5	2.1	6.4
Direct-selling companies	0.7	1.3	32.5	4.3	44.8	2.5	3.2	18.6
Drug & proprietary stores	1.1	2.7	15.0	3.5	24.1	1.7	5.0	14.1
Eating places	0.5	0.9	3.3	2.9	54.9	1.9	2.7	13.7
Family clothing stores	0.8	3.7	6.2	3.9	38.5	4.3	2.4	8.1
Florists	0.9	2.0	15.0	4.4	49.2	1.1	2.8	7.4
Furniture stores	0.7	2.4	17.2	4.8	40.5	1.3	2.5	5.9
Gasoline service stations	0.6	1.3	5.8	2.9	16.2	0.7	4.5	9.0
Gift, novelty, & souvenir shops	0.6	2.5	2.0	4.0	45.8	1.8	2.5	8.1
Grocery stores	0.5	1.6	2.9	3.1	24.1	0.8	5.0	8.4
Hardware stores	0.9	3.2	15.3	4.3	35.8	1.5	2.3	6.5
Hobby, toy, & game shops	0.4	2.6	1.5	5.4	43.5	0.7	2.6	5.8
Jewelry stores	0.5	2.9	15.2	8.0	44.6	1.3	1.6	4.6
Lumber & other materials dealers	1.2	2.7	34.7	4.4	27.0	1.5	2.8	9.1
Men's & boys' clothing stores	0.6	2.9	8.0	5.5	42.6	1.5	2.4	5.7
Radio, TV, & electronics stores	0.7	1.8	16.4	5.4	39.5	1.0	2.9	7.0
Sewing & needlework stores	0.3	3.2	2.6	6.1	45.1	1.5	2.4	5.0
Shoe stores	0.4	2.9	2.0	6.0	40.0	2.8	2.4	4.8
Sporting-goods & bicycle stores	0.3	2.0	3.7	8.2	36.6	1.2	2.6	7.0
Variety stores	0.5	2.9	2.6	3.6	37.5	0.9	2.9	5.1
Women's clothing stores	0.7	2.7	6.2	4.6	40.9	3.4	2.8	7.0

QR = Quick ratio
CR = Current ratio
CP = Collection period
AP = Accounts payable to net sales

OGP = Overall gross profit
NPM = Net profit margin after taxes
AT = Asset turnover
RONW = Return on net worth

[a] Gross profit is reported as means rather than medians and represents net figures, which take into account all deductions (such as markdowns, discounts, and shortages).

Source: Industry Norms and Key Business Ratios (New York: Dun & Bradstreet, 2003–04), pp. 125–142. Reprinted by permission.

is low for nonfood retailing. Asset turnover is conservative, 2.3, another indicator of the value of inventory. The return on net worth percentage of 6.5 is extremely low. In sum, hardware stores typically require high inventory and other investments and yield low to medium returns.

At our Web site (**www.prenhall.com/bermanevans**), we have links to each of the Yahoo! Finance sites related to retailers' financial performance.

Financial Trends in Retailing

Entrepreneur's "Money" section (**www. entrepreneurmag.com**) has a lot of valuable advice for small businesses.

Several trends relating to asset management merit discussion: the state of the U.S. economy; funding sources (including initial public offerings); mergers, consolidations, and spinoffs; bankruptcies and liquidations; and questionable accounting and financial reporting practices.

Many retailers are affected by the growth of the U.S. economy. During a strong economy, high consumer demand may mask retailer weaknesses. But when the economy is weak, sales stagnate, cash flow problems may occur, heavy markdowns may be needed (which cut profit margins), and consumers are more reluctant to buy big-ticket items. Furthermore, public firms may see their stock prices plummet, as happened in the early 2000s: "For much of the 1990s, retailers could mask operational issues and/or inefficiencies behind the booming market. Today, there is nowhere to hide. Those firms that best manage working capital and cash flow and remain focused on their business are well-positioned to withstand current market conditions. Others, unfortunately, will not survive."[4]

Three sources of funding are proving popular with retailers. First, because interest rates have remained quite low, many companies have refinanced their mortgages—which can dramatically decrease their monthly interest payments. Overall, refinancing is saving retailers billions of dollars yearly.[5]

Second, shopping center developers often use a real-estate investment trust (REIT) to fund construction. With this strategy, investors buy shares in an REIT as they would a stock. Investors like REITs because real-estate has historically been a good investment: "A REIT is a company that owns, and in most cases, operates income-producing real-estate such as shopping centers. Some REITs also engage in financing real-estate. Shares of many REITs are freely traded, usually on a major stock exchange. To qualify as a REIT, a firm must distribute at least 90 percent of taxable income to shareholders annually."[6]

Third, a funding source that has gained more retailing acceptance over the past 15 years is the initial public offering (IPO), whereby a firm raises money by selling stock. An IPO is typically used to fund expansion. What do investors look for in an IPO? "They want a company to have a history of profitability. They want to see revenue growth and strong backing. And they want a company to match up well against companies already trading." Among the retailers engaging in IPOs over the last several years are DSW (footwear), Petco, Kirkland's (home decorating products), Zumiez (sports-related apparel), and Overstock.com. Why? As 99 Cents Only Stores' president remarked: "Being public pushed us to grow faster. Having your firm traded at a stock exchange provides instant credibility with suppliers and manufacturers. Plus, the stock is a powerful motivational tool for employees in stock-option programs."[7]

Mergers and consolidations represent a way for retailers to add to their asset base without building new facilities or waiting for new business units to turn a profit. They also present a way for weak retailers to receive financial transfusions. For example, in recent years, Kmart acquired Sears, Dick's Sporting Goods acquired Gaylan's, Federated Department Stores acquired May Department Stores, and Foot Locker acquired Foot Action. All of these deals were driven by the weakness of the acquired firms. Typically mergers and consolidations lead to some stores being shut, particularly those with trading-area overlap, and cutbacks among management personnel.

The leveraged buyout (LBO) is a type of acquisition in which a retail owner-ship change is mostly financed by loans from banks, investors, and others. The LBO phenomenon has had a big effect on retail budgeting and cash flow. At times, because debts incurred with LBOs can be high, some well-known retailers have had to focus more on paying interest on their debts than on investing in their busi-nesses, run sales to generate enough cash to cover operating costs and buy new merchandise, and sell store units to pay off debt. One major retailer recently involved with an LBO was the weakened Toys "R" Us

Retailers sometimes consolidate their businesses to streamline operations and improve profits. In the past few years, Winn-Dixie, Eddie Bauer, Circuit City, Kmart, and several other firms have closed underperforming stores. Other times, retailers use spinoffs to generate more money or to sell a division that no longer meets expectations. Target sold off its Mervyn's and Marshall Field's divisions, Saks Inc. sold off Proffitt's and McRae's department store chains, and Viacom spun off its Blockbuster store division. See Figure 12-2. As the Saks chief executive stated at the time of the spinoff: "We believe it is appropriate to divide our depart-ment store businesses into distinct enterprises and permit each to have its own focused future. The decision to sell Proffitt's and McRae's was made very deliber-ately. We believe this strategy is in the long-term best interests of our shareholders, our customers, and our associates."[8]

When they want to continue in business, weak retailers file Chapter 11. If they want to liquidate, they file Chapter 7 (www.uscourts. gov/library/bankbasic.pdf).

To safeguard themselves against mounting debts, as well to continue in busi-ness, faltering retailers may seek bankruptcy protection under Chapter 11 of the Federal Bankruptcy Code (which was amended in 2005[9]). With bankruptcy pro-tection, retailers can renegotiate bills, get out of leases, and work with creditors to plan for the future. Declaring bankruptcy has major ramifications: "While some believe that filing for bankruptcy results in the loss of key executives, disruptions in supply, and demoralization on those who stay, others say it fends off creditors and lets firms pay off debt and survive what may be a temporary upheaval. Executives who are not in favor of filing also cite the cost of legal and financial advisory fees of bankruptcy protection."[10]

FIGURE 12-2
Rebuilding Mervyn's

Since being sold by Target Corporation, the Mervyn's (**www.mervyns.com**) value department store chain has been striving to improve its busi-ness. Mervyn's is now privately held: "Our stores have an aver-age of 50,000 retail square feet, smaller than most other mid-tier retailers and easier to shop, and are located primarily in regional malls, community shopping centers, and free-standing sites."

Photo reprinted by permission of Susan Berry, Retail Image Consulting, Inc.

Technology in RETAILING — Analyzing Data: The Wal-Mart Way

Wal-Mart's (**www.walmart.com**) data warehouse is capable of storing two years' worth of transactions that have been generated in over 5,000 of its stores. One of the special challenges to a Wal-Mart supplier is the massive quantity of data that are available through Wal-Mart's Retail Link data-sharing system.

The data base contains information that can help vendors better manage their inventory, see trends as they emerge, and improve markdown control. Wal-Mart also constantly reminds its suppliers to make better use of this information. Many suppliers blend the Retail Link data with research from such market research firms as Information Resources, Inc. (**www.infores.com**) and A.C.

Nielsen (**www.acnielsen.com**). Other firms produce software that facilitates data collection and analysis.

Five years ago, Northwest Arkansas Community College developed a program to train personnel in the dynamics of Retail Link. According to Shawn Beezley, coordinator of the marketing analyst certification program at the school, "If you get someone who really knows what they are doing, they are worth their weight in gold." Many of the students in this program already had four-year degrees when they enrolled.

Source: "Wanted: Skilled Marketing Analysts," *DSN Retailing Today* (February 10, 2005), pp. 13–15.

Here's a recent bankruptcy example. In 2005, Winn-Dixie, one of the largest supermarket chains in the United States, filed for bankruptcy protection:

> After suffering a "perfect storm" of bad conditions which forced Winn-Dixie Stores into bankruptcy, the supermarket giant's CEO said it is now trying to stabilize itself as it decides how many stores to close and how many of its 78,000 employees to lay off. Winn-Dixie, once one of the South's most prosperous supermarket chains, was hit by high inventories, low sales, tightening vendor credit, and a tarnished reputation. Those conditions forced Winn-Dixie and 23 of its subsidiaries to seek protection from its creditors. As the CEO noted, "We are stabilizing the ship, but at the end of the day we need to move the needle on sales. We have far too much overhead in the Jacksonville corporate offices. This thing is upside down, but we are headed in the right direction." The chain listed assets of $2.2 billion and liabilities of $1.9 billion in its bankruptcy filing.[11]

Not all bankruptcies end up with rejuvenated retailers. Many end up in liquidations, where the firms ultimately go out of business. This has happened with Montgomery Ward, Ames Department Stores, One Price Clothing, Frank's Nursery, Factory 2 You, and Scotty's. When a retailer goes out of business, it is painful for all parties: the owner/stockholders, employees, creditors, landlords (who then have vacant store sites), and customers.

As with several other sectors of business, over the last few years, some retailers have been heavily criticized for questionable accounting and financial practices. Here are two examples:

- At the Krispy Kreme donut chain, the Securities and Exchange Commission (SEC) started with an informal inquiry about the franchisor's buybacks of several franchises. The situation then quickly escalated: "As the stock price plunged, shareholders filed suit. Franchisees alleged channel stuffing, claiming that some stores were getting twice their regular shipments in the final weeks of a quarter so that headquarters could make its numbers." The SEC upgraded its investigation to formal. As a result, "Average weekly sales, a key retailing measure, fell even as the company continued to add stores. In early 2005, Krispy Kreme decided to restate its financials for much of fiscal 2004." Six senior executives were fired during June 2005.[12]

- In 2005, the CVS drugstore chain agreed to pay $110 million to shareholders to settle a lawsuit: "The lawsuit alleged that CVS violated accounting practices by delaying discounts on merchandise in an effort to prop up earnings. The complaint also accused CVS and its chief executive in 2001 of waiting several months to disclose that CVS intended to shutter 200 underperforming stores and that a pharmacist shortage would have a negative impact on the company." In a press release about the settlement, "CVS officials said the company 'continues to deny liability and entered into the settlement agreement solely to avoid the risk and diversion of resources associated with trial.'"[13]

To bolster public confidence and stockholder equity, retailers need to be as "transparent" as possible in their accounting and financial reporting practices:

In the aftermath of the Enron scandal, more retailers are being proactive in sharing their views on disclosure and accurate financial reporting with investors. Wal-Mart, in its annual report, noted that, "The financial results reported here will provide you, the stakeholders, with a review of our company, and will provide a detailed discussion about those financial matters that are significant to your company. Although it is not the most exciting reading, our team has worked hard to make these reports comprehensive, yet simple, and I would encourage you to review them." The increased disclosure now practiced by retailers and the relatively straightforward accounting involved in a retail business have made the industry attractive to investors looking for stability in turbulent times. Yet, retailers will almost certainly be forced to live with new and unknown finance-related requirements from elected officials and government regulators who don't want another Enron.[14]

BUDGETING

Why does a new business need a formal budget? Type "Budgeting" at this site (**www.entrepreneurmag. com**).

Budgeting outlines a retailer's planned expenditures for a given time based on expected performance. Costs are linked to satisfying target market, employee, and management goals. What should personnel costs be to attain a certain level of customer service? What compensation amount will motivate salespeople? What operating expenses will generate intended revenues and reach profit goals?

There are several benefits from a retailer's meticulously preparing a budget:

- Expenditures are clearly related to expected performance, and costs can be adjusted as goals are revised. This enhances productivity.
- Resources are allocated to the right departments, product categories, and so on.
- Spending for various departments, product categories, and so on is coordinated.
- Because planning is structured and integrated, the goal of efficiency is prominent.
- Cost standards are set, such as advertising equals 5 percent of sales.
- A firm prepares for the future rather than reacts to it.
- Expenditures are monitored during a budget cycle. If a firm allots $50,000 to buy new merchandise, and it has spent $33,000 halfway through a cycle, it has $17,000 remaining.
- A firm can analyze planned budgets versus actual budgets.
- Costs and performance can be compared with industry averages.

A retailer should be aware of the effort in the budgeting process, recognize that forecasts may not be fully accurate (due to unexpected demand, competitors' tactics, and so forth), and modify plans as needed. It should not be too conservative (or inflexible) or simply add a percentage to each expense category to arrive at

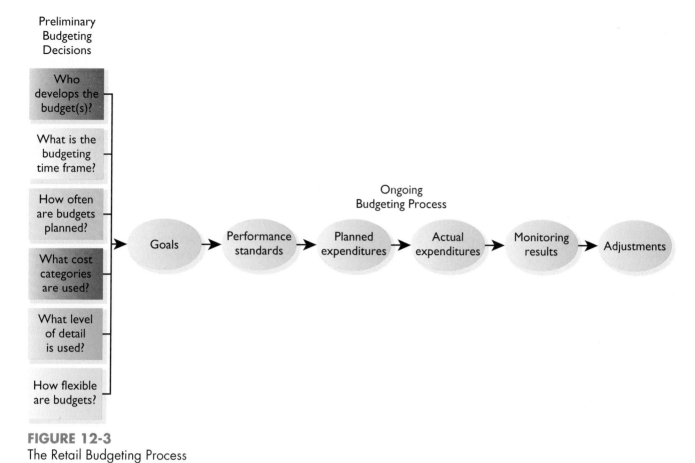

FIGURE 12-3
The Retail Budgeting Process

the next budget, such as increasing spending by 3 percent across the board based on anticipated sales growth of 3 percent. The budgeting process is shown in Figure 12-3 and described next.

Preliminary Budgeting Decisions

There are six preliminary decisions.

First, budgeting authority is specified. In top-down budgeting, senior executives make centralized financial decisions and communicate them down the line to succeeding levels of managers. In bottom-up budgeting, lower-level executives develop departmental budget requests; these requests are assembled, and a company budget is designed. Bottom-up budgeting includes varied perspectives, holds managers more accountable, and enhances employee morale. Many firms combine aspects of the two approaches.

Second, the time frame is defined. Most firms have budgets with yearly, quarterly, and monthly components. Annual spending is planned, while costs and performance are regularly reviewed. This responds to seasonal or other fluctuations. Sometimes the time frame is longer than a year or shorter than a month. When a firm opens new stores over a five-year period, it sets construction costs for the entire period. When a supermarket orders perishables, it has weekly budgets for each item.

Third, budgeting frequency is determined. Many firms review budgets on an ongoing basis, but most plan them yearly. In some firms, several months may be set aside each year for the budgeting process; this lets all participants have time to gather data and facilitates taking the budgets through several drafts.

Fourth, cost categories are established:

- *Capital expenditures* are long-term investments in land, buildings, fixtures, and equipment. *Operating expenditures* are the short-term expenses of running a business.
- *Fixed costs*, such as store security, remain constant for the budget period regardless of the retailer's performance. *Variable costs*, such as sales commissions, are based on performance. If performance is good, these expenses often rise.
- *Direct costs* are incurred by specific departments, product categories, and so on, such as the earnings of department based salespeople. *Indirect costs*, such as centralized cashiers, are shared by multiple departments, product categories, and so on.
- *Natural account expenses* are reported by the names of the costs, such as salaries, and not assigned by purpose. *Functional account expenses* are classified on the basis of the purpose or activity for which expenditures are made, such as cashier salaries.

Fifth, the level of detail is set. Should spending be assigned by department (produce), product category (fresh fruit), product subcategory (apples), or product item (McIntosh apples)? With a very detailed budget, every expense subcategory must be adequately covered.

Sixth, budget flexibility is prescribed. A budget should be strict enough to guide planned spending and link costs to goals. Yet, a budget that is too inflexible may not let a retailer adapt to changing market conditions, capitalize on new opportunities, or modify a poor strategy (if further spending is needed to improve matters). Budget flexibility is often expressed in quantitative terms, such as allowing a buyer to increase a quarterly budget by a certain maximum percentage if demand is higher than anticipated.

Ongoing Budgeting Process

After making preliminary budgeting decisions, the retailer engages in the ongoing budgeting process shown in Figure 12-3:

- Goals are set based on customer, employee, and management needs.
- Performance standards are specified, including customer service levels, the compensation needed to motivate employees, and the sales and profits

RETAILING Around the World — Offshore Outsourcing: What Is the Proper Balance?

Retailers must consider off-shore manufacturing's impact on revenues due to longer lead times. Two retailers that are commonly mentioned for their successful sourcing operations are World Co. Ltd. of Japan (**www.world.co.jp/english**) and Zara (**www.zara.com**), which is headquartered in Spain. Both of these fashion-based retailers have reduced lead times from six months to as little as six weeks.

World Co. Ltd.'s speedy supply chain is the result of careful planning, an information system that constantly updates forecasts, and flexible production processes. Although domestic labor is more costly than overseas, World Co. maintains domestic production due to its ability to more quickly respond to fashion trends.

Zara produces about 11,000 distinct items annually; in contrast, its key competitors produce from 2,000 to 4,000 items. Zara is able to design a new product and have the new product in its stores in four to five weeks; it can modify an existing item in as little as two weeks. Zara manufactures its riskiest items domestically so they can be produced in small quantities and reordered more frequently based on sales trends.

Sources: "Offshoring: Bringing Retailing Back into Balance," *Frontline Solutions* (July 2004), pp. 12-13; "World Investor Relations," **www.world.co.jp/english/ir/databook.html** (January 11, 2006); and "Zara: Business," **www.zara.com** (January 11, 2006).

needed to satisfy management. Typically, the budget is related to a sales forecast, which projects revenues for the next period. Forecasts are usually broken down by department or product category.

- Expenditures are planned in terms of performance goals. In **zero-based budgeting**, a firm starts each new budget from scratch and outlines the expenditures needed to reach that period's goals. All costs are justified each time a budget is done. With **incremental budgeting**, a firm uses current and past budgets as guides and adds to or subtracts from them to arrive at the coming period's expenditures. Most retailers use incremental budgeting because it is easier, less time-consuming, and not as risky.

- Actual expenditures are made. The retailer pays rent and employee salaries, buys merchandise, places ads, and so on.

- Results are monitored: (1) Actual expenditures are compared with planned spending for each expense category, and reasons for any deviations are reviewed. (2) The firm learns if performance standards have been met and tries to explain deviations.

- The budget is adjusted. Revisions are major or minor, depending on how closely a firm has come to reaching its goals. The funds allotted to some expense categories may be reduced, while greater funds may be provided to other categories.

Table 12-5 compares budgeted and actual revenues, expenses, and profits for Donna's Gift Shop during fiscal 2006. The actual data come from Table 12-1. The variance figures compare expected and actual results for each profit-and-loss item. Variances are positive if performance is better than expected and negative if it is worse.

TABLE 12-5	Donna's Gift Shop, Fiscal 2006 Budgeted versus Actual Profit-and-Loss Statement (in Dollars and Percent)					
	BUDGETED		**ACTUAL**		**VARIANCE**[a]	
	Dollars	Percent	Dollars	Percent	Dollars	Percent
Net sales	$300,000	100.00	$330,000	100.00	+$30,000	—
Cost of goods sold	$165,000	55.00	$180,000	54.55	−$15,000	+0.45
Gross profit	$135,000	45.00	$150,000	45.45	+$15,000	+0.45
Operating expenses:						
Salaries	$ 75,000	25.00	$ 75,000	22.73	—	+2.27
Advertising	5,250	1.75	4,950	1.50	+$ 300	+0.25
Supplies	1,800	0.60	1,650	0.50	+$ 150	+0.10
Shipping	1,350	0.45	1,500	0.45	−$ 150	—
Insurance	4,500	1.50	4,500	1.36	—	+0.14
Maintenance	5,100	1.70	5,100	1.55	—	+0.15
Other	3,000	1.00	2,550	0.77	+$ 450	+0.23
Total	$ 96,000	32.00	$ 95,250	28.86	+$ 750	+3.14
Other costs	$ 18,000	6.00	$ 20,000	6.06	−$ 2,000	−0.06
Total costs	$114,000	38.00	$115,250	34.92	−$ 1,250	+3.08
Net profit before taxes	$ 21,000	7.00	$ 34,750	10.53	+$13,750	+3.53
Taxes	$ 9,000	3.00	$ 15,500	4.70	−$ 6,500	−1.70
Net profit after taxes	$ 12,000	4.00	$ 19,250	5.83	+$ 7,250	+1.83

There are small rounding errors.

[a] Variance is a positive number if actual sales or profits are higher than expected or actual expenses are lower than expected. Variance is a negative number if actual sales or profits are lower than expected or actual expenses are higher than expected.

As Table 12-5 indicates, in *dollar terms*, net profit after taxes was $7,250 higher than budgeted. Sales were $30,000 higher than expected; thus, the cost of goods sold was $15,000 higher. Actual operating expenses were $750 lower than expected, while other costs were $2,000 higher. Table 12-5 also shows results in *percentage terms*. This lets a firm evaluate budgeted versus actual performance on a percent-of-sales basis. In Donna's case, actual net profit after taxes was 5.83 percent of sales—better than planned. The higher net profit was mostly due to the actual operating costs percentage being lower than planned.

Learn more about cash flow management by typing "Cash Flow" at this site (www.entrepreneurmag. com).

A firm must closely monitor its **cash flow**, which relates the amount and timing of revenues received to the amount and timing of expenditures for a specific time. In cash flow management, the usual intention is to make sure revenues are received before expenditures are made.[15] Otherwise, short-term loans may be needed or profits may be tied up in inventory and other expenses. For seasonal retailers, this may be unavoidable. Underestimating costs and overestimating revenues, both of which affect cash flow, are leading causes of new business failures. Table 12-6 has cash flow examples.

TABLE 12-6	The Effects of Cash Flow

A.

A retailer has rather consistent sales throughout the year. Therefore, the cash flow in any given month is positive. This means no short-term loans are needed, and the owner can withdraw funds from the firm if she so desires:

Linda's Luncheonette, Cash Flow for January

Cash inflow:		
Net sales		$11,000
Cash outflow:		
Cost of goods sold	$2,500	
Operating expenses	3,500	
Other costs	2,000	
Total		$ 8,000
Positive cash flow		$ 3,000

B.

A retailer has highly seasonal sales that peak in December. Yet, to have a good assortment of merchandise on hand during December, it must order merchandise in September and October and pay for it in November. As a result, it has a negative cash flow in November that must be financed by a short-term loan. All debts are paid off in January, after the peak selling season is completed:

Dave's Party Favors, Cash Flow for November

Cash inflow:		
Net sales		$14,000
Cash outflow:		
Cost of goods sold	$12,500	
Operating expenses	3,000	
Other costs	2,100	
Total		$17,600
Net cash flow		−$ 3,600
Short-term loan (to be paid off in January)		$ 3,600

RESOURCE ALLOCATION

In allotting financial resources, both the magnitude of various costs and productivity should be examined. Each has significance for asset management and budgeting.

The Magnitude of Various Costs

To easily study the financial operating performance of publicly owned retailers, go to AnnualReports.com (www.annualreports.com), enter a company name, and download its 10K report.

As noted before, spending can be divided into two categories. **Capital expenditures** are long-term investments in fixed assets. **Operating expenditures** are short-term selling and administrative costs in running a business. It is vital to have a sense of the magnitude of various capital and operating costs.

In 2005, these were the average capital expenditures (for the basic building shell; heating, ventilation, and air-conditioning; lighting; flooring; fixtures; ceilings; interior and exterior signage; and roofing) for erecting a single store for a range of retailers: department store—$11.8 million; supermarket—$6 million; big-box discount store—$5.2 million; home center—$2.5 million; apparel specialty store—$1.8 million; and drugstore—$1.2 million.[16] Thus, a typical home center chain must be prepared to invest $2.5 million to build each new outlet (which averaged 33,200 square feet industrywide in 2005), not including land and merchandise costs; the total could be higher if a bigger store is built.

Remodeling can also be expensive. It is prompted by competitive pressures, mergers and acquisitions, consumer trends, the requirement of complying with the Americans with Disabilities Act, environmental concerns, and other factors.

To reduce their investments, some retailers insist that real-estate developers help pay for building, renovating, and fixturing costs. These demands by retail tenants reflect some areas' oversaturation, the amount of retail space available due to the liquidation of some retailers (as well as mergers), and the interest of developers in gaining retailers that generate consumer traffic (such as category killers).

Operating expenses, usually expressed as a percentage of sales, range from 20 percent or so in supermarkets to over 40 percent in some specialty stores. To succeed, these costs must be in line with competitors'. Costco has an edge over many rivals due to lower SGA (selling, general, and administrative expenses as a percentage of sales): Costco, 10 percent; Wal-Mart, 18 percent; Kohl's, 25 percent; Target, 26 percent; and Dillard's, 33 percent. However, BJ's SGA is 8 percent.[17]

Ethics in RETAILING

Visa and MasterCard: Reimbursing Retailers for Transaction Fee Overcharges

As part of a $3.05 billion settlement in a class action suit involving 8 million retailers, Visa (www.visa.com) and MasterCard (www.mastercard.com) agreed to drop their "honor all" policy. Under the honor all plan, retailers had to accept both an issuer's debit and credit cards. Visa and MasterCard also agreed to more clearly label debit cards and to lower certain transaction fees for past debit card transactions (made in 2003).

According to George Green, vice-president of the Food Marketing Institute (www.fmi.org) in Washington, D.C., "Retailers were, and are in many cases, paying the banks more for the processing of transactions than they are making at the front end of the store. They might be making a penny on the dollar while the processing fee is greater than 1 percent."

The major impact of the settlement is the recognition by credit card providers that their fees to retailers are no longer "set in stone." Some retailers are now able to negotiate and obtain lower debit card transaction prices. To get the best rates, some merchants have threatened to stop accepting debit cards except on PIN-based transactions.

Source: Lamont Wood, "Credit-Card Settlement: Payments on the Way," *Retail Technology Quarterly* (January 2005), pp. 8A, 12A.

Resource allocation must also take into account **opportunity costs**—the possible benefits a retailer forgoes if it invests in one opportunity rather than another. If a supermarket chain renovates 25 existing stores at a total cost of $6 million, it cannot open a new outlet requiring a $6 million investment (excluding land and merchandise). Financial resources are finite, so firms often face either/or decisions.

Productivity

Look at the various ways in which retailers can improve their financial performance (**www.toolkit.cch.com/text/P06_0100.asp**).

Due to erratic sales, mixed economic growth, high labor costs, intense competition, and other factors, many retailers place great priority on improving **productivity**, the efficiency with which a retail strategy is carried out. Productivity can be described in terms of costs as a percentage of sales, the time it takes a cashier to complete a transaction, profit margins, sales per square foot, inventory turnover, and so forth. The key question is: How can sales and profit goals be reached while keeping control over costs?

Because different retail strategy mixes have distinct resource needs as to store location, fixtures, personnel, and other elements, productivity must be based on norms for each type of strategy mix (like department stores versus full-line discount stores). Sales growth should also be measured on the basis of comparable seasons, using the same stores. Otherwise, the data will be affected by seasonality and/or the increased square footage of stores.

There are two ways to enhance productivity: (1) A firm can improve employee performance, sales per foot of space, and other factors by upgrading training programs, increasing advertising, and so forth. (2) It can reduce costs by automating, having suppliers do certain tasks, and so forth. A retailer could use a small core of full-time workers during nonpeak times, supplemented with part-timers in peak periods.

Productivity must not be measured from a cost-cutting perspective alone. This may undermine customer loyalty. One of the more complex dilemmas for store retailers that are also online is how to handle customer returns. To control costs, some of them have decided not to allow online purchases to be returned at their stores. This policy has gotten a lot of customers upset.

These are two strategies that retailers have used to raise productivity:

- Department stores such as Sears are paying more attention to space productivity. Sears has cleared hundreds of thousands of square feet of space by removing some furniture departments, converting space that was previously used by its affiliated home improvement contractors to retail use, and better managing and displaying its merchandise categories.

Tuesday Morning has a unique customer service philosophy (**www.tuesdaymorning.com/ci/customer.asp**). It even saves money by offering online circulars.

- Tuesday Morning, a chain selling quality closeouts, shuts its stores for parts of several months. Operating costs are low because the stores save on labor expenses (part-time workers are used extensively), utilities, and insurance. The firm further reduces its costs by locating in low-rent sites. Tuesday Morning operates destination stores that are sought out by loyal customers. It does not offer online shopping: "We feel it is more economically beneficial to our customers at this time to shop the store and realize the full benefit of our 50 percent to 80 percent off retail discount, as opposed to paying additional shipping and handling charges online."[18]

Analysts say: "It turns out that what worked for manufacturers worked even better for retailers. In the second half of the 1990s, retail productivity skyrocketed. Almost all the growth came from closing old stores and opening more efficient ones with the latest equipment at the checkout and in the storeroom."[19]

Summary

1. *To define operations management.* Operations management involves efficiently and effectively implementing the tasks and policies to satisfy the retailer's customers, employees, and management. This chapter covered the financial aspects of operations management. Operational dimensions are studied in Chapter 13.

2. *To discuss profit planning.* The profit-and-loss (income) statement summarizes a retailer's revenues and expenses over a specific time, typically on a monthly, quarterly, and/or yearly basis. It consists of these major components: net sales, cost of goods sold, gross profit (margin), operating expenses, and net profit after taxes.

3. *To describe asset management, including the strategic profit model, other key business ratios, and financial trends in retailing.* Each retailer has assets and liabilities to manage. A balance sheet shows assets, liabilities, and net worth at a given time. Assets are items with a monetary value owned by a retailer; some appreciate and may have a hidden value. Liabilities are financial obligations. The retailer's net worth, also called owner's equity, is computed as assets minus liabilities.

    Asset management may be measured by reviewing the net profit margin, asset turnover, and financial leverage. Net profit margin equals net profit divided by net sales. Asset turnover equals net sales divided by total assets. By multiplying the net profit margin by asset turnover, a retailer can find its return on assets—which is based on net sales, net profit, and total assets. Financial leverage equals total assets divided by net worth. The strategic profit model incorporates asset turnover, profit margin, and financial leverage to yield the return on net worth. It allows a retailer to better plan and control its asset management.

    Other key ratios for retailers are the quick ratio, current ratio, collection period, accounts payable to net sales, and overall gross profit (in percent).

    Current financial trends involve the state of the economy; funding sources; mergers, consolidations, and spinoffs; bankruptcies and liquidations; and questionable accounting and financial reporting practices.

4. *To look at retail budgeting.* Budgeting outlines a retailer's planned expenditures for a given time based on expected performance; costs are linked to goals.

    There are six preliminary decisions: (1) Responsibility is defined by top-down and/or bottom-up methods. (2) The time frame is specified. (3) Budgeting frequency is set. (4) Cost categories are established. (5) The level of detail is ascertained. (6) Budgeting flexibility is determined.

    The ongoing budgeting process then proceeds: goals, performance standards, planned spending, actual expenditures, monitoring results, and adjustments. With zero-based budgeting, each budget starts from scratch; with incremental budgeting, current and past budgets are guides. The budgeted versus actual profit-and-loss statement and the percentage profit-and-loss statement are vital tools. In all budgeting decisions, cash flow, which relates the amount and timing of revenues received with the amount and timing of expenditures made, must be considered.

5. *To examine resource allocation.* Both the magnitude of costs and productivity need to be examined. Costs can be divided into capital and operating categories; both must be regularly reviewed. Opportunity costs mean forgoing possible benefits if a retailer invests in one opportunity rather than another. Productivity is the efficiency with which a retail strategy is carried out; the goal is to maximize sales and profits while keeping costs in check.

Key Terms

operations management (p. 356)

profit-and-loss (income) statement (p. 356)

net sales (p. 356)

cost of goods sold (p. 356)

gross profit (margin) (p. 356)

operating expenses (p. 356)

taxes (p. 356)

net profit after taxes (p. 356)

balance sheet (p. 357)

assets (p. 357)

hidden assets (p. 358)

liabilities (p. 358)

net worth (p. 358)

net profit margin (p. 358)

asset turnover (p. 359)

return on assets (ROA) (p. 359)

financial leverage (p. 359)

strategic profit model (p. 360)

return on net worth (RONW) (p. 360)

budgeting (p. 366)

zero-based budgeting (p. 369)

incremental budgeting (p. 369)

cash flow (p. 370)

capital expenditures (p. 371)

operating expenditures (p. 371)

opportunity costs (p. 372)

productivity (p. 372)

Questions for Discussion

1. Describe the relationship of assets, liabilities, and net worth for a retailer. How is a balance sheet useful in examining these items?

2. A retailer has net sales of $925,000, net profit of $145,000, total assets of $600,000, and a net worth of $225,000.
   a. Calculate net profit margin, asset turnover, and return on assets.
   b. Compute financial leverage and return on net worth.
   c. Evaluate the financial performance of this retailer.

3. How can a small grocery store increase its asset turnover?

4. Is too low a financial leverage ratio good or bad? Why?

5. Differentiate between an IPO and an LBO.

6. Present five recommendations for retailers to improve their accounting and financial reporting practices with regard to disclosure ("transparency") of all relevant information to stockholders and others.

7. What is zero-based budgeting? Why do most retailers utilize incremental budgeting, despite its limitations?

8. What is the value of a percentage profit-and-loss statement?

9. How could a seasonal retailer improve its cash flow during periods when it must buy goods for future selling periods?

10. Distinguish between capital spending and operating expenditures. Why is this distinction important to retailers?

11. What factors should retailers consider when assessing opportunity costs?

12. How can these retailers improve their productivity?
    a. Tree-trimming service.
    b. Restaurant.
    c. Movie theater.
    d. Upscale apparel store.

Note: At our Web site (**www.prenhall.com/ bermanevans**), there are several math problems related to the material in this chapter so that you may review these concepts.

Web-Based Exercise

Visit the Web site of QuickBooks (**www.quickbooks.intuit.com**), select one of its financial planning software products, and then "Take a Tour." What are benefits of a product such as this for a small retailer?

Note: Stop by our Web site (**www.prenhall.com/bermanevans**) to experience a number of highly interactive, appealing Web exercises based on actual company demonstrations and sample materials related to retailing.

Chapter Endnotes

1. Various company sources.

2. See Suzanne P. Nimocks, "Managing Overhead Costs," *McKinsey Quarterly* (Number 2, 2005), pp. 106–117.

3. *Industry Norms and Key Business Ratios* (New York: Dun & Bradstreet, 2003–04).

4. "Managing Working Capital," *Chain Store Age* (August 2001), p. 26A. See also "How to Spot Trouble in Your Financials," *Inc.* (October 2004), p. 96.

5. Charlyne H. McWilliams, "Retail Growth Spurt," *Mortgage Banking* (May 2002), pp. 24–29.

6. "What Is an REIT?" **www.investinreits.com/learn/ faq.cfm#1** (January 7, 2006).

7. Ken Clark, "Going Public: Down But Not Out," *Chain Store Age* (January 2002), pp. 55–56; Wayne Niemi, "Analysts Give DSW IPO Big Thumbs Up," *FN Online* (March 21, 2005); and Colleen O'Connor, "Specialty Retailers Poised for IPO Boom," *Investment Dealers Digest Online* (May 30, 2005).

8. "Saks Incorporated Agrees to Sell Proffitt's/McRae's to Belk, Inc. for $622 Million," *Business Wire* (April 29, 2005).

9. See Katherine Field, "Code Blue," *Chain Store Age* (June 2005), pp. 33–34.

10. Michael Hartnett, "Value of Chapter 11 Protections for Retailers Sparks Sharp Debate," *Stores* (April 1999), p. 92.

11. Matt Nannery, "Picking Up the Pieces," *Chain Store Age* (March 2002), pp. 54–62.

12. Kate O'Sullivan, "Kremed!" *CFO Online* (June 2005); and Paul Nowell, "Struggling Donut Chain Krispy Kreme Fires Six Top Executives," *Associated Press Worldstream* (June 21, 2005).

13. Jenn Abelson, "CVS Agrees to Pay $110M to Settle Suit," *Boston Globe Online* (June 7, 2005).

14. Mike Troy, "12 Hot Issues Facing Mass Retailing—2: Financial Reform," *DSN Retailing Today* (May 20, 2002), p. 21.

15. See Dennis McCafferty, "How to Manage Your Cash Flow," *VAR Business* (May 16, 2005), pp. 55–56; and Michael Hunstad, "Better Forecasting: Know Your Cash Flows," *Financial Executive* (May 2005), p. 60.

16. Computed by the authors from Marianne Wilson, "Physical Supports Census," *Chain Store Age Online* (July 2005).

17. Company annual reports.

18. "Online Shopping," **www.tuesdaymorning.com/ci/customer.asp#9** (January 26, 2006).

19. Margaret Popper, "Really Grand Openings: New Stores Boost Retail Productivity," *Business Week* (September 23, 2002), p. 32.

Chapter 13
OPERATIONS MANAGEMENT: OPERATIONAL DIMENSIONS

The term **black gold** is typically used to describe oil. However, this term is also appropriate for the coffee shops created by Howard Schultz, the chief executive of Starbucks (**www.starbucks. com**). While traveling in Italy in 1983, Schultz became excited over the coffee-bar culture there. He was very enthusiastic about the growth prospects in the United States since Milan, a city about the size of Philadelphia, supported 1,500 espresso bars.

Reprinted by permission.

Schultz was able to convince his Starbucks bosses to sell espresso at a new store in Seattle in 1984. However, they were reluctant to move into the prepared coffee business. As a result, Schultz began his own coffee-bar operation in 1985. Currently, Starbucks has over 12,500 stores in more than 35 countries. The company recently raised its worldwide target from 25,000 to 30,000 stores; this will include 15,000 stores in the United States. In fiscal 2004, Starbucks added 1,344 new stores and opened an additional 1,500 stores for fiscal year 2005. It serves over 30 million customers on a global basis each week.

In 2005, Starbucks was rated as 11th overall on the 2005 *Fortune's* "Best Places to Work" list and was number two among large companies on the same list. Retailing analysts believe that Starbucks' competitive advantages are based on the firm's superior training programs, employee stock option programs, and health and benefits packages (even for part-time employees), as well as the superiority of its coffee blends. Starbucks' executives also proclaim that its employees or "partners" have had a major impact on the positive in-store experience provided to customers.[1]

chapter objectives

1. To describe the operational scope of operations management
2. To examine several specific aspects of operating a retail business: operations blueprint; store format, size, and space allocation; personnel utilization; store maintenance, energy management, and renovations; inventory management; store security; insurance; credit management; computerization; outsourcing; and crisis management

OVERVIEW

For a good operations overview, go to About's Retail Industry site (http://retailindustry.about.com/sitesearch.htm?terms=operations).

As defined in Chapter 12, *operations management* is the efficient and effective implementation of the policies and tasks that satisfy a retailer's customers, employees, and management (and stockholders, if it is publicly owned). While Chapter 12 examined the financial dimensions of operations management, this chapter covers the operational aspects.

For firms to succeed in the long term, operational areas need to be managed well. A decision to change a store format or to introduce new anti-theft equipment must be carefully reviewed since these acts greatly affect performance. In running their businesses, retail executives must make a wide range of operational decisions, such as these:

- What operating guidelines are used?
- What is the optimal format and size of a store? What is the relationship among shelf space, shelf location, and sales for each item in the store?
- How can personnel best be matched to customer traffic flows? Would increased staffing improve or reduce productivity? What impact does self-service have on sales?
- What effect does the use of various building materials have on store maintenance? How can energy costs be better controlled? How often should facilities be renovated?
- How can inventory best be managed?
- How can the personal safety of shoppers and employees be ensured?
- What levels of insurance are required?
- How can credit transactions be managed most effectively?
- How can computer systems improve operating efficiency?
- Should any aspects of operations be outsourced?
- What kinds of crisis management plans should be in place?

OPERATING A RETAIL BUSINESS

To address these questions, we now look at the operations blueprint; store format, size, and space allocation; personnel utilization; store maintenance, energy management, and renovations; inventory management; store security; insurance; credit management; computerization; outsourcing; and crisis management.

Operations Blueprint

To encourage more compatibility among different retail hardware and software systems, the National Retail Federation has established its ARTS program (www.nrf-arts.org).

An **operations blueprint** systematically lists all the operating functions to be performed, their characteristics, and their timing. While developing a blueprint, the retailer specifies, in detail, every operating function from the store's opening to closing—and those responsible for them.[2] For example, who opens the store? When? What are the steps (turning off the alarm, turning on the power, setting up the computer, and so forth)? The performance of these tasks must not be left to chance.

A large or diversified retailer may use multiple blueprints and have separate blueprints for such areas as store maintenance, inventory management, credit management, and store displays. Whenever a retailer modifies its store format or operating procedures (such as relying more on self-service), it must also adjust the operations blueprint(s).

Figure 13-1 has an operations blueprint for a quick-oil-change firm. It identifies employee and customer tasks (in order) and expected performance times for each activity. Among the advantages of this blueprint—and others—are that it standardizes activities (within a location and between locations), isolates points at which operations may be weak or prone to failure (Do employees actually check transmission, brake, and power-steering fluids in one minute?), outlines a plan that can be evaluated for completeness (Should customers be offered different grades of oil?), shows personnel needs (Should one person change the oil and another wash the windshield?), and helps identify productivity improvements (Should the customer or an employee drive a car into and out of the service bay?).

Store Format, Size, and Space Allocation

With regard to store format, it should be determined whether productivity can be raised by such tactics as locating in a planned shopping center rather than in an unplanned business district, using prefabricated materials in construction, and applying certain kinds of store design and layouts.

A key store format decision for chain retailers is whether to use **prototype stores**, whereby multiple outlets conform to relatively uniform construction, layout, and operations standards. Such stores make centralized management control easier, reduce construction costs, standardize operations, facilitate the interchange of employees among outlets, allow fixtures and other materials to be bought in quantity, and display a consistent chain image. Yet, a strict reliance on prototypes may lead to inflexibility, failure to adapt to or capitalize on local customer needs, and too little creativity. Pep Boys, Office Depot, Starbucks, McDonald's, and most supermarket chains are among those with prototype stores.

Together with prototype stores, some chains use **rationalized retailing** programs to combine a high degree of centralized management control with strict operating procedures for every phase of business. Most of these chains' operations are performed in a virtually identical manner in all outlets. Rigid control and standardization make this technique easy to enact and manage, and a firm can add a significant number of stores in a short time. Radio Shack, Toys "R" Us, and Starbucks use rationalized retailing. They operate many stores that are similar in size, layout, and merchandising.

Many retailers use one or both of two contrasting store-size approaches to be distinctive and to deal with high rents in some metropolitan markets. Home Depot, Barnes & Noble, and Sports Authority have category killer stores with huge assortments that try to dominate smaller stores. Food-based warehouse stores and large discount-oriented stores often situate in secondary sites, where rents are low—confident that they can draw customers. Cub Foods (a warehouse chain) and Wal-Mart engage in this approach. At the same time, some retailers believe large stores are not efficient in serving saturated (or small) markets; they have been opening smaller stores or downsizing existing ones because of high rents:

> Best Buy's new "Escape" format, being tested on Chicago's North Side, is located in a converted police station and nestled among the cafés, bars, and countless boutiques. Escape essentially is an electronics toy boutique designed to entice young men. In the back of the store are several suites in which customers can test video equipment or rent it for private parties; local restaurants provide the catering for such events. In the front of the store is an Internet café; for an annual $10 membership fee, use of the computers in the café is free of charge. Instead of salespeople, in-store personnel offer guided tours to the store when a new customer enters—a

The Benchmark Group (**www.bgark.com**) has collaborated with a number of retailers to develop their stores. Click on "Project Experience."

Expected Average Time per Activity

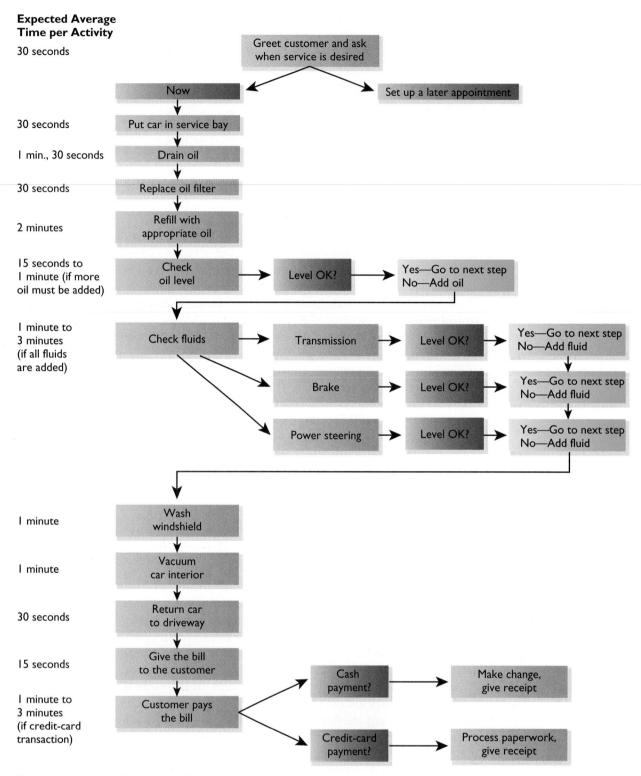

Total expected time = 10 minutes to 14 minutes, 45 seconds.

FIGURE 13-1

An Operations Blueprint for a Quick-Oil-Change Firm's Employees

Careers in RETAILING — Is Retail for Me? Store Management

Store management is where people skills and running a business meet. The store manager or management team has responsibility ranging from departmental to overall establishment. Managers at all levels supervise and assist sales and other employees. Additional responsibilities, depending upon store/company size and management level, include opening and closing the store, staffing, administration, and financial functions. Promotions to management positions can be earned through experience, or a college degree may afford direct entry to management trainee programs:

- *Store Manager:* Responsible for the overall sales, administration, and staffing of one store.
- *Assistant Store Manager:* This position is the "Number 2" person or level in the store, in charge of the whole store when the Store Manager is absent. Specific

duties and title will vary by the merchandise type and volume size of store.

- *Department Sales Manager:* This position supervises merchandising and staff in a department or zone in a large-square-footage store. May be a keyholder.
- *"Third Key"—Hourly Keyholder:* This position is a job level and not a title. A retail store typically has 12 to 14 shifts per week that require a keyholder to open or close. Since the manager and assistant are typically scheduled for 5 shifts each, for a total of 10, there has to be another Associate holding the "third key." In smaller-volume stores, this may be a part-time associate. In a big-box store, the third key may be held by a senior department sales manager.

Source: Reprinted by permission of the National Retail Federation.

---

far cry from the category killer environment of Best Buy's traditional units. Best Buy is also testing a store called Studio D in nearby Naperville that is targeted to women. It offers a variety of classes and has a small spa designed to relax customers intimidated by the high-tech equipment. The decision by Best Buy to test different formats is driven by several concerns. One has to do with real-estate; there are fewer places in which to put its traditional 50,000-square-foot-plus stores, so creating differentiated and smaller formats—from 3,500 to 5,000 square feet—is imperative. Perhaps more importantly, Best Buy understands that there is not one kind of consumer, and that in order to appeal to shoppers with different temperaments and interests, it needs to develop a wide range of approaches.[3]

See Figure 13-2.

Retailers often focus on allocating store space. They use facilities productively by determining the amount of space, and its placement, for each product category. Sometimes, retailers drop merchandise lines because they occupy too much space. That is why J.C. Penney eliminated home electronics, large sporting goods, and photo equipment from its department stores. With a **top-down space management approach**, a retailer starts with its total available store space (by outlet and for the overall firm, if a chain), divides the space into categories, and then works on product layouts. In contrast, a **bottom-up space management approach** begins planning at the individual product level and then proceeds to the category, total store, and overall company levels.

These are among the tactics that some retailers use to improve store space productivity: Vertical displays, which occupy less room, hang on store walls or from ceilings. Formerly free space now has small point-of-sale displays and vending machines; sometimes, product displays are in front of stores. Open doorways, mirrored walls, and vaulted ceilings give small stores a larger appearance. Up to 75 percent or more of total floor space may be used for selling; the rest is for storage, rest rooms, and so on. Scrambled merchandising (with high-profit, high-turnover items) occupies more space in stores, in catalogs, and at Web sites than before. By staying open longer, retailers use space better.

FIGURE 13-2
Escape: A New Store
Concept from Best Buy

Photo reprinted by permission
of Susan Berry, Retail Image
Consulting, Inc.

Our Web site (**www.prenhall.com/bermanevans**) has many links on these topics.

Personnel Utilization

From an operations perspective, efficiently utilizing retail personnel is vital: (1) Labor costs are high. For various retailers, wages and benefits may account for up to one-half of operating costs. (2) High employee turnover means increased recruitment, training, and supervision costs. (3) Poor personnel may have weak sales skills, mistreat shoppers, misring transactions, and make other errors. (4) Productivity gains in technology have exceeded those in labor; yet, some retailers are labor intensive. (5) Labor scheduling is often subject to unanticipated demand. Although retailers know they must increase staff in peak periods and reduce it in slow ones, they may still be over- or understaffed if weather changes, competitors run specials, or suppliers increase promotions. (6) There is less flexibility for firms with unionized employees. Working conditions, compensation, tasks, overtime pay, performance measures, termination procedures, seniority rights, and promotion criteria are generally specified in union contracts.

These are among the tactics that can maximize personnel productivity:

- Hiring process—By very carefully screening potential employees before they are offered jobs, turnover is reduced and better performance secured.

Kronos' Workforce Scheduler (**www.kronos. com/Products/wf_Scheduler. htm**) allows retailers to better manage employee scheduling.

- Workload forecasts—For each time period, the number and type of employees are pre-determined. A drugstore may have one pharmacist, one cashier, and one stockperson from 2 P.M. to 5 P.M. on weekdays and add a pharmacist and a cashier from 5 P.M. to 7:30 P.M. (to accommodate people shopping after work). In doing workload forecasts, costs must be balanced against the possibilities of lost sales if customer waiting time is excessive. The key is to be both efficient (cost-oriented) and effective (service-oriented). Many retailers use computer software as an aid in scheduling personnel.

FIGURE 13-3
Burger King: Fostering Job Standardization

Burger King employees are trained to perform specific tasks in a standardized manner, so that customers receive consistent, high-quality service each time they dine with Burger King.

Reprinted by permission of Douglas Brucker, Burger King franchisee.

- Job standardization and cross-training—Through **job standardization**, the tasks of personnel with similar positions in different departments, such as cashiers in clothing and candy departments, are rather uniform. See Figure 13-3. With **cross-training**, personnel learn tasks associated with more than one job, such as cashier, stockperson, and gift wrapper. A firm increases personnel flexibility and reduces the number of employees needed at any time by job standardization and cross-training. If one department is slow, a cashier could be assigned to a busy one; and a salesperson could process transactions, set up displays, and handle complaints. Cross-training even reduces employee boredom.

- Employee performance standards—Each worker is given clear goals and is accountable for them. Cashiers are judged on transaction speed and misrings, buyers on department revenues and markdowns, and senior executives on the firm's reaching sales and profit targets. Personnel are more productive when working toward specific goals.

- Compensation—Financial remuneration, promotions, and recognition that reward good performance help to motivate employees. A cashier is motivated to reduce misrings if there is a bonus for keeping mistakes under a certain percentage of all transactions.

- Self-service—Costs are reduced with self-service. However: (1) Self-service requires better displays, popular brands, ample assortments, and products with clear features. (2) By reducing sales personnel, some shoppers may feel service is inadequate. (3) There is no cross-selling (whereby customers are encouraged to buy complementary goods they may not have been thinking about).

- Length of employment—Generally, full-time workers who have been with a firm for an extended time are more productive than those who are part-time or who have worked there for a short time. They are often more knowledgeable, are more anxious to see the firm succeed, need less supervision, are popular with customers, can be promoted, and are adaptable to the work environment. The superior productivity of these workers normally far outweighs their higher compensation.

Store Maintenance, Energy Management, and Renovations

Store maintenance encompasses all the activities in managing physical facilities. These are just some of the facilities to be managed: exterior—parking lot, points of entry and exit, outside signs and display windows, and common areas adjacent to a store (e.g., sidewalks); interior—windows, walls, flooring, climate control and energy use, lighting, displays and signs, fixtures, and ceilings. See Figure 13-4.

Visit this Web site (www. bltllc.com/commercial_ industrial_floor.htm) to learn more about commercial flooring.

The quality of store maintenance affects consumer perceptions, the life span of facilities, and operating costs. Consumers do not like stores that are decaying or otherwise poorly maintained. This means promptly replacing burned-out lamps and periodically repainting room surfaces.

Thorough, ongoing maintenance may extend current facilities for a longer period before having to invest in new ones. At home centers, the heating, ventilation, and air-conditioning equipment lasts an average of 15 years; display fixtures an average of 12 years; and interior signs an average of 9 years. But maintenance is costly.[4] In a typical year, a home center spends $10,000 on floor maintenance alone.

Due to rising costs over the last 30-plus years, energy management is a major factor in retail operations. For firms with special needs, such as food stores, it is especially critical. To manage their energy resources more effectively, many retailers now:

- Use better insulation in constructing and renovating stores.
- Carefully adjust interior temperature levels during nonselling hours. In summer, air-conditioning is reduced at off-hours; in winter, heating is lowered at off-hours.
- Use computerized systems to monitor temperature levels. Some chains' systems even allow operators to adjust the temperature, lighting, heat, and air-conditioning in multiple stores from one office.
- Substitute high-efficiency bulbs and fluorescent ballasts for traditional lighting.
- Install special air-conditioning systems that control humidity levels in specific store areas, such as freezer locations—to minimize moisture condensation.

FIGURE 13-4
A Checklist of Selected Store Maintenance Decisions

✓ What responsibility should the retailer have for maintaining outside facilities? For instance, does a lease agreement make the retailer or the property owner accountable for snow removal in the parking lot?

✓ Should store maintenance activities be done by the retailer's personnel or by outside specialists? Will that decision differ by type of facility (e.g., air-conditioning versus flooring) and by type of service (e.g., maintenance versus repairs)?

✓ What repairs should be classified as emergencies? How promptly should nonemergency repairs be made?

✓ What should be the required frequency of store maintenance for each type of facility (e.g., daily vacuuming of floors versus weekly washing of exterior windows)? How often should special maintenance activities be done (e.g., restriping spaces in a parking lot)?

✓ How should store maintenance vary by season and by time of day (e.g., when a store is open versus when it is closed)?

✓ How long should existing facilities be utilized before acquiring new ones? What schedule should be followed?

✓ What performance standards should be set for each element of store maintenance? Do these standards adequately balance costs against a desired level of maintenance?

Ethics in RETAILING

Leadership in Energy and Environmental Design

Giant Eagle's (**www.gianteagle.com**) new store in Brunswick, Ohio, does not look unusual from either the inside (apart from the use of natural light) or outside. Yet, it is the first supermarket in the United States to secure LEED (Leadership in Energy and Environmental Design) certification. The U.S. Green Building Council (**www.usgbc.com**), a nonprofit group made up of all segments of the building industry, developed the LEED program to establish environmentally sensitive construction standards. Buildings that score above a given number of points are designated as LEED-certified.

Let's examine some of the energy-saving characteristics of Giant Eagle's LEED store. Since more than half of its electrical energy needs are supplied by wind generation, the store will use 30 percent less energy than a comparable supermarket. The store's 50 skylights also have electrical lighting sensors that automatically adjust the electric light based on natural light conditions. To reduce water consumption, drought-resistant plants have been used that require no water beyond natural rainfall. And recycled materials have been used in all of the store's cabinets and wallboard.

Source: Marianne Wilson, "Taking the LEED," *Chain Store Age* (March 2005), pp. 45–52.

Here is an example of how seriously some retailers take energy management:

Food Lion was recently honored with an Energy Star Award in the category of Sustained Excellence. "We are demonstrating a long-term commitment to the environment and to its bottom line, which benefits the environment, consumers, the firm, and its investors," said Food Lion's vice-president of construction and engineering. The chain has reduced its energy use by more than 25 percent, or 1.62 trillion BTUs, since 2000, primarily through new lighting, refrigeration, and heating and cooling technologies, and management efforts. Hundreds of Food Lion stores have earned the Energy Star designation, which means these stores are among the most energy-efficient retail facilities in the country. "Our goal is to be a world-class leader in energy management in the supermarket industry."[5]

Besides everyday maintenance and energy management, retailers need decision rules regarding renovations: How often are renovations necessary? What areas require renovations more frequently than others? How extensive will renovations be at any one time? Will the retailer be open for business as usual during renovations? How much money must be set aside in anticipation of future renovations? Will renovations result in higher revenues, lower operating costs, or both?

Sometimes, the complexities of store renovations are addressed quite cleverly:

Prime Outlets San Marcos, reputed to be one of Texas' biggest tourist draws along with the Alamo and the San Antonio River Walk, has undergone a $30-million expansion and renovation. The outlet shopping center is re-emerging with a Venetian theme that includes a 200,000-square-foot expansion featuring a bell tower, piazzas, a lagoon, and canals. The existing 658,000-square-foot center has been renovated to complement the expansion, and will introduce such upscale fashion outlet tenants as Neiman Marcus Last Call, Ferragamo, and Hugo Boss.[6]

Inventory Management

A retailer uses inventory management to maintain a proper merchandise assortment while ensuring that operations are efficient and effective. While the role of

FIGURE 13-5
Inventory Management at Costco

Costco has a very efficient approach to inventory management. Virtually all merchandise is displayed on the sales floor in a manner that makes maximum use of floor space. Many of its products are displayed in their original packing cartons, which reduces display and labor costs.

Reprinted by permission of Retail Forward, Inc.

inventory management in merchandising is covered in Chapter 15, these are some operational issues to consider:

- How can the handling of merchandise from different suppliers be coordinated?
- How much inventory should be on the sales floor versus in a warehouse or storeroom? See Figure 13-5.
- How often should inventory be moved from nonselling to selling areas of a store?
- What inventory functions can be done during nonstore hours?
- What are the trade-offs between faster supplier delivery and higher shipping costs?
- What supplier support is expected in storing merchandise or setting up displays?
- What level of in-store merchandise breakage is acceptable?
- Which items require customer delivery? When? By whom?

Store Security

Store security relates to two basic issues: personal security and merchandise security. Personal security is examined here. Merchandise security is covered in Chapter 15.

Many shoppers and employees feel less safe at retail establishments than they did before, with these results: Some people are unwilling to shop at night. Some people age 60 and older no longer go out at all during the night. Some shoppers believe malls are not as safe as they once were. Parking is a source of anxiety for people who worry about walking through a dimly lit parking lot. In response, retailers need to be proactive. For example, the Jersey Gardens Outlet Mall in Elizabeth, New Jersey, has a very sophisticated camera-surveillance network, complete with 220 cameras that monitor every inch of the center. As the manager noted, "We opened with a very strong security presence and have always taken a serious approach to security measures here. Since the center's opening, the system has been upgraded, and it can continue to be upgraded for years."[7]

These are among the practices retailers are utilizing to address this issue:

- Uniformed security guards provide a visible presence that reassures customers and employees, and it is a warning to potential thieves and muggers. Some malls even have horse-mounted guards. This is a big change: "Mall management wants us to be less ambassadors of goodwill and is asking us to take a more aggressive approach. They are asking us to not watch and wait too long if we spot suspicious behavior."[8]

- Undercover personnel are used to complement uniformed guards.
- Brighter lighting is used in parking lots, which are also patrolled more frequently by guards. These guards more often work in teams.
- TV cameras and other devices scan the areas frequented by shoppers and employees. 7-Eleven has an in-store cable TV and alarm monitoring system, complete with audio.
- Some shopping areas have curfews for teenagers. This is a controversial tactic.
- Access to store backroom facilities (such as storage rooms) has been tightened.
- Bank deposits are made more frequently—often by armed security guards.

Insurance

Among the types of insurance that retailers buy are workers' compensation, product liability, fire, accident, property, and officers' liability. Many firms also offer health insurance to full-time employees. Sometimes they pay the entire premiums; other times, employees pay part or all of the premiums.

Insurance decisions can have a big impact on a retailer: (1) In recent years, premiums have risen dramatically. (2) Several insurers have reduced the scope of their coverage; they now require higher deductibles or do not provide coverage on all aspects of operations (such as the professional liability of pharmacists). (3) There are fewer insurers servicing retailers today than a decade ago; this limits the choice of carrier. (4) Insurance against environmental risks (such as leaking tanks) is more important due to government rules.

To protect themselves financially, a number of retailers have enacted costly programs aimed at lessening their vulnerability to employee and customer insurance claims due to unsafe conditions, as well as to hold down premiums. These programs include no-slip carpeting, flooring, and rubber entrance mats; frequently mopping and inspecting wet floors; doing more elevator and escalator checks; having regular fire drills; building more fire-resistant facilities; setting up separate storage areas for dangerous items; discussing safety in employee training; and keeping records that proper maintenance has been done.

Credit Management

Visa presents a lot of advice (**www.visa.com/fb/merch/practice**) for retailers to reduce their administrative costs and the fraud associated with the use of credit and debit cards.

These are the operational decisions to be made in the area of credit management:

- What form of payment is acceptable? A retailer may accept cash only, cash and personal checks, cash and credit card(s), cash and debit cards, or all of these.
- Who administers the credit plan? The firm can have its own credit system and/or accept major credit cards (such as Visa, MasterCard, American Express, and Discover).
- What are customer eligibility requirements for a check or credit purchase? With a check purchase, a photo ID might be sufficient. To open a new charge account, a customer must meet age, employment, income, and other conditions; an existing customer would be evaluated in terms of the outstanding balance and credit limit. A minimum purchase amount may be specified for a credit transaction.
- What credit terms will be used? A retailer with its own plan must determine when interest charges begin to accrue, the rate of interest, and minimum monthly payments.

● How are late payments or nonpayments to be handled? Some retailers with their own credit plans rely on outside collection agencies to follow up on past-due accounts.

The retailer must weigh the ability of credit to increase revenues against the costs of processing payments—screening, transaction, and collection costs, as well as bad debts. If a retailer completes credit functions itself, it incurs these costs; if outside parties (such as Visa) are used, the retailer covers the costs by its fees to the credit organization.

The *Nilson Report* presents information on retail payment methods. At its site (**www.nilsonreport. com**), you can access highlights.

In the United States, there are 1.5 billion credit and debit cards in use. During the Christmas holiday season alone (the day after Thanksgiving until Christmas), there are more than 2 billion retail credit and debit card transactions yearly. The average sales transaction involving a credit/debit card or a check is far higher than a cash one. Overall, one-third of U.S. retail transactions are in cash, one-sixth are by check, and one-half are by credit and debit card. Among retailers accepting credit and debit cards, one-third have their own card, virtually all accept MasterCard and/or Visa, 80 percent accept Discover, and just over one-half accept American Express. Most firms that accept credit cards handle two or more cards.[9]

Credit card fees paid by retailers range from 1.5 percent to 5.0 percent of sales for Visa, MasterCard, Discover, and American Express—depending on credit volume and the card provider. There may also be transaction and monthly fees. The total costs of retailers' own credit operations as a percent of credit sales are usually lower, at 2.0 percent. Costco has a merchant credit processing program so that small firms may carry Visa or MasterCard. It charges a 1.67 percent of sale fee and a transaction charge of 20 cents for store retailers; the amounts are 2.02 percent and 27 cents per transaction for nonstore retailers.[10]

Many retailers—of all types—are now placing greater emphasis on a **debit card system**, whereby the purchase price of a good or service is immediately deducted from a consumer's bank account and entered into a retailer's account through a computer terminal. The retailer's risk of nonpayment is eliminated and its costs are reduced with debit rather than credit transactions. For traditional credit cards, monthly billing is employed; with debit cards, monetary account transfers are made at the time of the purchase. There is some resistance to debit transactions by consumers who like the delayed-payment benefit of conventional

Technology in RETAILING — At Piggly Wiggly, Biometrics Comes to Payment Systems

Piggly Wiggly (**www.pigglywiggly.com**) recently rolled out its Pay By Touch (**www.paybytouch.com**) technology in more than 30 of its stores. Through Pay By Touch, consumers register their fingerprints with the retailer and then swipe their fingers at a point-of-sale register (instead of their credit or debit card). Payment is then deducted through the customer's checking account.

According to Rich Farrell, Piggly Wiggly's vice-president of information services, the chain found this technology after searching through alternatives to soaring debit and credit card fees. The cost for deducting funds from a consumer's checking account averages 10 cents per transaction versus 75 cents for a credit card.

About 15 percent of the chain's eligible customers have enrolled in Pay By Touch. And 18 percent of its noncash transactions are now through the Pay By Touch network. Piggly Wiggly is contemplating using a loyalty rewards program to encourage credit card customers to use the new technology. One problem in enrolling new customers is that while the system requires that customers have a paper check when they enroll in the program, many debit card customers do not carry a paper check with them.

Sources: Ken Clark, "Pointing to Savings," *Chain Store Age* (February 2005), p. 140; and "Piggly Wiggly Wins Retail Systems Achievement Award for Implementation of Pay By Touch," **www.paybytouch.com/ news/pr_05-31-05.html** (May 31, 2005).

credit cards. On the other hand, the pre-paid gift card, a form of debit card, is booming in popularity.

Click on "About Deluxe" (www.deluxe.com) to learn about one of the premier payment systems support companies for retailers.

As the payment landscape evolves, new operational issues must be addressed:

- Retailers have more options for processing payments. For example, an E-commerce study of major online retailers found that 99 percent of them accept credit cards, nearly one-half sell gift certificates, one-quarter accept electronic checks, one-fifth offer instant credit, and one-seventh have their own credit cards.[11] For store-based retailers, training cashiers is more complex due to all the formats.

- Hardware and software are available to process paper checks electronically. This means cost savings for the retailer and faster payments from the bank.

- Visa and MasterCard have been sued for requiring retailers to accept both credit and debit cards, if the retailers want to continue carrying Visa and MasterCard credit cards.

- Nonstore retailers have less legal protection against credit card fraud than store retailers that secure written authorization.

- Credit card transactions on the Web must instantly take into account different sales tax rates and currencies (for global sales).

- In Europe, retailers have grappled with the intricacies of converting to the common euro currency.

Computerization

CAM Commerce Solutions (www.camcommerce.com) offers very inexpensive operations software to small retailers in the hope that as these retailers grow, they will upgrade to advanced software.

Many retailers have improved their operations productivity through computerization; and with the continuing decline in the prices of computer systems and related software, even more small firms will do so in the near future. At the same time, retailers must consider this observation: "The supply chain is no longer characterized by the old plan-buy-build-move-sell principle, but rather by a highly integrated and collaborative, sense-and-respond network. In this network, retailers and their supply partners sense changes in consumer demand in real time and react accordingly, so the right product is in the right place for the right customer."[12] Let us look at various examples of the operational benefits of computerization.

Retailers such as Home Depot, Wal-Mart, and J.C. Penney use videoconferencing. This lets them link store employees with central headquarters, as well as interact with vendors. Videoconferencing can be done through satellite technology and by computer (with special hardware and software). In both cases, audio/video communications train workers, spread news, stimulate employee morale, and so on.

SpectraLink (www.spectralink.com) has wireless "Solutions" for "Retail" businesses.

In-store telecommunications aid operations by offering low-cost, secure in-store transmissions. SpectraLink Corporation is one of the firms that markets lightweight pocket phones so personnel can talk to one another anywhere in a store. There are no air time charges or monthly fees. SpectraLink clients include Barnes & Noble, Ikea, Kmart, Neiman Marcus, Rite Aid, and Toys "R" Us. See Figure 13-6.

Software provides computerized inventory control and customer order tracking. For example, "One of the toughest challenges grocers face is matching perishable inventory supply to demand. Underestimate demand, and the shelves go bare. Overestimate demand, and you have a lot of spoiled goods on your hands. To strike an optimum balance between the two, Price Chopper turned to technology. The role of the software solution the grocer chose—Fresh Market Manager

FIGURE 13-6
Effective In-Store
Communications

Foot Locker employees are
equipped with battery-powered
headsets that enable them to
communicate easily within individual stores.

Photo reprinted by permission of
Foot Locker.

from Park City Group—was to measure day-to-day demand of fresh items based
on sales history and to manage the production of those items accordingly."[13] And
Icode's Everest Enterprise software lets retailers offer online order tracking to customers. See Figure 13-7.

Nowhere is computerization more critical than in the checkout process. Let us
examine the computerized checkout, the electronic point-of-sale system, and scanning formats.

The **computerized checkout** is used by both large and small retailers so they
can efficiently process transactions and monitor inventory. Firms rely on UPC-
based systems; cashiers manually ring up sales or pass items over or past scanners. Computerized registers instantly record and display sales, provide detailed
receipts, and store inventory data. See Figure 13-8. This type of checkout lowers
costs by reducing transaction time, employee training, misrings, and the need for
item pricing. Retailers also have better inventory control, reduced spoilage, and
improved ordering. They even get item-by-item data—which aid in determining
store layout and merchandise plans, shelf space, and inventory replenishment.
Recent technological developments related to computerized checkouts include
wireless scanners that let workers scan heavy items without lifting them, radio
frequency identification tags (RFID) that emit a radio frequency code when
placed near a receiver (which is faster than UPC codes and better for harsh cli-
mates), and speech recognition (that can tally an order on the basis of a clerk's verbal command).

Retailers do face two potential problems with computerized checkouts. First,
UPC-based systems do not reach peak efficiency unless all suppliers attach UPC
labels to merchandise; otherwise, retailers incur labeling costs. Second, because
UPC symbols are unreadable by humans, some states have laws that require price

FIGURE 13-7

Everest Enterprise: Integrated E-Commerce Software

This figure shows the order-tracking function of the software.

Reprinted by permission of Icode, Inc.

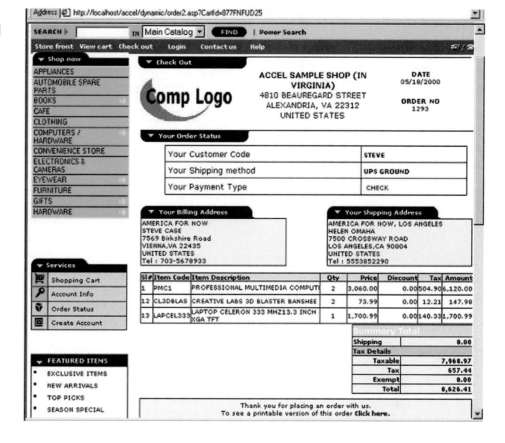

labeling on individual items. This lessens the labor savings of posting only shelf prices.

Many retailers have upgraded to an **electronic point-of-sale system**, which performs all the tasks of a computerized checkout and verifies check and charge transactions, provides instantaneous sales reports, monitors and changes prices, sends intra- and interstore messages, evaluates personnel and profitability, and stores data. A point-of-sale system is often used along with a retail information system. Point-of-sale terminals can stand alone or be integrated with an in-store or a headquarters computer.

Retailers have specific goals for their scanning equipment: "Scanning has been in use since the early 1970s and its use was limited then. The majority of products available at the time did not even include barcodes on their packaging. However, when retailers saw how scanners sped up their sales lanes, increased accuracy, and improved their customer service, they demanded that manufacturers include barcodes on all their merchandise. Today's scanners are faster, more versatile, more durable, and more accurate than their predecessors."[14] Among the recent advances in scanning technology are handheld scanners; wearable, hands-free scanners; and miniaturized data transceivers.

As noted in Chapter 2, one emerging scanning option with great retailer interest is **self-scanning**, whereby the consumer himself or herself scans the items being purchased at a checkout counter, pays by credit or debit card, and bags the items:

Symbol Technologies (www.symbol.com) is one of the leaders in retail scanning equipment, with an extensive product line.

> ATMs and pay-at-the-pump gas were mere baby steps for an industry now taking giant strides at airports, hotels, and elsewhere. Consumers scanned $70 billion worth of self-serve transactions in 2003. The amount will nearly quintuple to $330 billion by 2007, estimates IHL Consulting. Self-scan machines at Home Depot, Kroger, and Wal-Mart aren't just a

FIGURE 13-8
The Latest in Checkout Technology

State-of-the-art computerized checkout systems even feature color sales receipts for customers.

Reprinted by permission of TransAct Technologies, Inc.

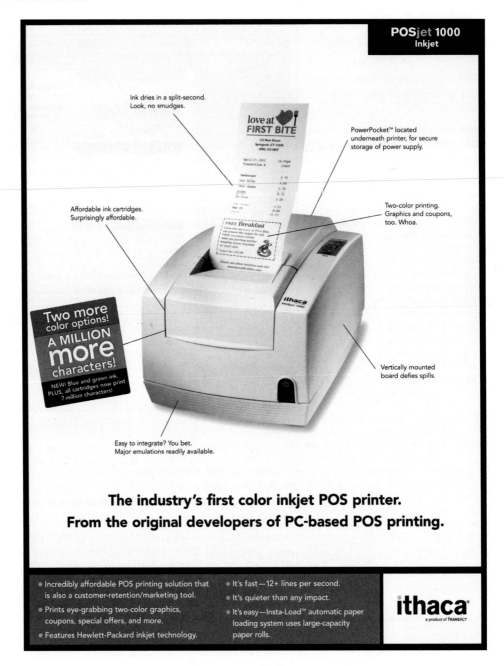

fad. In 1999, we scanned next to nothing. Today, it's part of our shopping trip. At Home Depot, shoppers scan 39 percent of all the chain's in-store transactions. Many Kroger stores in Atlanta report 40 percent of their transactions are scanned by customers. The units aren't cheap. At NCR, the list price for a typical installation, including four self-checkout units, an attendant station, and software, is $100,000.[15]

Outsourcing

More retailers have turned to outsourcing for some of the operating tasks they previously performed themselves. With **outsourcing**, a retailer pays an outside party to undertake one or more of its operating functions. The goals are to reduce the costs and employee time devoted to particular tasks. For example, Limited Brands uses outside firms to oversee its energy use and facilities maintenance.

A key consideration in the selection of a new point-of-sale (POS) system provider for Papa John's (**www.papa johns.com**), a pizza chain, was its ability to support and service Papa John's growing international operations. Especially important was the need to shift from a text-based interface to a graphics user interface for countries such as China and Korea, where text-based systems would not work. Lastly, Papa John's wanted to add several new functions to its POS system. These functions could not be handled by the firm's existing system.

Papa John's selected Wincor (**www.wincor-nixdorf. com**) as its POS provider. According to Terry Foster, Papa John's director of global systems architecture, "For now, we are using the Wincor hardware exclusively in our international restaurants, but we are looking toward developing it in the United States, as well." Papa John's currently has two types of POS systems: an "inexpensive, get-the-job-done system" and a "more costs, more features type." Its domestic restaurants have used a basic system, whereas the international systems offer newer technology with additional features.

Sources: "Papa John's Picks POS Provider," *Retail Technology Quarterly* (October 2004), p. 30A; and "Investor Relations," **www.papajohns.com/ investor/index.htm** (April 4, 2006).

Crate & Barrel outsources the management of its E-mail programs. Kmart uses logistics firms to consolidate small shipments and to process returned merchandise; it also outsources electronic data interchange tasks. Home Depot outsources most trucking operations. J.C. Penney, which for decades managed its credit operations, now has a long-term contract with GE Capital.

GE Consumer Financial Services (**www.geconsumerfinance. com**) handles the credit operations for a number of retailers.

This comment sums up the benefits of outsourcing:

In the past, retailers were guilty of outsourcing for negative reasons. Some simply moved a problem from in-house to outsourcer, handing over functions they didn't understand. Now, retailers appear to be outsourcing positively—to concentrate on what they are good at and what makes them different in a market where everyone is in competition. "Every retailer believes there are things that make them distinctive," says the business development director at outsourcing company Retail Assist. "If the retailer is all about having the right product at the right time then it wouldn't want to outsource its supply chain, but could outsource store systems, for example. Every retailer can't be good at everything, but if you're best at one thing, keep that close to the business."[16]

Crisis Management

Despite the best intentions, retailers may sometimes be faced with crisis situations that need to be managed as smoothly as feasible. Crises may be brought on by an in-store fire or broken water pipe, access to a store being partially blocked due to picketing by striking workers, a car accident in the parking lot, a burglary, a sudden illness by the owner or a key employee, a storm that knocks out a retailer's power, unexpectedly high or low consumer demand for a good or service, a sudden increase in a supplier's prices, a natural disaster such as a flood or an earthquake, or other factors.

Although many crises may be anticipated, and some adverse effects may occur regardless of retailer efforts, these principles are important:

1. There should be contingency plans for as many different types of crisis situations as possible. That is why retailers buy insurance, install backup generators, and prepare management succession plans. A firm can have a checklist to follow if there is an incident such as a store fire or a parking-lot accident.

2. Essential information should be communicated to all affected parties, such as the fire or police department, employees, customers, and the media, as soon as a crisis occurs.
3. Cooperation—not conflict—among the involved parties is essential.
4. Responses should be as swift as feasible; indecisiveness may worsen the situation.
5. The chain of command should be clear and decision makers given adequate authority.

Crisis management is a key task for both small and large retailers. As one expert notes, "The first thing we tell a company is that if you haven't thought about how to deal with customers before a crisis happens, you're actually too late if one occurs. You have to plan how messages and actions are taken to key constituents, and the customer is often overlooked as the key constituent."[17]

Visit our Web site (**www.prenhall.com/bermanevans**) for several links related to crisis management.

Summary

1. *To describe the operational scope of operations management.* Operations management efficiently and effectively seeks to enact the policies needed to satisfy customers, employees, and management. In contrast to Chapter 12, which dealt with financial aspects, Chapter 13 covered operational facets.

2. *To examine several specific aspects of operating a retail business.* An operations blueprint systematically lists all operating functions, their characteristics, and their timing, as well as the responsibility for performing the functions.

Store format and size considerations include the use of prototype stores and store dimensions. Firms often use prototype stores in conjunction with rationalized retailing. Some retailers emphasize category killer stores; others open smaller stores. In space allocation, retailers deploy a top-down or a bottom-up approach. They want to optimize the productivity of store space.

Personnel utilization activities that improve productivity range from better screening applicants to workload forecasts to job standardization and cross-training. Job standardization routinizes the tasks of people with similar positions in different departments. With cross-training, people learn tasks associated with more than one job. A firm can advance its personnel flexibility and minimize the total number of workers needed at any given time by these techniques.

Store maintenance includes all activities in managing physical facilities. It influences people's perceptions of the retailer, the life span of facilities, and operating costs. To better control energy resources, retailers are doing everything from using better-quality insulation materials when building and renovating stores to substituting high-efficiency bulbs. Besides everyday facilities management, retailers need decision rules as to the frequency and manner of store renovations.

Good inventory management requires that retailers acquire and maintain the proper merchandise while ensuring efficient and effective operations. This encompasses everything from coordinating different supplier shipments to planning customer deliveries (if needed).

Store security measures protect both personal and merchandise safety. Because of safety concerns, fewer people now shop at night and some avoid shopping in areas they view as unsafe. In response, retailers are employing security guards, using better lighting in parking lots, tightening access to facilities, and deploying other tactics.

Among the insurance that retailers buy are workers' compensation, product liability, fire, accident, property, and officers' liability. Many firms also have employee health insurance.

Most U.S. adults use credit cards. Check and credit payments generally mean larger transactions than cash payments. One-third of retail transactions are in cash, one-sixth by check, and one-half by credit or debit card. Retailers pay various fees to be able to offer noncash payment options to customers, and there is a wide range of payment systems available for retailers.

A growing number of retailers have computerized elements of operations. Videoconferencing and wireless in-store telephone communications are gaining in popularity. Computerized checkouts and electronic point-of-sale systems are quite useful. Electronic point-of-sale systems perform all the tasks of computerized checkouts and verify check and charge transactions, provide instant sales reports, monitor and change prices, send intra- and interstore messages, evaluate personnel and profitability, and store data. Self-scanning is gaining in popularity.

With outsourcing, the retailer pays another party to handle one or more operating functions.

The goals are to reduce costs and better utilize employees' time.

Crisis management must handle unexpected situations as smoothly as possible. There should be contingency plans, information should be communicated to those affected, all parties should cooperate, responses should be swift, and the chain of command for decisions should be clear.

Key Terms

operations blueprint (p. 378)
prototype stores (p. 379)
rationalized retailing (p. 379)
top-down space management approach (p. 381)

bottom-up space management approach (p. 381)
job standardization (p. 383)
cross-training (p. 383)
store maintenance (p. 384)

debit card system (p. 388)
computerized checkout (p. 390)
electronic point-of-sale system (p. 391)
self-scanning (p. 391)
outsourcing (p. 392)

Questions for Discussion

1. Present a brief operations blueprint for a fast-food restaurant.

2. What are the pros and cons of prototype stores? For which kind of firms is this type of store *least* desirable?

3. Why would a retailer be interested in job standardization and cross-training for its employees?

4. Comment on this statement: "The quality of store maintenance efforts affects consumer perceptions of the retailer, the life span of facilities, and operating expenses."

5. Talk to two local retailers and ask them what they have done to maximize their energy efficiency. Present your findings.

6. As a drugstore owner, you are planning a complete renovation of the greeting card section. What decisions must you make?

7. Present a five-step plan for a retailer to reassure customers that it is safe to shop there.

8. An appliance store does not accept checks because of the risks involved. However, it does accept Visa and MasterCard. Evaluate this strategy.

9. What potential problems may result if a retailer relies on its computer system to implement too many actions (such as employee scheduling or inventory reordering) automatically?

10. What operations criteria would you use to evaluate the success of self-scanning at Wal-Mart?

11. Are there any operating functions that should *never* be outsourced? Explain your answer.

12. Outline the contingency plan a retailer could have in the event of each of these occurrences:
    a. A shopper's tripping over an on-floor display in the store and sustaining an injury.
    b. A store fire.
    c. A firm's Web site inadvertently making personal customer information available to a mailing list company.
    d. The bankruptcy of a key supplier.

Web-Based Exercise

Visit the Web site of the Outsourcing Center (**www. outsourcing-center.com**) and type "Retail" in the search bar. What useful information do you find there?

Note: Stop by our Web site (**www.prenhall.com/ bermanevans**) to experience a number of highly

interactive, appealing Web exercises based on actual company demonstrations and sample materials related to retailing.

Chapter Endnotes

1. Various company sources.

2. See Steven Gray, "Coffee on the Double," *Wall Street Journal* (April 12, 2005), pp. B1, B7.

3. "Best Buy Tests Small Formats with Big Goals," **www.xr23.com/page.cfm/137** (May 15, 2005).

4. "Average Life Span of Physical Supports Systems," *Chain Store Age* (July 2005), p. 80.

5. Marianne Wilson, "Efficient Partners," *Chain Store Age* (June 2005), p. 76.

6. "Texas and Venice Meet in San Marcos," *Chain Store Age* (May 2005), p. 62.

7. Lauri Klepacki, "State-of-the-Art Security," *Chain Store Age* (September 2004), p. 129.

8. Leslie Kaufman, "Malls Are Tightening Security as the Holiday Rush Begins," *New York Times* (November 23, 2001), p. C7.

9. Compiled from various sources by the authors.

10. "Credit Card Processing," **www.costco.com/Service/FeaturePage.aspx?ProductNo=10166089** (February 28, 2006).

11. "More Ways to Pay," *Marketing Management* (November–December 2004), p. 7.

12. "Re-Inventing the Supply Chain," **www.xr23.com/page.cfm/141** (May 15, 2005).

13. Dan Scheraga, "Keeping It Fresh," *Chain Store Age* (May 2005), p. 111.

14. "POS Scanning," **www.adsretail.com/_ns/wireless/wireless.html** (February 23, 2006).

15. Marlon Manuel, "Scan-It-Yourself Part, Parcel of Life in Fast Lane," *Cox News Service* (January 26, 2005).

16. Natalie Stevenson, "Sourcing Out the Best Deal," *Retail Week Online* (April 29, 2005).

17. Don Peppers and Martha Rogers, "Crisis Management Seeks a Customer Center," *Inside 1to1 Strategy Online* (February 24, 2005).

part five
Short Cases

CASE 1: THE EMPLOYEE CULTURE AT UMPQUA BANK[c-1]

Umpqua Bank (**www.umpquabank.com**), with more than 90 branches (from Napa Valley, California, to Seattle) and $5 billion in assets, is committed to creating and maintaining a corporate culture that provides excellent customer service. A key component of its strategy is a universal associate program.

At Umpqua, every employee is trained to perform every task. A teller can take a loan application, and a mortgage officer is able to assist a customer in opening a safe-deposit box. According to Ray Davis, Umpqua's chief executive, "When a customer walks in, the only people there are people there to serve them." A significant side benefit of this employee culture is that Umpqua's employee turnover is one-half the industry average. Another benefit is that employee boredom is reduced as they perform multiple tasks each day. An employee's workday varies based on which departments are slow and/or busy.

In contrast, at a typical bank, employees specialize in certain tasks; as a result, many employees have a "it's not my job" mentality. Davis asks, "How many times have you walked into a bank where there's someone sitting behind a desk, busy—doing something—and you're waiting in line for a half-hour and they won't even look up to make eye contact?" Part of the reason for this, according to Davis, is that they have not been trained in the tasks necessary to help you.

Umpqua's employees are empowered to satisfy customers. Many branches place dog bowls full of water at the bank's entrance for clients with dogs. At a bank location in Portland, Oregon, employees have arranged to open the lobby of the bank for yoga lessons, movie nights, and a monthly knitting club. Umpqua's tellers also do not need a manager's approval to waive a fee. To foster the importance of customer service, every employee undertakes a daylong training program run by Ritz-Carlton (**www.ritzcarlton.com**), a hotel chain known for providing excellent customer service to its guests.

Umpqua believes that it needs to continually measure and reward customer service on a departmental level. "Banks have ratios like 'return on assets' and 'return on equity' to show how they're doing. We call this our 'return on quality,'" says Davis. Umpqua measures return on quality for 29 different departments on a monthly basis, including its back-office services (such as mortgage and loan processing) and marketing. The bank publishes each score on a monthly basis so that every department can see its relative performance. These scores are an important factor in bonuses and other incentives.

Ray Davis is determined to maintain this culture as the firm grows. He understands the major difficulties in sustaining its customer service strategy as Umpqua acquires banks that have had vastly different cultures and personnel who do not share Umpqua's customer-orientation philosophy. When it acquires a local bank, Umpqua seeks immediately to convey its culture to employees and customers. For example, when Umpqua acquired a local 27-unit bank, it announced its opening with ice-cream trucks filled with ice-cream sandwiches.

Questions

1. Discuss the pros and cons of Umpqua's universal associate program from the perspective of the bank's management.
2. Discuss the pros and cons of Umpqua's universal associate program from the perspective of the bank's employees.
3. Is a tall or flat organization most appropriate for Umpqua? Explain your answer.
4. Develop a goal-oriented job description for an Umpqua teller.

CASE 2: SONY LOOKS TO A SMALL-STORE FORMAT[c-2]

Sony (**www.sony.com**) is now gearing up to sell its TVs, DVD players, and other electronics through a number of small company-owned Sony Style (**www.sonystyle.com**) stores. Since it began this strategy, Sony has opened more than 25 U.S. stores, with plans to expand significantly. While apparel manufacturers such as Coach (**www.coach.com**), Burberry (**www.burberry.com**), and Ralph Lauren (**www.polo.com**) typically have hundreds of company-owned stores that compete with department and specialty stores, this strategy is uncommon for electronics manufacturers.

Due to its belief that many conventional electronics stores do a poor job in demonstrating its goods to women, Sony plans to place stores in upscale shopping centers and central business districts. It will open stores near such female-oriented firms as Sephora (**www.sephora.com**), Tiffany (**www.tiffany.com**), and Louis Vuitton (**www.vuitton.com**). Sony seeks out mall locations in the nation's largest 50 markets and bids for the best locations in these malls. This locational strategy is in sharp contrast with that of large electronics stores such as Best Buy (**www.bestbuy.com**), which are situated in smaller malls.

Sony's stores feature a concierge desk where each shopper is greeted. Aisles are designed to easily accommodate strollers. And unlike conventional electronics stores where competing brands are lined up in rows, each Sony model will be placed on a different stand. This gives consumers a better idea of what the TVs or home theaters will look like in their living room or den. And all TVs will be tuned into the

---

[c-1]The material in this case is drawn from Lucas Conley, "Cultural Phenomenon," *Fast Company* (April 2005), pp. 76–77.

[c-2]The material in this case is drawn from Elliott Spagat, "Sony Makes Big Changes with Small Stores," *Marketing News* (November 15, 2004), p. 12; and "Sony Style," **www.sonystyle.com** (April 2, 2006).

Discovery Channel or to movie clips from Sony Corporation movies, not to sports channels.

Sony's newest strategy focuses on using small-store formats. Its Cosa Mesa, California, store is 6,000 square feet in size; this is about one-seventh the size of a typical Best Buy. The store carries a wide assortment, ranging from $20 headphones to $20,000 televisions, but its selection is limited to about 18 different models of TVs, 15 computers, and 12 camcorders.

This strategy has created a significant concern among Sony's traditional retailers. Many fear that Sony will become a direct competitor, as well as their supplier. These retailers are further worried that manufacturer-retailer competition for the final consumer market will intensify as other electronics firms such as Panasonic (**www.panasonic.com**) and Samsung (**www.samsung.com**) copy this strategy.

To reduce their concerns, Sony invites retailers that have nearby stores to their newest locations prior to their opening. Sony has also undertaken marketing research studies showing that the new stores, by better educating customers about the features of a Sony model, increase the sales of all stores in the area. Some retail analysts, on the other hand, feel that Sony will probably take away sales more from smaller chains than larger ones.

Sony claims that it is not trying to undercut its retailers, and comparison shopping around a California store confirms this. As an example, Sony's price for a 42-inch plasma TV was $250 more than the price for the same set offered by a Circuit City (**www.circuitcity.com**) store located eight miles away. And Best Buy's (**www.bestbuy.com**) prices were within $10 of the Sony store's prices for two DVD players.

Questions

1. Identify the pros and cons of Sony's small-store format.
2. Should Sony use prototype stores? Should it use rationalized retailing? Explain your answers.
3. Describe the pros and cons of a top-down space management approach for Sony, as well a bottom-up space management system.
4. Discuss the inventory management issues Sony needs to understand in managing its stores.

CASE 3: IMPROVING PRODUCTIVITY AT ALBERTSON'S[c-3]

When Lawrence R. Johnston came to Albertson's (**www.albertsons.com**) in April 2001, the nation's second-largest supermarket chain had major problems. Albertson's did not properly integrate its merger with American Stores. And while Albertson's worked hard to win lawsuits and union battles, Wal-Mart, Target, and others gained market share at

[c-3]The material in this case is drawn from Stanley Holmes, "The Jack Welch of the Meat Aisle," *Business Week* (January 24, 2005), pp. 60–61; and "Albertson's Facts," **www.albertsons.com** (March 29, 2006).

its expense. A member of Albertson's board complained that, "It was clear we didn't know who we were."

Johnston is not a stranger to managing a complex organization. He turned around General Electric's (**www.ge.com**) medical services business in Europe in the late 1990s. As he began this assignment, the business was losing $100 million a year. Within three years, the division was earning an operating profit of $100 million. Jack Welch, then president of General Electric, commented, "Larry can lead people over the hill. He put us on the map in Europe."

Johnston's challenges at General Electric were so intense that he considered early retirement. But Albertson's piqued his interest: "This one intrigued me because it was very close to customers. It was big. It was complex. And it was broken."

Johnston's first objective was to make Albertson's more efficient by cutting $1 billion in annual costs and by closing 500 unprofitable stores. At the same time, he invested money to upgrade Albertson's supply chain and distribution technology and introduced financial controls and management training to the chain. As of mid-2007, shoppers in all of Albertson's 2,300 stores will be given hand-held scanners. These scanners will enable the shoppers to be directed to the shortest path to their groceries, alert them to specials based on their past purchase behavior, keep a running tab on their total purchases, and let them use self-scanning to avoid waiting on line at the checkout.

Although Albertson's has been increasingly profitable, the growth in earnings has largely occurred due to greater cost controls, not increased sales. The chain's recent same-store sales growth, for example, was only 0.3 percent. The chain has also had labor problems as evidenced by a four-month-long strike in Southern California that cost Albertson's $1.2 billion in lost sales and generated ill will among its employees. As the executive vice-president of the United Food & Commercial Workers union remarked, "You can't differentiate yourself from Wal-Mart through high-quality service at the same time you go to war with your work force demanding they give up their benefits."

Said Johnston, "[The strike] was very costly, but [the settlement] was one of the best investments our company ever made." One effect of the strike was that Johnston's tough position enabled Albertson's to more easily negotiate with other unions. The strike also showed Johnston's effectiveness in dealing directly with Albertson's workers. While their union was sitting on a new contract, Johnston sent a video to every worker's home explaining the terms of the contract. As a result, the proposed contract was quickly approved by the chain's union members.

Questions

1. What kind of difficulties arise when a firm such as Albertson's closes hundreds of unprofitable stores? How may they be overcome?
2. Discuss the implications of this statement: "Although Albertson's has been increasingly profitable, the growth

in earnings is largely due to greater cost controls, not increased sales."

3. List five suitable financial controls for Albertson's.
4. Discuss the implications of this statement: "You can't differentiate yourself from Wal-Mart through high-quality service at the same time you go to war with your work force demanding they give up their benefits."

CASE 4: EUROPEAN RETAILERS EXPERIMENT WITH RFID TECHNOLOGY[c-4]

In Europe, retailers such as Marks & Spencer (**www.marksandspencer.com**), Tesco (**www.tesco.com**), and Metro Group AG (**www.metrogroup.de**) have developed initiatives where RFID tags are attached to cases, containers, and pallets. These tags enable the retailer to know exactly where goods are located from the time they leave a manufacturer's plant until they arrive at a store's receiving docks. While Wal-Mart (**www.walmart.com**) is the leader of RFID technology in the United States, the European retailers' systems use tagging data in conjunction with their point-of-sale systems and for garment-sorting purposes. According to Metro's chief information officer (CIO), "It's [RFID is] about taking the technology deeper toward the customer, even after the sale, into warranty claims. It's about having the ability to track returns and trace merchandise to comply with regulatory issues and product recalls and safety."

Recently, Marks & Spencer has used radio-frequency identification devices (RFIDs) for men's shirts and suits. They will be used on women's clothing and lingerie. RFID technology is essential to track with 100 percent accuracy items that come in complex sizes, such as bras that have 68 different sizes. At Marks & Spencer, the RFID chips will store serial numbers that are unique to each product. The chips also enable clerks to complete a physical inventory at the end of each day using hand-held readers. As one observer notes, by

2007, Marks & Spencer will have "the potential to tag at the item level about 350 million individual pieces at a cost of about 20 cents for each tag."

At Tesco, a retailer with 2,400 stores in Europe and Asia, RFID chips are currently being used on items such as cosmetics and DVDs. The chips enable Tesco to more easily check stock levels, as well as to find DVDs that have been put back on incorrect shelves by customers and retail personnel. A retail analyst estimates that Tesco has had a 4 percent increase in DVD sales due to RFID technology alone. This increase in sales and profits resulted in Tesco's recovering its RFID investment in one year.

Metro Group AG (a conglomerate of convenience stores, electronics stores, and other retail businesses) has also used item-level tagging at some of its department stores. The RFID tagging has been integrated into Metro's point-of-sale and order-processing systems. When an RFID-tagged item is sold, a signal is sent to the order-processing system to alert clerks to restock the shelf and/or receive another shipment from a vendor or the retailer's distribution system.

Metro has been testing an RFID application that scans tags on merchandise that customers take into a dressing room, then finds other sizes and colors of the same item, and even recommends accessories that coordinate with the clothing. The recommended items are shown on a visual display located in the dressing room. It has also tested the use of RFIDs in its automatic replenishment systems. Metro's CIO says, "We're trying to understand where the technology will provide the biggest benefits. It's obvious with logistics and supply chain."

Questions

1. Describe the cost components of developing, testing, and implementing RFID technology.
2. Discuss the potential savings due to an effective RFID program.
3. What other applications of RFID are possible?
4. Describe how RFID technology can be used in warranty claims and in product recalls.

[c-4]The material in this case is drawn from Laurie Sullivan, "Europe Tries on RFID," *Informationweek.com* (March 7, 2005), pp. 36–42.

part five
Comprehensive Case

Dealing with Disengaged Employees*

INTRODUCTION

As customers, we've been waited on by people who quit but never left. As employees, we've been managed by bosses who quit but managed to stay. As managers, we have managed people who physically attend but mentally pretend. Disengaged workers cost U.S. firms more than $250 billion per year, as noted by a Gallup poll. Our own research shows that three out of four workers are disengaged. This price tag includes co-worker and customer dissatisfaction plus loss of loyalty on both sides. Who wants to work with a person who performs only enough to get by? Who wants to be served by a person who barely does what is expected?

Engaged Employee, Strong Asset

Consider what it means to be an engaged employee: involved, occupied, committed, meshed, participating. This also means "unavailable to anyone else"—as in other employers. When fully engaged in work, a person's energy and focus are a laser directed on outcome and satisfaction. They become a company's strongest asset, one that cannot be stolen.

Disconnected, Detached, Disheartened

Why do workers become disengaged? Here's an example. The chief executive of a successful specialty chain wanted to improve the hiring process and raise the bar on customer service. He said that he wanted to hire people who naturally understand what service means. He felt training was not the answer: "We have some terrific people. We need more of them." Was it a question of hiring or retaining and engaging? Were "terrific" people already on board and overlooked?

Our company conducted an online survey of frontline workers; supervisors; managers at the store, district, and regional levels; and executives. They were asked questions related to their perceptions of several job positions, as well as their view of company effectiveness in several areas, including employee development, recognition, communication, and performance issues.

The results were unexpected. Employees widely disagreed on what particular positions required in behaviors, attitudes, and values for a person to be successful. Qualifications for success in that firm were based on what exists rather than what is possible. This is like using the performance of a second-string team as the benchmark for top performers on the first team. Often top performers in one firm would be only average if in the same position with another company.

Another important discovery emerged from that survey. An individual who became a "good employee" was expected to remain at that level without much feedback, recognition, or involvement. The only way to get a raise or recognition was to try to be promoted to the next level, even though the employee might not want to leave a current position.

Final analysis showed that managers played the key role in employee retention, development, and satisfaction, yet they were never held accountable. This lack of accountability reduced efforts in employee development and took focus away from talented employees, letting them do what they had to do rather than motivating them to grow. Lack of accountability became a major cause of disengagement.

Disengagement in that company was widespread and the result of distorted perceptions about how and why people do what they do and about what workers expect from gainful employment.

Spreading Virus

Generally, the reasons for disengagement are both economic and behavioral. Mentally leaving a job where you're unhappy but get a paycheck is better than no job at all. For many disengaged workers, this makes total economic sense. Yet, the behavioral factor has even more power.

Forty-two percent of the North American population has a behavior style identified as "High S" or high steadiness. A few characteristics of this behavior preference are: prefers little or no change, avoids risk, tolerates ambiguity, evades confrontation, passively disagrees, prefers routine work: "I may be unhappy, I may complain (to friends and co-workers only). I may think of leaving, meanwhile, I'll put up with my frustrations until something else comes along."

At a specialty chain retailer, we found that disengagement took its toll on productivity, motivation, and customer service even though disengaged employees were relatively few. Two disengaged store managers had an adverse impact on supervisors and associates, causing these workers to reduce their customer service efforts. The result was an attitude of "why bother?" The low customer service scores and sales results over time caused a negative reaction from the entire region, which went from number one to number five. Two unhappy workers affected hundreds.

In a category chain operation, the disengaged director of advertising inadvertently caused her team to negatively impact certain buyers in the firm. Her lack of involvement led to a negative view of the entire marketing department. The senior vice-president of marketing eventually let the director go, only to learn from the rest of the team that the problem existed for almost two years.

Why would a CEO allow a bad employee to remain on the job for two years? Disengagement occurs in stages, and many disengaged workers are passively disengaged. By lack of involvement or interest, they do only what absolutely needs to get done so they seem to be working. Here's when it is critical to diagnose the problem: Within nine months to a year after the initial but hidden disengagement, the worker becomes actively disengaged: exhibiting harmful behavior— criticizing others' efforts, speaking negatively about co-workers and bosses, refusing to do what needs to be done, or undermining initiatives.

Turned Off, Yet Shining

All disengaged workers are not the same. During the course of an organizational survey, I asked Suzanne, a district manager in her late thirties, to explain confidentially why her colleagues were concerned about her loss of enthusiasm and involvement. Her answer: "My heart's not in it anymore." When she first started with the firm, she was considered a bright, fast-rising star. She was given challenges and then praise or criticism. She welcomed both because they helped her learn and grow, an important factor of her work. When a new boss arrived, the learning eventually stopped, and conversations with her boss became one-sided and solely numbers-focused. She was told to keep doing what she was doing because she was doing well. Several months later, Suzanne was given a bigger district to manage.

Suzanne's example expresses the soul of disengagement: (1) Disengaged workers usually were once engaged, caring workers. (2) Disengaged workers are not necessarily poor performers. (3) Disengagement usually begins with either a new boss or a boss who becomes disengaged. (4) Disengagement often occurs after changes in job position. (5) Disengagement begins when learning and development stop.

Suzanne is in the first stage of disengagement, *reactive disengagement*. Without intervention, this will turn to *active disengagement*. Reactive disengagement describes persons who *react* to their boredom and/or unhappiness with their job by simply doing nothing except what has to be done. They have lost initiative and interest. Active disengagement means they quietly begin involving others in their discontent through negative comments and begin to express their resentment of co-workers, leaders, and the firm.

Mediocrity Wins

All new employees go through a "honeymoon" period of adapting—when the newness of the job, the excitement of meeting new people, making new friends, and learning about the job and the company create adrenalin-filled days. Managers, co-workers, and reports pay more attention to a new worker than to seasoned ones. This is true whether the new employee is a line person or an executive. Problems begin when the honeymoon period ends and the expectations of fulfillment continue. The same people who lavished attention now begin taking the new worker for granted.

Managers spend too much time on mediocre and poor performers. Productive workers are left alone, or worse, given more responsibility and tasks because everyone knows they'll get it done. It's almost punishment—more work, fewer rewards, less attention. Disengaged and mediocre workers are "rewarded" with extra attention, lower expectations, and benefit of the doubt. The result? A confusing path that eventually leads productive workers into reactive disengagement.

Many companies mistakenly create incentive programs to boost mediocre productivity. The question I raise: "Why should these mediocre performers do better?" Do they suddenly know how to do a job better? In other words, is the employee's attitude, "I know how to perform better, but I choose not to unless I get an incentive or more money?"

"B" Workers Not Disengaged

Every organization today is searching for talent. Talent is exciting, energizing, and enveloping. Talented people draw you in with their creativity and innovation. Their ideas and commitment to making something happen are infectious. Talent comes in many different forms. Take what I call "A" players. They are hungry for results, impatient for promotions, willing to sacrifice life for work and its meaning in helping them identify who they are as individuals.

"B" players—loyal, dedicated, focused on helping others succeed—do not like the spotlight on themselves. They are "worker bees" with few demands. "B" players are balanced—an enigma to "A" players who do not understand them. As a result, "B" players and their value are overlooked. Their contributions are minimized. Hiring managers routinely pass on them primarily because they do so poorly in interviews. Highly developed listening skills make them, by default, the sounding board for others' issues and concerns. Due to their caring nature, they become the behind the-scenes counselors and coaches. Many "B" players are mistaken as disengaged—often the result of "A" players' perceptions.

The significant difference between "B" players and disengaged workers is their heart. "B" workers truly care about their co-workers, company, and customers. They are mentally present in contrast to disengaged workers who are mentally absent.

Identifying "Mental Absence"

How do you discover and fix the "mental absence" before disengagement takes its toll on morale, productivity, and integrity? The first step is to identify the signs and degree of disengagement.

Some of the initial external signs of reactive disengagement include:

- Increased absenteeism.
- Disconnection from boss.
- Disinterested.
- Uninvolved.
- Uncreative.
- Longer lunches and breaks.
- Less communication.
- Little initiative.

Additional signs when active disengagement sets in:

- Depression.
- Missed deadlines.
- Work-related accidents.
- No talk about the future.
- Anger.
- Poor or nonexistent discussions with boss.

- Undermining others' contributions.
- Late in, early out.

The second step is to understand what underlying personal and work factors must exist for disengagement to grow and spread. Chiefly, disengagement has become a coping mechanism for job-related stress, most often the result of several factors:

- People mismatched to positions.
- Little or no control over work patterns.
- No opportunity to grow, learn, develop, or contribute.
- Lack of pride in the job one does.
- No involvement in decisions or changes.
- Feeling unneeded.
- Lack of accountability.
- No recognition.
- Ineffective communication.
- Lack of future opportunities.
- Communication difficulties.
- Work pattern and behavior differences with boss.

Engaging the Disengaged

When a manager becomes aware of poor performance, what generally happens? He or she often waits too long to speak with the employees, hoping the negative behavior will fix itself. This is the biggest problem. *It's not about healing disengagement, it's about prevention.* By the time active disengagement becomes apparent, the damage is done.

Poor performance by co-workers is the leading reason that dedicated and caring—engaged—employees leave their jobs. More than 1,500 executives and frontline people were assessed. Ninety-two percent agreed that their firms do not identify or deal with poor performers. Most people spend 80 percent of their time doing tasks and 20 percent of their time achieving results.

It is critical for managers to be sensitive to and aware of every worker's job satisfaction. Frequent conversations and involvement with the employee's views, preferences, and goals are a must. If disengagement has set in, an assessment must be completed before any solution initiatives are prescribed. Trying to learn reasons for or causes of disengagement by asking an employee is like determining a heart condition by listening to the heart. Managers need to know the root of the disengagement and define the focus of improvement; and the worker must agree that the analyses are correct. Opinion has no role here.

Individual Matters

In *Principle-Centered Leadership*, Stephen Covey writes, "In a very real sense, there is no such thing as organizational behavior, there is only individual behavior."

How well do you really know and understand your employees? How do you approach those you must encourage, develop, teach, and coach while ensuring productivity and top performance? As human beings, we cannot avoid bringing our personal biases, opinions, and work style preferences to the workplace. This is why managers who rely on validated assessments are able to retain talent at far higher percentages than managers who rely solely on their instincts.

I have successfully used a particular survey process that identifies critical factors in three distinct areas specifically contributing to superior job performance. As we know, the key to successful individual excellence lies in the combination of a person's behavior, values, and personal skills—attributes. This survey provides a clear reading on *how* a person does what they do, *why* they do what they do, and *will* they do what they say they will do.

Each individual has a unique way of working. Each individual within the right job with the right guidance has incredible potential. Each person does not necessarily want to be a hard-driving, winner-takes-all "A" player. The steady doers who are consistent, loyal, dedicated, and helpful to others—the "B" players—are often overlooked. Decision makers who prefer assertive, energetic, or outgoing people rarely select a "B" player as a team leader. How wrong and unfair.

Many managers are so focused on results and tasks that they lose sight of a critical component for their success—their people and their impact on the organization. It is necessary to repeatedly identify the mixed messages sent to executives and managers about the importance of focus. Focus allows only one focal point—what needs to be accomplished. But without a wide-angle lens, you lose the surrounding elements that create the entirety of the landscape.

Motivating Engagement

Understanding each person's unique abilities, skills, motivators, and work styles is the key to engagement along with a managing style that focuses on the real individual rather than a manager's perception:

- Benchmark the job by focusing on the job requirements rather than the "type" of person.
- Match the person to the position by measuring individual behavior preferences, beliefs, values, and attributes.
- Understand the emotional requirements of a new employee by discussing with them their strengths and limitations, needs, and reasons for working.
- Watch for behavior changes during the first six months of employment. Job performance either improves or drops during this period.
- Provide informal feedback monthly by asking specific questions related to the employee's perceptions of how he or she is doing.

Firing Is a Favor

The damage that an unproductive, disengaged worker can cause is hard to tally. Typically, co-workers see disengagement much sooner than management. Thus, the impact on employee morale, as well as its effect on customers and productivity, can be devastating. The conversations about dissatisfaction, frustrations, griping, and complaining create such a vortex that it even sucks in the productive and engaged workers.

Because a manager may wait an average of 9 months to first recognize unacceptable work patterns and another 3 months to begin addressing the issue, the employee becomes actively disengaged during the 9 to 12 months since passive disengagement set in. Yet, it will normally take another 6 to 9 months for the manager to conclude that the individual needs to be separated. This totals 18 to 21 months during which a disengaged employee negatively affects co-workers, customers, and subordinates. This pattern exists at all levels—from frontline to executive.

If you make the wrong decision in hiring, recognize this early and deal with it. Either change the position or change the person. *Do the individual a favor*. Show them that the match is simply not there. *Do other employees a favor*. They know before you may know that a co-worker is ineffective or a detriment to the company. *Do yourself a favor*. How much time are you spending with the poor performer? Your time is costly—to you and your firm. Use your time to develop engaged employees with potential. *Do your customers a favor*. An unhappy worker does not deliver satisfying and happy service.

People Need Purpose

A chief marketing officer of a large Midwestern retailer says that his awareness of purpose began one evening with a sweet and simple question from his daughter. She asked, "Daddy, did you make anyone happy today?" He felt as if someone had hit him in the chest because the innocent question caused him to think about his effect on people and what actually makes people happy. What had he done lately to find out about his co-workers? He realized that focusing on tasks to accomplish leaves little time to understand one's purpose for taking a job, working long hours, putting up with conflicts. Why? He discovered in the process that it certainly is not money.

Do you know your purpose for doing what you do? What are your drivers? Do you receive a quiet satisfaction that causes you to go to work? Do your employees know their answers to these questions? If not, you'll never benefit from "purpose-driven engagement."

Questions

1. What are the major lessons to be learned from this case?
2. How can training and re-training be used to better engage retail employees when (a) they are new and (b) after they have been with a retailer for a while?
3. What supervision style do you believe is most likely to motivate retail employees? Explain your answer.
4. Suppose that a retailer decides to reduce its labor costs as a percentage of sales from 10 percent to 8 percent. Is this good or bad? Why?
5. Present five suggestions to improve labor productivity in retailing.
6. What are the pros and cons of cross-training a disengaged employee?
7. What labor-related functions could be outsourced by an auto dealer? Explain your answer.

*The material in this case is adapted by the authors from Terri Kabachnick, Chief Executive, Kabachnick Group, "I Quit But I Forgot to Tell You," *Retailing Issues Letter* (Number 1, 2004), pp. 1–6. Reprinted by permission.

Merchandise Management and Pricing

In Part Six, we present the merchandise management and pricing aspects of the retail strategy mix. Merchandise management consists of the buying, handling, and financial aspects of merchandising. Pricing decisions deal with the financial aspects of merchandise management and affect their interaction with other retailing elements.

- **Chapter 14** covers the development of merchandise plans. We begin by discussing the concept of a merchandising philosophy. We then look at buying organizations and their processes, as well as the major considerations in formulating merchandise plans. The chapter concludes by describing category management and merchandising software.

- **Chapter 15** focuses on implementing merchandise plans. We study each stage in the buying and handling process: gathering information, selecting and interacting with merchandise sources, evaluation, negotiation, concluding purchases, receiving and stocking merchandise, reordering, and re-evaluation. We also examine logistics and inventory management and their effects on merchandising.

- **Chapter 16** concentrates on financial merchandise management. We introduce the cost and retail methods of accounting. The merchandise forecasting and budgeting process is presented. Unit control systems are discussed. Dollar and unit financial inventory controls are integrated.

- **Chapter 17** deals with pricing. We review the outside factors affecting price decisions: consumers, government, suppliers, and competitors. A framework for developing a price strategy is then shown: objectives, broad policy, basic strategy, implementation, and adjustments.

Chapter 14
DEVELOPING MERCHANDISE PLANS

In 1993, the chief executive of Gap Inc. (**www.gap.com**) realized that his Gap and Banana Republic stores were ineffective in reaching consumers who did not want to spend much money on clothes. So, he converted 48 underperforming Gap stores into Gap Warehouse stores. Soon thereafter, these stores were renamed Old Navy (**www.oldnavy.com**).

Reprinted by permission.

Today, Old Navy is the most often purchased brand by two of the three generations that together account for about 80 percent of apparel spending by women and girls: the Millennials (aged 10–27) and Generation Xers (aged 28–38), according to a major market research firm. Old Navy is also the top-selling private-label retailer of sportswear with an 8 percent market share. Old Navy generates about $7 billion in annual sales from its more than 850 stores.

Old Navy has achieved its success through a strategy that combines value pricing, timely styling, an updated image, and sizing to fit Americans' growing waistlines. Old Navy is able to hold prices at low levels by using lower-cost materials. For example, while a Gap sweater is typically made from merino wool, an Old Navy sweater is more likely made with low-cost acrylic fabric. Despite its low prices, Old Navy apparel is stylish and well displayed, and the sales staff is well trained. Important components of its image include retro-style marketing. To appeal to larger Americans, close to one-fifth of Old Navy's stores now offer women's sizes 16–26.[1]

chapter objectives

1. To demonstrate the importance of a sound merchandising philosophy
2. To study various buying organization formats and the processes they use
3. To outline the considerations in devising merchandise plans: forecasts, innovativeness, assortment, brands, timing, and allocation
4. To discuss category management and merchandising software

OVERVIEW

GERS Merchandising (www.gers.com/solutions/merch.html) is one of the many software tools to help retailers make better merchandising decisions.

Retailers must have the proper product assortments and sell them in a manner consistent with their overall strategy. **Merchandising** consists of the activities involved in acquiring particular goods and/or services and making them available at the places, times, and prices and in the quantity that enable a retailer to reach its goals. Merchandising decisions can dramatically affect performance. Consider these observations of the late Stanley Marcus, former chief executive of Neiman Marcus:

I believe that retail merchandising is actually very simple: it consists of two factors, customers and products. If you take good care in the buying of the product, it doesn't come back. If you take good care of your customers, they do come back. It's just that simple and just that difficult. This is obviously an oversimplification of the problems of retailing. It's not quite that easy—but almost.

Yet, no wonder customer loyalty has dropped. There is little reason for a shopper to go across town to a store when it's a forgone conclusion that she'll find the same merchandise in store C that she has already seen in stores A and B. I fully expect to come upon a newspaper headline that proclaims, "Customers Found Bored to Death in the Sportswear Department of the XYZ Department Store."

Merchandise sameness emanates from the training of buyers who have been taught to play it safe by avoiding risky fashions, to play it cautiously by buying from a limited number of standard vendors who sell the same "packages" to all major accounts, to play it for profit by advertising only the goods supported by manufacturers' advertising allowances. Many retailers erroneously believe the goal is to make a profit and fail to realize that a profit is due to having goods or services that are so satisfactory that the customer is willing to pay a bonus, or a profit, over and above the distributor's cost.[2]

In this chapter, the *planning* aspects of merchandising are discussed. The *implementation* aspects of merchandising are examined in Chapter 15. The *financial* aspects of merchandising are described in Chapter 16. Retail *pricing* is covered in Chapter 17.

Visit our Web site (**www.prenhall.com/bermanevans**) for a broad selection of links related to merchandising strategies and tactics.

MERCHANDISING PHILOSOPHY

At Cost Plus World Market, you never know what you'll find (www.costplus.com).

A **merchandising philosophy** sets the guiding principles for all the merchandise decisions that a retailer makes. It must reflect target market desires, the retailer's institutional type, the marketplace positioning, the defined value chain, supplier capabilities, costs, competitors, product trends, and other factors. The retail merchandising philosophy drives every product decision, from what product lines to carry to the shelf space allotted to different products to inventory turnover to pricing—and more: "Retailers have to decide on the breadth of assortment across the store (narrow or wide) and the depth of the assortment within each category (deep or shallow). In addition, they must select the quality of the items within the assortment—high or low, national brands or store brands. They need to decide on their pricing policies, across categories and within. Finally, retailers must decide if

FIGURE 14-1

Nike's Merchandising Philosophy for Its Own Stores

At its company-owned stores, such as this one at the Rome airport, Nike has the ability to showcase its products in an environment free from other brands. It can offer a fuller product line and better control the introduction of new Nike products than it could through other resellers (which still account for the bulk of its business).

Photo reprinted by permission of Susan Berry, Retail Image Consulting, Inc.

assortments should generally be stable over time or whether there should be surprise, specials, or customization in assortments."[3] See Figure 14-1.

Costco, the membership club giant, flourishes with its individualistic merchandising philosophy:

> We want to provide the customer with a broad range of high-quality merchandise at prices consistently lower than at discount retailers or supermarkets. A key element of this strategy is to carry only those products on which we can provide members with significant cost savings. Items that members request but that cannot be bought at prices low enough to pass along meaningful cost savings are often not carried. We seek to limit specific items in each product line to fast-selling models, sizes, and colors. Thus, we carry about 4,000 active items per store, as opposed to discount retailers and supermarkets that usually have 40,000 to 60,000 items or more. Many consumable products are offered for sale in case, carton, or multiple-pack quantities only. In keeping with our customer satisfaction policy, we accept merchandise returns within a reasonable time after purchase.[4]

In forming a merchandising philosophy, the scope of responsibility for merchandise personnel must be stated. Are these personnel to be involved with the full array of *merchandising functions*, both buying and selling goods and services (including selection, pricing, display, and customer transactions)? Or are they to focus on the *buying function*, with others responsible for displays, personal selling, and so on? Many firms consider merchandising to be the foundation for their success, and buyers (or merchandise managers) engage in both buying and selling tasks. Other retailers consider their buyers to be skilled specialists who should not be active in the selling function, which is done by other skilled specialists. Store managers at full-line discount stores often have great influence on product displays but have little impact on whether to stock or promote particular brands.

With a merchandising-oriented philosophy, the buyer's expertise is used in selling, responsibility and authority are clear, the buyer ensures that items are properly displayed, costs are reduced (fewer specialists), and the buyer is close to

Merchandise buying and planning involves the intersection of retail art and statistics. Retail professionals select the merchandise to be sold. They facilitate order follow-up, inventory flow through, and allocation of merchandise to stores. Statistical development and analysis are woven into this retail career area, where team members also coordinate gross margin planning/analysis responsibilities, develop distribution plans for merchandise categories and subclasses, and balance stock unit ratios by store:

- *Head of Merchandise Buying/General Merchandise Manager (GMM):* Top executive in charge of all merchandise buying for a chain. This position will typically be a GMM position or, in very large volume chains, may be executive vice-president level with multiple GMMs reporting to him or her.
- *Divisional Merchandise Manager (DMM):* This position is one level above and directly supervises a group of buyers, typically in related merchandise categories.
- *Senior Merchandise Buyer:* These buyers are senior to merchandise buyers due to unusually high dollar volume or product complexity of the goods being bought. Senior buyers may train other buyers and may supervise a small staff but are ranked between buyer and DMM.
- *Merchandise Buyer:* This position selects the merchandise to be sold by sourcing vendors in the United States or overseas markets and/or by working with vendors to produce private labels.
- *Associate Merchandise Buyer:* This position assists the buyer but typically has an open-to-buy authority over a portion of the buyer's category or for reorders and test quantities. The buyer typically retains responsibility over the merchandise category.
- *Assistant Merchandise Buyer:* Supports the buyer in merchandise selection, order follow-up, and inventory flow through. May not have an open-to-buy, although some may have authority to make replenishment orders. This is a buyer trainee professional position, not clerical support.

Source: Reprinted by permission of the National Retail Federation.

consumers through his or her selling involvement. When buying and selling are separated, specialized skills are applied to each task, the morale of store personnel goes up as they get more authority, selling is not viewed as a secondary task, the interaction of salespeople with customers is better exploited, and buying and selling personnel are distinctly supervised. An individual firm must evaluate which format is better for its particular retail strategy.

To capitalize on opportunities, more retailers now use micromerchandising and cross-merchandising. With **micromerchandising**, a retailer adjusts shelf-space allocations to respond to customer and other differences among local markets. Dominick's supermarkets allot shelf space to children's and adults' cereals to reflect demand patterns at different stores. Wal-Mart adapts the space it assigns to product lines at various stores to reflect differences in demographics, weather, and customer activities. Micromerchandising is easier today because of the information generated through data warehouses. At Chico's, "instant electronic access to sales data has contributed substantially to its commitment of customizing each store to the specific buying habits of a particular store's clientele. Open-to-buys are better managed, and budgetary techniques and other planning efforts are more effective."[5]

In **cross-merchandising**, a retailer carries complementary goods and services to encourage shoppers to buy more. That is why apparel stores stock accessories and auto dealers offer extended warranties. Cross-merchandising, like scrambled merchandising, can be ineffective if taken too far. Yet, it has tremendous potential. Consider the creative approach of Whole Foods:

> This upscale, organic grocery store is a big believer in cross-merchandising kitchenware with food items. Salad spinners are found near organic lettuce. Grill tools are on endcap displays near the butcher shop, and Tetsubin teapots from Joyce Chen, at nearly $70, are positioned near

Asian ingredients. Assorted bakeware from Norpro has about 10 feet of space on an aisle filled with spices and various types of flour. Food storage containers from Snapware fill an endcap leading into the cereal aisle. Neoprene wine tote bags and corkscrews from builtNY fill another endcap near the wine and beer section, and a five-foot wall of water bottles is featured within the bottled water aisle.[6]

BUYING ORGANIZATION FORMATS AND PROCESSES

A merchandising plan cannot be properly devised unless the buying organization and its processes are well defined: Who is responsible for decisions? What are their tasks? Do they have sufficient authority? How does merchandising fit with overall operations? Figure 14-2 highlights the range of organizational attributes from which to choose.

Level of Formality

With a *formal buying organization*, merchandising (buying) is a distinct retail task and a separate department is set up. The functions involved in acquiring merchandise and making it available for sale are under the control of this department. A formal organization is most often used by larger firms and involves distinct personnel. In an *informal buying organization*, merchandising (buying) is not a distinct task. The same personnel handle both merchandising (buying) and other retail tasks; responsibility and authority are not always clear-cut. Informal organizations generally occur in smaller retailers.

The advantages of a formal organization are the clarity of responsibilities and the use of full-time, specialized merchandisers. The disadvantage is the cost of a separate department. The advantages of an informal format are the low costs and flexibility. The disadvantages are less-defined responsibilities and the lesser emphasis on merchandise planning. Both structures exist in great numbers. It is

FIGURE 14-2
The Attributes and Functions of Buying Organizations

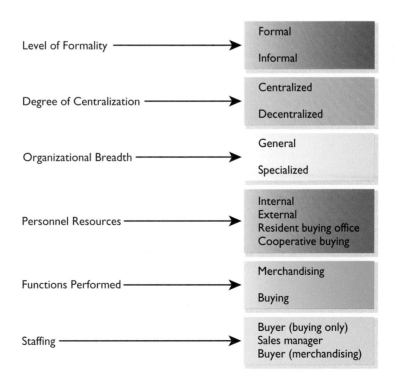

Level of Formality → Formal / Informal

Degree of Centralization → Centralized / Decentralized

Organizational Breadth → General / Specialized

Personnel Resources → Internal / External / Resident buying office / Cooperative buying

Functions Performed → Merchandising / Buying

Staffing → Buyer (buying only) / Sales manager / Buyer (merchandising)

not critical for a firm to use a formal department. It is crucial that the firm recognizes the role of merchandising (buying) and ensures that responsibility, activities, and operational relationships are aptly defined and enacted.

Degree of Centralization

Multi-unit retailers must choose whether to have a centralized buying organization or a decentralized one. In a *centralized buying organization*, all purchase decisions emanate from one office. A chain may have eight stores, with all merchandise decisions made at the headquarters store. In a *decentralized buying organization*, purchase decisions are made locally or regionally. A 40-store chain may allow each outlet to select its own merchandise or divide the branches into geographic territories (such as four branches per region) with regional decisions made by the headquarters store in each territory.

The advantages of centralized buying are the integration of effort, strict controls, consistent image, proximity to top management, staff support, and volume discounts. Possible disadvantages are the inflexibility, time delays, poor morale at local stores, and excessive uniformity. Decentralized buying has these advantages: adaptability to local conditions, quick order processing, and improved morale because of branch autonomy. Potential disadvantages are disjointed planning, an inconsistent image, limited controls, little staff support, and a loss of volume discounts.

Many chains combine the formats by deploying a centralized buying organization while also giving store managers some input. This is how Zara, the Madrid-based global apparel chain, operates:

> At Inditex's (the parent company of Zara) head office, 300 designers are in daily contact with store managers to discover best-selling items. Production is deliberately carried out in small batches to avoid over-supply. While there is some replenishment of stock, most lines are replaced quickly with new designs rather than with more of the same. Shoppers cannot be sure that something that has caught their eye will appear in the store again. They also know that everyone they meet will not be wearing it. Zara's production cycles are much faster than those of its nearest rival, Sweden's H&M. An entirely new Zara garment takes five weeks from design to delivery; a new version of an existing model can be in the shops within two weeks. In a typical year, Zara launches 11,000 new items, compared with 2,000 to 4,000 from firms like H&M or America's Gap.[7]

Organizational Breadth

In a general buying organization, one or several people buy all of a firm's merchandise. The owner of a small hardware store may buy the merchandise for his or her store. With a specialized organization, each buyer is responsible for a product category. A department store usually has separate buyers for girls', juniors', and women's clothes.

A general approach is better if the retailer is small or there are few products involved. A specialized approach is better if the retailer is large or many products are carried. By specializing, there is greater expertise and responsibility is well defined; however, costs are higher and extra personnel are required.

Personnel Resources

A retailer can choose an inside or outside buying organization. An *inside buying organization* is staffed by a retailer's personnel, and merchandise decisions are made by permanent employees. See Figure 14-3. With an *outside buying organization*, a

See what Zara's merchandisers think is "hot" (www.zara.com).

Melissa Davies

WAL★MART

TYPE OF STORE:
Mass Market

HEADQUARTERS:
Bentonville, Ark.

Networking helped Melissa Davies score a job as a buyer for the nation's largest retailer, Wal-Mart. While a student and basketball player at Eastern Washington University in Cheney, Wash., Davies was part of a group called Students in Free Enterprise. "The program allows you to network with businesses locally," explains Davies, a business administration marketing and management major. While giving a presentation, a Wal-Mart executive heard her speak and invited her to pursue a career with the chain's training program.

After starting as a buyer trainee, Davies rose through the ranks with four promotions. Now she is a buyer of outdoor decorative merchandise in the lawn and garden department.

"I love the challenge. I find it amazing that I'm 24 years old and have the responsibility for a category that is somewhere in the $300 million range," says Davies. What she finds refreshing at Wal-Mart is that the company is willing to let even young associates follow their gut instincts. "At Wal-Mart, it isn't about experience or tenure, it is about performance," adds Davies, who once vowed she'd never work in retail and wanted to pursue a career in sports marketing because of her college basketball experience. She is now a great supporter of a retail career path. "I've entrusted my career to Wal-Mart," she adds.

During a typical day, Davies finds herself meeting with suppliers, talking to store associates and answering at least 170 e-mails. "It is fast paced, and I find it exciting to work with suppliers on long-term ideas and strategies." Although she's young, she says she's earned the respect of top-level executives from major manufacturers who supply Wal-Mart.

What's her gameplan? "I'd like to stay in merchandising and ultimately have a leadership role in the company." She's still involved in Students in Free Enterprise, and she helps show others the opportunity presented by not only retailing, but Wal-Mart in particular. ■

FIGURE 14-3
At Wal-Mart: Developing an Inside Buying Organization

Reprinted by permission of *DSN Retailing Today.*

company or personnel external to the retailer are hired, usually on a fee basis. Most retailers use either an inside or an outside organization; some employ a combination.

An inside buying organization is most often used by large retailers and very small retailers. Large retailers do this to have greater control over merchandising decisions and to be more distinctive. They have the financial clout to employ their own specialists. At very small retailers, the owner or manager does all merchandising functions to save money and keep close to the market.

Ross Stores has merchandising career opportunities in New York and Los Angeles. Scroll down to "Buying Office" and click on a job category (www.rossstores.com/ jo_jb.jsp).

Ross Stores (**www.rossstores.com**), the off-price apparel chain with stores in 22 states, is an example of a retailer with an inside buying organization: "Off-price buying is a relationship business. Successful buying correlates directly to the quality and quantity of vendor contacts we maintain with a broad array of moderate and better name-brand resources." Ross has a merchandising staff of more than 200, 90 percent located in New York's garment district. It also has a smaller buying office in Los Angeles near the apparel and shoe markets: "The size of our buying organization, with its strategic locations, gives our staff daily access to an extensive selection of branded bargains sourced from a network of about 4,000 vendors and manufacturers."[8]

An outside organization is most frequently used by small or medium-sized retailers or those far from supply sources. It is more efficient for them to hire outside buyers than to use company personnel. An outside organization has purchase volume clout in dealing with suppliers, usually services noncompeting retailers, offers research, and may sponsor private brands. Outside buying organizations may be paid by retailers that subscribe to their services or by vendors that give commissions. An individual retailer may set up its own internal organization if it feels its outside group is dealing with direct competitors or the firm finds it can buy items more efficiently on its own.

Learn more at "About Doneger" (www.doneger.com/AboutDoneger), the world's largest outside buying organization.

The Doneger Group (**www.doneger.com**) is the leading independent resident buying office, with hundreds of retailer clients that operate more than 7,000 stores. As its Web site notes, "Advising clients throughout the world, we research, analyze, and evaluate all segments of the apparel and accessories markets, in women's wear, menswear, and children's wear. Member stores are supplied with the resources and information appropriate to their business."

Associated Merchandising Corporation (AMC) is a hybrid buying organization. For more than 70 years, it was a nonprofit organization co-owned by numerous retailers. Target Corporation acquired AMC in 1998, mostly to serve its own retail stores. AMC still provides merchandising functions for several other retailers, as well. It is involved with international trend identification, product design and development, global product sourcing, quality assurance, and production, delivery, and order tracking. It focuses on apparel, accessories, and home goods.

A **resident buying office**, which can be an inside or outside organization, is used when a retailer wants to keep in close touch with key market trends and cannot do so through just headquarters buying staff. Such offices are situated in important merchandise centers and provide valuable data and contacts. A few large specialized U.S. firms operate resident buying offices that serve several thousand retailers. Each organization just cited (Ross, Doneger, and AMC) has multiple resident buying offices to get a better sense of local markets and merchandise sources. Besides the major players, there are many smaller outside resident buying offices that assist retailers.

The Federation of Pharmacy Networks (www.fpn.org) provides many services for its members.

Today, independent retailers and small chains are involved with cooperative buying to a greater degree than before to compete with large chains. In **cooperative buying**, a group of retailers gets together to make quantity purchases from suppliers and obtain volume discounts. It is most popular among food, hardware, and drugstore retailers. As an illustration, the Federation of Pharmacy Networks (FPN) comprises 22 buying groups across the United States. It represents 13,000 independent drugstore owners: "FPN negotiates with selected vendors to establish favorable contracts based on the volume purchasing power achieved through our pharmacies. Many of our programs provide the independent pharmacist with significant net savings. Additionally, each member group office benefits from FPN's programs."[9]

Functions Performed

At this juncture, the responsibilities and functions of merchandise and in-store personnel are assigned. With a "merchandising" view, merchandise personnel oversee all buying and selling functions, including assortments, advertising, pricing, point-of-sale displays, employee utilization, and personal selling approaches. With a "buying" view, merchandise personnel oversee the buying of products, advertising, and pricing, while in-store personnel oversee assortments, displays, employee utilization, and sales presentations. The functions undertaken must reflect the retailer's level of formality, the degree of centralization, and personnel resources.

Staffing

The last organizational decision involves staffing. What positions must be filled and with what qualifications? Firms with a merchandising viewpoint are most concerned with hiring good buyers. Firms with a buying perspective are concerned about hiring sales managers, as well. Many large firms hire college graduates, train them, and promote them to buyers and sales managers.

A **buyer** is responsible for selecting the merchandise to be carried by a retailer and setting a strategy to market that merchandise. He or she devises and controls sales and profit projections for a product category (generally for all stores in a chain); plans proper merchandise assortments, styling, sizes, and quantities; negotiates with and evaluates vendors; and often oversees in-store displays. He or she must be attuned to the marketplace, be able to bargain with suppliers, and be capable of preparing detailed plans; and he or she may travel to the marketplace. A **sales manager** typically supervises the on-floor selling and operational activities for a specific retail department. He or she must be a good organizer, administrator, and motivator. A *merchandising buyer* must possess the attributes of each. Most retailers feel the critical qualification for good merchandisers is their ability to relate to customers and methodically anticipate future needs. In addition, to some extent, buyers are involved with many of the remaining tasks described in this and the next chapter.

Federated Department Stores, which operates such department store chains as Bloomingale's and Macy's, has career tracks that recognize the value of both merchandising and in-store personnel. Figure 14-4 shows two distinct career tracks.

Here's what it's like at the top of the merchandising world:

> As executive vice-president, general merchandise manager, Jay Wanamaker oversees the Guitar Center divisions that consist of buying, planning, marketing, advertising, in-store product training, and visual merchandising. He also leads Guitar Center's promotions

Federated Department Stores (www.retailology.com/college/career/paths.asp) has exciting career paths in both merchandising and operations.

FIGURE 14-4
Merchandising versus Store Management Career Tracks at Federated Department Stores

Source: Figure developed by the authors based on information at "Career Opportunities," **www.retailology.com/college/career** (February 9, 2006).

Merchandising Track

Divisional Merchandise Manager
Oversees merchandise selection and procurement for a particular business segment. Sets the merchandise direction to ensure continuity on the selling floor. Develops strategy to ensure customer satisfaction and maximize performance and profits.

Buyer
Expected to maximize sales and profitability of a given business area by developing and implementing a strategy, analyzing it, and reacting to trends. Overall support of company sales, gross margin, and turnover objectives.

Associate Buyer
Responsible for merchandise development, marketing, and financial management of a particular business area. This is a developmental step to buyer.

Assistant Buyer
Aids buyer in selecting and procuring merchandise, which supports overall sales, gross margin, and turnover goals. Provides operational support to buyers. Assumes some buying responsibility, once buyer determines proficiency.

Store Management Track

Store Manager
Responsible for all aspects of running a profitable store. Sets the tone to ensure success in customer service, profits, operations, people development, merchandise presentation, and merchandise assortment.

Assistant Store Manager
Directs merchandise flow, store maintenance, expense management, shortage prevention, and store sales support activities for a large portion of store volume. Acts as Store Manager in his or her absence.

Sales Manager
In charge of store activities in a specific merchandise area. Includes merchandise presentation, employee development, customer service, operations, and inventory control.

Assistant Sales Manager
Responsible for supervising daily store activities in a specific merchandise area. Includes selling and service management, selecting and developing associates, merchandising, and business management.

department—involved with direct mail, radio, and TV ads. A 25-year veteran in the music industry, Wanamaker joined Guitar Center in 2000 and has directed various of its divisions. Most recently, he oversaw the integration of the American Music Group and the Music & Arts Center into the Guitar Center organization.[10]

DEVISING MERCHANDISE PLANS

There are several factors to consider in devising merchandise plans, as discussed next. See Figure 14-5.

Forecasts

Forecasts are projections of expected retail sales for given periods. They are the foundation of merchandise plans and include these components: overall company projections, product category projections, item-by-item projections, and store-by-store projections (if a chain). Consider the process used by Ikea, the global furniture chain:

Ikea (www.ikea.com) scours the globe for interesting new items that will be popular in its stores.

Ikea manages production from raw materials to finished product. To do so, Ikea must coordinate with more than 1,600 suppliers in 55 nations. At any time, Ikea has more than 10,000 items to manage, 30 percent of which are less than 12 months old. Thus, forecasting is quite important: "We decided we needed a unified planning solution with a top-down approach. The idea was to have a system that would first forecast demand at the highest level, across continents. Then, to drill down to forecasts for individual countries, and then automatically break down those forecasts to the store level."[11]

In this section, forecasting is examined from a general planning perspective. In Chapter 16, the financial dimensions of forecasting are reviewed.

When preparing forecasts, it is essential to distinguish among different types of merchandise. **Staple merchandise** consists of the regular products carried by a retailer. For a supermarket, staples include milk, bread, canned soup, and facial tissues. For a department store, staples include everyday watches, jeans, glassware, and housewares. Because these items have relatively stable sales (sometimes

FIGURE 14-5
Considerations in Devising
Merchandise Plans

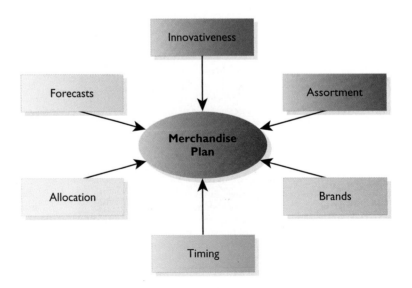

seasonal) and their nature may not change much over time, a retailer can clearly outline the quantities for these items. A **basic stock list** specifies the inventory level, color, brand, style category, size, package, and so on for every staple item carried by the retailer.

Assortment merchandise consists of apparel, furniture, autos, and other products for which the retailer must carry a variety of products in order to give customers a proper selection. This merchandise is harder to forecast than staples due to demand variations, style changes, and the number of sizes and colors to be carried. Decisions are two-pronged: (1) Product lines, styles, designs, and colors are projected. (2) A **model stock plan** is used to project specific items, such as the number of green, red, and blue pullover sweaters of a certain design by size. With a model stock plan, many items are ordered for popular sizes and colors, and small amounts of less popular sizes and colors fill out the assortment.

Fashion merchandise consists of products that may have cyclical sales due to changing tastes and lifestyles. For these items, forecasting can be hard since styles may change from year to year. "Hot" colors often change back and forth. **Seasonal merchandise** consists of products that sell well over nonconsecutive time periods. Items such as ski equipment and air-conditioner servicing have excellent sales during one season per year. Since the strongest sales of seasonal items usually occur at the same time each year, forecasting is straightforward.

With **fad merchandise**, high sales are generated for a short time. Often, toys and games are fads, such as Harry Potter toys that fly off store shelves each time a related movie is released. It is hard to forecast whether such products will reach specific sales targets and how long they will be popular. Sometimes fads turn into extended fads—and sales continue for a long period at a fraction of earlier sales. Trivial Pursuit board games are in the extended fad category.

In forecasting for best-sellers, many retailers use a **never-out list** to determine the amount of merchandise to purchase for resale. The goal is to purchase enough of these products so they are always in stock. Products are added to and deleted from the list as their popularity changes. Before a new Stephen King novel is released, stores order large quantities to be sure they meet anticipated demand. After it disappears from best-seller lists, smaller quantities are kept. It is a good strategy to use a combination of a basic stock list, a model stock plan, and a never-out list. These lists may overlap.

Ethics in RETAILING — Tom's of Maine: Bringing All-Natural Idealism to Retailers

Tom's of Maine (**www.tomsofmaine.com**) makes and markets more than 90 all-natural products that are sold at small health-food stores, mass merchants, and drugstores. The firm positions itself as a company with a conscience. Examples of its social responsibility include donating 10 percent of profits to charity and paying manufacturing employees 15 percent higher than the prevailing local wage rate.

Tom's of Maine has a Common Good Partnerships program that encourages retailers to work on community projects. For example, the company recently partnered with Brooks Pharmacy, a New England chain, to improve children's dental health via grants to dental clinics. Part of the program involved Brooks' preparing displays and promoting Tom's of Maine's products in newspaper inserts. The promotion enabled Tom's of Maine to meet its social responsibility objectives while increasing its business with Brooks Pharmacy. And Brooks Pharmacy has been able to project a socially conscious image while increasing sales of Tom's high-profit-margin items. Due in large part to this program, over a two-year period, Brooks almost tripled its annual purchases from Tom's.

Sources: "Tom's of Mainstream," *Business 2.0* (December 2004), pp. 72–73; and "The Tom's of Maine Story," **www.tomsofmaine.com/about** (March 4, 2006).

TABLE 14-1	Factors to Bear in Mind When Planning Merchandise Innovativeness
Factor	**Relevance for Planning**
Target market(s)	Evaluate whether the target market is conservative or innovative.
Goods/service growth potential	Consider each new offering on the basis of rapidity of initial sales, maximum sales potential per time period, and length of sales life.
Fashion trends	Understand vertical and horizontal fashion trends, if appropriate.
Retailer image	Carry goods/services that reinforce the firm's image. The level of innovativeness should be consistent with this image.
Competition	Lead or follow competition in the selection of new goods/services.
Customer segments	Segment customers by dividing merchandise into established-product displays and new-product displays.
Responsiveness to consumers	Carry new offerings when requested by the target market.
Amount of investment	Consider all of the possible investments for each new good/service: product costs, new fixtures, and additional personnel (or further training for existing personnel).
Profitability	Assess each new offering for potential profits.
Risk	Be aware of the possible tarnishing of the retailer's image, investment costs, and opportunity costs.
Constrained decision making	Restrict franchisees and chain branches from buying certain items.
Declining goods/services	Delete older goods/services if sales and/or profits are too low.

Innovativeness

The innovativeness of a merchandise plan depends on a number of factors. See Table 14-1.

An innovative retailer has a great opportunity—distinctiveness (by being first in the market)—and a great risk—possibly misreading customers and being stuck with large inventories. By assessing each factor in Table 14-1 and preparing a detailed plan for merchandising new goods and services, a firm can better capitalize on opportunities and reduce risks. As shown in Figure 14-6, Wendy's takes innovativeness quite seriously. So do companies such as Hammacher Schlemmer and 7-Eleven:

Check out Hammacher Schlemmer's (www. hammacher.com) list of current "Top Picks."

- Hammacher Schlemmer offers an eclectic mix of housewares, personal care products, home and office products, apparel, sports and leisure goods, and gift items. It has stores in major cities, as well as catalogs and a Web site. Its slogan is "Offering the Best, the Only, and the Unexpected." The firm carries such items as a $1,900 leather massage chair, a $1,460 transparent kayak, and a $100 iPod alarm clock radio.

FIGURE 14-6
R&D at Wendy's

Wendy's Research & Development Department is dedicated to continually improving products by refining cooking and serving procedures and ingredients. R&D regularly comes up with new products for testing and possible addition to the menu.

Photo reprinted by permission.

• Although the name "7-Eleven" may not conjure up "innovative retailer," it is extremely innovative. Recently, the firm has introduced innovative programs and brands "that are challenging many of the industry's tried-and-true processes with groundbreaking approaches to everything from merchandising to distribution." As its chief executive says, "We offer a broad array of products, including many not traditionally available in convenience stores."[12]

Retailers should assess the growth potential for each new good or service they carry: How fast will a new good or service generate sales? What are the most sales (dollars and units) to be reached in a season or year? Over what period will a good or service continue selling? One tool to assess potential is the **product life cycle**, which shows the expected behavior of a good or service over its life. The basic cycle comprises introduction, growth, maturity, and decline stages—shown in Figure 14-7 and described next.

During introduction, the retailer should anticipate a limited target market. The good or service will probably be supplied in one basic version. The manufacturer (supplier) may limit distribution to "finer" stores. Yet, new convenience items such as food and housewares products are normally mass distributed. Items initially distributed selectively tend to have high prices. Mass distributed products typically involve low prices to foster faster consumer acceptance. Early promotion must be explanatory, geared to informing shoppers. At this stage, there are very few possible suppliers.

As innovators buy a new product and recommend it to friends, sales increase rapidly and the growth stage is entered. The target market includes middle-income

FIGURE 14-7
The Traditional Product
Life Cycle

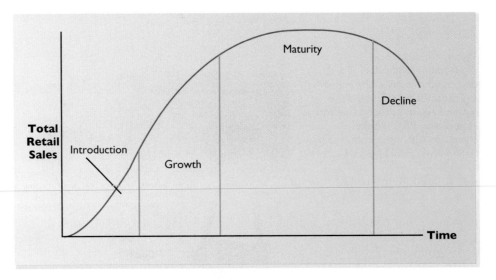

consumers who are more innovative than average. The assortment expands, as do the number of retailers carrying the product. Price discounting is not widely used, but competing retailers offer a range of prices and customer service. Promotion is more persuasive and aimed at acquainting shoppers with availability and services. There are more suppliers.

In maturity, sales reach their maximum, the largest portion of the target market is attracted, and shoppers select from very broad product offerings. All types of retailers (discount to upscale) carry the good or service in some form. Prestige retailers stress brand names and customer service, while others use active price competition. Price is more often cited in ads. Competition is intense.

The decline stage is brought on by a shrinking market (due to product obsolescence, newer substitutes, and boredom) and lower profit margins. The target market may become the lowest-income consumers and laggards. Some retailers cut back on the assortment; others drop the good or service. At retailers still carrying the items, promotion is reduced and geared to price. There are fewer suppliers.

Many retailers pay a lot of attention to new-product additions but not enough to deciding whether to drop existing items. Yet, because of limited resources and shelf space, some items have to be dropped when others are added. Instead of intuitively pruning products, a retailer should use structured guidelines:

- Select items for possible elimination on the basis of declining sales, prices, and profits, as well as the appearance of substitutes.
- Gather and analyze detailed financial and other data about these items.
- Consider nondeletion strategies such as cutting costs, revising promotion efforts, adjusting prices, and cooperating with other retailers.
- After making a deletion decision, do not overlook timing, parts and servicing, inventory, and holdover demand.

Sometimes a seemingly obsolete good or service can be revived. An innovative retailer recognizes the potential in this area and merchandises accordingly. Direct marketers heavily promote "greatest hits" recordings featuring individual music artists and compilations of multiple artists.

Apparel retailers must be familiar with fashion trends. A *vertical trend* occurs when a fashion is first accepted by upscale consumers and undergoes changes in its basic form before it is sold to the general public. A fashion goes through three stages: distinctive—original designs, designer stores, custom-made, worn by

FIGURE 14-8
A Selected Checklist for
Predicting Fashion Adoption

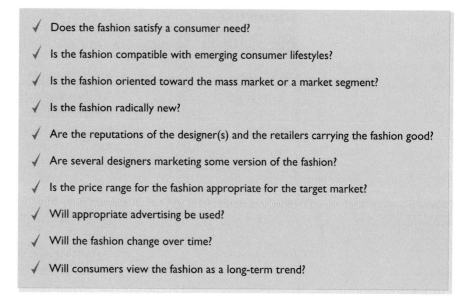

✓ Does the fashion satisfy a consumer need?

✓ Is the fashion compatible with emerging consumer lifestyles?

✓ Is the fashion oriented toward the mass market or a market segment?

✓ Is the fashion radically new?

✓ Are the reputations of the designer(s) and the retailers carrying the fashion good?

✓ Are several designers marketing some version of the fashion?

✓ Is the price range for the fashion appropriate for the target market?

✓ Will appropriate advertising be used?

✓ Will the fashion change over time?

✓ Will consumers view the fashion as a long-term trend?

upscale shoppers; emulation—modification of original designs, finer stores, alterations, worn by middle class; and economic emulation—simple copies, discount stores, mass produced, mass marketed.

With a *horizontal trend*, a new fashion is accepted by a broad spectrum of people upon its introduction while retaining its basic form. Within any social class, there are innovative customers who act as opinion leaders. New fashions must be accepted by these leaders, who then convince other members of the same social class (who are more conservative) to buy the items. Fashion is sold across the class and not from one class to another. Figure 14-8 has a checklist for predicting fashion adoption.

Assortment

An **assortment** is the selection of merchandise a retailer carries. It includes both the breadth of product categories and the variety within each category.

A firm first chooses the quality of merchandise. Should it carry top-line, expensive items and sell to upper-income customers? Or should it carry middle-of-the-line, moderately priced items and cater to middle-income customers? Or should it carry lesser-quality, inexpensive items and attract lower-income customers? Or should it try to draw more than one market segment by offering a variety, such as middle- and top-line items for middle- and upper-income shoppers? The firm must also decide whether to carry promotional products (low-priced closeout items or special buys used to generate store traffic). Several factors must be reviewed in choosing merchandise quality. See Table 14-2.

Dollar General has an overall merchandising strategy that is very consistent with its approach to merchandise quality:

Look at Dollar General's
(www.dollargeneral.com)
targeted merchandising
approach. Click on
"Merchandise."

We are a customer-driven retailer of consumable basics—items that are frequently used and replenished by our customers, such as milk, paper products, food, snacks, health and beauty aids, and cleaning supplies. We offer our customers convenience by carrying the most wanted items every day. We understand our customers require value. You will find value reflected in every item we carry—national brands and private label. These price points are the majority of our items: 4/$1, 3/$1, 2/$1, $1, 2/$3, $2, 2/$5, $3, $4, $5, $6, $7, $8, $10, $12, $15, and $20. Keep in

TABLE 14-2	Factors to Take into Account When Planning Merchandise Quality
Factor	**Relevance for Planning**
Target market(s)	Match merchandise quality to the wishes of the desired target market(s).
Competition	Sell similar quality (follow the competition) or different quality (to appeal to a different target market).
Retailer's image	Relate merchandise quality directly to the perception that customers have of retailer.
Store location	Consider the impact of location on the retailer's image and the number of competitors, which, in turn, relate to quality.
Stock turnover	Be aware that high quality and high prices usually yield a lower turnover than low quality and low prices.
Profitability	Recognize that high-quality goods generally bring greater profit per unit than lesser-quality goods; turnover may cause total profits to be greater for the latter.
Manufacturer versus private brands	Understand that, for many consumers, manufacturer brands connote higher quality than private brands.
Customer services offered	Know that high-quality goods require personal selling, alterations, delivery, and so on. Lesser-quality merchandise may not.
Personnel	Employ skilled, knowledgeable personnel for high-quality merchandise. Self-service may be used with lesser-quality merchandise.
Perceived goods/ service benefits	Analyze consumers. Lesser-quality goods attract customers who desire functional product benefits. High-quality goods attract customers who desire extended product benefits (e.g., status, services).
Constrained decision making	Face reality. a. Franchisees or chain store managers have limited or no control over products. b. Independent retailers that buy from a few large wholesalers are limited to the range of quality offered by those wholesalers.

mind most items sell for $5 and under. We're proud to serve lower- and lower-middle income customers[13]

After deciding on product quality, a retailer determines its width and depth of assortment. **Width of assortment** refers to the number of distinct goods/service categories (product lines) a retailer carries. **Depth of assortment** refers to the variety in any one goods/service category (product line) a retailer carries. As noted in Chapter 5, an assortment can range from wide and deep (department store) to narrow and shallow (box store). Figure 14-9 shows advantages and disadvantages for each basic strategy.

Assortment strategies vary widely. Web retailer Discount Art (**www.discountart. com**) says it is geared toward "the artist who demands good-quality art materials, but also appreciates good prices." KFC's thousands of worldwide outlets emphasize chicken and related quick-service products. They do not sell hamburgers, pizza, or many other popular fast-food items. Macy's department stores feature

Advantages   **Disadvantages**

Wide and Deep (many goods/service categories and a large assortment in each category)

Advantages	Disadvantages
Broad market	High inventory investment
Full selection of items	General image
High level of customer traffic	Many items with low turnover
Customer loyalty	Some obsolete merchandise
One-stop shopping	
No disappointed customers	

Wide and Shallow (many goods/service categories and a limited assortment in each category)

Advantages	Disadvantages
Broad market	Low variety within product lines
High level of customer traffic	Some disappointed customers
Emphasis on convenience customers	Weak image
Less costly than wide and deep	Many items with low turnover
One-stop shopping	Reduced customer loyalty

Narrow and Deep (few goods/service categories and a large assortment in each category)

Advantages	Disadvantages
Specialist image	Too much emphasis on one category
Good customer choice in category(ies)	No one-stop shopping
Specialized personnel	More susceptible to trends/cycles
Customer loyalty	Greater effort needed to enlarge the size of the trading area
No disappointed customers	Little (no) scrambled merchandising
Less costly than wide and deep	

Narrow and Shallow (few goods/service categories and a limited assortment in each category)

Advantages	Disadvantages
Aimed at convenience customers	Little width and depth
Least costly	No one-stop shopping
High turnover of items	Some disappointed customers
	Weak image
	Limited customer loyalty
	Small trading area
	Little (no) scrambled merchandising

FIGURE 14-9
Retail Assortment Strategies

thousands of general merchandise items, and Amazon.com is a Web-based department store with millions of items for sale. Figure 14-10 features Sephora, the cosmetics giant. This is the dilemma that retailers may face in determining how big an assortment to carry:

> A common strategy has been to compete by offering a wide variety of items within a category, designed to appeal to every consumer taste. This can backfire, however, if it causes such information overload that a customer feels overwhelmed or chooses not to make a choice at all. Research shows that dissatisfaction with the shopping process is attributed largely to the retailer, which can impact store traffic and the percentage of customers who purchase. We propose that retailers that offer a large variety in each category ask consumers to explicitly indicate attribute preferences

FIGURE 14-10

Sephora: A Very Deep Assortment of Cosmetics

Sephora offers 365 shades of lipstick, 150 shades of nail polish, and 150 shades of cosmetic pencils.

Photo reprinted by permission of Retail Forward, Inc.

as a way to help them sort through the variety and figure out which option best fits their needs.[14]

Retailers should take several factors into account in planning their assortment: If variety is increased, will overall sales go up? Will overall profits? How much space is required for each product category? How much space is available? Carrying 10 varieties of cat food will not necessarily yield greater sales or profits than stocking 4 varieties. The retailer must look at the investment costs that occur with a large variety. Because selling space is limited, it should be allocated to those goods and services generating the most customer traffic and sales. The inventory turnover rate should also be considered.

A distinction should be made among scrambled merchandising, complementary goods and services, and substitute goods and services. With *scrambled merchandising*, a retailer adds unrelated items to generate more revenues and lift profit

---

RETAILING
Around the World — At Vans, Mass Customization Comes to the Fore with a Global Supply Chain

When Vans Inc. (**www.vans.com**) started to custom-make shoes in the 1960s, its customers would ask the retailer to order sneakers made from the same fabric as their favorite surf shorts or piece of carpet. Now, Web surfers can order mass-customized sneakers in thousands of different ways for delivery in six weeks or less. What makes Vans' approach so special is that mass-customized shoes are manufactured in China and then shipped directly to each customer from the factory.

According to Jody Giles, the chief information officer at Vans, when the company started its mass-customization efforts, accepting an order was the easy part. "The hard part was getting the order information from our Web site through our ERP [Enterprise Resource Planning] system to generate a unique purchase order that would then be sent to China." Vans also had to modify its distribution-resource planning process to handle inventory that is not to be stocked in its distribution center. Direct shipping of individual orders from China also had to be accommodated.

Sources: Beth Bacheldor and Rick Whiting, "Closer Connections," *Informationweek.com* (September 6, 2004), pp. 20–22; and "Customs," **http://shop.vans.com** (March 30, 2006).

margins (such as a florist carrying umbrellas). Handling *complementary goods and services* lets the retailer sell basic items and related offerings (such as stereos and CDs) through cross-merchandising. Although scrambled merchandising and cross-merchandising both increase overall sales, carrying too many *substitute goods and services* (such as competing brands of toothpaste) may shift sales from one brand to another and have little impact on overall retail sales.

These factors are also key as a retailer considers a wider, deeper assortment: (1) Risks, merchandise investments, damages, and obsolescence may rise dramatically. (2) Personnel may be spread too thinly over dissimilar products. (3) Both the positive and negative ramifications of scrambled merchandising may occur. (4) Inventory control may be difficult; overall turnover probably will slow down.

A retailer may not have a choice about stocking a full assortment within a product line if a powerful supplier insists that the retailer carry its entire line or it will not sell at all to that retailer. But large retailers—and smaller ones belonging to cooperative buying groups—are now standing up to suppliers, and many retailers stock their own brands next to manufacturers'.

Brands

As part of its assortment planning, a retailer chooses the proper mix of manufacturer, private, and generic brands—a challenge made more complex with the proliferation of brands. **Manufacturer (national) brands** are produced and controlled by manufacturers. They are usually well known, supported by manufacturer ads, somewhat pre-sold to consumers, require limited retailer investment in marketing, and often represent maximum quality to consumers. Such brands dominate sales in many product categories. Popular manufacturer brands include Barbie, Liz Claiborne, Coke, Gillette, Microsoft, Nike, Revlon, and Sony. The retailers likely to rely most heavily on manufacturer brands are small firms, Web firms, discounters, and others that want the credibility associated with well-known brands or that have low-price strategies (so consumers can compare the prices of different retailers on name-brand items).

Although they face extensive competition from private bands, manufacturer brands remain the dominant type of brand, accounting for more than 80 percent of all retail sales worldwide: "What would a supermarket without national brands look like? I can describe it in one lonely word—empty. It's hard to imagine a store with no Pepsi, Cheerios, Fritos, or Tide. No Colgate, Oreos, Tylenol, or Hellmann's. No Hershey bars, Campbell's soup, Heinz ketchup, Quaker oatmeal, or Tropicana orange juice. Where are this imaginary store's shoppers? At a supermarket where the aisles are lined with national brands."[15]

Private (dealer) brands, also known as **store brands**, contain names designated by wholesalers or retailers, are more profitable to retailers, are better controlled by retailers, are not sold by competing retailers, are less expensive for consumers, and lead to customer loyalty to retailers. With most private labels, retailers must line up suppliers, arrange for distribution and warehousing, sponsor ads, create displays, and absorb losses from unsold items. This is why retailer interest in private brands is growing:

- Private brands account for nearly 20 percent of U.S. and Canadian retail sales. They represent one-half of apparel sales and one-sixth of food store sales. In Northern Europe, the figure exceeds one-quarter. Private brands account for only 2 percent of sales in Eastern Europe and under 1 percent in Brazil and Argentina.[16]

- Private brands are typically priced 20 to 30 percent below manufacturer brands. This benefits consumers, as well as retailers (costs are lower and revenues are shared by fewer parties). Retailer profits are higher from private brands, despite the lower prices.

- Most U.S. shoppers are aware of private brands—80 percent buy them regularly.
- At Gap, Old Navy, The Limited, and McDonald's, private brands represent most or all of company revenues.
- At virtually all large retailers, both private brands and manufacturer brands are strong. Sears' Kenmore appliance line is the market-leading brand—ahead of GE, Maytag, and others. J.C. Penney private brands include Stafford, Hunt Club, St. John's Bay, and Worthington. Amazon.com sells private brands along with millions of manufacturer-branded items. Great Britain's Tesco supermarkets have four different private brands that encompass at least 500 product items *each*. Take our private brand challenge in Table 14-3.

The best-selling appliance brand (**www.kenmore.com**) is not GE or Whirlpool.

In the past, private brands were only discount versions of mid-tier products. They are now seen in a different light: "When a consumer encounters an array of products on a Wegmans grocery store shelf, she does not think, 'Ah, these are private label brands, and these are not.' Rather, she considers that some are worth her time and money, and perhaps her patronage, while others are not, regardless of who owns the brand name, designs its package, or controls its placement in the store. Store brands cry out as loudly—and often, every bit as persuasively—as the name brands that appear alongside them do."[17] See Figure 14-11.

A new form of private branding has also emerged—the *premium private brand*. For example, Premier Selection is a popular brand by Harris Teeter (the supermarket chain). The brand is exclusive to the chain: "Try our Premier Selection Truly Chocolate Chip Cookies, an all butter recipe with 40 percent real chocolate chips, and you'll taste the difference. Or try our Premier Selection 100 percent juice line. In addition to cookies and juice, the Premier Selection line offers carbonated beverages, sparkling waters, cereal, breakfast bars, nuts, frozen fruit bars, frozen garlic breads, and frozen chicken."[18]

Care must be taken in deciding how much to emphasize private brands. As previously noted, many consumers are loyal to manufacturer brands and would

---

| **TABLE 14-3** | **The Berman/Evans Private Brand Test** |

Think you know a lot about private brands? Then take our test. Match the retailers and the brand names. The answers are at the bottom of the table. No peeking. First, take the test.

Please note: Retailers may have more than one brand on the list.

Retailer	Brand
1. A&P	a. America's Choice cookies
2. Bloomingdale's	b. Arizona jeans
3. Costco	c. Alfani men's apparel
4. Kmart	d. Craftsman tools
5. Macy's	e. Master Choice jams and preserves
6. J.C. Penney	f. Joseph & Lyman men's apparel
7. Saks Fifth Avenue	g. Kenmore appliances
8. Sears	h. Kirkland Signature film
9. Target	i. Martha Stewart home furnishings
10. Wal-Mart	j. Michael Graves home products
	k. Real Clothes apparel
	l. Ol' Roy dog food

Answers: 1 – a, e; 2 – f; 3 – h; 4 – i; 5 – c; 6 – b; 7 – k; 8 – d, g; 9 – j; 10 – l

FIGURE 14-11
Wal-Mart's New Approach
to Private Brands

Wal-Mart is well known for its
discount prices and value-
oriented private brands.
Through its George line, Wal-
Mart is now aggressively trying
to create more of a "designer"
look for its apparel to better
compete with Target's designer
brands.

Photo reprinted by permission of
Susan Berry, Retail Image
Consulting, Inc.

shop elsewhere if those brands are not stocked or their variety is pruned. See
Figure 14-12.

Generic brands feature products' generic names as brands (such as canned
peas); they are no-frills goods stocked by some retailers. They are a form of private
brand. These items usually receive secondary shelf locations, have little or no promotion support, may be of lesser quality, are stocked in limited assortments, and
have plain packages. Retailers control generics and price them well below other
brands. In supermarkets, generics account for less than 1 percent of sales. In the
prescription drug industry, where the quality of manufacturer brands and generics is similar, generics provide one-third of unit sales.

The competition between manufacturers and retailers for shelf space and
profits has led to a **battle of the brands**, whereby manufacturer, private, and
generic brands fight each other for more space and control. Nowhere is this battle
clearer than at large retail chains: "Walk down the aisle of a Staples store, and
you'll see a lot of big-name brands—Avery, Duracell, Hewlett-Packard, 3M, and
more. But you'll also find more than a thousand products sold under the retailer's
own brand: Staples' yellow self-stick notes, Staples' stainless-steel shears, even
Staples' ink cartridges for laser printers. This year, its brand is expected to exceed
17 percent of total sales."[19]

Timing

For new products, the retailer must decide when they are first purchased, displayed, and sold. For established products, the firm must plan the merchandise
flow during the year. The retailer should take into account its forecasts and other
factors: peak seasons, order and delivery time, routine versus special orders, stock
turnover, discounts, and the efficiency of inventory procedures.

FIGURE 14-12
Daffy's Distinctive Branding Strategy

This is an off-price chain that caters to brand-conscious shoppers who look for deals. As its Web site (**www. daffys. com**) notes, "Daffy's provides new meaning to the word bargain. For everyone. We offer a wide selection of apparel and accessories for men, women, and children. You don't have to hunt for a good deal here. We already pay people to do that for you. Our buyers load the racks every week with new merchandise from all over the world. From housewares to sportswear and every other type of 'wear,' you'll find the finest designer collections at savings up to 80 percent off the regular retail price. Look like a million without having to spend one."

Photo reprinted by permission of Retail Forward, Inc.

Some goods and services have peak seasons. These items (such as winter coats) require large inventories in peak times and less stock during off-seasons. Because some people like to shop during off-seasons, the retailer should not eliminate the items.

With regard to order and delivery time, how long does it take the retailer to process an order request? After the order is sent to the supplier, how long does it take to receive merchandise? By adding these two periods together, the retailer can get a good idea of the lead time to restock shelves. If it takes a retailer 7 days to process an order and the supplier another 14 days to deliver goods, the retailer should begin a new order at least 21 days before the old inventory runs out.

Routine orders involve restocking staples and other regularly sold items. Deliveries are received weekly, monthly, and so on. Planning and problems are minimized. Special orders involve merchandise not sold regularly, such as custom furniture. They need more planning and cooperation between retailer and supplier. Specific delivery dates are usually arranged.

Stock turnover (how quickly merchandise sells) greatly influences how often items must be ordered. Convenience items such as milk and bread (which are also highly perishable) have a high turnover rate and are restocked quite often. Shopping items such as refrigerators and color TVs have a lower turnover rate and are restocked less often.

In deciding when and how often to buy merchandise, the availability of quantity discounts should be considered. Large purchases may result in lower per-unit costs. Efficient inventory procedures, such as electronic data interchange and quick response planning procedures, also decrease costs and order times while raising merchandise productivity.

Allocation

The last part of merchandise planning is the allocation of products. A single-unit retailer chooses how much merchandise to place on the sales floor, how much to place in a stockroom, and whether to use a warehouse. A chain also apportions products among stores. Allocation is covered further in Chapter 15.

Some retailers rely on warehouses as distribution centers. Products are shipped from suppliers to these warehouses and then assigned and shipped to individual stores. Other retailers, including many supermarket chains, do not rely as much on warehouses. They have at least some goods shipped directly from suppliers to individual stores.

It is vital for chains, whether engaged in centralized or decentralized merchandising, to have a clear store-by-store allocation plan. Even if merchandise lines are standardized across the chain, store-by-store assortments must reflect the variations in the size and diversity of the customer base, in store size and location, in the climate, and in other factors.

CATEGORY MANAGEMENT

As noted in Chapter 2, **category management** is a merchandising technique that some firms—including several supermarkets, drugstores, hardware stores, and general merchandise retailers—use to improve productivity. It is a way to manage a retail business that focuses on the performance of product category results rather than individual brands. It arranges product groupings into strategic business units to better meet consumer needs and to achieve sales and profit goals. Retail managers make merchandising decisions that maximize the total return on the assets assigned to them.

Consider the category management goals of the Borders bookstore chain, which believes strongly in its "category marketing" team:

> Our mission is to be the best-loved provider of books, music, movies, and other educational and informational products and services. This team plays the chief role in implementing and refining our category marketing strategies. The category team is responsible for the selection, allocation, inventory management, and marketing of all products sold in our stores. The categories include books, music, movies, gifts, stationery, calendars, and periodicals. The types of positions available in category marketing include buying, allocation, and marketing.[20]

According to the A.C. Nielsen research company, good category management involves these steps:

1. The readiness of all participating firms to engage in the intricate process of category management.
2. The creation of a consumer-driven category definition.
3. A clearly stated role for each category. Some categories are more growth-oriented than others.
4. Establishment of a regular, in-depth category assessment process.
5. Up-to-data category objectives that are reviewed frequently.
6. Focused category strategies.
7. Tactics consistent with the strategies for each category.
8. Implementation of decisions.
9. Monitoring, reviewing, and revising category strategies.[21]

A fundamental premise is that a retailer must empower specific personnel to be responsible for the financial performance of each product category. As with micromerchandising, category management means adapting merchandise for each store or region to best satisfy customers. In deciding on the space per product category, there are several crucial measures of performance. Comparisons can be made by studying company data from period to period and by looking at categorical statistics in trade magazines:

- Sales per linear foot of shelf space—annual sales divided by the total linear footage devoted to the product category.
- Gross profit per linear foot of shelf space—annual gross profit divided by the total linear footage devoted to the product category.
- Return on inventory investment—annual gross profit divided by average inventory at cost.
- Inventory turnover—the number of times during a given period, usually one year, that the average inventory on hand is sold.
- Days' supply—the number of days of supply of an item on the shelf.
- Direct product profitability (DPP)—an item's gross profit less its direct retailing costs (warehouse and store support, occupancy, inventory, and direct labor costs, but not general overhead).

Some collaborative aspects of category management are working well, while other aspects are not working out as planned:[22]

What Manufacturers Feel About Retailers

SUCCESSFUL APPLICATIONS OF CATEGORY MANAGEMENT

- Retailers act as equal partners.
- Retailers get input from manufacturers so they put the best possible plan together.
- Retailers are open minded and willing to change.
- Retailers that give manufacturers proper lead time—and timely goals and suggestions—receive the highest-quality work.

UNSUCCESSFUL APPLICATIONS OF CATEGORY MANAGEMENT

- Different goals among the retailers' senior managers, category managers, and operations managers impede the process.
- Retailers have a "template fixation." Yet, a template alone cannot explain why shoppers choose a given product or category.
- Retailers expect manufacturers to do more than their share or to pay more than their share for gathering and analyzing data.

What Retailers Feel About Manufacturers

SUCCESSFUL APPLICATIONS OF CATEGORY MANAGEMENT

- Manufacturers gather data on consumer purchasing behavior and make recommendations to retailers.
- Manufacturers with clearly defined and supported plans are viewed favorably.
- Manufacturers help the retailers understand how to get more out of shopper traffic and build shopper loyalty, incremental volume, and return on merchandising assets.

UNSUCCESSFUL APPLICATIONS OF CATEGORY MANAGEMENT

- Manufacturers make recommendations that consistently favor their brands.
- Manufacturers just drop a completed template off with their retailers.
- Manufacturers do not maintain confidentiality for shared data or recommendations.

FIGURE 14-13
Applying Category
Management to Heavy-Duty
Liquid Detergent

Source: Walter H. Heller,
"Profitability; Where It's Really At,"
(December 1992), p. 27. Copyright
Progressive Grocer. Reprinted by
permission.

Note: The criteria are based on the
average profit and movement of the
items in the product category of
heavy-duty liquid detergent. The
averages change for each product
category.

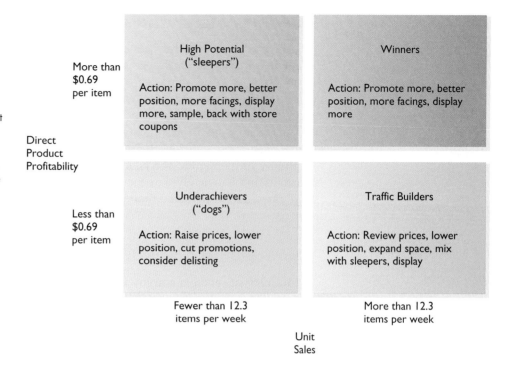

Figure 14-13 indicates how a retailer could use category management to better merchandise liquid detergent. One axis relates to direct product profitability. For the supermarket in this example, $0.69 per item is the average DPP for all liquid detergents. Those with higher amounts would be placed in the top half of the grid and those with lower amounts in the bottom half. The other axis classifies the detergents in terms of unit sales (an indicator of inventory turnover), with 12.3 items per week being the dividing line between slow- and fast-moving detergents. All detergents could be placed into one of four categories: high potential ("sleepers")— products with high profitability but low sales; winners—products with high profitability and high sales; underachievers ("dogs")—products with low profitability and low sales; and traffic builders—products with low profitability and high sales. Specific strategies are recommended in the figure.

MERCHANDISING SOFTWARE

Forseon's RMSA division has forecasting solutions for retailers in several different sectors (**www.forseon.com/ Pages/prod_body.htm**).

One of the most significant advances in merchandise planning is the widespread availability of computer software, which gives retailers an excellent support mechanism to systematically prepare forecasts, try out various assortment scenarios, coordinate the data for category management, and so forth. In an era when many retailers carry thousands of items, merchandising software is a part of everyday business life.

Some merchandising software is provided by suppliers and trade associations at no charge—as part of the value delivery chain and relationship retailing. Other software is sold by marketing firms, often for $1,500 or less (although some software sells for $25,000 or more). Let us now discuss the far-reaching nature of merchandising software. The links to several retail merchandising software products, including category management, may be found at our Web site (**www.prenhall. com/bermanevans**).

General Merchandise Planning Software

Some retailers prefer functionally driven software, while others use integrated software packages. Pacific Sunwear, a 900-store national chain, is an example of the latter. Its software package from Island Pacific Systems (**www.islandpacific. com**) encompasses merchandise planning and forecasting, purchase order management, allocation, inventory management, and price management. As Pacific Sun's vice-president of information systems says, "Retailers need intelligence to effectively run and grow their businesses. We recognized this early on when we initially implemented the Island Pacific merchandising solution. The software from Island Pacific gives us the information we need to manage the products that we carry, and understand their performance."[23]

Forecasting Software

A number of retailers employ their data warehouses to make merchandise forecasts. JDA Software (**www.jdasoftware.com**) is one of the firms that produces software that lets them do so. Ace Hardware is a major retail client. JDA's Seasonal Profiling by Intellect software helps Ace to ensure that its stores are appropriately stocked to handle seasonality issues, last-minute impulse purchases, and huge spikes in demand for the most popular items. Ace's goal "in applying this advanced data mining application is to uncover hidden seasonal demand for its 65,000 products, spanning 22 departments."[24]

Firms such as Khimetrics offer sophisticated software for retail forecasting purposes. Its software enables client retailers to prepare store-level demand forecasts by "modeling all the factors that affect unit movement including seasonality, price, promotion, cannibalization, affinity, product life cycle, and vendor deal impact."[25]

Innovativeness Software

Because today's software provides detailed data rapidly, it allows retailers to monitor and more quickly react to trends. Processes that once took months now

---

Technology in RETAILING — Enhanced Merchandise Planning at Nordstrom and J.C. Penney

Nordstrom's (**www.nordstrom.com**) executive vice-president and chief financial officer reports that Nordstrom's new perpetual inventory management system has had a major impact on the chain's gross margin, as well as inventory levels. Among the benefits of the system are more timely markdowns, the early identification of fast-selling items, and the reduction of less productive items. The perpetual inventory management system has enabled Nordstrom to reduce its inventory in every quarter since it was fully operational. And in some quarters, the reduction in inventory has been as much as 10 percent.

At J.C. Penney (**www.jcpenney.com**), merchandise planning was decentralized prior to 2000. As J.C. Penney's executive vice-president of planning and allocation noted, "The stores all chose their own assortments, and right around 2000 was when J.C. Penney realized that was going to have to change if we were to remain competitive. It became an issue of survival." Using software solutions from ProfitLogic (**www.profitlogic.com**), J.C. Penney centralized merchandise and assortment planning, purchase-order management, markdown planning, and supply chain management. The increased centralization has resulted in increased inventory turnover, fewer markdowns, and better in-stock performance.

Source: Dan Scheraga, "Sounds Like a Plan," *Chain Store Age* (March 2005), pp. 65–66.

are done in weeks or days. Instead of missing a selling season, retailers are prepared for the latest craze.

Target Corporation, among others, uses Web-based color control software from Datacolor International: "Colorite combines precise on-screen color with image and texture to produce life-like product simulations as a substitute for physical samples. You'll streamline workflow and shorten product development, while reducing the time, cost, and quality compromises of physical sampling. With accurate color reproduction, you can make color decisions by viewing digital samples on a monitor and even simulate the color under various lighting conditions without waiting for physical samples to arrive."[26]

Assortment Software

Learn more about SAS retail software (www.sas.com/industry/retail).

Many retailers employ merchandising software to better plan assortments. One application is Marketmax Assortment Planning software from SAS. A leading client is Bakers Footwear, with more than 200 stores. The chain makes 16,000 new style and color choices annually: "Bakers keeps a year's worth of store data on merchandise styles and colors. Using Marketmax Assortment Planning software, store planners analyze the previous year's data, identify the chain's hits and misses, and factor in fashion shifts to create a detailed assortment plan, by store cluster and 180 days out. Planners fine-tune the assortment plan until it is time for the merchandise to be received."[27]

Allocation Software

Chains of all sizes and types want to improve how they allocate merchandise to stores. There are several software programs to let them do so. Consider the Assortment Execution software from ProfitLogic. Most retail planners would like to better tailor their merchandise to local needs. Yet, they usually do not have the ability to "take local market needs into consideration for every item. Assortment Execution helps planners and allocators effectively execute the assortment to the store by providing decision support that maintains merchandising objectives, like color stories and assortment mix, within the constraints of the financial plan."[28]

Category Management Software

Spaceman Merchandiser (www.acnielsenspaceman.com/spcmnmer.asp) is Nielsen's entry-level software.

A wide range of software programs is available to help manufacturers and retailers deal with category management's complexities. A few retailers have even developed their own software. Programs typically base space allocation on sales, inventory turnover, and profits at individual stores. Because data are store specific, space allocations reflect actual sales. These are examples of category management software:

- A.C. Nielsen's programs include Category Business Planner (**www.acnielsen.com/products/reports/cbp_cm**) and Spaceman (**www.acnielsenspaceman.com**).
- MEMRB Retail Tracking Services offers several versions of the popular Apollo merchandising software (**www.memrb.com/products/technology/overview**).
- Logical Planning Systems (**www.shelflogic.com**) markets Shelf Logic Pro category management software for only $750 and Shelf Logic Quik plan for $479. See Figure 14-14.

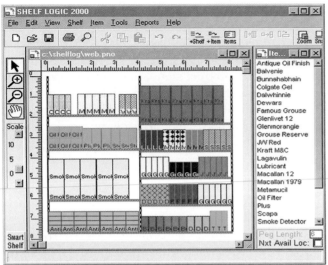
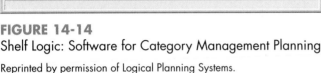
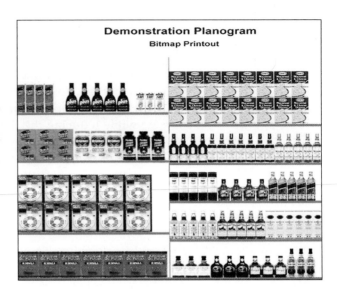

FIGURE 14-14
Shelf Logic: Software for Category Management Planning

Reprinted by permission of Logical Planning Systems.

Summary

1. *To demonstrate the importance of a sound merchandising philosophy.* Developing and implementing a merchandise plan is a key element in a successful retail strategy. Merchandising consists of the activities involved in a retailer's buying goods and services and making them available for sale. A merchandising philosophy sets the guiding principles for all merchandise decisions and must reflect the desires of the target market, the retailer's institutional type, its positioning, its defined value chain, supplier capabilities, costs, competitors, product trends, and other factors.

2. *To study various buying organization formats and the processes they use.* The buying organization and its processes must be defined in terms of its formality, degree of centralization, organizational breadth, personnel resources, functions performed, and staffing.

   With a formal buying organization, merchandising is a distinct task in a separate department. In an informal buying organization, the same personnel handle both merchandising and other retail tasks. Multi-unit retailers must choose whether to have a centralized or a decentralized buying organization. In a centralized organization, all purchases emanate from one office. In a decentralized organization, decisions are made locally or regionally. For a general organization, one person or a few people buy all merchandise. For a specialized organization, each buyer is responsible for a product category.

   An inside buying organization is staffed by a retailer's personnel and decisions are made by its permanent employees. An outside buying organization involves a company or personnel external to the retailer. Most retailers use either an inside or an outside buying organization; some employ a combination. A resident buying office, which can be an inside or outside organization, is used when a retailer wants to keep in close touch with key markets and cannot do so through headquarters buying staff. Independents and small chains often use cooperative buying to compete with large chains.

   If a retailer has a "merchandising" view, merchandise personnel oversee all buying and selling functions. If it has a "buying" view, merchandise personnel oversee buying, advertising, and pricing, while store personnel oversee assortments, displays, personnel deployment, and sales presentations.

   A buyer is responsible for selecting merchandise and setting a strategy to market that merchandise. He or she devises and controls sales and profit projections for a product category; plans assortments, styling, sizes, and quantities; negotiates with and evaluates vendors; and oversees store displays. A sales manager supervises the on-floor selling and operational activities for a specific retail department. He or she must be a good organizer, administrator, and motivator.

3. *To outline the considerations in devising merchandise plans: forecasts, innovativeness, assortment, brands,*

timing, and allocation. Forecasts are projections of expected retail sales and form the foundation of merchandise plans. Staple merchandise consists of the regular products a retailer carries. A basic stock list specifies the inventory level, color, brand, and so on for every staple item carried. Assortment merchandise consists of products for which there must be a variety so customers have a proper selection. A model stock plan projects levels of specific assortment merchandise. Fashion merchandise has cyclical sales due to changing tastes and lifestyles. Seasonal merchandise sells well over nonconsecutive periods. With fad merchandise, sales are high for a short time. When forecasting for best-sellers, many retailers use a never-out list.

A retailer's innovativeness is related to the target market(s), product growth potential, fashion trends, the retailer's image, competition, customer segments, responsiveness to consumers, investment costs, profitability, risk, constrained decision making, and declining goods and services. Three issues are of particular interest: How fast will a new good or service generate sales? What are the most sales to be achieved in a season or a year? Over what period will a good or service continue to sell? A useful tool is the product life cycle.

An assortment is the merchandise selection carried. The retailer first chooses the quality of merchandise. The assortment is then determined. Width of assortment refers to the number of distinct product categories carried. Depth of assortment refers to the variety in any category. As part of assortment planning, a retailer chooses its mix of brands. Manufacturer brands are produced and controlled by manufacturers. Private brands contain names designated by wholesalers or retailers. Generic brands feature generic names as brands and are a form of private brand. The competition between manufacturers and retailers is called the battle of the brands.

For new goods and services, it must be decided when they are first to be displayed and sold. For established goods and services, the firm must plan the merchandise flow during the year. In deciding when and how often to buy merchandise, quantity discounts should be considered. A single-unit retailer chooses how much merchandise to allocate to the sales floor and how much to the stockroom and whether to use a warehouse. A chain also allocates items among stores.

4. *To discuss category management and merchandising software.* Category management is a technique for managing a retail business that focuses on product category results rather than the performance of individual brands. It arranges product groups into strategic business units to better address consumer needs and meet financial goals. Category management helps retail personnel make the merchandising decisions that maximize the total return on the assets. There is now plentiful PC- and Web-based merchandising software available for retailers, in just about every aspect of merchandise planning.

Key Terms

merchandising (p. 408)
merchandising philosophy (p. 408)
micromerchandising (p. 410)
cross-merchandising (p. 410)
resident buying office (p. 414)
cooperative buying (p. 414)
buyer (p. 415)
sales manager (p. 415)
forecasts (p. 416)

staple merchandise (p. 416)
basic stock list (p. 417)
assortment merchandise (p. 417)
model stock plan (p. 417)
fashion merchandise (p. 417)
seasonal merchandise (p. 417)
fad merchandise (p. 417)
never-out list (p. 417)
product life cycle (p. 419)

assortment (p. 421)
width of assortment (p. 422)
depth of assortment (p. 422)
manufacturer (national) brands (p. 425)
private (dealer, store) brands (p. 425)
generic brands (p. 427)
battle of the brands (p. 428)
category management (p. 429)

Questions for Discussion

1. Describe and evaluate the merchandising philosophy of your favorite department store.

2. What is the distinction between *merchandising functions* and the *buying function*?

3. Is micromerchandising a good approach? Why or why not?

4. What are the advantages and disadvantages of a decentralized buying organization?

5. Interview a local store owner and determine how he or she makes merchandise decisions. Evaluate that approach.

6. How could a gift store use a basic stock list, a model stock plan, and a never-out list?

7. Under what circumstances could a retailer carry a wide range of merchandise quality without hurting its image? When should the quality of merchandise carried be quite narrow?

8. How should a consumer electronics retailer use the product life cycle concept?

9. What are the trade-offs in a retailer's deciding how much to emphasize private brands rather than manufacturer brands?

10. Present a checklist of five factors for a chain retailer to review in determining how to allocate merchandise among its stores.

11. What is the basic premise of category management? Why do you think that supermarkets have been at the forefront of the movement to use category management?

12. What do you think are the risks of placing too much reliance on merchandising software? Do the risks outweigh the benefits? Explain your answer.

Web-Based Exercise

Visit this section of the Planning Factory's Web site (**www.planfact.co.uk/mp_resources.htm**). Look at several of the merchandising resources listed there. Discuss what you learn from these resources.

Note: Stop by our Web site (**www.prenhall.com/ bermanevans**) to experience a number of highly

interactive, appealing Web exercises based on actual company demonstrations and sample materials related to retailing.

Chapter Endnotes

1. Various company sources.

2. Stanley Marcus, "Reflections on Retailing," *Retailing Issues Letter* (July 2000), p. 2.

3. Barbara E. Kahn, "Introduction to the Special Issue: Assortment Planning," *Journal of Retailing*, Vol. 75 (Fall 1999), p. 289.

4. *Costco 2005 Annual Report*.

5. "Case Study: Chico's Retail Clothing," **http:// www-1.ibm.com/servers/eserver/iseries/casest/ islandp.htm** (March 5, 2006).

6. Thyra Porter, "Super Marketing in Maine, Five Stores Across a Variety of Channels Break Out the Techniques to Attract Shoppers," *HFN* (May 9, 2005), p. 48.

7. "The Future of Fast Fashion," *Economist* (June 18, 2005), p. 57.

8. *Ross Stores 2004 Annual Report*.

9. "FPN History—Who We Are," **www.fpn.org/who. htm** (March 9, 2006).

10. "Guitar Center Appoints David Angress to EVP," *Mix Online* (June 27, 2005).

11. Dan Scheraga, "Balancing Act at Ikea," *Chain Store Age* (June 2005), p. 46.

12. "An Icon Continues to Improve Its Image," *Drugstore News* (May 2, 2005), p. 144.

13. "Our Products," **www.dollargeneral.com/merchan dise/products.aspx** (February 28, 2006).

14. Cynthia Huffman and Barbara E. Kahn, "Variety for Sale: Mass Customization or Mass Confusion?" *Journal of Retailing*, Vol. 74 (Fall 1998), pp. 491–492.

15. Gary Rodkin, "A Balancing Act," *Progressive Grocer* (June 1999), p. 29.

16. Mary Brett Whitehead, "The Surging Growth of Private Brands," *2005 Strategic Outlook Conference* (Columbus, OH: Retail Forward); and "Private Label Continues to Gain Share, A.C. Nielsen Study Shows," **www.acnielsen.com** (August 27, 2002).

17. William J. McEwen, "Private Labels Are Brands, Too," **http://gmj.gallup.com** (June 9, 2005).

18. "Premier Selection," **www.harristeeter.com/default. aspx?pageId=108** (March 1, 2006).

19. Laurie Sullivan, "Retailers Ply Their Own Brands," *Information Week* (April 18, 2005), pp. 61–65.

20. "Corporate Careers," **www.bordersgroupinc.com/ careers/corporate.htm#mm** (March 1, 2006).

21. "The Category Management Process," **www. acnielsen. com/services/category/ie.htm** (March 4, 2006).

22. Information Resources, Inc., "Manufacturer and Retailer Report Cards," *NeoBrief* (Issue 1, 1999), pp. 3–6.

23. "Pacific Sunwear: Customer Success Story," **www. islandpacific.com/images/PacSun.pdf** (February 23, 2006).

24. "Ace Hardware Is the Place with the Help of Seasonal Profiling by Intellect," **www.jda.com/ file_ bin/casestudies/AceHardware.pdf** (February 23, 2006).

25. "Demand Forecasting," **www.khimetrics.com/ retail/retail_forecast.html** (February 23, 2006).

26. "Colorite," **www.datacolor.com/uploads/colorite_ broch_eng.pdf** (February 23, 2006).

27. "Bakers Footwear Keeps a Step Ahead," **www.sas. com/news/feature/20oct04/bakers.html** (February 23, 2006).

28. ProfitLogic Fills Gap in Retail Planning Software with Unique Next-Generation Merchandise Optimization Solution for Assortment Execution," **www.profit logic.com/1_04_05_AssortmentExecution.htm** (January 4, 2005).

In 1961, Dr. Stanley Pearle had the idea to create a store that combined a complete eye exam, an extensive selection of frames and corrective lenses, and convenient store hours. Pearle could not possibly have foreseen that his first one-stop total eyecare center located in Savannah, Georgia, would grow into Pearle Vision Center.

Reprinted by permission.

Cole National Corporation (**www.colenational.com**) acquired Pearle Vision Center in 1996 from Grand Metropolitan. In 2004, Milan-based Luxottica Group SpA (the owner of LensCrafters Inc. and the Sunglass Hut International chains, as well as Ray-Ban, Revo, and other premium brands) purchased Cole National in a $441 million transaction. At the time of the merger, Cole National with its Pearle Vision franchises had close to 3,000 locations in the United States, Canada, Puerto Rico, and the Virgin Islands. This deal joined the two largest eyeglass retailing companies in America.

In addition to Pearle Vision, Luxottica Group SpA (the parent company) sells eyewear through its Sears Optical, BJ's Optical, Target Optical, and Cole Managed Vision (which markets eyecare directly to major employers) units. The large number of different types of sites gives Luxottica the ability to market its products to different segments, as well as clout in negotiating with its key vendors. Luxottica recently signed licensing agreements with Prada, Versace, Donna Karan, and Dolce & Gabbana.

Despite the large size of Luxottica and the power of mass retailers that sell optical products, the U.S. eyeglass/sunglass market is still highly fragmented, with independent retailers accounting for about 45 percent of sales.[1]

chapter objectives

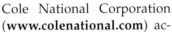

1. To describe the steps in the implementation of merchandise plans: gathering information, selecting and interacting with merchandise sources, evaluation, negotiation, concluding purchases, receiving and stocking merchandise, reordering, and re-evaluation
2. To examine the prominent roles of logistics and inventory management in the implementation of merchandise plans

OVERVIEW

Enter the Seven-Eleven Japan site (www.sej.co.jp/english/index.html) and click on "News Release" to find out what this creative retailer is doing.

This chapter builds on Chapter 14 and covers the implementation of merchandise plans, including logistics and inventory management. Sometimes it is simple to enact merchandise plans. Other times, it requires hard work and creativity. Mary Kay's supply chain management illustrates the latter situation:

> Mary Kay is quite gifted at making informed supply chain decisions, thanks to new technologies and process improvements. By understanding the logistical challenges of manufacturers, wholesale distributors, and retailers, Mary Kay has a unique perspective that spans the product life cycle from raw materials to consumer purchase. At the back end of the supply chain, raw goods are received at the Mary Kay manufacturing facility in Dallas, where they are developed into the company's signature cosmetics. Then products are shipped to the nearby inventory center. From the warehouse, Mary Kay products are sent to five distribution centers located throughout the United States. From there, products are shipped to more than 1 million Mary Kay beauty consultants, who maintain personal inventories to fill individual consumer orders. Approximately 400 SKUs comprise Mary Kay's product line, and the company processes approximately 24,000 orders per day.[2]

IMPLEMENTING MERCHANDISE PLANS

The implementation of merchandise plans comprises the eight sequential steps shown in Figure 15-1 and discussed next.

Gathering Information

See how mySimon (www.mysimon.com) can help retailers track competitors.

After overall merchandising plans are set, more information about target market needs and prospective suppliers is required before buying or rebuying merchandise. In gathering data *about the marketplace*, a retailer has several possible sources. The most valuable is the consumer. By regularly researching target market demographics, lifestyles, and potential shopping plans, a retailer can learn about consumer demand directly. Loyalty programs are especially useful in tracking consumer purchases and interests.

Other information sources can be used when direct consumer data are insufficient. Suppliers (manufacturers and wholesalers) usually do their own sales forecasts and marketing research (such as test marketing). They also know how much

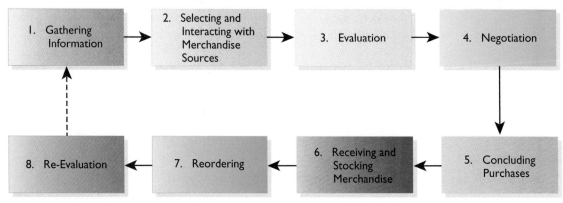

FIGURE 15-1
The Process for Implementing Merchandise Plans

outside promotional support a retailer will get. In closing a deal with the retailer, a supplier may present charts and graphs, showing forecasts and promotional support. Yet, the retailer should remember that it is the party with direct access to the target market and its needs.

Retail sales and display personnel interact with consumers and can pass their observations along to management. A **want book (want slip)** system is a formal way to record consumer requests for unstocked or out-of-stock merchandise. It is very helpful to a retailer's buyers. Outside of customers, salespeople may provide the most useful information for merchandising decisions.

Competitors represent another information source. A conservative retailer may not stock an item until competitors do and employ comparison shoppers to study the offerings and prices of competitors. The most sophisticated comparison shopping involves the use of Web-based shopping bots such as mySimon.com, whereby competitors' offerings and prices are tracked electronically. Buy.com, for one, constantly checks its prices to make sure that it is not undersold. In addition, trade publications report on trends in each aspect of retailing and provide another way of gathering data from competitors. See Figure 15-2 for an example of a competition shopping report.

In addition, government sources indicate unemployment, inflation, and product safety data; independent news sources conduct their own consumer polls and do investigative reporting; and commercial data can be purchased.

To learn about the attributes of *specific suppliers* and their merchandise, retailers can

- Talk to suppliers, get specification sheets, read trade publications, and seek references.

FIGURE 15-2
A Competition Shopping Report

COMPETITION SHOPPING REPORT

Store #_____ Date__________

Dept. #_____ Qualified Competition Shopped:

1.__________
2.__________

Our Style No.	Mfr. Model or Style	Description	Our Price	1st Compet. Price	2nd Compet. Price	Store's Recom. Price	Buyer's Recom. Price

Item Seen at Our Competitor's Store Which We Should Carry:					
Manufacturer	Mfr. Model or Style	Description	Reg. or List Price	Sale Price	Buyer's Comments

Signature of Shopper *Store Manager*

Learn why High Point (www.ihfc.com) is a world-class market.

- Attend trade shows with numerous exhibitors (suppliers). There are hundreds of trade shows yearly in New York. In Paris, the semi-annual Prêt À Porter show attracts 1,100 exhibitors and more than 40,000 attendees. The National Hardware Show in Las Vegas has 3,200 exhibitors and 35,000 attendees each year. The High Point Furniture Market in North Carolina has semi-annual shows that attract more than 3,000 manufacturers and 80,000 attendees—from all 50 states and 110 countries.

California Market Center (www.californiamarket center.com) offers a lot of online information for retailers. Click on "exhibitor/tenant."

- Visit year-round merchandise marts such as AmericasMart in Atlanta (www. americasmart.com), Merchandise Mart in Chicago (www.merchandisemart. com/mmart), California Market Center in Los Angeles (www.california marketcenter.com), and Dallas Market Center (www.dallasmarketcenter.com). These marts have daily hours for permanent vendor showrooms and large areas for trade shows.

- Search the Web. One newer application is Super Expo (www.superexpo.com): "Vendors exhibit to buyers and the press in their online showrooms. This allows buyers to preview the wholesaler's product line directly from their desktops. It also gives exhibitors a direct exposure of their products to the general public around the world. The shows let the public 'pre-shop' the items directly from the manufacturer and get detailed information such as new products, where sold, press releases, etc."

Whatever the information acquired, a retailer should feel comfortable that it is sufficient for making good decisions. For routine decisions (staple products), limited information may be adequate. On the other hand, new fashions' sales fluctuate widely and require extensive data for forecasts.

At our Web site (www.prenhall.com/bermanevans), we have more than a dozen links to leading trade shows and merchandise marts.

Selecting and Interacting with Merchandise Sources

The next step is to select sources of merchandise and to interact with them. Three major options exist:

- *Company-owned*—A large retailer owns a manufacturing and/or wholesaling facility. A company-owned supplier handles all or part of the merchandise the retailer requests.
- *Outside, regularly used supplier*—This supplier is not owned by the retailer but used regularly. A retailer knows the quality of merchandise and the reliability of the supplier from its experience.
- *Outside, new supplier*—This supplier is not owned by the retailer, which has not bought from it before. The retailer may be unfamiliar with merchandise quality and supplier reliability.

A retailer can rely on one kind of supplier or utilize a combination (the biggest retailers often use all three formats). The types of outside suppliers (regularly used and new) are described in Figure 15-3. In choosing vendors, the criteria listed in the Figure 15-4 checklist should be considered.

Big Lots places plenty of emphasis on supplier relations (www.biglots.com/aboutus/vendors.asp).

Big Lots, which buys merchandise to stock its national chain of closeout stores, is a good example of how complicated choosing suppliers can be:

An integral part of our business is buying quality, branded merchandise directly from manufacturers and other vendors at prices substantially

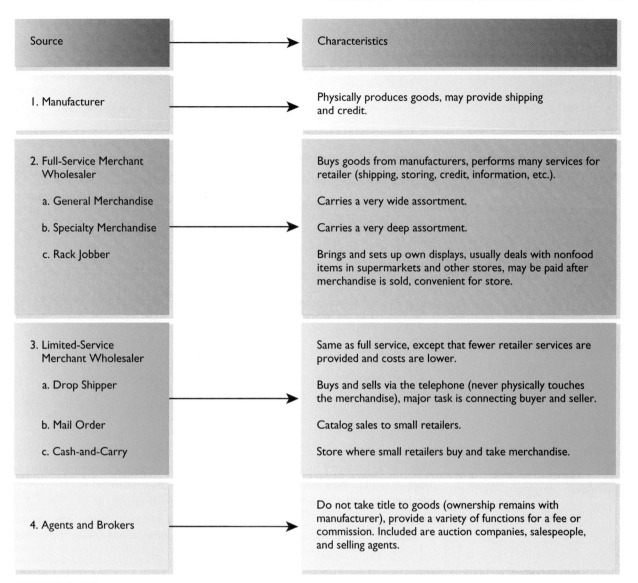

FIGURE 15-3
Outside Sources of Supply

below those paid by traditional retailers. We are able to buy significant quantities of a manufacturer's closeout merchandise in specific product categories and to control distribution in accordance with vendor instructions. In 2004, a wholly owned subsidiary was established to source merchandise outside of our customary channels. These expanded sourcing channels are expected to include bankruptcies, liquidations, and insurance claims. We supplement traditional brand-name closeout purchases with various direct import and domestically sourced merchandise in categories such as furniture, home décor, and seasonal. We buy about 30 percent of products directly from overseas suppliers. As a result, a significant portion of our merchandise supply is subject to certain risks including increased import duties and transportation delays.[3]

Retailers and suppliers often interact well together, as highlighted in Figure 15-5. Other times, there are conflicts. As noted earlier, relationship building can be invaluable. Yet, there remain sore points between retailers and suppliers. On the one hand, many retailers have beefed up their use of private brands because they

FIGURE 15-4
A Checklist of Points to Review in Choosing Vendors

✓ Reliability—Will a supplier consistently fulfill all written promises?

✓ Price–quality—Who provides the best merchandise at the lowest price?

✓ Order-processing time—How fast will deliveries be made?

✓ Exclusive rights—Will a supplier give exclusive selling rights or customize products?

✓ Functions provided—Will a supplier undertake shipping, storing, and other functions, if needed?

✓ Information—Will a supplier pass along important data?

✓ Ethics—Will a supplier fulfill all verbal promises and not engage in unfair business or labor practices?

✓ Guarantee—Does a supplier stand behind its offerings?

✓ Credit—Can credit purchases be made from a supplier? On what terms?

✓ Long-term relationships—Will a supplier be available over an extended period?

✓ Reorders—Can a supplier promptly fill reorders?

✓ Markup—Will markup (price margins) be adequate?

✓ Innovativeness—Is a supplier's line innovative or conservative?

✓ Local advertising—Does a supplier advertise in local media?

✓ Investment—How large are total investment costs with a supplier?

✓ Risk—How much risk is involved in dealing with a supplier?

are upset with firms such as Gucci for opening their own stores in the same shopping centers. Most Gucci sales now come from company-owned and franchised shops. On the other hand, many suppliers are distressed by what they believe is retailers' excessive use of **chargebacks**, whereby retailers, at their sole discretion, make deductions in their bills for infractions ranging from late shipments to damaged and expired goods. Some suppliers have even taken their retailers to

FIGURE 15-5
Zara: A Collaborative Supplier-Retailer Program

For its fast-paced merchandise planning and development processes to work properly, Zara personnel need to foster close relationships with suppliers around the world. As the retailer's Web site notes, "Zara offers the latest trends in international fashion in an environment of thought-out design."

Photo reprinted by permission of Susan Berry, Retail Image Consulting, Inc.

court: "The last thing a company wants to do is sue one of its biggest customers. But disputes over stores' payments to their suppliers are growing increasingly bitter, spawning at least two dozen lawsuits over the last few years, involving almost every large American department store chain."[4]

Selecting merchandise sources must be viewed as a two-way street. For example, in 2005, Nike announced that it would no longer distribute its products through Sears' stores, out of concern that Nike items would end up being sold at Sears' sister chain Kmart. At roughly the same time, Nike decided to make a new brand of sneakers available at Wal-Mart. The Starter brand sold at Wal-Mart does not carry the famous Nike name or its swoosh logo.[5]

Evaluating Merchandise

Whatever source is chosen, there must be a procedure to evaluate the merchandise under consideration. Three procedures are possible: inspection, sampling, and description. The technique depends on the item's cost, its attributes, and purchase regularity.

Inspection occurs when every single unit is examined before purchase and after delivery. Jewelry and art are examples of expensive, rather unique purchases for which the retailer carefully inspects all items.

Sampling is used with regular purchases of large quantities of breakable, perishable, or expensive items. Because inspection is inefficient, items are sampled for quality and condition. A retailer ready to buy several hundred light fixtures, bunches of bananas, or inexpensive watches does not inspect each item. A number of units are sampled, and the entire selection is bought if the sample is okay. An unsatisfactory sample might cause a whole shipment to be rejected (or a discount negotiated). Sampling may also occur upon receipt of merchandise.

Description buying is used with standardized, nonbreakable, and nonperishable merchandise. Items are not inspected or sampled; they are ordered in quantity based on a verbal, written, or pictorial description. A stationery store can order paper clips, pads, and printer paper from a catalog or Web site. After it receives an order, only a count of those items is conducted.

Negotiating the Purchase

Next, a retailer negotiates the purchase and its terms. A new or special order usually results in a negotiated contract, and a retailer and a supplier carefully discuss all aspects of the purchase. A regular order or reorder often involves a uniform contract, since terms are standard or have already been set and the order is handled routinely.

Off-price retailers and other deep discounters may require negotiated contracts for most purchases. These firms employ **opportunistic buying**, by which especially low prices are negotiated for merchandise whose sales have not lived up to expectations, end-of-season goods, items consumers have returned to the manufacturer or another retailer, and closeouts. At TJX, "unlike traditional retailers that order goods far in advance of the time they appear on the selling floor, TJX buyers are in the marketplace virtually every week. By maintaining a liquid inventory position, our buyers can buy close to need, enabling them to buy into current market trends and take advantage of the opportunities in the marketplace"[6]

Several purchase terms must be specified, whether a negotiated or a uniform contract is involved. These include the delivery date, quantity purchased, price and payment arrangements, discounts, form of delivery, and point of transfer of title, as well as special clauses.

The delivery date and the quantity purchased must be clear. A retailer should be able to cancel an order if either provision is not carried out. The purchase price, payment arrangements, and permissible discounts must also be addressed. What is the retailer's cost per item (including handling)? What forms of payment are permitted (cash and credit)? What discounts are given? Retailers' purchase prices are often discounted for early payments ("2/10/net 30" means there is a 2 percent discount if the full bill is paid in 10 days; the full bill is due in 30 days), support activities (setting up displays), and quantity purchases. Stipulations are needed for the form of delivery (truck, rail, and so on) and the party responsible for shipping fees (FOB factory—free on board—means a supplier places merchandise with the shipper, but the retailer pays the freight). Last, the point of transfer of title—when ownership changes from supplier to buyer—must be stated in a contract.

Special clauses may be inserted by either party. Sometimes they are beneficial to both parties (such as an agreement about the advertising support each party provides). Other times, the clauses are inserted by the more powerful party. As noted in Chapter 1, a major disagreement between vendors and large retailers is the latter's increasing use of **slotting allowances**—payments that retailers require of vendors for providing shelf space.

To learn more about the slotting allowance controversy, visit this Web site (**www.ftc.gov/opa/2003/11/slottingallowance.htm**).

> For small suppliers, the need to fund slotting allowances can severely limit distribution or cause the diversion of resources that could be better spent on other parts of the business. For consumers, the practice leads to artificially restricted product assortments. Category managers who decide which items to put on store shelves are often forced to choose between conflicting goals—maximizing profits by accepting slotting allowances or doing what is in the best interests of their customers.[7]

Unlike many other retailers, industry leader Wal-Mart does not charge any slotting allowances and often gets new products first from suppliers as a result of this policy.

Concluding Purchases

Many medium-sized and large retailers use computers to complete and process orders (based on electronic data interchange [EDI] and quick response [QR] inventory planning), and each purchase is fed into a computer data bank. Smaller retailers often write up and process orders manually, and purchase amounts are added to their inventory in the same way. Yet, with the advances in computerized ordering software, even small retailers may have the capability of placing orders electronically—especially if they buy from large wholesalers that use EDI and QR systems.

There is EDI/QR software (**www.gxs.com/solutions_smb.htm**) to fit almost any budget.

Multi-unit retailers must determine whether the final purchase decision is made by central or regional management or by local managers. Advantages and disadvantages accrue to each approach.

Several alternatives are possible regarding the transfer of title between parties. The retailer's responsibilities and rights differ in each case:

- The retailer takes title immediately on purchase.
- The retailer assumes ownership after items are loaded onto the mode of transportation.
- The retailer takes title when a shipment is received.
- The retailer does not take title until the end of a billing cycle, when the supplier is paid.

Careers in
RETAILING   Is Retail for Me? Merchandise Buying and Planning—Part 2

Besides the typical merchandising positions noted in Chapter 14, there are many other opportunities:

- *Head of Merchandise Planning and Allocation:* Top executive responsible for allocation of merchandise to stores. This position may advise the GMM (general merchandise manager) and buying staff on flow quantities and timing and assist in planning quantities needed for merchandise events. Does not buy goods but may have gross margin planning/analysis responsibilities.
- *Senior Merchandise Planner/Controller:* In very large chains, this position is between the head of planning and planners. This position supervises planners responsible for selected product categories, often corresponding to the DMM (divisional merchandise manager) merchandise groupings.
- *Merchandise Planner/Controller:* This position advises on flow quantities and timing and develops distribution plans for specific merchandise categories and subclasses. Responsible for balancing stock unit ratios by store. May directly supervise a crew of merchandise distributors/allocators.

- *Merchandise Distributor/Allocator/Analyst:* Responsible for allocating new merchandise into stores by replenishment needs or stock ratios. May also coordinate inter-store transfers of goods. Will generally do analysis only upon instruction from a planner. Primary duty is allocation, not planning.
- *Head of Import Coordination and Production:* Top executive over imports and/or offshore merchandise production, which includes licensing and monitoring production at offshore factories. May be responsible for quota management. May assist traffic department or third-party contractor with shipping arrangements through Customs.
- *Production Manager:* Monitors factory production of private label goods, ensuring conformity to specifications and quality. May coordinate shipping from factory to distribution centers. May work with overseas factories. May have responsibility for import shipping arrangements through Customs.

Source: Reprinted by permission of the National Retail Federation.

- The retailer accepts merchandise on consignment and does not own the items. The supplier is paid after merchandise is sold.

A consignment or memorandum deal may be possible if a vendor is in a weak position and wants to persuade retailers to carry its items. In a **consignment purchase**, a retailer has no risk because title is not taken; the supplier owns the goods until sold. An electronic version (scan-based trading) is being tried at some supermarkets. It saves time and money for all parties due to the paperless steps in a purchase. In a **memorandum purchase**, risk is still low, but a retailer takes title on delivery and is responsible for damages. In both options, retailers do not pay for items until they are sold and can return items.

Receiving and Stocking Merchandise

The retailer is now ready to receive and handle items. This involves receiving and storing, checking and paying invoices, price and inventory marking, setting up displays, figuring on-floor assortments, completing transactions, arranging delivery or pickup, processing returns and damaged goods, monitoring pilferage, and controlling merchandise. See Figure 15-6. Distribution management is key.

Items may be shipped from suppliers to warehouses (for storage and disbursement) or directly to retailers' store(s). The Walgreens drugstore chain has fully automated warehouses that stock thousands of products and speed their delivery to stores. Limited Brands orders some apparel by satellite and computer, uses common and contract carriers to pick it up from manufacturers in the United States and Asia (using chartered jets), ships items to its own warehouses in Columbus, Ohio, and then delivers them to stores. J.C. Penney has separate distribution centers for its store and catalog operations.

FIGURE 15-6
Receiving and Stocking
Merchandise at REI's
Category Killer Stores

With its wide and deep product
assortment, along with some
very tall vertical displays, in-
store merchandising at REI can
be quite challenging.

Photo reprinted by permission of
Susan Berry, Retail Image
Consulting, Inc.

One important emerging technology that may greatly advance the merchandise tracking and handling process for retailers involves **RFID (radio frequency identification)** systems. RFID "is a method of remotely storing and retrieving data using devices called RFID tags or transponders. An RFID tag is a small object, such as an adhesive sticker, that can be attached to or incorporated into a product or its shipping package. RFID tags contain tiny antennas to enable them to receive and respond to radio frequency queries from an RFID transceiver."[8]

At present, RFID utilization is quite limited. It is too early to predict how widespread RFID use will be or how long it will take to gain acceptance by the majority of retailers and their suppliers. The current costs for an RFID system are estimated at several million dollars per supplier (which is responsible for most of the work and investment):

> RFID is way beyond the now-ubiquitous barcodes found on products from candy to computers. Barcodes basically count products for retailers. RFID, with its more sophisticated tags and readers, can tell retailers and suppliers what's in a case, what's on a pallet, and where products are at any point along the supply chain. Recognizing that about $1.2 trillion worth of inventory is stuck at some point within the supply chain at any given point in time, there's massive room for improvement. According to one expert, "Wal-Mart, as any retailer, is basically a distributor of products. It has to be able to get products in and get them out extremely effectively and track them while it is doing that. And RFID is its attempt to track them better."[9]

When orders are received, they must be checked for completeness and product condition. Invoices must be reviewed for accuracy and payments made as specified. This step cannot be taken for granted.

At this point, prices and inventory information are marked on merchandise. Supermarkets estimate that price marking on individual items costs them an amount equal to their annual profits. Marking can be done in various ways. Small

FIGURE 15-7
The Monarch 1130 Series Labeler

The 1130 Series labelers represent a complete family of identification and pricing solutions. The labelers are simple and easy to use. They have ergonomic handle grips, lift-up covers for quick maintenance, label-viewing windows, and other features.

Photo reprinted by permission of Monarch Marking Systems.

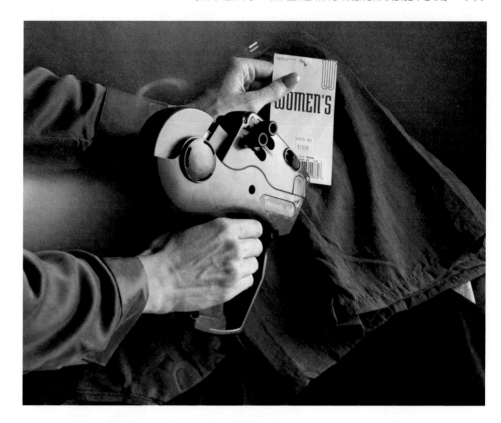

Monarch Marking (**www.monarch.com/products/retbarproducts.htm**) markets an extensive line of printing devices.

firms may hand-post prices and manually keep inventory records. Some retailers use their own computer-generated price tags and rely on pre-printed UPC data on packages to keep records. Others buy tags, with computer- and human-readable price and inventory data, from outside suppliers. Still others expect vendors to provide source tagging.

An inventory system works best when there is more data on labels or tags. With Monarch Marketing Systems' portable printers, hand-held devices print UPC-based labels and can be connected to store computers. Seagull Scientific's Bar Tender software (**www.seagullscientific.com**) lets firms easily print data-rich tags. See Figures 15-7 and 15-8.

Store displays and on-floor quantities and assortments depend on the retailer and products involved. Supermarkets usually have bin and rack displays and place most inventory on the sales floor. Traditional department stores have all kinds of interior displays and place a lot of inventory in the back room, off the sales floor. Displays and on-floor merchandising are discussed in Chapter 18.

Merchandise handling is not complete until the customer buys and receives it from a retailer. This means order taking, credit or cash transactions, packaging, and delivery or pickup. Automation has improved retailer performance in each of these areas.

A procedure for processing returns and damaged goods is also needed. The retailer must determine the party responsible for customer returns (supplier or retailer) and the situations in which damaged goods would be accepted for refund or exchange (such as the length of time a warranty is honored).

As discussed later in the chapter, more retailers are taking aggressive actions to monitor and reduce inventory losses. This is a major problem due to the high costs of merchandise theft.

Merchandise control involves assessing sales, profits, turnover, inventory shortages, seasonality, and costs for each product category and item carried. Control is usually achieved by preparing computerized inventory data and doing

physical inventories. A physical inventory must be adjusted to reflect damaged goods, pilferage, customer returns, and other factors. A discussion of this topic appears in Chapter 16.

Merchandise receiving and handling is covered further later in this chapter.

Reordering Merchandise

Four factors are critical in reordering merchandise that the retailer purchases more than once: order and delivery time, inventory turnover, financial outlays, and inventory versus ordering costs.

How long does it take for a retailer to process an order and a supplier to fulfill and deliver it? It is possible for delivery time to be so lengthy that a retailer must reorder while having a full inventory. On the other hand, overnight delivery may be available for some items.

How long does it take for a retailer to sell out its inventory? A fast-selling product gives a retailer two choices: order a surplus of items and spread out reorder periods, or keep a low inventory and order frequently. A slow-selling item may let a retailer reduce its initial inventory and spread out reorders.

What are the financial outlays under various purchase options? A large order, with a quantity discount, may require a big cash outlay. A small order, while more expensive per item, results in lower total costs at any one time since less inventory is held.

There are trade-offs between inventory holding and ordering costs. A large inventory fosters customer satisfaction, volume discounts, low per-item shipping costs, and easier handling. It also means high investments; greater obsolescence and damages; and storage, insurance, and opportunity costs. Placing many orders and keeping a small inventory mean a low investment, low opportunity costs, low storage costs, and little obsolescence. Yet, there may be higher unit costs, adverse effects from order delays, a need for partial shipments, service charges, complex handling, and disappointed customers (if items are out of stock). Retailers try to hold enough stock to satisfy customers while not having a high surplus. Quick response inventory planning lowers inventory and ordering costs via close retailer-supplier relationships.

Re-Evaluating on a Regular Basis

A merchandising plan should be re-evaluated regularly, with management reviewing the buying organization and that organization assessing the implementation. The overall procedure, as well as the handling of individual goods and services, should be monitored. Conclusions during this stage become part of the information-gathering stage for future efforts.

LOGISTICS

Logistics is the total process of planning, implementing, and coordinating the physical movement of merchandise from manufacturer (wholesaler) to retailer to customer in the most timely, effective, and cost-efficient manner possible. Logistics regards order processing and fulfillment, transportation, warehousing, customer service, and inventory management as interdependent functions in the value delivery chain. If a logistics system works well, firms reduce stockouts, hold down inventories, and improve customer service—all at the same time. See Figure 15-9. Logistics can also be quite challenging:

> When Nestlé Purina launches an item, it typically takes weeks for product information to be printed and sent to retailers. Grocers may need an

FIGURE 15-9
The Sophisticated Logistics System of Reitmans

As Canada's largest women's specially retailer, Reitmans Limited operates stores in several divisions, including Reitmans, Smart Set/Dalmys, Penningtons Superstores, Thyme Maternity, and RW & Co. The firm's distribution center consists of 566,000 square feet in Montreal. It is capable of annually shipping more than 55,000,000 garments and accessories to 1,100 stores across Canada. This requires sophisticated technology, proven conveyor systems, and dedicated employees. Automated receiving, processing, and shipping systems—with three flat-goods sorters, two hanging-goods sorters, and powered trolleys—have produced excellent results, including increased distribution accuracy, a 30 percent reduction in labor requirements, a 50 percent increase in peak processing throughput, and a two-day reduction in processing time.

Photos reprinted by permission of Reitmans.

Ethics in RETAILING
The Greening of Home Depot

Between 1997 and 1999, global activists organized several protests against Home Depot (**www.homedepot.com**), accusing it of purchasing wood from endangered forests. Concerned about the effect that these protests could have on its sales and image, Home Depot agreed to stop buying products from these forests. It also created an environmental global project manager position, staffed by Roland Jarvis, who was given the authority to stop contracts with any supplier whose practices endangered forests or otherwise hurt the environment.

Jarvis recently used this power to reduce Home Depot's purchase of tropical woods from Indonesia. Home Depot's main Indonesia-based supplier razed large parts of the country's rain forests to get the lum-

ber. According to Jarvis, "We asked them to stop, but they said they would continue." In response, he cut 90 percent of Home Depot's purchases of Indonesian lumber. The remaining amount comes from environmentally responsible Indonesian-based suppliers. Jarvis also recently convinced Chile's two largest lumber companies and environmentalists to meet for the first time. Home Depot attributes a modest increase in its sales from customers aware of its environment policies.

Sources: Jim Carlton, "Once Targeted by Protesters, Home Depot Plays Green Role," *Wall Street Journal* (August 6, 2004), pp. A1, A6; and "Protecting Our Environment," **www.homedepot.com/HDUS/EN_US/corporate/corp_respon/protect_environ.shtml** (April 3, 2006).

additional week or more before the data are typed into their procurement systems. Data also need to be entered into warehouse and inventory systems so stock handlers can accept a shipment when it arrives, and into the point-of-sale system so the retailer can price, stock, sell, and reorder an item. If a product arrives before the grocer has all that information, the delivery often sits on a loading dock until Nestlé Purina and the retailer work out the problem. Sometimes the product just gets sent back from a warehouse. That forces Nestlé Purina to return to the buyer who placed the order and fix the problem manually—an expensive, time-consuming effort. With new technology, the process of entering data into retailers' systems can be automated, so when new information is entered, it's added almost in real time to retailer systems.[10]

In this section, we discuss these logistics concepts: performance goals, the supply chain, order processing and fulfillment, transportation and warehousing, and customer transactions and customer service. Inventory management is covered in the final section of this chapter.

Performance Goals

Among retailers' major logistics goals are to

- Match the costs incurred to specific logistics activities, thereby fulfilling all activities as economically as possible, given the firms' other performance objectives.
- Place and receive orders as easily, accurately, and satisfactorily as possible.
- Minimize the time between ordering and receiving merchandise.
- Coordinate shipments from various suppliers.
- Have enough merchandise on hand to satisfy customer demand, without having so much inventory that heavy markdowns will be necessary.
- Place merchandise on the sales floor efficiently.
- Process customer orders efficiently and in a manner satisfactory to customers.
- Work collaboratively and communicate regularly with other supply chain members.

- Handle returns effectively and minimize damaged products.
- Monitor logistics performance.
- Have backup plans in case of breakdowns in the system.

At Sears, there is an entire division devoted to logistics. Sears Logistics Services is the sole point of contact for all of the logistical activity at Sears. It is responsible for the movement of apparel, appliances, home furnishings, hardware, automotive goods, and repair parts to Sears stores; and it performs millions of home deliveries to Sears customers. This division is responsible for developing and implementing programs to improve the efficiency and effectiveness of logistics at Sears. Quantifiable goals are set, such as reducing the cost of moving cartons through a distribution center by a given time.[11]

The Bon-Ton department store chain has a detailed *International Vendor Standards Guide*, as stated at its Web site (**www.bonton.com/pdfs/2005impguide. pdf**):

Bon-Ton (**www.bonton.com/scm_ main.asp**) is very serious about maximizing its logistics performance.

> In any partnership where a supplier and retailer have a working relationship, it is very important to define clear expectations. Product quality, shipping windows, production, and product availability are just some of the expectations that must be defined. In retail, the role of international logistics takes on significant importance in producing higher levels of productivity, improving product flow to the selling floor, reducing inventories, and overall cost reduction for both the retailer and supplier. To this end, these logistical requirements have been developed. They are clear and concise expectations consistent with standard practices prevalent throughout the retail industry. While critical to our mutual success, these provisions allow Bon-Ton to minimize costs and to receive and process merchandise in a timely cost-effective manner, thereby assuring a continuous flow of merchandise to the unit store. All instructions, terms, and expectations must be fully complied with and are applicable to all shipments consigned to Bon-Ton Department Stores.

Supply Chain Management

The **supply chain** is the logistics aspect of a value delivery chain. It comprises all of the parties that participate in the retail logistics process: manufacturers, wholesalers, third-party specialists (shippers, order-fulfillment houses, and so forth), and the retailer. Visit our Web site (**www.prenhall.com/bermanevans**) for numerous links related to supply chain management.

The CPFR Committee (**www.vics.org/committees/ cpfr**) is actively working to expand the use of integrated supply chain planning.

Many retailers and suppliers are seeking closer logistical relationships. One technique for larger retailers is **collaborative planning, forecasting, and replenishment (CPFR)**—a holistic approach to supply chain management among a network of trading partners. According to the Voluntary Interindustry Commerce Standards Association, more than 300 major firms (including Ace Hardware, Best Buy, Circuit City, Federated Department Stores, Meijer, J.C. Penney, Safeway, Staples, Target Corporation, Walgreens, and Wal-Mart) have participated in CPFR programs. Nonetheless, CPFR has not been an unqualified success:

> While CPFR was very much in vogue a few years back, among some commentators, it has now somewhat fallen into disrepute—perhaps this is because few initiatives have lived up to their initial hype. However, the key issue of collaboration between retailers and their suppliers still offers the best hope for a future in which both manufacturers and their retail customers will need to work more closely together to survive. The CPFR initiative, according to its Web site, is to "improve the partnership

between retailers and vendor merchants through shared information." All very laudable, but there is an inherent lack of trust between the two parties which has the potential to strangle any emerging signs of collaborative life at birth. The main fear of many suppliers with different retail customers to keep happy is that if they share too much information, then, when push comes to shove, those with the greatest muscle will demand preferential treatment at the expense of others.[12]

Third-party logistics (outsourcing) is becoming more popular. For example, many retailers (including Internet-based firms) rely on UPS Supply Chain Solutions, a division of United Parcel Service, as their logistics specialist: "In a retail environment where it is increasingly more difficult to show a competitive advantage while maintaining profit margins, you need to focus on your retail strategy rather than deal with supply chain issues." At UPS Supply Chain Solutions, "experienced professionals work closely with retail businesses to improve service, optimize distribution and transportation networks, and streamline their global supply chains."[13] Logistics specialists work with retailers of all sizes to ship and warehouse merchandise.

Target Corporation's Partners Online program (**www.partnersonline.com**) is a proactive relationship retailing activity.

The Web is a growing force in supplier-retailer communications. A number of manufacturers and retailers have set up dedicated sites exclusively to interact with their channel partners. For confidential information exchanges, passwords and secure encryption technology are utilized. Target Corporation has a very advanced Web site called Partners Online, which took several years to develop and test. At the Web site, vendors can access sales data and inventory reports, accounts payable figures, invoices, and report cards on their performance. There are also manuals and newsletters.

Order Processing and Fulfillment

To optimize order processing and fulfillment, many firms now engage in **quick response (QR) inventory planning**, by which a retailer reduces the amount of inventory it holds by ordering more frequently and in lower quantity. A QR system requires a retailer to have good relationships with suppliers, coordinate shipments, monitor inventory levels closely to avoid stockouts, and regularly communicate with suppliers by electronic data interchange (via the Web or direct PC connections) and other means.

For the retailer, a QR system reduces inventory costs, minimizes the space required for storage, and lets the firm better match orders with market conditions—by replenishing stock more quickly. For the manufacturer, a QR system can also improve inventory turnover and better match supply and demand by giving the vendor the data to track actual sales. These data were less available in the past. In addition, an effective QR system makes it more unlikely that a retailer would switch suppliers. The most active users of QR are department stores, full-line discount stores, apparel stores, home centers, supermarkets, and drugstores. Among the firms using QR are Dillard's, Federated Department Stores, Giant Food, Home Depot, Limited Brands, J.C. Penney, Sears, Target Corporation, and Wal-Mart.

A QR system works best in conjunction with floor-ready merchandise, lower minimum order sizes, properly formatted store fixtures, and electronic data interchange (EDI). **Floor-ready merchandise** refers to items that are received at the store in condition to be put directly on display without any preparation by retail workers. In this approach, apparel manufacturers are responsible for pre-ticketing garments (with information specified by the retailer) and placing them on hangers, and Wal-Mart requires that vendors ship apples "to stores in collapsible plastic trays that go straight from the truck on the loading dock to the sales floor. When the tray sells out, a full one is put in its place. Wal-Mart employees don't have to handle each apple to restock the display, which saves time and enables them to perform other tasks."[14]

Quick response also means suppliers need to rethink the minimum order sizes they will accept. While a minimum order size of 12 for a given size or color was once required by sheet and towel makers, minimum order size is now as low as 2 units. Minimum order sizes for men's shirts have been reduced from 6 to as few as 2 units.

The lower order sizes have led some retailers to refixture in-store departments. Previously, fixtures were often configured on the basis of a retailer's stocking full inventories. Today, the retailer must make a visual impact with smaller inventories.

Electronic data interchange, EDI (described in Chapter 8), lets retailers do QR inventory planning efficiently—via a paperless, computer-to-computer relationship between retailers and vendors. Research suggests that retail prices could be reduced by an average of 10 percent with the industrywide usage of QR and EDI. This illustration shows the value of QR and EDI:

> Implementing a Web-based, electronic data interchange system to communicate with most of its suppliers is saving United Supermarkets of Lubbock, Texas, up to $400,000 a year in transaction costs. "It's very easy to move into this [EDI] world today," said the chief information officer at the 44-store chain. By making the transition to EDI with suppliers, the retailer can now process purchase orders, receipts, and invoices much more efficiently. United is also able to have real-time communication and tracking capabilities. Moreover, the retailer has reduced per-transaction costs by $5 to $6. The implementation was done in two phases. United's 20 major suppliers—who provide about two-thirds of its goods—were put online first. This took about six months. Getting the second-tier suppliers to become EDI-compliant in accordance with United's system took a bit longer.[15]

ECR Europe (www.ecrnet. org) has taken a lead role in trying to popularize this business tool.

A number of firms in the food sector of retailing are striving to use **efficient consumer response (ECR)** planning, which permits supermarkets to incorporate aspects of quick response inventory planning, electronic data interchange, and logistics planning. The goal is "to develop a responsive, consumer-driven system in which manufacturers, brokers, and distributors work together to maximize consumer value and minimize supply chain cost. To meet this goal, we need a smooth, continual product flow matched to consumer consumption. And to support the flow of products, we need timely, accurate data flowing through a paperless system between the retail checkout and the manufacturing line."[16]Although ECR has enabled supermarkets to cut tens of billions of dollars in distribution costs, applying it has not been easy. Many supermarkets are still unwilling to trade their ability to negotiate short-term purchase terms with vendors in return for routine order fulfillment without special deals.

Retailers are also addressing two other aspects of order processing and fulfillment. (1) With *advanced ship notices*, retailers that utilize QR and EDI receive an alert when bills of lading are sent electronically as soon as a shipment leaves the vendor. This gives the retailers more time to efficiently receive and allocate merchandise. (2) Since more retailers are buying from multiple suppliers, from multilocation sources, and from overseas, they must better coordinate order placement and fulfillment. Home Depot, among others, has added an import logistics group to coordinate overseas forecasting, ordering, sourcing, and logistics. Supervalu is dealing with its practice of buying products from so many different countries around the globe.

Sometimes the order-processing-and-fulfillment process can be quite challenging:

> Tony Stallone works for Peapod, an online grocery-delivery service, near Chicago. His title is vice-president of perishables, so for him, a delicate strawberry has value beyond measure. "This is the most important item we sell. If customers receive mushy strawberries, they may never shop with us again." Online grocers have to work so hard to win new customers that any slipup—one bad strawberry, one late delivery—could send the recipient back to the store down the street.[17]

Transportation and Warehousing

Several transportation decisions are necessary:

- How often will merchandise be shipped to the retailer?
- How will small order quantities be handled?
- What shipper will be used (the manufacturer, the retailer, or a third-party specialist)?
- What transportation form will be used? Are multiple forms required (such as manufacturer trucks to retailer warehouses and retailer trucks to individual stores)?
- What are the special considerations for perishables and expensive merchandise?
- How often will special shipping arrangements be necessary (such as rush orders)?
- How are shipping terms negotiated with suppliers?
- What delivery options will be available for the retailer's customers? This is a critical decision for nonstore retailers, especially those selling through the Web.

Transportation effectiveness is influenced by the caliber of the logistics infrastructure (including access to refrigerated trucks, airports, waterway docking, and superhighways), traffic congestion, parking, and other factors. Retailers operating outside the United States must come to grips with the logistical problems in many foreign countries, where the transportation network and the existence of modern technology may be severely lacking.

Technology in RETAILING

Sportsman's Warehouse: Optimizing Logistics

Sportsman's Warehouse (**www.sportsmanswarehouse. com**) is an outdoor products retailer that sells hunting, fishing, and camping equipment. The chain operates about 40 stores in the Midwest and the western United States. With the objective of adding more stores, Sportsman's Warehouse recently revamped its information technology systems. Sportsman's also updated its picking system. According to Chris Utgaard, the retailer's chief operating officer, after an order was received, "pickers would then go around the warehouse and literally search for the product."

Sportsman's Warehouse moved to a much larger distribution center and completed the transition of two major information technology systems during its busiest season. Now, instead of a single person picking an order, picking is done in zones based on a product's characteristics.

In planning for these changes, Chris Utgaard used a "big bang" approach to speed up the changes. His objective was to make major changes quickly and then fine-tune the system when gaps were identified. With the new system in place, Sportsman's can now ship products to six stores in less time than it used to take to ship to four stores.

Sources: "Gearing Up for Growth," *Inbound Logistics* (January 2005), pp. 134–138; and "Store Locations & Information," **www.sportsmans warehouse.com/stores.htm** (March 14, 2006).

FIGURE 15-10
Claire's Aggressive Use of Central Warehousing

Claire's Stores has a central warehouse in Hoffman Estates, Illinois. The mammoth warehouse has been designed to accommodate a second level and can support up to 6,000 stores. At present, the firm operates 3,000 shops, mostly in shopping malls. They sell inexpensive jewelry and accessories for girls. Its stores include Claire's and Icing by Claire's

Photos reprinted by permission of Claire's Stores, Inc.

Descartes Systems Group (**www.descartes.com/ solutions/industries/direct_ delivery.html**) is a leader in DSD software.

With regard to warehousing, some retailers focus on warehouses as central or regional distribution centers. Products are shipped from suppliers to these warehouses and then allotted and shipped to individual outlets. Claire's Stores has its central buying and store operations offices, as well as its North American distribution center, in Hoffman Estates, Illinois. The distribution facility occupies 373,000 square feet of space. See Figure 15-10. Toys "R" Us uses separate regional distribution centers for U.S. Toys "R" Us stores and its international Toys "R" Us stores. Most centers are owned; some are leased.

Other retailers, including many supermarket chains, do not rely as much on central or regional warehouses. Instead, they have at least some goods shipped right from suppliers to individual stores through **direct store distribution (DSD)**. This approach works best with retailers that also utilize EDI. It is a way to move high turnover, high bulk, perishable products from the manufacturer directly to the store. The items most apt to involve DSD (such as beverages, bread, and snack foods) have an average shelf life of 70 days, while warehoused items have an average shelf life of more than a year. About 25 percent of the typical supermarket's sales are from items with DSD.[18]

The advantages of central warehousing are the efficiency in transportation and storage, mechanized processing of goods, improved security, efficient merchandise marking, ease of returns, and coordinated merchandise flow. Key disadvantages are the excessive centralized control, extra handling of perishables, high costs for small retailers, and potential ordering delays. Centralized warehousing may also reduce the capability of QR systems by adding another step. These are the pros and cons of DSD:

> Logistics managers constantly find themselves between a rock and a hard place, trying to balance customer service with the demands of chief financial officers for lower inventories and operating costs. Those demands are multiplied many times over when the products involved are perishable or have a limited shelf life due to other concerns. To get those products to market in a timely manner to avoid spoilage, the most practical answer is the implementation of direct store-delivery. However, DSD does not come without a price. One expert says, "There's no doubt that DSD, in terms of perishables, is the most efficient way to maximize the residual shelf life of a product. Without maximizing residual shelf life, you end up either throwing away product or losing sales. It's also

adding to your total costs." Another expert notes that "It's a high-cost system, but you're managing your brand and adding value to that brand. There's a trade-off between cost and control."[19]

Customer Transactions and Customer Service

Retailers must plan for outbound logistics (as well as inbound logistics): completing transactions by turning over merchandise to customers. This can be as simple as having a shopper take an item from a display area to the checkout counter or driving his or her car to a loading area. It can also be as complex as concluding a Web transaction that entails shipments from multiple vendors to the customer. A shopper's purchase of a computer, a fax machine, and an answering machine from Buy.com may result in three separate shipments. That is why UPS, Federal Express, DHL, and Airborne are doing more home deliveries. They can readily handle the diversity of shipping requests that retailers often cannot.

Even basic deliveries can have a breakdown. Think of the local pharmacy whose high school delivery person fails to come to work one day—or the pizzeria that gets no customer orders between 2:00 P.M. and 5:00 P.M. and 25 delivery orders between 5:00 P.M. and 7:00 P.M.

There are considerable differences between store-based and nonstore retailers. Most retail stores know that the customer wants to take the purchase or to pick it up when it is ready (such as a new car). All direct marketers, including Web retailers, are responsible for ensuring that products are delivered to the shopper's door or another convenient nearby location.

Customer service expectations are very much affected by logistical effectiveness. That is why Home Depot, in an effort to upgrade its in-store shopping experience, has implemented a Service Performance Improvement (SPI) initiative: "Through Service Performance Improvement, associates focus on serving customers while the store is open and turn to tasks like unloading trucks and restocking after hours."[20]

INVENTORY MANAGEMENT

As part of its logistics efforts, a retailer utilizes **inventory management** to acquire and maintain a proper merchandise assortment while ordering, shipping, handling, storing, displaying, and selling costs are kept in check. First, a retailer places an order based on a sales forecast or actual customer behavior. Both the number of items and their variety are requested when ordering. Order size and frequency depend on quantity discounts and inventory costs. Second, a supplier fills the order and sends merchandise to a warehouse or directly to the store(s). Third, the retailer receives products, makes items available for sale (by removing them from packing, marking prices, and placing them on the sales floor), and completes customer transactions. Some transactions are not concluded until items are delivered to the customer. The cycle starts anew as a retailer places another order. Let us look at these aspects of inventory management: retailer tasks, inventory levels, merchandise security, reverse logistics, and inventory analysis.

Retailer Tasks

Due to the comprehensive nature of inventory management, and to be more cost-effective, some retailers now expect suppliers to perform more tasks or they outsource at least part of their inventory management activities: "In 1990, producers

RETAILING Around the World   Dealing with Overloaded Ports of Entry

The Los Angeles-Long Beach ports are favored by importers since they are equipped to handle large freighters that can hold more than 4,000 containers. Many of these freighters are too big to pass through the Panama Canal to Eastern seaports. The Los Angeles-Long Beach ports handle 43 percent of America's imports. These two ports handle 24,000 containers a day, which amounts to 62 percent of all shipments to West Coast ports from Asian exporters. With the 12 percent increase in imports through these ports in 2004, the ports' capacity was strained. In November 2004, 94 cargo ships had to wait to be unloaded; some of these ships took as many as eight days to unload—twice the normal time period.

The overloaded situation has major ramifications for retailers. For example, Toys "R" Us (**www.tru.com**) had to add 10 extra days to its supply chain requirements. And Sharper Image (**www.sharperimage.com**) attributed part of a loss in the third quarter of 2004 to reduced inventory on hand, as well as extra costs for air freight to bypass these ports.

Sources: Barney Gimbel, "Yule Log Jam," *Fortune* (December 13, 2004), pp. 163–170; "Port of Los Angeles," **www.portoflosangeles.org** (January 11, 2006); and "Port of Long Beach," **www.polb.com** (January 11, 2006).

shipped products to retailers in a *warehouse-ready* mode. Retailers then reprocessed merchandise to package and price it for sale in the store where consumers make purchases. Today, in the era of *floor-ready*, producers ship products that have already been packaged and prepared for immediate movement to the sales floor. As we move further into the new millennium, there will be a shift to *consumer-ready* manufacturing where the links between producer and consumer are even more direct than traditionally."[21] Here are some examples:

- Wal-Mart and other retailers count on key suppliers to participate in their inventory management programs. Industrywide, this practice is known as **vendor-managed inventory (VMI)**. Procter & Gamble even has its own employees stationed at Wal-Mart headquarters to manage the inventory replenishment of that manufacturer's products.

- Target Corporation is at the forefront of another trend, store retailers outsourcing customer order fulfillment for their online businesses. Through its arrangement with Amazon.com, "Target.com utilizes Amazon.com technology and patented Web site capabilities such as 1-Click checkout to make shopping faster and more convenient for you. We also offer an extensive 'entertainment' product selection which is fulfilled by Amazon.com."[22]

The National Association for Retailing Merchandising Services offers a national online "JobBank" (www. narms.com/jobbank.html) by category and job location.

- According to the National Association for Retail Merchandising Services (**www.narms.com**), over $2 billion in retail merchandising services are annually provided by third-party specialists, ranging from reordering to display design. One such specialist is National In-Store Merchandisers (**www. nis-online.com/merchandising.asp**), which provides a variety of in-store merchandising services for such clients as Best Buy, Costco, Nordstrom, and Walgreens.

A contentious inventory management activity involves who is responsible for source tagging, the manufacturer or the retailer. In *source tagging*, anti-theft tags are put on items when they are produced, rather than at the store. Although both sides agree on the benefits of this, in terms of the reduced costs and the floor-readiness of merchandise, there are disagreements about who should pay for the tags.

Inventory Levels

Having the proper inventory on hand is a difficult balancing act:

1. The retailer wants to be appealing and never lose a sale by being out of stock. Yet, it does not want to be "stuck" with excess merchandise that must be marked down drastically.
2. The situation is more complicated for retailers that carry fad merchandise, that handle new items for which there is no track record, and that operate in new business formats where demand estimates are often inaccurate. Thus, inventory levels must be planned in relation to the products involved: staples, assortment merchandise, fashion merchandise, fads, and best-sellers.
3. Customer demand is *never* completely predictable—even for staples. Weather, special sales, and other factors can have an impact on even the most stable items.
4. Shelf space allocations should be linked to current revenues, which means that allocations must be regularly reviewed and adjusted.

One of the advantages of QR and EDI is that retailers hold "leaner" inventories since they receive new merchandise more often. Yet, when merchandise is especially popular or the supply chain breaks down, stockouts may still occur. A Food Marketing Institute study found that even supermarkets, which carry more staples than most other retailers, lose 3 percent of sales due to out-of-stock goods.

This illustration shows just how tough inventory management can be:

> Although the pharmacy in a typical chain drugstore may occupy only 10 or 20 percent of the total square footage, it usually accounts for at least 60 percent of the store's revenues. And an average pharmacy carries $175,000 in inventory, half of which is slow-moving items. Thus, inventory management is a critical concern for pharmacies—with carrying costs constantly rising across a carousel of moving targets as new drugs are brought to market, patented drugs become over-the-counter offerings, and the shelf life of every SKU has to be monitored without exception. Logistics processes are compounded because merchandise received in bulk cases and bottles are dispensed as ounces and doses when prescriptions are filled. Pharmacists, unlike other merchants, must determine inventory replenishment based upon SKUs being depleted through incremental percentages.[23]

Inventory level planning is discussed further in the next chapter.

Merchandise Security

Each year, $30 billion to $35 billion in U.S. retail sales are lost due to **inventory shrinkage** caused by employee theft, customer shoplifting, vendor fraud, and administrative errors. Of this amount, employees account for 47 percent, customers 32 percent, vendors 5 percent, and administrative errors (faulty paperwork and computer entries) 16 percent. As these figures show, employee theft is much higher than shopper theft.[24] Shrinkage typically ranges from under 1 percent of sales to more than 3 percent of sales at retail stores. This means that a small store with $500,000 in annual sales might lose up to $15,000 or more due to shrinkage, and a large store with $3 million in sales might lose up to $90,000 or more due to shrinkage. Thus, some form of merchandise security is needed by all retailers.

To reduce merchandise theft, there are three key points to consider. (1) Loss prevention measures should be included as stores are designed and built. The placement of entrances, dressing rooms, and delivery areas is critical. (2) A combination of security measures should be enacted, such as employee background checks, in-store guards, electronic security equipment, and merchandise tags. (3) Retailers must communicate the importance of loss prevention to employees, customers, and vendors—and the actions they will to take to reduce losses (such as firing workers and prosecuting shoplifters).

Here are some activities that are reducing losses from merchandise theft:

- Product tags, guards, video cameras, point-of-sale computers, employee surveillance, and burglar alarms are being used by more firms. Storefront protection is also popular.

Sensormatic (**www.sensormatic.com**) is a leader in electronic security.

- Many general merchandise retailers and some supermarkets use **electronic article surveillance**—whereby special tags are attached to products so that the tags can be sensed by electronic security devices at store exits. If the tags are not removed by store personnel or desensitized by scanning equipment, an alarm goes off. Retailers also have access to nonelectronic tags. These are snugly attached to products and must be removed by special detachers; otherwise, products are unusable. Dye tags permanently stain products, if not removed properly. See Figure 15-11.

- A number of retailers do detailed background checks for each prospective new employee. Some use loss prevention software that detects suspicious employee behavior.

- Various retailers have employee training programs and offer incentives for reducing merchandise losses. Others use written policies on ethical behavior that are signed by all personnel, including senior management. Target Stores has enrolled managers at problem stores in a Stock Shortage Institute. Neiman Marcus has shown workers a film with interviews of convicted shoplifters in prison to highlight the problem's seriousness.

- More retailers are apt to fire employees and prosecute shoplifters involved with theft. Courts are imposing stiffer penalties; in some areas, store detectives are empowered by police to make arrests. In over 40 states, there are civil restitution laws; shoplifters must pay for stolen goods or face arrests and criminal trials. In most states, fines are higher if goods are not returned or are damaged. Shoplifters must also contribute to court costs.

FIGURE 15-11
Sensormatic: The Leader in Store Security Systems

These aesthetically pleasing, acrylic pedestals (part of Sensormatic's Euro Pro Max system) provide an unobstructed vision of exits, as well as the ultimate electronic article surveillance system. An alarm goes off if a person tries to leave a store without a product's security tag being properly removed.

Photo reprinted by permission of Sensormatic Electronics Corporation.

FIGURE 15-12
Ways Retailers Can Deter
Employee and Shopper Theft

A. Employee Theft
- Use honesty tests as employee screening devices.
- Lock up trash to prevent merchandise from being thrown out and then retrieved.
- Verify through cameras and undercover personnel whether all sales are rung up.
- Centrally control all exterior doors to monitor opening and closing.
- Divide responsibilities—have one employee record sales and another make deposits.
- Give rewards for spotting thefts.
- Have training programs.
- Vigorously investigate all known losses and fire offenders immediately.

B. Shopper Theft While Store Is Open
- Use uniformed guards.
- Set up cameras and mirrors to increase visibility—especially in low-traffic areas.
- Use electronic article surveillance for high-value and theft-prone goods.
- Develop comprehensive employee training programs.
- Offer employee bonuses based on an overall reduction in shortages.
- Inspect all packages brought into store.
- Use self-locking showcases for high-value items such as jewelry.
- Attach expensive clothing together.
- Alternate the direction of hangers on clothing near doors.
- Limit the number of entrances and exits to the store, and the dollar value and quantity of merchandise displayed near exits.
- Prosecute all individuals charged with theft.

C. Employee/Shopper Theft While Store Is Closed
- Conduct a thorough building check at night to make sure no one is left in store.
- Lock all exits, even fire exits.
- Utilize ultrasonic/infrared detectors, burglar alarm traps, or guards with dogs.
- Place valuables in a safe.
- Install shatterproof glass and/or iron gates on windows and doors to prevent break-ins.
- Make sure exterior lighting is adequate.
- Periodically test burglar alarms.

- Some mystery shoppers are hired to watch for shoplifting, not just to research behavior.

Figure 15-12 presents a list of tactics retailers can use to combat employee and shopper theft, by far the leading causes of losses.

When devising a merchandise security plan, a retailer must assess the plan's impact on its image, employee morale, shopper comfort, and vendor relations. By setting strict rules for fitting rooms (by limiting the number of garments) or placing chains on very expensive coats, a retailer may cause some shoppers to avoid this merchandise—or visit another store.

Reverse Logistics

The term **reverse logistics** encompasses all merchandise flows from the retailer back through the supply channel. It typically involves items returned because of damages, defects, or less-than-anticipated sales. Sometimes retailers may use closeout firms that buy back unpopular merchandise (at a fraction of the original cost) that suppliers will not take back, and then these firms resell the goods at a deep discount. To avoid channel conflicts, the conditions for reverse logistics should be specified in advance.

According to one logistics expert, U.S. firms spend nearly $40 billion per year for the handling, transportation, and processing costs associated with returns. A recent study by the Boston Consulting Group and Shop.org found that the rate of customer returns is 6 percent for retailing overall.[25]

These are among the decisions that must be made for reverse logistics:

- Under what conditions (the permissible time, the condition of the product, and so forth) are customer returns accepted by the retailer and by the manufacturer?
- What is the customer refund policy? Is there a fee for returning an opened package?
- What party is responsible for shipping a returned product to the manufacturer?
- What customer documentation is needed to prove the date of purchase and the price paid?
- How are customer repairs handled (an immediate exchange, a third-party repair, or a refurbished product sent by the manufacturer)?
- To what extent are employees empowered to process customer returns?

Inventory Analysis

Inventory status and performance must be analyzed regularly to gauge the success of inventory management. Recent advances in computer software have made such analysis much more accurate and timely. According to surveys of retailers, these are the elements of inventory performance that are deemed most important: gross margin dollars, inventory turnover, gross profit percentage, gross margin return on inventory, the weeks of supply available, and the average in-stock position. See Figure 15-13.

Inventory analysis is discussed further in the next chapter.

Decorator's Warehouse (**www.the-showcase.com**) buys merchandise from failing retailers, estates, and other sources and sells the items at its store in Richmond, Virginia.

FIGURE 15-13
Ryder: A Solution for Reducing the Investment in Inventory

Reprinted by permission of Ryder Integrated Logistics.

Summary

1. *To describe the steps in the implementation of merchandise plans.* (1) Information is gathered about target market needs and prospective suppliers. Data about shopper needs can come from customers, suppliers, personnel, competitors, and others. A want book (want slip) is helpful. To acquire information about suppliers, the retailer can talk to prospects, attend trade shows, visit merchandise marts, and search the Web.

(2) The retailer chooses firm-owned; outside, regularly used; and/or outside, new supply sources. Relationships may become strained with suppliers because their goals differ from those of retailers.

(3) The merchandise under consideration is evaluated by inspection, sampling, and/or description. The method depends on the product and situation.

(4) Purchase terms may be negotiated (as with opportunistic buying) or uniform contracts may be used. Terms must be clear, including the delivery date, quantity purchased, price and payment arrangements, discounts, form of delivery, and point of transfer. There may also be special provisions.

(5) The purchase is concluded automatically or manually. Sometimes management approval is needed. The transfer of title may take place as soon as the order is shipped or not until after merchandise is sold by the retailer.

(6) Handling involves receiving and storing, price and inventory marking, displays, floor stocking, customer transactions, delivery or pickup, returns and damaged goods, monitoring pilferage, and control. RFID (radio frequency identification) is an emerging technology in this area.

(7) Reorder procedures depend on order and delivery time, inventory turnover, financial outlays, and inventory versus ordering costs.

(8) Both the overall merchandising procedure and specific goods and services must be reviewed.

2. *To examine the prominent roles of logistics and inventory management in the implementation of merchandise plans.* Logistics includes planning, implementing, and coordinating the movement of merchandise from supplier to retailer to customer. Logistics goals are to relate costs to activities, accurately place and receive orders, minimize ordering/receiving time, coordinate shipments, have proper merchandise levels, place merchandise on the sales floor, process customer orders, work well in the supply chain, handle returns effectively and minimize damaged goods, monitor performance, and have backup plans.

A supply chain covers all parties in the logistics process. Collaborative planning, forecasting, and replenishment (CPFR) uses a holistic approach. Third-party logistics is more popular than before. Many manufacturers and retailers have Web sites to interact with channel partners.

Some retailers engage in QR inventory planning. Floor-ready merchandise is received at the store ready to be displayed. EDI lets retailers use QR planning through computerized supply chain relationships. Numerous supermarkets use efficient consumer response. Several transportation decisions are needed, as are warehousing choices. Certain retailers have goods shipped by direct store distribution. Retailers must also plan outbound logistics: completing transactions by turning over merchandise to the customer.

As part of logistics, a retailer uses inventory management. Due to its complexity, and to reduce costs, retailers may expect suppliers to perform more tasks or they may outsource some inventory activities. Vendor-managed inventory (VMI) is growing in popularity.

Having the proper inventory is a balancing act: The retailer does not want to lose sales due to being out of stock. It also does not want to be stuck with excess merchandise. Each year, $30 billion to $35 billion in U.S. retail sales are lost due to employee theft, customer shoplifting, vendor fraud, and administrative errors. Many retailers use electronic article surveillance, with special tags attached to products.

Reverse logistics involves all merchandise flows from the retailer back through a supply channel. It includes returns due to damages, defects, or poor retail sales.

Inventory performance must be analyzed regularly.

Key Terms

want book (want slip) (p. 441)
chargebacks (p. 444)
opportunistic buying (p. 445)
slotting allowances (p. 446)
consignment purchase (p. 447)
memorandum purchase (p. 447)
RFID (radio frequency identification) (p. 448)
logistics (p. 451)

Questions for Discussion

1. What information should a membership club gather before adding a new stereo brand to its product mix?

2. What are the pros and cons of a retailer's relying too much on a want book?

3. Cite the advantages and disadvantages associated with these merchandise sources for your regular drugstore. How would your answers differ for a local deli?
   a. Company-owned.
   b. Outside, regularly used.
   c. Outside, new.

4. Devise a checklist a retailer could use to negotiate opportunistic buying terms with suppliers.

5. Under what circumstances should a retailer try to charge slotting allowances? How may this strategy backfire?

6. Which is more difficult, implementing a merchandise plan for a small music store or a music superstore? Explain your answer.

7. Distinguish between these two terms: *logistics* and *inventory management*. Give an example of each.

8. What are the benefits of quick response inventory planning? What do you think are the risks?

9. Why are some retailers convinced that distribution centers must be used as the shipping points for merchandise from manufacturers while other retailers favor direct store distribution?

10. How could a local restaurant be prepared for the variations in customer demand for home delivery during the day?

11. What is vendor-managed inventory? How do both manufacturers and retailers benefit from its use?

12. Present a seven-item checklist for a retailer to use with its reverse logistics.

Web-Based Exercise

Visit the Web site of UPS Supply Chain Solutions (**www.ups-scs.com/solutions/retail.html**). Describe the services that it offers for retailers. What are the benefits of using UPS Supply Chain Solutions?

Note: Stop by our Web site (**www.prenhall.com/ bermanevans**) to experience a number of highly

interactive, appealing Web exercises based on actual company demonstrations and sample materials related to retailing.

Chapter Endnotes

1. Various company sources.

2. Connie Robbins Gentry, "More Than Skin Deep," *Chain Store Age* (January 2005), p. 68.

3. *Big Lots 2005 Annual Report*.

4. Tracie Rozhon, "Stores and Vendors Take Their Haggling Over Payment to Court," *New York Times Online* (May 17, 2005).

5. "Nike Finds That Wal-Mart Fits Better Than Kmart," **www.bizjournals.com** (May 16, 2005); and Rich Thomaselli, "Nike Finds a Way to Go to Wal-Mart," *Advertising Age* (March 21, 2005), p. 1.

6. *TJX Companies 2004 Annual Report*.

7. "Getting the Real Story on Slotting Allowances," *MMR Online* (May 9, 2005).

8. "RFID," **http://en.wikipedia.org/wiki/RFID#The_RFID_system** (March 27, 2006).

9. John S. McClenahen, "Wal-Mart's Big Gamble," *IndustryWeek.com* (April 1, 2005).

10. Steve Konicki, "Shopping for Savings," *Informationweek* (July 1, 2002), pp. 36-45.

11. "About Sears: Careers—Sears Logistics Services, Inc.," **www.sears.com** (March 5, 2006).

12. Rick Pendrous, "Collaboration: Greater Trust Needed to Move Ahead," *Food Manufacture* (October 2004), p. 22.

13. "Retail," **http://ups-scs.com/solutions/retail.html** (January 30, 2006).

14. "Wal-Mart Rewrites Book on Cutting Costs," *DSN Retailing Today* (May 20, 2002), p. 26.

15. Peter Perrotta, "EDI Lowers Transaction Costs for Texas Grocer," *Supermarket News* (February 18, 2002), p. 19.

16. "What Is Efficient Consumer Response?" **www.ecr.ca/en/ecrinfo.html** (February 27, 2006).

17. Ted C. Fishman, "Click Here for Tomatoes," *Money* (April 2005), p. 143.

18. Grocery Manufacturers of America, "E-Commerce DSD Opportunities Provide Retailers and Manufacturers with Profit Growth," **www.gmabrands.com/news/docs/NewsRelease.cfm?DocID=915** (March 26, 2002).

19. "Delivering Just in Time: Trade Partner Collaboration Could Relieve Some of DSD's Headaches," *Food Logistics Online* (October 15, 2004).

20. "Growing the Business," **www.homedepot.com/HDUS/EN_US/corporate/media_relations/docs/growing.pdf** (July 8, 2005).

21. Kurt Salmon Associates, "Vision for the New Millennium," *KSA Brochure* (n.d.).

22. "Offered by Amazon.com," **www.target.com** (March 4, 2006).

23. "Druggists or Distributors?" *Chain Store Age* (December 2000), p. 148.

24. William George Shuster, "Winning the Battle Against Internal Theft," *JCK* (January 2005), pp. 98-104.

25. C. J. Charlton, "Reverse Logistics: Customer Satisfaction, Environment Key to Success in 21st Century," *Inbound Logistics* (January 2005), p. 28; and Joe Monteleone, "Moving in Return: Handling Returns," **www.ec.ups.com/ecommerce/solutions/c5c.html** (March 6, 2006).

Chapter 16
FINANCIAL MERCHANDISE MANAGEMENT

eBay (**www.ebay.com**) was founded in 1995 by Pierre Omidyar as a place for his girlfriend to trade Pez dispensers with fellow collectors. In its first years under Omidyar, eBay quickly grew by popularizing the online auction environment for a host of goods.

In 1998, Meg Whitman took over as eBay's chief executive. Under Whitman, more goods are sold at fixed prices, new

Reprinted by permission.

categories of merchandise have been added, and large retailers now sell goods at their own online eBay stores. eBay's number of confirmed registered users has grown from 2 million at the beginning of 1999 to 135 million by 2005. In 2005, eBay had approximately 60 million active users who bid on, bought, or listed an item during the prior 12-month period. And since 2000, the collective worth of merchandise sold on eBay has increased from $5.2 billion to $33.8 billion.

Even though eBay accounts for only a small fraction of Wal-Mart's sales, the difference in the two firms' operations is dramatic. Wal-Mart relies on several distribution centers, numerous trucks, thousands of stores, and 1.5 million employees. In comparison, eBay has less than 8,100 employees. And unlike Wal-Mart, eBay does not take title to or possession of a single item. eBay earns its profits by charging sellers a placement fee to list items for sale, an extra fee to highlight "Featured Auction" items, and a success fee, if a transaction is made. Some retailing analysts cite Wal-Mart as the model of the modern, centralized mass marketer, while eBay is the model of the decentralized, virtual marketing company.[1]

chapter objectives

1. To describe the major aspects of financial merchandise planning and management
2. To explain the cost and retail methods of accounting
3. To study the merchandise forecasting and budgeting process
4. To examine alternative methods of inventory unit control
5. To integrate dollar and unit merchandising control concepts

OVERVIEW

ACCPAC International (www.accpac.com) is one of many firms that offer integrated accounting software that is widely used by retailers.

Through **financial merchandise management**, a retailer specifies which products (goods and services) are purchased, when products are purchased, and how many products are purchased. **Dollar control** involves planning and monitoring a retailer's financial investment in merchandise over a stated period. **Unit control** relates to the quantities of merchandise a retailer handles during a stated period. The dollar investment is determined before assortment decisions are made.

Well-structured financial merchandise plans offer these benefits:

- The value and amount of inventory in each department and/or store unit during a given period are delineated. Stock is balanced, and fewer markdowns may be necessary.

- The amount of merchandise (in terms of investment) a buyer can purchase during a given period is stipulated. This gives a buyer direction.

- The inventory investment in relation to planned and actual revenues is studied. This improves the return on investment.

- The retailer's space requirements are partly determined by estimating beginning-of-month and end-of-month inventory levels.

- A buyer's performance is rated. Various measures may be used to set standards.

- Stock shortages are determined, and bookkeeping errors and pilferage are uncovered.

- Slow-moving items are classified—leading to increased sales efforts or markdowns.

- A proper balance between inventory and out-of-stock conditions is maintained.

As one expert noted, "Many firms suffer from poor inventory control which leads to inefficiency and wasted expenditures on products that sit on the shelf. With the right software and techniques, you can optimize inventory levels, eliminate stock-outs, lift sales, and squeeze the most out of a supply chain."[2]

This chapter divides financial merchandise management into four areas: methods of accounting, merchandise forecasting and budgeting, unit control systems, and financial inventory control. The hypothetical Handy Hardware Store illustrates the concepts.

INVENTORY VALUATION: THE COST AND RETAIL METHODS OF ACCOUNTING

The Small Business Administration has an excellent guide on inventory management (www.sba.gov/ library/pubs/mp-22.pdf).

Retail inventory accounting systems can be complex because they entail a great deal of data (due to the number of items sold). A typical retailer's dollar control system must provide such data as the sales and purchases made by that firm during a budget period, the value of beginning and ending inventory, markups and markdowns, and merchandise shortages.

Table 16-1 shows a profit-and-loss statement for Handy Hardware Store for the period from January 1, 2006, through June 30, 2006. The sales amount represents total receipts over this time. Beginning inventory was computed by counting the merchandise in stock on January 1, 2006—recorded at cost. Purchases (at cost) and transportation charges (costs incurred in shipping items from suppliers to the retailer) were derived by adding the invoice slips for all merchandise bought by Handy in the period.

TABLE 16-1	Handy Hardware Store Profit-and-Loss Statement, January 1, 2006–June 30, 2006		
Sales			$417,460
Less cost of goods sold:			
Beginning inventory (at cost)		$ 44,620	
Purchases (at cost)		289,400	
Transportation charges		2,600	
Merchandise available for sale		$336,620	
Ending inventory (at cost)		90,500	
Cost of goods sold			246,120
Gross profit			$171,340
Less operating expenses:			
Salaries		$ 70,000	
Advertising		25,000	
Rental		16,000	
Other		26,000	
Total operating expenses			137,000
Net profit before taxes			$ 34,340

Together, beginning inventory, purchases, and transportation charges equal the cost of **merchandise available for sale**. The **cost of goods sold** equals the cost of merchandise available for sale minus the cost value of ending inventory. Sales less cost of goods sold yields **gross profit**, while **net profit** is gross profit minus retail operating expenses. Because Handy does a physical inventory twice yearly, ending inventory was figured by counting the items in stock on June 30, 2006—recorded at cost (Handy codes each item).

Retailers have different data needs than manufacturers. Assortments are larger. Costs cannot be printed on cartons unless coded (due to customer inspection). Stock shortages are higher. Sales are more frequent. Retailers require monthly, not quarterly, profit data.

Two inventory accounting systems are available: (1) The cost accounting system values merchandise at cost plus inbound transportation charges. (2) The retail

Careers in RETAILING — Is Retail for Me? Distribution, Logistics, and Supply Chain Management

The logistics retail career area oversees the movement and storage of consumer products. Responsibilities include the management and facilitation of distribution centers, logistics traffic management, trucking, and other transportation operations. It may also include import/export shipping and related duties.

Here are three management-level jobs in logistics:

- *Head of (Physical) Distribution and Logistics:* Top executive position over all domestic distribution centers and logistics traffic management. May have some trucking operations for merchandise movement to and among stores. May handle import/export shipping.
- *Distribution Center Manager:* This position manages one distribution center in a firm with two or more centers. Typically will not supervise a full traffic

department function, because distribution is centrally run.

- *Traffic Manager (Head of Transport Logistics):* This position is responsible for selecting trucking firms, negotiating carrier rates, and managing inbound/outbound shipments in the United States. May be responsible for overseas merchandise only after it clears Customs. Does not run a distribution center. Variations to job description: (a) Position is generally as described; or (b) Doesn't negotiate the trucking contracts, just administers the shipping, damage claims, and carrier billings; or (c) Also handles overseas shipping and clearing goods through U.S. Customs.

Source: Reprinted by permission of the National Retail Federation.

accounting system values merchandise at current retail prices. Let us study both methods in terms of the frequency with which data are obtained, the difficulties of a physical inventory and record keeping, the ease of settling insurance claims (if there is inventory damage), the extent to which shortages can be computed, and system complexities.

At our Web site (**www.prenhall.com/bermanevans**), there are a number of links related to retail accounting and inventory valuation, including several from the Internal Revenue Service.

The Cost Method

With the **cost method of accounting**, the cost to the retailer of each item is recorded on an accounting sheet and/or is coded on a price tag or merchandise container. As a physical inventory is done, item costs must be learned, the quantity of every item in stock counted, and total inventory value at cost calculated. One way to code merchandise cost is to use a 10-letter equivalency system, such as M = 0, N = 1, O = 2, P = 3, Q = 4, R = 5, S = 6, T = 7, U = 8, and V = 9. An item coded with STOP has a cost value of $67.23. This technique is useful as an accounting tool and for retailers that allow price bargaining by customers (profit per item is easy to compute).

A retailer can use the cost method as it does physical or book inventories. A physical inventory means an actual merchandise count; a book inventory relies on record keeping.

A Physical Inventory System Using the Cost Method

In a **physical inventory system**, ending inventory—recorded at cost—is measured by counting the merchandise in stock at the close of a selling period. Gross profit is not computed until ending inventory is valued. A retailer using the cost method along with a physical inventory system derives gross profit only as often as it does a full merchandise count. Since most firms do so just once or twice yearly, a physical inventory system alone imposes limits on planning. In addition, a firm might be unable to compute inventory shortages (due to pilferage and unrecorded breakage) because ending inventory value is set by adding the costs of all items in stock. It does not compute what the ending inventory *should be*.

A Book Inventory System Using the Cost Method

View Skandata's online perpetual inventory screens (**www.skandata.com/invdemo.html**) or download a "Demo."

A **book (perpetual) inventory system** avoids the problem of infrequent financial analysis by keeping a running total of the value of all inventory on hand at cost at a given time. End-of-month inventory values can be computed without a physical inventory, and frequent financial statements can be prepared. In addition, a book inventory lets a retailer uncover stock shortages by comparing projected inventory values with actual inventory values through a physical inventory.[3]

At its Web site, LIFO Systems (**www.lifosystems.com/publications/educational.htm**) provides good background information.

A book inventory is kept by regularly recording purchases and adding them to existing inventory value; sales are subtracted to arrive at the new current inventory value (all at cost). Table 16-2 shows Handy Hardware's book inventory system for July 1, 2006, through December 31, 2006; the beginning inventory in Table 16-2 is the ending inventory from Table 16-1. Table 16-2 assumes that merchandise costs are rather constant and monthly sales at cost are easy to compute. Yet, suppose merchandise costs rise. How would inventory value then be computed?

FIFO and LIFO are two ways to value inventory. The **FIFO (first-in-first-out) method** logically assumes old merchandise is sold first, while newer items remain in inventory. The **LIFO (last-in-first-out) method** assumes new merchandise is sold first, while older stock remains in inventory. FIFO matches inventory value

TABLE 16-2	Handy Hardware Store Perpetual Inventory System, July 1, 2006–December 31, 2006ᵃ			
Date	Beginning-of-Month Inventory (at Cost)	+ Net Monthly Purchases (at Cost)	− Monthly Sales (at Cost)	= End-of-Month Inventory (at Cost)
7/1/06	$90,500	$ 40,000	$ 62,400	$ 68,100
8/1/06	68,100	28,000	38,400	57,700
9/1/06	57,700	27,600	28,800	56,500
10/1/06	56,500	44,000	28,800	71,700
11/1/06	71,700	50,400	40,800	81,300
12/1/06	81,300	15,900	61,200	36,000
	Total	$205,900	$260,400	(as of 12/31/06)

ᵃTransportation charges are not included in computing inventory value in this table.

with the current cost structure—the goods in inventory are the ones bought most recently, while LIFO matches current sales with the current cost structure—the goods sold first are the ones bought most recently. When inventory values rise, LIFO offers retailers a tax advantage because lower profits are shown.

In Figure 16-1, the FIFO and LIFO methods are illustrated for Handy Hardware's snow blowers for 2006; the store carries only one model of snow blower. Handy knows that it sold 220 snow blowers in 2006 at an average price of $320. It began 2006 with an inventory of 30 snow blowers, purchased for $150 each. During January 2006, it bought 100 snow blowers at $175 each; from October

FIGURE 16-1
Applying FIFO and LIFO Inventory Methods to Handy Hardware, January 1, 2006–December 31, 2006

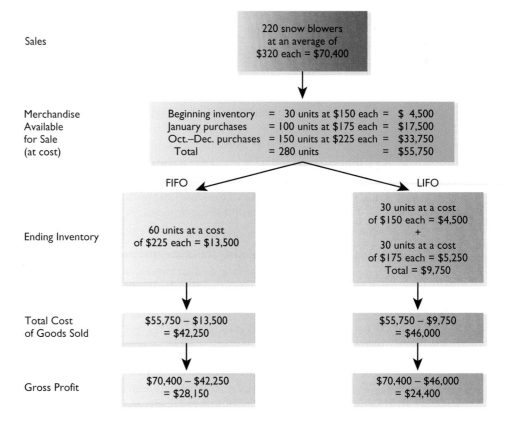

to December 2006, Handy bought another 150 snow blowers for $225 apiece. Because Handy sold 220 snow blowers in 2006, as of the close of business on December 31, it had 60 units remaining.

With the FIFO method, Handy assumes its beginning inventory and initial purchases were sold first. The 60 snow blowers remaining in inventory would have a cost value of $225 each, a total cost of goods sold of $42,250, and a gross profit of $28,150. With the LIFO method, Handy assumes the most recently purchased items were sold first and the remaining inventory would consist of beginning goods and early purchases. Of the snow blowers remaining in inventory, 30 would have a cost value of $150 each and 30 a cost value of $175 apiece, resulting in a total cost of goods sold of $46,000 and a gross profit of $24,400. The FIFO method presents a more accurate picture of the cost of goods sold and the true cost value of ending inventory. The LIFO method indicates a lower profit, leading to the payment of lower taxes but an understated ending inventory value at cost.

The retail method of inventory, which combines FIFO and LIFO concepts, is explained shortly.

Disadvantages of Cost-Based Inventory Systems

Cost-based physical and book systems have significant disadvantages. First, both require that a cost be assigned to each item in stock (and to each item sold). When merchandise costs change, cost-based valuation systems work best for firms with low inventory turnover, limited assortments, and high average prices—such as car dealers.

Second, neither cost-based method adjusts inventory values to reflect style changes, end-of-season markdowns, or sudden surges of demand (which may raise prices). Thus, ending inventory value based on merchandise cost may not reflect its actual worth. This discrepancy could be troublesome if inventory value is used in filing insurance claims for losses.

Despite these factors, retailers that make the products they sell—such as bakeries, restaurants, and furniture showrooms—often keep records on a cost basis. A department store with these operations can use the cost method for them and the retail method for other areas.

The Retail Method

See a retail-world application of the retail method (**www.reacct software.com/rm_over. html**).

With the **retail method of accounting**, closing inventory value is determined by calculating the average relationship between the cost and retail values of merchandise available for sale during a period. Though the retail method overcomes the disadvantages of the cost method, it requires detailed records and is more complex since ending inventory is first valued in retail dollars and then converted to compute gross margin (gross profit).

There are three basic steps to determine ending inventory value by the retail method:

1. Calculating the cost complement.
2. Calculating deductions from retail value.
3. Converting retail inventory value to cost.

Calculating the Cost Complement

The value of beginning inventory, net purchases, additional markups, and transportation charges are all included in the retail method. Beginning inventory and net purchase amounts (purchases less returns) are recorded at both cost and retail levels. Additional markups represent the extra revenues received when a retailer

TABLE 16-3	Handy Hardware Store, Calculating Merchandise Available for Sale at Cost and at Retail, July 1, 2006–December 31, 2006	

	At Cost	At Retail
Beginning inventory	$ 90,500	$139,200
Net purchases	205,900	340,526
Additional markups	—	16,400
Transportation charges	3,492	—
Total merchandise available for sale	$299,892	$496,126

increases selling prices, due to inflation or unexpectedly high demand. Transportation charges are the retailer's costs for shipping the goods it buys from suppliers to the retailer. Table 16-3 shows the total merchandise available for sale at cost and at retail for Handy Hardware from July 1, 2006, through December 31, 2006, using the costs in Table 16-2.

By using Table 16-3 data, the average relationship of cost to retail value for all merchandise available for sale by Handy Hardware—the **cost complement**—can be computed:

$$\text{Cost complement} = \frac{\text{Total cost valuation}}{\text{Total retail valuation}}$$

$$= \frac{\$299,892}{\$496,126} = 0.6045$$

Because the cost complement is 0.6045 (60.45 percent), on average, 60.45 cents of every retail sales dollar went to cover Handy Hardware's merchandise cost.

Calculating Deductions from Retail Value

The ending retail value of inventory must reflect all deductions from the total merchandise available for sale at retail. Besides sales, deductions include markdowns (for special sales and end-of-season goods), employee discounts, and stock shortages (due to pilferage and unrecorded breakage). Although sales, markdowns, and employee discounts can be recorded throughout an accounting period, a physical inventory is needed to learn about stock shortages.

From Table 16-3, it is known that Handy Hardware had a retail value of merchandise available for sale of $496,126 for the period from July 1, 2006, through December 31, 2006. As shown in Table 16-4, this was reduced by sales of $422,540

TABLE 16-4	Handy Hardware Store, Computing Ending Retail Book Value, as of December 31, 2006	

Merchandise available for sale (at retail)		$496,126
Less deductions:		
Sales	$422,540	
Markdowns	11,634	
Employee discounts	2,400	
Total deductions		436,574
Ending retail book value of inventory		$ 59,552

TABLE 16-5	Handy Hardware Store, Computing Stock Shortages and Adjusting Retail Book Value, as of December 31, 2006	
Ending retail book value of inventory		$59,552
Physical inventory (at retail)		56,470
Stock shortages (at retail)		3,082
Adjusted ending retail book value of inventory		$56,470

and recorded markdowns and employee discounts of $14,034. The ending book value of inventory at retail as of December 31, 2006, was $59,552.

To compute stock shortages, the retail book value of ending inventory is compared with the actual physical ending inventory at retail. If book inventory exceeds physical inventory, a shortage exists. Table 16-5 shows the results of Handy's physical inventory. Shortages were $3,082 (at retail), and book value was adjusted accordingly. While Handy knows the shortages were from pilferage, bookkeeping errors, and overshipments not billed to customers, it cannot learn the proportion of shortages from each factor.

Occasionally, a physical inventory may reveal a stock overage—an excess of physical inventory value over book value. This may be due to errors in a physical inventory or in keeping a book inventory. If overages occur, ending retail book value is adjusted upward. Inasmuch as a retailer has to conduct a physical inventory to compute shortages (overages), and a physical inventory is usually taken only once or twice a year, shortages (overages) are often estimated for monthly merchandise budgets.

Converting Retail Inventory Value to Cost

The retailer must next convert the adjusted ending retail book value of inventory to cost so as to compute dollar gross profit (gross margin). The ending inventory at cost equals the adjusted ending retail book value multiplied by the cost complement. For Handy Hardware, this was:

Ending inventory = Adjusted ending retail book value × Cost complement
  (at cost)
$$= \$56,470 \times .6045 = \$34,136$$

This computation does not yield the exact inventory cost. It shows the average relationship between cost and the retail selling price for all merchandise available for sale.

The adjusted ending inventory at cost can be used to find gross profit. As Table 16-6 shows, Handy's six-month cost of goods sold was $265,756, resulting in gross profit of $156,784. By deducting operating expenses of $139,000, Handy learns that the net profit before taxes for this period was $17,784.

Advantages of the Retail Method

Compared to other techniques, there are several advantages to the retail method of accounting:

- Valuation errors are reduced when conducting a physical inventory since merchandise value is recorded at retail and costs do not have to be decoded.

TABLE 16-6	Handy Hardware Store Profit-and-Loss Statement, July 1, 2006–December 31, 2006

Sales		$422,540
Less cost of goods sold:		
Total merchandise available for sale (at cost)	$299,892	
Adjusted ending inventory (at cost)[a]	34,136	
Cost of goods sold		265,756
Gross profit		$156,784
Less operating expenses:		
Salaries	$ 70,000	
Advertising	25,000	
Rental	16,000	
Other	28,000	
Total operating expenses		139,000
Net profit before taxes		$ 17,784

[a]Adjusted ending inventory (at cost) = Adjusted retail book value × Cost complement = $56,470 × .6045 = $34,136.

- Because the process is simpler, a physical inventory can be completed more often. This lets a firm be more aware of slow-moving items and stock shortages.

- The physical inventory method at cost requires a physical inventory to prepare a profit-and-loss statement. The retail method lets a firm set up a profit-and-loss statement based on book inventory. The retailer can then estimate the stock shortages between physical inventories and study departmental profit trends.

- A complete record of ending book values helps determine insurance coverage and settle insurance claims. The retail book method gives an estimate of inventory value throughout the year. Since physical inventories are usually taken when merchandise levels are low, the book value at retail lets retailers plan insurance coverage for peak periods and shows the values of goods on hand. The retail method is accepted in insurance claims.

Limitations of the Retail Method

The greatest weakness is the bookkeeping burden of recording data. Ending book inventory figures can be correctly computed only if the following are accurately noted: the value of beginning inventory (at cost and at retail), purchases (at cost and at retail), shipping charges, markups, markdowns, employee discounts, transfers from other departments or stores, returns, and sales. Although personnel are freed from taking many physical inventories, ending book value at retail may be inaccurate unless all required data are precisely recorded. With computerization, this potential problem is lessened.

Another limitation is that the cost complement is an average based on the total cost of merchandise available for sale and total retail value. The ending cost value only approximates the true inventory value. This may cause misinformation if fast-selling items have different markups from slow-selling items or if there are wide variations among the markups of different goods.

Familiarity with the retail and cost methods of inventory is essential for understanding the financial merchandise management material described in the balance of this chapter.

Ethics in
R E T A I L I N G

Auto Dealers and Ethics: Not an Oxymoron

Ethical behavior by auto dealers is increasingly important as consumers become more knowledgeable due to information on the Web—and as auto retailing becomes a more popular target of regulators and attorneys. Two ways for car dealers to instill ethical behavior among their sales personnel involve rethinking sales force compensation and re-examining how car dealers operate as business leaders.

Traditionally, many salespeople have been paid on the basis of the gross margin of each sale. That encourages a salesperson to inflate the sales price to an unsuspecting consumer or to push high-profit, dealer-installed options. Alternative methods are to place fixed prices on cars, to provide bonuses to sales staff based on customer satisfaction scores, or to link bonuses to referral and repeat business.

As the leader–manager, the owner of a dealership should set an example for the practices of his or her employees. The firm's code of ethics needs to reflect what behavior is unacceptable, including high-pressure tactics and misrepresentation of price or credit. Salespeople who continually violate the ethical code should be terminated regardless of their profitability.

Sources: Donna Harris, "Only Dealers Can Instill Ethics," *Automotive News* (September 20, 2004), p. 14; and "Find a Car: NADA Code of Ethics," **www.nada.org** (April 5, 2006).

MERCHANDISE FORECASTING AND BUDGETING: DOLLAR CONTROL

As we noted earlier, dollar control entails planning and monitoring a firm's inventory investment over time. Figure 16-2 shows the six-step dollar control process for merchandise forecasting and budgeting. This process should be followed sequentially since a change in one stage affects all the stages after it. If a sales forecast is too low, a firm may run out of items because it does not plan to have enough merchandise during a selling season and planned purchases will also be too low.

Visit our Web site (**www.prenhall.com/bermanevans**) for a detailed listing of links related to both dollar control and unit control in merchandise management.

Designating Control Units

Merchandise forecasting and budgeting requires the selection of **control units**, the merchandise categories for which data are gathered. Such classifications must be narrow enough to isolate opportunities and problems with specific merchandise lines. A retailer wishing to control goods within departments must record data on dollar allotments separately for each category.

Knowing that total markdowns in a department are 20 percent above last year's level is less valuable than knowing the specific merchandise lines in which large markdowns are being taken. A retailer can broaden its control system by combining categories that comprise a department. However, a broad category cannot be broken down into components.

It is helpful to select control units consistent with other company and trade association data. Internal comparisons are meaningful only when categories are

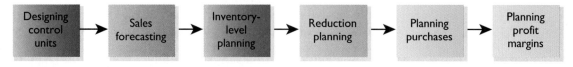

FIGURE 16-2
The Merchandise Forecasting and Budgeting Process: Dollar Control

stable. Classifications that shift over time do not permit comparisons. External comparisons are not meaningful if control units are dissimilar for a retailer and its trade associations. Control units may be based on departments, classifications within departments, price line classifications, and standard merchandise classifications. A discussion of each follows.

The broadest practical classification for financial record keeping is the department, which lets a retailer assess each general merchandise grouping or buyer. Even the small Handy Hardware needs to acquire data on a departmental basis (tools and equipment, supplies, housewares, and so on) for buying, inventory control, and markdown decisions.

To obtain more financial data, **classification merchandising** can be used, whereby each department is subdivided into further categories for related types of merchandise. In planning its tools and equipment department, Handy Hardware can keep financial records on both overall departmental performance and the results of such categories as lawn mowers/snow blowers, power tools, hand tools, and ladders.

A special form of classification merchandising uses *price line classifications*—sales, inventories, and purchases are analyzed by price category. This helps if different models of a product are sold at different prices to different target markets (such as Handy's having $20 power tools for do-it-yourselfers and $135 models for contractors). Retailers with deep assortments most often use price line control.

To best contrast its data with industry averages, a firm's merchandise categories should conform to those cited in trade publications. The National Retail Federation devised a *standard merchandise classification* with common reporting categories for a range of retailers and products. It annually produces *Retail Horizons*, using its classifications. Specific classifications are also popular for some retailers. *Progressive Grocer* regularly publishes data based on standard classifications for supermarkets.

Once appropriate dollar control units are set, all transactions—including sales, purchases, transfers, markdowns, and employee discounts—must be recorded under the proper classification number. Thus, if house paint is Department 25 and brushes are 25-1, all transactions must carry these designations.

Sales Forecasting

Manhattan Associates (**www.evant.com/library/ read.html**) has aided many retailers with forecasting.

A retailer estimates its expected future revenues for a given period by *sales forecasting*. Forecasts may be companywide, departmental, and for individual merchandise classifications. Perhaps the most important step in financial merchandise planning is accurate sales forecasting, because an incorrect projection of sales throws off the entire process. That is why many retailers have state-of-the art forecasting systems. Longs Drug Stores has dramatically improved its cash flow by using a system from Evant.[4]

Larger retailers often forecast total and department sales by techniques such as trend analysis, time series analysis, and multiple regression analysis. A discussion of these techniques is beyond the scope of this book. Small retailers rely more on "guesstimates," projections based on experience. Even for larger firms, sales forecasting for merchandise classifications within departments (or price lines) relies on more qualitative methods. One way to forecast sales for narrow categories is first to project sales on a company basis and by department, and then to break down figures judgmentally into merchandise classifications.

External factors, internal company factors, and seasonal trends must be anticipated and taken into account. Among the external factors that can affect projected sales are consumer trends, competitors' actions, the state of the economy, the weather, and new supplier offerings. For example, Planalytics offers a patented

TABLE 16-7	Handy Hardware Store, A Simple Sales Forecast Using Product Control Units		
Product Control Units	Actual Sales 2006	Projected Growth/ Decline (%)	Sales Forecast 2007
Lawn mowers/snow blowers	$200,000	+10.0	$220,000
Paint and supplies	128,000	+3.0	131,840
Hardware supplies	108,000	+8.0	116,640
Plumbing supplies	88,000	−4.0	84,480
Power tools	88,000	+6.0	93,280
Garden supplies/chemicals	68,000	+4.0	70,720
Housewares	48,000	−6.0	45,120
Electrical supplies	40,000	+4.0	41,600
Ladders	36,000	+6.0	38,160
Hand tools	36,000	+9.0	39,240
Total year	$840,000	+4.9[a]	$881,080

[a]There is a small rounding error.

methodology to analyze and forecast the relationship among consumer demand, store traffic, and the weather.[5] Internal company factors that can impact on future sales include additions and deletions of merchandise lines, revised promotion and credit policies, changes in hours, new outlets, and store remodeling. With many retailers, seasonality must be considered in setting monthly or quarterly sales forecasts. Handy's yearly snow blower sales should not be estimated from December sales alone.

A sales forecast can be developed by examining past trends and projecting future growth (based on external and internal factors). Table 16-7 shows a forecast for Handy Hardware. It is an estimate, subject to revisions. Various factors may be hard to incorporate when devising a forecast, such as merchandise shortages, consumer reactions to new products, the rate of inflation, and new government legislation. That is why a financial merchandise plan needs some flexibility.

After a yearly forecast is derived, it should be broken into quarters or months. In retailing, monthly forecasts are usually required. Jewelry stores know December accounts for nearly one-quarter of annual sales, while drugstores know December sales are slightly better than average. Stationery stores and card stores realize that Christmas cards generate 60 percent of seasonal greeting card sales, while Valentine's Day cards are second with about 25 percent.[6]

To acquire more specific estimates, a retailer could use a **monthly sales index**, which divides each month's actual sales by average monthly sales and multiplies the results by 100. Table 16-8 shows Handy Hardware's 2006 actual monthly sales and monthly sales indexes. The store is seasonal, with peaks in late spring and early summer (for lawn mowers, garden supplies, and so on), as well as December (for lighting fixtures, snow blowers, and gifts). Average monthly 2006 sales were $70,000 ($840,000/12). Thus, the monthly sales index for January is 67 [($46,800/ $70,000) × 100]; other monthly indexes are computed similarly. Each monthly index shows the percentage deviation of that month's sales from the average month's. A May index of 160 means May sales are 60 percent higher than average. An October index of 67 means sales in October are 33 percent below average.

TABLE 16-8	Handy Hardware Store, 2006 Sales by Month	
Month	Monthly Actual Sales	Sales Index[a]
January	$46,800	67
February	40,864	58
March	48,000	69
April	65,600	94
May	112,196	160
June	103,800	148
July	104,560	149
August	62,800	90
September	46,904	67
October	46,800	67
November	66,884	96
December	94,792	135
Total yearly sales	$840,000	
Average monthly sales	$ 70,000	
Average monthly index		100

[a]Monthly sales index = (Monthly sales/Average monthly sales) × 100.

Once monthly sales indexes are determined, a retailer can forecast monthly sales, based on the yearly sales forecast. Table 16-9 shows how Handy's 2007 monthly sales can be forecast if average monthly sales are expected to be $73,423.

Inventory-Level Planning

LogicTools (www.logic-tools.com) offers software such as Inventory Analyst to enhance inventory planning.

At this point, a retailer plans its inventory. The level must be sufficient to meet sales expectations, allowing a margin for error. Techniques to plan inventory levels are the basic stock, percentage variation, weeks' supply, and stock-to-sales methods.

With the **basic stock method**, a retailer carries more items than it expects to sell over a specified period. There is a cushion if sales are more than anticipated, shipments are delayed, or customers want to select from a variety of items. It is best when inventory turnover is low or sales are erratic over the year. Beginning-of-month planned inventory equals planned sales plus a basic stock amount:

Basic stock (at retail) = Average monthly stock at retail − Average monthly sales

Beginning-of-month planned inventory level (at retail) = Planned monthly sales + Basic stock

If Handy Hardware, with an average monthly 2007 forecast of $73,423, wants extra stock equal to 10 percent of its average monthly forecast and expects January 2007 sales to be $49,193:

Basic stock (at retail) = ($73,423 × 1.10) − $73,423 = $7,342

Beginning-of-January planned inventory level (at retail) = $49,193 + $7,342 = $56,535

TABLE 16-9	Handy Hardware Store, 2007 Sales Forecast by Month

Month	Actual Sales 2006	Monthly Sales Index	Monthly Sales Forecast for 2007[a]
January	$ 46,800	67	$73,423 × .67 = $ 49,193
February	40,864	58	73,423 × .58 = 42,585
March	48,000	69	73,423 × .69 = 50,662
April	65,600	94	73,423 × .94 = 69,018
May	112,196	160	73,423 × 1.60 = 117,477
June	103,800	148	73,423 × 1.48 = 108,666
July	104,560	149	73,423 × 1.49 = 109,400
August	62,800	90	73,423 × .90 = 66,081
September	46,904	67	73,423 × .67 = 49,193
October	46,800	67	73,423 × .67 = 49,193
November	66,884	96	73,423 × .96 = 70,486
December	94,792	135	73,423 × 1.35 = 99,121
Total sales	$840,000		Total sales forecast $881,080[b]
Average monthly sales	$70,000		Average monthly forecast $ 73,423

[a]Monthly sales forecast = Average monthly forecast × (Monthly index/100). In this equation, the monthly index is computed as a fraction of 1.00 rather than 100.
[b]There is a small rounding error.

In the **percentage variation method**, beginning-of-month planned inventory during any month differs from planned average monthly stock by only one-half of that month's variation from estimated average monthly sales. This method is recommended if stock turnover is more than six times a year or relatively stable, since it results in planned inventories closer to the monthly average than other techniques:

$$\begin{array}{c} \text{Beginning-of-month} \\ \text{planned inventory level} = \\ \text{(at retail)} \end{array} \begin{array}{c} \text{Planned average monthly stock at retail} \\ \times \; 1/2 \, [1 + (\text{Estimated monthly sales/} \\ \text{Estimated average monthly sales})] \end{array}$$

If Handy Hardware plans average monthly stock of $80,765 and November 2007 sales are expected to be 4 percent less than average monthly sales of $73,423, the store's planned inventory level at the beginning of November 2007 would be:

$$\begin{array}{c} \text{Beginning-of-November} \\ \text{planned inventory level} \\ \text{(at retail)} \end{array} = \$80{,}765 \times 1/2 \, [1 + (\$70{,}487/\$73{,}423)] = \$79{,}150$$

Handy Hardware should not use this method due to its variable sales. If it did, Handy would plan a beginning-of-December 2007 inventory of $94,899, less than expected sales ($99,121).

The **weeks' supply method** forecasts average sales weekly, so beginning inventory equals several weeks' expected sales. It assumes inventory is in proportion to sales. Too much merchandise may be stocked in peak periods and too little during slow periods:

$$\begin{array}{c} \text{Beginning-of-month} \\ \text{planned inventory level} = \\ \text{(at retail)} \end{array} \begin{array}{c} \text{Average estimated} \\ \text{weekly sales} \end{array} \times \begin{array}{c} \text{Number of weeks} \\ \text{to be stocked} \end{array}$$

If Handy Hardware forecasts average weekly sales of $10,956.92 from January 1, 2007, through March 31, 2007, and it wants to stock 13 weeks of merchandise (based on expected turnover), beginning inventory would be $142,440:

$$\begin{array}{c} \text{Beginning-of-January} \\ \text{planned inventory level} = \$10{,}956.92 \times 13 = \$142{,}440 \\ \text{(at retail)} \end{array}$$

With the **stock-to-sales method**, a retailer wants to maintain a specified ratio of goods on hand to sales. A ratio of 1.3 means that if Handy Hardware plans sales of $69,018 in April 2007, it should have $89,723 worth of merchandise (at retail) available during the month. Like the weeks' supply method, this approach tends to adjust inventory more drastically than changes in sales require.

Yearly stock-to-sales ratios by retail type are provided by sources such as *Industry Norms & Key Business Ratios* (New York: Dun & Bradstreet) and *Annual Statement Studies* (Philadelphia: RMA). A retailer can, thus, compare its ratios with other firms'.

Reduction Planning

Besides forecasting sales, a firm should estimate its expected **retail reductions**, which represent the difference between beginning inventory plus purchases during the period and sales plus ending inventory. Planned reductions incorporate anticipated markdowns (discounts to stimulate sales), employee and other discounts (price cuts to employees, senior citizens, and others), and stock shortages (pilferage, breakage, and bookkeeping errors):

$$\text{Planned reductions} = \begin{array}{c} (\text{Beginning inventory} + \text{Planned purchases}) \\ - (\text{Planned sales} + \text{Ending inventory}) \end{array}$$

Reduction planning revolves around two key factors: estimating expected total reductions by budget period and assigning the estimates monthly. The following should be considered in planning reductions: past experience, markdown data for similar retailers, changes in company policies, merchandise carryover from one budget period to another, price trends, and stock-shortage trends.

Past experience is a good starting point. This information can then be compared with the performance of similar firms—by reviewing data on markdowns, discounts, and stock shortages in trade publications. A retailer with higher markdowns than competitors could investigate and correct the situation by adjusting its buying practices and price levels or training sales personnel better.

A retailer must consider its own procedures in reviewing reductions. Policy changes often affect the quantity and timing of markdowns. If a firm expands its assortment of seasonal and fashion merchandise, this would probably lead to a rise in markdowns.

Merchandise carryover, price trends, and stock-shortage trends also affect planning. If such items as gloves and antifreeze are stocked in off seasons, markdowns are often not used to clear out inventory. Yet, the carryover of fad items merely postpones reductions. Price trends of product categories have a strong impact on reductions. Many full computer systems now sell for less than $1,000, down considerably from prior years. This means higher-priced computers must be marked down. Recent stock shortage trends (determined by comparing prior book and physical inventory values) can be used to project future reductions due to employee, customer, and vendor theft; breakage; and bookkeeping mistakes. If a firm has total stock shortages of less than 2 percent of annual sales, it is usually deemed to be doing well. Figure 16-3 shows a checklist to reduce shortages from clerical and handling errors. Suggestions for reducing shortages from theft were covered in Chapter 15.

After determining total reductions, they must be planned by month because reductions as a percentage of sales are not the same during each month. Stock shortages may be much higher during busy periods, when stores are more crowded and transactions happen more quickly.

Planning Purchases

The formula for calculating planned purchases for a period is:

$$\text{Planned purchases (at retail)} = \begin{array}{l} \text{Planned sales for the month} + \text{Planned reductions for the month} \\ + \text{Planned end-of-month stock} - \text{Beginning-of-month stock} \end{array}$$

If Handy Hardware projects June 2007 sales to be $108,666 and total planned reductions to be 5 percent of sales, plans end-of-month inventory at retail to be $72,000, and has a beginning-of-month inventory at retail of $80,000, planned purchases for June are

$$\text{Planned purchases (at retail)} = \$108,666 + \$5,433 + \$72,000 - \$80,000 = \$106,099$$

Because Handy Hardware expects 2007 merchandise costs to be about 60 percent of retail selling price, its plan is to purchase $63,659 of goods at cost in June 2007:

$$\begin{array}{l} \text{Planned purchases (at cost)} = \begin{array}{l} \text{Planned purchases at retail} \\ \times \text{Merchandise costs as a percentage of selling price} \end{array} \\ = \$106,099 \times 0.60 = \$63,659 \end{array}$$

Open-to-buy is the difference between planned purchases and the purchase commitments already made by a buyer for a given period, often a month. It

FIGURE 16-3
A Checklist to Reduce
Inventory Shortages Due to
Clerical and Handling Errors

Answer yes or no to each of the following questions. A no means corrective action must be taken.

Buying
1. Is the exact quantity of merchandise purchased always specified in the contract?
2. Are special purchase terms clearly noted?
3. Are returns to the vendor recorded properly?

Marking
4. Are retail prices clearly and correctly marked on merchandise?
5. Are markdowns and additional markups recorded by item number and quantity?
6. Does a cashier check with a manager if a price is not marked on an item?
7. Are old price tags removed when an item's price changes?

Handling
8. After receipt, are purchase quantities checked against the order?
9. Is merchandise handled in a systematic manner?
10. Are items sold in bulk (such as produce, sugar, candy) measured accurately?
11. Are damaged, soiled, returned, or other special goods handled separately?

Selling
12. Do sales personnel know correct prices or have easy access to them?
13. Are misrings by cashiers made on a very small percentage of sales?
14. Are special terms noted on sales receipts (such as employee discounts)?
15. Are sales receipts numbered and later checked for missing invoices?

Inventory Planning
16. Is a physical inventory conducted at least annually and is a book inventory kept throughout the year?
17. Are the differences between physical inventory and book inventory always explained?

Accounting
18. Are permanent records on all transactions kept and monitored for accuracy?
19. Are both retail and cost data maintained?
20. Are inventory shortages compared with industry averages?

Take an online tour of *The OTB Book* (www.otb-retail.com/tour1.htm).

represents the amount the buyer has left to spend for that month and is reduced each time a purchase is made. At the beginning of a month, a firm's planned purchases and open-to-buy are equal if no purchase commitments have been made before that month starts. Open-to-buy is recorded at cost.

At Handy Hardware, the buyer has made purchase commitments for June 2007 in the amount of $55,000 at retail. Accordingly, Handy's open-to-buy at retail for June is $51,099:

$$\text{Open-to-buy} \atop \text{(at retail)} = \begin{array}{l} \text{Planned purchases for the month} \\ - \text{ Purchase commitments for that month} \end{array}$$

$$= \$106,099 - \$55,000 = \$51,099$$

To calculate the June 2007 open-to-buy at cost, $51,099 is multiplied by Handy Hardware's merchandise costs as a percentage of selling price:

$$\text{Open-to-buy} \atop \text{(at cost)} = \begin{array}{l} \text{Open-to-buy at retail} \\ \times \text{ Merchandise costs as a percentage of selling price} \end{array}$$

$$= \$51,099 \times 0.60 = \$30,659$$

The open-to-buy concept has two major strengths: (1) It maintains a specified relationship between inventory and planned sales; this avoids overbuying and underbuying. (2) It lets a firm adjust purchases to reflect changes in sales, markdowns, and so on. If Handy revises its June 2007 sales forecast to $120,000 (from $108,666), it automatically increases planned purchases and open-to-buy by $11,334 at retail and $6,800 at cost.

It is advisable for a retailer to keep at least a small open-to-buy figure for as long as possible—to take advantage of special deals, purchase new models when introduced, and fill in items that sell out. An open-to-buy limit sometimes must be exceeded due to underestimated demand (low sales forecasts). A retailer should not be so rigid that merchandising personnel are unable to have the discretion (employee empowerment) to purchase below-average-priced items when the open-to-buy is not really open.

Planning Profit Margins

In preparing a profitable merchandise budget, a retailer must consider planned net sales, retail operating expenses, profit, and retail reductions in pricing merchandise:

$$\text{Required initial markup percentage} = \frac{\text{Planned retail expenses} + \text{Planned profit} + \text{Planned reductions}}{\text{Planned net sales} + \text{Planned reductions}}$$

The required markup is a companywide average. Individual items may be priced according to demand and other factors, as long as the average is met. A fuller markup discussion is in Chapter 17. The concept of initial markup is introduced here for continuity in the description of merchandise budgeting.

Handy has an overall 2007 sales forecast of $881,080 and expects annual expenses to be $290,000. Reductions are projected at $44,000. The total net dollar profit margin goal is $60,000 (6.8 percent of sales). Its required initial markup is 42.6 percent:

$$\text{Required initial markup percentage} = \frac{\$290,000 + \$60,000 + \$44,000}{\$881,080 + \$44,000} = 42.6\%$$

$$\text{Required initial markup percentage (all factors expressed as a percentage of net sales)} = \frac{32.9\% + 6.8\% + 5.0\%}{100.0\% + 5.0\%} = 42.6\%$$

UNIT CONTROL SYSTEMS

RWS Information Systems offers unit control software capabilities in its POS-IM program (**www.rwsinfo.com/ invcon2.html**).

Unit control systems deal with quantities of merchandise in units rather than in dollars. Information typically reveals

- Items selling well and those selling poorly.
- Opportunities and problems in terms of price, color, style, size, and so on.
- The quantity of goods on hand (if book inventory is used). This minimizes overstocking and understocking.
- An indication of inventory age, highlighting candidates for markdowns or promotions.

- The optimal time to reorder merchandise.
- Experiences with alternative sources (vendors) when problems arise.
- The level of inventory and sales for each item in every store branch. This improves the transfer of goods between branches and alerts salespeople as to which branches have desired products. Also, less stock can be held in individual stores, reducing costs.

Physical Inventory Systems

A *physical inventory unit control system* is similar to a physical inventory dollar control system. However, the latter is concerned with the financial value of inventory, while a unit control system looks at the number of units by item classification. With unit control, inventory levels are monitored either by visual inspection or actual count. See Figure 16-4.

In a visual inspection system, merchandise is placed on pegboard (or similar) displays, with each item numbered on the back or on a stock card. Minimum inventory quantities are noted, and sales personnel reorder when inventory reaches the minimum level. This is accurate only if items are placed in numerical

FIGURE 16-4
Physical Inventory Systems Made Simpler

Taking a physical inventory using a Retail Pro portable terminal takes only a fraction of the time required for a traditional manual count. It also yields a more accurate result. After each scan with the laser gun, the physical count is recorded in the portable terminal. Once a section of inventory is complete, an employee connects the portable terminal to a computer and Retail Pro compares the recorded inventory with the physical counts. Any discrepancies are immediately isolated and reported. When the firm is ready, it can automatically adjust the recorded inventory to reflect the physical counts and record this adjustment. The portable terminal can also perform quantity and price verifications by pre-loading inventory quantity and price information. When merchandise is scanned, the unit displays the correct retail price and the expected quantity on hand. This makes it easy to detect pricing errors and missing merchandise.

Photo reprinted by permission of Retail Technologies International.

order on displays (and sold accordingly). The system is used in the housewares and hardware displays of various discount and hardware stores. Although easy to maintain and inexpensive, it does not provide data on the rate of sales of individual items. And minimum stock quantities may be arbitrarily defined and not drawn from in-depth analysis.

The other physical inventory system, actual counting, means regularly compiling the number of units on hand. This approach records—in units—inventory on hand, purchases, sales volume, and shortages during specified periods. A stock-counting system requires more clerical work but lets a firm obtain sales data for given periods and stock-to-sales relationships as of the time of each count. A physical system is not as sophisticated as a book system. It is more useful with low-value items having predictable sales. Handy Hardware could use the system for its insulation tape:

	Number of Rolls of Tape for the Period 12/1/06–12/31/06
Beginning inventory, December 1, 2006	100
Total purchases for period	70
Total units available for sale	170
Closing inventory, December 31, 2006	60
Sales and shortages for period	110

Perpetual Inventory Systems

A *perpetual inventory unit control system* keeps a running total of the number of units handled by a retailer through record keeping entries that adjust for sales, returns, transfers to other departments or stores, receipt of shipments, and other transactions. All additions to and subtractions from beginning inventory are recorded. Such a system can be applied manually, use merchandise tags processed by computers, or rely on point-of-sale devices such as optical scanners.

A manual system requires employees to gather data by examining sales checks, merchandise receipts, transfer requests, and other documents. Data are then coded and tabulated. A merchandise tagging system relies on pre-printed tags with data by department, classification, vendor, style, date of receipt, color,

FIGURE 16-5
How Does a UPC-Based
Scanner System work?

When a scanner is passed over an item with a UPC symbol, that symbol is read by a low-energy laser. The UPC symbol consists of a series of vertical lines, with numbers below them. Each product has its own unique identification code, and the price is not in the symbol. Scanned information is transmitted to an in-store computer that identifies the item and searches its memory for the current price. This information is then sent back to the checkout terminal.

Photo reprinted by permission of Beeline Shopper.

Want to look up a UPC code? Go here (www. upcdatabase.com/item.pl).

and/or material. When an item is sold, a copy of the tag is removed and sent to a tabulating facility for computer analysis. Since pre-printed tags are processed in batches, they can be used by smaller retailers that subscribe to service bureaus and by branches of chains (with data processed at a central location). Point-of-sale (POS) systems feed data from merchandise tags or product labels directly to in-store computers for immediate data processing. Computer-based systems are quicker, more accurate, and of higher quality than manual ones.

Newer POS systems are easy to network, have battery backup capabilities, and run on standard components. Many of these systems use optical scanners to transfer data from products to computers by wands or other devices that pass over sensitized strips on the items. Figure 16-5 shows how barcoding works. As noted earlier, the UPC is the dominant format for coding data onto merchandise. This is how to interpret a barcode:

(1) The *number system* uses two digits (sometimes three digits) to identify the country (or economic region) numbering authority which assigns the manufacturer code. In the traditional UPC code, the first digit is 0, and it is not displayed on the label. (2) The *manufacturer code* is a unique code assigned to each manufacturer by the numbering authority indicated by the number system code. All products from a given firm use the same manufacturer code, which is typically 5 digits. (3) The *product code* is a unique code assigned by the manufacturer. Unlike its assigned manufacturer code, the manufacturer is free to assign 5-digit product codes to each of their products without consulting any other organization. (4) The *check digit* is an additional digit used to verify that a barcode has been scanned correctly. It is calculated based on the rest of the digits of the barcode.[7]

Many retailers combine perpetual and physical systems, whereby items accounting for a large proportion of sales are controlled by a perpetual system and other items are controlled by a physical inventory system. Thus, attention is properly placed on the retailer's most important products.

Unit Control Systems in Practice

Conducting a physical inventory is extremely time-consuming and labor-intensive. It is also crucial: "Having too much stock, or too little, is costly." The National Retail Federation has found that each year retailers in the United States lose about $225 billion due to excessive inventory and $45 billion from not having sufficient inventory on hand.[8] According to an inventory management practices survey of department stores, discount stores, specialty apparel stores, supermarkets, drugstores, and home centers:

- 94 percent of the firms engage in "wall to wall" physical inventories, with 40 percent doing so yearly, 24 percent semiannually, 20 percent quarterly, and 10 percent monthly.
- The majority (57 percent) use a cost inventory system, while 38 percent use the retail method.
- 68 percent of the firms use a perpetual inventory system.[9]

FINANCIAL INVENTORY CONTROL: INTEGRATING DOLLAR AND UNIT CONCEPTS

ProfitLogic (www. profitlogic.com/In_Season. htm) markets sophisticated inventory analysis software.

Until now, we have discussed dollar and unit control separately. In practice, they are linked. A decision on how many units to buy is affected by dollar investments, inventory turnover, quantity discounts, warehousing and insurance costs, and so on. Three aspects of financial inventory control are covered next: stock turnover and gross margin return on investment, when to reorder, and how much to reorder.

Stock Turnover and Gross Margin Return on Investment

Stock turnover represents the number of times during a specific period, usually one year, that the average inventory on hand is sold. It can be measured by store, product line, department, and vendor. With high turnover, inventory investments are productive on a per-dollar basis, items are fresh, there are fewer losses due to changes in styles, and interest, insurance, breakage, and warehousing costs are reduced. A retailer can raise stock turnover by reducing its assortment, eliminating or having little inventory for slow-selling items, buying in a timely way, applying QR inventory planning, and using reliable suppliers.

Stock turnover can be computed in units or dollars (at retail or cost). The choice of a formula depends on the retailer's accounting system:

$$\text{Annual rate of stock turnover (in units)} = \frac{\text{Number of units sold during year}}{\text{Average inventory on hand (in units)}}$$

$$\text{Annual rate of stock turnover (in retail dollars)} = \frac{\text{Net yearly sales}}{\text{Average inventory on hand (at retail)}}$$

$$\text{Annual rate of stock turnover (at cost)} = \frac{\text{Cost of goods sold during the year}}{\text{Average inventory on hand (at cost)}}$$

In computing turnover, the average inventory for the entire period needs to be reflected. Turnover rates are invalid if the true average is not used, as occurs if a

TABLE 16-10	Annual Median Stock Turnover Rates for Selected Types of Retailers

Type of Retailer	Annual Median Stock Turnover Rate (Times)
Auto & home supply stores	7.5
Car dealers (new and used)	5.8
Department stores	4.6
Drug & proprietary stores	12.4
Eating places	91.5
Family clothing stores	4.6
Furniture stores	5.2
Gasoline service stations	41.0
Grocery stores	19.1
Hardware stores	4.8
Household appliance stores	6.5
Jewelry stores	2.5
Lumber & other materials dealers	7.9
Men's & boys' clothing stores	4.7
Shoe stores	4.1
Women's clothing stores	6.1

Source: Industry Norms & Key Business Ratios (New York: Dun & Bradstreet, 2003–2004), pp. 125–142.

firm mistakenly views the inventory level of a peak or slow month as the yearly average. Table 16-10 shows annual turnover rates for various retailers. Eating places, gasoline service stations, and grocery stores have high rates. They rely on sales volume for their success. Jewelry stores, shoe stores, department stores, and some clothing stores have low rates. They require larger profit margins on each item sold and maintain a sizable assortment.

Despite the advantages of high turnover, buying items in small amounts may also result in the loss of quantity discounts and in higher transportation charges. Since high turnover might be due to a limited assortment, some sales may be lost, and profits may be lower if prices are reduced to move inventory quickly. The return on investment depends on both turnover and profit per unit.

Learn more about GMROI (http://rtfurniture.net/ worksheet.html).

Gross margin return on investment (GMROI) shows the relationship between the gross margin in dollars (total dollar operating profits) and the average inventory investment (at cost) by combining profitability and sales-to-stock measures:

$$\text{GMROI} = \frac{\text{Gross margin in dollars}}{\text{Net sales}} \times \frac{\text{Net sales}}{\text{Average inventory at cost}}$$

$$= \frac{\text{Gross margin in dollars}}{\text{Average inventory at cost}}$$

The gross margin in dollars equals net sales minus the cost of goods sold. The gross margin percentage is derived by dividing dollar gross margin by net sales.

A sales-to-stock ratio is derived by dividing net sales by average inventory at cost. That ratio may be converted to stock turnover by multiplying it by [(100 − Gross margin percentage)/100].

GMROI is a useful concept for several reasons:

- It shows how diverse retailers can prosper. A supermarket may have a gross margin of 20 percent and a sales-to-stock ratio of 25—a GMROI of 500 percent. A women's clothing store may have a gross margin of 50 percent and a sales-to-stock ratio of 10—a GMROI of 500 percent. Both firms have the same GMROI due to the trade-off between item profitability and turnover.

- It is a good indicator of a manager's performance since it focuses on factors controlled by that person. Interdepartmental comparisons can also be made.

- It is simple to plan and understand, and data collection is easy.

- It can be determined if GMROI performance is consistent with other company goals.

The gross margin percentage and the sales-to-stock ratio must be studied individually. If only overall GMROI is reviewed, performance may be assessed improperly.

When to Reorder

One way to control inventory investment is to systematically set stock levels at which new orders must be placed. Such a stock level is called a **reorder point**, and it is based on three factors. **Order lead time** is the period from the date an order is placed by a retailer to the date merchandise is ready for sale (received, price-marked, and put on the selling floor). **Usage rate** refers to average sales per day, in units, of merchandise. **Safety stock** is the extra inventory that protects against out-of-stock conditions due to unexpected demand and delays in delivery. It depends on the firm's policy toward running out of items.

This is the formula for a retailer that does not plan to carry safety stock. It believes customer demand is stable and that its orders are promptly filled by suppliers:

$$\text{Reorder point} = \text{Usage rate} \times \text{Lead time}$$

If Handy Hardware sells 10 paintbrushes a day and needs 8 days to order, receive, and display them, it has a reorder point of 80 brushes. It would reorder brushes once inventory on hand reaches 80. By the time brushes from that order are placed on shelves (8 days later), stock on hand will be 0, and the new stock will replenish the inventory.

This strategy is proper only when Handy has a steady customer demand of 10 paintbrushes daily and it takes exactly 8 days to complete all stages in the ordering process. This does not normally occur. If customers buy 15 brushes per day during the month, Handy would run out of stock in 5-1/3 days and be without brushes for 2-2/3 days. If an order takes 10 days to process, Handy would have no brushes for 2 days, despite correctly estimating demand. Figure 16-6 shows how stockouts may occur.

For a retailer interested in keeping a safety stock, the reorder formula becomes:

$$\text{Reorder point} = (\text{Usage rate} \times \text{Lead time}) + \text{Safety stock}$$

FIGURE 16-6
How Stockouts May Occur

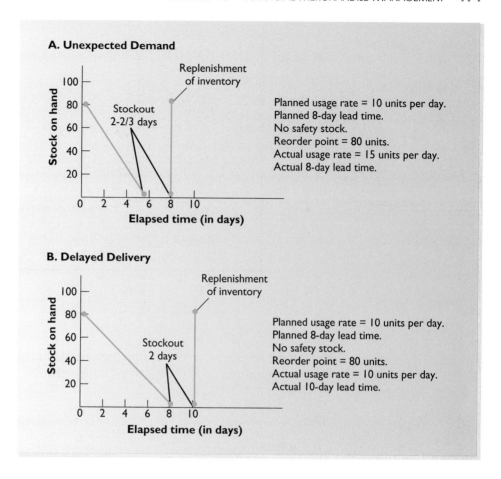

Suppose Handy Hardware decides on safety stock of 30 percent for paint-brushes; its reorder point is $(10 \times 8) + (.30 \times 80) = 80 + 24 = 104$. Handy still expects to sell an average of 10 brushes per day and receive orders in an average of 8 days. The safety stock of 24 extra brushes is kept on hand to protect against unexpected demand or a late shipment.

By combining a perpetual inventory system and reorder point calculations, ordering can be computerized and an **automatic reordering system** can be mechanically activated when stock-on-hand reaches the reorder point. However, intervention by a buyer or manager must be possible, especially if monthly sales fluctuate greatly.

How Much to Reorder

A firm placing large orders generally reduces ordering costs but increases inventory-holding costs. A firm placing small orders often minimizes inventory-holding costs while ordering costs may rise (unless EDI and a QR inventory system are used).

Economic order quantity (EOQ) is the quantity per order (in units) that minimizes the total costs of processing orders and holding inventory. Order-processing costs include computer time, order forms, labor, and handling new goods. Holding costs include warehousing, inventory investment, insurance, taxes, depreciation, deterioration, and pilferage. EOQ calculations can be done by large and small firms.

As Figure 16-7 shows, order-processing costs drop as the order quantity (in units) goes up because fewer orders are needed for the same total annual quantity, and inventory-holding costs rise as the order quantity goes up because more units

FIGURE 16-7
Economic Order Quantity

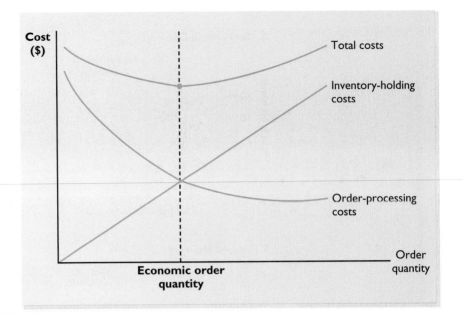

must be held in inventory and they are kept for longer periods. The two costs are summed into a total cost curve. Mathematically, the economic order quantity is

$$EOQ = \sqrt{\frac{2DS}{IC}}$$

where

EOQ = quantity per order (in units)
D = annual demand (in units)
S = costs to place an order (in dollars)
I = percentage of annual carrying cost to unit cost
C = unit cost of an item (in dollars)

Handy estimates it can sell 150 power tool sets per year. They cost $90 each. Breakage, insurance, tied-up capital, and pilferage equal 10 percent of the costs of the sets (or $9 each). Order costs are $25 per order. The economic order quantity is 29:

$$EOQ = \sqrt{\frac{2(150)(\$25)}{(0.10)(\$90)}} = \sqrt{\frac{\$7,500}{\$9}} = 29$$

The EOQ formula must often be modified to take into account changes in demand, quantity discounts, and variable ordering and holding costs.

Summary

1. *To describe the major aspects of financial merchandise planning and management.* The purpose of financial merchandise management is to stipulate which products are bought by the retailer, when, and in what quantity. Dollar control monitors inventory investment, while unit control relates to the amount of merchandise handled. Financial merchandise management encompasses accounting methods, merchandise forecasts and budgets, unit control, and integrated dollar and unit controls.

2. *To explain the cost and retail methods of accounting.* The two accounting techniques for retailers are the cost and retail methods of inventory valuation. Physical

and book (perpetual) procedures are possible with each. Physical inventory valuation requires counting merchandise at prescribed times. Book inventory valuation relies on accurate bookkeeping and a smooth data flow.

The cost method obligates a retailer to have careful records or to code costs on packages. This must be done to find the exact value of ending inventory at cost. Many firms use LIFO accounting to project that value, which lets them reduce taxes by having a low ending inventory value. In the retail method, closing inventory value is tied to the average relationship between the cost and retail value of merchandise. That more accurately reflects market conditions but can be complex.

3. *To study the merchandise forecasting and budgeting process.* This is a form of dollar control with six stages: designating control units, sales forecasting, inventory-level planning, reduction planning, planning purchases, and planning profit margins. Adjustments require all later stages to be modified.

Control units—merchandise categories for which data are gathered—must be narrow to isolate problems and opportunities with specific product lines. Sales forecasting may be the key stage in the merchandising and budgeting process. Through inventory-level planning, a firm sets merchandise quantities for specified periods through the basic stock, percentage variation, weeks' supply, and/or stock-to-sales methods. Reduction planning estimates expected markdowns, discounts, and stock shortages. Planned purchases are linked to planned sales, reductions, and ending and beginning inventory. Profit margins depend on planned net sales, operating expenses, profit, and reductions.

4. *To examine alternative methods of inventory unit control.* A unit control system involves physical units of merchandise. It monitors best-sellers and poor-sellers, the quantity of goods on hand, inventory age, reorder time, and so on. A physical inventory unit control system may use visual inspection or stock counting. A perpetual inventory unit control system keeps a running total of the units handled through record keeping entries that adjust for sales, returns, transfers, and so on. A perpetual system can be applied manually, by merchandise tags processed by computers, or by point-of-sale devices. Virtually all larger retailers conduct regular complete physical inventories; two-thirds use a perpetual inventory system.

5. *To integrate dollar and unit merchandising control concepts.* Three aspects of financial inventory management integrate dollar and unit control concepts: stock turnover and gross margin return on investment, when to reorder, and how much to reorder. Stock turnover is the number of times during a period that average inventory on hand is sold. Gross margin return on investment shows the relationship between gross margin in dollars (total dollar operating profits) and average inventory investment (at cost). A reorder point calculation—when to reorder—includes the retailer's usage rate, order lead time, and safety stock. The economic order quantity—how much to reorder—shows how big an order to place, based on both ordering and inventory costs.

Key Terms

financial merchandise management (p. 468)

dollar control (p. 468)

unit control (p. 468)

merchandise available for sale (p. 469)

cost of goods sold (p. 469)

gross profit (p. 469)

net profit (p. 469)

cost method of accounting (p. 470)

physical inventory system (p. 470)

book inventory system (perpetual inventory system) (p. 470)

FIFO method (p. 470)

LIFO method (p. 470)

retail method of accounting (p. 472)

cost complement (p. 473)

control units (p. 476)

classification merchandising (p. 477)

monthly sales index (p. 478)

basic stock method (p. 479)

percentage variation method (p. 480)

weeks' supply method (p. 481)

stock-to-sales method (p. 481)

retail reductions (p. 481)

open-to-buy (p. 482)

stock turnover (p. 488)

gross margin return on investment (GMROI) (p. 489)

reorder point (p. 490)

order lead time (p. 490)

usage rate (p. 490)

safety stock (p. 490)

automatic reordering system (p. 491)

economic order quantity (EOQ) (p. 491)

Questions for Discussion

1. Which retailers can best use a perpetual inventory system based on the cost method? Explain your answer.

2. The FIFO method seems more logical than the LIFO method, because it assumes the first merchandise purchased is the first merchandise sold. So, why do more retailers use LIFO?

3. Explain the basic premise of the retail method of accounting. Present an example.

4. Why should a small clothing store designate control units, even though this may be time-consuming?

5. Why use sophisticated weather forecasting services if daily weather predictions tend to be inaccurate?

6. Contrast the weeks' supply method and the percentage variation method of merchandise planning.

7. Present two situations in which it would be advisable for a retailer to take a markdown instead of carry over merchandise from one budget period to another.

8. A retailer has yearly sales of $750,000. Inventory on January 1 is $300,000 (at cost). During the year, $600,000 of merchandise (at cost) is purchased. The ending inventory is $275,000 (at cost). Operating costs are $90,000. Calculate the cost of goods sold and net profit, and set up a profit-and-loss statement. There are no retail reductions in this problem.

9. A retailer has a beginning monthly inventory valued at $90,000 at retail and $52,500 at cost. Net purchases during the month are $210,000 at retail and $105,000 at cost. Transportation charges are $10,500. Sales are $225,000. Markdowns and discounts equal $30,000. A physical inventory at the end of the month shows merchandise valued at $15,000 (at retail) on hand. Compute the following:

   a. Total merchandise available for sale—at cost and at retail.

   b. Cost complement.

   c. Ending retail book value of inventory.

   d. Stock shortages.

   e. Adjusted ending retail book value.

   f. Gross profit.

10. The sales of a full-line discount store are listed. Calculate the monthly sales indexes. What do they mean?

Jan.	$300,000	May	$360,000	Sept.	$360,000
Feb.	315,000	June	330,000	Oct.	300,000
Mar.	315,000	July	270,000	Nov.	390,000
Apr.	360,000	Aug.	330,000	Dec.	510,000

11. If the planned average monthly stock for the discount store in Question 10 is $420,000 (at retail), how much inventory should be planned for August if the retailer uses the percentage variation method? Comment on this retailer's choice of the percentage variation method.

12. The store in Questions 10 and 11 knows its cost complement for all merchandise purchased last year was 0.61; it projects this to remain constant. It expects to begin and end December with inventory valued at $240,000 at retail and estimates December reductions to be $18,000. The firm already has purchase commitments for December worth $180,000 (at retail). What is the open-to-buy at cost for December?

Note: At our Web site (**www.prenhall.com/ bermanevans**), there are several math problems related to the material in this chapter so that you may review these concepts.

Web-Based Exercise

Interactive Edge markets a computer software suite called XP3. In this software suite, there is a GMROI component. Visit the Web site (**www.interactiveedge. com/category_management/tips3_02.htm**) and read the GMROI tips. Comment on what a retailer could learn from the discussion. Be sure to include the tables at the site in your discussion.

Note: Stop by our Web site (**www.prenhall.com/bermanevans**) to experience a number of highly interactive, appealing Web exercises based on actual company demonstrations and sample materials related to retailing.

Chapter Endnotes

1. Various company sources.

2. "Inventory Management," **www.tech-encyclopedia. com/inventory-management.htm** (July 30, 2005).

3. For more information on inventory valuation, visit Investopedia.com's Web site, **www.investopedia. com/terms/p/perpetualinventory.asp**.

4. "Replenishment Is the Right Prescription for Increasing Working Capital at Longs Drugs," **www. evant.com/library/read.html** (December 29, 2005).

5. "Retail & Manufacturing Products/Applications," **www.planalytics.com/app/corp/start.jsp?p=retail_ products** (February 18, 2006).

6. "The Facts About Greeting Cards," **www.greeting card.org/pdf/FactsAboutGreetingCardsFactSheet. pdf** (August 25, 2005).

7. "EAN-13: Background Information," **www.barcode island.com/ean13.phtml** (March 15, 2006).

8. "Ready, Aim, Scan," *Business Wire* (May 2, 2005).

9. "Overview: Inventory Management," *Chain Store Age* (December 2001), pp. 3A–6A.

Chapter 17
PRICING IN RETAILING

During the 1950s, Sol Price founded FedMart, the nation's first membership club. Initially, FedMart was open only to government employees due to strict laws regarding discounting. In 1975, Price sold his interest in FedMart and a year later opened Price Club in an aircraft hanger in an industrial section of San Diego. In 1983, some former Price Club executives opened their own membership club and named it Costco. Price Club and Costco merged as Price Costco in 1993, and the name of the company was changed to Costco (**www.costco.com**) in 1995.

Reprinted by permission.

There are now 1,250 membership clubs in the United States, operated mostly by Costco, Sam's Club (**www.samsclub.com**), and BJ's (**www.bjswholesale.com**). Costco operates more than 450 membership clubs serving 42 million cardholders in 36 states and Puerto Rico, Canada, Japan, South Korea, Taiwan, and Great Britain. Costco averages $800 a square foot in sales, about 50 percent above Sam's Club's sales per square foot and over double the national average for shopping centers.

To attract upscale customers, Costco carries fine wines and charges a retail markup of no more than 14 percent. In contrast, local merchants may mark up wine as much as 50 percent. As a result, Costco is probably the largest retailer of premium wines in the United States. It also lures affluent shoppers with Ralph Lauren clothing, Waterford crystal, and even Dom Perignon champagne at deep discounts. It is known for stocking treasure-hunt items, such as Prada handbags, that are offered briefly to encourage bargain hunters to visit the store more frequently.[1]

chapter objectives

1. To describe the role of pricing in a retail strategy and to show that pricing decisions must be made in an integrated and adaptive manner

2. To examine the impact of consumers; government; manufacturers, wholesalers, and other suppliers; and current and potential competitors on pricing decisions

3. To present a framework for developing a retail price strategy: objectives, broad policy, basic strategy, implementation, and adjustments

OVERVIEW

Learn about the complexities of setting prices (http://retailindustry.about.com/od/retailpricing).

Goods and services must be priced in a way that both achieves profitability for the retailer and satisfies customers. A pricing strategy must be consistent with the retailer's overall image (positioning), sales, profit, and return on investment goals.

There are three basic pricing options for a retailer: (1) A *discount orientation* uses low prices as the major competitive advantage. A low-price image, fewer shopping frills, and low per-unit profit margins mean a target market of price-oriented customers, low operating costs, and high inventory turnover. Off-price retailers and full-line discount stores are in this category. (2) With an *at-the-market orientation*, the retailer has average prices. It offers solid service and a nice atmosphere to middle-class shoppers. Margins are moderate to good, and average to above-average quality products are stocked. This firm may find it hard to expand its price range, and it may be squeezed by retailers positioned as discounters or prestige stores. Traditional department stores and many drugstores are in this category. (3) Through an *upscale orientation*, a prestigious image is the retailer's major competitive advantage. A smaller target market, higher expenses, and lower turnover mean customer loyalty, distinctive services and products, and high per-unit profit margins. Upscale department stores and specialty stores are in this category.

Nordstrom is the world's largest online shoe retailer (http://store.nordstrom.com/category/default_shoes.asp), with its usual upscale prices and service.

As we have mentioned several times, a big key to successful retailing is providing a good *value* in the consumer's mind—for the price orientation chosen. That is why Sports Authority is shifting from its longtime good, better, and best three-tier pricing strategy to one that emphasizes better and best products in order to improve gross margins and achieve greater customer loyalty: "We don't want to be in the $199 treadmill business because we will never win that war."[2]

Every customer, whether buying an inexpensive $4 ream of paper or a $40 ream of embossed, personalized stationery, wants to feel the purchase represents a good value. The consumer is not necessarily looking only for the best price. He or she is often interested in the best value—which may be reflected in a superior shopping experience. See Figure 17-1.

FIGURE 17-1

The Classy Lord & Taylor

Even when it runs a sale, the fashionable Lord & Taylor does so in an impressive manner—consistent with the image and service for which it is famous: "The Signature of Style."

Photo reprinted by permission.

Consider the fast-growing Five Below store chain:

> Five Below combines the value positioning of a dollar store with the trend-right products of a cool teen store. All of the merchandise costs $5 or less, and is always priced in whole-dollar amounts. It's an eclectic mix that spans a hodgepodge of categories, including games, jewelry, temporary tattoos, makeup, hair accessories, candy, room décor, books, snacks, novelty items, sporting goods, and seasonal goods. Name brands are featured. More than just cheap, the merchandise is also fun and in sync with the interests of its pre-teen and young teen audience. Unlike traditional dollar stores, Five Below doesn't skimp on the store experience. Colorful murals, hip music, brightly colored banners, and fun slogans—featured on the walls and floors—contribute to the exuberant atmosphere. The noise, especially on Saturday, can be deafening.[3]

Another factor shaping today's pricing environment for retailers of all types is the ease by which a shopper can compare prices on the Web. When a consumer could only do price comparisons by visiting individual stores, the process was time-consuming—which limited many people's willingness to shop around. Now, with a few clicks of a computer mouse, a shopper can quickly gain online price information from several retailers in just minutes—without leaving home. Web sites such as Shopping.com, mySimon.com, and CNET make comparison shopping even simpler: "The growth of online comparison-shopping sites has leveled the retail playing field and permanently altered how consumers shop, both online and offline. Comparison shopping is a natural behavior for shoppers, given that a person can visit dozens of stores in a matter of minutes."[4] See Figure 17-2.

The interaction of price with other retailing mix elements can be shown by BE's Toy City, a hypothetical discounter. It has a broad strategy consisting of:

- A target market of price-conscious families that shop for inexpensive toys ($9 to $12).

- A limited range of merchandise quality ("better" merchandise consists of end-of-season closeouts and manufacturer overruns).

- Self-service in an outlet mall location.

FIGURE 17-2
Shopping.com: A Comparison-Shopping Web Site

Reprinted by permission.

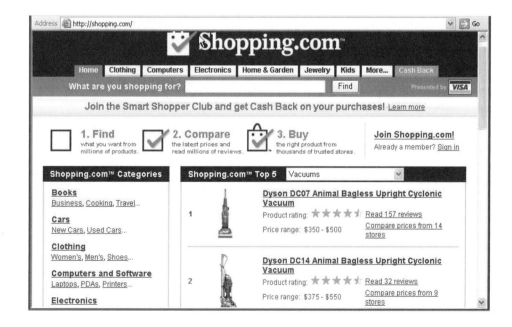

- A good assortment supported by quantity purchases at deep discounts from suppliers.
- An image of efficiency and variety.

In this chapter, we divide retail pricing into two major sections: the external factors affecting a price strategy and the steps in a price strategy. At our site (**www.prenhall.com/bermanevans**), there are several links to information on setting a price strategy.

EXTERNAL FACTORS AFFECTING A RETAIL PRICE STRATEGY

Several factors (discussed next) have an impact on a retail pricing strategy, as shown in Figure 17-3. Sometimes the factors have a minor effect. In other cases, they severely restrict a firm's pricing options.

The Consumer and Retail Pricing[5]

Retailers should understand the **price elasticity of demand**—the sensitivity of customers to price changes in terms of the quantities they will buy—because there is often a relationship between price and consumer purchases and perceptions. If small percentage changes in price lead to substantial percentage changes in the number of units bought, demand is *price elastic*. This occurs when the urgency to purchase is low or there are acceptable substitutes. If large percentage changes in price lead to small percentage changes in the number of units bought, demand is *price inelastic*. Then purchase urgency is high or there are no acceptable substitutes

FIGURE 17-3
Factors Affecting Retail Price Strategy

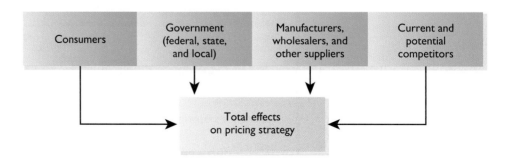

TABLE 17-1	A Movie Theater's Elasticity of Demand

Price	Tickets Sold (Saturday Night)	Total Ticket Receipts	Elasticity of Demand[a]
$ 6.00	1,000	$6,000	
			E = 0.68
7.00	900	6,300	
			E = 0.79
8.00	810	6,480	
			E = 1.00
9.00	720	6,480	
			E = 2.54
10.00	550	5,500	

Computation example = [(1,000 − 900)/(1,000 + 900)]/[($6.00 − $7.00)/($6.00 + $7.00)]
= 0.68

[a]Expressed as a positive number.

One look at Godiva's Web site (www.godiva.com) and you'll know why demand for its products is inelastic.

(as takes place with brand or retailer loyalty). *Unitary elasticity* occurs when percentage changes in price are directly offset by percentage changes in quantity.

Price elasticity is computed by dividing the percentage change in the quantity demanded by the percentage change in the price charged. Because purchases generally decline as prices go up, elasticity tends to be a negative number:

$$\text{Elasticity} = \frac{\dfrac{\text{Quantity 1} - \text{Quantity 2}}{\text{Quantity 1} + \text{Quantity 2}}}{\dfrac{\text{Price 1} - \text{Price 2}}{\text{Price 1} + \text{Price 2}}}$$

Table 17-1 shows the price elasticity for a 1,000-seat movie theater (with elasticities converted to positive numbers) that offers second-run movies. The quantity demanded (tickets sold) declines at every price from $6.00 to $10.00. Demand is inelastic from $6.00 to $7.00 and $7.00 to $8.00; ticket receipts increase since the percentage change in price is greater than the percentage change in tickets sold. Demand is unitary from $8.00 to $9.00; ticket receipts are constant since the percentage change in tickets sold exactly offsets the percentage change in price. Demand is elastic from $9.00 to $10.00; ticket receipts decline since the percentage change in tickets sold is greater than the percentage change in price.

For our movie theater example, total ticket receipts are highest at $8.00 or at $9.00. But what about total revenues? If patrons spend an average of $4.00 each at the concession stand, the best price is $6.00 (total overall revenues of $10,000). This theater is most interested in total revenues since its operating costs are the same whether there are 1,000 or 550 patrons. But typically, retailers should evaluate the costs, as well as the revenues, from serving additional customers.

In retailing, computing price elasticity is difficult. First, as with the movie theater, demand for individual events or items may be hard to predict. One week, the theater may attract 1,000 patrons to a movie, and the next week it may attract 400 patrons to a different movie. Second, many retailers carry thousands of items and cannot possibly compute elasticities for every one. As a result, they usually rely on average markup pricing, competition, tradition, and industrywide data to indicate price elasticity.

Price sensitivity varies by market segment, based on shopping orientation. After identifying potential segments, retailers determine which of them form their target market:

Dell (www.dell.com) appeals to multiple market segments—from novice to advanced computer user, with prices set accordingly.

- *Economic consumers*—They perceive competing retailers as similar and shop around for the lowest possible prices. This segment has grown dramatically in recent years.
- *Status-oriented consumers*—They perceive competing retailers as quite different. They are more interested in prestige brands and strong customer service than in price.
- *Assortment-oriented consumers*—They seek retailers with a strong selection in the product categories being considered. They want fair prices.
- *Personalizing consumers*—They shop where they are known and feel a bond with employees and the firm itself. These shoppers will pay slightly above-average prices.
- *Convenience-oriented consumers*—They shop because they must, want nearby stores with long hours, and may use catalogs or the Web. These people will pay higher prices for convenience.

The Government and Retail Pricing

Three levels of government may affect retail pricing decisions: federal, state, and local. When laws are federal, they apply to interstate commerce. A retailer operating only within the boundaries of one state may not be restricted by some federal legislation. Major government rules relate to horizontal price fixing, vertical price fixing, price discrimination, minimum price levels, unit pricing, item price removal, and price advertising. For retailers operating outside their home countries, a fourth level of government comes into play: international jurisdictions.

Horizontal Price Fixing

An agreement among manufacturers, among wholesalers, or among retailers to set prices is known as **horizontal price fixing**. Such agreements are illegal under the Sherman Antitrust Act and the Federal Trade Commission Act, regardless of how "reasonable" prices may be. It is also illegal for retailers to get together regarding the use of coupons, rebates, or other price-oriented tactics.

Although few large-scale legal actions have been taken in recent years, the penalties for horizontal price fixing can be severe:

> A few years ago, venerable auction houses Sotheby's and Christie's pled guilty to colluding to fix commission fees in the 1990s. The two firms paid more than $600 million in fines and to settle civil lawsuit damages. After a high-profile trial, Sotheby's chairman, A. Alfred Taubman, cooled his heels in prison for ten months and CEO Diana Brooks languished under house arrest in Manhattan.[6]

Vertical Price Fixing

When manufacturers or wholesalers seek to control the retail prices of their goods and services, **vertical price fixing** occurs. According to the Consumer Goods Pricing Act, retailers in the United States cannot be forced to adhere to *minimum retail prices* set by manufacturers and wholesalers. The Act encourages competition among retailers. However, as a result of a Supreme Court ruling, manufacturers and wholesalers are allowed to set *maximum retail prices*. This ruling "opened the door for manufacturers and wholesalers to cap the prices retailers charge for their products. It reversed a decision that barred such limits and left retailers and franchisees free to raise prices above suppliers' suggested prices. Now, manufacturers can set a maximum price as long as they show they aren't stifling competition."[7]

There have been various legal actions in this area. For example, in late 2002,

> The big-five recording companies and three of the biggest music retailers were found to be fixing CD prices. The industry was charged with keeping CD prices artificially high with a policy called "minimum advertised-pricing." The recording companies paid for retailers' ads; in return, the stores agreed to sell CDs at above retail prices. The lawsuit was led by state governments, and the companies agreed to pay $67.4 million and distribute $75 million in CDs to nonprofits. The record company participants were Universal Music, Sony Music, Warner Music, BMG Music, and EMI Group, and the retailers were Musicland Stores, Trans World Entertainment, and Tower Records.[8]

Other than by setting maximum prices, manufacturers and wholesalers can legally control retail prices only by one of these methods: They can screen retailers. They can set realistic list prices. They can pre-print prices on products (which retailers do not have to use). They can set regular prices that are accepted by consumers (such as 50 cents for a newspaper). They can use consignment selling, whereby the supplier owns items until they are sold and assumes costs normally associated with the retailer. They can own retail facilities. They can refuse to sell to retailers that advertise discount prices in violation of written policies. A supplier has a right to announce a policy for dealer pricing and can refuse to sell to those that do not comply. It cannot use coercion to prohibit a retailer from advertising low prices.

Price Discrimination

The **Robinson-Patman Act** bars manufacturers and wholesalers from discriminating in price or purchase terms in selling to individual retailers if these retailers are purchasing products of "like quality" and the effect of such discrimination is to injure competition. The intent of this act is to stop large retailers from using their power to gain discounts not justified by the cost savings achieved by suppliers due to big orders. There are exceptions that allow justifiable price discrimination when:

- Products are physically different.
- The retailers paying different prices are not competitors.
- Competition is not injured.
- Price differences are due to differences in supplier costs.
- Market conditions change—costs rise or fall, or competing suppliers shift their prices.

Discounts are not illegal, as long as suppliers follow the preceding rules, make discounts available to competing retailers on an equitable basis, and offer discounts sufficiently graduated so small retailers can also qualify. Discounts for cumulative purchases (total yearly orders) and for multistore purchases by chains may be hard to justify.

Although the Robinson-Patman Act restricts sellers more than buyers, retailers are covered under Section 2(F): "It shall be unlawful for any person engaged in commerce, in the course of such commerce, knowingly to induce or receive a discrimination in price which is prohibited in this section." Thus, a retail buyer must try to get the lowest prices charged to any competitor, yet not bargain so hard that discounts cannot be justified by acceptable exceptions.

Minimum-Price Laws

About half the states have **minimum-price laws** that prevent retailers from selling certain items for less than their cost plus a fixed percentage to cover overhead. Besides general laws, some state rules set minimum prices for specific products. For instance, in New Jersey and Connecticut, the retail price of liquor cannot be less than the wholesale cost (including taxes and delivery charges).

Minimum-price laws protect small retailers from **predatory pricing**, in which large retailers seek to reduce competition by selling goods and services at very low prices, thus causing small retailers to go out of business. In one widely watched case, three pharmacies in Arkansas filed a suit claiming Wal-Mart had sold selected items below cost in an attempt to reduce competition. Wal-Mart agreed it had priced some items below cost to meet or beat rivals' prices but not to harm competitors. The Arkansas Supreme Court ruled that Wal-Mart did not use predatory pricing since the three pharmacies were still profitable.

With **loss leaders**, retailers price selected items below cost to lure more customer traffic for those retailers. Supermarkets and other retailers use loss leaders to increase overall sales and profits because people buy more than one item once in a store. However, consider this: "The loss leader strategy is used primarily to attract customers to your business by introducing a bargain. Such bargains themselves are not profitable, but hopefully this will be made up through the sale of other goods/services that may or may not be related to the loss leader product. Implementing the loss leader strategy can be risky and therefore needs to be considered that it is the right approach to penetrating the market."[9]

Unit Pricing

In some states, the proliferation of package sizes has led to **unit pricing** laws—whereby some retailers must express both the total price of an item and its price per unit of measure. Food stores are most affected by unit price rules because grocery items are more regulated than nongrocery items.[10] There are exemptions for firms with low sales. The aim of unit pricing is to enable consumers to better compare the prices of products available in many sizes. Thus, a 6-ounce can of tuna fish priced at 99 cents would also have a shelf label showing this as $2.64 per pound. With unit pricing, a person learns that a 12-ounce can of soda selling for 35 cents (2.9 cents per ounce) costs more than a 67.6-ounce—2-liter—bottle for $1.49 (2.2 cents per ounce).

Retailer costs include computing per-unit prices, printing product and shelf labels, and keeping computer records. These costs are influenced by the way prices are attached to goods (by the supplier or the retailer), the number of items subject to unit pricing, the frequency of price changes, sales volume, and the number of stores in a chain.

Unit pricing can be a good strategy for retailers to follow, even when not required. Giant Food's unit pricing system more than pays for itself because of decreased price-marking errors, better inventory control, and improved space management.

Item Price Removal

The boom in computerized checkout systems has led many firms, especially supermarkets, to advocate **item price removal**—whereby prices are marked only on shelves or signs and not on individual items. Scanning equipment reads pre-marked product codes and enters price data at the checkout counter. This practice is banned in several states and local communities.

Many retailers oppose item pricing laws: "In the eyes of the typical retailer, item-pricing laws are relics of a bygone era, inappropriate for the world of scanners and shelf labeling, electronic or manual. And instead of serving customers and cutting costs, employees are forced to work the aisles with a sticker gun." Yet, consumer advocates support them: "Price tags help people shop and help reduce checkout errors. Consumers have the right to compare a price tag to the amount charged at the checkout."[11]

Price Advertising

The FTC has guidelines pertaining to advertising price reductions, advertising prices in relation to competitors' prices, and bait-and-switch advertising. To access several FTC publications on acceptable pricing practices, visit our Web site (**www.prenhall.com/bermanevans**).

A retailer cannot claim or imply that a price has been reduced from some former level (a suggested list price) unless the former price was one that the retailer had actually offered for a good or service on a regular basis during a reasonably substantial, recent period of time.

When a retailer says its prices are lower than competitors', it must make certain that its comparisons pertain to firms selling large quantities in the same trading area. A somewhat controversial, but legal, practice is price matching. For the most part, a retailer makes three assumptions when it "guarantees to match the lowest price of any competing retailer": (1) This guarantee gives shoppers the impression that the firm always offers low prices or else it would not make such a commitment. (2) Most shoppers will not return to a store after a purchase if they see a lower price advertised elsewhere. (3) The guarantee may exclude most deep discounters by stating they are not really competitors.

Bait-and-switch advertising is an illegal practice in which a retailer lures a customer by advertising goods and services at exceptionally low prices; once the customer contacts the retailer (by entering a store, calling a toll-free number, or going to a Web site), he or she is told the good/service of interest is out of stock or of inferior quality. A salesperson (or Web script) tries to convince the person to buy a more costly substitute. The retailer does not intend to sell the advertised item. In deciding if a promotion uses bait-and-switch advertising, the FTC considers how many sales are made at the advertised price, whether a sales commission is paid on sale items, and total sales relative to advertising costs.

Manufacturers, Wholesalers, and Other Suppliers—and Retail Pricing

There may be conflicts between manufacturers (and other suppliers) and retailers in setting final prices since each would like some control. Manufacturers usually want a certain image and to enable all retailers, even inefficient ones, to earn profits. In contrast, most retailers want to set prices based on their own image, goals, and so forth. A supplier can control prices by using exclusive distribution, not selling to price-cutting retailers, or being its own retailer. A retailer can gain control by being a vital customer, threatening to stop carrying suppliers' lines, stocking private brands, or selling gray market goods.

Many manufacturers set their prices to retailers by estimating final retail prices and then subtracting required retailer and wholesaler profit margins. In the men's apparel industry, the common retail markup is 50 percent of the final price. Thus, a man's shirt retailing at $50 can be sold to the retailer for no more than $25. If a wholesaler is involved, the manufacturer's wholesale price must be far less than $25.

Retailers sometimes carry manufacturers' brands and place high prices on them so rival brands (such as private labels) can be sold more easily. This is called "selling against the brand" and is disliked by manufacturers since sales of their brands are apt to decline. Some retailers also sell **gray market goods**, brand-name products bought in foreign markets or goods transshipped from other retailers. Manufacturers dislike gray market goods since they are often sold at low prices by unauthorized dealers. Some of them sue gray market goods resellers on the basis of copyright and trademark infringement.

When suppliers are unknown or products are new, retailers may seek price guarantees. For example, to get its radios stocked, a new supplier might have to guarantee the $30 suggested retail price. If the retailers cannot sell the radios for $30, the manufacturer pays a refund. Should the retailers have to sell the radios at $25, the manufacturer gives back $5. Another guarantee is one in which a supplier tells the retailer that no competitor will buy an item for a lower price. If anyone does, the retailer gets a rebate. The relative power of the retailer and its suppliers determines whether such guarantees are provided.

A retailer also has other suppliers: employees, fixtures manufacturers, landlords, and outside parties (such as ad agencies). Each has an effect on price because of their costs to the retailer.

Competition and Retail Pricing

See how differently Auto-by-Tel (www.autobytel.com) and CarsDirect.com (www.carsdirect.com) approach the selling of cars.

Market pricing occurs when shoppers have a large choice of retailers. In this instance, retailers often price similarly to each other and have less control over price because consumers can easily shop around. Supermarkets, fast-food firms, and gas stations may use market pricing due to their competitive industries. Demand for specific retailers may be weak enough so that some customers would switch to a competitor if prices are raised much.

With *administered pricing*, firms seek to attract consumers on the basis of distinctive retailing mixes. This occurs when people consider image, assortment, service, and so forth to be important and they are willing to pay above-average prices to unique retailers. Upscale department stores, fashion apparel stores, and expensive restaurants are among those with unique offerings and solid control over their prices.

Most price-oriented strategies can be quickly copied. Thus, the reaction of competitors is predictable if the leading firm is successful. This means a price strategy should be viewed from both short-run and long-run perspectives. If competition becomes too intense, a price war may erupt—whereby various firms continually lower prices below regular amounts and sometimes below their cost to lure consumers from competitors. Price wars are sometimes difficult to end and

Ethics in RETAILING — Is "Free" Really Free?

Two years ago, package goods suppliers bowed to pressure from Wal-Mart (www.walmart.com) and agreed to stop using the word "free" on special package sizes containing additional goods at no additional cost. Since Wal-Mart accounts for 35 percent of sales in many non-food categories, the expression "30% more free" has now been replaced by "30% bonus" or "30% more." Wal-Mart's sales executives feel that the word "free" could be misinterpreted as "free of charge," not just a larger size at the original price.

In contrast, Walgreens (www.walgreens.com), the largest drugstore chain in the United States, has asked its suppliers to use the word "free." Walgreens executives think that the word "free" has a greater impact than any of the customary alternatives.

Satisfying both Walgreens and Wal-Mart is costly since package goods suppliers need two different sets of labels, an additional UPC code, separate labeling production runs, and an additional set of inventory. Sending Wal-Mart an incorrect shipment with the word "free" could also result in chargebacks. These additional requirements could easily result in millions of dollars of unexpected costs.

Source: Jack Niff, "Free Becomes Fighting Word," *Advertising Age* (January 24, 2005), p. 14.

can lead to low profits, losses, or even bankruptcy for some competitors. This is especially so for Web retailers.

DEVELOPING A RETAIL PRICE STRATEGY

As Figure 17-4 shows, a retail price strategy has five steps: objectives, policy, strategy, implementation, and adjustments. Pricing policies must be integrated with the total retail mix, which occurs in the second step. The process can be complex due to the often erratic nature of demand, the number of items carried, and the impact of the external factors already noted.

Retail Objectives and Pricing

Nielsen's Priceman (http://us.acnielsen.com/products/ms_priceman.shtml) is a powerful software tool for strategic pricing.

A retailer's pricing strategy has to reflect its overall goals and be related to sales and profits. There must also be specific pricing goals to avoid such potential problems as confusing people by having too many prices, spending too much time bargaining with customers, offering frequent discounts to stimulate customer traffic, having inadequate profit margins, and placing too much emphasis on price.

Overall Objectives and Pricing

Find Used CDs (www.findusedcds.com) sells used and new music CDs at a discount. Tiffany (www.tiffany.com) has great jewelry—although it can be a little pricey.

Sales goals may be stated in terms of revenues and/or unit volume. An aggressive strategy, known as **market penetration pricing**, is used when a retailer seeks large revenues by setting low prices and selling many units. Profit per unit is low, but total profit is high if sales projections are reached. This approach is proper if customers are price sensitive, low prices discourage actual and potential competition, and retail costs do not rise much with volume.

With a **market skimming pricing** strategy, a firm sets premium prices and attracts customers less concerned with price than service, assortment, and prestige. It usually does not maximize sales but does achieve high profit per unit. It is proper if the targeted segment is price insensitive, new competitors are unlikely to enter the market, and added sales will greatly increase retail costs. See Figure 17-5.

Return on investment and early recovery of cash are other possible profit-based goals for retailers using a market skimming strategy. *Return on investment* is sought if a retailer wants profit to be a certain percentage of its investment, such as 20 percent of inventory investment. *Early recovery of cash* is used by retailers that may be short on funds, wish to expand, or be uncertain about the future.

BE's Toy City, the discounter we introduced earlier in this chapter, may be used to illustrate how a retailer sets sales, profit, and return-on-investment goals. The firm sells inexpensive toys and overruns to avoid competing with mainstream toy stores, has one price for all toys (to be set within the $9 to $12 range), minimizes operating costs, encourages self-service, and carries a good selection. Table 17-2 has

FIGURE 17-4
A Framework for Developing a Retail Price Strategy

FIGURE 17-5
Bulgari's Market Skimming Approach

As Hoovers.com (**www.hoovers.com**) notes, "If you have to ask, 'How much?' you probably can't afford Bulgari. The world's number three jewelry company (behind Cartier and Tiffany & Co.) has been crafting prized baubles for the rich and famous for more than a hundred years. Today Bulgari reaches a larger—but no less exclusive—market through more than 150 Bulgari stores, as well as select retailers worldwide."

Photo reprinted by permission of Susan Berry, Retail Image Consulting, Inc.

data on BE's Toy City pertaining to demand, costs, profit, and return-on-inventory investment at prices from $9 to $12. The firm must select the best price within that range. Table 17-3 shows how the figures in Table 17-2 were derived. Several conclusions can be drawn from Table 17-2:

- A sales goal would lead to a price of $10. Total sales are highest ($1,040,000).
- A dollar profit goal would lead to a price of $11. Total profit is highest ($132,000).

TABLE 17-2		BE's Toy City: Demand, Costs, Profit, and Return on Inventory Investment[a]							
Selling Price ($)	Demand (units)	Total Sales Revenue ($)	Average Cost of Goods ($)	Total Cost of Goods ($)	Total Operating Costs($)	Total Costs ($)	Average Total Costs ($)	Total Profit ($)	
9.00	114,000	1,026,000	7.60	866,400	104,000	970,400	8.51	55,600	
10.00	104,000	1,040,000	7.85	816,400	94,000	910,400	8.75	129,600	
11.00	80,000	880,000	8.25	660,000	88,000	748,000	9.35	132,000	
12.00	60,000	720,000	8.75	525,000	80,000	605,000	10.08	115,000	

Selling Price ($)	Profit/ Unit ($)	Markup at Retail (%)	Profit/ Sales (%)	Average Inventory on Hand (units)	Inventory Turnover (units)	Average Inventory Investment at Cost ($)	Inventory Turnover ($)	Return-on-Inventory Investment (%)
9.00	0.49	16	5.4	12,000	9.5	91,200	9.5	61
10.00	1.25	22	12.5	13,000	8.0	102,050	8.0	127
11.00	1.65	25	15.0	14,000	5.7	115,500	5.7	114
12.00	1.92	27	16.0	16,000	3.8	140,000	3.8	82

Note: Average cost of goods reflects quantity discounts. Total operating costs include all retail operating expenses.
[a]Numbers have been rounded.

TABLE 17-3	Derivation of BE's Toy City Data
Column in Table 17-2	**Source of Information or Method of Computation**
Selling price	Trade data, comparison shopping, experience
Demand (in units) at each price	Consumer surveys, trade data, experience
Total sales revenue	Selling price × Quantity demanded
Average cost of goods	Supplier contacts, quantity discount structure, estimates of order sizes
Total cost of goods	Average cost of goods × Quantity demanded
Total operating costs	Experience, trade data, estimation of individual retail expenses
Total costs	Total cost of goods + Total operating costs
Average total costs	Total costs/Quantity demanded
Total profit	Total sales revenue − Total costs
Profit per unit	Total profit/Quantity demanded
Markup (at retail)	(Selling price − Average cost of goods)/Selling price
Profit as a percentage of sales	Total profit/Total sales revenue
Average inventory on hand	Trade data, inventory turnover data (in units), experience
Inventory turnover (in units)	Quantity demanded/Average inventory on hand (in units)
Average inventory investment (at cost)	Average cost of goods × Average inventory on hand (in units)
Inventory turnover (in $)	Total cost of goods/Average inventory investment (at cost)
Return-on-inventory investment	Total profit/Average inventory investment (at cost)

- A return-on-inventory investment goal would also lead to a price of $10. Return-on-inventory investment is 127 percent.
- Although a lot can be sold at $9, that price would lead to the least profit ($55,600).
- A price of $12 would yield the highest profit per unit and as a percentage of sales, but total dollar profit is not maximized at this price.
- High inventory turnover would not necessarily lead to high profits.

As a result, BE's Toy City decides a price of $11 would earn the highest dollar profits, while generating good profit per unit and profit as a percentage of sales.

Specific Pricing Objectives

Figure 17-6 lists specific pricing goals other than sales and profits. Each retailer must determine their relative importance given its situation—and plan accordingly. Some goals may be incompatible, such as "to not encourage shoppers to be overly price-conscious" and a " 'we-will-not-be-undersold' philosophy."

Broad Price Policy

KSS (www.kssg.com) offers a lot of software solutions that enable retailers to better integrate their price strategies.

Through a broad price policy, a retailer generates an integrated price plan with short- and long-run perspectives (balancing immediate and future goals) and a consistent image (vital for chains and franchises). The retailer interrelates its price policy with the target market, the retail image, and the other elements of the retail mix. These are some of the price policies from which a firm could choose:

- No competitors will have lower prices; no competitors will have higher prices (for prestige purposes); or prices will be consistent with competitors'.

FIGURE 17-6
Specific Pricing Objectives from Which Retailers May Choose

✓ To maintain a proper image.

✓ To encourage shoppers not to be overly price-conscious.

✓ To be perceived as fair by all parties (including suppliers, employees, and customers).

✓ To be consistent in setting prices.

✓ To increase customer traffic during slow periods.

✓ To clear out seasonal merchandise.

✓ To match competitors' prices without starting a price war.

✓ To promote a "we-will-not-be-undersold" philosophy.

✓ To be regarded as the price leader in the market area by consumers.

✓ To provide ample customer service.

✓ To minimize the chance of government actions relating to price advertising and antitrust matters.

✓ To discourage potential competitors from entering the marketplace.

✓ To create and maintain customer interest.

✓ To encourage repeat business.

- All items will be priced independently, depending on the demand for each; or the prices for all items will be interrelated to maintain an image and ensure proper markups.
- Price leadership will be exerted; competitors will be price leaders and set prices first; or prices will be set independently of competitors.
- Prices will be constant over a year or season; or prices will change if costs change.

Price Strategy

See the Small Business Administration's tips on how to set prices (www.sba.gov/library/pubs/fm-13.doc).

In **demand-oriented pricing**, a retailer sets prices based on consumer desires. It determines the range of prices acceptable to the target market. The top of this range is called the demand ceiling, the most people will pay for a good or service. With **cost-oriented pricing**, a retailer sets a price floor, the minimum price acceptable to the firm so it can reach a specified profit goal. A retailer usually computes merchandise and operating costs and adds a profit margin to these figures. For **competition-oriented pricing**, a retailer sets its prices in accordance with competitors'. The price levels of key competitors are studied and applied.

As a rule, retailers should combine these approaches in enacting a price strategy. The approaches should not be viewed as operating independently.

Demand-Oriented Pricing

Retailers use demand-oriented pricing to estimate the quantities that customers would buy at various prices. This approach studies customer interests and the psychological implications of pricing. Two aspects of psychological pricing are the price-quality association and prestige pricing.

According to the **price-quality association** concept, many consumers feel high prices connote high quality and low prices connote low quality. This association is especially important if competing firms or products are hard to judge on bases other than price, consumers have little experience or confidence in judging quality (as with a new retailer), shoppers perceive large differences in quality among retailers or products, and brand names are insignificant in product choice. Though various studies have documented a price-quality relationship, research also indicates that if other quality cues, such as retailer atmospherics, customer service, and popular brands, are involved, these cues may be more important than price in a person's judgment of overall retailer or product quality.

Prestige pricing—which assumes that consumers will not buy goods and services at prices deemed too low—is based on the price-quality association. Its premise is that consumers may feel too low a price means poor quality and status. Some people look for prestige pricing when selecting retailers and do not patronize those with prices viewed as too low. Saks Fifth Avenue and Neiman Marcus do not generally carry low-end items because their customers may feel they are inferior. Prestige pricing does not apply to all shoppers. Some people may be economizers and always shop for bargains; and neither the price-quality association nor prestige pricing may be applicable for them.

Cost-Oriented Pricing

One form of cost-oriented pricing, markup pricing, is the most widely used pricing technique. In **markup pricing**, a retailer sets prices by adding per-unit merchandise costs, retail operating expenses, and desired profit. The difference between merchandise costs and selling price is the **markup**. If a retailer buys a desk for $200 and sells it for $300, the extra $100 covers operating costs and profit. The markup is 33-1/3 percent at retail or 50 percent at cost. The level of the markup depends on a product's traditional markup, the supplier's suggested list price, inventory turnover, competition, rent and other overhead costs, the extent to which the product must be serviced, and the selling effort.

Markups can be computed on the basis of retail selling price or cost but are typically calculated using the retail price. Why? (1) Retail expenses, markdowns, and profit are always stated as a percentage of sales. Thus, markups expressed as a percentage of sales are more meaningful. (2) Manufacturers quote selling prices and discounts to retailers as percentage reductions from retail list prices. (3) Retail price data are more readily available than cost data. (4) Profitability seems smaller if expressed on the basis of price. This can be useful in communicating with the government, employees, and consumers.

This is how a **markup percentage** is calculated. The difference is in the denominator:

$$\text{Markup percentage (at retail)} = \frac{\text{Retail selling price} - \text{Merchandise cost}}{\text{Retail selling price}}$$

$$\text{Markup percentage (at cost)} = \frac{\text{Retail selling price} - \text{Merchandise cost}}{\text{Merchandise cost}}$$

Table 17-4 shows several markup percentages at retail and at cost. As markups go up, the disparity between the percentages grows. Suppose a retailer buys a watch for $20 and considers whether to sell it for $25, $40, or $100. The $25 price yields a markup of 20 percent at retail and 25 percent at cost, the $40 price a markup of 50 percent at retail and 100 percent at cost, and the $80 price a markup of 80 percent at retail and 400 percent at cost.

These three examples indicate the usefulness of the markup concept in planning:

1. A discount clothing store can buy a shipment of men's jeans at $12 each and wants a 30 percent markup at retail.[12] What retail price should the store charge to achieve this markup?

TABLE 17-4	Markup Equivalents
Percentage at Retail	**Percentage at Cost**
10.0	11.1
20.0	25.0
30.0	42.9
40.0	66.7
50.0	100.0
60.0	150.0
70.0	233.3
80.0	400.0
90.0	900.0

$$\text{Markup percentage (at retail)} = \frac{\text{Retail selling price} - \text{Merchandise cost}}{\text{Retail selling price}}$$

$$0.30 = \frac{\text{Retail selling price} - \$12.00}{\text{Retail selling price}}$$

$$\text{Retail selling price} = \$17.14$$

2. A stationery store desires a minimum 40 percent markup at retail.[13] If one large box of manila envelopes retails at $7.99 per box, what is the maximum price the store can pay for each box?

$$\text{Markup percentage (at retail)} = \frac{\text{Retail selling price} - \text{Merchandise cost}}{\text{Retail selling price}}$$

$$0.40 = \frac{\$7.99 - \text{Merchandise cost}}{\$7.99}$$

$$\text{Merchandise cost} = \$4.794$$

3. A sporting goods store has been offered a closeout purchase for bicycles. The cost of each bike is $105, and it should retail for $160. What markup at retail would the store obtain?

$$\text{Markup percentage (at retail)} = \frac{\text{Retail selling price} - \text{Merchandise cost}}{\text{Retail selling price}}$$

$$= \frac{\$160.00 - \$105.00}{\$160.00} = 34.4$$

A retailer's markup percentage may also be determined by examining planned retail operating expenses, profit, and net sales. Suppose a florist estimates yearly operating expenses to be $55,000. The desired profit is $50,000 per year, including the owner's salary. Net sales are forecast to be $250,000. The planned markup would be:

$$\text{Markup percentage (at retail)} = \frac{\text{Planned retail operating expenses} + \text{Planned profit}}{\text{Planned net sales}}$$

$$= \frac{\$55,000 + \$50,000}{\$250,000} = 42$$

If potted plants cost the florist $8.00 each, the retailer's selling price would be:

$$\text{Retail selling price} = \frac{\text{Merchandise cost}}{1 - \text{Markup}}$$

$$= \frac{\$8.00}{1 - 0.42} = \$13.79$$

The florist must sell about 18,129 plants (assuming that this is the only item it carries) at $13.79 apiece to achieve sales and profit goals. To reach these goals, all plants must be sold at the $13.79 price.

Because it is rare for a retailer to sell all items in stock at their original prices, initial markup, maintained markup, and gross margin should each be computed. **Initial markup** is based on the original retail value assigned to merchandise less the costs of the merchandise. **Maintained markup** is based on the actual prices received for merchandise sold during a time period less merchandise cost. Maintained markups relate to actual prices received, so they can be hard to predict. The difference between the initial and maintained markups is that the latter reflect adjustments due to markdowns, added markups, shortages, and discounts.

The initial markup percentage depends on planned retail operating expenses, profit, reductions, and net sales:

$$\begin{array}{l}\text{Initial markup}\\ \text{percentage}\\ \text{(at retail)}\end{array} = \frac{\begin{array}{c}\text{Planned retail operating expenses} + \text{Planned profit}\\ + \text{Planned retail reductions}\end{array}}{\text{Planned net sales} + \text{Planned retail reductions}}$$

If planned retail reductions are 0, the initial markup percentage equals planned retail operating expenses plus profit, both divided by planned net sales. To resume the florist example, suppose the firm projects that retail reductions will be 20 percent of estimated sales, or $50,000. To reach its goals, the initial markup and the original selling price would be:

$$\begin{array}{l}\text{Initial markup}\\ \text{percentage}\\ \text{(at retail)}\end{array} = \frac{\$55,000 + \$50,000 + \$50,000}{\$250,000 + \$50,000} = 51.7$$

$$\text{Retail selling price} = \frac{\text{Merchandise cost}}{1 - \text{Markup}} = \frac{\$8.00}{1 - 0.517} = \$16.56$$

The original retail value of 18,129 plants is about $300,000. Retail reductions of $50,000 lead to net sales of $250,000. Thus, the retailer must begin by selling plants at $16.56 apiece if it wants an average selling price of $13.79 and a maintained markup of 42 percent.

The maintained markup percentage can be viewed as:

$$\begin{array}{l}\text{Maintained markup}\\ \text{percentage}\\ \text{(at retail)}\end{array} = \frac{\text{Actual retail operating expenses} + \text{Actual profit}}{\text{Actual net sales}}$$

or

$$\begin{array}{l}\text{Maintained markup}\\ \text{percentage}\\ \text{(at retail)}\end{array} = \frac{\text{Average selling price} - \text{Merchandise cost}}{\text{Average selling price}}$$

Gross margin is the difference between net sales and the total cost of goods sold (which adjusts for cash discounts and additional expenses):

$$\text{Gross margin (in \$)} = \text{Net sales} - \text{Total cost of goods}$$

Technology in RETAILING
Bozzuto's New Pricing System for Retailers

Bozzuto's (**www.bozzutos.com**) is a food distributor and wholesaler that delivers food and household products to about 800 stores in New England, New York, New Jersey, and Pennsylvania. It hopes to simplify its pricing decision making by supplying key data for its retailer customers.

Bozzuto's has faced a number of challenges in planning and implementing its pricing system. One, the system needs to support at least six different front-end systems since Bozzuto's customers have not adapted a standardized platform. Two, the data are constantly changing to reflect demand and market conditions. And three, all price changes have to be immediately reflected in retail signage, on shelf tags, and in the retailers' point-of-sale system.

To reduce potential problems, Bozzuto's first implemented its new pricing system with Adams Super Food Stores (**www.adamssuperfood.com**). According to Bozzuto's vice-president of information technology, "Once we learned from that and set up the technologies and controls, we could roll it out as an offering to our independent customer base." While Bozzuto's will encourage its customers to adopt a solution from one vendor, its use will not be mandatory.

Sources: Matthew Haeberle, "Price Empowered," *Chain Store Age* (October 2004), p. 76; and "Our Company," **www.bozzutos.com/com_ourcompany.htm** (March 25, 2006).

The florist's gross margin (the dollar equivalent of maintained markup) is roughly $105,000.

Although a retailer must set a companywide markup goal, markups for categories of merchandise or individual products may differ—sometimes dramatically. At many full-line discount stores, maintained markup as a percentage of sales ranges from under 20 percent for consumer electronics to more than 40 percent for jewelry and watches.

With a **variable markup policy**, a retailer purposely adjusts markups by merchandise category. Such a policy:

- Recognizes that the costs of different goods/service categories may fluctuate widely. Some items require alterations or installation. Even within a product line, expensive items may require greater end-of-year markdowns than inexpensive ones. The high-priced line needs a larger initial markup.

- Allows for differences in product investments. For major appliances, where the retailer orders regularly from a wholesaler, lower markups are needed than with fine jewelry, where the retailer must have a complete stock of unique merchandise.

- Accounts for differences in sales efforts and merchandising skills. A feature-laden food processor may require a substantial effort, whereas a standard toaster involves much less effort.

- May help a retailer to generate more customer traffic by advertising certain products at deep discounts. This entails leader pricing (discussed later in the chapter).

One way to plan variable markups is **direct product profitability (DPP)**, a technique that enables a retailer to find the profitability of each category of merchandise by computing adjusted per-unit gross margin and assigning direct product costs for such expense categories as warehousing, transportation, handling, and selling. The proper markup for each category or item is then set. DPP is used by some supermarkets, discounters, and other retailers. The major problem is the complexity of assigning costs.

Figure 17-7 illustrates DPP for two items with a selling price of $20. The retailer pays $12 for Item A, whose per-unit gross margin is $8. Since the retailer gets a $1 per unit allowance to set up a special display, the adjusted gross margin

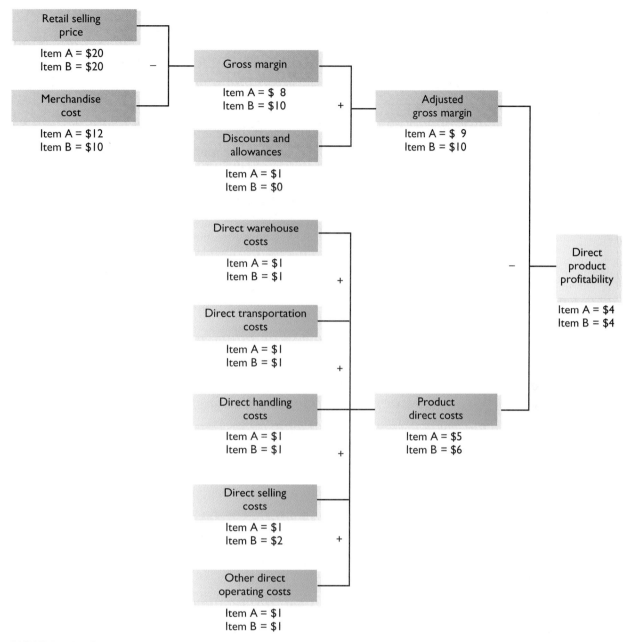

FIGURE 17-7
How to Determine Direct Product Profitability

is $9. Total direct retail costs are estimated at $5. Direct product profit is $4—20 percent of sales. The retailer pays $10 for Item B, whose per-unit gross margin is $10. There are no special discounts or allowances. Since Item B needs more selling effort, total direct retail costs are $6. The direct profit is $4—20 percent of sales. To attain the same direct profit per unit, Item A needs a 40 percent markup (per-unit gross margin/selling price), and Item B needs 50 percent.

Cost-oriented (markup) pricing is popular among retailers. It is simple, because a retailer can apply a standard markup for a product category more easily than it can estimate demand at various prices. The firm can also adjust prices according to demand or segment a market. Markup pricing has a sense of equity given that the retailer earns a fair profit. When retailers have similar markups, price competition is reduced. Markup pricing is efficient if it takes into account competition, seasonal factors, and the intricacies in selling some products.

TABLE 17-5	Competition-Oriented Pricing Alternatives		
	ALTERNATIVE PRICE STRATEGIES		
Retail Mix Variable	Pricing Below the Market	Pricing At the Market	Pricing Above the Market
Location	Poor, inconvenient site; low rent	Close to competitors, no location advantage	Few strong competitors, convenient to consumers
Customer service	Self-service, little salesperson support, limited displays	Moderate assistance by sales personnel	High levels of personal selling, delivery, etc.
Product assortment	More emphasis on best-sellers	Medium or large assortment	Small or large assortment
Atmosphere	Inexpensive fixtures, racks for merchandise	Moderate atmosphere	Attractive and pleasant décor
Innovativeness in assortment	Follower, conservative	Concentration on best-sellers	Leader
Special services	Not available	Not available or extra fee	Included in price
Product lines carried	Some name brands, private labels, closeouts	Selection of name brands, private labels	Exclusive name brands and private labels

Competition-Oriented Pricing

A retailer can use competitors' prices as a guide. That firm might not alter prices in reaction to changes in demand or costs unless competitors alter theirs. Similarly, it might change prices when competitors do, even if demand or costs remain the same.

As shown in Table 17-5, a competition-oriented retailer can price below, at, or above the market. A firm with a strong location, superior service, good assortments, a favorable image, and exclusive brands can set prices above competitors. However, above-market pricing is not suitable for a retailer that has an inconvenient location, relies on self-service, is not innovative, and offers no real product distinctiveness.

Competition-oriented pricing does not require calculations of demand curves or price elasticity. The average market price is assumed to be fair for both the consumer and the retailer. Pricing at the market level does not disrupt competition and therefore does not usually lead to retaliation.

Integration of Approaches to Price Strategy

To properly integrate the three approaches, questions such as these should be addressed:

- If prices are reduced, will revenues increase greatly? (Demand orientation)
- Should different prices be charged for a product based on negotiations with customers, seasonality, and so on? (Demand orientation)
- Will a given price level allow a traditional markup to be attained? (Cost orientation)
- What price level is necessary for a product requiring special costs in purchasing, selling, or delivery? (Cost orientation)
- What price levels are competitors setting? (Competitive orientation)
- Can above-market prices be set due to a superior image? (Competitive orientation)

FIGURE 17-8
A Checklist of Selected
Specific Pricing Decisions

✓ How important is price stability? How long should prices be maintained?

✓ Is everyday low pricing desirable?

✓ Should prices change if costs and/or customer demand vary?

✓ Should the same prices be charged to all customers buying under the same conditions?

✓ Should customer bargaining be permitted?

✓ Should odd pricing be used?

✓ Should leader pricing be utilized to draw customer traffic? If yes, should leader prices be above, at, or below costs?

✓ Should consumers be offered discounts for purchasing in quantity?

✓ Should price lining be used to provide a price range and price points within that range?

✓ Should pricing practices vary by department or product line?

Implementation of Price Strategy

Implementing a price strategy involves a variety of separate but interrelated specific decisions, in addition to those broad concepts already discussed. A checklist of selected decisions is shown in Figure 17-8. In this section, the specifics of a pricing strategy are detailed.

Customary and Variable Pricing

With **customary pricing**, a retailer sets prices for goods and services and seeks to maintain them for an extended period. Examples of items with customary prices are newspapers, candy, arcade games, vending machine items, and foods on restaurant menus. In each case, the retailer wants to establish set prices and have consumers take them for granted.

Careers in RETAILING   Is Retail for Me? Loss Prevention

Do you have an eye for detail, an appetite for solving puzzles, or a knack for proactivity? The loss prevention career area is responsible for safeguarding company assets and may include risk management issues, such as customer and employee safety. Loss prevention team members work together to prevent and handle merchandise loss due to shoplifting, employee theft, paperwork errors, and vendor fraud. Physical security of store and company buildings may also be included, as well as financial auditing responsibilities.

Here are three jobs in the area of loss prevention:

● *Head of Loss Prevention:* Top position responsible for safeguarding company assets. Primary emphasis is preventing merchandise shrinkage through theft or poor paperwork. May also be responsible for physical security of home office building(s) and warehouse(s).

May do executive investigations. May have an auditing department monitoring cash flow documents.

● *Regional Loss Prevention Manager:* Responsible for safeguarding company assets within a geographic area. May emphasize preventing merchandise loss through employee training and audits but will also investigate known losses and coordinate with police/courts on theft prosecutions.

● *Store Detective:* Primarily responsible for prevention of merchandise theft, apprehension, and prosecution of shoplifters. May do investigations of suspected employee theft. This is a "plain clothes" position, not a uniformed security guard or watchperson.

Source: Reprinted by permission of the National Retail Federation.

FIGURE 17-9
Ikea and Everyday Low Pricing

Ikea's use of EDLP even extends to its in-store restaurant.

Photo reprinted by permission.

Bi-Lo (www.bi-lo.com), the southeastern supermarket chain, offers everyday low prices and discounts. Click on "Weekly Ad."

A version of customary pricing is **everyday low pricing (EDLP)**, in which a retailer strives to sell its goods and services at consistently low prices throughout the selling season. Low prices are set initially; and there are few or no advertised specials, except on discontinued items or end-of-season closeouts. The retailer reduces its advertising and product repricing costs and increases the credibility of its prices in the consumer's mind. On the other hand, with EDLP, manufacturers tend to eliminate the special trade allowances designed to encourage retailers to offer price promotions during the year. Wal-Mart and Ikea are among the retailers successfully utilizing EDLP. See Figure 17-9.

In many instances, a retailer cannot or should not use customary pricing. A firm *cannot* maintain constant prices if its costs are rising. A firm *should not* hold prices constant if customer demand varies. Under **variable pricing**, a retailer alters its prices to coincide with fluctuations in costs or consumer demand. Variable pricing may also provide excitement due to special sales opportunities for customers.

Cost fluctuations can be seasonal or trend-related. Supermarket and florist prices vary over the year due to the seasonal nature of many food and floral products. When seasonal items are scarce, the cost to the retailer goes up. If costs continually rise (as with luxury cars) or fall (as with computers), the retailer must change prices permanently (unlike temporary seasonal changes).

Demand fluctuations can be place- or time-based. Place-based fluctuations exist for retailers selling seat locations (such as concert halls) or room locations (such as hotels). Different prices can be charged for different locations, such as tickets close to the stage commanding higher prices. Time-based fluctuations occur if consumer demand differs by hour, day, or season. Demand for a movie theater is greater on Saturday than on Wednesday. Prices should be lower during periods of less demand.

Yield management pricing is a computerized, demand-based, variable pricing technique, whereby a retailer (typically a service firm) determines the combination of prices that yield the greatest total revenues for a given period. It is widely used by airlines and hotels. A crucial airline decision is how many first-class, full-coach, intermediate-discount, and deep-discount tickets to sell on each flight. With this approach, an airline offers fewer discount tickets for flights during peak periods than for ones in off-peak times. The airline has two goals: to fill as many seats as possible on every flight and to sell as many full-fare tickets as it can ("You don't want to sell a seat for $99 when someone will pay $599"). Yield management pricing may be too complex for small retailers, and it requires complex software. Our Web site (**www.prenhall.com/bermanevans**) has many links that illustrate the uses of yield management and other pricing software.

It is possible to combine customary and variable pricing. A movie theater can charge $5 every Wednesday night and $9 every Saturday. A bookstore can lower prices by 20 percent for best-sellers that have been out for three months.

One-Price Policy and Flexible Pricing

Under a **one-price policy**, a retailer charges the same price to all customers buying an item under similar conditions. This policy may be used together with customary pricing or variable pricing. With variable pricing, all customers interested in a particular section of concert seats would pay the same price. This approach is easy to manage, does not require skilled salespeople, makes shopping quicker, permits self-service, puts consumers under less pressure, and is tied to price goals. One-price policies are the rule for most U.S. retailers, and bargaining is often not permitted.

Looking to bargain? Go to eBay (**www.ebay.com**) or Overstock Auctions (**www.auctions. overstock.com**).

Flexible pricing lets consumers bargain over prices; those who are good at it obtain lower prices. Many jewelry stores, auto dealers, and others use flexible pricing. They do not clearly post bottom-line prices; shoppers need prior knowledge to bargain successfully. Flexible pricing encourages consumers to spend more time, gives an impression the firm is discount-oriented, and generates high margins from shoppers who do not like haggling. It requires high initial prices and good salespeople.

A special form of flexible pricing is **contingency pricing**, whereby a service retailer does not get paid until after the service is performed and payment is contingent on the service's being satisfactory. In some cases, such as real-estate, consumers prefer contingency payments so they know the service is done properly. This represents some risk to the retailer since a lot of time and effort may be spent without payment. A real-estate broker may show a house 25 times, not sell it, and, therefore, not be paid.

Odd Pricing

Retail prices are set at levels below even dollar values, such as $0.49, $4.98, and $199, in **odd pricing**. The assumption is that people feel these prices represent discounts or that the amounts are beneath consumer price ceilings. Odd pricing is a form of psychological pricing. Realtors hope consumers with a price ceiling of less than $350,000 are attracted to houses selling for $349,500. See Figure 17-10.

Odd prices that are 1 cent or 2 cents below the next highest even price ($0.29, $0.99, $2.98) are common up to $10.00. Beyond that point and up to $50.00, 5-cent reductions from the highest even price ($19.95, $49.95) are more usual. For more expensive items, prices are in dollars ($399, $4,995).

Leader Pricing

In **leader pricing**, a retailer advertises and sells selected items in its goods/service assortment at less than the usual profit margins. The goal is to increase customer traffic for the retailer so that it can sell regularly priced goods and services in addition to the specially priced items. This is different from bait-and-switch, in which sale items are not sold.

FIGURE 17-10
Odd Pricing: A Popular
Retailing Tactic

At Aeropostale, odd pricing is
widely employed so that the
chain projects a value-driven
image to shoppers.

Photo reprinted by permission of
Susan Berry, Retail Image
Consulting, Inc.

Leader pricing typically involves frequently purchased, nationally branded, high turnover goods and services because it is easy for customers to detect low prices. Supermarkets, home centers, discount stores, drugstores, and fast-food restaurants are just some of the retailers that utilize leader pricing to draw shoppers. There are two kinds of leader pricing: loss leaders and sales at lower than regular prices (but higher than cost). Loss leaders are regulated on a statewide basis under minimum-price laws.

Multiple-Unit Pricing

With **multiple-unit pricing**, a retailer offers discounts to customers who buy in quantity or who buy a product bundle. By selling items at two for $0.75, a retailer attempts to sell more products than at $0.39 each. There are three reasons to use multiple-unit pricing: (1) A firm could seek to have shoppers increase their total purchases of an item. (If people buy multiple units to stockpile them, instead of consuming more, the firm's overall sales do not increase.) (2) This approach can help sell slow-moving and end-of-season merchandise. (3) Price bundling may increase sales of related items.

In **bundled pricing**, a retailer combines several elements in one basic price. A 35-mm camera bundle could include a camera, batteries, a telephoto lens, a case, and a tripod for $289. This approach increases overall sales and offers people a discount over unbundled prices. However, it is unresponsive to different customers. As an alternative, many retailers use **unbundled pricing**—they charge separate prices for each item sold. A TV rental firm could charge separately for TV set rental, home delivery, and a monthly service contract. This closely links prices with costs and gives people more choice. Unbundled pricing may be harder to manage and may result in people buying fewer related items.

Price Lining

Marriott International
(www.marriott.com/
corporateinfo/glance.mi)
really knows how to use
price lining.

Rather than stock merchandise at all different price levels, retailers often employ **price lining** and sell merchandise at a limited range of price points, with each point representing a distinct level of quality. Retailers first determine their price floors and ceilings in each product category. They then set a limited number of price points within the range.[14] Department stores generally carry good, better, and best versions of merchandise consistent with their overall price policy—and set individual prices accordingly.

Price lining benefits both consumers and retailers. If the price range for a box of handkerchiefs is $6 to $15 and the price points are $6, $9, and $15, consumers know that distinct product qualities exist. However, should a retailer have prices of $6, $7, $8, $9, $10, $11, $12, $13, $14, and $15, the consumer may be confused about product differences. For retailers, price lining aids merchandise planning. Retail buyers can seek those suppliers carrying products at appropriate prices, and they can better negotiate with suppliers. They can automatically disregard products not fitting within price lines and thereby reduce inventory investment. Also, stock turnover goes up when the number of models carried is limited.

Difficulties do exist: (1) Depending on the price points selected, price lining may leave excessive gaps. A parent shopping for a graduation gift might find a $30 briefcase to be too cheap and a $200 one to be too expensive. (2) Inflation can make it tough to keep price points and price ranges. (3) Markdowns may disrupt the balance in a price line, unless all items in a line are reduced proportionally. (4) Price lines must be coordinated for complementary product categories, such as blazers, skirts, and shoes.

Price Adjustments

Retailers need to be focused in making price adjustments (www.bizmove.com/general/m6h4.htm).

Price adjustments let retailers use price as an adaptive mechanism. Markdowns and additional markups may be needed due to competition, seasonality, demand patterns, merchandise costs, and pilferage. Figure 17-11 shows a price change authorization form.

A **markdown** from an item's original price is used to meet the lower price of another retailer, adapt to inventory overstocking, clear out shopworn merchandise, reduce assortments of odds and ends, and increase customer traffic. An

FIGURE 17-11
A Price Change Authorization Form

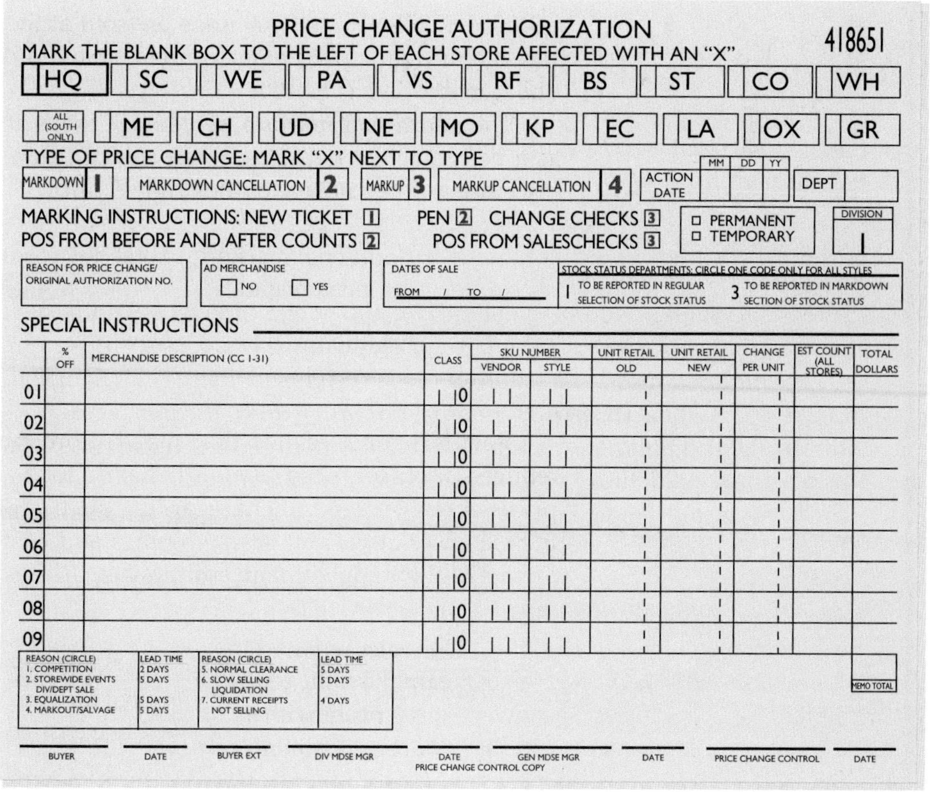
PRICE CHANGE AUTHORIZATION 418651

MARK THE BLANK BOX TO THE LEFT OF EACH STORE AFFECTED WITH AN "X"

HQ | SC | WE | PA | VS | RF | BS | ST | CO | WH

ALL (SOUTH ONLY) | ME | CH | UD | NE | MO | KP | EC | LA | OX | GR

TYPE OF PRICE CHANGE: MARK "X" NEXT TO TYPE

MARKDOWN 1 | MARKDOWN CANCELLATION 2 | MARKUP 3 | MARKUP CANCELLATION 4 | ACTION DATE MM DD YY | DEPT

MARKING INSTRUCTIONS: NEW TICKET 1 PEN 2 CHANGE CHECKS 3 | □ PERMANENT | DIVISION

POS FROM BEFORE AND AFTER COUNTS 2 POS FROM SALESCHECKS 3 | □ TEMPORARY | 1

REASON FOR PRICE CHANGE/ ORIGINAL AUTHORIZATION NO. | AD MERCHANDISE □ NO □ YES | DATES OF SALE FROM / TO /

STOCK STATUS DEPARTMENTS: CIRCLE ONE CODE ONLY FOR ALL STYLES
1 TO BE REPORTED IN REGULAR SELECTION OF STOCK STATUS
3 TO BE REPORTED IN MARKDOWN SECTION OF STOCK STATUS

SPECIAL INSTRUCTIONS

	% OFF	MERCHANDISE DESCRIPTION (CC 1-31)	CLASS	SKU NUMBER VENDOR	SKU NUMBER STYLE	UNIT RETAIL OLD	UNIT RETAIL NEW	CHANGE PER UNIT	EST COUNT (ALL STORES)	TOTAL DOLLARS
01			10							
02			10							
03			10							
04			10							
05			10							
06			10							
07			10							
08			10							
09			10							

REASON (CIRCLE)	LEAD TIME	REASON (CIRCLE)	LEAD TIME
1. COMPETITION	2 DAYS	5. NORMAL CLEARANCE	5 DAYS
2. STOREWIDE EVENTS DIV/DEPT SALE	5 DAYS	6. SLOW SELLING LIQUIDATION	5 DAYS
3. EQUALIZATION	5 DAYS	7. CURRENT RECEIPTS NOT SELLING	4 DAYS
4. MARKOUT/SALVAGE	5 DAYS		

MEMO TOTAL

BUYER | DATE | BUYER EXT | DIV MDSE MGR | DATE | GEN MDSE MGR | DATE | PRICE CHANGE CONTROL | DATE

PRICE CHANGE CONTROL COPY

additional markup increases an item's original price because demand is unexpectedly high or costs are rising. In today's competitive marketplace, markdowns are applied much more frequently than additional markups.

A third price adjustment, the employee discount, is noted here since it may affect the computation of markdowns and additional markups. Although an employee discount is not an adaptive mechanism, it influences morale. Some firms give employee discounts on all items and also let workers buy sale items before they are made available to the general public.

Computing Markdowns and Additional Markups

Markdowns and additional markups can be expressed in dollars or percentages.

The **markdown percentage** is the total dollar markdown as a percentage of net sales (in dollars):

$$\text{Markdown percentage} = \frac{\text{Total dollar markdown}}{\text{Net sales (in \$)}}$$

While it is simple to compute, this formula does not enable a retailer to learn the percentage of items that are marked down relative to those sold at the original price.

A complementary measure is the **off-retail markdown percentage**, which looks at the markdown for each item or category of items as a percentage of original retail price. The markdown percentage for every item can be computed, as well as the percentage of items marked down:

$$\text{Off-retail markdown percentage} = \frac{\text{Original price} - \text{New price}}{\text{Original price}}$$

Suppose a gas barbecue grill sells for $400 at the beginning of the summer and is reduced to $280 at the end of the summer. The off-retail markdown is 30 percent [($400 − $280)/$400]. If 100 grills are sold at the original price and 20 are sold at the sale price, the percentage of items marked down is 17 percent, and the total dollar markdown is $2,400.

The **additional markup percentage** looks at total dollar additional markups as a percentage of net sales, while the **addition to retail percentage** measures a price rise as a percentage of the original price:

$$\frac{\text{Additional markup}}{\text{percentage}} = \frac{\text{Total dollar additional markups}}{\text{Net sales (in \$)}}$$

$$\frac{\text{Addition to retail}}{\text{percentage}} = \frac{\text{New price} - \text{Original price}}{\text{Original price}}$$

Retailers must realize that many more customers would have to buy at reduced prices for those retailers to have a total gross profit equal to that at higher prices. A retailer's judgment regarding price adjustments is affected by its operating expenses at various sales volumes and customer price elasticities. The true impact of a markdown or an additional markup can be learned from this formula:

$$\begin{array}{c}\text{Unit sales required to} \\ \text{earn the same total} \\ \text{gross profit with a} \\ \text{price adjustment}\end{array} = \frac{\text{Original markup (\%)}}{\begin{array}{c}\text{Original markup (\%)} \times \\ +/- \text{ Price change (\%)}\end{array}} \begin{array}{c}\text{Expected unit} \\ \text{sales at} \\ \text{original price}\end{array}$$

Suppose a Sony Walkman with a cost of $50 has an original retail price of $100 (a markup of 50 percent). A retailer expects to sell 500 units over the next year, generating a total gross profit of $25,000 ($50 x 500). How many units does the retailer have to sell if it reduces the price to $85 or raises it to $110—and still earn a $25,000 gross profit? Here are the answers:

$$\text{Unit sales required (at \$85)} = \frac{50\%}{50\% - 15\%} \times 500 = 1.43 \times 500 = 714$$

$$\text{Unit sales required (at \$110)} = \frac{50\%}{50\% + 10\%} \times 500 = 0.83 \times 500 = 417$$

Markdown Control

Through markdown control, a retailer evaluates the number of markdowns, the proportion of sales involving markdowns, and the causes. The control must be such that buying plans can be altered in later periods to reflect markdowns. A good way to evaluate the cause of markdowns is to have retail buyers record the reasons for each markdown and then examine them periodically. Possible buyer notations are "end of season," "to match the price of a competitor," "worn merchandise," and "obsolete style."

Markdown control lets a retailer monitor its policies, such as the way items are displayed. Careful planning may also enable a retailer to avoid some markdowns by running more ads, training workers better, shipping goods more efficiently among branch units, and returning items to vendors.

The need for markdown control should not be interpreted as meaning that all markdowns can or should be minimized or eliminated. In fact, too low a markdown percentage may indicate that a retailer's buyers have not assumed enough risk in purchasing goods.

Timing Markdowns

Although there are different perspectives among retailers about the best markdown timing sequence, much can be said about the benefits of an *early markdown policy*: It requires lower markdowns to sell products than markdowns late in the season. Merchandise is offered at reduced prices while demand is still fairly active. Early markdowns free selling space for new merchandise. The retailer's cash flow position can be improved. The main advantage of a *late markdown policy* is that a retailer gives itself every opportunity to sell merchandise at original prices. Yet, the advantages associated with an early markdown policy cannot be achieved under a late markdown policy.

Retailers can also use a *staggered markdown policy* and discount prices throughout a selling period. One pre-planned staggered markdown policy is an *automatic markdown plan*, in which the amount and timing of markdowns are controlled by the length of time merchandise remains in stock. Syms, the off-price chain, uses this approach to ensure fresh stock and early markdowns:

> All garments are sold with the brand name as affixed by the manufacturer. Because women's dresses are vulnerable to considerable style fluctuation, Syms has long utilized a 10-day automatic markdown pricing policy to promote movement of merchandise. The date of placement on the selling floor of each women's dress is stamped on the back of the

price ticket. The front of each ticket contains what the company believes to be the nationally advertised price, the initial Syms price, and three reduced prices. Each reduced price becomes effective after the passage of 10 selling days. Syms also offers "dividend" prices consisting of additional price reductions on various types of merchandise.[15]

A *storewide clearance*, conducted once or twice a year, is another way to time markdowns. It often takes place after peak selling periods such as Christmas and Mother's Day. The goal is to clean out merchandise before taking a physical inventory and beginning the next season. The advantages of a storewide clearance are that a longer period is provided for selling merchandise at original prices and that frequent markdowns can destroy a consumer's confidence in regular prices: "Why buy now, when it will be on sale next week?" Clearance sales limit bargain hunting to once or twice a year. See Figure 17-12.

In the past, many retailers would introduce merchandise at high prices and then mark down many items by as much as 60 percent to increase store traffic and improve inventory turnover. This caused customers to wait for price reductions and treat initial prices skeptically. Today, more retailers start out with lower prices, run fewer sales, and apply fewer markdowns than before. Nonetheless, a big problem facing some retailers is that they have gotten consumers too used to buying when items are discounted.

FIGURE 17-12
Promoting Markdowns

Sometimes retailers are subtle when they offer special sales on merchandise. Other times, they want to make sure that shoppers are quite aware that a clearance sale is going on. It's pretty hard to miss this sign!

Photo reprinted by permission.

Summary

1. *To describe the role of pricing in a retail strategy and to show that pricing decisions must be made in an integrated and adaptive manner.* Pricing is crucial to a retailer because of its interrelationship with overall objectives and the other components of the retail strategy. A price plan must be integrated and responsive—and provide a good value to customers.

2. *To examine the impact of consumers; government; manufacturers, wholesalers, and other suppliers; and current and potential competitors on pricing decisions.* Before designing a price plan, a retailer must study the factors affecting its decisions. Sometimes the factors have a minor effect on pricing discretion; other times, they severely limit pricing options.

    Retailers should be familiar with the price elasticity of demand and the different market segments that are possible. Government restrictions deal with horizontal and vertical price fixing, price discrimination, minimum prices, unit pricing, item price removal, and price advertising. There may be conflicts about which party controls retail prices; and manufacturers, wholesalers, and other suppliers may be asked to provide price guarantees (if they are in a weak position). The competitive environment may foster market pricing, lead to price wars, or allow administered pricing.

3. *To present a framework for developing a retail price strategy.* This framework consists of five stages: objectives, broad price policy, price strategy, implementation of price strategy, and price adjustments.

    Retail pricing goals can be chosen from among sales, dollar profits, return on investment, and early recovery of cash. Next, a broad policy outlines a coordinated series of actions, consistent with the retailer's image and oriented to the short and long run.

    A good price strategy incorporates demand, cost, and competitive concepts. Each of these orientations must be understood separately and jointly. Psychological pricing, markup pricing, alternative ways of computing markups, gross margin, direct product profitability, and pricing below, at, or above the market are among the key aspects of strategy planning.

    When enacting a price strategy, specific tools can be used to supplement the broad base of the strategy. Retailers should know when to use customary and variable pricing, one-price policies and flexible pricing, odd pricing, leader pricing, multiple-unit pricing, and price lining.

    Price adjustments may be required to adapt to internal and external conditions. Adjustments include markdowns, additional markups, and employee discounts. It is important that adjustments are controlled by a budget, the causes of markdowns are noted, future company buying reflects prior performance, adjustments are properly timed, and excessive discounting is avoided.

Key Terms

price elasticity of demand (p. 500)
horizontal price fixing (p. 502)
vertical price fixing (p. 502)
Robinson-Patman Act (p. 503)
minimum-price laws (p. 504)
predatory pricing (p. 504)
loss leaders (p. 504)
unit pricing (p. 504)
item price removal (p. 504)
bait-and-switch advertising (p. 505)
gray market goods (p. 506)
market penetration pricing (p. 507)
market skimming pricing (p. 507)
demand-oriented pricing (p. 510)
cost-oriented pricing (p. 510)
competition-oriented pricing (p. 510)

price-quality association (p. 510)
prestige pricing (p. 511)
markup pricing (p. 511)
markup (p. 511)
markup percentage (p. 511)
initial markup (p. 513)
maintained markup (p. 513)
gross margin (p. 513)
variable markup policy (p. 514)
direct product profitability (DPP) (p. 514)
customary pricing (p. 517)
everyday low pricing (EDLP) (p. 518)
variable pricing (p. 518)
yield management pricing (p. 518)

one-price policy (p. 519)
flexible pricing (p. 519)
contingency pricing (p. 519)
odd pricing (p. 519)
leader pricing (p. 519)
multiple-unit pricing (p. 520)
bundled pricing (p. 520)
unbundled pricing (p. 520)
price lining (p. 520)
markdown (p. 521)
additional markup (p. 522)
markdown percentage (p. 522)
off-retail markdown percentage (p. 522)
additional markup percentage (p. 522)
addition to retail percentage (p. 522)

Questions for Discussion

1. Why is it important for retailers to understand the concept of price elasticity even if they are unable to compute it?

2. Comment on each of the following from the perspective of a small retailer:
   a. Horizontal price fixing.
   b. Vertical price fixing.
   c. Price discrimination.
   d. Minimum-price laws.
   e. Unit pricing.

3. Give an example of a price strategy that integrates demand, cost, and competitive criteria.

4. Explain why markups are usually computed as a percentage of selling price rather than of cost.

5. A floor tile retailer wants to receive a 45 percent markup (at retail) for all merchandise. If one style of tile retails for $11 per tile, what is the maximum that the retailer would be willing to pay for a tile?

6. A car dealer purchases multiple-disc CD players for $150 each and desires a 40 percent markup (at retail). What retail price should be charged?

7. A photo store charges $11.00 to process a roll of slides; its cost is $8.25. What is the markup percentage (at cost and at retail)?

8. A firm has planned operating expenses of $150,000, a profit goal of $110,000, and planned reductions of $35,000 and expects sales of $600,000. Compute the initial markup percentage.

9. At the end of the year, the retailer in Question 8 determines that actual operating expenses are $140,000, actual profit is $105,000, and actual sales are $590,000. What is the maintained markup percentage? Explain the difference in your answers to Questions 8 and 9.

10. What are the pros and cons of everyday low pricing to a retailer? To a manufacturer?

11. Under what circumstances do you think unbundled pricing is a good idea? A poor idea? Why?

12. A retailer buys items for $50. At an original retail price of $75, it expects to sell 1,000 units.
    a. If the price is marked down to $65, how many units must the retailer sell to earn the same total gross profit it would attain with a $75 price?
    b. If the price is marked up to $90, how many units must the retailer sell to earn the same total gross profit it would attain with a $75 price?

Note: At our Web site (**www.prenhall.com/bermanevans**), there are several math problems related to the material in this chapter so that you may review these concepts.

Web-Based Exercise

Visit the Web site of Sam's Club (**www.samsclub.com**). What are the least expensive consumer products sold through this site? The most expensive? Do you feel that this price range is consistent with Sam's image as a discount-oriented membership club chain? Explain your answer.

Note: Stop by our Web site (**www.prenhall.com/bermanevans**) to experience a number of highly interactive, appealing Web exercises based on actual company demonstrations and sample materials related to retailing.

Chapter Endnotes

1. Various company sources.

2. Mike Troy, "Got Game? The Sports Authority Gets It Together," *DSN Retailing Today* (April 11, 2005), p. 6.

3. Marianne Wilson, "Cheap Thrills for Teens," *Chain Store Age* (March 2005), p. 118.

4. LeeAnn Prescott, "Shopping Around Online," *Chain Store Age* (March 2005), p. 78.

5. See Lan Xia, Kent B. Monroe, and Jennifer L. Cox, *Journal of Marketing*, Vol. 68 (October 2004), pp. 1–15; and Christian Homburg, Wayne D Hoyer, and Nicole Koschate, "Customers' Reactions to Price Increases: Do Customer Satisfaction and Perceived Motive Fairness Matter?" *Journal of the Academy of Marketing Science*, Vol. 33 (Winter 2005), pp. 36–49.

6. Julie Creswell, "Sotheby's Is Back in Auction," *Fortune* (September 20, 2004), p. 18.

7. Edward Felsenthal, "Manufacturers Allowed to Cap Retail Prices," *Wall Street Journal* (November 5, 1997), pp. A3, A8.

8. "Oligopolies and Price Fixing," **www.oligopoly watch.com** (May 26, 2003).

9. "The Loss Leader," **www.bizhelp24.com/marketing/ loss_leader.shtml** (January 29, 2006).

10. See "Item and Unit Pricing," **www.fmi.org/gr/issues/ gr_issues_display.cfm?id=112** (September 28, 2004).

11. Ken Clark, "Sticker Shock," *Chain Store Age* (September 2000), p. 88.

12. Selling price may also be computed by transposing the markup formula into

$$\text{Retail selling price} = \frac{\text{Merchandise cost}}{1 - \text{Markup}} = \$17.14$$

13. Merchandise cost may also be computed by transposing the markup formula into

$$\text{Merchandise cost} = (\text{Retail selling price}) \times (1 - \text{Markup}) = \$4.794$$

14. See Joan Gunin, "Starting Price Points a Key Element in Leather," *Furniture Today* (February 14, 2005), pp. 12–13.

15. *Syms 2005 Annual Report.*

part six
Short Cases

CASE 1: THE ZUMIEZ MERCHANDISING APPROACH TO LURING TEENS[c-1]

Zumiez (**www.zumiez.com**) (pronounced as Zoo-meez) is a 150-store action-sports lifestyle chain that specializes in cutting-edge action-sports equipment and apparel for snow board, surf, skateboard, motocross, and BMX racing enthusiasts. Rick Brooks, Zumiez's president and chief executive officer, says that what sets Zumiez apart from most competitors is its selection.

Zumiez recently filed an offering to go public that could raise as much as $57.5 million. The offering will convert Zumiez from a privately held to a public corporation and will help finance the retailer's store expansion plans. Zumiez added 27 new stores in 2004, planned to add 35 stores in 2005, and may grow to as many as 600 stores within the next decade. Its stores typically have sales per square foot of between $450 and $500.

Zumiez's merchandising strategy differs from most other retailers that sell either apparel or action-based sports apparel. It not only carries more brands than either of these retailer types but also is often the first major chain to stock a good after the good has been successful in independent stores. Many retailers group similar products together regardless of their brand. In contrast, Zumiez's stores are organized by lifestyle and then by brand within that lifestyle category. Zumiez's stores are also dense by design. Brooks says that his strategy is to have a much more complete product assortment than its competitors.

Although soft goods such as apparel dominate Zumiez's product mix, the chain carries hard goods such as boards in each of its major merchandise categories: surfing, skateboarding, and snowboarding. In addition, unlike many competitors, Zumiez sells such services as fitting boards and boots to customers, as well as assembling skateboards. Zumiez sells mostly manufacturer brands; private-label products account for about 14 percent of its sales.

Its stores are organized in a hip and laid-back manner to make its 12- to 24-year-old customers feel comfortable. According to Brooks, "We want kids to come in and hang out with us." As part of that strategy, each Zumiez store unit contains a living room section where customers can play electronic games or watch videos depicting action-sports plays. To encourage customers to linger, each store also has an old sofa, coffee table, and an old television (that is outfitted with a new monitor). Many of the chain's employees are also sports enthusiasts. These employees possess excellent product knowledge and are enthusiastic about their job. Employees who sell over $100,000 in products win a company-sponsored snowboarding trip to the Rocky Mountains.

To increase consumer interest and generate store traffic, Zumiez constantly runs special promotions. These range from a "design-your-own-skateboard contest" to the Zumiez Couch Tour, a festival-style event held each summer. The Couch Tour features autograph signings by professional skateboarders and motocross racers, live music, and merchandise booths (many of which are co-sponsored by vendors). Zumiez's recent Mall of America Couch Tour drew more than 12,000 consumers.

Questions

1. Develop an appropriate merchandising philosophy for Zumiez.
2. What buying organization format and processes are most appropriate for Zumiez? Explain your answer.
3. What are the pros and cons of centralized buying for Zumiez?
4. How important is innovativeness for Zumiez? Explain your answer.

CASE 2: STARBUCKS: A LOT MORE THAN COFFEE[c-2]

Starbucks (**www.starbucks.com**) sells much more than espresso and cappuccino, even though coffee contributes more than 80 percent of the firm's total revenues,. The company is focused on three broad sources of growth: additional items that are now sold in traditional Starbucks coffeehouses, new locations (both within the United States and internationally), and food service (made up of restaurants, offices, schools, and hotels that purchase Starbucks products such as whole bean coffee and Frappucino) for resale. This case is limited to the first category.

Starbucks recently added Tazo tea to its stores, a hot breakfast sandwich menu, and a $5.95 gourmet selection of cheeses that is part of a larger lunch menu. All of these items are part of Starbucks' plan to get a larger share of each customer's food budget. Starbucks' Music CD division also sells products in its retail locations. For example, the CD division received exclusive rights to sell a remake of Alanis Morissette's *Jagged Little Pill.*

A major problem associated with Starbucks' adding new products to existing stores is the effect on waiting lines. According to research, 64 percent of Americans say that they choose a restaurant based on how much time they have. Since these new items require preparation, Starbucks becomes

---

[c-1]The material in this case is drawn from Kimberly Pfaff, "Board Teens," *Shopping Centers Today* (January 2005), pp. 9–10, 12; Monica Soto Ouchi, "Trendy Sports Chain Zumiez Files to Go Public," *The Seattle Times* (February 18, 2005); and "Zumiez 411," **www.zumiez.com/help/index.html** (April 2, 2006).

[c-2]The material in this case is drawn from John Gaffney, "Starbucks Adds Buzz to Food Service Sales," *1to1 Magazine* (November–December 2004); "Starbucks Is All Set to Say Cheese," *Daily News* (April 11, 2005); and Steven Gray, "Coffee on the Double," *Wall Street Journal* (April 12, 2005), pp. B1, B7.

more vulnerable to time-pressed consumers. Starbucks' director of store operations engineering acknowledges that, "This is a game of seconds." She and her 10 engineers constantly ask themselves: "How can we shave time off this?" Starbucks has focused on delivery speed since its growth spurt in the 1990s.

At Starbucks, it now takes, on average, about three minutes from the time a customer gets in line until he/she receives the final order. This compares favorably with the three-and-one-half minutes it took five years ago, when Starbucks began to measure this variable.

Let's consider some tactics to deal with the time issue. One solution is to stop requiring customer signatures for credit card purchases under $25. In the past, the processing of a credit card was the longest part of the cash register transaction. Eliminating the need for a signature can reduce the service transaction time by 22 seconds. Another time-saver involves the addition of "floaters," personnel who wait on customers, take orders, and run to the back room for necessary supplies. The chain is considering a floater who will work only on sandwiches at especially busy times. Starbucks' quest for increased speed has had no effect on its order accuracy rate that has remained constant at 99.4 percent. Starbucks' new sandwich items are warmed in a combination convection and microwave oven that meets the chain's need for speed, as well as taste.

Starbucks' organization also has to accommodate the chain's overall growth rate. Howard Schulz, Starbucks' chairman and chief global strategist, recently announced that Starbucks now has a long-term goal of having 30,000 locations on a worldwide basis, as compared with its current 12,500-plus stores. This new goal is for 5,000 more locations than the previous objective.

Questions

1. Identify Starbucks' major issues in selecting and interacting with merchandise sources.
2. How should Starbucks evaluate its merchandise?
3. Discuss supply chain management issues for Starbucks.
4. How else can Starbucks reduce transaction times within its stores?

CASE 3: THE GROWING POPULARITY OF "SLIGHTLY USED" MERCHANDISE[c-3]

The sales of used clothing and other items have grown dramatically in popularity. The National Association of Resale & Thrift Shops (**www.narts.org**) reports that there are more than 20,000 resale stores in the United States, with 750 new stores added each year. One obvious attraction of these stores is their low prices. For example, a Columbia Child's coat that generally sells for $150 new can be purchased at a used

[c-3]The material in this case is drawn from Maura K. Ammenheuser, "Slightly Used," *Shopping Centers Today* (January 2005), pp. 15–18; and "Industry Statistics & Trends," **www.narts.org/press/stats.htm** (April 9, 2006).

clothing store for $30. A second benefit is that many of the items available at these stores are "one-of-a-kind pieces" appealing to a shopper's need to be different.

Most stores have a similar business model in which consumers sell their used resellable merchandise to a store, the store's buyers pay for the merchandise in either cash or store credit (for other used merchandise), and the store sells used merchandise at a profit. Resale shops that sell clothing generally focus on women's apparel. Men's used clothing shops are very rare since men are generally harder on their clothes and have less enthusiasm for shopping.

The terms "resale" and "secondhand" stores are broad-based concepts that cover a wide variety of businesses. They include stores that sell inexpensive merchandise and others that sell used designer clothing, fur coats and jackets, and even used wedding gowns. While many used merchandise stores focus on clothing, others like Music Go Round (**www.musicgoround.com**) and Play It Again Sports (**www.playitagainsports.com**) focus exclusively on limited lines of merchandise such as music CDs and used sports equipment. There are also profit and nonprofit forms of ownership.

Children's Orchard (**www.childrensorchard.com**) is a for-profit chain with $20 million in annual sales. According to its chief executive, the chain had 85 franchises as of 2005 and commitments for another 15 stores from franchisees. Children's Orchard is testing another used clothing concept called Howie Mack that will sell used clothing aimed at the teen and college markets.

In addition to for-profit chains, nonprofits such as Goodwill Industries (**www.goodwill.org**), the Salvation Army (**www.salvationarmyusa.org**), and other charities typically operate secondhand stores. Goodwill Industries, for example, operates more than 2,000 stores in North America and has annual revenues of $1.4 billion.

Unlike the bleak appearance of used clothing and other merchandise stores of the past, many used clothing stores now feature lighting, store signage, and store fixtures that are similar to those used by many traditional retailers of new merchandise. The better appearance makes these stores much more appealing to property owners who do not want to adversely affect the image of their property or anger existing retail tenants. As the property manager of The Lab, a collection of 13 shops in 50,000 square feet in Costa Mesa, California, says, "I'd rather have a great secondhand store than a homogenized store."

Questions

1. Distinguish between the merchandise planning process for a new camera store versus a used camera store.
2. Distinguish between the merchandise planning process for a for-profit used clothing store versus a nonprofit used clothing store.
3. Aside from savings and uniqueness, what are some of the other benefits to a consumer's purchasing used merchandise?

4. Besides those cited in the case, what are the other benefits of a used clothing store's using upgraded signage, lighting, and fixtures?

CASE 4: RETAILER PRESSURE ON SUPPLIERS: THE MARKDOWN SHOWDOWN[c-4]

When major retail chains such as Saks Fifth Avenue (**www.saks.com**) and Macy's (**www.macys.com**) require substantial markdowns to clear out merchandise, they typically demand "markdown money" from their suppliers to make up for their lost profits. This means that suppliers such as Tommy Hilfiger (**www.tommy.com**), Liz Claiborne (**www.lizclaiborne.com**), and Jones Apparel Group (**www.jny.com**) have little choice but to pay.

Before markdown monies were introduced in the late 1980s, stores were responsible for excessive markdowns. The stores typically sold overstocked goods to off-price chains and accepted the losses as a cost of doing business. Now, the retailers want to pass off the risk of higher-than-planned markdowns to their suppliers. If a retailer's plan, for example, calls for a 42 percent initial markup percentage on a vendor's line of clothing and the retailer's maintained markup percentage is actually 32 percent, the retailer will ask the vendor to pay for the extra 10 percent of markdown money to "make them whole."

Many retail analysts agree that negotiations concerning markdown money between retailers and vendors have become more hostile. An executive for a major apparel manufacturer says that large retailers "are not taking 'no' for an answer. If you don't agree to the cuts they propose, they say we can forget the 5 percent raise in volume they promised us. They say it will be flat. If you still refuse, or try to argue, they say they'll order 5 percent less."

One reason for the increased conflict is the higher number of markdowns. One analyst found that the 2004 seasonal markdown index rose 12 percent, the highest increase since he began tracking markdowns. Some retailers have argued that markdown monies have increasingly been a bargaining issue due to some manufacturers not living up to their promises.

A Macy's executive noted that some large suppliers that required department stores to sell their goods at full price offered the same goods at a 30 percent discount to off-price retailers such as T.J. Maxx (**www.tjmaxx.com**). This move required Macy's to lower its prices. Manufacturers, on the other hand, state that retailers need to follow the markdown schedule agreed to in advance. For example, the schedule might call for a 25 percent markdown after 12 weeks and a 40 percent markdown after 16 weeks.

To make matters worse for vendors, mid-level department stores such as Kohl's (**www.kohls.com**) and J.C. Penney (**www.jcpenney.com**), as well as specialty stores, have begun to demand markdown money. Discounters such as Target (**www.target.com**) and even some retailers with private labels have begun to hit up their vendors.

Some analysts believe that smaller suppliers are most vulnerable to markdown money demands due to their lower bargaining power. Yet two major suppliers, Kellwood and Jones, have recently warned of lower earnings due to post-holiday payments by merchants.

One clothing manufacturer, Nicole Miller, refuses to pay markdown monies. Buyers are told that the vendor deals only on a "buy it and don't come back to me" basis. Despite this statement, a Nicole Miller executive concedes that the firm helps with cooperative advertising allowances to reduce a merchant's promotional expenses.

Questions

1. Develop a number of suggestions for a retailer to better control its use of markdowns.
2. Explain the role of outsourcing of production to the Far East on a retailer's need for additional markdowns.
3. Discuss how the payment of markdown money is affected by the Robinson-Patman Act.
4. What are the ethical implications of markdown money?

[c-4]The material in this case is drawn from Tracie Rozhon, "First the Markdown, Then the Showdown," *New York Times* (February 25, 2005), pp. C1, C3.

part six
Comprehensive Case
Pricing's Role in Merchandise Management*

Introduction

Retail pricing and promotion practices have come under increased scrutiny. Firms such as Wal-Mart (**www.walmart.com**), with its winning everyday low-pricing (EDLP) strategy, demonstrate that pricing and promotion can be done differently, causing many retailers to second-guess their established practices. Key retail sectors that grew a lot in the 1990s—home improvement, warehouse clubs, supercenters, manufacturer outlets—promoted everyday low or everyday fair pricing as an alternative to the time-honored high-low pricing format (high regular prices, frequent discounts).

Advocates say everyday pricing increases customer loyalty, improves inventory management, and reduces labor and advertising expenses. Retailers that use everyday pricing promote its benefits directly to consumers to show pricing integrity. Trader Joe's (**www.traderjoes.com**), a grocery store chain, features a large sign inside each store: "How We Keep Prices So Low: We buy direct from our suppliers, in large volume. We bargain hard and manage our costs carefully; we don't pay exorbitant amounts to create a fancy store; we're not open 24 hours a day; we don't conduct couponing wars or fancy promotions. And we don't borrow money. We pay in cash, and on time, so our suppliers like to do business with us."

Still, the practice of offering regular price promotions is deeply ingrained. Price promotions can increase store traffic, clear out time-sensitive merchandise, communicate a low-price image, and attract customers who will also buy higher-margin, regular-priced items. Fearing declines in profit margins and more direct price competition between national brands and their own store brands, many retailers have been reluctant to adopt everyday pricing. With few rules or guideposts to follow in making price promotion decisions, retail managers face the following questions:

- How should we balance everyday pricing and promotional pricing?
- How deeply should we discount promotional prices?
- How aggressively should we advertise everyday prices and price promotions?
- What are the effects of price promotion on financial performance?

To gain insight into how retailers might answer these questions, we studied the price promotion practices of 38 companies from 11 retail sectors. Table 1 identifies the companies and sectors we studied. It also charts their scores on three dimensions of promotional intensity that we tracked over a 12-month period—price variation (everyday versus promotional pricing), volume of promotional advertising, and depth of discount—and includes a composite score for overall promotional intensity. As a final step, we measured the degree to which our sample companies' price promotion practices affected their financial performance. Guided by the results of our study, we developed the retail price promotion matrix, a framework that retail managers can apply to price promotion decisions.

The Fundamental Traits

The retail price promotion matrix shows that the effectiveness of a retailer's price promotion strategy depends on how it is aligned with two fundamental traits that distinguish retail offerings: assortment overlap and assortment life span. See Figure 1.

Assortment overlap is the degree to which retailers' product assortments are similar to, rather than distinctive from, one another. Assortment life span is a function of the speed at which a typical assortment loses value or becomes obsolete over time. Assortments that are limited in life span can be said to be perishable; this affects many product categories, including food, fashion, and consumer electronics. For example, a bakery item may have a two-day life span, a fashion apparel item may have a three-month life span, and an electronics item, such as a personal computer, may have a 12-month life span.

Figure 1 identifies the sectors that benefit least from price promotion (low-gain promoters) and those that benefit most (high-gain promoters). Each position represents a different prescribed approach to retail price promotion. Retailers in the low-low position (differentiators) and high-high position (price point rivals) should limit use of price promotion by following everyday pricing strategies. Retailers on the high-low to low-high diagonal—variety promoters, broadscope promoters, and clear-out promoters—should follow more intensive price promotion strategies.

Everyday Pricing Strategies
Differentiators

Where life span and product overlap are both low and product assortments are relatively perishable and sharply distinctive from competitors, retailers use differentiation strategies. This downplays the role of price, continuously offering new products to spur demand and avoid head-to-head competition. This type of market includes high-end fashion department stores (e.g., Neiman Marcus, **www.neimanmarcus.com**) and specialty stores (e.g., Emporio Armani, **www.emporioarmani.com**) that rely on a high rate of product innovation. Defined by the uniqueness of their products, these firms sometimes are tied to a single designer (e.g., Donna Karan, Georgio Armani) and typically use everyday high pricing to reinforce the exclusivity and cachet of their stores. These retailers should not be dependent on price promotions, which would only detract from their positioning.

The marketing efforts of these elite retailers are directed at building and maintaining brand equity, which supports their image appeal and guarantees continued status. Coach Leather, which sells its products through catalogs, department

TABLE 1	Retail Sector Index Scores			

Retail Sectors and Companies	Price Variation Index	Price Promotion Ad Volume Index	Average Depth of Discount Index	Overall Promotional Intensity Index[a]
Bookstores Barnes & Noble, Borders	.00	.02	.00	.00
Discount stores Kmart, Service Merchandise, Target, Wal-Mart	1.44	2.98	1.00	2.96
Electronics stores Best Buy, Circuit City, CompUSA, Tandy	.87	2.31	1.00	1.38
Fashion department stores Neiman Marcus, Nordstrom, Saks Fifth Avenue	1.46	.08	1.40	.12
Furniture stores Bombay Company, Ethan Allen, Haverty's, Heilig-Meyers	1.44	.22	1.09	.24
Grocery stores Albertson's, Food Lion, Kroger, Whole Foods, Winn-Dixie	1.57	.67	1.45	1.06
Home improvement stores Home Depot, Lowes	.28	.35	.41	.03
Office supply stores Office Depot, OfficeMax, Staples	.57	.77	.95	.29
Off-price stores Men's Wearhouse, SteinMart, T.J. Maxx	1.02	.09	1.27	.08
Specialty clothing stores Ann Taylor, Gap, Talbots	.80	.06	1.13	.04
Traditional department stores Dillard's, J.C. Penney, Macy's, Montgomery Ward, Sears	1.54	3.45	1.31	4.80

[a]The index score is the sector mean divided by the average for all sectors, so an index of 1 represents the average. Overall promotional intensity was calculated as price variation times ad volume times depth of discount and then expressed as an index.

store boutiques, and Coach stores (**www.coach.com**), shuns promotions, with standard product prices published and maintained in all channels. Fashion department stores Barneys (**www.barneys.com**) and Nordstrom (**www.nordstrom.com**) deliberately advertise "annual" or "twice-annual" sales, the implication being: We don't have to put our products on sale, and we don't do it often.

Faced with pressure to move short-lived products, differentiators often use outlet stores or private shopping events (pre-sales for core customers), rather than widely advertised price promotions. When these retailers offer price promotions, they tend to use deep discounts. With their higher original margins and infrequent sales events, they can discount deeply to generate store traffic and move perishable inventory

without damaging their image and price credibility. Neiman Marcus is an exemplary differentiator: It was one of the first fashion retailers to develop an effective loyalty program, operate a successful high-volume outlet store, and publicize a famous annual-only clearance sale.

Price Point Rivals

Where overlap and life span are both high, large efficient chains follow a mass-marketing approach and depend on volume sales. These retailers include the office supply, home improvement, book superstore, discount store, and warehouse club sectors. When assortment life span and overlap are both at high levels, there is limited variation across retailers, price is the key to differential advantage, and companies

FIGURE 1
The Retail Price Promotion Mix

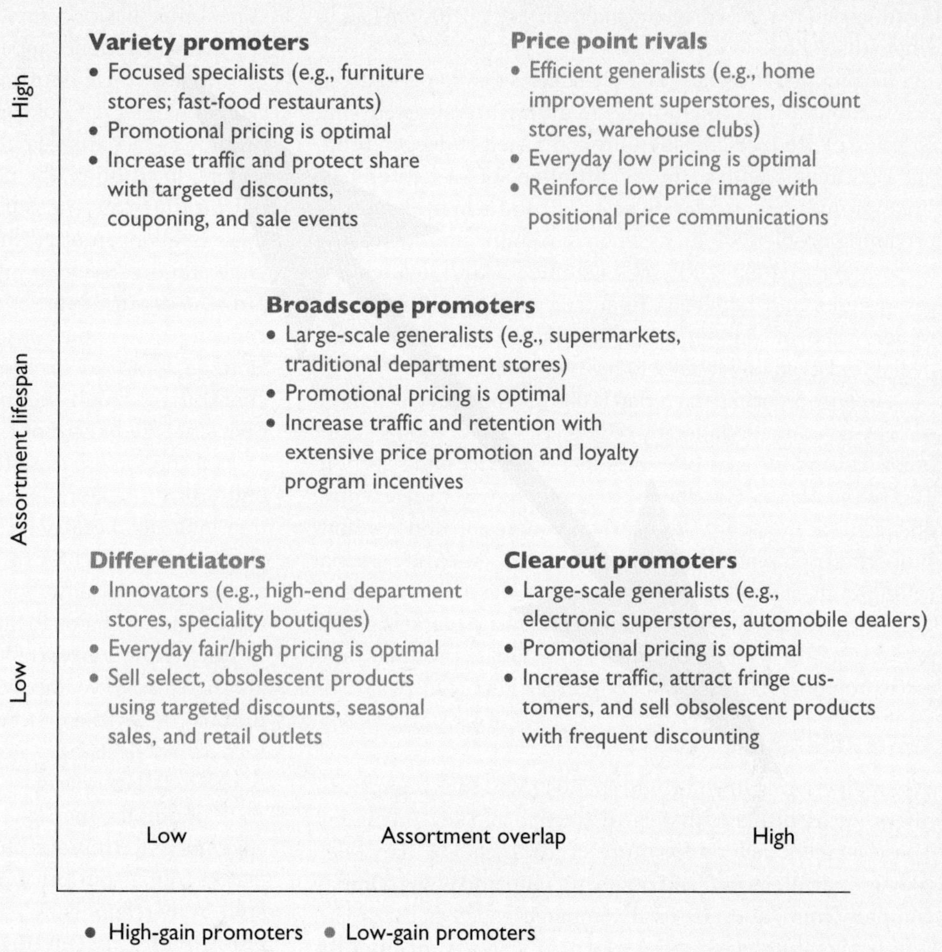

Assortment lifespan — High / Low

Variety promoters
- Focused specialists (e.g., furniture stores; fast-food restaurants)
- Promotional pricing is optimal
- Increase traffic and protect share with targeted discounts, couponing, and sale events

Price point rivals
- Efficient generalists (e.g., home improvement superstores, discount stores, warehouse clubs)
- Everyday low pricing is optimal
- Reinforce low price image with positional price communications

Broadscope promoters
- Large-scale generalists (e.g., supermarkets, traditional department stores)
- Promotional pricing is optimal
- Increase traffic and retention with extensive price promotion and loyalty program incentives

Differentiators
- Innovators (e.g., high-end department stores, speciality boutiques)
- Everyday fair/high pricing is optimal
- Sell select, obsolescent products using targeted discounts, seasonal sales, and retail outlets

Clearout promoters
- Large-scale generalists (e.g., electronic superstores, automobile dealers)
- Promotional pricing is optimal
- Increase traffic, attract fringe customers, and sell obsolescent products with frequent discounting

Low — Assortment overlap — High

● High-gain promoters   ● Low-gain promoters

rely on economies of scale or scope to lower expenses and support lower prices.

An optimal price point rival strategy conveys a favorable price image, emphasizing EDLP and including a relatively small number of price promotions. Differentiation is a challenge in these sectors: An Office Depot store (**www.officedepot.com**) can easily substitute for a Staples store (**www.staples.com**) and a Barnes & Noble (**www.bn.com**) for a Borders bookstore (**www.borders.com**). Because of the constant need to defend market share, these retailers often invest in high advertising. Widespread consolidation in these sectors has produced large retail chains with a constant need to defend market share. With their critical mass of stores and bargaining power, the companies benefit from investing in high-volume, price-oriented advertising, even if it promotes everyday low prices rather than sales.

Convenience is paramount when consumers shop for the basic, low-involvement products sold by price point rivals. By assuring lower average regular prices on a basket of items, everyday low price retailers attract time-constrained consumers who want to avoid "shopping around." However, low-cost leadership is a prerequisite for low price leadership. The lower gross margins associated with everyday low or even everyday fair pricing mandate strong volume increases for a retailer shifting to less promotional pricing. Wal-Mart's

supercenter concept—with its combined grocery and discount store assortment—is the quintessential retail format for this position.

In general, the low-gain promoters we examined exhibited much lower levels of price promotion intensity. Price promotion intensity had a negative financial impact for firms in the home improvement, specialty apparel, and fashion department sectors. Only one sector behaved counter to expectations. The intensity score for discounters was high—largely because of advertising—even though this sector received little financial benefit from its promotional practices. It should be noted that our results reflect a period of shakeout and repositioning within that sector, which likely triggered increased promotion.

Where It Makes Sense

Clear-Out Promoters

Where overlap is high and life span is low, retailers offer perishable assortments that are relatively undifferentiated across competitors. These sectors include auto dealerships and consumer electronics retailers, such as Best Buy (**www.bestbuy.com**) and Circuit City (**www.circuitcity.com**). Each retailer is fairly secure in a core market in which customers show a preference for the firm's offering, but there are many infrequent customers who are variety seekers or are indifferent as to where they shop.

The limited life span of assortments is tied to rapid product proliferation, including manufacturers' recurring redesign of products. Retailers are compelled to deepen product assortments with many modifications of basic products. Price promotions accelerate sales of products in danger of becoming obsolete by increasing store traffic and increasing the buying frequency of core customers. Auto dealers use promotions and generous financing terms to attract customers who may have little awareness of the individual dealer and even low loyalty to the manufacturer.

Because assortment overlap is high, some retailers in these sectors seek differentiation by selling "exclusive" models from branded vendors or by offering superior service and selection. The Tweeter Home Entertainment Group (**www. tweeter.com**), an electronics retailer with nearly 200 stores, includes a high proportion of top-shelf products in its mix, focuses on personal selling in its stores, and offers an automatic price protection policy. But in general, these retailers operate in markets where it is fairly difficult for consumers to evaluate products, and price promotion is a motivator of purchase decisions.

Variety Promoters

Where overlap is low and life span is high, each competitor offers an assortment that is distinctive on key attributes. These retailers include furniture stores, such as Ethan Allen (**www.ethanallen.com**) and Bombay Company (**www.bombaycompany.com**), and fast-food companies, such as Pizza Hut (**www.pizzahut.com**) and McDonald's (**www.mcdonalds.com**). Customers of these companies seek variety among substitutable alternatives. Someone shopping for a table, for instance, can choose a classic American reproduction from Ethan Allen or a Victorian-style item from Bombay Company.

Because consumer inertia can be an obstacle for variety promoters, the need for promotions that encourage trial and protect market share is ongoing. Firms try to increase store traffic with promotions that, ideally, target fringe customers who seek variety or are neutral or undecided as to their shopping destination. Fast-food companies frequently use weekly coupons, often featuring new menu items or value meals, which bypass core customers who do not search for coupons and so are not aware of the discounts.

Broadscope Promoters

The third group of retailers for whom promotional pricing strategies make sense are those with broad product assortments that are both low and high in life span and overlap. These sectors, which include traditional department stores and supermarkets, offer many product categories, some commoditylike in nature and some prone to obsolescence. Supermarkets offer national-brand (manufacturer) packaged goods (high life span, high overlap), store-brand packaged goods (high life span, low overlap), and perishable items such as those in the deli, seafood, and bakery departments (low life span, low overlap). Similarly, traditional department stores offer basic, commodity-type soft goods, store-brand apparel, and designer apparel items that follow fashion seasons.

Because their assortments include many types of product categories that are not especially differentiated, broad-scope promoters face intense competition both within and across sectors. In addition, the perishable categories create substantial product loss pressures. Promotional activity provides these retailers an opportunity to attract customers, control a large and diverse store inventory, and inspire frequent shopping. Most supermarket and department store retailers use general price promotions, including weekly circulars and in-store deals, as well as more targeted initiatives (delivered at checkout, through the mail, or online) supported by their own store credit card or loyalty card data.

Of the sectors classified as high-gain promoters, all but one—furniture stores—exhibited high levels of price promotion intensity. Because price promotion intensity had a positive financial effect for firms in this sector, we attribute this to a resource constraint. Some furniture retailers in our sample were regional chains that likely lacked the economies of scale to fully exploit advertising opportunities. Price promotion also had a positive impact on profitability for grocery and traditional department stores—the broad-scope promoter sectors. This reflects how effectively these retailers have institutionalized discounting.

Among the high-gain promoters we examined, only the consumer electronics sector failed to receive significant financial benefits from price promotion. We attribute this to the split in merchandising strategies within the sector. Best Buy and Circuit City sell higher lifespan household appliances and electronics, while CompUSA (**www.compusa.com**) and Radio Shack (**www.radioshack.com**) focus closely on more perishable electronics. Best Buy and Circuit City have far higher advertising volume but less price variation and more shallow discounts than their more specialized competitors.

Assessing Strategy

Retailers can use the price promotion matrix to evaluate their current practice and positioning. A starting point for determining an ideal level of price promotion is the retail sector's position relative to product assortment overlap and life span. Should a firm follow the norm suggested by its sector's position? Or should it refine its merchandising and price promotion strategies to break away from others in the sector?

We propose answering these seven questions—the first four serve to position the manager's company on the matrix, and the other three help to evaluate the firm's current price promotion strategy:

1. Which position defines our sector on the price promotion matrix? Is it clearly defined as one of the five positions or is it on a boundary?
2. What is the promotional norm in my company's sector? Is it consistent with the matrix?
3. Considering the three price promotion dimensions separately, what is my company's current strategy relative to

price variation, promotional advertising volume, and depth of discount? Does it follow the sector norm?

4. Will our current or future merchandising strategy likely change our position? Is our assortment likely to move higher or lower in overlap or life span in a way that might cause our position to shift?

5. How well is our current price promotion strategy working? How confident are we in this assessment?

6. If we were to fine-tune any of the three promotional dimensions, which would they be and why?

7. Is there a need or significant opportunity to pursue a radical shift in our price promotion strategy?

Questions

1. How would you characterize the relationship between merchandising and everyday low pricing? What are the ramifications of this?

2. What impact do you think that everyday low pricing has on merchandise sales forecasts? Explain your answer.

3. As a supplier, would you be happy or unhappy with a retailer's use of everyday low pricing for your products?

4. What are the implications of the findings reported in Table 1?

5. What are the implications of Figure 1?

6. As the owner of a new luggage store, which of the five strategies in Figure 1 would you pick? Why?

7. For the scenario in Question 6, what markdown approach would you use? Explain your answer.

*The material in this case is adapted by the authors from Kathleen Seiders and Glenn B. Ross, "From Price to Purchase," *Marketing Management* (November–December 2004), pp. 38–43. Reprinted by permission of the American Marketing Association.

part seven

Communicating with the Customer

In Part Seven, the elements involved in a retailer's communicating with its customers are discussed. First, we look at the role of a retail image and how it is developed and sustained. Various aspects of a promotional strategy are then detailed.

- **Chapter 18** discusses the importance of communications for a retailer. We review the significance of image in the communications effort and the components of a retailer's image. Creating an image depends heavily on a retailer's atmosphere—which is comprised of all of its physical characteristics, such as the store exterior, the general interior, layouts, and displays. This applies to both store and nonstore retailers. Ways of encouraging customers to spend more time shopping and the value of community relations are also described.

- **Chapter 19** focuses on promotional strategy, specifically how a retailer can inform, persuade, and remind its target market about its strategic mix. In the first part of the chapter, we deal with the four basic types of retail promotion: advertising, public relations, personal selling, and sales promotion. The second part describes the steps in a promotional strategy: objectives, budget, mix of forms, implementation of mix, and review and revision of the plan.

537

Chapter 18
ESTABLISHING AND MAINTAINING A RETAIL IMAGE

Target Stores (**www.target.com**) has been busy building its image as a fashion-forward full-line discount store chain. And it has succeeded. The firm has come a very long way since its 1962 founding. While many upper-middle-class customers feel uncomfortable shopping for clothing or housewares at Wal-Mart (**www.walmart.com**) or Kmart (**www.kmart.com**), their general view of Target can be summarized by the statement "Expect more, pay less."

Reprinted by permission.

Target's strategy was born from its realization that it could not compete against Wal-Mart on price alone. Instead, Target decided to use its department store roots to develop partnerships with leading designers and brands in order to attract upscale shoppers. These include housewares designed by architect Michael Graves (**www.michaelgraves.com**), pots made by Calphalon (**www.calphalon.com**), seating designed by architect Phillipe Starck, maternity apparel by Liz Lange (**www.lizlange.com**), and an exclusive line of apparel by Mossimo (**www.mossimo.com**). To increase store traffic, Target has begun to offer prepared foods, wine, and USDA Choice Angus beef in many stores. Yet, despite its upscale merchandising, Target is still clearly a discounter as seen by its optical, pharmacy, and photofinishing departments—as well as its self-service merchandising philosophy.

Target's success in refining its image can be seen by examining the demographics of its current target customer: typically a suburban, professional, well-educated female with a family and an average household annual income of $45,000 per year. This is significantly higher than the demographics of the average shopper at either Wal-Mart or Kmart.[1]

chapter objectives

1. To show the importance of communicating with customers and examine the concept of retail image
2. To describe how a retail store image is related to the atmosphere it creates via its exterior, general interior, layout, and displays, and to look at the special case of nonstore atmospherics
3. To discuss ways of encouraging customers to spend more time shopping
4. To consider the impact of community relations on a retailer's image

OVERVIEW

There are many trade associations (www.visualstore.com/index.php/channel/0/id/6094) in the retail image arena. Visit a few online.

A retailer needs a superior communications strategy to properly position itself in customers' minds, as well as to nurture their shopping behavior. Once customers are attracted, the retailer must strive to create a proper shopping mood for them. Various physical and symbolic cues can be used to do this. See Figure 18-1. It is imperative to maximize the total retail experience:

> The consumer/retailer relationship is simply all about perception. Consider some of the strong brands in retailing. Starbucks brings to mind, in one word, the concept "relax." Almost immediately, one thinks about a casual, albeit expensive, cup of coffee in a comfortable atmosphere. The single most important strategy for Wal-Mart is its everyday low price strategy which others have tried to establish, but very few have been able to execute. Wal-Mart's image is reinforced with one word—"rollback." When it comes to fashion and cool products, Target has nurtured its perception among consumers for being the destination for "cheap chic." Sears, one of the nation's oldest chains, is an example of how a retailer has tried time and again to alter its stodgy company image and become more contemporary, yet it is still known best for the quality and dependability of its private brands (Kenmore and Craftsman). Over the years, Eckerd has exploited its strength in photos while CVS has focused on healthcare to help differentiate the chains among consumers.[2]

This chapter describes how to establish and maintain an image. Retail atmosphere, storefronts, store layouts, and displays are examined. We also explore the challenge of how to encourage people to spend more time shopping and the role of community relations. Chapter 19 focuses on the common promotional tools available to retailers: advertising, public relations, personal selling, and sales promotion.

While our discussion looks more at store retailers, the basic principles do apply to nonstore retailers. For a mail-order firm, the catalog cover is its storefront,

FIGURE 18-1

Positioning and Retail Image

Both Hard Rock Cafe and McDonald's devote considerable resources for image reinforcement, such as these well-known corporate symbols.

Photos reprinted by permission.

Careers in RETAILING — Is Retail for Me? Marketing and Advertising—Part 1

Unleash your creativity (or your strategic side) in retail. Depending upon a firm's size, marketing functions may be centralized in one department, divided into different departments (such as advertising, sales promotion, art and visual merchandising, and public/press relations), or grouped in various combinations:

- *Head of Marketing/Advertising/Sales Promotion:* Depending on the firm's size, marketing, advertising, sales promotion, art, and visual merchandising tasks may all be in one department or divided into any combination. Marketing conducts focus groups and statistical analysis of customer buying patterns for a strategic overview of the company's market share and positioning. Advertising creates and places media to sell either the company image or specific goods. Sales promotion commonly puts emphasis on mailings, coupons, events, and point of purchase material. Visual merchandising focuses on in-store presentation of the merchandise. The art department creates the imagery to be used for advertising and sales promotion.

- *Head of Marketing (only):* Marketing conducts focus groups and statistical analysis of customer buying patterns for a strategic overview of the company's market share and positioning.
- *Head of Advertising:* Advertising creates and places media to sell either the company image or specific goods. Media placement and copywriting separate this position from the art department head below. The position of head of advertising and sales promotion adds extensive sales promotion activity to the advertising duties listed here.
- *Head of Advertising and Sales Promotion:* Advertising selects and places media to sell either the company image or specific goods. Sales promotion commonly puts emphasis on mailings, coupons, events, and point of purchase material.

Source: Reprinted by permission of the National Retail Federation.

and the interior layouts and displays are the pages devoted to product categories and the individual items within them. For a Web retailer, the home page is its storefront, and the interior layouts and displays are represented by the links within the site.

THE SIGNIFICANCE OF RETAIL IMAGE

Display & Design Ideas (www.ddimagazine.com) is a leading trade magazine that often deals with retail image topics.

As defined in Chapter 3, *image* refers to how a retailer is perceived by customers and others, and *positioning* refers to how a firm devises its strategy so as to project an image relative to its retail category and its competitors—and to elicit a positive consumer response. To succeed, a retailer must communicate a distinctive, clear, and consistent image. Once its image is established in consumers' minds, a retailer is placed in a niche relative to competitors. For global retailers, it can be challenging to convey a consistent image worldwide, given the different backgrounds of consumers.

Components of a Retail Image

Numerous factors contribute to a retailer's image, and it is the totality of them that forms an overall image. See Figure 18-2. We examined these factors in earlier chapters: target market, firm's positioning, customer service, store location, merchandise attributes, and pricing. Our focal points for Chapters 18 and 19 are the attributes of physical facilities, shopping experiences, community service, advertising, public relations, personal selling, and sales promotion.

FIGURE 18-2
The Elements of a Retail
Image

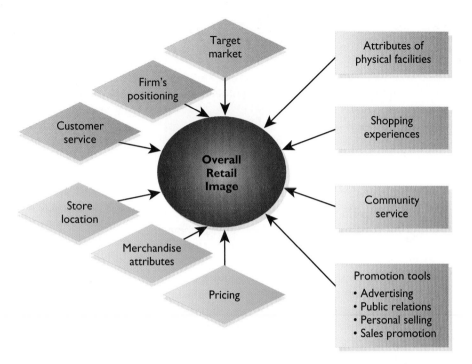

The Dynamics of Creating and Maintaining a Retail Image

Creating and maintaining a retail image is a complex, multi-step, ongoing process. It encompasses far more than store "atmosphere," which is discussed shortly. Furthermore, with so many people having little time for shopping and others having less interest in it, retailers must work hard to *entertain* shoppers:

See how Jungle Jim's Web site (www.junglejims.com) reinforces its retail image.

> James O. Bonaminio is an independent grocer with a capital "I." Today, if the mood strikes, Bonaminio might put on his wizard suit and roller-skate through his Jungle Jim's International Market performing "price magic." Or perhaps he'll go off "junking" for a few hours, returning with a ton or two of bargain-priced salvage that he eventually will incorporate into his sprawling, 280,000-square-foot supermarket in Fairfield, Ohio—just like he did with the animatronic Robin Hood and the monorail recycled from an amusement-park ride. Jungle Jim's might well be America's wackiest supermarket, but there is a method to Bonaminio's madness. Instead of trying to beat the big chains at their price-squeezing game, Bonaminio has built a funhouse maze of a store north of Cincinnati that draws 50,000 shoppers a week from as far away as Indianapolis and Lexington, Kentucky.[3]

As one industry expert says, "A shopper should be able to determine the following about a store *in three seconds*: its name, its line of trade, its claim to fame, its price position, and its personality." The expert adds, "Those who need what you are selling will find you. Everyone else must be enticed—in very short order—to enter your store. The glut of pitches out there only ups the ante. Without a distinct image, you don't have a chance of being seen or heard through all the clutter that is retailing."[4]

Let's highlight two other examples. At Prada, the upscale 250-store apparel and accessories chain, the goal is to turn shopping into a rewarding experience and not just a chore. Prada stores provide sales associates with high-tech, hand-held devices that are tied into the Prada data base, enabling the associates to have some expertise on every item sold. The devices even serve as remote controls that associates can use to display runway videos of fashion items upon the customer's request. There are video panels on clothing racks and elsewhere in the store. And for more excitement, "All dressing rooms are equipped with RFID-enabled touch-screen panels that scan all items, then provide shoppers with product information, runway videos, available sizes and colors, and suggestions on which accessories are 'must haves.' Dressing room glass doors change from clear (so the shopper may show the garment to others) to opaque (for privacy), by the wave of a hand. Dressing rooms also contain 'Magic Mirrors' which shoot digital video of the customers wearing the apparel so they may see how it looks from the back and other angles before purchasing." In addition, the stores have Wi-Fi technology.[5] See Figure 18-3.

Would you name a store Chapter 11? An Atlanta bookstore chain has. The founder, Barbara Babbit Kaufman, wanted to position her business as a deep discounter and to gain media attention because of the unique name. The slogan is "Prices so low, you'd think we were going bankrupt." Today, the firm has 16 stores and a Web site (**www.chapter11books.com**), and it offers regular book signing and special events. There are "no comfy couches or cappuccinos, but lots of great bargains. Markdown prices make this Atlanta bookstore chain a perennial favorite. Best-sellers are always 30 percent off, and Oprah's picks are reliably stocked, too." The books are priced at up to 75 percent off the list price. "Décor consists of walls painted 'Have a Nice Day' yellow, and there isn't much room to sit down and read. This no-frills approach pays off at the cash register."[6]

A key goal for chain retailers, franchisors, and global retailers is to maintain a consistent image among all branches. Yet, despite the best planning, a number of factors may vary widely among branch stores and affect the image. They include management and employee performance, consumer profiles, competitors, the convenience in reaching stores, parking, safety, the ease of finding merchandise, language and cultural diversity among customers in different countries, and the qualities of the surrounding area. Sometimes retailers with good images receive negative publicity. This must be countered in order for them to maintain their desired standing with the public.

FIGURE 18-3
Shopping at Prada: Not a Routine Experience

Photo reprinted by permission of Susan Berry, Retail Image Consulting, Inc.

ATMOSPHERE

The Visual Store (www. visualstore.com/resources. php) provides many useful online atmospherics resources.

A retailer's image depends heavily on its "atmosphere," the psychological feeling a customer gets when visiting that retailer. It is the personality of a store, catalog, vending machine, or Web site. "Retail image" is a much broader and all-encompassing term relative to the communication tools a retailer uses to position itself. For a store-based retailer, **atmosphere (atmospherics)** refers to the store's physical characteristics that project an image and draw customers. For a nonstore-based firm, atmosphere refers to the physical characteristics of catalogs, vending machines, Web sites, and so forth. A retailer's sights, sounds, smells, and other physical attributes all contribute to customer perceptions.

A retailer's atmosphere may influence people's shopping enjoyment, as well as their time spent browsing, willingness to converse with personnel, tendency to spend more than originally planned, and likelihood of future patronage. Many people even form impressions of a retailer before entering its facilities (due to the store location, storefront, and other factors) or just after entering (due to displays, width of aisles, and other things). They often judge the firm prior to examining merchandise and prices.

Check out the advantages of "Visual Simulation" (www.facit.co.uk/retail_ planning.htm) in planning atmospherics.

When a retailer takes a proactive, integrated atmospherics approach to create a certain "look," properly display products, stimulate shopping behavior, and enhance the physical environment, it engages in **visual merchandising**. It includes everything from store display windows to the width of aisles to the materials used for fixtures to merchandise presentation, as highlighted in Figure 18-4. This is how the Eddie Bauer chain has revamped and enhanced its visual merchandising efforts:

> "In our stores today, you'll see more emphasis on display, more romancing of the products," says the firm's creative director, visual presentation, apparel. "The graphics, the window displays are more important now,

FIGURE 18-4
Visual Merchandising and Eddie Bauer

The Eddie Bauer chain is placing greater reliance on its visual merchandising efforts.

Photo reprinted by permission of Susan Berry, Retail Image Consulting, Inc.

and we change them every three to four weeks." The new store design segments different collections, such as velvet or denim, into shops, through the use of architectural details and built-in fixtures. Graphics are also playing a larger role in the stores. "In the past, if we had graphics, they were portrait shots. Now we feature more full-body shots, more group shots, and more mixed-gender shots. We show more top to bottom because we have everything from shoes to outerwear."[7]

Visit our Web site (**www.prenhall.com/bermanevans**) for links related to visual merchandising.

A Store-Based Retailing Perspective

Store atmosphere (atmospherics) can be divided into these key elements: exterior, general interior, store layout, and displays. Figure 18-5 contains a detailed breakdown of them.

Exterior

A store's exterior has a powerful impact on its image and should be planned accordingly.

A **storefront** is the total physical exterior of the store itself. It includes the marquee, entrances, windows, lighting, and construction materials. With its storefront, a retailer can present a conservative, trendy, upscale, discount, or other image. Consumers who pass through an unfamiliar business district or shopping center often judge a store by its exterior. Besides the storefront itself, atmosphere can be enhanced by trees, fountains, and benches in front of the store. These intensify consumer feelings about shopping and about the store by establishing a relaxed environment. There are various alternatives in planning a basic storefront. Here are a few of them:

- Modular structure—a one-piece rectangle or square that may attach several stores.
- Prefabricated (prefab) structure—a frame built in a factory and assembled at the site.
- Prototype store—used by franchisors and chains to foster a consistent atmosphere.

FIGURE 18-5
The Elements of Atmosphere

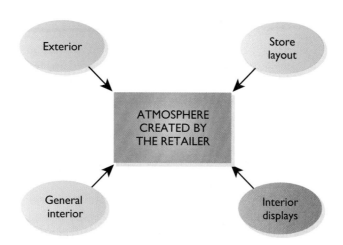

FIGURE 18-6
Using a Marquee to
Generate a Powerful Retail
Image

Photo reprinted by permission of
Goran Petrovic.

- Recessed storefront—lures people by being recessed from the level of other stores. Customers must walk in a number of feet to examine the storefront.
- Unique building design—a round structure, for example.

A **marquee** is a sign that displays the store's name. It can be painted or a neon light, printed or script, and set alone or mixed with a slogan (trademark) and other information. The marquee should attract attention, as Macy's Herald Square does. See Figure 18-6. Image is influenced because a marquee can be gaudy and flashy or subdued and subtle. The world's best-known marquee is McDonald's golden arch.

Store entrances require three major decisions. First, the number of entrances is determined. Many small stores have only one entrance. Department stores may have four to eight or more entrances. A store hoping to draw both vehicular and pedestrian traffic may need at least two entrances (one for pedestrians, another near the parking lot). Because front and back entrances serve different purposes, they should be designed separately. A factor that may limit the number of entrances is potential pilferage.

Second, the type of entrance(s) is chosen. The doorway can be revolving; electric, self-opening; regular, push-pull; or climate-controlled. The latter is an open entrance with a curtain of warm or cold air, set at the same temperature as inside the store. Entrance flooring can be cement, tile, or carpeting. Lighting can be traditional or fluorescent, white or colors, and/or flashing or constant. Look at how the 99¢ Dreams entrance reinforces its discount image, as depicted in Figure 18-7.

Third, walkways are considered. A wide, lavish walkway creates a different atmosphere and mood than a narrow one. Large window displays may be attractive, but customers would not be pleased if there is insufficient space for a comfortable entry into the store.

Display windows have two main purposes: to identify the store and its offerings and to induce people to enter. By showing a representative merchandise offering, a store can create an overall mood. By showing fashion or seasonal

Ethics in RETAILING
Enhancing the Ethical Image of Electronics Retailing

Not long ago, the Electronic Retailing Association's (**www.retailing.org**) (ERA) Board of Directors unanimously approved a strengthened Code of Ethics for its electronic retailer members. Even though the code does not have any enforcement mechanism, ERA hopes that members will voluntarily comply. The board will take action in cases involving clear and serious violations of this code.

Here is a summary of the ERA's ethical guidelines for members:

- To comply with ERA's marketing guidelines and all laws pertaining to the marketing of products.
- To honor all warranties, money-back guarantees, and to fairly handle all consumer complaints.
- To accurately reflect the nature of business operations and all ownership interests.

- To avoid false statements concerning competitors, their products, businesses, and business practices.
- To fulfill all contracts and legal obligations and to avoid interfering with the legal rights of others.
- To refrain from improper business conduct including discrimination based on race, color, religion, national origin, age, or sex.
- To support legislation that promotes fair competition and the protection of consumer rights, as well as oppose legislation that weakens the free market economic system.

Source: "Policies & Guidelines: Member Code of Ethics," **www. retailing.org/new_site/memresources/policies_procedures/policies_ procedures.htm** (January 29, 2006).

goods, it can show it is contemporary. By showing sale items, a store can lure price-conscious consumers. By showing eye-catching displays that have little to do with its merchandise offering, a store can attract pedestrians' attention. By showing public service messages (such as a sign for the Special Olympics), the store can indicate its community involvement.

A lot of planning is needed to develop good display windows, which leads many retailers to hire outside specialists. Decisions include the number, size, shape, color, and themes of display windows—and the frequency of changes per year. Retailers in shopping malls may not use display windows for the side of the building facing the parking lot; there are solid building exteriors. They feel vehicular patrons are not lured by expensive outside windows; they invest in displays for storefronts inside the malls.

FIGURE 18-7
How a Store Entrance Can Generate Shopper Interest

Photo reprinted by permission.

Exterior building height can be disguised or nondisguised. With disguised building height, part of a store or shopping center is beneath ground level. Such a building is not as intimidating to people who dislike a large structure. With nondisguised building height, the entire store or center can be seen by pedestrians. An intimate image cannot be fostered with a block-long building. Nor can a department store image be linked to a small site.

Few firms succeed with poor visibility. This means pedestrian and/or vehicular traffic must clearly see storefronts or marquees. A store located behind a bus stop has poor visibility for vehicular traffic and pedestrians across the street. Many firms near highways use billboards since drivers go by quickly.

In every case, the goal is to have the store or center appear unique and catch the shopper's eye. A distinctive storefront, an elaborate marquee, recessed open-air entrances, decorative windows, and unusual building height and size are one set of features that could attract consumers by their uniqueness. Nonetheless, uniqueness may not be without its shortcomings. An example is the multi-level "shopping-center-in-the-round." Because this center (which often occupies a square city block) is round, parking on each floor level makes the walking distances very short. Yet, a rectangular center may have greater floor space on a lot of the same size, on-floor parking may reduce shopping on other floors, added entrances increase chances for pilferage, many people dislike circular driving, and architectural costs are higher.

As a retailer plans its exterior, the surrounding stores and the surrounding area should be studied. Surrounding stores present image cues due to their price range, level of service, and so on. The surrounding area reflects the demographics and lifestyles of those who live nearby. An overall area image rubs off on individual retailers because people tend to have a general perception of a shopping center or a business district. An unfavorable atmosphere would exist if vandalism and crime are high, people living near the store are not in the target market, and the area is rundown.

Parking facilities can add to or detract from store atmosphere. Plentiful, free, nearby parking creates a more positive image than scarce, costly, distant parking. Some potential shoppers may never enter a store if they must drive around for parking. Other customers may rush in and out of a store to finish shopping before parking meters expire. A related potential problem is that of congestion. Atmospherics are diminished if the parking lot, sidewalks, and/or entrances are jammed. Consumers who feel crushed in the crowd spend less time shopping and are in poorer moods than those who feel comfortable.

General Interior

Once customers are inside a store, numerous elements affect their perceptions; and retailers need to plan accordingly:

- At Gander Mountain, the outdoor lifestyle chain, its merchandising philosophy guides store interior decisions. Its stores have "bare concrete floors, an open rafter ceiling, simple signage, and functional fixtures." Why? "The products in our industry are just so darn cool and interesting that we believe they are the heroes so we let the merchandise speak for itself," says the firm's chief executive.[8]

- At Apple Stores, owned by Apple Computer, "the most recent experiment is with mini-stores, which average 750 square feet. With their stainless steel walls, seamless white floors and ceilings, they are an extension of Apple's much-admired industrial design esthetic. Common design elements are used in full-line and mini-stores to maintain visual identity."[9]

● At the Toys "R" Us Times Square store in New York City, visitors "can take a ride on the only indoor Ferris wheel in Times Square. Only there will you see a dramatic 60-foot Ferris wheel—complete with flashing chevron neon lights. It features 14 cars, each inspired by a favorite children's toy or character. A portion of the proceeds from the ride goes to the Toys "R" Us Children's Fund."[10]

The general interior elements of store atmosphere were cited in Figure 18-5. They are described next.

Flooring can be cement, wood, linoleum, carpet, and so on. A plush, thick carpet creates one kind of atmosphere and a concrete floor another. Thus, virtually all traditional department stores have carpeted floors, 75 percent of full-line discount stores have vinyl floors, and 90 percent of home centers have concrete floors.[11]

Bright, vibrant colors contribute to a different atmosphere than light pastels or plain white walls. See Figure 18-8. Lighting can be direct or indirect, white or colors, constant or flashing. A teen-oriented apparel boutique might use bright colors and vibrant, flashing lights to foster one atmosphere, and a maternity dress shop could use pastel colors and indirect lighting to form a different atmosphere. Sometimes when colors are changed, customers may be initially uncomfortable until they get used to the new scheme: "At first, shoppers in a Southwest Florida town were mystified by their new Sweetbay Supermarket. Was it the same company as the former Kash n' Karry store? Or was it a new company altogether? Vibrant colors such as purple and apricot were splashed about the new Sweetbay store—unlike the teal coloring of Kash n' Karry. Years ago, Kash n' Karry stores even had yucky brown-and-orange colors." In fact, Sweetbay is "working to transform Tampa-based Kash n' Karry into the more elegant Sweetbay Supermarkets."[12]

Scents and sounds influence the customer's mood. A restaurant can use food aromas to increase people's appetites. A cosmetics store can use an array of perfume scents to attract shoppers. A pet store can let its animals' natural scents and sounds woo customers. A beauty salon can play soft music or rock, depending on

Maxey Hayse Design Studios (**www.maxeyhayse. com/design_portfolio.html**) has designed interiors for a variety of retailers. Several are profiled here.

FIGURE 18-8

Eye-Catching Displays from M&M World

"Four floors of retail space devoted to our favorite chocolate-covered candies? It just doesn't get much better than that! Located in the Showcase Mall in Las Vegas, the mouth-watering exhibit features Red, Yellow, and the rest of the brightly colored gang on everything from T-shirts and golf-club covers to calculators and martini glasses." [**from www.vegas.com**]

Photo reprinted by permission of Susan Berry, Retail Image Consulting, Inc.

its customers. Slow-tempo music in supermarkets encourages people to move more slowly.

Store fixtures can be planned on the basis of both their utility and aesthetics. Pipes, plumbing, beams, doors, storage rooms, and display racks and tables should be considered part of interior decorating. An upscale store usually dresses up its fixtures and disguises them. A discount store might leave fixtures exposed because this portrays the desired image.

Wall textures enhance or diminish atmospherics. Prestigious stores often use raised wallpaper. Department stores are more apt to use flat wallpaper, while discount stores may have barren walls. Chic stores might have chandeliers, while discounters have fluorescent lighting.

The customer's mood is affected by the store's temperature and how it is achieved. Insufficient heat in winter and no air-conditioning in summer can shorten a shopping trip. And image is influenced by the use of central air-conditioning, unit air-conditioning, fans, or open windows.

Wide, uncrowded aisles create a better atmosphere than narrow, crowded ones. People shop longer and spend more if they are not pushed while walking or looking at merchandise. In Boston and elsewhere, although Filene's Basement stores offer bargains, overcrowding keeps some customers away.

Dressing facilities can be elaborate, plain, or nonexistent. An upscale store has carpeted, private dressing rooms. An average-quality store has linoleum-floored, semiprivate rooms. A discount store has small stalls or no facilities. For some apparel shoppers, dressing facilities are a factor in store selection.

Multi-level stores must have vertical transportation: elevator, escalator, and/or stairs. Larger stores may have a combination of all three. Traditionally, finer stores relied on operator-run elevators and discount stores on stairs. Today, escalators are quite popular. They provide shoppers with a quiet ride and a panoramic view of the store. Finer stores decorate their escalators with fountains, shrubs, and trees. Stairs remain important for some discount and smaller stores.

Light fixtures, wood or metal beams, doors, rest rooms, dressing rooms, and vertical transportation can cause **dead areas** for the retailer. These are awkward spaces where normal displays cannot be set up. Sometimes it is not possible for such areas to be deployed profitably or attractively. However, retailers have learned to use dead areas better. Mirrors are attached to exit doors. Vending machines are located near rest rooms. Ads appear in dressing rooms. One creative use of a dead area involves the escalator. It lets shoppers view each floor, and sales of impulse items go up when placed at the escalator entrance or exit. Many firms plan escalators so customers must get off at each floor and pass by appealing displays.

Polite, well-groomed, knowledgeable personnel generate a positive atmosphere. Ill-mannered, poorly groomed, uninformed personnel engender a negative one. A store using self-service minimizes its personnel and creates a discount, impersonal image. A store cannot develop an upscale image if it is set up for self-service. As one expert puts it, "15 feet, 15 seconds. That's how quickly your customers should be greeted, welcomed, and treated like a guest in your store."[13]

The merchandise a retailer sells influences its image. Top-line items yield one kind of image, and lower-quality items yield another. The mood of the customer is affected accordingly.

Price levels foster a perception of retail image in consumers' minds; and the way prices are displayed is a vital part of atmosphere. Upscale stores have few or no price displays, rely on discrete price tags, and place cash registers in inconspicuous areas behind posts or in employee rooms. Discounters accentuate price displays, show prices in large print, and locate cash registers centrally, with signs pointing to them.

Technology in RETAILING — Digital Signs Flourish at Tesco

By mid-2005, Tesco (**www.tesco.com**), a huge supermarket chain based in Great Britain, had outfitted more than 100 of its stores with an in-store communication network. It planned to expand the network to include an additional 200 stores by the beginning of 2006.

A key aspect of the communication network is the use of 55 digital signs in each store that inform and entertain Tesco's customers. For example, in Tesco's wine department, a digital sign recommends a new wine to customers, noting that the wine is a "perfect complement to grilled red meat." And in the store's home entertainment area, a new Disney DVD might be featured.

There are different strategies for developing and implementing digital signage. In the "advertising-supported model," the store is viewed as the medium and the hardware and messages are produced by third parties. In a "captive model," the retailer funds the network and does not accept outside advertising. Tesco's model is a blend of both. While Tesco has invested its own capital to implement the program, it sells sponsorships, as well as advertising time.

Sources: Susan Reda, "Digital Signage Helps Tesco Inform, Entertain, and Boost Sales," *Stores* (March 2005); and "Tesco Corporate Web Site," **www.tesco.com/corporateinfo** (March 23, 2006).

A store with state-of-the-art technology impresses people with its operations efficiency and speed. One with slower, older technology may have impatient shoppers. A store with a modern building (new storefront and marquee) and new fixtures (lights, floors, and walls) fosters a more favorable atmosphere than one with older facilities. Remodeling can improve store appearance, update facilities, and reallocate space. It typically results in strong sales and profit increases after completion.

Last, but certainly not least, there must be a plan for keeping the store clean. No matter how impressive the exterior and interior, an unkempt store will be perceived poorly: "A restroom with broken or malfunctioning equipment appears sloppy. It's really important that restrooms look clean."[14]

Store Layout

At this point, the specifics of store layout are *sequentially* planned and enacted.

ALLOCATION OF FLOOR SPACE. Each store has a total amount of floor space to allot to selling, merchandise, personnel, and customers. Without this allocation, the retailer would have no idea of the space available for displays, signs, rest rooms, and so on:

- *Selling space* is used for displays of merchandise, interactions between salespeople and customers, demonstrations, and so on. Self-service retailers apportion most space to selling.

- *Merchandise space* is used to stock nondisplayed items. At a traditional shoe store, this area takes up a large percentage of total space.

- *Personnel space* is set aside for employees to change clothes and to take lunch and coffee breaks and for rest rooms. Because retail space is valuable, personnel space is strictly controlled. Yet, a retailer should consider the effect on employee morale.

- *Customer space* contributes to the shopping mood. It can include a lounge, benches and/or chairs, dressing rooms, rest rooms, a restaurant, a nursery, parking, and wide aisles. Discounters are more apt to skimp on these areas.

More firms now use planograms to assign space. A **planogram** is a visual (graphical) representation of the space for selling, merchandise, personnel, and

Visit Shelf Logic (**www.shelflogic.com/ movies.htm**) and click on "Creating a Planogram" to learn more about this tool.

customers—as well as for product categories. It also lays out their in-store placement. A planogram may be hand-drawn or computer-generated. Visit our Web site (**www.prenhall.com/bermanevans**) for several planogram links.

CLASSIFICATION OF STORE OFFERINGS. A store's offerings are next classified into product groupings. Many retailers use a combination of groupings and plan store layouts accordingly. Special provisions must be made to minimize shoplifting and pilferage. This means placing vulnerable products away from corners and doors. Four types of groupings (and combinations of them) are most commonly used:

- **Functional product groupings** display merchandise by common end use. A men's clothing store might group shirts, ties, cuff links, and tie pins; shoes, shoe trees, and shoe polish; T-shirts, undershorts, and socks; suits; and sports jackets and slacks.

- **Purchase motivation product groupings** appeal to the consumer's urge to buy products and the amount of time he or she is willing to spend on shopping. A committed customer with time to shop will visit a store's upper floors; a disinterested person with less time will look at displays on the first floor. Look at the first level of a department store. It includes impulse products and other rather quick purchases. The third floor has items encouraging and requiring more thoughtful shopping.

- **Market segment product groupings** place together various items that appeal to a given target market. A women's apparel store divides products into juniors', misses', and ladies' apparel. A music store separates CDs into rock, jazz, classical, R&B, country, and other sections. An art gallery places paintings into different price groups.

- **Storability product groupings** may be used for products needing special handling. A supermarket has freezer, refrigerator, and room-temperature sections. A florist keeps some flowers refrigerated and others at room temperature, as do a bakery and a fruit store.

DETERMINATION OF A TRAFFIC-FLOW PATTERN. The traffic-flow pattern of the store is then set. A **straight (gridiron) traffic flow** places displays and aisles in a rectangular or gridiron pattern, as shown in Figure 18-9. A **curving (free-flowing) traffic flow** places displays and aisles in a free-flowing pattern, as shown in Figure 18-10. Piggly Wiggly's innovative layout, which combines both approaches, is highlighted in Figure 18–11.

A straight traffic pattern is often used by food retailers, discount stores, drugstores, hardware stores, and stationery stores. It has several advantages:

- An efficient atmosphere is created.
- More floor space is devoted to product displays.
- People can shop quickly.
- Inventory control and security are simplified.
- Self-service is easy, thereby reducing labor costs.

The disadvantages are the impersonal atmosphere, the more limited browsing by customers, and the rushed shopping behavior.

A curving traffic pattern is used by department stores, apparel stores, and other shopping-oriented stores. This approach has several benefits:

- A friendly atmosphere is presented.
- Shoppers do not feel rushed and will browse around.

FIGURE 18-9
How a Supermarket Uses a Straight (Gridiron) Traffic Pattern

Illustration by Steve Cowden for *Progressive Grocer*. Reprinted by permission.

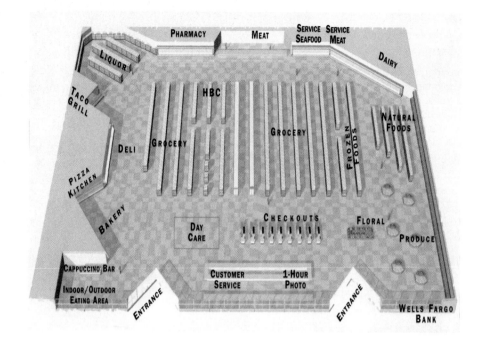

FIGURE 18-10
How a Department Store Uses a Curving (Free-Flowing) Traffic Pattern

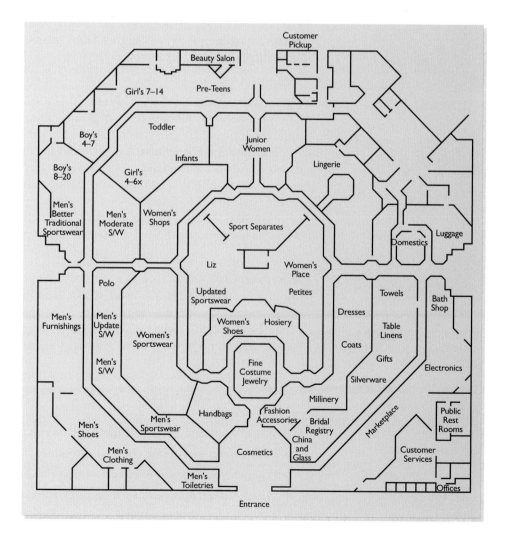

- People are encouraged to walk through the store in any direction or pattern.
- Impulse or unplanned purchases are enhanced.

The disadvantages are the possible customer confusion, wasted floor space, difficulties in inventory control, higher labor intensity, and potential loitering. Also,
these displays often cost more.

DETERMINATION OF SPACE NEEDS. The space for each product category is
now calculated, with both selling and nonselling space considered. There are two
different approaches: the model stock method and the space-productivity ratio.

The **model stock approach** determines the floor space necessary to carry and
display a proper merchandise assortment. Apparel stores and shoe stores are
among those using this method. The **sales-productivity ratio** assigns floor space
on the basis of sales or profit per foot. Highly profitable product categories get
large chunks of space; marginally profitable categories get less. Food stores and
bookstores are among those that use this technique.

MAPPING OUT IN-STORE LOCATIONS. At this juncture, department locations
are mapped out. For multi-level stores, that means assigning departments to
floors and laying out individual floors. What products should be on each floor?
What should be the layout of each floor? A single-level store addresses only the
second question. These are some questions to consider:

- What items should be placed on the first floor, on the second floor, and so on?
- How should groupings be placed relative to doors, vertical transportation,
  and so on?
- Where should impulse products and convenience products be situated?
- How should associated product categories be aligned?
- Where should seasonal and off-season products be placed?
- Where should space-consuming categories such as furniture be located?
- How close should product displays and stored inventory be to each other?

- What shopping patterns do consumers follow once they enter the store?
- How can the overall appearance of store crowding be averted?

In a recent study of supermarket shoppers, these interesting findings were uncovered:

1. "Grocery shoppers don't weave up and down all aisles—a pattern commonly thought to dominate store travel. Most shoppers tend only to travel select aisles, and rarely in the systematic up and down patterns most tend to consider the dominant travel pattern."
2. "Once they enter an aisle, shoppers rarely make it to the other end. They travel into and out of the aisle rather than traversing its entire length."
3. "Shoppers prefer a counter-clockwise shopping experience. They tend to shop more quickly as they approach the checkout counters. Behavior is driven more by their location in the store than the merchandise in front of them."
4. "The perimeter of the store—often called the 'racetrack'—is the shopper's home base, not just the space covered between aisles. Previous folklore perpetuated the myth that the perimeter was visited incidental to successive aisle traverses. We now know that it often serves as the main thoroughfare, effectively a home base from which shoppers take quick trips into the aisles."[15]

ARRANGEMENT OF INDIVIDUAL PRODUCTS. The last step in store layout planning is arranging individual products. The most profitable items and brands could be placed in the best locations; and products could be arranged by package size, price, color, brand, level of personal service required, and/or customer interest. End-aisle display positions, eye-level positions, and checkout-counter positions are the most likely to increase sales for individual items. Continuity of locations is also important; shifts in store layout may decrease sales by confusing shoppers. The least desirable display position is often knee or ankle level, because consumers do not like to bend down.

Retailer goals often differ from their manufacturers. While the latter want to maximize their brands' sales and push for eye-level, full-shelf, end-aisle locations, retailers seek to maximize total store sales and profit, regardless of brand. Self-service retailers have special considerations. Besides using a gridiron layout to minimize shopper confusion, they must clearly mark aisles, displays, and merchandise.

Consider some of the tactics that supermarkets have employed:

- Many have produce near the entrance; some others have flowers. "The idea is to tantalize the customer, to draw you in with eye-catching displays."
- "Cereal theory" means placing boxes on lower shelves, which are at eye level for children.
- People buy more soup if the varieties are not shelved in alphabetical order.
- Store brands do better when located to the left of manufacturer brands. "After seeing the name brand, the eye automatically moves left (as if on a new page) to compare prices."
- Since "the best viewing angle is 15 degrees below the horizontal, the choicest display level has been measured at 51 to 53 inches off the floor."[16]

Interior (Point-of-Purchase) Displays

Once store layout is fully detailed, a retailer devises its interior displays. Each **point-of-purchase (POP) display** provides shoppers with information, adds to

Cahill specializes in creative retail displays (www.cahilldisplay.com).

store atmosphere, and serves a substantial promotional role. Here's what Point-of-Purchase Advertising International (POPAI) has to say:

> *POP advertising is persuasive.* Serving as the last three feet of the marketing plan, it is the only mass medium executed at the critical point where products, consumers, and the money to purchase all meet at the same time. It is no coincidence that with 74 percent of all purchase decisions in mass merchandisers made in store, an increasing number of brand marketers and retailers invest in this medium. *POP advertising serves as the silent salesperson.* Signs and in-store media educate and draw attention to consumers about product availability and attributes. Coming at a time when most consumers want more information, and retailers have reduced staffing levels, POP performs a vital service and augments cost-reduction efforts. *POP advertising is flexible.* It is the only advertising medium that can convey the same overall strategic message in differing languages to varying audiences in the same village, city, or region. *POP advertising is increasingly sophisticated in its construction and utilization.* Today's displays are easily assembled, maintained, and more powerful in entertaining and informing in the retail environment. *POP advertising is used increasingly by retailers to enhance the shopping experience.* POP is used to help overhaul a store's image, re-direct store traffic, and bolster merchandising plans.[17]

At this site (http://dir.yahoo.com/Business_and_Economy), retailers can choose from many display firms. Click on "Business to Business," "Retail Management," and then "Point of Purchase Displays."

Several types of displays are described here. Most retailers use a combination of them.

An **assortment display** exhibits a wide range of merchandise. With an *open assortment*, the customer is encouraged to feel, look at, and/or try on products. Greeting cards, books, magazines, and apparel are the kinds of products for which retailers use open assortments. In addition, food stores have expanded their open displays for fruit, vegetables, and candy; and some department stores have opened up their cosmetics and perfume displays. With a *closed assortment*, the customer is encouraged to look at merchandise but not touch it or try it on. Computer software and CDs are pre-packaged items that cannot be opened before buying. Jewelry is usually kept in closed glass cases that employees must unlock.

A **theme-setting display** depicts a product offering in a thematic manner and sets a specific mood. Retailers often vary their displays to reflect seasons or special events; some even have employees dress for the occasion. All or part of a store may be adapted to a theme, such as Columbus Day, Valentine's Day, or another concept. Each special theme seeks to attract attention and make shopping more fun.

With an **ensemble display**, a complete product bundle (ensemble) is presented—rather than showing merchandise in separate categories (such as a shoe department, sock department, pants department, shirt department, and sports jacket department). Thus, a mannequin may be dressed in a matching combination of shoes, socks, pants, shirt, and sports jacket, and these items would be available in one department or adjacent departments. Customers like the ease of a purchase and envisioning an entire product bundle.

A **rack display** has a primarily functional use: to neatly hang or present products. It is often used by apparel retailers, housewares retailers, and others. This display must be carefully maintained because it may lead to product clutter and shoppers' returning items to the wrong place. Current technology enables retailers to use sliding, disconnecting, contracting/expanding, lightweight, attractive rack displays. A **case display** exhibits heavier, bulkier items than racks hold. Records, books, pre-packaged goods, and sweaters typically appear in case displays.

A **cut case** is an inexpensive display that leaves merchandise in the original carton. Supermarkets and discount stores frequently use cut cases, which do not create a warm atmosphere. Neither does a **dump bin**—a case that holds piles of sale clothing, marked-down books, or other products. Dump bins have open assortments of roughly handled items. Both cut cases and dump bins reduce display costs and project a low-price image.

Posters, signs, and cards can dress up all types of displays, including cut cases and dump bins. They provide information about product locations and stimulate customers to shop. A mobile, a hanging display with parts that move in response to air currents, serves the same purpose—but stands out more. Electronic displays are also widely used today. They can be interactive, be tailored to individual stores, provide product demonstrations, answer customer questions, and incorporate the latest in multi-media capabilities. These displays are much easier to reprogram than traditional displays are to remodel.

A Nonstore-Based Retailing Perspective

Interact with this demo E-store (**http://sm.kemford. com/webstore/store**) to experience many of the components of online retailing.

Many atmospherics' principles apply to both store and nonstore retailers. However, there are also some distinctions.[18] Let us look at the storefront, general interior, store layout, displays, and checkout counter from the vantage point of one type of direct marketer, the Web retailer.

Storefront

The storefront for a Web retailer is the home page. Thus, it is important that the home page:

- Prominently show the company name and indicate the positioning of the firm.
- Be inviting. A "virtual storefront" must encourage customers to enter.
- Make it easy to go into the store.
- Show the product lines carried.
- Use graphics as display windows and icons as access points.
- Have a distinctive look and feel.
- Include the retailer's E-mail address, mailing address, and phone number.
- Be highlighted at various search engines.

See Figure 18-12.

General Interior

As with store retailers, a Web retailer's general interior sets a shopping mood. Colors run the gamut from plain white backgrounds to stylish black backgrounds. Some firms use audio to generate shopper interest. "Fixtures" relate to how simple or elaborate the Web site looks. "Width of aisles" means how cluttered the site appears and the size of the text and images. The general interior also involves these elements:

- Instructions about how to use the site.
- Information about the company.
- Product icons.
- News items.
- The shopping cart (how orders are placed).
- A product search engine.

FIGURE 18-12

L.L. Bean's Online Storefront

L.L. Bean has devoted considerable attention to the design of its online storefront. This attractive, easy-to-use home page is consistent with the image created by the firm.

Photo reprinted by permission.

- Locations of physical stores (for multi-channel retailers).
- A shopper login for firms that use loyalty programs and track their customers.

Store Layout

A Web retailer's store layout has two components: the layout of each individual Web page and the links to move from page to page. Web retailers spend a lot of time planning the traffic flow for their stores. Online consumers want to shop efficiently, and they get impatient if the "store" is not laid out properly.

Some online firms use a gridiron approach, while others have more free-flowing Web pages and links. Web companies often have a directory on the home page that indicates product categories. Shoppers click on an icon to enter the area of the site housing the category (department) of interest. Many retailers encourage customers to shop for any product from any section of the Web site by providing an interactive search engine. In that case, a person types in the product name or category and is automatically sent to the relevant Web page. Like physical stores, online retailers allocate more display space to popular product categories and brands and give them a better position. On pages that require scrolling down, best-sellers usually appear at the top of the page and slower-sellers at the bottom.

Displays

Web retailers can display full product assortments or let shoppers choose from tailored assortments. This decision affects the open or cluttered appearance of a site, the level of choice, and possible shopper confusion. Online firms often use special themes, such as Valentine's Day. It is easy for them to show ensembles—and for shoppers to interactively mix and match to create their own ensembles. Through graphics and photos, a site can give the appearance of cut cases and dump bins for items on sale.

Checkout Counter

The checkout counter can be complicated for Web retailers: (1) Online shoppers tend to worry more about the security and privacy of purchase transactions than those who buy in a store. (2) Online shoppers often have to work harder to complete transactions. They must carefully enter the model number and quantity and their shipping address, E-mail address, shipping preference, and credit card number. They may also be asked for their phone number, job title, and so on, because some retailers want to build their data bases. (3) Online shoppers may feel surprised by shipping and handling fees, if these fees are not revealed until they go to checkout.

To simplify matters, Amazon.com has a patented checkout process—a major competitive advantage. Amazon.com's "1-Click" program lets shoppers securely store their shipping address, preferred shipping method, and credit card information. Each purchase requires just one click to set up an order form.

At the bottom of the home page, learn how Amazon.com (www.amazon.com) enables shoppers to use "1-Click Settings" for easy ordering.

Special Considerations

Let us examine two other issues: how to set up a proper Web site and the advantages and disadvantages of Web atmospherics versus those of traditional stores.

New online retailers often have little experience with Web design or the fundamentals of store design and layout. These firms typically hire specialists to design their sites. When business grows, they may take Web design in-house. Here is a sampling of specialists that design online stores for small retailers: Bigstep.com (**http://go.bigstep.com/**), Entrabase (**www.econgo.com**), and Yahoo! Small Business (**http://smallbusiness.yahoo.com/merchant**). In this grouping, design and hosting costs are as low as $29.95 monthly.

Compared with physical stores, online stores have several advantages. A Web site:

- Has almost unlimited space to present product assortments, displays, and information.
- Can be tailored to the individual customer.
- Can be modified daily (or even hourly) to reflect changes in demand, new offerings from suppliers, and competitors' actions.
- Can promote cross-merchandising and impulse purchases with little shopper effort.
- Enables a shopper to enter and exit an online store in a matter of minutes.

Online stores also have potential disadvantages. A Web site:

- Can be slow for dialup shoppers. The situation worsens as more graphics and video clips are added.
- Can be too complex. How many clicks must a shopper make from the time he or she enters a site until a purchase is made?
- Cannot display the three-dimensional aspects of products as well as physical stores.
- Requires constant updating to reflect stockouts, new merchandise, and price changes.
- Is more likely to be exited without a purchase. It is easy to visit another Web site.

ENCOURAGING CUSTOMERS TO SPEND MORE TIME SHOPPING

Underhill's Envirosell Inc. (www.envirosell.com) is a leader in shopping behavior research.

Paco Underhill, the guru of retail anthropology, has a simple explanation for why consumers should be encouraged to spend more time in a store or at a Web site: "The amount of time a shopper spends in a store (shopping, not waiting in a line) is perhaps the single most important factor in determining how much he or she will buy. In an electronics store that we studied, nonbuyers spent an average of 5 minutes and 6 seconds in the store, compared with the 9 minutes and 29 seconds

FIGURE 18-13
Making the Shopping
Experience More Pleasant

At Best Buy, shoppers can "test
drive" its consumer electronics—
especially the large-screen
TV sets.

Photo reprinted by permission of
Susan Berry, Retail Image
Consulting, Inc.

buyers spent there. In a toy store, buyers averaged more than 17 minutes, compared with 10 minutes for nonbuyers. In some stores, buyers are there three or four times longer."[19] Our Web site (**www.prenhall.com/bermanevans**) has links to a number of research projects and video clips from Underhill's company Envirosell.

Among the tactics to persuade people to spend more time shopping are experiential merchandising, solutions selling, an enhanced shopping experience, retailer co-branding, and wish list programs.

The aim of **experiential merchandising** is to convert shopping from a passive activity into a more interactive one, by better engaging customers. See Figure 18-13. Retailers must meet this challenge: "Many consumers are strapped for time, and shopping is an inconvenience."[20] A number of firms are doing so:

> The growing Urban Outfitters chain is blazing past the competition by rejecting just about every strategy typical of national retailers—from mass-produced merchandise to glitzy advertising and look-alike stores. Instead, every store has the feel of a boutique. New and recycled fashions are sold alongside housewares (think beaded curtains and cocktail shakers),

---

RETAILING
Around the World   Japan's Jomo: Making Service Stations "Fun" Is Introduced

Jomo (**www.j-energy.co.jp/english**), Japan's sixth-largest gas station chain, decided to inject more "fun" into the gas station experience. Its objective was to remodel its stations so that drivers would enjoy waiting while their cars were being serviced. Jomo decided to hire a leading restaurant designer who redesigned the stations with cafés, children's areas, and even massage chairs. The car wash was also upgraded. Now, two men dance around the vehicle using water hoses almost like samurai swords. The performance is so well done that Jomo's customers sometimes applaud and competitors call it "the car-wash dance."

Sales and profit levels at the recently remodeled stations are up significantly over the pre-remodeled levels.

At eight remodeled stations open for at least three months, the average monthly visits per vehicle are up 22 percent and sales are up 15 percent as compared with the previous year's levels. And each renovated station's profits increased by 82 percent. According to Jomo's sales director, the upscale atmosphere has attracted more customers, as well as more owners of expensive cars.

Sources: Mariko Mikami, "Where Filling Up Is a Gas," *Business 2.0* (October 2004), pp. 62–63; and "Japanese Petrol Station Adds a Little Entertainment to Their Service," **http://tigersleap.senseworldwide. net/archives/000593.php** (January 3, 2005).

creating a thrill-of-the-hunt vibe suited to a thrift store. Urban delivers small batches of new merchandise daily to keep things fresh, while a visual arts staff at each store overhauls the interior design twice a month. That gets customers stopping in often and staying for at least 45 minutes per visit—more than twice as long as shoppers linger in most clothing stores.[21]

I came across a cooking demonstration at a Sam's Club the other day. Actually, I smelled it from 30 yards, I saw it from 25 yards, and I heard it from 15 yards. They were showing how to make cheese and ham crepes. The cooks wore white chef hats and were tossing around a French accent as if it were a poorly dubbed foreign film. I was first in line to get a sample. Did I buy any crepe making material? No. But it did stick in my mind for the next store visit and it took my mood from robotically going down the aisles to having a pleasurable time. The more pleasant the customer finds the environment, the longer he/she will stay in the store, the more sections they will shop, the more items they will shop, and the more items they will purchase.[22]

Solutions selling takes a customer-centered approach and presents "solutions" rather than "products." It goes a step beyond cross-merchandising. At holiday times, some retailers group gift items by price ("under $25, under $50, under $100, $100 and above") rather than by product category. This provides a solution for the shopper who has a budget to spend but a fuzzy idea of what to buy. Many supermarkets sell fully prepared, complete meals that just have to be heated and served. This solves the problem of "What's for dinner?" without requiring the consumer to shop for meal components.

See how retailers can create an enhanced shopping experience (http://merchandiseconcepts.com/showBusiness.htm).

An *enhanced shopping experience* means the retailer does everything possible to make the shopping trip pleasant—and to minimize annoyances. Given all of the retail choices facing consumers, a pleasing experience is a must. For example, in a supermarket, "the average regular checkout lane wait is 3 minutes and 24 seconds (the average express checkout lane is 3 minutes 11 seconds)." As a result, retailers "have spent years trying to reduce actual wait time by shaving time off operations, when you can just as easily reduce perceived wait time by giving customers something to do. Taste, pleasure, and reducing perceived wait time are all connected."[23]

Retailers can provide an enhanced shopping experience by setting up wider aisles so people do not feel cramped, adding benches and chairs so those accompanying the main shopper can relax, using kiosks to stimulate impulse purchases and answer questions, having activities for children (such as Ikea's playroom), and opening more checkout counters. What 80-year-old shopping accessory is turning out to be one of the greatest enhancements of all? It is the humble shopping cart, as highlighted in Figure 18-14:

As old-fashioned as they seem, carts are perfectly suited for the way people shop today. They're pressed for time and buy more in fewer trips. Mothers struggling to corral children love them. The growing ranks of senior citizens lean on carts for support and appreciate not having to carry their purchases. Carts empower an impulse. From category killers such as Home Depot to mass merchandisers such as Target Stores and Kmart, stores are getting bigger, carrying a wider array of goods, and pushing prices lower. They need customers to stay longer, cruise through the whole store, and load up. Why would any sane retailer deny its customers a cart? Some, it seems, are just too classy to have stainless steel contraptions junking up their stores. "I'm not sure I could see someone buying a $2,000 suit and hanging it over a cart," says the director of stores for Saks Fifth Avenue.[24]

More firms participate in *co-branding*, whereby two or more well-known retailers situate under the same roof (or at one Web site) to share costs, stimulate consumers to visit more often, and attract people shopping together who have different preferences. Here are several examples: McDonald's in Wal-Mart stores, Starbucks in Barnes & Noble stores, joint Dunkin' Donuts and Baskin-Robbins outlets, and Amazon.com featuring Target and Toys "R" Us as partners at its Web site. For example, "Sean and Tina Berry often disagree on where to have lunch. But there was no dispute the other day, when they went to a combined Taco Bell and Long John Silver's restaurant not far from where they work. Mr. Berry had the Taco Bell grilled stuffed burrito while his wife opted for a fried fish platter from Long John Silver's. The combined restaurant is part of an increasingly popular trend in the fast-food industry. Restaurants say such combinations are preferred by customers, generate higher sales, and give the companies a chance to build lesser-known brands."[25]

Another tactic in use by a growing number of retailers is the *wish list program*. It is a technique borrowed from Web retailers that enables customers to prepare shopping lists for gift items they'd like to receive from a particular store or shopping center:

> Birthdays. Holidays. Graduations. The joy surrounding these occasions can be trumped by the stress of finding a great gift. And for those about to receive a bevy of gifts, it would be nice to actually get what you want, right? Online gift registries are the answer for both sides of the gift-giving process. The set-up is simple. You create an online wish list, which friends and relatives can easily access. And if your loved ones aren't the most computer-savvy, you can often E-mail your list to them. By viewing someone's wish list, you'll know exactly what they want. To find someone's "wish box," you simply enter some general information, such as their name, address, or home state.[26]

COMMUNITY RELATIONS

The way that retailers interact with the communities around them can have a significant impact on their image—and performance. Their stature can be enhanced by engaging in such community-oriented actions as these:

- Making sure that stores are barrier-free for disabled shoppers.
- Showing a concern for the environment by recycling trash and cleaning streets.
- Supporting charities and noting that support at the company Web site.
- Participating in anti-drug programs.
- Employing area residents.
- Running special sales for senior citizens and other groups.
- Sponsoring Little League and other youth activities.
- Cooperating with neighborhood planning groups.
- Donating money and/or equipment to schools.
- Carefully checking IDs for purchases with age minimums.

Each year, 7-Eleven makes substantial charitable contributions of cash and goods to support programs addressing issues such as literacy, reading, crime, and multi-cultural understanding. It also donates hundreds of thousands of pounds of food to local food banks throughout the United States. Wal-Mart, Kmart, and Big Lots are among the numerous retailers participating in some type of anti-drug program. Borders, Barnes & Noble, Target Stores, and others participate in national literacy programs. Safeway and Giant Food are just two of the supermarket chains that give money or equipment to schools in their neighborhoods.

As with any aspect of retail strategy planning, community relations efforts can be undertaken by companies and organizations of any size and format:

> On Good Hope Road in southeast Washington, D.C., a financial services education center run by the nonprofit Operation Hope Inc. opened just down the street from the Good Hope Marketplace. The Hope Center, as it is called, is largely backed by more than $5 million in grants from E-Trade. Community leaders hope the Hope Center can give an economic boost to the Anacostia neighborhood, long known for its poverty, low homeownership rates, and a dearth of businesses. The president of the online E-Trade Bank says the investment is also good business. He says it will help fulfill Community Reinvestment Act obligations and bring in customers in neighborhoods where few have bank accounts. E-Trade also hopes the partnership will turn some unbanked residents into customers. Through the Hope Center, it is offering a range of products aimed at low-income people, including no-minimum checking accounts with no monthly fee and $500-minimum certificates of deposit and money-market accounts with free checks.[27]

Summary

1. *To show the importance of communicating with customers and examine the concept of retail image.* Customer communications are crucial for a store or nonstore retailer to position itself in customers' minds. Various physical and symbolic cues can be used.

   Presenting the proper image—the way a firm is perceived by its customers and others—is an essential aspect of the retail strategy mix. The components of a firm's image are its target market characteristics, retail positioning and reputation, store location, merchandise assortment, price levels, physical facilities, shopping experiences, community service, advertising, public relations, personal selling, and sales promotion. A retail image requires a multi-step, ongoing approach. For chains, there must be a consistent image among branches.

2. *To describe how a retail store image is related to the atmosphere it creates via its exterior, general interior, layout, and displays, and to look at the special case of nonstore atmospherics.* For a store retailer, atmosphere (atmospherics) is based on the physical attributes of

the store utilized to develop an image; it is composed of the exterior, general interior, store layout, and displays. For a nonstore firm, the physical attributes of such elements as catalogs, vending machines, and Web sites affect the image.

The store exterior is comprised of the storefront, marquee, entrances, display windows, building height and size, visibility, uniqueness, surrounding stores and area, parking, and congestion. It sets a mood before a prospective customer even enters a store.

The general interior of a store encompasses its flooring, colors, lighting, scents and sounds, fixtures, wall textures, temperature, width of aisles, dressing facilities, vertical transportation, dead areas, personnel, self-service, merchandise, price displays, cash register placement, technology/modernization, and cleanliness. An upscale retailer's interior is far different from a discounter's—reflecting the image desired and the costs of doing business.

In laying out a store interior, six steps are necessary: (1) Floor space is allocated among selling, merchandise, personnel, and customers based on a firm's overall strategy. More firms now use planograms. (2) Product groupings are set, based on function, purchase motivation, market segment, and/or storability. (3) Traffic flows are planned, using a straight or curving pattern. (4) Space per product category is computed by a model stock approach or sales-productivity ratio. (5) Departments are located. (6) Individual products are arranged within departments.

Interior (point-of-purchase) displays provide information for consumers, add to the atmosphere, and have a promotional role. Interior display possibilities include assortment displays, theme displays, ensemble displays, rack and case displays, cut case and dump bin displays, posters, mobiles, and electronic displays.

For Web retailers, many principles of atmospherics are similar to those for store retailers. There are also key differences. The home page is the storefront. The general interior consists of site instructions, company information, product icons, the shopping cart, the product search engine, and other factors. The store layout includes individual Web pages, as well as the links that connect them. Displays can feature full or more selective assortments. Sales are lost if the checkout counter does not function well. There are specialists that help in Web site design. Compared to traditional stores, Web stores have various pros and cons.

3. *To discuss ways of encouraging customers to spend more time shopping.* To persuade consumers to devote more time with the retailer, these tactics are often employed: experiential merchandising, solutions selling, enhancing the shopping experience, retailer co-branding, and wish list programs.

4. *To consider the impact of community relations on a retailer's image.* Consumers react favorably to retailers involved in such activities as establishing stores that are barrier-free for persons with disabilities, supporting charities, and running special sales for senior citizens.

Key Terms

atmosphere (atmospherics) (p. 544)
visual merchandising (p. 544)
storefront (p. 545)
marquee (p. 546)
dead areas (p. 550)
planogram (p. 551)
functional product groupings
    (p. 552)
purchase motivation product groupings
    (p. 552)

market segment product groupings
    (p. 552)
storability product groupings (p. 552)
straight (gridiron) traffic flow (p. 552)
curving (free-flowing) traffic flow
    (p. 552)
model stock approach (p. 554)
sales-productivity ratio (p. 554)
point-of-purchase (POP) display
    (p. 555)

assortment display (p. 556)
theme-setting display (p. 556)
ensemble display (p. 556)
rack display (p. 556)
case display (p. 556)
cut case (p. 556)
dump bin (p. 557)
experiential merchandising (p. 560)
solutions selling (p. 561)

Questions for Discussion

1. Why is it sometimes difficult for a retailer to convey its image to consumers? Give an example of an apparel retailer with a fuzzy image.

2. How could a realtor selling new homes project a value-based retail image? How could a realtor selling 20-year-old homes project such an image?

3. Define the concept of *atmosphere*. How does this differ from that of *visual merchandising*?

4. Which aspects of a store's exterior are controllable by a retailer? Which are uncontrollable?

5. What are meant by *selling*, *merchandise*, *personnel*, and *customer space*?

6. Present a planogram for a nearby convenience store.

7. Develop a purchase motivation product grouping for an online consumer electronics store.

8. Which stores should *not* use a curving (free-flowing) layout? Explain your answer.

9. Visit the Web site of eToys (**www.etoys.com**) and then comment on its storefront, general interior, store layout, displays, and checkout counter.

10. How could a neighborhood carpeting store engage in solutions selling?

11. Do you agree with upscale retailers' decision not to provide in-store shopping carts? What realistic alternatives would you suggest? Explain your answers.

12. Present a community relations program for a local restaurant.

Web-Based Exercise

Visit the Web site of the Cheesecake Factory (**www.thecheesecakefactory.com**). How would you rate the atmospherics and ambience of this site? Why? Also comment on the Cheesecake Factory's use of multi-channel retailing.

Note: Stop by our Web site (**www.prenhall.com/bermanevans**) to experience a number of highly interactive, appealing Web exercises based on actual company demonstrations and sample materials related to retailing.

Chapter Endnotes

1. Various company sources.
2. Tony Lisanti, "Retailers, Too, Need to Build a Brand Image," *Drug Store News* (June 2002), p. 27.
3. Anthony Bianco, "The Wizard of Odd," *Business Week* (April 18, 2005), p. 82.
4. Edward O. Welles, "The Diva of Retail," *Inc.* (October 1999), p. 48.
5. "Prada—The Cutting Edge of Retail Technology," **www.xr23.com/Page.cfm/140** (May 15, 2005).
6. "Company Profile," **www.chapter11books.biz** (January 17, 2006); and Katie Caperton, "Citysearch Editorial Profile," **http://atlanta.citysearch.com/profile/2995005#editorialreview** (January 17, 2006).
7. "In a Well-Planned Store Display, Every Picture Tells a Fashion Story," **www.cottoninc.com/lsmarticles/?articleID=133** (January 2, 2002).
8. Mike Troy, "Strong Regional Mix Foundation for Gander Mountain Growth," *DSN Retailing Today* (May 23, 2005), p. 20.
9. Vilma Barr, "La Boutique Electronique," **www.retailtrafficmag.com/mag/retail_la_boutique_electronique** (March 1, 2005).
10. "Toys 'R' Us Times Square," **http://www5.toysrus.com/TimesSquare/dsp_home.cfm** (January 31, 2006).
11. "The Right Flooring for Your Store," *Chain Store Age* (July 2005), p. 100.
12. Michael Sasso, "Sweetbay's Bright Outlook," *Tampa Tribune Online* (June 26, 2005).
13. Steven Zarwell, "What's on Your Front Door?" *Dealernews* (March 2005), p. 38.
14. "Surface Beauty," *Chain Store Age* (July 2005), p. 94.
15. Peter S. Fader, Eric T. Bradlow, and Jeffrey S. Larson, "Tag Team: Tracking the Patterns of Supermarket Shoppers," **http://knowledge.wharton.upenn.edu/index.cfm?fa=viewArticle&id=1208** (June 1, 2005).
16. Jack Hitt, "The Theory of Supermarkets," *New York Times Magazine* (March 10, 1996), pp. 56–61, 94, 98.
17. "The Retail Marketing Industry," **www.popai.com/AM/Template.cfm?Section=Industry** (March 8, 2006).
18. See Pookie Sautter, Michael R. Hyman, and Vaidotas Lukŏius, "E-Tail Atmospherics: A Critique of the Literature and Model Extension," *Journal of Electronic Commerce Research*, Vol. 5 (Number 1, 2004), pp. 14–24.
19. Paco Underhill, *Why We Buy* (New York: Simon & Schuster, 1999). See also Paul Keegan, "The Architect of Happy Customers," *Business 2.0* (August 2002), pp. 85–87.

20. Lorrie Grant, "Last-Minute Buyers Push Sales Higher," *USA Today Online* (December 29, 2004).

21. Susanna Hamner, "Lessons from a Retail Rebel," *Business 2.0* (June 2005), p. 62.

22. Craig Childress, "Supermarkets Coming to Their Senses, All Five of Them," *Progressive Grocer: Equipment & Design Online* (June 4, 2004).

23. Ibid.

24. Joseph B. Cahill, "The Secret Weapon of Big Discounters: Lowly Shopping Cart," *Wall Street Journal* (November 24, 1999), pp. A1, A10. See also Renee DeGross, "Department Stores Try on New Ideas," *Atlanta Journal-Constitution* (August 18, 2002), p. F1.

25. Melanie Warner, "Diners Walk Through One Door and Visit Two Restaurants," *New York Times Online* (July 11, 2005).

26. Karalee Miller, "Online 'Wishes' Can Ease Gift Giving," *Fort Worth Star-Telegram Online* (June 7, 2005).

27. Hannah Bergman, "Online Bank Makes Inner-City Connection," *American Banker* (May 10, 2005), p. 5.

Chapter 19
PROMOTIONAL STRATEGY

In her second year selling Stanley Home Products, Mary Kay Ash was named "queen of sales." In 1963, when a younger male associate was promoted instead of her, Mary Kay Ash quit Stanley in frustration. One month later, with a $5,000 investment, Ash started her own skin care business with just five items for sale. Today, Mary Kay Inc. (**www.marykay.com**) has annual sales of $2 billion and is the second largest direct seller of skin products in the United States, with an independent sales force of more than 1 million consultants based in 33 countries.

Reprinted by permission of Mary Kay.

Associates characterized Mary Kay Ash as a tough businesswoman who stressed the empowerment of women, as well as positive thinking. Ash believed that "given the opportunity, encouragement, and awards, they will soar." Many of her employees feel that Mary Kay offered women with families career opportunities that were not otherwise available to them. A popular quote attributed to Mary Kay Ash is "if your mind can conceive it, and if you can believe it, you can achieve it." *Fortune* magazine has named Mary Kay as among the "Best Companies to Work for in America" and as one of the 10 best companies for women.

Ash is also remembered for her reward dinners where top sales consultants were (and still are) given jewelry and cars. The reward for the top independent sales consultants who purchase a specified amount of Mary Kay products in six months? A two-year lease of a new pink Cadillac. Currently, these consultants drive an estimated 2,000 "Mary Kay Pink Pearl Cadillacs."[1]

chapter objectives

1. To explore the scope of retail promotion
2. To study the elements of retail promotion: advertising, public relations, personal selling, and sales promotion
3. To discuss the strategic aspects of retail promotion: objectives, budgeting, the mix of forms, implementing the mix, and reviewing and revising the plan

OVERVIEW

Sephora, the European and U.S. beauty chain, has an integrated promotion plan—from its colorful Web site (www.sephora.com) to its stores.

Retail promotion includes any communication by a retailer that informs, persuades, and/or reminds the target market about any aspect of that firm. In the first part of this chapter, the elements of retail promotion are detailed. The second part centers on the strategic aspects of promotion.

Consider the effort that Best Buy puts into its promotion strategy:

Best Buy has crafted a three-tiered plan that balances mass, customized, and local marketing to reach its best customers in key audience segments. To further custom-fit, Best Buy is diving deeper to learn more about each shopper. Much of that data will come from its four million Reward Zone loyalty club members, and much will come from the Blue Shirts—Best Buy's in-store staff. "We want to reinvent retail marketing. That's our new mantra," says Best Buy's senior vice-president for consumer and brand marketing. "We want to get to co-creation, with marketing staff, store associates, and customers in a continuous loop talking to each other."[2]

Best Buy also plans aggressive use of customer-centric stores that tailor their merchandise mix to suit local shoppers. This dovetails with the firm's marketing strategy: first, to target offers by demographics and purchase history, and second, to shape local marketing by geography and by consumer group. Best Buy's chief marketing officer says that, "We're trying to spend our money on people who most want to shop the brand, versus just throwing it all out there." Mass marketing still gets the bulk of Best Buy's total promotion. But shopper data helps refine offers to make shoppers more loyal. "Figuring out how to balance marketing and shift money across the tools is an ongoing challenge." Take Geek Squad, the computer-repair service that Best Buy bought and rolled into all stores. Geeks make house calls and staff in-store help stations. The Geek Squad is "good as a brand by itself; it's great as a connection for Best Buy's brand, and it lets us offer something different for a select customer."[3]

ELEMENTS OF THE RETAIL PROMOTIONAL MIX

This site (www. entrepreneur.com) is a good place to start learning about retail promotion. Type in "Promotion Plan."

Advertising, public relations, personal selling, and sales promotion are the elements of promotion. In this section, we discuss each in terms of goals, advantages and disadvantages, and basic forms. A good plan integrates these elements—based on the overall strategy. A movie theater concentrates on ads and sales promotion (food displays), while an upscale specialty store stresses personal selling. See Figure 19-1.

Retailers devote significant sums to promotion. For example, a typical department store spends up to 4 percent of sales on ads and 8 to 10 percent on personal selling and support services. And most department store chains invest heavily in sales promotions and use public relations to generate favorable publicity and reply to media information requests. We have more than a dozen links related to the retail promotion mix at our Web site (**www.prenhall.com/bermanevans**).

Advertising

Advertising is paid, nonpersonal communication transmitted through out-of-store mass media by an identified sponsor. Four aspects of this definition merit clarification: (1) Paid form—This distinguishes advertising from publicity (an element of

FIGURE 19-1

Communicating Through the Retail Promotion Mix

In a good promotion mix, a full variety of promotion tools are used to communicate the retailer's message—even the side panels of service trucks.

Photo reprinted by permission.

public relations), for which no payment is made by the retailer for the time or space used to convey a message. (2) Nonpersonal presentation—A standard message is delivered to the entire audience, and it cannot be adapted to individual customers (except with the Web). (3) Out-of-store mass media—These include newspapers, radio, TV, the Web, and other mass channels, rather than personal contacts. In-store communications (such as displays) are considered sales promotion. (4) Identified sponsor—The sponsor's name is clearly divulged, unlike publicity. See Figure 19-2.

Sears has the highest annual dollar advertising expenditures among U.S. retailers—$1.8 billion, about 6 percent of its U.S. sales. On the other hand, Wal-Mart spends just 0.4 percent of sales on ads, relying more on word of mouth,

FIGURE 19-2

Lands' End's Dominant Business: Mail-Order Retailing

Lands' End is one of the leading mail-order retailers in the world, with a large and growing global presence. It regularly advertises its catalogs in a number of media. And its catalogs are the firm's best form of advertising.

Photo reprinted by permission.

TABLE 19-1	Selected U.S. Advertising-to-Sales Ratios by Type of Retailer	
Type of Retailer	Advertising Dollars as Percentage of Sales Dollars[a]	Advertising Dollars as Percentage of Margin[b]
Apparel and accessories stores	3.7	9.0
Auto and home supply stores	1.5	3.2
Department stores	3.5	10.4
Drug and proprietary stores	0.7	3.8
Eating places	3.2	14.3
Family clothing stores	2.3	6.3
Furniture stores	5.9	14.6
Grocery stores	1.0	3.8
Hobby, toy, and game shops	3.8	11.2
Hotels and motels	2.2	7.9
Lumber and building materials	1.1	3.3
Mail-order firms	3.2	13.4
Movie theaters	1.0	4.3
Radio, TV, and consumer electronics stores	2.8	10.6
Shoe stores	2.4	7.3

[a]Advertising dollars as percentage of sales = Advertising expenditures/Net company sales
[b]Advertising dollars as percentage of margin = Advertising expenditures/(Net company sales − Cost of goods sold)

Source: Schonfeld & Associates, "2004 Advertising-to-Sales Ratios for 200 Largest Ad Spending Industries," **www.adage.com/page.cms?pageId=1064**. Reprinted by permission. Copyright Crain Communications Inc.

in-store events, and everyday low prices.[4] Table 19-1 shows advertising ratios for several retailing categories.

Differences between Retailer and Manufacturer Advertising Strategies

Retailers usually have more geographically concentrated target markets than manufacturers. This means they can adapt better to local needs, habits, and preferences. However, many retailers are unable to utilize national media as readily as manufacturers. Only the largest retail chains and franchises can advertise on national TV programs. An exception is direct marketing (including the World Wide Web) because trading areas for even small firms can be geographically dispersed.

Retail ads stress immediacy. Individual items are placed for sale and advertised over short time periods. Manufacturers are more often concerned with developing favorable attitudes.

Many retailers stress prices in ads, whereas manufacturers usually emphasize key product attributes. In addition, retailers often display several different products in one ad, whereas manufacturers tend to minimize the number of products mentioned in a single ad.

Media rates tend to be lower for retailers. Because of this, and the desire of many manufacturers and wholesalers for wide distribution, the costs of retail advertising are sometimes shared by manufacturers or wholesalers and their retailers. Two or more retailers may also share costs. Both of these approaches entail **cooperative advertising**.

Objectives

Find out how to devise good ads (**www.inc.com/ articles_by_topic/marketing-pr-advertising**).

A retailer would select one or more of these goals and base advertising efforts on it (them):

- Lifting short-term sales.
- Increasing customer traffic.
- Developing and/or reinforcing a retail image.
- Informing customers about goods and services and/or company attributes.
- Easing the job for sales personnel.
- Developing demand for private brands.

Advantages and Disadvantages

The major advantages of advertising are that:

- A large audience is attracted. And for print media, circulation is supplemented by the passing of a copy from one reader to another.
- The costs per viewer, reader, or listener are low.
- A number of alternative media are available, so a retailer can match a medium to the target market.

Careers in RETAILING
Is Retail for Me? Marketing and Advertising—Part 2

In addition to the typical marketing and advertising positions noted in Chapter 18, there are many other opportunities:

- *Art Department Head:* Manager of the department of graphics artists and/or computer-aided designers (CAD), who create signage and imagery for the advertising, sales promotion, and store operating groups, among others.
- *Graphics Designer:* Graphics artists and/or computer-aided designers (CAD) who create signage and imagery for the advertising, sales promotion, and store operating groups, among others.
- *Print Production Coordinator:* This position is responsible for negotiating printer prices and coordinating the production and distribution of printed media such as sales promotion materials, published reports, benefits booklets, etc. Works closely with graphic artist and printer shops.
- *Head of Visual Merchandising:* Top position responsible for the overall "look" of the stores, including

windows, sales floor signage, and displays. May publish "planograms," indicating where and how to place merchandise on the sales floor for best visual advantage.
- *Visual Merchandiser (VM):* This position is typically one of three types, with similar skills and responsibilities, but different scope: (a) Regional VMs are typically found in boutique chains, responsible for visual presentation in a geographic area. This position may report to the head of visual or to a local district/regional manager of stores. (b) In-store VMs are found in big-box stores that need one or more associates per store, typically reporting to the store manager. This position is more doing and less training than the regional VM. (c) Home office-based VMs focus on training and monitoring but may be responsible for a brand or category nationwide.

Source: Reprinted by permission of the National Retail Federation.

- The retailer has control over message content, graphics, timing, and size (or length), so a standardized message in a chosen format can be delivered to the entire audience.
- In print media, a message can be studied and restudied by the target market.
- Editorial content (a TV show, a news story, and so on) often surrounds an ad. This may increase its credibility or the probability it will be read.
- Self-service or reduced-service operations are possible since a customer becomes aware of a retailer and its offerings before shopping.

The major disadvantages of advertising are that:

- Standardized messages lack flexibility (except for the Web and its interactive nature). They do not focus on the needs of individual customers.
- Some media require large investments. This may reduce the access of small firms.
- Media may reach large geographic areas, and for retailers, this may be wasteful. A small supermarket chain might find that only 40 percent of an audience resides in its trading area.
- Some media require a long lead time for placing ads. This reduces the ability to advertise fad items or to react to some current events themes.
- Some media have a high throwaway rate. Circulars may be discarded without being read.
- A 30-second TV commercial or small newspaper ad does not have many details.

The preceding are broad generalities. The pros and cons of specific media are covered next.

Media

Retailers can choose from the media highlighted in Table 19-2 and described here.

Papers (dailies, weeklies, and shoppers) represent the most preferred medium for retailers, having the advantages of market coverage, short lead time, reasonable costs, flexibility, longevity, graphics, and editorial association (ads near columns or articles). Disadvantages include the possible waste (circulation to a wider area than necessary), the competition among retailers, the black-and-white format, and the appeal to fewer senses than TV. To maintain a dominant position, many papers have revamped their graphics, and some run color ads. Free-distribution shopper papers ("penny savers"), with little news content and delivery to all households in a geographic area, are popular today.

The Yellow Pages (www.yellowpages.com) remain a key medium for retailers.

In a White Pages telephone directory, retailers get free alphabetical listings along with all other phone subscribers, commercial and noncommercial. The major advantage of the White over the Yellow Pages is that people who know a retailer's name are not exposed to competitors' names. The major disadvantage, in contrast with the Yellow Pages, is the alphabetical rather than type-of-business listing. A customer unfamiliar with repair services will usually look in the Yellow Pages under "Repair" and choose a firm. In the Yellow Pages, firms pay for listings (and larger display ads, if desired) in their business category. Most retailers advertise in the Yellow Pages. The advantages include their widespread usage by people who are ready to shop and their long life (one year or more). The disadvantages are that retailer awareness may not be stimulated and there is a lengthy lead time for new ads.

With direct mail, retailers send catalogs or ads to customers by the mail or private delivery firms. Advantages are the targeted audience, tailored format,

TABLE 19-2	Advertising Media Comparison Chart	
Medium	Market Coverage	Particular Suitability
Daily papers	Single community or entire metro area; local editions may be available.	All larger retailers.
Weekly papers	Single community usually; may be a metro area.	Retailers with a strictly local market.
Shopper papers	Most households in one community; chain shoppers can cover a metro area.	Neighborhood retailers and service businesses.
Phone directories	Geographic area or occupational field served by the directory.	All types of goods and service-oriented retailers.
Direct mail	Controlled by the retailer.	New and expanding firms, those using coupons or special offers, mail order.
Radio	Definable market area surrounding the station.	Retailers focusing on identifiable segments.
TV	Definable market area surrounding the station.	Retailers of goods and services with wide appeal.
World Wide Web	Global.	All types of goods and service-oriented retailers.
Transit	Urban or metro community served by transit system.	Retailers near transit routes, especially those appealing to commuters.
Outdoor	Entire metro area or single neighborhood.	Amusement and tourist-oriented retailers, well-known firms.
Local magazines	Entire metro area or region, zoned editions sometimes available.	Restaurants, entertainment-oriented firms, specialty shops, mail-order firms.
Flyers/circulars	Single neighborhood.	Restaurants, dry cleaners, service stations, and other neighborhood firms.

controlled costs, quick feedback, and tie-ins (including ads with bills). Among the disadvantages are the high throwaway rate ("junk mail"), poor image to some people, low response rate, and outdated mailing lists (addressees may have moved).

Radio is used by a variety of retailers. Advantages are the relatively low costs, its value as a medium for car drivers and riders, its ability to use segmentation, its rather short lead time, and its wide reach. Disadvantages include no visual impact, the need for repetition, the need for brevity, and waste. The use of radio by retailers has gone up in recent years.

TV ads, although increasing due to the rise of national and regional retailers, are far behind papers in retail promotion expenditures. Among the advantages are the dramatic effects of messages, the large market coverage, creativity, and program affiliation (for sponsors). Disadvantages include high minimum costs, audience waste, the need for brevity and repetition, and the limited availability of popular times for nonsponsors. Because cable TV is more focused than conventional stations, it appeals to local retailers.

From an advertising perspective, retailers use the Web to provide information to customers about store locations, to describe the products carried, to let people order catalogs, and so forth. Retailers have two opportunities to reach customers: advertising on search engines and other firms' Web sites; and communicating with customers at their own sites.

At the Outdoor Advertising Association Web site (www.oaaa.org), click on "Creative Library" and then type in "Retail."

Transit advertising is used in areas with mass transit systems. Ads are displayed on buses and in trains and taxis. Advantages are the captive audience, mass market, high level of repetitiveness, and geographically defined market. Disadvantages are the ad clutter, distracted audience, lack of availability in small areas, restricted travel paths, and graffiti. Many retailers also advertise on their delivery vehicles.

Outdoor (billboard) advertising is sometimes used by retailers. Posters and signs may be displayed in public places, on buildings, and alongside highways. Advantages are the large size of the ads, the frequency of exposure, the relatively low costs, and the assistance in directing new customers. Disadvantages include the clutter of ads, a distracted audience, the limited information, and some legislation banning outdoor ads. See Figure 19-3.

Magazine usage is growing for three reasons: the rise in retail chains, the creation of regional and local editions, and the use by nonstore firms. Advantages are the tailoring to specific markets, creative options, editorial associations, longevity of messages, and color. Disadvantages include the long lead time, less sense of consumer urgency, and waste.

Single-page (flyers) or multiple-page (circulars) ads are distributed in parking lots or to consumer homes. Advantages include the targeted audience, low costs, flexibility, and speed. Among the disadvantages are the level of throwaways, the poor image to some, and clutter. Flyers are good for smaller firms, while circulars are used by larger ones.

Types

Advertisements can be classified by content and payment method. See Figure 19-4.

Pioneer ads have awareness as a goal and offer information (usually on new firms or locations). *Competitive ads* have persuasion as a goal. *Reminder ads* are geared to loyal customers and stress the attributes that have made the retailers successful. *Institutional ads* strive to keep retailer names before the public without emphasizing the sale of goods or services. Public service messages are institutional.

Retailers may pay their own way or seek cooperative ventures in placing ads. Firms paying their own way have total control and incur all costs. With cooperative ventures, two or more parties share the costs and the decision making.[5] Billions of dollars are spent yearly on U.S. cooperative advertising, most in vertical agreements. Newspapers are preferred over other media for cooperative ads related to retailing.

FIGURE 19-3
Billboard Advertising for Pedestrians and Motorists

Around the globe, billboard advertising is a rather inexpensive and attention-getting medium. Shown here is a Burger King billboard in Lugano, Switzerland.

Photo reprinted by permission.

FIGURE 19-4
Types of Advertising

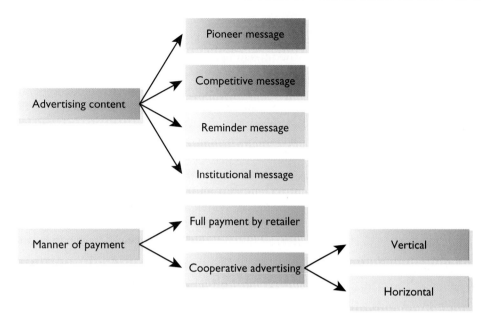

In a **vertical cooperative advertising agreement**, a manufacturer and a retailer or a wholesaler and a retailer share an ad. Responsibilities are specified contractually, and retailers are typically not reimbursed until after ads run. Vertical cooperative advertising is subject to the Robinson-Patman Act; similar arrangements must be offered to all retailers on a proportional basis. Advantages to a retailer are the reduced ad costs, assistance in preparing ads, greater market coverage, and less planning time. Disadvantages to a retailer include less control, flexibility, and distinctiveness. Some retailers are concerned about the eligibility requirements to participate and the emphasis on the supplier's name in ads. In response, manufacturers and other suppliers are being more flexible and understanding.

With a **horizontal cooperative advertising agreement**, two or more retailers share an ad. A horizontal agreement is most often used by small noncompeting retailers (such as independent hardware stores), retailers in the same shopping center, and franchisees of a given firm. Advantages and disadvantages are similar to those in a vertical agreement. Two further benefits are the bargaining power of retailers in dealing with the media and the synergies of multiple retailers working together.

When planning a cooperative strategy, these questions should be considered:

Carol Wright (**www.carolwright.com**) is a leader in horizontal cooperative promotions.

- What ads qualify, in terms of merchandise and special requirements?
- What percentage of advertising is paid by each party?
- When can ads be run? In what media?
- Are there special provisions regarding message content?
- What documentation is required for reimbursement?
- How does each party benefit?
- Do cooperative ads obscure the image of individual retailers?

At Wendy's (**www.wendys. com**), public relations means community relations. After entering the site, select "Community."

Public Relations

Public relations entails any communication that fosters a favorable image for the retailer among its publics (consumers, investors, government, channel members, employees, and the general public). It may be nonpersonal or personal, paid or nonpaid, and sponsor controlled or not controlled. **Publicity** is any nonpersonal form of public relations whereby messages are transmitted through mass media, the time or space provided by the media is not paid for, and there is no identified commercial sponsor.

The basic distinction between advertising and publicity is that publicity is non-paid. Thus, it is not as readily controllable. A story on a store opening may not appear at all, appear after the fact, or not appear in the form desired. Yet, to shoppers, publicity is often more credible and valuable. Advertising and publicity (public relations) should complement one other. Many times, publicity should precede ads.

Public relations can benefit both large and small retailers. While the former often spend a lot of money to publicize events such as the Macy's Thanksgiving Day Parade, small firms can creatively generate attention for themselves on a limited budget. They can feature book signings by authors, sponsor school sports teams, donate goods and services to charities, and so forth.

Objectives

Public relations seeks to accomplish one or more of these goals:

- Increase awareness of the retailer and its strategy mix.
- Maintain or improve the company image.
- Show the retailer as a contributor to the community's quality of life.
- Demonstrate innovativeness.
- Present a favorable message in a highly believable manner.
- Minimize total promotion costs.

Advantages and Disadvantages

The major advantages of public relations are that:

- An image can be presented or enhanced.
- A more credible source presents the message (such as a good restaurant review).
- There are no costs for message time or space.
- A mass audience is addressed.
- Carryover effects are possible (if a store is perceived as community-oriented, its value positioning is more apt to be perceived favorably).
- People pay more attention to news stories than to clearly identified ads.

The major disadvantages of public relations are that:

- Some retailers do not believe in spending any funds on image-related communication.
- There is little retailer control over a publicity message and its timing, placement, and coverage by a given medium.
- It may be more suitable for short-run, rather than long-run, planning.
- Although there are no media costs for publicity, there are costs for a public relations staff, planning activities, and the activities themselves (such as store openings).

Types

Public relations can be planned or unexpected and image enhancing or image detracting.

With planned public relations, a retailer outlines its activities in advance, strives to have media report on them, and anticipates certain coverage. Community services, such as donations and special sales; parades on holidays (such as the Macy's Thanksgiving Day Parade); the introduction of "hot" new goods and services; and a new store opening are activities a retailer hopes will gain media coverage. The release of quarterly sales figures and publication of the annual report are events a retailer knows will be covered.

When unexpected publicity occurs, the media report on a company without its having advance notice. TV and newspaper reporters may anonymously visit restaurants and other retailers to rate their performance and quality. A fire, an employee strike, or other newsworthy event may be mentioned in a story. Investigative reports on company practices may appear.

There is positive publicity when media reports are complimentary, with regard to the excellence of a retailer's practices, its community efforts, and so on. However, the media may also provide negative publicity. A story could describe a store opening in less than glowing terms, rap a firm's environmental record, or otherwise be critical. That is why public relations must be viewed as a component of the promotion mix, not as the whole mix.

Personal Selling

The communication tips at this Web site (www.inc. com/guides/sales/23032. html) are quite helpful.

Personal selling involves oral communication with one or more prospective customers for the purpose of making a sale. The level of personal selling used by a retailer depends on the image it wants to convey, the products sold, the amount of self-service, and the interest in long-term customer relationships—as well as customer expectations. Retail salespeople may work in a store, visit consumer homes or places of work, or engage in telemarketing.

J.C. Penney believes in training superior sales associates. Why? First, higher levels of selling are needed to reinforce its image as a fashion-oriented department store. Unlike self-service discounters, Penney wants its sales staff to give advice to customers. Second, Penney wants to stimulate cross-selling, whereby associates recommend related items to customers. Third, Penney wants sales associates to "save the sale," by suggesting that customers who return merchandise try different colors, styles, or quality. Four, Penney believes it can foster customer loyalty. Figure 19-5 highlights Penney's sales associate tips.

Objectives

The goals of personal selling are to:

- Persuade customers to buy (since they often enter a store after seeing an ad).
- Stimulate sales of impulse items or products related to customers' basic purchases.

FIGURE 19-5
J.C. Penney's Tips for Sales Associates

Source: J.C. Penney.

✓ Greet the customer. This sets the tone for the customer's visit to your department.
✓ Listen to customers to determine their needs.
✓ Know your merchandise. For example, describe the quality features of Penney's private brands.
✓ Know merchandise in related departments. This can increase sales and lessen a customer's shopping time.
✓ Learn to juggle several shoppers at once.
✓ Pack merchandise carefully. Ask if customer wants an item on a hanger to prevent creasing.
✓ Constantly work at keeping the department looking its best.
✓ Refer to the customer by his or her name; this can be gotten from the person's credit card.
✓ Stress Penney's "hassle-free" return policy.

- Complete customer transactions.
- Feed back information to company decision makers.
- Provide proper levels of customer service.
- Improve and maintain customer satisfaction.
- Create awareness of items also marketed through the Web, mail, and telemarketing.

Advantages and Disadvantages

The advantages of selling relate to its personal nature:

- A salesperson can adapt a message to the needs of the individual customer.
- A salesperson can be flexible in offering ways to address customer needs.
- The attention span of the customer is higher than with advertising.
- There is less waste; most people who walk into a store are potential customers.
- Customers respond more often to personal selling than to ads.
- Immediate feedback is provided.

The major disadvantages of personal selling are that:

- Only a limited number of customers can be handled at a given time.
- The costs of interacting with each customer can be high.
- Customers are not initially lured into a store through personal selling.
- Self-service may be discouraged.
- Some customers may view salespeople as unhelpful and as too aggressive.

Types

Most sales positions involve either order taking or order getting. An **order-taking salesperson** performs routine clerical and sales functions—setting up displays, stocking shelves, answering simple questions, and ringing up sales. This type of selling is most likely in stores that are strong in self-service but also have some personnel on the floor. An **order-getting salesperson** is actively involved with informing and persuading customers and in closing sales. This is a true "sales" employee. Order getters usually sell higher-priced or complex items, such as real-estate, autos, and consumer electronics. They are more skilled and better paid than order takers. See Figure 19-6.

A manufacturer may sometimes help fund personal selling by providing **PMs** (promotional or push monies) for retail salespeople selling its brand. PMs are in addition to regular salesperson compensation. Many retailers dislike this practice because their salespeople may be less responsive to actual customer desires (if customers desire brands not yielding PMs).

Functions

Store sales personnel may be responsible for all or many of the tasks shown in Figure 19-7 and described next. Nonstore sales personnel may also have to generate customer leads (by knocking on doors in residential areas or calling people who are listed in a local phone directory).

On entering a store or a department in it (or being contacted at home), a salesperson greets the customer. Typical in-store greetings are: "Hello, may I help you?" "Hi, is there anything in particular you are looking for?" With any greeting, the salesperson seeks to put the customer at ease and build rapport.

FIGURE 19-6
Personal Selling: When Self-Service Isn't Appropriate

Despite the greater emphasis on self-service retailing, many products (such as Goodyear tires) lend themselves to a more personal approach, where salespeople can present information and answer questions.

Photo reprinted by permission of Goodyear.

The salesperson next finds out what the person wants: Is the person just looking, or is there a specific good or service in mind? For what purpose is the item to be used? Is there a price range in mind? What other information can the shopper provide to help the salesperson?

At this point, the salesperson may show merchandise. He or she selects the product most apt to satisfy the customer. The salesperson may try to trade up (discuss a more expensive version) or offer a substitute (if the retailer does not carry or is out of the requested item).

The salesperson now makes a sales presentation to motivate the customer to purchase. The **canned sales presentation** is a memorized, repetitive speech given to all customers interested in a particular item. It works best if shoppers require little assistance and sales force turnover is high. The **need-satisfaction approach** is based on the principle that each customer has different wants; thus, a sales presentation should be geared to the demands of the individual customer. It is being utilized more in retailing.

A demonstration can show the utility of an item and allow customer participation. Demonstrations are often used with stereos, autos, health clubs, and watches.

A customer may have questions, and the salesperson must address them. Once all questions are answered, the salesperson tries to close the sale and get the shopper to buy. Typical closing lines are: "Will you take it with you or have it delivered?" "Cash or charge?" "Would you like this gift wrapped?"

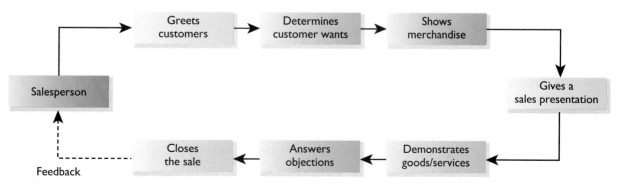

FIGURE 19-7
Typical Personal Selling Functions

FIGURE 19-8
Selected Reasons Why Retail
Sales Are Lost—and How to
Avoid Them

✗ *Poor qualification of the customer.* ✓ Obtain information from the customer so the sales presentation is properly tailored.
✗ *Salespersons not demonstrating the good or service.* ✓ Show the good or service in use so that benefits are visualized.
✗ *Failure to put feeling into the presentation.* ✓ Encourage salespeople to be sincere and consumer-oriented.
✗ *Poor knowledge.* ✓ Train salespeople to know the major advantages and disadvantages of the goods and services, as well as competitors', and be able to answer questions.
✗ *Arguing with a customer.* ✓ Avoid arguments in handling customer objections, even if the customer is wrong.
✗ *No suggestion selling.* ✓ Attempt to sell related items (such as service contracts, product supplies, and installation).
✗ *Giving up too early.* ✓ Try again if an attempt to close a sale is unsuccessful.
✗ *Inflexibility.* ✓ Be creative in offering alternative solutions to a customer's needs.
✗ *Poor follow-up.* ✓ Be sure that orders are correctly written, that deliveries arrive on time, and that customers are satisfied.

For personal selling to work well, salespeople must be enthusiastic, knowledgeable, interested in customers, and good communicators. Figure 19-8 cites several ways that retail sales can be lost through poor personal selling and how to avoid these problems.[6]

Sales Promotion

This Web site (http://en.wikipedia.org/wiki/Sales_promotion) offers a lot of information about sales promotion.

Sales promotion encompasses the paid communication activities other than advertising, public relations, and personal selling that stimulate consumer purchases and dealer effectiveness. It includes displays, contests, sweepstakes, coupons, frequent shopper programs, prizes, samples, demonstrations, referral gifts, and other limited-time selling efforts outside of the ordinary promotion routine. The value and complexity of sales promotion are clear from this commentary:

> In-store marketing—including POP, retail merchandising, and in-store services—is growing mostly via more (and more sophisticated) POP displays and in-store media such as TV and radio. In-store marketing agency Mass Connections has teamed with In-Store Broadcasting Network to launch Audio Connection to air product info via in-store radio during store events. Thousands of stores are using Audio Connection, including Kroger, Albertson's, Safeway, Ahold, Walgreens, and Rite Aid. Apparel and durables retailers (consumer electronics, appliances) are using more interactive displays that let shoppers interact with a brand before buying. (Nike Town displays let shoppers order custom shoes, delivered two weeks later by mail.) Packaged goods brands will adopt interactive displays as a bridge between static POP and speedy in-store demos. Sampling and demos are still strong.[7]

Objectives

Sales promotion goals include:

- Increasing short-term sales volume.
- Maintaining customer loyalty.
- Emphasizing novelty.
- Complementing other promotion tools.

RETAILING
Around the World | Europe's Trying to Ramp Up Customer Interest

As in the United States, European retailers are trying to extend the Christmas shopping season by starting the season earlier. An enclosed mall in Nantes, France, puts up decorations in the second week of November. German retailers have begun to offer pre-Christmas markdowns after the government revised laws that prohibited such sales.

In some European countries, price reductions are still restricted by law. France has two nationally legal periods of price discounting: January and July. Spain has a similar regulation, but the time periods vary by province. Because Christmas markdowns would be illegal in these countries, retailers have resorted to other methods of attracting shoppers. In France, gift certificates have become a popular means of attracting shoppers as they can redeem them in the legal sales period.

Some centers have also extended store hours and use special staff to greet shoppers and to even carry their bags as a means of reducing the stress associated with holiday shopping. Others have seasonal kiosks that offer crafts, toys, and decorations to generate excitement and to build and maintain customer traffic.

Source: Susan Thorne, "Hectic Holidays," *Shopping Centers Today* (December 2004), pp. 83–84.

Advantages and Disadvantages

The major advantages of sales promotion are that:

- It often has eye-catching appeal.
- Themes and tools can be distinctive.
- The consumer may receive something of value, such as coupons or free merchandise.
- It helps draw customer traffic and maintain loyalty to the retailer.
- Impulse purchases are increased.
- Customers can have fun, particularly with promotion tools such as contests and demonstrations.

The major disadvantages of sales promotion are that:

- It may be hard to terminate certain promotions without adverse customer reactions.
- The retailer's image may be hurt if trite promotions are used.
- Frivolous selling points may be stressed rather than the retailer's product assortment, prices, customer services, and other factors.
- Many sales promotions have only short-term effects.
- It should be used mostly as a supplement to other promotional forms.

Types

Figure 19-9 describes the major types of sales promotions. Each is explained here.

Point-of-purchase promotion consists of in-store displays designed to lift sales. From a promotional perspective, displays may remind customers, stimulate impulse behavior, facilitate self-service, and reduce retailer costs if manufacturers provide the displays. See Figure 19-10. These data show the extent of displays:

Visit the site of the leading point-of-purchase trade association (www.popai.org).

- U.S. manufacturers and retailers together annually spend $17 billion on in-store displays,[8] with retailers using about two-thirds of all displays provided by manufacturers.
- Virtually all retailers have some type of POP display.

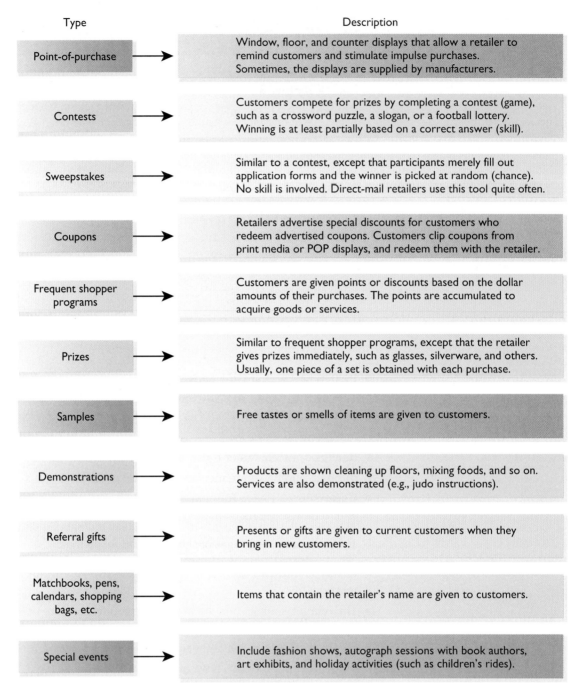

Type	Description
Point-of-purchase	Window, floor, and counter displays that allow a retailer to remind customers and stimulate impulse purchases. Sometimes, the displays are supplied by manufacturers.
Contests	Customers compete for prizes by completing a contest (game), such as a crossword puzzle, a slogan, or a football lottery. Winning is at least partially based on a correct answer (skill).
Sweepstakes	Similar to a contest, except that participants merely fill out application forms and the winner is picked at random (chance). No skill is involved. Direct-mail retailers use this tool quite often.
Coupons	Retailers advertise special discounts for customers who redeem advertised coupons. Customers clip coupons from print media or POP displays, and redeem them with the retailer.
Frequent shopper programs	Customers are given points or discounts based on the dollar amounts of their purchases. The points are accumulated to acquire goods or services.
Prizes	Similar to frequent shopper programs, except that the retailer gives prizes immediately, such as glasses, silverware, and others. Usually, one piece of a set is obtained with each purchase.
Samples	Free tastes or smells of items are given to customers.
Demonstrations	Products are shown cleaning up floors, mixing foods, and so on. Services are also demonstrated (e.g., judo instructions).
Referral gifts	Presents or gifts are given to current customers when they bring in new customers.
Matchbooks, pens, calendars, shopping bags, etc.	Items that contain the retailer's name are given to customers.
Special events	Include fashion shows, autograph sessions with book authors, art exhibits, and holiday activities (such as children's rides).

FIGURE 19-9
Types of Sales Promotion

- Restaurants, apparel stores, music/video stores, toy stores, and sporting-goods stores are among the retail categories with above-average use of in-store displays.
- Retailers spend one-sixth of their sales promotion budgets on displays.
- Display ads appear on shopping carts in most U.S. supermarkets. And thousands of supermarkets have electronic signs above their aisles promoting well-known brands.

Contests and sweepstakes are similar; they seek to attract customers who participate in events with large prizes. A contest requires a customer to show some

FIGURE 19-10
Using Point-of-Purchase
Displays to Generate
Consumer Enthusiasm

With the support of its suppliers,
Lord & Taylor knows how to use
appealing point-of-purchase displays to encourage impulse
shopping and make products
look attractive.

Photo reprinted by permission.

skill. A sweepstakes only requires participation, with the winner chosen at random. Disadvantages of contests and sweepstakes are their costs, customer reliance
on these tools for continued patronage, the customer effort, and entries by nonshoppers. Together, U.S. manufacturers and retailers spend nearly $2 billion
yearly on contests and sweepstakes.[9]

Each year, $250 billion worth of coupons—discounts from regular selling
prices—are distributed in the United States, with grocery products accounting for
75 percent of them. Consumers actually redeem $4 billion in coupons annually;
retailers receive several hundred million dollars for processing coupon redemptions. Coupons are offered through freestanding inserts in Sunday papers and
placements in daily papers, direct mail, Web sites, regular magazines, and Sunday
newspaper magazines. They are also placed in or on packages and dispensed
from in-store machines.[10]

Coupons have four key advantages: (1) In many cases, manufacturers pay to
advertise and redeem them. (2) According to surveys, more than three-quarters of
consumers redeem coupons at least once during the year. (3) They contribute to
the consumer's perception that a retailer offers good value. (4) Ad effectiveness
can be measured by counting redeemed coupons. Disadvantages include the possible negative effect on the retailer's image, consumers shopping only if coupons
are available, the low redemption rates, the clutter of coupons, retailer and consumer fraud, and handling costs. Less than 2 percent of coupons are redeemed by
consumers due to the large number of them that are received.

Frequent shopper programs foster customer relationships by awarding discounts or prizes to people for continued patronage. In most programs, customers
accumulate points (or their equivalent)—which are redeemed for cash, discounts,
or prizes. Programs that follow these principles are most apt to succeed:

> (1) Every good retention program begins with a data base of customers
> who share information with you during enrollment. By compiling cus-
> tomer data throughout the life of your program, you can tailor your
> offers based on customers' past preferences and purchase histories. If
> your original data base contains a large number of lapsed customers,
> offering an instant reward when they make their first purchase is a great
> way to bring them back. (2) Raise customer expectations. The best

programs build excitement by letting customers know exactly what rewards they can expect and how they can earn them. (3) Offer graduated rewards. To stimulate maximum participation, make rewards readily obtainable—and graduate them so you transform a higher percentage of your data base from low-value to high-value customers. This will help you avoid the pitfalls of programs that reward primarily on enrollment, which tend to attract low-value price-switchers who join to take advantage of first-time buyer rewards. Graduated rewards can also energize sales of higher-ticket items, including those customers might otherwise consider out of reach. (4) Communicate often.[11]

All sorts of retailers participate in online loyalty programs, such as e-Rewards (www.e-rewards.com/redeem/body.asp).

The advantages of frequent shopper programs for retailers are the loyalty (customers amass points only by shopping at a specific firm or firms), the increased shopping, and the competitive edge for a retailer similar to others. However, some consumers feel these programs are not really free and would rather shop at lower-priced stores without loyalty programs, it may take a while for shoppers to gather enough points to earn meaningful gifts, and their profit margins may be smaller if retailers with these programs try to price competitively with firms without the programs.

Prizes are similar to frequent shopper programs, but they are given with each purchase. They are most effective when sets of glasses, silverware, dishes, place mats, and so on are distributed one at a time to shoppers. These encourage loyalty. Problems are the cost of prizes, the difficulty of termination, and the possible impact on image.

Free samples (food tastings) and demonstrations (cooking lessons) can complement personal selling. About $2 billion is spent annually on sampling and demonstrations in U.S. stores[12]—mostly at supermarkets, membership clubs, specialty stores, and department stores. They are effective because customers become involved and impulse purchases increase. Loitering and costs may be problems.

Referral gifts may encourage existing customers to bring in new ones. Direct marketers, such as book and music clubs, often use this tool. It is a technique that has no important shortcomings and recognizes the value of friends in influencing purchases.

Matchbooks, pens, calendars, and shopping bags may be given to customers. They differ from prizes since they promote retailers' names. These items should be used as supplements. The advantage is longevity. There is no real disadvantage.

Retailers may use special events to generate consumer enthusiasm. Events can range from store grand openings to fashion shows. When new McDonald's stores open, there are typically giveaways and children's activities, and there is a guest appearance by the firm's Ronald McDonald (a human in a costume). Generally, in planning a special event, the potential increase in consumer awareness and store traffic needs to be weighed against that event's costs.

PLANNING A RETAIL PROMOTIONAL STRATEGY

A systematic approach to promotional planning is shown in Figure 19-11 and explained next. Our Web site (www.prenhall.com/bermanevans) has several links related to promotional strategy, including word of mouth.

Determining Promotional Objectives

A retailer's broad promotional goals may be drawn from this list:

- Increase sales.
- Stimulate impulse and reminder buying.

FIGURE 19-11
Planning a Retail
Promotional Strategy

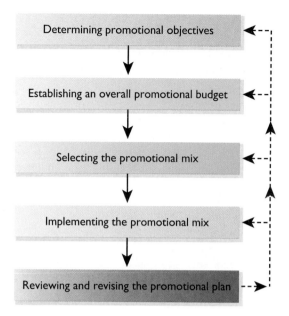

Determining promotional objectives

↓

Establishing an overall promotional budget

↓

Selecting the promotional mix

↓

Implementing the promotional mix

↓

Reviewing and revising the promotional plan

- Raise customer traffic.
- Get leads for sales personnel.
- Present and reinforce the retailer's image.
- Inform customers about goods and services.
- Popularize new stores and Web sites.
- Capitalize on manufacturer support.
- Enhance customer relations.
- Maintain customer loyalty.
- Have consumers pass along positive information to friends and others.

In developing a promotional strategy, the firm must determine which of these are most important. See Figure 19-12.

It is vital to state goals as precisely as possible to give direction to the choice of promotional types, media, and messages. Increasing sales is not a specific goal.

FIGURE 19-12
The Ikea Playroom

Since one of its goals is to attract parents with young children, Ikea actively promotes its glass-enclosed playrooms. Parents can shop in an undistracted manner while their children have a great time playing.

Photo reprinted by permission of Retail Forward, Inc.

Technology in RETAILING — Casual Male's In-Stock Guarantee

Casual Male (**www.casualmale.com**) is a clothing retailer that operates about 500 Big and Tall stores in 44 states. The chain offers an unusual guarantee: If an item is out of stock, the retailer will ship it to the customer at no additional charge within five days. If it is unable to meet this claim, the item is free.

For the typical retailer, this guarantee program could be costly. According to a recent study of 300 retailers sponsored by the National Retail Federation (**www.nrf.com**) and BearingPoint Inc. (**www.bearingpoint.com**), only a third of the respondents stated that they were in stock 91 percent of the time. The other two-thirds of respondents stated that out-of-stocks were more frequent.

Dennis Hernreich, Casual Male's executive vice-president, isn't too worried. Casual Male's system communicates with its suppliers on a daily (and sometimes even an hourly) basis using electronic data interchange (EDI). It also has an electronic link with United Parcel Service. Inventory is forecast on daily sales. These forecasts are then checked against inventory levels on a store-by-store basis. If inventory is too low, purchase orders are sent to suppliers via EDI.

Sources: Elena Malykhina, "Retailers Take Stock," *Informationweek.com* (February 7, 2005), pp. 20–21; and "About Us," **www.casualmale.com/store/en_US/static/aboutus.jsp** (February 17, 2006).

However, increasing sales by 10 percent is directional, quantitative, and measurable. With that goal, a firm could prepare a thorough promotional plan and evaluate its success. McDonald's, which has won numerous awards for creative advertising, wants its ads and promotions to drive sales, introduce new products, push special offers, create an emotional bond with customers, and deflect criticism about the firm's fast-food menu:

> McDonald's recently unveiled a major initiative centered on a multi-faceted education campaign to help consumers better understand the keys to balanced, active lives: "It's what I eat and what I do—I'm lovin' it." The theme underscores the important interplay between eating right and staying active. "One of the best things we can do is communicate the importance of energy balance in an engaging and simple way. Our entire worldwide system looks forward to bringing this balanced, active lifestyles commitment and education campaign to our customers." Ronald McDonald will continue to expand his role as a major advocate for balanced, active lifestyles. He will help inform children and parents around the world in a fun and meaningful way to eat well and stay active. McDonald's has refreshed its GoActive.com Web site with a new look and feel focusing on moms and families. The Web site includes relevant, balanced, active lifestyle tips and a Family Fitness Tool Kit. McDonald's Global Advisory Council on balanced, active lifestyles is comprised of outside experts in the areas of nutrition, wellness, and activity.[13]

See what leads to good WOM (**www.geocities.com/wallstreet/6246/tactics1.html**).

Perhaps the most vital long-term promotion goal for any retailer is to gain positive **word of mouth (WOM)**, which occurs when one consumer talks to others.[14] If a satisfied customer refers friends to a retailer, this can build into a chain of customers. No retailer can succeed if it receives extensive negative WOM (such as "The hotel advertised that everything was included in the price. Yet it cost me $50 to play golf"). Negative WOM will cause a firm to lose substantial business.

Service retailers, even more than goods-oriented retailers, must have positive word of mouth to attract and retain customers. They need WOM referrals to generate most new customers/clients/patients. As consultant Michael Cafferky says (**www.geocities.com/WallStreet/6246/main.html**): "We are bombarded with thousands of advertising messages every day. So many advertising messages rush at us daily, we cut through all that hype to get to the essence of the messages we need. Word of mouth (which usually we trust) allows us to sort it out."

Establishing an Overall Promotional Budget

There are five main procedures for setting the size of a retail promotional budget. Retailers should weigh the strengths and weaknesses of each technique in relation to their own requirements and constraints. To assist firms in their efforts, there is now computer software available.

With the **all-you-can-afford method**, a retailer first allots funds for each element of the retail strategy mix except promotion. The remaining funds go to promotion. This is the weakest technique. Its shortcomings are that little emphasis is placed on promotion as a strategic variable; expenditures are not linked to goals; and if little or no funds are left over, the promotion budget is too small or nonexistent. The method is used predominantly by small, conservative retailers.

The **incremental method** relies on prior promotion budgets to allocate funds. A percentage is either added to or subtracted from one year's budget to determine the next year's. If this year's promotion budget is $100,000, next year's would be calculated by adjusting that amount. A 10 percent rise means that next year's budget would be $110,000. This technique is useful for a small retailer. It provides a reference point. The budget is adjusted based on the firm's feelings about past successes and future trends. It is easy to apply. Yet, the budget is rarely tied to specific goals. "Gut feelings" are used.

With the **competitive parity method**, a retailer's promotion budget is raised or lowered based on competitors' actions. If the leading competitor raises its budget by 8 percent, other retailers in the area may follow. This method is useful for small and large firms, uses a comparison point, and is market-oriented and conservative. It is also imitative, takes for granted that tough-to-get competitive data are available, and assumes that competitors are similar (as to years in business, size, target market, location, merchandise, prices, and so on). That last point is critical because competitors often need very different promotional budgets.

In the **percentage-of-sales method**, a retailer ties its promotion budget to revenue. A promotion-to-sales ratio is developed. Then, during succeeding years, this ratio remains constant. A firm could set promotion costs at 10 percent of sales. Since this year's sales are $600,000, there is a $60,000 promotion budget. If next year's sales are estimated at $720,000, a $72,000 budget is planned. This process uses sales as a base, is adaptable, and correlates promotion and sales. Nonetheless, there is no relation to goals (for an established firm, sales growth may not require increased promotion); promotion is not used to lead sales; and promotion drops during poor periods, when increases might be helpful. This technique provides excess financing in times of high sales and too few funds in periods of low sales.

Under the **objective-and-task method**, a retailer clearly defines its promotion goals and prepares a budget to satisfy them. A goal might be to have 70 percent of the people in its trading area know a retailer's name by the end of a one-month promotion campaign, up from 50 percent. To do so, it would determine the tasks and costs required to achieve that goal:

Objective	Task	Cost
1. Gain awareness of working women.	Use eight 1/4-page ads in four successive Sunday editions of two area papers.	$20,000
2. Gain awareness of motorists.	Use twenty 30-second radio ads during prime time on local radio stations.	12,000
3. Gain awareness of pedestrians.	Give away 5,000 shopping bags.	10,000
	Total budget	$42,000

The objective-and-task method is the best budgeting technique. Goals are clear, spending relates to goal-oriented tasks, and performance can be assessed. It can be time-consuming and complex to set goals and specific tasks, especially for small retailers.

Selecting the Promotional Mix

After a budget is set, the promotional mix is determined: the retailer's combination of advertising, public relations, personal selling, and sales promotion. A firm with a limited budget may rely on store displays, flyers, targeted direct mail, and publicity to generate customer traffic. One with a big budget may rely more on newspaper and TV ads. Retailers often use an assortment of forms to reinforce each other. A melding of media ads and POP displays may be more effective than either form alone. See Figure 19-13.

The promotional mix is affected by the type of retailer involved. In supermarkets, sampling, frequent shopper promotions, theme sales, and bonus coupons are among the techniques used most. At upscale stores, there is more attention to personal selling and less to advertising and sales promotion as compared with discounters. Table 19-3 shows a number of small-retailer promotional mixes.

In reacting to a retailer's communication efforts, consumers often go through a sequence of steps known as the **hierarchy of effects**, which takes them from awareness to knowledge to liking to preference to conviction to purchase. Different promotional mixes are needed in each step. Ads and public relations are best to develop awareness; personal selling and sales promotion are best in changing attitudes and stimulating desires. This is especially true for expensive, complex goods and services. See Figure 19-14.

Freestanding inserts (**www.fsicouncil.org**) offer retailers many advertising and sales promotion possibilities.

FIGURE 19-13
Hi-Tech, In-Store Promotion

Photo reprinted by permission of Industrial Electronic Engineers (IEE).

IEE's color LCD dual input display, **ShopVue®**, is revolutionizing the way retail establishments present sales and advertising information to customers. The display will run advertising spots when not displaying a sales transaction. Retailers have the opportunity to sell advertising to their suppliers and thus the displays can become a source of revenue.

TABLE 19-3	The Promotional Mixes of Selected Small Retailers			
Type of Retailer	Favorite Media	Personal Selling Emphasis	Special Considerations	Promotional Opportunities
Apparel store	Weekly papers; direct mail; radio; Yellow Pages; exterior signs.	High.	Cooperative ads available from manufacturers.	Fashion shows for community groups and charities.
Auto supply store	Local papers; Yellow Pages; POP displays; exterior signs.	Moderate.	Cooperative ads available from manufacturers.	Direct mail.
Bookstore	Local papers; shoppers; Yellow Pages; radio; exterior signs.	Moderate.	Cooperative ads available from publishers.	Author-signing events.
Coin-operated laundry	Yellow Pages; flyers in area; local direct mail; exterior signs.	None.	None.	Coupons in newspaper ads.
Gift store	Weekly papers; Yellow Pages; radio; direct mail; exterior signs.	Moderate.	None.	Special events; Web ads.
Hair grooming/ beauty salon	Yellow Pages; mentions in feature articles; exterior signs.	Moderate.	Word-of-mouth communication key.	Participation in fashion shows; free beauty clinics.
Health food store	Local papers; shoppers; POP displays; exterior signs.	Moderate.	None.	Display windows.
Restaurant	Newspapers; radio; Yellow Pages; outdoor; entertainment guides; exterior signs.	Moderate.	Word-of-mouth communication key.	Write-ups in critics' columns; special events.

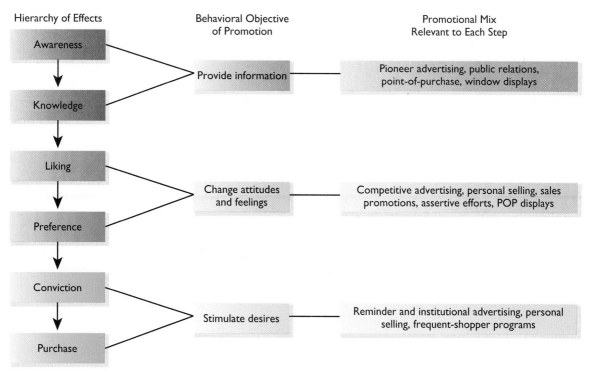

FIGURE 19-14
Promotion and the Hierarchy of Effects

Implementing the Promotional Mix

The implementation of a promotional mix involves choosing which specific media to use (such as Newspaper A and Newspaper B), timing, message content, the makeup of the sales force, specific sales promotion tools, and the responsibility for coordination. Consider this example:

> If you own an upscale jewelry store, you know from your sales history or marketing research that your target market is consumers earning more than $75,000 per year. Any print advertising should thus appear in publications in which readership income exceeds $75,000. To introduce new customers to your product, a direct-marketing technique, such as a direct-mail letter with a money-saving offer to first-time customers, might work. Or you can try a sales promotion, such as a free gift with a minimum purchase of $250. If your target market has a misconception about your store (say, that it's more expensive or less effective than rival stores), you can correct the perception by providing comparisons or testimonials.[15]

Media Decisions

Is 3D shopping on the Web ahead of its time or on target (www.3dshopper.net)?

The choice of specific media is based on their overall costs, efficiency (the cost to reach the target market), lead time, and editorial content. Overall costs are important since heavy use of one expensive medium may preclude a balanced promotional mix, and a firm may not be able to repeat a message in a costly medium.

A medium's efficiency relates to the cost of reaching a given number of target customers. Media rates are often expressed in terms of cost per 1,000 readers, watchers, or listeners:

$$\text{Cost per thousand} = \frac{\text{Cost per message} \times 1{,}000}{\text{Circulation}}$$

A newspaper with a circulation of 400,000 and a one-page advertising rate of $10,000 has a per-page cost per thousand of $25.

In this computation, total circulation was used to measure efficiency. Yet, because a retailer usually appeals to a limited target market, only the relevant portion of circulation should be considered. If 70 percent of readers are target customers for a particular firm (and the other 30 percent live outside the trading area), the real cost per thousand is

$$\begin{aligned}\text{Cost per thousand}\atop\text{(target market)} &= \frac{\text{Cost per page} \times 1{,}000}{\text{Circulation} \times \dfrac{\text{Target market}}{\text{Circulation}}} \\[2mm] &= \frac{\$10{,}000 \times 1{,}000}{400{,}000 \times 0.70} = \$35.71 \end{aligned}$$

Different media require different lead time. A newspaper ad can be placed shortly before publication, whereas a magazine ad sometimes must be placed months in advance. In addition, the retailer must decide what kind of editorial content it wants near ads (such as a sports story or a personal care column).

Media decisions are not simple. Despite spending billions of dollars on TV and radio commercials, banner ads at search engines, and other media, many Web retailers have found that the most valuable medium for them is E-mail. It is fast, inexpensive, and targeted. Consider the following.

To generate greater *awareness* of Web retailers, costly advertising may be necessary in today's competitive and cluttered landscape. As Netflix's chief executive says, "We will always be buying advertising from a wide range of online, radio, and TV."[16] Once customers have visited a Web site, E-mail can help *sustain relationships*:

> Opt-in marketing involves the customer giving permission for the retailer to send marketing materials and giving private information on where to send them. The customer is more likely to "read," "hear," or "see" a marketing message if he/she has already given prior permission. In the highest form, opt-in E-mail marketing involves an ongoing, evolving relationship between the retailer and the customer. The relationship is one that becomes increasingly focused, with the relevant exchange of information and value. In order to retain customers, the retailer must continually offer value. Customer loyalty cannot be taken for granted, it has to be earned.[17]

Timing of the Promotional Mix

Reach refers to the number of distinct people exposed to a retailer's promotion efforts in a specific period. **Frequency** is the average number of times each person reached is exposed to a retailer's promotion efforts in a specific period. A retailer can advertise extensively or intensively. Extensive media coverage often means ads reach many people but with relatively low frequency. Intensive media coverage generally means ads are placed in selected media and repeated frequently. Repetition is important, particularly for a retailer seeking to develop an image or sell new goods or services.

Decisions are needed about how to address peak selling seasons and whether to mass or distribute efforts. When peak seasons occur, all elements of the promotional mix are usually utilized; in slow periods, promotional efforts are typically reduced. A **massed promotion effort** is used by retailers, such as toy retailers, that promote seasonally. A **distributed promotion effort** is used by retailers, such as fast-food restaurants, that promote throughout the year. Although they are not affected by seasonality in the same way as other retailers, massed advertising is practiced by supermarkets, many of which use Wednesday or Thursday for weekly newspaper ads. This takes advantage of the fact that a high proportion of their consumers do their major shopping trip on Friday, Saturday, or Sunday.

Sales force size can vary by time (morning versus evening), day (weekdays versus weekends), and month (December versus January). Sales promotions also vary in their timing. Store openings and holidays are especially good times for sales promotions (and public relations).

Content of Messages

The CarMax (www.carmax.com) message: "The Way Car Buying *Should* Be" is clear and information packed. Click on "Company Info."

Whether written or spoken, personally or impersonally delivered, message content is important. Advertising themes, wording, headlines, the use of color, size, layout, and placement must be selected. Publicity releases must be written. In personal selling, the greeting, sales presentation, demonstration, and closing need to be applied. With sales promotion, the firm's message must be composed and placed on the promotional device.

To a large extent, the characteristics of the promotional form influence the message. A shopping bag often contains no more than a retailer's name, a billboard (seen at 55 miles per hour) is good for visual effect but can hold only limited information, and a salesperson may be able to hold a customer's attention for a while. Some shopping centers use a glossy magazine to communicate a community-oriented image, introduce new stores to consumers, and promote the goods and services carried at stores in the center. Cluttered ads displaying many products suggest a discounter's orientation, while fine pencil drawings and selective product displays suggest a specialty store focus.

Some retailers use comparative advertising to contrast their offerings with competitors'. These ads help position a retailer relative to competitors, increase awareness of the firm, maximize the efficiency of a limited budget, and offer credibility. Yet, they provide visibility for competitors, may confuse people, and may lead to legal action. Fast-food and off-price retailers are among those using comparative ads.

Makeup of Sales Force

Sales personnel qualifications must be detailed; and these personnel must be recruited, selected, trained, compensated, supervised, and monitored. Personnel should also be classified as order takers or order getters and assigned to the appropriate departments.

Sales Promotion Tools

Specific sales promotion tools must be chosen from among those cited in Figure 19-9. The combination of tools depends on short-term goals and the other aspects of the promotion mix. If possible, cooperative ventures should be sought. Tools inconsistent with the firm's image should never be used; and retailers should recognize the types of promotions that customers really want: "Store promotions are a way of life. Indeed, an intensive promotional activity allows the store to maintain/increase its sales by achieving a higher penetration rate in the market area, an increase in the frequency of visits, and/or an increase in the average amount spent in a store. Moreover, store-level promotions help reinforce a low-price positioning, a key to performance."[18]

Responsibility for Coordination

Regardless of the retailer's size or format, someone must be responsible for the promotion function. Larger retailers often assign this job to a vice-president, who oversees display personnel, works with the firm's ad agency, supervises the firm's advertising department (if there is one), and supplies branch outlets with POP materials. In a large retail setting, personal selling is usually under the jurisdiction of the store manager. For a promotional strategy to succeed, its components have to be coordinated with other retail mix elements. Sales personnel must be informed of special sales and know product attributes; featured items must be received, marked, and displayed; and accounting entries must be made. Often, a shopping center or a shopping district runs theme promotions, such as "Back to School." In those instances, someone must coordinate the activities of all participating retailers.

Reviewing and Revising the Promotional Plan

An analysis of the success of a promotional plan depends on its objectives. Revisions should be made if pre-set goals are not achieved. Here are some ways to test the effectiveness of a promotional effort:

Examples of Retail Promotion Goals	Approaches for Evaluating Promotion Effectiveness
Inform current customers about new credit plans; acquaint potential customers with new offerings.	Study company and product awareness before and after promotion; evaluate size of audience.
Develop and reinforce a particular image; maintain customer loyalty.	Study image through surveys before and after public relations and other promotion efforts.
Increase customer traffic; get leads for salespeople; increase revenues above last year's; reduce customer returns from prior year's.	Evaluate sales performance and the number of inquiries; study customer intentions to buy before and after promotion; study customer trading areas and average purchases; review coupon redemption.

NET-ADS (www.net-ads.com/articles/advertising) presents a lot of information on the status of Web advertising.

Although it may at times be tough to assess promotion efforts (for instance, increased revenues might be due to several factors, not just promotion), it is crucial for retailers to systematically study and adapt their promotional mixes. Wal-Mart provides suppliers with store-by-store data and sets up-front goals for cooperative promotion programs. Actual sales are then compared against the goals. Lowe's, the home center chain, applies computerized testing to review thousands of different ideas affecting the design of circulars and media mix options. And consider this:

Staples has turned to a statistic-driven solution: multi-variable testing (MVT). This complicated mathematics technique allows a company to test and measure the effectiveness of many changes in a procedure, service, or operation (from a store layout to an advertising insert) at once, as opposed to trying them out one at a time. Working with QualPro, Staples reviewed its circulars and came up with a list of 17 different items or variables to test. They ran the gamut from creative style and the percentage of promotions offered per circular to the size of the items pictured on the front page and circular size (page count). Staples created 20 different circular "recipes" or versions for the MVT test. They were tested per week over a period of six weeks. Depending on the version, some had lifestyle photos, for example, while others did not. Some had a more free-flow look compared to others. Everyone in Staples' marketing department was asked to vote as to which circular they thought would produce the best sales. There was an overwhelming response for one in particular. Surprisingly, it came in dead last in the MVT analysis.[19]

Summary

1. *To explore the scope of retail promotion.* Any communication by a retailer that informs, persuades, and/or reminds the target market about any aspect of the retailer through ads, public relations, personal selling, and sales promotion is retail promotion.

2. *To study the elements of retail promotion.* Advertising involves paid, nonpersonal communication. It has a large audience, low costs per person, many alternative media, and other factors. It also involves message inflexibility, high absolute costs, and a wasted

portion of the audience. Key advertising media are papers, phone directories, direct mail, radio, TV, the Web, transit, outdoor, magazines, and flyers/circulars. Especially useful are cooperative ads, in which a retailer shares costs and messages with manufacturers, wholesalers, or other retailers.

Public relations includes all communications fostering a favorable image. It may be nonpersonal or personal, paid or nonpaid, and sponsor controlled or not controlled. Publicity is the nonpersonal, nonpaid form of public relations. Public relations creates awareness, enhances the image, involves credible sources, and has no message costs. It also has little control over messages, is short term, and can entail nonmedia costs. Publicity can be expected or unexpected and positive or negative.

Personal selling uses oral communication with one or more potential customers and is critical for persuasion and in closing sales. It is adaptable, flexible, and provides immediate feedback. The audience is small, per-customer costs are high, and shoppers are not lured into the store. Order-taking and/or order-getting salespeople can be employed. Functions include greeting the customer, determining wants, showing merchandise, making a sales presentation, demonstrating products, answering objections, and closing the sale.

Sales promotion comprises the paid communication activities other than advertising, public relations, and personal selling. It may be eye-catching, unique, and valuable to the customer. It also may be hard to end, have a negative effect on image, and rely on frivolous selling points. Tools include POP displays, contests and sweepstakes, coupons, frequent shopper programs, prizes, samples, demonstrations, referral gifts, matchbooks, pens, calendars, shopping bags, and special events.

3. *To discuss the strategic aspects of retail promotion.* There are five steps in a promotion strategy: (1) Goals are stated in specific and measurable terms. Positive word of mouth (WOM) is an important long-term goal. (2) An overall promotion budget is set on the basis of one of these techniques: all you can afford, incremental, competitive parity, percentage of sales, and objective and task. (3) The promotional mix is outlined, based on the budget, the type of retailing, the coverage of the media, and the hierarchy of effects. (4) The promotional mix is enacted. Included are decisions involving specific media, promotional timing, message content, sales force composition, sales promotion tools, and the responsibility for coordination. (5) The retailer systematically reviews and adjusts the promotional plan, consistent with pre-set goals.

Key Terms

retail promotion (p. 568)
advertising (p. 568)
cooperative advertising (p. 571)
vertical cooperative advertising
   agreement (p. 575)
horizontal cooperative advertising
   agreement (p. 575)
public relations (p. 575)
publicity (p. 576)

personal selling (p. 577)
order-taking salesperson (p. 578)
order-getting salesperson (p. 578)
PMs (p. 578)
canned sales presentation (p. 579)
need-satisfaction approach (p. 579)
sales promotion (p. 580)
word of mouth (WOM) (p. 586)
all-you-can-afford method (p. 587)

incremental method (p. 587)
competitive parity method (p. 587)
percentage-of-sales method (p. 587)
objective-and-task method (p. 587)
hierarchy of effects (p. 588)
reach (p. 591)
frequency (p. 591)
massed promotion effort (p. 591)
distributed promotion effort (p. 591)

Questions for Discussion

1. How would an advertising plan for a Web retailer differ from that for a bricks-and-mortar chain?

2. How do manufacturer and retailer cooperative advertising goals overlap? How do they differ?

3. How may a local furniture store try to generate positive publicity?

4. Are there any retailers that should *not* use personal selling? Explain your answer.

5. Are there any retailers that should *not* use sales promotion? Explain your answer.

6. How can advertising, public relations, personal selling, and sales promotion complement each other for a retailer?

7. What are the pros and cons of coupons?

8. Develop sales promotions for each of the following:
   a. A nearby strip shopping center.
   b. A new laundromat.
   c. A pizzeria offering free delivery for the first time.

9. Which method of promotional budgeting should a small retailer use? A large retailer? Why?

10. Explain the hierarchy of effects from a retail perspective. Apply your answer to a new luggage store.

11. Develop a checklist for an upscale furniture store chain to coordinate its promotional plan.

12. For each of these promotional goals, explain how to evaluate promotional effectiveness:
    a. Increase customer traffic.
    b. Project an innovative image.
    c. Maintain customer loyalty rates.

Web-Based Exercise

Visit the Web site of Office.com (**www.office.com**) and click on "Promote Your Business." What could a retailer learn by surfing this site?

Note: Stop by our Web site (**www.prenhall.com/ bermanevans**) to experience a number of highly interactive, appealing Web exercises based on actual company demonstrations and sample materials related to retailing.

Chapter Endnotes

1. Various company sources.
2. Betsy Spethmann, "Mass in Transit," *Promo* (April 2005), p. 27.
3. Ibid., p. 28.
4. Computed by the authors from data in "100 Leading National Advertisers," *Advertising Age* (June 27, 2005), p. S-18.
5. See Don Doggett, "Shared Ad Can Lower Total Cost," *Houston Chronicle* (September 5, 2004), p. 4.
6. See also John R. Graham, "The Ten Most Deadly, Detrimental, and Destructive Sales Mistakes," *American Salesman* (October 2002), pp. 16–21.
7. Betsy Spethmann, "Tuning In at the Shelf," *Promo* (April 2005), pp. AR29, AR32.
8. Ibid., p. AR29.
9. "Spending," *Promo* (April 2005), p. AR3.
10. "All About Coupons," **www.couponmonth.com/ pages/allabout.htm** (December 16, 2005).
11. Kim T. Gordon, "Sweet Rewards," *Entrepreneur Online* (July 2005).
12. "Spending," p. AR3.
13. "McDonald's Launches New Worldwide Balanced, Active Lifestyles Public Awareness Campaign," *PR Newswire* (March 8, 2005).
14. See Tom J. Brown, Thomas E. Barry, Peter A. Dacin, and Richard F. Gunst, "Spreading the Word: Investigating Antecedents of Consumers' Positive Word-of-Mouth Intentions and Behaviors in a Retailing Context," *Journal of the Academy of Marketing Science*, Vol. 33 (Spring 2005), pp. 123–138.
15. "How to Establish a Promotion Mix," **www.peerspectives.org** (March 11, 2006).
16. "How Netflix Maintains Growth," **www.fool.com/ news/commentary/2005/commentary05013103.htm** (January 31, 2005).
17. Evelyn Lim, "How Opt-in Email Marketing Helps You in Your Online Business," **www.e-bizmap.com/ articles/opt-in.htm** (March 11, 2006).
18. Pierre Volle, "The Short-Term Effect of Store-Level Promotions on Store Choice, and the Moderating Role of Individual Variables," *Journal of Business Research*, Vol. 53 (August 2001), p. 63.
19. Marianne Wilson, "Solution Makes It Simple," *Chain Store Age* (June 2005), p. 69.

part seven
Short Cases

CASE 1: THE EVOLVING IMAGE OF AMAZON.COM[c-1]

Amazon.com's (**www.amazon.com**) recent revenues and profit growth have been quite strong. Its 2004 net sales of $6.9 billion were 31 percent higher than its 2003 sales level, and its profits jumped 16.7 times over 2003. For 2005, Amazon also posted strong results. In contrast, the company was not profitable prior to 2003.

Despite Amazon's success, some faculty at the University of Pennsylvania's Wharton School of Business have criticized the firm for its unclear "department store" image. This image stems from Amazon's business model being comprised of separate strategies for books and music and all other areas. Wharton professor Peter Fader says, "When you ask people what Amazon is, they will say it's a book and music store. I don't think Amazon is viewed as a broad retailer." According to William Cody, managing director of Wharton's *Jay H. Baker Retailing Initiative*, Amazon's "one-stop shopping works well in a [traditional] department store" where a consumer purchasing multiple unrelated products does not have to travel to multiple stores and park at multiple locations. Cody adds, "But online, another department store is just a click away."

Wharton professor Jerry Wind states that, "With Amazon, there is always a danger that it is spread too thin. The company is definitely established in books and music, but whether it is viewed as a place for other products remains to be seen." Some Wharton faculty members feel that it would be appropriate for Amazon to drop certain product lines—such as sporting goods—and focus more on its books and music business. Wind, for example, notes that "Amazon needs to find out its target market. It is competing with almost everyone in every market."

Amazon takes title to and ships its books and music merchandise. Much of Amazon's image is related to its success in books and the features offered in its book-based Web site. In this section, consumers can search for books by author, subject, and title. Other important features are a consumer's ability to view a book's table of contents and index, as well as its editorial and consumer reviews. The site will suggest other similar titles and even E-mail potential customers when a new title by a desired author becomes available.

In other departments, such as apparel, shoes and accessories, cameras and photography, consumer electronics, gourmet foods, jewelry and watches, and tools and hardware, Amazon handles promotion and order fulfillment functions for independent retailers such as Target (**www.target.com**), J&R Music and Computer World (**www.jr.com**), and Tiger Direct (**www.tigerdirect.com**), as well as many much smaller firms. As in the books and music categories, consumers are given easy access to customer reviews and technical data, as well as a comprehensive product description. Amazon feels that this arrangement is mutually beneficial for itself, its business partners, and consumers. Amazon is able to secure fixed fees and sales commissions without taking title to these goods. Its business partners are able to increase sales through the use of Amazon's search engine and the features of its site. Consumers are also able to benefit by purchasing products from multiple sellers through one checkout process.

Questions

1. Discuss the pros and cons of Amazon's "department store image."
2. How can Amazon ensure that its general merchandise business partners will not detract from its positive book- and music-based image?
3. Develop a questionnaire to assess Amazon's image.
4. Explain how the concept of store image differs between a store-based retailer and a clicks-only retailer.

CASE 2: BUILDING RETAIL BRANDS: THE GASOLINE EXPERIENCE[c-2]

Many consumers are brand loyal to a specific brand of gasoline or prefer to limit their purchases to a small number of gasoline brands, while other consumers believe "gasoline is gasoline" and that the brand has no bearing on quality. Several convenience store chains—including Racetrac (**www.racetrac.com**), Quik Trip (**www.quiktrip.com**), Wawa (**www.wawa.com**), and Sheetz (**www.sheetz.com**)—now appeal to gasoline consumers on the basis of their strong company image and customer service by offering their own gasoline brand. After viewing their success, other convenience store chains have followed this trend.

The process of developing and maintaining a store brand of gasoline is a tricky one. According to a brand consulting firm, "Anyone can open up a convenience [store] operation and get reasonable traffic just based on the geography of the location, but if the brand doesn't stand for something, it can't be expected to survive and thrive. As long as you stand for something and are able to differentiate yourself from the competition and meet or exceed the expectations of your customers, you will own the customer. It will be a lot harder for your competition to lure them away."

Kwik Trip (**www.kwiktrip.com**)—a 360-store convenience store chain with units located in Wisconsin, Minnesota, and Iowa—effectively promotes its own of brand of gasoline. In addition to guaranteeing the quality of its gasoline, Kwik Trip offers many of the advantages of a major gasoline chain.

[c-1]The material in this case is drawn from "Amazon's Multiple Personalities," *Strategic Management* (January 14, 2005); and *Amazon.com 2005 Annual Report*.

[c-2]The material in this case is drawn from Alison Embrey, "Brand X Marks the Spot," *Convenience Store News* (February 7, 2005); and "Where We Are," **www.kwiktrip.com/whereweare.asp** (April 12, 2006).

It has its own credit card that acts as a loyalty card by offering consumers an instant rebate of 3 cents a gallon on all gasoline purchases, as well as a 3 percent rebate on all in-store purchases (such as coffee, sandwiches, etc). Consumers who wish to donate the value of their rebate to charity will be matched by an additional 1 percent from Kwik Trip. According to Steve Loehr, Kwik Trip's vice-president of operations, "We have our own software and back-office systems in place. The value of what a branded supplier could give us is, we feel, pretty minimal."

Kwik Trip believes that it can differentiate its gasoline, not by national brand or price but through its quality, customer service, convenience, and safe and clean environment. To build customer-employee relationships, the firm has an extremely low employee turnover rate of only 38 percent. The low turnover rate better enables Kwik Trip's employees to forge relationships with customers. In addition, the firm's own gasoline brand benefits from its other successful private labels that include Café Karuba coffee, Hot Spot grill items, Kwikery Bakery, and Nature's Touch dairy items. Loehr says, "Our goal is to be the same quality as a national brand product at, in most cases, a much lower retail price."

One problem for Kwik Trip is the need to develop awareness for its brands when the chain expands to new geographic regions. To reduce this problem, the firm implements a well-integrated marketing program in new regions. Still, the company feels that word of mouth is its most effective form of promotion.

Questions

1. Describe the importance of atmosphere in the sale of gasoline.
2. Identify the pros and cons of a convenience store's developing its own brand of gasoline versus selling a national brand.
3. Discuss the advantages and disadvantages of Kwik Trip's loyalty card program.
4. Develop a promotional campaign that can be used by Kwik Trip to generate awareness as it expands to new regions.

CASE 3: LIMITED BRANDS BETS ON BIGELOW[c-3]

Limited Brands (**www.limitedbrands.com**) recently purchased the right to use the C.O. Bigelow brand name. C.O. Bigelow (**www.bigelowchemists.com**) is a New York City–based pharmacy that was established in 1838. It is the oldest apothecary in America. The store has a rich tradition as a Greenwich Village neighborhood pharmacy with patrons who have included Thomas Edison, Eleanor Roosevelt, and

[c-3]The material in this case is drawn from Fran Lefort, "New Rx," *Shopping Centers Today* (February 2005), pp. 17–18; "Cosmetics Retailer C.O. Bigelow Opens Store in Columbus, Ohio," *The Columbus Dispatch* (October 21, 2004); and Michelle Gilstrap, "A Modern Apothecary," *Display & Design Ideas* (May 2005), p. 16.

Mark Twain. Based on legend, Thomas Edison went to Bigelow seeking a remedy for a finger he injured while developing the lightbulb. The store has retained its status as a "hot spot" over the years with such current celebrities as Liv Tyler, Isaac Mizrahi, and Sarah Jessica Parker as customers. Aside from its clientele, C.O. Bigelow is well known for its natural "holistic" approach to beauty, skin, and healthcare; its use of simple packaging; and its extremely knowledgeable sales staff.

According to Anthony Hebron, Limited's vice-president of communications, "The Bigelow name has a lot of equity in the whole feel-good arena. And we want to take that name and pair it up with modern-day products." The Limited decided to purchase the right to the Bigelow name after hiring Ira Ginsberg, Bigelow's president, to help develop new cosmetics products for its Bath & Body Works (**www.bathand bodyworks.com**), Henri Bendel (**www.henribendel.com**), and Victoria's Secret (**www.victoriassecret.com**) chains. Although Limited has the exclusive right to use the Bigelow name for new stores, Ginsberg will retain ownership of the original New York store.

Limited opened its first Bigelow store in a former Bath & Body Works store in Easton Town Center in Columbus, Ohio. Eighty percent of the items at a typical Bath & Body Works store are made up of Bath & Body Works brands, and the remaining 20 percent are third-party products. However, the Bigelow store mostly sells upscale brands, such as Acqua Di Parma, L'Artisan Parfumeur, and Frédéric Fekkai.

Products range in price from a $12 jar of Lucky Girl Lip Shine to a $500 terra-cotta "Solid Perfume Amber Ball," with $125 refills. The store also offers facials, manicures, pedicures, and massages in its four private spa rooms. Hebron says, "What the store gives Columbus is a taste of New York and Los Angeles upscale brands that you would only find at exclusive locations."

The store's target audience will likely be older females who are more sophisticated and more willing to pay higher prices than the typical Bath & Body Works customer. Even though Limited Brands has not yet developed any expansion plans for Bigelow, the chief operating officer of Easton Town Center's developer puts the store concept on top of its wish list for seven other centers it is developing. These centers are located in Florida, Kentucky, Missouri, New Jersey, Ohio, and Wisconsin.

A retail strategist at a leading consulting firm believes the Bigelow purchase "is part of a pattern of bold, original thinking on Limited's part in developing new business and brands." Other similar examples are Victoria's Secret, Express, and Aura Science (a prestige beauty store).

Questions

1. Describe how the Columbus-based Bigelow store should allocate its 8,000 square feet among selling space, merchandise space, personnel space, and customer space.
2. Explain how the model stock approach and the sales-productivity ratio could be used in determining space needs for Bigelow's Columbus location.

3. What types of displays (assortment, theme, or ensemble) are most appropriate for Bigelow? Explain your answer.
4. How can Bigelow use experiential merchandising?

CASE 4: STOP & SHOP AND THE IBM PERSONAL SHOPPING ASSISTANT[c-4]

Stop & Shop (**www.stopandshop.com**) is an eastern U.S. chain with close to 350 supermarkets. Its stores have grocery items along with pharmacies, delis, and entertainment centers. Stop & Shop is a subsidiary of Ahold USA (**www.aholdusa. com**). It has a loyalty card program that provides members with targeted coupons based on behavior. These coupons are offered at the checkout, as well as through direct mail.

Until recently, according to Susan Shahroodi, Stop & Shop's director of development for information systems, "Our marketing efforts were targeting customers after the sale. Instead, we wanted to appeal to shoppers while they were in the aisle and actively making purchase decisions." By communicating with patrons while they shopped, Stop & Shop would be able to increase sales. At the same time, consumers would benefit from additional savings without having to save and clip coupons.

IBM's Personal Shopping Assistant solution, named "Shopping Buddy," is a device that is mounted on a shopping cart that helps guide customers through the store. Shopping Buddy enables customers to receive specialized promotions. These promotions are offered on an aisle-by-aisle basis. This approach enables customers to more easily locate any featured items. Shopping Buddy computes a customer's total bill at any point in time so that he or she can budget total expenditures and use self-scanning to avoid the checkout line. Shopping Buddy even has a direct linkage with the store's deli so that orders can be placed at the cart and picked up when ready.

There are multiple parts to IBM's Personal Shopping Assistant. The hardware consists of a touchscreen computer and a barcode scanner attached to each cart. The store's infrastructure consists of ceiling-mounted beacons that track a shopper's location in the store within each aisle. The system's user interface software gives shoppers the ability to place an order, locate products, and see relevant offers. This software was developed by Cuesol (**www.cuesol.com**), an IBM Business Partner. All of these systems are effectively integrated so that consumers receive Web-style displays as they walk through the store.

Stop & Shop has used IBM's Personal Shopping Assistant solution in three stores as a test and planned to roll out this solution to 20 more locations by mid-2005. The chain has already seen tangible results from shoppers that use Shopping Buddy. These include reduced waiting times, better ability to find merchandise, and enhanced use of special offers. Shahroodi reports that, "Customers will drive beyond their local Stop & Shop to get to one of these Shopping Buddy locations. They love how the technology gives them control over their shopping experience."

This system also saves Stop & Shop significant money that used to be spent for printing and distributing coupons. Stop & Shop's director of marketing says, "Instead of printing and mailing 15 variations of a marketing piece tailored to different audiences, we'll be able to develop and distribute messages electronically—for substantial savings."

Questions

1. Develop specific promotional goals for Shopping Buddy.
2. Describe how vertical cooperative advertising can be implemented with Shopping Buddy.
3. Discuss the advantages and disadvantages of the use of Shopping Buddy as compared with traditional coupons.
4. Develop a promotional campaign that would integrate the use of Shopping Buddy with other promotional media.

[c-4]The material in this case is drawn from "Stop & Shop Grocery Drives Sales and Boosts Customer Loyalty with IBM Personal Shopping Assistant," *On Demand Business* (2004); and "About Stop & Shop," **www.stopandshop.com** (April 30, 2006).

part seven
Comprehensive Case
The Role of Marketing in Retailing*

Introduction

For retail-brand chief financial officers, marketing has traditionally been one of the softest factors in the budget universe. Clearly, stores need a continual infusion of new customers to replace the 20 to 30 percent who fall out of the customer base each year. Just as clearly, the marketplace responds to news, specials, and offers that generate traffic and aim at closing a next-day sale. However, the ability to directly establish a hard return on investment (ROI) for most marketing expenditures is at best elusive and at worst totally confounding. Discovering the optimal spending and offer level in the context of bottom-line impact can feel like a search for the Holy Grail. Can a hard ROI for marketing ever be vouchsafed? Can the financial aspect of customer activation ever be truly managed? In short, they should be.

The Value of Transactional Analysis

The flood of data generated by the expansion of scanner technology and customer data bases has already fueled the emergence of transactional analysis as an essential approach in driving the growth of customer relationship management (CRM), E-commerce, and direct marketing as reliable, manageable program areas directly related to the bottom-line performance of the retail enterprise.

With the evolution of technology, media, and customer data, the opportunities that transactional analysis affords to retailers will increase. It could create a world where individual responses can be tracked and marketing dollars accounted for, down to the penny. And improvements to retail offers are even now being implemented faster than ever.

Ultimately, the power of transactional analysis will change the landscape of retail marketing, extending from the mass media programs down to the individual store trading area. The majority of customer activation expenditures in today's world, however, still seemingly lie beyond the financial pale. The scope of the issue can be gauged by the spending for local direct marketing and Internet media in the United States because it is a reasonable surrogate for advertising that attempts to attract the customer or make the sale today. Such spending totals 60 percent of all advertising expenditures.

Direct mail and Internet expenditures account for more than $50 billion of this total, and, for the most part, in their historically prime function of selling products directly, their sales and profitability performance can be reliably quantified and managed. For the remaining funds, linkages between expenditures and the resulting sales and profitability are minimal or nonexistent. While the impact of general customer activation expenditures can be estimated under controlled test conditions, albeit imperfectly, such efforts are made routinely. The statement that "I know half of my advertising is wasted, I just don't know which half" is, for many retailers, as true today as it was half a century ago. Retailers make few expenditures of similar magnitude with such limited ability to quantify ROI.

Transactional marketing and Internet expenditures, as noted above, are the exceptions. Early on, transactional marketing held out the promise of precise ROI measurement, and its realization of that promise has made it the most financially friendly element of the customer activation mix. From its inception as direct mail, it has had four advantages that mass media have lacked:

1. *Ability to track individual responses to a specific offer*: Response can be captured and tabulated. A direct relationship is established between the message/offer and the resulting sale on a respondent-by-respondent basis. This ability subsequently extended into telemarketing and E-marketing.

2. *Ability to evaluate the financial returns for a specific response*: The linkage between a sale and a specific individual allows not only the calculation of the actual dollar volume and profitability of that specific transaction but also the value of the additional transactions for that customer over time. The total of all sales and profits can be compared against the cost of the tactic generating the response to provide a tangible ROI for the tactic.

3. *Ability to control individual exposure to the specific offer*: Transactional marketing allows the retailer to address an individual customer with a specific message and/or offer different from those delivered to other customers. This targeting capability enables identification of the specific message/offer combination leading to a result and facilitates comparison of its performance with that of other messages/offers. Control-and-variable testing allows comparison of relative and incremental ROIs. These disciplines have been incorporated into the basic approach of direct mail and have been extended into direct response television and E-commerce.

4. *Ability to implement process improvements systematically*: Results from each effort can be incorporated rapidly and inexpensively in future tactics as a result of the relatively low production costs and control over the scheduling of direct mail exposures. While previously tested programs and offers were being run on a large scale, other test offers and programs were being conducted simultaneously to guide future strategy and tactics. The result of this process was a transactional marketing machine that exhibited manageability and predictability far beyond that available for other types of customer activation programs.

The manageability and reliability of transactional marketing have enabled the development of many successful retail enterprises based solely or primarily on direct marketing relationships with customers. The future for the use of similar disciplines by bricks-and-mortar retailers in an increasingly data-driven age looks bright as well. Perceptive analysis of robust transaction data generated through emerging information technologies has substantially increased their ability to manage their current customer relationships profitably and has led to their increasing use of CRM and loyalty programs. It has also resulted in productivity and profitability improvements for store design and merchandising.

The reliability of ROI calculations for direct marketing and Internet programs notwithstanding, ROI remains a mystery for most of the remaining $90 million of customer activation media. But retailers are making progress as information technology and the data explosion increasingly blur the line between transactional marketing and other mass media.

One early pathfinding effort began in 1992. Emergent technology at the inception of the transaction information revolution sparked the possibility of an accountability breakthrough by extending the same types of ROI management enjoyed by direct marketing to other customer activation tactics and programs. Barcoding was spawning a flood of data with the potential to yield new insights into retail transactions at the most basic level. The fundamental idea behind building accountability and ROI into general media customer activation, dubbed Tracer, was to apply barcoding technology to a coupon, thereby enabling the ability to track the individual response resulting from exposure to specific media, scheduling, and offers within a mass media mix. Sales and profitability of the trial device could be derived by matching this information and its cost to the size and profitability of the resulting sales transaction.

A leading quick-service restaurant (QSR) retailer was the subject of the first commercial test of this approach for the simple reason that coupons represented a substantial portion of total marketing expenditures across the QSR retailer category. In the early stages of Tracer deployment, barcoded redeemed coupons were stapled to order tickets representing the total transaction at the restaurant and then sent to a central location where the transaction information was coded manually. The results were eye-opening. Many commonly accepted coupon tactics did not generate enough profits to cover their costs. Others excessively cannibalized full-price sales for the same or similar items. The range of ROI, from the weakest to the strongest positive performers, was in excess of 500 percent.

Clearly, there was room for improvement and massive savings. For the first time, decisions could be based on ROI analysis generated from actual customer transactions on an ongoing basis. For coupon-driven brands, it was a giant step toward identifying "the 50 percent that is wasted," and this QSR retailer embarked on a journey of process and program improvement that continues to this day. The impact was startling and continuous. Several years after the initial implementation, coupon costs per restaurant decreased 32 percent, and coupon-generated traffic per restaurant increased 22 percent between 1998 and 1999. By eliminating lower-profit offers and focusing on more effective offers, redemption increased 12 percent and profitability for coupon-driven sales

increased 32 percent. These year-over-year profit gains were driven by decisions enabled by hard ROI tracking using the core Tracer methodology.

The immediate impact of the Tracer approach was to enable development of an ROI for any coupon-based tactic or offer. The greater potential of the Tracer approach was to deliver a hard ROI calculation on every customer activation expenditure. By approaching mass-marketing tactics as if they were transactional marketing tactics, some of the same accountability and response-based processes for improvement might be brought to customer activation management across the spectrum of activities. This potential is now surprisingly close to becoming a reality.

Over the last decade, the Tracer approach has continued to evolve with new developments in technology, media, and customer information. Today, the Tracer technology and methodology are among the technologies housed at Euro Retail and are being used on a recurring basis to closely replicate the ROI success formula of direct mail and to fuel development and execution of integrated customer activation programs for retail chains. It holds the promise of extending the power of the transactional marketing success formula to the mass media programs down to the individual store trading area.

Tracking Individual Responses

For direct mail and print advertising, the application of barcoding to specific offer components creates direct and comprehensive linkages or responses to specific tactics. The evolution of scanning technology at the point of sale is improving the efficiency and timeliness of data collection, eliminating the necessity for the physical transfer of paper records in many cases.

A further enhancement is the ability to fully integrate these processes with retailer loyalty program data bases. This has created the ability to track responsiveness of the individual customer and place the resulting transaction in the context of the total past and future transactions with the store— lifetime customer value.

One major finding of the transaction analysis undertaken by an increasing number of retailers is that 20 percent or fewer customers generate 50 percent or more of sales and an even higher percentage of profits. Tools such as CustomerTracer integrate with the customer data base to benchmark and identify changes in core customer frequency, recency, transaction size, and profitability due to customer activation tactics.

Evaluating Financial Returns

As Tracer-based systems have developed, multiple aspects of performance have been illuminated to create a financially oriented report card for program performance. See Table 1.

The integration of Tracer-based systems with retail point-of-sale systems can now be customized for integration with each retailer's transaction or customer data base to provide the financial report card for any type of tactic. Used in the context of traditional test/control research designs, it can readily provide accurate and tangible financial measurement

TABLE - 1	Tracer-Based System Financial Performance	
Tactical Elements	**Store Impact Elements**	**Financial Elements**
Trading Area Penetration	Transaction Mix	Cost of Tactic
Discount %/Price Point	Average Volume/Store	Cost of Goods
Distribution Date	Transactions/Store	Cannibalized Sales
Page/Vehicle Position		Break-Even Point
		Actual ROI

of any element or program of the customer activation mix, including broadcast and operational areas such as store design or in-store signage.

One interesting application of this type of analysis has been to identify the role and contribution of various elements in multi-product ads versus the value of the space devoted to them in newspaper ads and catalogs. This enables ongoing micro-tuning of content.

Controlling Exposure to Offers

Media claims the major part of the customer activation investments. Traditionally, mass media offer high efficiency in cost per impression, but they have lacked the targetability to focus on a store's best customers and prospects. Technology-based tracking methods apply new, rich, micro-geographic data on lifestyles, media habits, purchase behavior, and leisure activity to capture a level of targetability for mass media closely related to its direct media cousins.

On the horizon are methods to deliver very targeted broadcast content. A platform allowing variation in cable television content household by household is now being tested in 26 markets. If successful, this enhanced ability to track individual customer response to specific offers and content could yield both tangible ROI for television broadcast and significant increases in consumer activation productivity.

Implementing Process Improvements

New technologies for content production and distribution have removed cost and process barriers that prevented mass media from competing against direct media on a level playing field. Feedback on customer response and ROI performance for previous tactics and programs can be incorporated into upcoming programs much faster than ever before possible. Over the past five years, cycle time for content preparation has been reduced by more than 1,000 percent, cutting times from weeks and months to days.

Tracer and associated technologies and systems can be looked upon as being at the core of a learning cycle for application of customer activation intelligence that produces continual process and ROI improvement and a segmented view of the customer base that drives customer acquisition management.

Thinking Like a Retailer, Acting Like a Transactional Marketer

Retail enterprises tailor their marketing communications to a variety of objectives. Those targeting a behavioral response from the customer can gain by designing programs to capture as much of the transactional marketing success formula as possible: tracking individual response, evaluating total financial returns, controlling and focusing on individual exposure, and systematically implementing process and program improvements with fast cycle times. The resulting impact on improvements in customer activation management and productivity can be extraordinary.

Lessons for Customer Activation Management Improvement

To date, Tracer has assigned an ROI to more than 5 billion retail transactions and their associated tactics and programs, generating them across more than 50,000 retail outlets, as well as to millions of additional loyalty program data base records under its management. From this experience, some general basic guidelines have emerged:

- *Listen to what your customer does:* Years of analyzing transaction data make it clear that the classical view of customers voting with their feet and their pocketbooks is indeed still relevant. In many situations, what customers said about their behavior varied dramatically from their actions, and action is the ultimate predictor of the behavior of similar customers. Seeing activity patterns at the point of sale is critical to developing a closer and expanding relationship with current and potential customers.
- *The offer or event is king:* From its earliest days, direct marketing has emphasized the primacy of the specific offer over all other elements in tactics seeking to activate the customer. The ROI results from thousands of mass media tactics bear this out for customer activation across media, categories, and customer types. Typically, the difference between changing the creative context for an offer is much less than the change in offers in the same context. A great offer can perform in almost any creative context, while a great creative context cannot overcome a poor offer.

- *Focus on total cost*: To generate a total transactional ROI, go beyond the direct costs of the tactic, the dollar value of the offer, and the revenue directly attributed to the tactic. The direct and indirect costs and revenues of all goods or services included in the transaction should also be reflected. This broader context yields an ROI that can radically change customer activation decision making and yield much greater productivity to the store as an enterprise.

- *The ROI for every customer activation program can be improved*: Without exception, every program initially analyzed using transaction tracking had room for double-digit increases in customer activation productivity. From that base, the tracking of ROI yields continuous guidance as to what is working better and what is working worse as the customer changes based on previous and competitive tactical experiences. Tactics and offers have life cycles that show up in ROI trends and allow optimization of each tactic within the activation mix.

As POS technology continues to improve and retailers increasingly adopt it, the ability of transactional analysis to channel the resulting flood of information into productive tributaries connecting the customer with the sale and its actual profitability will become ever more crucial for improving customer activation productivity. And in the process, this important area of retail operations will become truly responsible for demonstrated and accountable performance.

Questions

1. How would you measure a retailer's image? State both criteria and techniques in your answer.
2. How would you determine the impact of store atmospherics? State both criteria and techniques in your answer.
3. Why is transactional analysis such an important tool for retailers?
4. What effect should transactional analysis have on the retailer's choice of promotion mix?
5. What are the risks of an overreliance on transactional analysis in choosing a promotion mix?
6. Visit this site (**www.nationalbarcode.com/Asset-Tracking/Tracer_Details.htm**). Describe the software products you find there.
7. Would you recommend the software you reviewed for Question 6 to retailers? Explain your answer.

*The material in this case is adapted by the authors from Robert Largen, Chief Executive, Longlow Consulting, and Patrick Furey, President, Euro RSCG Retail, "The Power of Transactional Marketing in Retailing," *Retailing Issues Letter* (Number 2, 2004), pp. 1–6. Reprinted by permission.

part eight

Putting It All Together

In Part Eight, we "put it all together."

- **Chapter 20** connects the elements of a retail strategy that have been described all through this book. We examine planning and opportunity analysis, productivity, performance measures, and scenario analysis. The value of data comparisons (benchmarking and gap analysis) is indicated. Strategic control via the retail audit is covered.

Bernard Marcus and Arthur Blank, the co-founders of Home Depot (**www.homedepot.com**), met while they worked for Handy Dan, a regional hardware store chain based in Los Angeles. After a personality clash with their boss, Marcus and Blank were both fired. The two executives were convinced that a store offering home improvement products (some of which were previously available only to contractors)

Reprinted by permission.

could provide excellent customer service and change the way these products were sold. In 1979, the partners opened their first Home Depot store in Atlanta. Today, Home Depot dominates the do-it-yourself home improvement market with annual sales exceeding $75 billion, more than 1,800 stores (including Expo Design Centers), and 300,000-plus associates.

Home Depot is not complacent with its success as the firm plans for the future. It is rolling out a larger appliance showroom format in many of its locations in an attempt to move up from its number three position (with an 8 percent market share) in the appliance business (after Sears with a 37 percent share and Lowe's with a 15 percent share). It has recently added LG Electronics as its third white-goods supplier in addition to GE and Maytag.

Home Depot is also working on a neighborhood store prototype intended for high-density market areas where full-size units are impractical. One of its Manhattan stores, for example, customizes services to meet the needs of interior designers. The paint department there has 11 mixers capable of producing 3,260 different colors.[1]

chapter objectives

1. To demonstrate the importance of integrating a retail strategy
2. To examine four key factors in the development and enactment of an integrated retail strategy: planning procedures and opportunity analysis, defining productivity, performance measures, and scenario analysis
3. To show how industry and company data can be used in strategy planning and analysis (benchmarking and gap analysis)
4. To show the value of a retail audit

OVERVIEW

This chapter focuses on integrating and controlling a retail strategy. We tie together the material detailed previously, show why retailers need coordinated strategies, and describe how to assess performance.

By integrating and regularly monitoring their strategies, firms of any size or format can take a proper view of the retailing concept and create a superior total retail experience. Consider how Dollar Tree competes with Wal-Mart—which is 100 times larger:

> Dollar Tree has devised an ingenious way to attack Wal-Mart's greatest strength: low prices. Dollar Tree is the nation's largest single-price retailer, meaning it doesn't carry anything priced at more than $1. From picture frames and pet supplies to frozen food and fine china, Dollar Tree sells every item on its shelves for a buck. The firm has grown from a single 3,000-square-foot store into a multi-billion dollar nationwide retailer. Because of its rapid growth and because of a desire to counter Wal-Mart's buying clout, consumer-products giants have begun to develop products for Dollar Tree. For instance, P&G designers came up with 18-ounce bottles of Dawn dish soap to sell at $1. A lot of what's on Dollar Tree's shelves, however, comes from the hundreds of its buyers who scour their territories. When a rival canceled an order for Pringles potato chips, Dollar Tree bought 2 tons of the product at pennies on the dollar and sold it all in a few weeks. The other big advantage over Wal-Mart is convenience. Dollar Tree's biggest stores are 17,000 square feet; Wal-Mart's cavernous supercenters can be 20 times as big. At Dollar Tree, the average store visit is 15 minutes.[2]

As today's retailers look to the future, they must deal with new strategic choices due to the globalization of world markets, evolving consumer lifestyles, competition among formats, and rapid technology changes. They would also be wise to study the strategies of both successful firms and those encountering significant challenges. Here are the observations of a retailing executive who worked for both Target and Kmart:

> While at Target, I saw a model of retailing efficiency. New programs were carefully planned and tested. Caution was the operating principle for all moves. Underperforming elements of the business, whether stores or strategies, were eradicated. Leadership was valued for its consistency and tenure. Idea sharing was encouraged on all levels. Speed in replenishment, service, and execution were ingrained in the company mind-set. At Kmart, top leadership was always impressive and I was surrounded by a sense of pride and tradition. But operations left much to be desired. The firm had many long-term, experienced, and dedicated employees. Turnover, however, was a huge issue, especially in mid-level to vice-president ranks. Training suffered because of the rapid turnover. The transition to Fleming food distribution was extremely rocky, even if the decision to use Fleming over Supervalu was a coup. Technology was archaic.[3]

INTEGRATING THE RETAIL STRATEGY

A major goal of *Retail Management* has been to describe the relationships among the elements of a retail strategy and show the need to act in an integrated way. Figures 20-1 and 20-2 highlight the integrated strategy of Chico's, the apparel chain. Chico's has been cited by Retail Forward and *Chain Store Age* as a leading

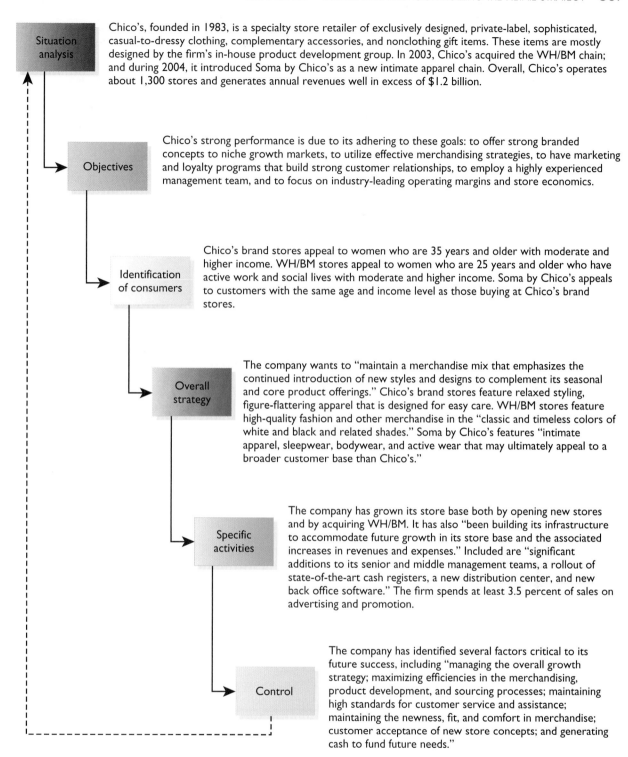

Situation analysis

Chico's, founded in 1983, is a specialty store retailer of exclusively designed, private-label, sophisticated, casual-to-dressy clothing, complementary accessories, and nonclothing gift items. These items are mostly designed by the firm's in-house product development group. In 2003, Chico's acquired the WH/BM chain; and during 2004, it introduced Soma by Chico's as a new intimate apparel chain. Overall, Chico's operates about 1,300 stores and generates annual revenues well in excess of $1.2 billion.

Objectives

Chico's strong performance is due to its adhering to these goals: to offer strong branded concepts to niche growth markets, to utilize effective merchandising strategies, to have marketing and loyalty programs that build strong customer relationships, to employ a highly experienced management team, and to focus on industry-leading operating margins and store economics.

Identification of consumers

Chico's brand stores appeal to women who are 35 years and older with moderate and higher income. WH/BM stores appeal to women who are 25 years and older who have active work and social lives with moderate and higher income. Soma by Chico's appeals to customers with the same age and income level as those buying at Chico's brand stores.

Overall strategy

The company wants to "maintain a merchandise mix that emphasizes the continued introduction of new styles and designs to complement its seasonal and core product offerings." Chico's brand stores feature relaxed styling, figure-flattering apparel that is designed for easy care. WH/BM stores feature high-quality fashion and other merchandise in the "classic and timeless colors of white and black and related shades." Soma by Chico's features "intimate apparel, sleepwear, bodywear, and active wear that may ultimately appeal to a broader customer base than Chico's."

Specific activities

The company has grown its store base both by opening new stores and by acquiring WH/BM. It has also "been building its infrastructure to accommodate future growth in its store base and the associated increases in revenues and expenses." Included are "significant additions to its senior and middle management teams, a rollout of state-of-the-art cash registers, a new distribution center, and new back office software." The firm spends at least 3.5 percent of sales on advertising and promotion.

Control

The company has identified several factors critical to its future success, including "managing the overall growth strategy; maximizing efficiencies in the merchandising, product development, and sourcing processes; maintaining high standards for customer service and assistance; maintaining the newness, fit, and comfort in merchandise; customer acceptance of new store concepts; and generating cash to fund future needs."

FIGURE 20-1
The Integrated Strategy of Chico's

Sources: Figure developed by the authors based on data from Chico's *Annual Reports* and Web site, **www.chicos.com** (January 30, 2006).

FIGURE 20-2
Chico's Visual Appearance:
Part of Its Integrated Strategy

Photo reprinted by permission of
Susan Berry, Retail Image
Consulting, Inc.

U.S. "high-performance retailer."[4] At our Web site (**www.prenhall.com/berman evans**), there are links to several integrated retail strategies using Bplans.com software templates.

Four fundamental factors especially need to be taken into account in devising and enacting an integrated retail strategy: planning procedures and opportunity analysis, defining productivity, performance measures, and scenario analysis. These factors are discussed next.

Planning Procedures and Opportunity Analysis

Planning procedures are enhanced by undertaking three coordinated activities. The process is then more systematic and reflects input from multiple parties:

1. Senior executives outline the firm's overall direction and goals. This provides written guidelines for middle- and lower-level managers, who get input from various internal and external sources. These managers are encouraged to generate ideas at an early stage.
2. Top-down plans and bottom-up or horizontal plans are combined.
3. Specific plans are enacted, including checkpoints and dates.

Opportunities need to be studied with regard to their impact on overall strategy and not in an isolated manner. See Figure 20-3. As noted by Retail Forward, "Retailers that apply innovative thinking to a growth market opportunity created by demographic, societal, economic, and technological trends can generate significant growth and financial performance. The needs of an aging population, ethnic consumers, and the pursuit of a healthy lifestyle provide fertile ground for innovative solutions."[5]

A useful retailer tool for evaluating opportunities is the **sales opportunity grid**, which rates the promise of new and established goods, services, procedures, and/or store outlets across a variety of criteria. It enables opportunities to be evaluated on the basis of the integrated strategies the firms would follow if the opportunities are pursued. Computerization makes it possible to apply such a grid.

Careers in RETAILING — Take Another Look!

Think there are few career opportunities in the retail industry? Take another look:

- *Marketing, Sales Promotion, and Advertising:* Develop creative and competitive ways to effectively present retail products to potential customers. Average salary $105,000.
- *Human Resources:* Use careful judgment to recruit, train, and develop employees, as well as manage payroll, benefits, and pensions. Average salary $95,000.
- *Store Manager:* Ensure that goals are met for financial success, merchandising and promotions, employees, customer relations, legal relations, and community involvement. Average salary $60,000.
- *Finance and Internal Auditing:* Oversee financial needs of a company, including accounting, budgeting, investments, and long- and short-term financial planning. Average salary $185,000.
- *Department Manager:* Supervise merchandise orders and displays, control inventories, schedule personnel, manage staff, and achieve financial goals. Average salary $45,000.

- *Vice-President/Director of Store Operations:* Supervise all stores, directing financial goals, strategic planning, marketing strategies, personnel development, and operations. Average salary $240,000.
- *Loss Prevention:* Save millions of dollars yearly for retailers using surveillance technology to ensure merchandise and facilities are not stolen or destroyed by misuse or abuse. Average salary $90,000.
- *E-Commerce, Information Technology, and Telecommunications:* Develop and maintain computer systems to increase efficiency, automate functions, and sell over the Web. Average salary $115,000.
- *Distribution, Logistics, and Supply Chain Management:* Use technology to manage the process of moving goods and information from raw material to supplier to customer. Average salary $110,000.
- *Merchandising and Buying:* Use expert understanding of consumer and market trends to predict what customers will want to buy. Average salary $105,000.

Source: Reprinted by permission of the National Retail Federation.

Table 20-1 shows a sales opportunity grid for a supermarket that wants to decide which of two salad dressing brands to carry. The store manager has outlined the integrated strategy for each brand; A is established; B is new. Due to its newness, the manager believes initial Brand B sales would be lower, but first-year sales would be similar. The brands would be priced the same and occupy identical space. Brand B requires higher display costs but offers a larger markup. Brand B would return a greater gross profit and net profit than Brand A by the end of the

FIGURE 20-3
Opportunity Analysis with the Small Business Administration

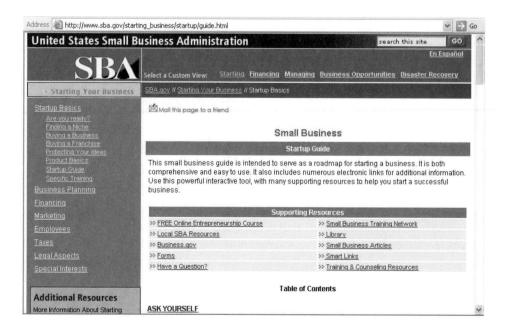

TABLE 20-1	Supermarket's Sales Opportunity Grid for Two Brands of Salad Dressing	
Criteria	Brand A (established)	Brand B (new)
Retail price	$1.29/8-ounce bottle	$1.29/8-ounce bottle
Floor space needed	8 square feet	8 square feet
Display costs	$10.00/month	$20.00/month for 6 mos. $10.00/month thereafter
Operating costs	$0.12/unit	$0.12/unit
Markup	19%	22%
Sales estimate		
During first month		
Units	250	50
Dollars	$323	$65
During first six months		
Units	1,400	500
Dollars	$1,806	$645
During first year		
Units	2,500	2,750
Dollars	$3,225	$3,548
Gross profit estimate		
During first month	$61	$14
During first six months	$343	$142
During first year	$613	$781
Net profit estimate		
During first month	$21	−$12
During first six months	$115	−$38
During first year	$193	$271

Example 1:
Gross profit estimate = Sales estimate − [(1.00 − Markup percentage) × (Sales estimate)]

Brand A gross profit estimate during first six months = $1,806 − [(1.00 − 0.19) × ($1,806)]
= $343

Example 2:
Net profit estimate = Gross profit estimate − (Display costs + Operating costs)

Brand A net profit estimate during first six months = $343 − ($60 + $168) = $115

first year. Based on the overall grid, the manager picks Brand B. Yet, if the store is more concerned about immediate profit, Brand A might be chosen.

Defining Productivity in a Manner Consistent with the Strategy

Intellilink (**www.intellilinksi. com/company/default.cfm**) can improve a retailer's productivity. See how.

As we noted in Chapters 12 and 13, productivity refers to the efficiency with which a retail strategy is carried out; it is in any retailer's interest to reach sales and profit goals while keeping control over costs. On the one hand, a retailer looks to avoid unnecessary costs. It does not want eight salespeople working at one time if four can satisfactorily handle all customers. And it does not want to pay high rent for a site in a regional shopping center if customers would willingly travel a few miles farther to a less costly site. On the other hand, a firm is not looking to lose customers because there are insufficient sales personnel to handle the rush of shoppers during peak hours. It also does not want a low rent site if this means a significant drop in customer traffic.

Potential trade-offs often mean neither the least expensive strategy nor the most expensive one is the most productive strategy; the former approach might not adequately service customers and the latter might be wasteful. An upscale retailer could not succeed with self-service, and it would be unnecessary for a discounter to have a large sales staff. The most productive approach applies a specific integrated retail strategy (such as a full-service jewelry store) as efficiently as possible.

Food Lion is a leading retailer due to its well-integrated, productive strategy:

> Food Lion's success is based on the principle of offering customers quality products at great prices and neighborly service in clean, conveniently located stores. These stores sell more than 28,000 different products and offer nationally and regionally advertised brand name merchandise, as well as a growing number of high-quality private label products manufactured and packaged for Food Lion. The company maintains its great prices and quality assurance through technological advances and operating efficiencies such as standard store formats, innovative warehouse design and management, energy-efficient facilities, and data synchronization and integration with suppliers. Food Lion's commitment to quality is evident in its 73,000 associates. The company actively supports them through ongoing training programs and continuing advancement opportunities.[6]

Performance Measures

By outlining relevant **performance measures**—the criteria used to assess effectiveness—and setting standards (goals) for each of them, a retailer can better develop and integrate its strategy. Among the measures frequently used by retailers are total sales, average sales per store, sales by goods/service category, sales per square foot, gross margins, gross margin return on investment, operating income, inventory turnover, markdown percentages, employee turnover, financial ratios, and profitability.

A retailer can gain insights from a visit to the Benchmarking Report Center (www. reportcenter.com).

To properly gauge a strategy's effectiveness, a firm should use **benchmarking**, whereby the retailer sets standards and measures its performance based on the achievements of its sector of retailing, specific competitors, high-performance firms, and/or the prior actions of the firm itself: "What company sets the standards in your industry, and what can you learn from them? Many executives sit around the table, beginning the budgeting process for the fiscal year and comparing performance from year to year. That is a good start but not enough. It is necessary to look at internal, as well as external, standards. The goal of benchmarking is to use peer operating results to improve the performance of all business processes."[7]

A good free source is the *Annual Benchmark Report for Retail Trade*, available from the U.S. Census Bureau (**www.census.gov/svsd/www/artstbl.html**). It shows more than 10 years of data involving a monthly comparison of sales, purchases, gross margins, inventories, and inventory-to-sales ratios by retail category.

Learn about best practices, both retail and nonretail, from APQC (www.apqc. org/best).

Retailers of varying sizes—and in different goods or service lines—can also obtain comparative data from such sources as the Small Business Administration, Internal Revenue Service, *Progressive Grocer, Stores, Chain Store Age, DSN Retailing Today*, Dun & Bradstreet, the National Retail Federation, RMA, and annual reports. Those retailers can then compare their performance with others.

Table 20-2 contains revenue, expense, and income benchmarking data for small retailers in 20 different business categories. The cost of goods sold as a percentage of revenues is highest for gas stations and grocery stores, gross profit is

TABLE 20-2	Benchmarking Through Annual Operating Statements of Typical Small Retailers (Expressed in Terms of Revenues = 100%)				
Type of Retailer	Total Revenues	Cost of Goods Sold	Gross Profit	Total Operating Expenses	Net Income
Apparel and accessory stores	100	66.7	33.3	29.2	4.1
Auto parking	100	32.9	67.1	59.1	8.0
Auto repair shops	100	53.9	46.1	33.7	12.4
Barbershops	100	4.1	95.9	41.3	54.6
Bars/drinking places	100	54.3	45.7	41.2	4.5
Beauty salons	100	20.0	80.0	54.0	26.0
Bicycle stores	100	69.8	30.2	24.5	5.7
Coin laundries	100	11.3	88.7	85.1	3.6
Dentists	100	8.5	91.5	49.6	41.9
Drugstores	100	69.0	31.0	22.5	8.5
Eating places	100	53.0	47.0	41.4	5.6
Gas stations	100	84.0	16.0	12.2	3.8
Gift stores	100	63.2	36.8	34.0	2.8
Grocery stores	100	83.1	16.9	14.4	2.5
Hardware stores	100	74.8	25.2	20.9	4.3
Motels	100	12.8	87.2	84.4	2.8
Photography studios	100	29.0	71.0	54.8	16.2
Real-estate brokers	100	9.1	90.9	52.2	38.7
Repair services	100	40.1	59.9	41.5	18.4
Used car dealers	100	83.5	16.5	14.3	2.2

Source: U.S. Internal Revenue Service, as reported at **www.score114.org/Docs/OpStmts/mTypOps.htm** (October 23, 2005).

greatest for barbershops and dentists, operating expenses are the most for coin laundries and motels, and net income is highest for barbershops and dentists.

One popular, independent, ongoing benchmarking survey is the American Customer Satisfaction Index (ACSI). It addresses two questions: (1) Are customer satisfaction and evaluations of quality improving or declining in the United States? (2) Are they improving or declining for particular sectors of industry and for specific companies? It is based on a scale of 0 to 100, with 100 the highest possible score. A national sample of 65,000 people takes part in phone interviews, with at least 250 interviews of current customers for each of the 200 firms studied (**www.theacsi.org**). Table 20-3 shows that the highest score by any listed retailer was 84 for Amazon.com, while the lowest was 62 for McDonald's.

There is now more interest in the benchmarking of service retailing. One well-known measurement tool is SERVQUAL, which lets service retailers assess their quality by asking customers to react to a series of statements in five areas of performance:

● *Reliability*—Providing services as promised. Dependability in handling service problems. Performing services right the first time. Providing services at the promised time. Maintaining error-free records.

TABLE 20-3	Benchmarking Through the American Customer Satisfaction Index			
Retailer	4th Quarter 1995 Index Score	4th Quarter 1998 Index Score	4th Quarter 2001 Index Score	4th Quarter 2004 Index Score[a]
Department/Discount Stores	**75**	**73**	**75**	**74**
Dillard's	74	71	75	77
Federated	71	67	69	74
J.C. Penney	77	75	75	76
Kmart	72	71	74	67
May	75	72	75	76
Sears	75	74	76	74
Target Corporation	76	74	77	75
Wal-Mart	81	75	75	73
Supermarkets	**75**	**73**	**75**	**73**
Albertson's	77	70	72	69
Kroger	76	73	75	73
Publix	82	79	81	81
Safeway	73	71	75	72
Supervalu	77	77	76	75
Winn-Dixie	75	74	72	72
Specialty Retail Stores	—	—	**73**	**74**
Best Buy	—	—	—	72
Circuit City	—	—	—	72
Costco	—	—	76	79
Home Depot	—	—	75	73
Lowe's	—	—	75	76
Sam's Club	—	—	78	75
Limited-Service Restaurants	**70**	**69**	**71**	**76**
KFC	68	64	63	69
McDonald's	63	61	62	62
Papa John's	—	—	78	78
Wendy's	73	73	72	75
E-Commerce	—	—	**74**	**79**
Amazon.com	—	—	84	84
eBay	—	—	82	80
Priceline	—	—	69	73

[a]First Quarter 2005 Index Score for Limited-Service Restaurants.

Sources: University of Michigan Business School, American Society for Quality Control, and CFI Group, "Fourth Quarter Scores 2004," **www.theacsi.org/industry_scores.htm** (July 25, 2005). Reprinted by permission.

- *Responsiveness*—Keeping customers informed about when services will be done. Prompt service. Willingness to help customers. Readiness to act on customer requests.
- *Assurance*—Employees who instill customer confidence and make customers feel safe in transactions. Employees who are consistently courteous and have the knowledge to answer questions.
- *Empathy*—Giving customers individual attention in a caring way. Having the customer's best interest at heart. Employees who understand the needs of their customers. Convenient business hours.
- *Tangibles* — Modern equipment. Visually appealing facilities. Employees who have a neat, professional appearance. Visually appealing materials associated with the service.[8]

In reviewing the performance of others, firms should look at the *best practices* in retailing—whether involving companies in its own business sector or other sectors. For example:

> Best Buy, J.C. Penney, Rite Aid, Safeway, and Target formed the Advisory Board for the 2005 Retail Supply Chain Best Practices Review. Distribution center operations, direct-to-consumer operations, and transportation (including international, ocean, and truck) were the primary topics the Advisory Board planned to review and analyze. The Advisory Board oversaw the collection and analysis of responses from participating firms through a Web-based interview tool. The data analysis was to be presented to participants in a series of reports and review meetings that would provide very specific insights into the current and best practices of retail companies within various industry segments.[9]

Retail Forward regularly produces a list of "high-performance U.S. retailers," derived from its own proprietary ranking system. It includes firms performing well above average on a **retail performance index,** encompassing 5-year trends in revenue growth and profit growth, and a 6-year average return on assets. Due to its importance, return on assets is weighted twice as much as revenue growth or profit growth. An overall performance index of 100 is average. Table 20-4 cites 20 high-performance retailers and reveals that there are various ways to be one. The leader, Chico's, was strong on all measures. On the other hand, Abercrombie & Fitch was first in return on assets but no higher than 18th for three other measures—among the 20 firms in Table 20-4. By learning about high-performance firms in different retail categories, a prospective or existing company can study the strategies of those retailers and try to emulate their best practices.

What makes a good retail Web site? Companies can close the gap by checking here (**www.waller.co.uk/ eval.htm**).

A retailer can also benchmark its own internal performance, conduct gap analysis, and plan for the future. Through **gap analysis,** a company compares its actual performance against its potential performance and then determines the areas in which it must improve. As Figure 20-4 indicates, gap analysis has four main steps.

Let us apply gap analysis to Home Depot. Table 20-5 indicates the firm's financial results for fiscal year 2001 through fiscal year 2005. The data in the table may be used to benchmark Home Depot in terms of its own performance. Between 2001 and 2005, Home Depot increased its gross margin percentage, while

Ethics in RETAILING
eBay: A Founder's Philanthropy

Pierre Omidyar, the founder of eBay (**www.ebay.com**), is one of the richest 30-something-year-olds in history. From the time be began acquiring his wealth, it was apparent to Omidyar's friends that he was uncomfortable, perhaps even embarrassed, by it. While Pierre and his wife Pam Omidyar have vowed to give away all their wealth, they want their philanthropy to have an impact as great as eBay's.

Several of Omidyar's concepts are unsettling to the philanthropic community since they disrupt many of the traditional rules of giving. For example, instead of investing only in nonprofits, the Omidyar Network will also invest in for-profit companies. Through one of the foundation's grants, 1,152 Ugandan women were able to develop a business selling wireless phones to villagers. This income enabled the grant getters to build homes and send their children to school.

Omidyar even focuses on giving grants to individuals who are already creating social change through the Internet. Through experience, he recognizes that the Internet enables people to initiate a global launch for small ideas, much the way he started eBay.

Sources: Michelle Conlin and Rob Hof, "The eBay Way," *Business Week* (November 29, 2004), pp. 96–98; and "Omidyar Network," **www. omidyar.net/home** (March 1, 2006).

TABLE 20-4	Benchmarking High-Performance U.S. Retailers						
Company	Compound Annual Revenue Growth, 1998–2003 (%)	Compound 5-Year Revenue Growth Index	Annual Profit Growth, 1998–2003 (%)	5-Year Profit Growth Index	Average Annual Return on Assets 1998–2003 (%)	5-Year Return on Assets Index	Retail Performance Index[a]
Chico's	48.4	499	61.4	480	21.8	437	463
Coach	21.1	217	73.4	573	18.7	375	385
Christopher & Banks	28.8	297	44.6	348	21.7	435	379
Hot Topic	40.8	421	51.6	403	16.1	323	367
Abercrombie & Fitch	15.9	164	15.0	117	25.0	502	321
Bed Bath & Beyond	26.2	271	32.6	255	14.3	287	275
Dollar Tree	25.0	258	20.9	163	16.0	320	265
Pacific Sunwear of California	26.5	273	27.8	217	13.5	271	258
Tuesday Morning	15.7	162	32.5	254	13.7	274	241
Charlotte Russe	27.8	286	14.8	116	11.7	235	218
99¢ Only	21.7	224	16.2	127	12.4	248	212
Home Depot	16.5	170	21.7	169	12.3	247	208
Urban Outfitters	21.3	220	25.1	197	10.2	205	206
Kohl's	22.8	235	25.2	197	9.6	192	204
Family Dollar	15.0	155	19.1	149	12.7	254	203
Hibbett Sporting Goods	17.5	180	24.5	192	10.7	215	201
Sharper Image	21.6	223	40.6	317	6.4	128	199
Lowe's	20.3	209	31.2	244	8.1	162	195
Williams-Sonoma	20.1	207	23.4	183	8.9	178	186
Tractor Supply	19.6	203	30.7	240	7.2	144	183
U.S. Retailing Medians	9.7	100	12.8	100	5.0	100	100

[a]Retail performance index = [Revenue growth index + Profit growth index + 2 (Return on assets index)]/4

Source: "2004 High Performance Retailers," www.retailforward.com (April 17, 2005). Reprinted by permission of Retail Forward, Inc.

both its selling and store operating expenses and its general and administrative expenses rose as a percent of sales. Net earnings in dollars and as a percent of sales increased as a result of the strong gross margins. The current ratio and inventory turnover declined, and return on invested capital rose. Overall, Home Depot's performance was impressive. However, the results still reflect some "gaps" that Home Depot must address to sustain its financial momentum.

To ensure that gaps are minimized in relationship retailing, firms should undertake the following:

1. *Customer Insight:* Analyze known consumer information, such as sales, cost, and profits by segment.
2. *Customer Profiling:* Regularly gather and merge transaction and lifestyle data to get a fuller picture of individual shoppers. Identify noncustomers who fit the profile of the firm's best segment.

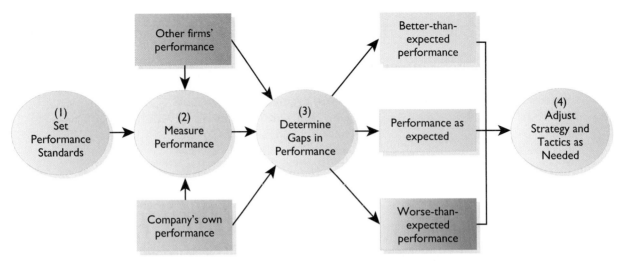

FIGURE 20-4
Utilizing Gap Analysis

3. *Customer Life-Cycle Model:* Study the firm's interactions with shoppers at various stages in the shoppers' life span. Analyze demographic data by market segment. Determine the cost of serving each life cycle within each segment and the resultant profitability.

4. *Extended Business Model:* Based on steps 3 and 4, draw conclusions about which customers to focus on, the best ways to interact with them, and the best strategy to foster relationships. Survey individual customers to find out how to tailor the retail strategy to best satisfy their needs.

5. *Relationship Program Planning and Design:* Identify all points of contact (in person, pick-up, delivery, kiosk, phone, fax, computer) between the firm and its customers, and the communications that should flow back and forth during each contact. Select processes that please existing customers and attract new ones, promote retention, increase spending, and lift profitability per customer.

6. *Implementation:* Integrate marketing, customer service, and selling efforts.[10]

At our Web site (**www.prenhall.com/bermanevans**), we have a number of links related to benchmarking and gap analysis.

Scenario Analysis

Retail Forward (**www.retail forward.com/FreeContent**) makes various forward-looking retail research reports available online. Click on "Free Info" and then "Free Newsletters."

In **scenario analysis**, a retailer projects the future by studying factors that affect long-run performance and then forms contingency ("what if") plans based on alternate scenarios (such as low, moderate, and high levels of competition). Planning for the future is not easy:

> The U.S. retailing business is a zero-sum game with low profit margins. Because the market is extremely competitive, each gain in sales for one store equals a loss for another. In this environment, retailers—especially department stores—have come to rely on frequent price promotions to attract customers, who now expect low prices. This dynamic keeps a lid on profits. Reinforcing this trend is Wal-Mart, whose everyday low prices policy offers discount prices all the time. Because of its size, Wal-Mart has

TABLE 20-5	Home Depot: Internal Benchmarking and Gap Analysis		
	Fiscal Year 2001	Fiscal Year 2003	Fiscal Year 2005
Statement of Earnings Data			
Net sales (in 000,000s)	$53,553	$58,247	$73,094
Earnings before taxes (in 000,000s)	$ 4,957	$ 5,830	$ 5,872
Net earnings (in 000,000s)	$ 3,044	$ 3,664	$ 5,001
Gross margin (% of sales)	30.2	31.1	33.4
Selling and store operating expenses (% of sales)	19.2	19.4	20.7
General and administrative expenses (% of sales)	1.7	1.7	1.9
Net earnings (% of sales)	5.7	6.3	6.8
Balance Sheet Data and Financial Ratios			
Total assets (in 000,000s)	$26,394	$30,011	$38,907
Working capital (in 000,000s)	$ 3,860	$ 3,882	$ 3,661
Merchandise inventories (in 000,000s)	$ 6,725	$ 9,076	$10,076
Current ratio (times)	1.59	1.48	1.35
Inventory turnover (times)	5.4	5.3	4.9
Return on invested capital (%)	18.3	18.8	21.5
Customer and Store Data			
Number of stores	1,333	1,532	1,890
Total square footage (in 000,000s)	109	166	201
Number of customer transactions (in 000,000s)	1,091	1,161	1,295
Average sale per transaction	$ 48.64	$ 49.43	$ 54.89
Comparable-store sales increase (%)	1	0	5
Weighted-average sales per square foot	$ 388	$ 370	$ 375

Source: Compiled by the authors from *Home Depot Annual Reports.*

gained power in its relationships with manufacturers, which it does not hesitate to wield. The world's largest retailer squeezes vendors for the greatest possible discount, which allows Wal-Mart to maintain and even lower its prices. The combination of a mature, highly saturated market, a slow sales growth environment, and merchants' inability to raise prices makes it imperative to drive down costs and/or improve economies of scale. Retailers' survival tactics include everything from closing weak units and cutting jobs, to instituting inventory controls and expanding stores.[11]

The consumer electronics industry in the United States continues to experience rapid technological innovation. This results in price deflation that's putting more products within the financial reach of many additional consumers. Consequently, household penetration rates are increasing for numerous goods and services, including DVD players, digital cameras, and broadband Internet access. Price remains a sizable barrier for only a few items, most notably high-definition televisions and satellite radio systems. The onus is on manufacturers and retailers to educate consumers about technological changes and drive consumer traffic to stimulate sales. While more shoppers feel they have a stronger grasp of technological changes than before, there are also more shoppers indicating they don't see a compelling need to buy the latest goods/services. There are significant purchase barriers for high-definition TVs, including price, confusion about technologies, and the shopping environment. Only 12 percent of shoppers enjoy shopping for the TVs, indicating a need to improve this experience.[12]

The opportunity in Mexico is bigger than it appears at first glance. It is a sizeable opportunity for retailers that can take away market share from Mexico's traditional retailers, as well as the large, informal market of mom-and-pop retailers. The retail opportunity is boosted by a youthful population driving demand for fashionable apparel and for housing and home goods. Suppliers, meanwhile, will be challenged to adapt and respond to growing pressure on retailers to push down costs, develop more private-label products, increase global sourcing, and improve supply chain efficiency. The growth of free trade poses both an opportunity and challenge for retailers and suppliers, particularly among those that already have unique synergies with the nearby U.S. market.[13]

Predicting the future is not easy (**www.futurist.com/ssp.htm**).

How are individual firms reacting to their environment? Let's look at Kohl's (**www.kohls.com**), whose well-conceived plan will continue in the future. Here are selected elements of the plan, as described by Kohl's chief executive:

- *Organizational Mission and Positioning:* "We have developed a new positioning statement for Kohl's targeting existing and new customers. Expect great things is our promise to the customer that she will have a great shopping experience and find great styles and brands—all in an easy, convenient shopping environment."
- *Goals:* "We want mid-single-digit comparable store sales increases. We want to maintain recent gross margin performance at a minimum, we want to continue to manage expenses while investing in areas that we need to support the future growth, and you put all those three things together and you get a 20 percent earnings increase for the year."
- *Store Strategy:* "We have made our stores easier to shop. Our current focus is improving visual presentation and making it easier for our customers to put together the looks that they want. We expanded our merchandise offerings to appeal to a broader range of customers with more offerings for our classic, updated, and contemporary customers. We differentiate our assortments by introducing new private brands such as Urban Pipeline and new exclusive brands such as Daisy Fuentes."
- *Merchandising:* "We are going to continue to be known as headquarters for wardrobe basics. We are committed and we always have been to remaining in stock on the basics that our customer needs for herself and her family throughout the year. We have developed from a brand standpoint a three-prong strategy for our merchandise brands. National, exclusive, and private label. National brands are still about 75 percent of our mix with classic brands representing the core of our strategy."

RETAILING
Around the World Wal-Mart: Enacting Global Best Practices

Wal-Mart's (**www.walmart.com**) international division is enormous with annual revenues that are higher than all but a handful of retailers. The firm operates nearly 2,000 store units in about 10 foreign countries. Wal-Mart's international retail strategy is based on adapting store formats to each market.

Wal-Mart operates an extremely large number of formats ranging from Sam's Clubs, department stores, and bodegas to appeal to customers of varying income levels. According to one retail analyst, "When you think of Wal-Mart in Mexico, don't think of the supercenter—think of the bodega. They are the ideal format for growth in mid-size and small-size Mexico."

Wal-Mart has also experimented with a number of formats in its British-based ASDA (**www.asda.co.uk**)

division. To complement ASDA's food-based stores, Wal-Mart has recently added dual-branded ASDA/Wal-Mart supercenters, ASDA Living stores featuring general merchandise, and George apparel stores.

The Chinese market is expected to have very high levels of growth for Wal-Mart over the next several years. To staff this growth, Wal-Mart has developed a "store of learning" concept wherein new employees are trained by Wal-Mart's best employees in a select group of stores.

Sources: Bernadette Casey, "Advancing Best Practices Throughout the World," *DSN Retailing Today* (February 28, 2005), pp. 50, 53; and "International Operations," **www.walmart.com** (April 9, 2006).

● *Marketing:* "We're focused on attracting new customers and increasing the frequency of our occasional customers. Our traditional marketing approach used inserts, direct-mail, radio, and TV. In addition to these traditional ways of reaching the customer, we now use more nontraditional means, such as magazines, Internet advertising, E-mail, in-store graphics, and public relations."[14]

At our Web site (**www.prenhall.com/bermanevans**), there are several links related to scenario analysis and future planning.

CONTROL: USING THE RETAIL AUDIT

After a retail strategy is devised and enacted, it must be continuously assessed and necessary adjustments made. A vital evaluation tool is the **retail audit**, which systematically examines and evaluates a firm's total retailing effort or a specific aspect of it. The purpose of an audit is to study what a retailer is presently doing, appraise performance, and make recommendations for the future. An audit investigates a retailer's objectives, strategy, implementation, and organization. Goals are reviewed and evaluated for their clarity, consistency, and appropriateness. The strategy and the methods for deriving it are analyzed. The application of the strategy and how it is received by customers are reviewed. The organizational structure is analyzed with regard to lines of command and other factors.

Good auditing includes these elements: Audits are conducted regularly. In-depth analysis is involved. Data are amassed and analyzed systematically. An open-minded, unbiased perspective is maintained. There is a willingness to uncover weaknesses to be corrected, as well as strengths to be exploited. After an audit is completed, decision makers are responsive to the recommendations made in the audit report.

Undertaking an Audit

There are six steps in retail auditing. See Figure 20-5 for an overview of the six-step retail auditing process, which is described next: (1) Determine who does an audit. (2) Decide when and how often an audit is done. (3) Establish the areas

FIGURE 20-5
The Retail Audit Process

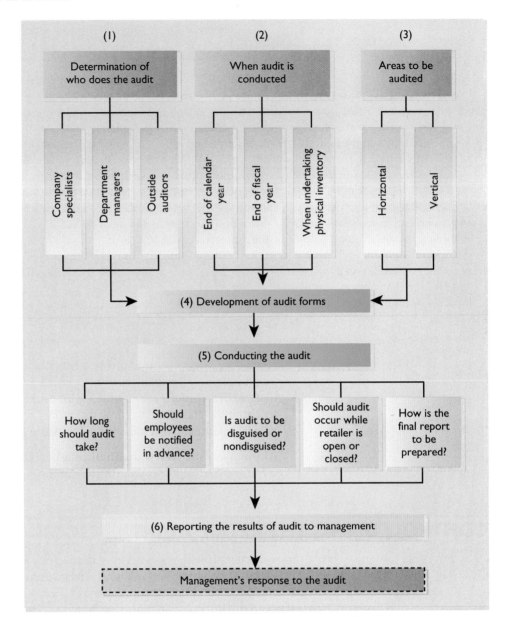

to be audited. (4) Develop audit form(s). (5) Conduct the audit. (6) Report to management.

Determining Who Does the Audit

One or a combination of three parties can be involved: a company audit specialist, a company department manager, and an outside auditor.

A company audit specialist is an internal employee whose prime responsibility is the retail audit. The advantages of this person include the auditing expertise, thoroughness, level of knowledge about the firm, and ongoing nature (no time lags). Disadvantages include the costs (especially for retailers that do not need full-time auditors) and the auditor's limited independence.

A company department manager is an internal employee whose prime job is operations management; that manager may also be asked to participate in the retail audit. The advantages are that there are no added personnel expenses and that the manager is knowledgeable about the firm and its operations. Disadvantages include the manager's time away from the primary job, the potential lack of objectivity, time pressure, and the complexity of companywide audits.

An outside auditor is not a retailer's employee but a paid consultant. Advantages are the auditor's broad experience, objectivity, and thoroughness. Disadvantages are the high costs per day or hour (for some retailers, it may be cheaper to hire per-diem consultants than full-time auditors; the opposite is true for larger firms), the time lag while a consultant gains familiarity with the firm, the failure of some firms to use outside specialists continuously, and the reluctance of some employees to cooperate.

Determining When and How Often the Audit Is Conducted

Logical times for auditing are the end of the calendar year, the end of the retailer's annual reporting year (fiscal year), or when a complete physical inventory is conducted. Each of these is appropriate for evaluating a retailer's operations during the previous period. An audit must be enacted at least annually, although some retailers desire more frequent analysis. It is important that the same period(s), such as January–December, be studied to make meaningful comparisons, projections, and adjustments.

Determining Areas to Be Audited

A retail audit typically includes more than financial analysis; it reviews various aspects of a firm's strategy and operations to identify strengths and weaknesses. There are two basic types of audits. They should be used in conjunction with one another because a horizontal audit often reveals areas that merit further investigation by a vertical audit.

A **horizontal retail audit** analyzes a firm's overall performance, from the organizational mission to goals to customer satisfaction to the basic retail strategy mix and its implementation in an integrated, consistent way. It is also known as a "retail strategy audit." A **vertical retail audit** analyzes—in depth—a firm's performance in one area of the strategy mix or operations, such as the credit function, customer service, merchandise assortment, or interior displays. A vertical audit is focused and specialized.

This site has a detailed online vertical pricing audit (**www.bizmove.com/marketing/m2y3.htm**) for retailers.

Developing Audit Forms

To be systematic, a retailer should use detailed audit forms. An audit form lists the area(s) to be studied and guides data collection. It usually resembles a questionnaire and is completed by the auditor. Without audit forms, analysis is more haphazard and subjective. Key questions may be omitted or poorly worded. Auditor biases may appear. Most significantly, questions may differ from one audit period to another, which limits comparisons. Examples of retail audit forms are presented shortly.

Conducting the Audit

Next, the audit itself is undertaken. Management specifies how long the audit will take. Prior notification of employees depends on management's perception of two factors: the need to compile some data in advance to save time versus the desire to get an objective picture and not a distorted one (which may occur if employees have too much notice). With a disguised audit, employees are unaware that it is taking place. It is useful if the auditor investigates an area such as personal selling and wishes to act as a customer to elicit employee responses. With a nondisguised audit, employees know an audit is being conducted. This is desirable if employees are asked specific operational questions and help in gathering data.

Some audits should be done while the retailer is open, such as assessing parking adequacy, in-store customer traffic patterns, the use of vertical transportation, and customer relations. Others should be done when the firm is closed, such as analyses of the condition of fixtures, inventory levels and turnover, financial statements, and employee records.

An audit report can be formal or informal, brief or long, oral or written, and a statement of findings or a statement of findings plus recommendations. It has a better chance of acceptance if presented in the format desired by management.

Reporting Audit Findings and Recommendations to Management

The last auditing step is to present findings and recommendations to management. It is the role of management—not the auditor—to see what adjustments (if any) to make. Decision makers must read the report thoroughly, consider each point, and enact the needed strategic changes. They should treat each audit seriously and react accordingly. No matter how well an audit is done, it is not a worthwhile activity if management fails to enact recommendations.

Responding to an Audit

TJX (www.tjx.com) is very open about its performance. Enter "About Our Company" and see how much information is available about the firm's plans and results.

After management studies audit findings, appropriate actions are taken. Areas of strength are continued and areas of weakness are revised. These actions must be consistent with the retail strategy and noted in the firm's retail information system (for further reference).

J.C. Penney, the veteran department store chain, places great reliance on its retail audits—especially during tough times:

> J.C. Penney still may not be the first choice of style-savvy teenagers. But the chain, which once seemed destined to join the ranks of dying chains, has benefited from one of the most aggressive turnaround initiatives in

---

Technology in RETAILING — Improving Online Checkout Systems

Forrester Research reports that about one-half of all Web-based transactions are terminated after consumers select the products but before the purchase button is pressed. As a result, retailers such as TJX (**www.tjx.com**), which owns T.J. Maxx (**www.tjmaxx.com**), Marshalls (**www.marshallsonline.com**), and HomeGoods (**www.homegoods.com**), are more closely examining their checkout procedures.

Until recently, T.J. Maxx's and HomeGoods' online stores used a traditional checkout that required customers to click through multiple screens as they input order quantities, shipping destinations, and credit card data. During one recent holiday season, these two chains tested a new system wherein all shipping and

billing information was contained on a single screen. TJX found that 50 percent more customers completed the one-screen versus the multiple-screen form.

The single-screen format is enabled by technology that feeds information from the Web site to a small software program that temporarily operates in the background when a consumer clicks on a particular Web page. The software is designed so that if a consumer types an incorrect ZIP code, a correction is immediately requested.

Source: Bob Tedeschi, "A Cure for Abandoned Shopping Carts: A Web Checkout System That Eliminates the Need for Multiple Screens," *New York Times* (February 14, 2005), p. C3.

the history of U.S. department stores. Since 2000, the retailer has overhauled its buying system, remodeled more than 100 stores, eliminated nearly half its clothing styles, and concentrated sales efforts on a smaller number of private labels that appeal to younger shoppers. So far, the makeover seems to be working. The strong results haven't generated much attention because they have become customary. J.C. Penney has posted higher same-store sales gains than its peers in 21 of the past 24 months. "Go back five years and this was just another ho-hum department store chain that was floundering around," said one consultant. "Now the stores are visually appealing and the merchandise has a real fashion sense."[15]

Possible Difficulties in Conducting a Retail Audit

AuditNet (www.auditnet. org) has a number of good examples of auditing applications. Click on "Audit Programs."

Several obstacles may occur in doing a retail audit. A retailer should be aware of them:

- An audit may be costly.
- It may be quite time-consuming.
- Performance measures may be inaccurate.
- Employees may feel threatened and not cooperate as much as desired.
- Incorrect data may be collected.
- Management may not be responsive to the findings.

At present, many retailers—particularly small ones—do not understand or perform systematic retail audits. But this must change if they are to assess themselves properly and plan correctly for the future.

Illustrations of Retail Audit Forms

Here, we present a management audit form and a retailing effectiveness checklist to show how small and large retailers can inexpensively, yet efficiently, conduct retail audits. An internal or external auditor (or department manager) could periodically complete one of these forms and then discuss the findings with management. The examples noted are both horizontal audits. A vertical audit would involve an in-depth analysis of any one area in the forms.

A Management Audit Form for Small Retailers

Under the auspices of the U.S. Small Business Administration, a *Marketing Checklist for Small Retailers* was developed. Although written for small firms, it is a comprehensive horizontal audit applicable to all retailers. Figure 20-6 shows selected questions from this audit form. "Yes" is the desired answer to each question. For questions answered negatively, the firm must learn the causes and adjust its strategy.

A Retailing Effectiveness Checklist

Figure 20-7 has another type of audit form to assess performance and prepare for the future: a retailing effectiveness checklist. It can be used by small and large firms alike. The checklist is more strategic than the *Management Audit for Small Retailers*—which is more tactical. Unlike the yes-no answers in Figure 20-6, the checklist lets a retailer rate its performance from 1 to 5 in each area; this provides more in-depth information. However, a total score should not be computed (unless items are weighted), because all items are not equally important. A simple summation would not be a meaningful score.

Planning

1. Have you thought about the long-term direction of your business?   _____
2. Have you developed a realistic set of plans for the year's operations?   _____
3. Do your plans provide methods to deal with competition?   _____
4. Is there a system for auditing your objectives?   _____

Customer Analysis (Who are your target customers and what are they seeking from you?)

1. Have you profiled your customers by age, income, education, occupation, etc.? _____
2. Are you aware of the reasons why customers shop with you?   _____
3. Do you ask your customers for suggestions on ways to improve your operation? _____
4. Do you know what goods and services your customers most prefer?   _____

Organization and Human Resources

1. Are job descriptions and authority for responsibilities clearly stated?   _____
2. Have you an effective system for communication with employees?   _____
3. Do you have a formal program for motivating employees?   _____
4. Have you taken steps to minimize shoplifting and internal theft?   _____

Operations and Special Services

1. Do you monitor every facet of your operations in terms of specific goals? _____
2. Do you provide time-saving services for greater customer convenience?   _____
3. Do you have a policy for handling merchandise returned by customers?   _____
4. Do you get feedback through customer surveys?   _____

Financial Analysis and Control

1. Do your financial records give you the information to make sound decisions? _____
2. Can sales be broken down by department?   _____
3. Do you understand the pros and cons of the retail method of accounting?   _____
4. Have you taken steps to minimize shoplifting and internal theft?   _____

Buying

1. Do you have a merchandise budget (planned purchases) for each season that is broken down by department and merchandise classification? _____
2. Does it take into consideration planned sales, planned gross margin, planned inventory turnover, and planned markdowns?   _____
3. Do you plan exclusive or private brand programs?   _____
4. Do you take advantage of cash discounts and allowances offered by your vendor/supplier? _____

Pricing

1. Have you determined whether to price below, at, or above the market?   _____
2. Do you set specific markups for each product category?   _____
3. Do you know which products are slow-movers and which are fast?   _____
4. Have you developed a markdown policy?   _____

Atmospherics

1. Are the unique appeals of your business reflected in your image?   _____
2. Have you figured out the best locations for displays?   _____
3. Do you know which items are bought on "impulse?"   _____
4. Do you use signs to aid your customers in shopping?   _____

Promotion

1. Are you familiar with the strengths and weaknesses of various promotional methods? _____
2. Do you participate in cooperative advertising?   _____
3. Do you ask customers to refer your business to friends and relatives?   _____
4. Do you make use of community projects or publicity?   _____

FIGURE 20-6

A Management Audit Form for Small Retailers—Selected Questions

These questions cover areas that are the basis for retailing. You can use this form to evaluate your current status and, perhaps, to rethink certain decisions. Answer YES or NO to each question.

Source: Adapted by the authors from Michael W. Little, *Marketing Checklist for Small Retailers* (Washington, DC: U.S. Small Business Administration, Management Aids Number 4.012).

✓ A long-term organizational mission is clearly articulated. _____

✓ The current status of the firm is taken into consideration when setting future plans. _____

✓ Sustainable competitive advantages are actively pursued. _____

✓ Company weaknesses have been identified and minimized. _____

✓ The management style is compatible with the firm's way of doing business. _____

✓ There is a logical short-run and long-run approach to the firm's chosen line of business. _____

✓ There are specific, realistic, and measurable short- and long-term goals. _____

✓ These goals guide strategy development and resource allocation. _____

✓ The characteristics and needs of the target market are known. _____

✓ The strategy is tailored to the chosen target market. _____

✓ Customers are extremely loyal. _____

✓ There are systematic plans prepared for each element of the strategy mix. _____

✓ All important uncontrollable factors are monitored. _____

✓ The overall strategy is integrated. _____

✓ Short-, moderate-, and long-term plans are compatible. _____

✓ The firm knows how each merchandise line, for-sale service, and business format stands in the marketplace. _____

✓ Tactics are carried out in a manner consistent with the strategic plan. _____

✓ The strategic plan and its elements are adequately communicated. _____

✓ Unbiased feedback is regularly sought for each aspect of the strategic plan. _____

✓ Information about new opportunities and threats is sought out. _____

✓ After enacting a strategic plan, company strengths and weaknesses, as well as successes and failures, are studied on an ongoing basis. _____

✓ Results are studied in a manner that reduces the firm's chances of overreacting to a situation. _____

✓ Strategic modifications are made when needed and before crises occur. _____

✓ The firm avoids strategy flip-flops (that confuse customers, employees, suppliers, and others). _____

✓ The company has a well-executed Web site or plans to have one shortly. _____

FIGURE 20-7

A Retailing Effectiveness Checklist

Rate your company's effectiveness in each of the following areas on a scale of 1 to 5, with 1 being strongly agree (excellent effort) and 5 being strongly disagree (poor effort). An answer of 3 or higher signifies that improvements are necessary.

Summary

1. *To demonstrate the importance of integrating a retail strategy.* This chapter shows why retailers need to plan and apply coordinated strategies and describes how to assess success or failure. The stages of a retail strategy must be viewed as an ongoing, integrated system of interrelated steps.

2. *To examine four key factors in the development and enactment of an integrated retail strategy: planning procedures and opportunity analysis, defining productivity, performance measures, and scenario analysis.* Planning procedures can be optimized by adhering to a series of specified actions, from situation analysis to control. Opportunities need to be studied in terms of their impact on overall strategy. The sales opportunity grid is good for comparing various strategic options.

To maximize productivity, retailers need to define exactly what productivity represents to them when they enact their strategies. Though firms should be efficient, this does not necessarily mean having the lowest possible operating costs (which may lead to customer dissatisfaction) but rather keying spending to the performance standards required by a retailer's chosen niche (such as upscale versus discount).

By applying the right performance measures and setting standards for them, a retailer can better integrate its strategy. Measures include total sales, average sales per store, sales by goods/service category, sales per square foot, gross margins, gross margin return on investment, operating income, inventory turnover, markdown percentages, employee turnover, financial ratios, and profitability. Retail

Forward's performance index combines sales growth, profit growth, and return on assets.

With scenario analysis, a retailer projects the future by examining the major factors that will have an impact on its long-term performance. Contingency plans are then keyed to alternative scenarios. This is not easy.

3. *To show how industry and company data can be used in strategy planning and analysis (benchmarking and gap analysis).* With benchmarking, a retailer sets its own standards and measures performance based on the achievements of its sector of retailing, specific competitors, the best companies, and/or its own prior actions. Through gap analysis, a retailer can compare its actual performance against its potential performance and see the areas in which it must improve.

4. *To show the value of a retail audit.* A retail strategy must be regularly monitored, evaluated, and fine-tuned or revised. The retail audit is one way to do this. It is a systematic, thorough, and unbiased review and appraisal.

The audit process has six sequential steps: (1) determining who does the audit, (2) deciding when and how often it is conducted, (3) setting the areas to be audited, (4) preparing forms, (5) conducting the audit, and (6) reporting results and recommendations to management. After the right executives read the audit report, necessary revisions in strategy should be made.

In a horizontal audit, a retailer's overall strategy and performance are assessed. In a vertical audit, one element of a strategy is reviewed in detail. Among the potential difficulties of auditing are the costs, the time commitment, the inaccuracy of performance standards, the poor cooperation from some employees, the collection of incorrect data, and unresponsive management. Some firms do not conduct audits; thus, they may find it difficult to evaluate their positions and plan for the future.

Two audit forms are presented in the chapter: a management audit for retailers and a retailing effectiveness checklist.

Key Terms

sales opportunity grid (p. 608)
performance measures (p. 611)
benchmarking (p. 611)

retail performance index (p. 614)
gap analysis (p. 614)
scenario analysis (p. 616)

retail audit (p. 619)
horizontal retail audit (p. 621)
vertical retail audit (p. 621)

Questions for Discussion

1. Why is it imperative for a firm to view its strategy as an integrated and ongoing process?

2. Develop a sales opportunity grid for a drugstore planning to add an ATM to its services mix.

3. Cite five performance measures commonly used by retailers, and explain what can be learned by studying each.

4. What is benchmarking? Present a five-step procedure to do retail benchmarking.

5. What do you think are the pros and cons of the retail performance index highlighted in Table 20-4?

6. How are the terms *gap analysis* and *scenario analysis* interrelated?

7. Distinguish between horizontal and vertical retail audits. Develop a vertical audit form for a TV repair store.

8. What are the attributes of good retail auditing?

9. Distinguish among these auditors. Under what circumstances would each be preferred?
   a. Outside auditor.
   b. Company audit specialist.
   c. Company department manager.

10. Under what circumstances should a disguised audit be used?

11. How should management respond to the findings of an audit? What can happen if the findings are ignored?

12. Why do many retailers not conduct any form of retail audit? Are these reasons valid? Explain your answer.

Web-Based Exercise

Visit the industry section of the Web site of the American Customer Satisfaction Index (**www.theacsi.org/industry_scores.htm**) and click on each of the current retailing industry links. What do you conclude from reviewing these scores?

Note: Stop by our Web site (**www.prenhall.com/bermanevans**) to experience a number of highly interactive, appealing Web exercises based on actual company demonstrations and sample materials related to retailing.

Chapter Endnotes

1. Various company sources.

2. Matthew Maier, "How to Beat Wal-Mart," *Business 2.0* (May 2005), pp. 111–112.

3. Rick Wingate, "Target vs. Kmart—A Store-Level View (Opinions from the Field)," *DSN Retailing Today* (May 6, 2002), p. 12.

4. To learn more about outstanding retail performers, look at the "High-Performance Retailers" issue of *Chain Store Age*, which appears every November.

5. "Ten Opportunities for Retail Innovation Revealed in New Retail Forward Report," **www.retailforward. com/freecontent/pressreleases/061305.asp** (June 13, 2005).

6. "Company Information," **www.foodlion.com/About FoodLion/CompanyInformation.asp** (February 9, 2006).

7. Thomas Angell, "Benchmarking Strategy Vital to Business Performance," *Financial Executive* (June 2005), p. 16.

8. A. Parasuraman, Valarie A. Zeithaml, and Leonard L. Berry, "Alternative Scales for Measuring Service Quality: A Comparative Assessment Based on Psychometric and Diagnostic Criteria," *Journal of Retailing*, Vol. 70 (Fall 1994), pp. 201–230. See also Lisa J. Morrison Coulthard, "Measuring Service Quality," *International Journal of Market Research*, Vol. 46 (Quarter 4, 2004), pp. 479–497; Anssi Mattila,

"Relationship Between Seamless Use Experience, Customer Satisfaction, and Recommendation," *Perspectives in Management* (Number 1, 2005), pp. 96–108; and Chien-Huang Lin and Ching-Huai Peng, "Cultural Dimension of Technology Readiness on Customer Value Chain in Technology-Based Service Encounters," *Journal of American Academy of Business*, Vol. 7 (September 2005), pp. 176–180.

9. Lynda Gratton and Sumantra Ghoshal, "Beyond Best Practice," *Sloan Management Review*, Vol. 46 (Spring 2005), pp. 49–57.

10. Austen Mulinder, "Hear Today . . . Or Gone Tomorrow? Winners Listen to Customers," *Retailing Issues Letter* (September 1999), p. 5.

11. "Retailing General," *Standard & Poor's Industry Surveys* (May 19, 2005), p. 8.

12. *Shopper Update: Consumer Electronics Point of View* (Columbus, OH: Retail Forward, April 2005), p. 1.

13. *Strategic Focus: Retailing in Mexico* (Columbus, OH: Retail Forward, December 2004), p. 1.

14. Larry Montgomery (Chairman and CEO, Kohl's), "Kohl's at Sanford C. Bernstein & Co. Strategic Decisions Conference," *Fair Disclosure Wire* (June 1, 2005).

15. Chris Serres, "Shining Up J.C. Penney," *Minneapolis Star Tribune Online* (June 6, 2005).

part eight
Short Cases

CASE 1: SAM ASH: A MUSICAL INSTRUMENT STORE ROLLS ON[c-1]

Privately held Sam Ash Music (**www.samashmusic.com**), with 45 stores in 14 states, is the number two retailer in the $7.5 billion U.S. musical instrument business [behind only publicly held Guitar Center (**www.guitarcenter.com**)]. Founded in 1924, Sam Ash raised money for his first Brooklyn, New York, store by pawning his wife's engagement ring. The chain is still a family business with Sam's sons and grandsons having active roles.

Sam Ash Music stores were considered to be destination stores for many years before the expression was coined. Famous musicians such as Bette Midler, Britney Spears, Bruce Springsteen, and Stevie Wonder have been customers of its stores in New York City, Nashville, Las Vegas, and Hollywood.

During the past decade, Sam Ash Music has almost tripled the number of stores it operates. In the 1990s, it decided to increase the size of all new store units to a big-box format. Although the chain's older stores ranged from 9,000 to 26,000 square feet, its newer stores average between 30,000 and 35,000 square feet. These newer stores are also in a broader variety of store location types. According to Paul Ash, Sam Ash Music's chairman, "If we fall in love with a location, it doesn't matter what kind of center. We're in strip malls. We're in two enclosed malls with entrances to the street. In some places, we're even downtown. We pick a city we want to be in and find a space that we like."

Its newer megastores are typically located near performing arts and entertainment centers so they are convenient for professional musicians. These megastores are generally located in high-traffic areas with good access to major highways. Four of these stores were formerly occupied by Mars Music, a competitor of Sam Ash Music that went bankrupt in 2002. Since these locations were formerly occupied by a music store, Sam Ash Music was quickly able to occupy these sites at a low renovation expense.

Sam Ash Music has also benefited from consolidation in the music retail industry. In 1999, it purchased five stores from Thoroughbred Music in Tennessee and Florida. In New Haven, Connecticut, Sam Ash Music took over the site of Bryan Music, a retailer that operated for 21 years before closing. And also in 1999, Sam Ash purchased Manny's (**www.mannysmusic.com**), a family-run business on West 48th Street in New York City. Due to Manny's excellent reputation, Sam Ash Music continues to run the store under its original name.

Aside from professional musicians, Sam Ash Music appeals to a broad target audience. Says Paul Ash, "There are families with young kids, teens and young adults, piano teachers, schools, DJs, and seniors who are going back to music." The retailer also sells speakers, microphones, and sound equipment to nonmusic-based organizations.

Unlike many other businesses where the growth of chain ownership is at the expense of independents, the music retail business is still largely individual or family owned. Guitar Center has 19 percent of the market, followed by Sam Ash Music's 5 percent share. Some retail analysts estimate that in time, the larger chains will grow as smaller firms either get acquired or go out of business.

Questions

1. Does Sam Ash Music have a well-integrated retail strategy? Explain your answer.
2. List 10 critical performance measures that Sam Ash Music needs to benchmark its performance against.
3. How can Sam Ash Music utilize scenario analysis?
4. Describe the strategic implications of the music industry's shift from individual and family-owned units to larger retail chain ownership.

CASE 2: NEIMAN MARCUS: HOW TO STAY AN ICON[c-2]

Neiman Marcus (**www.neimanmarcus.com**) had a wonderful year in 2004. Its earnings increased by 87 percent from the 2003 level. In addition, Neiman Marcus' sales per square foot hit $541, and its operating profit margin increased to 13.8 percent. Its same-store sales were up 10.6 percent at Neiman Marcus and 14.3 percent at its Bergdorf Goodman stores. This contrasts very highly with U.S. department store same-store sales growth of 1.7 percent over the same time period and with Nordstrom's and Saks Fifth Avenue's same-store sales growth of 9 percent and 5.2 percent, respectively. In addition to its stores, Neiman Marcus also operates print catalogs and Web sites for its Neiman Marcus and Bergdorf Goodman names, as well as for Horchow (an upscale retailer of home furnishings).

As Neiman Marcus' chief executive officer says, "Our merchants have done an outstanding job of filling our stores with the assortments that satisfy our customers' desire for the latest fashions and trends. The results have been more-satisfied customers and improved inventory returns." He also cites Neiman Marcus' full-price selling and its tight management of expenses and inventory levels as factors that have contributed to the chain's success.

There are several key components to Neiman Marcus' overall retail strategy; these relate to the chain's product, pricing, location, and store renovation and reconfiguring planning. "One of our key priorities is to differentiate our offerings from the competition. And we believe we have been successful in

---

[c-1]The material in this case is drawn from Jessica Roe, "Rock On," *Shopping Centers Today* (December 2004), pp. 25–28; and "Store Locations," **www.samashmusic.com/frameset.asp** (May 1, 2006).

[c-2]The material in this case is drawn from Molly Knight, "The Right Stuff," *Shopping Centers Today* (March 2005), pp. 9–10.

doing so," says the firm's chief executive. Neiman Marcus not only works closely with such top designers as Marc Jacobs and Prada but also has relationships with less exclusive designers that enable the store to get their best products. Neiman Marcus' ownership of a majority interest in Kate Spade accessories and Laura Mercier cosmetics also helps it get best-selling merchandise.

Neiman Marcus' exclusive merchandise enables it to sell a higher proportion of its goods at full price. Its focus on a highly affluent clientele also means that its target market has money to spend. According to Kurt Barnard, president of a retail consulting firm, "The economy may not be going very well overall, but it is going very well for these people."

Neiman is also noted for its proper execution of expansion plans. Many of its locations are anchors in upscale regional shopping centers. Unlike other department and specialty stores known for rapid expansion, there are only 35 Neiman Marcus locations (after a century in business). Over the next few years, Neiman Marcus is scheduled to open a handful of new stores. The low rate of expansion allows Neiman Marcus executives to devote most of their time to maximizing opportunities at existing stores, to choose only the most suitable locations, and to resolve promotion and distribution issues at its newer locations.

Neiman Marcus has focused its attention on remodeling and reconfiguring its existing stores as an alternative to additional store openings. By expanding its existing stores slowly, Neiman Marcus feels it can better promote and display the product lines with the greatest potential for profits and sales growth.

Questions

1. Visit Neiman Marcus' Web site and determine how successful the firm is today. Discuss why the firm is performing as it is.
2. Explain the pros and cons of Neiman Marcus' slow rate of store expansion.
3. Prepare a vertical retail audit form for Neiman Marcus to evaluate the effectiveness of its customer service.
4. Neiman Marcus was recently acquired by a private investment group. Do some library research and comment on whether or not you think this was a good idea. Explain your reasoning.

part eight

Comprehensive Case

Wal-Mart in the Year 2010*

INTRODUCTION

While the world waits for Wal-Mart (**www.walmart.com**) to collapse under its own weight, Wal-Mart waits for no one, demonstrating a remarkable capacity to manage the retail life cycle and keep right on rolling. If you thought Wal-Mart was an impetus for change during the last five years, watch out for the next five! Wal-Mart's strategy of innovation is not about creating incremental change. It is about creating new businesses that disrupt traditional businesses.

The Landscape

How Big Is It?

In 2003, total Wal-Mart Stores, Inc. sales topped $256 billion. They rose to nearly $290 billion in 2004. And sales zoomed past $300 billion in 2005. Wal-Mart is not just the biggest retailer (and largest company) on the planet, but it ranks as the leading retailer across several key product categories and retail sectors: number one food retailer, number one general merchandise retailer, number one health-and-beauty-care retailer, number one apparel retailer, number one home textiles retailer, number one home furnishings/housewares retailer, number one toy retailer, etc.

Wal-Mart's stores around the globe attract 138 million people weekly. Nearly half of U.S. households shop at Wal-Mart monthly. Wal-Mart is the largest private employer and real-estate developer in the United States. If Wal-Mart were a country, it would be the 21st-largest economy in the world.

How Did It Get There?

The history of Wal-Mart is a history of innovation—around business processes, products, formats, and geography. The company thinks big. Its strategy of innovation is not about creating incremental change. It is about creating new businesses that disrupt traditional businesses. Delivering low prices and value to consumers is the Wal-Mart way. The firm is the epitome of constant engineering, innovation, and improvement. It leverages its scalar economies across the supply chain in areas such as procurement, distribution, and information technology to create efficiencies and add value for the consumer.

Despite occasional missteps, Wal-Mart is a learning organization, applying lessons from one division or part of the globe to other parts of the business. It is a company that sticks with it. Wal-Mart has the proven ability to experiment with a concept until it gets it right and then expand it in rapid fashion—often taking out the competition along the way. Consider the Wal-Mart Supercenter.

Wal-Mart began its supercenter experiment in 1988. But it wasn't really until the mid-1990s that it got the formula right. In 1995, there were 239 Wal-Mart Supercenters. A decade later there are almost 1,700. And Wal-Mart remains committed to the supercenter as its growth vehicle largely because of the high revenue, productivity, and returns it gets on the investment.

As the firm continues to transition away from declining businesses like the discount department store, it is extending its reach with customers into a variety of new businesses, products, and service offers. To boost revenue and one-stop shopping appeal, Wal-Mart Supercenters and Sam's Club units are adding nontraditional offers such as financial, telecom, travel, and entertainment services. Expect Wal-Mart to continue to make plays that take it far beyond its conventional roots and national boundaries to capture a much larger share of the market for many goods and services worldwide.

What Is the Retail Impact?

Wal-Mart has been a key impetus of change across retailing. No industry sector or category has gone unscathed. Some examples of the kind of devastation Wal-Mart wreaks:

- The list of discount department store casualties is long. Today, only Wal-Mart, Target (**www.target.com**), and Kohl's (**www.kohls.com**) remain in expansion mode. Others are struggling to retain share. And Kmart (**www.kmart.com**), which emerged from Chapter 11 bankruptcy in 2003, is getting smaller as it continues to shed underperforming stores. More moves are likely given its intended merger with Sears (**www.sears.com**). Five years ago, Wal-Mart held 52 percent of mass channel sales. Today, it owns 62 percent and is growing.

- In 1997, 54 percent of supermarket industry sales were concentrated among the top 10 players. Wal-Mart had an estimated 10 percent of supermarket sector sales. Today, the top 10 controls two-thirds of supermarket sales. Wal-Mart has grown its share to 21 percent. More than 10,000 supermarkets have closed their doors in the past decade, often due to the rapid rollout of Wal-Mart supercenters. We estimate that for every domestic Wal-Mart supercenter that opens in the next five years, at least one more supermarket will close its doors.

- Traditional department stores continue to see their market share erode. The sector is caught in a vicious circle being propelled by escalating competition from a number of venues, including mass channel players such as Wal-Mart, specialty stores, and category killers.

- Wal-Mart alone owns 21 percent of toy spending in the United States. Price wars kicked some stalwart toy retailers such as Zany Brainy and Imaginarium right out of business. Other big names—Toys "R" Us (**www.toysrus.com**) and KB Toys (**www.kbtoys.com**)—continue to struggle.

What's Been the Supplier Impact?

An increasing number of suppliers report that Wal-Mart now accounts for more than 10 percent of their sales—for some, it is approaching 30 percent. By 2010, the typical consumer products manufacturer could have about 35 percent to 40 percent of its sales going through Wal-Mart registers.

Name brands will continue to rule—at least in food. To retain price leadership, Wal-Mart must do so through brand names. It will, however, continue to hone store brands to fill voids in its assortment. But expect brand-name products to continue to dominate Wal-Mart store shelves, especially for consumables/commodities. Expect more private-label emphasis in apparel, soft home, and hard lines to help create a differentiated offer vis-à-vis competitors and bolster gross margins.

Looking Ahead to 2010

Forecast

Wal-Mart's annual sales should reach $500 billion by 2010. Growth will come from multiple sources: more stores, more markets, and more exploration with formats and mix. We project that by 2010, 12 percent of all U.S. nonauto/nongasoline retail sales will go through Wal-Mart. The firm's goal is to grow square footage by at least 8 percent yearly. The primary growth vehicle will be the supercenter—it provides Wal-Mart with the most sales potential and greatest return on investment and shareholder value.

Wal-Mart has plans for its international division to account for one-third of its sales and profits in the coming years. Given that its sales account for only a small slice of the vast $8.5 trillion global retail marketplace, Wal-Mart has plenty of places around the world to conquer. We project international operations will contribute 30 percent of Wal-Mart's growth through 2010.

By 2010, Wal-Mart will have a broader portfolio of formats to satisfy more consumer needs and shopping occasions. We believe several venues—convenience stores, dollar stores, etc.—hold growth potential for Wal-Mart going forward. And none of these formats are foreign to Wal-Mart. It's been operating these businesses within its existing concepts for years.

Formats

We project that there will be more than 3,100 Wal-Mart supercenters by 2010. That's another 1,400 new Wal-Mart supercenters, which translates roughly into another $140 billion going through Wal-Mart cash registers. Wal-Mart is finding that a supercenter can play pretty much like a supermarket, i.e., fewer households needed to support one. Today, a typical Wal-Mart supercenter serves about 50,000 people. This means that supercenters can be placed closer together than previously thought without risking too much self-cannibalization. At present, two-thirds of Wal-Mart supercenters are located in just 15 southern states. This leaves plenty of domestic expansion possibilities.

The downsized "Urban 99" supercenter prototype (the 99,000-square-foot variety that debuted in Tampa in 2004) opens up even more possibilities, especially in metro areas where space is at a premium. We feel the potential exists for Wal-Mart to add another 2,500 U.S. Wal-Mart supercenters—a combination of full-sized and Urban 99 stores—during the next decade, the majority of which will open between now and 2010. As a result, the number of remaining conventional Wal-Mart discount department stores in operation will be cut in half by 2010.

Sam's Club will continue to roll out, but the format in its current state is likely to approach saturation by 2010. Sam's Club will likely add about another 100 net new units through 2010. But as the U.S. market approaches saturation, Wal-Mart will turn its attention toward global opportunities for the warehouse club model.

Neighborhood Markets is still not expected to contribute much by 2010. Wal-Mart's future growth strategy is clearly leveraging the supercenter concept—putting as many supercenters in as many places as it can. We anticipate that Neighborhood Market expansion will take a backseat until the time is right. We believe a couple of factors will drive the timing of a major rollout. First, a slowdown in supercenter expansion. Second, as today's generation of baby boomers becomes less mobile—making it harder to navigate a big-box supercenter—Neighborhood Market will take on an increasingly critical role in Wal-Mart's growth. Leading-edge boomers turn 60 in 2006 and 65 in 2011.

Wal-Mart will continue down the path of multi-channel retailer. It will figure out more ways to use the Web to drive shoppers to its stores (à la the drugstore pharmacy model—order online for in-store pickup). The firm recently launched one-hour online photofinishing—order digital prints online and pick up photos at a local Wal-Mart. After a three-year hiatus, it is again involved with online apparel retailing.

It is likely that many Wal-Mart shoppers who do not have Internet access today should by 2010, given Wal-Mart's foray into low-price PCs and Internet service. This should make walmart.com an even more popular destination site for the millions of products Wal-Mart offers exclusively online.

While the focus will remain on existing formats through 2010, expansion of supercenters is expected to drop off dramatically 5 to 10 years out. Consequently, expect Wal-Mart to begin cautiously testing additional concepts that could become the cornerstone of its growth initiatives post-2010. Here are some next steps to round out the portfolio:

- The convenience store industry is ripe. The gasoline market is huge. The sector is highly fragmented with no single dominant player. Freestanding c-stores are logical for Wal-Mart.
- Going after dollar stores would seem to be an easy call for Wal-Mart. Given its buying prowess and labor costs, it certainly seems likely that it could best Dollar General (**www.dollargeneral.com**) and Family Dollar (**www. familydollar.com**).
- Wal-Mart already has a huge pharmacy business. Freestanding units could be in the future.

New Categories

Consider the arenas where application of Wal-Mart's high-efficiency, low-cost business model could bring greater efficiency to fragmented, lumbering giants. It is interesting to note that Wal-Mart is currently dabbling in virtually all of these growth industries.

Wal-Mart continues to test the banking waters. In an October 2004 conference call, Wal-Mart listed financial services among the company's growth venues. The firm indicated that 20 percent of its shoppers do not have bank accounts. Besides offering its own store credit cards, other services available at Wal-Mart include credit reports, check printing, express bill payment, and money orders and money transfers. A key opportunity for Wal-Mart lies in the high-growth check-cashing business. In the face of stiff regulations and opposition, Wal-Mart will continue to pursue ways to break the bank.

Wal-Mart already offers travel packages and related services at **www.walmart.com/travel**, as well as inside select Wal-Mart supercenters. A test of car rental services is under way in a handful of stores in partnership with Budget (**www.budget.com**) and Enterprise (**www.enterprise.com**). In fall 2004, Wal-Mart promoted vacation packages, including a "Vacations on Layaway" option in an ad circular.

Wal-Mart is gaining traction as an entertainment destination. Shoppers can get hooked up with Internet access, cell phone service, and satellite TV. In 2004, Wal-Mart launched its online music download service—individual songs for the everyday low price of 88 cents. Most recently, Wal-Mart introduced a DVD rental subscription plan for $17.36 a month.

Domestic Markets

In the next 5 to 10 years, major mass channel players—particularly Wal-Mart—will likely run out of conventional location opportunities, i.e., suburban strip centers and small towns. Consequently, it will become increasingly critical to develop more flexible site strategies and/or smaller formats to fill in geographic gaps. Wal-Mart is cautiously experimenting with a handful of urban sites and mall locations.

Urban cores are virtually untapped by the supercenter format, largely due to their big-box size requirements. Wal-Mart supercenters will have a tough time penetrating remaining big metro areas. It will increasingly face battles with land scarcity, land-use laws, and land expense. Wal-Mart currently is experimenting with multi-level stores and downsized units for urban locations. This signals a company readying itself for alternative location types.

Although Wal-Mart currently operates only four mall stores, a company spokesperson has said that malls are now in the mix of real-estate properties Wal-Mart is reviewing. As more Wal-Mart supercenters start cropping up as mall anchors, it will not only bring new life to some malls but bring food into the mall as well—increased mall traffic means happy mall tenants. Given the number of vacant regional malls cropping up around the nation, we could also see more moves by Wal-Mart to bulldoze vacant and/or struggling malls and other shopping centers to construct stores, as it is doing in several areas.

Global Markets

Wal-Mart will look to get the biggest bang for its buck—concentrating on penetrating the largest markets, either in terms of the size of the economy or the population. It will also likely take an opportunistic approach to smaller markets, snatching up local retailers or real-estate when a good deal arises.

Progress will likely be measured and methodical as Wal-Mart applies lessons learned from its mixed international performance so far. Growth could also come in spurts—acquiring a large international retailer could give Wal-Mart a foothold across many countries at once. Among the more attractive retail opportunities that Wal-Mart may be tapping by 2010 are Spain, Russia, France, Italy, and Australia. Based on our analysis, Spain and Russia offer strong growth opportunities. The growth opportunities in France, Italy, and Australia are more modest; but these markets are characterized by relatively high living standards and low political and economic risk.

Capabilities

Wal-Mart's innovative use of information technology gives it a competitive leg up. The IT mantra is how to make it "easier, faster, and/or more efficient." Wal-Mart relies on data to run its business. It depends on technology as the enabler to meet customers' needs. It leverages IT to fine-tune the supply chain from factory floor to store shelf. Wal-Mart has developed its system in-house, which clearly is advantageous. The close alignment between the capabilities of Wal-Mart's systems and its unique business processes make it very difficult for competitors to get the same business benefit from similar technology systems. Because it does not outsource, Wal-Mart can deploy new technology at lightning speed. Several technology initiatives will drive Wal-Mart through 2010.

Whether it's speeding up inventory turnover, lowering out-of-stocks, or reducing costs associated with product handling, Wal-Mart continuously looks for ways to take inventory management to the next level. Improving inventory management will enable Wal-Mart to continuously lower prices and remain profitable in the future.

Wal-Mart is huge and becoming increasingly global. To drive the kind of growth anticipated by 2010, it will rely more heavily on global sourcing as a standard operating procedure. The idea behind global procurement is to find new, cheaper sources of goods that can give Wal-Mart an edge over the competition in any corner of the world. Global sourcing leads to lower cost of goods, boosting gross margins for Wal-Mart and allowing the company to pass more value onto consumers via lower prices.

Challenges

Wal-Mart will face some challenges that could affect its growth through the year 2010:

- There will be ongoing public relations obstacles as the firm confronts the barrage of negativity it receives. The company will continue to face questions regarding the political, economic, cultural, and social implications of its dominance.
- It may be difficult to find adequate real-estate for future development of its big-box supercenters.

- For continued growth, Wal-Mart will need to focus resources in new countries and new concepts—which may present a host of other complexities.
- The costs of doing business in urban areas are higher than in the small markets and rural areas that have historically been Wal-Mart's domain.
- As the largest private employer in the world, low labor costs are an important part of Wal-Mart's cost advantage. Company operating costs crept up in the past year, largely due to increasing labor wages, health and benefit costs, and added expenses associated with the company's pay equity program. Given Wal-Mart's growth goals, its labor force will increase dramatically in the coming years. Labor unrest certainly needs to be considered as a potential threat. Even small increases in labor costs could have a rippling effect, resulting in a big impact on the bottom line.

Questions

1. What do you believe are Wal-Mart's greatest strengths and weaknesses as a company? Explain your reasoning.

2. Describe the key *short-run* opportunities and threats facing Wal-Mart.
3. Describe the key *long-run* opportunities and threats facing Wal-Mart.
4. In planning for the future, why is it important that Wal-Mart distinguish between short-run and long-run opportunities and threats?
5. How can Wal-Mart maximize its productivity without sacrificing too much customer service?
6. In comparing itself to Target, what criteria should Wal-Mart use? Why?
7. What should Wal-Mart's future role be in the communities in which it operates? Explain your answer.

*The material in this case is adapted by the authors from *Wal-Mart 2010* (Columbus, OH: Retail Forward, December 2004). Reprinted by permission of Retail Forward, Inc. (**www.retailforward.com**).

Appendix A

CAREERS IN RETAILING

OVERVIEW

A person looking for a career in retailing has two broad possibilities: owning a business or working for a retailer. One alternative does not preclude the other. Many people open their own retail businesses after getting experience as employees. A person can also choose franchising, which has elements of both entrepreneurship and managerial assistance (as discussed in Chapter 4).

Regardless of the specific retail career path chosen, recent college graduates often gain personnel and profit-and-loss responsibilities faster in retailing than in any other major sector of business. After an initial training program, an entry-level manager supervises personnel, works on in-store displays, interacts with customers, and reviews sales and other data on a regular basis. An assistant buyer helps in planning merchandise assortments, interacting with suppliers, and outlining the promotion effort. Our Web site (**www.prenhall.com/bermanevans**) has loads of career-related materials. We

- Have a table describing dozens of positions in retailing.
- Present career paths for several leading retailers across a variety of formats.
- Offer advice on résumé writing (complete with a sample resumé), interviewing, and internships.
- Highlight retailing-related information from the *Occupational Outlook Handbook*.
- Present links to a number of popular career sites, including well over 100 retailers' sites.

THE BRIGHT FUTURE OF A CAREER IN RETAILING

Consider these observations from Careers in Business, Federated Department Stores, and the National Retail Federation. According to Careers in Business:

> Retail is one of the fastest growing parts of the world economy. Retailing is worth taking a good look at, particularly if you are interested in a service-oriented, entrepreneurial profession. The options are many, including store management, buying, merchandising, and central management. Because of constant contact with customers, retailing is a people-oriented business. Sales skills are also very important since many retail jobs involve selling or buying from sellers. It would be hard to find a profession which places a greater emphasis on enthusiasm. People with good attitudes and a willingness to be flexible and resourceful thrive in retail.[1]

Federated Department Stores is one of the world's leading retailers, and it has a very proactive approach with regard to long-term career opportunities:

> Our industry is a powerful economic force and an engine powering the American economy. That's why retailing, especially within a company like Federated, is such an attractive and exciting place to build a career right out of college, further develop the knowledge you've acquired during college, broaden your skill set through combined classroom and on-the-job experiences, be challenged every day in a dynamic environment, explore the vast number of opportunities for your future, build new relationships, and make an impact on a large-scale business!!!

> That spells opportunity for you to build a career in a field with virtually unlimited potential, and with the sophistication and resources to support your initiative. This is a place where you can have the best of both worlds. On one hand, we offer great careers with competitive pay, great benefits, flexibility in balancing work and home, and outstanding opportunity for advancement. On the other hand, the nature of what we do is fun, fast-paced, and interesting. We're the leading department store retailer—bringing new looks, styles, and fashions to our customers every day. Ours is a firm that's all about people, brands, innovation. If you are looking for a career that offers promotions and advancement, ours is a company filled with potential. You can pursue a myriad of opportunities across the U.S. without ever leaving the company. We believe strongly in advancement from within and provide extensive training to prepare you for the next level.[2]

The National Retail Federation, through its Retail Employer Link to Education program, makes these points regarding some of the negative perceptions of retailing careers:[3]

> **Myth:** Retail jobs only consist of cashier and sales clerk positions. **Fact:** Retailing offers perhaps the greatest variety of opportunities for ambitious and hardworking employees. With dedication and commitment, a sales associate can be promoted into many retail career path options, such as merchandising and buying; store, regional, and corporate management; inventory control; distribution; finance and internal auditing; marketing, sales promotion, and public relations; information systems; E-commerce; and human resources.

> **Myth:** Retail positions do not prepare young people for challenging, upwardly mobile careers. **Fact:** Career paths in the dynamic, expanding retail industry are exciting, varied, and lucrative. At the store level alone, a general manager of a mass-merchandiser department store oversees an average sales volume of $25 million to $30 million and employs an average of 150 people. Some department store manager salaries start at $80,000 and exceed $100,000. In addition, most of the skills needed to succeed in the retail industry are necessary to succeed in any industry.

> **Myth:** College and university degrees do not apply to retail careers. **Fact:** While some individuals are promoted based solely on retail experience, most retail career-level positions, from store manager to corporate executive, are easier to attain with a college degree.

OWNING A BUSINESS

Owning a retail business is popular, and many opportunities exist. Three-quarters of retail outlets are sole proprietorships; and many of today's giants began as independents, including Wal-Mart, Home Depot, J.C. Penney, McDonald's, Sears,

Cheesecake Factory, and Mrs. Fields. Consider the saga of Wendy's (**www. wendys.com/wendys_story.pdf**):

> When Dave Thomas opened the first "Wendy's Old Fashioned Hamburgers" restaurant, he had created something new and different in the restaurant industry. He offered high-quality food made with the freshest ingredients and served the way the customer wanted it. To Dave, quality was so important that he put the phrase "Quality is our Recipe" on the logo. Dave had an uncompromising passion for quality—food, people, and the way we run our business. His passion for quality remains our number one priority at every Wendy's restaurant around the world. And it all began in 1969 with one restaurant in Columbus, Ohio. In 1970, Wendy's broke new ground by opening a second restaurant in Columbus, featuring a Pick-Up Window with a separate grill, a unique feature in quick-service restaurants. Wendy's is credited with creating the first modern-day, Drive-Thru Window. During 1972, Wendy's first franchisee, L.S. Hartzog, signed an agreement for Indianapolis, Indiana. As of 2006, Wendy's was the third largest quick-service hamburger restaurant chain in the world, with nearly 7,000 restaurants in the United States, Canada, and 18 other countries.

Too often, people overlook the possibility of owning a retail business. Initial investments can be quite modest (several thousand dollars). Direct marketing (both mail order and Web retailing), direct selling, and service retailing often require relatively low initial investments—as do various franchises. Financing may also be available from banks, suppliers, store-fixture firms, and equipment companies.

OPPORTUNITIES AS A RETAIL EMPLOYEE

As we've noted before, in the United States, 25 million people work for traditional retailers. This does not include millions of others employed by firms such as banks, insurance companies, and airlines. More people work in retailing than in any other industry.

Career opportunities are plentiful because of the number of new retail businesses that open and the labor intensity of retailing. Thousands of new outlets open each year in the United States, and certain segments of retailing are growing at particularly rapid rates. Retailers such as Wal-Mart and Costco also plan to open many new stores in foreign markets. The increased employment from new store openings and the sales growth of retail formats (such as supercenters) also mean there are significant opportunities for personal advancement for talented retail personnel. Every time a chain opens a new outlet, there is a need for a store manager and other management-level people.

Selected retailing positions, career paths, and compensation ranges are described next.

Types of Positions in Retailing

Employment is not confined to buying and merchandising. Retail career opportunities also encompass advertising, public relations, credit analysis, marketing research, warehouse management, data processing, personnel management, accounting, and real-estate. Look at the table ("Selected Positions in Retailing") in the career section of our Web site for a list and description of a wide range of retailing positions. Some highly specialized jobs may be available only in large retail firms.

The type of position a person seeks should be matched with the type of retailer likely to have such a position. Chain stores and franchises typically have real-estate divisions. Department stores and chain stores usually have large human resource departments. Mail-order firms often have advertising production departments. If one is interested in travel, a buying position or a job with a retailer having geographically dispersed operations should be sought.

Figures 1 and 2 show the retailing experiences of two diverse college graduates.

Career Paths and Compensation in Retailing

For college graduates, executive training programs at larger retailers offer good learning experiences and advancement potential. These firms often offer careers in merchandising and nonmerchandising areas.

Here is how a new college graduate could progress in a career path at a typical department store or specialty store chain: He or she usually begins with a training program (lasting from three months to a year or more) on how to run a merchandise department. That program often involves on-the-job and classroom experiences. On-the-job training includes working with records, reordering stock, planning displays, and supervising salespeople. Classroom activities include learning how to evaluate vendors, analyze computer reports, forecast fashion trends, and administer store policy.

After initial training, the person becomes an entry-level operations manager (often called a sales manager, assistant department manager, or department manager—depending on the firm) or an assistant buyer. An entry-level manager or assistant buyer works under the direction of a seasoned department (group) manager or buyer and analyzes sales, assists in purchasing goods, handles reorders, and helps with displays. The new manager supervises personnel and learns store operations; the assistant buyer is more involved in purchases than

Glorie Delamin

TYPE OF STORE:
Office Superstore

HEADQUARTERS:
Framingham, Mass.

Glorie Delamin knew what she wanted before graduating last May, and she got it. She went from a career fair to a career at Staples. Originally an accounting major, she realized she wanted to pursue the retail route after a good experience as an assistant manager at a Conroy's store. She switched to a major in business administration with an emphasis in retail and earned a certificate in marketing at California State University in Los Angeles.

She started last June, and is presently operations manager at a Staples store in Glendale, Calif. "Staples is currently a great opportunity. I'm fortunate that I got in at such a good time. We're expanding and growing at a rapid rate. There's new Web site opportunities now as well."

Like many in retail, she loves that she's not anchored down to a desk from 9 to 5. Her workday is flexible. One day she works on plan-o-grams and store layouts; another, she is hiring people and always making sure everyone's duties are completed. About 60 percent of the time, she's roaming the sales floor, and she enjoys this one-on-one contact with customers.

"The most challenging part of my job is being able to satisfy customers' needs, but it's one of the best parts as well," she adds. "Our store is in an area where we get a lot of regular customers, and we're constantly talking to them. We feel really close to them because of the personal contact we get on a daily basis."

Recruits learn about satisfying customer's needs in the in-store manager trainee program that also covers merchandising and taking inventory—basically the ropes of the operation. Staples' program features workshops where trainees role-play in-store scenarios. Stores usually have three managers—general, sales and operations—and trainees see firsthand what the different positions entail.

Delamin's advice to upcoming graduates? "Take advantage of your school's career fairs, career center, and contacts. They're really useful and could lead you right into a job after school."

It worked for her. ■

FIGURE 1
Staples

Reprinted by permission of *DSN Retailing Today.*

Michael Hines

TYPE OF STORE:
Consumer Electronics Chain

HEADQUARTERS:
Eden Prairie, Minn.

After teaching abroad, working in real estate and getting his MBA, retail was the last place Michael Hines thought he would end up. But, he's found it to be the perfect career for him.

He earned his bachelor's degree in psychology from the University of Notre Dame and his MBA from Vanderbilt University before working for Best Buy, where he is presently project manager for small business development. He's proof that there's a lot of room to move up in retail, even with an advanced degree. In fact, Best Buy offers scholarships to help workers pay for MBAs. And getting your MBA pays: according to Hines, starting salaries, not including the stock options, are around $70,000 to $80,000 annually with this additional degree.

As school ended, he took advantage of an alumni contact at Best Buy, adding that many college Web sites and career centers make similar information available.

"The best part of my job is that I get to work with bright, dynamic people from very diverse backgrounds," says Hines. "It's very intellectually stimulating and very rewarding."

Hines works on cross-functional teams, addressing issues like logistics, advertising, development and brand management. There's a lot to retail that's behind-the-scenes. He's only been with the company a few months, but he's already well into the swing of things.

"It's very challenging. The company puts a lot of trust in me and really respects my opinion. What we're doing is very entrepreneurial, and I get a lot of hands-on assignments on different sides of the company."

What kind of people fit in at Best Buy? "You have to be a fun-loving person, not take yourself too seriously, enjoy life outside of the workplace," adds Hines. "Best Buy wants its employees to have time to play. They feel it makes employees well rounded and more productive overall."

Respect, fun, challenges, growth opportunity all at one job? Hines should know, that's why he's sticking with retail. ■

FIGURE 2
Best Buy

Reprinted by permission of *DSN Retailing Today.*

operations. Depending on the retailer, either person may follow the same type of career path, or the entry-level operations manager may progress up the store management ladder and the assistant buyer up the buying ladder.

During this time, the responsibilities and duties depend on the department (group) manager's or buyer's willingness to delegate and teach. In a situation where a manager or buyer has authority to make decisions, the entry-level manager or assistant buyer will usually be given more responsibility. If a firm has centralized management, a manager (buyer) is more limited in his or her responsibilities, as is the entry-level manager or assistant buyer. Further, an assistant buyer will gain more experience if he or she is in a firm near a wholesale market center and can make trips to the market to buy merchandise.

The next step in a department store or specialty store chain's career path is promotion to department (group) manager or buyer. This position is entrepreneurial—running a business. The manager or buyer selects merchandise, develops a promotional campaign, decides which items to reorder, and oversees personnel and record keeping. For some retailers, *manager* and *buyer* are synonymous. For others, the distinction is as just explained for entry-level positions. Generally, a person is considered for promotion to manager or buyer after two years.

Large department store and specialty store chains have additional levels of personnel to plan, supervise, and assess merchandise departments. On the store management side, there can be group managers, store managers, branch vice-presidents, and others. On the buying side, there can be divisional managers, merchandising vice-presidents, and others.

At many firms, advancement is indicated by specific career paths. This lets employees monitor their performance, know the next career step, and progress in a clear manner. Several retail career paths are shown in the careers section of our Web site.

Table 1 lists compensation ranges for personnel in a number of retailing positions.

TABLE 1	Typical Compensation Ranges for Personnel in Selected Retailing Positions

Position	Compensation Range
Operations	
Department manager—soft-line retailer	$18,000–$35,000+
Store management trainee	$22,000–$35,000+
Department manager—department store	$25,000–$35,000+
Department manager—mass merchandiser	$25,000–$35,000+
Department manager—hard-line retailer	$25,000–$35,000+
Customer service representative	$25,000–$50,000+
Warehouse director	$30,000–$90,000+
Store manager—specialty store, home center, drugstore	$32,000–$70,000+
Store manager—soft-line retailer	$35,000–$75,000+
Customer service supervisor	$40,000–$60,000+
Security director	$42,000–$70,000+
Store manager—department store	$45,000–$85,000+
Operations director	$60,000–$100,000+
Merchandising	
Assistant buyer	$25,000–$40,000+
Buyer—specialty store, home center, drugstore, department store	$32,000–$80,000+
Buyer—discount store	$35,000–$85,000+
Buyer—national chain	$45,000–$85,000+
Divisional merchandise manager	$60,000–$90,000+
General merchandise manager—drugstore, home center	$65,000–$90,000+
General merchandise manager—specialty store, department store	$70,000–$125,000+
General merchandise manager—discount store, national chain	$70,000–$125,000+
Senior merchandising executive	$80,000–$250,000+
Marketing Research	
Market research junior analyst	$30,000–$35,000+
Market research analyst	$35,000–$45,000+
Market research senior analyst	$40,000–$55,000+
Market research assistant director	$45,000–$65,000+
Market research director	$55,000–$75,000+
Top Management	
Senior human resources executive	$60,000–$140,000+
Senior advertising executive	$65,000–$110,000+
Senior real-estate executive	$65,000–$120,000+
Senior financial executive	$85,000–$200,000+
President	$250,000–$3,000,000+
Chairman of the board	$350,000–$10,000,000+
Other	
Public relations specialist	$35,000–$85,000+
Retail sales analyst	$38,000–$90,000+

Source: Estimated by the authors from various sources.

GETTING YOUR FIRST POSITION AS A RETAIL PROFESSIONAL

The key steps in getting your first professional position in retailing are the search for opportunities, interview preparation, and the evaluation of options. You must devote sufficient time to these steps so your job hunt progresses as well as possible.

Searching for Career Opportunities in Retailing

Various sources should be consulted. These include your school placement office, company directories and Web sites, classified ads in your local newspapers, Web job sites, and networking (with professors, friends, neighbors, and family members). Here are some hints to consider:

- *Do not "place all your eggs in one basket."* Do not rely too much on friends and relatives. They may be able to get you an interview but not a guaranteed job offer.

- *Be serious and systematic in your career search.* Plan in advance and do not wait until the recruiting season starts at your school to generate a list of retail employers.

- *Use directories with lists of retailers and current job openings.* Online listings include CareerBuilder.com Retail Jobs (**http://retail.careerbuilder.com**), AllRetailJobs.com (**www.allretailjobs.com**), My Retail Jobs (**www.myretailjobs. net**), and RetailManager.net (**www.retailmanager.net**). Also visit our Web site (**www.prenhall.com/bermanevans**).

- *Rely on the "law of large numbers."* In sending out résumés, you may have to contact at least 10 to 20 retailers to get just two to four interviews.

- *Make sure your résumé and accompanying cover letter highlight your best qualities.* These may include school honors, officer status in an organization, work experience, special computer expertise, and the proportion of college tuition you paid. Our Web site shows a sample résumé geared to an entry-level position in retailing.

- *Show your résumé to at least one professor.* Be receptive to constructive comments. Remember, your professor's goal is to help you get the best possible first job.

Preparing for the Interview

The initial and subsequent interviews for a position, which may last for 20 to 30 minutes or longer, play a large part in determining if you get a job offer. For that reason, you should be prepared for all interviews:

- *Adequately research each firm.* Be aware of its goods/service category, current size, overall retail strategy, competitive developments, and so on.

- *Anticipate questions and plan general responses:* "Tell me about yourself." "Why are you interested in a retailing career?" "Why do you want a job with us?" "What are your major strengths?" "Your major weaknesses?" "What do you want to be doing five years from now?" "What would your prior boss say about you?" In preparation, role-play your answers to these questions with someone.

- *Treat every interview as if it is the most important one.* Otherwise, you may not be properly prepared if the position turns out to be more desirable than you originally thought. And remember that you represent both your college and yourself at all interviews.

- *Be prepared to raise your own questions when asked to do so in the interview.* They should relate to career paths, training, and opportunities for advancement.

- *Dress appropriately and be well groomed.*

- *Verify the date and place of the interview.* Be prompt.

- *Have a pen and pad available to record information after the interview is over.*

- *Write a note to the interviewer within a week to thank him or her for spending time with you and to express a continuing interest in the company.*

Evaluating Retail Career Opportunities

Job seekers often place too much emphasis on initial salary or the firm's image in assessing career opportunities. Many other factors should be considered, as well:

- What activities do you like?
- What are your personal strengths and weaknesses?
- What are your current and long-term goals?
- Do you want to work for an independent, a chain, or a franchise operation?
- Does the opportunity offer an acceptable and clear career path?
- Does the opportunity include a formal training program?
- Will the opportunity enable you to be rewarded for good performance?
- Will you have to relocate?
- Will each promotion in the company result in greater authority and responsibility?
- Is the compensation level fair relative to other offers?
- Can a good employee move up the career path much faster than an average one?
- If owning a retail firm is a long-term goal, which opportunity is the best preparation?

ENDNOTES

1. "Retailing Careers," **www.careers-in-business.com/retail.htm** (April 2, 2006).
2. "Is Retailing Right for Me?" **www.retailology.com/college/career/rightcareer/retailright.asp** (April 2, 2006).
3. "Retail Industry Myths and Facts," **www.nrf.com/download/mythsandfacts.pdf** (September 2000).

Appendix B

ABOUT THE WEB SITE THAT ACCOMPANIES *RETAIL MANAGEMENT*

(WWW.PRENHALL.COM/BERMANEVANS)

OVERVIEW

Retail Management: A Strategic Approach is accompanied by a comprehensive, dynamic, interactive Web site that includes everything from chapter links to career data to a comprehensive listing of retail company sites on the World Wide Web. Once you have connected to the Internet, it is designed to easily run on your Web browser. Our site is user-friendly, real-world in nature, and keyed to the concepts covered in *Retail Management*. In this appendix, we present an overview of the site's components.

From within your browser, enter our home page by going to **www.prenhall. com/bermanevans**. All of the components of the site can be accessed from this home page. The first time you visit the site, read the description. It explains each of the various components. You can print this (or any) material for later reference by clicking on the "Print" icon at the top of the screen. All necessary instructions appear at the home page or in the various sections. From the menu screen, you can click your mouse on the icon of any of the components of the Web site. You then enter that specific section.

WEB SITE COMPONENTS

Our site has these components:

- There is a chapter-by-chapter listing (including the appendixes).
- For each of the 20 chapters in *Retail Management*, there are chapter objectives, a chapter overview (summary), a listing of key terms (with their definitions), interactive study guide questions, hot links to relevant Web sites (several hundred in all), and more.
- For each of the eight parts in *Retail Management*, there are four real-world exercises drawn from company Web sites. These exercises ask you to apply a variety of retailing concepts in an interactive manner. In addition, each part has dozens of other links to free downloads and demonstrations.
- In the sections of our Web site devoted to Chapters 9, 12, 16, and 17, there are a number of extra online math problems so that you may enhance your understanding of the mathematical concepts in these chapters.
- We provide the full glossary in an easily scrollable manner.

- There is a plethora of career material, including a directory of hundreds of retailers—complete with links to their home pages.
- Author biographies and photos are shown.
- There are numerous resources for professors, including a large packet of PowerPoint slides, teaching notes, and a lot more.

Interactive Study Guide

The interactive study guide contains 15 multiple-choice questions for each chapter (with answers and text references). And you can look at the glossary section of the Web site to further brush up on key terms. You may even E-mail your results to yourself or your professor.

Chapter Objectives/Chapter Overviews

These two sections enable you to view the objectives and overviews of each of the book's 20 chapters.

Key Terms and Glossary

There is a listing of key terms (with their definitions) by chapter. These terms are presented in the order in which we covered them in the chapter. You may also access glossary terms alphabetically.

Text-Related Web Site Links

This section has links to well over 1,000 retailing-related Web sites, divided by category. Click on the link to any of the Web sites and you are immediately transported there.

Careers in Retailing

This section contains advice on résumé writing, how to take an interview, and internships. There is a lot of information from the *Occupational Outlook Handbook*, as well as actual career paths and links to popular career sites. There are also a listing of positions in retailing, a listing of retail career search engines, and links to the career sections of retailers' Web sites.

Retail Resources on the Web

Still more information on the world of retailing is contained here: a retailer directory, Federal Trade Commission business tips, and Small Business Administration business tips.

Web Exercises

At the end of each chapter in *Retail Management*, there is a short Web exercise. In addition, our site offers 32 more in-depth Web-based exercises (4 per part). Look at our site for more information on applying these exercises, which are divided by text part. The exercises contain links to actual company Web sites, as well as questions for you to answer.

Computer Exercises

Sixteen user-friendly computer exercises, noted by a computer symbol throughout this book, can be downloaded from our Web site. The exercises are divided by text part.

Trade Associations

This section lists about 50 retail-related associations, complete with mailing addresses and URLs.

Appendix C

Additional Markup Increase in a retail price above the original markup when demand is unexpectedly high or costs are rising.

Additional Markup Percentage Looks at total dollar additional markups as a percentage of net sales:

$$\text{Additional markup percentage} = \frac{\text{Total dollar additional markups}}{\text{Net sales (in \$)}}$$

Addition to Retail Percentage Measures a price rise as a percentage of the original price:

$$\text{Addition to retail percentage} = \frac{\text{New price} - \text{Original price}}{\text{Original price}}$$

Advertising Paid, nonpersonal communication transmitted through out-of-store mass media by an identified sponsor.

Affinity Exists when the stores at a given location complement, blend, and cooperate with one another, and each benefits from the others' presence.

All-You-Can-Afford Method Promotional budgeting procedure in which a retailer first allots funds for each element of the strategy mix except promotion. The funds that are left go to the promotional budget.

Americans with Disabilities Act (ADA) Mandates that persons with disabilities be given appropriate access to retailing facilities.

Analog Model Computerized site selection tool in which potential sales for a new store are estimated based on sales of similar stores in existing areas, competition at a prospective location, the new store's expected market share at that location, and the size and density of a location's primary trading area.

Application Blank Usually the first tool used to screen applicants. It provides data on education, experience, health, reasons for leaving prior jobs, outside activities, hobbies, and references.

Assets Any items a retailer owns with a monetary value.

Asset Turnover Performance measure based on a retailer's net sales and total assets. It is equal to net sales divided by total assets.

Assortment Selection of merchandise carried by a retailer. It includes both the breadth of product categories and the variety within each category.

Assortment Display An open or closed display in which a retailer exhibits a wide range of merchandise.

Assortment Merchandise Apparel, furniture, autos, and other products for which the retailer must carry a variety of products in order to give customers a proper selection.

Atmosphere (Atmospherics) Reflection of a store's physical characteristics that are used to develop an image and draw customers. The concept is also applicable to nonstore retailers.

Attitudes (Opinions) Positive, neutral, or negative feelings a person has about different topics.

Augmented Customer Service Encompasses the actions that enhance the shopping experience and give retailers a competitive advantage.

Automatic Reordering System Computerized approach that combines a perpetual inventory and reorder point calculations.

Bait-and-Switch Advertising Illegal practice in which a retailer lures a customer by advertising goods and services at exceptionally low prices and then tries to convince the person to buy a better, more expensive substitute that is available. The retailer has no intention of selling the advertised item.

Balanced Tenancy Occurs when stores in a planned shopping center complement each other as to the quality and variety of their product offerings.

Balance Sheet Itemizes a retailer's assets, liabilities, and net worth at a specific time—based on the principle that assets equal liabilities plus net worth.

Basic Stock List Specifies the inventory level, color, brand, style category, size, package, and so on for every staple item carried by a retailer.

Basic Stock Method Inventory level planning tool wherein a retailer carries more items than it expects to sell over a specified period:

$$\text{Basic stock} = \text{Average monthly stock at retail} - \text{Average monthly sales}$$

Battle of the Brands The competition between manufacturers and retailers for shelf space and profits, whereby manufacturer, private, and generic brands fight each other for more space and control.

Benchmarking Occurs when the retailer sets its own standards and measures performance based on the achievements in its sector, specific competitors, high-performance firms, and/or its own prior actions.

Bifurcated Retailing Denotes the decline of middle-of-the-market retailing due to the popularity of both mass merchandising and niche retailing.

Book Inventory System Keeps a running total of the value of all inventory at cost as of a given time. This is done by recording purchases and adding them to existing inventory value; sales are subtracted to arrive at the new current inventory value (all at cost). It is also known as a perpetual inventory system.

Bottom-Up Space Management Approach Exists when planning starts at the individual product level and then proceeds to the category, total store, and overall company levels.

Box (Limited-Line) Store Food-based discounter that focuses on a small selection of items, moderate hours of operation (compared to supermarkets), few services, and limited manufacturer brands.

Budgeting Outlines a retailer's planned expenditures for a given time based on expected performance.

Bundled Pricing Involves a retailer combining several elements in one basic price.

Business Format Franchising Arrangement in which the franchisee receives assistance in site location, quality control, accounting, startup practices, management training, and responding to problems—besides the right to sell goods and services.

Buyer Person responsible for selecting the merchandise to be carried by a retailer and setting a strategy to market that merchandise.

Canned Sales Presentation Memorized, repetitive speech given to all customers interested in a particular item.

Capital Expenditures Retail expenditures that are long-term investments in fixed assets.

Case Display Interior display that exhibits heavier, bulkier items than racks hold.

Cash Flow Relates the amount and timing of revenues received to the amount and timing of expenditures made during a specific time.

Category Killer (Power Retailer) Very large specialty store featuring an enormous selection in its product category and relatively low prices. It draws consumers from wide geographic areas.

Category Management Merchandising technique that improves productivity. It focuses on product category results rather than the performance of individual brands or models.

Census of Population Supplies a wide range of demographic data for all U.S. cities and surrounding vicinities. These data are organized on a geographic basis.

Central Business District (CBD) Hub of retailing in a city. It is synonymous with "downtown." The CBD has the greatest density of office buildings and stores.

Chain Retailer that operates multiple outlets (store units) under common ownership. It usually engages in some level of centralized (or coordinated) purchasing and decision making.

Channel Control Occurs when one member of a distribution channel can dominate the decisions made in that channel by the power it possesses.

Channel of Distribution All of the businesses and people involved in the physical movement and transfer of ownership of goods and services from producer to consumer.

Chargebacks Practice of retailers, at their discretion, making deductions in the manufacturers' bills for infractions ranging from late shipments to damaged and expired merchandise.

Class Consciousness Extent to which a person desires and pursues social status.

Classification Merchandising Allows firms to obtain more financial data by subdividing each specified department into further categories for related types of merchandise.

Cognitive Dissonance Doubt that occurs after a purchase is made, which can be alleviated by customer aftercare, money-back guarantees, and realistic sales presentations and advertising campaigns.

Collaborative Planning, Forecasting, and Replenishment (CPFR) Emerging technique for larger firms whereby there is a holistic approach to supply chain management among a network of trading partners.

Combination Store Unites supermarket and general merchandise sales in one facility, with general merchandise typically accounting for 25 to 40 percent of total sales.

Community Shopping Center Moderate-sized, planned shopping facility with a branch department store and/or a category killer store, in addition to several smaller stores. About 20,000 to 100,000 people, who live or work within 10 to 20 minutes of the center, are served by this location.

Compensation Includes direct monetary payments to employees (such as salaries, commissions, and bonuses) and indirect payments (such as paid vacations, health and life insurance benefits, and retirement plans).

Competition-Oriented Pricing Approach in which a firm sets prices in accordance with competitors'.

Competitive Advantages Distinct competencies of a retailer relative to competitors.

Competitive Parity Method Promotional budgeting procedure by which a retailer's budget is raised or lowered based on competitors' actions.

Computerized Checkout Used by large and small retailers to efficiently process transactions and monitor inventory. Cashiers ring up sales or pass items by scanners. Computerized registers instantly record and display sales, customers get detailed receipts, and inventory data are stored in a memory bank.

Concentrated Marketing Selling goods and services to one specific group.

Consignment Purchase Items not paid for by a retailer until they are sold. The retailer can return unsold merchandise. Title is not taken by the retailer; the supplier owns the goods until sold.

Constrained Decision Making Limits franchisee involvement in the strategic planning process.

Consumer Behavior The process by which people determine whether, what, when, where, how, from whom, and how often to purchase goods and services.

Consumer Cooperative Retail firm owned by its customer members. A group of consumers invests in the company, elects officers, manages operations, and shares the profits or savings that accrue.

Consumer Decision Process Stages a consumer goes through in buying a good or service: stimulus, problem awareness, information search, evaluation of alternatives, purchase, and post-purchase behavior. Demographics and lifestyle factors affect this decision process.

Consumerism Involves the activities of government, business, and other organizations that protect people from practices infringing on their rights as consumers.

Consumer Loyalty (Frequent Shopper) Programs Reward a retailer's best customers, those with whom it wants long-lasting relationships.

Contingency Pricing Arrangement by which a service retailer does not get paid until after the service is satisfactorily performed. This is a special form of flexible pricing.

Control Phase in the evaluation of a firm's strategy and tactics in which a semiannual or annual review of the retailer takes place.

Controllable Variables Aspects of business that the retailer can directly affect (such as hours of operation and sales personnel).

Control Units Merchandise categories for which data are gathered.

Convenience Store Well-located food-oriented retailer that is open long hours and carries a moderate number of items. It is small, with average to above-average prices and average atmosphere and services.

Conventional Supermarket Departmentalized food store with a wide range of food and related products; sales of general merchandise are rather limited.

Cooperative Advertising Occurs when manufacturers or wholesalers and their retailers, or two or more retailers, share the costs of retail advertising.

Cooperative Buying Procedure used when a group of retailers make quantity purchases from suppliers.

Core Customers Consumers with whom retailers seek to nurture long relationships. They should be singled out in a firm's data base.

Corporation Retail firm that is formally incorporated under state law. It is a legal entity apart from individual officers (or stockholders).

Cost Complement Average relationship of cost to retail value for all merchandise available for sale during a given time period.

Cost Method of Accounting Requires the retailer's cost of each item to be recorded on an accounting sheet and/or coded on a price tag or merchandise container. When a physical inventory is done, item costs must be learned, the quantity of every item in stock counted, and total inventory value at cost calculated.

Cost of Goods Sold Amount a retailer has paid to acquire the merchandise sold during a given time period. It equals the cost of merchandise available for sale minus the cost value of ending inventory.

Cost-Oriented Pricing Approach in which a retailer sets a price floor, the minimum price acceptable to the firm so it can reach a specified profit goal. A retailer usually computes merchandise and retail operating costs and adds a profit margin to these figures.

Cross-Merchandising Exists when a retailer carries complementary goods and services so that shoppers are encouraged to buy more.

Cross-Shopping Occurs when consumers shop for a product category through more than one retail format during the year or visit multiple retailers on one shopping trip.

Cross-Training Enables personnel to learn tasks associated with more than one job.

Culture Distinctive heritage shared by a group of people. It passes on beliefs, norms, and customs.

Curving (Free-Flowing) Traffic Flow Presents displays and aisles in a free-flowing pattern.

Customary Pricing Used when a retailer sets prices for goods and services and seeks to maintain them for an extended period.

Customer Loyalty Exists when a person regularly patronizes a particular retailer (store or nonstore) that he or she knows, likes, and trusts.

Customer Satisfaction Occurs when the value and customer service provided through a retailing experience meet or exceed consumer expectations.

Customer Service Identifiable, but sometimes intangible, activities undertaken by a retailer in conjunction with the basic goods and services it sells.

Cut Case Inexpensive display, in which merchandise is left in the original carton.

Data-Base Management Procedure a retailer uses to gather, integrate, apply, and store information related to specific subject areas. It is a key element in a retail information system.

Data-Base Retailing Way to collect, store, and use relevant information on customers.

Data Mining Involves the in-depth analysis of information so as to gain specific insights about customers, product categories, vendors, and so forth.

Data Warehousing Advance in data-base management whereby copies of all the data bases in a company are maintained in one location and accessible to employees at any locale.

Dead Areas Awkward spaces where normal displays cannot be set up.

Debit Card System Computerized process whereby the purchase price of a good or service is immediately deducted from a consumer's bank account and entered into a retailer's account.

Demand-Oriented Pricing Approach by which a retailer sets prices based on consumer desires. It determines the range of prices acceptable to the target market.

Demographics Objective, quantifiable, easily identifiable, and measurable population data.

Department Store Large store with an extensive assortment (width and depth) of goods and services that has separate departments for purposes of buying, promotion, customer service, and control.

Depth of Assortment The variety in any one goods/service category (product line) with which a retailer is involved.

Destination Retailer Firm that consumers view as distinctive enough to become loyal to it. Consumers go out of their way to shop there.

Destination Store Retail outlet with a trading area much larger than that of a competitor with a less unique appeal. It offers a better merchandise assortment in its product category(ies), promotes more extensively, and/or creates a stronger image.

Differentiated Marketing Aims at two or more distinct consumer groups, with different retailing approaches for each group.

Direct Marketing Form of retailing in which a customer is first exposed to a good or service through a nonpersonal medium and then orders by mail, phone, or fax—and increasingly by computer.

Direct Product Profitability (DPP) Method for planning variable markups whereby a retailer finds the profitability of each category or unit of merchandise by computing adjusted per-unit gross margin and assigning direct product costs for such expenses as warehousing, transportation, handling, and selling.

Direct Selling Includes both personal contact with consumers in their homes (and other nonstore locations such as offices) and phone solicitations initiated by a retailer.

Direct Store Distribution (DSD) Exists when retailers have at least some goods shipped directly from suppliers to individual stores. It works best with retailers that also utilize EDI.

Discretionary Income Money left after paying taxes and buying necessities.

Distributed Promotion Effort Used by retailers that promote throughout the year.

Diversification Way in which retailers become active in business outside their normal operations—and add stores in different goods/service categories.

Diversified Retailer Multi-line firm with central ownership. It is also known as a retail conglomerate.

Dollar Control Planning and monitoring the financial merchandise investment over a stated period.

Downsizing Unprofitable stores closed or divisions sold off by retailers unhappy with performance.

Dual Marketing Involves firms engaged in more than one type of distribution arrangement. This enables those firms to appeal to different consumers, increase sales, share some costs, and maintain a good degree of strategic control.

Dump Bin Case display that houses piles of sale clothing, marked-down books, or other products.

Ease of Entry Occurs due to low capital requirements and no, or relatively simple, licensing provisions.

Economic Base Area's industrial and commercial structure—the companies and industries that residents depend on to earn a living.

Economic Order Quantity (EOQ) Quantity per order (in units) that minimizes the total costs of processing orders and holding inventory:

$$EOQ = \sqrt{\frac{2DS}{IC}}$$

Efficient Consumer Response (ECR) Form of order processing and fulfillment by which supermarkets are incorporating aspects of QR inventory planning, EDI, and logistics planning.

Electronic Article Surveillance Involves special tags that are attached to products so that the tags can be sensed by electronic security devices at store exits.

Electronic Banking Includes both automatic teller machines (ATMs) and the instant processing of retail purchases.

Electronic Data Interchange (EDI) Lets retailers and suppliers regularly exchange information through their computers with regard to inventory levels, delivery times, unit sales, and so on, of particular items.

Electronic Point-of-Sale System Performs all the tasks of a computerized checkout and also verifies check and charge transactions, provides instantaneous sales reports, monitors and changes prices, sends intra- and interstore messages, evaluates personnel and profitability, and stores data.

Employee Empowerment Way of improving customer service in which workers have discretion to do what they feel is needed—within reason—to satisfy the customer, even if this means bending some rules.

Ensemble Display Interior display whereby a complete product bundle (ensemble) is presented rather than showing merchandise in separate categories.

Equal Store Organization Centralizes the buying function. Branch stores become sales units with equal operational status.

Ethics Involves activities that are trustworthy, fair, honest, and respectful for each retailer constituency.

Evaluation of Alternatives Stage in the decision process where a consumer selects one good or service to buy from a list of alternatives.

Everyday Low Pricing (EDLP) Version of customary pricing whereby a retailer strives to sell its goods and services at consistently low prices throughout the selling season.

Exclusive Distribution Takes place when suppliers enter agreements with one or a few retailers to designate the latter as the only firms in specified geographic areas to carry certain brands or product lines.

Expected Customer Service Level of service that customers want to receive from any retailer, such as basic employee courtesy.

Experiential Merchandising Tactic whose intent is to convert shopping from a passive activity into a more interactive one, by better engaging the customer.

Experiment Type of research in which one or more elements of a retail strategy mix are manipulated under controlled conditions.

Extended Decision Making Occurs when a consumer makes full use of the decision process, usually for expensive, complex items with which the person has had little or no experience.

External Secondary Data Available from sources outside a firm.

Factory Outlet Manufacturer-owned store selling its closeouts, discontinued merchandise, irregulars, canceled orders, and, sometimes, in-season, first-quality merchandise.

Fad Merchandise Items that generate a high level of sales for a short time.

Family Life Cycle How a traditional family moves from bachelorhood to children to solitary retirement.

Fashion Merchandise Products that may have cyclical sales due to changing tastes and lifestyles.

Feedback Signals or cues as to the success or failure of part of a retail strategy.

FIFO Method Logically assumes old merchandise is sold first, while newer items remain in inventory. It matches inventory value with the current cost structure.

Financial Leverage Performance measure based on the relationship between a retailer's total assets and net worth. It is equal to total assets divided by net worth.

Financial Merchandise Management Occurs when a retailer specifies exactly which products (goods and services) are purchased, when products are purchased, and how many products are purchased.

Flea Market Location where many vendors offer a range of products at discount prices in plain surroundings. Many flea markets are located in nontraditional sites not normally associated with retailing.

Flexible Pricing Strategy that lets consumers bargain over selling prices; those consumers who are good at bargaining obtain lower prices than those who are not.

Floor-Ready Merchandise Items that are received at the store in condition to be put directly on display without any preparation by retail workers.

Food-Based Superstore Retailer that is larger and more diversified than a conventional supermarket but usually smaller and less diversified than a combination store. It caters to consumers' complete grocery needs and offers them the ability to buy fill-in general merchandise.

Forecasts Projections of expected retail sales for given time periods.

Franchising Contractual arrangement between a franchisor (a manufacturer, a wholesaler, or a service sponsor) and a retail franchisee, which allows the franchisee to conduct a given form of business under an established name and according to a given pattern of business.

Frequency Average number of times each person who is reached by a message is exposed to a retailer's promotion efforts in a specific period.

Fringe Trading Area Includes customers not found in primary and secondary trading areas. These are the most widely dispersed customers.

Full-Line Discount Store Type of department store with a broad, low-priced product assortment; all of the range of products expected at department stores; centralized checkout service; self-service; private-brand nondurables and well-known manufacturer-brand durables; less fashion-sensitive merchandise; relatively inexpensive building, equipment, and fixtures; and less emphasis on credit.

Functional Product Groupings Categorize and display a store's merchandise by common end use.

Gap Analysis Enables a company to compare its actual performance against its potential performance and then determine the areas in which it must improve.

Generic Brands No-frills goods stocked by some retailers. These items usually receive secondary shelf locations, have little or no promotion support, are sometimes of less quality than other brands, are stocked in limited assortments, and have plain packages. They are a form of private brand.

Geographic Information Systems (GIS) Combine digitized mapping with key locational data to graphically depict such trading-area characteristics as the demographic attributes of the population, data on customer purchases, and listings of current, proposed, and competitor locations.

Goal-Oriented Job Description Enumerates a position's basic functions, the relationship of each job to overall goals, the interdependence of positions, and information flows.

Goods Retailing Focuses on the sale of tangible (physical) products.

Goods/Service Category Retail firm's line of business.

Graduated Lease Calls for precise rent increases over a stated period of time.

Gravity Model Computerized site selection tool based on the premise that people are drawn to stores that are closer and more attractive than competitors'.

Gray Market Goods Brand-name products bought in foreign markets or goods transshipped from other retailers. They are often sold at low prices by unauthorized dealers.

Gross Margin Difference between net sales and the total cost of goods sold. It is also called gross profit.

Gross Margin Return on Investment (GMROI) Shows relationship between total dollar operating profits and the average inventory investment (at cost) by combining profitability and sales-to-stock measures:

$$\text{GMROI} = \frac{\text{Gross margin in dollars}}{\text{Net sales}}$$
$$\times \frac{\text{Net sales}}{\text{Average inventory at cost}}$$
$$= \frac{\text{Gross margin in dollars}}{\text{Average inventory at cost}}$$

Gross Profit Difference between net sales and the total cost of goods sold. It is also known as *gross margin*.

Hidden Assets Depreciated assets, such as store buildings and warehouses, that are reflected on a retailer's balance sheet at low values relative to their actual worth.

Hierarchy of Authority Outlines the job interactions within a company by describing the reporting relationships among employees. Coordination and control are provided.

Hierarchy of Effects Sequence of steps a consumer goes through in reacting to retail communications, which leads him or her from awareness to knowledge to liking to preference to conviction to purchase.

Horizontal Cooperative Advertising Agreement Enables two or more retailers (most often small, situated together, or franchisees of the same company) to share an ad.

Horizontal Price Fixing Agreement among manufacturers, among wholesalers, or among retailers to set certain prices. This is illegal, regardless of how "reasonable" prices may be.

Horizontal Retail Audit Analyzes a retail firm's overall performance, from mission to goals to customer satisfaction to basic retail strategy mix and its implementation in an integrated, consistent way.

Household Life Cycle Incorporates the life stages of both family and nonfamily households.

Huff's Law of Shopper Attraction Delineates trading areas on the basis of the product assortment carried at various shopping locations, travel times from the shopper's home to alternative locations, and the sensitivity of the kind of shopping to travel time.

Human Resource Management Recruiting, selecting, training, compensating, and supervising personnel in a manner consistent with the retailer's organization structure and strategy mix.

Human Resource Management Process Consists of these interrelated activities: recruitment, selection, training, compensation, and supervision. The goals are to obtain, develop, and retain employees.

Hypermarket Combination store pioneered in Europe that blends an economy supermarket with a discount department store. It is even larger than a supercenter.

Image Represents how a given retailer is perceived by consumers and others.

Impulse Purchases Occur when consumers buy products and/or brands they had not planned to before entering a store, reading a catalog, seeing a TV shopping show, turning to the Web, and so forth.

Incremental Budgeting Process whereby a firm uses current and past budgets as guides and adds to or subtracts from them to arrive at the coming period's expenditures.

Incremental Method Promotional budgeting procedure by which a percentage is either added to or subtracted from one year's budget to determine the next year's.

Independent Retailer that owns one retail unit.

Infomercial Program-length TV commercial (most often, 30 minutes in length) for a specific good or service that airs on cable television or on broadcast television, often at a fringe time. It is particularly worthwhile for products that benefit from visual demonstrations.

Information Search Consists of two parts: determining alternatives to solve the problem at hand (and where they can be bought) and learning the characteristics of alternatives. It may be internal or external.

Initial Markup (at Retail) Based on the original retail value assigned to merchandise less the merchandise costs, expressed as a percentage of the original retail price:

$$\text{Initial markup percentage (at retail)} =$$
$$\frac{\begin{array}{c}\text{Planned retail operating expenses} \\ + \text{Planned profit} + \text{Planned retail reductions}\end{array}}{\begin{array}{c}\text{Planned net sales} \\ + \text{Planned retail reductions}\end{array}}$$

Intensive Distribution Takes place when suppliers sell through as many retailers as possible. This often maximizes suppliers' sales and lets retailers offer many brands and product versions.

Internal Secondary Data Available within a company, sometimes from the data bank of a retail information system.

Internet Global electronic superhighway of computer networks that use a common protocol and that are linked by telecommunications lines and satellite.

Inventory Management Process whereby a firm seeks to acquire and maintain a proper merchandise assortment while ordering, shipping, handling, storing, displaying, and selling costs are kept in check.

Inventory Shrinkage Encompasses employee theft, customer shoplifting, vendor fraud, and administrative errors.

Isolated Store Freestanding retail outlet located on either a highway or a street. There are no adjacent retailers with which this type of store shares traffic.

Issue (Problem) Definition Step in the marketing research process that involves a clear statement of the topic to be studied.

Item Price Removal Practice whereby prices are marked only on shelves or signs and not on individual items. It is banned in several states and local communities.

Job Analysis Consists of gathering information about each job's functions and requirements: duties, responsibilities, aptitude, interest, education, experience, and physical tasks.

Job Motivation Drive within people to attain work-related goals.

Job Standardization Keeps tasks of employees with similar positions in different departments rather uniform.

Leader Pricing Occurs when a retailer advertises and sells selected items in its goods/service assortment at less than the usual profit margins. The goal is to increase customer traffic so as to sell regularly priced goods and services in addition to the specially priced items.

Leased Department Site in a retail store—usually a department, discount, or specialty store—that is rented to an outside party.

Liabilities Financial obligations a retailer incurs in operating a business.

Lifestyle Center An open-air shopping site that typically includes 150,000 to 500,000 square feet of space dedicated to upscale, well-known specialty stores.

Lifestyles Ways that individual consumers and families (households) live and spend time and money.

LIFO Method Assumes new merchandise is sold first, while older stock remains in inventory. It matches current sales with the current cost structure.

Limited Decision Making Occurs when a consumer uses every step in the purchase process but does not spend a great deal of time on each of them.

Logistics Total process of planning, enacting, and coordinating the physical movement of merchandise from supplier to retailer to customer in the most timely, effective, and cost-efficient manner possible.

Loss Leaders Items priced below cost to lure more customer traffic. Loss leaders are restricted by some state minimum price laws.

Maintained Markup (at Retail) Based on the actual prices received for merchandise sold during a time period less merchandise cost, expressed as a percentage:

$$\text{Maintained markup percentage (at retail)} = \frac{\text{Actual retail operating expenses} + \text{Actual profit}}{\text{Actual net sales}}$$

or

$$\frac{\text{Average selling price} - \text{Merchandise cost}}{\text{Average selling price}}$$

Maintenance-Increase-Recoupment Lease Has a provision allowing rent to increase if a property owner's taxes, heating bills, insurance, or other expenses rise beyond a certain point.

Manufacturer (National) Brands Produced and controlled by manufacturers. They are usually well known, supported by manufacturer ads, somewhat pre-sold to consumers, require limited retailer investment in marketing, and often represent maximum product quality to consumers.

Markdown Reduction from the original retail price of an item to meet the lower price of another retailer, adapt to inventory overstocking, clear out shopworn merchandise, reduce assortments of odds and ends, and increase customer traffic.

Markdown Percentage Total dollar markdown as a percentage of net sales (in dollars):

$$\text{Markdown percentage} = \frac{\text{Total dollar markdown}}{\text{Net sales (in \$)}}$$

Marketing Research in Retailing Collection and analysis of information relating to specific issues or problems facing a retailer.

Marketing Research Process Embodies a series of activities: defining the issue or problem, examining secondary data, generating primary data (if needed), analyzing data, making recommendations, and implementing findings.

Market Penetration Pricing Strategy in which a retailer seeks to achieve large revenues by setting low prices and selling a high unit volume.

Market Segment Product Groupings Place together various items that appeal to a given target market.

Market Skimming Pricing Strategy wherein a firm charges premium prices and attracts customers less concerned with price than service, assortment, and status.

Markup Difference between merchandise costs and retail selling price.

Markup Percentage (at Cost) Difference between retail price and merchandise cost expressed as a percentage of merchandise cost:

$$\text{Markup percentage (at cost)} = \frac{\text{Retail selling price} - \text{Merchandise cost}}{\text{Merchandise cost}}$$

Markup Percentage (at Retail) Difference between retail price and merchandise cost expressed as a percentage of retail price:

$$\text{Markup percentage (at retail)} = \frac{\text{Retail selling price} - \text{Merchandise cost}}{\text{Retail selling price}}$$

Markup Pricing Form of cost-oriented pricing in which a retailer sets prices by adding per-unit merchandise costs, retail operating expenses, and desired profit.

Marquee Sign used to display a store's name and/or logo.

Massed Promotion Effort Used by retailers that promote mostly in one or two seasons.

Mass Marketing Selling goods and services to a broad spectrum of consumers.

Mass Merchandising Positioning approach whereby retailers offer a discount or value-oriented image, a wide and/or deep merchandise selection, and large store facilities.

Mazur Plan Divides all retail activities into four functional areas: merchandising, publicity, store management, and accounting and control.

Megamall Enormous planned shopping center with at least 1-million square feet of retail space, multiple anchor stores, up to several hundred specialty stores, food courts, and entertainment facilities.

Membership (Warehouse) Club Appeals to price-conscious consumers, who must be members to shop.

Memorandum Purchase Occurs when items are not paid for by the retailer until they are sold. The retailer can return unsold merchandise. However, it takes title on delivery and is responsible for damages.

Merchandise Available for Sale Equals beginning inventory, purchases, and transportation charges.

Merchandising Activities involved in acquiring particular goods and/or services and making them available at the places, times, and prices and in the quantity to enable a retailer to reach its goals.

Merchandising Philosophy Sets the guiding principles for all the merchandise decisions a retailer makes.

Mergers The combinations of separately owned retail firms.

Micromarketing Application of data mining whereby the retailer uses differentiated marketing and focused strategy mixes for specific segments, sometimes fine-tuned for the individual shopper.

Micromerchandising Strategy whereby a retailer adjusts its shelf-space allocations to respond to customer and other differences among local markets.

Minimum Price Laws State regulations preventing retailers from selling certain items for less than their cost plus a fixed percentage to cover overhead. These laws restrict loss leaders and predatory pricing.

Model Stock Approach Method of determining the amount of floor space necessary to carry and display a proper merchandise assortment.

Model Stock Plan Planned composition of fashion goods, which reflects the mix of merchandise available based on expected sales. It indicates product lines, colors, and size distributions.

Monthly Sales Index Measure of sales seasonality that is calculated by dividing each month's actual sales by average monthly sales and then multiplying the results by 100.

Motives Reasons for consumer behavior.

Multi-Channel Retailing A distribution approach whereby a retailer sells to consumers through multiple retail formats (points of contact).

Multiple-Unit Pricing Discounts offered to customers who buy in quantity or who buy a product bundle.

Mystery Shoppers People hired by retailers to pose as customers and observe their operations, from sales presentations to how well displays are maintained to service calls.

Need-Satisfaction Approach Sales technique based on the principle that each customer has a different set of wants; thus, a sales presentation should be geared to the demands of the individual customer.

Neighborhood Business District (NBD) Unplanned shopping area that appeals to the convenience shopping and service needs of a single residential area. The leading retailer is typically a supermarket or a large drugstore, and it is situated on the major street(s) of its residential area.

Neighborhood Shopping Center Planned shopping facility with the largest store being a supermarket or a drugstore. It serves 3,000 to 50,000 people within a 15-minute drive (usually less than 10 minutes).

Net Lease Calls for all maintenance costs, such as heating, electricity, insurance, and interior repair, to be paid by the retailer.

Net Profit Equals gross profit minus retail operating expenses.

Net Profit After Taxes The profit earned after all costs and taxes have been deducted.

Net Profit Margin Performance measure based on a retailer's net profit and net sales. It is equal to net profit divided by net sales.

Net Sales Revenues received by a retailer during a given time period after deducting customer returns, markdowns, and employee discounts.

Net Worth Retailer's assets minus its liabilities.

Never-Out List Used when a retailer plans stock levels for best-sellers. The goal is to purchase enough of these products so they are always in stock.

Niche Retailing Enables retailers to identify customer segments and deploy unique strategies to address the desires of those segments.

Nongoods Services Area of service retailing in which intangible personal services are offered to consumers—who experience the services rather than possess them.

Nonprobability Sample Approach in which stores, products, or customers are chosen by the researcher—based on judgment or convenience.

Nonstore Retailing Utilizes strategy mixes that are not store-based to reach consumers and complete transactions. It occurs via direct marketing, direct selling, and vending machines.

Objective-and-Task Method Promotional budgeting procedure by which a retailer clearly defines its promotional goals and prepares a budget to satisfy them.

Objectives Long-term and short-term performance targets that a retailer hopes to attain. Goals can involve sales, profit, satisfaction of publics, and image.

Observation Form of research in which present behavior or the results of past behavior are observed and recorded. It can be human or mechanical.

Odd Pricing Retail prices set at levels below even dollar values, such as $0.49, $4.98, and $199.

Off-Price Chain Features brand-name apparel and accessories, footwear, linens, fabrics, cosmetics, and/or housewares and sells them at everyday low prices in an efficient, limited-service environment.

Off-Retail Markdown Percentage Markdown for each item or category of items computed as a percentage of original retail price:

$$\frac{\text{Off-retail markdown}}{\text{percentage}} = \frac{\text{Original price} - \text{New price}}{\text{Original price}}$$

One-Hundred Percent Location Optimum site for a particular store. A location labeled as 100 percent for one firm may be less than optimal for another.

One-Price Policy Strategy wherein a retailer charges the same price to all customers buying an item under similar conditions.

Open Credit Account Requires a consumer to pay his or her bill in full when it is due.

Open-to-Buy Difference between planned purchases and the purchase commitments already made by a buyer for a given time period, often a month. It represents the amount the buyer has left to spend for that month and is reduced each time a purchase is made.

Operating Expenditures (Expenses) Short-term selling and administrative costs of running a business.

Operations Blueprint Systematically lists all the operating functions to be performed, their characteristics, and their timing.

Operations Management Process used to efficiently and effectively enact the policies and tasks to satisfy a firm's customers, employees, and management (and stockholders, if a publicly owned company).

Opportunistic Buying Negotiates low prices for merchandise whose sales have not met expectations, end-of-season goods, items returned to the manufacturer or another retailer, and closeouts.

Opportunities Marketplace openings that exist because other retailers have not yet capitalized on them.

Opportunity Costs Possible benefits a retailer forgoes if it invests in one opportunity rather than another.

Option Credit Account Form of revolving account that allows partial payments. No interest is assessed if a person pays a bill in full when it is due.

Order-Getting Salesperson Actively involved with informing and persuading customers and in closing sales. This is a true "sales" employee.

Order Lead Time Period from when an order is placed by a retailer to the date merchandise is ready for sale (received, price marked, and put on the selling floor).

Order-Taking Salesperson Engages in routine clerical and sales functions, such as setting up displays, placing inventory on shelves, answering simple questions, filling orders, and ringing up sales.

Organizational Mission Retailer's commitment to a type of business and a distinctive marketplace role. It is reflected in the attitude to consumers, employees, suppliers, competitors, government, and others.

Organization Chart Graphically displays the hierarchical relationships within a firm.

Outshopping When a person goes out of his or her hometown to shop.

Outsourcing Situation whereby a retailer pays an outside party to undertake one or more operating tasks.

Overstored Trading Area Geographic area with so many stores selling a specific good or service that some retailers will be unable to earn an adequate profit.

Owned-Goods Services Area of service retailing in which goods owned by consumers are repaired, improved, or maintained.

Parasite Store Outlet that does not create its own traffic and has no real trading area of its own.

Partnership Unincorporated retail firm owned by two or more persons, each with a financial interest.

Perceived Risk Level of risk a consumer believes exists regarding the purchase of a specific good or service from a given retailer, whether or not the belief is actually correct.

Percentage Lease Stipulates that rent is related to a retailer's sales or profits.

Percentage-of-Sales Method Promotional budgeting method in which a retailer ties its budget to revenue.

Percentage Variation Method Inventory level planning method where beginning-of-month planned inventory during any month differs from planned average monthly stock by only one-half of that month's variation from estimated average monthly sales. Under this method:

$$\frac{\text{Beginning-of-month}}{\text{planned inventory}} = \frac{\text{Planned average monthly}}{\text{stock at retail} \times 1/2}$$
$$\text{level (at retail)} \quad [1 + (\text{Estimatd emonthly sales}/ \text{Estimated average monthly sales})]$$

Performance Measures Criteria used to assess effectiveness, including total sales, sales per store, sales by product category, sales per square foot, gross margins, gross margin return on investment, operating income, inventory turnover, markdown percentages, employee turnover, financial ratios, and profitability.

Personality Sum total of an individual's traits, which make that individual unique.

Personal Selling Oral communication with one or more prospective customers to make sales.

Physical Inventory System Actual counting of merchandise. A firm using the cost method of inventory valuation and relying on a physical inventory can derive gross profit only when it does a full inventory.

Planned Shopping Center Group of architecturally unified commercial facilities on a site that is centrally owned or managed, designed and operated as a unit, based on balanced tenancy, and accompanied by parking.

Planogram Visual (graphical) representation of the space for selling, merchandise, personnel, and customers—as well as for product categories.

PMs Promotional money, push money, or prize money that a manufacturer provides for retail salespeople selling that manufacturer's brand.

Point of Indifference Geographic breaking point between two cities (communities), so that the trading area of each can be determined. At this point, consumers would be indifferent to shopping at either area.

Point-of-Purchase (POP) Display Interior display that provides shoppers with information, adds to store atmosphere, and serves a substantial promotional role.

Positioning Enables a retailer to devise its strategy in a way that projects an image relative to its retail category and its competitors and elicits consumer responses to that image.

Post-Purchase Behavior Further purchases or re-evaluation based on a purchase.

Power Center Shopping site with (a) up to a half dozen or so category killer stores and a mix of smaller stores or (b) several complementary stores specializing in one product category.

Predatory Pricing Involves large retailers that seek to reduce competition by selling goods and services at very low prices, thus causing small retailers to go out of business.

Prestige Pricing Assumes consumers will not buy goods and services at prices deemed too low. It is based on the price-quality association.

Pre-Training Indoctrination on the history and policies of the retailer and a job orientation on hours, compensation, the chain of command, and job duties.

Price Elasticity of Demand Sensitivity of customers to price changes in terms of the quantities bought:

$$\text{Elasticity} = \frac{\dfrac{\text{Quantity 1} - \text{Quantity 2}}{\text{Quantity 1} + \text{Quantity 2}}}{\dfrac{\text{Price 1} - \text{Price 2}}{\text{Price 1} + \text{Price 2}}}$$

Price Lining Practice whereby retailers sell merchandise at a limited range of price points, with each point representing a distinct level of quality.

Price-Quality Association Concept stating that many consumers feel high prices connote high quality and low prices connote low quality.

Primary Data Those collected to address the specific issue or problem under study. This type of data may be gathered via surveys, observations, experiments, and simulation.

Primary Trading Area Encompasses 50 to 80 percent of a store's customers. It is the area closest to the store and possesses the highest density of customers to population and the highest per-capita sales.

Private (Dealer, Store) Brands Contain names designated by wholesalers or retailers, are more profitable to retailers, are better controlled by retailers, are not sold by competing retailers, are less expensive for consumers, and lead to customer loyalty to retailers (rather than to manufacturers)

Probability (Random) Sample Approach whereby every store, product, or customer has an equal or known chance of being chosen for study.

Problem Awareness Stage in the decision process at which the consumer not only has been aroused by social, commercial, and/or physical stimuli but also recognizes that the good or service under consideration may solve a problem of shortage or unfulfilled desire.

Productivity Efficiency with which a retail strategy is carried out.

Product Life Cycle Shows the expected behavior of a good or service over its life. The traditional cycle has four stages: introduction, growth, maturity, and decline.

Product/Trademark Franchising Arrangement in which the franchisee acquires the identity of the franchisor by agreeing to sell the latter's products and/or operate under the latter's name.

Profit-and-Loss (Income) Statement Summary of a retailer's revenues and expenses over a particular period of time, usually a month, quarter, or year.

Prototype Stores Used with an operations strategy that requires multiple outlets in a chain to conform to relatively uniform construction, layout, and operations standards.

Publicity Any nonpersonal form of public relations whereby messages are transmitted by mass media, the time or space provided by the media is not paid for, and there is no identified commercial sponsor.

Public Relations Any communication that fosters a favorable image for the retailer among its publics (consumers, investors, government, channel members, employees, and the general public).

Purchase Act Exchange of money or a promise to pay for the ownership or use of a good or service. Purchase variables include the place of purchase, terms, and availability of merchandise.

Purchase Motivation Product Groupings Appeal to the consumer's urge to buy products and the amount of time he or she is willing to spend in shopping.

Quick Response (QR) Inventory Planning Enables a retailer to reduce the amount of inventory it keeps on hand by ordering more frequently and in lower quantity.

Rack Display Interior display that neatly hangs or presents products.

Rationalized Retailing Combines a high degree of centralized management control with strict operating procedures for every phase of business.

Reach Number of distinct people exposed to a retailer's promotional efforts during a specified period.

Recruitment Activity whereby a retailer generates a list of job applicants.

Reference Groups Influence people's thoughts and behavior. They may be classified as aspirational, membership, and dissociative.

Regional Shopping Center Large, planned shopping facility appealing to a geographically dispersed market. It has at least one or two full-sized department stores and 50 to 150 or more smaller retailers. The market for this center is 100,000+ people who live or work up to a 30-minute drive time from the center.

Regression Model Computerized site selection tool that uses equations showing the association between potential store sales and several independent variables at each location under consideration.

Reilly's Law of Retail Gravitation Traditional means of trading-area delineation that establishes a point of indifference between two cities or communities, so the trading area of each can be determined.

Relationship Retailing Exists when retailers seek to establish and maintain long-term bonds with customers, rather than act as if each sales transaction is a completely new encounter with them.

Rented-Goods Services Area of service retailing in which consumers lease and use goods for specified periods of time.

Reorder Point Stock level at which new orders must be placed:

$$\text{Reorder point} = \frac{(\text{Usage rate} \times \text{Lead time})}{+ \text{Safety stock}}$$

Resident Buying Office Inside or outside buying organization used when a retailer wants to keep in close touch with market trends and cannot do so with just its headquarters buying staff. Such offices are usually situated in important merchandise centers (sources of supply) and provide valuable data and contacts.

Retail Audit Systematically examines the total retailing effort or a specific aspect of it to study what a retailer is presently doing, appraise how well it is performing, and make recommendations.

Retail Balance The mix of stores within a district or shopping center.

Retail Information System (RIS) Anticipates the information needs of managers; collects, organizes, and stores relevant data on a continuous basis; and directs the flow of information to proper decision makers.

Retailing Business activities involved in selling goods and services to consumers for their personal, family, or household use.

Retailing Concept An approach to business that is customer-oriented, coordinated, value-driven, and goal-oriented.

Retail Institution Basic format or structure of a business. Institutions can be classified by ownership, store-based retail strategy mix, and nonstore-based, electronic, and nontraditional retailing.

Retail Life Cycle Theory asserting that institutions—like the goods and services they sell—pass through identifiable life stages: introduction (early growth), growth (accelerated development), maturity, and decline.

Retail Method of Accounting Determines closing inventory value by calculating the average relationship between the cost and retail values of merchandise available for sale during a period.

Retail Organization How a firm structures and assigns tasks, policies, resources, authority, responsibilities, and rewards so as to efficiently and effectively satisfy the needs of its target market, employees, and management.

Retail Performance Index Encompasses five-year trends in revenue growth and profit growth, and a six-year average return on assets.

Retail Promotion Any communication by a retailer that informs, persuades, and/or reminds the target market about any aspect of that firm.

Retail Reductions Difference between beginning inventory plus purchases during the period and sales plus ending inventory. They encompass anticipated markdowns, employee and other discounts, and stock shortages.

Retail Strategy Overall plan guiding a retail firm. It influences the firm's business activities and its response to market forces, such as competition and the economy.

Return on Assets (ROA) Performance ratio based on net sales, net profit, and total assets:

$$\frac{\text{Return}}{\text{on assets}} = \frac{\text{Net profit}}{\text{Net sales}} \times \frac{\text{Net sales}}{\text{Total assets}} = \frac{\text{Net profit}}{\text{Total assets}}$$

Return on Net Worth (RONW) Performance measure based on net profit, net sales, total assets, and net worth:

$$\frac{\text{Return on}}{\text{net worth}} = \frac{\text{Net profit}}{\text{Net sales}} \times \frac{\text{Net sales}}{\text{Total assets}} \times \frac{\text{Total assets}}{\text{Net worth}}$$

Reverse Logistics Encompasses all merchandise flows from the retailer back through the supply channel.

Revolving Credit Account Allows a customer to charge items and be billed monthly on the basis of the outstanding cumulative balance.

RFID (Radio Frequency Identifaction) A method of remotely storing and retrieving data using devices called RFID tags or transponders.

Robinson-Patman Act Bars manufacturers and wholesalers from discriminating in price or purchase terms in selling to individual retailers if these retailers are purchasing products of "like quality" and the effect of such discrimination is to injure competition.

Routine Decision Making Takes place when a consumer buys out of habit and skips steps in the purchase process.

Safety Stock Extra inventory to protect against out-of-stock conditions due to unexpected demand and delays in delivery.

Sales Manager Person who typically supervises the on-floor selling and operational activities for a specific retail department.

Sales Opportunity Grid Rates the promise of new and established goods, services, procedures, and/or store outlets across a variety of criteria.

Sales-Productivity Ratio Method for assigning floor space on the basis of sales or profit per foot.

Sales Promotion Encompasses the paid communication activities other than advertising, public relations, and personal selling that stimulate consumer purchases and dealer effectiveness.

Saturated Trading Area Geographic area with the proper amount of retail facilities to satisfy the needs of its population for a specific good or service, as well as to enable retailers to prosper.

Scenario Analysis Lets a retailer project the future by studying factors that affect long-term performance and then forming contingency plans based on alternate scenarios.

Scrambled Merchandising Occurs when a retailer adds goods and services that may be unrelated to each other and to the firm's original business.

Seasonal Merchandise Products that sell well over non-consecutive time periods.

Secondary Business District (SBD) Unplanned shopping area in a city or town that is usually bounded by the intersection of two major streets. It has at least a junior department store and/or some larger specialty stores—in addition to many smaller stores.

Secondary Data Those gathered for purposes other than addressing the issue or problem currently under study.

Secondary Trading Area Geographic area that contains an additional 15 to 25 percent of a store's customers. It is located outside the primary area, and customers are more widely dispersed.

Selective Distribution Takes place when suppliers sell through a moderate number of retailers. This lets suppliers have higher sales than in exclusive distribution and lets retailers carry some competing brands.

Self-Scanning Enables the consumer himself or herself to scan the items being purchased at a checkout counter, pay electronically by credit or debit card, and bag the items.

Semantic Differential Disguised or nondisguised survey technique, whereby a respondent is asked to rate one or more retailers on several criteria; each criterion is evaluated along a bipolar adjective scale.

Service Retailing Involves transactions in which consumers do not purchase or acquire ownership of tangible products. It encompasses rented goods, owned goods, and nongoods.

Simulation Type of experiment whereby a computer program is used to manipulate the elements of a retail strategy mix rather than test them in a real setting.

Single-Channel Retailing A distribution approach whereby a retailer sells to consumers through one retail format.

Situation Analysis Candid evaluation of the opportunities and threats facing a prospective or existing retailer.

Slotting Allowances Payments that retailers require of vendors for providing shelf space in stores.

Social Class Informal ranking of people based on income, occupation, education, and other factors.

Social Responsibility Occurs when a retailer acts in society's best interests—as well as its own. The challenge is to balance corporate citizenship with fair profits.

Sole Proprietorship Unincorporated retail firm owned by one person.

Solutions Selling Takes a customer-centered approach and presents "solutions" rather than "products." It goes a step beyond cross-merchandising.

Sorting Process Involves the retailer's collecting an assortment of goods and services from various sources, buying them in large quantity, and offering to sell them in small quantities to consumers.

Specialog Enables a retailer to cater to the specific needs of customer segments, emphasize a limited number of items, and reduce catalog production and postage costs.

Specialty Store Retailer that concentrates on selling one good or service line.

Staple Merchandise Consists of the regular products carried by a retailer.

Stimulus Cue (social or commercial) or a drive (physical) meant to motivate or arouse a person to act.

Stock-to-Sales Method Inventory level planning technique wherein a retailer wants to maintain a specified ratio of goods on hand to sales.

Stock Turnover Number of times during a specific period, usually one year, that the average inventory on hand is sold. It can be computed in units or dollars (at retail or cost):

$$\text{Annual rate of stock turnover (in units)} = \frac{\text{Number of units sold during year}}{\text{Average inventory on hand (in units)}}$$

$$\text{Annual rate of stock turnover (in retail dollars)} = \frac{\text{Net yearly sales}}{\text{Average inventory on hand (at retail)}}$$

$$\text{Annual rate of stock turnover (at cost)} = \frac{\text{Cost of goods sold during the year}}{\text{Average inventory on hand (at cost)}}$$

Storability Product Groupings Used for products that need special handling.

Storefront Total physical exterior of a store, including the marquee, entrances, windows, lighting, and construction materials.

Store Maintenance Encompasses all the activities in managing a retailer's physical facilities.

Straight (Gridiron) Traffic Flow Presents displays and aisles in a rectangular or gridiron pattern.

Straight Lease Requires the retailer to pay a fixed dollar amount per month over the life of a lease. It is the simplest, most direct leasing arrangement.

Strategic Profit Model Expresses the numerical relationship among net profit margin, asset turnover, and financial leverage. It can be used in planning or controlling a retailer's assets.

Strategy Mix Firm's particular combination of store location, operating procedures, goods/services offered, pricing tactics, store atmosphere and customer services, and promotional methods.

String Unplanned shopping area comprising a group of retail stores, often with similar or compatible product lines, located along a street or highway.

Supercenter Combination store blending an economy supermarket with a discount department store.

Supermarket Self-service food store with grocery, meat, and produce departments and minimum annual sales of $2 million. The category includes conventional supermarkets, food-based superstores, combination stores, box (limited-line) stores, and warehouse stores.

Supervision Manner of providing a job environment that encourages employee accomplishment.

Supply Chain Logistics aspect of a value delivery chain. It comprises all of the parties that participate in the retail logistics process: manufacturers, wholesalers, third-party specialists, and the retailer.

Survey Research technique that systematically gathers information from respondents by communicating with them.

Tactics Actions that encompass a retailer's daily and short-term operations.

Target Market Customer group that a retailer seeks to attract and satisfy.

Taxes The portion of revenues turned over to the federal, state, and/or local government.

Terms of Occupancy Consist of ownership versus leasing, the type of lease, operations and maintenance costs, taxes, zoning restrictions, and voluntary regulations.

Theme-Setting Display Interior display that depicts a product offering in a thematic manner and portrays a specific atmosphere or mood.

Threats Environmental and marketplace factors that can adversely affect retailers if they do not react to them (and sometimes, even if they do).

Top-Down Space Management Approach Exists when a retailer starts with its total available store space, divides the space into categories, and then works on in-store product layouts.

Total Retail Experience All the elements in a retail offering that encourage or inhibit consumers during their contact with a retailer.

Trading Area Geographic area containing the customers of a particular firm or group of firms for specific goods or services.

Trading-Area Overlap Occurs when the trading areas of stores in different locations encroach on one another. In the overlap area, the same customers are served by both stores.

Traditional Department Store Type of department store in which merchandise quality ranges from average to quite good, pricing is moderate to above average, and customer service ranges from medium levels of sales help, credit, delivery, and so forth to high levels of each.

Traditional Job Description Contains each position's title, supervisory relationships (superior and subordinate), committee assignments, and the specific ongoing roles and tasks.

Training Programs Used to teach new (and existing) personnel how best to perform their jobs or how to improve themselves.

Unbundled Pricing Involves a retailer's charging separate prices for each item sold.

Uncontrollable Variables Aspects of business to which the retailer must adapt (such as competition, the economy, and laws).

Understored Trading Area Geographic area that has too few stores selling a specific good or service to satisfy the needs of its population.

Unit Control Looks at the quantities of merchandise a retailer handles during a stated period.

Unit Pricing Practice required by many states, whereby retailers (mostly food stores) must express both the total price of an item and its price per unit of measure.

Universal Product Code (UPC) Classification for coding data onto products via a series of thick and thin vertical lines. It lets retailers record information instantaneously on a product's model number, size, color, and other factors when it is sold, as well as send the information to a computer that monitors unit sales, inventory levels, and other factors. The UPC is not readable by humans.

Unplanned Business District Type of retail location where two or more stores situate together (or nearby) in such a way that the total arrangement or mix of stores is not due to prior long-range planning.

Usage Rate Average sales per day, in units, of merchandise.

Value Embodied by the activities and processes (a value chain) that provide a given level of value for the consumer—from manufacturer, wholesaler, and retailer perspectives. From the customer's perspective, it is the perception the shopper has of a value chain.

Value Chain Total bundle of benefits offered to consumers through a channel of distribution.

Value Delivery System All the parties that develop, produce, deliver, and sell and service particular goods and services.

Variable Markup Policy Strategy whereby a firm purposely adjusts markups by merchandise category.

Variable Pricing Strategy wherein a retailer alters prices to coincide with fluctuations in costs or consumer demand.

Variety Store Outlet that handles a wide assortment of inexpensive and popularly priced goods and services, such as apparel and accessories, costume jewelry, notions and small wares, candy, toys, and other items in the price range.

Vending Machine Format involving the cash- or card-operated dispensing of goods and services. It eliminates the use of sales personnel and allows around-the-clock sales.

Vendor-Managed Inventory (VMI) Practice of retailers counting on key suppliers to actively participate in their inventory management programs. Suppliers have their own employees stationed at retailers' headquarters to manage the inventory replenishment of the suppliers' products.

Vertical Cooperative Advertising Agreement Enables a manufacturer and a retailer or a wholesaler and a retailer to share an ad.

Vertical Marketing System All the levels of independently owned businesses along a channel of distribution. Goods and services are normally distributed through one of three types of systems: independent, partially integrated, and fully integrated.

Vertical Price Fixing Occurs when manufacturers or wholesalers seek to control the retail prices of their goods and services.

Vertical Retail Audit Analyzes—in depth—performance in one area of the strategy mix or operations.

Video Kiosk Freestanding, interactive, electronic computer terminal that displays products and related information on a video screen; it often uses a touch-screen for consumers to make selections.

Visual Merchandising Proactive, integrated approach to atmospherics taken by a retailer to create a certain "look," properly display products, stimulate shopping, and enhance the physical environment.

Want Book Notebook in which retail store employees record requests for unstocked or out-of-stock merchandise.

Want Slip Slip on which retail store employees enter requests for unstocked or out-of-stock merchandise.

Warehouse Store Food-based discounter offering a moderate number of food items in a no-frills setting.

Weeks' Supply Method An inventory level planning method wherein beginning inventory equals several weeks' expected sales. It assumes inventory is in direct proportion to sales. Under this method:

$$\begin{array}{l}\text{Beginning-of-month} \\ \text{planned inventory} \\ \text{level (at retail)}\end{array} = \begin{array}{l}\text{Average estimated weekly sales} \\ \times \text{Number of weeks} \\ \text{to be stocked}\end{array}$$

Weighted Application Blank Form whereby criteria best correlating with job success get more weight than others. A minimum total score becomes a cutoff point for hiring.

Wheel of Retailing Theory stating that retail innovators often first appear as low-price operators with low costs and low profit margins. Over time, they upgrade the products carried and improve facilities and customer services. They then become vulnerable to new discounters with lower-cost structures.

Width of Assortment Number of distinct goods/service categories (product lines) a retailer carries.

Word of Mouth (WOM) Occurs when one consumer talks to others.

World Wide Web (Web) Way of accessing the Internet, whereby people work with easy-to-use Web addresses and pages. Users see words, colorful charts, pictures, and video, and hear audio.

Yield Management Pricing Computerized, demand-based, variable pricing technique whereby a retailer (typically a service firm) determines the combination of prices that yield the greatest total revenues for a given period.

Zero-Based Budgeting Practice followed when a firm starts each new budget from scratch and outlines the expenditures needed to reach that period's goals. All costs are justified each time a budget is done.

Name Index

Subject Index